Computer & Telecommunications Acronyms

Gale's publications in the acronyms and abbreviations field include:

Acronyms, Initialisms & Abbreviations Dictionary series:

Acronyms, Initialisms & Abbreviations Dictionary (Volume 1). A guide to acronyms, initialisms, abbreviations, and similar contractions, arranged alphabetically by abbreviation.

New Acronyms, Initialisms & Abbreviations (Volume 2). Two interedition supplements in which terms are arranged alphabetically both by abbreviation and by meaning.

Reverse Acronyms, Initialisms & Abbreviations Dictionary (Volume 3). A companion to Volume 1 in which terms are arranged alphabetically by meaning of the acronym, initialism, or abbreviation.

International Acronyms, Initialisms & Abbreviations Dictionary series:

International Acronyms, Initialisms & Abbreviations Dictionary (Volume 1). A guide to foreign and international acronyms, initialisms, abbreviations, and similar contractions, arranged alphabetically by abbreviation.

New International Acronyms, Initialisms & Abbreviations (Volume 2). Two interedition supplements in which terms are arranged alphabetically both by abbreviation and by meaning.

Reverse International Acronyms, Initialisms & Abbreviations Dictionary (Volume 3). A companion to Volume 1 in which terms are arranged alphabetically by meaning of the acronym, initialism, or abbreviation.

Periodical Title Abbreviations series:

Periodical Title Abbreviations: By Abbreviation (Volume 1). A guide to abbreviations commonly used for periodical titles, arranged alphabetically by abbreviation.

Periodical Title Abbreviations: By Title (Volume 2). A guide to abbreviations commonly used for periodical titles, arranged alphabetically by title.

New Periodical Title Abbreviations (Volume 3). Two interedition supplements in which terms are arranged alphabetically both by abbreviation and by title.

Computer & Telecommunications Acronyms

A Selection of Approximately 25,000 Acronyms, Initialisms, Abbreviations, Contractions, Alphabetic Symbols, and Similar Condensed Appellations from Acronyms, Initialisms & Abbreviations Dictionary, *Tenth Edition, and Other Selected Sources*

Covering: Associations, Computers, Data Processing, Information Services, Information Technology, Institutions, Online Databases, Periodicals, Programming Languages, Telecommunications Services, and Other Fields

Volume 1 of the
Acronyms, Initialisms & Abbreviations Dictionary Subject Guide Series

First Edition

Julie E. Towell
and
Helen E. Sheppard
Editors

GALE RESEARCH COMPANY • BOOK TOWER • DETROIT, MICHIGAN 48226

Editors:	Julie E. Towell, Helen E. Sheppard
Senior Assistant Editor:	Prindle LaBarge
Assistant Editors:	Pamela Dear, Anthony J. Scolaro, Peter A. Smith
Editorial Assistants:	Barbara J. Cameron, Claire A. Selestow
Production Supervisor:	Mary Beth Trimper
Production Assistant:	Darlene K. Maxey
Art Director:	Arthur Chartow
Editorial Data Systems Director:	Dennis LaBeau
Supervisor of Programming and Systems:	Diane H. Belickas
Program Design:	Donald G. Dillaman, Barry M. Trute
Publisher:	Frederick G. Ruffner
Editorial Director:	Dedria Bryfonski
Associate Editorial Director:	Ellen T. Crowley
Senior Editor, Dictionaries:	Donna Wood

TRADEMARKS AND PROPRIETARY RIGHTS

Computer and Telecommunications Acronyms and its parent series, *Acronyms, Initialisms, and Abbreviations Dictionary,* are not, and are not intended to be in any way, sources of legal authority. The inclusion of an acronym, initialism, or abbreviation (acronym) does not represent an expression of the publisher's opinion as to any legal rights, trademark or otherwise, in such acronym, nor should it be relied upon as having any bearing on the validity or ownership of any trademark. The failure to indicate that an acronym is a trademark is not intended as a representation by the publisher that no trademark right exists in the acronym and does not affect any legal rights in such acronym. A reference to an owner of an acronym or to an acronym as a trademark likewise should not be relied upon for legal authority.

Errors brought to the attention of the publisher and verified to the satisfaction of the publisher will be corrected in future editions.

Library of Congress Cataloging-in-Publication Data

Computer & telecommunications acronyms.

(Acronyms, initialisms & abbreviations dictionary subject guide series ; v. 1)
All entries also appear in: Acronyms, initialisms & abbreviations dictionary. Detroit, Mich. : Gale Research Co., 1976-
Bibliography: p. 13
1. Computers--Acronyms. 2. Telecommunication--Acronyms. I. Towell, Julie E. II. Sheppard, Helen E. III. Gale Research Company. IV. Title: Computer and telecommunications acronyms. V. Series.
QA76.15.C6 1986   004'.0148   86-19503
ISBN 0-8103-2491-1

Copyright © 1986 by Gale Research Company

Computerized photocomposition by
Computer Composition Corporation
Madison Heights, Michigan

Printed in the United States of America

Contents

Preface 7
Editorial Policies 11
    Arrangement of Terms 11
List of Sources Cited 13
Computer and Telecommunications Acronyms
    By Acronym 19
    By Meaning 209

Preface

For over twenty-five years, *Acronyms, Initialisms, and Abbreviations Dictionary (AIAD)* has been the comprehensive source for deciphering acronyms and similar terms, and this tradition will continue. Arranged in a single A-to-Z alphabet, *AIAD* is used for easy identification of terms in a wide range of subject areas—or when the subject area of a term is unclear.

In an age of increasing specialization, however, subject-specific collections of these terms might better suit the research needs and budgets of some users. To meet these needs, Gale is establishing a series of specialized acronyms dictionaries extracted mainly from *AIAD* and covering areas of high interest.

Computer and Telecommunications Acronyms (CTA) is the first volume of the *AIAD* Subject Guide Series. The rapidly developing field of computers and telecommunications affects nearly every aspect of modern life, including banking, shopping, education, and entertainment; and the terminology of this dynamic subject area is especially rich in acronyms. For these reasons, the editors have chosen this significant and timely topic for the first volume of the Subject Guide Series. *CTA* contains approximately 25,000 acronyms, initialisms, and abbreviations, the majority borrowed from the *AIAD* database but with several thousand additional terms newly collected for this edition.

Scope and Coverage

CTA is principally a selection of terms from the *AIAD* database. Among the areas included are data processing and computer terminology, information services, telecommunications services, online databases, programming languages, companies, associations and institutions, and periodicals.

The primary purpose of this volume is to define terms that currently appear in computer and information-technology literature and that are in general use in this field. Terms of limited or local interest are not included. Every effort has been made to make the coverage as complete and up-to-date as possible.

Many entries of international interest have been included (e.g., universally used computer items; Russian data processing terms; foreign databases, companies, and associations; international information services; and general terms). Coverage of foreign terms of primarily local interest, however, is minimal.

Not all entries are newly formed or even in common current use. Many are listed for their historical interest. When additional information is discovered, changes or corrections will be made to existing entries. Old or obsolete entries will not be deleted, but will have their current status indicated during updating procedures. As in *AIAD*, entries will be deleted only if found to be incorrect.

Types of Entries Included

The term "acronym" in the title of this publication actually represents several alphabetic short forms. The types of entries included are acronyms, initialisms, abbreviations, alphabetic symbols, and other short forms.

A primary issue that concerned the editors was that no user of the book should be disappointed because the term for which an explanation was sought was omitted on a technicality. It was decided, therefore, to include in *CTA* all terms of the types described above as well as terms that *appear* to be of those types and may be thought to be acronyms, initialisms, or abbreviations when encountered in reading or conversation.

Thus, one will find in *CTA* some entries that might be considered alphabetical *symbols* rather than acronyms, initialisms, or abbreviations. These include online databases, software programs, computer names, and programming languages. For example, there is an entry for LOGO, a programming language designed for young people, because it is nearly always written in uppercase and appears to be an acronym. Actually, the word is not an acronym and the letters do not represent other words.

Entries Enhanced during Compilation

Extensive editorial work was done to locate and augment the entries in *AIAD* that have been included in *CTA*. During this search process, many entries have been enhanced by adding brief explanations, geographic information, and cross-references to other entries.

Thus, *CTA* is more than just an extraction of entries from the *AIAD* database. Considerable effort was made to ensure complete coverage in the specific field of computers and telecommunications. New entries have been added to round out the collection extracted from *AIAD*.

Further, the entries in *AIAD* eventually will be enhanced by this Subject Guide Series. Specialized research done for *CTA* will allow more information to be added to existing entries in future editions of *Acronyms, Initialisms, and Abbreviations Dictionary* and will promote accuracy and complete coverage in many fields.

Contents and Format

Access to terms is provided both *By Acronym* and *By Meaning*. Therefore, a user can easily locate the correct definition of an acronym by using the *By Acronym* section. A typical entry in this section will include: an acronym, its definition, and a category or subject area. The *By Meaning* section allows the user to locate the acronym or acronyms that are associated with a specific phrase, name, or term. The meaning of the term (as well as its category or explanation) is presented first, followed by the acronym or abbreviation. In both sections, many entries will have a mnemonic code indicating the source of the information.

Major Sources Cited

CTA contains entries from a wide variety of published sources, miscellaneous newspaper and newsmagazine references, terms provided by outside contributors, and independent research by the editorial staff. A code for the source of the entry (represented in small capital letters within parentheses) is given only for those print sources that provided at least 50 items. A key to these symbols and bibliographical information about the publications cited can be found in the List of Sources Cited, following the Editorial Policies. For sources used on an ongoing basis, only the latest edition is listed. For most of the remaining sources, the edition that was used is cited. The editors will provide further information upon request.

All Entries Eventually Included in *AIAD*

Coverage of computer and telecommunications terms will continue in the original *AIAD* series. Any additional entries and all supplemental information added to existing entries during the production of the *CTA* Subject Guide volume will be retained in the next main edition of *AIAD*. Thus, the publication of *Computer and Telecommunications Acronyms* and the other volumes in the Subject Guide Series enhance rather than diminish the scope and usefulness of *Acronyms, Initialisms, and Abbreviations Dictionary*.

Other Volumes in Series

Subject areas for future volumes of the *AIAD* Subject Guide Series will include business and trade, health and medicine, associations and institutions, and military and government.

In each case, the majority of terms will be extracted from the current *AIAD* database. Extensive editorial effort will be made to ensure that entries are accurate and that the subject field is covered comprehensively. As with *CTA*, new entries gathered to provide comprehensive coverage for any of the volumes in the Subject Guide Series will be included in the next main edition of *AIAD*.

For each volume, the number of new entries will vary. The goal is not a specific number of entries but complete coverage of a field. In the current volume, approximately 18% of the entries were newly located for this edition.

Editorial guidelines have been designed to ensure that overlap between subject volumes is minimal.

Acknowledgments

For research suggestions or contributions of terms and for other courtesies during the preparation of this first edition, the editors are indebted to Leland G. Alkire, David Glagovsky, Jack Gordon, Mildred Hunt, Steven Krems, the late Harry Schecter, Ed Schmerler, Peter Sikli, Edwin Steen, Miriam Steinert, Don Weeks, and Harvey Wolf, whose contributions to *Acronyms, Initialisms, and Abbreviations Dictionary* are reflected in this special subject volume.

Comments and Suggestions Are Welcome

Users of *CTA* can make unique and important contributions to future editions by notifying the editors of subject fields that are not adequately covered, by suggesting sources for covering such fields, and even by sending lists of terms they feel should be included.

Although every effort has been made to ensure accuracy, errors may occasionally occur. The editors will be grateful if these are brought to their attention.

Editorial Policies

The editorial practices followed in preparing *Computer and Telecommunications Acronyms* are much the same as those applied to *Acronyms, Initialisms, and Abbreviations Dictionary*. These include collecting as comprehensively as possible in one reference the abbreviated terms in the field of computers and telecommunications; listing and deciphering these terms; and keeping criteria for inclusion broad enough that terms are not excluded on subtle technicalities.

Access to terms is provided both *By Acronym* and *By Meaning*. Therefore, a user can easily locate the correct definition of an acronym by using the *By Acronym* section. A typical entry in this section will include: an acronym, its meaning and a category or subject area. The *By Meaning* section allows the user to locate the acronym or acronyms that are associated with a specific phrase, name, or term. The meaning of the term (as well as its category or explanation) is presented first, followed by the acronym or abbreviation. In both sections, many entries will have a mnemonic code indicating the source of the information. If additional information becomes available during future research, an entry will be revised.

Arrangement of Terms

The following summaries and examples outline the alphabetical arrangement in each of the two sections of *Computer and Telecommunications Acronyms*.

By Acronym Section

Acronyms, initialisms, and abbreviations are arranged alphabetically in letter-by-letter sequence, regardless of spacing, punctuation, or capitalization. Neither ampersands, articles, conjunctions, nor prepositions are considered in the alphabetizing. If the same abbreviation has more than one meaning, the various *meanings* are then subarranged alphabetically, in word-by-word sequence.

After this principal arrangement of terms will follow any forms of the entry using Arabic numerals. (Roman numerals sort as alphabetics.) These numeric forms are, in turn, followed by pluralized forms (usually indicated by an apostrophe and lowercase "s" to emphasize that the "s" is not part of the initialism). Finally come entries in which a parenthetical explanatory word is an integral part of the term: A (Bomb), C (Section), D (Day), etc.

For example:

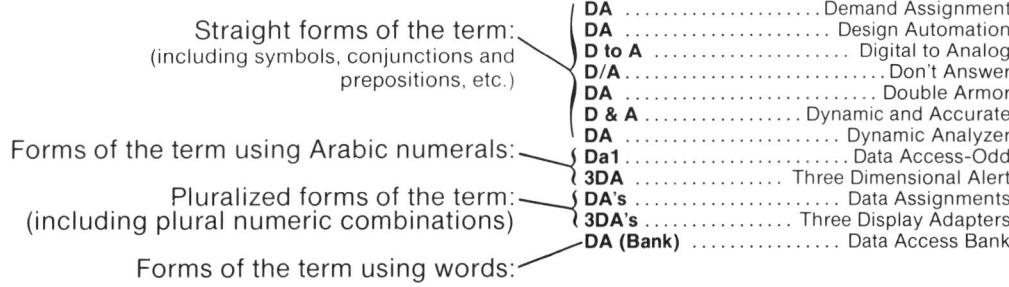

With respect to arrangement of terms and their meanings, it should be kept in mind that the point of reference for the user is the *abbreviation* rather than its meaning. Therefore, it is deliberate when there are several listings for Data Management, for example, under slightly different initialisms, all of which were encountered in one or another of the various sources used to compile this dictionary.

By Meaning Section

Terms are arranged alphabetically in word-by-word sequence according to the translation of the acronym, initialism, or abbreviation. If a particular translation has more than one initialism representing it, the various choices are then subarranged alphabetically, letter-by-letter, as they are in the *By Acronym* section.

Neither ampersands, articles, conjunctions, nor prepositions are considered in the alphabetizing; hyphenated terms are treated as separate words.

Material within brackets, such as categories or explanations, is not considered in alphabetizing. Material within parentheses *is* alphabetized, usually because it is considered to be an integral part of the term and important to the logical placement of the term.

Digits precede all alphabetic forms; entries in which the number is spelled out are filed alphabetically; Roman numerals are filed as letters.

For example:

Digital	D
Digital	DGTL
Digital	DI
Digital 3	D3
Digital Accession Document	DAD
Digital Hardware	DH
Digital II Control	DC
Digital in Isolation	DII
Digital & Magnetic	D & M
Digital to Output	DO
Digital Twelve Computer	DTC
Digitalization	D
Disk Monitor	DM
Disk Operating System	DOSY
Disk Operating System (Automatic)	DOS(A)
Disk Storage Unit	DSU
Disk Tape	DT
Disk [Storage] Utility	DSU
Display/Keyboard	d/K
Displayed Logic Unit	DLUN

List of Sources Cited

Unless further described in an annotation, the publications listed here contain no additional information about the acronym, initialism, or abbreviation cited in *Computer & Telecommunications Acronyms*.

Each of these sources contributed at least 50 terms. A number of other sources, contributing only a few terms each, have not been included.

(AFM) *Air Force Manual of Abbreviations*. Washington, D.C.: Department of the Air Force, 1975. [Use of source began in 1969]

(BUR) *Computer Acronyms and Abbreviations Handbook*. Tokyo: Burroughs Co. Ltd., 1978.

(CAA) *Computer Acronyms, Abbreviations, Etc.* By Claude P. Wrathall. New York: Petrocelli Books, Inc., 1981.
    Appendix.

(CAAL) *CAAL COMOPTEVFOR Acronym and Abbreviation List.* (CAAL) (U) Operational Test and Evaluation Force. Norfolk, Va.: 1981.

(CAH) *Computer Acronym Handbook.* By Donald D. Spencer. Englewood Cliffs, N.J.: Prentice-Hall, Inc., 1974.

(CBSS) *Abbreviations, Acronyms, and Symbols Common to Communication and Broadcast Satellite Systems.* 1st ed. Comp. by Communication and Broadcast Satellite Systems Committee of the IEEE Aerospace and Electronic Systems Society. New York: The Institute of Electrical and Electronics Engineers, Inc., 1977.

(CCD) *CAD/CAM Dictionary.* By Edward J. Preston, George W. Crawford, and Mark E. Coticchia. New York: Marcel Dekker, Inc., 1985.
    Includes over 500 general computer definitions and application-specific terminology.

(CDH) *Computer Dictionary and Handbook.* 3rd ed. By Charles J. Sippl. Slough, Buckinghamshire, England: W. Foulsham & Co. Ltd., 1980.

(CET) *Communications-Electronics Terminology.* AFM II-I. Vol. 3. Department of the Air Force, 1973.

(CGC) *Many Computer Acronyms for Defining Your Terms Easily.* New York: Computer Guidance Corp., 1971.

(CIT) *Abbreviations and Acronyms Guide.* Comp. by the Office of the Assistant Laboratory Director for Technical Divisions and the Technical Information and Documentation Division, Jet Propulsion Laboratory, California Institute of Technology, 1971.

(CMD) *Complete Multilingual Dictionary of Computer Terminology.* Comp. by Georges Nania. Chicago: National Textbook Co., 1984.
    Computer-related terms in Spanish, French, Italian, Portuguese, and English. Indexes in French, Italian, Spanish, and Portuguese are also provided.

(CSR) *Computer Science Resources.* A Guide to Professional Literature. Ed. by Darlene Myers. White Plains, N.Y.: Knowledge Industry Publications, Inc., 1981.
> Covers several types of computer-related literature including journals, technical reports, directories, dictionaries, handbooks, and university computer center newsletters. Five appendices cover career and salary trends in the computer industry, user group acronyms, university computer libraries, and trade fairs and shows.

(CUAD) *Directory of Online Databases.* Vol. 7, Number 3. New York: Cuadra/Elsevier, July, 1986.
> Entries include database name and address, producer, online service, subject area, and a brief description of database contents.

(DASO) *Data Sources.* Hardware-Data Communications/4th Quarter. Cherry Hill, N.J.: Ziff-Davis Publishing Co., 1984.
> A quarterly guide to available data processing/data communications equipment, software, and companies.

(DASOS) *Data Sources.* Software/4th Quarter. Cherry Hill, N.J.: Ziff-Davis Publishing Co., 1984.
> A quarterly guide to available data processing/data communications equipment, software, and companies.

(DDI) *Directory of Aerospace and Military and Technology Abbreviations.* "Dictionary of the Defense Industry." La Jolla, Calif.: U.S. Organization Chart Service, 1978.

(DEEC) *Dictionary of Electrical, Electronics and Computer Abbreviations.* By Phil Brown. Boston: Butterworths, 1985.
> Extensive definitions of each term are included.

(DEN) *Dictionary of Electronics and Nucleonics.* By L. E. C. Hughes, R. W. B. Stephens, and L. D. Brown. New York: Barnes & Noble, 1969.

(DIT) *Dictionary of Informatics Terms in Russian and English.* By G. S. Zhdanov, E. S. Kolobrodov, V. A. Polushkin, and A. I. Cherny. Moscow: Nauka, 1971.

(EANO) *Encyclopedia of Associations.* 21st ed. Ed. by Katherine Gruber. Vol. 1, *National Organizations of the U.S.* Detroit: Gale Research Co., 1986. [Use of source began in 1960]
> A guide to trade, professional, and other nonprofit associations that are national and international in scope and membership and that are headquartered in the United States. Entries include name and address, telephone and telex number, chief official, and a description of the purpose, activities, and structure of the organization.

(EISS) *Encyclopedia of Information Systems and Services.* 6th ed. Ed. by John Schmittroth, Jr. Detroit: Gale Research Co., 1985. [Use of source began in 1976]
> An international guide to computer-readable databases, database producers and publishers, online vendors and time-sharing companies, telecommunications networks, and many other information systems and services. Entries include name and address, telephone number, chief official, and a detailed description of the purpose and function of the system or service.

(FAAC) *Contractions Handbook.* Changes. Department of Transportation. Federal Aviation Administration, 1985. [Use of source began in 1969]

(FDB) *The Federal Data Base Finder.* A Directory of Free and Fee-Based Data Bases and Files Available from the Federal Government. By Sharon Zarozny and Monica Horner. Potomac, Md.: Information USA, Inc., 1984.
> Entries include name and address, telephone number, principal contact, database producer, and a description of the contents of each database.

(IBMDP)   *IBM Data Processing Glossary.* 6th ed. White Plains, N.Y.: IBM Corp., 1977.

(IDA)   *International Directory of Acronyms in Library, Information and Computer Sciences.* By Pauline M. Vaillancourt. New York: R. R. Bowker Co., 1980.
> Acronyms in nine subject areas, including associations, information sciences, publications, information centers, and commercial firms. The index provides access to entries by key words in the phrase.

(IEEE)   *IEEE Standard Dictionary of Electrical and Electronics Terms.* Ed. by Frank Jay. New York: The Institute of Electrical and Electronics Engineers, Inc., 1977, 1984.
> Includes definitions for thousands of electrical and electronics terms. Each entry includes a numeric source code.

(KSC)   *A Selective List of Acronyms and Abbreviations.* Comp. by the Documents Department, Kennedy Space Center Library, 1971, 1973.

(MCD)   *Acronyms, Abbreviations, and Initialisms.* Comp. by Carl Lauer. St. Louis: McDonnell Douglas Corp., 1982. [Use of source began in 1969]

(MDG)   *Microcomputer Dictionary and Guide.* By Charles J. Sippl. Champaign, Ill.: Matrix Publishers, Inc., 1975.
> A listing of definitions for over 5,000 microelectronics terms. Seven appendices.

(MSA)   *Military Standard Abbreviations for Use on Drawings, and in Specifications, Standards, and Technical Documents.* MIL-STD-12D. Department of Defense, 1981. [Use of source began in 1975]

(MUGU)   *The Mugu Book of Acronyms & Abbreviations.* Management Engineering Office, Pacific Missile Range, California, 1963, 1964.

(NASA)   *Glossary, Acronyms, Abbreviations.* Space Transportation System and Associated Payloads. Prep. by A. M. Koller, Jr. National Aeronautics and Space Administration, N.p., 1971.

(NATG)   *Glossary of Abbreviations Used in NATO Documents.* AAP 15 (B)., N.p., 1979. [Use of source began in 1976]

(NCC)   *NCC The National Centre for Information Technology.* Guide to Computer Aided Engineering, Manufacturing and Construction Software. Manchester, England: NCC Publications, The National Computing Centre Ltd., 1985.
> Includes software classifications and descriptions, names and addresses of suppliers, processor manufacturers, and operating systems.

(NG)   *NAVAIR Glossary of Unclassified Common-Use Abbreviated Titles and Phrases.* NAVAIRNOTE 5216 AIR-6031., N.p., July, 1969.

(NITA)   *Dictionary of New Information Technology Acronyms.* By M. Gordon, A. Singleton, and C. Rickards. London: Kogan Page Ltd., 1984; distributed in U.S. by Gale Research Co., Detroit.

(NQ)   *NASDAQ/CQS Symbol Directory.* New York: NASDAQ, Inc., 1983.

(NVT)   *Naval Terminology.* NWP3 (Rev. B). Department of the Navy. Office of the Chief of Naval Operations, 1978, 1980.
> Includes a section on definitions of naval terminology.

(OA)   *Ocran's Acronyms.* A Dictionary of Abbreviations and Acronyms Used in Scientific and Technical Writing. By Emanuel Benjamin Ocran. Boston: Routledge & Kegan Paul, 1978.

(OBD)   *Online Bibliographic Databases.* A Directory and Sourcebook. 3rd ed. By James L. Hall and Marjorie J. Brown. London: Aslib, 1983; distributed in U.S. by Gale Research Co., Detroit.

(ODIN) *ODIN Database Guide.* Heidelberg: Gesellschaft fuer Information und Dokumentation MBH (GID), 1981.
> Entries include database name, host database (one of four European DIANE networks), subject coverage, search aids, and size of each database.

(RCD) *Research Centers Directory.* 10th ed. Ed. by Mary Michelle Watkins. Detroit: Gale Research Co., 1985 (And first and second supplements, 1985).
> A guide to university-related and other nonprofit research organizations carrying on research in agriculture, astronomy and space sciences, behavioral and social sciences, computers and mathematics, engineering and technology, physical and earth sciences, and regional and area studies.

(RDA) *Army RD & A Magazine.* Alexandria, Va.: Development, Engineering, and Acquisition Directorate, Army Materiel Command, 1985. [Use of source began in 1979]

(SKY) *Skylab Astronyms.* Acronyms and Space Terms Used in Air-to-Ground Communication. Houston: Philco-Ford Corp. Aerospace and Defense Systems Operations WDL Division, Houston Operation., N.d.

(TEL) *Telephony's Dictionary.* 1st ed. By Graham Langley. Chicago: Telephony Publishing Corp., 1982.
> Includes definitions for over 14,000 U.S. and international terms. Ten appendices.

(TSSD) *Telecommunications Systems and Services Directory.* 2nd ed. Ed. by Martin Connors. Detroit: Gale Research Co., 1985.
> An international descriptive guide to approximately 2,000 telecommunications organizations, systems, and services. Entries include name and address, telephone number, chief official, and a description of the purposes, technical structure, and background of the service or system.

(TUT) *Acronyms.* 2nd ed. Ed. by John P. Tutunjian, N.p., 1971.

(VIT) *Glossary of Abbreviations.* Ballistic and Guided Missiles. Silver Spring, Md.: Vitro Laboratories, 1968.

Computer & Telecommunications Acronyms

By Acronym

A

A	....	Accessed BIT [*Binary Digit*] [*Data processing*]
A	....	Accumulator [*Data processing*] (MDG)
A	....	Address [*Computer character*] [*Data processing*]
A	....	Alphabetic
A	....	Ammeter (MDG)
A	....	Ampere [*Unit of electric current*] [*SI symbol*]
A	....	Amplitude [*Physics*]
A	....	Anaconda Co. [*NYSE symbol*] [*Delisted*]
A	....	Angstrom [*Also, AU*]
A	....	Anode [*Technical drawings*]
A	....	Area
a	....	Atto [*A prefix meaning divided by 10 to the 18th power*] [*SI symbol*]
AA	....	Absolute Address
AA	....	Advanced Analytical [*In company name, AA Computer Systems*] [*Tarzana, CA*] [*Software manufacturer*] (DASOS)
AA	....	Automatic Answer [*Telecommunications*] (TEL)
AAAI	....	American Association for Artificial Intelligence (EANO)
AAAS	....	American Academy of Arts and Sciences [*Boston, MA*]
AAAS	....	American Association for the Advancement of Science [*Washington, DC*]
AABP	....	Aptitude Assessment Battery Programing [*Data processing*] (IEEE)
AAC	....	Anacomp, Inc. [*NYSE symbol*]
AAC	....	Anglo-American Code [*Cataloging*] (DIT)
AAC	....	Automatic Amplitude Control (CET)
AACC	....	American Automatic Control Council [*Wickliffe, OH*]
AACC	....	Association of Agricultural Computer Companies (EANO)
AACP	....	American Association of Computer Professionals [*Stockbridge, GA*] (EANO)
AACS	....	Asynchronous Address Communications Systems (OA)
AAEDC	......	American Agricultural Economics Documentation Center [*Department of Agriculture*] [*Washington, DC*] (EISS)
AAHDS	......	American Association of Health Data Systems [*Ann Arbor, MI*] (EANO)
AAI	....	AUTODIN/AUTOVON Interface (CET)
AAL	....	Absolute Assembly Language [*Programing language*] (BUR)
AAL	....	Alexander & Alexander Services, Inc. [*NYSE symbol*]
AAME	....	American Association of Microprocessor Engineers (CAA)
AAMI	....	American Association of Microcomputer Investors (EANO)
AAMSI	....	American Association for Medical Systems and Informatics [*Bethesda, MD*] (EANO)
AAP	....	Analog Antenna Positioner
AAP	....	Associative Array Processor (MCD)
AAP	....	Attached Applications Processor (CAA)
AAPL	....	Apple Computer, Inc. [*NASDAQ symbol*] (NQ)
AAPL	....	[*An*] Array Processing Language [*Programing language*] (CAA)
AAPWISM	...	American Association of Public Welfare Information Systems Management (EANO)
A/AR	....	Aero/Acoustic Rotor (RDA)
AARS	....	Automatic Address Recognition System [*or Subsystem*] [*Data processing*] (CAA)
AAS	....	Advanced Accounting System (TUT)
AAS	....	Analog Alarm Section
AAS	....	Arithmetic Assignment Statement
AAS	....	Automated Accounting System (BUR)
AAS	....	Automatic Addressing System [*Data processing*]
AAS	....	Automatic Announcement Subsystem [*Telecommunications*] (TEL)
AAT	....	Automatic Antenna Timer
AATC	....	Automatic Air Traffic Control [*System*] (IEEE)
AAU	....	Address Arithmetic Unit [*Data processing*] (CAA)
AAU/BNA	...	Association of Atlantic Universities/Blackwell North America [*Project*] [*Lake Oswego, OR*] [*Information service*] (EISS)
AAVD	....	Automatic Alternate Voice/Data [*Data processing*]
AB	....	Abstract [*Online database field identifier*]
AB	....	Abstracting Board [*International Council of Scientific Unions*] [*Information service*] (EISS)
AB	....	Address Bus [*Data processing*]
AB	....	All [*Text*] Before [*Specified Point*] [*Message handling*]
AB	....	Automated Bibliography (DEEC)
ABACUS	.....	Aktiebolaget Atomenergi Computer-Based User-Oriented Service
ABBS	....	Apple Bulletin Board System [*Pronounced "abbies"*]
ABC	....	Adaptable Board Computer [*Signetics*] (CAA)
ABC	....	Alpha Block Control Number [*Data processing*]
ABC	....	American Broadcasting Companies, Inc. [*New York, NY*] [*NYSE symbol*]
ABC	....	Answer-Back Code [*Telecommunications*] (TEL)
ABC	....	Apparel Business Control [*System*] [*Data processing*]
ABC	....	Applied Business Telecommunications [*San Ramon, CA*] [*Information service*] [*Telecommunications*] (TSSD)
ABC	....	Approach by Concept [*Information retrieval*]
ABC	....	Atanasoff-Berry Computer [*Early computer*]
ABC	....	Australian Business Computer [*A publication*]
ABC	....	Automatic Bass Compensation [*Radio*]
ABC	....	Automatic Bass Control
ABC	....	Automatic Bill Calling [*Later, MCCS*] [*Telecommunications*]
ABC	....	Automatic Binary Computer
ABC	....	Automatic Brightness Control [*Telecommunications*] (TEL)
ABC	....	Automation of Bibliography through Computerization [*ABC-Clio Press*]
ABCD	....	Add BCD [*Binary Coded Decimal*] Number with Extend [*Data processing*]
ABCD	....	Association of Better Computer Dealers [*Lexington, KY*] (EANO)
ABCI	....	Advanced Business Communications, Incorporated [*McLean, VA*] [*Telecommunications*] (TSSD)
ABCI	....	Airport Business Center, Incorporated [*Minneapolis, MN*] [*Telecommunications*] (TSSD)
ABCS	....	Automatic Broadcasting Control System [*Japan*]
ABCST	....	Automatic Broadcast (FAAC)
ABD	....	Access Block Diagram
ABD	....	Average Business Day [*Bell System*]
ABDA	....	Arbeitsgemeinschaft der Berufsvertretungen Deutscher Apotheker [*Information retrieval*] (ODIN)
ABDL	....	Automatic Binary Data Link [*Data processing*] (CET)
ABE	....	Arithmetic Building Element [*Data processing*] (CAA)
ABEND	....	Abnormal End [*Data processing*]
ABERT	....	Automatic BIT [*Binary Digit*] Error Rate Test [*Data processing*] (MCD)
ABES	....	Aerospace Business Environment Simulator [*Computer-programed management game*]
ABI	....	Abstracted Business Information [*Data Courier, Inc.*]
ABI	....	American Bell, Incorporated
ABI	....	Audit Bureau of Circulations [*Database producer*]
ABIR	....	All-Band Intercept Receiver
ABL	....	Adaption Binary Load [*Program*] (CET)
ABL	....	All Busy Low [*AT & T*]
ABL	....	Architectural Block Diagram Language (CAA)
ABL	....	Atlas Basic Language [*Data processing*] (CGC)
ABL	....	Automatic Bootstrap Loader [*Data processing*] (CAA)
ABLE	....	[*A*] programing language [*1966*] (CSR)
ABM	....	Acquisition Bus Monitor [*Data processing*] (MCD)
ABM	....	Asynchronous Balanced Mode (CCD)
ABM	....	Automated Batch Mixing [*Data processing*]
ABN	....	Associated Broadcast News [*Cable-television system*]
ABN	....	Australian Bibliographic Network [*National Library of Australia*] [*Canberra, Australia*] [*Information service*] (EISS)
ABOL	....	Adviser Business Oriented Language [*Programing language*] (CAA)
ABOS	....	Advanced Banking On-Line System (BUR)
ABP	....	Actual Block Processor [*IBM Corp.*] [*Data processing*] (BUR)
ABP	....	Advanced Business Processor [*Datapoint Corp.*] (CAA)
ABR	....	Active Business Records [*Bell & Howell Co.*]
ABR	....	Automatic Band Rate (IEEE)
ABS	....	Absolute [*Flowchart*]
ABSBH	....	Average Busy Season Busy Hour [*Telecommunications*] (TEL)
ABSC	....	Automatic Bass Compensation [*Radio*] (MSA)
Abstr Comput Lit	...	Abstracts of Computer Literature [*A publication*]
ABT	....	Applied Business Technology Corp.
ABT	....	Brazilian Association of Tele-Education
ABTD	....	Automatic Bulk Tape Degausser
ABU	....	Asia Pacific Broadcasting Union [*Kuala Lumpur, Malaysia*] [*Telecommunications*] (EANO)
ABV	....	Absolute Value (BUR)
ABWC	....	Automatic Bandwidth Control (MSA)

Acronym	Expansion
AC	Access [*Telecommunications*] (TEL)
AC	Accumulator [*Data processing*]
AC	Acoustic Coupler [*Computer MODEM*]
AC	Advice of Charge [*Telecommunications*] (TEL)
A-C	Allied Corporation [*Initialism is trademark*]
AC	Alternate Call Listing [*Telecommunications*] (TEL)
AC	Alternating Current
AC	Analog Computer
AC	Answer Complete [*Telecommunications*] (TEL)
AC	Automatic Checkout (BUR)
AC	Automatic Computer
AC	Awaiting Connection [*Telecommunications*] (TEL)
ACA	Agricultural Computer Association [*Elk Grove, CA*] (EANO)
ACA	American Communications Association
ACA	Automatic Circuit Analyzer
ACA	Automatic Conference Arranger (CET)
ACAD	Alarm Communications and Display System (MCD)
ACADE	Association for Computer Art and Design Education (EANO)
ACADS	Alarm Communications and Display Segment (MCD)
ACAF	Automatic Circuit Assurance Feature (CET)
ACAM	Augmented Content-Addressed Memory (CAA)
ACAP	Advanced Computer for Array Processing
ACAP	Automatic Circuit Analysis Program
ACARS	ARINC Communication Addressing Reporting System (IEEE)
ACAS	AUTOVON Centralized Alarm System
ACB	Access Method Control Block [*Data processing*] (BUR)
ACB	Adapter Control Block [*Data processing*] (IBMDP)
ACB	Annoyance Call Bureau [*Telephone-pest control*]
ACB	Australian Computer Bulletin [*A publication*]
ACBCT	Automatic Circuit Board Card Tester
ACBT	Automatic Circuit Board Tester
ACC	Academic Computation Center [*Georgetown University*] [*Research center*] (RCD)
ACC	Academic Computer Center [*University of Washington*] [*Research center*] (RCD)
ACC	Academic Computing Center [*University of Vermont*] [*Research center*] (RCD)
ACC	Academic Computing Center [*University of California, Riverside*] [*Research center*] (RCD)
ACC	Accumulator [*Flowchart*] (MSA)
ACC	Advanced Computer Communications [*Santa Barbara, CA*] [*Hardware manufacturer*] (DASO)
ACC	Alternating Current Circuit
ACC	Antenna Control Console
ACC	Argonne Code Center [*Department of Energy*] (EISS)
ACC	Asynchronous Communications Control (CAA)
ACC	Automatic Carrier Control [*Telecommunications*] (TEL)
ACC	Automatic Control Console (NASA)
ACCA	Asynchronous Communications Control Attachment (OA)
ACCAP	Autocoder to COBOL Conversion Aid Program [*IBM Corp.*] [*Data processing*]
ACCEL	Automated Circuit Card Etching Layout [*Data processing*]
ACCESS	Automated Computer Controlled Editing Sound System
ACCESS	Automated Control and Checking of Electrical Systems Support (MCD)
ACCESS	Automatic Card Control Entrance Security System [*Data processing*] (TUT)
ACCESS	Automatic Computer-Controlled Electronic Scanning System [*National Bureau of Standards*]
ACCESS	[A] Complete Computerized Examination System [*Anatomy and physiology*]
ACCIS	Advisory Committee for the Co-Ordination of Information Systems [*Database producer*] (CUAD)
ACCOMP	Academic Computing Group
ACCS	Advanced Communications Control System (CAAL)
ACCS	Automated Circulation Control System [*Library management*]
ACCS	Automatic Checkout and Control System
ACCT	Account [*or Accountant*] (AFM)
ACCT	American Council for Competitive Telecommunications [*Formerly, Ad Hoc Committee for Competitive Telecommunications*] [*Washington, DC*] (EANO)
ACCTID	Account Identifier [*Data processing*]
ACD	Allied Corporation [*Toronto Stock Exchange symbol*]
ACD	Alternating Current Dump
ACD	Antenna Control Display
ACD	Associative Computer Device
ACD	Automatic Call Distribution [*Switching system*] [*Telecommunications*]
ACD	Automatic Contour Digitizer
ACDB	International Airport Characteristics Data Bank [*International Civil Aviation Organization*] [*Information service*] (EISS)
A-C/D-C	Alternating Current/Direct Current
ACD-ESS	Automatic Call Distributor - Electronic Switching System [*Telecommunications*] (TEL)
ACDMS	Automated Control of a Document Management System [*Data processing*] (DIT)
ACDP	Antenna Control and Display Panel (MCD)
ACDP	Association of Compact Disk Publishers (EANO)
ACDS	Advanced Command Data System (NG)
ACDS	Automatic Comprehensive Display System [*Data processing*]
ACE	Advanced Compilation Equipment (MCD)
ACE	Animated Computer Education (CGC)
ACE	Automatic Calling Equipment [*Telecommunications*] (BUR)
ACE	Automatic Checkout Equipment
ACE	Automatic Circuit Exchange
ACE	Automatic Computer Evaluation (BUR)
ACE	Automatic Computing Engine [*Early computer*] [*National Physical Laboratory*]
ACED	Advanced Communications Equipment Depot (NATG)
ACES	Automated Code Evaluation System (CAA)
ACES	Automatic Checkout Equipment Sequencer (NASA)
ACESS	Advanced Computer Environmental Systems Support, Inc. [*Silver Spring, MD*] [*Hardware manufacturer*] (DASO)
ACET	Association Canadienne des Entreprises de Telecommunications [*Canadian Association of Telecommunication Businesses*]
ACF	Academic Computer Facility [*Roosevelt University*] [*Research center*] (RCD)
ACF	Access Control Facility
ACF	Advanced Communications Function [*IBM Corp.*] [*Data processing*]
ACF	Analog Computer Facility (CIT)
ACF	Area Computing Facilities (CET)
ACFG	Automatic Continuous Function Generation [*Data processing*]
ACG	Address Coding Guide
ACG	Adjacent Charging Group [*Telecommunications*] (TEL)
ACG	Automatic Code Generator (CAA)
ACH	Association for Computers and the Humanities [*University of Minnesota*] [*Minneapolis, MN*] (EANO)
ACH	Attempts per Circuit per Hour [*Telecommunications*] (TEL)
ACH	Automated Clearinghouse [*Banking*]
ACHPIRST	Australian Clearing House for Publications in Recreation Sport and Tourism [*Information service*] (EISS)
ACHS	Automatic Checkout System
ACHV	Archive Corp. [*NASDAQ symbol*] (NQ)
ACI	Adjacent Channel Interference
ACI	Amplifier-Control Intercommunications (MCD)
ACI	Arlen Communications, Incorporated [*Bethesda, MD*] [*Information service*] [*Telecommunications*] (TSSD)
ACI	Association Canadienne de l'Informatique [*Canadian Information Processing Society - CIPS*]
ACIA	Asynchronous Communications Interface Adapter [*Data processing*] (MDG)
ACID	Automatic Classification and Interpretation of Data (BUR)
ACIM	Auxiliary Computer Input Multiplexer (SKY)
ACIP	Active Certificate Information Program [*for stock certificates*] [*Data processing*]
ACIS	Avionics, Control, and Information Systems (MCD)
ACK	Acknowledgment Character [*Keyboard*] [*Data processing*]
ACK0	Even Positive Acknowledgment [*Data processing*] (IBMDP)
ACK1	Odd Positive Acknowledgment [*Data processing*] (IBMDP)
ACKTX	Automatic Circuit Exchange (MSA)
ACL	Application Control Language [*Data processing*] (BUR)
ACL	Association for Computational Linguistics [*Bell Communications Research*] [*Morristown, NJ*]
ACL	Atlas Commercial Language [*Data processing*] (BUR)
ACL	Audit Command Language (IDA)
ACM	Advanced Circuit Module
ACM	Alarm Control Module [*Telecommunications*] (TEL)
ACM	Alterable Control Memory (CAA)
ACM	Association for Computing Machinery [*New York, NY*]
ACM	Associative Communication Multiplexer (OA)
ACM	Auxiliary Core Memory [*Data processing*] (MCD)
ACMAC	ACM [*Association for Computing Machinery*] Accreditation Committee (CAH)
ACME	Advanced Computer for Medical Research [*Stanford University*]
ACME	Antenna Contour Measuring Equipment
ACM-GAMM	Association for Computing Machinery - German Association for Applied Mathematics and Mechanics [*Frankfurt/Main, Germany*]
ACMIC	Application of Computer Methods in the Mineral Industry. Proceedings of the International Symposium [*A publication*]
ACM Proc	ACM [*Association for Computing Machinery*] National Conference Proceedings [*A publication*]
ACMRU	Audio Commercial Message Repeating Unit [*Device delivering a recorded commercial from cigarette vending machines*]
ACMSC	ACM [*Association for Computing Machinery*] Standards Committee (CAH)
ACM Trans Database Syst	ACM [*Association for Computing Machinery*] Transactions on Database Systems [*A publication*]
ACM Trans Database Systems	ACM [*Association for Computing Machinery*] Transactions on Database Systems [*A publication*]
ACM Trans Math Softw	ACM [*Association for Computing Machinery*] Transactions on Mathematical Software [*A publication*]
ACM Trans Math Software	ACM [*Association for Computing Machinery*] Transactions on Mathematical Software [*A publication*]
ACM Trans Off Inf Syst	ACM [*Association for Computing Machinery*] Transactions on Office Information Systems [*A publication*]
ACN	Accession Number [*Online database field identifier*] (OBD)
ACO	Automatic Call Origination [*Telecommunications*] (CAA)
ACOB	ASCII COBOL [*Data processing*]
ACOC	Area Communications Operations Center [*Telecommunications*] (TEL)
ACODAC	Acoustic Data Capsule
ACOE	Automatic Checkout Equipment

Computer & Telecommunications Acronyms

ACOLI......... Advance Circuit Order and Layout Information [*Telecommunications*] (TEL)
ACOM......... Astrocom Corp. [*NASDAQ symbol*] (NQ)
ACOM......... Automatic Coding Machine [*Data processing*] (CET)
ACOMPLINE ... [A] Computerised London Information System Online [*Greater London Council Research Library*] [*Bibliographic database*] [*British*] (OBD)
ACOMPLIS ... [A] Computerised London Information Service [*Greater London Council Research Library*] [*British*] (DEEC)
ACOPP....... Abbreviated COBOL Preprocessor [*Data processing*] (IEEE)
ACORN....... Associative Content Retrieval Network [*A. D. Little, Inc.*] [*Information service*] (IDA)
ACORN....... Automated Coder of Report Narrative [*Data processing*] (DIT)
ACORN....... Automatic Checkout and Recording Equipment
ACOS......... Advanced Computer Oriented System (BUR)
ACOS......... Automatic Checkout Set
ACOS......... [A] Computer Series [*Nippon Electric Company*] [*Japan*] (CAA)
A & CP....... Access and Control Point [*Telecommunications*] (TEL)
ACP .... Advanced Computational Processor
ACP .... Analytical Computer Program
ACP .... Ancillary Control Processor (CAA)
ACP .... Arithmetic and Control Processor (CAA)
ACP .... Associate Client Program [*Business International Corp.*] [*Information service*] (EISS)
ACP .... Association of Computer Professionals [*New York, NY*] (EANO)
ACP .... Automated Chemistry Program [*Data processing*]
ACP .... Automated Communications Publications
ACPA......... Association of Computer Programmers and Analysts [*Kensington, MD*] (EANO)
ACPIC........ American Council for Private International Communications, Inc. [*Proposed corporation to replace Radio Free Europe*]
ACPU......... Auxiliary Computer Power Unit
ACQE......... Acquisition and Control Query Executive [*Programing language*] (DDI)
ACR .... Abandon Call and Retry [*Telecommunications*]
ACR .... Access Control Register (CAA)
ACR .... Alternate CPU [*Central Processing Unit*] Recovery [*IBM Corp.*] [*Data processing*] (BUR)
AC & R....... American Cable & Radio Corp.
ACR .... Antenna Coupler Receiver (MCD)
ACR .... Antenna Coupling Regulator (IEEE)
ACR .... Applied Communication Research, Inc. [*Information service*] (EISS)
ACR .... Applied Computer Research [*Phoenix, AZ*] [*Information service*] (EISS)
ACR .... Association of Computer Retailers (EANO)
ACR .... Audio Cassette Recorder (RDA)
ACR .... Automatic Call Recording [*Telecommunications*] (CMD)
ACRA......... Accuray Corp. [*NASDAQ symbol*] (NQ)
ACRE......... Automatic Checkout and Readiness Equipment
ACRODABA ... Acronym Data Base
ACRT......... Applied Circuit Technology [*Anaheim, CA*] [*Hardware manufacturer*] (DASO)
ACRV......... Audio Center - Receiver (KSC)
ACS .... Academic Computer Service [*Miami University*] [*Research center*] (RCD)
ACS .... Academic Computer Services [*Northeastern University*] [*Research center*] (RCD)
ACS .... Academic Computer Services [*University of Calgary*] [*Research center*] (RCD)
ACS .... Academic Computer Services [*Michigan Technological University*] [*Research center*] (RCD)
ACS .... Academic Computing Services [*Syracuse University*] [*Research center*] (RCD)
ACS .... Academic Computing Services [*University of Colorado - Boulder*] [*Research center*] (RCD)
ACS .... Academic Computing Services [*University of Wisconsin - Eau Claire*] [*Research center*] (RCD)
ACS .... Access [*Telecommunications*] (MSA)
ACS .... Accounting Control System (TUT)
ACS .... Accumulator Switch [*Data processing*]
ACS .... Adaptive Control System
ACS .... Administrative Computing Service (CIT)
ACS .... Administrative Control System [*Telecommunications*] (TEL)
ACS .... Advance Count Switch
ACS .... Advanced Communications Service [*Later, AIS*] [*AT & T*]
ACS .... Advanced Computer Services [*Honeywell Information Systems*] (IEEE)
ACS .... Advanced Computer System [*IBM Corp.*] (IEEE)
ACS .... Affiliated Computer Systems [*Dallas, TX*] [*Telecommunications*] (TSSD)
ACS .... Alarm and Control System [*Telecommunications*] (TEL)
ACS .... American Cable Supply Corp. [*Fort Lauderdale, FL*] [*Hardware manufacturer*] (DASO)
ACS .... American Communication Services [*Evanston, IL*] [*Telecommunications*] (TSSD)
ACS .... Analog Computer System
ACS .... Analysis Computer System (CIT)
ACS .... Anisotropically Conductive Silicone [*Rubber*]
ACS .... Applied Color Systems, Inc. [*Princeton, NJ*] [*Software manufacturer*] (DASOS)
ACS .... Assembly Control System [*IBM Corp.*] (BUR)
ACS .... Attitude Command System (IEEE)
ACS .... Attitude Control System [*Telecommunications*] (TEL)
ACS .... Audio Communications System
ACS .... Australian Computer Society (CAA)
ACS .... Automated Circulation System [*Data processing*]
ACS .... Automated Communications Set (BUR)
ACS .... Automatic Control System
ACS .... Automatic Counter System
ACS .... Auxiliary Core Storage [*Data processing*] (BUR)
ACSAP....... Automated Cross-Section Analysis Program [*Data processing*]
ACSB......... Amplitude Companded Single Sideband [*Electronics*]
ACSC......... Applied Communications Systems Center [*AT & T*]
ACSD......... Academic Computer Services Division [*Milwaukee School of Engineering*] [*Research center*] (RCD)
ACSD......... Automatic Color-Scanned Device (MCD)
ACSED....... Automated Computer Science Education
ACSES....... Automated Computer Science Education System (IDA)
ACSL......... Advanced Continuous Simulation Language [*Pronounced "axle"*] [*Data processing*] (CSR)
ACSN......... Appalachian Community Service Network [*Cable-television system*]
ACSR......... Aluminum Cable Steel Reinforced
ACSR......... Aluminum Conductor Steel Reinforced
ACSS......... Analog Computer Subsystem
ACSTI....... Advisory Committee for Scientific and Technical Information [*British*] (DIT)
ACSYS....... Accounting Computer System [*Burroughs Corp.*] (CAA)
ACT .... Accounting Control Table (CMD)
ACT .... Actuarial Data Base [*I. P. Sharp Associates*] [*Database*] (CUAD)
ACT .... Adaptive Computer Technologies
ACT .... Adaptive Control of Thought [*Computer simulation program*]
ACT .... Advanced Color Technology, Inc. [*Chelmsford, MA*] [*Printer manufacturer*]
ACT .... Advanced Communications Technology [*Tymshare, Inc.*] (CAA)
ACT .... Advertised Computer Technologies [*Data Courier, Inc.*] [*Database*] [*Information service*] (EISS)
ACT .... Algebraic Compiler and Translator [*Data processing*]
ACT .... Antenna Cross Talk
ACT .... Asset Control Techniques
ACT .... Auto-Lock Channel Tuning [*Television technology*]
ACT .... Automated Contingency Translator [*Data processing*]
ACT .... Automatic Cable Tester
ACT .... Automatic Channel and Time [*Toshiba Corp.*] [*Programable television set*]
ACT .... Automatic Circuit Tester
ACT .... Automatic Code Translation [*Data processing*]
ACTA......... Automatic Computerized Transverse Axial [*Computer X-ray system*]
Acta Polytech Scand Math Comput Mach Ser ... Acta Polytechnica Scandinavica. Mathematics and Computing Machinery Series [*Finland*] [*A publication*]
Acta Polytech Scand Math and Comput Mach Ser ... Acta Polytechnica Scandinavica. Mathematics and Computing Machinery Series [*A publication*]
Acta Polytech Scand Math Comput Sci Ser ... Acta Polytechnica Scandinavica. Mathematics and Computer Science Series [*A publication*]
ACTE......... Automatic Checkout Test Equipment
ACTM........ Audio Center - Transmitter (KSC)
ACTO........ Automatic Computing Transfer Oscillator (IEEE)
ACTP......... Advanced Computer Techniques Corp. [*NASDAQ symbol*] (NQ)
ACTP......... Advanced Computer Techniques Project (KSC)
ACTRAN..... Analog Computer Translator
ACTRAN..... Autocoder-to-COBOL Translating Service [*Data processing*] (IEEE)
ACTS......... Acoustic Control and Telemetry System
ACTS......... American Christian Television [*Cable-television system*]
ACTS......... Analog Conditioning and Test System (CIT)
ACTS......... Automated Custom Terminal System
ACTS......... Automatic Coin Telephone Service
ACTS......... Automatic Computer Telex Services
ACTSU....... Association of Computer Time-Sharing Users (CAA)
ACU .... Acknowledgement Unit [*Telecommunications*] (TEL)
ACU .... Address Control Unit [*Data processing*] (MDG)
ACU .... Alarm Control Unit [*Bell System*] [*Telecommunications*]
ACU .... Antenna Control Unit
ACU .... Arithmetic Computer (VIT)
ACU .... Arithmetic and Control Unit (BUR)
ACU .... Association of Computer Users [*Formerly, ATSU, ASCU*] [*Boulder, CO*] (EANO)
ACU .... Automatic Calling Unit [*Telecommunications*] (TEL)
ACUI......... Automatic Calling Unit Interface [*Telecommunications*] (IEEE)
ACUTA....... Association of College and University Telecommunications Administrators [*Madison, WI*] (EANO)
ACUTE....... Accountants Computer Users Technical Exchange [*Indianapolis, IN*]
ACVP........ Additive Color Viewer Printer
ACW .... Alternating Continuous Waves [*Radio*]
ACWS........ All-Canada Weekly Summaries [*Canada Law Book Ltd.*] [*Database*]
A-to-D....... Analog-to-Digital [*Converter*] [*Data processing*]
AD .... Analog-to-Digital [*Converter*] [*Data processing*] (AFM)
AD .... Assignment Date [*Telecommunications*] (TEL)
AD .... Attendant [*Telecommunications*] (TEL)

Computer & Telecommunications Acronyms

AD	Attention Display [*Communications device*]
AD	Automatic Depositor [*Banking*] (BUR)
AD	Automatic Display [*Data processing*]
AD	Awaiting Disconnection [*Telecommunications*] (TEL)
ADA	Action Data Automation [*British*] (NATG)
ADA	After Date of Award of Contract [*Telecommunications*] (TEL)
ADA	Automatic Data Acquisition
ADA	Automatic Document Analysis (DIT)
ADA	[*A*] programing language [*1979*] [*Named after Ada Augusta Byron, 1815-52, who wrote coded instructions for Charles Babbage's mechanical calculators and is considered the first computer programer*] (CSR)
ADABAS	Adaptable Data Base System [*Database management system*]
ADAC	Acoustic Data Analysis Center
ADAC	Automatic Direct Analog Computer (BUR)
ADAIS	Aerodynamic Data Analysis and Integration System [*Data processing*]
ADAM	Adaptive Arithmetical Method
ADAM	Advanced Data Management [*Kingston, NJ*]
ADAM	Analog Data Acquisition Module
ADAM	Assocometrics Data Management System (IEEE)
ADAPS	Automatic Display and Plotting System (BUR)
ADAPSO	Association of Data Processing Service Organizations [*Also, ADPSO*] [*Includes American and Canadian companies*] [*Arlington, VA*]
ADAPT	Adoption of Automatically Programed Tools [*Data processing*] (IEEE)
ADAPT	Analog-Digital Automatic Program Tester [*Data processing*]
ADAPT	Automated Data Analysis and Presentation Techniques (MCD)
ADAR	Analog Data Reduction System (CAAL)
ADAS	Automated Data Acquisition System [*GCA Corp.*]
ADAS	Auxiliary Data Annotation Set [*or System*]
ADASP	Automatic Data and Select Program (KSC)
ADAT	Automatic Data Accumulation and Transfer
ADATE	Automatic Digital Assembly Test Equipment (MCD)
ADBMS	Available Database Management System (OA)
ADBS	Advanced Database System (CAA)
ADC	Address Complete, Charge [*Telecommunications*] (TEL)
AD and C	Advise Duration and Charge [*British telephone term*]
ADC	Air Data Computers [*or Computing*] (MCD)
ADC	Air Data Converter
ADC	Analog-to-Digital Converter [*Data processing*] (MUGU)
ADC	Antenna Dish Control
ADC	Assistive Device Center [*California State University, Sacramento*] [*Research center*] (RCD)
ADC	Automatic Digital Calculator [*Data processing*]
ADCC	Applied Data Communications [*NASDAQ symbol*] (NQ)
ADCC	Asynchronous Data Communications Channel (CAA)
ADCCP	Advanced Data Communications Control Procedure [*American National Standards Institute*]
ADCIS	Association for Development of Computer-Based Instructional Systems [*Formerly, ADIS*] [*Western Washington State College*] [*Bellingham, WA*] (EANO)
ADCON	Address Constant [*Data processing*]
ADCON	Analog-to-Digital Converter [*Data processing*]
ADCS	Air Data Computing System
ADCS	AUTODIN Coordination Station (CET)
ADCS	Automated Document Control System [*Data processing*] (MCD)
ADCS	Automatic Data Collection System (RDA)
ADCSPC	Air Data Computer Static Pressure Compensator (MCD)
ADCU	Alarm Display and Control Unit [*Telecommunications*] (TEL)
ADCU	Association of Data Communications Users [*Bloomington, MN*] [*Telecommunications*] (EANO)
ADD	Acoustic Deception Device (CAAL)
ADD	Acoustic Detection Device (MCD)
ADD	Addendum (KSC)
ADD	Addition
ADD	Analog Data Digitizer
ADD	Analog-Digital-Designer [*Trademark*]
ADD	Automatic Data Descriptor
ADD	Automatic Drawing Device (DIT)
AD/DA	Analog Digital/Digital Analog (RDA)
ADDAC	Analog Data Distributor and Control [*Data processing*] (KSC)
ADDAR	Automatic Digital Data Acquisition and Recording [*Data processing*]
ADDAS	Automatic Digital Data Assembly System [*Data processing*] (DDI)
ADDC	Addmaster Corporation [*NASDAQ symbol*] (NQ)
ADDDS	Automatic Direct-Distance Dialing System [*Telecommunications*] (IEEE)
ADDER	Automatic Digital-Data-Error Recorder [*Data processing*]
Addison-Wesley Ser Comput Sci Inform Process	Addison-Wesley Series in Computer Science and Information Processing [*A publication*]
ADDL	Additional (KSC)
ADDL	Anti-Digit Dialing League
ADDM	Automated Drafting and Digitizing Machine [*Data packaging*] (RDA)
ADDR	Adder [*Computer device*]
ADDR	Address [*Computer character*] [*Data processing*]
ADDRESOR	Analog-to-Digital Data Reduction System for Oceanographic Research
ADDS	Applied Digital Data Systems, Inc. [*NASDAQ symbol*]
ADDS	Automated Digital Design System [*Raytheon Co.*]
ADDT	All-Digital Data Tape (KSC)
ADDT	Angular Distribution Data Tape
ADE	Advanced Data Entry (CAA)
ADE	Approved Data Element (AFM)
ADE	Audible Doppler Enhancer [*Telecommunications*] (TEL)
ADE	Automated Data Exchange [*Berkeley, CA*] [*Software manufacturer*] (DASOS)
ADE	Automated Debugging Environment [*Applied Data Research, Inc.*] (CAA)
ADE	Automated Design Engineering [*Telecommunications*] (TEL)
ADE	Automatic Data Evaluation
ADEC	Aiken Dahlgren Electronic Calculator
ADEM	Automatic Data Equalized Modem
ADEPT	Automated Direct Entry Packaging Technique (OA)
ADEPT	Automatic Data Extractor and Plotting Table
ADEPT	Automatic Dynamic Evaluation by Programed Test
ADER	Automatic Data Extraction Routine (CAAL)
ADES	Automatic Digital Encoding System [*Data processing*]
ADEU	Automatic Data Entry Unit
ADF	Application Development Facility [*IBM Corp.*] [*Data processing*]
ADF	Automatic Display Finder [*Data processing*] (NASA)
ADFS	Automatic Direction Finding System
ADGE	Adage, Inc. [*NASDAQ symbol*] (NQ)
ADH	Automatic Data Handling [*Data processing*]
ADHS	Analog Data Handling System
ADI	Address Incomplete [*Telecommunications*] (TEL)
AD/I	Air Density/Injun [*Explorer satellite*]
ADI	Alternating Direction Implicit [*Algorithm*]
ADI	American Documentation Institute [*Later, American Society for Information Science*]
ADI	Area of Dominant Influence [*Telecommunications*]
ADIC	Analog-to-Digital Conversion System [*Data processing*]
ADIE	Acquisition Data Input Equipment
ADIGE	Archive of Italian Data of Geology [*Center for Stratigraphy and Petrology of the Central Alps*] [*Database*] (CUAD)
ADIOS	Analog-Digital Input/Output System [*Data processing*] (CAA)
ADIOS	Automatic Diagnostic Input/Output System [*Data processing*] (CAA)
ADIOS	Automatic Digital Input/Output System [*Data processing*]
ADIS	Association for Development of Instructional Systems [*Later, ADCIS*] [*Western Washington University*] [*Bellingham, WA*] (BUR)
ADIS	Automatic Data Interchange System [*International Civil Aviation Organization*]
ADIT	Analog-Digital Integrating Translator [*Data processing*]
ADJ	Angle Deception Jamming
ADJMOM	Adjoint Gamma-Ray Moments [*Computer code*]
ADJS	Angle Deception Jamming System
ADL	Antenna Dummy Load
ADL	Architecture Description Language [*Data processing*] (CSR)
ADL	Arthur D. Little, Inc. [*Cambridge, MA*] [*Research code symbol*]
ADL	Automatic Data Link [*Data processing*]
ADLC	Advanced Data Link Control [*Data processing*] (CAA)
ADLIB	[*A*] Design Language for Indicating Behavior [*1967*] [*Data processing*] (CSR)
ADM	Acoustic Digital Memory
ADM	Activity Data Method (IEEE)
ADM	Adaptable Data Manager [*Hitachi Ltd.*] [*Japan*] (CAA)
ADM	Asynchronous Disconnected Mode (CCD)
ADM	Automatic Display Mode [*Data processing*] (BUR)
ADM	Automatic Distribution of Microfiche
ADMA	Automatic Drafting Machine (DIT)
ADMD	Adjust Mode [*Data processing*]
ADMIN	Administration [*or Administrator*]
ADMIRAL	Automatic and Dynamic Monitor with Immediate Relocation, Allocation, and Loading (IEEE)
ADMIRE	Automatic Diagnostic Maintenance Information Retrieval [*Data processing*] (MCD)
ADMIS	Automated Data Management Information System
ADML	Advanced Design Methods Laboratory [*Ohio State University*] [*Research center*] (RCD)
ADMLP	ASCII COBOL Data Manipulation Language-Preprocessor [*Data processing*]
ADMS	Analog and Digital Monitoring System [*Data processing*] (MCD)
ADMS	Asynchronous Data Multiplexer Synchronizer
ADMS	Automatic Digital Message Switching
ADMSC	Automatic Digital Message Switching Center [*AUTODIN*]
ADN	Address Complete, No-Charge [*Telecommunications*] (TEL)
ADOIT	Automatically Directed Outgoing Intertoll Trunk [*Bell System*]
ADONIS	Automatic Digital On-Line Instrumentation System
ADOS	Advanced Diskette Operating System (CAA)
ADOT	Automatically Directed Outgoing Trunk [*Bell System*]
ADP	Acceptance Data Package (KSC)
ADP	Accountability Data Package (MCD)
ADP	Acoustic Data Processor (MCD)
ADP	Administrative Data Processing (KSC)
ADP	Air Data Package
ADP	Air Data Probe (MCD)
ADP	Association of Database Producers [*Oxford, England*] (EISS)
ADP	Automatic Data Plotter
ADP	Automatic Data Processing

Computer & Telecommunications Acronyms

ADP............ Automatic Data Processing, Inc. [*Trademark for data processing services*]
ADPA......... Accounting and Data Processing Abstracts [*A publication*]
ADPBCT..... Automatic Data Processing Budget Control Totals   (DDI)
ADPC......... Automatic Data Processing Center
ADPCM...... Adaptive Differential Pulse Code Modulation   (MCD)
ADPE......... Automatic Data Processing Engineering   (DDI)
ADPE......... Automatic Data Processing Equipment
ADPE......... Auxiliary Data Processing Equipment
ADPEP....... Automated Data Preparation by Electronic Photocomposition   (MCD)
ADPEP...... Automated Data Preparation Evaluation Program   (MCD)
ADPES....... Automatic Data Processing by Equipment Systems
ADPFB....... Automatic Data Processing Field Branch [*BUPERS*]   (DDI)
ADPLL....... All-Digital Phase-Locked Loop   (KSC)
ADPM........ Automatic Data Processing Machine
ADPMIS..... Automatic Data Processing Management Information System
ADPMO...... Automatic Data Processing Modification Order
ADPP......... Automatic Data Processing Programs   (FAAC)
ADPREP..... Automatic Data Processing Resource Estimating Procedures
ADPS......... Automatic Data Processing System [*or Subsystem*]
ADPSO....... Association of Data Processing Service Organizations [*Also, ADAPSO*] [*Includes American and Canadian companies*] [*Arlington, VA*]
ADPSS........ Archivio Dati e Programmi per le Scienze Sociali [*Data and Program Archive for the Social Sciences*] [*University of Milan*] [*Milan, Italy*] [*Information service*]   (EISS)
ADQ........... Almost Differential Quasiternary Code [*Telecommunications*]   (TEL)
ADR........... Adder [*Computer device*]   (MDG)
ADR........... Address [*Computer character*] [*Data processing*]
ADR........... Address Register   (BUR)
ADR........... Analog-Digital Recorder [*Data processing*]
ADR........... Angle Data Recorder
ADR........... Applied Data Research, Inc. [*Software supplier*] [*American Stock Exchange symbol*]
ADRAC....... Automatic Digital Recording and Control
ADRC......... Automatic Data Rate Changer
ADREP....... Automatic Data Processing Resource Estimating Procedure
ADRG......... Automatic Data Routing Group
ADRK......... Auxiliary Display Request Keyboard   (SKY)
ADRMP...... Automated Dialer and Recorded Message Player   (IEEE)
ADRP......... Acoustic Data Reduction Program   (CAAL)
ADRS......... Address [*Computer character*] [*Data processing*]   (AFM)
ADRS......... Analog-to-Digital Data Recording System [*Data processing*]   (IEEE)
ADRS......... Automatic Data Reporting System   (NATG)
ADRS......... Automatic Document Request Service [*or System*]   (DEEC)
ADRS......... [*A*] Departmental Reporting System [*IBM Corp.*]
ADRSA....... Assistant Data Recording System Analyst   (MUGU)
ADRSS....... Automated Data Reports Submission System
ADRT......... Analog Data Recorder Transcriber
ADS........... Accessory Drive System   (NG)
ADS........... Accounting System   (TUT)
ADS........... Accurately Defined System [*Data processing*]
ADS........... Activity Data Sheet   (IEEE)
ADS........... Address [*Message handling*]
ADS........... Administration of Designed Services   (TEL)
ADS........... Administrative Data Systems
ADS........... Advanced Data Scalar   (CIT)
ADS........... Advanced Debugging System   (CAA)
ADS........... Advanced Display System
ADS........... Aerospace Data Systems   (MCD)
ADS........... Air Data Sensor   (MCD)
ADS........... Air Data Subsystem   (RDA)
ADS........... All-Digital Simulator
ADS........... Angle Data Subsystem   (CIT)
ADS........... Application Design Service [*IBM Corp.*]
ADS........... Application Development Systems [*Data processing*]
ADS........... Applied Decision Systems [*Lexington, MA*] [*Information service*]   (EISS)
ADS........... Applied Digital Data Systems, Inc. [*NYSE symbol*] [*Delisted*]
ADS........... Attitude Display System   (MCD)
ADS........... Automated Design System   (MCD)
ADS........... Automated Documentation Systems [*Data processing*]
ADS........... Automated Drafting System
ADS........... Automatic Data System [*Data processing*]
ADS........... Automatic Development System   (MCD)
ADS........... Automatic Digital Switch
ADS........... Aviation Data Service, Inc. [*Information service*]   (EISS)
ADSC......... Automatic Data Service Center
ADSCOM.... Advanced Shipboard Communications
ADSEL....... Address-Selective [*British*]   (MCD)
ADSNB...... Addison Wesley Publishers [*NASDAQ symbol*]   (NQ)
ADSO........ Automatic Display Switching Oscilloscope
ADSP......... Advanced Digital Signal Processor
ADSR......... Attack/Decay/Sustain/Release [*Audio programming parameters*]
ADSS......... Analysis of Digitized Seismic Signals [*Data processing*]
ADSS......... Automated Data Subsystem
ADSS......... Automatic Data Switching System [*Deep Space Network*]   (CIT)
ADST......... AUTODIN Digital Subscriber Terminal
ADSTAR.... Automatic Document Storage and Retrieval [*Data processing*]
ADS-TP..... Administrative Data Systems - Teleprocessing   (IEEE)

ADSUP....... Automatic Data System Uniform Practices
ADT............ Active Disk Table [*Data processing*]   (IBMDP)
ADT............ Air Data Transducer   (MCD)
ADT............ Asynchronous Data Transceiver   (CAA)
ADT............ Automatic Data Translator [*or Transmitter*]
ADT............ Automatic Debit Transfer [*Banking*]
ADT............ Automatic Detection and Tracking   (MCD)
ADT............ Autonomous Data Transfer   (CAA)
ADTA......... Air Data Transducer Assembly   (NASA)
ADTAC...... Automatic Digital Tracking Analyzer Computer [*Data processing*]   (FAAC)
ADTD......... Association of Data Terminal Distributors   (CAA)
ADTS......... Automated Data and Telecommunications Service [*Later, Office of Information and Resources Management*]
ADTS......... Automatic Data Test System [*Bell System*]
ADTU......... Automatic Digital Test Unit
ADTU......... Auxiliary Data Translator Unit
ADU........... Accumulation Distribution Unit [*Data processing*]
ADU........... Analog Delay Unit
ADU........... Analog Display Unit
ADU........... Annunciator Display Unit   (MCD)
ADU........... Automatic Data Unit   (CAA)
ADU........... Automatic Dialing Unit [*Telecommunications*]
ADUM........ Automated Data Unit Movement
ADV........... Advance [*Flowchart*]   (AFM)
ADV........... Arbeitsgemeinschaft fuer Daten Verarbeitung [*Data Processing Association of Austria*] [*Vienna, Austria*]
Advan Electron and Electron Phys ... Advances in Electronics and Electron Physics [*A publication*]
Adv Electron Electron Phys ... Advances in Electronics and Electron Physics [*A publication*]
Adv Electron Electron Phys Suppl ... Advances in Electronics and Electron Physics. Supplement [*A publication*]
Adv Engng Software ... Advances in Engineering Software [*A publication*]
Adv Eng Software ... Advances in Engineering Software [*A publication*]
ADVISOR.... Advanced Integrated Safety and Optimizing Computer
ADVOCNET ... Adult and Vocational Educational Electronic Mail Network [*National Center for Research in Vocational Education*] [*Columbus, OH*] [*Telecommunications*]   (TSSD)
ADW........... Aerial Distribution Wire [*Telecommunications*]   (TEL)
ADW........... Automated Data Wiring
ADX........... Address Complete, Coin-Box [*Telecommunications*]   (TEL)
ADX........... Asymmetric Data Exchange   (CAA)
ADX........... Automatic Data Exchange
AE.............. Added Entry [*Online database field identifier*]
AE.............. Arithmetic Element   (BUR)
AE.............. Arithmetic Expression   (IEEE)
A & E.......... Arts & Entertainment Network [*Cable-television system*]
AE.............. Audit Entry   (BUR)
AEA........... American Electronics Association [*Formerly, WEMA*]
AEA........... Automatic Error Analysis
AEAS......... Automatic Equalization/Analyzation System
AEC........... Analog Electronic Computer
AEC........... Association of Electronic Cottagers [*Sierra Madre, CA*]   (EANO)
AECT......... Association for Educational Communications and Technology [*Washington, DC*]
AED............ Academy for Educational Development [*Washington, DC*] [*Telecommunications*]
AED............ Advanced Electronic Design
AED............ ALGOL Extended for Design [*1967*] [*Data processing*]
AED............ Automated Engineering Design [*Programing language*] [*1960*] [*Data processing*]
AEDCAP..... Automated Engineering Design Circuit Analysis Program
AEDP......... Association for Educational Data Processing   (CAH)
AEDS......... Analog Event Distribution System [*Data processing*]   (MCD)
AEDS......... Association for Educational Data Systems [*Washington, DC*]
AEGIS........ Agricultural, Ecological, and Geographical Information System   (CAA)
AEGIS........ [*An*] Existing Generalized Information System [*Data processing*]
AEI............. Australian Education Index [*Australian Council for Educational Research*] [*Information service*]   (EISS)
AEICP........ Association of Entertainment Industry Computer Professionals [*Los Angeles, CA*]   (EANO)
AEIDC........ Arctic Environmental Information and Data Center [*University of Alaska*] [*Research center*]   (EISS)
AEIMS....... Administrative Engineering Information Management System
AEL............ Audit Entry Language [*Burroughs Corp.*]   (CAA)
AEM........... Analytical Electron Microscopy
AEM........... Automatic Environment Monitoring   (BUR)
AEMIS....... Aerospace and Environmental Medicine Information System   (EISS)
AEP............ Automated Environmental Prediction   (CAAL)
AEPS......... Automated Environmental Prediction System   (MCD)
AERIC........ Applied Economic Research & Information Center [*Canada*]   (CUAD)
AEROS....... Artificial Earth Research and Orbiting Satellite   (NATG)
AEROSAT... Aeronautical Communications Satellite System [*Proposed*]
AEROS-NATE ... Aeronomy Satellite - Neutral Atmosphere Temperature Experiment
AEROSPACECOM ... Aerospace Communications
AERTC........ Association pour les Etudes sur la Radio-Television Canadienne [*Association for the Study of Canadian Radio and Television - ASCRT*]

Acronym	Definition
AES	Analog Event System [*Data processing*] (MCD)
AES	Applications Environment System
AES	Auxiliary Encoder System
AESC	Automatic Electronic Switching Center
AESOP	Automated Educational Services On-Line Processing (MCD)
AESOP	[*An*] Evolutionary System for On-Line Processing [*Data processing*] (TUT)
AESP	Auxiliary Engineering Signal Processor
AEVS	Automatic Electronic Voice Switch (RDA)
AF	Affiliation of Author [*Online database field identifier*] (OBD)
AF	Audio Frequency [*Data transmission*]
AF	Availability Factor [*Generating time ratio*] (IEEE)
AFA	Analog Filter Assembly (MCD)
AFA	Audio Frequency Amplifier
AFA	Audio Frequency Apparatus
AFAC	Automatic Field Analog Computer
AFAM	Automatic Frequency Assignment Model [*Telecommunications*]
AFAS	Air Flow Actuated Switch
AFAS	Automated Frequency Assignment System [*Telecommunications*]
AFC	Analog to Frequency Converter
AFC	Antenna for Communications
AFC	Area Frequency Coordinator (MUGU)
AFC	Audio Frequency Change
AFC	Audio Frequency Choke
AFC	Audio Frequency Coder
AFC	Automated Fare Collection
AFC	Automatic Flight Control
AFC	Automatic Frequency Control [*Electronics*]
AFCAL	Association Francaise de Calcul [*French computing association*] (OA)
AFCAN	Analog Factor Calibration Network
AFCCE	Association of Federal Communications Consulting Engineers [*Bloomfield Hills, MI*]
AFCET	Association Francaise pour la Cybernetique Economique et Technique [*Paris, France*]
AFCOM	AFTN [*Aeronautical Fixed Telecommunications Network*] Communications Center [*FAA*] (FAAC)
AFD	Amplitude-Frequency Distortion
AFDB	Alternative Fuel Data Bank [*Bartlesville Energy Technology Center*] (FDB)
AFDCS	Automatic Film Data Collection System (MCD)
AFFIL	Affiliate
AFFIRM	Association for Federal Information Resources Management (EANO)
AFG	Analog Function Generator
AFG	Antenna Field Gain
AFG	Arbitrary Function Generator (MUGU)
AFI	Automatic Fault Isolation
AFIN	Association Francaise des Informaticiens [*Paris, France*]
AFIP	American Federation of Information Processing [*Formerly, AFIPS*] (CAH)
AFIPS	American Federation of Information Processing Societies [*Reston, VA*]
AFIPS Conf Proc Fall Jt Comput Conf	American Federation of Information Processing Societies. Conference Proceedings. Fall Joint Computer Conference [*A publication*]
AFIPS Conf Proc Fall Spring Jt Comput Conf	American Federation of Information Processing Societies. Conference Proceedings. Fall and Spring Joint Computer Conferences [*A publication*]
AFIPS Conf Proc Spring Jt Comput Conf	American Federation of Information Processing Societies. Conference Proceedings. Spring Joint Computer Conference [*A publication*]
AFIPS Nat Comput Conf Expo Conf Proc	AFIPS [*American Federation of Information Processing Societies*] National Computer Conference and Exposition. Conference Proceedings [*A publication*]
AFIPS Natl Comp Conf Expo Conf Proc	American Federation of Information Processing Societies. National Computer Conference and Exposition. Conference Proceedings [*A publication*]
AFL	Abstract Family of Languages [*Data processing*]
AFL	Animated Film Language (BUR)
AFM	Application Functions Module [*Data processing*]
AFN	Address Complete, Subscriber Free, No-Charge [*Telecommunications*] (TEL)
AFN	All Figure Number [*Telecommunications*] (TEL)
AFNOR	Association Francaise de Normalisation [*French Standardization Association*] [*Paris, France*] [*Database producer*]
AFO	Advanced File Organization (CAA)
AFOS	Automation of Field Operations and Services [*National Weather Service*]
AFP	Attached FORTRAN Processor [*Burroughs Corp.*] [*Data processing*] (BUR)
AF/PC	Automatic Frequency/Phase-Controlled [*Loop*] (IEEE)
AFR	Automatic Format Recognition [*Data processing*]
AFR	Awaiting Forward Release [*Telecommunications*] (TEL)
AFRTS	Armed Forces Radio-Television [*Cable-television system*]
AFS	Antenna Feed System
AFS	Audio Frequency Shift (IEEE)
AFSARI	Automation for Storage and Retrieval of Information (IDA)
AFSK	Audio Frequency Shift Key
AFT	Active File Table [*Data processing*] (IBMDP)
AFT	Analog Facility Terminal [*Data processing*] (TEL)
AFT	Audio Frequency Transformer
AFT	Automatic Fine Tuning
AFT	Automatic Frequency Tuner
AFT	Automatic Funds Transfer
AFTN	Aeronautical Fixed Telecommunications Network
AFTP	Advanced Fault Tree Analysis Program [*SIA Computer Services*] [*Software package*] [*British*] (NCC)
AFTS	Aeronautical Fixed Telecommunications Service
AFTS	Automatic Flexible Test Station
AFTS	Automatic Frequency Tone Shift
AFU	Auxiliary Functional Unit [*Data link*] (NG)
AFUA	ARMS/FIRMS Users Association [*Toledo, OH*] (EANO)
AFVCS	Automatic Fingerprint Verification Computer System
AFX	Address Complete, Subscriber Free, Coin-Box [*Telecommunications*] (TEL)
AG	Again [*Telecommunications*] (TEL)
AG	Allegheny International, Inc. [*NYSE symbol*]
AG	And Gate [*Logic element*] [*Data processing*]
AG	Try Again [*Telecommunications*] (TEL)
AGA	Alcatel-Thomson Gigadisk
AGACS	Air-Ground-Air Communications System
AGACS	Automatic Ground-to-Air Communications System
AGAMP	Automatic Gain Adjusting Amplifier [*Telecommunications*] (TEL)
AGARD	Advisory Group for Aerospace Research and Development [*Paris, France*]
AGBUS	Analog Ground Bus (VIT)
AGC	Automatech Graphics Corporation [*New York, NY*] [*Information service*] (EISS)
AGC	Automatic Gain Control [*Electronics*]
AGCC	Air-Ground Communications Channel
AGCS	Automatic Ground Checkout System (KSC)
AGCS	Automatic Ground Computer System (KSC)
AGCS	Automatic Ground Control Station (KSC)
AGCSC	Automatic Ground Control System Computer (KSC)
AGCU	Autopilot Ground Control Unit
AGDIC	Astro Guidance Digital Computer (IEEE)
AGE	Asian Information Center for Geotechnical Engineering [*Asian Institute of Technology*] [*Bangkok, Thailand*] (EISS)
AGE	Automatic Guidance Electronics
AGF	Automatic Guided Flight (MUGU)
AGIC	Andrus Gerontological Information Center [*University of Southern California*] [*Los Angeles, CA*] (EISS)
AGIFORS	Airline Group of International Federation of Operational Research Societies [*Lyngby, Denmark*]
AGL	Computation Center-Advanced Graphics Laboratory [*University of Texas at Austin*] [*Research center*] (RCD)
AGMIS	Adjutant General Management Information System
AGP	Automatic Guidance Programing (NATG)
AGREP	Permanent Inventory of Agricultural Research Projects [*Commission of the European Communities*] [*Database*] (ODIN)
AGRICOLA	Agricultural On-Line Access [*Formerly, CAIN*] [*National Agricultural Library, Information Systems Division*] [*Beltsville, MD*] [*Bibliographic database*] [*Information service*] (EISS)
AGRIS	Agricultural Research Information System [*United Nations*]
AGS	AGS Computers, Inc. [*NYSE symbol*]
AGSC	AGS Computers, Inc. [*NASDAQ symbol*] (NQ)
AGSP	Atlas General Survey Program (IEEE)
AGT	Audiographic Teleconference (CAA)
AGV	Automated Guided Vehicle [*Robotics*]
AGVS	Automatic Guided Vehicle Systems (EANO)
AH	Accumulator High [*Data processing*]
A h	Ampere Hour
AHC	American Health Consultants [*Atlanta, GA*] [*Information service*] (EISS)
AHCS	Advanced Hybrid Computer System
AHDC	Atari Hard-Disk Controller
AHI	Augmented Human Intellect (KSC)
AHIS	Automated Hospital Information System [*Washington, DC*] [*Veterans Administration*] (EISS)
AHL	America: History and Life [*ABC-Clio Information Services*] [*Database*]
AHPL	[*A*] Hardware Programing Language [*1971*] [*Data processing*] (CSR)
AHRS	Attitude Heading Reference System (NG)
AHRS	Automatic Heading Reference System (DDI)
AHS	Antenna Homing System
AHTN	Association of Hospital Television Networks [*Pittsburgh, PA*] [*Telecommunications*] (EANO)
AHVN	American Hospital Video Network [*Satellite television system*]
AI	Address Incomplete [*Telecommunications*] (TEL)
AI	Antenna Impedance
AI	Artificial Intelligence
AI	Automatic Input [*Data processing*] (BUR)
AIAA	American Institute of Aeronautics and Astronautics [*New York, NY*]
AIB	Automatic Intercept Bureau [*Telecommunications*] (TEL)
AIBA	Agricultural Information Bank for Asia [*Southeast Asian Regional Center for Graduate Study and Research in Agriculture*] [*Laguna, Philippines*] [*Information service*] (EISS)
AIC	American International Communications Corp.

Computer & Telecommunications Acronyms

Acronym	Definition
AIC	Analysts International Corporation [*Minneapolis, MN*] [*Software manufacturer*] (DASOS)
AIC	Association Internationale de Cybernetique [*International Association for Cybernetics - IAC*]
AIC	Automatic Initiation Circuit (IEEE)
AIC	Automatic Intercept Center [*Bell System*]
AIC	Awaiting Incoming Continuity [*Telecommunications*] (TEL)
AIC	Ayer Information Center [*N. W. Ayer, Inc.*] [*Information service*] (EISS)
AICA	Association Internationale pour le Calcul Analogique [*International Association for Analogue Computation*] [*Later, IMACS*]
AICA	Associazione Italiana per il Calcolo Automatico [*Italian Association for Automatic Data Processing*]
AICA	Automatico Associazione Italiana per il Calcolo [*Italian computing association*] (CAH)
AICCP	Association of the Institute for Certification of Computer Professionals [*Des Plaines, IL*] (EANO)
AICPA	American Institute of Certified Public Accountants [*New York, NY*]
AICS	Adaptive Interference Cancellation System (CAAL)
AICS	Advanced Interior Communication System
AICS	Automatic Inlet Control System (NG)
AICT	Automatic Integrated Circuit Tester
AID	Advanced Integrated Diagnostics (BUR)
AID	Advanced Interactive Draughting [*McGrane Computer Systems Ltd.*] [*Software package*] [*British*] (NCC)
AID	Algebraic Interpretive Dialogue [*Data processing*] (BUR)
AID	Applied Information Development, Inc. [*Oak Brook, IL*] [*Software manufacturer*] (DASOS)
AID	Artikkel-Indeks Database [*Norwegian Center for Informatics*] [*Database*] (CUAD)
AID	Associative Interactive Dictionary [*for databases*] [*National Library of Medicine*]
AID	Auditory Information Display
AID	Auto-Interactive Design [*Combines operator-executed and automatic features*] [*Data processing*] (CCD)
AID	Automatic Interaction Detection [*or Detector*] [*Data processing*]
AIDA	Automated Inspection of Data
AIDAS	Advanced Instrumentation and Data Analysis System
AIDE	Automated Image Device Evaluator [*Electronics*]
AIDES	Analyst Intelligence Display and Exploitation System
AIDES	Automated Image Data Extraction System (MCD)
AIDMS	Applied Information and Data Management Systems Section [*Battelle Memorial Institute*] [*Information service*] (EISS)
AIDS	Abstract Information Digest Service [*Forest Products Research Society*] [*Madison, WI*] [*Information service*] (EISS)
AIDS	Account Identification and Description Services [*Dun & Bradstreet*] (EISS)
AIDS	Action Information Display System
AIDS	Administrative Information Data System (AFM)
AIDS	Advanced Integrated Data System (AFM)
AIDS	Advanced Interactive Debugging System (CAA)
AIDS	Aerospace Intelligence Data System [*IBM Corp.*] (DIT)
AIDS	Agricultural Information and Documentation Section [*Royal Tropical Institute*] [*Amsterdam, Netherlands*] [*Information service*] (EISS)
AIDS	Amdahl Internally Developed Software (CAA)
AIDS	American Institute for Decision Sciences (EANO)
AIDS	Attitudinal Information Data System (NVT)
AIDS	Automated Information Data System
AIDS	Automatic Illustrated Documentation System [*Information International, Inc.*]
AIDS	Automatic Integrated Debugging System [*Data processing*] (BUR)
AIDS	Automation Instrument Data Service [*Computer-based industrial information system*] [*Indata Ltd.*] [*British*]
AIEE	American Institute of Electrical Engineers [*Later, IEEE*]
AIENDF	Atomics International Evaluated Nuclear Data Files (KSC)
AIERI	Association Internationale des Etudes et Recherches sur l'Information [*International Association of Mass Communications Research*]
AIET	Average Instruction Execution Time [*Computer parameter*] (OA)
AIFM	Automatic Integrating Fluctuation Meter
AIFT	Audio Input Frequency Tolerance
AIG	Address Indicating Group [*Data processing*] [*NATO*]
AIG	Association pour l'Informatique de Gestion [*Paris, France*]
AIGS	Acoustic Intelligence Gathering System (CAAL)
AII	Automatic Imagery Interpretation
AIIDC	Authorized Item Identification Data Collaborator Code
AIIDR	Authorized Item Identification Data Receiver Code
AIIDS	Authorized Item Identification Data Submitter Code
AIIE	American Institute of Industrial Engineers [*Later, IIE*]
AIIM	Association for Information and Image Management [*Silver Spring, MD*] (EANO)
AIL	Array Interconnection Logic [*Data processing*] (CAA)
AIL	Artificial Intelligence Laboratory [*Massachusetts Institute of Technology*] [*Research center*] (RCD)
AIM	Advanced Information Manager [*Fujitsu Ltd.*] [*Japan*] (CAA)
AIM	Air Isolated Monolithic [*Circuit*]
AIM	American Interactive Media, Inc. [*Software manufacturer*]
AIM	Analog Input Module [*Data processing*] (CIT)
AIM	Arbeitsgemeinschaft Information Meeresforschung und Meerestechnik eV [*Hannover*] [*Information retrieval*] (ODIN)
AIM	Artificial Intelligence in Medicine
AIM	Assembly Instruction Mnemonics [*Data processing*]
AIM	Associated Information Managers [*Formerly, PRIM*] [*Rockville, MD*] (EANO)
AIM	Association of Independent Microdealers (EANO)
AIM	Association of Information Managers for Financial Institutions (EANO)
AIM	Associative Index Method (CAA)
AIM	Automated Information Management (NASA)
AIM	Automated Intelligent Microscope
AIM	Avalanche-Induced Migration (MCD)
AIM	Awaiting Incoming Message [*Telecommunications*] (TEL)
AIM/ARM	Abstracts of Instructional Materials/Abstracts of Research Materials
AIMC	Auto-Initiate Manual-Confirm (CAAL)
AIMES	Automated Information and Management Systems (MCD)
AIMES	Automated Inventory Management Evaluation System (IEEE)
AIMIS	Advanced Integrated Modular Instrumentation System (MCD)
AIMS	Advanced Image Management Software [*Data processing*]
AIMS	Advanced Integrated Magnetic Anomaly Detection System (MCD)
AIMS	Analysis of Internal Management Systems
AIMS	Applied Information Management Sciences, Inc. [*Monroe, LA*] [*Software manufacturer*] (DASOS)
AIMS	Applied Information Management System [*Data processing*] (DIT)
AIMS	Automated Industrial Management System
AIMS	Automated Information and Management System (BUR)
AIMS	Automated Instructional Materials Services [*Developed by the System Development Corp.*] (EISS)
AIMT	Association for Integrated Manufacturing Technology (EANO)
AIM-TWX	Abridged Index Medicus Accessed by Teletypewriter Exchange Service [*National Library of Medicine*]
AIN	Alternative Information Network (EANO)
AIOD	Automatic Identified Outward Dialing
AIOP	Analog Input/Output Package [*Data processing*]
AIP	Alphanumeric Impact Printer (CAA)
AIP	Automated Implementation Plan
AIP	Average Instructions per Second [*Data processing*]
AIPS	Advanced Interactive Presentation System
AIPS	Astronomical Image Processing System
AIPS	Automated Intelligence Processing System (MCD)
AIPS	Automatic Indexing and Proofreading System
AIR	Adaptive Intercommunication Requirement (NASA)
AIR	Antenna Input Resistance
AIRCOMNET	Air Communications Network
AIRCON	Automated Information and Reservation Computer Operated Network
AIRL	Automation Industries Research Laboratory (KSC)
AIRLOC	Air Lines of Communication
AIRMAP	Air Monitoring Analysis and Prediction [*System*]
AIRMICS	Army Institute for Research in Management Information and Computer Science (IEEE)
AIRPAP	Air Pressure Analysis Program [*Bell System*]
AIRS	Accident Information Retrieval System (RDA)
AIRS	Accounting Incomplete Records System [*Software package*] [*British*] (NCC)
AIRS	Alliance of Information and Referral Systems [*Indianapolis, IN*] (EANO)
AIRS	Automated Insurance Rating Services, Inc. [*Naperville, IL*] [*Software manufacturer*] (DASOS)
AIRS	Automatic Image Retrieval System (MCD)
AIRS	Automatic Information Retrieval System [*Data processing*] (BUR)
AIS	Accounting Information System (BUR)
AIS	Advanced Information System/Net 1 Service [*Formerly, ACS*] [*American Bell, Inc.*]
AIS	Advanced Instructional System (MCD)
AIS	Alarm Indication Signal [*Telecommunications*] (TEL)
AIS	Alarm Inhibit Signal [*Telecommunications*] (TEL)
AIS	Altitude Indication System
AIS	Amron Information Services [*Union, NJ*] (EISS)
AIS	Analog Input System (CAA)
AIS	Analog Instrumentation Subsystem (CIT)
AIS	Antenna Interface Subsystem (CAAL)
AIS	Automated Information System
AIS	Automated Instrumentation System
AIS	Automated Insurance Service
AIS	Automatic Intercept System [*Bell System*]
AIS	Automatic Intermediate Station (MCD)
AIS	Automatic Interplanetary Station [*USSR*]
AISC	Association of Independent Software Companies [*Later, ADAPSO*] (EANO)
AISF	Avionic Integration Support Facility (MCD)
AISL	Aviation Information Services Limited [*Hounslow, Middlesex, England*]
AISP	Association of Information Systems Professionals [*Willow Grove, PA*] (EANO)
AISP	Association of Information Systems Professionals [*Canada*]
AISS	Automatic Intercom Switching System
AIST	Agency of Industrial Science and Technology [*Japanese*] (NASA)
AIST	Automatic Information Station [*or System*] (BUR)

By Acronym

Computer & Telecommunications Acronyms

AIT .... Agency for Instructional Television
AIT .... Automotive Information Test
AITI .... Artikkel-Indeks Tidsskrifter [*Norwegian Center for Informatics*] [*Database*] (CUAD)
AITRC .... Applied Information Technologies Research Center [*Columbus, OH*] [*Information service*] (EISS)
AITS .... Automated Information Transfer System [*Department of Commerce*] [*Database*] (FDB)
AITU .... Alliance of Independent Telephone Unions [*Later, TIU*]
AIU .... Alarm Interface Unit [*Telecommunications*] (TEL)
AIU .... Array Interface Unit [*Data processing*] (CAAL)
AIU .... Avionics Interface Unit (MCD)
AJ .... Analog Junction (TEL)
AJ .... Anderson Jacobson, Inc. [*Terminal manufacturer*] [*American Stock Exchange symbol*]
AJAC .... Automatic Jamming Avoidance Circuitry
AJ/AI .... Antijamming/Anti-Interference (CET)
AJBO .... Antijamming Blackout
AJCC .... Alternate Joint Communications Center
AJD .... Antijam Display
AJE .... Antijam Equipment
AJF .... Antijam Frequency
AJFH .... Antijam Frequency Hopper
AJH .... Antijam Hopper
AJI .... Antijamming Improvements
AJLO .... Avalanching Junction Light Output
AJM .... Analog Junction Module (TEL)
AJO .... Antijam Operator (CET)
AJPO .... Ada Joint Program Office [*Data processing*] (RDA)
AJS .... Angle Jamming System
AJS .... Antijam Synthesizer
AJT .... Antijam Technique
AJVD .... Abrupt Junction Varactor Doubler
AK .... Amplitude Keyed
AKI .... Automix Keyboards, Incorporated
AKR .... Address Key Register (CAA)
AKRO .... Acknowledge Receipt Of [*Telecommunications*] (TEL)
AKWIC .... Author and Keyword in Context (DEEC)
AL .... Accumulator Low [*Data processing*]
AL .... Additional Listing [*Telecommunications*] (TEL)
AL .... Aeronautical Radionavigation Land Station [*ITU designation*]
AL .... Alarm [*Telecommunications*] (TEL)
AL .... Analog Link [*Telecommunications*] (TEL)
AL .... Analog Loop-Back [*Telecommunications*] (TEL)
AL .... Antenna Laboratory (MCD)
A/L .... Assemble/Load [*Data processing*] (VIT)
AL .... Assembly Language [*Data processing*] (CGC)
AL .... Astronuclear Laboratory [*Westinghouse Electric Corp.*] (MCD)
ALA .... Al Lee & Associates, Inc. [*Dallas, TX*] [*Software manufacturer*] (DASOS)
ALA .... American Library Association [*Chicago, IL*]
ALABOL .... Algorithmic and Business Oriented Language [*Data processing*]
ALANET .... American Library Association's Electronic Information Service
ALAP .... Associative Linear Array Processor [*Data processing*] (CAA)
ALARM .... Automatic Light Aircraft Readiness Monitor
ALAS .... Asynchronous Look-Ahead Simulator (IEEE)
ALAS .... Automated Library Acquisitions System [*Suggested name for the Library of Congress computer system*]
ALAS .... Automated Literature Alerting System [*Data processing*] (DIT)
ALBO .... Automatic Line Buildout [*Bell Laboratories*]
ALC .... Adaptive Logic Circuit (OA)
ALC .... Advanced Library Concepts, Inc. [*Honolulu, HI*] [*Information service*] (EISS)
ALC .... Antenna Loading Coil
ALC .... Assembly Language Coding [*Data processing*]
ALC .... Automatic Load Control
ALCAPP .... Automatic List Classification and Profile Production
ALCKT .... All stations or offices having send-receive teletypewriter service on circuit [*FAA*] (FAAC)
ALCOM .... Algebraic Compiler [*Data processing*]
ALCOM .... ALGOL Compiler [*Data processing*] (DIT)
ALCU .... Arithmetic Logic and Control Unit [*Data processing*] (CAA)
ALCU .... Asynchronous Line Control Unit [*Telecommunications*] (CAA)
ALD .... American Library Directory [*Online database*]
ALD .... Analog Line Driver [*Data processing*] (BUR)
ALD .... Asynchronous Line Driver [*Prentice Corp.*] (CAA)
ALD .... Automated Logic Diagram [*Data processing*] (IBMDP)
ALDEP .... Automated Layout Design Program [*IBM Corp.*]
ALDI .... Associated Long-Distance Interstate Message [*Telecommunications*] (TEL)
ALDP .... Automatic Language Data Processing
ALDPS .... Automated Logistics Data Processing System
ALDRI .... Automatic Low Date Rate Input
ALDS .... Automatic Lightning Detection System [*To aid in the prevention of forest fires*]
ALE .... Address Latch Enable [*Data processing*]
ALE .... Automatic LASER Encoder
ALERT .... Automated Linguistic Extraction and Retrieval Technique
ALERT .... Automated Local Evaluations in Real Time [*National Oceanic and Atmospheric Administration*]
ALERT .... Automatic Logging Electronic Reporting and Telemetering System [*Maintains surveillance over petroleum wells and pipelines*]

ALERT .... Automatic Logical Equipment Readiness Tester
ALF .... Absorption Limiting Frequency (DEN)
ALF .... Application Library File [*Data processing*] (CAA)
ALF .... Automatic Lead Former
ALF .... Automatic Letter Facer
ALF .... Automatic Line Feed [*Telecommunications*] (CAA)
ALFC .... Automatic Local Frequency Control
ALFGL .... Automatic Low-Frequency Gain-Limiting Circuit (RDA)
ALFTRAN .... ALGOL-to-FORTRAN Translator [*Data processing*] (MCD)
ALGEC .... Algorithmic Language for Economic Calculations [*Data processing*]
ALGO .... Algorithm (MSA)
ALGOL .... Algorithmic Language [*1958*] [*Formerly, IAL*] [*Data processing*]
ALI .... Asynchronous Line Interface [*Telecommunications*] (CAA)
ALI .... Automated Logic Implementation [*Data processing*] (IEEE)
ALI .... Automatic Line Integration (NVT)
ALI .... Automatic Location Identification [*Street crime locator*]
ALICE .... Adaptive Line Canceller and Enhancer (CAAL)
ALICE .... Alaskan Integrated Communications Exchange
ALICE .... Applicative Language Idealized Computing Engine
ALICE .... Automated Location of Isolation and Continuity Error [*Module*] [*Raytheon Co.*]
ALID .... Automated Library Issue Document (NVT)
ALIS .... Advanced Life Information System [*Data processing*]
ALIS .... Arid Lands Information System [*University of Arizona*] [*Tucson, AZ*] (EISS)
ALIS .... Automated Library Information System [*Dataphase Systems, Inc.*] [*Shawnee Mission, KS*] (EISS)
ALIT .... Automatic Line Insulation Test [*or Tester*] [*Bell System*]
ALL .... Accelerated Learning of Logic
ALL .... Address Locator Logic [*Data processing*]
ALLC .... Association for Literary and Linguistic Computing (EANO)
ALLCB .... ALLC [*Association for Literary and Linguistic Computing*] Bulletin [*A publication*]
ALLC J .... ALLC [*Association for Literary and Linguistic Computing*] Journal [*A publication*]
ALLOC .... Allocate [*or Allocation*] (AFM)
ALLP .... Audiolingual Language Programing [*Data processing*]
ALM .... Assembler Language for MULTICS (CAA)
ALM .... Asynchronous Line Module (CAA)
ALM .... Asynchronous Line Multiplexer [*Telecommunications*] (CAA)
ALMI .... Alpha Microsystems [*NASDAQ symbol*] (NQ)
ALMIDO .... Amplitude and Latency Measuring Instrument with Digital Output
ALMS .... Analytic Language Manipulation System
ALN .... Accounting Line Number
ALN .... Adaptive Learning Network [*Data processing*]
ALNICO .... Aluminum, Nickel, Cobalt [*Alloy*]
ALO .... Automatic Lock-On (MCD)
ALOG .... Analogic Corp. [*NASDAQ symbol*] (NQ)
ALP .... Arithmetic Logic Processor (CAA)
ALP .... Assembly Language Preprocessor [*Data processing*] (IEEE)
ALP .... Assembly Language Program [*Data processing*] (CGC)
ALP .... Automated Learning Process
ALP .... Automated Library Program [*Data processing*] (DIT)
ALPAC .... Automatic Language Processing Advisory Committee [*National Research Council*]
ALPAK .... Algebra Package [*Data processing*]
ALPC .... Adaptive Linear Predictive Coding (TEL)
ALPETH .... Aluminum and Polyethylene [*Components of a type of telecommunications cable*]
ALPHA .... Alphabetical [*Flowchart*]
ALPHA .... Automatic Literature Processing, Handling, and Analysis
ALPS .... Advanced Linear Programing System [*Operational research technique*]
ALPS .... Approach and Landing Procedures Simulator (MCD)
ALPS .... Associated Logic Parallel System (BUR)
ALPS .... Automated Language Processing Systems [*Provo, UT*] [*Software manufacturer*] (DASOS)
ALPS .... Automated Library Processing Services [*System Development Corp.*] (EISS)
ALPS .... Automatic License Plate Scanning
ALPS .... Automatic Linear Positioning System (DDI)
ALPTA .... American Low Power Television Association (EANO)
ALPURCOMS ... All-Purpose Communications System
ALR .... Automatic Level Recorder
ALR .... Automatic Load Regulator
ALRU .... Automated Line Record Update [*Telecommunications*] (TEL)
ALS .... Advanced Library Systems, Inc. [*Andover, MA*] [*Information service*] (EISS)
ALS .... Approach and Landing Simulator
ALS .... Arithmetic Logic Section [*Data processing*] (CAA)
ALS .... Augmented Logistics Support (MCD)
ALS .... Automated Library System [*Foundation for Library Research, Inc.*] [*Information service*] (EISS)
ALS .... Automatic Level Setting
ALSU .... Autonomous Line Scanning Unit (MCD)
ALT .... Alternate
ALTAC .... Algebraic Translator and Compiler [*Data processing*] (MCD)
ALTAIR .... Automatic Logical Translation and Information Retrieval [*Data processing*] (DIT)
ALTAPE .... Automatic Line Tracer and Programing Equipment
ALTARE .... Automatic Logic Testing and Recording Equipment

Acronym	Expansion
ALTEL	Association of Long Distance Telephone Companies [*Washington, DC*] (EANO)
ALTO	Altos Computer Systems [*NASDAQ symbol*] (NQ)
ALTP	Automatic Linear Temperature Programer
ALTRAN	Algebraic Translator [*Programing language*] [*1969*]
ALTRAN	Assembly Language Translator [*Xerox Corp.*] (CAH)
ALTREC	Automatic Life Testing and Recording of Electronic Components [*Canada*] (CDH)
ALTS	Analog Line Termination Subsystem [*Telecommunications*] (TEL)
ALTS	Automated Library Technical Services [*Program*] [*Los Angeles Public Library*]
ALTS	Automatic Line Test Set [*Telecommunications*] (TEL)
ALTU	Adder, Logical, and Transfer Unit [*Computer*]
A & LU	Arithmetic and Logic Unit [*Data processing*]
ALU	Arithmetic and Logic Unit [*Data processing*]
ALU	Asynchronous Line Unit [*Telecommunications*] (CAA)
ALVIN	Antenna Lobe for Variable Ionospheric Nimbus (IEEE)
AM	Access Method [*Data processing*]
AM	Adaptive Multiplexer (CAAL)
AM	Address Mark [*Microprocessors*]
AM	Address Mode [*Data processing*] (CAA)
AM	Address Modifier (CAA)
AM	Aeronautical Radionavigation Mobile Station [*ITU designation*]
AM	Alternate Mode (CAAL)
AM	AM International, Inc. [*Formerly, Addressograph-Multigraph Corp.*] [*American Stock Exchange symbol*]
A/M	Amperes per Meter
AM	Amplitude Modulation [*Electronics*]
AM	Analog Module [*Telecommunications*] (TEL)
AM	Area Multiplexer (CAAL)
AM	Associative Memory [*Data processing*]
AM	Asynchronous MODEM (CAA)
A/M	Auto/Manual (MDG)
AM	Automatic Monitoring (CET)
AM	Auxiliary Marker [*Telecommunications*] (TEL)
A²M	Auxiliary Memory
A²M	Automated Auger Microprobe
AMA	American Management Associations [*New York, NY*]
AMA	American Medical Association [*Chicago, IL*]
AMA	Analog Major Alarm (MCD)
AMA	Associative Memory Address [*Data processing*] (CAA)
AMA	Associative Memory Array [*Data processing*] (CAA)
AMA	Automated Modification Analyzer [*Data processing*]
AMA	Automatic Memory Allocation [*Data processing*] (BUR)
AMA	Automatic Message Accounting [*Bell Laboratories*] [*Telecommunications*]
AMANDA	Automized Medical Anamnesis Dialog Assistant [*Computer*]
AMARS	Automatic Message Accounting Recording System [*Bell System*]
AMARS	Automatic Message Address Routing System
AMAS	Automatic Message Accounting System (MCD)
AMB	Antarctic Meteorite Bibliography [*Lunar and Planetary Institute*] [*Database*] (FDB)
AMB	Auto-Manual Bridge Control [*Telecommunications*] (TEL)
AMBEL	Ambiguity Eliminator [*Electronics*]
AMBERS	A. M. Best Electronic Retrieval Services [*A. M. Best Co.*] [*Database*] (CUAD)
AMBIT	Algebraic Manipulation by Identity Translation (TUT)
AMBIT/L	Acronym May Be Ignored Totally [*Data processing*] (CSR)
AMBUSH	Advanced Model Builder Shell [*Programing language*] [*1970*] (CSR)
AMC	Account Manager Code (TEL)
AMC	Advanced Minuteman Computer
AMC	Alarm Monitor Computer
AMC	Alberta Microelectronic Centre [*University of Alberta*] [*Research center*] (RCD)
AMC	Alternate Media Center [*New York University*] [*Telecommunications*]
AMC	Associative Memory Computer [*Data processing*]
AMC	Auto-Manual Center [*Telecommunications*] (TEL)
AMC	Automatic Message Counting
AMC	Autonomous Multiplexer Channel (CAA)
AMCD	Addressograph-Multigraph Copier Duplicator
AMCEE	Association for Media-Based Continuing Education for Engineers [*Atlanta, GA*] [*Telecommunications*] (EANO)
AMCI	Ameritech Mobile Communications, Incorporated [*Schaumburg, IL*] [*Telecommunications*] (TSSD)
AMCODE	AMEX [*American Stock Exchange*] Computerized Order Display and Execution System
AMCOM	AMEX [*American Stock Exchange*] Communications [*Network*]
AMD	Advanced Micro Devices, Inc. [*Computer manufacturer*] [*NYSE symbol*]
AMD	Associative Memory Device [*Data processing*] (DIT)
AMD	Atomic and Molecular Physical Data Program [*American Society for Testing and Materials*] (EISS)
AMD	Automatic Map Display
AMD	Auxiliary Memory Drum
AMDA	American Microcomputer Dealers Association [*Tustin, CA*] (EANO)
AMDA	Associated Minicomputer Dealers of America (EANO)
AMDAC	Amdahl Diagnostics Assistance Center (CAA)
AMDAPS	Automatic Meteorological Data Acquisition and Processing System (MCD)
AMDL	Abstract Machine Description Language [*1977*] [*Data processing*] (CSR)
AMDS	Agri-Markets Data Service [*Capitol Publications, Inc.*] [*Database*] (FDB)
AMDS	Automatic Message Distribution System (CET)
AMDSB	Amplitude Modulation, Double Sideband [*Electronics*]
AMDSB/SC	Amplitude Modulation, Double Sideband, Suppressed Carrier [*Electronics*] (CET)
AMDT	Active Maintenance Downtime
AME	Amplitude Modulation Equivalent [*Telecommunications*] (TEL)
AME	Automatic Microfiche Editor (IDA)
AMECOS	Automatic Measuring Computing and Sorting
AMEDPC	Automotive Manufacturers EDP [*Electronic Data Processing*] Council [*Teaneck, NJ*] (EANO)
AMERITECH	American Information Technologies [*Telecommunications*]
AMES	Automatic Message Entry System [*Data processing*] (MCD)
AMEX	American Express Co.
AMEXCO	American Express Company
AMF	Analog Matched Filter
AMFIS	Automatic Microfilm Information System
AMFV	[*A*] Mind Forever Voyaging [*Infocom*] [*Computer gaming*]
AMG	Automatic Magnetic Guidance
AMH	Amdahl Corp. [*American Stock Exchange symbol*]
AMHS	Automated Materials Handling System [*Data processing*] (DDI)
AMHS	Automated Message Handling System
AMI	Advertising and Marketing Intelligence Service [*Mead Data Central*] [*Database*] (EISS)
AMI	Alternate Mark Inversion [*Telecommunications*] (IEEE)
AMI	American Microsystems, Incorporated (MCD)
AMICA	Automatic Module for Industrial Control Analysis
AMIGOS	Access Method for Indexed Data Generalized for Operating System [*Data processing*] (TUT)
AMIQ	Association pour l'Avancement de la Micro-Informatique [*Association for the Advancement of Micro-Information*] [*Canada*]
AMIS	Atari Message and Information System [*Computer-based bulletin board system*]
AMIS	Automated Management Information System (DIT)
AMIS	Automated Minerals Information System [*Bureau of Mines*] [*Database*] (FDB)
AML	Actual Measured Loss [*Telecommunications*] (TEL)
AML	Amplitude Modulated Link [*Electronics*]
AML	Animated Movie Language (BUR)
AML	Application Module Library [*IBM Corp.*]
AML	Array Machine Language [*Data processing*] (CAA)
AML	[*A*] Manufacturing Language [*Data processing*]
AMLC	Asynchronous Multiline Controller [*Telecommunications*] (CAA)
AMLP	Amplitude Modulation Link Program
AMM	Additional Memory Module (CAA)
AMM	Analog Monitor Module [*Data processing*] (CAA)
AMM	Associated Maintenance Module [*Telecommunications*] (TEL)
AMMS	Automatic Multimode Mass Spectrometry
AMNIP	Adaptive Man-Machine Nonarithmetic Information Processing [*Documentation*]
AMO	Answering Machine Owner
AMOS	Alpha Microsystems Operating System (CAA)
AMOS	Assembly Management Operating System (MCD)
AMOS	Automatic Computer, Ministry of Supply [*British*] (DEN)
AMOS	Automatic Meteorological Observation [*or Observing*] Station [*or System*]
AMOSS	Adaptive Mission-Oriented Software System (MCD)
AMP	Adaptation Mathematical Processor
AMP	AMP, Inc. [*NYSE symbol*]
AMP	Ampere [*Unit of electric current*] (AFM)
AMP	Amplifier (KSC)
AMP	Amplitude
AMP	Argonne Microprocessor
AMP	Associative Memory Processor [*Data processing*] (BUR)
AMPC	Automatic Message Processing Center
AMP-HR	Ampere-Hour (MDG)
AMPL	Advanced Microprocessor Programing Language [*Texas Instruments, Inc.*] (CAA)
AMPL	Advanced Microprocessor Prototyping Laboratory [*Texas Instruments, Inc.*] (CAA)
AMPL	Amplifier
AMPL	[*A*] Macro Programing Language [*Data processing*]
AMPOL	[*The*] Almanac of American Politics [*National Journal Inc.*] [*Database*] [*A publication*] (CUAD)
AMPP	Advanced Microprogramable Processors (MCD)
AMPS	Adaptive Mode Planning System [*Computer program*] (CIT)
AMPS	Advanced Mobile Phone Service [*Bell System*]
AMPS	Amperes (KSC)
AMPS	Automated Material Processing System [*Data processing*] (TUT)
AMPSIN	Adaptive Mode Planning System Input [*Computer program*] (CIT)
AMQ	Analog Multiplexer Quantizer [*Data processing*] (KSC)
AMR	Automated Management Reports (BUR)
AMR	Automatic Message Recording
AMR	Automatic Message Registering
AMR	Automatic Message Routing (BUR)
AMR	Automatic Meter Reading
AMS	Access Method Service [*Data processing*] (BUR)

AMS	Advanced Memory Systems, Inc. (IEEE)
AMS	American Management Systems, Inc. [*Arlington, VA*] [*Information service*] (EISS)
AMS	American Mathematical Society [*Providence, RI*]
AMS	American Meteorological Society [*Boston, MA*]
AMS	Amplifier Subsystem (NASA)
AMS	Asymmetric Multiprocessing System [*IBM Corp.*] (CAA)
AMS	Atmospheric Monitor System (IEEE)
AMS	Automatic Mode Status (CAAL)
AMS	Auxiliary Memory Set (MCD)
AMSAT	Radio Amateur Satellite Corp. [*An association*] (EANO)
Am Soc Eng Educ COED Trans	American Society for Engineering Education. Computers in Education Division. Transactions [*A publication*]
Am Soc Eng Educ Comput Educ Div Trans	American Society for Engineering Education. Computers in Education Division. Transactions [*A publication*]
Am Soc Info Science Bul	Bulletin. American Society for Information Science [*A publication*]
AMSSB	Amplitude Modulation, Single Sideband [*Electronics*]
AMSSB/SC	Amplitude Modulation, Single Sideband, Suppressed Carrier [*Electronics*] (CET)
AMSSS	Actron Microprocessor Softwear Support System (MCD)
AMSWA	American Software Cl A [*NASDAQ symbol*] (NQ)
AMSY	American Management Systems [*NASDAQ symbol*] (NQ)
AMT	American Telecommunications Corp. [*Vancouver Stock Exchange symbol*]
AMT	Amplitude-Modulated Transmitter [*Electronics*]
AMT	Angular Mapping Transformation [*Data processing*]
AMT	AUTODIN Multimedia Terminal (NVT)
AMTAS	Automatic Modal Tuning and Analysis System (NASA)
AMTCL	Association for Machine Translation and Computational Linguistics [*Later, Association for Computational Linguistics*]
AMTD	Automatic Magnetic Tape Dissemination [*Defense Documentation Center*] (CIT)
AMTR	Ammeter (DDI)
AMTRAN	Automatic Mathematical Translator [*Programing language*] [1970]
AMTS	Advanced Mobile Telephone System (MCD)
AMU	Alarm Monitor Unit [*Telecommunications*] (TEL)
AMU	Antenna Matching Unit
AMU	Association of Minicomputer Users [*Framingham, MA*] (EANO)
AMU	Auxiliary Memory Unit
AMUX	Avionics Multiplex
AMW	Active Microwave Workshop
AMWS	American Men and Women of Science [*R. R. Bowker Co., 1979*] [*New York, NY*] [*A publication*] (EISS)
AMX	Automatic Message Exchange
AN	Accession Number [*Online database field identifier*] (OBD)
AN	Alphanumeric
ANA	Adaptive Null Antenna
ANA	Assigned Night Answer [*Telecommunications*] (TEL)
ANA	Automatic Network Analyzer
ANA	Automatic Number Announcer [*Telecommunications*] (TEL)
ANACOM	Analog Computer
ANALIT	Analysis of Automatic Line Insulation Test [*Bell System*]
ANATRAN	Analog Translator [*Data processing*] (CGC)
ANBFM	Adaptive Narrowband FM [*Frequency Modulation*] MODEM [*Telecommunications*] (TEL)
ANC	All Numbers Calling [*Telephone*]
AND	Automatic Network Dialing [*Telecommunications*] (TEL)
ANDAS	Automatic Navigation and Data Acquisition System
ANDIP	American National Dictionary for Information Processing [*A publication*] (IEEE)
ANDIPS	American National Dictionary for Information Processing Systems [*A publication*]
ANDVT	Advanced Narrowband Digital Voice Terminal (MCD)
ANF	Automatic Number Identification Failure [*Telecommunications*] (TEL)
ANI	Association Nationale pour l'Infographie [*National Computer Graphics Association of Canada*]
ANI	Automatic Number Identification [*Telecommunications*]
ANIPLA	Associazione Nazionale Italiana per l'Automazione [*Milan, Italy*]
ANL	American National Standard Labels (BUR)
ANL	Analog (NASA)
ANL	Argonne National Laboratory [*Argonne, IL*]
ANL	Automatic Noise Limiter [*Electronics*]
ANLG	Analog (MSA)
ANLG	Antilogarithmic Function
ANLY	Analysts International Corp. [*NASDAQ symbol*] (NQ)
ANN	Annunciator [*Electronically controlled signal board*] (KSC)
ANN	Answer, No-Charge [*Telecommunications*] (TEL)
Annu Rev Autom Program	Annual Review in Automatic Programming [*A publication*]
Annu Rev Inf Sci Technol	Annual Review of Information Science and Technology [*Encyclopedia Britannica*] [*A publication*]
ANOV	Analysis of Variance [*Also, ANOVA*]
ANOVA	Analysis of Variance [*Also, ANOV*]
ANPOD	Antenna Positioning Device
ANR	Awaiting Number Received [*Telecommunications*] (TEL)
ANRA	Air Navigation Radio Aids
ANRT	Association Nationale de la Recherche Technique [*Database producer*] (CUAD)
ANS	American National Standard [*ANSI*] (MCD)
ANS	Answer (AFM)
ANSA	Advanced Network System Architecture (BUR)
ANSC	American National Standards (Institute) Committee
ANSCII	American National Standard Code for Information Interchange (MCD)
ANSER	Agricultural Network Serving Extension and Research [*University of Kentucky*] [*Information service*] [*Research center*] (EISS)
ANSI	American National Standards Institute [*New York, NY*]
ANSSIR	[A] Network of Social Security Information Resources [*Canada*] (EISS)
ANSVIP	American National Standard Vocabulary for Information Processing
ANSWER	Automated Network Schedule with Evaluation of Resources (MCD)
ANT	Antenna (AFM)
ANTILOG	Antilogarithm
ANTIOPE	L'Acquisition Numerique et Televisualisation d'Images Organisees en Pages d'Ecriture [*French videotex system*] (CAA)
ANTS	Any Tape Search [*Computer program*] (KSC)
ANTS	ARPA [*Advanced Research Projects Agency*] Network Terminal System (CAA)
AN-WSC-3	Whiskey-3 [*Shipboard radio*]
AO	Absolute Output [*Data processing*]
AO	Adjusted Output [*Data processing*]
AO	Amplifier Output [*Data processing*]
AO	Analog Output [*Data processing*] (NASA)
AO	Anodal Opening
AOC	Automatic Operation Control
AOC	Automatic Output Control
AOC	Automatic Overload Circuit
AOC	Automatic Overload Control (IEEE)
AOC	Average Operating Cost (KSC)
AOC	Awaiting Outgoing Continuity [*Telecommunications*] (TEL)
AOCR	Advanced Optical Character Reader
AOCS	Alpha Omega Computer System (IEEE)
AOCU	Arithmetic Output Control Unit (CAA)
AOCU	Associative Output Control Unit (CAA)
AOD	Analog Output Differential [*Data processing*] (MCD)
AOD	Arithmetic Output Data [*Data processing*] (CAA)
AOF	Advanced Operating Facility [*Computer Technology, Inc.*] (CAA)
AOI	Accent on Information [*Data bank for the handicapped and rehabilitation professionals sponsored by association of the same name*] [*Bloomington, IL*] (EISS)
AOIPS	Atmospheric and Oceanographic Information Processing System [*Satellite image enhancing system*] (MCD)
AOL	Application Oriented Language [*Data processing*] (BUR)
AOM	Add One to Memory [*Data processing*]
AOMPS	Automatic Outgoing Message Processor System (NVT)
AONALS	Type "A" Off-Network Access Lines [*Telecommunications*] (TEL)
AONET	American Osteopathic Network [*Chicago, IL*] [*Information service*] (EISS)
AOP	Advanced On-Board Processor [*Computer*]
AOR	Album Oriented Rock
AOR	Antenna Ohmic Resistance
AOR	Atlantic Ocean Region [*INTELSAT*] (CBSS)
AORF	Amplifier Oscillator, Radiofrequency (DDI)
AOS	Advanced Operating System [*Data General Corp.*] (CAA)
AOS	Algebraic Operating System [*Texas Instruments, Inc.*] [*Data processing*]
AOS	Amplifier Output Stage
AOSP	Atlantic Ocean Ship [*INTELSAT*] (CBSS)
AOSP	Automatic Operating and Scheduling Program [*Data processing*]
AOTT	Automatic Outgoing Trunk Test [*Bell System*]
AOU	Arithmetic Output Unit (CAA)
AOU	Associative Output Unit [*Data processing*] (CAA)
AOVC	Automatic Overload Circuit (MSA)
AP	Access Point [*Telecommunications*] (TEL)
AP	Add Packed [*Data processing*]
AP	Advance Payment [*Telecommunications*] (TEL)
AP	Anomalous Propagation [*Telecommunications*] (TEL)
A/P	Antennas and Propagation
AP	Application Program [*Data processing*] (BUR)
AP	Argument Programing (MSA)
AP	Arithmetic Processor (CAA)
AP	Arithmetic Progression
AP	Array Processor [*Data processing*] (BUR)
AP	Assembly of Parties [*INTELSAT*] (CBSS)
AP	Associated Press [*Online news wire service*]
AP	Associated Press Network
AP	Associative Processor [*Data processing*] (BUR)
AP	Attached Processor [*Data processing*] (BUR)
AP	Automatic Programing [*Data processing*]
APA	All Points Addressable [*Data processing*]
APA	American Psychological Association [*Database producer*]
APA	Antenna Pattern Analyzer
APA	Augmented Predictive Analyzer [*Data processing*] (DIT)
APAC	Antenna Pointing Angle Change (CIT)
APACHE	Accelerated Project to Automate Critical Hardware Hardcore Systems

Computer & Telecommunications Acronyms

Acronym	Expansion
APACHE	Analog Programing and Checking [*Data processing*]
APADAS	Automatic Phase and Amplitude Data System (MCD)
APAL	Array Processor Assembly Language [*Data processing*] (CAA)
APAM	Array Processor Access Method [*Data processing*] (BUR)
APAR	Authorized Program Analysis Report [*Data processing*] (IBMDP)
APAR	Automatic Program Analysis Report [*Data processing*] (BUR)
APAR	Automatic Programing and Recording [*Data processing*]
APAS	Automated Programable Assembly System [*Data processing*]
APAS	Automatic Performance Analysis System
APC	Accounting Processing Code
APC	Adaptive Predictive Coding [*Telecommunications*] (TEL)
APC	Advanced Performance Computer
APC	Advanced Programing Course [*Data processing*]
APC	Analog to Pressure Converter
APC	Antenna Pattern Correction [*for spacecraft data*]
APC	Associative Processor Control [*Data processing*] (CAA)
APC	Australian Personal Computer [*A publication*]
APC	Automated Packaging Code (MCD)
APC	Automatic Phase Control [*Telecommunications*] (TEL)
APC	Average Power Control [*Telecommunications*] (TEL)
APCA	Audio Peak Clipping Amplifier
APCHE	Automatic Programed Checkout Equipment
APCI	Apollo Computer, Incorporated [*NASDAQ symbol*] (NQ)
APCM	Adaptive Pulse Code Modulation [*Telecommunications*] (TEL)
APCOM	International Symposium on the Application of Computers and Operations Research in the Mineral Industries
APCS	Associative Processor Computer System (IDA)
APD	Amplitude Probability Distribution [*Telecommunications*]
APD	Analog-to-Pulse Duration
APD	Avalanche Photodiode Detector
APDS	Advanced Personnel Data System (MCD)
APDU	Association of Public Data Users [*Princeton University*] [*Princeton, NJ*] (EANO)
APEA	Antenna Pattern Error Analysis
APEC	All-Purpose Electronic Computer (IEEE)
APEC	Automated Procedures for Engineering Consultants, Inc.
APEX	Automated Procurement Planning, Execution, and Control
APExC	All Purpose Electronic x Computer [*Early computer*] [*Birkbeck College*] [*British*] (CAH)
APF	Authorized Program Facility [*Data processing*] (BUR)
APF	Automatic Program Finding [*Electronics*]
APG	American Programmers Guild
APG	Antenna Power Gain
APG	Application Program Generator [*Data processing*]
APG	Automatic Priority Group [*Fujitsu Ltd.*] [*Japanese*] (MCD)
API	Antenna Position Indicator
API	Application Program Interface [*Data processing*] (BUR)
API	Architectural Periodicals Index [*Royal Institute of British Architects*] [*London, England*] [*Information service*] (EISS)
API	Automatic Priority Interrupt [*Data processing*]
API	Automatic Programing Instruction [*Data processing*]
APIC	Automatic Power Input Controller
APIC	Automatic Programing Information Centre [*British*]
APICS	Air Pollution Information and Computation System
APICS	American Production and Inventory Control Society, Inc. [*Washington, DC*]
APIE	[*The*] American Psycho/Info Exchange [*New York, NY*] [*Information service*] (EISS)
APIF	Automated Process Information File [*Library of Congress*]
APILIT	API [*American Petroleum Institute*] Literature [*New York, NY*] [*Bibliographic database*] (OBD)
APIS	Array Processing Instruction Set [*Data processing*] (MSA)
APK	Amplitude Phase Shift Keying (MCD)
APL	Advanced Programing Language [*Data processing*]
APL	Assembly Programing Language [*Data processing*]
APL	Association of Programmed Learning [*London, England*] (MCD)
APL	Associative Programing Language [*Data processing*] (BUR)
APL	Automatic Programing Language [*Data processing*] (CMD)
APL	Average Picture Level
APL	[*A*] Programing Language [*1960*] [*Data processing*] (CSR)
APLAC	Analysis Program Linear Active Circuits (NASA)
APLET	Association for Programmed Learning and Educational Technology
APLS	American Private Line Services, Inc. [*Newton, MA*] [*Telecommunications*] (TSSD)
APL/S	[*A*] Programing Language/Structured [*Data processing*] (CSR)
APLSTATPACK	Advanced Programing Language Statistical Package (MCD)
APLSV	[*A*] Programing Language Shared Variable [*Data processing*]
APLU	Automatic Program Loading Unit [*Data processing*]
APLUM	[*A*] Programing Language/University of Massachusetts [*Data processing*] (CSR)
APM	Analog Panel Meter (IEEE)
APM	Antenna Positioning Mechanism
APM	Automatic Programing Machine [*Data processing*]
APMIS	Automated Project Management Information System [*Data processing*]
APMMRI	Automatic Point Marking, Measuring, and Recording Instrument
APOJI	Automatic Processing of Jezebel [*Sonobuoy System*] Information (DDI)
APOL	Australian Political Register [*Australian Consolidated Press*] [*Database*] (CUAD)
APOLLO	Article Procurement with Online Local Ordering [*Document delivery system*] [*Telecommunications*]
APOTA	Automatic Positioning Telemetering Antenna
APP	Application Date [*Bell System*] (TEL)
APP	Associative Parallel Processor [*Data processing*]
APP	Automatic Plate Processor
APPECS	Adaptive Pattern Perceiving Electronic Computer System
APPLE	Applied Parallel Programing Language Experiment [*Data processing*] (MCD)
APPLE	Associative Processor Programing Language Evaluation (OA)
AP & PO	Advance Programing and Proposal Operations (MCD)
APPROX	Approximately
APPS	Automated Packaging Planning System (MCD)
APR	Alternate Path Reentry [*Fujitsu Ltd.*] [*Data processing*] (MCD)
APR	Antenna Position Recorder
APR	Automatic Passbook Reader (BUR)
APR	Automatic Pattern Recognition
APR	Automatic Programing and Recording [*Data processing*] (MCD)
APRIL	Automatically Programed Remote Indication Logged
APS	Alphanumeric Photocomposer System (IEEE)
APS	Amplifier Power Supply
APS	Antenna Pointing Subsystem (CIT)
AP(S)	Application Process [*or Program*] (Structure) [*Telecommunications*] (TEL)
APS	Application Process Subsystem [*Telecommunications*] (TEL)
APS	Arc-Plasma Spraying [*Magnetic film*]
APS	Array Processor Software [*Data processing*] (IEEE)
APS	Assembly Programing System [*Data processing*] (IEEE)
APS	Automatic Patching System (IEEE)
APS	Automatic Program System [*Data processing*] (DDI)
APS	Auxiliary Program Storage [*Data processing*] (BUR)
APS	Avionics Processing System
APSE	Ada Programing Support Environments [*Data processing*] (RDA)
APSI	Allstates-Programming & Systems, Incorporated
APSI	Automated Professional Systems [*NASDAQ symbol*] (NQ)
APSN	Association Package Sequence Number (MCD)
APSP	Array Processor Subroutine Package [*Data processing*] (BUR)
APSS	Automated Program Support System [*Data processing*]
APT	Adaptive Programing Technology
APT	Advanced Patent Technique (TUT)
APT	All-Purpose Terminal [*Computer technology*]
APT	Allarcom Pay Television Ltd. [*Canada*]
APT	Analog Pressure Transducer
APT	Analog Program Tape [*Data processing*]
APT	Asia-Pacific Telecommunity [*Bangkok, Thailand*] [*Telecommunications*] (TSSD)
APT	Augmented Programing Training [*Data processing*] (IEEE)
APT	Automatic Picture Taking (IEEE)
APT	Automatic Position Telemetering
APT	Automatically Programed Tools [*Computer software*] [*Data processing*] (TUT)
APTIC	Air Pollution Technical Information Center [*Also, NAPTIC*] [*Environmental Protection Agency*] [*Bibliographic database*]
APTP	Arithmetic Proficiency Training Program [*Computer-assisted training program*]
APU	Analytic Processing Unit (CCD)
APU	Arithmetic Processing Unit [*Data processing*]
APU	Auxiliary Processing Unit
APUG	AutoPrep 5000 Users Group [*South Windsor, CT*] (EANO)
APUHS	Automatic Program Unit High-Speed [*Component of ADIS*]
APULS	Automatic Program Unit Low-Speed [*Component of ADIS*]
A/PW	Analog-to-Pulse Width Converter (CIT)
APX	Ampex Corp. [*NYSE symbol*] [*Delisted*]
AQCL	Analytical Quality Control Laboratory (EISS)
AQI	Automated Quill, Incorporated [*Englewood, CO*] [*Software manufacturer*] (DASOS)
AQL	Acceptable Quality Level [*Quality control*]
AQUARIUS	[*A*] Query and Retrieval Interactive Utility System [*Data processing*]
AQUIRE	Aquatic Information Retrieval Database [*Database*] [*Environmental Protection Agency*] (FDB)
AR	Accounts Register [*Data processing*]
AR	Accumulator Register (CAA)
AR	Acknowledgment of Receipt [*Message handling*] [*Telecommunications*]
AR	Address Register (CMD)
A/R	Alternate Route [*Telecommunications*] (TEL)
AR	Amateur (Radio) Station [*ITU designation*] (CET)
AR	Argus Corp. Ltd. [*Toronto Stock Exchange symbol*]
AR	Arithmetic Register (OA)
AR	Associative Register [*Data processing*] (OA)
AR	Awaiting Reply [*Telecommunications*] (TEL)
ARA	Average Response Amplitude
ARABSAT	Arab Satellite Communications Organization [*Riyadh, Saudi Arabia*] [*Telecommunications*] (TSSD)
ARAD	Automated Requirements Allocation Data (MCD)
ARAD	Average Response Amplitude Data
ARAL	Automatic Record Analysis Language [*Data processing*]
ARAMIS	American Rheumatism Association Medical Information System [*Palo Alto, CA*] [*Database producer*] (EISS)
ARAND	Analysis of Random Data [*System documentation*] [*Oregon State University*]
ARAT	Automatic Random Access Transport

Computer & Telecommunications Acronyms

Acronym	Expansion
ARB	All Routes Busy [*Telecommunications*] (TEL)
ARB	APCHE [*Automatic Program Checkout Equipment*] Relay Box
ARBITER	Access Refusal and Barrier Interface Terminal [*Hardware-based security device from Computer Security Systems*]
ARC	Amplitude and Rise Time Compensation (IEEE)
ARC	Analog Response Conditioner (MCD)
ARC	Analyzer-Recorder-Controller
ARC	Applied Research Corporation
ARC	Argonne Reactor Computation (IEEE)
ARC	Atlantic Research Corporation
ARC	Audio Response Control (BUR)
ARC	Automated Rent Collections (TUT)
ARC	Automatic Ram Control (CAAL)
ARC	Automatic Relay Calculator [*Early computer*] [*Birkbeck College*] [*British*] (MCD)
ARC	Average Response Computer
ARCADE	Argonne Computer-Aided Diffraction Equipment
ARCH	Articulated Computing Hierarchy [*British*]
ARCOMSAT	Arabian Communication Satellite (CBSS)
ARCOS	Architects Job Costing [*ICS*] [*Software package*] [*British*] (NCC)
ARCS	Advanced Reconfigurable Computer System
ARCS	Automatic Route Control System [*Truck-delivery computer system*]
ARCSS	Center for Social Science Research and Documentation for the Arab Region [*UNESCO*] [*Information service*] (EISS)
ARD	Answering, Recording, and Dialing (CAA)
ARDA	Analog Recording Dynamic Analyzer [*Data processing*]
ARDC	Applied Research and Design Center [*California State University, Sacramento*] [*Research center*] (RCD)
ARE	Advanced Real-Time Executive (BUR)
ARE	Antenna Range Equipment (CIT)
ARE	Automated Responsive Environment (BUR)
ARE	Automatic Record Evaluation
AREG	Apparatus Repair - Strategy Evaluation Guidelines [*Telecommunications*] (TEL)
ARES	Amateur Radio Emergency Service
ARF	Area Resource File [*Public Health Service*] [*Rockville, MD*] [*Information service*] (EISS)
ARF	Automatic Reporting Feature (MCD)
ARG	Argument
ARGA	Appliance, Range, Adjust [*Data processing*]
ARGUS	Associative Registers for Generalized User Switching [*Computer typesetting system*]
ARGUS	Automatic Routine Generating and Updating System [*Compiler*] [*Data processing*]
ARI	Astronomisches Recheninstitut [*Information retrieval*] (ODIN)
ARI	Automatic Radio Information [*System which relays traffic information through car radios*]
ARIC	Agricultural Research Information Centre [*New Delhi, India*] (EISS)
ARIES	Automated Reliability Estimation Program [*Data processing*]
ARINC	Aeronautical Radio, Incorporated [*Annapolis, MD*] [*Telecommunications*]
ARIS	Automatic Recording Infrared Spectrometer
ARITH	Arithmetic
ARJCC	Andrew R. Jennings Computing Center [*Case Western Reserve University*] [*Research center*] (RCD)
ARL	Acceptable Reliability Level [*Quality control*]
ARM	Acorn RISC [*Reduced Instruction Set Computer*]
ARM	Algorithmic Remote Manipulation [*Programing language*]
ARM	Amateur Radio Monitor
ARM	Asynchronous Response Mode [*Data processing*] (CAA)
ARM	Automated Route Management (DEN)
ARM	Availability, Reliability, and Maintainability [*Computer performance*] (CAA)
ARMA	Association of Records Managers and Administrators, Inc. [*Prairie Village, KS*]
ARMA	Autoregressive Moving Average [*Statistics*]
ARMMS	Automatically Reconfigurable Modular Multiprocessor [*or Multiprocessing*] System [*Data processing*]
ARMS	ADPE [*Automatic Data Processing Equipment*] Resources Management System (AFM)
ARMU	Addressable Remote Multiplexer Unit (MCD)
ARO	After Receipt of Order
ARO	Algonquin Radio Observatory [*Herzberg Institute of Astrophysics, National Research Council of Canada*] [*Research center*] (RCD)
AROM	Alterable Read-Only Memory [*Data processing*]
AROS	Alterable Read-Only Operating System (CAA)
ARP	Antenna Radiation Pattern
ARPA	Advanced Research Projects Agency
ARPDP	Association of Rehabilitation Programs in Data Processing (EANO)
ARPSC	Amateur Radio Public Service Corps
ARQ	Automatic Repeat Request [*Data processing*] (MCD)
ARQ	Automatic Request for Repetition [*Data transmission*] (CMD)
ARR	Antenna Radiation Resistance
ARR	Antenna Rotation Rate
ARR	Automatic Rerouting [*Telecommunications*] (TEL)
ARRE	Alarm Receiving and Reporting Equipment [*Telecommunications*] (TEL)
ARRL	American Radio Relay League [*Newington, CT*]
ARS	Advanced Reconnaissance Satellite
ARS	Aerospace Research Satellite
ARS	Analog Recording System (CIT)
ARS	Audio Response System (CAA)
ARS	Automatic Route Selection [*Also, MERS*] [*Bell System*] [*Telecommunications*]
ARSB	Automated Repair Service Bureau (TEL)
ARSC	Analog Rotation Speed Control
ART	Additional Reference Carrier Transmission [*Telecommunications*] (TEL)
AR & T	Advanced Research and Technology (MUGU)
ART	Advanced Research and Technology
ART	Alarm Reporting Telephone [*Telecommunications*] (TEL)
ART	Artificial [*Telecommunications*] (TEL)
ART	Automatic Reporting Telephone [*Telecommunications*] (TEL)
ARTEC	Association of Radio and Television Employees of Canada
ARTEMIS	Automatic Retrieval of Text from Europe's Multinational Information Service
ARTIC	Assocometrics Remote Terminal Inquiry Control System (IEEE)
ARTIS	ALPHA [*AMC Logistics Program - Hardcore Automated*] Remote Terminal Interactive System
ARTS	Adventist Radio Television Services [*Canada*]
ARTS	Alpha Repertory Television Service [*Cable-television system*]
ARU	Address Recognition Unit (CAA)
ARU	Analog Remote Unit
ARU	Analog Response Unit (SKY)
ARU	Audio Response Unit
ARW	Arrow Electronics, Inc. [*NYSE symbol*]
AS	Advanced System [*NAS*] (CAA)
AS	Ammeter Switch (MSA)
As	Ampere Second
AS	Articulation Score [*Percentage of words correctly understood over a radio channel perturbed by interference*] [*Telecommunications*]
AS	Artificial Satellite
AS	Auxiliary Storage [*Data processing*] (CAA)
AS	Start of Answer [*Telecommunications*] (TEL)
AS	Wait [*Morse telephony*] (FAAC)
ASA	Acoustical Society of America [*New York, NY*]
ASA	American Standards Association [*Later, USASI, ANSI*]
ASA	American Statistical Association [*Washington, DC*]
ASA	Amplifier and Switch Assembly (MCD)
ASA	Andrew Sipos Associates [*New York, NY*] [*Software manufacturer*] (DASOS)
ASA	Automatic Steering Antenna
ASA	Automatic Systems Analysis (KSC)
ASAAS	Asymmetric Stress Analysis of Axisymmetric Solids [*Computer program*]
ASAC	Active Satellite Attitude Control
ASAP	Analog System Assembly Pack
ASAP	Applied Systems and Personnel (BUR)
ASAP	Automated Statistical Analysis Program
ASAS	Atkins Stress Analysis System [*Atkins Research & Development*] [*Software package*] [*British*] (NCC)
ASBAL	[*A*] Stack Based Abstraction Language [*1978*] [*Data processing*] (CSR)
ASC	Advanced Scientific Computer [*Texas Instruments, Inc.*]
ASC	Advanced System Concept (MCD)
ASC	American Satellite Company [*Rockville, MD*] [*Telecommunications*] (TSSD)
ASC	American Society for Cybernetics
ASC	Analog Signal Converter (DDI)
ASC	Analog Signal Correlator
ASC	Analog Strip Chart
ASC	Associative Structure Computer (BUR)
ASC	Asynchronous Communication Procedure (BUR)
ASC	AUTODIN Switching Center
ASC	Automatic Scan Counter
ASC	Automatic Sensitivity Control
ASC	Automatic Switching Center
ASCA	Automatic Subject Citation Alert [*A publication*]
ASCAT	Analog Self-Checking Automatic Tester
ASCC	Automatic Sequence Controlled Calculator [*First all-automatic calculating machine*]
ASCD	American Society of Computer Dealers [*Dallas, TX*] (EANO)
ASCE	Abrupt Space Charge Edge [*Algorithm*]
ASCE	American Society of Civil Engineers [*New York, NY*]
ASCEND	Advanced System for Communications and Education in National Development (MCD)
ASCENT	Assembly System for Central Processor [*Data processing*]
ASCII	American Standard Code for Information Interchange [*Pronounced "ask-ee"*] [*American National Standards Institute*] [*Data processing*]
ASCON	Automated Switched Communications Network (MCD)
ASCOP	[*A*] Statistical Computing Procedure
ASCOT	Analogue Simulation of Competitive Operational Tactics [*Game*]
ASCP	Automatic System Checkout Program (CAA)
ASCR	Analog Strip Chart Recorder
ASCS	Automatic Scan Counter System
ASCU	Association of Small Computer Users [*Later, ACU*] (EANO)
ASCUE	Association of Small Computer Users [*Later, ACU*]
ASD	Advanced Systems Division [*IBM Corp.*]
ASDEC	Automatic Selection of Digital Electronic Computers
ASDL	Automated Ship Data Library (IEEE)

Computer & Telecommunications Acronyms

Acronym	Expansion
ASDPSIM	Advanced System Data Processing Simulation
ASDSRS	Automatic Spectrum Display and Signal Recognition System (IEEE)
ASD (T)	Assistant Secretary of Defense (Telecommunications)
ASE	Advanced Systems Engineering (DDI)
ASEE	American Society for Engineering Education [*Washington, DC*]
ASES	Automated Software Evaluation System (CAA)
ASF	Amperes per Square Foot
ASF	Automatic Sheet Feeder (CAA)
ASFA	Aquatic Sciences and Fisheries Abstracts [*Information Retrieval Ltd.*] [*Bibliographic database*] [*A publication*]
ASFIS	Aquatic Sciences and Fisheries Information System [*Rome, Italy*] [*United Nations*] (EISS)
ASG	Antenna Steering Group
ASI	Action Surveys, Incorporated [*Silver Spring, MD*] [*Information service*] (EISS)
ASI	American Statistics Index [*Congressional Information Service, Inc.*] [*Bibliographic database*] [*A publication*]
ASIC	Application Specific Integrated Circuit [*National Semiconductor Corp.*]
ASID	Address Space Identifier (BUR)
ASIDIC	Association of Information and Dissemination Centers [*Athens, GA*]
ASIM	Alpha-Comp Simulation Package [*Alpha-Comp Ltd.*] [*Software package*] [*British*] (NCC)
ASIS	American Society for Industrial Security
ASIS	American Society for Information Science [*Washington, DC*]
ASIS	Arbeitsschutzinformationssystem [*Information System for Occupational Safety and Health*] [*West Germany*] (EISS)
ASIST	Advanced Scientific Instruments Symbolic Translator [*Assembly program*] (DEN)
ASIST	Alberta Statistical Information System [*Alberta Treasury, Bureau of Statistics*] [*Database*] (CUAD)
ASIT	Adaptable Surface Interface Terminal (MCD)
ASK	Actively Shared Knowledge [*Data processing system*]
ASK	Alerting Search Service from Kinokuniya [*Kinokuniya Co. Ltd.*] [*Tokyo, Japan*] [*Information service*] (EISS)
ASK	Amplitude Shift Keying
ASK	Analog Select Keyboard [*Data processing*] (KSC)
ASKI	Ask Computer Systems [*NASDAQ symbol*] (NQ)
ASL	Arithmetic Shift Left [*Data processing*]
ASL	Available Space List [*Data processing*]
ASLT	Advanced Solid Logic Technology [*Data processing*]
ASLU	Antenna Select Logic Unit (NASA)
ASM	Antenna Switching Matrix
ASM	Assembler [*Sperry UNIVAC*] [*Data processing*]
ASM	Association for Systems Management [*Formerly, SPA*] [*Cleveland, OH*] (TUT)
ASM	Asynchronous State Machine (IEEE)
ASM	Automatic Space Management
ASM	Auxiliary Storage Manager [*Data processing*]
ASMC	AUTODIN Station Maintenance Console
ASME	American Society of Mechanical Engineers [*New York, NY*]
ASN	Atlantic Satellite Network [*Cable-television system*]
ASNA	Amalgamated Software of North America, Inc. [*Malibu, CA*] [*Software manufacturer*] (DASOS)
ASNA	American SMR [*Special Mobile Radio*] Network Association (EANO)
ASNAP	Automatic Steerable Null Antenna Processor
ASOP	Automatic Scheduling and Operating Program (BUR)
ASP	Advanced Signal Processor [*Data processing*]
ASP	Advanced Software Products, Inc. [*Delray Beach, FL*] [*Software manufacturer*] (DASOS)
ASP	Association for Software Protection [*Computer software developers and vendors*] (EANO)
ASP	Association-Storing Processor [*Data processing*]
ASP	Associative Structures Package (BUR)
ASP	Attached Support Processor [*Data processing*] (CGC)
ASP	Automated Spooling Priority [*Data processing*] (CGC)
ASP	Automatic Switching Panel
ASP	[*A*] System for Programers
ASPDE	Automatic Shaft-Position Data Encoder
ASPER	Assembly System for the Peripheral Processors [*Data processing*]
ASPI	Asynchronous Synchronous Programable Interface [*Data processing*] (CAA)
ASPOL	[*A*] Simulation Process Oriented Language [*1972*] [*Data processing*] (CSR)
ASPP	Antenna Solar Panel Positioner (CIT)
ASQC	American Society for Quality Control [*Milwaukee, WI*]
ASR	Accumulators Shift Right [*Data processing*] (BUR)
ASR	Active Status Register (CAA)
ASR	Analog Shift Register [*Data processing*]
ASR	Arithmetic Shift Right [*Data processing*]
ASR	Australasian Software Report [*A publication*]
AS/R	Automatic Send/Receive Teletypewriter [*Communications equipment*]
ASR	Automatic Speech Recognition
ASRA	ADP [*Automatic Data Processing*] Systems Resources Analysis
ASRM	Antenna System Readiness Monitor (MCD)
AS/RS	Automated Storage/Retrieval Systems
ASS	Analog Simulation System
ASS	Assembler Language [*Data processing*] (CMD)
ASSIST	[*A*] Simple Systematic Integration of Statistical Techniques (BUR)
ASSN	Association
Assn Comp Mach J	Association for Computing Machinery Journal [*A publication*]
AST	Advanced Simulation Technology (IEEE)
AST	Antisidetone [*Telecommunications*] (TEL)
ASTAP	Advanced Statistical Analysis Program [*Data processing*] (MCD)
ASTEC	Advanced Systems Technology (IEEE)
ASTIS	Arctic Science and Technology Information System [*Arctic Institute of North America*] [*University of Calgary*] [*Calgary, AB, Canada*] (EISS)
ASTM	American Society for Testing and Materials [*Philadelphia, PA*] [*Research center*]
ASTMS	Association of Scientific, Technical, and Managerial Staffs [*British*]
ASTRA	Application of Space Techniques Relating to Aviation [*International Civil Aviation Organization*]
ASTRA	Automatic Scheduling with Time-Integrated Resource Allocation
ASTRAC	Arizona Statistical Repetitive Analog Computer
ASTRAL	Analog Schematic Translator to Algebraic Language [*Data processing*] (IEEE)
ASTRO	Artificial Satellite Time and Radio Orbit (MCD)
ASTROC	Automatic Stellar Tracking, Recognition, and Orientation Computer
ASTUTE	Association of System 2000 Users for Technical Exchange
ASTV	American Communications & TV [*NASDAQ symbol*] (NQ)
ASU	Acknowledgement Signal Unit [*Telecommunications*] (TEL)
ASU	Analog Stimulus Unit (SKY)
ASU	Automatic Switching Unit [*Telecommunications*] (OA)
ASUG	American Software Users Group [*Franklin Park, IL*] (EANO)
ASUP	AUTODIN Switch Upgrade Project (MCD)
ASV	Automatic Self-Verification
ASVC	Automatic Secure Voice Communications (CAAL)
ASVIP	American Standard Vocabulary for Information Processing (BUR)
ASVS	Automatic Signature Verification System (CAA)
ASWLC	American Shortwave Listeners Club
ASYMP	Asymptote [*Mathematics*]
ASYN	Asynchronous (MSA)
ASYNC	Asynchronous
ASYNCH	Asynchronous
AT	Address Translator [*Data processing*] (CAA)
AT	Advanced Technology [*In PC AT, model name of a computer*] [*IBM Corp.*]
AT	Aerial Tape Armor [*Telecommunications*] (TEL)
AT	Amateur Station [*ITU designation*]
AT	Audit Trail (OA)
AT	Automated Teller
ATA	Administrative Telecommunications Agency [*Canada*]
ATA	Agence des Telecommunications Administratives [*Administrative Telecommunications Agency*] [*Canada*]
ATA	Albanian Telegraph Agency
ATA	American Telemarketing Association [*Glenview, IL*] (EANO)
ATA	Asynchronous Terminal Adapter [*Telecommunications*] (CAA)
ATA	Automated Testing Analyzer [*Data processing*]
ATA	Automatic Trouble Analysis (TEL)
ATA	Average Turnaround [*Data processing*]
ATAC	Air Transportable Acoustic Communications (CAAL)
ATAC	All Tariffs Computerized [*Project*]
ATACC J	ATACC [*Alberta Teachers' Association, Computer Council*] Journal [*A publication*]
ATAE	Associated Telephone Answering Exchanges [*Formerly, ATE*] [*Alexandria, VA*]
ATALA	Association for Automatic Language Processing
ATAR	Automated Travel Agents Reservation (CGC)
ATAS	Association of Telephone Answering Services [*New York, NY*]
ATAS	Automatic Tracking Antenna System
A.TAS	Thermal Analysis Software/Architects [*Amazon Energy Ltd.*] [*Software package*] [*British*] (NCC)
ATASCII	Atari-Version American Standard Code for Information Interchange [*Character code*]
ATB	Access Type BITS [*Data processing*] (OA)
ATB	All Trunks Busy [*Telecommunications*]
ATBA	Automatic Test Break and Access [*Telecommunications*] (TEL)
ATC	Address Translation Chip
ATC	Aetna Telecommunications Consultants [*Centerville, MA*] [*Telecommunications*] (TSSD)
ATC	Analog Technology Company (CIT)
ATC	Architecture Technology Corporation [*Minneapolis, MN*] [*Information service*] [*Telecommunications*] (TSSD)
ATCAA	Automatica [*United States*] [*A publication*]
ATD	Acceptance and Takeover Date [*Telecommunications*] (TEL)
ATD	Analog to Time to Digital [*Data processing*]
ATDG	Automated Test Data Generator [*Data processing*]
ATDM	Asynchronous Time-Division Multiplexing [*Data processing*]
ATDMA	Advanced Time-Division Multiple Access (IEEE)
ATDP	Air Traffic Data Processor
ATDS	Automatic Telemetry Decommutation System
ATE	Associated Telephone Exchanges [*Later, ATAE*]
ATE	Automatic Test Equipment
ATEC	Agence Transequatoriale des Communications [*Trans-Equatorial Communications Agency*] [*or CCEAE*]

By Acronym

Computer & Telecommunications Acronyms

ATEC	Automated Technical Control [System] [Honeywell, Inc.]
ATECO	Automatic Telegram Transmission with Computers [Telecommunications] (TEL)
ATEL	All Type Equipment Leasing, Inc. [San Francisco, CA] [Software manufacturer] (DASOS)
ATF	Algebraic Technological Function [Data processing]
ATF	Antenna Test Facility
ATF	Automatic Text Formatter (CAA)
ATG	Agence des Telecommunications Gouvernementales [Government Telecommunications Agency] [Canada]
ATG	Alcatel Thomson Gigadisc [Optical disk]
ATG	Automated Test-Case Guidance [Data processing]
ATI	Amtel, Inc. [NYSE symbol] [Delisted]
ATI	Associated Telemanagement, Incorporated [Boston, MA] [Telecommunications] (TSSD)
ATI	Audiometer Telephone Interface [for the hearing-impaired]
ATIS	Antenna and Transmitter Improvement Study
ATIS	AT & T [American Telephone & Telegraph Co.] Information Systems
ATIS	Automatic Transmitter Identification System [Citizens band radio]
ATL	Active Time List [Data processing]
AT/L	Advanced Technology/Libraries [Information service]
ATL	Analog Threshold Logic
ATL	Automated Tape Library
ATLAS	Abbreviated Test Language for All Systems [Data processing]
ATLAS	Abbreviated Test Language for Avionics Systems (CAA)
ATLAS	Automated Tape Label Assignment System
ATLAS	Automatic Tabulating, Listing, and Sorting System [Software] (DEEC)
ATLAS	Automatic Tape Load Audit System
AT/M	Ampere-Turn per Meter (MCD)
ATM	Antenna Test Model (CIT)
ATM	Automated [or Automatic] Teller Machine [Banking]
ATM	Auxiliary Tape Memory [Spacecraft guidance]
ATMAC	Advanced Technology Microelectronic Array Computer (MCD)
ATME	Automatic Transmission Measuring Equipment [Telecommunications] (TEL)
ATMG	Angus Telemanagement Group, Inc. [Toronto, ON] [Information service] [Telecommunications] (TSSD)
ATMS	Advanced Text Management System [IBM Corp.]
ATMS	Automatic Transmission Measuring System
ATMS	Automatic Trunk Measuring System [Bell System]
ATN	Augmented Transition Network [Language analysis]
ATO	Aeronautical Telecommunications Operator
ATOM	Analog Tree-Organized Multiplexer
ATOM	Automatic Transmission of Mail [Early electronic mail system] (CAA)
ATP	Acceptance Test Plan [or Procedure]
ATP	Automated Test Plan (BUR)
ATPSD	ACM [Association for Computing Machinery] Transactions on Programming Languages and Systems [A publication]
ATR	Analog Tape Recorder
ATR	Angle, Time, Range [Data processing]
ATR	Answering Time Recorder [Telecommunications] (TEL)
ATR	Anti-Transmit-Receive
ATR	Australian Telecommunication Research [A publication]
ATR	Automatic Trunk Routiner (MCD)
ATR Aust Telecommun Res	ATR: Australian Telecommunication Research [A publication]
ATRAX	Air Transportable Communications Complex
ATRC	Atlantic Research Corporation [NASDAQ symbol] (NQ)
ATRIB	Average Transfer Rate of Information BITS [Binary Digits] [Data processing] (IEEE)
ATRT	Anti-Transmit-Receive Tube
ATS	Acoustic Telemetry Subsystem (MCD)
ATS	Acoustic Transmission System
ATS	Active Television System (MCD)
ATS	Administrative Terminal System [IBM Corp.]
ATS	Advanced Technology Satellite
ATS	Advanced Technology Systems, Inc. [Arlington, VA] [Telecommunications] (TSSD)
ATS	Alarm Termination Subsystem [Telecommunications] (TEL)
ATS	Automated Trading System [NYSE computer]
ATS	Automatic Telemetry System
ATS	Automatic Telephone Set
ATS	Automatic Terminal System (NASA)
ATS	Automatic Test System
ATS	Automatic Trunk Synchronizer [Telecommunications] (TEL)
ATS	[A] Tutorial System [1971] [Data processing] (CSR)
ATSS	Auto Tracking Scan System [for television video quality] [Sony Corp.]
ATSS	Automatic Telecommunications Switching System (CAA)
ATSU	Association of Time-Sharing Users [Later, ACU] (EANO)
AT & T	American Telephone & Telegraph Co. [New York, NY]
ATT	American Telephone & Telegraph Co. [New York, NY]
ATT	Application Transfer Teams [IBM Corp.]
ATT	Attachment [Telecommunications] (TEL)
ATT	Attended Public Telephone [Telecommunications] (TEL)
ATT	Automatic Toll Ticketing (TEL)
ATTC	Auto-Trol Technology [NASDAQ symbol] (NQ)
ATTC	Automatic Transmission Test and Control [Telecommunications] (TEL)
ATTCOM	AT & T [American Telephone & Telegraph Co.] Communications [Bedminster, NJ] [Telecommunications] (TSSD)
ATTN	Attention (AFM)
ATTRA	Automatic Telemetry Tracking Receiving Antenna
ATTS	Automatic Telemetry Tracking System
ATU	Alliance of Independent Telephone Unions [Later, TIU]
ATU	Antenna Tuning Unit (MSA)
ATU	Application Terminal Unit [Telecommunications] (TEL)
ATU	Autonome Transfer Unit [Data processing] (DIT)
ATUG	Australian Telecommunications Users Group [Sydney, Australia] (TSSD)
ATURS	Automatic Traffic Usage Recording System (TEL)
ATVS	Advanced Television Seeker (MCD)
ATVSC	Advanced TV Systems Committee (EANO)
ATWDDS	Automated Terminal Weather Dissemination Display System (MCD)
ATX	Automatic TELEX Exchange [Telecommunications] (TEL)
AU	Address Unit [Data processing]
AU	Angstrom Unit [Also, A]
AU	Arithmetic Unit [Data processing]
AU	Astronomical Unit [Equal to average distance from earth to sun]
AU	Author [Online database field identifier] [Data processing]
AUCBE	Advisory Unit for Computer Based Education [Hatfield, England] [Information service] [Telecommunications] (TSSD)
AUD	Automatic Data Processing, Inc. [NYSE symbol]
AUDACIOUS	Automatic Direct Access to Information with the On-Line UDC [Universal Decimal Classification] System [American Institute of Physics] [Information retrieval]
Audiov Commun	Audio Visual Communications [A publication]
AUDIT	Auditory Input Task [Data processing]
AUDIT	Automatic Unattended Detection Inspection Transmitter [Raytheon Co.]
AUDRE	Audio Response [International Harvester Co. computer]
AUDREY	Audio Reply (IEEE)
AUDREY	Automatic Digit Recognition
Auerbach Data Base Manage	Auerbach Data Base Management [A publication]
Auerbach Rep	Auerbach Reporter [A publication]
AUG	Amdahl Users Group (EANO)
AUI	Applied Urbanetics, Incorporated [Information service] (EISS)
AUJS	Advanced Universal Jamming System
AUR	Aural
AURCA	Automation and Remote Control [A publication]
AUSB	Australian Business [Australian Consolidated Press] [Database] (CUAD)
Aust Comput Bull	Australian Computer Bulletin [A publication]
Aust Comput J	Australian Computer Journal [A publication]
Aust Comput Sci Commun	Australian Computer Science Communications [A publication]
Aust Telecomm Res	Australian Telecommunication Research [A publication]
Aust Telecomm Research	Australian Telecommunication Research [A publication]
Aust Telecommun Dev Assoc	Australian Telecommunications Development Association. Annual Report [A publication]
Aust Telecommun Res	Australian Telecommunication Research [A publication]
AUT	Author [Online database field identifier] [Data processing] (OBD)
AUTOBUS	Automated Budget System
AUTOCAT	Automatic Control of Air Transmissions (NATG)
AUTOCOM	Automated Combustor [Computer code]
AUTODIN	Automatic Digital Information Network
AUTODIN	Automatic Digital Network [DoD]
AUTOGRAF	[A] programing language [1972] (CSR)
AUTOLING	Automated Linguistic Fieldworker [Data processing] (DIT)
AUTOMAP	Automatic Machining Program
AUTOMAST	Automatic Mathematical Analysis and Symbolic Translation [Data processing]
Automat Control and Computer Sci	Automatic Control and Computer Sciences [A publication]
Automat Control Comput Sci	Automatic Control and Computer Sciences [A publication]
Automat Control Theory Appl	Automatic Control Theory and Applications [A publication]
Automat Data Process Inform B	Automatic Data Processing Information Bulletin [A publication]
Automatic Control Theory Appl	Automatic Control Theory and Applications [A publication]
Automat Remote Contr	Automation and Remote Control [USSR] [A publication]
Automat Remote Control	Automation and Remote Control [A publication]
Autom Control Comput Sci	Automatic Control and Computer Sciences [A publication]
Autom Control and Comput Sci	Automatic Control and Computer Sciences [A publication]
Autom Control Theory & Appl	Automatic Control Theory and Applications [A publication]
Autom Data Process Inf Bull	Automatic Data Processing Information Bulletin [A publication]
AUTOMEX	Automatic Message Exchange Service (CAA)
Autom & Remote Control	Automation and Remote Control [USSR] [A publication]

Computer & Telecommunications Acronyms

Autom Remote Control ... Automation and Remote Control [*USSR*] [*A publication*]
AUTONEST ... Automatic Nesting Program [*Kongsberg UK*] [*Software package*] [*British*]   (NCC)
AUTONET ... Automatic Network Display   (CGC)
AUTOPIC .... Automatic Personal Identification Code [*IBM Corp.*]
AUTOPROD ... Automated Projective Drawing [*GMW Computers Ltd.*] [*Software package*] [*British*]   (NCC)
AUTOPROMT ... Automatic Programing of Machine Tools [*IBM Corp.*]
AUTOPSY ... Automatic Operating System [*IBM Corp.*]
AUTOQEST ... Automatic Generation of Requests [*Data processing*]   (DIT)
AUTOSATE ... Automated Data System Analysis Technique
AUTOSCRIPT ... Automated System for Composing, Revising, Illustrating, and Phototypesetting
AUTOSEVOCOM ... Automatic Secure Voice Communications
AUTOSPEC ... Automated Specifications [*Data processing*]   (DIT)
AUTOVON ... Automatic Voice Network [*DoD*]
Aut Remot R ... Automation and Remote Control (USSR) [*A publication*]
AUUA .... Americas UNIVAC [*Universal Automatic Computer*] Users Association [*Formerly, UUA*] [*Winston-Salem, NC*]   (EANO)
AUX .... Auxiliary   (AFM)
AUXRC .... Auxiliary Recording Control [*Circuit*] [*Bell System*]
AUXT .... Auxton Computer Enterprises [*NASDAQ symbol*]   (NQ)
AV .... Audiovisual
AV .... Available [*or Availability*] [*Online database field identifier*] [*Data processing*]
AV .... Average
AVA .... Absolute Virtual Address [*Data processing*]   (CAA)
AVAIL .... Available [*or Availability*]   (KSC)
AVB .... Analog Video Bandwidth
AVBS .... Absolute Value BIT [*Binary Digit*] Synchronizer   (CIT)
AVC .... American Video Channels, Inc. [*New York, NY*] [*Telecommunications*]   (TSSD)
AVC .... Automatic Volume Control [*Radio*]
AVCCOA .... Audiovisual, Computer, and Communication Office Automation
AVCS .... Advanced Vidicon Camera System
AVD .... Alternate Voice Data
AVD .... Anode Voltage Drop
AVD .... Automatic Voice Data   (MCD)
AVE .... Average
AVEBD .... Average Blank Data [*Data processing*]
AVEXS .... Aviation Electronic Equipment Information Exchange System   (MCD)
AVG .... Average   (AFM)
AVGA .... Avant-Garde Computing [*NASDAQ symbol*]   (NQ)
AVID .... Advanced Visual Information Display
AVL .... Adelson-Velskii and Landis Trees [*Data processing*]
AVL .... Angle Versus Length [*Data processing*]
AVLINE ...... Audiovisuals On-Line [*National Library of Medicine*] [*Rockville Pike, MD*] [*Database*]
AVLSI .... Advanced Very-Large-Scale Integration [*Electronics*]
AVMC .... AVM Corporation [*NASDAQ symbol*]   (NQ)
AVOCON .... Automated Vocabulary Control [*Subsystem of PLIS*] [*Data processing*]
AVR .... Automatic Volume Recognition   (MCD)
AVS .... American Videotext Services, Inc. [*Peekskill, NY*] [*Telecommunications*]   (TSSD)
AVS .... Automated Verification System [*Data processing*]   (MCD)
A/VSA .... Altimeter/Velocity Sensor Antenna   (CIT)
AVSM .... Auxiliary Video Switching Matrix   (SKY)
AVT .... Applications Vertical Test Program [*Communication Satellite program*]
AVTC .... American Video Teleconferencing Corporation [*Oceanside, NY*] [*Telecommunications*]   (TSSD)
AWA .... Acoustic Wave Analysis
AWA .... All Wave Antenna
AWA .... Audio Wave Analyzer
AWAS .... Acoustic Wave Analysis System
AWC .... Association for Women in Computing [*Silver Spring, MD*]   (EANO)
AWGN .... Additive White Gaussian Noise [*Telecommunications*]   (TEL)
AWT .... Actual Work Time [*Bell System*]
AWWS .... Automated Want and Warrant System [*Data processing system used in police work*]
AWYDC ..... All-Weather Yaw Damper Computer
AX .... Accumulator Register [*Data processing*]
AXFOR1 ..... Axisymmetric Forging [*Leeds University*] [*Software package*] [*British*]   (NCC)
AXIS .... Auxiliary System for Interactive Statistics [*Sweden*] [*Information service*]   (EISS)
AXP .... American Express Co. [*NYSE symbol*] [*Toronto Stock Exchange symbol*]
AXXX .... Artel Communications [*NASDAQ symbol*]   (NQ)
AYD .... Aydin Corp. [*NYSE symbol*]

B

B	Bandwidth [*Frequency range*]	
B	Base	
B	Baud [*Unit of data transmission speed*]	(MCD)
B	Bel [*Ten decibels*]	
B	Bias [*Telecommunications*]	(CDH)
B	Binary	(BUR)
B	BIT [*Binary Digit*] [*Data transmission speed*] [*Data processing*]	(DIT)
B	Blank	(BUR)
B	Break [*Electronics*]	
B	Broadcasting	
B	Broadcasting [*A publication*]	
B	Byte [*Usually 8 BITS*] [*Data processing*]	
b	Magnetic Flux Density	(CDH)
BA	Binary Add [*Data processing*]	
BA	Buffer Amplifier [*Data processing*]	
BA	Bus Available [*Data processing*]	
BAA	Broadband Active Analyzer	
BAAS	Broadband Acoustic Array Section	
BABT	British Approvals Board for Telecommunications	
BAC	Binary-Analog Conversion [*Data processing*]	(DIT)
BAC	Binary Asymmetric Channel	
BAC	Buffer Access Card [*Data processing*]	(NASA)
BACAIC	Boeing Airplane Company [*later, Boeing Co.*] Algebraic Interpretive Computing System	
BACE	Basic Automatic Checkout Equipment	
BACIS	Budget Accounting Information System [*IBM Corp.*]	
BACS	Bankers' Automated Clearing Service [*British*]	(CAA)
BACS	Bloomington Academic Computer Services [*Indiana University*] [*Research center*]	(RCD)
BADAS	Binary Automatic Data Annotation System	
BADB	Boating Accident Data Base [*Coast Guard*] [*Database*]	(FDB)
BADC	Binary Asymmetric Dependent Channel	
BADSA	Backup Air Data Sensor Assembly	(MCD)
BAE	Beacon Antenna Equipment	
BAEDS	Best Alternative Equally Effective Data System	
BAH	Basic Adaptive Hardware	
BAI	Bank Administration Institute [*Formerly, National Association for Bank Audit, Control, and Operation*] [*Arlington Heights, IL*]	
BAIC	Binary Asymmetric Independent Channel	
BAIS	Bulletin Articles Information Subsystem [*Data processing*]	
BAK	Broadband Antenna Kit	
BAL	Basic Assembly Language [*Programing language*] [*Sperry UNIVAC*] [*Data processing*]	
BAL	Business Application Language	(CAA)
BALGOL	Burroughs Algebraic Compiler	(IEEE)
BALIS	Bayerisches Landwirtschaftliches Informationssystem [*Bavarian Agricultural Information System*] [*Databank*] [*West Germany*]	(EISS)
BALITAC	Basic Literal Automatic Coding	
BALLOTS	Bibliographic Automation of Large Library Operations Using a Time-Sharing System [*Later, RLIN*] [*Stanford University*]	
BALM	Block and List Manipulator [*Data processing*]	(CSR)
BALUN	Balanced-to-Unbalanced Line Transformer [*Telecommunications*]	(TEL)
BAM	Basic Access Method [*Data processing*]	
BAM	Block Access Method [*Data processing*]	(CAA)
BAM	Broadcasting Amplitude Modulation	
BAM	Bundesanstalt fuer Materialpruefung [*Database producer*] [*Information retrieval*]	(ODIN)
BAMBI	Bayesian Analysis Modified by Inspection [*Data processing*]	
BANCS	Bell Administrative Network Communication System [*Telecommunications*]	(TEL)
BANSDOC	Bangladesh National Scientific and Technical Documentation Centre [*Information service*]	(EISS)
BAP	Band Amplitude Product	
BAP	Basic Assembler Program [*Data processing*]	
BAR	Base Address Register [*Data processing*]	(BUR)
BAR	Buffer Address Register [*Data processing*]	
BARS	Bell Audit Relate System [*Bell Laboratories*]	
BARS	Boating Accident Reports System [*Washington, DC*] [*Coast Guard*] [*Information service*]	(EISS)
BARSA	Billing, Accounts Receivable, Sales Analysis	(IBMDP)
BARZREX	Bartok Archives Z-Symbol Rhythm Extraction [*Data processing*]	
BAS	Bell Audit System [*Bell Laboratories*]	
BAS	Block Automation System [*NYSE trading computer*]	
BASE	Basic Semantic Element [*Data processing*]	(DIT)
BASE	Brokerage Accounting System Elements [*IBM computer program*]	
BASEMAG	Base de Datos Geomagneticos [*Instituto Geografico Nacional*] [*Database*]	(CUAD)
BASIC	Basic Algebraic Symbolic Interpretive Compiler	(IEEE)
BASIC	Basic Automatic Stored Instruction Computer	(BUR)
BASIC	Beginner's All-Purpose Symbolic Instruction Code [*Programing language invented by T. E. Kurtz and J. G. Kemeny at Dartmouth College in 1963-64*]	
BASIC	Bulletin. American Society for Information Science [*A publication*]	
BASICPAC	BASIC [*Beginner's All-Purpose Symbolic Instruction Code*] Processor and Computer	(CDH)
BASIS	Bank Automated Service Information System	(BUR)
BASIS	Battelle Automated Search Information System [*Database management system*] [*Battelle Memorial Institute*] [*Information service*]	
BASIS	Bulletin. American Society for Information Science [*A publication*]	
BASIS	Burroughs Advanced Statistical Inquiry System [*Data processing*]	(BUR)
BASR	Bureau of Applied Social Research [*Columbia University*]	(EISS)
BASS	Belgian Archives for the Social Sciences [*Information service*]	(EISS)
BASYS	Basic System	(IEEE)
BATAB	Baker and Taylor's Automated Buying System [*Teleordering system*] [*Baker & Taylor Companies*] [*Information service*]	(EISS)
BaTaSYSTEMS	Baker & Taylor Electronic Book Ordering Service [*Baker & Taylor Companies*] [*Trademark*]	
BATELCO	Bahrain Telecommunications Company [*Manama, Bahrain*]	(TSSD)
BATHY	Bathythermograph Report [*Radio message*]	
BATS	Basic Additional Teleprocessing Support [*Data processing*]	(BUR)
BAUD	Baudot Code	(DEEC)
BAUFO	Bauforschungsprojekte [*Research Projects in Civil Engineering*] [*Information Center for Regional Planning and Building Construction of the Fraunhofer Society*] [*Database*]	(ODIN)
BAVIP	British Association of Viewdata Information Providers	(DEEC)
BB	Backboard [*Telecommunications*]	(TEL)
BB	Begin Bracket [*Indicator*] [*Data processing*]	(IBMDP)
BB	BIT [*Binary Digit*]/Byte Conversion [*Telecommunications*]	(TEL)
BB	Broadband [*Communications channel description*]	(IEEE)
BB	Broadcast Bureau [*of FCC*]	
BB	Bulletin Board [*Computer online message system*]	
BB	Bunching Block	(MSA)
BB	Bus-Bar Layout Drawing [*Data processing*]	(TEL)
BBA	Bogart-Brociner Associates, Inc. [*Annapolis, MD*] [*Information service*]	(EISS)
BBC	Backup Bus Controller [*Data processing*]	
BBC	Broadband Conducted	(IEEE)
BBC	Browne, Bortz & Coddington, Inc. [*Denver, CO*] [*Telecommunications*]	(TSSD)
BBD	Bucket-Brigade Device [*Electronics*]	
BBG	Board of Broadcast Governors [*Later, Canadian Radio-Television Commission*]	
BBL	Basic Business Language [*Data processing*]	(IEEE)
BBL	Branch Back and Load [*Data processing*]	
BBMIP	Branch-Bound Mixed Integer Programing [*Data processing*]	
BBN	Bolt, Beranek & Newman, Inc. [*NYSE symbol*]	
BBR	Broadband Radiated	(IEEE)
BBR	Bureau of Business Research [*University of Texas, Austin*] [*Information service*]	(EISS)
BBRC	Burr-Brown Corporation [*NASDAQ symbol*]	(NQ)
BBS	Bulletin Board Systems [*Personal computer message network system*]	
BBU	BIT [*Binary Digit*] Buffer Unit [*Data processing*]	(CET)
BC	Basic Control [*Mode*] [*Data processing*]	
BC	Before Computer	
BC	Billing Cease Date	(TEL)

Acronym	Expansion
BC	Binary Code
BC	Block Count [*Data processing*]
BC	Broadcasting (MCD)
BC	Burroughs Corporation
BC	Bus Coupler [*Data processing*] (MCD)
BCB	BIT [*Binary Digit*] Control Block [*Data processing*] (IBMDP)
BCB	Broadcast Band
BCC	Baylor Computing Center [*Baylor College of Medicine*] [*Research center*] (RCD)
BCC	Block Check Character [*Data processing*]
BCC	Branch Conditionally [*Data processing*]
BCC	Broadcast Control Center
BCC	Business Communications Company, Inc. [*Stamford, CT*] [*Information service*] [*Telecommunications*] (TSSD)
BCC-52	BASIC-52 Computer/Controller
BCCD	Bulk-Channel Charge-Coupled Device [*Electronics*] (TEL)
BCCL	Birkbeck College Computation Laboratory [*British*] (CAH)
BCD	Binary-Coded Data [*or Decimal*] [*Data processing*]
BCD/B	Binary-Coded Decimal/Binary (DEN)
BCDC	Binary-Coded Decimal Counter
BCDIC	Binary-Coded Decimal Interchange Code (IEEE)
BCD/Q	Binary-Coded Decimal/Quaternary (DEN)
BCE	Boston Computer Exchange
BCE	Bus Control Electronics (MCD)
BCF	Bandpass Crystal Filter
BCF	Basic Control Frequency
BCF	Billion Conductor Feet [*Telecommunications*] (TEL)
BCF	FM Broadcasting Station [*ITU designation*] (CET)
BCFSK	Binary Code Frequency Shift Keying [*SAGE*]
BCH	Block Control Header [*Data processing*] (IBMDP)
BCH	Bose-Chaudhuri-Hocquenghem [*Cyclic codes*] [*Telecommunications*]
BCHG	Test a BIT [*Binary Digit*] and Change [*Data processing*]
BCI	Bell Canada International, Inc. [*Ottawa, ON*] [*Telecommunications*] (TSSD)
BCI	Binary-Coded Information
BCI	BIT [*Binary Digit*] Count Integrity [*Telecommunications*] (TEL)
BCIP	Belgian Centre for Information Processing (CAH)
BCIU	Bus Control Interface Unit (MCD)
BCJS	Buffer Control Junction Switch [*Data processing*]
BCL	Burroughs Common Language [*Data processing*] (BUR)
BCLR	Test a BIT [*Binary Digit*] and Clear [*Data processing*]
BCM	Basic Control Monitor (BUR)
BCM	Binary Coded Matrix [*Telecommunications*] (TEL)
BCML	Burroughs Current Mode Logic (CAA)
BCN	Biomedical Communications Network [*Proposed*] [*National Library of Medicine*]
BCN	Broadband Communication Network (BUR)
BCN	Business Computer Network [*San Antonio, TX*] [*Telecommunications*] (TSSD)
BCO	Battery Cutoff [*Telecommunications*] (TEL)
BCO	Bill in Care Of [*Telecommunications*] (TEL)
BCO	Binary-Coded Octal [*Data processing*]
BCOM	Burroughs Computer Output to Microfilm (IEEE)
BCP	BIT [*Binary Digit*] Control Panel [*Data processing*] (MCD)
BCPL	Basic Combined Programing Language
BCPL	Bootstrap Combined Programing Language [*Data processing*] (CSR)
BCR	Bibliographical Center for Research, Inc., Rocky Mountain Region [*Denver, CO*] [*Research center*] (RCD)
BCR	Billing-Collecting-Remitting (TEL)
BCREQ	Broadcast Requested (FAAC)
BCRT	Bright Cathode-Ray Tube (DEN)
BCS	Basic Control System [*For satellites*] (MDG)
BCS	Beam Communications Set
BCS	Biomedical Computing Society [*Later, SIGBIO*] (BUR)
BCS	Block Control Sheet [*Data processing*]
BCS	Block Control Signal [*Telecommunications*] (TEL)
BCS	Boeing Computer Services Co. [*Vienna, VA*]
BCS	British Computer Society
BCS	Broadcast Communications System
BCS	Bucknell Computer Services [*Bucknell University*] [*Research center*] (RCD)
BCS	Business Communications Service [*British Telecommunications International*] [*London*] (TSSD)
BCS	Business Communications Systems [*Telecommunications*] (TEL)
BCS	Business Customer Services [*Telecommunications*] (TEL)
BCSI	Biometric Computer Service, Incorporated (OA)
BCST	Broadcast [*Information transmission*] (AFM)
BCSTG	Broadcasting
BCSTN	Broadcast Station (FAAC)
BCSTR	Broadcaster
BCT	Between Commands Testing [*Data processing*] (CAA)
BCT	Television Broadcasting Station [*ITU designation*] (CET)
BCTIC	Biomedical Computing Technology Information Center [*Oak Ridge National Laboratory*] [*Department of Energy*] (EISS)
BCTV	Berks Community Television [*Reading, PA*] [*Telecommunications*] (TSSD)
BCU	Basic Computer Unit (SKY)
BCU	Binary Counting Unit (IEEE)
BCU	Block Control Unit [*Data processing*] (IBMDP)
BCU	Buffer Control Unit [*Data processing*] (CET)
BCV	Brightness Contrast Value
BCW	Buffer Control Word [*Data processing*] (CGC)
Bd	Baud [*Unit of data transmission*] (CET)
B/D	Binary to Decimal [*Data processing*]
BD	Binary Decoder [*Data processing*]
BD	BIT [*Binary Digit*] Density [*Data processing*]
BD	Board
BDAM	Basic Direct Access Method [*IBM Corp.*] [*Data processing*] (BUR)
BDC	Backup Digital Computer
BDC	Binary Decimal Counter [*Data processing*]
BDC	Block Downconverter [*Satellite communications*]
BDCB	Buffered Data and Control Bus (CAA)
BDD	Binary-to-Decimal Decoder [*Data processing*]
BDD	Binary Digital Data [*Data processing*]
BDE	Bright Display Equipment
BDI	Bank Descriptor Index [*Data processing*]
BDIC	Binary-Coded Decimal Interchange Code (CAH)
BDIR	Bus Direction [*Data processing*] (TEL)
BDIS	Birth Defects Information System [*Tufts University*] [*Boston, MA*] [*Information service*] (EISS)
BDL	Bad Data Lister (CIT)
BDLC	Burroughs Data Link Control [*Data processing*] (BUR)
BDM	Banque de Donnees Macroeconomiques [*Institut National de la Statistique et des Etudes Economiques*] [*Database*] (CUAD)
BDM	Binary Delta Modulation
BDM	Binary Digital Multiplier [*Data processing*]
BDN	Bank Draft Number (TEL)
BDN	Bell Data Network [*Telecommunications*]
BDO	Base de Donnees des Obligations Francaises [*DAFSA*] [*Database*] (CUAD)
BDOS	Basic Disk Operating System
BDOS	Batch Disk Operating System (CAA)
BDP	Business Data Processing (CIT)
BDPA	Black Data Processing Associates [*Philadelphia, PA*] (EANO)
BDPSK	Binary Differential Phase-Shift Keying [*Telecommunications*] (TEL)
BDR	Bank Descriptor Registers [*Data processing*]
BDR	Bell Doesn't Ring [*Telecommunications*] (TEL)
BDR	Bi-Duplexed Redundancy [*Telecommunications*] (CAA)
BDR	Binary Dump Routine (CAA)
BDR	Bradford National Corp. [*American Stock Exchange symbol*] [*Delisted*]
BDRS	Business Development Report System [*Department of Commerce*] [*Database*] (FDB)
BDRT	Baud Rate [*Data transmission speed*] [*Data processing*]
BDRY	Boundary
BDS	Binary Decode Scaler [*Data processing*]
BDS	Building Design System [*Applied Research of Cambridge Ltd.*] [*Software package*] [*British*] (NCC)
BDS	Bulk Data Switching (CAA)
BDT	Binary Deck-to-Tape [*Data processing*]
BDTS	Batch Data Transmission System
BDTS	Buffered Data Transmission Simulator (CAA)
BDTS	Bulk Data Transfer Subsystem [*Telecommunications*] (TEL)
BDU	Basic Device Unit [*Data processing*] (IBMDP)
BDU	Basic Display Unit [*Data processing*] (CGC)
BDV	Breakdown Voltage [*Telecommunications*] (TEL)
BDW	Bank Descriptor Word [*Data processing*]
BDW	Buried Distribution Wire [*Telecommunications*] (TEL)
BE	Back End (MSA)
BE	Band Elimination
BEA	Bureau of Economic Analysis [*Department of Commerce*] (EISS)
BEAC	Boeing Electronic Analog Computer (CDH)
BEAC	Boeing Engineering Analog Computer (IEEE)
BEAM	Burroughs Electronic Accounting Machine (BUR)
BEAMOS	Beam Addressed Metal Oxide Semiconductor [*Memory technology*] (CAA)
BEAMS	Basic Education Assistance Material Service [*National Multimedia Center for Adult Basic Education*] (EISS)
BEAST	Brookings Economics and Statistical Translator [*Data processing*] (TUT)
BEASY	Boundary Element Analysis System [*Computational Mechanics Ltd.*] [*Software package*] [*British*] (NCC)
BEAT	Best Execution Analysis Tabulation [*Data processing*]
BEBA	Bilingual Education Bibliographic Abstracts [*National Clearinghouse for Bilingual Education*] [*Rosslyn, VA*] [*Database*]
BEC	Background Equivalent Concentration [*Data processing*]
BEC	Boston Educational Computing, Inc. [*Boston, MA*] [*Software manufacturer*] (DASOS)
BEC	Business Electronics Computer [*Used in training*]
BECA	Bureau of Educational and Cultural Affairs [*Later Known as USIA, then as ICA or USICA, then again as USIA*]
BECAN	Biomedical Engineering Current Awareness Notification [*England*] [*A publication*] (EISS)
BECKTRAN	Beckman Translation [*Programing language*] [*Beckman Instruments, Inc.*]
BECS	Basic Error Control System (CAA)
BECUN	Battelle's Educational Computer User's Network [*Battelle Memorial Institute*] [*Columbus, OH*] [*Information service*] (EISS)
BEEC	Binary Error Erasure Channel (IEEE)

Computer & Telecommunications Acronyms

BEEF	Business and Engineering Enriched FORTRAN [*Programing language*] [*Sperry UNIVAC*]
BEF	Band Elimination Filter
BEFAP	Bell Laboratories FORTRAN Assembly Program [*Data processing*] (IEEE)
BEFLIX	Bell FLICKS [*Programing language*] [*1973*] (CSR)
BEL	Bell Character [*Keyboard*]
BELINDIS	Belgian Information and Dissemination Service [*European host database system*] [*Brussels, Belgium*] (EISS)
Bell Lab Re	Bell Laboratories Record [*A publication*]
Bell Lab Rec	Bell Laboratories Record [*A publication*]
BELLMATIC	Bell Laboratories Machine-Aided Technical Information Center (DIT)
Bell System Tech J	Bell System Technical Journal [*A publication*]
Bell Syst T	Bell System Technical Journal [*A publication*]
Bell Syst Tech J	Bell System Technical Journal [*A publication*]
BELLTEL	Bell Telephone
Bell Telephone Mag	Bell Telephone Magazine [*A publication*]
Bell Teleph Syst Tech Publ Monogr	Bell Telephone System. Technical Publications. Monographs [*A publication*]
BELR	Bell Laboratories Record [*A publication*]
BEMA	Business Equipment Manufacturers Association [*Later, CBEMA*]
BEP	Back-End Processor [*Computer*] (TSSD)
BEP	BIT [*Binary Digit*] Error Probability [*Data processing*] (KSC)
BEPOC	Burrough's Electrographic Printer-Plotter for Ordnance Computing
BER	BIT [*Binary Digit*] Effectiveness Report (CAAL)
BER	BIT [*Binary Digit*] Error Rate [*Data processing*]
BERM	Basic Encyclopedic Redundancy Media (IEEE)
BERM	BIT [*Binary Digit*] Error Rate Monitor (CAA)
BERPM	Basic Exchange Rate Planning Model [*Telecommunications*] (TEL)
BERS	Bureau of Educational Research and Service [*Memphis State University*] [*Research center*] (RCD)
BERT	BIT [*Binary Digit*] Error-Rate-Test [*Set*] [*Data processing*]
BES	Basic Executive System [*Honeywell, Inc.*] (CAA)
BESCO	Business Equipment & Supply Company [*Columbus, MS*] [*Software manufacturer*] (DASOS)
BESS	Biomedical Experiment Scientific Satellite (NASA)
BEST	Business EDP [*Electronic Data Processing*] Systems Technique [*NCR Corp.*]
BEST	Business Equipment Software Techniques [*Data processing*]
BET	Between (KSC)
BET	Black Entertainment Television [*Cable-television system*]
BET	Boundary Element Tape [*Computational Mechanics Ltd.*] [*Software package*] [*British*] (NCC)
BETA	Business Equipment Trade Association [*London, England*]
BETC	Bartlesville Energy Technology Center [*Later, NIPER*] [*Department of Energy*] [*Information service*]
BETNET	Bilingual Education Telecommunications Network [*National Clearinghouse for Bilingual Education*] [*Rosslyn, VA*] (TSSD)
BEU	Basic Encoding Unit (OA)
BeV	Billion Electron Volts
BEX	Broadband Exchange [*Western Union communication system*]
BF	Bandpass Filter
BF	Base File (CAH)
B/F	Blip/Frame (CET)
BF	Branching Filter [*Telecommunications*] (TEL)
BfA	Bundesstelle fuer Aussenhandelsinformation [*Foreign Trade Information Office*] [*West Germany*] [*Information service*] (EISS)
BFAI	Bundesstelle fuer Aussenhandelsinformation [*Foreign Trade Information Office*] [*West Germany*] [*Information service*] (EISS)
BFAS	Basic File Access System (CAA)
BFCO	Band Filter Cutoff (MSA)
BFD	Basic Floppy Disk (CAA)
BFE	Bundesforschungsanstalt fuer Ernaehrung [*Karlsruhe*] [*Information retrieval*] (ODIN)
BFF	Buffered Flip-Flop [*Data processing*]
BFF	Bundesforschungsanstalt fuer Fischerei [*Database producer*] (ODIN)
BFG	Binary Frequency Generator (IEEE)
BFH	Bundesforschungsanstalt fuer Forst- und Holzwirtschaft [*Hamburg*] [*Information retrieval*] (ODIN)
BFLOPS	Billion Floating-Point Operations per Second [*Data processing*]
BFMA	Business Forms Management Association, Inc.
BFO	Beat-Frequency Oscillator
BFPDDA	Binary Floating-Point Digital Differential Analyzer (IEEE)
BFR	Bridged Frequency Ringing [*Telecommunications*] (TEL)
BFR	Buffer [*Data storage device*] (MSA)
BFTSC	Brassboard Fault Tolerant Spaceborne Computer (MCD)
BG	Background [*Low-priority processing*]
BG	Billing Group [*Telecommunications*] (TEL)
BGA	Bundesgesundheitsamt [*Database producer*] (ODIN)
BGH	Burroughs Corp. [*NYSE symbol*]
BGR	Bundesanstalt fuer Geowissenschaften und Rohstoffe [*Hannover*] [*Information retrieval*] (ODIN)
BGSS	BGS Systems, Inc. [*NASDAQ symbol*] (NQ)
B & H	Becker & Hayes, Inc. [*Santa Monica, CA*] [*Information service*] (EISS)
BH	Bell & Howell Co.
BH	Bibliographia Huntiana [*Computer-based bibliography*]
BH	Binary to Hexadecimal (BUR)
BH	Block Handler [*Data processing*]
BHAS	Burroughs Hospital Administrative System [*Data processing*] (BUR)
BHC	Beam-Heated Cathode
BHC	Busy Hour Call [*Telecommunications*] (TEL)
BHCA	Busy Hour Call Attempts [*Telecommunications*]
BHI	Beehive International [*American Stock Exchange symbol*] [*Delisted*]
BHL	Busy Hour Load [*Telecommunications*] (TEL)
BHM	Busy Hour Model [*Data processing*]
BHR	Block Handler Routine [*Data processing*] (BUR)
BHR	Block Header Record [*Data processing*]
BHTD	Bureau of Hygiene and Tropical Diseases [*Database producer*] (CUAD)
BHW	Bell & Howell Co. [*NYSE symbol*]
BI	Backward Indicator [*Telecommunications*] (TEL)
BI	Billing Instructions [*Telecommunications*] (TEL)
BI	Blanking Input (IEEE)
BI	Buffer Index [*Data processing*]
B/I	Bus Interface [*Data processing*]
BI	Input Blocking Factor [*Data processing*] (IBMDP)
BIAC	BI, Inc. [*NASDAQ symbol*] (NQ)
BIAT	Business Information Analysis and Integration Technique [*Data processing*]
BIB	Backward Indicator BIT [*Binary Digit*] [*Telecommunications*] (TEL)
BIBLIO-DATA	National Bibliographic Data Base [*Deutsche Bibliothek*] [*Database*] (ODIN)
BIBNET	Bibliographic Network [*OCLC retrieval system*] [*Data processing*]
BIC	Bus Interface Circuit [*Data processing*] (MDG)
BIC	Byte Input Control [*Data processing*]
BICARSA	Billing, Inventory Control, Accounts Receivable, Sales Analysis (IBMDP)
BICEPT	Book Indexing with Context and Entry Points from Text [*Indexing method*] [*Data processing*] (DIT)
BICS	Building Industry Consulting Service [*Telecommunications*] (TEL)
BICS	Burroughs Inventory Control System [*Data processing*] (BUR)
BICSI	Building Industry Consulting Service International [*Telecommunications*]
BIDAP	Bibliographic Data Processing Program [*For keyword indexing*] [*Information retrieval software*]
BIDEC	Binary-to-Decimal Converter [*Data processing*]
BIEN	Billings Corp. [*NASDAQ symbol*] (NQ)
BIG	BCS [*Boeing Computer Services*] Interactive Graphics
BII	Battery Information Index [*Battelle Memorial Institute*] (EISS)
BIL	Basic Impulse Insulation Level [*Electronics*]
BIL	Block Input Length [*Data processing*] (BUR)
BILA	Battelle Institute Learning Automation [*Battelle Memorial Institute*] (IEEE)
BILD	Bibliographic Index of Library Documents [*Helsinki School of Economics*] [*Database*] (CUAD)
BIM	Beginning of Information Marker [*Data processing*]
BIM	BIT [*Binary Digit*] Image Memory [*Data processing*]
BIM	Branch If Multiplexer (OA)
BIM	Bus Interface Module (CAA)
BIMAC	Bistable Magnetic Core [*Data processing*] (CGC)
BIMAG	Bistable Magnetic Core (OA)
BiMOS	Bipolar Metal-Oxide Semiconductor (IEEE)
BIN	Bell Information Network
BIN	Billboard Information Network [*Billboard Publications, Inc.*] [*New York, NY*] [*Information service*] (EISS)
BIN	Binary (AFM)
BIN	Business Information Network [*Telecommunications*] (TEL)
BINAC	Binary Automatic Computer [*Eckert-Maudely Computer Corp.*]
BINAGRI	Biblioteca Nacional de Agricultura [*National Library of Agriculture*] [*Brazil*] [*Information service*] (EISS)
BINSS	Binary to Seven Segment [*Data processing*]
BIO	Biological Information Processing Organization [*Later, SIGBIO*]
BIOETHICSLINE	Bioethics Online [*Database*]
BIOM	Buffer Input-Output Memory [*Data processing*]
BIOMOD	Biochemical Modeling [*Data processing*]
BIOR	Business Input/Output Rerun [*UNIVAC compiling system*]
BIOS	Basic Input/Output System [*IBM Corp.*]
BIOSIS	BioScience Information Service [*Database producer*] [*Philadelphia, PA*]
BIP	BASIC Interpreter Package (CAA)
BIP	Binary Image Processor [*Data processing*] (OA)
BIP	Books in Print [*Bibliographic database*] [*R. R. Bowker Co.*] [*A publication*]
B-I-P	Business Intelligence Program [*SRI International*] [*Menlo Park, CA*] [*Information service*] (EISS)
BIPA	Banque d'Informations Politiques et d'Actualites [*Political and Current Events Information Bank*] [*Database*] [*Telesystems - Questel*] [*Paris, France*] [*Information service*] (EISS)
BIPASS	Burroughs Inventory Planning Analysis and Simulation System [*Data processing*] (BUR)
BIPM	Bureau International des Poids et Mesures [*International Bureau of Weights and Measures*]
BIPS	Banking Information Processing System (BUR)

By Acronym

Computer & Telecommunications Acronyms

BIPS............ Billion Instructions per Second [*Computing power measurement*] [*Data processing*]
B-IR............ Bell-Independent Relations [*Telecommunications*]   (TEL)
BIRD........... Banque d'Information Robert Debre [*Centre International de l'Enfance*] [*Database*]   (CUAD)
BIRS........... Basic Indexing and Retrieval System [*Data processing*]   (DIT)
BIS .... Bechtel Information Services [*Gaithersburg, MD*]   (EISS)
BIS .... Bibliotheks- und Informationssystem [*Library and Information System*] [*German*]   (ODIN)
BIS .... Brought into Service [*Telecommunications*]   (TEL)
BIS .... Business Information Service [*Financial Times Business Information Ltd.*] [*British*]   (EISS)
BIS .... Business Information Systems [*Bell System*]
BISA........... Bibliographic Information on Southeast Asia [*Database*] [*Australia*] [*Information service*]   (EISS)
BISAD......... Business Information Systems Analysis and Design [*Bell System*]   (DIT)
BISAM .... Basic Indexed Sequential Access Method [*IBM Corp.*] [*Data processing*]
BISCOM...... Business Information Systems Communications [*Bell System*]
BISCUS .... Business Information Systems Customer Service [*Bell System*]
BISCUS/FACS ... Business Information Systems Customer Service/Facilities Assignment and Control System [*Bell System*]   (MCD)
BISMAC...... Business Machine Computer   (TUT)
BISNET....... Bank Information System Network   (CAA)
BISP........... Bundesinstitut fuer Sportwissenschaft [*Cologne, West Germany*] [*Information retrieval*]   (ODIN)
BISTSS....... Business Information System/Trunks and Special Services [*Telecommunications*]   (TEL)
BISYNC ...... Binary Synchronous Transmission [*Data processing*]
BIT .... Binary Digit [*Data processing*]
BIT .... Built-In Test [*or Testing*] [*Data processing*]
BITE........... Backward Interworking Telephony Event [*Telecommunications*]   (TEL)
BITE........... Built-In Test Equipment
BITS........... Binary Digits [*Data processing*]
BITS........... Binary Intersystem Transmission Standard
BITS........... BITS [*Binary Digits*] per Second [*Data processing*]   (OA)
BIU .... Basic Information Unit   (BUR)
BIU .... Buffer Interface Unit [*Data processing*]   (NASA)
BIU .... Bus Interface Unit [*Data processing*]
BIX .... Byte Information Exchange [*Electronic conferencing system provided by McGraw-Hill's Byte magazine*]
BIZNET .... American Business Network [*US Chamber of Commerce*] [*Washington, DC*] [*Cable-television system*] [*Telecommunications*]   (TSSD)
BJF............. Batch Job Foreground [*Data processing*]   (CAH)
BJM........... Between Job Monitor [*Data processing*]   (CAH)
BJS .... Bureau of Justice Statistics [*Department of Justice*] [*Information service*]   (EISS)
BJT .... Bipolar Junction Transistor [*Electronics*]
BK .... Break Signal [*Used to interrupt a transmission in progress*] [*Communications*]   (FAAC)
BKF............. Blocking Factor   (CMD)
BKI............. Break-In [*Telecommunications*]   (TEL)
BKS............. Broadcast Keying Station   (NVT)
BKSP.......... Backspace Character [*Keyboard*] [*Data processing*]   (BUR)
BKUP .... Backup   (KSC)
BL .... Bell   (IEEE)
BL .... Blank Line [*Data processing*]
BL .... Blanking   (DEN)
BL .... Block Length   (CAA)
BLA............. Binary Logical Association   (CAA)
BLA............. Blocking Acknowledgment [*Telecommunications*]   (TEL)
BLADE........ Basic Level Automation of Data through Electronics
BLADE........ Bell Laboratories Automatic Device
BLADES...... Bell Laboratories Automatic Design System [*Computer program*]
BLADS........ Bell Laboratories Automatic Design System [*Computer program*]
BLAISE .... British Library Automated Information Service [*European host database system*] [*London*]   (EISS)
BLCK .... Block   (BUR)
BLDIS .... Blood Information Service [*Information service*]   (EISS)
BLE .... Binary Logic Element [*Data processing*]   (BUR)
BLERT .... Block Error Rate Test   (CAA)
BLESSED ... Bell Little Electrodata Symbolic System for the Electrodata [*Symbolic assembly program*]
BLF............. Busy Lamp Field [*Phone console*] [*Bell System*]
BLI .... Bibliothekar-Lehrinstitut [*Information retrieval*]   (ODIN)
BLIS .... Bell Laboratories Interpretive System [*Computer program*]
BLIS .... Business Lead Identification System [*Timeplace, Inc.*] [*Database*]   (CUAD)
BLISS.......... Basic Language for the Implementation of System Software [*Data processing*]
BLISS.......... Basic Library Inquiry Subsystem [*Data processing*]
BLISS.......... Bibliographic and Library Information Search Service
BLK .... Block [*Unit of data*]
BLL .... Bibliographie Linguistischer Literatur [*Bibliography of Linguistic Literature*] [*Database*] [*Information retrieval*]   (ODIN)
BLL .... Bibliography of Linguistic Literature [*Database*] [*Information retrieval*]   (ODIN)
BLM .... Basic Language Machine [*Computer*]   (BUR)
BLM .... Blinking Light Monitor
BLO............. Blocking [*Telecommunications*]   (TEL)

BLOC .... Booth Library On-Line Circulation [*Data processing system*] [*Eastern Illinois University*] [*Charleston, IL*]
BLODI .... Block Diagram Compiler
BLODIB...... Block Diagram Compiler B   (IEEE)
BLP .... Bypass Label Processing [*Data processing*]
BLRCA....... Bell Laboratories Record [*A publication*]
BLS .... Band-Limited Signal
BLS .... Bell Log System
BLT .... BASIC Language Translator [*Data processing*]   (MCD)
BLU .... Basic Link Unit [*Data processing*]   (BUR)
BLU .... Basic Logic Unit   (IEEE)
BM .... Benchmark [*Computer system evaluation*]
BM .... Breakdown Maintenance
BM .... Bubble Memory [*Data storage device*] [*Data processing*]   (BUR)
BM .... Buffer Module [*Data processing*]
B/M .... Buffer/Multiplexer [*Data processing*]   (CET)
BMAP......... Buffer Map [*Data processing*]   (NASA)
BMC............ Battelle Monte Carlo [*Data processing*]
BMC............ Block Multiplexer Channel   (CAA)
BMC............ Bubble Memory Controller   (CAA)
BMC............ Bulk Media Conversion   (CAA)
BMC............ Burst Multiplexer Channel [*Telecommunications*]   (CAA)
BMD........... Benchmark Monitor Display System [*Sperry UNIVAC*]   (CAA)
BMD........... Biomedical
BMD........... Bubble Memory Device   (CAA)
BMEU......... Biomedical Engineering Unit [*McGill University*] [*Canada*] [*Research center*]   (RCD)
BMF .... Basic Main Frame   (NATG)
BMG........... Business Machines Group [*Burroughs Corp.*]   (CAA)
BMI .... Biography Master Index [*Bibliographic database*] [*Gale Research Co.*] [*A publication*]   (EISS)
BMIS .... Bank Management Information System   (CAA)
BMMG........ British Micro Manufacturer Group
BMOC .... Big Machine on Campus [*Computer*]
BMS .... Basic Mapping Support [*Data processing*]
BMS .... Biomedical Studies Section [*Oak Ridge National Laboratory*]   (EISS)
BMS .... Business Management System   (BUR)
BMT .... Beginning of Magnetic Tape [*Data processing*]   (MDG)
BMTI .... Block Mode Terminal Interface [*Data processing*]   (CAA)
BN .... Binary Number [*Data processing*]
BNDO......... Bureau National des Donnees Oceaniques [*National Bureau for Ocean Data*] [*European host database system*] [*France*] [*Information service*]   (EISS)
BNF............. Backus Naur [*or Normal*] Form [*ALGOL*] [*Data processing*]   (BUR)
BNF............. Boolean Normal Form [*Mathematics*]
BNG............ Branch No Group [*Data processing*]   (MDG)
BNIST .... Bureau National de l'Information Scientifique et Technique [*National Scientific and Technical Information Bureau*] [*France*] [*Information service*]   (EISS)
BNPF.......... Beginning, Negative, Positive, Finish [*ASCII subset*]   (DEEC)
BNR............ Bell-Northern Research [*Telecommunications*]   (TEL)
BNS............. Bell Number Screening [*Telecommunications*]   (TEL)
BNS............. Binary Number System [*Data processing*]   (CGC)
BO .... Binary to Octal [*Data processing*]   (BUR)
BO .... Output Blocking Factor [*Data processing*]   (IBMDP)
BOADICEA ... British Overseas Airways [*later, British Airways*] Digital Information Computer for Electronic Automation
BOAM .... Bell Owned and Maintained [*Telecommunications*]   (TEL)
BOAMP...... Bulletin Officiel des Annonces des Marches Publics [*Direction des Journaux Officiels*] [*Database*]   (CUAD)
BOC .... Bell Operating Company [*Also, BSOC*] [*Post-divestiture division of American Telephone & Telegraph Co.*]
BOC .... Block-Oriented Computer
BOC .... Build Out Capacitor [*Telecommunications*]   (TEL)
BOC .... Byte Output Control [*Data processing*]
BOCOL ...... Basic Operating Consumer-Oriented Language [*Data processing*]   (CGC)
BOCS.......... Bendix Optimum Configuration Satellite   (IEEE)
BOCS.......... Box-Office Computer System
BODO......... Bauobjektdokumentation [*Information Centre for Regional Planning and Building Construction of the Fraunhofer-Society*] [*Database*]   (CUAD)
BOF............. Beginning of File   (NASA)
BOF............. Billing and Ordering Forum [*Exchange Carriers Standards Association*] [*Telecommunications*]
BOI............. Bolt-On Intelligence [*Proposed use for the biochip*]
BOI............. Branch Output Interrupt [*Data processing*]   (MDG)
BOL............. Build Out Lattice [*Telecommunications*]   (TEL)
BOLD .... Bibliographic On-Line Display [*Document storage and retrieval system*] [*Data processing*]
BOLDS....... Burroughs Optical Lens Docking System   (MCD)
BOM........... Basic Operating Monitor   (TUT)
BOM........... Bill of Materials [*Digital Dynamics Ltd.*] [*Software package*]
BOM........... Binary Order of Magnitude [*Data processing*]
BOM........... BIT [*Binary Digit*]-Oriented Message   (RDA)
BOMP........ Base Organization and Maintenance Processor   (IEEE)
BOMP........ Bill of Material Processor
B-ONALS.... Type "B" Off-Network Access Lines [*Telecommunications*]   (TEL)
BOOB......... Block out of Balance [*Data processing*]
BOOK........ Bibliographic On-Line Organized Knowledge [*Data processing*]   (KSC)

Computer & Telecommunications Acronyms

BOP............ Binary Output Program
BOP............ BIT-Oriented Protocol   (DEEC)
BOP............ Building Optimization Program [*Data processing*]
BOPS......... Banking On-Line Package System   (BUR)
BOR............ Belady Optimum Replacement [*Algorithm*] [*Data processing*]
BOR............ Bus Out Register [*Data processing*]   (CAA)
BORAM....... Block-Oriented Random-Access Memory [*Data processing*]
BOS............ Background Operating System   (IEEE)
BOS............ Basic Operating System [*IBM Corp.*] [*Data processing*]
BOS............ Batch Operating System [*Data processing*]   (CAA)
BOS............ Bell Operating System [*Telecommunications*]   (TEL)
BOS............ Book Order and Selection [*Data processing*]
BOS............ Business Office Supervisor [*Telecommunications*]   (TEL)
BOSS......... Basic Operating System Software [*Toshiba Corp.*] [*Japan*]   (CAA)
BOSS......... Batch Operating Software System   (CAA)
BOSS......... Business-Oriented Software System [*Digital Equipment Corp.*] [*Data processing*]   (BUR)
BOT............ Beginning of Tape [*Data processing*]   (CGC)
BOTTS....... Busy Tone Trunks [*Telecommunications*]   (TEL)
BOWI......... Bibliographie zur Offentlichen Unternehmung und Verwaltung [*NOMOS Datapool*] [*Database*]   (CUAD)
BP .... Bandpass
BP .... Base Pointer [*Data processing*]
BP .... Batch Processing   (CAA)
BP .... Binding Post   (KSC)
BP .... BIOSIS Previews [*Information retrieval*]   (ODIN)
BP .... Block Parity [*Error checking method*] [*Telecommunications*]   (TEL)
BP .... Breakpoint [*Telecommunications*]   (TEL)
BP .... Buffered Printing   (CAA)
BPAM......... Basic Partitioned Access Method [*IBM Corp.*] [*Data processing*]   (TUT)
BPC............ Basic Peripheral Channel   (CAA)
BPC............ Binding Post Chamber [*Telecommunications*]   (TEL)
BPE............ BIT [*Binary Digit*]-Plane Encoding [*Data processing*]
BPF............ Bandpass Filter
BPI............. BITS [*Binary Digits*] per Inch [*Data density measurement*] [*Data processing*]
BPI............. Bytes per Inch [*Data processing*]   (CGC)
BPII............ BPI Systems, Incorporated [*NASDAQ symbol*]   (NQ)
BPILE......... Bored Insitu Piles [*Camutek*] [*Software package*] [*British*]   (NCC)
BPKT......... Basic Programing Knowledge Test   (MCD)
BPL............ Binary Program Loader   (CAA)
BPL............ Block Proof List [*Data processing*]
BPM............ Batch Processing Monitor [*Xerox Corp.*] [*Data processing*]   (MCD)
BPM............ BITS [*Binary Digits*] per Minute [*Data processing*]   (SKY)
BPMM........ BITS [*Binary Digits*] per Millimeter   (CAA)
BPN............ Bandpass Network
BPO............ British Post Office
BPR............ Block Proof Record [*Data processing*]
BPS............ Basic Programing Support [*IBM Corp.*]   (BUR)
BPS............ Basic Programing System   (TUT)
BPS............ Batch Processing System   (OA)
BPS............ BITS [*Binary Digits*] per Second [*Data transmission speed*] [*Data processing*]
BPS............ Bytes per Second [*Data processing*]   (BUR)
BPSA......... Business Products Standards Association   (CAA)
BPSI........... BITS per Square Inch   (CAA)
BPSK......... Binary Phase-Shift Keying [*Data processing*]   (IEEE)
BPT............ Bandpass Transformer
BPU............ Basic Processing Unit   (CET)
BQ2............ Bill of Quantities [*Contract Data Research*] [*Software package*] [*British*]   (NCC)
BQL............ Basic Query Language [*Data processing*]   (BUR)
BQL............ Batch Query Language [*Programing language*]   (CAA)
BR .... Base Register   (CMD)
BR .... BIT [*Binary Digit*] Rate [*Data transmission speed*] [*Data processing*]   (MCD)
BR .... Break Request [*Data processing*]   (MDG)
BR .... Bridge [*Interconnects computer networks*]
BR .... Bridging Key [*on Dial Assistance Switchboard*]   (CET)
BR .... Brown
BR .... Buffer Register [*Data processing*]
BRA............ Base Rate Area [*Telecommunications*]   (TEL)
BRA............ Branch Always [*Data processing*]
BRAID........ Bidirectional Reference Array, Internally Derived [*Data processing*]   (DIT)
BRAIN........ Baruch Retrieval of Automated Information for Negotiations [*City University of New York*] [*Information service*]   (EISS)
BRB............ Base Rate Boundary [*Telecommunications*]   (TEL)
BRC............ Biological Records Centre [*British*] [*Information service*]   (EISS)
BRC............ Branch Conditional   (OA)
BRC............ Burroughs Corporation
Br Commun Electron ...   British Communications and Electronics [*England*] [*A publication*]
BRD............ Binary Rate Divider   (OA)
BRD............ Broadband Subsystem   (CIT)
BRDT......... Bayesian Reliability Demonstration Test [*Data processing*]
BREF......... Book Review Editors File [*University Press of New England*] [*Information service*]   (EISS)
BRF............ Bell Rings Faintly [*Telecommunications*]   (TEL)
BRG........... Baud Rate Generator   (CAA)
BRG........... Bridge [*or Bridging*] [*Telecommunications*]   (TEL)
BRICS......... Black Resources Information Coordinating Services [*Information service*]   (EISS)
BRL............ Balance Return Loss [*Telecommunications*]   (TEL)
BRN............ Broadcast Net   (NATG)
BROWSER ...   Browsing On-Line with Selective Retrieval   (DEEC)
BRS............ B-Mode Receiving Station [*Telecommunications*]   (TEL)
BRS............ Bible Research Systems [*Austin, TX*] [*Information service*]   (EISS)
BRS............ Bibliographic Retrieval Services, Inc. [*Database host system*] [*Scotia, NY*]
BRS............ Block Received Signal [*Telecommunications*]   (TEL)
BRS............ Break Request Signal [*Data processing*]   (CGC)
BRT............ Binary Run Tape [*Data processing*]   (BUR)
Br Telecom J ...   British Telecom Journal [*A publication*]
BRUIN......... Brown University Interpreter [*Data processing*]   (TUT)
BS .... Backspace Character [*Keyboard*] [*Data processing*]
BS .... Backward Signaling [*Telecommunications*]   (TEL)
BS .... Bank-Switching [*Computer technology*]
BS .... Beam Splitter [*Instrumentation*]
BS .... Biosystematic Code [*Online database field identifier*]   (OBD)
BS .... BIT [*Binary Digit*] Sync [*Data processing*]   (CIT)
B/S .... BITS [*Binary Digits*] per Second [*Data transmission speed*] [*Data processing*]   (CET)
BS .... Broadcast Satellite [*Japan*]   (CBSS)
BS .... Broadcasting Station
BSA............ BIT [*Binary Digit*] Sync Acquisition [*Data processing*]
BSAL......... Block Structured Assembly Language   (CAA)
BSAM........ Basic Sequential Access Method [*IBM Corp.*] [*Data processing*]   (TUT)
BSB............ Bayerische Staatsbibliothek [*Information retrieval*]   (ODIN)
BSB............ Both Sideband
BSC............ Basic Message Switching Center [*Data processing*]   (CGC)
BSC............ Bibliographic Systems Center [*Case Western Reserve University*]   (EISS)
BSC............ Binary Symmetric Channel [*Data processing*]
BSC............ Binary Synchronous Communication [*IBM Corp.*] [*Data processing*]
BSC............ BIT [*Binary Digit*] Scan Command [*Data processing*]
BSC............ Building Services Calculations [*Amazon Computers*] [*Software package*] [*British*]   (NCC)
BSCA......... Binary Synchronous Communications Adapter [*Data processing*]
BSCL......... Bell System Common Language [*Telecommunications*]   (TEL)
BSCM......... Binary Synchronous Communications Macro   (CAA)
BSCN......... BIT [*Binary Digit*] Scan [*Data processing*]   (BUR)
BSC/SS..... Binary Synchronous Communications/Start-Stop   (CAA)
BSCTE...... Bell System Center for Technical Education
BSD............ BIT [*Binary Digit*] Storage Density [*Data processing*]
BSD............ Bulk Storage Device   (IEEE)
BSDC......... Binary Symmetric Dependent Channel [*Data processing*]
BSDC......... British Standard Data Code   (BUR)
BSE............ Backscatter Electron
BSE............ Broadcasting Satellite Experimental [*Japan*]   (MCD)
BSE............ Building Services Estimating [*Tipdata Ltd.*] [*Software package*] [*British*]   (NCC)
BSELCH .....   Buffered Selector Channel   (CAH)
BSET........ Test a BIT [*Binary Digit*] and Set
BSF............ Backspace File   (BUR)
BSG........... BIT [*Binary Digit*] Sync Generator [*Data processing*]   (CIT)
BSG........... British Standard Gauge [*Telecommunications*]   (TEL)
BSI............. Biblio Service Informatique [*Informatics Biblio Service*] [*France*] [*Information service*]   (EISS)
BSI............. Branch and Store Instruction [*Data processing*]   (MDG)
BSI............. British Standards Institution [*Promulgates manufacturing standards and specifications*] [*London*]
BSI............. Broker Services, Incorporated [*Englewood, CO*] [*Information service*]   (EISS)
BSIC.......... Binary Symmetric Independent Channel [*Data processing*]   (CGC)
BSIE.......... Banking Systems Information Exchange   (CAA)
BSL............ BIT [*Binary Digit*] Serial Link   (CAA)
BSLR......... Bus Selector [*Data processing*]
BSM........... Basic System Memory [*Data processing*]   (BUR)
BSMD......... Bulk Store Memory Device   (MCD)
BSMF......... BIT [*Binary Digit*] Sync Matched Filter [*Data processing*]   (CIT)
BSN............ Backward Sequence Number [*Telecommunications*]   (TEL)
BSOC......... Bell System Operating Company [*Also, BOC*] [*Post-divestiture division of American Telephone & Telegraph Co.*]
BSP............ Bell System Practices
BSP............ Building Services Programs [*Amazon Computers*] [*Software package*] [*British*]   (NCC)
BSP............ Burroughs Scientific Processor [*Data processing*]   (BUR)
BSP............ Business Systems Planning
BSPL......... Behavioral Science Programing Language [*Data processing*]
BSR............ Backspace Recorder
BSR............ BIT [*Binary Digit*] Slippage Rate [*Data processing*]
BSR............ Board of Standards Review [*American National Standards Institute*]
BSR............ Branch to Subroutine [*Data processing*]
BSR............ Buffered Send/Receive   (CAA)
BSRFS....... Bell System Reference Frequency Standard [*Telecommunications*]   (TEL)
BSRS......... Bell System Repair Specification [*Telecommunications*]   (TEL)
BSS............ Bulk Storage System   (CAA)

BST	Business Systems Technology, Inc. (CAA)		BV	Before Video
BSTJ	Bell System Technical Journal [*A publication*]		BV	Busy Verification [*Telecommunications*] (TEL)
BSTJA	Bell System Technical Journal [*A publication*]		BVW	Backward Volume Wave [*Telecommunications*] (TEL)
BSU	Basic Sounding Unit [*Telecommunications*] (TEL)		BW	Bandwidth [*Frequency range*]
BSU	Business Service Unit [*Telecommunications*] (TEL)		BW	Buried Wire [*Telecommunications*] (TEL)
BSUG	Bedford Systems Users Group [*Salt Lake City, UT*] (EANO)		BWC	Buffer Word Counter [*Data processing*] (CAA)
BT	Break Transmission (NVT)		BWCS	Bob White Computing & Software, Inc. [*Oak Brook, IL*] [*Software manufacturer*] (DASOS)
BT	British Telecom [*or Telecommunications*] [*Common carrier*]		BWD	Backward [*Telecommunications*] (TEL)
BT	Broadcasting Station, Television [*ITU designation*]		BWG	Birmingham Wire Gauge
BT	Buried Tape Armor [*Telecommunications*] (TEL)		BWN	Brown [*Telecommunications*] (TEL)
BT	Busy Tone [*Telecommunications*] (TEL)		BWO	Backward Wave Oscillator
BTAM	Basic Tape Access Method [*Data processing*] (CAA)		BWR	Bandwidth Ratio
BTAM	Basic Telecommunications Access Method [*IBM Corp.*] [*Data processing*] (CGC)		BX	Base Register [*Data processing*]
BTAM	Basic Teleprocessing Access Method [*IBM Corp.*] (CAH)		BX	Branch Exchange [*Telecommunications*] (CAA)
BTAM	Basic Terminal Access Method [*Data processing*] (IDA)		BY	Busy [*Telecommunications*] (TEL)
BTAS	Thermal Analysis Software/Building Services [*Amazon Energy Ltd.*] [*Software package*] [*British*] (NCC)		BYMUX	Byte-Multiplexer Channel (CAA)
BTB	Bus Tie Breaker		BYP	Bypass (KSC)
BTC	BIT [*Binary Digit*] Time Counter [*Data processing*]			
BTC	Block Transfer Controller [*Data processing*] (CAA)			
BTC	Business and Technology Center [*Control Data Corp.*] [*British*] (CAA)			
BTC	Business Telecommunications Corporation [*Chicago, IL*] (TSSD)			
BTD	Binary to Decimal [*Data processing*] (BUR)			
BTDL	Basic Transient Diode Logic [*Data processing*] (BUR)			
BTE	Bidirectional Transceiver Element [*Telecommunications*] (CAA)			
BTE	Business Telecommunications Equipment [*Canada*]			
BTE	Business Terminal Equipment [*Telecommunications*] (TEL)			
BTEC	Banctec, Inc. [*NASDAQ symbol*] (NQ)			
BTelE	Bachelor of Telecommunications Engineering			
BTF	Bulk Transfer Facility (CAA)			
BTH	Basic Transmission Header [*Data processing*] (IBMDP)			
BTI	British Telecommunications International (TSSD)			
BTI	BTI Computer Systems [*Formerly, Basic Timesharing, Inc.*] (CAA)			
BTIS	Bankers Trust Information Service [*Database producer*] (CUAD)			
BTL	Beginning Tape Label [*Data processing*] (BUR)			
BTL	Bell Telephone Laboratories, Inc. [*Murray Hill, NJ*]			
BTM	Batch Time-Sharing Monitor [*Xerox Corp.*] [*Data processing*] (MCD)			
BTMF	Block Type Manipulation Facility (OA)			
BTN	Baptist Telecommunications Network [*Cable-television system*]			
BTN	Billing Telephone Number [*Telecommunications*] (TEL)			
BTP	Batch Transfer Program (DEEC)			
BTP	British Telecom Phonecards [*Prepaid cards for use in noncoin pay telephones*]			
BTQ	Banque de Terminologie du Quebec [*Terminology Bank of Quebec*] [*French Language Board*] [*Information service*] (EISS)			
BTR	Back Tape Reader (CCD)			
BTR	Broadcast and Television Receivers (MCD)			
BTRY	Battery (AFM)			
BTS	Batch Terminal Simulator [*Data processing*]			
BTS	British Telecommunications Systems Ltd. (TEL)			
BTS	Broadcast Transmission Systems (MCD)			
BTSS	Basic Time-Sharing System (BUR)			
BTSS	Braille Time-Sharing System (CAA)			
BTST	BIT [*Binary Digit*] Test [*Data processing*]			
BTU	Basic Transmission Unit [*Data processing*]			
BTU	British Thermal Unit [*Also, BTHU*]			
BTX	Bildschirmtext [*Viewdata system*] [*Federal Ministry of Posts and Telecommunications*] [*Bonn, WG*] (TSSD)			
BTY	British Telecommunications [*Toronto Stock Exchange symbol*]			
BU	Bottom Up (CAA)			
BU	Bus Unit [*Data processing*]			
BUBMEM	Bubble Memory [*Data storage device*] [*Data processing*] (MSA)			
BUDC	Backup Digital Computer			
BUDS	Backup Digital System			
BUDWSR	Brown University Display for Working Set References (OA)			
BUEC	Backup Emergency Communications			
BUF	Buffer (CAH)			
BUFVC	British Universities Film & Video Council [*Database producer*] (CUAD)			
BUG	Business User Group [*Data processing*]			
BUGS	Brown University Graphic System (OA)			
BUGSYS	[*A*] programing language (CSR)			
BUILD	Base for Uniform Language Definition [*Data processing*] (IEEE)			
Bull Am Soc Inform Sci	Bulletin. American Society for Information Science [*A publication*]			
Bull Am Soc Inf Sci	Bulletin. American Society for Information Science [*A publication*]			
BUMP	Bottom-Up Modular Programing (CAA)			
BUNCH	Burroughs, UNIVAC, NCR, Control Data, Honeywell [*IBM competitors in computer manufacture*]			
BUR	Back Up Register (CAA)			
BUR	Buried			
BURDS	Burroughs Distribution Scheduling System [*Data processing*] (BUR)			
BUSAK	Bus Acknowledgement [*Data processing*] (TEL)			
BUSED	Base and User [*A publication*]			
BUSRQ	Bus Request [*Data processing*] (TEL)			
BUV	Backscatter Ultraviolet [*Spectrometry*]			

C

C	Cable		CAD	Character Assemble/Disassemble (CAA)
C	Capacitor (CET)		CAD	Communications Access Device (CET)
C	Cathode		CAD	Computer Access Device
c	Centi [*A prefix meaning divided by 100*] [*SI symbol*]		CAD	Computer-Aided Design
C	Character (BUR)		CAD	Computer-Aided Detection
C	Clear [*Calculators*]		CAD	Computer-Aided Drafting
C	Collector [*Electronics*]		CAD	Computer Applications Digest [*A publication*]
C	Communications		CAD	Computer-Assisted Design
C	Compute [*or Computer*] (MDG)		CAD	Computer-Assisted Diagnosis
C	Constant		CAD	Computer-Assisted Dialog
C	Continuous Operation during Hours Shown [*Broadcasting*]		CAD	Computer-Associated [*or -Assisted*] Device (SKY)
C	Control		CADA	Computer-Aided Design and Analysis
C	Creosote [*Telecommunications*] (TEL)		CADA	Computer-Assisted Development Aids
C	[*A*] programing language [*Bell Telephone Laboratories*] [*1974*] (CSR)		CADA	Computer-Assisted Distribution and Assignment (NVT)
C²	Command and Control [*Pronounced "see-squared"*]		CADAM	Computer-Graphics Augmented Design and Manufacturing [*Software package*] [*British*] (NCC)
C³	Command, Control, and Communications [*Pronounced "see-cubed"*]		CADANCE	Computer-Aided Design and Numerical Control Effort
C⁴	Command, Control, Communications, and Computer Systems (NVT)		CADAR	Computer-Aided Design, Analysis, and Reliability (IEEE)
CA	Cable (MSA)		CADAT	Computer-Aided Design and Test [*System*]
CA	Cathode		CADB	Climate Assessment Data Base [*National Meteorological Center*] [*Database*] (FDB)
CA	Channel Adapter [*Data processing*] (IBMDP)		CADC	Cambridge Automatic Digital Computer (IEEE)
CA	Chemical Abstracts [*Chemical Abstracts Service*] [*Database*] [*A publication*]		CADC	Central Air Data Computer
CA	Coaxial		CAD/CAM	Computer-Aided Design/Computer-Aided Manufacturing
CA	Communications Adapter (CAA)		CAD/CAM Tech	CAD/CAM [*Computer-Aided Design/Computer-Aided Manufacturing*] Technology [*A publication*]
CA	Computer Automation, Inc. [*Richardson, TX*] (TSSD)		CADD	Computer-Aided Design Development
CA	Computers and Automation (BUR)		CADD	Computer-Aided Design and Drafting [*Software package*] (MCD)
CA	Continue-Any [*Mode*] [*Data processing*] (IBMDP)		CADDA	Computer-Aided Design and Design Automation
CA	Courant Alternatif [*Alternating Current*] [*French*]		CADDAC	Central Analog Data Distributing and Computing System (KSC)
CAA	Computer Amplifier Alarm		CADE	Computer-Aided Design Engineering (RDA)
CAA	Computer-Assisted Accounting (BUR)		CADE	Computer-Aided Design and Evaluation (MCD)
CAA	Computing Across America [*From book title, "Computing Across America: The Bicycle Odyssey of a High-Tech Nomad" by Steven K. Roberts*]		CADEC	Computer-Aided Design of Electronic Circuits [*Elsevier Book Series*] [*A publication*]
CAAC	Center for Academic & Administrative Computing [*George Washington University*] [*Research center*] (RCD)		CADEP	Computer-Aided Design of Electronic Products (IEEE)
CAAS	Computer-Aided Alerting Subsystem (CAAL)		CADET	Can't Add, Doesn't Even Try [*Data processing*]
CAAS	Computer-Assisted Acquisition System [*for libraries*] (DEEC)		CADET	Computer-Aided Design and Electrical Test
CAB	Cabletelevision Advertising Bureau (EANO)		CADET	Computer-Aided Design Experiment Translator
CAB	Commonwealth Agricultural Bureaux [*Buchs, England*] [*Database producer*] (EANO)		CADET	Computer-Associated Diagnostic and Evaluation Tests (CAAL)
Cablecast Cable TV Eng	Cablecasting, Cable TV Engineering [*A publication*]		CADETS	Classroom-Aided Dynamic Educational Time-Sharing System (IEEE)
Cable Rpt	Cable Report [*A publication*]		CADF	Cathode-Ray Tube Automatic Direction Finding (IEEE)
Cables & Transm	Cables and Transmission [*A publication*]		CADI	Computer Access Device Input (CET)
Cables Transm	Cables and Transmission [*A publication*]		CADIC	Computer-Aided Design of Integrated Circuits
Cable Telev Eng	Cable Television Engineering [*A publication*]		CADISIM	Computer-Assisted Disposal Simulation [*Game*]
CABS	Computer-Aided Batch Scheduling		CADL	Communications and Data Link (KSC)
CABS	Computerized Annotated Bibliography System [*Alberta University*] [*Canada*]		CADLAB	Computer Aided Design and Graphics Laboratory [*Purdue University*] [*Research center*] (RCD)
CABSADS	Computerized, Automated, Bus Spacing and Dispatching System		CAD-LAB	Computer-Aided Design Laboratory [*Pennsylvania State University*] [*Research center*] (RCD)
CAC	Cable Access Cover		CADMAT	Computer-Aided Design, Manufacture, and Test (DEEC)
CAC	Chemical Abstracts Condensates [*A publication*] (EISS)		CADMINI	Computer Administrative Instruction
CAC	Communications Analysis Corporation [*Framingham, MA*] [*Telecommunications*] (TSSD)		CADO	Computer Access Device Output (CET)
CAC	Computer-Aided Classification (CAA)		CADOS	Computer Aided Design of Optical Systems [*Energy Soft Computer Systems Ltd.*] [*Software package*] [*British*] (NCC)
CAC	Current Abstracts of Chemistry [*Institute for Scientific Information*] [*Database*] [*A publication*]		CADPO	Communications and Data Processing Operation
CACC	Communications and Configuration Console (MCD)		CADRE	Complete ADR [*Applied Data Research, Inc.*] Environment (EANO)
CACD	Computer-Aided Circuit Design		CADRE	Current Awareness and Document Retrieval for Engineers (DIT)
CACHE	Chicago Area Computer Hobbyist Exchange		CADS	Computer-Assisted Dispatching System [*IBM Corp.*]
CACI	CACI, Inc. [*NASDAQ symbol*] (NQ)		CADSI	Communications and Data Systems Integration (NASA)
CACM	Communications. ACM [*Association for Computing Machinery*] [*A publication*]		CADSS	Combined Analog-Digital Systems Simulator [*Data processing*] (CGC)
CACON	Chemical Abstracts Condensates [*Database*] (CAA)		CAE	Computer-Aided Education (BUR)
CAC/PL	Canadian Advisory Committee on Programming Languages		CAE	Computer-Aided Engineering
CACS	Centralized Alarm and Control System [*Telecommunications*] (TEL)		CAE	Computer-Aided Engineering Center [*University of Wisconsin - Madison*] [*Research center*] (RCD)
CACS	Computer-Aided [*or -Assisted*] Communication System (CAA)		CAE	Computer-Assisted Enrollment [*IBM Corp.*] (IEEE)
CACS	Content Addressable Computing System (CAA)		CAE	Computer-Assisted Entry (CIT)
CACTOS	Computation and Communication Trade-Off Study [*ARPA*]		CAE	Computer-Assisted Estimating
			CAEEA	Canadian Electronics Engineering [*A publication*]

Computer & Telecommunications Acronyms

CAE LAB .... Computer-Aided Engineering Laboratory [*Lawrence Institute of Technology*] [*Research center*]   (RCD)
CAEX .... Community Automatic Exchange [*Telephone*]   (BUR)
CAFE .... Computer Aided Design of Fire Escapes [*Micro Core Ltd.*] [*Software package*] [*British*]   (NCC)
CAFE .... Computer-Aided Film Editor   (TUT)
CAFS .... Content-Addressable File Store [*Data processing*]   (IEEE)
CAGE .... Compiler and Assembler by General Electric
CAI .... Century Analysis, Incorporated [*Pacheco, CA*] [*Software manufacturer*]   (DASOS)
CAI .... Communication Advisors, Incorporated [*Southfield, MI*] [*Telecommunications*]   (TSSD)
CAI .... Computer-Administered Instruction   (RDA)
CAI .... Computer-Aided [*or -Assisted*] Instruction
CAI .... Computer Automation, Incorporated   (CAH)
CAI .... Connectionless Acknowledged Information   (CCD)
CAIC .... Computer-Assisted Indexing and Categorizing [*or Classification*]   (IDA)
CAIC .... Computer-Assisted Instruction Center   (DDI)
CAICYT ...... Centro Argentino de Informacion Cientifica y Tecnologica [*Argentine Center for Scientific and Technological Information*] [*Information service*]   (EISS)
CAIN .... Cataloging and Indexing Number [*Later, AGRICOLA*] [*National Agricultural Library*] [*Database*]
CAIN .... Computerized AIDS [*Acquired Immune Deficiency Syndrome*] Information Network [*Los Angeles Gay and Lesbian Community Services Center*] [*Database*]   (CUAD)
CAIOP .... Computer Analog Input/Output   (CGC)
CAIRS .... Computer-Aided Analysis and Information Recovery Systems   (MCD)
CAIRS .... Computer-Assisted Information Retrieval System   (DEEC)
CAIRS .... Computer-Assisted Interactive Resources Scheduling System
CAIS .... Canadian Association for Information Science [*Ottawa, ON*]
CAIS .... Central Abstracting and Indexing Service [*American Petroleum Institute*] [*New York, NY*] [*Information service*]   (EISS)
CAIS .... Computer-Administered Instructional System
CAIS .... Computer-Aided Instruction   (IEEE)
CAIS .... Computer-Assisted Action Information System [*NATO*]
CAIS/ACSI ... Canadian Association for Information Science/Association Canadienne des Sciences de l'Information [*Ottawa, ON*]   (EISS)
CAISF .... Chemical Abstracts Integrated Subject File [*Chemical Abstracts Service*] [*Database*] [*A publication*]   (EISS)
CAISMS ...... Computer-Assisted Instruction Study Management System   (MCD)
CAISR .... Center for Automation and Intelligent Systems Research [*Case Western Reserve University*] [*Research center*]   (RCD)
CAISYS ...... Computer-Aided Instruction System [*Programing language*] [*1971*]   (CSR)
CAITS .... Computerized Automatic Inertial Test Set   (MCD)
CAK .... Command Access Keys   (OA)
CAK .... Command Acknowledge   (BUR)
CAL .... Calibrate   (CET)
CAL .... Computer-Aided [*or -Assisted*] Learning   (BUR)
CAL .... Computer Animation Language   (TUT)
CAL .... Computer Augmented Learning   (CMD)
CAL .... Conversational Algebraic Language [*Adaptation of JOSS language*] [*Data processing*]
CAL .... Course Author Language [*Data processing*]   (CGC)
CALB .... Computer-Aided Line Balance
CALC .... Calculated
CALCOMP ... California Computer Products, Inc.   (CAH)
CALDOC ..... Calgary Public Library Government Documents [*Calgary, AB*] [*Information service*]   (EISS)
CALL .... Computer-Augmented Loft Lines [*Graphic arts*]   (MCD)
CALM .... COBOL [*Common Business-Oriented Language*] Automatic Language Modifier [*Data processing*]   (TUT)
CALM .... Collected Algorithm for Learning Machines [*Data processing*]
CALM .... Computer-Assisted Library Mechanization   (CGC)
CALMS ...... Continuous Automatic Line Monitoring System
CALN .... Computer-Assisted Learning Network
CALRS .... Centralized Automatic Loop Reporting System [*Telecommunications*]   (TEL)
CAM .... Central Address Memory [*Data processing*]   (CGC)
CAM .... Computer Achievement Monitoring   (MCD)
CAM .... Computer Address Matrix
CAM .... Computer-Aided Makeup [*Graphic arts*]
CAM .... Computer-Aided Manufacturing
CAM .... Computer Annunciation Matrix   (MCD)
CAM .... Computer-Assisted Maintenance
CAM .... Computer-Assisted Makeup [*Graphic arts*]
CAM .... Content-Addressable Memory [*Data processing*]
CAM .... Control Access Manager   (BUR)
CAM .... Engineering Center for Automated Manufacturing Technology [*Clemson University*] [*Research center*]   (RCD)
CAMA .... Centralized Automatic Message Accounting [*Bell System*]
CAMA .... Computer-Assisted Method Assembly [*Analytical method writing*]
CAMA-C ..... Centralized Automatic Message Accounting - Computerized [*Bell System*]   (TEL)
CAMAC .... Computer-Automated Measurement and Control   (MSA)
CAMAL .... Cambridge Algebraic System [*Programing language*] [*1975*]   (CSR)

CAMA-ONI ... Centralized Automatic Message Accounting - Operator Number Identification [*Telecommunications*]   (TEL)
Cambridge Comput Sci Texts ... Cambridge Computer Science Texts [*A publication*]
CAMCOS.... Computer-Assisted Maintenance Planning and Control System
CAMD .... Computer-Aided Mechanical Drafting
CAM-I .... Computer Aided Manufacturing International [*Arlington, TX*] [*An association*]   (EANO)
CAMIL .... Computer-Assisted/Managed Instructional Language   (CSR)
CAMP .... Compiler for Automatic Machine Programing   (BUR)
CAMP .... Computer Applications of Military Problems [*Computer users' group*]
CAMP .... Computer-Assisted Management of Portfolios   (CGC)
CAMP .... Computer-Assisted Mathematics Program [*Scott, Foresman, 1968-1969*] [*Textbook series*]   (BUR)
CAMP .... Computer-Assisted Menu Planning
CAMP .... Computer-Assisted Movie Production   (IEEE)
CAMP .... Controls and Monitoring Processor   (IEEE)
CAMRAS .... Computer-Assisted Mapping and Records Activities System   (IEEE)
CAN .... Cancel Character [*Keyboard*] [*Data processing*]
CANAL .... Command Analysis [*Telecommunications*]   (TEL)
CANC .... Canceled
CANCERLIT ... Cancer Literature [*National Library of Medicine*] [*Database*]
CANCERPROJ ... Cancer Research Projects [*National Library of Medicine*] [*Database*]
CANCOM.... Canadian Satellite Communications, Inc. [*Mississauga, ON*] [*Telecommunications*]   (TSSD)
Can Commun Power Conf Proc ... Canadian Communications and Power Conference. Proceedings [*A publication*]
CAN/CRS... Canadian Computer-Based Reference Service [*National Library of Canada*] [*Information service*]   (EISS)
Can Datasyst ... Canadian Datasystems [*A publication*]
CANDE .... Command and Edit Program [*Burroughs Corp.*] [*Data processing*]   (BUR)
CAN DO ...... Computer Analyzed Newspaper Data On-Line [*Newspaper Advertising Bureau, Inc.*] [*Information service*]   (EISS)
Can Electr Eng J ... Canadian Electrical Engineering Journal [*A publication*]
Can Electron Eng ... Canadian Electronics Engineering [*A publication*]
Can J Info Science ... Canadian Journal of Information Science [*A publication*]
CANMINDEX ... Canadian Mineral Occurrence Index [*Ottawa, ON*] [*Information service*]   (EISS)
CANS.......... Computer-Assisted Network Scheduling System   (IEEE)
CANSIM...... Canadian Socio-Economic Information Management System [*Statistics Canada*] [*Database*]   (EISS)
CANTAT ..... Canadian Transatlantic Telephone Cable [*Between Canada and England*]
CANTRAN ... Canceled Transmission   (CET)
CAOCI .... Commercially Available Organic Chemicals Index [*Chemical Notation Association*] [*Databank*] [*British*]
CAOS.......... Completely Automatic Operational System [*UNIVAC*]
CAP .... Capacity   (AFM)
CAP .... Circuit Access Point [*Telecommunications*]   (TEL)
CAP .... Computational Arithmetic Program
CAP .... Computer Address Panel   (CAAL)
CAP .... Computer-Aided Planning   (CCD)
CAP .... Computer-Aided [*or Assisted*] Production
CAP .... Computer-Aided Programing   (CAA)
CAP .... Computer Analysts & Programmers Ltd. [*British*]   (CAH)
CAP .... Computer-Assisted Printing
CAP .... Computers and People [*A publication*]
CAP .... Computing Assistance Program [*Taylor University*] [*Information service*]   (EISS)
CAP .... Concurrent Algorithmic Programing Language [*Data processing*]   (CSR)
CAP .... Continuous Audit Program [*Data processing*]   (IEEE)
CAP .... Control Assembly Program   (BUR)
CAP .... Council on Advanced Programing
CAP .... Cryotron Associative Processor   (IEEE)
CAPAL .... Computer and Photographic Assisted Learning
CAPD.......... Computer-Aided Process Design   (MCD)
CAPDAC ..... Computer-Aided Piping Design and Construction   (MCD)
CAPE .... Communication Automatic Processing Equipment
CAPE .... Computer Aided Planning and Estimating [*Marlow Microplan National Engineering Laboratory*] [*Software package*] [*British*]   (NCC)
CAPER........ Computer-Aided Pattern Evaluation and Recognition   (KSC)
CAPES........ Computer Aided Planning and Estimating [*Inbucon Productivity Services Ltd.*] [*Software package*] [*British*]   (NCC)
CAPF .... Chemical Age Project File [*Pergamon InfoLine Inc.*] [*Database*]   (CUAD)
CAPM .... Computer-Aided Patient Management
CAPOSS..... Capacity Planning and Operations Sequencing System [*IBM Corp.*]
CAPOSS-E ... Capacity Planning and Operations Sequencing System - Extended [*IBM Corp.*]
CAPP .... Computer-Aided Process Planning   (MCD)
CAPP .... Content-Addressable Parallel Processor [*Data processing*]
CAPPAC..... Computer Aided Production Planning and Control [*John Yates & Associates*] [*Software package*] [*British*]   (NCC)
CAPR .... Catalog of Programs   (OA)
CAPRI......... Card and Printer Remote Interface   (CAA)
CAPRI......... Coded Address Private Radio Intercommunications

Computer & Telecommunications Acronyms

CAPRI	Computerized Area Pricing [*Telecommunications*] (TEL)
CAPS	Call Attempts per Second [*Telecommunications*] (TEL)
CAPS	Cashiers' Automatic Processing System (DIT)
CAPS	Cassette Programing System [*Digital Equipment Corp.*] (IDA)
CAPS	Command Automated Procurement System (MCD)
CAPS	Computer-Aided Pipe Sketching [*System*] [*Du Pont*]
CAPS	Computer-Aided Programing System
CAPS	Computer-Assisted Placement Service [*British*]
CAPS	Computer-Assisted Problem Solving (IEEE)
CAPS	Computer-Assisted Prosthesis Selection [*Orthopedic surgery*]
CAPS	Computing and Data Processing Services [*University of Maine*] [*Research center*] (RCD)
CAPS	Continuous Automated Placement Survey [*Department of Labor*]
CAPS	Courtauld's All-Purpose Simulator (IEEE)
CAPSK	Combined Amplitude Phase Shift Keying (MCD)
CAPT	Conversational Parts Programing Language [*Data processing*] (IEEE)
CAPTAIN	Character and Pattern Telephone Access Information Network [*Viewdata system*] [*Japan*] [*Telecommunications*] (TEL)
CAPTAIN	Computer-Aided Processing and Terminal Access Information Network [*Rutgers University*] [*New Brunswick, NJ*] [*Library computer network*]
CAPTALC	Control and Protection of Transoceanic Air Lanes of Communication
CAPTIS	Computer-Assisted Prisoner Transportation Index Service [*National Sheriffs' Association*]
CAQA	Computer-Aided Quality Assurance
CAR	Channel Address Register [*Data processing*] (CGC)
CAR	Check Authorization Record (IBMDP)
CAR	Community Antenna Relay [*Service*] [*FCC*]
CAR	Computer-Assisted Research (BUR)
CAR	Computer-Assisted Retrieval
CARBINE	Computer-Automated Real-Time Betting Information Network (IEEE)
CARD	Channel Allocation and Routing Data (IEEE)
CARD	Coded Automatic Reading Device
CARD	Compact Automatic Retrieval Device [*Massachusetts Institute of Technology*] [*Data processing*]
CARD	Compact Automatic Retrieval Display [*Data processing*] (EISS)
CARDCODER	Card Automatic Code System [*IBM Corp.*] (IEEE)
CARDIAC	Cardboard Illustrative Aid to Computation [*Bell Telephone Co.*] [*Data processing*]
CARDS	Card-Automated Reproduction and Distribution System [*Library of Congress*]
CARDS	Computer-Aided Reliability Data Systems [*Bell System*]
CARDS	Computer-Aided Requirements Definition Software
CARE	Computer-Aided Reliability Estimation
CARES	Computer-Aided Railway Engineering System (MCD)
CARESIM	Computer-Assisted Repair Simulation [*Game*]
CARIN	Car Information and Navigation System [*Compact disc technology*]
CARIS	Computerized Agricultural Research Information System [*United Nations Food and Agricultural organization information system*]
CARIS	Current Agricultural Research Information System [*United Nations*] [*Information service*] (EISS)
CARISMA	Computer-Aided Research into Stock Market Applications
CARISMA	Corrections to Applied Research Laboratories Ion-Sputtering Mass Analyzers [*Data processing*]
CARL	Computer Audio Research Laboratory [*University of California, San Diego*] [*Research center*] (RCD)
CARLA	Center for Applied Research in the Language Arts [*Texas Tech University*] [*Research center*] (RCD)
CARLA	Code Actuated Random Load Apparatus (MCD)
CARMSIM	Computer-Assisted Reliability and Maintainability Simulation [*Game*]
CAROT	Centralized Automatic Recording on Trunks [*Bell System*]
CARP	Call Accounting Reconciliation Process [*Telecommunications*] (TEL)
CARR	Carrier [*Telecommunications*] (AFM)
CARS	Cable Relay Service [*or Station*] [*Television transmission*]
CARS	Community Antenna Relay Service [*FCC*] [*Telecommunications*]
CARS	Computer-Aided Reference Service [*Information service*]
CARS	Computer-Aided Routing System (CGC)
CARS	Computer Audit Retrieval System [*Trade name for Sage Systems, Inc., computer software product*]
CARS	Computerized Automotive Replacement Scheduling [*Bell System*]
CARS	Computerized Automotive Reporting Service (BUR)
CARS	Continuous Alarm Reporting Service [*Telecommunications*] (TEL)
CART	Complete Automatic Reliable Testing (CDH)
CART	Computerized Automatic Rating Technique (DEN)
CARTA	Computer-Aided Reorder Trap Analysis [*Bell Laboratories*]
CARU	Computer Architecture Research Unit [*York University*] [*Canada*] [*Research center*] (RCD)
CAS	Cable Activity System [*Telecommunications*] (TEL)
CAS	Call Accounting System [*or Subsystem*] [*Telecommunications*]
CAS	Centralized Attendants Service [*Bell System*]
CAS	Chemical Abstracts Service [*Database producer*]
CAS	Column-Address Strobe (IEEE)
CAS	Combined Antenna System (CAAL)
CAS	Communications Antenna Sleeve
CAS	Computer Accounting System [*Boole & Babbage, Inc.*] (IDA)
CAS	Computer Arts Society (EANO)
CAS	Computer-Assisted Search (CAAL)
CAS	Computer Audit Specialist [*IRS*]
CAS	Control Automation System [*IBM Corp.*] (CAA)
CASA	Computer-Associated Self-Assessment [*British*]
CASA	Computer and Automated Systems Association [*Later, CASA/SME*] [*Dearborn, MI*]
CASA/SME	Computer and Automated Systems Association of Society of Manufacturing Engineers [*Formerly, CASA*] [*Dearborn, MI*] (EANO)
CASD	Computer-Aided Structural Design (MCD)
CASD	Computer-Aided System Design [*Programing language*] (BUR)
CASE	Computer-Aided Software Engineering (CAA)
CASE	Computer-Aided System Evaluation (TUT)
CASE	Computer-Automated Support Equipment
CASE	Computer & Software Enterprises, Inc. [*San Luis Obispo, CA*] [*Software manufacturer*] (DASOS)
CASE	New York State Center for Advanced Technology in Computer Applications and Software Engineering [*Syracuse University*] [*Research center*] (RCD)
CASI	Computer Application Services, Incorporated [*Los Alamitos, CA*] [*Telecommunications*] (TSSD)
CASI	Computer Associates International [*NASDAQ symbol*] (NQ)
CASIA	Chemical Abstracts Subject Index Alert [*Database*] [*A publication*]
CASL	Computer Architecture Specification Language (CSR)
CASMS	Computer-Controlled Area Sterilization Multisensor System
CASP	Computer-Assisted Search Planning (MCD)
CASPAR	Cambridge Analog Simulator for Predicting Atomic Reactions [*British*] (DIT)
CASS	Computer Applications in Shipping and Shipbuilding [*Elsevier Book Series*] [*A publication*]
CASS	Computer-Automated Social Simulation
CASS	Computer Automatic Scheduling System
CASSANDRA	Chromatogram Automatic Soaking Scanning and Digital Recording Apparatus
CASSARS	Computer-Assisted Simulation of Supply and Related Systems
CASSI	Chemical Abstracts Service Source Index [*Online database*]
CASSIS	Classification and Search Support Information System [*Patent and Trademark Office*] [*Information service*]
CASSM	Context Addressed Segment Sequential Memory (CAA)
CAST	Chemical Automated Search Terminal [*Computer Corp. of America*] [*Information service*] (EISS)
CAST	Common Access Security Terminal
CAST	Computer-Aided Structural Technology (MCD)
CAST	Computer-Assisted Scanning Techniques
CAST	Computerized Automatic Systems Tester (MCD)
CASTOR	College Applicant Status Report [*Honeywell, Inc.*] [*Data processing*] (CDH)
CAT	Compile and Test (BUR)
CAT	Computer-Aided Teaching (CGC)
CAT	Computer-Aided Technology (MCD)
CAT	Computer-Aided Test [*Telecommunications*] (TEL)
CAT	Computer Aided Testing [*Hoskyns Group Ltd.*] [*Software package*] [*British*] (NCC)
CAT	Computer-Aided Translation (IEEE)
CAT	Computer-Assisted Testing (BUR)
CAT	Computer-Assisted Tomography
CAT	Computer of Average Transients
CAT	Credit Authorization Terminal
CAT	Cumulative Abbreviated Trouble File [*Telecommunications*] (TEL)
CATCH	Computer Analysis of Thermochemical Data Tables [*University of Sussex*] [*Sussex, England*]
CATE	Computer-Aided Test Equipment (MSA)
CATE	Computer-Controlled Automatic Test Equipment (DDI)
CATED	Centre d'Assistance Technique et de Documentation [*Center for Technical Assistance and Documentation*] [*Database producer*] [*France*] [*Information service*] (EISS)
CATI	Computer-Assisted Telephone Interviewing
CATIA	Computer Graphics Aided 3D Interactive [*IBM UK Ltd.*] [*Software package*] [*British*] (NCC)
CATIS	Computer-Aided Tactical Information System (IEEE)
CATLAS	Centralized Automatic Trouble-Locating and Analysis System [*AT & T*] (TEL)
CATLG	Catalog (BUR)
CATLINE	Catalog On-Line [*National Library of Medicine*] [*Bibliographic database*]
CATNIP	Computer-Assisted Technique for Numerical Indexing Purposes
CATNYP	Catalog of the New York Public Library
CATO	Compiler for Automatic Teaching Operation (IEEE)
CATP	Computer-Aided Typesetting Process
CATS	Catalog Access System [*Project for automated library systems*]
CATS	Communications and Tracking System [*or Subsystem*]
CATS	Compute Air-Trans Systems, Inc.
CATS	Computer-Accessed [*or-Aided*] Telemetry System (CIT)
CATS	Computer-Aided Teaching System (IEEE)
CATS	Computer-Aided Troubleshooting
CATS	Computer-Assisted Test Shop
CATS	Computer-Assisted Trading System
CATS	Computer-Assisted Training System [*IRS*]
CATS	Computer-Automated Test System [*AT & T*]

Computer & Telecommunications Acronyms

CATS	Computer-Automated Transit Systems
CATscan	Computerized Axial Tomography Scanner [*Roentgenography*]
CATSS	Cataloging Support Service [*UTLAS International*]
CATT	Centralized Automatic Toll Ticketing [*Telecommunications*] (TEL)
CATT	Controlled Avalanche Transit Time [*Electronics*]
CATT	Conveyorized Automatic Tube Tester [*Data processing*] (CGC)
CATV	Cable Television [*Later, CTV*]
CATV	Community Antenna Television [*Later, CTV*]
CAU	Command Arithmetic Unit
CAU	Computer Applications Unlimited, Inc. [*Portchester, NY*] [*Software manufacturer*] (DASOS)
CAU	Converter Amplifier Unit (MCD)
CAU	Customer Acquisition Unit (NASA)
CAUML	Computers and Automation Universal Mailing List (IEEE)
CAUPR	Center for Architecture and Urban Planning Research [*University of Wisconsin - Milwaukee*] [*Research center*] (RCD)
CAUSE	College and University Systems Exchange [*Acronym is now used as name of association*]
CAUT	Computer Automation [*NASDAQ symbol*] (NQ)
CAV	Composite Analog Video (CIT)
CAVALCADE	Calibrating, Amplitude-Variation, and Level-Correcting Analog-Digital Equipment (DEN)
CAVEAT	Code and Visual Entry Authorization Technique [*Closed-circuit TV*] (MCD)
CAVS	Center for Advanced Visual Studies [*Massachusetts Institute of Technology*] [*Research center*] (RCD)
CAW	Channel Address Word [*Data processing*] (CGC)
CAW	Common Aerial Working [*Telecommunications*] (TEL)
CAWG	Coaxial Adapter Waveguide
CAWS	Computer-Aided Work Sampling
CAX	Community Automatic Exchange [*Telephone*]
CAX	Conrac Corp. [*NYSE symbol*]
CB	Call Back [*Word processing*]
CB	Cataclysmic Binary [*Data processing*]
Cb	Centibels [*Telecommunications*] (CDH)
CB	Citizens Band [*A radio frequency band for limited-range, two-way voice communications by persons without technical training or standard operator licenses*]
CB	Clear Back [*Telecommunications*] (TEL)
CB	Coin Box [*Telecommunications*] (TEL)
CB	Common Base [*Data processing*] (MSA)
CB	Common Battery [*Electronics; technical drawings*]
CB	Communications Buffer [*Data processing*] (CAA)
CB	Comparator Buffer [*Data processing*] (MUGU)
CB	Condition BIT [*Binary Digit*] [*Data processing*]
CB	Conduction Band [*Electronics*]
CB	Connecting Block [*Telecommunications*] (TEL)
CB	Constant Bandwidth (MCD)
CBA	C-Band Transponder Antenna [*Radio*] (CET)
CBA	Continuous-Beam Analysis [*Jacys Computing Services*] [*Software package*] [*British*] (NCC)
C-BASIC	Commercial BASIC (CAA)
CBAT	Central Bureau for Astronomical Telegrams (EANO)
CBB	Computerized Bulletin Board
CBBS	Computer-Based Behavioral Studies (MCD)
CBBS	Computer-Based Bibliographic Search Service
CBBS	Computer Bulletin Board System
CBC	Canadian Broadcasting Corporation [*Telecommunications*]
CBC	Can't Be Called [*Telecommunications*] (TEL)
CBCS	Chemical-Biological Computer System
CBCT	Circuit Board Card Tester
CBCT	Customer-Bank Communication Terminal [*Computerized banking*]
CBD	Call Box Discrimination [*Telecommunications*] (TEL)
CBD	Commerce Business Daily [*Department of Commerce*] [*Database*] [*A publication*]
CBD	Configuration Block Diagram [*Telecommunications*] (TEL)
CBD	Constant BIT [*Binary Digit*] Density [*Control feature of magnetic tape recorders*] [*Data processing*]
CBDS	Carcinogenesis Bioassay Data System [*National Cancer Institute*] (EISS)
CBDT	Can't Break Dial Tone [*Telecommunications*] (TEL)
CBE	Centralized Branch Exchange [*Telecommunications*] (TEL)
CBE	Circuit Board Extractor
C-BE	Computer-Based Education [*Project*]
CBEC	Canadian Book Exchange Centre [*Ottawa, ON*] (EISS)
CBEMA	Computer and Business Equipment Manufacturers Association [*Washington, DC*]
CBER	Center for Business & Economics Research [*University of Nevada - Las Vegas*] [*Research center*] (RCD)
CBH	Can't Be Heard [*Telecommunications*] (TEL)
CBH	Circuit Board Holder
CBI	Canadian Business Index [*Micromedia Ltd.*] [*Database*] [*A publication*]
CBI	Center for Business Information [*Information service*] (EISS)
CBI	Charles Babbage Institute for the History of Information Processing [*University of Minnesota*] [*Research center*] (EANO)
CBI	Compound Batch Identification [*Data processing*] (CGC)
CBI	Computer-Based Instruction [*Education*]
CBIC	Complementary Bipolar Integrated Circuit [*Telecommunications*] (TEL)
CBIS	Computer-Based Instructional System (IEEE)
CBL	Computer-Based Learning
CBM	Ceramic-Based Microcircuit
CBM	Communications Buffer Memory [*Data processing*]
CBMS	Computer-Based Message System [*Electronic mail*]
CBMU	Current BIT [*Binary Digit*] Monitor Unit [*Data processing*]
CBN	Christian Broadcasting Network [*Cable-television system*]
CBNB	Chemical Business NewsBase [*Database*]
CBO	Computer Burst Order
CBOA	Citizens Band Operating Area
CBOSS	Count Back Order and Sample Select [*Data processing*] (CAA)
CBRP	CB Radio Patrol (EANO)
CBRS	Computer-Based Reference Service [*Information service*]
CBRU	Computer-Based Resource Units [*Education*]
CBS	Call Box Station (MSA)
CBS	Central Bureau of Statistics [*Netherlands*] [*Information service*] (EISS)
CBS	Columbia Broadcasting System [*Later, CBS, Inc.*]
CBS	Common Battery Signaling [*Telecommunications*] (TEL)
CBS	Computer Business Systems [*Youngstown, OH*] [*Software manufacturer*] (DASOS)
CBT	Central Battery Telephone [*Telecommunications*]
CBT	Coin Box Telephone [*Telecommunications*]
CBT	Computer-Based Terminal
CBT	Computer-Based Training
CBTA	Central Battery Telephone Apparatus [*Telecommunications*]
CBTS	Central Battery Telephone Set [*Telecommunications*]
CBUIVTF	Concerned Broadcasters Using Inter-City Video Transmission Facilities (EANO)
CBW	Constant Bandwidth
CBW	Critical Bandwidth [*of noise*]
CBX	C-Band Transponder [*Radio*]
CBX	Computerized Private Branch Exchange [*Telecommunications*]
CC	Calculator (MDG)
CC	Card Count [*Data processing*] (TUT)
CC	Category Code [*Online database field identifier*] (OBD)
CC	Central Computer
CC	Central Control (KSC)
CC	Circuit Closing
C/C	Circuit Control
CC	Classification Code [*IRS*] [*Online database field identifier*]
CC	Closed Captioning
CC	Code Control (AFM)
CC	Coin Collect [*Telecommunications*] (TEL)
CC	Coin Completing [*Telecommunications*] (TEL)
CC	Collect Call [*Telecommunications*] (TEL)
CC	Command Computer
C & C	Command and Control (CGC)
CC	Common Carrier
CC	Common Control [*Telecommunications*] (TEL)
CC	Communications Control (MCD)
CC	Computer Calculator
CC	Computer Center [*Telecommunications*] (TEL)
CC	Computer Community (IEEE)
CC	Computer Complex (VIT)
C-to-C	Computer-to-Computer (NASA)
CC	Computer Conferencing
C & C	Computers and Communications
CC	Concurrent Concession (MDG)
CC	Condition Code
CC	Control Computer (KSC)
CC	Coordinates Computed (MUGU)
CC	Corporate Conversions [*Dobbs Ferry, NY*] [*Information service*] (EISS)
CC	Coupled Channel [*Electronics*]
CC	Cursor Control [*Data processing*] (BUR)
CC	Custom Chip [*Personal computers*]
CC	Cyclic Code (BUR)
CCA	Canadian Communication Association
CCA	Central Computer Accounting
CCA	Channel-to-Channel Adapter (CAA)
CCA	Common Communication Adapter [*Data processing*]
CCA	Computer and Control Abstracts [*IEE*] [*A publication*]
CCA	Computer Corporation of America [*Cambridge, MA*]
CCA	Cooperative Communicators Association (EANO)
CCAB	Communications and Cable [*NASDAQ symbol*] (NQ)
CCAC	Central Computer Accounting Corporation
CCAD	Center for Computer Aided Design [*University of Iowa*] [*Research center*] (RCD)
CCAI	Creative Computer Applications [*NASDAQ symbol*] (NQ)
CCALI	Center for Computer-Assisted Legal Instruction [*Minneapolis, MN*] (EANO)
CCAM	Conversational Communication Access Method (CAA)
CCAP	Communications Control Applications Program (CGC)
CCB	Character Control Block [*Data processing*] (IBMDP)
CCB	Circuit Concentration Bay
CCB	Command Control Block [*Data processing*] (BUR)
CCB	Common Carrier Bureau [*of FCC*]
CCB	Communications Control Block [*Data processing*] (CAA)
CCB	Console to Computer Buffer (MUGU)
CCBMM	Comac Condition Base Monitor Module [*Comac Systems PLC.*] [*Software package*] [*British*] (NCC)

Computer & Telecommunications Acronyms

CCBS	Center for Computer-Based Behavioral Studies [*University of California, Los Angeles*] [*Research center*]	(RCD)
CCC	Canadian Criminal Cases [*Database*]	
CCC	Carriage Control Character [*Data processing*]	(TUT)
CCC	Central Communications Controller	(CAA)
CCC	Central Computational Computer	(OA)
CCC	Central Computer Complex	
CCC	Communication Center Console	(CIT)
CCC	Communications Center of Clarksburg [*Clarksburg, MD*] [*Telecommunications*]	(TSSD)
CCC	Communications Control Center	(FAAC)
CCC	Compucats' Computer Club [*Aberdeen, MD*]	(EANO)
CCC	Computer Command Control [*General Motors Corp.*]	
CCC	Computer Communications Console	(AFM)
CCC	Computer Communications Converter	(MCD)
CCC	Computer Composition Corporation [*Madison Heights, MI*]	
CCC	Computer Control Communication	(BUR)
CCC	Computer Control Complex	(OA)
CCC	Computer Control Corporation	(CIT)
CCC	Console Control Circuit	
CCC	Controller Checkout Console	(NASA)
CCC	Coordinate Conversion Computer	(MCD)
CCC	Cyclic Check Character [*Data processing*]	(TUT)
CCCC	Computerized Conferencing and Communications Center [*New Jersey Institute of Technology*] [*Research center*]	(RCD)
CCCC	Consolidated Computer and Control Center	
CCCC	Coordinating Council for Computers in Construction [*New York, NY*]	(EANO)
CCCI	Capital Cities Communications, Incorporated	
CCCI	Command, Control, Communications, and Intelligence [*Telecommunications*]	(TEL)
CCCL	Complementary Constant Current Logic [*Data processing*]	(BUR)
CCCS	Central Control Computer System	
CCD	Center for Curriculum Design [*Information service*] [*Defunct*]	(EISS)
CCD	Charge-Coupled Device [*Data storage device*]	
CCD	Computer-Controlled Display	(CGC)
CCD	Contract Completion Date [*Telecommunications*]	(TEL)
CCDB	Carbon-Carbon Data Base [*Battelle Columbus Laboratories*] [*Database*]	(FDB)
CCDC	Central Control and Display Console	
CCDF	Cambridge Crystallographic Data File [*Database*]	(ODIN)
CCDN	Centre de Compilation de Donnees Neutroniques [*Neutron Data Compilation Center*] [*France*] [*Information service*]	(EISS)
CCDN	Corporate Consolidated Data Network [*IBM Corp.*] [*Telecommunications*]	
CCE	Centro de Calculo Electronico Universidad Nacional Autonoma de Mexico [*National Autonomous University of Mexico, Data Processing Center*] [*Villa Obregon, Mexico*]	
CCE	Communications Control Equipment	(MCD)
CCE	Computer Command Engineer	(MCD)
CCEA	Center for Climatic and Environmental Assessment [*National Oceanic and Atmospheric Administration*]	(EISS)
CCES	Common Command Echo Suppressor [*Telecommunications*]	(TEL)
CCETT	Centre Commun d'Etudes de Television et de Telecommunications [*Videotex research center*] [*French*]	(DEEC)
CCF	Communications Control Field	
CCF	Configuration Control Function [*Telecommunications*]	(TEL)
CCFM	Cryogenic Continuous Film Memory [*Data processing*]	(DIT)
CCFX	ContiCurrency Foreign Exchange and Money Market Database [*No longer available online*]	(CUAD)
CCG	Computer Communications Group [*Canada*]	
CCH	Channel-Check Handler [*Japanese*]	(MCD)
CCH	Computerized Criminal History [*FBI*]	
CCH	Connections per Circuit per Hour [*Telecommunications*]	(TEL)
CCHS	Cylinder-Cylinder-Head-Sector [*Data processing*]	(IBMDP)
CCI	Card Computer Interface [*Data processing*]	(EISS)
CCI	CCI Corp. [*NYSE symbol*] [*Delisted*]	
CCI	Communications Carrier, Incorporated [*Austin, TX*] [*Telecommunications*]	(TSSD)
CCI	Communications Concepts, Incorporated [*Newport Beach, CA*] [*Telecommunications*]	(TSSD)
CCI	Communications Consultants, Incorporated [*Asbury, NJ*] [*Telecommunications*]	(TSSD)
CCI	Computer Communications, Incorporated	(CAA)
CCI	Computer Control Indicator	(CAAL)
CCI	Consortium Communications International, Inc. [*New York, NY*] [*Telecommunications*]	(TSSD)
CCIA	Cellular Communications Industry Association [*Washington, DC*] [*Telecommunications*]	(EANO)
CCIA	Computer and Communications Industry Association [*Arlington, VA*]	(EANO)
CCIA	Console Computer Interface Adapter	
CCIF	Comite Consultatif International Telephonique des Frequences [*International Telephone Consultative Committee*]	(NATG)
CCIM	Command Computer Input Multiplexer	(MCD)
CCIR	Comite Consultatif International des Radiocommunications [*International Radio Consultative Committee*] [*Switzerland*]	
CCIRD	Computers and Computing Information Resources Directory [*In preparation*] [*A publication*]	
CCIS	Common Channel Interoffice Signaling [*System*] [*Bell System*]	
CCIS	Computer-Controlled Interconnect System	(MCD)
CCIS	Computerized Clinical Information System [*Micromedex, Inc.*] [*Database*]	
CCIT	Consultative Committee on International Telephony [*Later, CCITT*] [*ITU*]	
CCITT	Comite Consultatif International Telegraphique et Telephonique [*Consultative Committee on International Telegraphy and Telephony*] [*Geneva, Switzerland*]	
CCITT	Consultative Committee on International Telegraphy and Telephony [*ITU*]	
CCL	Center for Computer/Law [*Manhattan Beach, CA*]	(EANO)
CCL	Communications Control Language	
CCL	Computer Control Loading	
CCL	Consultec Canada Limited [*Vancouver, BC*] [*Telecommunications*]	(TSSD)
CCL	Control Card Listing [*Data processing*]	
CCLN	Council for Computerized Library Networks	(EISS)
CCLR	Commerce Clearing House [*NASDAQ symbol*]	(NQ)
CCM	Center for Composite Materials [*University of Delaware*] [*Research center*]	(RCD)
CCM	Communications Control Module [*Telecommunications*]	(TEL)
CCM	Communications Controller Multichannel [*Data processing*]	
CCMPTC	Central Computer Center	
CCMS	Central Control and Monitoring System [*for managing buildings' heating, ventilation, and security needs*]	
CCMSS	Computer-Controlled Microfilm Search System	(MCD)
CCMU	Computer Controller Multiplexer Unit	(SKY)
CCN	Campus Conference Network [*Services by Satellite, Inc.*] [*Washington, DC*] [*Telecommunications*]	(TSSD)
CC-NDT	Can't Call - No Dial Tone [*Telecommunications*]	(TEL)
CCNG	Computer Communications Networks Group [*University of Waterloo*] [*Canada*] [*Information service*] [*Research center*]	(EISS)
CCO	Circuit Control Office [*Automatic Digital Information Network*]	(CET)
CCO	Current-Controlled Oscillator	(IEEE)
CCP	Call Control Processing [*Telecommunications*]	(TEL)
CCP	Certificate in Computer Programing [*Designation awarded by Institute for the Certification of Computer Professionals*]	
CCP	Communication Control Program	(BUR)
CCP	Communications Control Processor	(CAA)
CCP	Computer Central Processing [*Telecommunications*]	(TEL)
CCP	Computer Control Panel	(SKY)
CCP	Console Command Processor [*Digital Research*]	(DEEC)
CCP	Console Control Package	(OA)
CCP	Continuous Correlation Processing	
CCP	Contract Configuration Process [*Telecommunications*]	(TEL)
CCP	Coordinated Commentary Programing [*Data processing*]	
CCP	Cross Connection Point [*Telecommunications*]	(TEL)
CCPA	Court of Customs and Patent Appeals	
CCPC	Communication Computer Programing Center	(AFM)
CCR	Closed-Circuit Radio	(DDI)
CCR	Computer Character Recognition	
CCR	Condition Code Register	(CAA)
CCR	Control Contactor	
CCRESPAC	Current Cancer Research Project Analysis Center [*Database producer*]	
CCRIS	Chemical Carcinogenous Research Information System [*SRI International*] [*Database*]	(FDB)
CCRMA	Center for Computer Research in Music and Acoustics [*Pronounced "karma"*] [*Stanford University*]	
CCROS	Card Capacitor Read-Only Storage [*Data processing*]	(IEEE)
CCS	Call Control Systems [*San Clemente, CA*] [*Telecommunications*]	(TSSD)
CCS	Calling Card Service [*Bell System*]	
CCS	Canadian Computer Show	(CAA)
CCS	Center for Cybernetic Studies [*University of Texas at Austin*] [*Research center*]	(RCD)
CCS	Central Computer Station	(OA)
CCS	Chanin Consulting Services, Inc. [*New York, NY*] [*Software manufacturer*]	(DASOS)
CCS	Collective Call Sign [*Radio*]	
CCS	Commercial Communications Satellite [*Japan*]	(CBSS)
CCS	Common Channel Signaling [*Telecommunications*]	(TEL)
CCS	Communication Control System	
CCS	Computer Campaign Services [*Data processing firm in field of politics*]	
CCS	Computer Consoles, Inc. [*American Stock Exchange symbol*]	
CCS	Computer Consulting Service	(BUR)
CCS	Computer Core Segment	(NASA)
CCS	Continuous Color Sequence [*Telecommunications*]	
CCS	Controlled Communications Systems [*Chicago, IL*] [*Telecommunications*]	(TSSD)
CCS	Conversational Compiling System [*Xerox Corp.*]	(IEEE)
CCS	Cooperative Computing System [*Echo detection*]	
CCS	Custom Computer System	(IEEE)
CCS	One Hundred Call-Seconds [*Also, UC*] [*Bell System*]	(TSSD)
CCS^2	Command, Control, and Subordinate Systems [*Telecommunications*]	(TEL)
CCSA	Common Carrier Special Application	(CAH)
CCSA	Common Control Switching Arrangement [*AT & T*] [*Telecommunications*]	

Computer & Telecommunications Acronyms

CCSD.......... Center for Computer Systems Design [*Washington University*] [*Research center*]   (RCD)
CCSD.......... Command Communications Service Designator   (CET)
CCSG .... Computer Components and System Group
CCSL .... Communications and Control Systems Laboratory
CCSP .... Communications Concentrator Software Package [*Data processing*]
CCSP .... University/Industry Cooperative Research Center for Communications and Signal Processing [*North Carolina State University*] [*Research center*]   (RCD)
CCSR .... Canadian Consortium for Social Research   (EISS)
CCSS .... Cali Computer Systems [*NASDAQ symbol*]   (NQ)
CCST .... Center for Computer Sciences and Technology [*Later, ICST*] [*National Bureau of Standards*]
CCSU .... Computer Cross Select Unit
CCT .... C-Band Communications Transponder
CCT .... Comite de Coordination des Telecommunications [*Coordinating Committee for Communications*] [*NATO*]   (NATG)
CCT .... Commodore Corporation [*American Stock Exchange symbol*]
CCT .... Complete Calls To [*Telecommunications*]   (TEL)
CCT .... Computer-Compatible Tape
CCT .... Coupler Cut-Through
CCTA .... Central Computer and Telecommunications Agency [*British*]
CCTC .... Computer & Commercial Technology [*NASDAQ symbol*]   (NQ)
CCTU .... Corporate Committee of Telecommunications Users   (EANO)
CCTV .... Closed-Circuit Television
CCU .... Central Computer Unit
CCU .... Central Control Unit
CCU .... Channel Control Unit   (CMD)
CCU .... Christian Computer Users [*Christian Ministries Management Association*] [*Diamond Bur, CA*]   (EANO)
CCU .... Communication Control Unit
CCU .... Communications Coupling Unit   (CET)
CCU .... Computer Control Unit
CCU .... Conversion Computer Unit   (VIT)
CCU .... Coronary Care Unit [*University of Southern California*] [*Research center*]   (RCD)
CCUAP .... Computerized Cable Upkeep Administrative Program [*Bell System*]
CCUP .... Compucorp [*NASDAQ symbol*]   (NQ)
CCVS .... COBOL [*Common Business-Oriented Language*] Compiler Validation System [*Data processing*]
CCW .... Channel Command [*or Control*] Word [*Data processing*]   (CGC)
CCX .... Customer Communications Exchange [*Bell System*]
CD .... Calling Device [*Telecommunications*]
CD .... Card   (MSA)
CD .... Carrier Detector   (BUR)
CD .... Cash Dispenser   (BUR)
CD .... Circuit Description   (MSA)
CD .... Coden [*Online database field identifier*]   (OBD)
C & D .... Communications and Data
CD .... Compact Disk [*Audio/video technology*] [*Philips*]
CD .... Computer Design [*A publication*]
C3D .... Cascade Charge Coupled Device [*Electronics*]
CDA .... Command Data Acquisition   (MSA)
CDA .... Computer Dealers Association   (CAA)
CDA .... Computer Directions Advisors, Inc. [*Information service*]   (EISS)
CDA .... Control Data Corp. [*NYSE symbol*]
CDAS .... Computer Design and Architecture Series [*Elsevier Book Series*] [*A publication*]
CDAT .... Cordatum, Inc. [*NASDAQ symbol*]   (NQ)
CDB .... Central Data Bank
CDB .... Central Data Buffer [*Data processing*]   (MCD)
CDB .... Common Data Bus [*Data processing*]
CDB .... Common Database [*Data processing*]   (CAAL)
CDB .... Corporate Database [*Data processing*]   (TUT)
CDB .... Current Data BIT [*Binary Digit*] [*Data processing*]
CDBN .... Column-Digit Binary Network
CDC .... Call Directing Code
CDC .... Central Digital Computer
CDC .... Characteristic Distortion Compensation [*Telecommunications*]   (TEL)
CDC .... Chemical Data Center, Inc. [*Columbus, OH*] [*Information service*]   (EISS)
CDC .... Code Directing Character [*Data processing*]
CDC .... Command and Data-Handling Console   (CIT)
CDC .... Command Decoder Coaxial   (MCD)
CDC .... Computer Development Center   (KSC)
CDC .... Computer Directions Corporation
CDC .... Computer Display Channel
CDC .... Configuration Data Control
CDC .... Construction Design Criteria [*Telecommunications*]   (TEL)
CDC .... Control Data Corporation
CDCCP .... Control Data Communications Control Procedure [*Telecommunications*]   (TEL)
CDCE .... Central Data-Conversion Equipment
CDCP .... Command Display and Control Processor
CDCS .... Central Data Collection System   (AFM)
CDCS .... Construction Dollar Control System [*AT & T*]
CDCT .... Centro de Documentacao Cientifica e Tecnica [*Scientific and Technical Documentation Center*] [*Portugal*] [*Information service*]   (EISS)
CDD .... Central Data Display
CDD .... Color Data Display
CDD .... Computer-Directed Drawing
CDDA .... Compact Data Disk Association [*Philadelphia, PA*]   (EANO)
CDDI .... Computer-Directed Drawing Instrument
CDDP .... Console Digital Display Programer   (MUGU)
CDDR .... CD [*Compact Disc*] Data Report [*McClean, VA*] [*A publication*]   (EISS)
CDE .... Certificate in Data Education   (BUR)
CDEI .... Control Data Education Institutes
CDEK .... Computer Data Entry Keyboard
CDEVC .... Computer Development Center   (KSC)
CDF .... Communications-Data Field
CDF & TDS ... Circuit Design, Fabrication, and Test Data Systems   (NASA)
CDG .... Compact Disc Group [*New York, NY*]   (EANO)
CDH .... Command and Data Handling   (DEN)
CDHC .... Command and Data-Handling Console   (KSC)
CDI .... Command Display Indicator   (MCD)
CD-I .... Compact Disc - Interactive
CDI .... Comprehensive Dissertation Index [*University Microfilms International*] [*Ann Arbor, MI*] [*Bibliographic database*] [*A publication*]
CDI .... Computer-Developed Instruction
CDI .... Computer Devices, Incorporated   (CAA)
CDI .... Computer-Directed Instrument
CDI .... Consumer Demographics, Incorporated [*Information service*]   (EISS)
CDI .... Control Data Institute   (DDI)
CDIC .... Carbon Dioxide Information Center [*Oak Ridge National Laboratory*] [*Database*]   (FDB)
CDID .... Consumer Drug Information on Disk [*American Society of Hospital Pharmacists*] [*Database*]
CDIDC .... Committee on Data Interchange and Data Centers
CDIF .... Consumer Drug Information [*American Society of Hospital Pharmacists*] [*Database*] [*Information service*]   (EISS)
CDIF .... Controller/Director Information File
CDIS .... Commodities Data Information Service [*MJK Associates*] [*Information service*]   (EISS)
CDIS .... Commodity Data Information System [*MJK Associates*] [*Database*]   (CUAD)
CDIUPA ...... Centre de Documentation Internationale des Industries Utilisatrices de Produits Agricoles [*International Documentation Center for Industries Using Agricultural Products*] [*France*] [*Database producer*] [*Information service*]   (EISS)
CDK .... Channel Data Check   (OA)
CDK .... Communication Desk   (BUR)
CDL .... Capacitor-Diode Logic   (MSA)
CDL .... Common Display Logic [*Data processing*]   (CGC)
CDL .... Computer Description Language   (BUR)
CDL .... Computer Design Language   (CSR)
CDL .... Computer Development Laboratory [*Fujitsu Ltd., Hitachi Ltd., and Mitsubishi Corp.*] [*Japan*]   (CAA)
CDL .... Core Diode Logic
CDLA .... Computer Dealers and Lessors Association [*Washington, DC*]   (EANO)
CDLRD .... Confirming Design Layout Report Date [*Bell System*]   (TEL)
CDM .... Central Data Management
CDM .... Centre de Documentation de la Mecanique [*Documentation Center for Mechanics*] [*France*] [*Information service*]   (EISS)
CDM .... Coded Division Multiplex
CDM .... Companded Delta Modulation [*Telecommunications*]   (TEL)
CDMA .... Cartridge Direct Memory Access   (CAA)
CDMA .... Code Division Multiple Access
CDMR .... Command Data Management Routine [*Data processing*]
CDMR .... Cyclic Data Management Routine [*Data processing*]
CDMS .... Command Data Management System   (NASA)
CDMS .... COMRADE [*Computer-Aided Design Environment*] Data Management System   (OA)
CD/NC .... Computer-Aided Design/Numerical Control
Cdn Data .... Canadian Datasystems [*A publication*]
Cdn Elec E ... Canadian Electronics Engineering [*A publication*]
CDO .... Community Dial Office [*Small switching system*] [*Telecommunications*]
CDP .... Centralized Data Processing   (IEEE)
CDP .... Certificate in Data Processing [*Designation awarded by Institute for Certification of Computer Professionals*]
CDP .... Command Data Processor   (CIT)
CDP .... Communications Data Processor [*Electronics*]
CDP .... Control Data Panel   (VIT)
CDP .... Control and Display Panel   (MCD)
CDP .... Correlated Data Processor
CDPC .... Central Data Processing Computer
CDPC .... Commercial Data Processing Center   (IEEE)
CDPC .... Computation and Data Processing Center   (DIT)
CDPIE .... Command Data Processing Interface Equipment
CDPR .... Customer Dial Pulse Receiver [*Telecommunications*]   (TEL)
CDPS .... Communications Data Processing System   (NVT)
CDR .... Call Detail Recording [*Telecommunications*]   (TEL)
CDR .... Critical Design Review   (AFM)
CD-ROM .... Compact Disk Read-Only Memory [*Data processing*]
CDRS .... Computer Data Recording System   (KSC)
CDS .... Central Data Station
CDS .... Central Data Subsystem   (NASA)

Computer & Telecommunications Acronyms

CDS	Centre de Donnees Stellaires [*Stellar Data Center*] [*France*] [*Information service*] (EISS)
CDS	Comprehensive Display System
CDS	Compressed Data Storage
CDS	Computer Data Switchboard
CDS	Computer Data System (CIT)
CDS	Computer Duplex System (BUR)
CDS	Computerized Dispersive Spectroscopy
CDS	Computerized Documentation System [*UNESCO*] (EISS)
CDS	Construction Dollar Spreading [*System*] [*AT & T*]
CDS	Control Data System (NASA)
CDS	CUNY [*City University of New York*] Data Service [*Information service*] (EISS)
CDSA	Center for Data Systems and Analysis [*Montana State University*] [*Research center*] (RCD)
CDSE	Computer-Driven Simulation Environment [*FAA*]
CDSF	COMRADE [*Computer-Aided Design Environment*] Data Storage Facility (OA)
CDSH	Centre de Documentation Sciences Humaines [*Documentation Center for Human Sciences*] [*France*] [*Information service*] (EISS)
CDSI	Computer Data Systems, Incorporated [*Information service*] (EISS)
CDSI	Computer Designed Systems [*NASDAQ symbol*] (NQ)
CDSI	Contemporary Digital Services, Incorporated [*New Rochelle, NY*] [*Telecommunications*] (TSSD)
CDSIDS	Command and Decision Sensor Interface Data System (MCD)
CDS/ISIS	Computerized Documentation System/Integrated Set of Information Systems [*UNESCO*] (EISS)
CDSS	Compressed Data Storage System
CDT	Compressed Data Tape
CDT	Control Data Terminal
CDTL	Common Data Translation Language (CAA)
CDTLBS	Computer-Directed Training Lesson Building System
CDTS	Computer-Directed Training System
CDU	Central Display Unit
CDU	Computer Display Unit (MCD)
CDU	Control Data Unit
CDU	Control and Diagnostic Unit [*Data processing*]
CDU	Control Display Unit
CDU	Coupling Data Unit
CDU	CRT [*Cathode-Ray Tube*] Display Unit (MCD)
CDV	Check Digit Verification (CMD)
CDW	Computer Data Word (CET)
CDX	Control Differential Transmitter
CE	Chip Enable [*Input*] [*Data processing*]
C & E	Communications and Electronics
C-E	Communications-Electronics
CE	Communications Equipment
CE	Computer Engineer (CGC)
CE	Conducted Emission (IEEE)
CE	Custom Electronics, Inc. [*Chicopee, MA*] [*Software manufacturer*] (DASOS)
CE	Customer Engineer [*Data processing*]
CEA	Chemical Engineering Abstracts [*Royal Society of Chemistry*] [*Bibliographic database*] [*British*] (OBD)
CEAI	Chase Econometrics Associates, Incorporated [*Cynwyd, PA*] [*Information service*] (EISS)
CEAS	Center for Environmental Assessment Services [*National Oceanic and Atmospheric Administration*] [*Rochester, NY*] [*Information service*] (EISS)
CEC	Capital Equipment Corporation [*Burlington, MA*]
CEC	Controlled Element Computer
CECMRL	Communications-Electronics Consolidated Mobilization Reserve List
CECS	Communications-Electronics Coordinating Section [*NATO*]
CED	Capacitance Electronic Disk
CEDAR	Center for Engineering Development and Research [*University of South Florida*] [*Research center*] (RCD)
CEDPA	California Educational Data Processing Association (CAH)
CEDS	Center for Econometrics and Decision Sciences [*University of Florida*] [*Research center*] (RCD)
CEDS	Comptamation Electronics Designer System [*COMPUTAMION*] [*Software package*] [*British*] (NCC)
CEE	International Commission for Conformity of Certification of Electrical Equipment
CEEDE	Center for Educational Experimentation, Development, and Evaluation [*University of Iowa*] [*Research center*] (RCD)
CEF	Computer Execute Function (KSC)
CEFIP	Communications-Electronics Facility Inoperative for Parts (MCD)
CEGL	Cause-Effect Graph Language [*Data processing*] (IBMDP)
CEH	Chemical Economics Handbook [*SRI International*] [*Database*]
CEI	Commission Electrotechnique Internationale [*International Electrotechnical Commission*] [*See also IEC*]
CEI	Communication Electronic Instructions
CEI	Comparably Efficient Interconnection [*Telecommunications*]
CEI	Computer-Extended Instruction (IEEE)
CEIC	Chemical Effects Information Center [*Oak Ridge, TN*] [*Department of Energy*] (EISS)
CE/IDC	Chase Econometrics/Interactive Data Corporation
CEIRD	Confirming Engineering Information Report Date [*Bell System*] (TEL)
CEIRS	Conservation and Renewable Energy Inquiry and Referral Service [*Database*] (FDB)
CEK	Computer Entry Keyboard (SKY)
CEL	Conversational Extensible Language [*Data processing*] (CSR)
CEL	Cooley Electronics Laboratory [*University of Michigan*] [*Research center*] (RCD)
CELCA	Commutation et Electronique [*A publication*]
CELEX	Communitatis Europeae Lex [*European Community Law*] [*Information service*] (EISS)
CELLSIM	Cell Simulation [*Programing language*] [1973] (CSR)
CELTIC	Concentrateur Exploitant les Temps d'Inactivite des Circuits [*French*] [*Telecommunications*] (TEL)
CEM	Cement Conduit [*Telecommunications*] (TEL)
CEM	Communications-Electronics-Meteorological [*Equipment*]
CEM	Computer Education for Management (OA)
CEMA	Canadian Electrical Manufacturers' Association
CEMF	Counter Electromotive Force (MCD)
CEMTEX	Central Magnetic Tape Exchange [*Data processing*]
CEN	Centronics Data Computer Corp. [*NYSE symbol*]
CEN	Comite Europeen de Coordination des Normes [*European Committee for Coordination of Standards*]
CENADEM	Centro Nacional de Desenvolvimento Micrografico [*National Center for Micrographic Development*] [*Brazil*] [*Information service*] (EISS)
CENEL	Comite Europeen de Coordination des Normes Electriques [*European Electrical Standards Coordinating Committee*]
CENIDS	Centro Nacional de Informacion y Documentacion en Salud [*National Center for Health Information and Documentation*] [*Mexico*] [*Information service*] (EISS)
CENTREX	Central Exchange
CEO	Chip Enable Output [*Data processing*]
CEOI	Communications-Electronics Operating Instruction
CEP	Computer Entry Punch
CEP	Continuous Expression Processor, Inc. [*Medfield, MA*] [*Hardware manufacturer*] (DASO)
CEPA	Society for Computer Applications in Engineering, Planning, and Architecture [*Rockville, MD*] [*Formerly, Civil Engineering Program Applications*] [*Later, SCAEPA*]
CEPER	Combined Engineering Plant Exchange Record [*Telecommunications*] (TEL)
CEPII	Centre d'Etudes Prospectives et d'Informations Internationales [*Database producer*] (CUAD)
CEPO	Central Eastern Personnel Organization [*Computerized scouting combine for professional football teams*]
CEPS	Color Electronic Prepress Systems [*Printing technology*]
CEPT	Conference Europeenne des Administrations des Postes et des Telecommunications [*Conference of European Postal and Telecommunications Administrations*] [*Berne, Switzerland*] [*Telecommunications*] (EANO)
CERDIC	Centre de Recherches et de Documentation des Institutions Chretiennes [*Christian Institutions Research and Documentation Center*] [*France*] [*Information service*] (EISS)
CER-DIP	Ceramic Dual In-Line Package (DEEC)
CERE	Computer Entry and Readout Equipment (KSC)
CERL	Computer-Based Education Research Laboratory [*University of Illinois*] [*Research center*]
CERT	Character Error Rate Test (CAA)
CES	Communications Errors Statistics (CMD)
CES	Computer Election Systems, Inc.
CES	Computer Engineering Service
CES	Computer Enhanced Spectroscopy [*A publication*]
CES	Consumer Electronics Show [*Computer industry*]
CESA	Canadian Engineering Standards Association [*Later, Canadian Standards Association*]
CESAR	Center for Engineering Systems Advanced Research [*Oak Ridge National Laboratory*]
CESARS	Chemical Evaluation Search and Retrieval System [*Database*] [*Michigan Department of Natural Resources*] (FDB)
CESC	Computer Entry Systems [*NASDAQ symbol*] (NQ)
CESD	Composite External Symbol Dictionary (BUR)
CESEMI	Computer Evaluation of Scanning Electron Microscope Image
CESI	Communications-Electronics Standing Instruction
CESP	Centre d'Etude des Supports Publicitaires [*Database producer*] (CUAD)
CET	Council for Educational Technology [*London, England*] [*Telecommunications*] (TSSD)
CETIA	Computer Electronics Telecommunications Instruments Automation
CETIM	Centre Technique des Industries Mecaniques [*Database producer*] (CUAD)
CEU	Channel Extension Unit (CAA)
CEU	Communications Expansion Unit (OA)
CF	Call Finder [*Telecommunications*]
CF	Central Files
CF	Change [*or Changing*] to Frequency [*Followed by number*] [*Communications*] (FAAC)
CF	Context Free (BUR)
CF	Control Footing (CAH)
CF	Conversation Factor [*Data processing*] (CDH)
CF	Count Forward [*Data processing*] (CGC)
CFA	Carrier Frequency Alarm [*Telecommunications*] (TEL)
CFA	Cascade-Failure Analysis (IEEE)

Computer & Telecommunications Acronyms

CFA	Computer Factory, Inc. [*American Stock Exchange symbol*]
CFA	Computer Family Architecture (CAA)
CfAR	Center for Automation Research [*University of Maryland*] [*Research center*] (RCD)
CFB	Cipher Feedback (CAA)
CFC	C-Band Frequency Converter
CFC	Centre Francais de la Couleur [*Online service*] (CUAD)
CFC	Channel Flow Control (CAA)
CFC	Coin and Fee Checking [*Telecommunications*] (TEL)
CFCA	Communications Fraud Control Association (EANO)
CFCB	Computer Format Control Buffer
CFD	Canadian Financial Database [*Toronto, ON*] [*Information service*] (EISS)
CFET	Common Field Effect Transistor [*Data processing*]
CFF	Counter Flip-Flop [*Data processing*] (VIT)
CFF	Current Fault File [*Telecommunications*] (TEL)
CFH	Cubic Feet per Hour
CFIA	Component Failure Impact Analysis [*IBM Corp.*]
CFL	Call Failed [*or Failure*] [*Telecommunications*] (TEL)
CFL	Context Free Language
CFM	Christiane Fabre de Morlhon [*In information service name CFM Documentazione*] [*Information service*] (EISS)
CFM	Closed Flux Memory [*Data processing*]
CFM	Companding and Frequency Modulation [*Telecommunications*] (TEL)
CFM	Computer Facilities Management (MCD)
CFM	Cubic Feet per Minute
CFMS	Chained File Management System [*IBM Corp.*]
CFMS	Computer-Based Financial Management System [*Harper & Shuman, Inc.*] [*Information service*] (EISS)
CFO	Consolidated Function Ordinary [*IBM Corp.*]
CFO	Critical Flashover [*Voltage*] (IEEE)
CFP	Creation Facilities Program [*Data processing*] (IBMDP)
C-F/PCM	Coarse-Fine/Pulse Code Modulator (DDI)
CFS	Calls for Service Signal [*Telecommunications*] (TEL)
CFS	Combined File Search [*IBM program*] [*Data processing*]
CFS	Common File System [*Data processing*]
CFSK	Coherent Frequency Shift Keying
CFSS	Combined File Search Strategy [*Data processing*]
CFU	Control Functional Unit [*Data link*] (NG)
CG	Character Generator [*Telecommunications*]
CG	Common Ground [*A publication*]
CG	Computer Graphics (MCD)
CG	Course Generator (TUT)
CGA	Carrier Group Alarm [*Telephone communications*]
CGA	Color/Graphics Monitor Adapter [*Computer technology*]
CGAC	CGA Computer Association [*NASDAQ symbol*] (NQ)
CGB	Convert Gray to Binary
CGC	Circuit Group Congestion [*Telecommunications*] (TEL)
CGC	Command Guidance Computer (NASA)
CGC	Computer Guidance Corporation (CGC)
CGE	Compagnie Generale d'Electricite [*General Electric Company*] [*French*]
CGF	Computer Graphics Forum [*A publication*]
CGH	Computer-Generated Hologram
CGI	Communications Group, Incorporated [*Concord, MA*] [*Telecommunications*] (TSSD)
CGI	Computer-Generated Imagery
CGIS	Canada Geographic Information System [*Ottawa, ON*] (EISS)
CGL	Computer Generated Letter (CAA)
CGP	Color Graphics Printer (CAA)
CGPC	Cellular General Purpose Computer (CAA)
CGPR	Computer-Generated Purchase Request
CGRG	Computer Graphics Research Group [*Ohio State University*] [*Research center*] (RCD)
CGRP	Circuit Group [*Telecommunications*] (TEL)
CGS	Centimeter-Gram-Second [*System of units*]
CGSA	Computer Graphics Structural Analysis
CH	Can't Hear [*Telecommunications*] (TEL)
CH	Change
CH	Channel
CH	Channel Continuity Check Transmission [*Communications*] (FAAC)
CH	Character [*Data processing*] (BUR)
CH	Coastal Harbor [*Telecommunications*] (TEL)
CH	Control Heading (BUR)
CH	Control Hole (BUR)
CH	Critical Hours [*Broadcasting term*]
CHAD	Code to Handle Angular Data (IEEE)
CHAMIL	Chameleon Micro Implementation Language [*1978*] [*Data processing*] (CSR)
CHAMP	Character Manipulation Procedures (CAH)
CHAMP	Communications Handler for Automatic Multiple Programs (CAA)
CHAN	Channel [*Data processing*]
CHAN	Clearing House Accession Number [*Online database field identifier*] (OBD)
CHAOTIC	Computer and Human-Assisted Organization of a Technical Information Center [*National Bureau of Standards*]
CHAR	Character (KSC)
CHART	Computerized Hierarchy and Relationship Table
CHASE	Cornell Hotel Administration Simulation Exercise [*Computer-programed management game*]
CHC	Channel Control (BUR)
CHC	Community Health Computing
CHCC	Chancellor Computer [*NASDAQ symbol*] (NQ)
CHCU	Channel Control Unit (CAA)
CHDB	Compatible High-Density Bipolar Code [*Telecommunications*] (TEL)
CHDL	Computer Hardware Description Language
CHE	Channel End (BUR)
CHEC	Channel Evaluation and Call (IEEE)
CHEMDEX	Chemical Index [*Database*] (CAA)
CHEMLAB	Chemical Modeling Laboratory
CHEMLINE	Chemical Dictionary On-Line [*National Library of Medicine*] [*Bethesda, MD*] [*Database*]
CHEMNAME	Chemical Name Dictionary [*Dialog Information Services, Inc.*] [*Database*]
CHEMRiC	Chemical Monograph Referral Center [*Consumer Product Safety Commission*] [*Information service*] (EISS)
CHEMSAFE	Safe Computing Chemical Factory System [*Safe Computing Ltd.*] [*Software package*] [*British*] (NCC)
CHEMSIS	CHEM Singly Indexed Substances [*DIALOG Information Services, Inc.*] [*Database*] (CUAD)
CHEOPS	Chemical Information Systems Operators [*Later, EUSIDIC*] (IDA)
CHER	Cherry Electronic Products Corp. [*NASDAQ symbol*] (NQ)
CHI	Computer-Human Interaction (BUR)
CHICS	Computerized Hospital Information System (MCD)
CHIF	Channel Interface (CAA)
CHIL	Current Hogging Injection Logic [*Electronics*] (IEEE)
CHILI	[*A*] programing language [*1970*] (CSR)
CHILL	CCITT [*Consultative Committee on International Telegraphy and Telephony*] High-Level Language [*Telecommunications*] (TEL)
CHIP	Chip Hermeticity in Plastic [*Electronics*] (MDG)
CHIPS	Clearing House Interbank Payment System (BUR)
CHIRP	Chemical Engineering Investigation of Reaction Paths [*Data processing*]
CHK	Check (KSC)
CHK	Check Register Against Bounds [*Data processing*]
CHKPT	Checkpoint [*Data processing*] (BUR)
CHL	Current-Hogging Logic [*Electronics*]
CHMOS	Complementary High-Performance Metal-Oxide Semiconductor
CHN	Change [*Telecommunications*] (TEL)
CHNL	Channel [*Electrical transmission*] (AFM)
CHOL	Common High-Order Language (DEEC)
CHP	Channel Processor (CAA)
CHPI	Characters per Inch [*Data processing*] (CMD)
CHPS	Characters per Second [*Data processing*] (CMD)
CHR	Character (BUR)
CHSI	Continental Health Care [*NASDAQ symbol*] (NQ)
CHT	Call Hold and Trace [*Telecommunications*] (TEL)
CHT	Call Holding Time [*Telecommunications*] (TEL)
CHum	Computers and the Humanities [*Database*] [*A publication*]
CI	Call Indicator [*Data processing*] (CGC)
CI	Card Input [*Data processing*] (BUR)
C/I	Carrier-to-Interference Ratio [*Data processing*] (CGC)
CI	Cast Iron [*Telecommunications*] (TEL)
CI	Characteristic Independence (CGC)
CI	Communications Interface (CAA)
CI	Community of Interest [*Telecommunications*] (TEL)
CI	Computer Indicator (AFM)
CI	Computer Inquiries
CI	Configuration Item
CI2	Second Computer Inquiry (TSSD)
C³I	Computer-Controlled Coil Ignition
C⁴I²	Command, Control, Communications, Computing/Information and Intelligence
CIA	Communications Interface Assembly [*Data processing*] (CIT)
CIA	Communications Interrupt Analysis [*Sperry UNIVAC*] (IEEE)
CIA	Computer Industry Association (CAH)
CIA	Computer Interface Adapter (CGC)
CIAJ	Communications Industries Association of Japan [*Tokyo*] [*Telecommunications*] (TSSD)
CIB	Centralized Intercept Bureau [*Bell System*]
CIB	Centrum voor Informatie Beleid [*Netherlands Center for Information Policy*] [*Information service*] (EISS)
CIB	Command Input Block [*Data processing*]
CIB	Command Input Buffer [*Data processing*] (IBMDP)
CIC	Cancer Information Clearinghouse [*National Cancer Institute*] [*Database*] (FDB)
CIC	Centre for Industrial Control [*Concordia University*] [*Canada*] [*Research center*] (RCD)
CIC	Cobalt Information Center [*Battelle Memorial Institute*] [*Information service*] (EISS)
CIC	Communications Intelligence Channel (OA)
CIC	Computer Innovations Distribution, Inc. [*Toronto Stock Exchange symbol*]
CIC	Computer Instruments Corporation
CIC	Computer Interface Control [*Part of digital television computer*] (CIT)
CIC	Core Image Converter [*Data processing*] (TUT)
CIC	Cross Information Company [*Boulder, CO*] [*Telecommunications*] (TSSD)
CICG	Center for Interactive Computer Graphics [*Rensselaer Polytechnic Institute*] [*Research center*] (RCD)

Computer & Telecommunications Acronyms

CICH .... Centro de Informacion Cientifica/Humanistica [*Center for Scientific and Humanistic Information*] [*Mexico*] [*Information service*]   (EISS)
CICI............ Confederation of Information Communication Industries [*British*]
CICIN .... Conference on Interlibrary Communications and Information Networks [*September 28 - October 2, 1970*]
CICP .... Communication Interrupt Control Program [*Data processing*]   (IBMDP)
CICS .... Customer Information Control System [*Pronounced "kicks"*] [*IBM Corp.*]
CICS/VS ..... Customer Information Control System Virtual Storage [*IBM Corp.*] [*Data processing*]
CICU .... Computer Interface Conditioning Unit   (MCD)
CID............. Cable Interconnection Diagram   (KSC)
CID............. Cabling Interface Drawing   (MCD)
CID............. Charge-Injection Device [*Electronics*]
CID............. Communication Identifier [*Data processing*]   (IBMDP)
CID............. Computer Integrated Draughting [*Terminal Display Systems Ltd.*] [*Software package*] [*British*]   (NCC)
CID............. Computer Interface Device   (NASA)
CID............. Creative Industries of Detroit, Inc. [*Warren, MI*] [*Telecommunications*]   (TSSD)
CIDA .... Centre d'Informatique et Documentation Automatique [*Center for Automated Information and Documentation*] [*France*] [*Information service*]   (EISS)
CIDA .... Channel Indirect Data Addressing   (IBMDP)
CIDAS........ Conversational Interactive Digital/Analog Simulator [*IBM Corp.*]   (IEEE)
CIDF........... Control Interval Definition Field [*Data processing*]   (BUR)
CIDN .... Computer Identics Corp. [*NASDAQ symbol*]   (NQ)
CIDP .... Centre International de Documentation Parlementaire [*International Center for Parliamentary Documentation*] [*Switzerland*] [*Information service*]   (EISS)
CIDST .... Advisory Committee on Information Dissemination in Science and Technology
CIE............. C. Itoh Electronics [*In company name, CIE Systems, Inc.*] [*Irvine, CA*] [*Software manufacturer*]   (DASOS)
CIE............. Center for Integrated Electronics [*Rensselaer Polytechnic Institute*] [*Research center*]   (RCD)
CIF .... Captive Installation Function [*Telecommunications*]   (TEL)
CIF .... Carriage, Insurance, and Freight   (CDH)
CIF .... Central Information File
CIF .... Computer-Integrated Factory
CIF .... Customer Information File [*Data processing*]   (BUR)
CIFAR .... Center for International Financial Analysis and Research, Inc. [*Princeton, NJ*] [*Information service*]   (EISS)
CIFR........... Cipher Data Products [*NASDAQ symbol*]   (NQ)
CIG............. Computer Image Generator   (MCD)
CIG............. Computer-Informationsdienst Graz [*Graz Computer-Information Service*] [*Austria*]   (EISS)
CIG............. Computer Investors Group, Inc. [*American Stock Exchange symbol*] [*Delisted*]
CIG............. Computerized Interactive Graphics   (MCD)
CIHB .... Canadian Inventory of Historic Building [*Ottawa, ON*] [*Information service*]   (EISS)
CII.............. Computer-Integrated Instruction   (NVT)
CII.............. George M. Low Center for Industrial Innovation [*Rensselaer Polytechnic Institute*] [*Research center*]   (RCD)
CIIA............ Canadian Information Industry Association [*Ottawa, ON*]   (EISS)
CIIHB .... Compagnie Internationale pour l'Informatique Honeywell-Bull [*Computer manufacturer*] [*French*]   (CAA)
C/I/L........... Computer-Information/Library Sciences [*Abstracts*]
CIL .... Core Image Library   (CMD)
CIL .... Current Injection Logic [*Data processing*]   (CAA)
CILEA .... Consorzio Interuniversitario Lombardo per l'Elaborazione Automatica [*Lombard Interuniversity Consortium for Data Processing*] [*Italy*] [*Information service*]   (EISS)
CILES .... Central Information, Library, and Editorial Section [*CSIRO*] [*Information service*]   (EISS)
CIM .... Canadian Institute of Metalworking [*McMaster University*] [*Research center*]   (RCD)
CIM .... Communication Interface Monitor   (CAA)
CIM .... Communications Interface Modules [*Data processing*]   (CGC)
CIM .... Computer Input Matrix   (KSC)
CIM .... Computer Input Microfilming
CIM .... Computer Input Multiplexer   (KSC)
CIM .... Computer-Integrated Manufacturing
CIMAR .... Center for Intelligent Machines and Robotics [*University of Florida*] [*Research center*]   (RCD)
CIMCO .... Card Image Correction [*Data processing*]
CIMI .... Chemical Information Management, Incorporated [*Information service*]   (EISS)
CIMS.......... Courant Institute of Mathematical Sciences [*New York University*] [*Research center*]   (RCD)
CIMTECH ... National Centre for Information Media and Technology [*British*]
CIN............. Centro de Informacoes Nucleares [*Center for Nuclear Information*] [*Brazil*] [*Information service*]   (EISS)
CIN............. Chemical Industry Notes [*Chemical Abstracts Service*] [*Bibliographic database*] [*A publication*]
CIN............. Commodore Information Network [*Commodore Business Machines*] [*West Chester, PA*] [*Telecommunications*]   (TSSD)
CINCH .... Computerised Information from National Criminological Holdings [*Australian Institute of Criminology Library*] [*Database*] [*Information service*]   (EISS)
CIND .... Computer Index of Neutron Data [*Atomic Energy Authority*] [*Databank*] [*British*]
CINDA........ Chrysler Improved Numerical Differencing Analyzer [*Data processing*]
CINDA........ Computer Index of Neutron Data [*Atomic Energy Authority*] [*Databank*] [*British*]
CINDA-3G ... Chrysler Improved Numerical Differencing Analyzer for Third-Generation Computers [*Data processing*]
CINDAS ...... Center for Information and Numerical Data Analysis and Synthesis [*Purdue*] [*National Bureau of Standards*] [*Research center*]   (MCD)
CINDI .... Central Information Dispatch [*Genesis Electronics Corp.*] [*Folsom, CA*] [*Telecommunications*]   (TSSD)
CINTEL ...... Computer Interface for Television   (MCD)
CINUD........ Computers in Industry [*A publication*]
CIO............. Central Input-Output Multiplexer [*Data processing*]   (CGC)
CIO............. Confirming Informal Order [*Telecommunications*]   (TEL)
CIO............. Corporate Information Officer
CIOCS .... Communications Input and Output Control System   (BUR)
CIOM .... Communications Input/Output Multiplexer
CIOP .... CAMAC [*Computer-Aided Measurement and Control*] Input-Output Processor [*Computer*]
CIOU .... Custom Input/Output Unit [*Data processing*]   (IEEE)
CIP .... Center for Interactive Programs [*University of Wisconsin-Extension*] [*Madison*] [*Information service*] [*Telecommunications*]   (TSSD)
CIP .... Central Information Processor   (MCD)
CIP .... COBOL [*Common Business-Oriented Language*] Instrumentation Package [*Data processing*]
CIP .... Commercial Instruction Processor [*Honeywell, Inc.*]   (CAA)
CIP .... Common Input Processor
CIP .... Communications Interrupt Program   (CAA)
CIP .... Compatible Independent Peripherals   (IEEE)
CIPG .... Communications and Information Processing Group [*Rensselaer Polytechnic Institute*] [*Research center*]   (RCD)
CIPHER...... Calculations of Patient and Hospital Education Resources [*Data processing*]
CIPOM .... Computers, Information Processing, and Office Machines
CIPP........... Context, Input, Process, Product [*Data processing*]
CIPS........... Canadian Information Processing Society [*Toronto, ON*]   (CGC)
CIPS Rev .... CIPS [*Canadian Information Processing Society*] Review [*A publication*]
CIPT........... Comite International des Telecommunications de Presse [*International Press Telecommunications - IPTC*]
CIR............. Center for Information Research [*Drexel University, University of Florida*] [*Research center*]   (EISS)
CIR............. Color Infrared [*Image*]
CIR............. Current Instruction Register
CIRA .... Computerised Instrumented Residential Audit [*Energy auditing*]
CIRC .... Circulation Input Recording Center [*Data processing system*]
CIRC .... Cross-Interleaved Reed-Solomon Code [*Data processing*]
CIRCA........ Center for Instructional and Research Computing Activities {*University of Florida*] [*Research center*]   (RCD)
CIRCAL...... Circuit Analysis [*Data processing*]
CIRCL .... Center for Interdisciplinary Research in Computer-Based Learning [*University of Delaware*] [*Research center*]   (RCD)
Circuits Manuf ... Circuits Manufacturing [*A publication*]
Circuits Mfg ... Circuits Manufacturing [*A publication*]
CIRCUS ...... Calculation of Indirect Resources and Conversion to Unit Staff [*Data processing*]
CIRM.......... Comite International Radio Maritime [*International Maritime Radio Committee*]
CIRR .... Corporate and Industry Research Reports [*JA Micropublishing, Inc.*] [*Database*]   (CUAD)
CIRS .... Chesapeake Information Retrieval Service [*Edgewater, MD*]   (EISS)
CIS............. Center for Instructional Services [*Purdue University*] [*Research center*]   (RCD)
CIS............. Center for Integrated Systems [*Stanford University*] [*Research center*]   (RCD)
CIS............. Centre d'Information Spectroscopique et Physico-Chimique d'Analyse [*Information Center for Spectroscopic and Physicochemical Analysis*] [*France*] [*Information service*]   (EISS)
CIS............. Centre International d'Informations de Securite et d'Hygiene du Travail [*International Occupational Safety and Health Information Center*]   (EISS)
CIS............. Channel and Isolation Supervision [*Telecommunications*]   (TEL)
CIS............. Character Instruction Set   (IEEE)
CIS............. Chemical Information Services [*Stanford Research Institute*]   (EISS)
CIS............. Chemical Information System [*Computer Sciences Corp.*] [*Falls Church, VA*]
CIS............. Commercial Instruction Set   (CAA)
CIS............. Communication Industrial Services
CIS............. Communication Information System   (IEEE)
CIS............. Communications Interface System   (MCD)
CIS............. CompuServe Information Service [*CompuServe, Inc.*]   (EISS)

CIS	Computer and Information Sciences Research Laboratory [*University of Alabama in Birmingham*] [*Research center*] (RCD)
CIS	Computer and Information Services [*Corporation for Public Broadcasting*] (EISS)
CIS	Computer and Information Systems [*A publication*]
CIS	Computing & Information Systems [*East Carolina University*] [*Research center*] (RCD)
CIS	Congressional Information Service [*Washington, DC*] [*Database producer*] [*Information service*]
CIS	Current Information Selection [*IBM Technical Information Retrieval Center*] [*White Plains, NY*]
CIS	Customer Information System [*IBM Corp.*]
CISAM	Compressed Index Sequential Access Method (CAA)
CISCO	Commodity Information Services Company (EISS)
CISCO	Compass Integrated System Compiler (IEEE)
CIS & DB	Comprehensive Information System and Database
CISI	Compagnie Internationale de Services en Informatique [*International Information Services Co.*] [*French*] [*Information service*] (EISS)
CISPR	Comite International Special des Perturbations Radioelectriques [*International Special Committee on Radio Interference*]
CISR	Center for Instructional Services and Research [*Memphis State University*] [*Research center*] (RCD)
CISTI	Canada Institute for Scientific and Technical Information [*Ottawa, ON*] (EISS)
CIT	Center for Information Technology [*Stanford University*] [*Stanford, CA*]
CIT	Command Interface Test (KSC)
CIT	Compagnie Industrielle de Telecommunication [*Computer manufacturer*] [*French*] (CAH)
CIT	Computer Interface Technology (IEEE)
CIT	Computer Interface Terminal (CET)
CITAB	Computer Instruction and Training Assistance for the Blind
CITCA	Committee of Inquiry into Technological Change in Australia (CAA)
CITE	Computer-Integrated Test Equipment
CITE	Controller Input Test Equipment
CITE	Council of Institute of Telecommunication Engineers
CITECH	Cawkell Information & Technology Services, Ltd. [*Uxbridge, England*] [*Telecommunications*] (EISS)
CITEL	Conference on Inter-American Telecommunications [*Organization of American States*] [*Telecommunications*] (TSSD)
CITERE	Centre d'Information en Temps Reel pour l'Europe [*European Center for Information in Real Time*] [*France*] [*Information service*] (EISS)
CITIBASE	Citibank Economic Database [*Citibank, NA*] [*New York, NY*] [*Information service*] (EISS)
CITP	Conseil International des Telecommunications de Press [*International Press Telecommunications Council*]
CIU	Communications Interface Unit (CAA)
CIU	Community Information Utility (BUR)
CIU	Computer Interface Unit
CIU	Controller Interface Unit (MCD)
CIVITEX	Civic Information & Techniques Exchange [*Citizens Forum on Self-Government/National Municipal League*] [*New York, NY*] [*Information service*] (EISS)
CIWS	Concentrator Isolation Working Subsystem [*Telecommunications*] (TEL)
CJ	Computer Journal [*British*] [*A publication*]
CJIS	Criminal Justice Information System
CJP	Communication Jamming Processor (IEEE)
CJPI	Criminal Justice Periodical Index [*University Microfilms International*] [*Bibliographic database*] [*A publication*]
CK	Call Key [*Telecommunications*]
CKO	Check Operator (DEN)
CKT	Circuit
CKT-ID	Circuit Identification [*Telecommunications*] (TEL)
CL	Circuit Layout [*AT & T*]
CL	Command Language (CAA)
CL	Compiler Language (DIT)
CL	Computational Linguistics (IEEE)
CL	Control Language [*Data processing*] (BUR)
CL	Control Leader [*Data processing*]
CL	Control Logic
C & L	Coopers & Lybrand USA [*New York, NY*] [*Telecommunications*] (TSSD)
CL	Cutter Location File (CCD)
C³L	Complementary Constant Current Logic (MCD)
CL9	Cloud Nine [*Manufacturer of remote control devices for home electronics*] [*Company founded by Stephen Wozniak*]
CLA	Communication Line Adapters
CLA	Communication Link Analyzer (IEEE)
CLA	Computer Law Association [*Falls Church, VA*] (EANO)
CLA	Computer Lessors Association [*Later, CDLA*] (EANO)
CLA	Computers Lawyers Association (EANO)
CLA	Control Logic Array
CLADES	Centro Latinoamericano de Documentacion Economica y Social [*Latin American Center for Economic and Social Documentation*] [*United Nations*] [*Information service*] (EISS)
CLAIM	Centre for Library and Information Management [*Loughborough University of Technology*] [*British*] [*Information service*] (EISS)
CLAIR	Computerised Library of Analysed Igneous Rocks [*Australia*] [*Information service*] (EISS)
CLAM	Command Load Acceptance Message (SKY)
CLAND	Computer Languages [*A publication*]
CLANS	Computerized Link Analysis System
CLARA	Computer Load and Resource Analysis (MCD)
CLAS	Chromatography Laboratory Automatic Software
CLAS	Communications Link Analyzer System
CLAS	Computerized Library Acquisitions System [*Lukac Data Systems*] [*Lewis and Clark College*] [*Information service*] (EISS)
CLASIX	Computer/LASER Access Systems for Information Exchange
CLASS	Closed Loop Accounting for Stores Sales (IEEE)
CLASS	Computer-Based Laboratory for Automated School Systems [*System Development Corp. project*]
CLASS	Computerized Literature Access Search Service
CLASS	Cooperative Library Agency for Systems and Services [*San Jose, CA*] [*Telecommunications*] (TSSD)
CLASS	Current Literature Awareness Search Service [*BIOSIS*] [*Database*]
CLASSIC	Circulation Library Automated System for Inventory Control [*Cincinnati Electronics Corp.*] [*Information service*] (EISS)
CLASSMATE	Computer Language to Aid and Stimulate Scientific, Mathematical, and Technical Education
CLAT	Communication Line Adapters for Teletype
CLB	Central Logic Bus [*Data processing*] (CAA)
CLB	Clear Both [*Data processing*]
CLBW	Closed-Loop Bandwidth
CLC	Central Logic Control [*Data processing*] (OA)
CLC	Claritas Corporation [*Alexandria, VA*] [*Information service*] (EISS)
CLC	Command Load Controller (SKY)
CLC	Communications Line Control (CAA)
CLC	Communications Link Controller [*International Computers Ltd.*] [*Telecommunications*] (CAA)
CLC	Computerized Lubrication Control [*Sun Oil Co.*]
CLCE	Communications Link Characterization Experiment [*Communications Technology Satellite*] (MCD)
CLCL	Computational Linguistics and Computer Languages [*A publication*]
CL & CL Comput Linguist Comput Lang	CL & CL. Computational Linguistics and Computer Languages [*Budapest*] [*A publication*]
CLD	Computer Logic Demonstrator
CLDA	Control Logic and Drive Assembly
CLDAS	Clinical Laboratory Data Acquisition System [*Data processing*]
CLE	Communications Line Expander [*Electrodata, Inc.*] [*Telecommunications*] (CAA)
CLE	Key Word [*Online database field identifier*] (OBD)
CLEO	Clear Language for Expressing Orders [*Data processing*] (IEEE)
CLEO	Computer Listings of Employment Opportunities [*The Copley Press, Inc.*] [*Database*] (CUAD)
CLETS	California Law Enforcement Telecommunications System
CLF	Clear Forward [*Telecommunications*] (TEL)
CLG	Compile, Load, and Go [*Data processing*] (BUR)
CLHU	Computer Laboratory of Harvard University
CLI	Calling Line Identification [*or Identity*] [*Telecommunications*] (TEL)
CLI	Coin Level Indicator [*Telephone communications*]
CLI	Command Language Interpreter [*Data processing*] (OA)
CLI	Command Line Interface [*For Amiga computers*]
CLI	Compression Labs, Incorporated [*San Jose, CA*] [*Telecommunications*] (TSSD)
CLIBOC	Chinese Linguistics Bibliography on Computer [*Cambridge University Press*] [*England*]
CLIC	Canadian Law Information Council [*Ottawa, ON*] (EISS)
CLIC	Command Language for Interrogating Computers [*Royal Radar Establishment*] [*British*]
CLIC	Conversational Language for Interactive Computing (CAA)
CLINPROT	Clinical Cancer Protocols [*National Library of Medicine*] [*Database*]
CLIO	Conversational Language for Input/Output [*Data processing*] (CAA)
CLIP	Cellular Logic Image Processor [*Telecommunications*] (TEL)
CLIP	Compiler Language for Information Processing [*System Development Corp.*] [*Programing language*]
CLIPR	Computer Laboratory for Instruction in Psychological Research [*University of Colorado - Boulder*] [*Research center*] (RCD)
CLIS	Criminalistic Laboratory Information Systems [*FBI*]
CLK	Clerk (AFM)
CLK	Clock
CLLT	Collation [*Online database field identifier*] (OBD)
CLM	Communications Line Multiplexer (CAA)
CLMS	Clinical Laboratory Management System [*Data processing*]
CLO	Computer Lock-On
CLOAX	Corrugated-Laminated Coaxial [*Cable*]
CLOB	Core Load Overlay Builder [*General Automation, Inc.*] (CAA)
CLP	Command Language Processor
CLP	Communication Line Processor (CAA)
CLP	Cornell List Processor [*Data processing*] (TUT)
CLP	Current Line Pointer [*Data processing*] (IBMDP)

Acronym	Definition
CLR	Central Logic Rack [*Telecommunications*] (TEL)
CLR	Clear (KSC)
CLR	Clear to Zero [*Data processing*]
CLR	Clearance (FAAC)
CLR	Combined Line and Recording [*Telecommunications*] (TEL)
CLR	Computer Language Recorder
CLR	Computer Language Research (IEEE)
CLRC	Circuit Layout Record Card [*Telecommunications*] (TEL)
CLRI	Computer Language Research, Incorporated [*NASDAQ symbol*] (NQ)
CLS	Carolina Library Services, Inc. (EISS)
CLS	Clear and Subtract (IEEE)
CLS	Close [*Data processing*] (BUR)
CLS	Common Language System [*Data processing*] (BUR)
CLS	Communications Line Switch (CAA)
CLS	Computer Listing Service, Inc. [*Round Rock, TX*] [*Information service*] (EISS)
CLS	Concept Learning System [*Data processing*] (BUR)
CLSI	Computer Library Services, Incorporated [*Wellesley Hills, MA*]
CLSR	Computer Law Service Reporter
CLSS	Communication Link Subsystem
CLSS	Computerized Literature Searching Service
CLT	Communication Line Terminal [*Data processing*] (CGC)
CLT	Computer Language Translator
CLTV	Closed-Loop Television (VIT)
CLU	Central Logic Unit
CLU	Cluster [*Programing language*] [*1973*] (CSR)
CLU	Command Logic Unit (MCD)
CLUT	Computer Logic Unit Tester (MCD)
CM	Cards per Minute (CAH)
cm	Centimeter
CM	Central Memory [*Data processing*] (BUR)
CM	Chart Maker [*Computer Design*] [*Software package*] [*British*] (NCC)
CM	Circuit Modeller [*Seasim Engineering Software Ltd.*] [*Software package*] [*British*] (NCC)
CM	Class Marks [*Telecommunications*] (TEL)
CM	Communications Multiplexer [*Data processing*]
CM	Component Manufacturer [*Foundry Business Systems*] [*Software package*] [*British*] (NCC)
CM	Computer Management [*British*] [*A publication*] (CAH)
CM	Computer Module
CM	Computing Media
CM	Configuration Management
CM	Continuity Message [*Telecommunications*] (TEL)
CM	Control Mark (DEN)
CM	Control Memory [*Telecommunications*] (TEL)
CM	Control Monitor (MCD)
CM	Core Memory
CMA	Channel Multiplier Array
CMA	Communication Managers Association
CMA	Communications Market Association (EANO)
CMA	Computer Management Association (CAA)
CMA	Computer-Marked Assignment [*Education*] [*British*]
CMA	Computer Monitor Adapter (CAA)
CMA	Conical Monopole Antenna
CMAP	Central Memory Access Priority [*Data processing*] (CAA)
CMAR	Control Memory Address Register [*Data processing*] (CAA)
CMB	Conductivity Modulated Bipolar [*Data processing*]
CMC	Cable Maintenance Center [*Telecommunications*] (TEL)
CMC	Center for Mass Communication [*Columbia University*]
CMC	Code for Magnetic Characters (IEEE)
CMC	Communications Mode Control
CMC	Crew Module Computer (MCD)
CMCA	Character Mode Communications Adapter (CAA)
CMCC	Computer Monitor and Control Console (CAAL)
CMCI	CMC International [*NASDAQ symbol*] (NQ)
CMCS	Canadian Man-Computer Communications Society
CMCS	Communications Monitoring and Control Subsystem (NVT)
CMCS	COMSAT [*Communications Satellite Corp.*] Maritime Communications Satellite (MCD)
CMCT	Communicate (MDG)
CMCT	Communicating Magnetic Card Typewriter
CMCTL	Current Mode Complementary Transistor Logic (IEEE)
CMD	Command
CMDAC	Current-Mode Digital-to-Analog Converter [*Data processing*]
CMDC	Compucom Development [*NASDAQ symbol*] (NQ)
CMDCC	Command Computer Console (CIT)
CMDS	Centralized Message Data System [*Bell System*]
CMDS	Command Manpower Data System
CME	Central Memory Extension [*Data processing*] (CAA)
CME	Computer Measurement and Evaluation (CAA)
CME	Computer Memory Element
CME	Computerizing Medical Examination [*IBM Corp.*]
CMF	Combined Master File [*Data processing*]
CMF	Continuous Multibay Frames [*Jacys Computing Services*] [*Software package*] [*British*] (NCC)
CMF	Cymotive Force [*Telecommunications*] (TEL)
C/MFI	Conversion, Memory, and Fault Indication [*Telecommunications*] (TEL)
CMG	Computer Modelling Group [*Calgary, AB*] [*Research center*] (RCD)
CMI	Cambridge Memories, Incorporated (CAA)
CMI	Canadian Magazine Index [*Micromedia, Ltd.*] [*Information service*] (EISS)
CMI	Center for Machine Intelligence [*University of Michigan, Electronic Data Systems*] [*Research center*] (RCD)
CMI	Code Mark Inversion [*Telecommunications*] (TEL)
CMI	Commission Mixte Internationale pour les Experiences Relatives a la Protection des Lignes de Telecommunication et des Canalisations Souterraines
CMI	Computer-Managed Instruction
CMIC	California Microwave, Inc. [*NASDAQ symbol*] (NQ)
CMIC	Computer Microfilm International Corporation [*Information service*] (EISS)
CMIN	Computer Memories [*NASDAQ symbol*] (NQ)
CMIR	Common Mode Input Resistance
CML	Common Machine Language [*Data processing*]
CML	Common Mode Logic (CAA)
CML	Computer-Managed Laboratory
CML	Conversational Modeling Language [*Data processing*]
CML	Current-Mode Logic [*Data processing*]
CMLC	Computer Maintenance & Leasing Corp. [*Minneapolis, MN*] [*Hardware manufacturer*] (DASO)
CMLS	Computer Multiple Listing Service [*Fairfax, VA*] [*Information service*] (EISS)
CMM	Coherent Microwave Memory
CMM	Communications Multiplexer Module (CAA)
CMM	Computer Main Memory [*Telecommunications*] (TEL)
CMM	Concentration Module Main [*Telecommunications*] (TEL)
CMMP	Carnegie Multi-Mini Processor
CMN	Computerized Management Network [*For Agricultural Cooperative Extension Service Education*] [*Virginia Polytechnic Institute*] [*Database*] (FDB)
CMND	Command (IBMDP)
CMO	Common Mode Operation [*Telecommunications*] (TEL)
CMO	Computers and Operations Research [*A publication*]
CMORA	Computers and Operations Research [*A publication*]
CMOS	Complementary Magnetic Oxide on Silicone [*Data processing*]
CMOS	Complementary Metal-Oxide Semiconductor [*Transistor*] [*Electronics*]
CMOS/SOS	Complementary Metal-Oxide Semiconductor/Silicon-on-Sapphire [*Electronics*]
CMOST	Complementary Metal-Oxide Semiconductor Transistor [*Electronics*]
CMP	Camp-On [*Telecommunications*] (TEL)
CMP	Center for Manufacturing Productivity and Technology Transfer [*Rensselaer Polytechnic Institute*] [*Research center*] (RCD)
CMP	Circuit Modeller Plus [*Seasim Engineering Software Ltd.*] [*Software package*] [*British*] (NCC)
CMP	Compare [*Data processing*]
CMP	Computational (MDG)
CMP	Computer (MUGU)
CMP	Console Message Processor [*Data processing*]
CMPC	Compucare, Inc. [*NASDAQ symbol*] (NQ)
CMPCTR	Computer Center (DDI)
CMPQ	Compaq Computer Corp. [*NASDAQ symbol*] (NQ)
CMPSCTY	Computer Security (MSA)
CMPT	Compute [*or Computer*]
CMPTD	Computed
CMPTG	Computing
CMPTR	Computer (KSC)
CMPX	Complex (DDI)
CMR	Centralized Mail Remittance [*Telecommunications*] (TEL)
CMR	Common Mode Rejection
CMRR	Common Mode Rejection Ratio
CMS	Cambridge Monitor System
CMS	Center for Migration Studies [*City University of New York*] (EISS)
CMS	Centralized Maintenance System [*Telecommunications*]
CMS	Circuit Maintenance System [*AT & T*]
CMS	Communication Management System [*Data processing*]
CM & S	Communications Maintenance and Storage (NASA)
CMS	Compiler Monitor System (BUR)
CMS	Complete Management Systems
CMS	Computer Management System [*Burroughs Corp.*] (BUR)
CMS	Computer Marketing Services [*Anaheim, CA*] [*Information service*] (EISS)
CMS	Computer Modelling System [*Computer Modelling International Ltd.*] [*Software package*] [*British*] (NCC)
CMS	Conversational Monitor System [*IBM Corp.*] [*Data processing*]
CMS	Current-Mode Switching [*Data processing*] (MSA)
CM/SEC	Centimeters per Second [*Telecommunications*] (TEL)
CMSG	"C" Message Weighting [*Telecommunications*] (TEL)
CMSV	Comserv Corp. [*NASDAQ symbol*] (NQ)
CMT	Cassette Magnetic Tape (CAA)
CM/T	Change Management/Tracking [*IBM Corp.*]
CMT	Computer Memory Tester
CMT	Computer Micrographics Technology [*An association*] (EANO)
CMT	Comtech, Inc. [*Toronto Stock Exchange symbol*]
CMT	Conversational Mode Terminal [*Friden, Inc.*] (IEEE)
CMTK	Comptek Research, Inc. [*NASDAQ symbol*] (NQ)
CMTL	Comtech Telecommunications [*NASDAQ symbol*] (NQ)
CMTM	Communications and Telemetry
CMTS	Computer Maintenance Test Set
CMTT	Joint Committee on Television Transmission
CMTV	Country Music Television [*Cable-television system*]

Computer & Telecommunications Acronyms

CMU .... Computer Memory Unit (OA)
CMU .... Control Maintenance Unit (CAA)
CMU .... Core Memory Unit (MCD)
CMUC .... Comp-U-Check, Inc. [*NASDAQ symbol*] (NQ)
CMX .... Character Multiplexer [*Telecommunications*] (CAA)
CMX .... Concentration Module Extension [*Telecommunications*] (TEL)
CN .... Call Number [*Online database field identifier*] (OBD)
C/N .... Carrier-to-Noise [*Ratio*] (CIT)
CN .... Check Not OK [*Telecommunications*] (TEL)
CN .... Coin Trunk [*Telecommunications*] (TEL)
CN .... Communications Network (CAA)
CN .... Contract Number [*Data processing*]
CNA .... Communications Network Architecture (CAA)
CNC .... Computer Numerical Control [*Data processing*]
CNCC .... Customer Network Control Center [*Telecommunications*] (TEL)
CNCE .... Communications Network Control Element (MCD)
CNCL .... Cancel (FAAC)
CNCT .... Connect (FAAC)
C/N)d .... Carrier-to-Noise, Downlink (CBSS)
CND .... Centre National de Documentation [*National Documentation Center*] [*Morocco*] [*Information service*] (EISS)
CND .... Condition (MDG)
CNDDB ...... California Natural Diversity Data Base [*California State Department of Fish and Game*] [*Information service*] (EISS)
CNDP .... Communications Network Design Program
CNDST ...... Centre National de Documentation Scientifique et Technique [*National Scientific and Technical Documentation Center*] [*Senegal*] [*Information service*] (EISS)
CNE .... Communications Network Emulator (CAA)
CNE .... Compare Numeric Equal (OA)
CNEP .... Cable Network Engineering Program [*Bell System*]
CNET .... Computer Network Corp. [*NASDAQ symbol*] (NQ)
C-NET ...... Cromemco Local Area Network [*Cromemco, Inc.*] [*Mountain View, CA*] [*Telecommunications*] (TSSD)
CNGI .... Comite des Normes Gouvernementales en Informatique [*Government Electronic Data Processing Standards Committee*] [*Canada*]
CNI .... Canadian News Index [*Micromedia Ltd.*] [*Database*] [*A publication*]
CNI .... Changed Number Interception [*Telecommunications*] (TEL)
CNIC .... Centre National de l'Information Chimique de France [*National Center for Chemical Information of France*] [*Information service*] (EISS)
C/N)im ..... Carrier-to-Noise, Intermodulation (CBSS)
CNIPTG ..... Communications, Networks, and Information Processing Theory Group [*MIT*]
CNL .... Constant Net Loss [*Telecommunications*] (TEL)
CNMI .... Communications Network Management Interface (CAA)
CNMR .... Carbon-13 Nuclear Magnetic Resonance Search System [*Netherlands Information Combine*] [*Database*] (CUAD)
CNN .... Cable News Network [*Cable-television system*]
C/No .... Carrier-to-Noise Density (CBSS)
C/No)d .... Carrier-to-Noise Density, Downlink (CBSS)
C/No)im ... Carrier-to-Noise Density, Intermodulation (CBSS)
C/No)t ..... Carrier-to-Noise Density, Total (CBSS)
C/No)u .... Carrier-to-Noise Density, Uplink (CBSS)
CNP .... Communications Network Processor (CAA)
CNPPSDP ... Cooperative National Plant Pest Survey and Detection Program [*Database*] (FDB)
CNPTI .... Centre National de Prevention et de Traitement des Intoxications [*National Poison Control Center*] [*Information service*] (EISS)
CNR .... Carrier-to-Noise Ratio
CNR .... COMSAT [*Communications Satellite Corp.*] Nonreflecting [*Solar cell*]
C N Report ... Computer Negotiations Report [*A publication*]
CNRS .... Centre National de la Recherche Scientifique [*Database producer*] (CUAD)
CNS .... Center for Nuclear Studies [*Memphis State University*] [*Research center*] (RCD)
CNS .... Commodity News Services, Inc. [*Information service*] (EISS)
CNS .... Communications Network Service [*Satellite Business Systems*] [*McLean, VA*] [*Telecommunications*] (TSSD)
CNS .... CompuServe Network Services [*CompuServe, Inc.*] [*Columbus, OH*] [*Telecommunications*] (TSSD)
CNSO .... Consco Enterprises [*NASDAQ symbol*] (NQ)
CNT .... Canadian National Telecommunications
C/N)t .... Carrier-to-Noise, Total (CBSS)
CNT .... Count (CAH)
CNT .... Counter (MDG)
CNTA .... Contact [*A publication*]
CNTL .... Control (KSC)
CNTR .... Counter (MSA)
CNTRL ...... Control
C/N)u .... Carrier-to-Noise, Uplink (CBSS)
CNU .... Compare Numeric Unequal (OA)
CO .... Check OK [*Telecommunications*] (TEL)
CO .... Coden [*Online database field identifier*] (OBD)
CO .... Coinbox Line [*Telecommunications*] (TEL)
CO .... Collation [*Online database field identifier*] (OBD)
CO .... Command Output
CO .... Crystal Oscillator
COA .... Constant-Output Amplifier (MUGU)
COA .... Crude Oil Analysis Data Bank [*Department of Energy*] [*Database*] (FDB)
COACH ...... Computer-Aided Chartroom
COALDATA ... European Coal Data Bank [*Frankfurt am Main, FRG*] [*Information service*] (EISS)
COALPRO ... Coal Research Projects [*IEA Coal Research*] [*Database*] (CUAD)
COAM .... Customer-Owned and Maintained [*Equipment*]
COATS .... Communications-Oriented Automatic Test (MCD)
COAX .... Coaxial
COB .... COBOL [*Common Business-Oriented Language*] Element Subtype [*Data processing*]
COB .... Communications Office Building (NASA)
COBESTCO ... Computer-Based Estimating Technique for Contractors
COBIDOC ... Commissie voor Bibliografie en Documentatie [*Netherlands Bibliographical and Documentary Committee*] [*Information service*] (EISS)
COBIS .... Computer-Based Instruction System (IEEE)
COBLIB ...... COBOL [*Common Business-Oriented Language*] Library [*Data processing*] (MCD)
COBLOC .... CODAP [*Control Data Assembly Program*] Language Block-Oriented Compiler (MCD)
COBOL ...... Common Business-Oriented Language [*1959*] [*Data processing*]
COBRA ...... Computerized Boolean Reliability Analysis [*Boeing*]
COBRD ...... Communication and Broadcasting [*A publication*]
COC .... Coded Optical Character [*Data processing*] (BUR)
COC .... Compiler Object Code [*Telecommunications*] (TEL)
COC .... Computer Communications [*A publication*]
COC .... Computer Operators' Course
COC .... Computer Oriented Classicists (EANO)
CO-CO ...... Central Office to Central Office [*Bell System*]
COCO .... COBOL [*Common Business-Oriented Language*] Conversion [*Data processing*] (MCD)
COCO .... Color Computer
COCOS ...... Corporate Communications System [*Bell-Northern Research Ltd.*] [*Data processing*]
COD .... Constrained Optimal Design [*Data processing*] (RDA)
CODA .... Chemical On-Line Data Analyzer [*Interactive Elements, Inc.*]
CODAC ...... Coordination of Operating Data by Automatic Computer
CODAN ...... Carrier-Operated Device, Antinoise [*Radio*]
CODAP ...... Client-Oriented Data Acquisition Process [*FDA*]
CODAP ...... Control Data Assembly Program [*Control Data Corp.*]
CODAR ...... Correlation Data Analyzer Recorder (CAAL)
CODAR ...... Correlation Display Analyzing and Recording
CODAS ...... Current Operational Data System (DDI)
CODAS ...... Customer-Oriented Data System (DIT)
CODASYL ... Conference on Data Systems Languages [*Washington, DC*]
CODATA Bull ... CODATA [*Committee on Data for Science and Technology*] Bulletin [*A publication*]
CODATA Newsl ... CODATA [*Committee on Data for Science and Technology*] Newsletter [*France*] [*A publication*]
CODE .... Cable On-Line Data Exchange [*A. C. Nielson Co.*] [*Database*] (CUAD)
CODEC ...... Coder-Decoder (MCD)
CODED ...... Computer-Oriented Design of Electronic Devices
CODEIN ..... Computerized Drawing Electrical Information (NG)
CODEL .... Computer Developments Limited Automatic Coding System (IEEE)
CODES ...... Computer Design and Education System (OA)
CODES ...... Computer Design and Evaluation System (IEEE)
CODES ...... Computerized Deployment Execution System
CODIC .... Color Difference Computer (MUGU)
CODIC .... Computer-Directed Communications
CODICOM ... Computerized Distribution and Control of Microfilm [*American Motors Corp.*]
CODIL .... Content Dependent Information Language (CAA)
CODIL .... Control Diagram Language [*Data processing*] (IEEE)
CODILS ...... Commodity-Oriented Digital Label Input System
CODIS .... Controlled Digital Simulator
CODIT .... Computer Direct to Telegraph
CODN .... Codenoll Technology [*NASDAQ symbol*] (NQ)
CODOC ...... Cooperative Documents Network Project [*University of Guelph Library*] [*Database*]
COEBRA ..... Computerized Optimization of Elastic Booster Autopilot
COED .... Computer-Operated [*or -Oriented*] Electronic Display
COEES .... Central Office Equipment Estimation System [*Bell System*]
COF .... Cause of Failure [*Telecommunications*] (TEL)
COF .... Computer Operations Facility
COF .... Computer Optimized Fabrication [*Sheet metal*] [*Raytheon Co.*]
COFIL .... Core File (IEEE)
COFRS .... Computerized Freight Remittance System [*Pronounced "coffers"*]
COG .... Computer Operations Group
COGENT ..... Compiler and Generalized Translator [*Argonne National Laboratory*] [*List processor*] (IEEE)
COGEODATA ... Committee on Storage, Automatic Processing, and Retrieval of Geological Data [*International Union of Geological Sciences*] [*Information service*] (EISS)
COGO .... Coordinated Geometry [*Programing language*] [*1957*] (CSR)
COGS .... Consumer Goods System [*Data processing*]
COH .... Computer Operator Handbook
COIN .... Coin Phone Operational and Information Network System [*Telecommunications*] (TEL)
COIN .... Complete Operating Information [*Data processing*]

Computer & Telecommunications Acronyms

COIN .... Coordinated Occupational Information Network [*Bell & Howell Co.*] (EISS)
CO IN HES ... Communications and Information Handling Equipment and Services
COINS .... Calspan On-Line Information Service [*Calspan Corp.*] [*Information service*] (EISS)
COINS .... Community On-Line Intelligence Network System [*Computer network*] [*National Science Administration and Central Intelligence Agency*]
COINS .... Computer and Information Sciences
COINS .... Control in Information Systems
COL .... Column
COL .... Communications-Oriented Language (CAA)
COL .... Computer-Oriented Language [*Programing language*] [*Data processing*]
COLA .... Constant-Output Level Adapter
COLEX .... CIRC [*Central Information Reference and Control*] Online Experiment
COLINGO ... Compile Online and Go [*Data processing*]
COLL .... Collator
COLLECT ... Connecticut On-Line Law-Enforcement Communications and Teleprocessing [*Computer law-enforcement system*]
COLR .... Circuit Order Layout Record [*Telecommunications*] (TEL)
COLT .... Communication Line Terminator [*IBM Corp.*]
COLT .... Computer-Oriented Language Translator (IEEE)
COLT .... Computerized Online Testing
COLT .... Control Language Translator (IEEE)
COM .... Cassette Operating Monitor (CAA)
COM .... Communicate [*or Communications*]
COM .... Communications Processor
COM .... Computer Output Microfilm [*or Microfiche or Microform*] (BUR)
COMA .... Computer Operations Management Association (CAH)
ComAb .... Computer Abstracts [*A publication*]
COMAC ...... Communications Advisory Committee
COMAC ...... Continuous Multiple Access Collator [*Proposed by Mortimer Taube, 1957*] [*Data processing*]
COMARC .... Cooperative Machine-Readable Cataloging Program [*Library of Congress*]
COMASIII ... Computerized Maintenance and Administration Support III [*Telecommunications*] (TEL)
COMAT .... Computer-Assisted Training (IEEE)
COMB .... Console-Oriented Model Building [*Data processing*]
COMBASE ... Communications Data Base [*Canada*] [*Information service*] (EISS)
COMCAS .... Computer-Oriented Modal Control and Appraisal System
COMCAT .... Computer Output Microform Catalog
COMCM ...... Communication Countermeasures
COMDEX .... Computer Dealer Exposition
COME .... Computer Output Microfilm Equipment
COMEINDORS ... Composite Mechanized Information and Document Retrieval System
COMEPP ..... Cornell Manufacturing Engineering and Productivity Program [*Cornell University*] [*Research center*] (RCD)
COMET .... Computer Message Transmission (CAA)
COMET .... Meteorological Office Computer [*British*] (DEN)
COMETS ..... Community Electronic Teller System
COMETS ..... Computer-Operated Multifunction Electronic Test System (MCD)
COMFOR .... Commercial Wire Center Forecast Program [*Telecommunications*] (TEL)
COMI .... Computer Microfilm Corp. [*NASDAQ symbol*] (NQ)
COMIC .... Colorant Mixture Computer [*Du Pont trademark*]
COMISS ...... Computerized Medical Information Support System [*Veterans Administration*]
COMIT .... Compiler/Massachusetts Institute of Technology (IEEE)
COMLOGNET ... Communications Logistics Network (IEEE)
COMM .... Communication (AFM)
Com M .... Communication Monographs [*A publication*]
Comm ACM ... Communications. ACM [*Association for Computing Machinery*] [*A publication*]
COMMCEN ... Communications Center
Comm Educ ... Communication Education [*A publication*]
COMMEL .... Communications-Electronics
COMMEN ... Compiler Oriented for Multiprogramming and Multiprocessing Environments (IEEE)
COMMEND ... Computer-Oriented Mechanical Design (MCD)
Comm Monogr ... Communication Monographs [*A publication*]
Comm Q ...... Communication Quarterly [*A publication*]
Comm Res ... Communication Research [*A publication*]
Comm Res Trends ... Communication Research Trends [*A publication*]
Comm Roy Soc Edinburgh Phys Sci ... Communications. Royal Society of Edinburgh. Physical Science [*A publication*]
COMMS ...... Central Office Maintenance Management System [*Telecommunications*] (TEL)
COMMS ...... Communications
Comms N ... Communications News [*A publication*]
COMMS-PM ... Central Office Maintenance Management System - Preventive Maintenance [*Telecommunications*] (TEL)
COMM-STOR ... Communications Storage Unit (DEEC)
COMMSWITCH ... Communications-Failure Detecting and Switching Equipment (MDG)
COMMUN ... Communications
Commun ACM ... Communications. ACM [*Association for Computing Machinery*] [*A publication*]
Commun Broadcast ... Communication and Broadcasting [*England*] [*A publication*]
Commun Electron ... Communications and Electronics [*England*] [*A publication*]
Commun Eng ... Communication Engineering [*A publication*]
Commun Equip & Syst Des ... Communications Equipment and Systems Design [*A publication*]
COMMUNICAT ... Communications Satellite (MUGU)
Communication Tech Impact ... Communications Technology Impact [*A publication*]
Commun News ... Communications News [*A publication*]
Commun Quart ... Communication Quarterly [*A publication*]
COMMZ ...... Communications Zone (MUGU)
COMN .... Communication
COMNEED ... Communications Need
COMNET .... Communications Network (AFM)
COMNET .... Computer Network Corp. [*Information service*] (EISS)
COMOPTIONS ... Commodity Options [*I. P. Sharp Associates*] [*Database*] (CUAD)
COMP .... Comparator (CET)
COMP .... Compatible
COMP .... Compiler
COMP .... Computation (AFM)
COMP .... Computer (AFM)
COMPAC .... Computer Output Microfilm Package (DEEC)
COMPAC .... Computer Packages (MCD)
COMPAC .... Computer Program for Automatic Control
COMPACT ... Compatible Algebraic Compiler and Translator
COMPACT ... Computer Planning and Control Technique (BUR)
COMPACT ... Computer-Programed Automatic Checkout and Test System
COMPACT ... Computerization of World Facts [*Stanford Research Institute*] [*Databank*]
COMPANDER ... Compressor Expander [*Telecommunications*] (IEEE)
COMPARE ... Computerized Performance and Analysis Response Evaluator (IEEE)
COMPASS ... Automotive Competitive Assessment Data Bank [*Ward's Research*] [*Database*] (CUAD)
COMPASS ... Compiler-Assembler
COMPASS ... Comprehensive Assembler System [*Programing language*] [*1964*] [*Control Data Corp.*] (CGC)
COMPASS ... Computer-Assisted Classification and Assignment System (IEEE)
COMPASS ... Computer-Assisted Surveillance Subsystem (MCD)
Comp & Automation ... Computers and Automation [*Later, Computers and People*] [*A publication*]
COMPAY .... Computer Payroll (BUR)
Comp Bul ... Computer Bulletin [*A publication*]
Comp Chem ... Computers and Chemistry [*A publication*]
Comp Comm ... Computer Communications [*A publication*]
COMPCON ... Computer Conference
Comp Data ... Computer Data [*A publication*]
Comp Dec ... Computer Decisions [*A publication*]
Comp Decisions ... Computer Decisions [*A publication*]
COMPDES ... Compensator Design [*Data processing*]
Comp Des ... Computer Design [*A publication*]
Comp & Educ ... Computers and Education [*A publication*]
COMPEL ..... Compute Parallel (IEEE)
COMPELS ... Computer Electrical System [*Davy Computing Ltd.*] [*Software package*] [*British*] (NCC)
COMPENDEX ... Computerized Engineering Index [*Engineering Index, Inc.*] [*New York, NY*] [*Bibliographic database*]
Comp Fluids ... Computers and Fluids [*A publication*]
Comp J .... Computer Journal [*A publication*]
Comp Law ... Computer Law and Tax Report [*A publication*]
COMPMARK ... Computer Marketing [*Standard & Poor's*]
Comp & Med ... Computers and Medicine [*A publication*]
Comp Methods Appl Mech Eng ... Computer Methods in Applied Mechanics and Engineering [*A publication*]
Comp Mgmt ... Computer Management [*A publication*]
Comp Net ... Computer Networks [*A publication*]
Comp Oper Res ... Computers and Operations Research [*A publication*]
Comp & People ... Computers and People [*A publication*]
Comp Pers ... Computer Personnel [*A publication*]
Comp Phys Comm ... Computer Physics Communications [*A publication*]
COMPRESS ... Computer Research, Systems, and Software (IEEE)
Comp Rev ... Computing Reviews [*A publication*]
COMPROG ... Computer Program (IEEE)
COMPSAC ... Computer Software and Applications Conference (CAA)
COMPSO .... Computer Software and Peripheral Show (IEEE)
Comp Surv ... Computing Surveys [*A publication*]
COMPTEL ... Competitive Telecommunications Association [*Washington, DC*] [*Telecommunications*] (TSSD)
COMPTR ..... Comparator [*Data processing*]
COMPUNICATIONS ... Computers and Communications (DEEC)
Comput ...... Computer [*A publication*]
Comput Abstr ... Computer Abstracts [*A publication*]
Comput Acquis Syst Ser ... Computerized Acquisitions Systems Series [*A publication*]
Comput Aided Des ... Computer-Aided Design [*A publication*]
Comput Appl ... Computer Applications [*A publication*]
Comput Appl ... Computers and Their Applications [*A publication*]
Comput Appl Archaeol ... Computer Applications in Archaeology [*A publication*]

Comput Appl Chem (China) ... Computers and Applied Chemistry (China) [*A publication*]
Comput Appl Nat and Soc Sci ... Computer Applications in the Natural and Social Sciences [*A publication*]
Comput Appl Serv ... Computer Applications Service [*A publication*]
Comput Arch Elektron Rechn ... Computing. Archiv fuer Elektronisches Rechnen [*A publication*]
Comput Arch Inf Num ... Computing. Archiv fuer Informatik und Numerik [*A publication*]
Comput Archit News ... Computer Architecture News [*A publication*]
Comput Autom ... Computers and Automation [*Later, Computers and People*] [*A publication*]
Comput and Autom and People ... Computers and Automation and People [*A publication*]
Comput Biol Med ... Computers in Biology and Medicine [*A publication*]
Comput Biol and Med ... Computers in Biology and Medicine [*A publication*]
Comput Biom ... Computers and Biomedical Research [*A publication*]
Comput Biomed Res ... Computers and Biomedical Research [*A publication*]
Comput and Biomed Res ... Computers and Biomedical Research [*A publication*]
Comput Bull ... Computer Bulletin [*A publication*]
Comput Busn ... Computer Business News [*A publication*]
Comput Bus News ... Computer Business News [*A publication*]
Comput Cardiol ... Computers in Cardiology [*A publication*]
Comput Cat Syst Ser ... Computerized Cataloging Systems Series [*A publication*]
Comput Chem ... Computers and Chemistry [*A publication*]
Comput Chem Biochem Res ... Computers in Chemical and Biochemical Research [*A publication*]
Comput & Chem Eng ... Computers and Chemical Engineering [*A publication*]
Comput Chem Eng ... Computers and Chemical Engineering [*A publication*]
Comput Chem Instrum ... Computers in Chemistry and Instrumentation [*A publication*]
Comput Circ Syst Ser ... Computerized Circulation Systems Series [*A publication*]
Comput Commun ... Computer Communications [*A publication*]
Comput & Contr Abstr ... Computer and Control Abstracts [*IEE*] [*A publication*]
Comput Contrib ... Computer Contributions [*A publication*]
Comput Control Abstr ... Computer and Control Abstracts [*IEE*] [*A publication*]
Comput Control Abstracts ... Computer and Control Abstracts [*IEE*] [*A publication*]
Comput Control Inf Theory ... Computers, Control, and Information Theory [*A publication*]
Comput Decis ... Computer Decisions [*A publication*]
Comput Des ... Computer Design [*A publication*]
Comput & Electr Eng ... Computers and Electrical Engineering [*A publication*]
Comput Electr Eng ... Computers and Electrical Engineering [*A publication*]
Comput Electr Engrg ... Computers and Electrical Engineering [*A publication*]
Comput Elem Syst ... Computer Elements and Systems [*A publication*]
Comput Enhanc Spectrosc ... Computer Enhanced Spectroscopy [*A publication*]
Comput Environ Urban Syst ... Computers, Environment, and Urban Systems [*England*] [*A publication*]
Computer Ed ... Computer Education Conference [*A publication*]
Computer Engrg Ser ... Computer Engineering Series [*A publication*]
Computer Hu ... Computers and the Humanities [*Database*] [*A publication*]
Computer J ... Computer Journal [*A publication*]
Computer Mus J ... Computer Music Journal [*A publication*]
Computer Pe ... Computers and People [*A publication*]
Computer Ph ... Computer Physics Communications [*A publication*]
Computer Pr ... Computer Programs in Biomedicine [*A publication*]
Computers Geosci ... Computers and Geosciences [*A publication*]
Computer Wkly ... Computer Weekly [*A publication*]
Comput & Fluids ... Computers and Fluids [*A publication*]
Comput Fluids ... Computers and Fluids [*A publication*]
Comput and Fluids ... Computers and Fluids [*A publication*]
Comput Fraud and Secur Bull ... Computer Fraud and Security Bulletin [*A publication*]
Comput & Geosci ... Computers and Geosciences [*A publication*]
Comput Geosci ... Computers and Geosciences [*A publication*]
Comput Graphics ... Computers and Graphics [*A publication*]
Comput & Graphics ... Computers and Graphics [*A publication*]
Comput Graphics and Art ... Computer Graphics and Art [*A publication*]
Comput Graphics Image Process ... Computer Graphics and Image Processing [*A publication*]
Comput Graphics and Image Process ... Computer Graphics and Image Processing [*A publication*]
Comput Graphics World ... Computer Graphics World [*A publication*]
Comput Hum ... Computers and the Humanities [*Database*] [*A publication*]
Comput & Humanities ... Computers and the Humanities [*Database*] [*A publication*]
Comput Ind ... Computers in Industry [*Netherlands*] [*A publication*]
Comput Ind Eng ... Computers and Industrial Engineering [*A publication*]
Comput Inf ... Computer Information [*A publication*]
Comput & Info Sys ... Computer and Information Systems [*A publication*]
Computing J Abs ... Computing Journal Abstracts [*A publication*]
Comput J ... Computer Journal [*A publication*]
Comput L ... Computational Linguistics [*A publication*]
Comput Lang ... Computer Languages [*A publication*]
Comput Manage ... Computer Management [*A publication*]
Comput Math Appl ... Computers and Mathematics with Applications [*A publication*]
Comput & Math with Appl ... Computers and Mathematics with Applications [*A publication*]
Comput Med ... Computers and Medicine [*A publication*]
Comput Methods Appl Mech Eng ... Computer Methods in Applied Mechanics and Engineering [*A publication*]
Comput Methods Appl Mech & Eng ... Computer Methods in Applied Mechanics and Engineering [*A publication*]
Comput Methods Appl Mech & Engng ... Computer Methods in Applied Mechanics and Engineering [*A publication*]
Comput Methods Appl Mech Engrg ... Computer Methods in Applied Mechanics and Engineering [*A publication*]
Comput Mgmt ... Computer Management [*A publication*]
Comput Mus ... Computer Music Journal [*A publication*]
Comput Music J ... Computer Music Journal [*A publication*]
Comput Networks ... Computer Networks [*A publication*]
Comput Newsl Schools Bus ... Computing Newsletter for Schools of Business [*A publication*]
Comput Oper Res ... Computers and Operations Research [*A publication*]
Comput & Oper Res ... Computers and Operations Research [*A publication*]
Comput and People ... Computers and People [*A publication*]
Comput Performance ... Computer Performance [*A publication*]
Comput Peripherals Rev ... Computer Peripherals Review [*A publication*]
Comput Pers ... Computer Personnel [*A publication*]
Comput Phys Comm ... Computer Physics Communications [*A publication*]
Comput Phys Commun ... Computer Physics Communications [*A publication*]
Comput Phys Rep ... Computer Physics Reports [*A publication*]
Comput Prax ... Computer Praxis [*A publication*]
Comput Program Abstr ... Computer Program Abstracts [*A publication*]
Comput Programs Biomed ... Computer Programs in Biomedicine [*A publication*]
Comput Programs Chem ... Computer Programs for Chemistry [*A publication*]
Comput Rep Dep Archit Sci Syd Univ ... Computer Report. Department of Architectural Science. University of Sydney [*A publication*]
Comput Rev ... Computing Reviews [*A publication*]
Comput S Afr ... Computing South Africa [*A publication*]
Comput Sci Appl Math ... Computer Science and Applied Mathematics [*A publication*]
Comput Sci Monographs (Tokyo) ... Computer Science Monographs (Tokyo) [*A publication*]
Comput and Secur ... Computers and Security [*A publication*]
Comput Ser Syst Ser ... Computerized Serials Systems Series [*A publication*]
Comput and Soc ... Computers and Society [*A publication*]
Comput Stat and Data Anal ... Computational Statistics and Data Analysis [*A publication*]
Comput Struct ... Computers and Structures [*A publication*]
Comput and Struct ... Computers and Structures [*A publication*]
Comput and Structures ... Computers and Structures [*A publication*]
Comput Stud Hum & Verbal Behav ... Computer Studies in the Humanities and Verbal Behavior [*A publication*]
Comput Suppl ... Computing. Supplementum [*Vienna*] [*A publication*]
Comput Surv ... Computer Survey [*A publication*]
Comput Surv ... Computing Surveys [*A publication*]
Comput Survey ... Computing Surveys [*A publication*]
Comput Talk ... Computer Talk [*A publication*]
Comput Terminals Rev ... Computer Terminals Review [*A publication*]
Comput Times with Computacards ... Computer Times with Computacards [*A publication*]
Comput Today ... Computing Today [*A publication*]
Comput Tomogr ... Computerized Tomography [*A publication*]
Comput Vision Graphics and Image Process ... Computer Vision. Graphics and Image Processing [*A publication*]
Comput Week ... Computer Week [*A publication*]
Comput Wkly ... Computer Weekly [*A publication*]
Comput Wkly Int ... Computer Weekly International [*A publication*]
Comput World ... Computer World [*A publication*]
Computwrld ... Computerworld [*A publication*]
Comp Wkly ... Computer Weekly [*A publication*]
COMRADE ... Computer-Aided Design Environment [*Software system*] (IEEE)
COMRAZ .... Communication, Range, and Azimuth Unit [*Data processing*]
ComRev...... Computing Reviews [*A publication*]
COMRI........ Communications Routing Indicator
COMSAT .... Communications Satellite Corp. [*Assignee of operational and developmental responsibilities for Telstar and other international communications space devices*] [*Washington, DC*]
COMSATCOM ... Commercial Satellite Communications System
COMSATCORP ... Communications Satellite Corporation [*See also COMSAT*]
COMSAT Tech Rev ... COMSAT [*Communications Satellite Corp.*] Technical Review [*A publication*]
COMSEC .... Communications Security Association (EANO)
COMSL....... Communication System Simulation Language [*Data processing*] (IEEE)
COMSOAL ... Computer Method of Sequencing Operations for Assembly Lines (MCD)
COM-STAT ... Computer Stock Timing and Analysis Technique
COM-STEP ... Computerized Spot Television Evaluation and Processing [*Advertising*]
COMSYS .... Communication Systems Ltd. [*London, England*] [*Telecommunications*] (TSSD)
COMTEC .... Computer Micrographics Technology [*An association*] [*Northbrook, IL*] (EANO)

Computer & Telecommunications Acronyms

COMTEL ..... International Computer and Telecommunications Conference [*International Conference Management, Inc.*] [*Dallas, TX*] [*Telecommunications*] (TSSD)
COMTRAC ... Computer-Based Case Tracing [*Medicine*]
COMTRAN ... [*A*] programing language (CSR)
COMUSE .... Conference on Computers in Undergraduate Science Education
Con .... Contact [*A publication*]
CONCA .... Continue Calling Until (FAAC)
COND .... Condition (AFM)
COND .... Conductor (KSC)
CONDUIT .... Computers at Oregon State University, North Carolina Educational Computing Service, Dartmouth College, and the Universities of Iowa and Texas at Austin [*An educational consortium*]
CONECS ..... Connectorized Exchange Cable Splicing [*Telecommunications*] (TEL)
CONF .... Conference (AFM)
CONFG .... Configuration Process [*Telecommunications*] (TEL)
CONFIRM ... Conversational File Information Retrieval and Management System [*Data processing*] (MCD)
CONFLEX ... Conditioned Reflex [*Machine*] (IEEE)
CONG .... Congestion [*Telecommunications*] (TEL)
CONIO .... Console Input/Output (CAA)
CONIT .... Connector for Networked Information Transfer [*Massachusetts Institute of Technology*] [*Information service*] (EISS)
CONNIVER ... [*A*] programing language [*1973*] (CSR)
CO/NO .... Current Operator - Next Operator [*Data processing*] (MDG)
CONRAD .... Computerized National Range Documentation
CONS .... Carrier-Operated Noise Suppression
CONS .... Console [*Data processing*]
CONSAS ..... Constrado Structural Analysis System [*Structures & Computers Ltd.*] [*Software package*] [*British*] (NCC)
CONSIM ..... Console Simulator [*Data processing*]
CONSORT ... Conversational System with On-Line Remote Terminals [*Data processing*] (IEEE)
CONST .... Constant
CONSUL ..... Control Subroutine Language [*Data processing*] (IEEE)
CONT .... Control (MSA)
CONT .... Controller (KSC)
CONTB .... Continuous Beam [*Camutek*] [*Software package*] [*British*] (NCC)
CONTRAN ... Control Translator [*Honeywell, Inc.*] [*Data processing*]
CONTU .... National Commission on New Technological Uses of Copyrighted Works [*Terminated, 1978*] [*Library of Congress*]
CONV .... Conversion
CONV .... Converter (KSC)
CONVERT ... [*A*] programing language [*1965*] (CSR)
CON-VID ..... Concerned Broadcasters Using Inter-City Video Transmission Facilities (EANO)
COOL .... Checkout-Oriented Language [*Data processing*] (IEEE)
COOL .... Control-Oriented Language [*Data processing*] (IEEE)
COP .... Code of Practice [*Telecommunications*] (TEL)
COP .... Common On-Line Package [*Fujitsu Ltd.*] [*Japan*] (CAA)
COP .... Communication Output Printer (CAA)
COP .... Computer Optimization Package [*or Program*] [*General Electric Co.*]
COP .... Computermarkt [*A publication*]
COP .... Continuous Operation Program [*Data processing*] (MDG)
COP .... Crisis-Oriented Program (TUT)
COP .... Customer Order Processing (BUR)
COP .... Customer-Orienting Program (TUT)
COPAC .... Continuous Operation Production Allocation and Control [*Data processing*]
COPAR .... Computerized Operational Audit Routine
COPE .... Communications-Oriented Processing Equipment
COPE .... Console Operator Proficiency Examination [*Computer Usage Co.*] (CDH)
COPI .... Computer-Oriented Programed Instruction (IEEE)
COPIC .... Computer Information Center (MCD)
COPICS ...... Communications-Oriented Production Information and Control System [*IBM Corp.*]
COPR .... Computerized Outside Plant Records [*Telecommunications*] (TEL)
COPR .... Copyright (TEL)
COPS .... Circuit Order Preparation [*or Processing*] System [*AT & T*]
COPS .... Computer-Oriented Partial Sum (NVT)
COPS .... Customer Order Processing System (TUT)
COR .... Contracting Officer's Representative [*Telecommunications*] (TEL)
COR .... Corporate Source [*Online database field identifier*] (OBD)
CORA .... Conditioned Reflex Analog (IEEE)
CORAL .... Class-Oriented Ring-Associative Language [*Data processing*]
CORAL .... Comparison of Recognition Algorithms [*US Postal Service*]
CORAL .... Computer On-Line Real-Time Applications Language [*Data processing*] (IEEE)
CORC .... Cornell Computing Language [*Data processing*]
CORCOM .... Correcting Computer (MCD)
CORD .... Canadian On-Line Record Database
CORD .... Computer with On-Line Remote Devices [*National Bureau of Standards*]
CORDAT ..... Coordinate Data Set (CDH)
CORDIC ...... Coordinate Rotation Digital Computer
CORDS .... Coordination of Record and Data Base System [*Telecommunications*] (TEL)

CORE .... Computer-Oriented Reporting Efficiency (AFM)
CORE .... Computer Research [*NASDAQ symbol*] (NQ)
COREDITOR ... Computer Retrieval Editor [*Used to manage CORKIPER file family*]
CORELAP ... Computerized Relationship Layout Planning
CORESCEL ... Communications Requirements Systems Configuration and Equipment List (NVT)
CORIS .... Computerized Operating Room Information System
CORKIPER ... Computer Retrieval of Kinetic Parameters of Electrode Reactions
CORN .... Canadian Clearinghouse for Ongoing Research in Nursing [*University of Alberta*] [*Edmonton, AB*] (EISS)
CORODIM ... Correlation of the Recognition of Degradation with Intelligibility Measurements [*Telecommunications*] (TEL)
CORPS .... Customs Optical Reader Passport Systems [*A scanning device capable of reading the latest US passports*]
CORRAL ..... Computer-Oriented Retrieval of Auto Larcenists
CORREGATE ... Correctable Gate [*Data processing*] (MDG)
CORS .... Canadian Operational Research Society
CORSA .... Cosmic Ray Satellite [*Japan*]
CORSAIR .... Computer-Oriented Reference System for Automatic Information Retrieval [*Forsvarets Forskningsamsalt*] [*Swedish*]
CORTEX ...... Communications-Oriented Real-Time Executive (OA)
CORTEX ...... Computer-Based Optimization Routines and Techniques for Effective X (DIT)
COS .... Cassette-Operated System (MSA)
COS .... Change of Subscribers [*Telecommunications*] (TEL)
COS .... Class of Service [*Telecommunications*] (TEL)
COS .... Communications Operating System (CAA)
COS .... Communications Oriented Software (CAA)
COS .... Compatibility Operating System [*Data processing*] (CGC)
COS .... Concurrent Operating System [*Sperry UNIVAC*] [*Data processing*] (IEEE)
COS .... Customer's Other Service [*Telecommunications*] (TEL)
COSAM ...... COBOL Shared Access Method [*Pertec*] (CAA)
COSAM ...... Cosite Analysis Model [*Data processing*]
COSATI ...... Committee on Scientific and Technical Information [*Defunct*] [*Federal Council for Science and Technology*]
COSBA .... Computer Service and Bureaux Association [*British*] (OA)
COSCL .... Common Operating System Control Language (CAA)
COSH .... Cosine, Hyperbolic
COSHI .... Clearinghouse for Occupational Safety and Health Information [*Cincinnati, OH*] [*HEW*] (EISS)
COSIE .... Commission on Software Issues in the 80s (EANO)
COSMIC ..... Common Systems Main Interconnecting [*Frame system*] [*Bell System*]
COSMIC ..... Computer Software Management and Information Center [*University of Georgia*] [*NASA*] [*Research center*] (RCD)
COSMIS ..... Computer System for Medical Information Services (DIT)
COS/MOS ... Complementary Symmetry/Metal Oxide Semiconductor
COSMOS .... Computer-Oriented System for Management Order Synthesis [*IBM Corp.*] (BUR)
COSMOS .... Computer System for Main Frame Operations [*Bell System*]
COSMOS .... Console-Oriented Statistical Matrix Operator System [*Data processing*]
COSNOSTRA ... Computer-Oriented System - Newly Organized Storage-to-Retrieval Apparatus (KSC)
COSOS .... Conference on Self-Operating Systems [*Data processing*]
COSP .... Central Office Signaling Panel [*Telecommunications*] (TEL)
COSSTA ...... Computer for Special Small Tactical Application
COST .... Coalition Opposed to Signal Theft (EANO)
COST .... Committee on Office Systems and Technology [*Stanford University*] [*Stanford, CA*]
COST .... Computer Optimized Sheetmetal Technology [*Raytheon Co.*]
COSTAR ..... Computer-Stored Ambulatory Record (MCD)
CO-STAR .... Covert Submarine Transmitter and Receiver (MCD)
COSTI .... National Center of Scientific and Technological Information [*National Council for Research and Development*] [*Tel Aviv, Israel*] [*Also, CSTI*] (EISS)
COSY .... Compiler System (OA)
COSY .... Compressed Symbolic [*Programing language*] [*Control Data Corp.*]
COSY .... Correction System (OA)
COT .... Central Office Terminal [*Telecommunications*] (TEL)
COT .... Continuity [*Telecommunications*] (TEL)
COT .... Customer-Operated Terminal [*Data processing*]
COT .... Customer-Oriented Terminal [*Data processing*] (CAA)
COTA .... Confirming Telephone [*or message*] Authority Of
COTC .... Canadian Overseas Telecommunications Corporation
COTM .... Customer Owned and Telephone Company Maintained [*Telecommunications*] (TEL)
COTRAN ..... COBOL-to-COBOL Translator (IEEE)
COUNT .... Computer-Operated Universal Test
COUPLE ...... Communications-Oriented User Programing Language (CAA)
COURSEWRITER ... [*A*] programing language [*1965*] (CSR)
CP .... Calendar Process [*Telecommunications*] (TEL)
CP .... Call Paid [*Telecommunications*]
CP .... Card Punch [*Data processing*] (BUR)
CP .... Central Processor [*Data processing*] (CGC)
CP .... Character Printer [*Data processing*]
CP .... Clock Pulse
CP .... Command Processor [*Data processing*] (BUR)
CP .... Common Process [*Telecommunications*] (TEL)

Computer & Telecommunications Acronyms

CP	Communications Processor
CP	Computer Paragraph
CP	Connection Pending [*Telecommunications*] (TEL)
CP	Connection Point [*Data processing*] (IBMDP)
CP	Console Processor (NASA)
CP	Construction Permit [*Broadcasting term*]
CP	Control Processor (IEEE)
CP	Control Program [*Data processing*]
C/P	Converter/Programer (MCD)
CP	Corrosion Protection [*Telecommunications*] (TEL)
CP	Customized Processor [*IBM Corp.*] (IEEE)
CP	General Call to Two or More Specified Stations [*Telecommunications*] (FAAC)
CP	Station Open to Public Correspondence [*ITU designation*]
CPA	Carry Propagate Adder [*Computer*]
CPA	Computer Performance Analysis [*Boole & Babbage, Inc.*] (CAA)
CPA	Computer Press Association [*Homewood, IL*] (EANO)
CPA	Control Program Assist [*IBM Corp.*] (CAA)
CPA	Copolar Attenuation [*Telecommunications*] (TEL)
CPA	Cross Program Auditor [*Applied Data Research, Inc.*] (CAA)
CPAC	Center for Process Analytical Chemistry [*University of Washington*] [*Research center*] (RCD)
CPAC	Computer Program Associated Contractor
CPAS	Construction Program Administration System [*Telecommunications*] (TEL)
CPAWS	Computer-Planning and Aircraft-Weighing Scales
CPB	Channel Program Block [*Data processing*]
CPB	Computer Program Book
CPBX	Computerized Private Branch Exchange [*Telecommunications*]
CPC	Calling Party's Category [*Telecommunications*] (TEL)
CPC	Card Programed Calculator [*Early IBM machine - late 1940's*] [*Data processing*]
CPC	Carolina Population Center [*University of North Carolina*] [*Research center*] (EISS)
CPC	Channel Program Commands (OA)
CPC	Clock Pulsed Control
CPC	Communication Planning Corporation [*Jacksonville, FL*] [*Telecommunications*] (TSSD)
CPC	Communications Processing Center (CET)
CPC	Computer Power Center (DEEC)
CPC	Computer Print Console
CPC	Computer Process Control
CPC	Computer Program Components (MCD)
CPC	Computer Programing Concepts (BUR)
CPC	Continuous Process Control [*Design Software Ltd.*] [*Software package*] [*British*] (NCC)
CPC	Current Papers on Computers and Control [*A publication*]
CPC	Cycle Program Control (MCD)
CPC	Cycle Program Counter (IEEE)
CPCC	Communications Processor Conversion Center (CIT)
CPCEI	Computer Program Contract End Item
CPCH	Calling Party Cannot Hear [*Telecommunications*] (TEL)
CPCI	Ciprico, Incorporated [*NASDAQ symbol*] (NQ)
CPCI	Computer Program Configured Item (MCD)
CPCI	CPU Power Calibration Instrument (CAA)
CPCR	Computer Program Change Request (NASA)
CPCS	Check Processing Control System [*IBM Corp.*] (BUR)
CPCUG	Capital PC [*Personal Computer*] User Group [*Gaithersburg, MD*] (EANO)
CPD	Cards per Day [*Data processing*] (BUR)
CPD	Central Pulse Distributor [*Telecommunications*] (TEL)
CPD	Charge Priming Device
CPDAMS	Computer Program Development and Management System (CAA)
CPDT	Centre de Preparation Documentaire a la Traduction [*Center for Translation Documentation*] [*France*] [*Information service*] (EISS)
CPE	Central Processing Element [*Data processing*]
CPE	Central Programer and Evaluator
CPE	Computer Performance Evaluation
CPE	Computer Peripheral Equipment (KSC)
CPE	Customer Premises Equipment [*Telecommunications*]
CPE	Customer Provided Equipment [*Telecommunications*]
CPEI	Computer Program End Item (NASA)
CPEUG	Computer Performance Evaluation Users Group [*National Bureau of Standards*] [*Gaithersburg, MD*]
CPF	Control Program Facility (MCD)
CPFA	Custom Packages for Automation [*3D Digital Design & Development Ltd.*] [*Software package*] [*British*] (NCC)
CPFMS	COMRADE [*Computer-Aided Design Environment*] Permanent File Management System (OA)
CPFR	Calling Party Forced Release [*Telecommunications*] (TEL)
CPFSK	Continuous Phase Frequency Shift Keying (CAA)
CPFT	Customer-Premises Facility Terminal [*Telecommunications*] (TEL)
CPG	Clock Pulse Generator
CPG	Communications Publishing Group, Inc. [*Boston, MA*] [*Information service*] [*Telecommunications*] (TSSD)
CPH	Cards per Hour [*Data processing*]
CPH	Characters per Hour [*Data processing*]
CPHCC	Computers and the Humanities [*Database*] [*A publication*]
CPI	Cable Pair Identification [*Telecommunications*] (TEL)
CPI	California Computer Products, Incorporated [*American Stock Exchange symbol*] [*Delisted*]
CPI	Call Progress Indicator [*Telecommunications*] (TEL)
CPI	Canadian Periodical Index [*Canadian Library Association*] [*Ottawa, ON*] [*Information service*] (EISS)
CPI	Capital Planning Information Ltd. [*British*] [*Information service*] (EISS)
CPI	Center of Programed Instruction (DIT)
CPI	Characters per Inch [*Typesetting*]
CPI	Coherent Processing Interval [*Data processing*]
CPI	Computer-Prescribed Instruction (IEEE)
CPI	Computer Projects, Incorporated [*Greensboro, NC*] [*Telecommunications*] (TSSD)
CPI	Consumer Price Index [*Department of Labor*] [*Database*]
CPI	Cost per Instruction [*Data processing*]
CPIC	Computer Program Integration Contractor
CPIC	CPI Corporation [*NASDAQ symbol*] (NQ)
CPIN	Computer Program Identification Number (MCD)
CPIP	Computer Pneumatic Input Panel
CPIP	Computer Program Implementation Process
CPI/PPI	Consumer and Producer Price Indexes [*Department of Labor*] [*Database*] (CUAD)
CPL	Capability Password Level [*Telecommunications*] (TEL)
CPL	CAST [*Computerized Automatic System Tester*] Programing Language (OA)
CPL	Combined Programing Language [*Data processing*]
CPL	Common Program Language [*Data processing*]
CPL	Computer Program Library (BUR)
CPL	Computer Projects Limited (OA)
CPL	Conversational Programing Language [*High-level language*] [*Digital Equipment Corp.*] [*Data processing*]
CPM	Call Protocol Message [*Telecommunications*] (TEL)
CPM	Cards per Minute [*Data processing*]
CPM	Central Path Method [*Data processing*]
CPM	Central Processing Modules [*Data processing*] (MCD)
CPM	Characters per Minute [*Data processing*]
CPM	Computer Performance Management (CAA)
CPM	Computer Program Module (NASA)
CP/M	Control Program for Microcomputers [*Operating system*]
CP/M	Control Program/Monitor [*Data processing*]
CPM	Conversational Program Module [*Fujitsu Ltd.*] [*Japan*] (CAA)
CPM	Critical Path Method [*Graph theory*] [*Telecommunications*] (TEL)
CPM	Current Processor Mode
CPMA	Central Processor Memory Address (CAA)
CPMA	Computer Peripheral Manufacturers Association
CPMS	Cable Pressure Monitoring System [*Bell System*]
CPNS	CP National Network Services [*Concord, CA*] [*Telecommunications*] (TSSD)
CPO	Concurrent Peripheral Operations (BUR)
CPODA	Contention Priority-Oriented Demand Assignment [*Protocol*] [*Data processing*]
CPOL	Communications Procedure-Oriented Language [*Data processing*]
CPP	Card Punching Printer [*Computer output device*] [*Data processing*] (BUR)
CPP	Central Processing Point [*Data processing*]
CPP	Computer Program Package (CAAL)
CPP	Conductive Plastic Potentiometer
CPPI	Computer Peripheral Products [*NASDAQ symbol*] (NQ)
CPPI	Consultative Panel on Public Information [*United Nations*] [*Telecommunications*] (TEL)
CPPS	Computer Programing Performance Specification (MCD)
CP/R	Card Punch and Reader [*Data processing*] (CAA)
CPR	Career Placement Registry, Inc. [*Database producer*] [*Alexandria, VA*] [*Information service*] (EISS)
CPR	Computerized Performance Rating [*of a horse*]
CPR	Continuous Progress Indicator [*Telecommunications*] (TEL)
CP-R	Control Program - Real-Time [*Xerox Corp.*] (CAA)
CPRD	Computer Products [*NASDAQ symbol*] (NQ)
CPRG	Computer Personnel Research Group [*Later, Special Interest Group for Computer Personnel Research*]
CPR Proc	Computer Personnel Research Proceedings [*A publication*]
CPRS	Centralized Personnel Record System [*Telecommunications*] (TEL)
CPS	Calling Processing Subsystem [*Telecommunications*] (TEL)
CPS	Card Programing System (CMD)
CPS	Cards per Second [*Data processing*]
CPS	Central Processing System [*Data processing*]
CPS	Characters per Second [*Data processing*] (CGC)
CPS	Circuit Provision System [*AT & T*]
CPS	Communications Processing System (CIT)
CPS	Computer Power Supply
CPS	Computer Program Specification (AFM)
CPS	Computer Programing Service
CPS	Control Programs Support (IEEE)
CPS	Conversational Programing System [*Data processing*]
CPS	Customer Premises System [*Bell System*]
CPS	Cycles per Second [*See also Hz*]
CPSK	Coherent Phase Shift Keyed [*System*] [*Data processing*]
CPSM	Critical Path Scheduling Method [*Management*] (OA)
CPSR	Computer Professionals for Social Responsibility (EANO)
CPSR	Central Processing Subsystem [*Data processing*]
CPSS	Common Program Support System (CGC)

Computer & Telecommunications Acronyms

CPSS	Computer Power Support System (CAA)
CPSU	Central Processor Subunit [*Data processing*]
CPT	Computer Program Tapes (MCD)
CPTA	Computer Programing and Testing Activity (IEEE)
CPTC	Central Processor Test Console [*Data processing*]
CPTC	CPT Corporation [*NASDAQ symbol*] (NQ)
CPTD	Computer Data Systems, Inc. [*NASDAQ symbol*] (NQ)
CPT & E	Computer Program Test and Evaluation (CAA)
CPTPL	Computer Program Test Plan (CAAL)
CPTPR	Computer Program Test Procedures (CAAL)
CPU	Central Processing Unit [*Data processing*]
CPU	Communications Processing Unit (CET)
CPU	Communications Processor Utility [*Telecommunications*] (TEL)
CPU	Compugraphic Corp. [*NYSE symbol*]
CPU	Computer Peripheral Unit (IEEE)
CPU	Computer Printer Unit (MCD)
CPU	Computer Process Utility, Inc. [*Muskegon, MI*] [*Software manufacturer*] (DASOS)
CPU	Computer Processor Unit (OA)
CPU	Computer Program Update (TUT)
CPU	Control Processing Unit (OA)
CPU	ME Compu Software, Inc. [*Vancouver Stock Exchange symbol*]
CP-V	Control Program-Five [*Operating system*] [*Xerox Corp.*] (CAA)
CPW	Coplanar Waveguide
CPY	Copy (BUR)
CQ	Communications Satellite Corp. [*See also COMSAT*] [*NYSE symbol*]
CQMS	Circuit Quality Monitoring System
CQT	Correct [*British*] (CDH)
CR	Canadian Restricted [*Broadcasting term*]
CR	Card Reader [*Data processing*] (NVT)
CR	Carriage Return [*Keyboard*]
CR	Cited Reference [*Online database field identifier*] (OBD)
CR	Clear Record [*Telecommunications*] (TEL)
CR	Command Register
CR	Communication Representative
CR	Communication Resources [*Haddonfield, NJ*] [*Telecommunications*] (TSSD)
CR	Communications Register (OA)
CR	Computing Reviews [*A publication*]
CR	Control Routine (OA)
CR	Count Reverse [*Data processing*]
CR	Customer's Report [*Telecommunications*] (TEL)
CRA	Catalog Recovery Area [*Data processing*]
CRA	Charles River Associates, Inc. [*Boston, MA*] [*Telecommunications*] (TSSD)
CRAB	Communications Research Advisory Board [*Canada*]
CRAFT	Computerized Relative Allocation of Facilities Technique [*IBM Corp.*]
CRAGS	Chemistry Records and Grading System [*Data processing*]
CRAM	Card Random-Access Memory [*NCR Corp.*] [*Data processing*]
CRAM	Computerized Reliability Analysis Method
CRAM	CONRAIL [*Consolidated Rail Corp.*] Analysis Model [*Data processing*]
CRAM	Core and Random Access Manager [*General Automation, Inc.*] (CAA)
CRAR	Control ROM [*Read-Only Memory*] Address Register [*Data processing*] (CAA)
CRAS	Coder and Random Access Switch
CRATT	Covered Radio Teletype (NVT)
CRATTZ	Communication Radio and Teletype (Secure) System
CRAZI	Count Routine Applied to Zero Input [*Computer program*]
CRB	Customer Records and Billing [*Bell System*]
CRBE	Conversational Remote Batch Entry [*Data processing*]
CRBO	Centralized Records Business Office [*Telecommunications*] (TEL)
CRC	Cable Communications Resource Center (EANO)
CRC	Communication Research Center [*Florida State University*] [*Research center*] (RCD)
CRC	Communication Research Center [*University of Florida*] [*Research center*] (RCD)
CRC	Communication Research Center [*Boston University*] [*Research center*] (RCD)
CRC	Communications Regulatory Commission (CAA)
CRC	Communications Research Center [*University of Tennessee at Knoxville*] [*Research center*] (RCD)
CRC	Communications Research Centre [*Defunct*] [*Canada*]
CRC	Computer Response Corporation
CRC	Cyclic Redundancy Check [*Data processing*]
CRCC	Cyclic Redundancy Check Character [*Data processing*] (IEEE)
CRCS	Centre de Recherches sur les Communications [*Sherbrooke University*] [*Canada*] [*Research center*] (RCD)
CRCS	CR [*Christian Rovsing*] Computer Systems, Inc. [*Los Angeles, CA*] [*Telecommunications*] (TSSD)
CRCT	Center for Research in Computing Technology [*Harvard University*] [*Research center*] (RCD)
CRD	Card Reader [*Data processing*] (OA)
CRDS	Chemical Reactions Documentation Service [*Derwent Publications Ltd.*] [*Bibliographic database*] [*England*]
CRE	Communications Research Establishment (NATG)
Creatv Comp	Creative Computing [*A publication*]
CRECORD	Congressional Record On-Line [*Capitol Services, Inc.*] [*Washington, DC*] [*Bibliographic database*]
CREF	Cross Reference (AFM)
CREG	Concentrated Range Extension with Gain [*Telecommunications*] (TEL)
CRESS	Computerized Reader Enquiry Service System (IEEE)
CRESTS	Courtauld's Rapid Extract, Sort, and Tabulate System (IEEE)
CRF	Carrier Frequency Telephone Repeater [*Telecommunications*] (CDH)
CRF	Current Research File [*NIOSH*] [*Database*] (FDB)
CRFT	Computer Craft, Inc. [*NASDAQ symbol*] (NQ)
CRFW	Catalyst Resources for Women [*New York, NY*] [*Bibliographic database*]
CRGS	Chemical Regulations and Guidelines System [*CRC Systems, Inc.*] [*Fairfax, VA*] [*Information service*] (EISS)
CRI	Communications Research Institute (MCD)
CRI	Cray Research, Incorporated (CAA)
CRIB	Computerized Resources Information Bank [*United States Geological Survey*] (EISS)
CRID	Centro di Riferimento Italiano DIANE [*Italian Reference Center for EURONET DIANE*] [*Information service*] (EISS)
CRII	Computer Resources [*NASDAQ symbol*] (NQ)
CRIM	Center for Research [*formerly, Robotics*] in Integrated Manufacturing [*University of Michigan*] [*Research center*] (RCD)
CRINC	University of Kansas Center for Research, Incorporated [*Research center*] (RCD)
CRIS	Combined Retrospective Index Sets [*Carrollton Press, Inc.*] [*Information service*] (EISS)
CRIS	Command Retrieval Information System
CRIS	Computerized Recall Identification System [*Automobile industry*]
CRIS	Corporate Research Information Service [*Frederick Research*]
CRIS	Current Research Information System [*Department of Agriculture*] [*Washington, DC*] [*Database*]
CRISP	Computer Retrieval of Information on Scientific Projects (EISS)
CRIT	Critical [*Telecommunications*] (TEL)
CRJE	Conversational Remote Job Entry [*Data processing*]
CRL	Centre for Research in Librarianship [*University of Toronto*] [*Research center*] (RCD)
CRL	Communications Research Laboratory [*McMaster University*] [*Canada*] [*Research center*] (RCD)
CRL	Computing Research Laboratory [*New Mexico State University*] [*Research center*] (RCD)
CR/LF	Carriage Return/Line Feed
CRLT	Center for Research on Learning and Teaching [*University of Michigan*] [*Research center*] (RCD)
CRM	Communications/Research/Machines, Inc. [*Publisher*]
CRM	Control and Reproducibility Monitor (IEEE)
CRMK	Cermetek Microelectronics [*NASDAQ symbol*] (NQ)
CRNL	Chalk River Nuclear Laboratories [*Atomic Energy of Canada Ltd.*] [*Information service*] [*Research center*] (EISS)
CRO	Cathode-Ray Oscilloscope [*or Oscillograph*]
CRO	Central Radio Office [*Telecommunications*] (TEL)
CRO	Complete with Related Order [*Telecommunications*] (TEL)
CRO	Continuous Receiver On [*Electronic device*]
CROC	Computer Review and Orientation Course
CROM	Capacitive Read-Only Memory [*Data processing*] (IEEE)
CROM	Control Read-Only Memory [*Data processing*]
CROS	Capacitor Read-Only Storage [*Data processing*] (CAA)
CROS	Computerized Reliability Organization System
CROS	Contralateral Routing of Signal [*Audiometry*]
CROSS	Computerized Rearrangements of Special Subjects [*or Subject Specialties*]
CROSSBOW	Computer Retrieval of Organic Structures Based on Wiswesser
CROSSPATE	Coordinative Retrieval of Selectively Sorted Permuted Analogue-Title Entries [*Data processing*]
CROSSTABS	[*A*] programing language (CSR)
CRP	Card Reader/Punch [*Data processing*] (CAA)
CRP	Chopp Computer Corp. [*Vancouver Stock Exchange symbol*]
CRP	Command Read Pulse (KSC)
CRP	Computer Reset Pulse (KSC)
CRQ	Call Request [*Telecommunications*] (TEL)
CRQ	Console Reply Queuing (CAA)
CRR	Computer Run Report (NASA)
CRRERIS	Commonwealth Regional Renewable Energy Resources Information System (EISS)
CRS	Centralized Results System [*Telecommunications*] (TEL)
CRS	Computerized Retrieval Service
CRSA	Centralized Repair Service Attendants [*Telecommunications*] (TEL)
CRSC	Center for Research in Scientific Communication [*Johns Hopkins University*] (EISS)
CRSM	Center for Robotic Systems in Microelectronics [*University of California, Santa Barbara*] [*Research center*] (RCD)
CRSP	Center for Research in Security Prices [*University of Chicago*] [*Information service*] (EISS)
CRT	Cathode-Ray Tube
CRT	Cathode-Ray Typesetting
CRT	Continuous Ring Tone [*Telecommunications*] (TEL)
CRTC	Canadian Radio and Telecommunications Commission [*Conseil de la Radiodiffusion et des Telecommunications Canadiennes*] [*Ottawa, ON*] [*Telecommunications*]
CRTC	Cathode-Ray Tube Controller (CAA)

Computer & Telecommunications Acronyms

CRTU	Combined Receiving and Transmitting Unit
CRU	Card Reader Unit [*Data processing*] (CAA)
CRU	Commodities Research Unit Ltd. [*Originator and Databank*] [*Information service*] [*British*] (EISS)
CRU	Computer Resource Unit (CGC)
CRV	Contact Resistance Variation [*Telecommunications*] (TEL)
CRVR	Computerized Register of Voice Research [*Southern Illinois University at Carbondale*] [*Information service*] (EISS)
CRVS	Corvus Systems, Inc. [*NASDAQ symbol*] (NQ)
CRW	Carrier Wave [*A form of radio transmission in code*] (KSC)
CRYPTONET	Crypto-Communication Network (MDG)
CRYSNET	Crystallographic Computing Network [*AEC*] (EISS)
CS	Call Sign [*or Signal*] [*Radio*]
CS	Call Store [*Telecommunications*] (TEL)
CS	Calls per Second [*Telecommunications*] (TEL)
CS	Card Station [*Data processing*] (BUR)
CS	Chip Select [*Input*] [*Data processing*]
CS	Class of Service [*Telecommunications*] (TEL)
CS	Clear and Subtract
CS	Code Segment [*Data processing*]
CS	Coding Specification (CAH)
CS	Commercial System [*Data General Corp.*] (CAA)
CS	Communication Station
CS	Communications Satellite [*Japan*] (CBSS)
CS	Communications Simulator [*Sperry UNIVAC*] (CAA)
CS	Communications Switcher (CIT)
CS	Communications System
CS	Computer Science (BUR)
CS	Computer Simulation (RDA)
CS	Computers and Standards [*A publication*]
CS	Computers and Systems (MCD)
C & S	Computers and Systems (IEEE)
CS	Conducted Susceptibility (IEEE)
CS	Congressional Session [*Online database field identifier*] (OBD)
CS	Continue-Specific [*Mode*] [*Data processing*] (IBMDP)
CS	Control Store (CAA)
CS	Corporate Source [*Online database field identifier*]
CS	Currency Sign [*Telecommunications*] (TEL)
CS	Customer Service (BUR)
CS	Customer Support (BUR)
CSA	Called Subscriber Answer [*Telecommunications*] (TEL)
CSA	Cambridge Scientific Abstracts [*Bethesda, MD*] [*Information service*] (EISS)
CSA	Canadian Standards Association
CSA	Character Scan or Alternate [*Data processing*] (CIT)
CSA	Commercial Service Authorization [*Telecommunications*] (TEL)
CSA	Common Service Area [*Data processing*] (BUR)
CSA	Computer Services Association [*British*]
CSA	Computer System Analyst (BUR)
CSA	Computer Systems Association (CAH)
CSA	Conical Scan Antenna
CSACCS	Customer Service Administration Control Center System [*Telecommunications*] (TEL)
CSACS	Centralized Status, Alarm, and Control System [*Bell System*]
CSAM	Circular Sequential Access Memory (CAA)
CSAR	Communications Satellite Advanced Research [*AFSC*]
CSAR	Control Store Address Register (CAA)
CSB	Communication Scanner Base (IBMDP)
CSB	Computer Support Base
CSC	Central Switching Center [*Telecommunications*] (TEL)
CSC	Centralized Supervisory and Control (BUR)
CSC	Circuit Switching Center [*Telecommunications*] (TEL)
CSC	Common Signaling Channel (IEEE)
CSC	Communications Satellite Corp. [*See also COMSAT*]
CSC	Communications Switchboard Console
CSC	Communications Systems Center
CSC	Comprehensive Self-Check [*Computer*]
CSC	Computer Science Center [*North Carolina A & T State University*] [*Research center*] (RCD)
CSC	Computer Science Center [*University of Maryland*] [*Research center*] (RCD)
CSC	Computer Sciences Corporation [*El Segundo, CA*] [*Database originator*] [*NYSE symbol*]
CSC	Computer Search Center [*Illinois Institute of Technology Research Center*] [*Chicago, IL*]
CSC	Computer Service Center
CSC	Computer Set Control (CAAL)
CSC	Computer Society of Canada (CAH)
CSC	Computer Subsystem Controller
CSC	Computing Services Center [*Texas A & M University*] [*Research center*] (RCD)
CSC	Construction Scheduling and Coordination [*AT & T*]
CSCB	Command Scheduling Control Block [*Data processing*] (BUR)
CSCC	Communications System Control Console (SKY)
CSCD	Character Set Computer Development
CSCE	Communication System Control Element [*of TCCF*] (MCD)
CSCN	Character Scan Command [*Data processing*]
CSCSAT	Commercial Synchronous Communication Satellite (NASA)
CSD	Circuit Switched Data (CAA)
CSD	Committee on Statistics of Drilling [*American Association of Petroleum Geologists*] (EISS)
CSD	Computer Science Division (CAH)
CSD	Computer Services Division [*University of South Carolina at Columbia*] [*Research center*] (RCD)
CSD	Computer Systems Development Ltd. [*London, England*] [*Software supplier*] (NCC)
CSD	Computer Systems Director (KSC)
CSD	Computing Services Division [*Seton Hall University*] [*Research center*] (RCD)
CSDC	Circuit Switched Digital Capability [*AT & T*]
CSDM	Continuous Slope Delta Modulation [*Telecommunications*] (CAA)
CSDP	Center for the Study of Data Processing [*Washington University*] [*Research center*] (RCD)
CSDR	Control Store Data Register (CAA)
CSDS	Communication Signal Distribution System
CSDT	Computer Software Data Tapes (MCD)
CSE	Cold Start Entry [*Data processing*]
CSE	Communications Satellite for Experimental Purposes [*Japanese*] [*Telecommunications*] (TEL)
CSE	Communications Systems Engineer (KSC)
CSE	Computer Science and Engineering
CSE	Computer Support Equipment (MCD)
CSEC	Computer Security Evaluation Center
CSEE	Canadian Society for Electrical Engineers (MCD)
CSEEB	Communications Security Equipment Engineering Bulletin (MCD)
CSEP	Communications Security Education Program (AFM)
CSERB	Computer Systems and Electronics Requirements Board [*British*] (CAA)
CSESAS	Center for State Employment Security Automated Systems
CSF	Central Switching Facility
CSF	Character Scan or Fail [*Data processing*] (CIT)
CSG	Canada Systems Group [*Database producer*] [*Information service*]
CSG	Capital Systems Group, Inc. [*Kensington, MD*] [*Information service*] (EISS)
CSH	Cableshare, Inc. [*Toronto Stock Exchange symbol*]
CSH	Called Subscriber Held [*Telecommunications*] (TEL)
CSHP	CompuShop, Inc. [*NASDAQ symbol*] (NQ)
CSHVB	Computer Studies in the Humanities and Verbal Behavior [*A publication*]
CSI	Capitol Services, Incorporated [*Bethesda, MD*] [*Database producer*] [*Information service*] (EISS)
CSI	Command String Interpreter [*Digital Equipment Corp.*] (CAA)
CSI	Commodity Systems, Incorporated [*Information service*] (EISS)
CSI	Communications Solutions, Incorporated [*San Jose, CA*] [*Information service*] [*Telecommunications*] (TSSD)
CSI	Communications Systems, Incorporated
CSI	Computer Search International Corp. [*Database producer*] (CUAD)
CSI	Computer Security Institute [*Northboro, MA*] (EANO)
CSI	Computer Systems International (OA)
CSI	Crew Software Interface (MCD)
CSIC	Computer Stock Inventory Control (MCD)
CSIC	Computer System Interface Circuits (IEEE)
CSIE	Center for the Study of Information and Education [*Syracuse University*] (EISS)
CSII	Communications Systems [*NASDAQ symbol*] (NQ)
CSIN	Chemical Substances Information Network [*Federal Interagency Toxic Substances Data Committee*] [*Information service*]
CS:IP	Code Segment:Instruction Pointer [*Data processing*]
CSIR	Computer Systems Integration Review (NASA)
CSIRO Computing Res Sect Memo	CSIRO [*Commonwealth Scientific and Industrial Research Organisation*] Computing Research Section. Memorandum [*A publication*]
CSIRO Div Appl Geomech Prog Circ	Computer Program Users Manual CSIRO [*Commonwealth Scientific and Industrial Research Organisation. Division of Applied Geomechanics*] [*A publication*]
CSK	Cable Splicing Kit
CSKKY	Computer Service Corp. ADR [*NASDAQ symbol*] (NQ)
CSL	Code Selection Language [*Data processing*] (BUR)
CSL	Communication Sciences Laboratory [*University of Florida*]
CSL	Communication Services Limited [*Hong Kong*] [*Telecommunications*] (TSSD)
CSL	Computer Sensitive Language [*Programing language*]
CSL	Computer Simulation Language (BUR)
CSL	Computer Status Lights (MCD)
CSL	Computer Structure Language [*1974*] [*Data processing*] (CSR)
CSL	Computer System Language
CSL	Control and Simulation Language [*Data processing*]
CSL	Control and Status Logic (KSC)
CSL	Coordinated Science Laboratory [*University of Illinois*] [*Research center*]
CSL	Current Switch Logic (IEEE)
CSLB	Computer Services - Long Beach (MCD)
CSLI	Center for the Study of Language & Information [*Stanford University*] [*Research center*] (RCD)
CSM	Call Supervision Module [*Telecommunications*] (TEL)
CSM	Computer Status Matrix (MCD)
CSM	Computer System Manual
CSM	Continuous Sheet Memory [*Data processing*] (BUR)
CSMA	Carrier Sense Multiple Access (DEEC)
CSMA	Communications Systems Management Association (MCD)

Computer & Telecommunications Acronyms

CSMA/CD	Carrier Sense Multiple Access with Collision Detection [*Data processing*]
CSMP	Continuous System Modeling Program [*Data processing*]
CSMPS	Computerized Scientific Management Planning System
CSN	Circuit Switching Network
CSN	Common Services Network [*Telecommunications*] (TEL)
CSN	Computer Sequence Number
CSO	Centralized Service Observation [*Telecommunications*] (TEL)
CSOS	Communications Switch Operating System (MCD)
CSP	Center for Space Policy, Inc. [*Cambridge, MA*] [*Telecommunications*] (TSSD)
CSP	Central Signal Processor
CSP	Coder Sequential Pulse
CSP	Coherent Signal Processor
CSP	Commercial Subroutine Package [*IBM Corp.*] (BUR)
CSP	Communications Security Publication
C/SP	Communications/Symbiont Processor [*Sperry UNIVAC*] (CAA)
CSP	Computer Simulation Program
CSP	Control Signal Processor [*for spacecraft*]
CSP	Control Switching Point (BUR)
C-SPAN	Cable Satellite Public Affairs Network [*Cable-television system*]
CSPC	Communication Satellite Planning Center [*Stanford University*] [*Research center*] (RCD)
CSPO	Communications Satellite Project Office
CSR	Center for Space Research [*Massachusetts Institute of Technology*] [*Research center*] (RCD)
CSR	Center for Space Research and Applications [*University of Texas at Austin*] [*Research center*] (RCD)
CSR	Coaxial Single-Pole Relay
CSR	Common Services Rack [*Telecommunications*] (TEL)
CSR	Communications Satellite Relay (NG)
CSR	Control Status Register (CAA)
CSR	Customer Service Representative
CSRE	Comshare, Inc. [*NASDAQ symbol*] (NQ)
CSRI	Computer Systems Research Institute [*University of Toronto*] [*Research center*] (RCD)
CSRI	Customer Satisfaction Research Institute [*Lenexa, KS*] [*Telecommunications*] (TSSD)
CSRMP	Communications Sales Results Measurement Plan [*Telecommunications*] (TEL)
CSS	Caribbean Super Station
CSS	Center for the Social Sciences [*Columbia University*] [*Research center*] (RCD)
CSS	Character Start-Stop (CAA)
CSS	Character String Scanner [*Computer program*]
CSS	Circuit Switching Station (CET)
CSS	Cognitive Science Society (EANO)
CSS	College Selection Service [*Peterson's Guides*] [*Princeton, NJ*] [*Information service*] (EISS)
CSS	Commercial Satellite Systems [*Berkeley, CA*] [*Telecommunications*] (TSSD)
CSS	Common Services Subsystem [*Telecommunications*] (TEL)
CSS	Communications Security System (MCD)
CSS	Communications Subsystem
CSS	Computer Search Services
CSS	Computer Sharing Services, Inc. [*Information service*] (EISS)
CSS	Computer Subsystem (NASA)
CSS	Computer System Simulator [*Programing language*] [1969]
CSS	Computing Support Services [*California Institute of Technology*] [*Research center*] (RCD)
CSS	Control Signaling Subsystem [*Telecommunications*] (TEL)
CSS	Conversational Software System [*National CSS, Inc.*] (CAA)
CSS	Customer Switching System [*Telecommunications*] (TEL)
CSSD	Communications System Status Display (KSC)
CSSEC	Computer Systems Support and Evaluation Command
CSSER	Center for Solid State Electronics [*Arizona State University*] [*Research center*] (RCD)
CSSL	Continuous System Simulation Language [*Data processing*]
CSSP	Circuits, Systems, and Signal Processing [*A publication*]
CSST	Computer System Science Training [*IBM Corp.*]
CSSU	Converter Simulator Signal Unit (MCD)
CST	Carrier Power Supply, Transistorized [*Telecommunications*] (TEL)
CST	Channel Status Indicator [*Data processing*] (MDG)
CST	Code Segment Table (CAA)
CST	Communications Surveillance Transistor
CSTA	Crew Software Training Aid (MCD)
CSTD	Council on Science and Technology for Development (EANO)
CSTI	Committee on Scientific and Technical Information [*Defunct*] [*Federal Council for Science and Technology*] (IEEE)
CSTRC	COMSAT [*Communications Satellite Corp.*] Technical Review [*A publication*]
CSTS	Combined System Test Stand (IEEE)
CSTT	Core Storage Terminal Table [*Data processing*]
CSU	Central Switching Unit
CSU	Channel Service Unit [*Telecommunications*] (TEL)
CSU	Channel Synchronizer Unit [*Data processing*] (TUT)
CSU	Check Signal Unit [*Telecommunications*] (TEL)
CSU	Circuit Switching Unit (CET)
CSU	Common Services Unit [*Telecommunications*] (TEL)
CSU	Communications Switching Unit (CAAL)
CSU	Customer Set-Up [*Data processing*]
CSU	Customer Support Unit
CSV	Circuit Switched Voice [*Telecommunications*] (CAA)
CSW	Channel Status Word [*Data processing*] (BUR)
CSW	Computer Sports World [*Boulder City, NV*] [*Information service*] (EISS)
CSW	Computing & Software, Inc. [*NYSE symbol*] [*Delisted*]
C/T	Cable Transfer [*of funds*]
CT	Carrier Telephone Channel
CT	Cassette Tape (CAA)
CT	Certron Corp. [*American Stock Exchange symbol*] [*Delisted*]
CT	Circuit
CT	Coastal Telegraph Station [*ITU designation*] (CET)
CT	Code Telegram
C/T	Command Transmitter (KSC)
CT	Commercial Translator (IEEE)
CT	Communications Terminal [*Data processing*]
CT	Complete Translation [*Telecommunications*] (TEL)
CT	Computer Technology (IEEE)
CT	Computer Transponder (MCD)
CT	Connectivity Table [*Data processing*]
CT	Continuity Transceiver [*Telecommunications*] (TEL)
CT	Controlled Term [*Online database field identifier*] (OBD)
CT	Counter (CDH)
CT	Current Transformer
CT	Transit Switching Center [*Telecommunications*] (TEL)
CTA	Center for Technology and Administration [*American University*] [*Research center*] (RCD)
CTA	Circuit Terminating Arrangement
CTA	Computerized Travel Aid [*Mobility device for the blind*]
CTAK	Cipher Text Auto Key [*Data processing*]
CTAM	Cable Television Administration and Marketing Society (EANO)
CTB	Code Table Buffer (CAA)
CTB	Commonwealth Telecommunications Board [*British*] (DEN)
CTB	Computer Time Bookers (OA)
CTB	Concentrator Terminal Buffer [*Data processing*] (IBMDP)
CTBM	Chief Testboard Man [*Telecommunications*] (TEL)
CTC	Central Traffic Control
CTC	Channel to Channel (CAA)
CTC	Communication Training Consultants, Inc. [*New York, NY*] [*Telecommunications*] (TSSD)
CTC	Compaq Telecommunications Corporation [*Dallas, TX*]
CTC	Computer Technology Center
CTC	Conditional Transfer of Control (CAH)
CTC	Continental Telecom [*Formerly, Continental Telephone Corporation*] [*NYSE symbol*]
CTC	Counter/Timer Circuit [*Data processing*] (CAA)
CTC	Counter-Timer Controller
CTCA	Canadian Telecommunications Carriers Association
CTCA	Channel-to-Channel Adapter [*Data processing*] (IBMDP)
CTCCC	Close Type Control Circuit Contact (MSA)
CTCP	Clinical Toxicology of Commercial Products [*Dartmouth Medical School; University of Rochester*] [*Database*] [*A publication*]
C/T)d	Carrier-to-Noise Temperature, Downlink (CBSS)
CTD	Charge-Transfer Device [*Electronics*]
CTD	Continuity Tone Detector [*Telecommunications*] (TEL)
CTD	Control Data Corp. [*Toronto Stock Exchange symbol*]
CTDC	Control Track Direction Computer
CTDF	Community Telecommunications Development Foundation [*Washington, DC*] (TSSD)
CTDH	Command and Telemetry Data Handling (IEEE)
C/TDS	Count/Time Data System (IEEE)
CTE	Cable Termination Equipment (CET)
CTE	Center for Teaching Effectiveness [*University of Texas at Austin*] [*Research center*] (RCD)
CTE	Channel Translating Equipment [*Telecommunications*] (TEL)
CTE	Computer TELEX Exchange [*RCA Corp.*] (CAA)
CTEC	Communication Technical Evaluation Console (KSC)
CTELP	Central Telephone Pfd [*NASDAQ symbol*] (NQ)
CTF	Contrast Transfer Function
CTG	Communications Task Group [*CODASYL*] (CAA)
CTG	Comtech Group International Ltd. [*Toronto Stock Exchange symbol*]
CTHS	Comite des Travaux Historiques et Scientifiques [*Ministere de l'Education Nationale*] [*Database*] (CUAD)
CTI	Center for Telephone Information [*Laguna Hills, CA*] [*Telecommunications*] (TSSD)
CTI	Centralized Ticket Investigation [*Telecommunications*]
CTI	Computer Translation, Incorporated [*Information service*] (EISS)
CTIC	Cable Television Information Center
CTI Commun Technol Impact	CTI. Communication Technology Impact [*A publication*]
CTIF	Centre Technique des Industries de la Fonderie [*Database producer*] (CUAD)
CTII	Computrac Instruments [*NASDAQ symbol*] (NQ)
C/T)im	Carrier-to-Noise Temperature, Intermodulation (CBSS)
CT J Comput Tomography	CT. Journal of Computed Tomography [*A publication*]
CTL	CAGE [*Computerized Aerospace Ground Equipment*] Test Language [*Data processing*] (KSC)
CTL	Cassette Tape Loader (CAA)
CTL	Checkout Test Language [*Data processing*] (TUT)
CTL	Complementary Transistor Logic [*Data processing*]
CTL	Control
CTL	Core Transistor Logic [*Data processing*]

Computer & Telecommunications Acronyms

CTM .... Communications Technology Management, Inc. [*McLean, VA*] [*Telecommunications*] (TSSD)
CTM .... Communications Terminal Module [*Data processing*] (CGC)
CTM .... Complete Treatment Module [*Telecommunications*] (TEL)
CTM .... Configuration and Tuning Module [*Data processing*]
CTM .... Continuity Transceiver Module [*Telecommunications*] (TEL)
CTMC .... Communications Terminal Module Controller [*Data processing*] (CGC)
CTML .... Computer Terminal Systems [*NASDAQ symbol*] (NQ)
CTMS .... Carrier Transmission Maintenance System [*Bell System*]
CTN .... Cable Termination Network
CTN .... Canadian Teleconference Network, Inc. [*Toronto, ON*] [*Telecommunications*] (TSSD)
CTN .... Catholic Television Network [*Cable-television system*]
CT/N .... Counter, n Stages [*Electronics*] (DEN)
CTNA .... Catholic Telecommunications Network of America [*New York, NY*] (TSSD)
CTNE .... Compania Telefonica Nacional de Espana [*National Telephone Company of Spain*] [*Madrid*] [*Telecommunications*] (TSSD)
CTO .... Central Telegraph Office [*British*]
CTO .... Central Telephone Operator [*British*]
CTO .... Charge Transforming Operator (IEEE)
CTO .... Commonwealth Telecommunications Organization (CBSS)
CTO .... Cutoff [*Telecommunications*] (TEL)
CTOMD ..... Computerized Tomography [*A publication*]
CTON .... Computone Systems [*NASDAQ symbol*] (NQ)
CTOS .... Cassette Tape Operating System (IEEE)
CTP .... Charge Transforming Parameter (IEEE)
CTP .... Command Translator and Programer
CTP .... Communications Timing Procedure (NASA)
CTP .... Consolidated Telecommunications Program
CTR .... Carrier Telegraph Receiver
CTR .... Computer Tape Recorder
CTR .... COMSAT [*Communications Satellite Corp.*] Technical Review [*A publication*]
CTR .... Consolidate Time Rate
CTR .... Counter (KSC)
CTR .... Current Transfer Ratio [*Bell System*]
CTRAP .... Customer Trouble Report Analysis Plan [*Telecommunications*] (TEL)
CTRC .... Colorado Technical Reference Center [*University of Colorado - Boulder*] [*Information service*] (EISS)
CTRC .... Computer Transceiver [*NASDAQ symbol*] (NQ)
CTRL .... Control Character [*Keyboard*]
CTS .... Cable Telemetry System
CTS .... Cable Terminal Section [*Telecommunications*] (TEL)
CTS .... Cable Turning Section [*Telecommunications*] (TEL)
CTS .... Canadian Technology Satellite (CAA)
CTS .... Card-to-Magnetic Tape Conversion System [*Data processing*] (DIT)
CTS .... Center for Telecommunications Studies [*Formerly, Broadcast Research Center*] [*Ohio University*] [*Research center*] (RCD)
CTS .... Centralized Translation System [*Communications*]
CTS .... Circuit Test Set
CTS .... Clear to Send
CTS .... Common Test Subroutine [*Data processing*] (OA)
CTS .... Communications Technology Satellite
CTS .... Communications Terminal, Synchronous [*Data processing*]
CTS .... Communications and Tracking System [*or Subsystem*]
CTS .... Computer Telewriter Systems (MCD)
CTS .... Computer Test Set (VIT)
CTS .... Computer Training System
CTS .... Computer Typing System
CTS .... Computerized Tomography Society (EANO)
CTS .... Conversational Terminal System [*Data processing*] (BUR)
CTS .... Conversational Time-Sharing [*Data processing*] (IEEE)
CTS .... Crescomm Transmission Services, Inc. [*Fairfield, NJ*] [*Telecommunications*] (TSSD)
CTS .... CTS Corp. [*NYSE symbol*]
CTSI .... Central Terminal Signaling Interface [*Telecommunications*] (TEL)
CTSI .... Computer Transceiver Systems, Incorporated (CAA)
CTSK .... Computer Task Group [*NASDAQ symbol*] (NQ)
CTSRTS ..... Clear to Send/Request to Send (OA)
CTSS .... Compatible Time-Sharing System [*Massachusetts Institute of Technology*] [*Data processing*]
CTT .... Cable Trouble Ticket [*Telecommunications*] (TEL)
CTT .... Card-to-Tape Tape [*Data processing*]
C/T)t .... Carrier-to-Noise Temperature, Total (CBSS)
CTT .... Central Trunk Terminals
CTTL .... Complementary Transistor-Transistor Logic
CTTX .... Computrac, Inc. [*NASDAQ symbol*] (NQ)
C/T)u .... Carrier-to-Noise Temperature, Uplink (CBSS)
CTU .... Cartridge Tape Unit [*Telecommunications*] (TEL)
CTU .... Central Telephone & Utilities Corp. [*NYSE symbol*] [*Delisted*]
CTU .... Central Terminal Unit [*Telecommunications*]
CTU .... Commercial Telegraphers' Union [*Later, UTW*]
CTU .... Control and Timing Unit [*Data processing*]
CTUC .... [*The*] Continuum Company [*NASDAQ symbol*] (NQ)
CTUSA .... ComputerTown, USA! [*San Ramon, CA*] [*An association*] (EANO)
CTV .... Cable Television [*Formerly, CATV*]
CTV .... Cockpit Television Sensor (MCD)
CTV .... Color Television (DEN)

CTV .... Commercial Television
CTVD .... Cinema Television Digest
CTX .... Centrex [*Bell System*]
CTX .... Centrex System Number [*Telecommunications*] (TEL)
CTXCO .... Centrex Central Office [*Telecommunications*] (TEL)
CTXCU .... Centrex Customer [*Telecommunications*] (TEL)
CU .... Communications Unlimited [*Charlotte, NC*] [*Telecommunications*] (TSSD)
CU .... Computer Unit [*American Topical Association*] [*Rockville, MD*] (EANO)
CU .... Construction Unit [*Data processing*]
CU .... Control Unit [*Data processing*]
CU .... Cross-Talk Unit
CU .... Cubic
CUA .... Compugraphics Users Association [*Bend, OR*] (EANO)
CUA .... Computer Users Association (CAA)
CUAS .... Computer Utilization Accounting System (IEEE)
CUB .... Control Unit Busy (CMD)
CUB .... Council for UHF [*Ultrahigh Frequency*] Broadcasting (EANO)
CUBE .... Cooperating Users of Burroughs Equipment [*Detroit, MI*] [*Data processing*]
CUBOL ...... Computer Usage's Business-Oriented Language [*Data processing*] (TUT)
CUC .... Communications Union Canada
CUC .... Computer Usage Control (NASA)
CUC .... Computers Users' Committee [*United Nations Development Program*]
CUCD .... Comp-U-Card International [*NASDAQ symbol*] (NQ)
CUDAT .... Common User Data [*Telecommunications*] (TEL)
CUDIX .... Common User Digital Information Exchange [*Satellite communication*] (NVT)
CUDIXS ..... Common User Digital Information Exchange System [*or Subsystem*] [*Satellite communication*] (MCD)
CUDN .... Common User Data Network
CUDOS ...... Continuously Updated Dynamic Optimizing Systems (IEEE)
CUE .... Communications Unit Executor
CUE .... Computer Update Equipment
CUE .... Computer User Education [*An association*]
CUE .... Configuration Utilization Efficiency (BUR)
CUE .... Control Unit End (CMD)
CUEFS .... Cooperative Users of Equimatics Financial Systems (CSR)
CUE J .... Computer Using Educators of BC [*British Columbia*] Journal [*Canada*] [*A publication*]
CUES .... Computer Utility Educational System (MCD)
CUFAM ...... Cooperative Users of FICS and MARS [*Atlanta, GA*]
CUFOS ...... Center for UFO [*Unidentified Flying Object*] Studies [*Lima, OH*] [*Information service*] (EISS)
CUG .... Closed User Group [*Communications*]
CUHS .... Computer Use in the Health Service [*British*]
CUI .... Cincinnati Uplink, Incorporated [*Cincinnati, OH*] [*Telecommunications*] (TSSD)
CUI .... Computer Instruments Corp. [*American Stock Exchange symbol*] [*Delisted*]
CUJT .... Complementary Unijunction Transistor (IEEE)
CUL .... See You Later [*Telegrapher's slang*]
CULL .... Cross Reference Utility [*Data processing*]
CULP .... California Union List of Periodicals [*Cooperative Library Agency for Systems and Services*] [*Database*] (CUAD)
CULP .... Computer Usage List Processor (IEEE)
CUM .... Central Unit-Memory
Cum Comput Abstr ... Cumulative Computer Abstracts [*A publication*]
CUMD .... Continuous Update Memory Display
CUME .... Cumulative Audience [*Telecommunications*]
CUMP .... Central Unit-Memory Programer (MCD)
CUMREC .... College and University Machine Records Conference (EANO)
CUP .... Code Universel de Produit [*Universal Product Code*] [*Canada*]
CUP .... Communications User Program [*Sperry UNIVAC*]
CUR .... Complex Utility Routine
CUR .... Current
CURES .... Computer Utilization Reporting System (IEEE)
CURFCOE ... Common Usage Radio Frequency Checkout Equipment (KSC)
CURTS .... Common User Radio Transmission Sounding System (MCD)
CUS .... Common User System [*Telecommunications*] (TEL)
CUS .... Customer Code [*Telecommunications*] (TEL)
CUSE .... Computer Usage Co. [*NASDAQ symbol*] (NQ)
CUSP .... Commonly Used System Programs [*Digital Equipment Corp.*] (CAA)
CUSSN ...... Computer Use in Social Services Network [*University of Texas at Arlington*] (EANO)
CUT .... Circuit under Test (IEEE)
CUT .... Control Unit Tester [*Sperry UNIVAC*] (BUR)
CUTS .... Cassette User Tape System (DEEC)
CV .... Cellular Ventures, Inc. [*Atlanta, GA*] [*Telecommunications*] (TSSD)
CVB .... Combined VHF [*Very-High-Frequency*]-Band
CVC .... Carrier Virtual Circuit [*Telecommunications*] (CAA)
CVCF .... Constant Voltage and Constant Frequency (BUR)
CVGT .... Convergent Technology [*NASDAQ symbol*] (NQ)
CVI .... Colorado Video, Incorporated
CVIC .... Conditional Variable Incremental Computer (IEEE)
CVIS .... Computerized Vocational Information System [*Guidance program*]

CVL	Computer Vision Laboratory [*University of Maryland*] [*Research center*] (RCD)
CVM	COBOL Virtual Machine (CAA)
CVN	Computervision Corp. [*NYSE symbol*]
CVO	Communications Validating Office (CET)
CVR	Computer Voice Response (CAA)
CVRTC	Nora Eccles Harrison Cardiovascular Research and Training Center [*University of Utah*] [*Research center*] (RCD)
CVSD	Continuous Variable Slope Delta [*Modulation*]
CVSDM	Continuously Variable Slope Delta Modulation [*Telecommunications*] (TEL)
CVSG	Channel Verification Signal Generator
CVT	Communication Vector Table (BUR)
CVT	Constant Voltage Transformer
C & W	Cable and Wireless Ltd. [*Telecommunications*] (TEL)
CW	Calls Waiting [*Telephone communication*]
CW	Carrier Wave [*A form of radio transmission in code*]
CW	Clockwise
CW	Command Word [*Data processing*] (MCD)
CW	Computerworld [*A publication*]
CW	Continuous Wave [*A form of radio transmission*]
CW	Control Word
C & W	Country and Western
CW	Coursewriter [*IBM Corp. programing language*]
CWA	Communications Workers of America [*Formerly, NFTW*]
CWA	Control Word Address (CAA)
CWC	Communications, Electronic, Technical, and Salaried Workers of Canada
CWD	Creosoted Wood Duct [*Telecommunications*] (TEL)
CWFM	Continuous Wave Frequency-Modulated (MSA)
CWI	Call Waiting Indication [*Telecommunications*] (TEL)
CWIC	Chase World Information Corporation [*Information service*] (EISS)
CWK	Cam-Net Communications Network, Inc. [*Vancouver Stock Exchange symbol*]
CWNS	C & W [*Cable & Wireless North America, Inc.*] Network Services [*Dallas, TX*] [*Telecommunications*] (TSSD)
CWO	Custom Work Order [*Telecommunications*] (TEL)
CWP	Communicating Word Processor (DEEC)
CWP	Current Word Pointer (CAA)
CWPS	Communicating Word Processing System
CWS	Copper Weld Steel [*Telecommunications*] (TEL)
CWTE	Commonwealth Telephone Enterprises, Inc. [*NASDAQ symbol*] (NQ)
CWTG	Computer World Trade Group [*British*] (OA)
CWV	Continuous Wave Video
CWX	Continuous Wave Transmitter (CAAL)
CX	Coin Collecting Box, Pay Station [*Telecommunications*] (TEL)
CX	Coinbox Set [*Telecommunications*] (TEL)
CX	Composite Signaling [*Telecommunications*] (TEL)
CX	Control Transmitter (MUGU)
CX	Count Register [*Data processing*]
CXC	Computrex Centres [*Vancouver Stock Exchange symbol*]
CXC	Cox Cable Communications, Inc. [*of Cox Broadcasting Corp.*] [*American Stock Exchange symbol*] [*Delisted*]
CXR	Carrier [*Telecommunications*]
CY	Calendar Year (TEL)
CY	Carry
CY	Case Copy [*Data processing*] (CDH)
CY	Country [*Online database field identifier*] (OBD)
Cybernet Systems	Cybernetics and Systems [*A publication*]
CYL	Cylinder
CYPHERTEXT	Cyphernetics Text Processing Language [*1970*] [*Data processing*] (CSR)
CYR	Cray Research [*NYSE symbol*]
CZ	Communications Zone (MCD)
CZCS	Coastal Zone Color Scanner
CZE	Compare Zone Equal [*Data processing*] (OA)
CZU	Compare Zone Unequal [*Data processing*] (OA)

D

D	Arithmetic Factor Register [*Data processing*] (CDH)	
D	Day [*Broadcasting term*]	
d	Deci [*A prefix meaning divided by ten*] [*SI symbol*]	
D	Decimal (BUR)	
D	Delay [*Electronics*]	
D	Density	
D	Depth	
D	Digit [*or Digital*] (MDG)	
D	Diode (MDG)	
D	Display (MDG)	
D	Drum (MDG)	
D	Intermediate Dialing Center on a Toll Ticket [*Telecommunications*] (TEL)	
2-D	Two-Dimensional	
3-D	Three-Dimensional [*Pictures or films*]	
3-D	Triple-Diffusion Process (MDG)	
DA	Data Acquisition (MDG)	
DA	Data Adapter (MCD)	
DA	Data Administrator (CAA)	
DA	Data Analysis (AFM)	
DA	Data Assembler	
DA	Data Automation (AFM)	
DA	Data Available	
DA	Date [*Online database field identifier*] (OBD)	
DA	Decimal-to-Analog (CET)	
DA	Define Area	
DA	Demand Assignment [*Telecommunications*] (TEL)	
DA	Design Automation (BUR)	
DA	Destination Address (CAA)	
DA	Differential Analyzer (IEEE)	
D-to-A	Digital-to-Analog [*Converter*] [*Data processing*]	
D-A	Digital-to-Analog [*Converter*] [*Data processing*] (CIT)	
DA	Direct Access (BUR)	
DA	Directional Antenna	
DA	Directory Assistance [*Telecommunications*] (TEL)	
DA	Discrete Address	
DA	Display Adapter (CAA)	
DA	Documentation Associates Information Services, Inc. (EISS)	
DA	Doesn't Answer	
DA	Don't Answer	
DA	Double Armor [*Telecommunications*] (TEL)	
DA-1	Directional Antenna Day and Night [*Broadcasting term*]	
DA-2	Directional Antenna with Changing Patterns, Day and Night [*Broadcasting term*]	
DA-3	Directional Antenna with Changing Patterns, Day and Night with Additional Pattern Change [*Broadcasting term*]	
DAA	Data Access Arrangement [*Telecommunications*] [*Obsolete*]	
DAA	Data Automation Activity (AFM)	
DAA	Digital Automatic Acquisition (MCD)	
DAA	Direct Access Arrangement [*Telecommunications*] (CAA)	
DAB	Display Assignment BITS [*Binary Digits*] (IDA)	
DAB	Display Attention BITS [*Binary Digits*] [*Data processing*]	
DABAWAS	Datenbank fuer Wassergefahrdende Stoffe [*Databank on Substances Harmful to Water*] [*West German*] [*Information service*] (EISS)	
DABS	Direct Access Beacon System (MCD)	
DAC	Data Access Systems, Inc. [*American Stock Exchange symbol*] [*Delisted*]	
DAC	Data Acquisition Camera	
DAC	Data Acquisition Chassis	
DAC	Data Acquisition Computer	
DAC	Data Acquisition and Control (NASA)	
DAC	Data Acquisition Controller	
DAC	Data Analysis Computer	
DAC	Data Analysis Console (AFM)	
DAC	Data Analysis Control (MCD)	
DAC	Demand Assignment Controller (CAA)	
DAC	Design Augmented by Computer [*General Motors Corp.*]	
DAC	Digital-to-Analog Converter [*Data processing*]	
DAC	Digital Arithmetic Center	
DAC	Direct Access Computing (MCD)	
DAC	Directory of Associations in Canada [*Micromedia, Ltd.*] [*A publication*] [*Information service*] (EISS)	
DAC	Display Analysis Console	
DAC	Distribution Automation and Control (MCD)	
DACB	Data Acquisition Control and Buffer (MCD)	
DACBU	Data Acquisition and Control Buffer Unit (NASA)	
DACE	Data Acquisition and Control Executive [*Hewlett-Packard Co.*] (CAH)	
DACE	Data Administration Center Equipment [*Telecommunications*] (TEL)	
DACEMS	Data Communications Equipment Monitoring and Switching (MCD)	
Da-Com	Data Communications, Inc. [*Information service*] (EISS)	
DACOM	Datascope Computer Output Microfilmer [*Eastman Kodak Co.*]	
DACON	Data Controller	
DACON	Digital-to-Analog Converter [*Data processing*]	
DACOR	Data Correction [*IBM Corp.*]	
DACOR	Data Correlator	
DACOS	Data Communication Operating System (CAA)	
DACPO	Data Count Printout [*Data processing*]	
DACS	Data Acquisition, Control, and Simulation Centre [*University of Alberta*] [*Research center*] (RCD)	
DACS	Data Acquisition Control System (IEEE)	
DACS	Data and Analysis Center for Software [*Illinois Institute of Technology*] [*Information service*] (EISS)	
DACS	Digital Access and Crossconnect System [*Telecommunications*] (TEL)	
DACS	Digital Animated Control System	
DACS	Discrete Address Communications System	
DACU	Data Acquisition and Control Unit (TUT)	
DACU	Digital-to-Analog Converter Unit [*Data processing*] (SKY)	
DACU	Digitizing and Control Unit (OA)	
DAD	Data Automation Digest [*A publication*]	
DAD	Data Description Language [*Data processing*]	
DA-D	Directional Antenna Daytime Only [*Broadcasting term*]	
DAD	Drums and Displays [*Data processing*]	
DADB	Data Analysis Database (OA)	
DADC	Digital Air Data Computer	
DADCOK	Digital Air Data Computer Status	
DADCTS	Digital Air Data Computer Test Set	
DADE	Data Acquisition and Decommutation Equipment	
DADE	Digital Acquisition and Documentation Equipment (KSC)	
DADEE	Dynamic Analog Differential Equation Equalizer	
DADiSP	Data Acquisition and Digital Signal Processing	
DADIT	Daystrom Analog-to-Digital Integrating Translator	
DADR	Digital Angle Data Recorder	
DADS	Data Acquisition Display Subsystem (OA)	
DADS	Data Acquisition and Display System	
DADS	Digital Air Data System	
DADS	Digital Analog Data System (CAAL)	
DADSM	Direct Access Device Space Management (MCD)	
DAEDAC	Drug Abuse Epidemiology Data Center [*Texas Christian University*] (EISS)	
DAF	Data Acquisition Facility [*of STADAN*]	
DAF	Data Analysis Facility (CIT)	
DAF	Destination Address Field [*Data processing*] (IBMDP)	
DAFM	Direct Access File Manager (CAA)	
DAFT	Digital-to-Analog Function Table [*Packard Bell Computer Corp.*]	
DAGC	Delayed Automatic Gain Control (MSA)	
DAGC	Digital Automatic Gain Control (MCD)	
DAI	Dittberner Associates, Incorporated [*Bethesda, MD*] [*Information service*] [*Telecommunications*] (TSSD)	
DAIM	Dynamic Active Index Matrix (BUR)	
DAIR	Driver Aid, Information, and Routing [*Data processing*]	
DAIR	Dynamic Allocation Interface Routine [*Data processing*] (BUR)	
DAIRS	Dial Access Information Retrieval System [*Shippensburg State College, Shippensburg, PA*]	
DAIS	Directory of Automated Information Systems (MCD)	
DAISY	Data Acquisition and Interpretation System	
DAISY	Decision Aiding Information System	
DAIU	Digital-to-Analog Interface Unit [*Data processing*]	
DAIV	Data Area Initializer and Verifier [*Telecommunications*] (TEL)	
DAK	Decision Acknowledge (BUR)	
DAK	Deny All Knowledge [*Telecommunications*] (TEL)	
DAL	Data Access Line	

Computer & Telecommunications Acronyms

DAL............ Data Accession List   (NASA)
DAL............ Data Acquisition Language [Data processing]   (CSR)
DAL............ Data Acquisition List   (MCD)
DAL............ Data Address Line   (CAA)
DAL............ Data Analysis Laboratory [Temple University] [Research center]   (CIT)
DAL............ Digital Analysis Library [Computer Design] [Software package] [British]   (NCC)
DALATS...... Data Logging and Transmission System   (MCD)
DALC......... Divided Access Line Circuit
DALIS......... Directory of Automated Library and Information Systems in Australia [A publication]
DALS......... Data Acquisition Logging System   (DDI)
DALTS....... Data Link Test Set
DAM.......... Data Addressed Memory [Data processing]
DAM.......... Data Association Message
DAM.......... Descriptor Attribute Matrix
DAM.......... Digital-to-Analog Multiplier   (IEEE)
DAM.......... Direct Access Memory [Data processing]   (BUR)
DAM.......... Direct Access Method [Sperry UNIVAC] [Data processing]   (TUT)
DAMA........ Demand-Assignment Multiple Access   (CBSS)
DAMAS...... Data Management Systems, Inc. [Portland, OR] [Software manufacturer]   (DASOS)
DAME........ Data Acquisition and Monitoring Equipment [Electronics]
DAMIT....... Data Analysis [Program] of Massachusetts Institute of Technology
DAMPS...... Data Acquisition Multiprograming System [IBM Corp.] [Data processing]
DAMS........ Direct Access Management System   (CAA)
DAMSU...... Digital Automanual Switching Unit [Telecommunications]   (TEL)
DA-N......... Directional Antenna Nighttime Only [Broadcasting term]
DANFIP...... Danish Federation for Information Processing and Management [Copenhagen, Denmark]
DAO......... Dial Assist Operator   (CET)
DAP......... Data Access Protocol [Digital Equipment Corp.]
DAP......... Data Acquisition Plan   (MCD)
DA & P....... Data Acquisition and Processing   (SKY)
DAP......... Data Analysis Program   (VIT)
DAP......... Data Automation Proposal   (AFM)
DAP......... Deformation of Aligned Phase   (MCD)
DAP......... Digital Assembly Program   (MCD)
DAP......... Distributed Array Processor [Sperry UNIVAC] [Telecommunications]
DAP......... Dynamic Assertion Processor [Data processing]
DAPF........ Data Analysis and Processing Facility   (DDI)
DAPN........ Directional Antenna Phasing Network
DAPO........ Digital Advance Production Order [Telecommunications]   (TEL)
DAPR........ Digital Automatic Pattern Recognition   (IEEE)
DAPRU...... Drug Abuse Prevention Resource Unit [National Institute on Drug Abuse] [Databank]
DAPS........ Data Acquisition and Processing System
DAPS........ Data Processing Automatic Publication Service   (TUT)
DAPS........ Direct Access Programing System [Data processing]
DAPS........ Distributed Application Processing System   (CAA)
DAQC........ Data Acquisition Center   (KSC)
DAR......... Damage Assessment Routines   (MDG)
DAR......... Data Access Register [Data processing]   (MDG)
DAR......... Driver Augmented Readout [Data processing]
DARA........ Deutsche Arbeitsgemeinschaft fuer Rechen-Anlagen [German Working Committee for Computing Machines] [German]   (CDH)
DARD........ Data Acquisition Requirements Document   (KSC)
DARDO...... Direct Access to Remote Data Bases Overseas [Rome, Italy] [Telecommunications]   (TSSD)
DARE........ Data Automatic Reduction Equipment   (CET)
DARE........ Data Automation Research and Experimentation   (CET)
DARE........ Differential Analyzer Replacement [Programing language] [1967]   (CSR)
DARE........ Document Abstract Retrieval Equipment   (IEEE)
DARES...... Data Analysis and Reduction System
DARMS..... Digital Alternate Representation of Musical Symbols   (OA)
DARS........ Data Accumulating and Reporting Sheet
DARS........ Data Acquisition Recording System
DARS........ Data Acquisition and Reduction System
DARS........ Decommutation and Readout System [Data processing]
DART........ Daily Automatic Rescheduling Technique [Data processing]
DART........ Data Analysis Recording Tape
DART........ Data Reduction Translator
DART........ Dynamic Acoustic Response Trigger   (IEEE)
DARYL...... Data Analysing Robot Youth Lifeform [From the movie entitled "D.A.R.Y.L."]
DAS .... Data Access Security   (CAA)
DAS .... Data Accountability System   (CIT)
DAS .... Data Acquisition Station   (DDI)
DAS .... Data Acquisition System
DAS .... Data Administration Section
DAS .... Data Amplification Sheet   (KSC)
DAS .... Data Analysis Software [Telecommunications]   (TEL)
DAS .... Data Analysis Station   (NASA)
DAS .... Data Auxiliary Set [Telecommunications]   (TEL)
DAS .... Datatron Assembly System [Burroughs Corp.]
DAS .... Dial Assistance Switchboard   (CET)
DAS .... Digital Address System   (MCD)
DAS .... Digital Aircraft Simulator   (MCD)
DAS .... Digital Altimeter Scanner
DAS .... Digital Analog Simulator [Data processing]
DAS .... Digital Attenuator System
DAS .... Digital Avionics System   (MCD)
DAS .... Dipole Antenna System
DAS .... Directory Assistance System [Telecommunications]   (TEL)
DAS .... Division of Applied Sciences [Harvard University] [Research center]   (RCD)
DASD........ Data Acquisition Support Document   (KSC)
DASD........ Direct Access Storage Device [Pronounced "daz-dee"] [Data processing]   (CGC)
DASDL...... Data and Structure Definition Language [Data processing]   (BUR)
DASDR...... Direct Access Storage Dump Restore   (CAA)
DASF........ Direct Access Storage Facility [Data processing]   (TUT)
DASG........ Data Acquisition Subsystem Group
DASH....... Database Acquisition for Student Health
DASH....... Direct Access Storage Handler [Telecommunications]   (TEL)
DASH....... Dual Access Storage Handling   (CAA)
DASL........ Data Access System Language   (CAA)
DAS/M...... Directory Assistance System/Microfilm [Bell System]
DASR........ Data Acquisition Statistical Recorder
DASS........ Demand-Assignment Signaling and Switching Unit
DASS........ Digital Acoustic Simulation System   (MCD)
DASSO...... Data Systems Support Office   (MCD)
DAST........ Design, Architecture, Software, and Testing   (MCD)
DASW....... Data Switch Corp. [NASDAQ symbol]   (NQ)
DASY........ Data Analysis System
DAT.......... Data Acquisition Test [Later, DST]
DAT.......... Data General Corp., Westboro, MA [OCLC symbol]
DAT.......... Digital Audio Tape
DAT.......... Disk Allocation Table [Data processing]   (IBMDP)
DAT.......... Dynamic Address Translation [Data processing]
DATA........ Derivation & Tabulation Associates, Inc. [Information service]   (EISS)
DATA........ Dial a Teacher Assistance [Telephone service]
DATA........ Direct Access Terminal Application [Data processing]   (BUR)
DATA........ Display Automated Telemetry Analyzer   (MCD)
DATA........ Endata, Inc. [NASDAQ symbol]   (NQ)
Data Acquis Process Biol Med ... Data Acquisition and Processing in Biology and Medicine [A publication]
Data Acquis Process Biol Med Proc Rochester Conf ... Data Acquisition and Processing in Biology and Medicine. Proceedings of the Rochester Conference [A publication]
Database J ... Database Journal [A publication]
Database Jrnl ... Database Journal [A publication]
Data Bus..... Data Business [A publication]
DATAC....... Data Analog Computer
Data C........ Data Communications [A publication]
Data Chan ... Data Channels [A publication]
DATACOL ... Data Collection
DATACOM ... Data Communications
Data Comm ... Data Communications [A publication]
Data Commun ... Data Communications [A publication]
DATACORTS ... Data Correlation and Transfer System   (DDI)
Data Dyn ... Data Dynamics [A publication]
Data Ed....... Data Education [A publication]
DATAFIT..... [A] programing language [1973]   (CSR)
DATAMAN ... Data Management System [Data processing]   (MCD)
Data Manage ... Data Management [A publication]
Data Mgmt ... Data Management [A publication]
Data Mgt..... Data Management [A publication]
DATAN .... Data Analysis   (IEEE)
DATANET... Data Network   (CET)
DATAP........ Data Transmission and Processing   (NATG)
Data Proc ... Data Processing [A publication]
Data Proces ... Data Processing [A publication]
Data Process ... Data Processing Digest [A publication]
Data Process Educ ... Data Processing for Education [North American Publishing Co.] [A publication]
Data Process Mag ... Data Processing Magazine [A publication]
Data Process Med ... Data Processing in Medicine [A publication]
Data Process Pract ... Data Processing Practitioner [A publication]
Datapro Rep Data Commun ... Datapro Reports on Data Communications [A publication]
Datapro Rep Minicomput ... Datapro Reports on Minicomputers [A publication]
Datapro Rep Office Syst ... Datapro Reports on Office Systems [A publication]
DATAR....... Digital Autotransducer and Recorder   (IEEE)
Data Sys ..... Data Systems [A publication]
Data Syst.... Data Systems [A publication]
Data Systems N ... Data Systems News [A publication]
DATA-TEXT ... [A] programing language   (CSR)
DATC......... Data Card Corp. [NASDAQ symbol]   (NQ)
DATE .... Digital Angular Torquing Equipment
DATE .... Digital Audio for Television [System to improve sound] [Public Broadcasting Service]
DATEC....... Data Technical Support Group [Telecommunications]   (TEL)
DATEL .... Data Telecommunications [RCA Global Communications Data Transmission Service over Telephone Circuits] [Telecommunications]   (TEL)
DATICO...... Data Analysis and Technique Development Center [Alexandria, VA]   (CDH)

Computer & Telecommunications Acronyms

DATICO	Digital Automatic Tape Intelligence Checkout
DATIN	Data Inserter
DATM	Datum, Inc. [*NASDAQ symbol*] (NQ)
DATN	Datricon Corp. [*NASDAQ symbol*] (NQ)
DATOM	Data Aids for Training, Operations, and Maintenance (VIT)
DATOS	Detection and Tracking of Satellites
DATR	Datron Corp. [*NASDAQ symbol*] (NQ)
DATRAN	Data Transmission Co. [*Defunct*]
DATREC	Data Recording (CET)
DATRIX	Direct Access to Reference Information [*Xerox Corp.*]
DATS	Data Accumulation and Transfer Sheet
DATS	Data Acquisition and Transmission System (MCD)
DATS	Data Transmission System
DAU	Data Acquisition Unit
DAU	Data Adapter Unit
DAU	Datamation [*A publication*]
DAV	Data Valid (IEEE)
DAV	Data above Voice [*Telecommunications*] (TEL)
DAVC	Delayed Automatic Volume Control
DAWID	Device for Automatic Word Identification and Discrimination [*Data processing*]
DAWN	Digital Automatic Weather Network
DAWNS	Design of Aircraft Wing Structures [*Computer program*]
DAX	Data Acquisition and Control
DAX	Data Exchange (CCD)
DAXI	Digital Auxiliary Information Code [*Data processing*]
DAY	Dayco Corp. [*NYSE symbol*]
DB	Data Bank
DB	Data Bus [*Data processing*] (MCD)
DB	Database [*Data processing*] (TUT)
dB	Decibel [*Symbol*] [*SI unit of sound level*]
D/B	Decimal to Binary [*Data processing*] (KSC)
DB	Delayed Broadcast [*Television*]
DB	Deutsche Bibliothek [*Database producer*] (ODIN)
DB	Digital Block [*Data processing*]
DB	Display Buffer [*Data processing*]
D & B	Dun & Bradstreet, Inc.
DBA	Database Administration [*or Administrator*] [*Data processing*] (BUR)
dBA	Decibels, Adjusted
DBAAM	Disk Buffer Area Access Method (CAA)
DBACS	Database Administrator Control System (CAA)
DBAF	Database Access Facility (CAA)
DBAM	Database Access Method (IDA)
DBAO	Digital Block And-Or Gate [*Data processing*] (IEEE)
DBAWG	Database Administration Working Group [*CODASYL*] (CAA)
DBC	Data Bibliography Card
DBC	Data Bus Control [*Data processing*] (MCD)
DBC	Data Bus Coupler [*Data processing*] (MCD)
DBC	Database Computer (MCD)
DBC	Digital-to-Binary Converter [*Data processing*]
DBC	Duck Book Communications Ltd. [*Vancouver Stock Exchange symbol*]
DBCB	Database Control Block (CAA)
DBCC	Decrement, Test, Branch if Condition True [*Data processing*]
DBCL	Database Command Language (CAA)
DBCO	Digital Block Clock Oscillator [*Data processing*]
DBCS	Database Control System (CAA)
DBCU	Data Bus Control Unit [*Data processing*] (KSC)
DBD	Database Description [*Data processing*] (BUR)
DBD	Diebold, Inc. [*NYSE symbol*]
DBDA	Database Design Aid [*Data processing*] (BUR)
DB/DC	Database/Data Communications [*IBM Corp.*]
DBDL	Database Definition Language (CAA)
DBDS	Data Base Directory Service [*Formerly, Data Base User Service*] [*Knowledge Industry Publications, Inc.*] [*Database*] (CUAD)
DBE	Data Bus Enable [*Data processing*]
DBF	Dansk Databehandlinsforening [*Danish Data Processing Association*] [*Copenhagen, Denmark*]
DBFF	Digital Block Flip-Flop [*Data processing*]
DBFN	Database File Numbers (MCD)
DBG	Data Bus Group [*Data processing*] (MCD)
DBG	Database Generator (CAA)
DBGEN	Database Generation [*Data processing*] (TUT)
DBGMP	Data Bus Generation and Maintenance Package [*Data processing*] (MCD)
DBHS	Database Handling System (DDI)
DBI	Data Base Index
DBI	Data Bus Interface Unit-Launch [*Data processing*] (MCD)
DBI	Double Byte Interleaved (CAA)
DBIA	Data Bus Interface Adapter [*Data processing*] (MCD)
DBIA	Data Bus Isolation Amplifier [*Data processing*] (MCD)
DBIA	Digital Block Inverter Amplifier [*Data processing*]
DBIL	Database Input Languages [*Data processing*]
DBIN	Data Bus In [*Data processing*]
DBIOC	Database Input/Output Control (CAA)
DBIS	Designers & Builders of Information Systems, Inc. [*New Rochelle, NY*] [*Software manufacturer*] (DASOS)
DBIU	Data Bus Interface Unit [*Data processing*] (MCD)
DBK	Data Bank
DBL	Database List
DBL	Database Load [*Data processing*]
DBLTG	Database Language Task Group [*CODASYL*] (CAA)
DBM	Data Buffer Module (IEEE)
DBM	Data Bus Monitor [*Data processing*]
DBM	Database Management [*or Manager*] [*Data processing*] (NVT)
DBM	Decibel Meter (KSC)
dBM	Decibels above One Milliwatt
DBM	Direct Branch Mode (CAA)
DBMAD	Auerbach Data Base Management [*A publication*]
DBMS	Database Management Software
DBMS	Database Management System [*Data processing*] (BUR)
DBMSPSM	Database Management System Problem Specification Model (OA)
DBMV	Digital Block Multivibrator [*Data processing*]
DBN	Data Bus Network [*Data processing*] (MCD)
DBNA	Digital Block Noninverting Amplifier [*Data processing*]
DBNK	Data Bank
DBO	Drop Build-Out Capacitor [*Telecommunications*] (TEL)
DBOMP	Database Organization and Maintenance Processor
DBOS	Disk-Based Operating System (IEEE)
DBP	Database Processor (CAA)
DBR	Database Retrieval (CAA)
DBRN	Data Bank Release Notice (NASA)
dBRN	Decibels above Reference Noise
DBS	Database System (MCD)
DBS	Direct Broadcast Satellite [*Television transmission system in which signals are transmitted by satellite directly to individual locations*]
DBSC	Digital Block Slave Clock [*Data processing*]
DBSC	Direct Broadcast Satellite Corporation [*Bethesda, MD*] [*Telecommunications*] (TSSD)
DBST	Digital Block Schmitt Trigger [*Data processing*]
DBTG	Database Task Group [*CODASYL*]
DBU	Digital Buffer Unit (OA)
DBUR	Databank Update Request (NASA)
DBUT	Database Update Time
DC	Data Call
DC	Data Camera
DC	Data Cartridge (CAA)
DC	Data Cell [*Data processing*] (TUT)
DC	Data Center (KSC)
DC	Data Channel [*Data processing*] (TUT)
DC	Data Check (BUR)
DC	Data Classifier (IEEE)
DC	Data Code
DC	Data Collection
DC	Data Communication [*Data processing*] (BUR)
DC	Data Concentrator [*Data processing*] (BUR)
DC	Data Control (AFM)
D/C	Data Conversion [*Data processing*] (KSC)
DC	Data Coordinator (MCD)
DC	Define Constant (MDG)
DC	Detail Condition (MDG)
DC	Device Control
DC	Device Coordinate (CCD)
DC	Dewey Decimal Classification [*Also, DDC*]
DC	Digital Comparator
DC	Digital Computer
DC	Direct Current
DC	Direction Cycle (MDG)
DC	Directional Coupler
DC	Director Deputy of Communications-Electronics
DC	Disk Controller [*Data processing*] (IEEE)
DC	Display Code (CAH)
DC	Display Computer
DC	Display Console (KSC)
DC	Document Code [*Data processing*]
DC	Document Control (VIT)
DC	Downconverter [*Satellite communications*]
DCA	Data Communications Administrator (CAA)
DCA	Data Correction Amplifier
DCA	Defense Communications Agency [*DoD*] [*Washington, DC*] [*Telecommunications*]
DCA	Digital Communications Associates, Inc. [*Norcross, GA*] [*Software manufacturer*] [*Telecommunications*] (TSSD)
DCA	Digital Computer Association (MUGU)
DCA	Distributed Communications Architecture (BUR)
DCA	Document Content Architecture [*IBM Corp.*]
DCA	Driver Control Area (BUR)
DCAI	Digital Communications Associates, Incorporated [*NASDAQ symbol*] (NQ)
DCAI	Digital Consulting Associates, Incorporated [*Andover, MA*] [*Telecommunications*] (TSSD)
DCAI	Direct-Current Analog Input (MCD)
DCAM	Data Collection Access Method (CAA)
DCAO	Digital Card And-Or Gate [*Data processing*]
DCARE	Driver Control Area Region Extension (BUR)
DCB	Data Control Block [*Data processing*]
DCB	Decimal Code Binaire [*Binary Coded Decimal*] [*Data processing*]
DCC	Data Circuit Concentration
DCC	Data Communications Channel
DCC	Data Communications Controller [*Data processing*] (CAA)
DCC	Data Communications Corporation [*Information service*] (EISS)
DCC	Data Condition Code
DCC	Data Control Characters (CMD)

Computer & Telecommunications Acronyms

Acronym	Definition
DCC	Device Control Character (IEEE)
DCC	Digital Control Computer
DCC	Digital Cross Current (OA)
DCC	Direct Computer Control (OA)
DCC	Direct Control Channel (CAA)
DCC	Discrimination and Control Computer (MUGU)
DCC	Display Control Console (KSC)
DCC	Double Cotton Covered [Wire insulation]
DCC	Downtown Copy Center [Washington, DC] [Telecommunications] (TSSD)
DCCC	Data Communication Control Character (IEEE)
DCCC	Double Current Cable Code [Telecommunications]
DCCO	Digital Card Clock Oscillator [Data processing]
DCCP	Digital Computer Control Panel
DCCS	Digital Command Communications System
DCCSA	Dictionary of Computer and Control Systems Abbreviations, Signs, and Symbols [New York: Odyssey Press, 1965] [A publication]
DCCU	Data Communications Control Unit (DEN)
DCCU	Data Correlation Control Unit (DDI)
DCCU	Digital Communications and Control Unit (MCD)
DCCU	Display Computer Control Unit (MCD)
DCD	Data Carrier Detect [or Detector] [Data communication signal] [Telecommunications] (TEL)
DCD	Digital Compact Disk
DCD	Digital Countdown Display [Data processing]
DCD	Direct-Current Dump
DCD	Dynamic Computer Display (IEEE)
DC/DC	Data Communication to Disk Control (CAA)
DC/DC	Direct Current to Direct Current [Telecommunications]
DCDL	Digital Control Design Language [1968] [Data processing] (CSR)
DCDR	Data Collection and Data Relay [Telecommunications] (TEL)
DCDS	Digital Control Design System (IEEE)
DCDS	Digital Countdown Display System [Data processing]
DCE	Data Circuit Equipment
DCE	Data Circuit-Terminating Equipment [Data processing] (BUR)
DCE	Data Communication Equipment
DCE	Data Conversion Equipment [Data processing]
DCES	Data Collection and Evaluation System (NVT)
DCES	Discretionary Capital Expenditure System [Bell System]
DCES	DSS [Deep Space Station] Communications Equipment Subsystem (CIT)
DCF	Data Channel Filter [Data processing]
DCF	Data Correlation Facility
DCF	Direct Control Feature (CMD)
DCF	Disk Controller/Formatter (CAA)
DCF	Document Composition Facility [IBM Corp.]
DCFF	Digital Card Flip-Flop [Data processing]
DCFL	Direct-Coupled FET [Field Effect Transistor] Logic [Integrated circuitry]
DCG	Dependent Charge Group [Telecommunications] (TEL)
DCG	Designs Coordination Group [Telecommunications] (TEL)
DCI	Data Courier, Inc. [Louisville, KY] (EISS)
DCI	Defense Computer Institute
DCI	Dialing Code Information [Telecommunications] [British]
DCI	Direct Channel Interface (CAA)
DCI	Direct Computer Input (MCD)
DCI	Director of Corporate Information
DCI	Disk Core Image (CMD)
DCIA	Digital Card Inverting Amplifier [Data processing]
DCIB	Data Communication Input Buffer
DCILM	Direct Computer Input Load Module (MCD)
DCIM	Display System Computer Input Multiplexer (MCD)
DCIO	Direct Channel Interface Option (CAA)
DCIP	Data Correction Indicator Panel (MUGU)
DCIP	Disk Cartridge Initialization Program (CMD)
DCIS	Downrange Computer Input System (MUGU)
DCIST	Directory of Computerized Information in Science and Technology [Leonard Cohen, ed., New York: Science Associates International, 1968] [A publication]
DCIU	Digital Control and Interface Unit (MCD)
DCKP	Direct-Current Key Pulsing (IEEE)
DCL	Delayed Call Limited [Telecommunications] (TEL)
DCL	Designate Command Line [Data processing]
DCL	Designer Choice Logic
DCL	Digital Channel Link
DCL	Digital Computer Laboratory [Massachusetts Institute of Technology]
DCL	Direct Communications Link [US/USSR]
DCLN	Direct Coupled Loop Network [Data processing]
DCM	Data Communications Multiplexer (CAA)
DCM	Diagnostic Controlled MODEM [Data processing] (BUR)
DCM	Digital Circuit Module [Data processing]
DCM	Direct Connection Module [Data processing]
DCM	Display and Control Module (MCD)
DCMH	Data Collection Module, High Speed
DCML	Data Collection Module, Low Speed
DCMPTR	Degaussing Computer (VIT)
DCMS	Data Control Multiplex System
DCMS	Dedicated Computer Message Switching (CAA)
DCMV	Digital Card Multivibrator [Data processing]
DCN	Distributed Computer Network (CAA)
DCNA	Data Communication Network Architecture (BUR)
DCNA	Digital Card Noninverting Amplifier [Data processing]
DCO	Digital Central Office [Trademark of the Stromberg-Carlson Corp.] [Telecommunications]
DCOM	Dicomed Corp. [NASDAQ symbol] (NQ)
DCOM	Disk Communications Area (CMD)
DCOS	Data Collection Operating System (CAA)
DCOS	Data Communication Output Selector (KSC)
DCOS	Direct Couple Operating System (CIT)
DCOS	Downrange Computer Output System (MUGU)
DCP	Data Collection Platform [National Weather Service] [Weather satellite system]
DCP	Data Communication Processor [Data processing] (BUR)
DCP	Design Change Package (IEEE)
DCP	Design Criteria Plan (IEEE)
DCP	Differential Computing Potentiometer
DCP	Digital Computer Processor (IEEE)
DCP	Digital Computer Programing [Data processing] (BUR)
DCP	Display Control Panel
DCP	Distributed Communications Processor [Sperry UNIVAC] (CAA)
DCP	Distribution Common Point [Telecommunications] (TEL)
DCPCM	Differentially Coherent Pulse Code Modulation (CAA)
DCPL	Distributed Control Programing Language [Data processing] (CSR)
DCPP	Data Communication Preprocessor (CAA)
DCPS	Data Communication Processing System
DCPS	Data Control Panel Submodule
DCPS	Digitally Controlled Power Source (IEEE)
DCPSK	Differential Coherent Phase Shift Keyed [System] [Data processing]
DCPY	Datacopy Corp. [NASDAQ symbol] (NQ)
DCQM	Digital Circuit Quality Monitor [Data processing]
DC/R	Data Collection/Relay (MCD)
DCR	Data Conversion Receiver [Data processing]
DCR	Data Coordinator and Retriever [Data processing] (CGC)
DCR	Design Change Request
DCR	Digital Cassette Recorder (CAA)
DCR	Digital Concentration Readout [Data processing]
DCR	Division of Computer Research [Formerly, OCA] [National Science Foundation]
DCRABS	Disk Copy Restore and Backup System (CAA)
DCRS	Data Collection and Reduction System
DCRT	Division of Computer Research and Technology [National Institutes of Health]
DCS	Data Collection System [or Subsystem] [Data processing] (TUT)
DCS	Data Communication System
DCS	Data Control Services (BUR)
DCS	Data Control System [Burroughs Corp.]
DCS	Data Conversion System [Data processing]
DCS	Davis Computer Systems, Inc.
DCS	Department of Computer Science [University of Illinois] [Research center] (RCD)
DCS	Department of Computing Service [University of Waterloo] [Research center] (RCD)
DCS	Diagnostic Control Store (CAA)
DCS	Digital Command System [or Subsystem]
DCS	Digital Communication System [Data processing] (CGC)
DCS	Digital Control Station [Data processing]
DCS	Digital Control System
DCS	Digital Countdown System [Data processing]
DCS	Direct Couple System
DCS	Distributed Computer Systems (MDG)
DCS	Document Control System [Data processing] (TUT)
DCSC	Digital Card Slave Clock [Data processing]
DCSG	Data Computation Subsystem Group
DCSI	Distributed Computer Systems [NASDAQ symbol] (NQ)
DCSNC	Decision Systems, Inc. [NASDAQ symbol] (NQ)
DCSP	Digital Control Signal Processor (NASA)
DCSS	Defense Communications Satellite System [Telecommunications] (TEL)
DCST	Digital Card Schmitt Trigger [Data processing]
DCSU	Digital Computer Switching Unit (MCD)
DCT	Data Communications Terminal (CIT)
DCT	Data Conversion Transmitter [Data processing]
DCT	Deaf Communicating Terminal [Telephone for the deaf]
DCT	Decimal Code Translator
DCT	Device Characteristics Table [Data processing] (IBMDP)
DCT	DSS [Deep Space Station] Communications Terminal Subsystem (CIT)
DCTL	Direct-Coupled Transistor Logic
DCTL	Docutel/Olivetti Corp. [NASDAQ symbol] (NQ)
DCTLC	Direct-Coupling Transistor Logic Circuit
DCTS	Digital Coordinate Transformation System
DCTV	Digital Color Television
DCU	Data Collection Unit
DCU	Data Command Unit
DCU	Data Communications Unit (CAA)
DCU	Data Communications Utility [Social Security Administration]
DCU	Data Control Unit
DCU	Decimal Counting Unit
DCU	Device Control Unit (OA)
DCU	Digital Coefficient Unit [Data processing] (RDA)
DCU	Digital Control Unit (KSC)
DCU	Digital Counting Unit

Computer & Telecommunications Acronyms

DCU	Display and Control Unit (CET)
DCUTL	Direct-Coupled Unipolar Transistor Logic
DCW	Data Control Word (CMD)
DCX	Device Control Character (CMD)
DD	Data Definition [*Data processing*] (BUR)
DD	Data Demand (IDA)
DD	Data Description (MCD)
DD	Data Dictionary [*Data processing*]
DD	Decimal Display (IDA)
DD	Dewey Decimal Number [*Online database field identifier*] (OBD)
DD	Digital Data (CET)
D-to-D	Digital-to-Digital
DD	Digital Display
DD	Direct Dialing [*or Dialed*] [*Telecommunications*] (TEL)
DD	Discriminating Digit [*Telecommunications*] (TEL)
DD	Double Dacron Braid Lacquered (MDG)
DD	Double Density (CAA)
DDA	Demand Deposit Accounting [*Banking*] (MDG)
DDA	Digital Differential Analyzer
DDA	Digital Display Alarm (IDA)
DDA	Digitally Directed Analog (MSA)
DDA	Direct Data Attachment (CAA)
DDA	Direct Disk Attachment (CAA)
DDA	Dr. Dvorkovitz & Associates [*Information service*] (EISS)
DDA	Dynamics Differential Analyzer (IEEE)
DDAPS	Digital Data Acquisition and Processing System
DDAS	Digital Data Acquisition System
DDAS	Digital Data Archives System
DDB	Data Display Board
DDB	Data Display Buffer
DDB	Design Data Book
DDB	Digital Data Buffer
DDB	Distributed Database (CAA)
DDB	Dortmund Data Bank [*Universitaet Dortmund*] [*Chemical databank*] [*Information service*] [*West German*] (EISS)
DDBS	Descriptor Database System (CAA)
DDC	Data Display Central
DDC	Data Distribution Center
DDC	Data Documentation Costs
DDC	Decision, Design, and the Computer [*Symposium*]
DDC	Dewey Decimal Classification [*Also, DC*]
DDC	Digital Data Converter
DDC	Digital Display Converter (BUR)
DDC	Digitally Directed Control (MSA)
DDC	Direct Data Channel (CIT)
DDC	Direct Digital Control
DDC	Distributed Digital Control [*Data processing*]
DDCC	Decision Data Computer Corporation [*Horsham, PA*] [*NASDAQ symbol*] (NQ)
DDCE	Digital Data Conversion Equipment
DDCMP	Digital Data Communications Message Protocol [*Digital Equipment Corp.*]
DDCS	Data Definition Control System (CAA)
DD & CS	Dedicated Display and Control Subsystem (NASA)
DDCS	Digital Data Calibration System (KSC)
DDCS	Direct Digital Control System
DD/D	Data Dictionary/Directory
DDD	Detailed Data Display
DDD	Digital Data Distributor (CET)
DDD	Digital Display Driver (KSC)
DDD	Direct Distance Dialing [*of telephone numbers for toll calls*]
DDD	Display Decoder Drive (MCD)
DDD	Duplexed Display Distributor
DDDA	Decimal Digital Differential Analyzer
DDDL	Digital Data Down Link [*Data processing*] (MCD)
DDDP	Discrete Differential Dynamic Programing [*Data processing*]
DD/DS	Data Dictionary/Directory System
DDDU	Digital Decoder Driver Unit (MCD)
DDE	Decentralized Data Entry (IEEE)
DDE	Direct Data Entry [*Data processing*] (BUR)
DDE	Direct Digital Encoder
DDE	Distributed Data Entry (CAA)
DDERS	Direct Data Entry Replacement System
DDES	Data-Design Laboratories [*NASDAQ symbol*] (NQ)
DDES	Direct Data Entry System
DDF	Digital Distribution Frame [*Telecommunications*] (TEL)
DDG	Data Display Generator
DDG	Digital Data Generator (IEEE)
DDG	Digital Data Group
DDG	Digital Display Generator
DDGE	Digital Display Generator Element
DDH	Digital Data Handling
DDH & DS	Digital Data Handling and Display System
DDI	Data Display Indicator
DDI	Digital Display Indicator (MCD)
DDI	Direct Dial In (BUR)
DDI	Direct Digital Interface (CBSS)
DDI	Discrete Data Input (MCD)
DDI	Discrete Digital Input (NASA)
DDIE	Direct Digital Interface Equipment [*Telecommunications*] (TEL)
DDII	Digital Datacom, Incorporated [*NASDAQ symbol*] (NQ)
DDIS	Data Display
DDIS	Document Data Indexing Set
DDJ	Digital Differencing Junction (CIT)
DDL	Data Definition Language
DDL	Data Description Language
DDL	Data-Design Laboratories [*NYSE symbol*]
DDL	Data Distribution List
DDL	Data Down Link [*Data processing*] (MCD)
DDL	Data Drawing List
DDL	Digital Data Link
DDL	Digital Data Logger
DDL	Digital System Design Language [*Data processing*] (CSR)
DDLC	Data Description Language Committee [*CODASYL*] (CAA)
DDLT	Diagnostic Decision Logic Table [*Data processing*]
DDM	Data Demand Module (IEEE)
DDM	Data Display Module (MCD)
DDM	Difference in Depth of Modulation (IEEE)
DDM	Digital Display Machine
DDM	Digital Display Makeup
DDMA	Disk Direct Memory Access (CAA)
DDMC	Design and Drafting Management Council (EANO)
DDMS	Digital Data Measuring System
DDN	Digital Data Network
DDNC	Direct Digital Numerical Controller
DDO	Discrete Data Output (MCD)
DDOCE	Digital Data Output Conversion Equipment
DDP	Data Distribution Panel (KSC)
DDP	Design Data Package
DDP	Digital Data Processor
DDP	Digital Display Processor (CMD)
DDP	Distributed Data Processing
DDPC	Departmental Data Processing Center [*Department of Labor*]
DDPC	Digital Data Processing Center [*or Complex*] (MCD)
DDPE	Digital Data Processing Equipment
DDPS	Data Directed Programing System [*British*] (DIT)
DDPS	Digital Data Processing System
DDPS	Discrimination Data Processing System
DDPU	Digital Data Processing Unit (IEEE)
DDR	DASD [*Direct Access Storage Device*] Dump Restore [*Data processing*] (IBMDP)
DDR	Data Direction Register [*Microcomputer*]
DDR	Device Dependent Routine (CAA)
DDR	Dialed Digit Receiver [*Telecommunications*] (TEL)
DDR	Digital Data Receiver
DDR	Direct Drive
DDR	Dynamic Device Reconfiguration [*IBM Corp.*] [*Data processing*] (MDG)
DDRH	Digital Data Recording Head
DDRS	Demographic Data Retrieval System [*Census Bureau*] [*Information service*] (EISS)
DDRS	Digital Data Recording System
DDS	Data Dialog System (MCD)
DDS	Data Dictionary System (CAA)
DDS	Data Display Set (MCD)
DDS	Data Display System
DDS	Data Distribution System [*or Subsystem*]
DDS	Data-Phone Digital Service [*Trademark of the American Telephone & Telegraph Co.*]
DDS	Digital Data Servo
DDS	Digital Data System
DDS	Digital Display Scope
DDS	Digital Drafting System
DDS	Digital Dynamics Simulator (IEEE)
DDS	Direct Distance Service
DDSG	Digital Data Switching Group (CAAL)
DDSM	Digital Data Switching Matrix
DDSOT	Digital Daily System Operability Test (VIT)
DDSU	Digital Data Storage Unit
DDT	Data Description Table (BUR)
DDT	Delayed Dialing Tone [*Telecommunications*] (TEL)
DDT	Design Data Transmittal
DDT	Diagnostic Decision Table [*Data processing*] (TUT)
DDT	DIBOL Debugging Technique [*Digital Equipment Corp.*] (CAA)
DDT	Digital Data Terminal (MCD)
DDT	Digital Data Transceiver (CDH)
DDT	Digital Data Transmitter
DDT	Digital Debugging Tape
DDT	Digital Demodulation Technique (CIT)
DDT	Doppler Data Translator
DDT	Double Deflection Tube (BUR)
DDT	Dynamic Debugging Technique (DEN)
DDTE	Digital Data Terminal Equipment
DDTESM	Digital Data Terminal Equipment Service Module
DDTS	Digital Data Transmission System (KSC)
DDTS	Direct Dial Telephone System
DDU	Data Display Unit (NASA)
DDU	Decommutator Distribution Unit (MCD)
DDU	Diagnostic Display Unit (MCD)
DDU	Digital Data Unit (MUGU)
DDU	Digital Display Unit
DDU	Digital Distributing Unit
DDU	Disk Data Unit
DDU	Display and Debug Unit [*Data processing*] (MDG)
DDU	Display Driver Unit (NASA)
DDX	Digital Data Exchange [*Telecommunications*] (TEL)

Computer & Telecommunications Acronyms

DE .... Data Element [*Data processing*]
DE .... Data Encoder   (CIT)
DE .... Data Entry   (CAA)
DE .... Decision Element
DE .... Descriptor [*Online database field identifier*]
DE .... Device End   (CAH)
DE .... Digital Element   (IEEE)
DE .... Digital Encoder   (MSA)
DE .... Display Element   (CAH)
DE .... Display Equipment   (CAH)
DE .... Distant Element   (MDG)
DE .... Division Entry   (BUR)
DEA .... Data Encryption Algorithm   (CAA)
DEA .... Data Exchange Agreement
DEA .... Data Exchange Annex
DEAC .... Data Exchange Auxiliary Console   (CAAL)
DEACON ..... Direct English Access and Control [*Data processing*]
DEACS .... Data Exchange Auxiliary Consoles   (MCD)
DEAG .... Data Extraction and Analysis Group
DEAL .... Data Entry Application Language   (CAA)
DEAL .... Decision Evaluation and Logic
DEB .... Data Extent Block   (MCD)
DEB .... Digital European Backbone [*System*]   (MCD)
DEBE .... Does Everything but Eat [*Superseded by DITTO*] [*Data processing*]
DEBS .... Digital Electron Beam Scanner
DEC .... Decimal   (KSC)
DEC .... Digital Equipment Corporation [*Maynard, MA*] [*NYSE symbol*]
DEC .... Digital Evaluation Computer   (VIT)
DECA .... Digital Electronic Countermeasures Analyzer   (MCD)
DECA .... Display/AGAP [*Attitude Gyro Accelerometer Package*] Electronic Control Assembly   (KSC)
DECAL .... Detailed Experimental Computer-Assisted Language
DECAL .... Digital Equipment Corporation Author Language [*Data processing*]   (CSR)
DECALC ..... DECHEMA [*Deutsche Gesellschaft fuer Chemisches Apparatewesen, Chemische Technik, und Biotechnologie eV*] Data Calculation System [*Information retrieval*]   (ODIN)
DECB .... Data Event Control Block [*Data processing*]   (BUR)
Dec-FB .... Decrease Feedback
DECHEMA ... Deutsche Gesellschaft fuer Chemisches Apparatewesen, Chemische Technik, und Biotechnologie eV [*Database producer*]   (EISS)
DECIT .... Decimal Digit   (DIT)
DECLAB ..... Digital Equipment Company Laboratory   (OA)
DECNET ..... Digital Equipment Corporation Telecommunications Network
DECOMP .... Decomposition
DECOMP .... Decomposition Mathematical Programing System
DECPSK ..... Differentially Encoded Coherent Phase Shift Keying [*Telecommunications*]   (TEL)
DECR .... Decrement   (MDG)
DECS .... Data Entry Control System   (CAA)
DECU .... Data Exchange Control Unit   (NASA)
DECUS .... Digital Equipment Computer Users Society [*Marlboro, MA*]
DED .... Distant End Disconnect [*Telecommunications*]   (TEL)
DED .... Double Error Detection   (CAA)
DEDAAS ..... Digital Electrophysiological Data Acquisition and Analysis System [*Neurometrics*]
DEDARS ..... DECHEMA [*Deutsche Gesellschaft fuer Chemisches Apparatewesen, Chemische Technik, und Biotechnologie eV*] Data Retrieval System [*Information retrieval*]   (ODIN)
DEDB .... Digital Elevation Database   (RDA)
DEDL .... Data Element Description List [*Data processing*]
DEDP .... Data Entry and Display Panel   (MCD)
DEDS .... Data Entry and Display Subsystem
DEDS .... Digital Error Detection Subsystem [*Data processing*]
DEDUCOM ... Deductive Communicator   (IEEE)
DEE .... Digital Evaluation Equipment
DEE .... Digital Events Evaluator   (MCD)
DEE .... Discrete Event Evaluator   (KSC)
DEEC .... Digital Electronic Engine Control   (MCD)
DEEP .... Data Exception Error Protection   (CAA)
DEES .... Dynamic Electromagnetic Environment Simulator
DEF .... Data Entry Facility   (CAA)
DEF .... Defective   (MSA)
DEF .... Definition
3DEFL .... Triple Diffused Emitter-Follower Logic   (MDG)
DEFT .... Definite-Time [*Relay*]
DEFT .... Direct Electronic Fourier Transform [*Camera*]
DEFT .... Display Evaluation Flight Testing   (MCD)
DEFT .... Dynamic Error-Free Transmission
DEG .... Degree   (AFM)
DEH .... Digital Encoder Handbook
DEHB .... Digital Encoder Handbook
DEIC .... Diver Equipment Information Center [*Battelle Memorial Institute*] [*Information service*]   (EISS)
DEIS .... Design Evaluation Inspection Simulator   (NASA)
DEK .... Data Entry Keyboard [*Data processing*]   (MCD)
DEL .... Data Entry Language   (CAA)
DEL .... Delay   (DDI)
DEL .... Delay Message [*Aviation code*]   (FAAC)
DEL .... Delete Character [*Keyboard*]   (CMD)
DEL .... Direct Exchange Line [*Telecommunications*]   (DEEC)

DELMAR ...... Data Element Management Accounting/Reporting
DELPHO ..... Deliver by Telephone [*Message handling*]
DELTA .... Determination Effective Levels of Task Automation [*Data processing*]
DELTA .... Distributed Electronic Test and Analysis   (CAA)
DELTABANK ... Drug Effects on Laboratory Tests: Attention [*Worldwide Medical Information Ltd.*] [*Database*]   (CUAD)
DEM .... Delta Modulation [*Telecommunications*]   (TEL)
DEM .... Demodulator [*Telecommunications*]   (KSC)
DEMA .... Data Entry Management Association [*Stamford, CT*]   (EANO)
DEMAC .... Diesel Engine Monitoring and Control [*ASMAP Electronics Ltd.*] [*Software package*] [*British*]   (NCC)
DEMAND .... Digitalized Electronics MARC [*Machine-Readable Cataloging*] and Non-MARC [*Machine-Readable Cataloging*] Display [*Library of Congress*]
DEMAR .... Data Element Management Accounting and Reporting   (MCD)
DE-ME-DRIVE ... Decoding Memory Drive [*Data processing*]   (MDG)
DEM/LAB ... Demographics Laboratory [*Information service*]   (EISS)
DEMOD ...... Demodulator [*Telecommunications*]
DEMON ...... Decision Mapping via Optimum Go-No Networks
DEMON ...... Digital Electric Monitor
DEMON ...... Diminishing Error Method of Optimization for Networks [*Data processing*]   (RDA)
DEMS .... Digital Electronic Message Systems
DEMS .... Digital Error Monitoring System   (MCD)
DEMUX .... Demultiplexer [*Data processing*]   (CIT)
DEN .... Data Element Number   (MCD)
DENALT ..... Density Altitude [*Computer*]
DEO .... Digital End Office [*Telecommunications*]
DEOT .... Disconnect, End of Transmission   (CAA)
DEP .... Data Entry Panel   (MCD)
DEP .... Data Exchange Program
DEPDA .... Deployment Data File
DEPIC .... Dual-Expanded Plastic-Insulated Conductor [*Telecommunications*]   (TEL)
DEPSK .... Differential Encoding Phase Shift Keying   (MCD)
DEQUIP ...... DECHEMA [*Deutsche Gesellschaft fuer Chemisches Apparatewesen Chemische Technik und Biotechnologie eV*] Equipment Suppliers Databank [*Database*]   (CUAD)
DER .... Directly Executable Representation   (CAA)
DER .... Distributed Energy Release [*Computer program*]
DER .... Division of Engineering Research [*Michigan State University*] [*Research center*]   (RCD)
DERP .... Defective Equipment Repair Program [*Telephone company*]
DERS .... Data Entry Reporting System   (CAA)
DERS .... Division of Educational Research Services [*University of Alberta*] [*Research center*]   (RCD)
DES .... Data Encryption Standard [*National Bureau of Standards*]
DES .... Data Engineering Section
DE/S .... Data Entry/Separation   (MCD)
DES .... Data Entry System   (CAA)
DES .... Data Exchange System   (NASA)
DES .... Digital Expansion System
DES .... Discrete Elastic System
DESC .... Data Entry System Controller   (CAA)
DESC .... Defense Electronics Supply Center [*DSA*]
DESC .... Digital Equation-Solving Computer   (IEEE)
DESSIM ...... Design Simulator
DEST .... Destination
DET .... Digital Event Timer   (KSC)
DETAB .... Decision Table [*Data processing*]
DETAB-X .... Decision Table Experimental [*Data processing*]
DETAP .... Decision Table Processor [*IBM Corp.*]   (CGC)
DETEQ .... DECHEMA [*Deutsche Gesellschaft fuer Chemisches Apparatewesen, Chemische Technik, und Biotechnologie eV*] Environmental Technology Equipment Databank [*Frankfurt am Main*] [*Information service*] [*West German*]   (EISS)
DETHERM-SDC ... DECHEMA [*Deutsche Gesellschaft fuer Chemisches Apparatewesen, Chemische Technik, und Biotechnologie eV*] Thermophysical Property Data Bank - Data Evaluation System [*Database*]   (ODIN)
DETHERM-SDR ... DECHEMA [*Deutsche Gesellschaft fuer Chemisches Apparatewesen, Chemische Technik, und Biotechnologie eV*] Thermophysical Property Data Bank - Data Retrieval System [*Database*]   (ODIN)
DETOC .... Decision Table to COBOL [*Common Business-Oriented Language*] Processor [*Data processing*]   (CGC)
DETOL .... Directly Executable Test-Oriented Language [*1968*] [*Data processing*]   (CSR)
DETRAN ..... Decision Table Translator [*Data processing*]   (CGC)
DETS .... Digital Element Test Set
DETX .... Detector Electronics [*NASDAQ symbol*]   (NQ)
DEU .... Data Encoder Unit   (SKY)
DEU .... Data Encryption Unit   (CAA)
DEU .... Data Entry Unit   (OA)
DEU .... Data Exchange Unit
DEU .... Digital Evaluation Unit   (VIT)
DEU .... Display Electronics Unit   (NASA)
DEUA .... Digitronics Equipment Users Association   (CAH)
DEUCE .... Digital Electronic Universal Calculating Engine
DEUT .... Data Encoder Unit Transmitter   (SKY)
DEV .... Device   (KSC)

Computer & Telecommunications Acronyms

Acronym	Definition
DEVSIS	Development Sciences Information System [*Information service*] [*Canada*] (EISS)
DEX	Data Exchange (CAA)
DEX	Deferred Execution (OA)
DEXAN	Digital Experimental Airborne Navigator
DF	Data Folder
DF	Decimal Fraction (MDG)
DF	Deflection Factor (IEEE)
DF	Destination Field (CAA)
DF	Direction Finder [*or Finding*] [*Radio aid to navigation*]
DF	Disk File [*Data processing*] (BUR)
DF	Distribution Frame (KSC)
DF	Double Frequency (DEEC)
DF	Douglas Fir (MSA)
DF	Dual Facility
DF	I am connecting you to the station you request [*Telecommunications*] (FAAC)
DFA	Digital Fault Analysis
DFA	Digital Frequency Analyzer
DFA	Distributed Function Architecture (CAA)
DFAST	Dynamic File Allocation System (CAA)
DFB	Distributed Feedback
DFC	Data Flow Control (IBMDP)
DFC	Data Format Converter (VIT)
DFC	Diagnostic Flow Chart [*Data processing*] (IEEE)
DFC	Digital Flight Controller
DFC	Disk File Check (OA)
DFC	Disk File Control [*Data processing*]
DFC	Dual-Feed Coupler
DFCLS	Digital Flight Control and Landing System
DFCNV	Disk Data File Conversion Program [*IBM Corp.*] (CAA)
DFCS	Digital Flight Control System
DFCU	Disk File Control Unit (OA)
DFD	Data Flow Diagram
DFD	Digital Flight Display
DFD	Digital Frequency Display
DFDC	Disk File Descriptor Control [*Data processing*]
DFDR	Digital Flight Data Recorder (MCD)
DFDSS	Data Facility Data Set Services
DFE	Data Facility Extended
DFE	Data Flow Engineer (MCD)
DFEU	Disk File Electronics Unit (CAA)
DFF	Display Format Facility (CAA)
DFG	Digital Function Generator
DFG	Discrete Frequency Generator
DFG	Display Format Generator (MCD)
DFGS	Digital Flight Guidance System (IEEE)
DFI	Disk File Interrogate (OA)
DFIB	Data Function Information Book (VIT)
DFIS	Digital Facsimile Interface System
DFL	Display Formatting Language (CIT)
DFLX	Division of Foreign Labor Conditions [*Department of Labor*]
DFLX	Dataflex Corp. [*NASDAQ symbol*] (NQ)
DFM	Digital Frequency Meter [*or Monitor*]
DFM	Dual-Frequency Method (CIT)
DFMMS	Data File/Media Management System
DFMO	Doppler Filter Mixer-Oscillator [*Electronics*]
DFN	Data File Number (CAA)
DFO	Directed Format Option [*Rapid access management information system*] (CAA)
DFO	Disk File Optimizer [*Data processing*] (BUR)
DFP	Data Facility Product
DFP	Define File Processor [*Data processing*]
DFP	Demand Forecasting Program (BUR)
DFPL	Data Flow Programing Language (CAA)
DFPS	Digital Ferrite Phase Shifter
DFR	Dual-Frequency Receiver
DFR	Dun's Financial Records [*Dun's Marketing Services*] [*Information Service*] (EISS)
DfS	Dataflow Systems, Inc. [*Bethesda, MD*] [*Information service*] (EISS)
DFS	Digital Field System
DFS	Digital Frequency Synthesizer
DFS	Display Formatting System (SKY)
DFS	Distributed File System (CAA)
DFS	Dynamic Flight Simulator
DFSG	Direct Formed Supergroup [*Telecommunications*] (TEL)
DFSK	Double Frequency Shift Keying [*Radio*]
DFSU	Disk File Storage Unit (OA)
DFT	Diagnostic Function Test [*Data processing*]
DFT	Digital Facility Terminal [*Telecommunications*] (TEL)
DFT	Discrete Fourier Transform
DFU	Data File Utility [*Data processing*] (IBMDP)
DFV	Dokumentationsstelle fuer Veterinaermedizin [*Information retrieval*] (ODIN)
DFWT	Dallas Fort Worth Teleport Ltd. [*Irving, TX*] [*Telecommunications*] (TSSD)
DG	Data General Corp. [*Computer manufacturer*] (CAA)
DG	Differential Gain
DGBUS	Digital Ground Bus (VIT)
DGC	Data General Corporation [*Computer manufacturer*] (CAH)
DGC	Data Graphics Corporation
DGD	Deutsche Gesellschaft fuer Dokumentation [*German Society for Documentation*] [*Information service*] (EISS)
DGEN	Data Generation (SKY)
DGK	Deutsche Gesellschaft fuer Kybernetik [*German Society for Cybernetics*] [*Uber Starnberg, Germany*]
DG/L	Data General's System Programing Language (CAA)
DGM	Data Gathering Monitoring [*System*]
DGM	Deutsche Gesellschaft fuer Metallkunde [*Information retrieval*] (ODIN)
DGN	Data General Corp. [*NYSE symbol*]
DGOR	Deutsche Gesellschaft fuer Operations Research [*German Society for Operational Research*] [*Frankfurt, Germany*]
DGP	Data Generating Program
DGS	Data Gathering System (MCD)
DGS	Digital Ground System
DGT	Digital Equipment Corp. [*Maynard, MA*] [*FAA designator*] (FAAC)
DGT	Direction Generale des Telecommunications [*General Management of Telecommunications*] [*Paris, France*] [*Telecommunications*] (TSSD)
DGTC	Digitech, Inc. [*NASDAQ symbol*] (NQ)
D-H	Decimal to Hexadecimal (IEEE)
DH	Device Handler (CAA)
DHDD	Digital High-Definition Display (KSC)
DHDS	Data Handling and Display Subsystem
DHE	Data Handling Equipment
DHISF	Document Handling and Information Services Facility [*General Accounting Office*] (EISS)
DHLLP	Direct High-Level Language Processor (IDA)
DHP	Document Handler Processor (CAA)
DHS	Data Handling System
DHS	Discrete Horizon Sensor (MCD)
DHSS	Data Handling Subsystem (NATG)
DHT	Discrete Hilbert Transform (IEEE)
DHU	Document Handler Unit (CAA)
DHVM	Digital Hardware Voter Monitor (MCD)
DI	Data Input [*Data processing*] (IEEE)
DI	Data Integrator (MCD)
DI	Data Interface
DI	Data Item
DI	Destination Index [*Data processing*]
DI	Device Independence (CAA)
DI	Digital Input [*Data processing*] (CGC)
DI	Discrete Input [*Data processing*] (KSC)
DIA	Diameter
DIA	Digital Interface Adapter [*Data processing*] (MCD)
DIA	Digital Isolation Amplifier (CIT)
DIA	Direct Interface Adapter (CAA)
DIA	Documents Information Accessing (BUR)
DIA	Dual Interface Adapter (CAA)
DIAD	Data Immediate Access Diagram (CCD)
DIADS	Digital Image Analysis and Display System [*Data processing*]
DIAG	Diagram (KSC)
DIAL	Data Independent Analysis Library (CAAL)
DIAL	Digital Image Analysis Laboratory [*University of Arizona*] [*Research center*] (RCD)
DIAL	Display Interactive Assembly Language [*Data processing*] (IEEE)
DIAL	Drum Interrogation, Alteration, and Loading System [*Honeywell, Inc.*] (IEEE)
DIALGOL	Dialect of Algorithmic Language
DIALS	Defense Information Automated Locator System
DIAM	Data Independent Architecture Model (OA)
DIAM	Diameter
DIAMON	Diagnostic Monitor [*Data processing*] (CIT)
DIAN	Digital Analog [*Data processing*] (IEEE)
DIANE	Direct Information Access Network for Europe [*Commission of the European Communities*] [*Information service*] (EISS)
DIAS	DUNS [*Data Universal Numbering System*] Industrial Affiliations Service [*Dun & Bradstreet, Inc.*] (EISS)
DIAS	Dynamic Inventory Analysis System [*Data processing*]
DIB	Data Input Bus [*Data processing*] (MDG)
DIB	Data Inspection Board [*Europe*] (CAA)
DIBIT	Di-Binary Digit [*Two consecutive binary digits*] (TEL)
DIBOL	Digital Equipment's Business-Oriented Language [*Data processing*] (TUT)
DIBS	Digital Integrated Business System [*Digital Equipment Corp.*] (CAA)
DIC	Data Input Clerk [*Data processing*]
DIC	Data Input Consoles [*Data processing*]
DIC	Data Insertion Converter
DIC	Data Item Category
DIC	Digital Input [*or Integrating*] Computer [*Data processing*]
DIC	Digital Integrated Circuit [*Data processing*]
DICAM	Datasystem Interactive Communications Access Method [*Digital Equipment Corp.*] (CAA)
DICAP	Direct-Current Circuit Analysis Program [*Data processing*]
DICC	Digital Interface Code Converter [*Data processing*]
DICE	Digital Integrated Circuit Element [*Data processing*]
DICE	Digital Intercontinental Conversion Equipment (MCD)
DICE	Digitally Implemented Communications Experiment (MCD)
DICODE	Digital Correlation Demonstrator
DICOMTA	Documentation Informatisee pour les Comptables [*CEDIC*] [*Database*] (CUAD)

By Acronym

Acronym	Definition
DICON	Digital Communication through Orbiting Needles
DICOSE	Digital Communications System Evaluator
DICU	Digital Interface and Control Unit (SKY)
DID	Data Identification (CIT)
DID	Data Input Display [*Data processing*]
DID	Data Item Description
DID	Datamation Industry Directory (MCD)
DID	Device Identifier (CAA)
DID	Digital Information Display [*Data processing*]
DID	Direct Inward Dialing [*Telecommunications*]
DID	Display Interface Device [*Telecommunications*] (TEL)
DIDA	Dynamic Instrumentation Digital Analyzer
DIDAC	Digital Data Computer
DIDACS	Digital Data Communications System (MCD)
DIDAD	Digital Data Display (CGC)
DIDAP	Digital Data Processor
DIDAS	Dynamic Instrumentation Data Automobile System [*Telemetering system for auto test tracks*]
DIDC	Data Input Display Console [*Data processing*]
DIDD	Dynamic Integrated Data Display
DIDDS	Dynamic Integrated Data Display System
DIDF	Dual Input Describing Function [*Data processing*]
DIDL	Digital Integrated Design Language [*Data processing*] (CSR)
DIDM	Document Identification and Description Macros [*IBM Corp.*] (CAA)
DI/DO	Data Input/Data Output [*Data processing*]
DIDO	Digital Input/Digital Output [*Data processing*] (CAA)
DIDOCS	Device Independent Display Operator Console Support (BUR)
DIDS	Decision Information Distribution System
DIDS	Digital Information Display System [*Data processing*]
DIDS	Document Information Directory System [*NIOSH*] [*Database*] (FDB)
DIDS	Domestic Information Display System [*Computer graphics*]
DIF	Data Interchange Format
DIF	Device Input Format (CAA)
DIF	Document Interchange Format
DIF	Drug Information Fulltext [*American Society of Hospital Pharmacists*] [*Database*]
DIFA	Differential Amplifier (MSA)
DIFAR	Directional Frequency Analysis and Recording System
DIFF	Difference (KSC)
DIFFTR	Differential Time Relay (IEEE)
DIFU	Deutsches Institut fuer Urbanistik [*Vereins fuer Kommunalwissenschaften eV*] [*Database producer*] (ODIN)
DIG	Design Implementation Guide [*Telecommunications*] (TEL)
DIG	Digital-Image-Generated [*Data processing*] (IEEE)
DIG	Digital Input Gate (OA)
DIGAC	Digital Avionics Control
DIGACC	Digital Guidance and Control Computer
DIGATEC	Digital Gas Turbine Engine Control (MCD)
DIGCOM	Digital Computer (IEEE)
DIGICOM	Digital Communications
DIGIDOPS	Digital Doppler System (MCD)
DIGINESS	Digital Network Simulation System (MCD)
DIGISAT	Digital Data Satellite Service [*Communications Satellite Corp.*]
DIGISMAC	Digital Scene Matching Area Correlator (MCD)
DIGISPLAY	Digitally Scanned Image Display (MCD)
DIGITAC	Digital Tactical Automatic Control (IEEE)
DIGITAR	Digital Airborne Computer (IEEE)
DIGRM	Digit/Record Mark (MDG)
DIGRMGM	Digit/Record Mark Group/Mark (MDG)
DIGRO	Digital Readout [*Data processing*]
DIH	Discrete Input High (MCD)
DIL	Discrete Input Low (MCD)
DIL	Displayed Impact Line (MCD)
DIL	Dual In-Line [*Electronic components*]
DILEP	Digital Line Engineering Program [*Telecommunications*] (TEL)
DILO	Digilog, Inc. [*NASDAQ symbol*] (NQ)
DILP	Dual In-Line Package [*Data processing*]
DIM	Data Interpretation Module (CAA)
DIM	Design Interface Meeting (NASA)
DIM	Device Interface Module (OA)
DIM	Digital Ignorant Mechanism [*Pocket calculator facetiously described by T. R. Reid in his book, "The Chip"*]
DIM	Digital Input Module [*Data processing*]
DIM	Digital Input Multiplexer (CAAL)
DIMA	Direct Imaging Mass Analyzer
DIMDI	Deutsches Institut fuer Medizinische Dokumentation und Information [*German Institute for Medical Documentation and Information*] [*Information service*] (EISS)
DIMES	Digital Image Manipulation and Enhancement Systems
DIMS	Distributed Intelligence Microcomputer System (DEEC)
DIMUS	Digital Multibeam Steering
DIN	Data Identification Number (AFM)
DIN	Deutsches Institut fuer Normung [*German Standards Institute*] [*Formerly, DNA*] [*Berlin, WG*]
DIN	Digital Input [*Data processing*] (KSC)
DINA	Digital Network Analyzer
DINA	Distributed Information Processing Network Architecture (CAA)
DIN/DCSS	Digital Network-Defense Special Security Communications System [*National Security Agency*]
DINN	Dual Input Null Network
DIO	Data Input/Output (CAA)
DIO	Direct Input/Output [*Telecommunications*] (TEL)
DIOB	Digital Input/Output Buffer [*Data processing*]
DIOC	Digital Input/Output Control (CAA)
DIODE	Digital Input/Output Display Equipment (IDA)
DIOI	Digital Input/Output Interface [*Data processing*] (KSC)
DIOP	Digital Input/Output Package [*Data processing*]
DIOS	Distributed Input/Output System (CAA)
DIP	Data Input Processor [*Data processing*] (SKY)
DIP	Digital Incremental Plotter
DIP	Digital Instrumentation Programer (VIT)
DIP	Display Interface Processing (MCD)
DIP	Distributed Information Processing (CAA)
DIP	Double In-Line Package [*Data processing*]
DIP	Dual In-Line Pin
DipCompSc	Diploma in Computer Science
DIPDOP	Disc and Drum Input/Output Routines [*Honeywell, Inc.*] (CDH)
DipInfmProcessing	Diploma in Information Processing
DIPLXR	Diplexer [*Electronics*]
DipNA & AC	Diploma in Numerical Analysis and Automatic Computing
DIPPA	Digital Parallel Processing Array
DipTech(InfProc)	Diploma in Technology (Information Processing)
DIPX	Diplex [*Electronics*] (MSA)
DIQD	Disk-Insulated Quad [*Telecommunications*] (TEL)
DIR	Data Input Register (CAA)
DIR	Directory
DIRLINE	Directory of Information Sources Online [*National Library of Medicine*] [*Database*]
Dir Online Databases	Directory of Online Databases [*United States*] [*A publication*]
DIRSLEARN	Datenbank fuer Schulung von GRIPS/DIRS3-Anwendern [*Database for Training of GRIPS/DIRS3 Users*] [*Database*] [*Information retrieval*] (ODIN)
DIRT	Director's Instant Reversible Talkback [*Device enabling contact between director in control room and crew in studio*]
DIRVIR	Directory Verification Processor [*Data processing*]
DIS	Data Input System [*Data processing*] (CIT)
DIS	Data Inspection Station (VIT)
DIS	Database Information System
DIS	Decision Information Services Ltd. [*Information service*] (EISS)
DIS	Digital Instrumentation Subsystem (CIT)
DIS	Digital Integration System (IEEE)
DIS	Display (KSC)
DIS	Distributed Information System [*Data processing*]
DIS	Draft International Standard [*International Standards Organization*]
DIS	Drug Information Services [*University of Minnesota*] (EISS)
DISAC	Digital Simulator and Computer (IEEE)
DISC	Data Processing and Information Science Contents
DISC	Digital Information Systems Corporation [*Sacramento, CA*] [*Software manufacturer*] (DASOS)
DISC	Digital International Switching Center [*Telecommunications*] (TEL)
DISC	Disconnect (KSC)
DISC	Drilling Information Service Company [*Houston, TX*] [*Telecommunications*] (TSSD)
DISC	Dynamic Interface Systems Corporation [*Los Angeles, CA*] [*Software manufacturer*] (DASOS)
DISCOM	Digital Selective Communications
DISCON	Defense Integrated Secure Communications Network [*Australia*] [*Telecommunications*] (TEL)
DISIM	Digital Input Simulator [*Data processing*] (VIT)
DISP	Display (KSC)
DISPLAY	Digital Service Planning Analysis [*Telecommunications*] (TEL)
DISS	Digital Interface Switching System (OA)
DISSCO	DISSPLA and TELL-A-GRAF User Community [*Argonne National Laboratory*] [*Argonne, IL*]
DISSPLA	Display Integrated Software System and Plotting Language [*Data processing*]
DIST	Distributed Time (KSC)
DIST	Distributor (KSC)
DISTAN	Distributed Interactive Secure Telecommunications Area Network (MCD)
Dist Proc	Distributed Processing Newsletter [*A publication*]
DISTR	Distribution [*or Distributor*] (AFM)
DISU	Digital International Switching Unit [*Telecommunications*] (TEL)
DIT	Data Identification Table (MCD)
DIT	Data Inquiry Terminal
DIT	Dual Input Transponder
DITAR	Digital Telemetry Analog Recording (VIT)
DITEC	Digital Television Camera (MCD)
DITEC	Digital Television Encoding (CBSS)
DITMCO	Data Information Test Material Checkout (VIT)
DITRAN	Diagnostic FORTRAN [*Data processing*] (IEEE)
DITS	Digital Information Transfer Set (CAAL)
DITS	Digital Television Spectrometer (NG)
DITTO	Data Interfile Transfer, Testing, and Operations Utility [*IBM program product*]
DITU	Digital Interface Test Unit [*Data processing*] (KSC)
DIU	Data Interface Unit
DIU	Digital Input Unit [*Data processing*]
DIU	Digital Insertion Unit [*Data processing*]
DIU	Digital Interface Unit [*Data processing*] (KSC)

Computer & Telecommunications Acronyms

DIU .... Office of Development Information and Utilization [*Agency for International Development*] [*Information service*] (EISS)
DIVA .... Digital Inquiry - Voice Answerback [*Touch-tone*] [*Bell System*] [*Telecommunications*]
DIVIC .... Digital Variable Increment Computer
DIVOT .... Digital-to-Voice Translator
DIVOTS ...... Data Input Voice Output Telephone System
DIVS .... Signed Division [*Data processing*]
DIVU .... Unsigned Division [*Data processing*]
DIW .... Deutsches Institut fuer Wirtschaftsforschung [*Data Resources, Inc.*] [*Database*] (CUAD)
DIWT .... Dokumentations - und Informationsgesellschaft fuer Wirtschaft und Touristik mbH [*Database producer*] (CUAD)
DJ .... Digital Junction [*Telecommunications*] (TEL)
DJCN .... Dow Jones Cable News [*Cable-television system*]
DJNR .... Dow Jones News/Retrieval [*Princeton, NJ*] [*Bibliographic database*] [*Information service*] (OBD)
DK .... Display/Keyboard
DKB .... Decimal Keyboard [*Data processing*]
DKF .... Dokumentation Kraftfahrwesen eV [*Database producer and database*] [*Information retrieval*] (ODIN)
DKFZ .... Deutsches Krebsforschungszentrum [*Heidelberg*] [*Information retrieval*] (ODIN)
DKI .... Data Key Idle (OA)
DKI .... Deutsches Krankenhausinstitut [*Dusseldorf*] [*Information retrieval*] (ODIN)
DKI .... Deutsches Kunststoffinstitut [*Database producer*] (ODIN)
DKSEN ...... Don King Sports and Entertainment Network [*Cable-television system*]
DL .... Dacron Braid Lacquered (MDG)
DL .... Data Language
DL .... Data Link
DL .... Day Letter [*Telegraphy*]
DL .... Direct Line [*Followed by telephone number*]
DL .... Distributed Lab (MDG)
DL .... Down Link [*Data processing*]
DL .... Dual Language (CAA)
DL .... Dynamic Load Characteristic (MDG)
DL/1 .... Data Language Version 1 [*Data processing*] (MCD)
DLA .... Data Link Adapter (CAA)
DLA .... Data Link Address
DLA .... Delay Message [*Aviation code*]
DLBI .... Differential Long-Baseline Interferometer [*Radio interferometry*]
DLC .... Data Link Control [*Data processing*] (BUR)
DLC .... Develcon Electronics Ltd. [*Toronto Stock Exchange symbol*]
DLC .... Digital Logic Circuit
DLC .... Duplex Line Control (BUR)
DLCF .... Data Link Control Field [*Data processing*]
DLCP .... Data Link Control Panel [*Data processing*] (MCD)
DLCS .... Data-Line Concentration System [*Bell System*]
DLD .... Data Link Decoder (MCD)
DLD .... Discount Long Distance [*Larose, LA*] [*Telecommunications*] (TSSD)
DLE .... Data Link Equipment
DLE .... Data Link Escape Character [*Keyboard*] (CMD)
DLF .... Document Library Facility [*Data processing*]
DLFDU ...... Data Line Flight Direction Unit (MCD)
DLIMP .... Descriptive Language Implemented by Macroprocessors (IDA)
DLK .... Data Link (KSC)
DLL .... Dial Long Line [*Bell System*]
DLM .... Data Line Monitor (CAA)
DLM .... Delay Line Memory
DLM .... Digital Logic Module
DLMCP ..... Distributed Loop Message Communication Protocol (CAA)
DLN .... Document Locator Number [*Data processing*]
DLO .... Delayed Output [*Data processing*]
DLOG .... Distributed Logic Corp. [*NASDAQ symbol*] (NQ)
DLOS .... Distributed Loop Operating System (CAA)
DLP .... Data Link Processor [*Burroughs Corp.*] [*Data processing*] (BUR)
DLP .... Data Link Programs (MCD)
DLP .... Data Listing Programs (IEEE)
DLR .... Data Link Receiver [*Data processing*] (MCD)
DLR .... Dominion Law Reports [*Canada Book Ltd.*] [*Database*]
DLRD .... Design Layout Report Date [*Telecommunications*] (TEL)
DLRP .... Data Link Reference Point
DLS .... Data Link Set
DLS .... Data Link Simulator
DLS .... Data Logging System
DLS .... Digital Line System [*Telecommunications*] (TEL)
DLS .... Digital Logic System
DLSM .... Data Link Summary Message (MCD)
DLSO .... Dial Line Service Observing [*Telecommunications*] (TEL)
DLT .... Data Link Terminal
DLT .... Data Link Translator
DLT .... Data Loop Transceiver [*Data processing*]
DLT .... Decision Logic Translator (CAA)
DLT .... Depletion-Layer Transistor (IEEE)
DLT .... Digital Line Termination [*Telecommunications*] (TEL)
DLTK .... Deltak Corp. [*NASDAQ symbol*] (NQ)
DLTM .... Data Link Test Message
DLTR .... Data Link Terminal Repeater (NASA)
DLTR .... Data Link Transmission Repeater (NASA)
DLTS .... Deep Level Transient Spectroscopy

DLTT .... Down-Link Television Terminal
DLU .... Data Line Unit (OA)
DLU .... Digitizer Logic Unit
DLU .... Display Logic Unit
DLY .... Delay (KSC)
DM .... Data Management (KSC)
DM .... Data Manager (CAH)
DM .... Data Master
DM .... Data Memory (CAA)
DM .... Debugging Mode
DM .... Delta Modulation
DM .... Demand Meter
DM .... Digital Module [*Telecommunications*] (TEL)
DM .... Disconnected Mode (CCD)
DM .... Magnetic Drum Module [*Data processing*] (CDH)
DMA .... Data Management Analysis
DMA .... Designated Market Area
DMA .... Digital Major Alarm (MCD)
DMA .... Direct Memory Access [*Computing method*]
DMA .... Direct Memory Address [*Data processing*] (CDH)
DMA .... Drum Memory Assembly [*Data processing*]
DMAC .... Direct Memory Access Control [*Data processing*]
DMACP ..... Direct Memory Access Communications Processor (CAA)
DMAD .... Diagnostic Machine Aid Digital [*Programing language*] (CSR)
DMAHTC .... Defense Mapping Agency Hydrographic/Topographic Center [*Database*] (FDB)
DMAI .... Direct Memory Access Interface (CAA)
DMAN .... Data Manager (KSC)
DMAS .... Distribution Management Accounting System (IEEE)
DMAT .... Digital Module Automatic Tester
DMB .... Data Management Block (CAA)
DMB .... Disconnect and Make Busy [*Telecommunications*] (TEL)
DMBC .... Double Mark Blank Column (BUR)
DMC .... Data Management Center (CAAL)
DMC .... Data Management Channel
DMC .... Data Management Computer (KSC)
DMC .... Digital Microcircuit
DMC .... Digital Monitor Computer (VIT)
DMC .... Direct Memory Channel (CAA)
DMC .... Direct Multiplexed Control (OA)
DMC .... Direct Multiplexor Channel
DMC .... Discrete Memoryless Channel [*Data processing*]
DMC .... Disk Memory Controller [*Data processing*]
DMCL .... Device Media Control Language [*CODASYL/Honeywell, Inc.*] (DEEC)
DMCM .... Double Density Modular Core Memory (MCD)
DMDC .... Diffusion in Metals and Alloys Data Center [*National Bureau of Standards*] (EISS)
DMDP .... Data Maintenance Diagnostic Program
DME .... Diagnostic Monitor Executive [*Data processing*] (TUT)
DME .... Digital Motor Electronics
DME .... Digital Multiplex Equipment [*Telecommunications*] (DEEC)
DME .... Direct Machine Environment (CAA)
DME .... Distance Measuring Equipment [*Navigation*]
DMED .... Digital Message Entry Device [*Data processing*]
DMEP .... Data Network Modified Emulator Program [*Telecommunications*] (TEL)
DMES .... Digital Message Entry System
DMET .... Distance Measuring Equipment TACAN (NG)
DMET .... Distance Measuring Equipment Terminal (CET)
DMF .... Data Management Facility (CAA)
DMF .... Digital Multiplexing and Formatting [*Data processing*] (MCD)
DMF .... Disk Management Facility (CAA)
DMG .... Data Management [*A publication*]
DMG .... Data Management Group (MCD)
DMGT .... Data Management (MSA)
D/M/I .... Decision/Making/Information [*Information service*] (EISS)
DMI .... Direct Memory Interface (CAA)
DMI .... Dun's Market Identifier [*Dun & Bradstreet, Inc.*] [*Database*] (EISS)
DMIS .... Data Management Information System [*DoD*]
DMIS .... Donnelley Marketing Information Services [*Stamford, CT*] (EISS)
DML .... Data Management Language [*Digital Equipment Corp.*] (CAA)
DML .... Data Manipulation Language [*Digital Equipment Corp.*] [*Data processing*]
DMM .... Data Manipulation Mode (OA)
DMM .... Digital Multimeter
DMNI .... Device Multiplexing Nonsynchronized Inputs [*Data processing*]
DMNO .... Device Multiplexing Nonsynchronized Outputs [*Data processing*] (CET)
DMOS .... Data Management Operating System (CAA)
DMOS .... Depletion Metal-Oxide Semiconductor (BUR)
DMOS .... Diffusion Metal-Oxide Semiconductor [*Telecommunications*] (TEL)
DMOS .... Double-Diffused Metal-Oxide Semiconductor [*Microelectronics*] (MCD)
DMP .... Direct Memory Processor (CAA)
DMQ .... Direct Memory Queue [*Data processing*] (CAA)
DMR .... Data Management Routine
DMR .... Date Material Required
DMR .... Demultiplexing/Mixing/Remultiplexing [*Device*] [*Telecommunications*] (TEL)
DMS .... Data Management Service (IEEE)

By Acronym

Computer & Telecommunications Acronyms

DMS............ Data Management System [*Data processing*]
DMS............ Data Measuring System
DMS............ Data Monitoring System
DMS............ Data Multiplex System [*Data processing*]
DMS............ Database Management System
DMS............ Development Management System [*IBM Corp.*]
DMS............ Digital Microsystems [*Digital Microsystems Ltd.*] [*Software package*] [*British*]   (NCC)
DMS............ Digital Multiplex Switch
DMS............ Digital Multiplexing Synchronizer [*Data processing*]
DMS............ Disk Monitor System [*Data processing*]
DMS............ Display Management System [*IBM Corp.*]
DMS............ Drum Memory System [*Data processing*]
DMS............ Dun's Marketing Services [*Dun & Bradstreet, Inc.*] [*Parsippany, NJ*] [*Information service*]   (EISS)
DMS............ Dynamic Mapping System [*Hewlett-Packard Co.*]
DMS/CS..... Data Management System/Computer Subsystem [*Data processing*]
DMSP......... Data Management Summary Processor   (KSC)
DMSS......... Data Multiplex Subsystem [*Data processing*]
DMSS......... Digital Multibeam Steering System
DM & T....... Defense Markets & Technology [*Predicasts, Inc.*] [*Database*]
DMT........... Digital Message Terminal   (MCD)
DMT........... Direct Memory Transfer [*Data processing*]   (CAA)
DMTC......... Digital Magnetic Tape Controller   (CAAL)
DMTC......... Digital Message Terminal Computer   (IEEE)
DMTI.......... Digitized Moving Target Indicator   (CET)
DMTPS....... Digital Magnetic Tape Plotting System
DMTS......... Digital Magnetic Tape System   (CAAL)
DMTS......... Digital Module Test Set
DMTU........ Digital Magnetic Tape Unit   (MCD)
DMTU........ Dual Modular Magnetic Tape Unit   (CAAL)
DMU.......... Data Management Unit [*Data processing*]
DMU.......... Digital Management Unit   (MCD)
DMU.......... Digital Message Unit   (MCD)
DMU.......... Digital Monitor Unit   (VIT)
DMU.......... Distributed Microprocessor Unit   (CAA)
DMUS........ Data Management Utility System   (CAA)
DMUX........ Demultiplexer [*Data processing*]
DMW......... Digital Milliwatt [*Telecommunications*]   (TEL)
DMX.......... Data Multiplex [*Computer*]
DMX.......... Direct Memory Exchange   (CAA)
DN............. Data Name
DN............. Data Number   (CIT)
DN............. Date Number
DNA........... Deutscher Normenausschuss [*German Standards Committee*] [*Later, DIN*]
DNA........... Digital Network Architecture [*Digital Equipment Corp.*] [*Data processing*]
DNA........... Does Not Answer [*Telephone operator's designation*]
DNAM........ Data Network Access Method   (CAA)
DNB........... Dun & Bradstreet, Inc. [*NYSE symbol*]
DNC........... Direct Numerical Control [*Automation method*] [*Data processing*]
DNCS......... Distributed Network Control System   (CAA)
DNET......... Data-Net [*Data-Net, Inc.*] [*Rochester, NY*] [*Telecommunications*]   (TSSD)
DNIC.......... Data Network Identification Code [*Telecommunications*]   (TEL)
DNR........... Digital Noise Reduction [*Television*]
DNS........... Decentralized Data Processing Network System   (BUR)
DNS........... Decimal Number System
DNS........... Discrete Network Simulation
DNS........... Distributed Network System   (CAA)
DNSW........ Day Night Switching Equipment [*Telecommunications*]
DNT........... Digital Network Terminator   (CAA)
DNT........... Downtime [*Data processing*] [*Telecommunications*]
DNVT......... Digital Nonsecure Voice Terminal   (MCD)
DNWS........ Discrete Network Simulation
DO............. Data Output [*Data processing*]   (IEEE)
D-O............ Decimal to Octal [*Data processing*]   (IEEE)
DO............. Design Objective   (IEEE)
DO............. Digital Output [*Data processing*]
DO............. Discrete Output [*Data processing*]   (KSC)
DOA........... Digital Output Adapter   (CAA)
DOB........... Data Output Bus   (CAA)
DOC........... Data, Operations, and Control
DOC........... Data Optimizing Computer
DOC........... Data Output Channel   (MSA)
DOC........... Decimal to Octal Conversion
DOC........... Department of Communications [*Canada*]
DOC........... Digital Output Control   (CAA)
DOC........... Document [*or Documentation*]   (AFM)
DOC........... Dynamic Overload Controls
DOCDEL..... Document Delivery [*Information service*]
DOCGEN.... Document Generator
DOCL......... Department of Commerce Library   (EISS)
DOCS......... Disk-Oriented Computer System   (IEEE)
DOCS......... Document Organization and Control System [*Telecommunications*]   (TEL)
DOCSYS.... Display of Chromosome Statistics System   (OA)
DOCUS...... Display-Oriented Computer Usage System
DOD.......... Direct Outward Dialing [*Telecommunications*]
DOD.......... Directory on Disk [*Los Gatos, CA*] [*Information service*]   (EISS)
DODAS...... Digital Oceanographic Data Acquisition System   (MCD)

DODCI....... Department of Defense Computer Institute
DODT........ Display Octal Debugging Technique   (CAA)
DOE........... Department of Energy [*Washington, DC*] [*Database producer*]
DOE/RECON ... Department of Energy's Remote Console Information System [*Department of Energy*] [*Database*]   (FDB)
DOES......... Decision-Oriented Evaluation System
DOES......... Disk-Oriented Engineering System [*Data processing*]
DOE-TIC..... Department of Energy Technical Information Center [*Database producer*]   (ODIN)
DOF........... Device Output Format   (CAA)
DOFIC....... Domain-Originated Functional Integrated Circuit   (IEEE)
DOGS......... Drawing Office Graphics System [*Deltacam Systems Ltd.*] [*Software package*] [*British*]   (NCC)
DOH........... Discrete Output High   (CAA)
DOIO......... Directly Operable Input/Output   (CAA)
DOIT.......... Database Oriented Interrogation Technique [*Comserv Corp.*]   (CAA)
DO/IT........ Digital Output/Input Translator [*Data processing*]
DOL........... Display-Oriented Language [*Data processing*]   (IEEE)
DOL........... Dynamic Octal Load
DOLARS .... Digital Offline Automatic Recording System
DOM.......... Data Output Multiplexer [*Data processing*]   (KSC)
DOM.......... Digital Ohmmeter
DOM.......... Digital Output Multiplexer   (CAAL)
DOM.......... Disk Operating Monitor   (CAA)
DOMA........ Dokumentation Maschinenbau [*FIZ Technik*] [*Database producer*]   (ODIN)
DOMAIN..... Distributed Operating Multi-Access Interactive Network [*Apollo Computer, Inc.*] [*Chelmsford, MA*] [*Telecommunications*]   (TSSD)
DOMESTIC ... Development of Minicomputers in an Environment of Scientific and Technological Information Centers [*Data processing*]
DOMLIB...... Domestic Library Automation Functions [*Data processing*]
DOMPRINT ... DOMESTIC [*Development of Microcomputers in an Environment of Scientific and Technological Information Centers*] Print Generator [*Data processing*]
DOMSAT .... Domestic Satellite [*Communications satellite*] [*Australia*]
DON........... Delayed Order Notice [*Telecommunications*]   (TEL)
DONA........ Decentralized Open Network Architecture   (BUR)
DOPE......... Databank of Program Evaluations [*University of California, Los Angeles*]   (EISS)
DOPE......... Display, Oral, Printed, and Electronic [*Media*]   (DDI)
DOPIC....... Documentation of Programs in Core [*Data processing*]   (IEEE)
DOPS......... Digital Optical Projection System   (IEEE)
DOR........... Data Output Register   (CAA)
DOR........... Digital Output Relay   (OA)
DORAN...... Doppler Range and Navigation [*Electronics*]
DORIS........ Demographic Online Retrieval Information System [*CACI, Inc.*]
DORIS........ Direct Order Recording and Invoicing System [*A computer-based system of British petroleum companies*]
DOS........... Decision Outstanding [*Data processing*]   (BUR)
DOS........... Digital Operation System   (IEEE)
DOS........... Discrete Orthonormal Sequence
DOS........... Disk Operating System [*IBM Corp.*] [*Data processing*]   (EISS)
DOSK......... Distributed Operating System Kernel [*Data processing*]
DOS-LV..... Disk Operating System - Large Volumes
DOS-SV..... Disk Operating System - Small Volumes
DOS/VS..... Disk Operating System/Virtual Storage [*IBM Corp.*] [*Data processing*]   (MCD)
DOT........... Digital Output Timer [*Data processing*]
DOT........... Discrete Ordinate Transport
DOTC......... Data Observing Testing Console
DOTS......... Digital Optical Technology System [*3-D television system*]
DOUDDAS ... Deep Ocean Untended Digital Data Acquisition System
DOV........... Data over Voice [*Telecommunications*]   (TEL)
DOWM....... Database of Off-Site Waste Management [*Public Data Access, Inc.*] [*Database*]   (CUAD)
DP.............. Data Pointer   (CAA)
DP.............. Data Printer
DP.............. Data Processing
DP.............. Data Processing and/or Computer Programing Programs [*Association of Independent Colleges and Schools specialization code*]
DP.............. Date of Publication [*Online database field identifier*]   (OBD)
DP.............. Datum Point
DP.............. Dial Pulse [*Telecommunications*]
DP.............. Differential Phase [*Telecommunications*]
DP.............. Digit Present
DP.............. Digital Plotter   (CAA)
DP.............. Dipole   (DEN)
DP.............. Disconnection Pending [*Telecommunications*]   (TEL)
DP.............. Disk Pack [*Data processing*]   (IEEE)
DP.............. Display Package
DP.............. Display Panel
DP.............. Distribution Point
DP.............. Double Pole [*Switch*]
DP.............. Drum Processor [*Data processing*]   (IEEE)
DP.............. Dynamic Programing [*Data processing*]
DPA........... Black Data Processing Associates   (EANO)
DPA........... Data Processing Activities
DPA........... Data Processing Agency   (VIT)
DPA........... Data Processing Algorithm
DPA........... Data Processing Area   (CIT)

Computer & Telecommunications Acronyms

Acronym	Expansion
DPA	Data Processing Assembly (MCD)
DPA	Data Protection Agency [*British*] (CAA)
DPA	Detailed Performance Analysis [*Bell System*]
DPA	Deutsches Patentamt [*Information retrieval*] (ODIN)
DPA	Dial Pulse Access [*Telecommunications*] (TEL)
DPA	Different Premises Address [*Telecommunications*] (TEL)
DPARS	Data Processing Automatic Record Standardization
D-PAT	Drum-Programed Automatic Tester
DPB	Data Plotting Board
DPB	Data Processing Branch (IEEE)
DPC	Data Processing Center
DPC	Data Processing Central
DPC	Data Processing Computer (CAAL)
DPC	Data Processing Control (AFM)
DPC	Data Protection Committee [*British*]
DPC	Dataproducts Corporation [*American Stock Exchange symbol*]
DPC	Destination Point Code [*Telecommunications*] (TEL)
DPC	Digital Phase Comparator
DPC	Digital Pressure Converter
DPC	Digital Process Controller
DPC	Direct Program Control (BUR)
DPC	Display Power Control
DPC	Display Processor Code (OA)
DPCE	Data Processing Customer Engineering
DPCM	Differential Pulse Code Modulation [*Transmission technique*]
DPCM	Distributed Processing Communications Module (CAA)
DPCS	Desktop Page Composition System [*Vision Research*]
DPCTE	Data Processor and Computer Test Equipment
DPCTG	Database Program Conversion Task Group [*CODASYL*] (CAA)
DPCU	Digital Processing and Control Unit
DPCX	Distributed Processing Control Executive [*IBM Corp.*]
DPCZ	Diagnostic Products Corporation [*NASDAQ symbol*] (NQ)
DPD	Data Processing Department
DPD	Data Processing Design, Inc. [*Anaheim, CA*] [*Software manufacturer*] (DASOS)
DPD	Data Processing Detachment
DPD	Data Processing Division [*IBM Corp.*] (CDH)
DPD	Digit Plane Driver [*Data processing*] (IEEE)
DPD	Digital Phase Difference
DPDL	Distributed Program Design Language (CAA)
DPDM	Double Pulse Duration Modulation (KSC)
DPDT	Double Pole, Double Throw [*Switch*]
DPDTSW	Double-Pole, Double-Throw Switch
DPE	Data Processing Equipment
DPE	Distributed Processing Environment (CAA)
DPE	Distributor-to-Printer Electronics
DPE	Dynamic Phase Error (CIT)
DPEK	Differential Phase Exchange Keying (IEEE)
DPEX	Distributed Processing Executive Program (CAA)
DPF	Data Processing Facility
DPF	Differential Pressure Feedback (KSC)
DPF	Dual Program Feature (CAA)
DPF	Dynamic Pressure Feedback
DPG	Digital Pattern Generator
DPH	Disintegrations per Hour
DPI	Data Processing Installation
DPI	Data Publishing International [*Netherlands*] [*Information service*] (EISS)
DPI	Detail Program Interrelationships (NASA)
DPI	Detected Pulse Interference (CET)
DPI	Different Premises Information [*Telecommunications*] (TEL)
DPI	Digital Process Instrument [*Data processing*] (IEEE)
DPI	Digital Pseudorandom Inspection (IEEE)
DPIF	Drug Product Information File [*American Society of Hospital Pharmacists*] [*Information service*] (EISS)
DPIR	Data Processing and Information Retrieval (DIT)
DPKG	Data Packaging Corp. [*NASDAQ symbol*] (NQ)
DPL	Data Processing Language (CAA)
DPLF	Data [*or Digital*] Phone Line Formatter (CIT)
DPLM	Domestic Public Land Mobile [*Telecommunications*] (TEL)
DPM	Data Preparation and Maintenance (CAAL)
DPM	Data Processing Machine
DPM	Data Processing Manager (CAH)
DPM	Digital Panel Meter [*Data processing*]
DPM	Disintegrations per Minute
DPM	Documents per Minute [*Data processing*] (BUR)
DPMA	Data Processing Management Association [*Formerly, NMAA*] [*Park Ridge, IL*]
DPMAA	Data Processing Magazine [*A publication*]
DPMC	Dual Port Memory Control (CAA)
DPMIAC	Defense Pest Management Information Analysis Center [*Database*] (FDB)
DPMOAP	Society of Data Processing Machine Operators and Programmers
DPMS	Data Project Management System (IEEE)
DPM/S	Disintegrations per Minute/Second (DEN)
DPO	Data Processing Operation
DPO	Dial Pulse Originating [*Telecommunications*] (TEL)
DPO	Digital Processing Oscilloscope (MCD)
DPO	Double Pulse Operation
DPOC	Dynamic Processor Overload Control [*Telephone technology*]
DPOIR	Dial Pulse Originating Incoming Register [*Telecommunications*]
DPP	Data Project Plan
DPP	Digital Parallel Processor (CAA)
DPPC	Data Processing Products Contract
DPPE	Data Processing Project Engineer (CIT)
DPPX	Distributed Processing Programing Executive Base [*IBM Corp.*]
DPR	Data Processing Request
DPR	Double Pulse Ranging (NG)
DPREP	Disk Preparation Processor [*Data processing*]
DPRO	Digital Projection Readout (CAAL)
DPS	Data Package Set (CAAL)
DP(S)	Data Packet (Subsystem) [*Telecommunications*] (TEL)
DPS	Data Present Signal
DP & S	Data Processing and Software (NASA)
DPS	Data Processing and Software (NASA)
DPS	Data Processing System
DPS	Delayed Printer Simulator
DPS	Different Premises Subscriber [*Telecommunications*] (TEL)
DPS	Digital Phase Shifter
DPS	Digital Plotter System
DPS	Digital Power Supply (VIT)
DPS	Disintegrations per Second
DPS	Disk Programing System [*IBM Corp.*] (IEEE)
DPS	Distributed Presentation Services [*IBM Corp.*]
DPS	Distributed Processing System [*Honeywell, Inc.*] (IDA)
DPS	Document Processing System [*IBM Corp.*] [*Data processing*]
DPSA	Data Processing Supplies Association [*Later, IOSA*]
DPSC	Data Processing Service Center (DDI)
DPSK	Differential Phase Shift Keying
DPSR	Data Processing Service Request (NVT)
DPSS	Data Processing Subsystem
DPSS	Data Processing System Simulator (IEEE)
DPST	Double Pole, Single Throw [*Switch*]
DPT	Datapoint Corp. [*NYSE symbol*]
DPT	Dedicated Planning Terminal (CAAL)
DPT	Dial Pulse Terminating [*Telecommunications*] (TEL)
DPT	Different Premises Telephone Number [*Telecommunications*] (TEL)
DPT	Digital Pressure Transducer
DPTSI	Design Professions Technical Specialty Index [*National Society of Professional Engineers*] [*Information service*] (EISS)
DPU	Data Processing Unit
DPU	Digital Patch Unit (CAA)
DPU	Digital Processing Unit
DPU	Disk Pack Unit (CAA)
DPWM	Double-Sided Pulse-Width Modulation [*Telecommunications*] (OA)
DPWR	Data Process Work Request
DQ	Destination Queues [*Data processing*] (MDG)
DQ	Directory Enquiry Service [*Telecommunications*] (TEL)
DQA	Design Quality Assurance [*Telecommunications*] (TEL)
DQC	Data Quality Control
DQC	Dynamic Quality Control
DQCM	Data Quality Control Monitor
DQD	Digital Quadrature Detection [*Instrumentation*]
DQM	Data Quality Monitors (MDG)
DQM	Digital Quality Monitor
DR	Data Rate [*Telecommunications*] (TEL)
DR	Data Receiver [*or Recorder*]
DR	Data Reduction (KSC)
DR	Data Register (CAA)
DR	Data Report
DR	Designator Register [*Data processing*]
DR	Discrete Register (MCD)
DR	Disk Recorder (DEN)
DR & A	Data Reduction and Analysis
DRA	Data Reformatter Assembly (SKY)
DR & A	Data Reporting and Accounting (AFM)
DR & A	Data Requirements and Analysis (MCD)
DRA	Data Resource Administrator (CAA)
DRA	Digital Read-In Assembly [*Data processing*] (VIT)
DRA	Digital Recorder Analyzer [*Data processing*]
DRA	Discrete Recovery Area (KSC)
DRA	Drum-Read Amplifier [*Data processing*] (CET)
DRAC	Distributed Read Address Counter
DRACO	Dead Reckoning Automatic Computer [*Obsolete*] (DDI)
DRAFT	Document Read and Format Translator (CAA)
DRAM	Dynamic Random Access Mechanization
d-RAM	Dynamic Random Access Memory [*Data processing*]
DRAMA	Digital Radio and Multiplexer Acquisition (MCD)
DRAMS	Digital Recording and Measuring System
DRAN	Dranetz Technologies [*NASDAQ symbol*] (NQ)
DRANS	Data Reduction and Analysis System
DRAPE	Data Recording and Processing Equipment
DRAPE	Digital Recording and Playback Equipment (MCD)
DRAT	Demonstration Reliability Acceptance Test
DRAW	Direct Read after Write [*Data processing*]
DRAW	Direct Read-and-Write [*Data processing*]
DRB	Decimal Register Binary
DRC	Data Rate Changer
DRC	Data Recording Camera
DRC	Data Recording Controller [*Data processing*] (BUR)
DRC	Data Reduction Center [*or Complex*]
DRC	Data Reduction Compiler (MCD)
DRC	Data Return Capsule [*or Container*]
DRC	Demographic Research Company [*Information service*] (EISS)

By Acronym

Computer & Telecommunications Acronyms

Acronym	Definition
DRC	Design Research Center [*Carnegie-Mellon University*] [*Research center*] (RCD)
DRC	Discrete Rate Command (MCD)
DRCDG	Data Recording (MSA)
DRCH	Data Architects, Inc. [*NASDAQ symbol*] (NQ)
DRCS	Distress Radio Call System [*Telecommunications*] (TEL)
DRD	Data Recording Device [*Data processing*] (BUR)
DRD	Data Resources Directory Publications Subsystem [*Department of Energy*] [*Database*] (FDB)
DRD	Drum-Read Driver [*Data processing*]
DRDCN	Data Reduction (MSA)
Dr Dobb's J	Dr. Dobb's Journal [*A publication*]
Dr Dobb's J Comput Calisthenics and Orthod	Dr. Dobb's Journal of Computer Calisthenics and Orthodontia [*A publication*]
DRE	Data Reduction Equipment
DRE	Direct Reading Encoder
DRE	Directional Reservation Equipment [*Telecommunications*] (TEL)
DRE	Dokumentationsring Elektrotechnik [*Database*] (ODIN)
DREAM	Data Retrieval, Entry, and Management (CAA)
DRED	Data Routing and Error Detecting
DREG	Data Regulations (KSC)
DREME	Division of Research and Evaluation in Medical Education [*Ohio State University*] [*Research center*] (RCD)
DREWS	Direct Readout Equatorial Weather Satellite
DRF	Data Reporting Form
DRF	Data Requirement Form (KSC)
DRGS	Direct Readout Ground Station
DRH	Digital Readout Head [*Data processing*]
DRH	Driver-Harris Co. [*American Stock Exchange symbol*]
DRI	Data Rate Indicator (NASA)
DRI	Data Recording Interface (MCD)
DRI	Data Reduction Interpreter
DRI	Data Resources, Incorporated [*Lexington, MA*] [*Database originator and operator*] [*Information service*] (EISS)
DRI	Data Routing Indicator
DRI	Digital Research, Incorporated
DRI	Document Retrieval Index (CAA)
DRID	Direct Readout Image Dissector [*Camera system*]
DRIDAC	Drum Input to Digital Automatic Computer (OA)
DRIG	Digital Rate-Integrating Gyro (MCD)
DRIP	Data Reduction Input Program [*Data processing*]
DRIP	Digital Ray and Intensity Projector
DRIPS	Dynamic Real-Time Information Processing System (MCD)
DRIR	Direct Readout Infrared Radiometer
DRISS	Digital Read-In Subsystem [*Data processing*]
DRIVE	Document Read, Information Verify, and Edit (CAA)
DRK	Data Request Keyboard (CIT)
DRK	Display Request Keyboard (KSC)
DRL	Data Reduction Laboratory
DRL	Data Requirement List (KSC)
DRL	Data Requirements Language (CAA)
DRL	Data Retrieval Language [*National Bureau of Standards*]
DRL	Digital Readout Light [*Data processing*]
DRM	Data Records Management (MCD)
DRM	Digital Radiometer (CDH)
DRM	Digital Range Machine
DRMI	Dual Radio Magnetic Indicator (MCD)
DRMS	Data Resources Management System
DRN	Data Record Number (MCD)
DRN	Data Reference Number
DRO	Destructive Readout
DRO	Digital Readout [*Data processing*] (DDI)
DRO	Digital Readout Oscilloscope [*Data processing*]
DRO	Doubly Resonant Oscillator (IEEE)
DROM	Decoder Read-Only Memory (CAA)
DROMDI	Direct Readout Miss Distance Indicator
DRON	Data Reduction
DROO	Digital Readout Oscilloscope [*Data processing*]
DROP	Data Printout Program
DROS	Direct Readout Satellite
DROS	Disk Resident Operating System [*Data processing*] (IEEE)
DROWS	Direct Readout Weather Satellite
DRP	Data Reception Process [*Telecommunications*] (TEL)
DRP	Data Reduction Procedure [*or Program*]
DRP	Data Retrieval Program (CAAL)
DRP	Digital Recording Process
DRP	Directional Radiated Power [*Telecommunications*] (TEL)
DRPS	Disk Real-Time and Programing System (CAA)
DRQ	Data Ready Queue [*IBM Corp.*] (IBMDP)
DRQ	Data Request (CAA)
DRR	Data Recorder/Reproducer (MCD)
DRR	Data Redundancy Removal (KSC)
DRR	Direct Reading Receiver
DRR	Diversity Reception Receiver
DRS	Data Rate Selector
DRS	Data Reaction System
DRS	Data Receiving Station (KSC)
DRS	Data Recording Set
DRS	Data Recording System (MUGU)
DRS	Data Reduction System [*Data processing*]
DRS	Data Relay Station (NASA)
DRS	Data Relay System (CAAL)
DRS	Data Requirements Specification (KSC)
DRS	Data Retrieval System [*Data processing*] (BUR)
DRS	Development Reference Service [*Society for International Development*] (EISS)
DRS	Digital Range Safety (NASA)
DRS	Digital Readout System [*Data processing*]
DRS	Digital Receiver Station [*Data processing*]
DRS	Digital Recording System (CIT)
DRS	Document Retrieval System
DRSA	Data Recording System Analyst (MUGU)
DRSG	Digital Recorder Signal Generator [*Data processing*]
DRT	Data Reckoning Tracer (MSA)
DRT	Data Review Technician
DRT	Device Reference Table (CAA)
DRT	Device Rise Time [*Photomultipliers for scintillation counting*] (IEEE)
DRT	Digital Readout Timer [*Data processing*]
DRT	Digital Rotary Transducer
DRT	Direct Reading Totalizer
DRTC	Diabetes Research and Training Center [*Yeshiva University*] [*Research center*] (RCD)
DRTM	Disk Real-Time Monitor (CAA)
DRU	Data Reference Unit (CAA)
DRU	Data Reorganization Utility [*Data processing*]
DRU	Digital Range Unit
DRU	Digital Register Unit (VIT)
DRU	Digital Remote Unit [*Data processing*]
DRU	Drive Unit
DRUB	Digital Remote Unit Buffer [*Data processing*]
DRV	Data Recovery Vehicle
DRWG	Data Reduction Working Group (MUGU)
DS	Data Scanning (BUR)
DS	Data Segment
DS	Data Set [*Data processing*]
DS	Data Sheet (NATG)
DS	Data Storage [*Data processing*] (NASA)
DS	Data Synchronization (DEN)
DS	Data System
DS	Debugging System (CAA)
DS	Define Storage (CAH)
DS	Digit Select (BUR)
DS	Digital Signal (OA)
DS	Direct Sequence [*Telecommunications*] (TEL)
DS	Discontinue (BUR)
D/S	Disintegrations per Second
DS	Disk Storage [*Data processing*] (NASA)
DS	Disk System (CAA)
D & S	Display and Storage (MSA)
DS	Distributed System (CAA)
DS	Dokumentation Schweisstechnik [*Welding Documentation*] [*Germany*] [*Information service*] (EISS)
DS	Drum Storage [*Data processing*] (IEEE)
DSA	Data Set Adapter [*Data processing*] (DEEC)
DSA	Data Systems Administration
DSA	Dataroute Serving Area [*TransCanada Telephone System/Computer Communications Group*] (CAA)
DSA	Dial Service Analysis [*Telecommunications*] (TEL)
DSA	Dial Service Assistance (CET)
DSA	Digital Serving Area [*Telecommunications*] (TEL)
DSA	Digital Signal Analyzer (IEEE)
DSA	Digital Spectrum Analyzer (NVT)
DSA	Direct Storage Access (CAA)
DSA	Discrete Sample Analyzer
DSA	Dynamic Signal Analyzer
DSA	Dynamic Storage Area (CMD)
DSAD	Data Systems and Analysis Directorate (MCD)
DSAD	Data Systems Application Division [*Agricultural Research Service*]
DSAD	Data Systems Authorization Directory
DSAMOS	Diffusion Self-Aligned Metal-Oxide Semiconductor (BUR)
DSAN	Debug Syntax Analysis [*Telecommunications*] (TEL)
DSAP	Destination Service Access Point (CCD)
DSAP	Directory Scope Analysis Program [*Bell System*]
DSAR	Data Sampling Automatic Receiver
DSAS	Dial Service Assistance Switchboard (CET)
DSB	Data Set Block (CAA)
DSB	Device Status Byte [*Data processing*] (BUR)
DSB	Double Sideband
DSBAM	Double-Sideband Amplitude Modulation [*Telecommunications*] (TEL)
DSBAMRC	Double-Sideband Amplitude Modulation Reduced Carrier (IEEE)
DSBEC	Double-Sideband Emitted Carrier [*Telecommunications*] (TEL)
DSBRC	Double-Sideband Reduced Carrier [*Telecommunications*] (TEL)
DSBSC	Double-Sideband Suppressed Carrier
DSBTC	Double-Sideband Transmitted Carrier
DSC	Data Services Center [*International City Management Association*] [*Information service*] (EISS)
DSC	Data Set Controller (CAA)
DSC	Data Synchronizer Channel
DSC	Data System Console (CAAL)
DSC	Decision Sciences Corporation (EISS)
DSC	Digital Scan Converter (MCD)
DSC	Digital Signal Conditioner (MCD)
DSC	Digital Stabilization Console (DDI)

Computer & Telecommunications Acronyms

Acronym	Expansion
DSC	Direct Satellite Communications
DSC	Discone Antenna
DSC	Discrete System Concept
DSC	Disk Storage Controller (CMD)
DSC	Distant Station Connected [*Data processing*] (BUR)
DSC	District Switching Center [*Telecommunications*] (DEEC)
DSC	Double Silk Covered [*Wire insulation*]
DSC	Dynamic Standby Computer (KSC)
DSCB	Data Set Control Block [*Data processing*]
DSCC	Datasouth Computer [*NASDAQ symbol*] (NQ)
DSCG	Digital Scan Converter Group (MCD)
DSCS	Desk Side Computer System [*General Electric Co.*]
DSD	Data Set Definition (IBMDP)
DSD	Data Status Display (CIT)
DSD	Data Storage Device
DSD	Data Structure Diagram
DSD	Data Systems Designator (AFM)
DSD	DECHEMA [*Deutsche Gesellschaft fuer Chemisches Apparatewesen, Chemische Technik, und Biotechnologie eV*] Stoffdaten Dienst [*DECHEMA Data Service*] [*Information service*] [*West German*] (EISS)
DSD	Digital System Design (IEEE)
DSD	Digital System Diagram (CAA)
DSD	Disk Storage Device
DSDD	Double-Sided, Double-Density Disk [*Data processing*]
DS & DH	Data Switching and Data Handling (AFM)
DSDL	Data Storage Description Language (CAA)
DSDP	Data System Development Plan (CIT)
DSDS	Dataphone Switched Digital Service [*AT & T*]
DSDS	Digital Synchro Data Source (VIT)
DSDT	Deformographic Storage Display Tube [*IBM Corp.*]
DSDT	Discrete Space and Discrete Time
DSDU	Data Storage Distribution Unit (MCD)
DSE	Data Set Extension [*IBM Corp.*] [*Data processing*] (BUR)
DSE	Data Storage Equipment
DSE	Data Switching Exchange [*Telecommunications*]
DSE	Data Systems Engineering
DSE	Digital Shaft Encoder
DSE	Distributed Systems Environment [*Honeywell, Inc.*] (BUR)
DSE	Dynamic System Electronics
DSE/FAD	Data Systems Environment Functions and Application Design [*Course*] [*Data processing*]
DSF	Data Scanning and Formatting
DSF	Disk Storage Facility (CAA)
DSFT	Detection Scheme with Fixed Thresholds [*Communication signal*]
DSG	Digital Signal Generator
DSI	Data Set Identifier
DSI	Data Submitted Information (KSC)
DSI	Data Systems Inquiry
DSI	Digital Speech Interpolation [*Telephone channels*]
DSI	Digital Strain Indicator
DSI	Division of Science Information [*National Science Foundation*] (EISS)
DSID	Data Set Identification (IBMDP)
DSIR	Department of Scientific and Industrial Research [*of the Privy Council for Scientific and Industrial Research*] [*Later, SRC*] [*British*]
DSIS	Defence Scientific Information Service [*Canada*] [*Information service*] (EISS)
DSK	Dvorak Simplified Keyboard [*Typewriter keyboard developed by August Dvorak in the 1920's*]
DSKY	Display and Keyboard [*Data processing*]
DSL	Data Set Label [*Data processing*]
DSL	Data Structures Language [*Data processing*] (BUR)
DSL	Digital Simulation Language [*Data processing*] (CSR)
DSLO	Distributed Systems Licensing Option [*IBM Corp.*] (CAA)
DSLT	Detection Scheme with Learning of Thresholds [*Communication signal*]
DSM	Data Status Messages (KSC)
DSM	Data Storage Memory (CIT)
DSM	Data Systems Modernization
DSM	Digital Select Matrix (SKY)
DSM	Digital Select Module (KSC)
DSM	Digital Simulation Model (KSC)
DSM	Direct Signal Monitoring [*Telecommunications*] (TEL)
DSM	Disk Space Management (CAA)
DSM	Dynamic Scattering Mode (IEEE)
DSMS	Data Systems and Mathematics Staff [*Bureau of Radiological Health*] (EISS)
DSMT	Dual-Speed Magnetic Transducer
DSN	Data Set Name
DSN	Data Smoothing Network [*Telecommunications*]
DSN	Detroit Suburban Network [*Radio*]
DSN	Distributed Systems Network [*Hewlett-Packard Co.*] (CAA)
DSNI	[*The*] DocketSearch Network, Incorporated [*Chicago, IL*] [*Information service*] (EISS)
DSO	Data Services Operations [*Informatics, Inc.*] (EISS)
DSO	Data Set Optimizer [*Boole & Babbage, Inc.*] (CAA)
DSO	Data Systems Office
DSO	Direct System Output [*Data processing*] (MCD)
DSO	Display Switching Oscilloscope
DSOS	Data Switch Operating System (CAA)
DSP	Data Source Panel (MCD)
DSP	Display Simulation Program
DSP	Distributed System Program [*Data processing*]
DSP	Dynamic Subscription Promotion
DSP	Dynamic Support Program [*Data processing*]
DSPF	Data Services Planning Form
DSPL	Display
DSPS	Digital Signal Processing System
DSQD	Double-Sided Quad-Density [*Scottsdale Systems*] [*Data processing*]
DSR	Data Scanning and Routing
DSR	Data Set Ready [*Model signal*]
DSR	Data Specification Request
DSR	Data Storage and Retrieval (MCD)
DS & R	Data Storage and Retrieval (MSA)
DSR	Data Survey Report
DSR	Digit Storage Relay
DSR	Digital Shift Register
DSR	Digital Stepping Recorder
DSR	Discriminating Selector Repeater (DEN)
DSR	Dynamic Shift Register
DSR	Dynamic Sideband Regulator
DSS	Data Storage System
DSS	Data Summary Sheets (MCD)
DSS	Data Switching System (CAA)
DSS	Data Systems Specification
DS & S	Data Systems and Statistics (AFM)
DSS	Data Systems Supervisor (MCD)
DSS	Decision Support System
DSS	Digital Signal Synchronizer
DSS	Digital Simulator System
DSS	Digital Storage System
DSS	Digital Subset [*or Subsystem*]
DSS	Digital Switching System [*Telecommunications*] (TEL)
DSS	Draughting Software System [*Gould Electronics Ltd. Computer Systems*] [*Software package*] [*British*] (NCC)
DSS	Drum Storage System
DSS	Dynamic Simulation System (MCD)
DSS	Dynamic Support System (MCD)
DSSC	Double-Sideband Suppressed Carrier [*Modulation*] (IEEE)
DST	Data Source Terminal (MCD)
DST	Data Systems Test [*Formerly, DAT*]
DST	Digital Subscriber Terminal
DST	Display Storage Tube (CET)
DSTE	Digital Subscriber Terminal Equipment (AFM)
DSTP	Data Self-Test Program
DSTS	Desk Side Time Shared [*Data processing*] [*General Electric Co.*]
DSU	Data Service Unit [*Telecommunications*]
DSU	Data Storage Unit (DDI)
DSU	Data Synchronization [*or Synchronizer*] Unit
DSU	Digital Service Unit [*Signal converting device*] [*Telecommunications*] (TSSD)
DSU	Digital Storage Unit (DIT)
DSU	Disk Storage Unit [*Data processing*] (MSA)
DSU	Drum Storage Unit
DSU/GSU	Direct Support Unit/General Support Unit [*Computer system*]
DSV	Digital Sum Variation [*Telecommunications*] (DEEC)
DSVT	Digital Secure Voice Telephone [*Telecommunications*] (TEL)
DSW	Data Status Word
DSW	Device Status Word (CMD)
DSX	Distributed Systems Executive [*IBM Corp.*]
DT	Data Terminal (CAA)
DT	Data Transcriber
DT	Data Translator (IEEE)
DT	Data Transmission
DT	Dead Time
DT	Decision Table [*Data processing*]
DT	Dial Tone [*Telecommunications*] (TEL)
DT	Differential Time (IEEE)
DT	Digit Tube (IEEE)
DT	Digital Technique
DT	Digital Tracker (CIT)
DT	Digroup Terminal [*Telecommunications*] (TEL)
D/T	Disk Tape [*Data processing*] (IEEE)
DT	Document Type [*Online database field identifier*] (OBD)
DT	Downtime [*Data processing*] [*Telecommunications*]
DT	Dump Telemetry (SKY)
DTA	Detailed Traffic Analysis [*Telecommunications*] (TEL)
DTA	Disk Turbine Assembly
DTA	Distributing Terminal Assembly [*Electronics*]
DTA	Double Tape Armored [*Heavy-duty telephone buried cable*]
DTABL	Decision Table Processor [*IBM Corp.*]
DTACCS	Director/Telecommunications and Command and Control System (MCD)
DTARS	Digital Transmitting and Routing System (IEEE)
DTAS	Data Transmission and Switching
DTB	Danmarks Tekniske Bibliotek [*National Technological Library of Denmark*] [*Information service*] (EISS)
DTB	Decimal to Binary [*Data processing*] (BUR)
DTB	Dynamic Translation Buffer (CAA)
DT BIOL	Deutsche Biologische Literatur [*German Biological Literature*] [*Database*] (ODIN)
DTBP	Dedicated Total Buried Plant [*Telecommunications*] (TEL)
DTBSD	Database [*United States*] [*A publication*]

Computer & Telecommunications Acronyms

DTC .... Data Terminals & Communications, Inc. (CAA)
DTC .... Data Test Center [*Telecommunications*] (TEL)
DTC .... Data Transmission Center (KSC)
DTC .... Data Transmission Channel (CMD)
DTC .... Detection Threshold Computer [*Telecommunications*] (TEL)
DTC .... Digital Tape Conversion
DTC .... Digital Television Camera
DTC .... Digital to Tone Converter
DTC .... Display Timing Control (CIT)
DTCR .... Data Transfer and Certification Record (KSC)
DTCS .... Data Transmission and Control System
DTCU .... Data Transmission Control Unit [*Burroughs Corp.*] (OA)
DTCW .... Data Transfer Command Word (NASA)
DTD .... Data Transfer Done (OA)
DTDS .... Digital Television Display System
DT/DV .... Deposit Ticket/Debit Voucher [*Data processing*]
DTE .... Data Terminal Equipment [*Data processing*]
DTE .... Data Transmitting Equipment
DTE .... Database [*A publication*]
DTE .... Digital Television Encoder
DTE .... Digital Television Equipment (KSC)
DTEA .... Data Telemetry Exploitation Aid (MCD)
DTEV .... Deutsche Telecom EV [*Cologne, WG*]
                 [*Telecommunications*] (TSSD)
DTF .... Data Transmission Factor
DTF .... Data Transmission Feature
DTF .... Data Transmission Function
DTF .... Data Transmittal Form (MCD)
DTF .... Date to Follow [*Telecommunications*] (TEL)
DTF .... Define the File [*Data processing*] (BUR)
DTF .... Dial Tone First [*Telecommunications*] (TEL)
DTG .... Data Transmission Generator (MCD)
DTG .... Date-Time Group [*Group of figures at head of radio or Teletype
                 message indicating filing time*]
DTG .... Display Transmission Generator
DTH .... Direct to Home [*Satellite broadcast mode*] [*Canada*]
DTI .... Display Terminal Interchange (CAA)
DTI .... Distortion Transmission Impairment [*Telecommunications*] (TEL)
DTK .... Datatech Systems Ltd. [*Toronto Stock Exchange symbol*]
                 [*Vancouver Stock Exchange symbol*]
DTL .... Dead Time Log
DTL .... Diode-Transistor Logic
DTM .... Dataram Corp. [*American Stock Exchange symbol*]
DTM .... Delay Timer Multiplier (IEEE)
DTM .... Digital Television Monitor
DTMF .... Dual-Tone Multifrequency [*Telecommunications*]
DTMI .... Diversified Technology Management [*NASDAQ symbol*] (NQ)
DTMNA .... Datamation [*A publication*]
DTMS .... Data Base and Transaction Management System [*IBM Corp.*]
DTMS .... Digital Test Measurement [*or Monitor*] System
DTN .... Data Transporting Network (CAA)
DTO .... Decentralized Toll Office [*Telecommunications*] (TEL)
DTO .... Digital Testing Oscilloscope (IEEE)
DTP .... Data Transfer Protocol (CAA)
DTPL .... Domain Tip Propagation Logic (MCD)
DTPS .... Diffusion Transfer Processing System
DTR .... Daily Transaction Registering [*or Reporting*] [*Data processing*]
DTR .... Data Telemetering Register
DTR .... Data Terminal Reader
DTR .... Data Terminal Ready
DTR .... Data Transfer Rate
DTR .... Data Transfer Register (CAA)
DTR .... Definite-Time Relay (MSA)
DTR .... Digital Tape Recorder (CIT)
DTR .... Digital Telemetering Register
DTR .... Disposable Tape Reel [*Data processing*] (OA)
DTR .... Distribution Tape Reel [*Data processing*]
DTR .... Downtime Ratio [*Data processing*] [*Telecommunications*] (TEL)
DTRF .... Daily Transaction Register File [*Data processing*]
DTRF .... Data Transmittal and Routing Form
DT/RSS .... Data Transmission/Recording Subsystem
DTRT .... Do the Right Thing [*Also, DWIM*] [*In data processing context,
                 translates as "Guess at the meaning of poorly worded
                 instructions"*]
DTS .... Data Terminal Set (NVT)
DTS .... Data Terminal Systems, Inc. [*NYSE symbol*] [*Delisted*]
DTS .... Data Test Station
DTS .... Defense Telephone Service [*DoD*]
DTS .... Detailed Test Specification (VIT)
DTS .... Detailed Type Specification (MCD)
DTS .... Digital Tandem Switch
DTS .... Digital Telemetry System
DTS .... Digital Termination Systems [*Telecommunications*]
DTS .... Digital Titration System
DTS .... Digital Tracking System [*or Subsystem*] (CIT)
DTS .... Diplomatic Telecommunications Service (FAAC)
DTS .... Domestic Transmission System [*ITT*]
                 [*Telecommunications*]
DTSS .... Dartmouth Time-Sharing System [*Data processing*]
DTS-W .... Defense Telephone Service - Washington [*DoD*]
DTSY .... Digital Transmission System (DDI)
DTT .... Data Transfer Timing (VIT)
DTT .... Data Transition Tracking (CAA)

DTTL .... Data-Transition Tracking Loop (CIT)
DT/TM .... Delayed Time/Telemetry (KSC)
DTTU .... Data Transmission Terminal Unit [*Burroughs Corp.*] (OA)
DTTY .... Digital-to-Teletype (SKY)
DTU .... Data Terminal Unit [*Telecommunications*]
DTU .... Data Terminating Unit (TEL)
DTU .... Data Transfer Unit (DDI)
DTU .... Data Transmission Unit (CIT)
DTU .... Dial Terminal Unit (CAAL)
DTU .... Digital Tape Unit (IEEE)
DTU .... Digital Telemetry Unit
DTU .... Digital Transmission Unit (IEEE)
DTU .... Display Terminal Unit (CMD)
DTVC .... Digital Transmission and Verification Converter (KSC)
DTWX .... Dial Teletypewriter Exchange
D/U .... Delay Unit [*Telecommunications*] (TEL)
DU .... Digital Unit
DU .... Dimensioning Unit [*Telecommunications*] (TEL)
DU .... Display Unit (NASA)
DU .... Display, Upper (VIT)
DU .... Distribution Unit (KSC)
DUA .... Digital Uplink Assembly
DUA .... Digitronics Users Association [*Later, IUA*] (EANO)
DUAL .... Dynamic Universal Assembly Language [*Data processing*] (TUT)
DUALABS .... Data Use and Access Laboratories [*Information service*] (EANO)
DUCE .... Denied Usage Channel Evaluator [*Telecommunications*] (TEL)
DUCS .... Department of University Computer Systems [*University of
                 Connecticut*] [*Research center*] (RCD)
DUCTS .... Ductwork Services [*Focus Software Consultants*] [*Software
                 package*] [*British*] (NCC)
DUE .... Detection of Unauthorized Equipment [*Bell Laboratories*]
DUEL .... Data Update Edit Language [*Data processing*]
DUET .... Dual Emitter Transistor [*Electronics*]
DUETS .... Duo-Mode Electric Transport System, Inc.
DUF .... Diffusion under [*Epitaxial*] Film (IEEE)
DUI .... Data Use Identifier (AFM)
DUNDIS .... Directory of United Nations Databases and Information Systems
                 [*United Nations*] [*Database*] (CUAD)
DUNS .... Data Universal Numbering System (CGC)
DUO .... Datatron Users' Organization
DUO .... DOS [*Disk Operating System*] under OS [*Operating
                 System*] (CAA)
DUP .... Disk Utility Program [*IBM Corp.*] [*Data processing*] (TUT)
DUP .... Duplicate (AFM)
DUPC .... Displayed under Program Control
DUS .... Data Utilization Station
DUS .... Diagnostic Utility System (CAA)
DUT .... Device under Test
DUTA .... Display Unit Test Assembly (MCD)
DUTE .... Digital Universal Test Equipment (MCD)
DUV .... Data Under Voice [*Bell System*]
DV .... Data Vetting
DVA .... Designed, Verified, and Assigned Date
                 [*Telecommunications*] (TEL)
DVB .... Device Base Control Block [*Data processing*] (IBMDP)
DVB .... Digital Video Bandwidth
DVC .... Device (MSA)
DVC .... Digital Voice Communications
D/VD .... Data/Voice Data (MCD)
DVDS .... Digital Video Display System
DVFO .... Digital Variable-Frequency Oscillator (IEEE)
DVG .... Digital Video Generator [*Data processing*]
DVI .... Digital Vascular Imaging [*Roentgenology*]
DVIP .... Digital Video Integrator and Processor (MCD)
DVJB .... Danish Veterinary and Agricultural Library Catalogue
                 [*Database*] (CUAD)
DVL .... Direct Voice Line (CET)
DVM .... Digital Velocity Meter (CIT)
DVM .... Digital Voltmeter
DVO .... Decimal Voltage Output
DVOM .... Digital Volt-Ohmmeter
DVS .... Digital Voice System (MCD)
DVST .... Direct-View Storage Tube [*Princeton Electronic Products*]
DVT .... Design Verification Test
DVX .... Digital Voice Exchange [*Telecommunications*] (TEL)
DW .... Daisy Wheel [*Printer*] (CAA)
DW .... Data Word Buffer [*Data processing*] (MDG)
DW .... Don't Want [*Telecommunications*] (TEL)
DW .... Double Word [*Data processing*] (CAA)
DW .... Drop and Block Wire [*Telecommunications*] (TEL)
DW .... Drum Write [*Data processing*]
DWAC .... Distributed Write Address Counter
DWB .... Designers' Workbench (TEL)
DWD .... Drum Write Driver [*Data processing*]
DWG .... Digital Waveform Generator (MCD)
DWIM .... Do What I Mean [*Also, DTRT*] [*In data processing context,
                 translates as "Guess at the meaning of poorly worded
                 instructions"*]
DWM .... Destination Warning Marker (DEEC)
DWM .... Destination Word Marker (CMD)
DX .... Data Extraction (CAAL)
DX .... Distance [*Radio term*] (EANO)
DX .... Duplex (MSA)

DXC	Data Exchange Control
DXE	Data Transmitting Equipment (MSA)
DXS	Data Exchange System [*Texas Instruments, Inc.*] (CAA)
DXSST	Data Exchange System Statement Translator [*Texas Instruments, Inc.*] (CAA)
DYANA	Dynamic Analyzer
DYCON	Dynamic Control
DYCOP	Dynamic Console for Operations Planners
DYNAMO	Dynamic Automatic Monitoring (CET)
DYNAMO	Dynamic Model Continuous Time Simulation (BUR)
DYNARM	Dynamic Arm Programer [*Data processing*]
DYP	Directory Yellow Pages [*Telecommunications*] (TEL)
DYSAC	Digital Simulated Analog Computer
DYSAC	Dynamic Storage Analog Computer (IEEE)
DYSEAC	Digital High-Speed Standard Eastern Automatic Computer
DYSN	Dysan Corp. [*NASDAQ symbol*] (NQ)
DYSTAC	Dynamic Storage Analog Computer
DYSTAL	Dynamic Storage Allocation Language [*in FORTRAN*] [*Data processing*]
DYTC	Dynatech Corporation [*NASDAQ symbol*] (NQ)
DYTR	Dyatron Corp. [*NASDAQ symbol*] (NQ)
DZF	Dokumentationszentrale Feinwerktechnik [*Precision Technology Documentation Center*] [*Originator, operator, and database*] [*Information service*] [*West German*] (EISS)
DZF	Dokumentationszentrale Feinwerktechnik im Fachinformationszentrum Technik [*Database*] (ODIN)

E

E .... Erlang [*Unit*] [*Statistics*] [*Telecommunications*]
E .... Error [*Data processing*]   (BUR)
E .... Voltage   (CET)
E (Mail) ...... Electronic Mail [*Telecommunications*]
EA .... Effective Address [*Data processing*]   (MDG)
EA .... Electronic Associates, Inc. [*NYSE symbol*]
EABS .... Euro-Abstracts [*Commission of the European Communities*] [*Luxembourg*] [*Bibliographic database*]   (OBD)
EAC .... Educational Assessment Center [*University of Washington*] [*Research center*]   (RCD)
EACC .... Electronic Asset Control Center   (AFM)
EACC .... Error Adaptive Control Computer   (IEEE)
EAD .... Economic Analysis Division [*Federal Emergency Management Agency*] [*Information service*]   (EISS)
EAD .... Electrically Alterable Device   (NASA)
EADAS .... Engineering and Administrative Data Acquisition System [*Bell System*]
EADS .... Engineering Administrative Data Systems   (MCD)
EAE .... Extended Arithmetic Element
EAGLE .... European Association for Grey Literature Exploitation [*Database producer*]   (CUAD)
EAI .... Electronic Associates, Incorporated
EAM .... Electric Accounting Machine [*or Methods*]
EAM .... Electrically Alterable Memory [*Data processing*]
EAM .... Electronic Accounting Machine [*Processes punched cards*]
EAM .... Electronic Automatic Machinery   (CIT)
EAM .... Evanescent Access Method [*Sperry UNIVAC*]   (CAA)
EAMEDPM ... Electric Accounting Machine and Electronic Data Processing Machine   (VIT)
EAMU .... Electric Accounting Machine Unit
EAN .... European Article Number [*Equivalent of Universal Product Code*]
EAP .... Expenditure Analysis Plan   (TEL)
EAPROM .... Electrically Alterable Programable Read-Only Memory [*Data processing*]
EAPSS .... Electronic Intelligence Analysis Processing Subsystem   (MCD)
EAR .... Electronic Audio Recognition
EARC .... Extraordinary Administrative Radio Conference [*ITU*]
EARN .... European Academic Research Network [*A computer network*]
EAROM .... Electrically Alterable Read-Only Memory [*Data processing*]   (TUT)
EAROS .... Electrically Alterable Read-Only Store [*Data processing*]
EARS .... Environmental Analog Recording System
EAS .... Educational Analog Simulator
EAS .... Extended Area Service [*Telecommunications*]
EASE .... Electronic Analog Simulating Equipment [*Data processing*]
EASI .... Electrical Accounting for the Security Industry [*IBM Corp.*]   (IEEE)
EASL .... Electroacoustic Systems Laboratory
EASL .... Engineering Analysis and Simulation Language [*Data processing*]
EASY .... Efficient Assembly System [*Honeywell, Inc.*] [*Assembler language*]
EAT .... Encoder Address Translator
EATMS .... Electroacoustic Transmission Measuring System [*Telecommunications*]
EAX .... Electronic Automatic Exchange [*See also ESS*] [*General Telephone & Electronics*] [*Telecommunications*]
EBBS .... Engineering Bulletin Board System
EBC .... Electronic Batch Control
EBCA .... External Branch Condition Address [*Telecommunications*]   (TEL)
EBCD .... Extended Binary-Coded Decimal [*Data processing*]   (CIT)
EBCDIC ...... Extended Binary-Coded Decimal Interchange Code [*Data processing*]
EBCI .... External Branch Condition Input [*Telecommunications*]   (TEL)
EBCS .... Electronic Business Communications System
EBD .... Effective Billing Date   (TEL)
EBD .... Equivalent Binary Digit
EBERAS ...... Event-by-Event Recording and Sorting [*Electronics*]
EBES .... Electric Beam Exposure System [*Integrated circuit*] [*Bell Laboratories*]
EB & F .... Equipment Blockages and Failures [*Telecommunications*]   (TEL)
EBI .... Electronic Business [*A publication*]
EBIB .... Energy Bibliography and Index [*Center for Energy and Mineral Resources - Texas A & M University*] [*College Station, TX*] [*Bibliographic database*]   (OBD)
EBIC .... Electron-Bombardment-Induced Conductivity
EBICON ...... Electron-Bombardment-Induced Conductivity
EBL .... Event-Based Language [*1979*] [*Data processing*]   (CSR)
EBM .... Early-Break-Make [*Data processing*]
EBM .... Extended Branch Mode   (CAA)
EBR .... Electron Beam Readout
EBR .... Electron Beam Recorder [*or Recording*]
EBR .... Electron Beam Regulator
EBRG .... Earth-Based Radio Guidance   (CIT)
EBS .... Electron Beam Semiconductor
EBS .... Electron Beam System
EBS .... Electron-Bombarded Semiconductor
EBS .... Electron-Bombardment Silicon   (KSC)
EBTR .... Electronic Bearing-Time Recorder
EBU .... European Broadcasting Union [*Geneva, Switzerland*]
EBU Rev ..... EBU [*European Broadcasting Union*] Review [*A publication*]
EBU Rev A ... EBU [*European Broadcasting Union*] Review. Part A [*A publication*]
EBW .... Effective Bandwidth
EC .... Eastern Cedar [*Utility pole*] [*Telecommunications*]   (TEL)
EC .... Echo Controller [*Telecommunications*]   (TEL)
EC .... Electron Coupled   (DEN)
EC .... Electronic Calculator   (BUR)
EC .... Electronic Calibration   (DDI)
EC .... Electronic Coding   (DDI)
EC .... Electronic Comparator   (VIT)
EC .... Electronic Computer   (MCD)
EC .... Electronic Conductivity
EC .... Electronic Counter
E/C .... Encoder Coupler   (NASA)
EC .... Engineering Change   (MCD)
EC .... Entry Code [*Data processing*]
EC .... Equation Cruncher [*Data processing*]
EC .... Equipment Controller   (CET)
EC .... Erection Computer   (VIT)
EC .... Error Code [*Data processing*]
E/C .... Error Correcting [*or Correction*] [*Data processing*]
EC .... Events Controller   (MCD)
EC .... Experiment Computer   (MCD)
EC .... Extended Control [*Mode*] [*Data processing*]
EC .... Extra Control [*Wire*] [*Telecommunications*]   (TEL)
ECA .... Electronic Confusion Area
ECA .... Electronic Control Amplifier   (MCD)
ECA .... Electronics Control Assembly
ECA .... Engineering Change Announcement   (TUT)
ECA .... Exchange Carrier Association   (EANO)
ECAM .... Electronic Centralized Aircraft Monitoring System
ECAN .... Electronic Calibration and Normalization   (KSC)
ECAN .... Electronic Consumer Advertising Network [*Data Corp. of America*]
ECAP .... Electrical [*or Electronic*] Circuit Analysis Program   (CIT)
ECARS .... Electronic Coordinatograph and Readout System
ECAS .... Experiment Computer Application Software   (MCD)
ECASS .... Electronically Controlled Automatic-Switching System   (DEN)
ECATS .... Expandable Computerized Automatic Test System   (MCD)
ECB .... Electrically Controlled Birefringence [*Telecommunications*]   (TEL)
ECB .... Event Control Block [*Data processing*]   (BUR)
ECC .... Electronic Common Control [*Telecommunications*]   (TEL)
ECC .... Electronic Components Code   (NATG)
ECC .... Electronic Components Conference   (CAH)
ECC .... Equatorial Communications Company [*Mountain View, CA*] [*Telecommunications*]   (TSSD)
ECC .... Error Checking and Correction [*Data processing*]
ECC .... Error-Correcting Circuitry [*Data processing*]   (MCD)
ECC .... Error Correction Code
ECC .... Expanded Community Calling [*Telecommunications*]   (TEL)
ECC .... Experimental Computer Complex
ECCS .... Economic Hundred Call Seconds [*Telecommunications*]   (TEL)
ECCSL .... Emitter-Coupled Current-Steered Logic   (MSA)
ECD .... Electric Control Drive
ECD .... Electron-Capture Detection [*Instrumentation*]
ECD .... Error Control Device   (TEL)

Computer & Telecommunications Acronyms

ECDIN......... Environmental Chemicals Data and Information Network [*Commission of the European Communities*] [*Chemical databank*] [*Italy*]   (EISS)
ECDO.......... Electronic Community Deal Office [*Telecommunications*]   (TEL)
ECE............ Echo Control Equipment [*Telecommunications*]   (TEL)
ECE............ Element Characteristics Equation
ECER .... Exceptional Child Education Resources [*Council for Exceptional Children*] [*Bibliographic database*]   (OBD)
ECF............ Echo Control Factor [*Telecommunications*]   (TEL)
ECH .... Earth Coverage Horn [*Satellite communications*]
ECHO......... Electronic Computing, Hospital-Oriented   (IEEE)
ECHO.......... European Commission Host Organization [*Commission of the European Communities*] [*Information service*] [*Host system*] [*Luxembourg*]   (EISS)
ECI............. Electronic Control Instrumentation
ECID .... En Route Computer Identification   (KSC)
ECL............ Emitter-Coupled Logic
ECL............ Engineering Computer Laboratory [*University of Southern California*] [*Research center*]   (RCD)
ECL............ Exchange Control Logic   (KSC)
ECL............ Executive Control Language [*Data processing*]
ECLA .... Economic Commission for Latin America [*Database originator*] [*United Nations*]
ECLIPS .... Expanded Calculator Link Processing System [*Data processing*]
ECLO .... Emitter-Coupled Logic Operator
ECM........... Electric [*or Electronic*] Cipher [*or Coding*] Machine
ECM........... Electronic Control Module [*Instrumentation*]
ECM........... Extended Core Memory [*Data processing*]   (MCD)
ECMA .... European Computer Manufacturers Association [*Geneva, Switzerland*]
ECMALGOL ... European Computer Manufacturers Association Algorithmic Language
ECME......... Electronic Circuit-Making Equipment [*Data processing*]
ECMU .... Extended Core Memory Unit [*Data processing*]   (NVT)
ECN .... Emergency Communication Network [*Highway*] [*Telecommunications*]   (TEL)
ECN .... Environmental Communications Network [*Proposed environmental information exchange network*]
ECO .... Electron-Coupled Oscillator
ECO .... Electronic Central Office [*Within network*] [*Telecommunications*]   (TEL)
ECO .... Electronic Checkout
ECO .... Engineering Change Order
ECODU ...... Engineering Control Office [*Telecommunications*]   (TEL)
ECODU ...... European Control Data Users [*Brussels, Belgium*]
E-COM....... Electronic Computer-Originated Mail [*Postal Service*]
ECOMA...... European Computer Measurement Association   (CAA)
ECOS......... Experiment Computer Operating System   (MCD)
ECP........... Electronic Calculating Punch
ECP........... Electronic Circuit Protector
ECP........... Equipment Conversion Package [*Telecommunications*]   (TEL)
ECPI.......... Electronic Computer Programming Institute [*Ceased operation, 1976*]
ECPIU .... Electronic Circuit Plug-In Unit   (VIT)
ECPR .... European Consortium for Political Research   (EISS)
ECPS .... Extended Control Program Support [*IBM Corp.*]   (CAA)
ECR........... Electronic Cash Register
ECR........... Electronic Control Relay   (IEEE)
ECR........... Embedded Computer Resources   (MCD)
ECR........... Error Control Receiver   (IEEE)
ECR........... External Channels Ratio
ECS........... Echo Control Subsystem [*Telecommunications*]   (TEL)
ECS........... Electronic Composing System
ECS........... Electronic Control Sensor   (MCD)
ECS........... Electronic Control Switch   (IEEE)
ECS........... Electronics Control System
ECS........... Embedded Computer Systems
ECS........... Emergency Call System [*AT & T*]
ECS........... Engineering Control System   (TUT)
ECS........... European Communication Satellite
ECS........... Extended Core Storage [*Data processing*]   (CGC)
ECSA .... European Computing Services Association   (CAA)
ECSA .... Exchange Carriers Standards Association [*Parisippany, NJ*] [*Telecommunications*]   (EANO)
ECS/API .... Enhanced Character Set/All Purpose Interface [*Xerox Corp.*]
ECSP .... Electronic Command Signal Programer   (MCD)
ECSS .... Extendable Computer System Simulator [*Programing language*] [*1973*]
ECSSL .... [*A*] programing language   (CSR)
ECSTASY... Economical Storage and Access System [*Data processing*]
ECT........... Error Control Translator
ECT........... Error Control Transmitter
ECTA .... Error-Correcting Tree Automation [*Data processing*]
ECTL......... Emitter-Coupled Transistor Logic
ECTS .... European Conference on Telecommunications by Satellite
ECU .... Electronic Cabling Unit
ECU .... Electronic Control Unit
ECU .... Entry Computer   (VIT)
ECU .... Extreme Close-Up [*Television*]
ECX........... Electronically Controlled Telephone Exchange   (DEN)
ED .... Electrodynamic   (DEN)
ED .... Electron Device   (MCD)
ED .... Electronic Differential [*Analyzer*]   (CDH)

ED .... Electronic Digital [*Analyzer*]   (CDH)
ED .... Electronic Display
ED .... Error Detecting [*or Detection*] [*Data processing*]
ED .... Expanded Display
ED .... External Device [*Data processing*]
EDA........... Electronic Differential Analyzer
EDA........... Electronic Digital Analyzer   (MCD)
EDA........... Electronic Display Assembly   (NASA)
EDA........... Erection Digital Assembly   (VIT)
EDA........... Error Detector Assembly
EDA........... Error and Dispersion Analysis   (MCD)
EDAC .... Error Detection and Correction
EDAPS....... Electronic Data Processing System
EDAS .... Engineering Design and Simulation System [*Graphic Data Ltd.*] [*Software package*] [*British*]   (NCC)
EDB........... Educational Data Bank   (IEEE)
EDB........... End of Data Block [*Data processing*]   (CET)
EDB........... Energy Information Database [*Department of Energy*] [*Database*]   (ODIN)
EDB........... Engineering Data Bank [*GIDEP*]
EDBD .... Environmental Data Base Directory [*National Oceanographic Data Center*] [*Database*]
EDC .... Electronic Data Communications   (DDI)
EDC .... Electronic Desk Calculator   (IEEE)
EDC .... Electronic Digital Computer
EDC .... Emergency Digital Computer
EDC .... Engineering Data Control
EDC .... Error Detecting Code
EDC .... Error Detection and Correction   (NATG)
EDC .... External-Device Code [*Data processing*]   (MDG)
EDCC......... External Disk/Drum Channel   (CAA)
EDCC......... Educational Computer Corporation [*NASDAQ symbol*]   (NQ)
EDCG......... Error Detection Code Generator
EDCN......... Experimental Data Communications Network   (MCD)
EDCW......... External-Device Control Word [*Data processing*]
EDD .... Electronic Data Display
EDDD .... Expanded Direct Distance Dialing [*Telecommunications*]
EDDF .... Error Detection and Decision Feedback
EDE........... Emitter Dip Effect   (IEEE)
EDET .... Elevation Data Edit Terminals   (RDA)
EDF........... External Delay Factor [*Data processing*]
EDFA .... Electronic Differential Analyzer   (MSA)
EDF-DOC... Electricite de France [*Bibliographic database*] [*French*]   (OBD)
EDFG .... Extended Data Flow Graph
EDGAR ...... Electronic Data Gathering, Analysis, and Retrieval [*Securities and Exchange Commission pilot project*]   (EISS)
EDGE .... Electronic Data Gathering Equipment
EDGE .... Experimental Display Generator
EDHE .... Experimental Data Handling Equipment
EDI............ Electronic Data Interchange
EDIS.......... Engineering Data Information System   (IEEE)
EDIT .... Error Deletion by Iterative Transmission
EDITAR ..... Electronic Digital Tracking and Ranging
EDITS .... Electronic Data Information Technical Service   (DIT)
EDITS .... Experimental Digital Television System
EDLCC....... Electronic Data Local Communications Central
EDM........... Electronic Distance Measuring
EDM........... Engineering Data Management
EDMA .... Extended Direct Memory Access   (CAA)
EDMARS.... Educational Document Management and Retrieval System [*Japanese*] [*Database*]   (CUAD)
EDME......... Electronic Distance Measuring Equipment   (MCD)
EDMF .... Extended Data Management Facility
EDMS......... Electra Data Management System
EDMS......... Extended Data Management System [*Xerox Corp.*]   (CAA)
EDO .... Error Demodulator [*or Determination*] Output   (MCD)
EDOS......... Extended Disk Operating System   (BUR)
EDP............ EDP [*Electronic Data Processing*] Industry Report [*A publication*]
EDP............ Electronic Data Processing
EDP............ Electronic Display Panel
EDPAA....... EDP [*Electronic Data Processing*] Analyzer [*A publication*]
EDPAA....... EDP [*Electronic Data Processing*] Auditors Association [*Carol Stream, IL*]   (EANO)
EDP A C S ... EDP [*Electronic Data Processing*] Audit, Control, and Security Newsletter [*A publication*]
EDP Anal .... EDP [*Electronic Data Processing*] Analyzer [*A publication*]
EDP Aud .... EDP [*Electronic Data Processing*] Auditor [*A publication*]
EDPC .... Electronic Data Processing Center
EDPE .... Electronic Data Processing Equipment
EDP Europa ... EDP [*Electronic Data Processing*] Europa Report [*A publication*]
EDP In-Depth Rep ... EDP [*Electronic Data Processing*] In-Depth Reports [*A publication*]
EDP Indus Rep ... EDP [*Electronic Data Processing*] Industry Report [*A publication*]
EDP/IR....... Electronic Data Processing/Industry Report   (CAH)
EDPLOT...... Engineering Data Plotting [*Data processing*]   (CIT)
EDPM......... Electronic Data Processing Machine [*Also translated by some users of such equipment as "Every Damn Problem Multiplied"*]
EDPM......... Electronic Data Processing Magnetic [*Tape*]   (DDI)
EDP Performance Rev ... EDP [*Electronic Data Processing*] Performance Review [*A publication*]

Computer & Telecommunications Acronyms

EDP Perf Rev ... EDP [*Electronic Data Processing*] Performance Review [*A publication*]
EDPS .... Electronic Data Processing System
EDPT .... Electronic Data Processing Test   (AFM)
EDQA .... Electronic Devices Quality Assurance
EDRAS .... Economic Data Retrieval and Application System   (BUR)
EDRCC ...... Electronic Data Remote Communications Complex
EDS .... Editorial Data Systems
EDS .... Electron Devices Society   (EANO)
EDS .... Electronic Data Switching System [*Data processing*]   (TEL)
EDS .... Electronic Data System   (IEEE)
EDS .... Electronic Data Systems Corp. [*NYSE symbol*] [*Delisted*]
EDS .... Electronic Data Systems Federal Corporation
EDS .... Energy Data System [*Environmental Protection Agency*] [*Databank*]   (EISS)
EDS .... Engineering Drafting Software [*Calcomp Ltd.*] [*Software package*] [*British*]   (NCC)
EDS .... Entry Data Subsystem   (CIT)
EDS .... Exchangeable Disk Storage [*Data processing*]
EDSAC .... Electronic Delay Storage Automatic Calculator [*or Computer*] [*1949*]
EDSAC .... Electronic Discrete Sequential Automatic Computer [*University of Manchester, 1949*] [*British*]   (IEEE)
EDSAT .... [*Center for*] Educational Diffusion and Social Application of Satellite Telecommunications [*University of Wisconsin*]
EDSFC .... Electronic Data Systems Federal Corporation
EDST .... Elastic Diaphragm Switch Technology [*IBM Corp.*]   (MCD)
EDT .... Electronic Data Transmission
EDTCC ...... Electronic Data Traffic Control Center
EDTCC ...... Electronic Data Transmission Communications Central
EDTSR .... Electronic Dial Tone Speed Register [*Bell System*]
EDU .... Electronic Display Unit
Educ Comm & Tech J ... Educational Communication and Technology Journal [*A publication*]
Educ Comput ... Educational Computing [*A publication*]
EDUCOM .... Educational Communications [*Inter-University Communications Council*]
EDUG .... European Datamanager Users Group [*London, England*]
EDUNET ..... Education Network [*EDUCOM*]   (CAA)
EDUSAT ..... Educational Satellite   (KSC)
EDV .... Elektronische Datenverarbeitung [*Electronic Data Processing*] [*German*]
EDX .... Event Driven Executive [*IBM Corp.*]   (CAA)
EE .... Electronic Editing [*Telecommunications*]
EE .... Energy Enterprises [*Denver, CO*] [*Information service*]   (EISS)
EE .... Enter Exponent [*Data processing*]
EE .... External Entity   (CCD)
EEA .... Electrical and Electronic Abstracts [*United Kingdom*] [*A publication*]
EEA .... Electronic Engineering Association [*British*]   (CAH)
EEC .... EECO, Inc. [*American Stock Exchange symbol*]
EEC .... Emerson Electric Company
EECL .... Emitter-Emitter Coupled Logic   (IEEE)
EECM .... Electronic Engine Control Module
EEDB .... Energy and Environment Data Base [*Oak Ridge National Laboratory*] [*Database*]   (FDB)
EEDM .... External Event Detection Module [*Data processing*]   (MDG)
EEEU .... End Effector Electronics Unit   (MCD)
EEI .... Evans Economics, Incorporated [*Database producer*] [*Information service*]   (EISS)
EEL .... Exclusive Exchange Line [*Telecommunications*]   (DEEC)
EEM .... Electronic Equipment Modification
EEMS .... Enhanced Expanded Memory Specifications [*AST, Quadram*]
EEMTIC ...... Electrical and Electronic Measurement and Test Instrumentation Conference   (MCD)
EEN .... Eastern Educational Network [*Television*]
EEP .... Elliptical Error Probability   (CAAL)
EEPROM .... Electrically Erasable, Programable, Read-Only Memory [*Data processing*]
EEQEA .... Electronic Equipment Engineering [*A publication*]
EEROM ...... Electrically Erasable Read-Only Memory [*Data processing*]   (MDG)
EES .... Engineering Experiment Station [*University of Missouri - Columbia*] [*Research center*]   (RCD)
EES .... Engineering Experiment Station [*University of Arkansas, University of Alaska, Fairbanks*] [*Research center*]
EESB .... Electrical and Electronics Standards Board [*American National Standards Institute*] [*Telecommunications*]
EET .... Equipment Engaged Tone [*Telecommunications*]   (TEL)
EET .... Explosive-to-Electric Transducer
EEX .... Electronic Egg Exchange [*Computer program*]
EF .... Emitter Follower   (MCD)
EF .... Error Factor   (IEEE)
EF .... Extended Facility [*IBM Corp.*]   (CAA)
EFAP .... Elastic Frame Analysis Program [*Structures & Computers Ltd.*] [*Software package*] [*British*]   (NCC)
EFAR .... Economic Feeder Administration and Relief [*Telecommunications*]   (TEL)
EFC .... Electronic Frequency Control
EFCS .... Electronic Flight Control System
EFD .... Early Failure Detection
EFDARS ..... Electronic Flight Data and Recording System   (MCD)
EFDAS .... Electronic Flight Data Accumulation Service

EFE .... External Field Emission
EFFGRO ..... Efficient Growth [*Computer program*]   (NASA)
EFL .... Emitter Follower Logic
EFPH .... Equivalent Full Power Hour [*FCC*]
EFR .... Electronic Failure Report
EFRAP .... Exchange Feeder Route Analysis Program [*Bell System*]
EFRIS .... External Finished Reports Information Subsystem [*Data processing*]
EFRO .... Electronic Failure Report Only   (DDI)
EFS .... Electronic Frequency Selection   (IEEE)
EFS .... Error Free Seconds   (TEL)
EFT .... Electronic Funds Transfer [*Banking*]
EFTPOS ..... Electronic Funds Transfer at Point-of-Sale
EFTS .... Electronic Funds Transfer System [*Banking*] [*National Science Foundation*]
EG .... Electronic Guidance
EG .... Europaeische Gemeinschaften [*European Community*] [*German*] [*Information retrieval*]   (ODIN)
EGA .... Enhanced Graphics Adapter [*Computer technology*]
E/GCR .... Extended Group Coded Recording [*Data processing*]   (IBMDP)
EGG .... EG & G, Inc. [*NYSE symbol*]
EGIF .... Equipment Group Interface   (OA)
EGLC .... Eagle Computer, Inc. [*NASDAQ symbol*]   (NQ)
EGM .... Electronic Governor Module   (IEEE)
EGM .... Enhanced Graphics Monitor [*Computer technology*]
EGPS .... Extended General Purpose Simulator [*National Electronics Conference*]   (IEEE)
EGR .... Electronic Governor Regulator   (IEEE)
EHF .... Extremely High Frequency [*Electronics, radio wave*]
EHN .... European Host Network [*Data processing*]
EHS .... Extra-High Strength [*Steel*] [*Telecommunications*]   (TEL)
EHT .... Extra-High Tension
EI .... Electronic Interface   (MCD)
EIA .... Electronic Industries Association [*Washington, DC*] [*Telecommunications*]
EIA .... Energy Information Administration [*Department of Energy*]   (EISS)
EIAC .... Environmental Information Analysis Center [*Battelle Memorial Institute*]   (EISS)
EIB .... Elektro-Information Berlin [*Information retrieval*]   (ODIN)
EIC .... Embar Information Consultants [*Wheaton, IL*] [*Information service*]   (EISS)
EIC .... Energy Information Center [*Battelle Memorial Institute*]   (EISS)
EIC .... Environment Information Center, Inc.
EICS .... Electromagnetic Intelligence Collection System
EID .... Electronic Intrusion Detection
EID .... End Item Delivery
EID .... End Item Description
EID .... End Item Designators
EID .... End Item Documentation   (MCD)
EIDAP .... Emitter Isolated Difference Amplifier Paralleling [*Bell System*]
EIDD .... Experiment Interface Definition Document   (MCD)
EIES .... Electronic Information Exchange System [*Pronounced "eyes"*] [*New Jersey Institute of Technology*] [*Computer network*] [*Telecommunications*]
EIF .... Electronic Industries Foundation   (EANO)
EIG .... Electronic Image Generator
EIG .... Emitter Identification Guide   (NG)
EII .... Encoded Item Identifier   (CAAL)
EIIS .... Energy Industry Information System   (IEEE)
EIM .... End Item Manager
EIMF .... End Item Maintenance Form
EIMS .... End Item Maintenance Sheets
EIMTS .... End Item Maintenance Transmittal Sheet
EIN .... Educational Information Network [*Princeton, NJ*]
EIN .... European Information Network [*Telecommunications*]   (TEL)
EIP .... Electronic Installation Plan   (NG)
EIP .... End Item Parameter
EIP .... Equipment Installation Procedure [*Telecommunications*]   (TEL)
EIR .... End Item Requirement
EIR .... Engineering Information Report [*Telecommunications*]   (TEL)
EIRD .... Engineering Information Report Date [*Telecommunications*]   (TEL)
EIRP .... Equivalent Isotropically Radiated Power [*Microwave transmission*]
EIS .... Economic Information Systems, Inc. [*Database originator*]   (NG)
EIS .... End Interruption Sequence [*Data processing*]
EIS .... End Item Specification
EIS .... Executive Information Services [*Data processing system*]
EIS .... Expanded Inband Signaling [*Telecommunications*]   (TEL)
EIS .... Extended Instruction Set [*Honeywell, Inc.*]   (CAA)
EIT .... Electromagnetic Interference Testing
EIT .... Entry Interface Time   (MCD)
EITP .... End Item Test Plan   (MCD)
EIU .... Electronic Interface Unit
EIU .... Equipment Inventory Update [*Telecommunications*]   (TEL)
EJ .... Electronic Jamming
EJ .... Electronic Journalism
EJC .... Eccles-Jordan Circuit [*Electronics*]
EJCC .... Eastern Joint Computer Conference
EJF .... Estimated Junction Frequency [*Telecommunications*]   (TEL)
EJT .... Eccles-Jordan Trigger [*Electronics*]
EK .... Eastman Kodak Co. [*NYSE symbol*]

EKB............ Electronic Keyboard
EKB............ Electronic Knowledge Bank
EKBS.......... Electronic Keyboard System
EKC............ Eastman Kodak Company
EKI............. Electronic Keyboarding, Incorporated [*Information service*] (EISS)
EKN............ Ecology of Knowledge Network (EANO)
EKOL.......... European Kompass Online [*Reed Publishing Ltd.*] [*Database*] (CUAD)
EKS............ Electronic Keyboard System
EKTS.......... Electronic Key Telephone System
EL.............. Electronic Lover
EL.............. Engineering Letter [*Telecommunications*] (TEL)
EL.............. Exchange Line [*Telecommunications*] (TEL)
ELATE........ Engineers' Language for Automatic Test Equipment
ELCO.......... Eliminate and Count [*Coding*] [*Data processing*]
ELCOM....... Electronics and Computers [*Cambridge Scientific Abstracts*] [*Bethesda, MD*] [*Bibliographic database*] (OBD)
ELD............ Economic Load Dispatching (BUR)
ELD............ Electronic Lie Detector
ELD............ Engineering Logic Diagram
ELD............ Error Logging Device
ELE............ Equivalent Logic Element (OA)
ELE............ European Electronics [*A publication*]
ELECA........ Electronics [*A publication*]
Elec Busns... Electronic Business [*A publication*]
ELECD........ Element Code (MCD)
Elec Des..... Electronic Design [*A publication*]
Elec Desgn... Electronic Design [*A publication*]
Elec Ed....... Electronic Education [*A publication*]
Elec & Electron Abstr... Electrical and Electronic Abstracts [*A publication*]
Elec Engrg Electron... Electrical Engineering and Electronics [*A publication*]
Elec Eng T... Electronic Engineering Times [*A publication*]
Elec Mkt T... Electronic Market Trends [*A publication*]
Elec News... Electronic News [*A publication*]
ELECOM...... Electronic Computing
Elec Prog.... Electronic Progress [*A publication*]
Elec T Intnl... Electronics Today International [*A publication*]
Elec Tod..... Electronics Today International [*A publication*]
Electr Co J... Electronics and Communications in Japan [*A publication*]
ELECTRO... Electronics (KSC)
Electron...... Electronics [*A publication*]
Electron Bus... Electronic Business [*A publication*]
Electron Comm Japan... Electronics and Communications in Japan [*A publication*]
Electron Commun... Electronic Communicator [*A publication*]
Electron & Communic Abstr J... Electronics and Communications Abstracts Journal [*A publication*]
Electron Commun Japan... Electronics and Communications in Japan [*A publication*]
Electron Commun Jpn... Electronics and Communications in Japan [*A publication*]
Electron Des... Electronic Design [*A publication*]
Electronic N... Electronic News [*A publication*]
Electronics Today... Electronics Today International [*A publication*]
Electron Packag Prod... Electronic Packaging and Production [*A publication*]
Electron Prod... Electronic Products Magazine [*A publication*]
Electron Prog... Electronic Progress [*A publication*]
Electron Publishing Rev... Electronic Publishing Review [*A publication*]
Electron Test... Electronics Test [*A publication*]
Electron Today Int... Electronics Today International [*A publication*]
Electron Wkly... Electronics Weekly [*A publication*]
Electr Prod... Electronic Products Magazine [*A publication*]
Elec Week... Electronics Weekly [*A publication*]
Elektr Nachr Tech... Elektrische Nachrichten Technik [*A publication*]
ELEM.......... Element (MSA)
ELF............. Extensible Language Facility [*Data processing*] (IEEE)
ELF............. Extremely Low Frequency [*Electronics, radio wave*]
ELFIS.......... Ernahrungs-, Land- und Forstwissenschaftliches Informationssystem [*Zentralstelle fuer Agrardokumentation und -information*] [*Database*] (CUAD)
ELI............. Electronic Line Indicator [*Tennis*]
ELI............. Equitable Life Interpreter [*Computer*]
ELI............. Extensible Language I [*Data processing*]
ELIAS......... Entry Level Interactive Applications Systems [*Data processing*]
ELIAS......... Environment Libraries Automated System [*Environment Canada*] [*Database*] [*Information service*] (EISS)
ELINT......... Electronic Intelligence [*or Intercept*] [*Meaning of ELINT determined by reference to before (Intercept) and after (Intelligence) analysis of reconnaissance mission results*]
Ellis Horwood Ser Comput Appl... Ellis Horwood Series. Computers and Their Applications [*A publication*]
ELM............ Element Load Model
ELMAP....... Exchange Line Multiplexing Analysis Program (TEL)
ELODA........ Electronic Design [*A publication*]
ELPPA........ Electronic Packaging and Production [*A publication*]
ELS............ Error Likely Situation (IEEE)
ELSA........... Electronic Selective Archives [*Swiss News Agency*] [*Information service*] (EISS)
ELSI........... Extra-Large-Scale Integration [*Data processing*] (TEL)
ELSIE......... Electronic Letter Sorting and Indicator Equipment
ELSIE......... Electronic Signaling and Indicating Equipment (IEEE)

ELSS.......... Electronic Legislative Search System [*Commerce Clearing House*] [*Database*] [*Information service*]
EL-SSC....... Electronic Switching System Control [*Telecommunications*] (TEL)
ELT............ Element
ELT............ Emergency Locator Transmitter
ELT............ European Letter Telegram
ELTPA........ Electronic Progress [*A publication*]
ELTR.......... Emergency Locator Transmitter Receiver
ELWYA...... Electronics Weekly [*A publication*]
EM............. Electronic Mail [*Telecommunications*]
EM............. Emergency Maintenance (BUR)
EM............. End of Medium [*Data processing*]
EM............. Entity Module [*Data processing*]
EM............. Erasable Memory [*Data processing*] (KSC)
EM............. Error Multiplier
EM............. Excerpta Medica Foundation [*Database producer*] (ODIN)
EMA........... Effective Mass Approximation
EMA........... Electronic Mail Association [*Washington, DC*] [*Telecommunications*] (EANO)
EMAR......... Experimental Memory - Address Register
EMB........... Early-Make-Break [*Data processing*]
EMBASE..... Excerpta Medica Database [*Trademark*] [*Elsevier*] [*Bibliographic database*]
EMBERS..... Emergency Bed Request System [*Data processing*]
EMBRATEL... Empresa Brasileira de Telecomunicacoes [*Brazilian Telecommunications Enterprises*] [*Rio De Janeiro*] (TSSD)
EMC........... Electromagnetic Compatibility
EMC........... Electromagnetic Control
EMC........... Electronic Mail Courier
EMC........... Electronic Material Change
EMC........... Engine Monitor Computer
EMCA......... Electronic Mail Corporation of America [*NASDAQ symbol*] (NQ)
EMCC......... Electromagnetic Control Compatibility
EMCC......... Emergency Medicine and Crisis Care [*Database*] (FDB)
EMCFOM.... Electromagnetic Compatibility Figure of Merit [*Telecommunications*] (TEL)
EMCON...... Electronic Emission Control (MCD)
EMCS......... Electromagnetic Compatibility Standardization [*Program*] [*Telecommunications*] (IEEE)
EMD........... Electronic Map Display
EMDS......... Electronic Material Data Service (MUGU)
EMEA......... Electronic Maintenance Engineering Association
EMEC......... Electromagnetic Effects Capability (NASA)
EMEG......... Electromagnetic Environment Generator
EMER......... Electromagnetic Environment Recorder (MCD)
EMF........... Electronic Mail Facility [*Postal Service*]
EMFC......... EMF Corporation [*NASDAQ symbol*] (NQ)
EMH........... Electronic Mail Handling
EMI............ Electromagnetic Interference
EMIC.......... Electromagnetic Interference and Compatibility
EMIDEC..... EMI [*formerly, Electric & Musical Industries Ltd.*] Data Electronic Computer [*Made by EMI Industries - Great Britain*]
EMINT........ Electromagnetic Intelligence (MSA)
EMIRTEL.... Emirates Telecommunications Corp. (TEL)
EMIS.......... Electronic Markets and Information [*McGraw-Hill Publications Co.*] [*Database*] (CUAD)
EMIS.......... Electronic Materials Information Service [*Institution of Electrical Engineers*] [*Database*] (EISS)
EMIT.......... Emergency Message Initiation Terminal (MCD)
EML........... Expected Measured Loss [*Telecommunications*] (TEL)
EMLX......... Emulex Corp. [*NASDAQ symbol*] (NQ)
EMM.......... Electronic Memories & Magnetics Corp. [*NYSE symbol*]
EMMS........ Electronic Mail and Message Systems (DEEC)
EMOD........ Erasable Memory Octal Dump [*Data processing*] (SKY)
EMOS........ Enhancement Metal-Oxide Semiconductor (BUR)
EMP........... Electromagnetic Pulse
EMP........... Electron Microprobe
EMP........... Electronic Multiplying Punches (DEN)
EMP........... Erasable Memory Program [*Data processing*]
EMPS......... Electromagnetic Pulse Simulator (MCD)
EMPT......... Electronic Maintenance Proficiency Test
EMR........... Electromechanical Relay [*Power switchgear*] (IEEE)
EMR........... Electromechanical Research (IEEE)
EMR........... Electronic Moisture Recorder
EMR........... Emerson Electric Co. [*NYSE symbol*]
EMR........... Error Monitor Register (KSC)
EMRP......... Effective Monopole-Radiated Power (TEL)
EMRRI....... Energy and Mineral Resources Research Institute [*Iowa State University*] [*Research center*] (RCD)
EMRT......... Electronic Market-Research Terminal
EMS........... Electromyosignal [*Data processing*]
EMS........... Electron Multiplex Switch
EMS........... Electronic Mail Service [*Telecommunications*]
EMS........... Electronic Mail System [*Postal Service*]
EMS........... Electronic Management System
EMS........... Electronic Meeting Services [*Clinton, MD*] [*Telecommunications*] (TSSD)
EMS........... Electronic Message System (DEEC)
EMS........... Elephant Memory System [*Data processing*]
EMS........... Emergency Signal (BUR)
EMS........... Equilibrium Mode Simulator (TEL)
EMS........... Error Mean Square

Computer & Telecommunications Acronyms

EMS	Expanded Memory Specification [Data processing]
EMS	Experimental Monitoring Satellite
EMSO	Electronic Memory Systems Organization [Burroughs Corp.]
EMSS	Electronic Message Service System [Telecommunications] (TEL)
EMSU	Electromagnetic Simulation Unit (MCD)
EMT	End of Magnetic Tape [Data processing] (MDG)
EMTEDS	Electromagnetic Test Environment Data System (MCD)
EMTH	Energy Methods Corp. [NASDAQ symbol] (NQ)
EMTU	Enhanced Master Terminal Unit
EMU	Electromagnetic Unit
EMU	Extended Memory Unit (NASA)
EMUX	Electrical Multiplex
EMX	Electron Microprobe X-Ray Analyzer
EMXA	Electron Microprobe X-Ray Analyzer
EMXRF	Electron Microprobe X-Ray Fluorescence
EN	Electronic News [A publication]
EN	Element Number [Data processing]
ENA	Electronic Networking Association [Philadelphia, PA] [Information service] (EISS)
ENADS	Enhanced Network Administration System [Telecommunications] (TEL)
ENBL	Enable (MSA)
ENCD	Encode (MSA)
ENCDR	Encoder (MSA)
ENCYA	Engineering Cybernetics [English Translation] [A publication]
ENDF	Evaluated Nuclear Data File [AEC] [Databank]
ENEA	European Nuclear Energy Agency [Paris, France]
ENEC	Energy and Economics Data Bank [Fachinformationszentrum Energie, Physik, Mathematik GmbH] [Database] (CUAD)
ENFIA	Exchange Network Facilities for Interstate Access [Telecommunications]
ENG	Electronic News Gathering [Television news coverage]
Eng Comput	Engineering Computers [A publication]
Eng Cybern	Engineering Cybernetics [A publication]
ENGR	Engineer
ENGRG	Engineering
ENI	Evans Newton, Incorporated [Scottsdale, AZ] [Software manufacturer] (DASOS)
ENIAC	Electronic Numerical Integrator and Calculator [Early computer, 1946]
ENQ	Enquiry [Transmission control character]
ENR	Enertec Corp. [Toronto Stock Exchange symbol]
ENSB	Equivalent Noise Sideband (DDI)
ENSDF	Evaluated Nuclear Structure Data File [Brookhaven National Laboratory] [Database] (ODIN)
ENSI	Equivalent Noise Sideband Input (MCD)
ENT	Equivalent Noise Temperature
ENTELEC	Energy Telecommunications and Electrical Association [Formerly, PIEA] (EANO)
ENTR	Enterprise Technology [NASDAQ symbol] (NQ)
ENT/SAT	Entertainment Satellite [Proposed] (MCD)
ENU	Essential/Nonessential/Update [Telecommunications] (TEL)
ENVIROBIB	Environmental Bibliography [Environmental Studies Institute] [Santa Barbara, CA] [Bibliographic database] (OBD)
ENVIRON	Environmental Information Retrieval On-Line [Environmental Protection Agency]
EO	End Office [Telecommunications] (TEL)
EO	Exclusive Or [Gates] [Data processing]
EO	Expected Output
EOA	End of Address [Data processing]
EOAU	Electro-Optical Alignment Unit
EOB	End of Block [Data processing]
EOC	End of Card [Data processing] (CMD)
EOC	End of Conversion
EOCA	Electronic Office Centers of America, Inc. [Schaumburg, IL] [Telecommunications] (TSSD)
EOD	Electro-Optic Display
EOD	Elements of Data (MSA)
EOD	End of Data [Data processing]
EOD	End of Dialing [Telecommunications] (TEL)
EODD	Electro-Optic Digital Deflector (IEEE)
EODS	Electro-Optic Direction Sensor
EODTC	Electro-Optic Display Test Chamber
EOE	End of Extent [Data processing] (IBMDP)
EOEM	Electronic Original Equipment Market
EOF	End of File [Data processing]
EOI	End of Input [Data processing]
EOI	End of Inquiry [Data processing] (CAA)
EOIS	Electro-Optical Imaging System (IEEE)
EOJ	End of Job [Data processing]
EOL	End of Line [Telecommunications] (FAAC)
EOL	Expression-Oriented Language [Data processing] (TUT)
EOLB	End of Line Block [Data processing] (CET)
EOLR	Electrical Objective Loudness Rating (IEEE)
EOLT	End of Logical Tape [Data processing]
EOM	Electro-Optical Modulator
EOM	End of Medium [Data processing] (BUR)
EOM	End of Message [Data processing]
EOMS	End of Message Sequence [Data processing] (CET)
EOP	End Output [Data processing] (IEEE)
EOP	End of Program [Data processing] (CGC)
EOPC	Electro-Optic Phase Change (IEEE)
EOR	End of Record [Data processing] (TUT)
EOR	End of Reel
EOR	End of Run [Telecommunications] (TEL)
EOR	Exclusive Or [Data processing]
EORSAT	ELINT [Electronic Intelligence] - Ocean Reconnaissance Satellite (MCD)
EOS	Electro-Optical Systems, Inc. [Subsidiary of Xerox Corp.]
EOT	End of Tape [Data processing]
EOT	End of Task [Data processing] (TUT)
EOT	End of Test [Data processing] (CIT)
EOT	End of Text [Data processing]
EOT	End of Transmission [Data processing]
EOV	End of Volume [Data processing] (TUT)
EOW	End of Word [Data processing]
EP	Electrically Polarized [Relay]
EP	Electron Paramagnetic
EP	Emulation Program [IBM Corp.] (BUR)
EP	End of Program [Data processing]
EP	Entry Point (BUR)
EP	Epitaxial Planar [Electronics]
EP	Equipment Practice [Telecommunications] (TEL)
EPA	Electronic Publishing Abstracts [The Research Association for the Paper and Board, Printing and Packaging Industries] [Database] (CUAD)
EPABX	Electronic Private Automatic Branch Exchange [Telecommunications] (MCD)
EPACASR	Environmental Protection Agency Chemical Activities Status Report [Environmental Protection Agency] [Database] (FDB)
EPAM	Elementary Perceiver and Memorizer [University of California] [Learning theory] [Computer device]
EPAN	Electronic Purchasing Agent Network [Service of Data Corp. of America]
EPB	Environmental Periodicals Bibliography [Environmental Studies Institute, International Academy at Santa Barbara] [Bibliographic Database]
EPBX	Electronic Private Branch Exchange [Telecommunications]
EPC	Earth Potential Compensation [Telecommunications] (TEL)
EPC	Editorial Processing Center (CAA)
EPC	Electronic Program Control
EPCA	European Petrochemical Association [Database producer] (CUAD)
EPCCS	Emergency Positive Control Communications System
EPD	Exchange Parameter Definitions [Telecommunications] (TEL)
EPDB	Environmental Protection Data Base [Environmental Protection Agency]
EPDCC	Elementary Potential Digital Computing Component
EPD/RDIS	Electric Power Database [Research and Development Information System] [Electric Power Research Institute] [Information service] (EISS)
EPDT	Estimated Project Duration Time (OA)
EPEC	Emerson Programer-Evaluator-Controller [Data processing] (CDH)
EPG	Edit Program Generator (TUT)
EPG	Electronic Program Guide [Cable-television system]
EPI	Electronic Position Indicator
EPIA	Electric Power Industry Abstracts [Edison Electric Institute] [Washington, DC] [Bibliographic database] (OBD)
EPIC	Earth-Pointing Instrument Carrier [A satellite]
EPIC	Emergency Programs Information Center [Database] (FDB)
EPIC	Estimate of Properties for Industrial Chemistry [Universite de Liege] [Database] (CUAD)
EPIC	Exchange Price Indicators [Database] [British] (DEEC)
EPICS	European Petrochemical Industry Computerized System [Parpinelli Tecnon] [Italy] [Information service] (EISS)
EPIN	Electronic Personnel Information Network [Data Corp. of America]
EPIRB	Emergency Position-Indicating Radio Beacon (MCD)
EPK	Electronic Press Kit
EPL	Early Programing Language [Data processing] (CGC)
EPL	Encoder Programing Language [Data processing] (CAA)
EPLANS	Engineering, Planning, and Analysis Systems [Telecommunications] (TEL)
EPM	External Polarization Modulation (IEEE)
EPO	Emergency Power Off (SKY)
EPOS	Electronic Point-of-Sale [Data processing]
EPPI	Electronic Programed Procurement Information (NG)
EPR	Electronic Publishing Review [A publication]
EPR	Error Pattern Register (CAA)
EPRL	Electric Power Research Laboratory [Arizona State University] [Research center] (RCD)
EPROM	Electrically Programable Read-Only Memory [Data processing]
EPROM	Erasable Programable Read-Only Memory [Data processing] (MCD)
EPS	Encoder Power Supply
EPS	Equilibrium Problem Solver (IEEE)
EPS	Evaluation & Planning Systems, Inc. [Windham, NH] [Software manufacturer] (DASOS)
EPS	Even Parity Select (CAA)
EPS	Extensible Programing System [Data processing] (CSR)
EPS	External Page Storage (BUR)
EPSCS	Enhanced Private Switched Communications Service [Pronounced "ep-sis"] [AT & T]
EPSL	Emergency Power Switching Logic (IEEE)

Computer & Telecommunications Acronyms

EPSS .... Experimental Packet Switching System [*Telecommunications*]
EP & T .... Electronic Products & Technology [*Canada*] [*A publication*]
EPTW .... Educational Programs That Work [*Department of Education*] [*Information service*]   (EISS)
EPU .... Emergency Power Unit
EPU .... Executive Processing Unit   (CAA)
EPUB .... Electronic Publishing System [*ITT Dialcom*] [*Database*]
EQ .... Enquiries [*Telecommunications*]   (TEL)
EQ .... Equal
EQ .... Equalization [*Electronics*]
EQ .... Equipment   (BUR)
EQCC .... Entry Query Control Console [*Data processing*]
EQE .... Event Queue Element [*Data processing*]   (MCD)
EQL .... Equal   (MSA)
EQPMT ...... Equipment   (MDG)
EQPT .... Equipment
EQU .... Equate   (MDG)
EQUA .... Equatorial Communications [*NASDAQ symbol*]   (NQ)
EQUIP .... Equipment
ER .... Easy to Reach [*Telecommunications*]   (TEL)
ER .... Engineering Route [*Telecommunications*]   (TEL)
ER .... Error Rate [*Statistics*]
ER .... Error Recorder   (VIT)
ER .... Error Recovery   (BUR)
ER .... Executive Request [*Data processing*]
ERA .... Electronic Reading Automation [*Information retrieval*]
ERA .... Electronic Representatives Association
ERB .... Electronic Recording Beam   (MDG)
ERC .... Educational Research Center [*New Mexico State University*] [*Research center*]   (RCD)
ERC .... Engineering Research Center [*New Mexico State University*] [*Research center*]   (RCD)
ERC .... Events Recorder Console   (MCD)
ERCC .... Error Checking and Correction   (CAA)
ERCR .... Electronic Retina Computing Reader
ERD .... Error Recording Device
ERDS .... Equipment Recall Data System   (MCD)
ERE .... Edison Responsive Environment [*Automated learning system*]
EREP .... Environmental Recording, Editing, and Printing Program   (BUR)
EREP .... Equipment Replacement and Enhancement Program [*Data processing*]
ERES .... Erlanger Rechner-Entwurfs-Sprache [*Programing language*] [*1974*]   (CSR)
ERF .... Error Function
ERF .... Exchange Reference File
ERFI .... Error Function, Inverse
ERFPI .... Extended-Range Floating Point Interpretive System
ERG .... Erase Gap [*Data processing*]   (TUT)
ERI .... Electronics Research Laboratory [*Montana State University*] [*Research center*]   (RCD)
ERI .... End of Recorded Information [*Data processing*]
ERIC .... Educational Resources [*formerly, Research*] Information Center [*Office of Education*] [*Bibliographic database*] [*Washington, DC*]
ERIC/ACVE ... Educational Resources Information Center/Clearinghouse on Adult, Career, and Vocational Education   (EISS)
ERIC/CAPS ... Educational Resources Information Center/Clearinghouse on Counseling and Personnel Services [*University of Michigan*] [*Research center*]   (EISS)
ERIC/CE ..... Educational Resources Information Center/Clearinghouse in Career Education [*Ohio State University*] [*Columbus, OH*]   (EISS)
ERIC/CHE ... Educational Resources Information Center/Clearinghouse on Higher Education   (EISS)
ERIC/CHESS ... Educational Resources Information Center/Clearinghouse for Social Studies/Social Science Education [*Social Science Education Consortium, Inc.*] [*Boulder, CO*]   (EISS)
ERIC/CLL ... Educational Resources Information Center/Clearinghouse on Languages and Linguistics [*Center for Applied Liguistics*] [*Arlington, VA*]   (EISS)
ERIC/CRESS ... Educational Resources Information Center/Clearinghouse on Rural Education and Small Schools [*New Mexico State University*] [*Research center*]   (EISS)
ERIC/CUE ... Educational Resources Information Center/Clearinghouse on Urban Education [*Columbia University*] [*New York, NY*]   (EISS)
ERIC/EECE ... Educational Resources Information Center/Clearinghouse on Elementary and Early Childhood Education [*University of Illinois*] [*Urbana, IL*]   (EISS)
ERIC/IR ...... Educational Resources Information Center/Clearinghouse for Information Resources [*Syracuse University*] [*Research center*]   (EISS)
ERIC/TM ..... Educational Resources Information Center/Clearinghouse on Tests, Measurement, and Evaluation [*Educational Testing Service*] [*Princeton, NJ*]   (EISS)
ERJE .... Extended Remote Job Entry   (CAA)
ERL .... Echo Return Loss [*Telecommunications*]
ERL .... Electronics Research Laboratory [*University of California, Berkeley*] [*Research center*]   (RCD)
ERMA .... Electrical Reproduction Method of Accounting
ERMA .... Electronic Recording Machine Accounting
ERMAC ...... Echo-Ranging Masked Acoustic Communications   (DDI)

ERNIE .... Electronic Random Number and Indicating Equipment [*Used for selecting winning premium bond numbers*] [*British*]
EROM .... Electron Readout Measurement   (MCD)
EROM .... Erasable Read-Only Memory [*Data processing*]
EROS .... Engineering Records Organisation System [*Applied Research of Cambridge Ltd.*] [*Software package*] [*British*]   (NCC)
EROW .... Executive Right of Way [*Telecommunications*]   (TEL)
ERP .... Effective Radiated Power [*Radio transmitting*]
ERP .... Equipment Replacement Program [*Data processing*]
ERP .... Error-Recovery Package [*Data processing*]   (MDG)
ERP .... Error-Recovery Procedure [*Data processing*]   (TUT)
ERPLD .... Extended Range Phase-Locked Demodulator   (IEEE)
ERR .... Error   (MCD)
ERRC .... Error Correction
ERRS .... Environmental Response and Referral Service [*Oak Ridge National Laboratory*]   (EISS)
ERS .... Electronic Register-Sender [*Telecommunications*]   (TEL)
ERS .... Electronic Remote Switching   (MCD)
ERS .... Emergency Reporting System [*Telecommunications*]   (TEL)
ERS .... Entry and Recovery Simulation   (MCD)
ERSC .... Extended-Range and Space Communication   (MCD)
ERSOS ...... Earth Resource Survey Operational System   (TEL)
ERSS .... Earth Resources Satellite System   (IEEE)
ERT .... Estimated Repair Time [*Telecommunications*]   (TEL)
ERT .... Expected Run-Time   (CAA)
ERTS .... ELINT [*Electronic Intelligence*] Receiver Test System   (MCD)
ERTS .... Environmental Resources Technology Satellite
ERTS .... Error Rate Test Set   (TEL)
ES .... Echo Suppressor [*Telecommunications*]   (TEL)
ES .... Electromagnetic Storage
ES .... Electronic Switching [*Telecommunications*]
ES .... Electronic Systems
ES .... External Store   (CAA)
ES .... Extra Segment [*Data processing*]
ES² .... European Silicon Structures
ESA .... Externally Specified Address   (CAAL)
ESAC .... Electronic Systems Assistance Center [*Telecommunications*]   (TEL)
ESAFT .... Electrically Steerable Antenna Feed Techniques   (NG)
ESA-IRS ..... European Space Agency Information Retrieval Service [*Frascati, Italy*]
ESAP .... Employment Security Automation Project [*Department of Labor*]
ESAS-2 ...... Elastic Structural Analysis System - Two Dimensional [*Structures & Computers Ltd.*] [*Software package*] [*British*]   (NCC)
ESC .... Echo Suppressor Control [*Telecommunications*]   (TEL)
ESC .... Escape Character [*Keyboard*]   (KSC)
ESC .... Exchange Servicing Center [*Telecommunications*]   (TEL)
ESCAD ...... Energy Soft Computer Aided Design [*Energy Soft Computer Systems Ltd.*] [*Software package*] [*British*]   (NCC)
ESCAPE ..... Expansion Symbolic Compiling Assembly Program for Engineers
ESCC .... Evans & Sutherland Computer Corporation [*NASDAQ symbol*]   (NQ)
ESCES .... Experimental Space Communication Earth Station [*Telecommunications*]   (TEL)
ESCG .... Energy Sciences Corporation [*NASDAQ symbol*]   (NQ)
ESCO .... European Satellite Consulting Organization [*Montrouge, France*] [*Telecommunications*]   (TSSD)
ESCON ...... Estimated Consumption [*of gasoline*] [*Computer model*]
ESCORT .... Electronic System for Control of Receipt Transactions   (MCD)
ESCS .... Emergency Satellite Communications System   (CAA)
ESD .... Ending Sequence Done   (OA)
ESD .... External Symbol Dictionary [*A publication*]
ES:DI .... Extra Segment:Destination Index [*Data processing*]
ESDS .... Economic and Social Data System [*Agency for International Development*] [*Database*]   (FDB)
ESG .... Education Service Group [*Bibliographic Retrieval Services*] [*Information service*]   (EISS)
ESG .... Exchange Software Generator   (TEL)
ESI .... Electronic Systems Integration   (KSC)
ESI .... Externally Specified Index
ESIS .... European Shielding Information Service [*EURATOM*] [*Databank*]   (EISS)
ESL .... Electroscience Laboratory [*Ohio State University*] [*Research center*]   (RCD)
ESL .... Essential Service Line [*Telecommunications*]   (TEL)
ESLR .... Events Select Logic and Rates   (MCD)
ESN .... Error Sequence Number [*Data processing*]
ESO .... Echo Suppressor, Originating End [*Telecommunications*]   (TEL)
ESO .... Event Sequence Override   (SKY)
ESOPS .... Employment Service Online Placement System [*Data processing*]
ESP .... Environmental Sketches in Perspective [*Computer program*]
ESPES .... Especialidades Farmaceuticas Espanolas Data Bank [*Spanish Pharmaceutical Specialities Data Bank*] [*Information service*]   (EISS)
ESPL .... Electronic Switching Programing Language   (CAA)
ESPL .... Extensible Structure Processing Language [*1969-71*] [*Data processing*]   (CSR)
ESPN .... Entertainment and Sports Programing Network, Inc. [*Cable-television system*]
ESPOL .... Executive System Problem-Oriented Language [*Burroughs Corp.*] [*Data processing*]   (BUR)
ESR .... Electronic Send/Receive   (CAA)
ESR .... Equipment Supervisory Rack [*Telecommunications*]   (TEL)

Computer & Telecommunications Acronyms

ESR .... Equivalent Series Resistance
ESS .... Echo Suppression Subsystem [*Telecommunications*]   (TEL)
ESS .... Electronic Security Surveillance
ESS .... Electronic Security System
ESS .... Electronic Sequence Switching
ESS .... Electronic Surveillance System
ESS .... Electronic Switching System [*See also EAX*] [*Telecommunications*]
ESS .... Event Scheduling System   (CAA)
ESSA .... Electronic Scanning and Stabilizing Antenna
ESSA .... Emergency Safeguards System Activation   (IEEE)
ESSA .... Environmental Survey Satellite   (TEL)
ESSEX .... Experimental Solid-State Exchange [*Communication system*]   (MCD)
EST .... Echo Suppressor, Terminating End [*Telecommunications*]   (TEL)
EST .... Estimate
ESTC .... Eighteenth Century Short Title Catalogue [*Bibliographic database*]   (OBD)
ESTRACK ... European Space Tracking and Telemetry Network   (MCD)
ESTS .... Echo Suppressor Testing System [*Telecommunications*]   (TEL)
ESTV .... Error Statistics by Tape Volume [*Data processing*]   (IBMDP)
ESU .... Electronic Switching Unit [*Telecommunications*]   (MCD)
ESU .... Electronics Services Unlimited [*New York, NY*] [*Telecommunications*]   (TSSD)
ESU .... Empty Signal Unit [*Telecommunications*]   (TEL)
ESV .... Error Statistics by Volume [*Data processing*]   (BUR)
ESV .... Essential Service Value [*Telecommunications*]   (IEEE)
ESW .... Error Status Word [*Data processing*]   (BUR)
ET .... Electrical Typewriter   (CMD)
ET .... Electronic Typewriter
ET .... EMCLASS Terms [*Online database field identifier*]   (OBD)
ET .... End of Tape [*Data processing*]   (CET)
ET .... End of Text [*Data processing*]   (CAA)
ET .... Engaged Tone [*Telecommunications*]   (TEL)
ET .... Engineering Technology   (MCD)
ET .... English Title [*Online database field identifier*]   (OBD)
ETA .... Expected Turnaround [*Data processing*]
ETAIRS ...... Employment and Training Automated Information and Retrieval System [*Department of Labor*] [*Database*]   (FDB)
ETAN .... Yugoslav Committee for Electronics and Automation [*Beograd, Yugoslavia*]
ETB .... Electronic Test Block
ETB .... End of Transmission Block [*Data processing*]
ETC .... Educational Technology Center [*Harvard University*] [*Research center*]   (RCD)
ETC .... Educational Travel Connection [*Oracle Corp.*] [*Information service*]   (EISS)
ETC .... Electronic Toll Center [*AT & T*]
ETC .... Extended Text Compositor [*Applied Data Research, Inc.*]   (CAA)
ETCRRM ..... Electronic Teleprinter Cryptographic Regenerative Repeater Mixer   (NATG)
ETD .... Electrical Terminal Distributor   (KSC)
ETD .... Event Time Digitizer
ETDC .... EADAS [*Engineering and Administrative Data Acquisition System*] Traffic Data Center [*Bell System*]
ETE .... Electromagnetic Test Environment   (MCD)
ETGTS .... Electronic Text and Graphics Transfer System   (CAA)
ETH .... Eidgenossische Technische Hochschule Zurich [*Swiss Federal Institute of Technology*]
ETI .... Electronics Today International [*A publication*]
ETI .... Esprit Systems [*American Stock Exchange symbol*]
ETIC .... Environmental Teratology Information Center [*Department of Energy*]   (EISS)
ETL .... Effective Testing Loss [*Telecommunications*]   (TEL)
ETL .... Ending Tape Label [*Data processing*]   (BUR)
ETM .... Electrically Transmitted Message
ETM .... Enhanced Timing Module   (IEEE)
ETMF .... Elapsed Time Multiprogramming Factor   (CAA)
ETN .... Eaton Corp. [*NYSE symbol*]
ETN .... Educational Telecommunications Network
ETN .... Elektrotechniek. Technisch-Economisch Tijdschrift [*A publication*]
ETOS .... Extended Tape Operating System   (BUR)
ETP .... Estimated Turnaround Point
ETP .... Extended Term Plan   (BUR)
ETPI .... Eastern Telecommunications Philippines, Incorporated [*Manila*]   (TSSD)
ETR .... Expected Time of Response   (CAA)
ETRE .... Entre' Computer Centers [*NASDAQ symbol*]   (NQ)
ETRMD .... Electromagnetics [*A publication*]
ETS .... Educational Teleconference System [*University of Missouri - Columbia*] [*Telecommunications*]   (TSSD)
ETS .... Educational Testing Service
ETS .... Electronic Tandem Switching [*Telecommunications*]   (TEL)
ETS .... Electronic Translator System [*Bell System*]
ETS .... Empire Telecommunications [*British*] [*World War II*]
ETS .... Engineering Test Satellite
ETS .... Enquiry Terminal System [*International Computers Ltd.*]   (CAA)
ETSAL .... Electronic Terms for Space Age Language
ETSS .... Electronic Telecommunication Switching System   (MCD)
ETSS .... Entry Time-Sharing System [*Data processing*] [*IBM Corp.*]
ETSTC .... Educational Testing Service Test Collection   (EISS)
ETT .... End of Tape Test [*Data processing*]

ETU .... Electronic Translator Unit [*Telecommunications*]
ETU .... Enhanced Telephone Unit
ETV .... Educational Television
ETW .... End of Tape Warning [*Data processing*]   (CET)
ETW .... Error Time Word   (KSC)
ETX .... End of Text [*Data processing*]
EU .... Electronic Unit
EU .... Error Unavoidable
EU .... Execution Unit [*Data processing*]
EUA .... Exchange Users Association   (EANO)
EUC .... End Use Check
EUCC .... Computing Center [*Emory University*] [*Research center*]   (RCD)
EUCLID .... Experimental Use Computer, London Integrated Display
EUDISED .... European Documentation and Information System for Education [*Council of Europe*] [*Database*]   (EISS)
EUDS .... Electronic Unit Design Section
EUF .... End User Facility   (CAA)
EURATOM ... Europaeische Atomgemeinschaft [*European Atomic Energy Community*] [*German*] [*Information retrieval*]   (ODIN)
EUROBIT .... European Association of Manufacturers of Business Machines and Data Processing Equipment   (EANO)
EUROCOMP ... European Computing Congress   (IEEE)
EURODICAUTOM ... European Automated Dictionary   (DEEC)
EURONET .... European On-Line Information Network [*Commission of the European Communities*] [*Information service*]   (EISS)
EUSIDIC ..... European Association of Scientific Information Dissemination Studies
EUSIREF ..... European Scientific Information Referral [*EUSIDIC*] [*Information service*]   (EISS)
EUTELSAT ... European Telecommunications Satellite Organization [*Paris, France*] [*Telecommunications*]   (TSSD)
EVA .... Error Volume Analysis [*Data processing*]   (IBMDP)
EVC .... Error Vector Computer   (NG)
EVD .... Economische Voorlichtingsdienst [*Economic Information Service*] [*Netherlands*] [*Information service*]   (EISS)
EVDS .... Electronic Visual Display Subsystem   (CAA)
EVIL .... Extensible Video Interactive Language   (CAA)
EVM .... Extended Virtual Machine   (CAA)
EVR .... Electronic Video Recording [*CBS Laboratories' brand name for tape cartridges of TV programs*]
EVX .... Electronic Voice Exchange [*Commterm, Inc.*] [*Billerica, MA*] [*Telecommunications*]   (TSSD)
EWA .... End Warning Area [*Data processing*]   (BUR)
EW-CLI .... East-West Institute of Culture and Communication [*Research center*]   (RCD)
EWG .... Ernaehrungswissenschaften Giessen [*Nutrition Sciences - Giessen University*] [*Database*]   (ODIN)
EWL .... Exchange Work List [*Telecommunications*]   (TEL)
EWTMI .... European Wideband Transmission Media Improvement Program   (IEEE)
EWTN .... Eternal Word Television Network [*Cable-television system*]
EX .... Execute   (CAH)
EXC .... Exchange Key [*Word processing*]
EXCH .... Exchange [*Telecommunications*]   (AFM)
EXCITE .... Expanded with Computers and Information Technology
EXCLU .... Exclusive   (MDG)
EXCP .... Execute Channel Program [*Data processing*]
EXD .... External Device [*Data processing*]
EXDAMS ..... Extendable Debugging and Monitoring System [*Data processing*]
EXEC .... Execute   (MSA)
EXG .... Exchange Two Registers [*Data processing*]
EXLST .... Exit List [*Data processing*]
EXOR .... Exclusive Or [*Data processing*]   (CAA)
EXPLOR ...... Explicit 2-D Patterns Local Operations and Randomness [*Programing language*] [*1975*]   (CSR)
EXR .... Execute and Repeat   (OA)
EXTHEO ...... Extra-Theoretical [*Telecommunications*]   (TEL)
EXTM .... Extended Telecommunications Modules
EXTRN .... External Reference   (BUR)
EXTSN .... Extension   (MDG)
EXU .... Executone, Inc. [*American Stock Exchange symbol*] [*Delisted*]
E/Z .... Equal Zero   (MDG)

F

F	Failure		FAP	Fault Analysis Process (TEL)
F	Farad [Symbol] [Unit of electric capacitance]		FAP	Financial Analysis Program [IBM Corp.]
f	Femto [A prefix meaning divided by 10 to the 15th power] [SI symbol]		FAP	Floating-Point Arithmetic Package [Data processing]
			FAP	FORTRAN Assembly Program [Data processing]
F	Filament		FAQS	Fast Queuing System [Data processing] (CAA)
F	Final [Telecommunications] (TEL)		FAR	File Address Register (CAA)
F	Flash [Precedence] [Telecommunications] (TEL)		FARGO	Forty Automatic Report Generating Operation (MCD)
F	Flat [Telecommunications] (TEL)		FARMS	Farm Audience Readership Measurement Service [Starch INRA Hooper, Inc.] [Information service] (EISS)
F	Frequency		FARS	Failure Analysis Report Summary [Bell System]
F	Function		FAS	File Access Subsystem [Data processing] (TEL)
FA	Field Address (CAA)		FAS	Frame Alignment Signal [Telecommunications] (TEL)
FA	Final Address Register [Data processing] (MDG)		FAS	Frame Analysis System [IBM UK Ltd.] [Software package] [British] (NCC)
FA	Full Adder [Data processing]		FASE	Fundamentally Analyzable Simplified English [Data processing]
FA	Fuse Alarm (TEL)		FASSC	Ford Aerospace Satellite Services Corporation [Washington, DC] [Telecommunications] (TSSD)
FAA	Forschungsgesellschaft fuer Agrarpolitik und Agrarsoziologie [Information retrieval] (ODIN)		FASST	Fly Around Saturated Sectors and Terminals [Recorded phone message tells callers where air traffic delays are occurring] [National Business Aircraft Association]
FAACS	Fully Automated Accounting Computer System (MCD)			
FAAP	Fixed Asset Accounting Package [Data processing] (TUT)		FAST	Facility for Automatic Sorting and Testing
FAC	Facsimile		FAST	Factory Automation Systems Technology [British]
FAC	File Access Channel (CAA)		FAST	Failure Analysis by Statistical Techniques [Data processing code]
FAC	Filter Address Correction		FAST	Federation Against Software Theft
FAC	Floating Accumulator (CAA)		FAST	Fiduciary Activity Simulation Training [Investment banking simulation game]
FACD	Foreign Area Consumer Dialing [Telecommunications]			
FACE	Field Alterable Control Element (MDG)		FAST	Field Data Applications, Systems, and Techniques [Data processing]
FACE	International Federation of Associations of Computer Users in Engineering Architecture and Related Fields (EANO)		FAST	File Analysis and Selection Technique [Data processing] (TUT)
			FAST	Fleet-Sizing Analysis and Sensitivity Technique [Bell System]
FACS	Federal Automated Career System		FAST	Flexible Algebraic Scientific Translator [NCR Corp.]
FACS	Flexible Accounting Control System [Data processing] (BUR)		FAST	Formal Auto-Indexing of Scientific Texts [Data processing] (IEEE)
FACS	Floating Decimal Abstract Coding System			
FACS	Fully Automatic Compiling System		FAST	Formula and Statement Translator [Data processing] (MCD)
FACT	Facility for the Analysis of Chemical Thermodynamics [Thermfact Ltd.] [Database] [Information service] (EISS)		FAST	Four-Address to SOAP [Self-Optimizing Automatic Pilot] Translator [Data processing] (IEEE)
FACT	Factory Automation, Control, and Test Facility (IDA)		FAST	Fundamentals of Application and System Training [Course] [Data processing]
FACT	Fast Access Current Text (DEEC)			
FACT	Federation of Automated Coding Technologies (EANO)		FASTEL	Fast Economic Language [Data processing] (BUR)
FACT	Fingerprint Automatic Classification Technique [Data processing]		FASTI	Fast Access to Systems Technical Information
FACT	Flexible Automatic Circuit Tester		FAT	Fast Automatic Transfer
FACT	Foundation for Advanced Computer Technology (CAH)		FAT	Foreign Area Toll [Telecommunications] (TEL)
FACT	Fully Automatic Compiler [or Computer]-Translator		FAT	Foreign Area Translation [Telecommunications] (TEL)
FACT	Fully Automatic Compiling Technique [Data processing]		FAT	Formula Assembler Translator [Data processing] (BUR)
FACTS	Facilities Administration Consolidated Tape System (MCD)		FATAR	Fast Analysis of Tape and Recovery (IDA)
FACTS	Fast Access to Computerized Technical Sources [Mill Valley, CA] [Information service] (EISS)		FATDL	Frequency and Time-Division Data Link
			FATS	FORTRAN Automatic Timing System [Data processing] (TUT)
FACTS	FORTRAN Analytical Cross Reference Tabulation System [Data processing] (TUT)		FAV	Full Analog Video (CIT)
			FAX	Facsimile (AFM)
FAD	Floating Add [Data processing] (IEEE)		FAX	Facsimile Transmission [Telecommunications] (MCD)
FADEC	Full Authority Digital Engine Control		FAXDIN	Facsimile Transmission over AUTODIN
FADPUG	Federal ADP [Automatic Data Processing] Users Group		FAXPAK	Facsimile Packet [ITT] [Telecommunications] (TEL)
FADS	Force Administration Data System [Bell System]		FB	File Block (CAA)
FADS	FORTRAN Automatic Debugging System (CAA)		FB	Fixed Block (CAA)
FAHQMT	Fully Automatic High-Quality Machine Translation [Data processing] (DIT)		FB	Function Button [Data processing]
			FBA	Fixed Block Architecture (CAA)
FAHQT	Fully Automatic High-Quality Translation [Data processing]		FBC	Fully Buffered Channel
FAIF	Field Automated Intelligence File (AFM)		FBCS	Fellow of the British Computer Society
FAIR	Fast Access Information Retrieval		FBD	Full Business Day (TEL)
FAIREC	Fruits Agro-Industrie Regions Chaudes [Institut de Recherches sur les Fruits et Agrumes] [Database] (CUAD)		FBD	Functional Block Diagram [Telecommunications] (TEL)
			FBFM	Feedback Frequency Modulation
FAIRS	Federal Aviation Information Retrieval System (IDA)		FBM	Foreground and Background Monitor (CAA)
FAL	File Access Listener (CAA)		FBN	Feedback Network
FAL	Finite Automation Language [Data processing]		FBP	Financial Business Package [Data processing] (TUT)
FALTRAN	FORTRAN-to-ALGOL Translator [Data processing] (IEEE)		FBR	Feedback Resistance (IEEE)
FAM	Facilities Analysis Model [Data processing]		FBRX	Fibronics International [NASDAQ symbol] (NQ)
FAM	Fast Auxiliary Memory (IEEE)		FBS	Feedback Signal
FAM	File Access Manager		FBS	Feedback System
FAM	Final Address Message [Telecommunications] (TEL)		FBS	Foundry Business System [Foundry Business Systems] [Software package] [British] (NCC)
FAMAS	Flutter and Matrix Algebra System [Data processing]			
FAMOS	Fast Multitasking Operating System [MVT Microcomputer Systems, Inc.] (CAA)		FC	Feature Count [Data processing]
			FC	File Code [Data processing] (IEEE)
FAMOS	Floating-Gate Avalanche-Injection Metal-Oxide Semiconductor [Data processing]		FC	File Control
FAMS	Forecasting and Modeling System [Data processing] (BUR)			
FAP	Facility Analysis Plan [Telecommunications] (TEL)			
FAP	Failure Analysis Program (IDA)			

87

Computer & Telecommunications Acronyms

FC	File Conversion [*Data processing*] (BUR)
FC	Find Called [*or Calling*] Party [*Telecommunications*] (TEL)
FC	Font Change [*Data processing*] (BUR)
FC	Forecast Center Station [*Telecommunications*] (TEL)
F/C	Format Code [*Data processing*]
FC	Frequency Converter
FC	Fuse Chamber (TEL)
FCA	French Computing Association
FCA	Frequency Control and Analysis
FCA	Full-Coverage Area [*Radio and TV*]
FCAF	Frequency Control Analysis Facility
FCAS	Frequency Control Analysis Subsystem (MCD)
FCB	File Control Block [*Data processing*] (BUR)
FCB	Format Control Buffer
FCB	Forms Control Buffer [*Data processing*] (IBMDP)
FCB	Function Control Block [*Data processing*] (IBMDP)
FCBA	Federal Communications Bar Association [*Washington, DC*] [*Telecommunications*]
FCC	Facilities Control Console
FCC	Federal Communications Commission [*Independent government agency*]
FCC	Fire Control Computer
FCC	Flight Control Computer (KSC)
FCC	Flight Control Console (VIT)
FCC	Fuel Control Computer
FCCTS	Federal COBOL [*Common Business-Oriented Language*] Compiler Testing Service [*National Bureau of Standards*]
FCDB	Flight Control Data Bus (MCD)
FCDC	Fire Control Data Converter (MCD)
FCDC	Fixed Ceramic Disk Capacitor
FCF	Frequency Compressive Feedback
FCFO	Full Cycling File Organization (CAA)
FCFS	First Come, First Served [*Data processing*] (DDI)
FCI	Flux Changes per Inch (CAA)
FCIM	Flight Control Interface Module (MCD)
FCL	Feedback Control Loop [*Data processing*] (BUR)
FCL	Flux Current Loop
FCL	Format Control Language (CAA)
FCM	Fault Control Module (TEL)
FCM	Firmware Control Memory (CAA)
FCNL	Frequently-Called-Numbers List [*Bell System*]
FCOS	Flight Control Operational Software (MCD)
FCP	File Control Processor [*Data processing*] (BUR)
FCP	File Control Program (CAA)
FCP	Fixed Code Processor
FCP	Function Control Package [*Data processing*]
FCPI	Flux Changes per Inch [*Data processing*]
FCR	France Cables & Radio Co. [*Paris, France*] [*Telecommunications*] (TSSD)
FCS	Facsimile Communications System [*Telecommunications*]
FCS	Federal Communications Systems (MCD)
FCS	Feedback Control System
FCS	File Control Services [*Digital Equipment Corp.*] (CAA)
FCS	First Customer Shipment [*IBM Corp.*] [*Data processing*]
FCS	Fixed Control Storage (CAA)
FCS	Frame Check Sequence [*Data processing*] (IBMDP)
FCS	Frequency Coded System (MCD)
FCSU	Fire Control Simulator Unit (VIT)
FCT	Function (DDI)
FCU	File Control Unit (CAA)
FCU	Frequency Converter Unit
FCVS	FORTRAN Compiler Validation System (CAA)
FD	Fiber Duct [*Telecommunications*] (TEL)
FD	File Definition [*Data processing*]
FD	File Description (CAH)
FD	File Directory (OA)
FD	Finished Dialing [*Telecommunications*] (TEL)
FD	Flexible Disk (CAA)
FD	Floppy Disk [*Data processing*] (BUR)
FD	Frequency Demodulator (OA)
FD	Frequency Distance [*Telecommunications*] (TEL)
FD	Frequency Diversity
FD	Frequency Division
FD	Full Duplex [*Telecommunications*]
FD	Functional Description
FDAS	Flight Data Acquisition System
FDAU	Flight Data Acquisition Unit
FDB	Field Descriptor Block (CAA)
FDB	File Data Block (CAA)
FDB	Functional Description Block [*Telecommunications*] (TEL)
FDC	Field Data Computer
FDC	Flight Data Center (FAAC)
FDC	Flight Director Computer (MCD)
FDC	Floppy Disk Controller [*Data processing*] (MDG)
FDC	Fluid Digital Computer
FDC	Frequency Domain Coding
FDC	Functional Data Coordinator (MCD)
FDCS	Functionally Distributed Computing System (CAA)
FDCT	Fast Discrete Cosine Transform (MCD)
FDCT	Frequency Domain Coding Technique
FDD	Flexible Disk Drive (CAA)
FDD	Floating Digital Drive
FDD	Floppy Disk Drive [*Data processing*]
FDDB	Function Designator Database (MCD)
FDDL	Frequency-Division Data Link [*Radio*]
FDDS	Flight Data Distribution System
FDEP	Formatted Data Entry Program [*Mohawk Data Systems*] (CAA)
FDG	Fractional Doppler Gate
FDH	Floating Divide or Halt
FDI	Feeder Distribution Interface [*Bell System*]
FDIC	Federal Deposit Insurance Corporation [*Independent government agency*] [*Database*]
FDIIR	Fault Detection, Isolation, Identification, and Recompensation (NASA)
FDIS	Flight Displays and Interface System (NVT)
FDL	Fixed Delay Line
FDM	Faraday Disc Machine
FDM	Frequency Data Multiplexer (NASA)
FDM	Frequency Deviation Meter
FDM	Frequency-Division Multiplex [*Telecommunications*]
FDMA	Frequency-Division Multiple Access
FDM/FM	Frequency Division Multiplex/Frequency Modulation [*Telecommunications*] (TEL)
FDMS	Frequency-Division Multiplexing System [*Radio*]
FDMVC	Frequency-Division Multiplex Voice Communication
FDN	Foreign Directory Name [*Telecommunications*] (TEL)
FDOP	Filtered Detection Only Processor (CAAL)
FDOS	Floppy Disk Operating System [*Data processing*] (IEEE)
FDP	Fast Digital Processor [*Data processing*]
FDP	Field Data Processing
FDP	Flight Data Processing (KSC)
FDPC	Federal Data Processing Centers
FDPS	Field Developed Programs [*Data processing*]
FD/PSK	Frequency-Differential/Phase-Shift Keyed System [*Data processing*] (TEL)
FDR	Federal Document Retrievals, Inc. [*Information service*] (EISS)
FDR	Feeder
FDR	File Data Register (CAA)
FDR	Flight Data Recorder
FDR	Frequency Dependent Rejection [*Telecommunications*] (TEL)
FDRS	Flight Data Recording System
FDRS	Flight Display Research System
FDRT	Flexible Digital Receiving Terminal
FDS	Flexible Disk System (CAA)
FDS	Floppy Disk System (CAA)
FDS	Frequency Division Separator [*Multiplexing*] (OA)
FDS	Frequency Division Switching [*Radio and television broadcasting*]
FDSR	Floppy Disk Send/Receive (CAA)
FDSU	Flight Data Storage Unit
FDT	Formatted Data Tapes (OA)
FDT	Full Duplex Teletype
FDT	Functional Description Table (CAA)
FDV	Fault Detect Verification (OA)
FDX	Full Duplex [*Telecommunications*]
FE	Format Effector [*Data processing*]
FE	Functional Entity [*Telecommunications*] (TEL)
FEAS	Finite Element Analysis System [*IBM UK Ltd.*] [*Software package*] [*British*] (NCC)
FEAT	Frequency of Every Allowable Term [*Data processing*]
FEB's	Functional Electronic Blocks
FEC	Floating Error Code [*Digital Equipment Corp.*] (CAA)
FEC	Forward Error Correction [*Computer code*]
FEC	Forward Events Controller (MCD)
FECB	File Extended Control Block [*Data processing*] (BUR)
FECP	Front End Communications Processor (CAA)
FED	Field Effect Device
FED	Final Estimation of Data [*Data processing*]
FEDAC	Forward Error Detection and Correction
FEDB	Failure Experience Data Bank [*GIDEP*]
Fed Com B J	Federal Communications Bar Journal [*Later, Federal Communications Law Journal*] [*A publication*]
FEDEX	Federal Index [*Capitol Services, Inc.*] [*Washington, DC*] [*Bibliographic database*] (OBD)
FEDGE	Finite Element Data Generation [*Data processing*] (CIT)
FEDNET	Federal Information Network (CAA)
FEDRAN-2	Feed Drive Analysis [*Machine Tool Industry Research Association*] [*Software package*] [*British*] (NCC)
FEDREG	Federal Register Abstracts [*Capitol Services, Inc.*] [*Washington, DC*] [*Database*]
FEDS	Fixed/Exchangeable Disk Store (CAA)
FEDSIM	Federal Computer Performance Evaluation and Simulation Center [*General Services Administration*]
FEE	Fill Exit Entry [*Data processing*]
FEER	Fast Eigensolution Extraction Routine [*Computer program*]
FEFO	First-Ended First-Out [*Data processing*]
FEK	Frequency Exchange Keying
FEM	Finite Element Method
FEMF	Foreign Electromotive Force (TEL)
FEMGEN	Finite Element Mesh Generation Program [*Fegs Ltd.*] [*Software package*] [*British*] (NCC)
FEMO	Finite Element Modeling Optimization
FEMP	Free Energy Minimization Procedure [*Data processing*]
FEMVIEW	Finite Element Mesh & Result Viewing [*Fegs Ltd.*] [*Software package*] [*British*] (NCC)
FEN	Frequency-Emphasizing Network (IEEE)
FEP	Financial Evaluation Program [*IBM Corp.*]

Computer & Telecommunications Acronyms

FEP	Front-End Processor [*Computer*] (NASA)
FERROD	Ferrite-Rod Antenna (IEEE)
FERST	Freight and Equipment Reporting System for Transportation [*IBM Corp.*]
FERST/VS	Freight and Equipment Reporting System for Transportation/Virtual Storage [*IBM Corp.*]
FES	Forms Entry System (CAA)
FESAP	Finite Element Structures Analysis Program [*Data processing*]
FET	Field Effect Transistor
FETO	Field Engineering Theory of Operations (TUT)
FEX	Foreign Exchange [*Telecommunications*] (TEL)
FEXT	Far-End Crosstalk [*Bell System*]
FF	Field Function [*Telecommunications*] (TEL)
F-F	Flip-Flop [*Data processing*] (CIT)
FF	Form Feed [*Data processing*]
FFA	Fast Fourier Analyzer (MCD)
FFC	Flip-Flop Complementary [*Data processing*] (MSA)
FFD	Fixed Format Display (MCD)
FFE	Forced Fault Entry [*Data processing*]
FFL	First Financial Language [*Data processing*]
FFL	Flip-Flop Latch [*Data processing*] (MSA)
FFNC	First Fix Not Converted
FF-NM	Flip-Flop - National Module [*Data processing*]
FFP	Fast Field Program (KSC)
FFPI	Flip-Flop Position Indicator [*Data processing*] (CIT)
FFRD	Flip-Flop Relay Driver [*Data processing*]
FFS	Formatted File System [*Data processing*] (TUT)
FFSCUG	Formatted File System Commercial Users' Group [*Data processing*] (TUT)
FFSK	Fast Frequency Shift Keying (MCD)
FFT	Fast Fourier Transform
FFT	Finite Fourier Transform
FFTO	Free-Flying Teleoperator [*Program*] [*Electronics*]
FG	File Gap [*Data processing*] (BUR)
FG	Forward Gate
FG	Frame Ground [*Data processing*] (BUR)
FG	Function Generator [*Data processing*] (IEEE)
F & GA	Frame and Grillage Analysis [*Modray Ltd.*] [*Software package*] [*British*] (NCC)
FGIPCI	Federation of Government Information Processing Councils, Incorporated [*Fair Oaks, CA*] (EANO)
FGRAAL	FORTRAN Extended Graph Algorithmic Language [*1972*] [*Data processing*] (CSR)
FGSS	Flexible Guidance Software System (MCD)
FH	Frequency Hopping [*Modulation*]
FHD	Fixed-Head Disk [*Data processing*]
FHL	Forward Half-Line [*Feed*]
FHSF	Fixed-Head Storage Facility [*Data processing*] (CAA)
FI	Field Intensity
FI	Flow Indicator
FI	Forecasting International Ltd. [*Information service*] (EISS)
FIACC	Five International Associations Coordinating Committee [*Budapest, Hungary*]
FIB	File Information Block (CAA)
FIB	Foreground Initiated Batch [*Data processing*]
FIB	FORTRAN Information Bulletin [*Data processing*] (IEEE)
FIB	Forward Indicator BIT [*Binary Digit*] (TEL)
Fiber Integr Opt	Fiber and Integrated Optics [*A publication*]
Fiber Laser	Fiber Laser News [*A publication*]
Fiberoptcs	Fiberoptics Report [*A publication*]
FIBR	American Fiber Optics [*NASDAQ symbol*] (NQ)
FIC	Fault Isolation Code
FICS	Fault Isolation Checkout System
FICS	Financial Information Control System
FID	Federation Internationale de Documentation [*International Federation for Documentation - IFD*]
FID	Format Identification [*Data processing*] (IBMDP)
FIDAC	Film Input to Digital Automatic Computer
FIDACSYS	Film Input to Digital Automatic Computer System
FIDAS	Formularorientiertes Interaktives Datenbanksystem [*Forms-Oriented Interactive Database System*] [*West German*] (CAA)
FIDO	Fugitive Information Data Organizer [*Database*]
FIFO	First In, First Out [*Queuing technique*]
FIFO	Floating Input - Floating Output [*Data processing*]
FIG	Figure (AFM)
FIG	FORTH Interest Group [*San Jose, CA*] (EANO)
FIGS	Figures Shift [*Teleprinters*]
FIL	Filament (KSC)
FILER	File Information Language Executive Routine [*Data processing*]
FILEX	File Exchange (CAA)
FILU	Four-BIT [*Binary Digit*] Interface Logic Unit (CAA)
FIM	Failure Indication Modules
FIM	Fault Isolation Module (CAAL)
FIMPACS	Fashion Integrated Merchandising Planning and Control System (BUR)
FINAC	Fast Interline Nonactivate Automatic Control [*AT & T*]
FINAL	Financial Analysis Language [*Data processing*]
FIND	File of Industrial Data [*Data processing*]
FIND	File Interrogation of Nineteen-Hundred Data [*Data processing*] (DIT)
FINP	Finnish Periodicals Index in Economics and Business [*Helsinki School of Economics*] [*Database*] (CUAD)
FINST	Final Station [*Data processing*]
FINTEL	Financial Times Company Information Database [*Financial Times Business Information Ltd. and Predicasts*] [*Bibliographic database*] [*British*] (OBD)
FIOP	FORTRAN Input-Output Package [*Data processing*] (IEEE)
FIP	Finance Image Processor [*Data processing*] (IBMDP)
FIPS	Federal Information Processing Standards [*National Bureau of Standards*]
FIPSCAC	Federal Information Processing Standards Coordinating and Advisory Committee [*National Bureau of Standards*]
FIPS-PUB	Federal Information Processing Standards Publication [*National Bureau of Standards*]
FIR	File Indirect Register (CAA)
FIRM	Financial Institutions Resource Management [*Computer service*]
FIRMS	Forecasting Information Retrieval of Management System (IEEE)
FIRS	File Interrogation and Reporting System [*Data processing*] (TUT)
FIRST	Fast Interactive Retrieval System Technology (DEEC)
FIRST	Financial Information Reporting System [*Data processing*] (CGC)
FIRST	Futures Information Retrieval System [*Congressional Research Service*]
FIS	Fault Isolation Software (CAAL)
FIS	Field Information System [*Data processing*]
FIS	Floating-Point Instruction Set [*Data processing*] (MSA)
FIS	Functional Interface Specification [*Telecommunications*] (TEL)
FISLIB	FORTRAN Interactive Subroutine Library [*Data processing*]
FIST	Field Intelligence Simulation Test (NATG)
FIT	Failure in Time [*Telecommunications*] (TEL)
FIT	File Information Table [*Data processing*]
FIT	File Inquiry Technique (CAA)
FIT	First Computer Interface Tester (MCD)
FITCE	Federation des Ingenieurs des Telecommunications de la Communaute Europeenne [*Federation of Telecommunications Engineers in the European Community*]
FITE	Forward Interworking Telephony Event [*Telecommunications*] (TEL)
FITGO	Floating Input to Ground Output
FIU	Facility Interface Unit [*Telecommunications*]
FIU	Federation of Information Users [*Pittsburgh, PA*] (EANO)
FIZ	Fachinformationszentrum [*Information retrieval*] (ODIN)
FJCC	Fall Joint Computer Conference [*Replaced by National Computer Conference - NCC*]
FKM	Fluke [*John*] Manufacturing Co., Inc. [*American Stock Exchange symbol*]
F/L	Fetch/Load [*Data processing*] (MDG)
FL	Field Length (CAA)
FL	Foreign Listing [*Telecommunications*] (TEL)
FL1	Function Language One (CAH)
FLAG	FORTRAN Load and Go [*Xerox Corp.*] (CAA)
FLAN	Factory Layout Analysis [*PERA*] [*Software package*] [*British*] (NCC)
FLAP	First Level Adaptive Program
FLAP	Flores Assembly Program [*Data processing*]
FLAP	Flow Analysis Program [*Data processing*]
FLAP	Formula Algebraic Processor [*Data processing*] (CSR)
FLASH	Facts Location and Summarized History [*General Motors Corp.*] [*Data processing*]
FLBIN	Floating-Point Binary [*Data processing*]
FLC	File Location Code [*Data processing*]
FLC	Forward Load Control (MCD)
FLC	Frequency and Load Controller
FLCA	Forward Load Control Assembly (MCD)
FLCB	Frequency and Load Control Box (MCD)
FLD	Fault Logic Diagram (VIT)
FLD	Field [*Data processing*] (AFM)
FLDEC	Floating-Point Decimal [*Data processing*]
FLEA	Flux Logic Element Array
FLEX	Flexowriter Equipment
FLF	Fixed-Length Field [*Data processing*] (BUR)
FLF	Flip-Flop [*Data processing*] (DEN)
FLF	Follow-the-Leader Feedback [*Circuit theory*] (IEEE)
FLG	Flag [*Data processing*] (MDG)
FLIM	Fast Library Maintenance (CAA)
FLINK	Flash/Wink Signal [*Telecommunications*] (TEL)
FLINT	Floating Interpretive Language [*Princeton University*]
FLIP	Film Library Instantaneous Presentation [*Data processing*]
FLIP	Floating Indexed Point Arithmetic [*Data processing*]
FLIP	Floating-Point Interpretive Program [*Data processing*]
FLIPS	Future Language Information Processing System (BUR)
FLIRT	FORTRAN Logical Information Retrieval Technique [*Data processing*] (TUT)
FLIST	File List Processor [*Data processing*]
FLIT	Fault Location through Interpretive Testing [*Data processing*]
FLIT	Flexowriter Interrogation Tape (CAH)
FLM	Fluidic Logic Module
FLO	Fault-Location Oscillator [*Bell System*]
FLODAC	Fluid-Operated Digital Automatic Computer [*Sperry UNIVAC*]
FLOP	Floating Octal Point [*IBM Corp.*]
FLOPS	Floating-Point Operations per Second [*Data processing*]
FLOTRAN	Flowcharting FORTRAN [*Data processing*] (IEEE)
FLP	Floating Point [*Data processing*]
FLP	Floating Point Systems, Inc. [*NYSE symbol*]
FLPAU	Floating Point Arithmetic Unit (CAA)

FLPL	FORTRAN List Processing Language [*Data processing*] (IEEE)
FLS	Free Line Signal [*Telecommunications*] (TEL)
FLT	Filing Time [*Time a message is presented for transmission*]
FLW	Fault Location Word (MCD)
FM	Facilities Management (TUT)
FM	Fault Monitor (TEL)
FM	Feedback Mechanism
FM	File Maintenance [*Data processing*] (BUR)
FM	File Management (CAA)
FM	Frequency Meter
FM	Frequency Modulation [*Radio*]
FM	Frequency Multiplex
FMA	Failure Mode Analysis
FMA	Foxon-Maddocks Associates [*Reston, VA*] (EISS)
FM & C	Factory Management & Control [*Computer Automation Ltd.*] [*Software package*] [*British*] (NCC)
FMC	Ferrite Memory Core
FMC	Fixed Message Cycle [*Telecommunications*] (TEL)
FMC	Flexible Monte Carlo [*Data processing*]
FMC	Fuel Management Computer (NG)
FMCS	Flight Management Computer System
FMD	Function Management Data (IBMDP)
FMDM	Flex Multiplexer/Demultiplexer (MCD)
FMDM	Frequency Modulation Deviation Meter
FMEA	Failure Mode and Effects Analysis
FMECA	Failure Mode, Effects, and Criticality Analyses
FMFB	Frequency Modulation with Feedback
FMFD	Frequency Modulation Feedback Discriminator (CIT)
FM-FM	Frequency Modulation - Frequency Modulation
FMI	Failure Mode Indicator (MUGU)
FMI	First Market Intelligence Ltd. [*London, England*] [*Information service*] (EISS)
FMIC	Frequency Monitoring and Interference Control [*Radio*]
FMIS	Farm Market Infodata Service [*Department of Agriculture*] [*Database*] (FDB)
FMIS	Fiscal Management Information System (OA)
FML	Feedback, Multiple Loop
FML	File Manipulation Language (CAA)
FMLF	File Management Loading Facility (CAA)
FMOP	Frequency Modulation on the Pulse (NG)
FMPP	Flexible Multipipeline Processor (CAA)
FMPS	FORTRAN Mathematical Programing System [*Data processing*] (IEEE)
FMPS	Functional Mathematical Programing System [*Data processing*] (CGC)
FMR	Frequency-Modulated Ranging (MCD)
FMR	Frequency-Modulated Receiver
FMRL	Functional Machine Representation Language [*Data processing*] (CSR)
FMS	File Management Supervisor [*Honeywell, Inc.*] (CAA)
FMS	File Management System
FMS	Fleet Management System [*Arrencross Ltd.*] [*Software package*] [*British*] (NCC)
FMS	FORTRAN Monitor System [*Data processing*]
FMS	Frequency Mixer Stage
FMS	Frequency-Multiplexed Subcarrier (CIT)
FMS	Frequency Multiplier Storer
FMS	Fuel Monitoring System [*Cheshire County Council*] [*Software package*] [*British*] (NCC)
FMSP	Frequency Modulation Signal Processor (NASA)
FMT	Frequency-Modulated Transmitter
FMTP	File Management Transaction Processor
FMU	Files Management Unit [*Data processing*]
FMX	Frequency-Modulated Transmitter (KSC)
FN	Functional Network (CAA)
FNA	Frequency Network Analyzer
FNA	Fujitsu Network Architecture [*Fujitsu Ltd.*] [*Japan*] (CAA)
FNM	Financial Network Manager (BUR)
FNN	Financial News Network [*Cable-television system*]
FNP	Front-End Network Processor
FNPA	Foreign Numbering Plan Area [*AT & T*] [*Telecommunications*] (TEL)
FNR	File Next Register (CAA)
FNS	Feedback Node Set
FNUG	Federation of NCR [*NCR Corp.*] User Groups [*Dayton, OH*] (EANO)
FO	Fiber Optics [*Data transmission*] (TEL)
FO	Flash Override [*Telecommunications*] (TEL)
FOB	Fiber Optics Board (MCD)
FOBS	Fiber Optics Borescope
FOC	Fiber Optics Communications [*Data transmission*] (TEL)
FOCAL	Formula Calculator [*Digital Equipment Corp.*] (CSR)
FOCAS	Fiber Optic Communications for Aerospace Systems (MCD)
FOCC	Fiber Optic Coordinating Committee [*American National Standards Institute*] [*Telecommunications*]
FOCUS	Fire Operational Characteristics Using Simulation [*System for comparing organizations for wildland fire protection services in cost-effective terms*] [*Department of Agriculture, Forest Services*]
FOCUS	Form of Control Users System
FOCUS	Forum of Control Data Users [*Later, VIM, Inc.*] (TUT)
FOD	Fluidic Output Device
FOD	Functional Operational Design (CAA)
FODAAS	Field Online Data Acquisition and Analysis System
FOG	First Osborne Group [*Daly City, CA*] [*Computer users*] (EANO)
FOGD	Fiber Optics Guidance Demonstration (RDA)
FOIL	File-Oriented Interpretive Language [*1969*] [*Data processing*] (TUT)
FOL	Fiber Optics LASER
FOL	Fiber Optics Light
FOLG	Fiber Optics LASER Gyros (MCD)
FOM	Factor of Merit [*Telecommunications*] (TEL)
FOM	Fiber Optic MODEM [*Modulator-Demodulator*] (CAA)
FONCON	Telephone Conversation (MCD)
FONE	Telephone (FAAC)
FONECON	Telephone Conference [*or Conversation*]
FOOS	Force Out of Service [*Telecommunications*] (TEL)
FOP	Fiber Optics Probe
FOPP	Fiber Optics Photo Pickup
FOPT	Fiber Optics Photo Transfer
FORAST	Formula Assembler Translator [*Data processing*]
FORBLOC	FORTRAN Compiled Block-Oriented Simulation Language [*Data processing*] (IEEE)
FORC	Formula Coder [*Data processing*]
FORCE	FORTRAN Conversational Environment (CAH)
FORDACS	Fuel Oil Route Delivery and Control System [*Computer-based system*]
FORDAD	Foreign Disclosure Automated Data [*System*]
FORDAP	FORTRAN Debugging Aid Program (CAA)
FOREM	File Organization Evaluation Model (CAA)
FOREMAN	Form Retrieval and Manipulation Language
FORGE	File Organization Generator (CAA)
FORGO	FORTRAN Load and Go System [*University of Wisconsin*] [*Data processing*] (IEEE)
FORIMS	FORTRAN-Oriented Information Management System (CAA)
FORIS	Forschungsinformationssystem Sozialwissenschaften [*Informationszentrum Sozialwissenschaften*] [*Database*] (CUAD)
FORM	Ferromagnetic Object Recognition Matrix
FORMA	FORTRAN Matrix Analysis [*Data processing*]
FORMAC	Formula Manipulation Compiler [*Programing language*] [*1962*] [*Data processing*]
FORMAL	Formula Manipulation Language [*1970*] [*Data processing*] (MDG)
FORMAT	FORTRAN Matrix Abstraction Technique [*Data processing*] (MCD)
FORMAT-FORTRAN	FORTRAN Matrix Abstraction Technique-FORTRAN [*Data processing*] (CSR)
FORS	Fiber-Optic Rate Sensors [*Instrumentation*]
FORS	Forschungsprojekte Raumordnung, Staedtebau, Wohnungswesen [*Research Projects on Regional Policy, Urban Development and Housing*] [*Database*] (ODIN)
FORTE	File Organization Technique (BUR)
FORTEL	Formatted Teletypewriter (CET)
FORTH	[*A*] programing language [*1968*] (CSR)
FORTRAN	Formula Translating System [*Programing language*] [*1953-54*] (CSR)
FORTRANSIT	FORTRAN and Internal Translator System [*Data processing*] (IEEE)
FORTRUNCIBLE	FORTRAN Style Runcible [*Data processing*]
FORUM	Formula for Optimizing through Real-Time Utilization of Multiprograming
FOS	File Organization System (DIT)
FOS	FORTRAN Operating System [*Data processing*] (TUT)
FOSDIC	Film Optical Sensing Device for Input to Computers [*National Bureau of Standards*]
FOSOL	Florian's Own Statistically Oriented Language [*Data processing*] (CSR)
FOT	Forward Transfer [*Telecommunications*] (TEL)
FOT	Frequency Optimum Traffic
FOTS	Fiber Optic Transmission System [*Consists of modulated light signals sent through glass fibers and demodulated by photo-diodes*] [*Data transmission*] (CCD)
FP	Faceplate (IEEE)
FP	Fast Processor [*Instrumentation*]
FP	Feedback Positive [*Data processing*]
FP	Feedback Potentiometer
FP	File Processor [*Data processing*] (BUR)
FP	File Protect (CAH)
FP	Fischer & Porter Co. [*American Stock Exchange symbol*]
FP	Floating Point [*Data processing*] (BUR)
FP	Frame Pointer
FPA	Floating-Point Arithmetic
FPAA	Flat-Plate Array Antenna
FPAP	Floating-Point Array Processor [*Data processing*]
FPC	Fixed Point Calculation
FPC	Fixed Program Computer
FPC	Flight Programer Computer
FPC	Floating-Point Calculation
FPC	Functional Progression Chart [*Telecommunications*] (TEL)
FPCS	Full-Page Composition System [*Data processing*]
FPDC	Federal Procurement Data Center [*Database*] (FDB)
FPEB	Family Planning Evaluation Branch [*Public Health Service*] (EISS)
FPED	Family Planning Evaluation Division [*HEW*] (EISS)
FPEG	Fast Pulse Electron Gun (MCD)
FPGA	Field Programable Gate Array [*Data processing*] (CAA)
FPH	Floating Point Hardware [*Data processing*] (OA)

Computer & Telecommunications Acronyms

FPI	Frames per Inch [*Data processing*]
FPIC	Financial Post Information Centre [*MacLean-Hunter Ltd.*] [*Information service*] (EISS)
FPIS	Forward Propagation by Ionospheric Scatter [*Radio communications technique*]
FPK	Fixed Position Keyboard
FPL	Fox Programing Language (OA)
FPL	Frequency Phase Lock
FPLA	Field-Programable Logic Array [*Data processing*]
FPLF	Field Programable Logic Family (TEL)
FPM	File Protect Memory [*Data processing*] (BUR)
FPM	Frequency Position Modulation [*Telecommunications*] (IEEE)
FPMH	Failures per Million Hours [*Telecommunications*] (TEL)
FPO	Fixed Path of Operation
FPO	Fixed Point Operation
FPOT	Feedback Potentiometer (MSA)
FPP	Floating-Point Processor [*Data processing*]
FPQA	Fixed Portion Queue Area [*Data processing*] (OA)
FPR	Flat-Plate Radiometer
FPR	Floating-Point Register (CAA)
FPR	Floating-Point Routine
F-PROM	Field-Programable Read-Only Memory [*Data processing*] (MCD)
FPS	Financial Planning System [*IBM Corp.*]
FPS	Floating-Point System, Inc.
FPS	Four-Phase Systems, Inc. [*NYSE symbol*] [*Delisted*]
FPS	Frames per Second [*Data processing*]
FPSK	Frequency and Phase Shift Keying (OA)
FPTS	Forward Propagation by Tropospheric Scatter [*Radio communications technique*]
FPU	Floating-Point Unit [*Data processing*] (MCD)
FPY	Failures per Year [*Telecommunications*] (TEL)
FQ	Frequency [*Online database field identifier*] (OBD)
FQL	Functional Query Language [*1978*] [*Data processing*] (CSR)
FQPR	Frequency Programer (IEEE)
FR	File Register (CAA)
FR	Flow Recorder
FR	Force Release [*Telecommunications*] (TEL)
FR	Frame Reset [*Telecommunications*] (TEL)
FR	Frequency Range
FR	Frequency Response
FR	Receiving station only, connected with the general network of telecommunications channels [*ITU designation*] (CET)
FRAC	Fractionator Reflux Analog Computer
FRAGNET	Fragmented Network (MCD)
FRANCIS	Fichier de Recherches Automatisees sur les Nouvautes, la Communication et l'Information en Sciences Sociales et Humaines [*French Retrieval Automated Network for Current Information in Social and Human Sciences*] [*Database*]
FRANCIS: DOGE	FRANCIS: Documentation Automatisee en Gestion des Entreprises [*Database*] (CUAD)
FRANCIS: RESHUS	FRANCIS: Reseau Documentaire en Sciences Humaines de la Sante [*French*] [*Database*] (CUAD)
FRANK	Frequency Regulation and Network Keying (IEEE)
FRAP	Flat Response Audio Pickup
FRC	Federal Radio Commission [*Functions transferred to FCC, 1934*]
FRC	Final Routing Center [*Telecommunications*] (TEL)
FRC	Fixed Radio Communication
FRC	Flow Recorder Controller
FRD	Failure Rate Data (KSC)
FRE	Frequency
FREC	Federal Radio Education Committee
FRED	Fast Realistic Editor [*Word processing program*]
FRED	Fiendishly Rapid Electronic Device
FRED	Figure Reading Electronic Device [*Information retrieval*]
FRED	Fractionally Rapid Electronic Device (OA)
FRED	Friendly Robot Educational Device [*Androbot, Inc.*]
FRED	Front End for Databases [*GTE usage*]
FREDI	Flight Range and Endurance Data Indicator
FREJID	Frequency Jumper Identification
FRELATOR	Frequency Translator (DDI)
FREQ	Frequency [*or Frequent*] (AFM)
FREQCONV	Frequency Converter (MCD)
FREQDIV	Frequency Divider (MCD)
FREQM	Frequency Meter
FREQMULT	Frequency Multiplier (KSC)
FRETURN	Function Return
FRF	Free Running Frequency
FRF	Frequency Response Function [*Statistics*]
FRIA	Finnish Radio Industries Association
FRIMP	Flexible Reconfigurable Interconnected Multiprocessor (CAA)
FRINGE	File and Report Information Processing Generator [*Data processing*]
FRL	Frame Representation Language [*Data processing*]
FRM	Fault Reporting Module (TEL)
FRM	Film Reading Machine
FRM	Frequency Meter
FRMR	Frame Reject (CCD)
FRN	Feminist Radio Network [*Defunct*] (EANO)
FROM	Fusable Read-Only Memory [*Data processing*] (MDG)
FRP	Fault Report Point (TEL)
FRP	Feature Recognition Processor (DDI)
FRP	Flag Register Processing
FRP	Frequency Reference Protection
FRP	Frequency Response Plotter
FRQMULT	Frequency Multiplier (KSC)
FRR	False Removal Rate (CAAL)
FRR	Functional Recovery Routine [*Data processing*] (BUR)
FR & RC	Family Resource and Referral Center [*National Council on Family Relations*] [*Information service*] (EISS)
FRS	Fast Retrieval Storage [*Data processing*]
FRS	Fault Repair Service [*Telecommunications*] [*British*]
FRS	Flight Radio Subsystem (CIT)
FRS	Forward Ready Signal [*Telecommunications*] (TEL)
FRS	Frequency Response Survey (CET)
FRSAS	Fast-Response Solar Array Simulator
FRSS	Federal Register Search System [*National Institutes of Health and Environmental Protection Agency*] [*Database*] (FDB)
FRSS	Federal Regulatory Search System [*Database*] [*Environmental Protection Agency*] (FDB)
FRT	Flow Recording Transmitter
FRT	Front [*Telecommunications*] (TEL)
FRTF	Fixed Radio Transmission Facility
FRTISO	Floating-Point Root Isolation [*Data processing*] (MDG)
FRU	Field Replaceable Unit [*IBM Corp.*]
FRUGAL	FORTRAN Rules Used as a General Applications Language [*Data processing*]
FRXD	Fully Automatic Reperforator Transmitter Distributor [*Telecommunications*] (TEL)
FRYA	Frey Associates, Inc. [*NASDAQ symbol*] (NQ)
FS	Fast Store [*Data processing*] (TEL)
FS	Feedback, Stabilized
FS	Fernschreiben [*Teletype message*] or Fernschreiber [*Teletype*] [*German military - World War II*]
F/S	Fetch and Send [*Telecommunications*] (TEL)
FS	Field Separator (OA)
FS	File Separator [*Data processing*]
FS	File Source [*Data processing*]
FS	Final Selector [*Telecommunications*] (DEEC)
FS	Follow Sender [*Telecommunications*] (TEL)
FS	Frame Scan (DEN)
FS	Frequency Shift (BUR)
FS	Frequency Stability
FS	Frequency Standard (DDI)
F & S	Frost & Sullivan, Inc. [*Information service*] (EISS)
FS	Full Scale [*Analog computers*]
FS	Functional Specification [*Telecommunications*] (TEL)
FS	Future System [*IBM Corp.*] [*Data processing*]
FS	Land station established solely for the safety of life [*ITU designation*] (CET)
FSA	Frequency Stability Analyzer
FSB	Forward Space Block (CMD)
FSB	Functional Specification Block [*Telecommunications*] (TEL)
FSC	Fault Simulation Comparator
FSC	File System Control [*Data processing*]
FSC	Frequency Shift Converter
FSCB	File System Control Block [*Data processing*] (IBMDP)
FSCR	Field Select Command Register (CAA)
FSCS	Flight Service Communications System
FSCS	Frequency Shift Communications System
FSCT	Floyd Satellite Communications Terminal
FSCU	Frequency Select Control Unit (MCD)
FSD	Functional Sequence Diagram [*Data processing*]
FSE	Fill Start Entry [*Data processing*]
FSEC	Federal Software Exchange Center (CAA)
FSF	Fading Safety Factor [*Telecommunications*] (TEL)
FSF	Fixed Sequence Format
FSF	Forward Space File (CMD)
FSI	Financial Software, Incorporated [*Norcross, GA*] [*Software manufacturer*] (DASOS)
FSIM	Functional Simulator (NASA)
FSJ	Feedback Summing Junction [*Data processing*]
FSK	Frequency Shift Keying [*Telecommunications*]
FSKLF	Frequency Shift Keying Low-Frequency [*Converter*] (NATG)
FSL	Formal Semantic Language [*Data processing*]
FSM	Field Strength Meter
FSM	Finite State Machine
FSM	Frequency Shift Modulation [*Radio*]
FSMWI	Free Space Microwave Interferometer
FSN	Forward Sequence Number [*Telecommunications*] (TEL)
FSO	Frequency Sweep Oscillator
FSO	Full-Scale Output
FSOS	Free-Standing Operating System [*General Automation, Inc.*] (CAA)
FSP	Fault Servicing Process (TEL)
FSP	Ford Satellite Plan [*Telecommunications*]
FSP	Frequency Shift Pulsing
FSP	Frequency Standard, Primary
FSP	Functional Specification Package [*Data processing*]
FSR	Feedback Shift Register
FSR	File Storage Region [*Digital Equipment Corp.*] (CAA)
FSR	Forward Space Record (OA)
FSR	Frequency Shift Receiver
FSR	Frequency Shift Reflector
FSRS	Frequency Selective Receiver System (MCD)
FSS	Flying Spot Scanner [*Optical character recognition*]
FSS	Frame Storage System [*Television*]

Computer & Telecommunications Acronyms

FSSR .... Flight Systems Software Requirement   (MCD)
FSSR .... Functional Subsystem Software Requirements   (NASA)
FST .... File Status Table [*Data processing*]   (IBMDP)
FST .... Flatter, Squarer Tube [*Television picture tube*]
FST .... Frequency Shift Transmission
FST .... Functional Simulator and Translator [*Data processing*]   (CSR)
FST .... Funkstelle [*Radio Station*] [*German military - World War II*]
FSTA .... Food Science and Technology Abstracts [*International Food Information Service*] [*Bibliographic database*] [*A publication*]
FSTD .... Flight Simulation Test Data
FSTS .... Financial Services Terminals Support [*IBM Corp.*]
FSU .... Facsimile Switching Unit   (CAA)
FSU .... Field Select Unit   (OA)
FSU .... Final Signal Unit [*Telecommunications*]   (TEL)
FSV .... Frequency Selective Voltmeter
FSW .... Flight Software   (MCD)
FSWEC ...... Federal Software Exchange Center
FSYS .... Fortune Systems Corp. [*NASDAQ symbol*]   (NQ)
FT .... Filing Time [*Time a message is presented for transmission*]
FT .... Forward Transfer [*Telecommunications*]   (TEL)
FT .... French Title [*Online database field identifier*]   (OBD)
FT .... Frequency Tolerance
FT .... Frequency Tracker   (MSA)
FT .... Functional Test [*Data processing*]
FTA .... Fault Tree Analysis   (NASA)
FTA .... Field to Advise [*Telecommunications*]   (TEL)
FTAR .... Following Transmitted as Received   (FAAC)
FTAS .... Fast Time Analyzer System
FTB .... Frequency Time Base   (DEN)
FTC .... Fault-Tolerant Computing
FTC .... Frequency Threshold Curve
FTC .... Frequency Time Control
FTD .... Frequency Translation Distortion
FTDR .... Flight Test Data Recorder   (MCD)
FTDS .... Flag Tactical Data System   (MUGU)
FTDS .... Formal Training Data System   (NVT)
FTE .... Frame Table Entry [*Data processing*]   (IBMDP)
FTE .... Full-Time Equivalent
FTET .... Full Time Equivalent Terminals [*Data processing*]   (DEEC)
FTI .... Foreign Traders Index [*Department of Commerce*] [*Information service*]   (EISS)
FTL .... Fast Transient Loader   (CAA)
FTM .... Frequency Time Modulation   (DEN)
FTMC .... Frequency and Time Measurement Counter
FTMP .... Fault Tolerant Multiprocessor System [*Data processing*]
FTP .... File Transfer Protocol   (DEEC)
FTPI .... Flux Transitions per Inch   (CAA)
FTR .... Federal Telephone and Radio
FTR .... Functional Test Requirement   (IEEE)
FTRC .... Federal Telecommunications Records Center
FT/RF .... Frequency Translator/Recursive Filter   (CAAL)
FTS .... Federal Telecommunications System [*of GSA*]
FTS .... Federal Telephone System   (KSC)
FTS .... Frequency Time Schedule   (NVT)
FTS .... Frequency Time Standard
FTS .... Funeral Telegraph Service
FTSC .... Fault Tolerant Spaceborne Computer
FTSC .... Federal Telecommunications Standards Committee
FTU .... Frequency Transfer Unit
FTV .... Fashion Television [*Video sales technique in the apparel industry*]
FTW .... Federation of Telephone Workers
FU .... Freie Universitaet Berlin [*Information retrieval*]   (ODIN)
FUD .... Fear, Uncertainty, and Doubt [*Factors hindering sales of lesser-known computers*]
FUDR .... Failure and Usage Data Report   (IEEE)
FUINCA ..... Fundacion para el Fomento de la Informacion Automatizada [*Foundation for the Automated Information Industry*] [*Madrid, Spain*] [*Information service*]   (EISS)
FUJIY .... Fuji Photo Film ADR [*NASDAQ symbol*]   (NQ)
FUN .... Fantasy Unrestricted Network [*Cable-television system*]
FUN .... Fifty Upward Network [*Cleveland, OH*]   (EANO)
FUN .... Free University Network [*Later, LERN*]   (EANO)
FUN .... Function   (MDG)
FUNC .... Function
FUNOP .... Full Normal Plot [*Data processing*]
FUO .... Follow-Up Output   (NASA)
FUR .... File Utility Routines [*Data processing*]
FURPUR ..... File Utility Routines, Program Utility Routines [*Data processing*]
FUS .... FORTRAN Utility System   (CAA)
FUTU .... Futures Information Service [*Institute for Futures Studies*] [*Database*]   (CUAD)
FV .... Femtovolt   (MDG)
F/V .... Frequency to Voltage   (IEEE)
FVU .... File Verification Utility   (CAA)
FVW .... Forward Volume Wave [*Telecommunications*]   (TEL)
FW .... First Word   (CAA)
FW .... Full Wave
FWA .... First Word Address [*Data processing*]
FWA .... Forward Wave Amplifier
FWA .... Full-Wave Amplifier
FWBR .... Full-Wave Bridge Rectifier
FWD .... Forward   (AFM)

FWDC .... Full-Wave Direct Current
FWG .... Flexible Waveguide
FWL .... Fixed Word Length [*Data processing*]
FWRS .... Fish and Wildlife Reference Service [*Database*]
FWT .... Forward Wave Tube
FX .... Fixed Area [*of magnetic disk*]   (DEEC)
FX .... Fixed Station [*ITU designation*]   (CET)
FX .... Foreign Exchange [*ADP Data Services*] [*Database*]   (CUAD)
FX .... Foreign Exchange Rate Service [*ContiCurrency*] [*Information service*]   (EISS)
FXC .... Ferrox Cube [*Telecommunications*]   (TEL)

G

G	Gain (CBSS)	GB	Gigabyte (10^9 bytes)
G	Gate [*Electronics*]	GB	Good-By [*Amateur radio*]
G	Giga [*A prefix meaning multiplied by 10^9*] [*SI symbol*]	GBA	Give Better Address [*Communications*]
g	Gram	GBC	Ground-Based Computer
G	Grid [*Electronics*]	GBCC	GBC Closed Circuit TV [*NASDAQ symbol*] (NQ)
G	Ground	GBH	Group Busy Hour [*Telecommunications*] (TEL)
G	Group [*Data processing*]	GBI	Gesellschaft fuer Betriebswirtschaftliche Information mbH [*Online service*] (CUAD)
G3	Gadolinium, Gallium, Garnet (DEEC)	GBP	Gain-Bandwidth Product
GA	Gain of Antenna (IEEE)	GBPS	GigaBITS [*Binary Digits*] per Second [*Transmission rate*] [*Data processing*] (TSSD)
GA	Gated Attenuation [*Data processing*]	GBR	Give Better Reference [*Communications*]
GA	General Automation, Inc.	GBS	Ground-Based Software (MCD)
GA	Global Address (CAA)	GBT	Generalized Burst Trapping (CAA)
GA	Go Ahead [*or resume sending*] [*Communications*]	GC	Garbage Collection [*Slang*] [*Data processing*]
GaAs	Gallium Arsenide [*Semiconductor*]	Gc	Gigacycle [*Measurement*]
GAB	Graphic Adapter Board (CAA)	GC	Government Communications (TEL)
GAC	Geac Computer Corporation Ltd. [*Toronto Stock Exchange symbol*]	GC	Guidance Computer
G/A COMM	Ground-to-Air Communications (MCD)	GCAP	Generalized Circuit Analysis Program (IEEE)
GAELIC	Grumman Aerospace Engineering Language for Instructional Checkout (OA)	GCC	Ground Communications Controller (SKY)
GAEO	Galileo Electro-Optics [*NASDAQ symbol*] (NQ)	GCC	Ground Computer Controller (SKY)
GAI	Gilbert Associates, Incorporated	GCC	Guidance Checkout Computer
GALPAT	Galloping Pattern Memory (DEEC)	GCC	Guidance and Control Computer (CIT)
GAM	Graphics Access Method (BUR)	GCCA	Graphic Communications Computer Association [*Printing Industries of America*] [*Later, GCA*]
GAMA	Graphics-Assisted Management Application [*Data processing*] (BUR)	GCCC	Ground-Control Computer Center (MCD)
GAMM	Gesellschaft fuer Angewandte Mathematik und Mechanik [*German Association for Applied Mathematics and Mechanics*]	GCD	Greatest Common Divisor
		GCF	Generation Control Function [*Telecommunications*] (TEL)
GAMMA	[*A*] programing language (CSR)	GCH	Gigacharacters (CAA)
GAN	Gandalf Technologies, Inc. [*Toronto Stock Exchange symbol*]	GCI	General Communication, Incorporated [*Anchorage, AK*] [*Telecommunications*] (TSSD)
GAN	Generating and Analyzing Networks [*Data processing*] (TUT)	GCI	Generalized Communication Interface (CAA)
GANDALF	General Alpha-Numeric Direct Access Library Facility [*Search system*]	GCI	Gnostic Concepts, Incorporated [*San Mateo, CA*] [*Database producer*] [*Information service*] [*Telecommunications*] (TSSD)
GANDF	Gandalf Technologies [*NASDAQ symbol*] (NQ)	GCI	Groupe des Communications Informatiques [*Computer Communications Group*] [*Canada*]
GAP	General Antenna Package [*COMSAT*]		
GAP	General Assembly Program [*Data processing*]	GCIL	Ground-Control Interface Logic (MCD)
GAP	General and Practical Energy Information Data Base (MCD)	GCILC	Ground-Control Interface Logic Controller (MCD)
GAP	Goodyear Associative Processor [*Data processing*]	GCILU	Ground-Control Interface Logic Unit (MCD)
GAP	Graphics Application Program (CAA)	GCIU	Graphic Communications International Union [*Washington, DC*] (EANO)
GAPHYOR	Gaz-Physique-Orsay [*Universite Paris-Sud*] [*Database*] (CUAD)		
GAPT	Graphical Automatically Programed Tools [*Data processing*]	GCIU	Graphic Communications International Union [*Canada*]
GAR	Growth Analysis and Review (BUR)	GCL	Generic Control Language [*Data processing*] (TEL)
GARADE	Gathers Alarms, Reports, Displays, and Evaluates [*General Electric Co.*]	GC LISP	Golden Common LISP [*Artificial intelligence language*]
GARD	General Address Reading Devices [*Data processing*] (DDI)	GCM	General Circulation Model [*Data processing*]
GAS	Generalized Audit Software [*Data processing*]	GCNED	Government Computer News [*A publication*]
GASKET	Graphic Surface Kinetics [*Computer program*] (KSC)	GCOM	Gray Communications Systems [*NASDAQ symbol*] (NQ)
GASL	General Activity Simulation Language [*Data processing*]	GCOS	General Comprehensive Operating Supervisor [*Data processing*]
GASP	General Activity Simulation Program [*Programing language*] [*1970*] [*Data processing*] (BUR)	GCP	Generalized Computer Program
		GCR	Geneva Consultants Registry [*Alpha Systems Resource*] [*Database*] (CUAD)
GASP	General All-Purpose Simulation Package [*McDonnell Douglas Automation Co.*] (MCD)	GCR	Group Coded Recording [*Data processing*] (BUR)
GASP	Generalized Academic Simulation Program [*Data processing*] (IEEE)	GCS	General Communication Subsystem [*Data processing*]
		GCS	General Computer Systems, Inc. (CAA)
GASP	Graphic Applications Subroutine Package [*Data processing*] (BUR)	GCS	Geostationary Communications Satellite [*WARC*]
		GCS	Graphic Compatibility System (CAA)
GASS	Generalized Assembly System [*Data processing*] (IEEE)	GCS	Ground Communications System
GAT	Generalized Algebraic Translator [*Data processing*]	GCSC	Guidance Control and Sequencing Computer (CIT)
GAT	Georgetown Automatic Translator [*Data processing*]	GCSS	Global Communications Satellite System
GATAC	General Assessment Tridimensional Analog Computer (IEEE)	GCT	Graphics Communications Terminal (CAA)
GATD	Graphic Analysis of Three-Dimensional Data	GCT	Guidance Computer Test (VIT)
GATE	Generalized Algebraic Translator Extended [*Data processing*]	GCTE	Guidance Computer Test Equipment (VIT)
GATR	Ground-to-Air Transmitting-Receiving [*Station*]	GD	Graphic Display (CAA)
GATS	General Acceptance Test Software (CAA)	GDAP	GEOS [*Geodetic Earth-Orbiting Satellite*] Data Adjustment Program
GATT	General Agreement on Tariffs and Trade [*Danish Standards Association*] [*Database*] (CUAD)		
		GDAS	Ground Data Acquisition System
GATT	Ground-to-Air Transmitter Terminal	GDAU	General Data Acquisition Unit (MCD)
GAUGE	General Automation Users Group Exchange [*Defunct*] (EANO)	GDB	Global Database (CAA)
GAUSS	[*A*] programing language [*Named after German mathematician Karl Friedrich Gauss, 1777-1855*] (CSR)	GDBS	Generalized Database System (NASA)
		GDC	General DataComm Industries, Inc. [*NYSE symbol*]
GB	Gain Bandwidth (DEN)	GDC	General [*Purpose*] Digital Computer
Gb	GigaBIT [*Binary Digit*] [*10^9 BITs*]		

Computer & Telecommunications Acronyms

GDC .... Geological Data Center [*Scripps Institution of Oceanography*] (EISS)
GDDL .... Graphical Data Definition Language (CAA)
GDDM .... Graphical Data Display Manager [*Data processing*]
GDE .... Generalized Data Entry
GDE .... Ground Data Equipment [*Electronics*]
GDF .... Geographic Data File [*List Processing Co.*] [*Information service*] (EISS)
GDF .... Group Distributing Frames
GDFF .... Geographic Distribution of Federal Funds Information System [*Comptroller General of the United States*]
GDG .... Generation Data Group [*Data processing*] (BUR)
GDI .... Graphics Device Interface
GDL .... Graphic Display Library (CAA)
GDL1 .... Graphic Drawing Library [*Graphic Data Ltd.*] [*Software package*] [*British*] (NCC)
GDL 2 .... Graphics Display List [*Graphic Data Ltd.*] [*Software package*] [*British*] (NCC)
GDM .... Global Data Manager (CAA)
GDMS .... Generalized Data Management System [*Data processing*] (BUR)
GDOA .... Graphic Data Output Area (CMD)
GDOC .... University of Guelph Document Holdings [*Database*] [*No longer available online*] (CUAD)
GDP .... Generalized Distributor Program [*Data processing*] (TUT)
GDP .... Generalized Drawing Primitive (CCD)
GDP .... Goal-Directed Programing (CAA)
GDP .... Graphic Display Processor
GDPS .... Global Data Processing System [*World Meteorological Organization*]
GDR .... Geodetic Data Reduction
GDS .... General Drafting System [*Applied Research of Cambridge Ltd.*] [*Software package*] [*British*] (NCC)
GDS .... Graphic Data System
GDS .... Graphic Design System (CAA)
GDS .... Graphical Display System [*Station control and data acquisition*] (IEEE)
GD/T .... General Dynamics/Telecommunications
GDT .... Geographic Data Technology, Inc. [*Information service*] (EISS)
GDT .... Global Descriptor Table [*Data processing*]
GDT .... Graphic Display Terminal
GDT .... Ground Data Terminal
GDTI .... General Database Technology [*NASDAQ symbol*] (NQ)
GDU .... Graphic Display Unit
GE .... Gateway Exchange [*Telecommunications*] (DEEC)
GE .... General Electric Co. [*NYSE symbol*]
GE .... Good Evening [*Amateur radio*]
GE .... Greater than or Equal To [*FORTRAN*]
GEASCOP ... General Asymptotic Composition Program [*Data processing*]
GEC .... General Electric Company Ltd.
GECOM .... Generalized Compiler [*Data processing*]
GECOS .... General Comprehensive Operating Supervisor [*Data processing*]
GECOS .... General Comprehensive Operating System
GEC Telecommun ... GEC [*General Electric Company*] Telecommunications [*A publication*]
GEEP .... General Electric Electronic Processor
GEESE .... General Electric Electronic System Evaluator
GEFRC .... General File/Record Control [*Honeywell, Inc.*] (CAH)
GEIS .... General Electric Information Services (OA)
GEISCO .... General Electric Information Services Company [*Rockville, MD*] [*Software manufacturer*] [*Information service*] [*Telecommunications*] (EISS)
GEL .... General Emulation Language (CAA)
GEM .... Graphics Environment Manager [*Data processing*]
GEMCO .... Global Electronic Markets Company [*Joint venture of Citicorp and McGraw-Hill, Inc. to provide computerized buying, selling, shipping, and insuring services for commodities traders*]
GEMCOS ..... Generalized Message Control System (BUR)
GEMDOS ..... Graphics Environment Manager/Disk Operating System
GEMS .... General Education Management System [*Data processing*] (IEEE)
GEMS .... General Electric Manufacturing Simulator (IEEE)
GEMSERVICE ... Global Electronic Mail Service [*Electronic Mail Corp. of America*] [*Old Greenwich, CT*] [*Telecommunications*] (TSSD)
GEN .... General Electric Network [*Data processing*]
GEN .... Generate (CAH)
GEN .... Generation (MSA)
GEN .... Generator [*Data processing*]
GEN .... GenRad, Inc. [*NYSE symbol*]
GENA .... General Automation, Inc. [*NASDAQ symbol*] (NQ)
GENBANK ... Genetic Sequence Databank [*Bolt, Beranek & Newman, Inc.*] [*Database*] [*Information service*] (EISS)
GEND .... Generated Data File [*Data processing*]
GENDARME ... Generalized Data Reduction, Manipulation, Evaluation
GENESIS .... [*A*] programing language [*1978*] (CSR)
GENESYS ... General Engineering System
GENFAP ...... General Non-Linear Frame Analysis Program [*Structures & Computers Ltd.*] [*Software package*] [*British*] (NCC)
GEnie .... General Electric Network for Information Exchange [*Rockville, MD*] [*Online Information Service*]
GENIE .... General Information Extractor (CAA)
GENTEL ...... General Telephone & Electronics Corp.

GEOMOD .... Geometric Modeller [*GE CAE International*] [*Software package*] [*British*] (NCC)
GEOREF ..... Geological Reference File [*American Geological Institute*] [*Bibliographic database*] [*Information service*] (EISS)
GEORGE .... General Organizational Environment [*Data processing*] (BUR)
GEOS .... Graphic Environment Operating System
GEOSCAN ... Ground-Based Electronic Omnidirectional Satellite Communications Antenna
GEPAC .... General Electric Process Automation Computer
GEPAC .... General Electric Programable Automatic Comparator (CDH)
GEPURS ..... General Electric General Purpose (CDH)
GERT .... Graphical Evaluation and Review Technique
GERTS .... General Electric Remote Terminal Supervisor (CAH)
GERTS .... General Electric Remote Terminal System (IEEE)
GES .... Genisco Technology Corp. [*American Stock Exchange symbol*]
GESC .... Government EDP [*Electronic Data Processing*] Standards Committee [*Canada*]
GESHUA ..... General Electric Six Hundred Users' Association [*Later, HLSUA*] [*Data processing*] (TUT)
GE/TAC .... General Electric Telemetering and Control (IEEE)
GETEL .... General Electric Test Engineering Language [*Data processing*] (IEEE)
GETOL .... General Electric Training Operational Logic [*Data processing*] (IEEE)
GEVIC .... General Electric Variable Increment Computer
GF .... Gain Factor [*Data processing*]
GFAM .... Graphics Flutter Analysis Methods [*Data processing*]
GFE .... Government-Furnished Equipment
GFI .... Guided Fault Isolation (CAA)
GFP .... General Forecasting Program (BUR)
GFP .... Generalized File Processor (CAA)
GFPBBD ...... Groupement Francais des Producteurs de Bases et Banques de Donnees [*French Federation of Data Base Producers*] [*Information service*] (EISS)
GFS .... Government-Furnished Software (NASA)
G-G .... Ground-to-Ground [*Communications, weapons, etc.*] (MSA)
GGG .... Gadolinium Gallium Garnet [*Substrate for magnetic film*]
GGP .... Golden Gate Productions [*San Francisco, CA*] [*Telecommunications*] (TSSD)
GHC .... Gating Half-Cycle [*Data processing*]
GH/LCD .... Guest-Host/Liquid Crystal Display [*Telecommunications*] (TEL)
GHS .... Gesamthochschule [*General High School*] [*Information retrieval*] [*German*] (ODIN)
GHz .... Gigahertz [*1,000 megahertz*]
GI .... General Instruments
GI .... Generic Identifier [*Telecommunications*] (TEL)
GIANT .... Genealogical Information and Name Tabulating System [*Data processing*] (IEEE)
GIANT .... General Information and Analysis Tool (TUT)
GIC .... General Input/Output Channel (CAA)
GID .... Gesellschaft fuer Information und Dokumentation mbH [*Society for Information and Documentation*] [*West Germany*] [*Information service*] (EISS)
GIDAS .... Geoanomaly Interactive Data Analysis System (MCD)
GIDEP .... Government-Industry Data Exchange Program [*Later, IDEP*] [*Department of the Navy*] [*Database*] [*Information service*]
GIF .... Gulf It to FORTRAN [*Translator*] [*Data processing*]
GIFT .... General Internal FORTRAN Translator [*Data processing*] (IEEE)
GIFTPOOL ... Datenbank ueber Gifte und Vergiftungen [*Databank for Poisons and Poisoning*] [*German*] (ODIN)
GIGO .... Garbage In, Garbage Out [*Data processing*]
GILBA .... Gilbert Associates, Inc. Cl A [*NASDAQ symbol*] (NQ)
GIM .... Generalized Information Management [*Language*] (CGC)
GIMIC .... Guard Ring Isolated Monolithic Integrated Circuit (CAA)
GINO .... Graphical Input/Output (CAA)
GINO-F .... Graphical Input and Output in FORTRAN [*GST Computer Systems Ltd.*] [*Software package*] [*Data processing*] [*British*]
GIOC .... Generalized Input/Output Controller [*Data processing*] (IEEE)
GIOP .... General Purpose Input/Output Processor (CAA)
GIPSY .... Generalized Information Processing System
GIRAFFE ..... Graphic Interface for Finite Elements [*Graphics data processing*]
GIRAS .... Geographic Information Retrieval and Analysis System [*Department of the Interior*]
GIRL .... Generalized Information Retrieval Language [*US Defense Nuclear Agency*] (IDA)
GIRL .... Graph Information Retrieval Language [*1970*] [*Data processing*] (CSR)
GIRLS .... Generalized Information Retrieval and Listing System
GIRS .... Gallaudet Information Retrieval Service
GIRSS .... General Information Retrieval System Simulation
GIS .... Generalized Information System [*IBM Corp.*]
GIS .... Generalized Inquiry System [*Data processing*] (TUT)
GIS .... Geographic Information Systems [*United States Geological Survey*] (EISS)
GIS .... Global Information Services, Inc. [*Flushing, NY*] [*Telecommunications*] (TSSD)
GIS .... Grant Information System [*Oryx Press*] (EISS)
GIS .... Guidance Information System [*Time Share Corp.*] [*Information service*] (EISS)
GISL .... Graphic Imaging Specification Language [*Printing technology*]
GJP .... Graphic Job Processor (MCD)
GKI .... General Kinetics, Incorporated

Computer & Telecommunications Acronyms

GLANCE	Global Lightweight Airborne Navigation Computer Equipment
GLD	Gould, Inc. [*NYSE symbol*]
GLF	General Telephone Co. of Florida [*NYSE symbol*]
GLITCH	Goblin Loose in the Computer Hut [*Data processing*]
GLOBE	Global Lending and Overseas Banking Evaluator [*Chase Econometrics*] [*Database*] (CUAD)
GLOC	Ground Line of Communications (AFM)
GLOMR	Global Low-Orbiting Message Relay [*Satellite*]
GLP	GOAL [*Ground Operations Aerospace Language*] Language Processor (MCD)
GLS	Gaylord Circulation Control System [*Gaylord Bros., Inc.*] [*Information service*] (EISS)
GLT	Greeting Letter Telegram
GLYPNIR	[*A*] programing language [*1970*] (CSR)
GM	Good Morning [*Amateur radio*]
GM	Group Mark [*Data processing*]
Gm	Mutual Conductance (CDH)
GMA	Geomechanics Abstracts [*Rock Mechanics Information Service*] [*Bibliographic database*] [*British*] (OBD)
GMAL	General Electric Macro Assembly Language (NASA)
GMAP	General Macroassembly Program [*Honeywell, Inc.*] (CAH)
GMAP	Generalized Macroprocessor (CAA)
GMC	General Monte Carlo Code [*Data processing*]
GMCR	Globe Mackay Cable and Radio Corp. [*Manila, Philippines*] [*Telecommunications*] (TSSD)
GMD	Gesellschaft fuer Mathematik und Datenverarbeitung [*Society for Mathematics and Data Processing*] [*West Germany*] [*Information service*] (EISS)
GME	Generic Macro Expander [*Telecommunications*] (TEL)
GMF	Generalized Mainline Framework [*Data processing*]
GMIS	Generalized Management Information System (CAA)
GML	Generalized Markup Language [*Data processing*]
GML	Graphic Machine Language (CAA)
GMR	General Modular Redundancy (CAA)
GMS	General Maintenance System [*Data processing*] (BUR)
GMS	Geostationary Meteorological Satellite [*Japan*]
GMSS	Graphical Modeling and Simulation System (CAA)
GMT	General Machine Test [*Data processing*] (BUR)
GMT	Generalized Multitasking (CAA)
GMT	Greenwich Mean Time
GN	Good Night [*Amateur radio*]
GNA	Graphics Network Architecture (CCD)
GNAT	General Numerical Analysis of Transport [*Computer program*]
GNATS	General Nonlinear Analysis of Two-Dimensional Structures [*Computer program*]
GNC	Graphic Numerical Control [*Deltacam Systems Ltd.*] [*Software package*] [*British*] (MCD)
GND	Ground
GNG	Generation Gather Group [*Data processing*]
GNIC	Gay News Information and Communication Network [*Woodbury, NY*] [*Information service*] (EISS)
GNT	Great Northern Telegraph Co. [*Denmark*] [*Telecommunications*] (TEL)
GO	Generated Output (CAA)
GOAM	Government Owned and Maintained [*Telecommunications*] (TEL)
GOATS	Group Operational Access Tester System [*AT & T*]
GOC	Greatest Overall Coefficient (TEL)
GOCI	General Operator-Computer Interaction (IEEE)
GODAS	Graphically Oriented Design and Analysis System [*Data processing*]
GOES	Geostationary Operational [*or Orbit*] Environmental Satellite [*National Oceanic and Atmospheric Administration*]
GOES/DCP	Geostationary Operational Environmental Satellite Data Collection Platform
GOL	General Operating Language [*Data processing*] (IEEE)
GOL	Goal-Oriented Language (CAA)
GOLD	Graphic Online Language [*Data processing*] (IEEE)
GOLEM	Grosspeicherorientierte Listenorganisierte Ermittlungsmethode [*Information retrieval*] (ODIN)
GOMAC	Government Microcircuit Applications Conference
GORX	Graphite Oxidation from Reactor Excursion [*Engineering computer code*]
GOS	Grade of Service [*Telecommunications*]
GOS	Graphics Operating System [*Tektronix*] (CAA)
GOTRAN	Load and Go FORTRAN [*Data processing*] (CDH)
Gov Data Syst	Government Data Systems [*United States*] [*A publication*]
Govt Data Sys	Government Data Systems [*A publication*]
GP	Gang Punch [*Data processing*] (TUT)
GP	General Processor (IDA)
GP	General Product (BUR)
GP	Generalized Programing [*Data processing*]
GP	Graphics Processor (CAA)
GPA	General-Purpose Amplifier
GPA	General-Purpose Analysis (IEEE)
GPA	General-Purpose Array (CAA)
GPA	Graphical PERT [*Program Evaluation and Review Technique*] Analog [*Data processing*] (IEEE)
GPAC	General-Purpose Analog Computer (DEN)
GPBIM	General-Purpose Buffer Interface Module [*Data processing*]
GPC	General Peripheral Controller (CAA)
GPC	General-Purpose Computer
GPCA	General-Purpose Communications Adapter (CAA)
GPCP	General-Purpose Contouring Program (CAH)
GPCP	Generalized Process Control Programing [*Data processing*] (IEEE)
GPD	General-Purpose Discipline [*IBM Corp.*]
GPDC	General-Purpose Digital Computer
GPDM	Geopotential Decameter [*Telecommunications*] (TEL)
GPGL	General-Purpose Graphic Language [*Data processing*] (IEEE)
GPI	General-Purpose Interface
GPI	Ground Position Indicator [*Dead-reckoning computer*]
GPIA	General-Purpose Interface Adapter (IEEE)
GPIB	General-Purpose Interface Bus [*Data processing*]
GPIC	General-Purpose Intercomputer [*Test*] (NVT)
GPIO	General-Purpose Input/Output [*Data processing*]
GPKD	General-Purpose Keyboard and Display Control [*Data processing*] (MDG)
GPL	General-Purpose Language [*Data processing*] (CSR)
GPL	Generalized Programing Language [*Data processing*] (TUT)
GPL	GOAL [*Ground Operations Aerospace Language*] Processing Language (MCD)
GPL	Group Processing Logic (TEL)
GPLAN	Generalized Database Planning System (CAH)
GPLP	General-Purpose Linear Programing [*Data processing*] (IEEE)
GPM	General-Purpose Macrogenerator [*Data processing*] (IEEE)
GPM	Groups [*of code transmitted*] per Minute [*or Message*] [*Telecommunications*]
GPMS	General-Purpose Microprogram Simulator [*Data processing*] (IEEE)
GPOS	General Purpose Operating System
GPP	General-Purpose Programing [*Data processing*]
GPR	General-Purpose Register [*Data processing*] (MDG)
GPRR	General-Purpose Radio Receiver
GPRT	General-Purpose Radio Transmitter
GPS	General Problem Solver [*Data processing*]
GPS	General Processing Subsystem (MCD)
GPS	Generic Processing System [*Data processing*] (TEL)
GPS	GigaBITS [*Binary Digits*] per Second [*Transmission rate*] [*Data processing*]
GPS	Global Positioning Satellite
GPS	Graphic Programing Services [*Data processing*] (IBMDP)
GPSCS	General-Purpose Satellite Communication System (MCD)
GPSE	General-Purpose Simulation Environment [*Data processing*]
GPSP	General-Purpose Software Program [*Data processing*] (CIT)
GPSS	General [*or Generic*] Problem Statement Simulator (IDA)
GPSS	General Process Simulation Studies (VIT)
GPSS	General-Purpose Simulation System [*formerly, Systems Simulator*] [*IBM Corp.*] [*1961*] [*Data processing*]
GPTI	General-Purpose Terminal Interchanges [*Airline communication system*] [*Raytheon Co.*]
GPX	Generalized Programing Extended [*Livermore Atomic Research Computer*] [*Sperry UNIVAC*]
GQ	Grumman Corp. [*NYSE symbol*]
GQA	Get Quick Answer [*Communications*]
GQA	Give Quick Answer [*Communications*]
GQE	Generalized Queue Entry [*Data processing*] (OA)
GRA	Government Reports Announcements [*Department of Commerce*] [*Database producer*]
GRAAL	Graph Algorithmic Language [*Data processing*]
GRAD	Generalized Remote Access Database (TUT)
GRAD	Graduate Resume Accumulation and Distribution [*Data processing*]
GRADB	Generalized Remote Access Database (IEEE)
GRADS	Generalized Remote Access Database System (IEEE)
GRAF	Graphic Addition to FORTRAN [*Data processing*]
GRAID	Graphical Aid [*Data processing*]
GRAIN	Graphics-Oriented Relational Algebraic Interpreter (CAA)
GRAMPA	General Analytical Model for Process Analysis (IEEE)
GRAMPS	Graphics for the Multipicture System [*Computer graphics*]
GRANADA	Grammatical Nonalgorithmic Data Description (CAA)
GRANIS	Graphical Natural Inference System (CAA)
GRAPDEN	Graphic Data Entry Unit [*Data processing*] (CDH)
GRAPE	Graphical Analysis of Program Execution [*Data processing*]
GRAPHDEN	Graphical Data Entry [*Data processing*] (MUGU)
GRASP	Generalized Read and Simulate Program (CAA)
GRASP	Generalized Remote Acquisition and Sensor Processing (CAA)
GRASP	Generalized Retrieval and Storage Program [*Data processing*]
GRASP	Graphic Service Program (IEEE)
GRASP	Graphical Robot Applications Simulation [*BYG Systems Ltd.*] [*Software package*] [*British*] (NCC)
GRASP	Graphics-Augmented Structural Post-Processing [*Module*]
GRASP Lab	General Robotics and Active Sensory Processing Laboratory [*University of Pennsylvania*] [*Research center*] (RCD)
GRATIS	Generation, Reduction, and Training Input System (IEEE)
GRC	Government Research Corporation [*Information service*] (EISS)
GRDSR	Geographically Referenced Data Storage and Retrieval System [*Canada*]
GRED	Generalized Random Extract Device [*Data processing*]
GREFICOR	Groupe de Recherche sur l'Efficacite Organisationnelle [*University of Quebec at Hull*] [*Research center*] (RCD)
GRG	GR Gordetsky Telecommunications and General Management Consulting [*San Diego, CA*] [*Telecommunications*] (TSSD)
GRG	Graphical Rewriting Grammar (CAA)
GRID	Graphic Interactive Display (IEEE)

Computer & Telecommunications Acronyms

GRID .... Graphic Reproduction by Integrated Design
GRID .... Graphic Retrieval and Information Display   (NASA)
GRIF .... Griffin Technology [*NASDAQ symbol*]   (NQ)
GRIN .... Graphical Input [*Language*] [*Data processing*]
GRIN-2 .... Graphical Interaction [*Language*] [*Data processing*]
GRINDER .... Graphical Interactive Network Designer   (CAA)
GRIP .... General Retrieval of Information Program [*Data processing*]
GRIP .... Grandmet Information Processing [*British*]   (OA)
GRIP .... Graphics Interaction with Proteins [*Computer graphics*]
GRIP .... Graphics Interactive Programing   (CAA)
GRIPHOS .... General Retrieval and Information Processor for Humanities Oriented Studies
GRL .... General Instrument Corp. [*NYSE symbol*]
GRM .... Generalized Report Module Program [*Data processing*]
GROOVE ..... Generated Real-Time Output Operations on Voltage-Controlled Equipment [*Data processing*]
GRP .... Group Reference Pilot [*Telecommunications*]   (TEL)
GRS .... General Register Set/Stack [*Data processing*]
GRS .... General Reporting System   (CAA)
GRS .... Generalized Retrieval System [*Data processing*]   (TUT)
GRTS .... General Remote Terminal Supervisor   (CAA)
GRW .... Galactic Radio Wave
GS .... Galvanized Steel [*Telecommunications*]
GS .... Group Selector [*Telecommunications*]   (TEL)
GS .... Group Separator [*Data processing*]
GSA .... General Services Administration
GSA .... General Syntax Analyzer [*Sperry UNIVAC*]   (CAA)
GSAM .... Generalized Sequential Access Method [*Data processing*]
GSC .... Group Switching Center [*British*] [*Telecommunications*]   (TEL)
GSD .... General Systems Division [*IBM Corp.*]
GSD .... Generic Structure Diagram [*Telecommunications*]   (TEL)
GSI .... Geographic Systems, Incorporated [*Information service*]   (EISS)
GSI .... Grand Scale Integration   (BUR)
GSI .... Graphic Structure Input   (DEEC)
GSIDC .... Gulf States Information Documentation Center [*Baghdad, Iraq*] [*Information service*]   (EISS)
GSIU .... Ground Standard Interface Unit   (MCD)
GSL .... Generalized Simulation Language [*Data processing*]   (MDG)
GSL .... Generation Strategy Language [*Data processing*]   (IEEE)
GSM .... Generalized Sequential Machine [*Data processing*]
GSM .... Generalized Sort/Merge [*Data processing*]
GSM .... Graphics System Module   (CAA)
GSP .... General Simulation Program [*Programing language*]   (IEEE)
GSP .... General Syntactic Processor   (OA)
GSP .... Graphic Subroutine Package [*Data processing*]
GSR .... Global Shared Resources [*Data processing*]   (IBMDP)
GSS .... Galvanized Steel Strand [*Telecommunications*]   (TEL)
GSS .... Graphic Support Software   (CAA)
GST .... Government Securities Trading [*Computer*]
GSTI .... Gerber Systems Technology [*NASDAQ symbol*]   (NQ)
GSVC .... Generalized Supervisor Calls [*Data processing*]   (IBMDP)
G/T .... [*Antenna*] Gain-to-Noise Temperature Ratio   (CBSS)
GT .... Gopher Tape Armor [*Telecommunications*]   (TEL)
GT .... Graphics Terminal   (CAA)
GT .... Greater Than [*FORTRAN*]
GT .... Green Thumbs [*National Weather Service and Department of Agriculture Extension Service telecommunication system*]
GTA .... Government Telecommunications Agency [*Canada*]
GTA .... Groupement Technique de Assureurs du Canada [*Government Telecommunications Agency*] [*Canada*]
GTCP .... General Telephone Call Processing
GTD .... Geometric and Technical Draughting [*British Olivetti Ltd.*] [*Software package*] [*British*]   (NCC)
GTD .... Graphic Tablet Display [*Data processing*]   (IEEE)
GTDPL .... Generalized Top-Down Parsing Language   (CAA)
GT & E .... General Telephone & Electronics Corp.
GTE .... Group Translating Equipment   (CBSS)
GTE .... GTE Corp. [*Formerly, General Telephone & Electronics Corp.*] [*NYSE symbol*]
GTE Auto .... GTE [*General Telephone and Electronics Corp.*] Automatic Electric Technical Journal [*A publication*]
GTE Autom Electr World-Wide Commun J ... GTE [*General Telephone and Electronics Corp.*] Automatic Electric World-Wide Communications Journal [*A publication*]
GTELN .... General Telephone of California [*NASDAQ symbol*]   (NQ)
GTEP .... General Telephone and Electronics Practice [*Telecommunications*]   (TEL)
GTF .... Generalized Trace Facility [*Data processing*]   (MCD)
GTG .... Ground-to-Ground [*Communications, weapons, etc.*]
GTI .... GTI Corp. [*American Stock Exchange symbol*]
GTL .... Geometric and Technical Language [*British Olivetti Ltd.*] [*Software package*] [*British*]   (NCC)
GTL .... Georgia Tech Language [*Data processing*]   (CSR)
GTO .... Gate Turn Off [*Data processing*]
GTO .... Graphics Text Organizer [*Data processing*]
GTRI .... Georgia Tech Research Institute [*Georgia Institute of Technology*] [*Research center*]   (RCD)
GTRP .... General Transpose [*Data processing*]   (CDH)
GTS .... Geostationary Technology Satellite
GTS .... Global Telecommunication System [*World Meteorological Organization*]   (EISS)
GTSA .... German Telecommunications Statistics Agency
GTSS .... General Time Sharing System [*Data processing*]

GTX .... Ground Transport Express [*Airport baggage computer*]
GU .... Generic Unit   (TEL)
GUARDSMAN ... Guidelines and Rules for Data Systems Management   (TEL)
GUB .... Generalized Upper Bounding [*Data processing*]
GUB .... Greatest Upper Bound [*Data processing*]   (CIT)
GUCCO ...... Guidance Computer Control Subsystem   (VIT)
GUHA .... General Unary Hypothesis Automation   (IEEE)
GUIDE .... Guidance for Users of Integrated Data Processing Equipment
GUL .... Gulton Industries, Inc. [*NYSE symbol*]
GULP .... General Utility Library Program [*Data processing*]
GUS .... Generic User System [*Data processing*]
GUTS .... Game on Urban Transport System [*Kins Developments Ltd.*] [*Software package*] [*British*]   (NCC)
GVC .... General Videotex Corporation
GVDSB ...... Government Data Systems [*A publication*]
GVP .... Gravis Computer Peripherals, Inc. [*Vancouver Stock Exchange symbol*]
GVP .... Group Visionary Productions, Inc. [*Studio City, CA*] [*Telecommunications*]   (TSSD)
GWIGWO .... Good Will In, Good Will Out [*Data processing*]
GWSTV ...... Golden West Subscription Television [*Cable TV programing service*]
GY .... GenCorp, Inc. [*NYSE symbol*]

H

H	Half-Word Designator [*Data processing*]	
H	Halt [*Data processing*]	(MDG)
H	Hardware [*Data processing*]	(MDG)
h	Hecto [*A prefix meaning multiplied by 10²*] [*SI symbol*]	
H	Height	
H	Henry [*Symbol*] [*SI unit of inductance*]	
H	Hexadecimal	(BUR)
H	Horizontal	
H	Hour [*Also, h*]	
H	Magnetizing Force [*Symbol*]	(DEN)
HA	Half Adder [*Circuitry*]	(MSA)
HA	Home Address	
HAAT	Height Above Average Terrain	
HAB	Home Address Block	(CAA)
HAD	Half Amplitude Duration [*Telecommunications*]	(TEL)
HA-DEC	Hour Angle-Declination [*Type of antenna mounting*]	(CIT)
HADTS	High-Accuracy Data Transmission System	(MUGU)
HAIT	Hash Algorithm Information Table	(CAA)
HAL	Harwell Automated Loans [*Library circulation system*]	(DEEC)
HAL	Hash Algorithm Library	(CAA)
HAL	Heuristically-Programed Algorithmic [*Name of computer in film, "2001: A Space Odyssey." Acronym is also considered to have been formed by combining the letters preceding IBM in the alphabet*]	
HAL	High-Order Articulated Language [*Data processing*]	(MCD)
HAL	High-Order Assembly Language [*Data processing*]	(NASA)
HAL	Highly Automated Logic [*Data processing*]	(TUT)
HAL	VCR [*Video Cassette Recorder*] device allowing programming via telephone [*Advanced Video Dynamics*]	
HAL-PC	Houston Area League of PC [*Personal Computer*] Users	
HALSIM	Hardware Logic Simulator [*Data processing*]	(IEEE)
HAM	Hardware Associative Memory [*Data processing*]	(DIT)
HAM	Hierarchical Access Method	(CAA)
HAM	Home Amateur [*Radio*]	
HAMT	Human-Aided Machine Translation	(DEEC)
HANDE	Hydrofoil Analysis and Design [*Data processing*]	
HAN/LCD	Hybrid Assigned Nematic/Liquid Crystal Display	(TEL)
HAPPE	Honeywell Associative Parallel Processing Ensemble	(CAA)
HAPS	Houston Automatic Priority Spooling [*Data processing*]	
HAPUB	High-Speed Arithmetic Processing Unit Board	(CAA)
HAR	Home Address Register	(CAA)
HARG	High-Speed Autoradiography	
HARP	Hitachi Arithmetic Processor [*Data processing*]	(IEEE)
HART	Hayden Analysis and Reporting Tool [*Data processing*]	(TUT)
HARTRAN	Hardwell FORTRAN [*Data processing*]	(IEEE)
HARU	Handbuch fuer Rundfunk und Fernsehen [*NOMOS Datapool*] [*Database*]	(CUAD)
HASP	High-Level Automatic Scheduling Program	(BUR)
HASP	Houston Automatic Spooling Priority System	(CAH)
HASQ	Hardware-Assisted Software Queue	(CAA)
HAT	High-Altitude Transmitter	
HAT	Home Area Toll [*Telecommunications*]	(TEL)
HAU	Horizontal Arithmetic Unit	(CAA)
HAU	Hybrid Arithmetic Unit	(CAA)
HAVC	Health Audiovisual On-Line Catalog [*Northeastern Ohio Universities College of Medicine*] [*Database*]	
HAVE	Heating and Ventilation Estimating [*Tipdata Ltd.*] [*Software package*] [*British*]	(NCC)
HAWC	Homing and Warning Computer	(MCD)
H-B	Hexadecimal-to-Binary [*Data processing*]	(IEEE)
HB	Honeywell-Bull	
HBC	Honeywell Business Computer	
HBEN	High Byte Enable	(CAA)
HBO	Home Box Office [*Cable-television system*]	
HBR	Harvard Business Review [*John Wiley & Sons, Inc.*] [*Bibliographic database*] [*A publication*]	
HBR	High BIT [*Binary Digit*] Rate	(KSC)
HBT	Harbor Bay Telecommunications [*Alameda, CA*]	(TSSD)
HBWA	High-Band Warning Antenna	(MCD)
HBWR	High-Band Warning Receiver	(MCD)
HC	Hard Copy [*Data processing*]	
HC	Heuristic Concepts	(IEEE)
HC	Host Computer	(CAA)
HC	House Cable [*Telecommunications*]	(TEL)
HC	Hybrid Computer [*for processing both analog and digital data*]	(NASA)
HCC	Heliax Coaxial Cable	
HCC	[*The*] Hoberman-Castello Company [*Reading, PA*] [*Software manufacturer*]	(DASOS)
HCCC	Computer Center [*Haverford College*] [*Research center*]	(RCD)
HCD	Hot-Carrier Diode	(IEEE)
HCF	Host Command Facility	(CAA)
HCG	Hardware Character Generator	(OA)
HCI	Host Computer Interface	(CAA)
HCI	Hughes Communications International [*Hughes Aircraft Co.*]	
HCMTS	High-Capacity Mobile Telecommunications System	(TEL)
HCN	Health Communications Network [*Medical University of South Carolina*] [*Charleston*] [*Telecommunications*]	(TSSD)
HCP	Hard Copy Printer [*Data processing*]	
HCP	Host Communications Processor	(CAA)
HCR	Hardware Check Routine	(CAA)
HCS	Health Care Support [*System*] [*IBM Corp.*]	
HCS	Homogeneous Computer System	
HCSS	Hospital Computer Sharing System	(IEEE)
HD	Half Duplex Transmission [*Data communication*]	(CET)
H-D	Hexadecimal-to-Decimal [*Data processing*]	(IEEE)
HD	Hierarchical Direct	(CAA)
HD	High Density	
HDA	Head Disk Assembly	(CAA)
HDA	Housekeeping Data Acquisition	(MCD)
HDAM	Hierarchical Direct Access Method [*Data processing*]	(MCD)
HDAS	Hybrid Data Acquisition System	(CAA)
HDAS	Hydrographic Data Acquisition System	
HDB	High-Density Binary	(TEL)
HDB	High-Density Bipolar Code [*Telecommunications*]	(TEL)
HDB3	High-Density Binary Three Level Signal	(TEL)
HDC	Hierarchical Distributed Control [*Data processing*]	
HDC	Hospital Data Center [*American Hospital Association*] [*Information service*]	(EISS)
HDDR	High-Density Digital Recording	
HDDS	High-Density Data System [*Data processing*]	
HDF	High-Density Flexible	(CAA)
HDF	Horizontal Distributing Frame	
HDL	Hardware Description Language [*Data processing*]	
HDLC	High-Level Data Link Control [*International Standards Organization*] [*Data communication*]	
HDMR	High-Density Multitrack Recording	(MCD)
HDMS	Honeywells Distributed Manufacturing [*Honeywell Information Systems Ltd.*] [*Software package*] [*British*]	(NCC)
HDOC	Handy Dandy Orbital Computer	(IEEE)
HDOS	Hard Disk Operating System	(CAA)
HDP	Horizontal Data Processing	
HDR	Header [*Data processing*]	
HDS	Head Set [*Telecommunications*]	(TEL)
HDS	Hybrid Development System	(CAA)
HDSHK	Handshake [*Computers*]	(MSA)
HDTV	High-Definition Television [*Broadcasting term*]	
HDW	Hardware [*Data processing*]	(KSC)
HDX	Half Duplex Transmission [*Data communication*]	
HE	Housekeeping Element	(TEL)
HEALS	Honeywell Error Analysis and Logging System	(CAA)
HEALTHLINE	Health Planning and Administration [*National Library of Medicine*] [*Database*]	
HEBIS-BIB	Hessische Bibliographie [*Hessian Bibliography*] [*Database*] [*Information retrieval*]	(ODIN)
HEC	Hollerith Electronic Computer	
HECI	Human-Interface Equipment Catalog Item	(TEL)
HECLINET	Health Care Literature Information Network [*Technische Universitaet Berlin*] [*West Germany*] [*Database*] [*Information service*]	(EISS)
HEEP	Highway Engineering Exchange Program [*Users group*]	
HEIC	HEI Corporation [*NASDAQ symbol*]	(NQ)
HEII	HEI, Incorporated [*NASDAQ symbol*]	(NQ)
HELP	Highly Extendable Language Processor [*Data processing*]	(TUT)
HELP	Honeywell Equipment Lease Plan	

Computer & Telecommunications Acronyms

HELPIS .... Higher Education Learning Programmes Information Service [*British Universities Film & Video Council*] [*Database*] (CUAD)
HELPS .... Handicapped Education Learner's Planning System [*Battelle Memorial Institute*] [*Information service*] (EISS)
HELPS .... Health Environment Long-Range Planning Support [*A computer model*]
HEMAC ...... Hybrid Electromagnetic Antenna Coupler
HEMT .... High Electron Mobility Transistor [*Data processing*]
HEN .... Home Entertainment Network [*Cable-television system*]
HEOS .... Highly Eccentric [*or Elliptical*] Orbit Satellite
HEP .... Heterogeneous Element Processor [*Data processing*] (RDA)
HERI .... Heavy Oil/Enhanced Recovery Index [*Alberta Oil Sands Information Centre*] [*Database*] (CUAD)
HERS .... Hardware Error Recovery System [*Sperry UNIVAC*] (CAA)
HETC .... Hetra Computer Commercial [*NASDAQ symbol*] (NQ)
HEX .... Hexadecimal [*System*]
HEX .... Hexagon
HF .... High Frequency [*Electronics*]
HFA .... High-Frequency Accelerometer (NASA)
HFA .... High-Frequency Recovery Antenna (KSC)
HFAA .... High-Frequency Airborne Antenna
HFAS .... High-Frequency Antenna System (KSC)
HFAS .... Honeywell File Access System (CAA)
HFC .... High-Frequency Correction
HFC .... High-Frequency Current
HFO .... Heavy Fuel Oils [*Database*] [*Department of Energy*] (FDB)
HFPS .... High-Frequency Phase Shifter [*Telecommunications*] (OA)
HFRA .... High-Frequency Recovery Antenna (KSC)
HFRT .... High-Frequency Radio Transmitter
HFSSB .... High-Frequency Single Sideband [*Telecommunications*]
HFWA .... High-Frequency Wave Analyzer
HFX .... High-Frequency Transceiver [*or Transducer*]
HGA .... High Gain Antenna
HGAC .... High Gain Antenna Controller (CIT)
HGAS .... High Gain Antenna System (IEEE)
HGI .... Hi-G, Incorporated [*American Stock Exchange symbol*] [*Delisted*]
HGL .... High Gain Link
HH .... Hanging Handset [*Telecommunications*] (TEL)
HH .... Home Radio Beacon - High Power (FAAC)
HHC .... Handheld Computer
HHF .... Hyper-High-Frequency (DEN)
HHIP .... Hand-Held Information Processor (DDI)
HHN .... Harte-Hanks Communications, Inc. [*NYSE symbol*]
HI .... High [*Data processing*]
HI .... Honeywell, Incorporated (NASA)
HIC .... Hybrid Integrated Circuit
HICAPCOM .. High-Capacity Communication System
HICS .... Hierarchical Information Control System [*Japanese*] (CAA)
HIDAM .... Hierarchical Indexed Direct Access Method [*Data processing*] (BUR)
HIDF .... Horizontal Side of an Intermediate Distribution Frame [*Telecommunications*] (TEL)
HiD/LoD ..... High-Density/Low-Density Tariff
HIDM .... High Information Delta Modulation [*Data processing*] (BUR)
HIFAM .... High-Fidelity Amplitude Modulation (DEN)
HIFT .... Hardware Implemented Fault Tolerance (CAA)
High Technol ... High Technology [*United States*] [*A publication*]
HIHAT .... High-Resolution Hemispherical Reflector Antenna Technique
HIIS .... Honeywell Institute for Information Science (IEEE)
HIN .... Hybrid Integrated Network [*Bell System*] [*Telecommunications*]
HING .... High-Intensity Noise Generator
HIPAC .... Hitachi Parametron Automatic Computer
HIPO .... Hierarchy plus Input-Process-Output [*Data processing*]
HI-RES .... High Resolution [*Data processing*]
HIS .... Homogeneous Information Sets (CAA)
HIS .... Honeywell Information System, Inc. (IEEE)
HIS .... Hospital Information System [*Data processing*]
HIS .... House Information Systems [*US House of Representatives*]
HISAM .... Hierarchical Indexed Sequential Access Method [*Data processing*] (BUR)
HISDAM ..... Hierarchical Indexed Sequential Direct Access Method [*Data processing*] (CAA)
HISI .... Health Information Systems [*NASDAQ symbol*] (NQ)
HISI .... Honeywell Information Systems, Incorporated (CAA)
HISSG .... Hospital Information Systems Sharing Group [*Reston, VA*] (EANO)
HISTLINE .... History of Medicine On-Line [*National Library of Medicine*] [*Bibliographic database*] (EISS)
HIT .... High Incidence Target [*Crime computer*]
HIT .... Houston International Teleport [*Houston, TX*] [*Telecommunications*] (TSSD)
HITAC .... Hitachi Computer (DIT)
HITLS .... Hardware in the Loop Simulation [*Data processing*] (MCD)
Hi-U .... High-Usage [*Telecommunications*]
HJ .... Halt and Jump [*Data processing*] (BUR)
HL .... Host Language (CAA)
HL .... Hot Line [*Alert system*]
HLAF .... High-Level Arithmetic Function (CAA)
HLBV .... Hessische Landesbibliothek - Versuchsversion [*Hessische Bibliographie*] [*Information retrieval*] (ODIN)
HLDA .... Hold Acknowledge [*Data processing*]

HLHB .... Hessische Landes- und Hochschulbibliothek [*Darmstadt*] [*Information retrieval*] (ODIN)
HLI .... Host Language Interface (CAA)
HLL .... High-Level Language [*Data processing*]
HLML .... High-Level Microprograming Language (CAA)
HLPI .... High-Level Programing Interface (CAA)
HLQL .... High-Level Query Language (CAA)
HLR .... High-Level Representation (CAA)
HLSUA .... Honeywell Large Systems Users Association
HLT .... Halt [*Data processing*] (MDG)
HLT .... Heterodyne Look-Thru [*Telecommunications*] (TEL)
HLTA .... Halt Acknowledge [*Data processing*]
HLTL .... High-Level Transistor Logic
HLTTL .... High-Level Transistor Translator Logic
HLU .... House Logic Unit (OA)
HMDF .... Horizontal Side of Main Distribution Frame (TEL)
HMG .... Hardware Message Generator [*Telecommunications*] (TEL)
HMI .... Hardware Monitor Interface (CAA)
HMI .... Horizontal Motion Index [*Printer technology*]
HMM .... Hardware Multiply Module (CAA)
HMO .... Hardware Microcode Optimizer (CAA)
HMOS .... High-Speed Metal-Oxide Semiconductor [*ROM*] (DEEC)
HMR .... Hybrid Modular Redundancy (CAA)
HMS .... Hierarchical Memory Storage [*Data processing*]
HMS .... Honeywells Manufacturing System [*Honeywell Information Systems Ltd.*] [*Software package*] [*British*] (NCC)
HN .... Host to Network [*Data processing*]
HNA .... Hierarchical Network Architecture (CAA)
HNA .... Hitachi Network Architecture (CAA)
HNDST .... Handset
HNE .... HN Engineering, Inc. [*Burnaby, BC, Canada*] [*Telecommunications*] (TSSD)
HNIL .... High-Noise-Immunity Logic
HNL .... Hourly Noise Level
HNLM .... High Noise-Level Margin
HNPA .... Home Numbering Plan Area [*AT & T*]
HO .... Hotel (TEL)
HOBIS .... Hotel Billing Information System [*Telecommunications*] (TEL)
HOCUS .... Hand or Computer Universal Simulation [*PE Computer Services Ltd.*] [*Software package*] [*British*]
HOGN .... Hogan Systems, Inc. [*NASDAQ symbol*] (NQ)
HOL .... High- [*or Higher-*] Order Language [*Data processing*]
HOLM .... Higher-Order Language Machine [*Data processing*] (KSC)
HOLWG ...... High- [*or Higher-*] Order Language Working Group [*Data processing*] (RDA)
HOMS .... Hydrological Operational Multipurpose Subprogramme [*World Meteorological Organization*] [*Information service*] (EISS)
HON .... Honeywell, Inc. [*Formerly, MH, M-H*] [*NYSE symbol*]
HONI .... Hon Industries, Inc. [*NASDAQ symbol*] (NQ)
HOP .... House Operating Tape [*Telecommunications*] (TEL)
HOP .... Hybrid Operating Program [*Data processing*] (IEEE)
HOPL .... History of Programing Languages
HOR .... Horizontal
HORIZ .... Horizontal Polarization
HOS .... High-Order Software [*Data processing*] (NASA)
HOS-STPL ... Hospital Operating System - Structured Programing Language [*Data processing*] (CSR)
HOT .... Hand Over Transmitter
HP .... Hewlett-Packard Co. (CIT)
HP .... High Pass [*Electronics*]
H/P .... High Position (MDG)
HP .... High-Positive (MDG)
HP .... Horsepower
HP .... Host Processor (CAA)
HPA .... Heuristic Path Algorithm (CAA)
HPA .... High-Power Amplifier
HPBW .... Half-Power Beamwidth (IEEE)
HPC .... Helicopter Performance Computer (NG)
HPCA .... High-Performance Communications Adapter (CAA)
HPDC .... High Pressure Data Center [*National Bureau of Standards*] [*Information service*] (EISS)
HPF .... High Pass Filter
HPF .... Highest Possible Frequency [*Electronics*]
HPI .... Height-Position Indicator (DEN)
HP-IB .... Hewlett-Packard Interface Bus [*Instrumentation*]
HPIR .... High-Probability-of-Intercept Receiver [*Telecommunications*] (IEEE)
HPL .... Hybrid Programing Language [*Data processing*]
HPT .... Head per Track (BUR)
HQ .... High Quality [*Home video systems*]
HR .... Hit Ratio (CAA)
HR .... Holding Register (CAA)
HR .... Hour
HRA .... Hemispherical Reflective Antenna
HRA .... HF [*High-Frequency*] Recovery Antenna (SKY)
HRC .... Hypothetical Reference Circuit [*Telecommunications*] (TEL)
HRFAX .... High-Resolution Facsimile [*Telecommunications*] (TEL)
HRIS .... House of Representatives Information System (CAA)
HRM .... Hardware Read-In Mode (CAA)
HRMR .... Human Read/Machine Read [*Microfilm memory system*]
HRNES .... Host Remote Node Entry System (CAA)
HRS .... Harris Corp. [*NYSE symbol*]
HRS .... Host Resident Software (OA)

HRSS	Host Resident Software System (CAA)
HRT	High-Resolution Tracker
HS	Half Subtractor [*Circuitry*]
HS	Handset
HSAC	High-Speed Analog Computer (DEN)
HSAM	Hierarchical Sequential Access Method [*Data processing*]
HSB	High-Speed Buffer (CAA)
HSB	High-Speed Bus [*Data processing*]
HSC	Hardware-Software Configuration [*Data processing*]
HSC	High-Speed Concentrator (CAA)
HSCF	Health Sciences Computing Facility [*UCLA*] (CIT)
HSCP	High-Speed Card Punch [*Data processing*]
HSCR	High-Speed Card Reader [*Data processing*]
HSCT	High-Speed Compound Terminal [*Data processing*] (MCD)
HSCT	Hughes Satellite Communications Terminal
HSCTT	High-Speed Card Teletypewriter Terminal [*Data processing*] (CET)
HSD	High-Speed Displacement (IEEE)
HSDA	High-Speed Data Acquisition [*Data processing*]
HSDB	High-Speed Data Buffer (CAA)
HSDL	High-Speed Data Line (CIT)
HSE	Home Sports Entertainment [*Cable-television system*]
HSEL	High-Speed Selector Channel (CAA)
HSELINE	Health and Safety Executive Online [*Health and Safety Executive*] [*Bibliographic database*] [*British*] (OBD)
H/SIR	Hardware/Software Integration Review (MCD)
HSM	Hierarchical Storage Manager
HSM	High-Speed Memory [*Data processing*] (TUT)
HSMIMP	High-Speed Modular Interface Message Processor
HSN	Hospital Satellite Network [*Los Angeles, CA*] [*Cable-television system*]
HSNP	High-Speed Nonimpact Printer [*Acronym pronounced "hisnip"*] [*Data processing*]
HSP	High-Speed Printer [*Data processing*]
HSPTAL	High-Speed Paper Tape Absolute Loader [*Data processing*] (MDG)
HSPTP	High-Speed Paper Tape Punch [*Data processing*]
HSPTR	High-Speed Paper Tape Reader [*Data processing*] (CET)
HSR	High-Speed Reader [*Data processing*]
HSS	Hierarchy Service System [*Toshiba Corp.*] (CAA)
HSS	High-Speed Storage [*Data processing*] (IEEE)
HSTTL	High-Speed Transistor-Transistor Logic
HSYS	Hale Systems, Inc. [*NASDAQ symbol*] (NQ)
HT	Hawaiian Telephone Co. [*NYSE symbol*] [*Delisted*]
H/T	Head per Track (CAA)
HT	High Tension
HT	Holding Time [*Telecommunications*] (TEL)
HT	Horizontal Tabulation [*Data processing*]
HTB	Hexadecimal to Binary (CAA)
HTC	Hybrid Technology Computer (CAA)
HTL	High Threshold Logic
HTL	Hotel Call, Time, and Charges Mandatory [*Telecommunications*] (TEL)
HTM	Hard Tube Modulator [*Electronics*]
HTN	Home Theatre Network [*In network name "HTN Plus"*] [*Cable-television system*]
HTN	Hughes Television Network [*New York, NY*] [*Cable-television system*]
HTS	Head, Track, and Selector (CAA)
HTS	Home Team Sports [*Cable-television system*]
HTS	Host-to-Satellite (CAA)
HTSS	Honeywell Time-Sharing System [*Data processing*] (IEEE)
HTTL	High-Power Transistor-Transistor Logic (IEEE)
HU	Hangup [*Telecommunications*] (TEL)
HU	High Usage [*Telecommunications*] (TEL)
HUCR	Harvard University Character Recognizer [*Data processing*]
HUD	Department of Housing and Urban Development
HUG	Hastech Users Group (EANO)
HUG	Honeywell Users Group (CAA)
HUG's	Home User Groups [*Data processing*]
HUG-SMS	Honeywell Users Group - Small and Medium Systems [*Later, NAHU*]
HUMARIS	Human Materials Resources Information System (DIT)
HUPATS	Heuristic Paper Trimming System (BUR)
HUT	Households Using Television [*Television ratings*]
HV	Hardware Virtualizer [*Data processing*] (IEEE)
HV	High Voltage
HVC	Hardened Voice Circuit (CET)
HVCH	Hardened Voice Channel (MSA)
HVG	High-Voltage Generator (OA)
HVIC	High-Voltage Integrated Circuit [*Data processing*]
HVN	Home View Network [*Cable-television system*]
HVP	Hayes Verification Protocol [*Data processing*]
HVR	Hardware Vector to Raster (CAA)
HVSF	Honeywell Verification Simulation Facility (NASA)
HVTS	High-Volume Time Sharing (CAA)
HW	Handset, Wall Model (TEL)
HW	Hardware [*Data processing*] (NASA)
HW	Howler [*Communications; electronics*]
HWI	Hardware Interpreter (CAA)
HWP	Hewlett-Packard Co. [*NYSE symbol*]
HWY	Highway
HYB	Hybrid (MSA)
HYBALL	Hybrid Analog Logic Language (MCD)
HYCOL	Hybrid Computer Link
HYCOTRAN	Hybrid Computer Translator
HYDAC	Hybrid Digital-Analog Computing [*System*] [*Satellite*]
HYDAPT	Hybrid Digital-Analog and Pulse Time
HYTRESS	High-Test Recorder and Simulator System (IEEE)
Hz	Hertz [*Symbol*] [*SI unit of frequency*]

I

I	Current [*Electronics*] (CDH)	
I	Input	
I	Instantaneous	
I	Instruction (CAA)	
I	Interference [*Broadcasting*]	
I	Intermittent Operation during the Time Indicated [*Broadcasting*]	
I (Bank)	Instruction Bank [*Data processing*]	
IA	Infra-Audible [*Sound*]	
IA	Integrated Adapter (CAA)	
IA	Intelligent Assistant [*Data processing*]	
IA	Intermediate Amplifier	
IAAB	Inter-American Association of Broadcasters	
IAB	Interrupt Address to Bus [*Data processing*] (CAA)	
IABC	International Association of Business Communicators	
IAC	Industry Advisory Conference [*Underwriters Laboratories*] [*Telecommunications*]	
IAC	Information Access Corporation [*Information service*] (EISS)	
IAC	Interactive Array Computer (CAA)	
IAC	Interarray Communications (NVT)	
IAC	International Accounting Center (TEL)	
IAC	International Advisory Committee [*ANSI*]	
IAC	International Apple Core	
IAC	International Association for Cybernetics [*See also AIC*] (EANO)	
IAC/ADP	Interagency Committee on Automatic Data Processing [*Office of Management and Budget*]	
IACCI	International Association of Computer Crime Investigators [*Oakland, CA*] (EANO)	
IACDLA	International Advisory Committee on Documentation, Libraries, and Archives [*UNESCO*] (DIT)	
IACP	International Association of Computer Programers (CAH)	
IACS	IAL Consultancy Services [*Southall, England*] [*Telecommunications*] (TSSD)	
IACS	Integrated Acoustic Communication System (NVT)	
IACS	Interactive Computer System [*Information science*]	
IAD	Initial Address Designator (CAA)	
IADIC	Integration Analog-to-Digital Converter (IEEE)	
IADPC	Interagency Data Processing Committee	
IADPG	Intelligence Automatic Data Processing Group	
IAEA	International Atomic Energy Agency [*United Nations*] [*Vienna, Austria*] [*Database originator and operator*]	
IAER	Institute of Applied Economic Research [*Concordia University*] [*Canada*] [*Research center*] (RCD)	
IAF	Interactive Facility [*Control Data Corp.*] (CAA)	
IAG	Industry Advisory Group [*Underwriters Laboratories*] [*Telecommunications*]	
IAG	International Applications Group [*IFIP*]	
IAI	Information Associates of Ithaca [*Information service*] (EISS)	
IAI	Initial Address Information [*Telecommunications*] (TEL)	
IAIS	Industrial Aerodynamics Information Service [*British*] (EISS)	
IAL	International Algebraic Language [*Programing language*] [*Replaced by ALGOL*]	
IAL	International Algorithmic Language [*Data processing*] (BUR)	
IAL	Investment Analysis Language [*Data processing*] (BUR)	
IALE	Instrumented Architectural Level Emulation (CAA)	
IAM	ILA [*Instruction Look Ahead*] Associative Memory [*Data processing*]	
IAM	Indefinite Admittance Matrix [*Network analysis*] (IEEE)	
IAM	Initial Address Message (TEL)	
IAM	Interactive Algebraic Manipulation [*Data processing*]	
IAMACS	International Association for Mathematics and Computers in Simulation (CAA)	
IAP	Image Array Processor (CAA)	
IAP	Industry Application Program [*Data processing*] (IBMDP)	
IAP	Interactive Programing [*Data processing*]	
IAP	Interarray Processor (NVT)	
IAP	Internal Array Processor [*Data General Corp.*] (CAA)	
IAPR	International Association for Pattern Recognition (EANO)	
IAR	Instruction Address Register [*Data processing*] (MDG)	
IAR	Interrupt Address Register (CAA)	
IARU	International Amateur Radio Union	
IAS	Interactive Applications Supervisor (CAH)	
IASC	International Association for Statistical Computing (EANO)	
IASSIST	International Association for Social Science Information Service and Technology	
IASTED	International Association of Science and Technology for Development	
IASU	International Association of Satellite Users [*Later, IASUS*] (EANO)	
IASUS	International Association of Satellite Users and Suppliers [*Mclean, VA*] [*Formerly, IASU*] [*Telecommunications*] (EANO)	
IAT	Institute for Advanced Technology [*Control Data Corp.*] [*Rockville, MD*] [*Telecommunications*]	
IAT	International Atomic Time	
IATA	International Air Transport [*formerly, Traffic*] Association	
IATC	International Air Traffic Communications	
IATCR	International Air Traffic Communications Receiver Station	
IATCS	International Air Traffic Communications Station	
IATCS	International Air Traffic Communications System (MCD)	
IATCT	International Air Traffic Communications Transmitter Station	
IATE	International Accounting and Traffic Analysis Equipment [*Telecommunications*] (TEL)	
IATN	International Association of Telecomputer Networks [*Winter Springs, FL*] [*Telecommunications*] (EANO)	
IATSC	International Aeronautical Telecommunications Switching Center	
IATV	Interactive Alphanumeric Television (CIT)	
IAV	Vidion/International Association of Video (EANO)	
IAVC	Instantaneous Automatic Video Control (IEEE)	
IAVC	Instantaneous Automatic Volume Control [*Electronics*]	
IAVTC	International Audio-Visual Technical Centre [*Netherlands*] (DIT)	
IB	Identifier Block (CAA)	
IB	Information Bureau [*Telecommunications*] (TEL)	
IB	Input Buffer [*Telecommunications*] (TEL)	
IB	Input Bus [*Data processing*] (CAA)	
IB	Instruction Bank [*Data processing*]	
IB	Instruction Bus [*Data processing*] (CAA)	
IB	Interface Bus [*Data processing*]	
IB	Internal Bus [*Data processing*] (CAA)	
IB	International Broadcasting	
IBA	Independent Broadcasting Authority [*Formerly, ITA*] [*British*]	
IBC	Integrated Business Computers [*Chatsworth, CA*] [*Software manufacturer*] (DASOS)	
IBES	Institutional Brokers Estimate System [*Lynch, Jones & Ryan*] [*Database*] [*Information service*] (EISS)	
IBES	International Business Earth Stations [*Communications Satellite Corp.*]	
IBEW	International Brotherhood of Electrical Workers	
IBFI	International Business Forms Industries [*Arlington, VA*]	
IBG	Inter Block Gap	
IBI	Intergovernmental Bureau for Informatics [*Rome, Italy*] [*Telecommunications*] (EANO)	
IBI	International Bureau for Informatics	
IBICT	Instituto Brasileiro de Informacao em Ciencia e Tecnologia [*Brazilian Institute for Information in Science and Technology*] [*Information service*] (EISS)	
IBI-ICC	Intergovernmental Bureau for Informatics - International Computation Center	
IBIS	Interactive Business Information Systems [*Santa Ana, CA*] [*Software manufacturer*] (DASOS)	
IBIS	International Bank Information System (CAA)	
IBIS	International Book Information Service (NITA)	
IBM	I Buy Money [*Humorous translation of the letters in IBM Corp., and referring to the appeal of investing in its stocks*]	
IBM	International Business Machines Corp. [*White Plains, NY*] [*Computer manufacturer*] [*NYSE symbol*] [*Toronto Stock Exchange symbol*]	
IBM J	IBM [*International Business Machines Corp.*] Journal of Research and Development [*A publication*]	
IBM J R D	IBM [*International Business Machines Corp.*] Journal of Research and Development [*A publication*]	
IBM J Res	IBM [*International Business Machines Corp.*] Journal of Research and Development [*A publication*]	
IBM J Res Dev	IBM [*International Business Machines Corp.*] Journal of Research and Development [*A publication*]	

Computer & Telecommunications Acronyms

IBM J Res and Dev ... IBM [*International Business Machines Corp.*] Journal of Research and Development [*A publication*]
IBM J Res Develop ... IBM [*International Business Machines Corp.*] Journal of Research and Development [*A publication*]
IBM Systems J ... IBM [*International Business Machines Corp.*] Systems Journal [*A publication*]
IBM Syst J ... IBM [*International Business Machines Corp.*] Systems Journal [*A publication*]
IBM Tech Discl Bull ... IBM [*International Business Machines Corp.*] Technical Disclosure Bulletin [*A publication*]
IBM Tech Disclosure Bull ... IBM [*International Business Machines Corp.*] Technical Disclosure Bulletin [*A publication*]
IBM TSS ..... International Business Machine's Timesharing System   (TEL)
IBM User ..... IBM [*International Business Machines Corp.*] System User [*A publication*]
IBOL .... Interactive Business-Oriented Language   (CAA)
IBR .... Institute for Behavioral Research [*York University*] [*Canada*] [*Research center*]   (EISS)
IBRD .... International Bank for Reconstruction and Development [*Also known as World Bank*]
IBS .... Independent Business Systems, Inc. [*Livermore, CA*] [*Hardware manufacturer*]   (DASO)
IBS .... Intercollegiate Broadcasting System
IBST .... International Bureau of Software Test
IBU .... International Business Unit [*British*] [*Information service*]   (EISS)
IBW .... Impulse Bandwidth   (MCD)
IC .... Identification Code   (CAA)
I/C .... Incoming [*Telecommunications*]   (TEL)
IC .... Instruction Cell   (CAA)
IC .... Instruction Counter [*Data processing*]
I & C .... Instrumentation and Communications [*Cable system*]   (KSC)
IC .... Integrated Circuit [*Electronics*]
IC .... Intercommunications
IC .... Intercomputer   (MCD)
IC .... Intercomputer Channel   (KSC)
IC .... Interfaces in Computing [*A publication*]
IC .... Internal Connection [*Electronics*]
ICA .... Immediate Constituent Analyzer [*Data processing*]   (DIT)
ICA .... Integrated Circuit Array
ICA .... Integrated Communications Adapter   (MCD)
ICA .... Intercomputer Adapter   (CAA)
ICA .... Intergovernmental Council for ADP [*Automatic Data Processing*]
ICA .... International Communication Agency [*Also, USICA*] [*Formerly called BECA and USIA, it later became known again as USIA*]
ICA .... International Communication Association [*Formerly, Industrial Communication Association*] [*Austin, TX*]
ICA .... International Communications Association [*Dallas, TX*] [*Telecommunications*]   (CSR)
ICAD .... Integrated Control and Display
ICADE .... Interactive Computer-Aided Design Evaluation
ICAE .... Integrated Communications Adapter Extended   (BUR)
ICAI .... Intelligent Computer-Assisted Instruction
ICAM .... Integrated Communications Access Method [*Data processing*]
ICAM .... Integrated Computer-Aided Manufacturing
ICAMRS ..... International Civil Aviation Message Routing System
ICAN .... Individual Circuit Analysis [*Telecommunications*]   (TEL)
ICAN .... Integrated Circuit Analysis [*Data processing*]
ICAR .... Inventory of Canadian Agri-Food Research [*Agriculture Canada*] [*Database*]   (CUAD)
ICASE .... Institute for Computer Applications in Science and Engineering [*Universities Space Research Association*] [*Research center*]   (RCD)
ICB .... Incoming Call Barred [*Telecommunications*]   (TEL)
ICB .... Individual Case Basis   (TEL)
ICB .... Internal Common Bus [*Data processing*]   (CAA)
ICB .... International Computer Bibliography [*A publication of National Computing Center*]
ICBRSD ...... International Council for Building Research, Studies, and Documentation   (DIT)
ICC .... Integrated Chip Circuit
ICC .... Integrated Communications Control   (MCD)
ICC .... Interchannel Communicator   (MCD)
ICC .... Intercomputer Channel   (NASA)
ICC .... Intercomputer Communication   (MCD)
ICC .... Interface Control Chart   (NASA)
ICC .... International Communications Corporation [*Miami, FL*]
ICC .... International Computaprint Corporation
ICC .... International Computation Center [*Sponsored by UNESCO*] [*Rome, Italy*]
ICC .... International Conference on Communications [*IEEE*]
ICC .... Interprocessor Communication and Control Routine   (MCD)
ICC .... Invitational Computer Conference   (CAA)
ICCA .... Independent Computer Consultants Association [*Database producer*]   (EANO)
ICCA .... International Computer Chess Association
ICCA .... International Conference on Computer Applications [*in developing countries*] [*1977*]
ICCB .... Intermediate Configuration Control Board [*Western Electric*]
ICCC .... International Color Computer Club   (EANO)
ICCC .... International Council for Computer Communication [*Washington, DC*]   (EANO)
ICCE .... International Council for Computers in Education [*University of Oregon*] [*Eugene, OR*]   (EANO)
ICCF .... Interactive Computing and Control Facility [*IBM Corp. program product*]
ICCF .... Interexchange Carrier and Carrier Forum [*Exchange Carriers Standards Association*] [*Telecommunications*]
ICCH .... International Conference on Computers and the Humanities
ICCL .... Interface Control Configuration List   (DDI)
ICCP .... Institute for Certification of Computer Professionals [*Des Plaines, IL*]   (EANO)
ICCP .... Integrated Communication Control Panel   (MCD)
ICCP .... Interface Coordination and Control Procedure   (NASA)
ICCPC .... International Computing Center's Preparatory Committee
ICCS .... Intercomputer Communication System
ICCU .... Intercomputer Compatibility Unit [*Data processing*]
ICD .... International Congress for Data Processing   (CAA)
ICDB .... Integrated Corporate Database   (IDA)
ICDDB .... Internal Control Description Database   (CAA)
ICDL .... Integrated Circuit Description Language   (CAA)
ICDL .... Interface Control Documentation Log   (KSC)
ICDL .... Internal Control Description Language   (CAA)
ICDR .... Inward Call Detail Recording [*Telecommunications*]   (TEL)
IC DRUM .... Intercommunication Drum   (MSA)
ICE .... In-Circuit Emulator
ICE .... Instrumentation Communication Equipment   (NASA)
ICE .... Interference Cancellation Equipment [*Telecommunications*]
ICE .... Intermediate Cable Equalizers   (IEEE)
ICECAN ..... Iceland-Canada Submarine Cable System [*Telecommunications*]   (TEL)
ICEEC .... International Congress of Electrical and Electronic Communications
ICES .... Integrated Civil Engineering System [*Programing language*] [*Data processing*]
ICF .... Integrated Control Facility [*Sperry UNIVAC*]   (CAA)
ICF .... Interactive Communications Feature [*IBM Corp.*]   (CAA)
ICF .... Intercommunication Flip-Flop [*Data processing*]
ICFAR .... Indianapolis Center for Advanced Research [*Indiana University - Purdue University at Indianapolis*] [*Research center*]   (RCD)
ICG .... Interactive Computer Graphics
ICGAD .... IEEE. Computer Graphics and Applications [*A publication*]
ICI .... Information Concepts, Incorporated
ICI .... Information Consultants, Incorporated [*Information service*]   (EISS)
ICI .... Intelligent Communications Interface   (IEEE)
ICIP .... International Conference on Information Processing [*Paris, 1959*]
ICIS .... Interactive Construction Industry System [*NCR Ltd.*] [*Software package*] [*British*]   (NCC)
ICJ .... Incoming Junction [*Telecommunications*]   (TEL)
ICJL .... Institute for Computers in Jewish Life [*Chicago, IL*]   (EANO)
ICKCMX ..... Integrated Circuit Keyset Central Multiplexer   (CAAL)
ICL .... Inserted Connection Losses [*Telecommunications*]
ICL .... Integrated Circuit Logic
ICL .... Intercommunication Logic   (CAA)
ICL .... International Computers Limited [*Great Britain*] [*Computer manufacturer*]
ICL .... Interpretive Coding Language   (CAA)
ICL Tech J .... ICL [*International Computers Limited*] Technical Journal [*A publication*]
ICM .... Instruction Control Memory   (CAA)
ICM .... Instrumentation and Communications Monitor
ICM .... Integrated Circuit Mask
ICM .... Intercommunication   (MSA)
ICM .... Interface Coordination Memo   (MCD)
ICM .... Interference Control Monitor
ICMA .... Institute for Computational Mathematics and Applications [*University of Pittsburgh*] [*Research center*]   (RCD)
ICMS .... Integrated Circuit and Message Switch
ICMST .... International Conference on Machine Searching and Translation
ICN .... Integrated Computer Network   (CAA)
ICN .... Interface Change Notice   (MCD)
ICN .... Intromogenous Computer Network
ICO .... Input Current Offset [*Data processing*]
ICO .... International Computer Orphanage [*Mississauga, ON*]   (EANO)
ICOCS .... Interim Circuit Order Control System [*Bell System*]
ICON .... [*A*] programing language [*1977*]   (CSR)
ICONDA ..... International Construction Database [*Information Centre for Regional Planning and Building Construction of the Fraunhofer-Society*] [*Database*]   (CUAD)
ICOS .... Interactive COBOL Operating System   (CAA)
ICOT .... ICOT Corp. [*NASDAQ symbol*]   (NQ)
ICP .... Incoming [*Message*] Process [*Telecommunications*]   (TEL)
ICP .... Initial Connection Protocol   (CAA)
IC-P .... Intelligent Copier-Printer [*Electrophotography*]
ICP .... Interface Control Panel   (MCD)
ICP .... International Computer Programs, Inc. [*Information service*]
ICP .... International Congress of Publishers   (DIT)
ICPAC .... Instantaneous Compressor Performance Analysis Computer
ICP Admin ... ICP [*International Computer Programs, Inc.*] Interface Administrative and Accounting [*A publication*]
ICP Bank Indus ... ICP [*International Computer Programs, Inc.*] Interface Banking Industry [*A publication*]
ICP DP Mgmt ... ICP [*International Computer Programs, Inc.*] Interface Data Processing Management [*A publication*]

Computer & Telecommunications Acronyms

ICPR	Integrated Circuit Parameter Retrieval [*Information Handling Services*] [*Database*] (CUAD)
ICPSR	Interuniversity Consortium for Political and Social Research [*University of Michigan*] [*Ann Arbor, MI*]
ICR	Independent Component Release [*Data processing*] (IBMDP)
ICR	Indirect Control Register [*Data processing*] (CAA)
ICR	Input Control Register [*Data processing*] (CAA)
ICR	Institute for Communications Research [*Texas Tech University*] [*Research center*] (RCD)
ICR	Institute for Computer Research [*University of Waterloo*] [*Canada*] [*Research center*] (RCD)
ICR	Interface Compatibility Record (NASA)
ICR	International Consumer Reports [*Consumers' Association*] [*London, England*] [*Information service*] (EISS)
ICR	Interrupt Control Register [*Data processing*]
ICRDB	International Cancer Research Data Bank [*National Cancer Institute*] [*Bethesda, MD*] [*Database producer*] (EISS)
ICRH	Institute for Computer Research in the Humanities [*New York University*]
ICS	Induction Communications System
ICS	Industrial Control System
ICS	Information Centers Service [*United States Information Agency*] (EISS)
ICS	Infrared Communications System
ICS	Inland Computer Service (IEEE)
ICS	Input Control Subsystem (OA)
ICS	Institute for Cognitive Science [*University of California, San Diego*] [*Research center*] (RCD)
ICS	Institute of Cognitive Science [*University of Colorado - Boulder*] [*Research center*] (RCD)
ICS	Institution of Computer Sciences [*British*] (DIT)
I & C(S)	Instrumentation and Communication (System) (SKY)
ICS	Insurance Communication Service [*IBM Information Network*] [*Tampa, FL*] [*Telecommunications*] (TSSD)
ICS	Integrated Communication Systems, Inc. [*Atlanta, GA*] [*Telecommunications*] (IEEE)
ICS	Integrated Control Storage [*Data processing*]
ICS	Interactive Communications Software (CAA)
ICS	Intercommunication Control Station (KSC)
ICS	Intercommunications System
ICS	Interlinked Computerized Storage and Processing System of Food and Agricultural Data [*United Nations*] [*Databank*] [*Information service*] (EISS)
ICS	International Chamber of Shipping
ICS	International Communications Sciences
ICS	Interphone Control Station
ICS	Interphone Control System (DDI)
ICS	Interpretive Computer Simulator
ICS	Intracommunication System (CIT)
ICS	Inventory Control System [*Data processing*] (TUT)
ICSC	Interim Communications Satellite Committee
ICSC	International Communications Satellite Consortium (MCD)
ICSCA	Institute for Computing Science and Computer Applications [*University of Texas at Austin*] [*Research center*] (RCD)
ICS/DMC	Institute for Continuing Studies in Design, Management and Communication [*University of Cincinnati*] [*Research center*] (RCD)
ICSMP	Interactive Continuous Systems Modeling Program (OA)
ICSRI	Intelligent Computer Systems Research Institute [*University of Miami*] [*Research center*] (RCD)
ICSSID	International Committee for Social Science Information and Documentation [*France*] [*Information service*] (EISS)
ICST	Institute [*formerly, Center*] for Computer Sciences and Technology [*National Bureau of Standards*]
ICSU	International Council of Scientific Unions [*Paris, France*] [*Sponsors CODATA*]
ICSWBD	Interior Communications Switchboard (VIT)
ICT	Incoming Trunk [*Telecommunications*] (BUR)
ICT	Institute of Computer Technology
ICT	Integrated Computer Telemetry
ICT	International Computers and Tabulators Ltd. [*Later, ICL*]
ICTV	Interactive Cable Television
ICU	Instruction Control Unit
ICU	Integrated Control Unit (CAA)
ICU	International [*or Internal*] Communication Unit [*Telecommunications*] (TEL)
ICUP	Individual Circuit Usage and Peg Count [*Telecommunications*] (TEL)
ICW	Initial Condition Word [*Data processing*] (CAA)
ICW	Input Control Word [*Data processing*] (MCD)
ICW	Interface Control Word [*Data processing*] (CAA)
ICW	Interrupted Continuous Waves [*Electronics*]
ICYT	Instituto de Informacion y Documentacion en Ciencia y Tecnologia [*Institute for Information and Documentation in Science and Technology*] [*Spain*] [*Database originator and host*] [*Information service*] (EISS)
ID	Identification [*Data processing*]
ID	Identifier [*Online database field identifier*]
ID	Image Digitizer [*Data processing*]
ID	Indicating Device (CDH)
ID	Inside Diameter
I/D	Instruction/Data (IEEE)
ID	Insulation Displacement (DEEC)
I & D	Integrate and Dump Detection [*Telecommunications*] (TEL)
ID	Intelligent Digitizer (CAA)
ID	Interactive Debugging (IEEE)
ID	Intercommunication Devices (MCD)
ID	Interconnection Device (MCD)
ID	Interdigital [*Telecommunications*] (IEEE)
ID	Item Description
IDA	Input Data Assembler
IDA	Integrated Digital Access [*Telecommunications*]
IDA	Integrated Disk Adapter [*Sperry UNIVAC*] (CAA)
IDA	Intelligent Data Access (CAA)
IDA	Interactive Debugging Aid (CAA)
IDA	International Database Association [*Defunct*] (EANO)
IDAC	Instant Data Access Control [*National Design Center, Inc.*] [*Information service*] (EISS)
IDAC	Integrated Digital-Analog Converter (MCD)
IDAC	Interconnecting Digital-Analog Converter (NG)
IDAC	Interim Digital-Analog Converter (VIT)
IDAM	Indexed Direct Access Method (CAA)
IDAPS	Image Data Processing System
IDAS	Information Displays Automatic Drafting System (IEEE)
IDAS	Integrated Data Acquisition System (MCD)
IDAST	Interpolated Data and Speech Transmission [*Data processing*]
IDB	Industrial Data Bank Department [*Gulf Organization for Industrial Consulting*] [*Information service*] (EISS)
IDB	Input Data Buffer (CAA)
IDB	Integrated Data Base [*Data processing*] (TUT)
IDB	International Data Base [*Bureau of Census*] [*Database*] (FDB)
IDBMS	Integrated Database Management System (CAA)
IDC	Image Dissector Camera
IDC	IMBLMS [*Integrated Medical Behavioral Measurement System*] Digital Computer (MCD)
IDC	Information Dynamics Corporation
IDC	Input Display Console [*Data processing*]
IDC	Integrated Disk Control [*NCR Corp.*] (CAA)
IDC	Integrated Displays and Controls (MCD)
IDC	Interceptor Distance Computer
IDC	Internal Data Channel (CAA)
IDC	International Data Corporation [*Waltham, MA*] [*Information service*] (EISS)
IDCC	Integrated Data Communications Controller (CAA)
IDCCC	Interim Data Communications Collection Center
IDCMA	Independent Data Communications Manufacturers Association
IDCP	International Data Collecting Platform (TEL)
IDCS	Image Dissector Camera System
IDCS	Initial Defense Communications Satellite (MCD)
IDCS	Instrumentation/Data Collection System
IDCS	Integrated Data Coding System (NG)
IDCS	International Digital Channel Service [*Federal Trade Commission*] (CAA)
IDD	Integrated Data Dictionary (CAA)
IDD	International Direct Dialing [*Telecommunications*]
IDDC	International Demographic Data Center [*Bureau of the Census*] [*Washington, DC*] [*Database*] [*Information service*] (EISS)
IDDD	International Demographic Data Directory [*Agency for International Development*] (EISS)
IDDD	International Direct Distance Dialing [*AT & T*]
IDDF	Intermediate Digital Distribution Frame [*Telecommunications*] (TEL)
IDDS	Improved Data Display System
IDDS	Instrumentation Data Distribution System (MUGU)
IDDS	Integrated Data Display System
IDDS	International Digital Data Service [*Western Union Corp.*] [*Data transmission service*]
IDE	Interactive Data Entry (CAA)
IDEA	Ideassociates, Inc. [*Billerica, MA*] [*Telecommunications*] (TSSD)
IDEA	Index for Design Engineering Applications [*Data retrieval service*] [*Product engineering*]
IDEA	Inductive Data Exploration and Analysis [*Data processing*]
IDEA	Interactive Data Entry Access [*Data General Corp.*] (CAA)
IDEA	Interface and Display Electronics Assembly
IDEAS	Integrated Design and Engineering Automated System (IEEE)
IDEDS	International Development Education Documentation Service [*University of Pittsburgh*] (EISS)
IDEF	Integrated System Definition Language [*Data processing*] (IEEE)
IDENT	Identification (AFM)
IDF	Image Description File (CAA)
IDF	Integrated Data File
IDF	Interactive Dialogue Facility [*Programing language*] (CSR)
IDF	Intermediate Distributing Frame [*Telecommunications*]
IDF	Internal Delay Factor [*Data processing*]
IDFT	Inverse Discrete Fourier Transform [*Electronics*] (IEEE)
IDG	International Data Group [*Publisher of computer magazines*]
IDHS	Information Data Handling System (DDI)
IDHS	Integrated Data Handling System (DDI)
IDHS	Intelligence Data Handling System (AFM)
IDI	Improved Data Interchange
IDI	Intelligent Dual Interface (CAA)
IDI	Intercomp Design, Incorporated [*Neshanic Station, NJ*] [*Telecommunications*] (TSSD)
IDID	Industrial Documentation and Information Department [*Industrial Development Center for Arab States*] [*Information service*] (EISS)

Acronym	Definition
IDIIOM	Information Displays, Incorporated, Input-Output Machine
IDIMS	Interactive Digital Image Manipulation System [*Minicomputer*]
IDIOT	Instrumentation Digital On-Line Transcriber [*Data processing*]
IDIPS	Intelligence Data Input Packages (MCD)
IDIS	Institut fuer Dokumentation und Information ueber Sozialmedizin und Offentliches Gesundheitswesen [*Information retrieval*] (ODIN)
IDIS	Institut fuer Dokumentation, Information, und Statistik [*Institute for Documentation, Information, and Statistics*] [*Information service on cancer research*] [*Germany*] (EISS)
IDL	Information Description Language (CAA)
IDL	Instruction Definition Language (CAA)
IDLC	Integrated Digital Logic Circuit
IDMAS	Interactive Database Manipulator and Summarizer (CAA)
IDMH	Input Destination Message Handler (CAA)
IDMS	Integrated Database Management System
IDN	Integrated Digital Network [*Telecommunications*]
IDN	Intelligent Data Network (CAA)
IDNC	Integrated Direct Numerical Control [*Burroughs Machines Ltd.*] [*Software package*] [*British*] (NCC)
IDOS	Interactive Disk Operating System [*Computer Associates, Inc.*] (CAA)
IDOS	Interrupt Disk Operating System (CAA)
IDP	Image Data Processor
IDP	Industrial Data Processing
IDP	Information Data Processing (VIT)
IDP	Input Data Processor (CET)
IDP	Institute of Data Processing [*London, England*]
IDP	Integrated Data Presentation
IDP	Integrated Data Processing
IDP	Interdigit Pause [*Telecommunications*] (TEL)
IDPC	Integrated Data Processing Center
IDPI	International Data Processing Institute (MCD)
IDPM	Institute of Data Processing Management [*British*] (DEEC)
IDP Rep	IDP [*Information and Data Base Publishing*] Report [*United States*] [*A publication*]
IDPS	Instrument Data Processing System
IDPS	Integrated Data Processing System
IDPS	Interactive Direct Processing System [*NCR Corp.*] (CAA)
IDPS	Interface Digital Processor (MCD)
IDPY	Information Displays [*NASDAQ symbol*] (NQ)
IDR	Identification Record [*Data processing*] (MCD)
IDR	Incremental Digital Recorder
IDR	Input Data Request
IDRC	International Development Research Centre [*Canada*] [*Information service*]
IDS	Image Display System
IDS	Information Data Search, Inc. [*Information service*] (EISS)
IDS	Information Display System (CAA)
IDS	Input Data Strobe
IDS	Integrated Data Store [*or System*] [*Honeywell, Inc.*] [*Data processing*]
IDS	Integrated Display Situation
IDS	Intelligence Data System (DDI)
IDS	Interactive Data System [*Data processing*]
IDS	Interactive Display System (CAA)
IDS	Interagency Dialing System [*Telephones*]
IDS	Interdepartmental Dial System [*Telephones*]
IDS	Interface Data Sheet (NASA)
IDS	Interface Design Specification (CAAL)
IDS	Internal Distribution System [*Television*]
IDS	International Data Sciences, Inc. [*Lincoln, RI*] [*Hardware manufacturer*] (DASO)
IDSCP	Initial Defense Satellite Communications Project [*Telecommunications*] (TEL)
IDSI	Interactive Data Services, Incorporated [*Database producer*] [*Information service*] (EISS)
IDSS	ICAM [*Integrated Computer-Aided Manufacturing*] Decision Support System (IEEE)
IDT	Intelligent Data Terminal (CAA)
IDT	Interactive Display Terminal (MCD)
IDT	Interdigital Transducer [*Physics*]
IDT	International Data Technology, Inc. [*Chicago, IL*] [*Software manufacturer*] (DASOS)
IDT	Interrupt-Descriptor Table [*Data processing*]
IDTP	Integrated Data Transmittal Package
IDU	Interface Demonstration Unit (NASA)
IDU	Intermittent Drive Unit
IDVM	Integrating Digital Voltmeter
IDW	Institut fuer Dokumentationswesen [*West German*] (OA)
IDWD	Input Data Word (MCD)
IDYN	Interdyne Co. [*NASDAQ symbol*] (NQ)
IE	Interrupt Enable [*Data processing*] (CAA)
IEC	Integrated Electronic Components (BUR)
IEC	International Electronics Corporation (MUGU)
IEC	International Electrotechnical Commission [*Standards body*] [*Geneva, Switzerland*] [*See also CEI*]
IECI	Industrial Electronics and Control Instrumentation (MCD)
IECMB	IEEE. Transactions on Communications [*A publication*]
IEE	Institution of Electrical Engineers [*London, England*] [*Database producer*]
IEEE	Institute of Electrical and Electronics Engineers [*New York, NY*] [*Document publisher*]
IEEE Acoust	IEEE. Transactions on Acoustics, Speech, and Signal Processing [*A publication*]
IEEE Antenn	IEEE. Transactions on Antennas and Propagation [*A publication*]
IEEE Circ S	IEEE. Transactions on Circuits and Systems [*A publication*]
IEEE Commun	IEEE. Transactions on Communications [*A publication*]
IEEE Commun Mag	IEEE. Communications Magazine [*A publication*]
IEEE Commun Soc Mag	IEEE. Communications Society Magazine [*A publication*]
IEEE Comput	IEEE. Transactions on Computers [*A publication*]
IEEE Comput Graphics and Appl	IEEE. Computer Graphics and Applications [*A publication*]
IEEE Comput Group News	IEEE. Computer Group News [*A publication*]
IEEE-CS	Institute of Electrical and Electronics Engineers - Computer Society
IEEE Device	IEEE. Transactions on Electron Devices [*A publication*]
IEEE Elmagn	IEEE. Transactions on Electromagnetic Compatibility [*A publication*]
IEEE Info T	IEEE. Transactions on Information Theory [*A publication*]
IEEE Instr	IEEE. Transactions on Instrumentation and Measurement [*A publication*]
IEEE J Q El	IEEE. Journal of Quantum Electronics [*A publication*]
IEEE J Quantum Electron	IEEE. Journal of Quantum Electronics [*A publication*]
IEEE J Sel Areas Commun	IEEE. Journal on Selected Areas in Communications [*A publication*]
IEEE J Soli	IEEE. Journal of Solid-State Circuits [*A publication*]
IEEE J Solid-State Circuits	IEEE. Journal of Solid-State Circuits [*A publication*]
IEEE Magnet	IEEE. Transactions on Magnetics [*A publication*]
IEEE Micr T	IEEE. Transactions on Microwave Theory and Techniques [*A publication*]
IEEE Prof C	IEEE. Transactions on Professional Communications [*A publication*]
IEEE Reliab	IEEE. Transactions on Reliability [*A publication*]
IEEE S	IEEE. Spectrum [*A publication*]
IEEE Spectr	IEEE. Spectrum [*A publication*]
IEEE Spectrum	IEEE. Spectrum [*A publication*]
IEEE Syst M	IEEE. Transactions on Systems, Man, and Cybernetics [*A publication*]
IEEE T El Dev	IEEE. Transactions on Electron Devices [*A publication*]
IEEE Trans	IEEE. Transactions on Computers [*A publication*]
IEEE Trans Acoust Speech Signal Process	IEEE. Transactions on Acoustics, Speech, and Signal Processing [*A publication*]
IEEE Trans Antennas Propag	IEEE. Transactions on Antennas and Propagation [*A publication*]
IEEE Trans Antennas Propagat	IEEE. Transactions on Antennas and Propagation [*A publication*]
IEEE Trans Antennas and Propagation	IEEE. Transactions on Antennas and Propagation [*A publication*]
IEEE Trans ASSP	IEEE. Transactions on Acoustics, Speech, and Signal Processing [*A publication*]
IEEE Trans CAS	IEEE. Transactions on Circuits and Systems [*A publication*]
IEEE Trans Circuits & Syst	IEEE. Transactions on Circuits and Systems [*A publication*]
IEEE Trans Circuits and Syst	IEEE. Transactions on Circuits and Systems [*A publication*]
IEEE Trans Circuits and Systems	IEEE. Transactions on Circuits and Systems [*A publication*]
IEEE Trans Com	IEEE. Transactions on Communications [*A publication*]
IEEE Trans Comm	IEEE. Transactions on Communications [*A publication*]
IEEE Trans Commun Electron	IEEE. Transactions on Communication and Electronics [*A publication*]
IEEE Trans Commun Syst	IEEE. Transactions on Communications Systems [*A publication*]
IEEE Trans Commun Technol	IEEE. Transactions on Communication Technology [*Later, IEEE Transactions on Communications*] [*A publication*]
IEEE Trans Components Hybrids Manuf Technol	IEEE. Transactions on Components, Hybrids, and Manufacturing Technology [*A publication*]
IEEE Trans Components Hybrids and Manuf Technol	IEEE. Transactions on Components, Hybrids, and Manufacturing Technology [*A publication*]
IEEE Trans Comput	IEEE. Transactions on Computers [*A publication*]
IEEE Trans Computers	IEEE. Transactions on Computers [*A publication*]
IEEE Trans Com Tech	IEEE. Transactions on Communication Technology [*Later, IEEE Transactions on Communications*] [*A publication*]
IEEE Trans Electromagn Compat	IEEE. Transactions on Electromagnetic Compatibility [*A publication*]
IEEE Trans Electron Comput	IEEE. Transactions on Electronic Computers [*United States*] [*A publication*]
IEEE Trans Electron Devices	IEEE. Transactions on Electron Devices [*A publication*]
IEEE Trans Information Theory	IEEE. Transactions on Information Theory [*A publication*]
IEEE Trans Inf Theory	IEEE. Transactions on Information Theory [*A publication*]
IEEE Trans Instrum Meas	IEEE. Transactions on Instrumentation and Measurement [*A publication*]
IEEE Trans Instrum and Meas	IEEE. Transactions on Instrumentation and Measurement [*A publication*]

Computer & Telecommunications Acronyms

IEEE Trans Magn ... IEEE. Transactions on Magnetics [*A publication*]
IEEE Trans Microwave Theory Tech ... IEEE. Transactions on Microwave Theory and Techniques [*A publication*]
IEEE Trans Microwave Theory and Tech ... IEEE. Transactions on Microwave Theory and Techniques [*A publication*]
IEEE Trans Prof Commun ... IEEE. Transactions on Professional Communications [*A publication*]
IEEE Trans Rel ... IEEE. Transactions on Reliability [*A publication*]
IEEE Trans Reliab ... IEEE. Transactions on Reliability [*A publication*]
IEEE Trans SE ... IEEE. Transactions on Software Engineering [*A publication*]
IEEE Trans Software Eng ... IEEE. Transactions on Software Engineering [*A publication*]
IEEE Trans Software Engrg ... IEEE. Transactions on Software Engineering [*A publication*]
IEEE Trans Syst Man Cybern ... IEEE. Transactions on Systems, Man, and Cybernetics [*A publication*]
IEEE Trans Syst Man and Cybern ... IEEE. Transactions on Systems, Man, and Cybernetics [*A publication*]
IEE J Comput Digital Tech ... IEE [*Institution of Electrical Engineers*] Journal on Computers and Digital Techniques [*A publication*]
IEE J Comput and Digital Tech ... IEE [*Institution of Electrical Engineers*] Journal on Computers and Digital Techniques [*A publication*]
IEE Proc E ... IEE [*Institution of Electrical Engineers*] Proceedings. Part E. Computers and Digital Techniques [*A publication*]
IEE Proc E Comput Digit Tech ... IEE [*Institution of Electrical Engineers*] Proceedings. Part E. Computers and Digital Techniques [*A publication*]
IEE Proc Part E ... IEE [*Institution of Electrical Engineers*] Proceedings. Part E. Computers and Digital Techniques [*England*] [*A publication*]
IEMATS ...... Improved Emergency Message Automatic Transmission System (MCD)
IEOCS .... Interim Equipment Order Control System [*Bell System*]
IER .... Installation Enhancement Release [*Data processing*]
IERE .... Institute of Electronics and Radio Engineers [*British*] (TEL)
IES .... Illuminating Engineering Society
IES .... Incoming Echo Suppressor [*Telecommunications*] (TEL)
IES .... Institute for Environmental Studies [*University of Washington*] [*Research center*] (RCD)
IESP .... Integrated Electronic Signal Processor
IETAB .... IEEE. Transactions on Acoustics, Speech, and Signal Processing [*A publication*]
IF .... Instruction Field (CAA)
I/F .... Interface [*Data processing*] (KSC)
IF .... Intermediate Frequency [*Electronics*]
IFA .... Imero Fiorentino Associates, Inc. [*New York, NY*] [*Telecommunications*] (TSSD)
IFA .... Integrated Feed Antenna
IFA .... Integrated File Adapter [*Data processing*] (BUR)
IFAC........... International Federation on Automatic Control [*Dusseldorf, WG*]
IFAM .... Initial-Final Address Message [*Telecommunications*] (TEL)
IFAM .... Inverted File Access Method (CAA)
IFAMS........ Integrated Force Administration System [*Bell System*]
IFAX .... International Facsimile Service [*Telecommunications*] (TEL)
IFB .... Institut fuer Bauforschung [*Information retrieval*] (ODIN)
IFCN........... Interfacility Communication Network
IFCNA .... Information and Control [*A publication*]
IFCS .... International Federation of Computer Sciences
IFD .... Instantaneous Frequency Discriminator (IEEE)
IFD .... International Federation for Documentation [*Also, FID*]
IFDO .... International Federation of Data Organizations for the Social Sciences [*West Germany*] [*Information service*] (EISS)
IFF .... Intensity Fluctuation Factor [*Telecommunications*] (TEL)
IFGL........... Initial File Generation Language (CAH)
IFIC .... International Ferrocement Information Center (EISS)
IFIP .... International Federation for Information Processing [*Formerly, IFIPS*] [*London, England*]
IFIPS .... International Federation of Information Processing Societies [*Later, IFIP*]
IFK .... Institut fuer Krankenhausbau der TU [*Technische Universitaet*] Berlin [*Information retrieval*] (ODIN)
IFL.............. International Frequency List (NATG)
IFLA .... International Federation of Library Associations and Institutions [*Tokyo, Japan*]
IFM .... Interactive File Manager [*Data processing*] (CAA)
IFM .... Intermediate Frame Memory [*Data processing*]
IFMS .... Integrated Financial Management System
IFN .... Information [*Data processing*] (MDG)
IFO .... Interphone (FAAC)
IFOC .... International Fiber Optics and Communications [*A publication*]
IFORS .... International Federation of Operational Research Societies
IFOTES ...... International Federation of Telephone Emergency Services (EANO)
IFOTES ...... International Federation of Telephonic Emergency Services
IFOV........... Individual Field of View
IFOV........... Instantaneous Field of View
IFP .... Integrated File Processor (CAA)
IFPS .... Interactive Financial Planning System [*Harris Systems Ltd.*] [*Software package*] [*British*] (NCC)
IFPS .... [*A*] programing language [*1979*] (CSR)
IFPTS........ Intertype Fototronic Photographic System (DIT)
IFR .... Instantaneous Frequency [*Indicating*] Receivers (IEEE)
IFR .... Interface Register (CAA)
IFRB........... International Frequency Registration Board [*ITU*]
IFRIS .... Intelligence Finished Reports Information Subsystem [*Data processing*]
IFS .... Interactive File Sharing (CAA)
IFS .... Interactive Flow Simulator (TEL)
IFS .... Interchange File Separator [*Data processing*] (BUR)
IFS .... Investment Feasibility Studies (TEL)
IFS .... Ionospheric Forward Scatter (TEL)
IFSRA .... Information Storage and Retrieval [*A publication*]
IFT.............. Input Frequency Tolerance [*Data processing*]
IFT.............. Intermediate Frequency Transformer
IFTC .... International Film and Television Council [*Rome, Italy*]
IFTF .... Institute for the Future [*Menlo Park, CA*] [*Research center*] [*Telecommunications*] (RCD)
IFTPP.......... International Federation of the Technical and Periodical Press (DIT)
IFU .... Instruction Fetch Unit [*Data processing*] (CAA)
IFU .... Integrated Fluorescence Unit [*Image formation*]
I/FU............ Interface Unit [*Data processing*] (NASA)
IFW .... Institut fuer Nationale und Internationale Fleischwirtschaft [*Heidelberg*] [*Information retrieval*] (ODIN)
IG .... Informatics General Corp. [*NYSE symbol*]
IG .... Interconnect Group (CAAL)
IGC .... Institute for Graphic Communication, Inc. [*Boston, MA*] [*Telecommunications*]
IGD............. Interaction Graphics Display
IGD............. Interactive Grafics Digitizer [*Data processing*]
IGFET .... Insulated-Gate Field-Effect Transistor [*Electronics*]
IGFET .... Isolated-Gate Field-Effect Transistor [*Electronics*]
IGI .... Information Gatekeepers, Incorporated [*Boston, MA*] [*Telecommunications*] [*Information service*] (EISS)
IGI .... Information General, Incorporated [*Needham, MA*] [*Information service*] (EISS)
IGIS .... International Group of Users of Information Systems   (EISS)
IGL .... Information Grouping Logic [*Data processing*]
IGL .... Interactive Graphics Language (CAA)
IGP .... Intelligent Gateway Processor [*Data processing*]
IGPP........... Interactive Graphics Packaging Program [*Data processing*]
IGS .... Information Group Separator (CAA)
IGS .... Integrated Graphics System [*Data processing*] (BUR)
IGS .... Interactive Graphics System [*Data processing*]
IGS .... Interchange Group Separator [*Data processing*] (BUR)
IGT .... Interactive Graphics Terminal [*Data processing*]
IGUC .... Information Gained per Unit Cost [*Data processing*]
IGV .... International Gravis Computer Technology, Inc. [*Formerly, Gravis Computer Peripherals, Inc.*] [*Vancouver Stock Exchange symbol*]
IH .... Information Hotline [*A publication*]
IHDRT .... Interim High-Data Rate Terminal (CAAL)
IHETS .... Indiana Higher Education Telecommunication System [*Indianapolis*] [*Telecommunications*] (TSSD)
IHF .... Inhibit Halt Flip-Flop [*Data processing*]
IHFAS .... Integrated High-Frequency Antenna System
IHFF .... Inhibit Halt Flip-Flop [*Data processing*] (MSA)
IHP .... Information Handling Project (DIT)
IH/SR .... Integration Hardware and Software Review (MCD)
II .... Interrupt Inhibit (CAA)
IIA .... ILA [*Instruction Look Ahead*] Interrupt Address [*Data processing*]
IIA .... Information Industry Association [*Washington, DC*] [*Affiliated with AIM*] [*Database producer*]
IIA .... Intelligence Industries Association [*Los Angeles, CA*] (EANO)
IIB .... Information Industry Bulletin [*Digital Information Group*] [*Information service*] (EISS)
IIC .... Iron Information Center [*Battelle Memorial Institute*] [*Information service*] (EISS)
IIF .... Independent Investors Forum [*Penn Yan, NY*] [*Information service*] (EISS)
III .... Information Intelligence, Incorporated [*Information service*] (EISS)
III .... Information International, Incorporated [*Phoenix, AZ*] [*Information broker*]
IIIC .... International Irrigation Information Center (EISS)
IIL .... Integrated Injection Logic [*Microprocessing*] (BUR)
IINT .... Information International, Inc. [*NASDAQ symbol*] (NQ)
IINTE.......... Instytut Informacji Naukowej, Technicznej, i Ekonomicznej [*Institute of Scientific, Technical, and Economic Information*] [*Poland*] [*Information service*] (EISS)
IIOP .... Integrated Input/Output Processor (CAA)
IIP .... Implementation/Installation Plan [*Telecommunications*] (TEL)
IIR .... Intercom Information Resources, Inc. [*Austin, TX*] [*Information service*] (EISS)
IIRMS .... Industrial Information's Record Management System [*Data processing*] (TUT)
IIS .... Institute of Information Scientists [*British*] (DIT)
IIS .... Interactive Instructional System [*IBM Corp.*]
IIST .... Institute for Information Storage Technology [*University of Santa Clara*] [*Research center*] (RCD)
IITRAN ...... [*A*] programing language (CSR)
IITRI .... IIT Research Institute [*Illinois Institute of Technology*] [*Research center*] (RCD)
IIU .... Input Interface Unit [*Data processing*]
IIU .... Instruction Input Unit (CAA)

IIWPA	International Information/Word Processing Association [Formerly, IWPA] [Later, IWP] (EANO)
IJCAI	International Joint Conference on Artificial Intelligence
IJCIS	International Journal of Computer and Information Sciences [A publication]
IJS	Interactive Job Submission [Data processing] (CAA)
IKAT	Interactive Keyboard and Terminal [Data processing] (MCD)
IKBD	Intelligent Keyboard Device
IKBS	Intelligent Knowledge-Based System [Using artificial intelligence] [Data processing]
IKS	Integrated Key Set [Data processing]
IKU	Interface Keying Unit [Data processing] (KSC)
IL	Idle (BUR)
IL	Insertion Loss (CIT)
IL	Instruction List (CAA)
IL	Intermediate Language [Data processing] (BUR)
I²L	Integrated Injection Logic [Microprocessing]
I²L	Isoplanar Integrated Injection Logic (CAA)
ILA	Instruction Look-Ahead [Unit] [Data processing]
ILA	Intelligent Line Adapter (CAA)
ILA	International Listening Association (EANO)
ILAS	Interrelated Logic Accumulating Scanner
ILB	Initial Load Block (CAA)
ILB	Inner Lead Bond [Integrated circuit technology]
ILC	Instruction Length Code [Data processing] (BUR)
ILC	Instruction Location Counter (CAA)
ILC	Integrated Logic Circuit
ILC	International Licensed Carrier [Telecommunications]
ILCS	Induction Loop Communications System
ILDS	Integrated Logistics Data System
ILDT	Item Logistics Data Transmittal
ILDTF	Item Logistics Data Transmittal Form (NATG)
ILE	Interface Latching Element (CAA)
ILF	Infra Low-Frequency [Telecommunications] (TEL)
ILI	Institute for Land Information [Washington, DC] [Research center] [Information service] (RCD)
ILIC	In-Line Integrated Circuit
I-LITE	Iowa Library Information Teletype Exchange [Des Moines, IA] [Telecommunications] [Library network]
ILL	Input Logic Level
ILL	Interstate Loan Library [Council of State Governments] (EISS)
ILLIAC	Illinois Institute for Advanced Computing
ILLIAC	Illinois Integrator and Automatic Computer [University of Illinois] (BUR)
ILM	Information Logic Machine (IEEE)
ILM	Intermediate Language Machine (CAA)
ILO	Individual Load Operation (CAA)
ILP	In-Line Printer
ILP	Integrated Logistics Panel (NASA)
ILP	Intermediate Language Processor [Data processing] (BUR)
ILP	Intermediate Language Program [Data processing] (CAA)
ILR	Institute of Library Research [University of California] (DIT)
ILR	International Luggage Registry [Computer system for recovery of airline luggage]
ILS	Information & Library Services [Information service] (EISS)
ILS	Institut fuer Landes- und Stadtentwicklungsforschung [Dortmund] [Information retrieval] (ODIN)
ILS	Integrated Library System [National Library of Medicine] [Information service] (EISS)
ILS	International Line Selector (CAA)
ILS	Interrupt Level Subroutine (CMD)
ILSUS	Integrated Library System Users Society (EANO)
ILTMS	International Leased Telegraph Message Switching Service [British Telecom] [Telecommunications] (TEL)
ILV	Fraunhofer-Institut fuer Lebensmitteltechnologie und Verpackung [Munich] [Information retrieval] (ODIN)
IM	Instruction Memory (CAA)
IM	Instrumentation (MDG)
IM	Integrated MODEM (CAA)
IM	Interface Module (MCD)
IM	Interrupt Mask (CAA)
IM	Item Mark (BUR)
IMA	Input Message Acknowledgment [Data processing] (CAA)
IMA	Institute of Mathematics and Its Applications [South-End-On-Sea, England]
IMA	International MIDI [Musical Instrument Digital Interface] Association (EANO)
IMA	Invalid Memory Address [Data processing] (CAA)
IMACS	International Association for Mathematics and Computers in Simulation [Formerly, AICA] [Rutgers University] [New Brunswick, NJ] (CSR)
IMANCO	Image Analysing Computers, Inc.
IMB	Input Memory Buffer [Data processing]
IMC	Integrated Multiplexer Channel (CAA)
IMC	Intelligent Matrix Control [T-Bar, Inc.] (CAA)
IMC	Interactive Module Controller (CAA)
IMC	International Information Management Congress [Bethesda, MD] (EANO)
IMC	International Maintenance Control [Telecommunications]
IMC	International Management Communications, Inc. [Database producer] (CUAD)
IMC	International Micrographic Congress
IMCAS	Interactive Man/Computer Augmentation System
IMCC	Integrated Mission Control Center (CDH)
IMC Jrnl	IMC [International Information Management Congress] Journal [A publication]
IMCO	International Metered Communications
IMCS II	Interactive Manufacturing Control System [NCR Ltd.] [Software package] [British] (NCC)
IME	International Microcomputer Exposition (CAA)
IMEKO	Internationale Messtichnische Konfoederation [International Measurement Confederation] [Budapest, Hungary]
IMET	Intermetrics [NASDAQ symbol] (NQ)
IMFK	Integrated Multifunction Keyboard (MCD)
IMG	Image
IMI	Intermediate Machine Instruction (CAA)
IMI	Interrogation Sign [Question mark] [Communications] (FAAC)
IMI	Invention Marketing, Incorporated [Information service] (EISS)
IMIA	International Medical Informatics Association [IFIP special interest group] (EANO)
IMIS	Integrated Motorists' Information System [Computerized guidance system to speed traffic and avoid tie-ups]
IMITAC	Image Input to Automatic Computers
IML	Incoming Matching Loss [Telecommunications] (TEL)
IML	Information Manipulation Language (CAA)
IML	Initial Machine Load [Data processing] (IBMDP)
IML	Initial Microprogram Load [Also, IMPL] [Data processing] (IBMDP)
IML	Intermediate Language [Data processing] (TEL)
IMM	Immediate (DDI)
IMM	Intelligent Memory Manager [Data processing]
IMM	International Mobile Machines Corp.
IMMY	Information Marketing Achievement Award [Information Industry Association]
IMNET	International MarketNet [System of broker work stations created by IBM Corp. and Merrill Lynch & Co.]
IMOS	Interactive Multiprograming Operating System [NCR Corp.] (CAA)
IMP	Image Processing Program [Computer program] (CIT)
IMP	Implementation Language [Edinburgh multiaccess system] (CSR)
IMP	Initial Memory Protection (MCD)
IMP	Input Message Processor
IMP	Integrated Memory Processor
IMP	Integrated Microprocessor [National Semiconductor] (CAA)
IMP	Interactive Microprogramable Control (MCD)
IMP	Interface Message Processor [Data processing]
IMP	Intrinsic Multiprocessing (IEEE)
IMPA	Information Management and Processing Association [Lansing, MI] (EANO)
IMPACS	International Packet-Switching Service [MCI International, Inc.] [Rye Brook, NY] [Telecommunications] (TSSD)
IMPACT	Implementation Planning and Control Technique [Data processing]
IMPACT	Inventory Management Program and Control Technique [IBM Corp.] [Data processing]
IMPATT	Impact Ionization Avalanche Transit Time [Solid state diodes] [Transistor technology]
IMPCON	Inventory Management & Production Control [ISTEL] [Software package] [British] (NCC)
IMPIS	Integrated Management Planning Information Systems [Data processing]
IMPL	Initial Microprogram Load [Also, IML] [Data processing]
IMPR	Imprint [Online database field identifier] (OBD)
IMPREG	Impregnated (TEL)
IMPRESS	Interdisciplinary Machine Processing for Research and Education in Social Sciences [Dartmouth College, Hanover, NH] [Data processing system]
IMPRINT	Imbricated Program for Information Transfer [Data processing]
IMPS	Industry Media Publishing System [Omni Industry Corp.] [Information service] (EISS)
IMPS	Integrated Modular Panel System
IMPS	International Microprogrammers' Society (CAA)
IMPTS	Improved Programer Test Station (IEEE)
IMR	Interrupt-Mask Register [Data processing]
IMRADS	Information Management, Retrieval, and Dissemination System (DIT)
IMS	Information Management Specialists [Information service] (EISS)
IMS	Information Management System [IBM Corp.] [Data processing] (CGC)
IMS	Integrated Microcomputer Systems, Inc.
IMS	Interactive Market Systems, Inc. [Host] [Information service] (EISS)
IMS	International Management Services, Inc. [Information service] (EISS)
IMS	Inventory Management and Simulator (CGC)
IMS	Inventory Management System (NASA)
IMSDD	Institut fuer Medizinische Statistik, Dokumentation, und Datenverarbeitung der Universitaet Bonn [Information retrieval] (ODIN)
IMSI	IMS International [NASDAQ symbol] (NQ)
IMSI	Information Management System Interface (CAA)
IMSL	International Mathematical and Statistical Libraries, Inc.
IMSP	Integrated Mass Storage Processor (CAA)
IMSSS	Institute for Mathematical Studies in the Social Sciences [Stanford University] [Research center] (RCD)

Computer & Telecommunications Acronyms

IMT............. Intelligent Microimage Terminal [*Kodak*]
IMT............. Intermachine Trunk [*Telecommunications*] (TEL)
IMT............. Intermediate Tape [*Telecommunications*] (TEL)
IMTS .... Improved Mobile Telephone Service
IMU .... Increment Memory Unit (CAA)
IMU .... Instruction Memory Unit (CAA)
IMX .... Inquiry Message Exchange (CAA)
IN .... Inch
IN .... Input (MDG)
IN .... Institution [*Online database field identifier*] (OBD)
IN .... Interference-to-Noise Ratio (IEEE)
INA............. Integrated Network Architecture (CAA)
INC............. Incoming [*Telecommunications*] (KSC)
INC............. Incoming Trunk [*Telecommunications*] (TEL)
INC............. Increment
INC............. Inertial Navigation Computer (MCD)
INCC .... International Network Controlling Center [*Telecommunications*] (TEL)
INCL........... Inclusive
INCM.......... InteCom, Inc. [*NASDAQ symbol*] (NQ)
INCOMEX ... International Computer Exhibition
INCR .... Increment (AFM)
INCR .... Interrupt Control Register [*Data processing*] (MSA)
IND............. Indicate [*or Indicator*] (KSC)
IND............. Induction (MSA)
IND............. International Number Dialing [*Telecommunications*] (TEL)
Ind Robot..... Industrial Robot [*A publication*]
INDUS......... Interactive Duct Sizing [*Facet Ltd.*] [*Software package*] [*British*] (NCC)
INF .... Information [*Data processing*]
INF .... Informationszentrum und Bibliotheken [*Information retrieval*] (ODIN)
Inf C .... Information and Control [*A publication*]
Inf Contr ..... Information and Control [*A publication*]
Inf Control ... Information and Control [*A publication*]
Inf and Control ... Information and Control [*A publication*]
Inf Disp .... Information Display [*A publication*]
Inf Display ... Information Display [*A publication*]
Inf Hotline... Information Hotline [*United States*] [*A publication*]
Inf Intell Online Newsl ... Information Intelligence Online Newsletter [*A publication*]
INFN........... Infotron Systems Corp. [*NASDAQ symbol*] (NQ)
INFO .... Information [*Data processing*] (AFM)
INFO .... Information Network and File Organization [*Data processing*] (BUR)
INFO .... Information Network for Operations [*Data processing*]
INFO .... Integrated Network Fiber Optics (MCD)
Info Age ...... Information Age [*A publication*]
INFOBANK ... [*The*] Information Bank [*Computer Sciences of Australia Pty. Ltd.*] [*Database*]
INFODATA ... Database Information Science and Practice [*Database*] (ODIN)
INFODATA ... Datenbank Informationswissenschaft und -Praxis [*Database Information Science and Practice*] [*Database*] [*Information retrieval*] (ODIN)
INFO/DOC ... Information/Documentation [*Information service*] (EISS)
INFOHOST ... Database Guide to German Host Operators [*Database*] (ODIN)
INFOL .... Information Oriented Language [*Information retrieval*]
INFONET..... Information Network [*British*] [*Telecommunications*] (TEL)
INFOREM..... Inventory Forecasting and Replenishment Modules [*IBM Corp.*]
INFORM...... Information Network for Freight Overhead Billing, Rating, and Message Switching
Information Syst ... Information Systems [*A publication*]
Inform Contr ... Information and Control [*A publication*]
INFOS .... Informationszentrum fuer Schnittwertemachning [*Information Center for Machining*] [*Germany*] [*Rheinische-Westfaelische Hochschule*] [*Database*] (EISS)
INFOSOR.... Information Sources [*Virginia Beach, VA*] [*Information service*] (EISS)
Infosys........ Infosystems [*Wheaton, IL*] [*A publication*]
Info Sys New ... Information Systems News [*A publication*]
Info Systems ... Information Systems [*Elmsford, NY*] [*A publication*]
INFOTERM ... International Information Centre for Terminology [*Austria*] [*UNESCO*] (EISS)
INFOTEX..... Information via Telex [*Telecommunications*] (TEL)
Inf Pr Man ... Information Processing and Management [*A publication*]
Inf Processing & Mgt ... Information Processing and Management [*A publication*]
Inf Process Manage ... Information Processing and Management [*A publication*]
Inf Process and Manage ... Information Processing and Management [*A publication*]
Inf Proc Man ... Information Processing and Management [*A publication*]
INFRAL....... Information Retrieval Automatic Language [*Data processing*]
INFROSS.... Information Requirements of the Social Sciences [*British*] (DIT)
Inf-Spektrum ... Informatik-Spektrum [*A publication*]
Inf Storage ... Information Storage and Retrieval [*A publication*]
Inf Storage & Retr ... Information Storage and Retrieval [*A publication*]
Inf Storage Retr ... Information Storage and Retrieval [*A publication*]
Inf Stor Retr ... Information Storage and Retrieval [*A publication*]
Inf Syst .... Information Systems [*A publication*]
Inf Technol and Libr ... Information Technology and Libraries [*A publication*]
INGA .... Interactive Graphics Analysis (CAA)
INGRES ...... Interactive Graphic and Retrieval System (CAA)

INI .... Interface Noise Inverter
INI .... Intervideo Network, Incorporated [*Los Angeles, CA*] [*Telecommunications*] (TSSD)
INIC .... Ideal Current Negative Immittance Converter
INIP .... Institute of Non-Numerical Information Processing [*Switzerland*] [*Information service*] (EISS)
INIS ATOMINDEX ... International Nuclear Information System [*International Atomic Energy Agency*] [*Vienna, Austria*] [*Bibliographic database*] (OBD)
INKA .... Informationssystem Karlsruhe [*Karlsruhe Information System*] [*Information service*] [*West German*]
INKA-CONF ... Information System Karlsruhe - Conference [*Database*] (ODIN)
INKA-CORP ... Information System Karlsruhe - Corporates in Energy [*Database*] (ODIN)
INKA-DATACOMP ... Information System Karlsruhe - Data Compilations in Energy and Physics [*Database*] (ODIN)
INKA-MATH ... Information System Karlsruhe - Mathematics [*Database*] (ODIN)
INKA-MATHDI ... Information System Karlsruhe - Mathematical Education [*Database*] (ODIN)
INKA-NUCLEAR PART INIS ... Information System Karlsruhe - Nuclear Database Part: International Nuclear Information System [*Database*] (ODIN)
INKA-NUCLEAR PART KKK ... Information System Karlsruhe - Nuclear Database Part: Conference Papers: Nuclear Research, Nuclear Technology [*Database*] (ODIN)
INKA-NUCLEAR PART NSA ... Information System Karlsruhe - Nuclear Database Part: Nuclear Science Abstracts [*Database*] (ODIN)
INKA-PHYS ... Information System Karlsruhe - Physics [*Database*] (ODIN)
INLAN .... Instant Language [*Trademark*] [*Data processing*]
INMAC .... International Minicomputer Accessories Corp. [*Santa Clara, CA*] [*Hardware manufacturer*] (DASO)
INMARISAT ... International Maritime Satellite System [*Department of Commerce*]
INMARSAT ... International Maritime Satellite Organization [*London, England*] [*Telecommunications*] (TSSD)
INMARSAT ... International Maritime Satellite System [*Department of Commerce*]
INMC.......... International Network Management Center [*Telecommunications*] (TEL)
INN .... Independent Network News [*Television*]
INODC .... Indian National Oceanographic Data Centre [*Information service*] (EISS)
INP .... Initial Program Load [*Data processing*]
INP .... Input (MSA)
INP .... Integrated Network Processor (CAA)
INP .... Intelligent Network Processor (CAA)
INPADOC.... International Patent Documentation Center [*Information service*] [*Austrian*]
INPH........... Interphone (VIT)
INPI............ Institut National de la Propriete Industrielle
INR .... Interference-to-Noise Ratio
INRES/TCDC ... Information Referral System for Technical Cooperation among Developing Countries [*United Nations*] [*Information service*] (EISS)
INRIA .... Institut National de Recherche en Informatique et en Automatique [*National Institute for Research in Informatics and Automation*] [*France*] [*Research center and database originator*] [*Information service*] (EISS)
INS .... Information Network System [*Japanese*]
INS .... Insulate (DDI)
INS .... Integrated Network Systems, Inc.
INS .... Interstation Noise Suppression
INSACS ...... Interstate Airways Communications Station
INSAR .... Instruction Address Register (CAA)
INSAT .... Indian National Satellite System [*Bangalore, India*] [*Telecommunications*]
InSci .... Information Science, Inc. [*Information service*] (EISS)
INSIS .... Inter-Institutional Integrated Services Information System (DEEC)
INSITE .... Institutional Space Inventory Technique [*Data processing*]
INSO .... Innovative Software [*NASDAQ symbol*] (NQ)
INST........... Instruction [*or Instructor*] (AFM)
INSTAB....... Information Service on Toxicity and Biodegradability [*Water Pollution Research Laboratory*] [*British*] (EISS)
INSTAL....... Installation
INSTARS .... Information Storage and Retrieval System [*Data processing*]
INST/COMM ... Instrumentation and Communication (MCD)
INSTN .... Instruction [*Data processing*] (TEL)
INSTN .... Instrumentation (MUGU)
INSTR .... Instruction (CAH)
Insul/Circuits ... Insulation/Circuits [*A publication*]
INT .... Integer (CAH)
INT .... Interphone (MDG)
INT .... Interrogate (MDG)
INT .... Interrupt (DEEC)
INTA........... Interrupt Acknowledge [*Data processing*]
INTC .... Intel Corporation [*NASDAQ symbol*] (NQ)
Int Comp .... Interactive Computing [*A publication*]
INTD........... Institut National des Techniques de la Documentation [*National Institute for Documentation Techniques*] [*France*] [*Information service*] (EISS)

INTE............ Interrupt Enable [Data processing]
INTEC.......... Interference [Telecommunications]   (MDG)
INTECOM ... International Council for Technical Communication
INTELLIVISION ... Intelligent Television [Home video game] [Mattel, Inc.]
INTELPOST ... International Electronic Post [Postal service]
INTELSAT ... International Telecommunications Satellite [Acronym is service mark and trade name of the International Telecommunications Satellite Organization and is used for communications services via satellite]
INTEN .... Intensity   (MSA)
INTER .... Interphone   (MCD)
INTERACT ... Interactive Television Network [Dartmouth-Hitchcock Medical Center] [Hanover, NH] [Telecommunications]   (TSSD)
INTERALIS ... International Advanced Life Information System   (BUR)
INTERCOM ... Intercommunication System
INTERCON ... Interconnection   (KSC)
INTERDACO ... Intercontinental Data Control Corp. Ltd. [Ottawa, ON] [Telecommunications]   (TSSD)
INTEREST ... Interactive Estimating [Camic Ltd.] [Software package] [British]   (NCC)
Interfaces Comput ... Interfaces in Computing [A publication]
INTERLISP ... [A] programing language [1974]   (CSR)
INTERMAG ... International Conference on Magnetics   (MCD)
INTERMAMA ... International Congress for Measurement and Automation   (IEEE)
INTERMARC ... International Machine Readable Catalogue   (DEEC)
Internat J Bio-Med Comput ... International Journal of Bio-Medical Computing [A publication]
Internat J Circuit Theory Appl ... International Journal of Circuit Theory and Applications [A publication]
Internat J Comput and Fluids ... International Journal. Computers and Fluids [A publication]
Internat J Comput Information Sci ... International Journal of Computer and Information Sciences [A publication]
Internat J Comput Inform Sci ... International Journal of Computer and Information Sciences [A publication]
Internat J Comput Math ... International Journal of Computer Mathematics. Section A [A publication]
Internat J Man-Machine Studies ... International Journal of Man-Machine Studies [A publication]
Internat J Man-Mach Stud ... International Journal of Man-Machine Studies [A publication]
INTERP .... Interpreter
INTF............ Interface Systems [NASDAQ symbol]   (NQ)
INTFU .... Interface Unit   (CAA)
INTGEN ...... Interpreter Generator   (CAA)
INTIB........... Industrial and Technological Information Bank [UNIDO]   (EISS)
INTIM .... Interrupt and Timing [Telecommunications]   (TEL)
INTIP .... Integrated Information Processing
INTIPS .... Integrated Information Processing System [Air Development Center, Rome, NY]
Int J Bio-M ... International Journal of Bio-Medical Computing [A publication]
Int J Bio-Med Comput ... International Journal of Bio-Medical Computing [A publication]
Int J C Inf .... International Journal of Computer and Information Sciences [A publication]
Int J Com M ... International Journal of Computer Mathematics [A publication]
Int J Comput & Inf Sci ... International Journal of Computer and Information Sciences [A publication]
Int J Comput Math ... International Journal of Computer Mathematics [A publication]
Int J Comput Math Sect A ... International Journal of Computer Mathematics. Section A. Programming Languages. Theory and Methods [A publication]
Int J Comput Math Sect B ... International Journal of Computer Mathematics. Section B. Computational Methods [A publication]
Int J Man-M ... International Journal of Man-Machine Studies [A publication]
Int J Man-Mach Stud ... International Journal of Man-Machine Studies [A publication]
Int J Microgr and Video Technol ... International Journal of Micrographics and Video Technology [A publication]
Int J Mini and Microcomput ... International Journal of Mini and Microcomputers [A publication]
INTL .... Inter-Tel, Inc. [NASDAQ symbol]   (NQ)
Intl Comp Symp ... International Computer Symposium Proceedings [A publication]
INTLINE ...... International Online Data Base [Chase Econometrics] [Database]   (CUAD)
INTPH .... Interphone
INTR............ Intermec Corp. [NASDAQ symbol]   (NQ)
INTR............ Interrupt [Data processing] [Telecommunications]
INTRAN....... Input Translator [IBM Corp.] [Data processing]
INTREX....... Information Transfer Experiment [Massachusetts Institute of Technology]   (DIT)
INTRF.......... Interference [Telecommunications]   (MSA)
INTRO .... Introduction   (MSA)
Int Tracts Comput Sci Technol Their Appl ... International Tracts in Computer Science and Technology and Their Application [A publication]
INTUG......... International Telecommunications Users Group [Leatherhead, England] [Telecommunications] [Information service]   (EISS)
INTV........... Association of Independent Television Stations   (EANO)

INV............. Inverter   (KSC)
INWATS...... Inward Wide Area Telephone Service [Bell System]
INWG .... International Network Working Group [International Federation for Information Processing]   (DEEC)
INXLTR .... Input Translator [IBM Corp.] [Data processing]   (MSA)
I/O............. Input/Output [Data processing]
IOA............ Input-Output Adapter [Data processing]   (NASA)
IOA............ Input-Output Address [Data processing]   (KSC)
IOA............ Input-Output Assembly [Data processing]   (MCD)
IOAU .... Input/Output Access Unit [Data processing]
IOB............ Input-Output Block [Data processing]   (CMD)
IOB............ Input-Output Box [Data processing]   (MCD)
IOB............ Input-Output Buffer [Data processing]
IOB............ Inter-Organization Board for Information Systems [United Nations]   (EISS)
IOBPS .... Input-Output Box and Peripheral Simulator [Data processing]   (MCD)
IOBS .... Input-Output Buffering System [Data processing]   (OA)
IOC............ Input-Output Channel [Data processing]   (DIT)
IOC............ Input-Output Comparator [Data processing]
I/OC .... Input/Output Console [Data processing]   (CAAL)
IOC............ Input-Output Controller [Data processing]
IOC............ Input-Output Converter [Data processing]
IOC............ Integrated Optical Circuit
IOC............ Integrated Optoelectronic Circuit
IOC............ INTELSAT [International Telecommunications Satellite] Operations Center   (CBSS)
IOC............ Interim Operational Capability   (CIT)
IOCC .... Input-Output Control Center [or Command] [Data processing]
I/OCC .... Input/Output Control Console [Data processing]   (CAAL)
IOCI .... Interstate Organized Crime Index [Computer databank]
IOCS .... Input-Output Control System [Data processing]
IOCU .... Input-Output Control Unit [Data processing]
IOD............ Identified Outward Dialing [Telecommunications]   (TEL)
IOD............ Information on Demand [Information service]   (EISS)
IOD............ Input/Output Device [Telecommunications]   (TEL)
IODC.......... Input-Output Data Channel [Data processing]
IODC.......... Input-Output Delay Counter [Data processing]
IODD .... Input-Output Data Document [Data processing]   (MCD)
IOE............ Input-Output Error Log Table [Data processing]   (MCD)
IOF............ Input/Output Front End [Data processing]   (CAA)
IOF............ Interactive Operations Facility [Honeywell, Inc.]   (CAA)
IOG .... Input-Output Gate [Data processing]
IOIH........... Input/Output Interrupt Handler [Data processing]   (CAA)
IOLA........... Input/Output Link Adapter [Data processing]   (CAA)
IOLC .... Input/Output Link Control [Data processing]   (CAA)
IOLIM......... International Online Information Meeting
IOLS........... Integrated Online Library Systems
IOM .... Input-Output Module [Data processing]   (MCD)
I/OM .... Input-Output Multiplexer [Data processing]
IOMG .... Iomega Corp. [NASDAQ symbol]   (NQ)
ION-M .... Integrated On-Line Non-Stop Manufacturing [Safe Computing Ltd.] [Software package] [British]   (NCC)
IOOP .... Input/Output Operation [Data processing]
I & OP........ In and Out Processing [Data processing]   (AFM)
IOP............ Initial Operating Production   (MCD)
IOP............ Input-Output Package [IBM Corp.] [Data processing]
IOP............ Input-Output Port [Data processing]   (MCD)
IOP............ Input-Output Processor [Data processing]
IOP............ Input-Output Pulse [Data processing]
IOPKG......... Input/Output Package [IBM Corp.] [Data processing]   (CAH)
IOPS .... Input/Output Programing System [Data processing]
IOQ .... Input-Output Queue [Data processing]   (IBMDP)
IOQE.......... Input-Output Queue Element [Data processing]   (MCD)
IORB .... Input/Output Record Block [Data processing]
IOREQ......... Input/Output Request [Data processing]   (OA)
IOS............ Input-Output Selector [Data processing]   (IEEE)
IOS............ Input-Output Sense [Data processing]   (KSC)
IOS............ Input-Output Skip [Data processing]
IOS............ Input-Output Supervision [Data processing]   (NASA)
IOS............ Input-Output Switch [Data processing]
IOS............ Input-Output System [General Automation] [Data processing]   (CAA)
IOS............ Integrated Operator System [Telecommunications]
IOS............ Interactive Operating System [Data processing]   (CAA)
IOSA .... Input/Output Systems Association
IOS/OSI...... International Organization for Standardization Open Systems Interconnection Model
IOSS .... Input/Output Subsystem [NCR Corp.]   (CAA)
IOT............ Input-Output Termination [Data processing]
IOT............ Input-Output Transfer [Data processing]
IOTA .... Integrated On-Line Text Arrangement
IOTC .... International Originating Toll Center [Bell System]
IOTG .... Input/Output Task Group [CODASYL]   (CAA)
IOU............ Input-Output Unit [Data processing]
IOU............ Input-Output Utility [Data processing]   (CIT)
IOWIT........ International Organization of Wo/Men in Telecommunications [Arlington, TX]   (TSSD)
IOWT .... International Organization of Wo/Men in Telecommunications [Arlington, TX]   (EANO)
IP.............. Impact Printer [Data processing]   (CAA)
IP.............. Information Processing   (BUR)
IP.............. Initial Phase   (IEEE)

Computer & Telecommunications Acronyms

Acronym	Expansion
I/P	Input [*Data processing*]
IP	Input Power [*Data processing*]
IP	Input Processor [*Data processing*] (CIT)
IP	Instruction Pointer [*Data processing*] (CAA)
IP	Instruction Processor [*Data processing*]
IP	Interdigital Pause [*Telecommunications*] (TEL)
IP	Interface Processor [*Data processing*] (CAA)
IP	Internet Protocol [*Facilitates data communications among networks*] (CCD)
I/P	Irregular Input Process [*Telecommunications*] (TEL)
IPA	Information Process Analysis (BUR)
IPA	Information Processing Association [*Israel*] (CAH)
IPA	Innovative Programming Associates, Inc. [*Princeton, NJ*] [*Software manufacturer*] (DASOS)
IPA	Integrated Peripheral Adapter (CAA)
IPA	Integrated Printer Adapter (CAA)
IPA	International Packaging Abstracts [*Database*] [*Information retrieval*] (ODIN)
IPA	International Patent Agreement (IEEE)
IPA	International Petroleum Annual [*Department of Energy*] [*Database*] (FDB)
IPA	International Pharmaceutical Abstracts [*American Society of Hospital Pharmacists*] [*Bibliographic database*] [*A publication*]
IPARS	International Passenger Airline Reservations System
IPB	Integrated Processor Board (CAA)
IPB	Interprocessor Buffer (CAA)
IPC	Image Processing Center [*Drexel University*] [*Research center*] (RCD)
IPC	Industrial Process Control [*by computers*]
IPC	Information Processing Code (DIT)
IPC	Institute for Personal Computing [*Miami, FL*] (EANO)
IPC	Integrated Peripheral Channel (CAA)
IPC	Intelligent Peripheral Controller [*Data processing*]
IPC	International PBX [*Private Branch Exchange*] Telecommunicators [*Richmond, VA*] (EANO)
IPC	Interplanetary Communications
IPC	Interprocess Controller (CAA)
IPC	Interprocessor Communication (BUR)
IPCF	Interprocess Communication Facility [*Digital Equipment Corp.*] (CAA)
IPCF	Interprogram Communication Facility [*Prime Computer, Inc.*] (CAA)
IPCS	Interactive Problem-Control System [*IBM Corp.*]
IPDC	International Program for the Development of Communications [*UNESCO*]
IPFM	Integral Pulse Frequency Modulation (IEEE)
IPG	INPADOC Patent Gazette [*Information retrieval*] (ODIN)
IPH	Inches per Hour [*Telecommunications*] (TEL)
IPI	Insurance Periodicals Index [*NILS Publishing Co.*] [*Information service*] (EISS)
IPI	Intelligent Printer Interface (CAA)
IPI	International Patent Institute (DIT)
IPL	Image Processing Laboratory [*University of Houston*] [*Research center*] (RCD)
IPL	Information Processing Language [*Data processing*]
IPL	Initial Program Load [*Data processing*] (CGC)
IPL	Interrupt Priority Level (CAA)
IPLSA	IPL Systems, Inc. Cl A [*NASDAQ symbol*] (NQ)
IPLV	Information Processing Language Five (CAH)
IPM	Impulses per Minute [*Telecommunications*]
IPM	Inches per Minute
IPM	Internal Polarization Modulation (IEEE)
IPN	Impulse Noise
IPN	Instant Private Network
IPO	Installation Productivity Option [*IBM Corp.*]
IPO/E	Installation Productivity Option/Extended [*IBM Corp.*]
IPOT	Inductive Potentiometer (MDG)
IPP	Infrared Pointer Package
IPP	Input Processor Programs (CIT)
IPP	Integrated Plotting Package
IPP	Interface Program Plan (MCD)
IPP	International Phototelegraph Position [*Telecommunications*] (TEL)
IPP	Interprocessor Process [*Telecommunications*] (TEL)
IPPF	Instruction Preprocessing Function (CAA)
IPR	In Pulse to Register [*Telecommunications*] (TEL)
IPS	Image Processing System (MCD)
IPS	Improved Processing System
IPS	Impulses per Second [*Telecommunications*] (TEL)
IPS	In Pulse to Sender [*Telecommunications*] (TEL)
IPS	Inches per Second
IPS	Index Preparation System [*Foxon-Maddocks Associates*] [*Information service*] (EISS)
IPS	Information Processing System
IPS	Information Products Systems, Inc. [*Houston, TX*] [*Hardware manufacturer*] (DASO)
IPS	Installation Performance Specification [*Data processing*] (IBMDP)
IPS	Instructions per Second [*Data processing*]
IPS	Intelligent Printing System [*Dataroyal, Inc.*] (CAA)
IPS	Interpretive Programing System
IPS	Ionospheric Prediction Service [*Telecommunications*] (TEL)
IPS	Item Processing System (BUR)
IPSB	Interprocessor Signal Bus (CAA)
IPSC	Information Processing Standards for Computers
IPSJ	Information Processing Society of Japan [*Information service*] (EISS)
IPSL	Interface Problem Status Log (NASA)
IPSOC	Information Processing Society of Canada (CAH)
IPSS	International Packet Switch Stream [*Data processing*]
IPSS	International Packet Switching Service [*British Post Office*] (DEEC)
IPSS	Interprocessor Signaling System [*Telecommunications*] (TEL)
IPSSB	Information Processing Systems Standards Board [*Later, Board of Standards Review of ANSI*] [*American Standards Association*]
IPST	In-Process Self Test (MCD)
IPT	Improved Programing Technologies (BUR)
IPT	Information Processing Techniques Corp. [*Palo Alto, CA*] [*Software manufacturer*] (DASOS)
IPTC	International Press Telecommunications Council [*See also CIPT*] [*London, England*] [*Telecommunications*] [*An association*] (EANO)
IPTEA	Internacia Postista kaj Telekomunikista Esperanto-Asocio [*International Esperanto Association of Post and Telecommunication Workers*] (EANO)
IPTLF	International Phasor Telecom [*NASDAQ symbol*] (NQ)
IPTM	Interval Pulse Time Modulation (OA)
IPTT	Internationale du Personnel des Postes, Telegraphes, et Telephones [*Postal, Telegraph, and Telephone International*] [*See also PTTI*]
IPU	Instruction Processing Unit (BUR)
IPU	Interface and Priority Unit
IPU	Interphase Unit
IPU	Interprocessor Unit (CAA)
IPY	International Polar Year
IQF	Interactive Query Facility [*Data processing*] (CAA)
IQL	Interactive Query Language [*Digital Equipment Corp.*] [*Data processing*] (CAA)
IQL	Intermediate Query Language [*Data processing*]
IQMH	Input Queue Message Handler [*Data processing*] (CAA)
IQRC	Institut Quebecois de la Recherche sur la Culture [*Database producer*] (CUAD)
IQRP	Interactive Query and Report Processor [*IBM Corp.*] [*Data processing*]
IR	Information Retrieval [*Data processing*]
IR	Infrared
IR	Instruction Register [*Data processing*]
IRA	Information Resource Administration (CAA)
IRA	Input Reference Axis (IEEE)
IRAM	Integrated Random-Access Memory [*Data processing*]
IRASA	International Radio Air Safety Association
IRB	Informationszentrum Raum und Bau [*Fraunhofer-Gesellschaft*] [*Information Center for Building and Space Planning*] [*West Germany*] [*Database producer*] [*Information service*] (EISS)
IRB	Interrupt Request Block (CMD)
IRBEL	Indexed References to Biomedical Engineering Literature [*A publication*] (EISS)
IRC	Information Research Center (DIT)
IRC	Information Retrieval Center [*BBDO International*] [*Information service*] (EISS)
IRC	Integrated Radio Control (NVT)
IRC	International Record Carrier [*Telecommunication companies providing international service*] (TSSD)
IRC	International Record Carrier, Inc. [*New York, NY*] [*Telecommunications*]
IRCAR	International Reference Center for Abortion Research (EISS)
IRCC	Instruction and Research Computer Center [*Ohio State University*] [*Research center*] (RCD)
IRCD	Information Retrieval Center on the Disadvantaged [*ERIC*]
IRCIHE	International Referral Center for Information Handling Equipment [*Yugoslavia*] [*UNESCO*] (EISS)
IRCS	Infrared Communications System
IRCS	International Radio Call Sign (DDI)
IRCS	International Research Communications System [*Electronic journal publisher*] [*British*]
IRCS	Intersite Radio Communications System (MCD)
IR & D	Independent Research and Development
IRD	International Resource Development, Inc. [*Norwalk, CT*] [*Telecommunications*] [*Information service*] (EISS)
IRDB	Information Retrieval Databank (IEEE)
IRDL	Information Retrieval and Display Language [*Data processing*]
IRDS	Integrated Reliability Data System
IRE	Institute of Radio Engineers [*Later, IEEE*]
IRE	International Research & Evaluation [*Information service*] [*Research center*] (EISS)
IREX	Ideas, Resources, Exchange [*Computer*] [*British*]
IRF	Input Register Full (CAA)
IRFA	Institut de Recherches sur les Fruits et Agrumes [*Database producer*] (CUAD)
IRFB	International Radio Frequency Board
IRFITS	Infrared Fault Isolation Test System (CAA)
IRG	Inter-Record Gap [*Data processing*] [*Telecommunications*] (MCD)
IRH	Inductive Recording Head (CAA)

Computer & Telecommunications Acronyms

IRI .... Image Resources, Incorporated [*Winter Park, FL*] [*Telecommunications*] (TSSD)
IRI .... Industrial Research Institute [*Canada*] [*Research center*] (RCD)
IRI .... Information Researchers, Incorporated [*Information service*] (EISS)
IRI .... International Relay, Incorporated [*New York, NY*] [*Telecommunications*] (TSSD)
IRIA .... Institut de Recherche d'Informatique et d'Automatique [*French*] [*Research center*]
IRIC .... Information Resources [*NASDAQ symbol*] (NQ)
IRIE .... Infrared Information Exchange
IRIS .... IBM Recruitment Information System
IRIS .... Increased Readiness Information System
IRIS .... Information Relayed Instantly from the Source [*Project*]
IRIS .... Information Resources Information System [*Library of Congress*]
IRIS .... Infrared Information System [*Sadtler Research Laboratories, Inc.*] [*Philadelphia, PA*] [*Database*] (FDB)
IRIS .... Instant Response Information System [*IEEE*]
IRIS .... Instructional Resources Information System [*EPA Instructional Resources Center*] [*Bibliographic database*] (OBD)
IRIS .... Intelligence Reports Information Subsystem [*Data processing*]
IRIS .... Interactive Real-Time Information System
IRIS .... Interactive Recorded Information Service [*British*] [*Telecommunications*] (TEL)
IRIS .... International Relations Information System [*West Germany*] (EISS)
IRIS .... International Reporting and Information Services [*International Private Intelligence Service*] [*Terminated, 1983*]
IRIS .... International Reporting Information Systems
IRJE .... Interactive Remote Job Entry (CAA)
IRL .... Information Retrieval Language [*Data processing*]
IRL .... Information Retrieval Limited [*Database originator*] [*British*] [*Information service*]
IRLS .... Interrogation, Recording, and Locating System [*Naval Oceanographic Office*]
IRM .... Information and Records Management
IRM .... Information Resource Management [*Data processing*]
IRN .... Internal Routing Network (CAA)
IROR .... Internal Rate of Return [*Telecommunications*] (TEL)
IROS .... Instant Response Ordering System [*Brodart, Inc.*] [*Teleordering system*] [*Information service*] (EISS)
IRP .... Information Returns Processing [*Data processing*]
IRP .... International Routing Plan [*Telecommunications*] (TEL)
IRPL .... Index to Religious Periodical Literature [*Database*]
IRQ .... Interrupt Request [*Data processing*]
IRR .... Integrated Radio Room (MCD)
IRR .... Interrupt Return Register (CAA)
IRRD .... International Road Research Documentation [*OECD*] [*Bibliographic database*] (OBD)
IRRI .... Industrial Relations Research Institute [*University of Wisconsin - Madison*] [*Research center*] (RCD)
IRRIS .... International Rehabilitation Research Information System [*National Institute of Handicapped Research*] [*Database*] (CUAD)
IRS .... Indian Remote-Sensing Satellite
IRS .... Information Recovery [*or Retrieval*] System [*or Subsystem*]
IRS .... Information Resources Specialists [*San Francisco, CA*] [*Information service*] (EISS)
IRS .... Information Retrieval Service [*European Space Agency*] [*Host*] (EISS)
IRS .... Input Read Submodule
IRS .... Inquiry and Reporting System
IRS .... Interchange Record Separator [*Data processing*] (BUR)
IRS .... Internal Revenue Service [*Department of the Treasury*] [*Washington, DC*]
IRS .... International Repeater Station [*Telecommunications*] (TEL)
IRSS .... Infrared Search System [*Environmental Protection Agency*] [*Database*] (CUAD)
IRT .... Information Retrieval Technique
IRT .... Input Revision Typewriter
IRT .... Interrupted Ring Tone [*Telecommunications*] (TEL)
IRTE .... Institut de Radio-Telediffusion pour Enfants [*Children's Broadcast Institute*] [*Canada*]
IRTU .... Intelligent Remote Terminal Unit (CAA)
IRU .... Indefeasible Right of User [*Telecommunications*] (TEL)
IRV .... Interrupt Request Vector (CAA)
IRW .... Indirect Reference Word (BUR)
IRX .... Interactive Resource Executive [*NCR Corp.*] (CAA)
IS .... In Service [*Telecommunications*] (TEL)
IS .... Indexed Sequential [*Data processing*] (DEEC)
IS .... Information Science (IEEE)
IS .... Information Separator [*Control character*] [*Data processing*]
IS .... Information Service
IS .... Information System (CAA)
IS .... Input Secondary [*Electronics*]
IS .... Installation Start [*Telecommunications*] (TEL)
IS .... Interference Suppressor (IEEE)
IS .... International Standard
IS .... ISSN [*International Standard Serial Number*] [*Online database field identifier*] (OBD)
IS .... Issue Code [*Online database field identifier*] (OBD)
I2S .... Imagerie, Industrie, Systeme [*Machine vision manufacturer*] [*Bordeaux, France*]

ISA .... Information Systems Architecture [*AT & T*]
ISA .... Instrument Society of America [*Pittsburgh, PA*]
ISA .... Interrupt Storage Area (OA)
ISAAC .... Integrated System for Automated Acquisition and Control
IS/A AMPE ... Inter-Service Agency Automated Message Processing Exchange
ISABEL .... ISO [*International Organization for Standardization*] Status Accumulating Binaries [*Using*] Extraordinary Logic
ISACCC .... Initial Satellite Communications Control Center (MCD)
ISACMETU ... International Secretariat of Arts, Communications Media, and Entertainment Trade Unions (EANO)
ISAD .... Information Science and Automation Division [*Later, LITA*] [*American Library Association*]
ISADPM ...... International Society for the Abolition of Data Processing Machines (EANO)
ISAGA .... International Simulation and Gaming Association (EANO)
ISAGUG ...... International Software AG Users Group [*Reston, VA*] (EANO)
ISAL .... Information System Access Lines [*Data processing*] (TUT)
ISAM .... Indexed Sequential Access Method [*Pronounced "i-sam"*] [*Data processing*] (CIT)
ISAM .... Integrated Switching and Multiplexing [*IBM Corp.*]
ISAP .... Information Sort and Predict
ISAR .... Information Storage and Retrieval [*Data processing*] (DII)
ISB .... Independent Sideband
ISB .... Intermediate Sideband (NATG)
ISBF .... Interactive Search of Bibliographic Files (CAA)
ISBL .... Information System Base Language (CAA)
ISBN .... International Standard Book Number [*Library of Congress*]
ISC .... Initial Software Configuration Map (MCD)
ISC .... Integrated Storage Control
ISC .... Intelligent Systems Corporation (CAA)
ISC .... Interactive Sciences Corporation [*Information service*] (EISS)
ISC .... Intercompany Services Coordination [*Telecommunications*] (TEL)
ISC .... Interface Signal Chart
ISC .... International Switching Center [*Communications*] (CBSS)
ISC .... Interstellar Communications
ISC .... Interval Selection Circuit
ISC .... Intrasite Cabling (CET)
ISCAN .... Inertialess Steerable Communications Antenna
ISCAS .... International Symposium on Circuits and Systems [*IEEE*] (MCD)
ISCC .... International Service Coordination Center [*Communications*] (CBSS)
ISCD .... Interface Specification Control Document (KSC)
ISCET .... International Society of Certified Electronics Technicians (EANO)
ISCI .... Information Systems Consultants, Incorporated [*Information service*] (EISS)
ISCII .... International Standard Code for Information Interchange (NATG)
ISCO .... Interactive Systems Corporation [*NASDAQ symbol*] (NQ)
ISCO .... Istituto Nazionale per lo Studio della Congiuntura [*Data Resources, Inc.*] [*Database*] (CUAD)
ISCS .... Information Service Computer System (DIT)
ISC/USO ..... Intercompany Services Coordination/Universal Service Order [*Telecommunications*] (TEL)
ISCX .... Integrated Software Systems Corporation [*NASDAQ symbol*] (NQ)
ISD .... Information Structure Design (CAA)
ISD .... Information System Development [*Telecommunications*] (TEL)
ISD .... Initial Selection Done (OA)
ISD .... Integrated Symbolic Debugger [*Data processing*] (EISS)
ISD .... Integrated Systems Demonstrator (MCD)
ISD .... Intermediate Storage Device (CAA)
ISD .... International Subscriber Dialing [*Later, IDD*] [*Telecommunications*]
ISDN .... Integrated Services Digital Network [*Telecommunications*]
ISDO .... Institute for Systems Design and Optimization
ISDOS .... Information Systems Design Optimization System
ISDS .... Integrated Software Development System (CAA)
ISDS .... Integrated Switched Data Service [*Telecommunications*] (TEL)
ISDS .... International Serials Data System [*Paris, France*] [*Database*] (EANO)
ISE .... Information Services to Education [*American Society for Information Science*]
ISE .... Institute for Software Engineering [*Sunnyvale, CA*] (EANO)
ISE .... Interrupt System Enable (CAA)
ISER .... Integral Systems Experimental Requirements
ISF .... Individual Store and Forward (CAA)
ISF .... Infrasonic Frequency
ISFD .... Integrated Software Functional Design (CAA)
ISFM .... Indexed Sequential File Manager [*Data processing*] (CAA)
ISFMS .... Indexed Sequential File Management System [*Data processing*] (BUR)
ISG .... Intersubblock Gap (CAA)
ISHTCP .... Inventory of Sources for History of Twentieth Century Physics [*University of California, Berkeley*] [*Information service*] (EISS)
ISI .... Infodata Systems, Incorporated [*Information service*] (EISS)
ISI .... Information Storage, Incorporated
ISI .... Institute for Scientific Information [*Database producer*]
ISI .... Internally Specified Index
ISI .... Intersymbol Interference
ISI/ISTP & B ... ISI/Index to Scientific and Technical Proceedings and Books [*Institute for Scientific Information*] [*Philadelphia, PA*] [*Bibliographic database*] (OBD)

Computer & Telecommunications Acronyms

Acronym	Expansion
ISIS	Information System Indexing System [*Federal Judicial Center*] [*Database*] (FDB)
ISIS	Integrated Safeguard Information System
ISIS	Integrated Scientific Information System
ISIS	Integriertes Statistisches Informationssystem [*Central Statistical Office*] [*Database*] [*Austrian*] (CUAD)
ISIS	Internally Switched Interface System [*Tymnet, Inc.*] (CAA)
ISIS	International Satellite for Ionospheric Studies [*NASA-Canada*]
ISIS	International Science Information Services [*Earth sciences data center*] [*Dallas, TX*]
ISIS	International Species Inventory System [*Data processing for animal mating*]
ISIS	Interstate Settlement Information System [*AT & T*]
ISIS	Investigative Support Information System [*Federal Bureau of Investigation*]
ISK	Instruction Space Key (CAA)
ISL	Information Search Language
ISL	Information System Language [*Data processing*] (IEEE)
ISL	Initial System Loading
ISL	Instructional Systems Language [*Data processing*] (IEEE)
ISL	Integrated Schottky Logic (IEEE)
ISL	Interactive Simulation Language [*Data processing*] (IEEE)
ISL	Intersatellite Link (DEEC)
ISL	Intersystem Link (CAA)
ISM	Information System Manager (NATG)
ISM	Information Systems for Management (IEEE)
ISM	Information Systems Marketing, Inc. [*Information service*] (EISS)
ISM	International Systems Meeting [*Data processing*] (TUT)
ISM	Interpretive Structural Modeling [*A computer-assisted learning process for structuring information*]
ISMC	International Switching Maintenance Center [*Communications*] (CBSS)
ISMEC	Information Service in Mechanical Engineering [*Cambridge Scientific Abstracts*] [*IEE*] [*British*] [*Bibliographic database*] (EISS)
ISMH	Input Source Message Handler (CAA)
ISMM	International Society of Mini- and Micro-Computers (EANO)
ISMS	Image Store Management System (CAA)
ISMS	Interactive Solids Modeling System [*Gould Electronics Ltd. Computer Systems*] [*Software package*] [*British*] (NCC)
ISMX	Integrated Subrate Data Multiplexer (TEL)
ISN	Instron Corp. [*American Stock Exchange symbol*] [*Delisted*]
ISN	International Software Network, Inc. [*Milwaukee, WI*] [*Software manufacturer*] (DASOS)
ISO	Information Systems Office [*Library of Congress*]
ISO	Internal Standard Organization Code (CMD)
ISO	International Organization for Standardization [*Geneva, Switzerland*] [*United Nations*]
ISO-CMOS	Isolated Fully Recessed Complementary Metal-Oxide Semiconductor (TEL)
ISODATA	Iterative Self-Organizing Data Analysis Technique A [*Data processing*]
ISOL	Information Solutions [*NASDAQ symbol*] (NQ)
ISONET	ISO [*International Organization for Standardization*] Information Network [*Information service*] (EISS)
I2S(OPS)	Integrated Information System (Operational) [*Marine Corps*] (DDI)
ISORID	International Information System on Research in Documentation [*Paris, France*] [*UNESCO*] (EISS)
ISP	Image Store Processor [*Data processing*]
ISP	Indexed Sequential Processor (CAA)
ISP	Information System Plan (MCD)
ISP	Information Systems Program [*National Science Foundation*]
ISP	Instruction Set Processor [*1971*] [*Data processing*]
ISP	Instructional System Package (MCD)
ISP	Internally Stored Program
ISPC	International Sound Programing Center [*Telecommunications*] (CBSS)
ISPC	International Statistical Program Center [*Agency for International Development*] (EISS)
ISPF	Interactive System Productivity Facility [*Data processing*]
ISPF/PDF	Interactive System Productivity Facility/Program Development Facility [*Data processing*]
ISPL	Incremental System Programing Language [*Data processing*]
ISPL	Instruction Set Processor Language [*Data processing*]
ISPN	International Standard Program Number [*Numbering system for software*]
ISPR	International Special Commission on Radio Interference (MCD)
ISPS	Instruction Set Processor Specification [*1977*] [*Data processing*] (CSR)
ISR	Image Storage Retrieval (OA)
ISR	Information Processing and Management [*A publication*]
IS & R	Information Storage and Retrieval [*Data processing*]
ISR	Information Storage and Retrieval [*Data processing*]
ISR	Interrupt Service Routine (IEEE)
ISRAC	ITT [*International Telephone & Telegraph Corp.*] Secure Ranging and Communications System
ISRM	Information Systems Resource Manager (CAA)
ISRU	International Scientific Radio Union [*Also, URSI*]
ISS	Information Storage System (IEEE)
ISS	Information Systems [*Subdivision*] (MCD)
ISS	Information Systems Security
ISS	Information Systems Services [*Brigham Young University*] [*Research center*] (RCD)
ISS	Intelligent Support System (CAA)
ISS	Interface Simulation System (CAAL)
ISS	Interrupt Service Subroutine (CMD)
ISS	Interstellar Scattering [*of radio waves in the galaxy*]
ISS	Ionospheric Sounding Satellite [*Japan*]
ISSA	Information Systems Security Association (EANO)
ISSAS	Interactive Structural Sizing and Analysis System [*Data processing*]
ISSB	Information Systems Standards Board [*American National Standards Institute*] [*Telecommunications*]
ISSCC	International Solid State Circuits Conference
ISSCO	Integrated Software Systems Corporation
ISSD	Information Systems and Services Division [*Department of Commerce*] (EISS)
ISSDN	Integrated Services Satellite Digital Network (MCD)
ISSLS	International Symposium on Subscribers' Loops and Services [*Telecommunications*] (TEL)
ISSMB	Information Systems Standards Management Board
ISSN	International Standard Serial Number [*Library of Congress*]
ISSR	Information Storage, Selection, and Retrieval [*Data processing*]
ISSUE	Information System Software Update Environment (CAA)
IST	Information Science and Technology (BUR)
IST	Institute of Science and Technology [*University of Michigan*] [*Research center*] (RCD)
IST	Institute for Simulation and Training [*University of Central Florida*] [*Research center*] (RCD)
IST	Integrated Switching and Transmission [*Telecommunications*] (TEL)
IST	Integrated System Transformer (IEEE)
IST	Interstation Transmission (KSC)
ISTAR	Image Storage Translation and Reproduction
ISTC	Incunable Short Title Catalogue [*British Library*] [*Information service*] (EISS)
ISTC	International Switching and Testing Center [*Communications*] (CBSS)
ISTIM	Interchange of Scientific and Technical Information in Machine Language [*Office of Science and Technology*]
ISTN	Integrated Switching and Transmission Network [*Telecommunications*] (TEL)
ISTP & B	Index to Scientific and Technical Proceedings and Books [*Institute for Scientific Information*]
ISTR	Indexed Sequential Table Retrieval (CAA)
ISU	Independent Signal Unit [*Telecommunications*] (TEL)
ISU	Initial Signal Unit [*Telecommunications*] (TEL)
ISU	Instruction Storage Unit (CAA)
ISU	Interface Sharing Unit (CAA)
ISU	Interface Switching Unit (BUR)
ISV	Independent Software Vendor [*Data processing*]
ISV	Interval Service Value (BUR)
ISWU	International Society of Wang Users [*Lowell, MA*] (EANO)
ISY	IBM [*International Business Machines Corp.*] Systems Journal [*A publication*]
ISZ	Increment and Skip on Zero [*Data processing*]
IT	Incomplete Translation [*Telecommunications*] (TEL)
IT	Index Term [*Data processing*]
IT	Industry Telephone Maintenance [*FCC*] (IEEE)
IT	Information Technology
IT	Information Transform [*Information service*] (EISS)
IT	Input Terminal (CAA)
IT	Input Translator [*IBM Corp.*] [*Data processing*]
IT	Intelligent Terminal [*Data processing*]
IT	Internal Translator [*Carnegie Institute*] [*IBM Corp.*]
IT	Intertoll [*Trunk*] [*Telecommunications*] (TEL)
IT	Interval Timer [*Data processing*] (TUT)
IT	Island Telephone Co. Ltd. [*Toronto Stock Exchange symbol*]
ITA	Independent Telecommunications Analysts [*Boulder, CO*] (TSSD)
ITA	Independent Television Authority [*Later, IBA*] [*British*]
ITA	Institute for Telecommunications and Aeronomy [*ESSA*] (MCD)
ITA	Interface Test Adapters (MCD)
ITA	International Telegraph Alphabet (NATG)
ITAMA	Information Technology Acquisition and Marketing Association (EANO)
ITAVS	Integrated Testing, Analysis, and Verification System (CAA)
ITB	Integral Terminal Block
ITB	Integrated Test Block
ITB	Intermediate Text Block (CAA)
ITB	Intermediate Transmission Block [*Data processing*] (BUR)
ITB	Internal Transfer Bus (CAA)
ITC	Instructional Telecommunications Consortium [*Washington, DC*] (EANO)
ITC	Integrated Trajectory Computations (SKY)
ITC	Intercept [*Telecommunications*] (TEL)
ITC	Interdata Transaction Controller [*Perkin-Elmer*] (CAA)
ITC	Intermediate Toll Center [*Telecommunications*] (TEL)
ITC	International Telemetering Conference (CAA)
ITC	International Teletraffic Congress [*Telecommunications*]
ITC	International Television Center [*Communications*] (CBSS)
ITC	International Trade Commission [*Databank originator*]
ITCA	Inter-American Technical Council on Archives (DIT)

Computer & Telecommunications Acronyms

Acronym	Expansion
IT/CA	International Teleconferencing Association [*McLean, VA*] [*Telecommunications*] (EANO)
ITCC	International Technical Communications Conference [*Society for Technical Communication*]
ITDE	Interchannel Time Displacement Error [*Magnetic recording*]
ITDM	Intelligent Time-Division Multiplexer
ITE	Institute of Telecommunications Engineers (CAH)
ITE	International Telephone Exchange [*Telecommunications*] (TEL)
ITEC	Information Technology Electronics and Computers [*A publication*]
ITEL	Joint WMO/IOC Group of Experts on Telecommunications
ITEMS	INCOTERM [*International Commerce Term*] Transaction Entry Management System (CAA)
ITEP	Interim Tactical ELINT [*Electronic Intelligence*] Processor
ITF	Impulse Transfer Function (KSC)
ITF	Integrated Test Facility [*Data processing*]
ITF	Interactive Terminal Facility
ITFS	Instructional Television Fixed Service [*Educational TV*]
ITI	Industrial Technology Institute [*Ann Arbor, MI*] [*Research center*] (RCD)
ITI	Infosystems Technology, Incorporated [*Greenbelt, MD*] [*Software manufacturer*] (DASOS)
ITI	Interactive Terminal Interface [*Data processing*] (IEEE)
ITI	Intermittent Trouble Indication [*Telecommunications*] (TEL)
ITIPI	Interim Tactical Information Processing and Interpretation
ITIRC	IBM Technical Information Retrieval Center
ITIS	Industrial Technical Information Service [*Singapore*] (EISS)
ITIS	Internal Translation Information Subsystem [*Data processing*]
ITL	Interactive Technology Laboratory [*New York Institute of Technology*] [*Research center*] (RCD)
ITL	Intermediate Transfer Language (CAA)
ITLS	International Thomson Library Services
ITM	Indirect Tag Memory (CAA)
ITMA	Investigation on Teaching Using Microcomputers as an Aid
ITMC	International Transmission Maintenance Center [*Communications*] (CBSS)
ITN	Integrated Teleprocessing Network (CAA)
ITOS	Improved TIROS [*Television Infrared Observation Satellite*] Operational Satellite [*National Oceanic and Atmospheric Administration*]
ITP	Input Translator Program [*Data processing*]
ITP	Interactive Terminal Protocol (CAA)
ITPA	Independent Telephone Pioneer Association
ITPC	International Television Program Center [*Telecommunications*] (TEL)
ITPS	Integrated Teleprocessing System (IEEE)
ITPS	Internal Teleprocessing System (CMD)
ITR	Information Technology Research [*Framingham, MA*] [*Telecommunications*] (TSSD)
ITR	Integrated Telephone Recorder [*Telecommunications*] (TEL)
ITRDB	International Tree-Ring Data Bank [*University of Arizona*] (EISS)
ITS	Information Processing Services [*California State University, Long Beach*] [*Research center*] (RCD)
ITS	Information Technology Systems
ITS	Information Transfer Satellite (KSC)
ITS	Information Transfer [*or Transmission*] System
ITS	Insertion Test Signal [*Telecommunications*] (TEL)
ITS	Institute for Telecommunication Sciences [*Formerly, ITSA*] [*Department of Commerce*]
ITS	Institute of Telecommunications Services
ITS	Integrated Test Software (CAAL)
ITS	Intelligent Terminal System [*IBM Corp.*] (CAA)
ITS	Interactive Terminal Support (CAA)
ITS	Interim Teleprinter System
ITS	International Telecom Systems, Inc. [*Madison, WI*] [*Telecommunications*] (TSSD)
ITS	Intertime Switch [*Connection or Call*] [*Telecommunications*] (TEL)
ITS	Invitation to Send [*Western Union*] [*Data communications*]
ITS	ITT [*International Telephone & Telegraph Corp.*] Consumer Services Corp. [*NYSE symbol*] [*Delisted*]
ITSA	Institute for Telecommunication Sciences and Aeronomy [*Later, ITS*] [*National Oceanic and Atmospheric Administration*]
ITSC	International Telecommunications Satellite Consortium [*Superseded by International Telecommunications Satellite Organization*]
ITSC	International Telephone Services Center [*Telecommunications*] (TEL)
ITT	Incoming Teletype
IT and T	International Telephone & Telegraph Corp. [*New York, NY*]
ITT	International Telephone & Telegraph Corp. [*NYSE symbol*] [*Wall Street slang name: "It Girl," the sobriquet for early movie star Clara Bow*]
ITTAC	International Telegraph and Telephonic Advisory Committee
ITTCCS	ITT Corporate Communications Services, Inc. (CAA)
ITTCOM	International Telephone & Telegraph World Communications, Inc.
ITTCS	International Telephone and Telegraph Communication System
ITTD	Information and Technology Transfer Database [*International Research and Evaluation*]
ITTF	International Telephone and Telegraph Federal Laboratories
ITTFL	International Telephone and Telegraph Federal Laboratories
ITU	International Telecommunications Union [*A specialized agency of the United Nations*] [*Geneva, Switzerland*]
ITU	International Telegraphic Union [*United Nations*]
ITUG	Information Technology Users Group [*Exxon Corp.*]
ITUG	International Tandem Users' Group (EANO)
ITUSA	Information Technology Users' Standards Association
ITV	Independent Television
ITV	Industrial Television
ITV	Instructional Television
ITV	Israel Television
ITVA	International Television Association [*Formerly, International Industrial Television Association*] [*Irving, TX*] [*Telecommunications*] [*Information service*] (EANO)
ITVAC	Industrial Transistor Value Automatic Computer
ITVB	International Television Broadcasting
ITY	Information Technology Year [*1982*]
IU	Information Unit (CAA)
IU	Information Unlimited [*Berkeley, CA*] [*Information service*] (EISS)
IU	Input Unit (CAA)
IU	Instant Update [*Professional Farmers of America*] [*Cedar Falls, IA*] [*Telecommunications*] (TSSD)
IU	Instruction Unit [*Data processing*]
IU	Interface Unit [*Data processing*] (MCD)
IUA	Interface Unit Adapter [*Data processing*] (MCD)
IUA	IOMEC Users Association [*Formerly, DUA*] [*Defunct*]
IUC	International University of Communication [*Washington, DC*]
IUC	International University Consortium for Telecommunications in Learning [*Owings Mill, MD*] (EANO)
IUCAF	Interunion Commission on Allocation of Frequencies [*Telecommunications*] (TEL)
IUD	Information und Dokumentation [*Information and Documentation*] [*German*] [*Information retrieval*] (ODIN)
IUG	ICES [*Integrated Civil Engineering System*] Users Group [*Cranston, RI*] (EANO)
IUG	Intercomm User Group [*Later, SDAUG*] (EANO)
IUP	Installed User Program [*Data processing*]
IURC	International Union for Research of Communication (EANO)
IURP	Integrated Unit Record Processor (CAA)
IUS	Information Unit Separator [*Data processing*] (CAA)
IUS	Interchange Unit Separator [*Data processing*] (BUR)
IUWDS	International URSI [*Union Radio Scientifique Internationale*]-gram and World Day Service
IVA	Interactive Video Association [*Evanston, IL*] [*Information service*] (EISS)
IVAG	Institutionenverzeichnis Auslaendischer Gesellschaften [*Nomos Verlagsgesellschaft*] [*Database*] (CUAD)
IVC	Interactive Videodisc Consortium (EANO)
IVC	Intervehicular Communication (KSC)
IVCS	Integrated Vehicular Communication System (MCD)
IVCS	Integrated [*or Interior*] Voice Communications System (MCD)
IVG	Interrupt Vector Generator (CAA)
IVIPA	International Videotex Information Providers' Association [*British*] [*Information service*] (EISS)
IVL	Inventory Validation Listing [*Data processing*]
IVLV	Industrievereinigung fuer Lebensmitteltechnologie und Verpackung [*Information retrieval*] (ODIN)
IVM	Initial Virtual Memory (OA)
IVM	Interface Virtual Machine [*Data processing*] (CAA)
IVP	Installation Verification Procedure (MCD)
IVS	Informationsvermittelungsstelle [*Information retrieval*] (ODIN)
IVSN	Initial Voice Switched Network [*NATO integrated communications system*] (NATG)
IVT	Integrated Video Terminal (CAA)
IV & V	Independent Validation and Verification (CAAL)
IW	Index Word [*Online database field identifier*] (OA)
IW	Inside Wire [*Telecommunications*] (TEL)
IWCA	Inside Wiring Cable [*Telecommunications*] (TEL)
IWCS/SEA	Integrated Wideband Communications System/Southeast Asia (IEEE)
IWP	International Information/Word Processing Association [*Formerly, IWPA*] (EANO)
IWPA	International Word Processing Association [*Later, IIWPA, IWP*]
IWR	Information World Review [*Oxford, England*] [*A publication*] [*Information service*] (EISS)
IWU	Isolation Working Unit [*Telecommunications*] (TEL)
IX	Index [*Data processing*] (BUR)
IXT	Interaction Cross Talk [*Telecommunications*] (TEL)
IZ	Informationszentrum [*Information Center*] [*German*] [*Information retrieval*] (ODIN)
IZB	Informationszentrum fuer Biologie [*Forschungsinstitut Senckenberg*] [*Frankfurt*] [*Information retrieval*] (ODIN)

J

J	Job (IEEE)
J	Joule [Symbol] [SI unit of energy]
J	Jour [Day] [Telegram not to be delivered during the night time] [French]
JABOWA	Janak-Botkin-Wallis [Data processing program regarding forest growth; named for three men involved in program]
JACC	Joint Automatic Control Conference
JACM	Journal. Association for Computing Machinery [A publication]
JAF	Job Accounting Facility (CAA)
JAFF	Electronic and Chaff Jamming (IEEE)
JAI	Job Accounting Interface (CAA)
JAKIS	Japanese Keyword Indexing Simulator
JALPG	Joint Automatic Language Processing Group
JAM	Jail Accounting Microcomputer System
JANET	Joint Academic Network [Proposed supercomputer network]
JANUS	Joint Analog Numeric Understanding System
JAPATIC	Japan Patient Information Center [Information service] (EISS)
JAPIO	Japan Patent Information Organization [Database producer] (CUAD)
JAR	Jump Address Register (CAA)
JAS	Job Analysis System [Computer program]
JASIS	Journal. American Society for Information Science [A publication]
J Ass Comput Mach	Journal. Association for Computing Machinery [A publication]
J Assoc Comput Mach	Journal. Association for Computing Machinery [A publication]
J Assoc Pers Comput Chem	Journal. Association of Personal Computers for Chemists [A publication]
JAT	Job Accounting Table (CAA)
JAWS	Josephson AttoWeber Switch [Data processor circuitry]
JAWS	Junk Acronyms When Speaking [Program]
JC	Journal Code [Online database field identifier] (OBD)
JC	Journal of Communication [A publication]
JC	JOVIAL [Joule's Own Version of the International Algorithmic Language] Compiler [Data processing]
JC	Jump on Condition [Data processing] (BUR)
JCB	Job Control Block [Data processing] (BUR)
JCC	Job Control Card (MCD)
JCC	Joint Communications Center (MCD)
JCC	Joint Computer Conference
JCCOMNET	Joint Coordination Center Communications Network
JCENS	Joint Communications-Electronics Nomenclature System
JCET	Joint Council on Educational Telecommunications [Corporation for Public Broadcasting] [Washington, DC]
JCEWG	Joint Communications and Electronics Working Group [NATO] (NATG)
JCGS	Joint Center for Graduate Study [Washington State University, University of Washington, and Oregon State University] [Research center] (RCD)
J Chem Inf Comp Sci	Journal of Chemical Information and Computer Sciences [A publication]
JCICS	Journal of Chemical Information and Computer Sciences [A publication]
JCL	Job Control Language [High-level programing language] [1979] [Data processing] (CGC)
JCM	Job Cylinder Map [Data processing] (IBMDP)
JCMNA	Journal of Communication [A publication]
JCN	Jump on Condition [Data processing]
J Comm	Journal of Communication [A publication]
J Communication	Journal of Communication [A publication]
J Comput Appl Math	Journal of Computational and Applied Mathematics [A publication]
J Comput Assisted Tomogr	Journal of Computer Assisted Tomography [A publication]
J Comput Assist Tomogr	Journal of Computer Assisted Tomography [A publication]
J Computational Phys	Journal of Computational Physics [A publication]
J Comput Chem	Journal of Computational Chemistry [A publication]
J Comput Ph	Journal of Computational Physics [A publication]
J Comput Phys	Journal of Computational Physics [A publication]
J Comput Soc India	Journal. Computer Society of India [A publication]
J Comput Sy	Journal of Computer and System Sciences [A publication]
J Comput Syst Sci	Journal of Computer and System Sciences [A publication]
J Comput and Syst Sci	Journal of Computer and System Sciences [A publication]
JCP	Job Control Program (CMD)
JCP	John Crowe Productions, Inc. [Houston, TX] [Telecommunications] (TSSD)
JCP	JOVIAL [Joule's Own Version of the International Algorithmic Language] Control Program [Data processing]
JCSS	Journal of Computer and System Sciences [A publication]
JCSTC	Joint Council for Scientific and Technical Communication [British]
JCT	Job Control Table (CMD)
JCT	Junction (AFM)
J Curr Laser Abstr	Journal of Current Laser Abstracts [A publication]
JCVS	JOVIAL [Joule's Own Version of the International Algorithmic Language] Compiler Validation System [Data processing]
J Cybern Inf Sci	Journal of Cybernetics and Information Science [A publication]
J Cybern and Inf Sci	Journal of Cybernetics and Information Science [A publication]
J Data Ed	Journal of Data Education [A publication]
JDC	Junction Diode Circuit
JDL	Job Description Language [Data processing]
JDL	Job Description Library (CAA)
JDS	Job Data Sheet (IEEE)
JE	Jamming Equipment
JEBG	Japan Electronics Buyers' Guide
JECC	Japanese Electronic Computer Company (CAH)
JECL	Job Entry Control Language (CAA)
JECS	Job Entry Central Services (MCD)
JEDEC	Joint Electron Device Engineering Council [Computer standards]
JEFF	Judiciously Efficient Fixed Frame [Data processing] (MCD)
JEIA	Joint Electronics Information Agency
JEIDA	Japanese Electronic Industries Development Association
JEIPAC	Japanese Electronic Information Processing Automatic Computer
J Elec Mat	Journal of Electronic Materials [A publication]
J Electron Mater	Journal of Electronic Materials [A publication]
JEMC	Joint Engineering Management Conference
JEOCN	Joint European Operations Communications Network
JEPS	Job Entry Peripheral Services [IBM Corp.] (MCD)
JES	Job Entry System [or Subsystem] [IBM Corp.] [Data processing]
JETS	Jet Express Ticketing System (TUT)
JETS	Job Executive and Transport Satellite [NCR Corp.] (CAA)
JF	Junction Frequency [Telecommunications] (TEL)
JF	Junctor Frame [Telecommunications] (TEL)
JFCB	Job File Control Block [Data processing] (BUR)
JFET	Junction Field-Effect Transistor
JFG	Jumbogroup Frequency Generator [Bell System]
JFN	Job File Number (CAA)
JFS	Jumbogroup Frequency Supply [Bell System]
JG	Junction Grammar [Data processing] (DEEC)
JGA	Joseph Guzman & Associates, Inc. [Palatine, IL] [Telecommunications] (TSSD)
JGF	Junctor Grouping Frame [Telecommunications] (TEL)
JHMCO	J. H. Morgan Consultants [Morristown, NJ] [Information service] [Telecommunications] (TSSD)
JIB	Job Information Block [Data processing] (BUR)
JICST	Japan Information Center of Science and Technology [Tokyo, Japan]
JICTAR	Joint Industry Committee for Television Advertising Research [Database producer] (CUAD)
JIN	Jump Indirectly [Data processing]
J Info Mgmt	Journal of Information Management [A publication]
J Information Processing	Journal of Information Processing [A publication]
J Inform Process	Journal of Information Processing [A publication]
J Inst Electr Eng Part 3	Journal. Institution of Electrical Engineers. Part 3. Radio and Communication Engineering [A publication]
J Inst Electron Commun Eng Jap	Journal. Institute of Electronics and Communication Engineers of Japan [A publication]
J Inst Electron and Commun Eng Jpn	Journal. Institute of Electronics and Communication Engineers of Japan [A publication]

Computer & Telecommunications Acronyms

J Inst Electron Telecommun Eng ... Journal. Institution of Electronics and Telecommunication Engineers [*A publication*]
J Inst Eng (India) Electron Telecommun Eng Div ... Journal. Institution of Engineers (India). Electronics and Telecommunication Engineering Division [*A publication*]
J Inst (India) Electron Telecommun Eng Div ... Journal. Institution of Engineers (India). Electronics and Telecommunication Engineering Division [*A publication*]
J Inst Telecommun Eng ... Journal. Institution of Telecommunication Engineers [*A publication*]
J Inst Telecommun Eng (New Delhi) ... Journal. Institution of Telecommunication Engineers (New Delhi) [*A publication*]
JIP............ Joint Input Processing   (IEEE)
JIS............. Japanese Industrial Standard
JIS............. Job Information Service [*Department of Labor*]
JISC.......... Japanese Industrial Standards Committee [*Agency of Industrial Science and Technology, Ministry of International Trade and Industry*] [*Tokyo, Japan*]
JISO........... Japanese International Satellite Organization [*Cable-television system*]
JK............... Flip-Flop Circuit [*Data processing*]   (DFFC)
JL............... Journal [*Online database field identifier*]   (OBD)
JLMPA....... Journal of Microwave Power [*A publication*]
J Microcomput Appl ... Journal of Microcomputer Applications [*A publication*]
J Microgr.... Journal of Micrographics [*A publication*]
J Micrographics ... Journal of Micrographics [*A publication*]
J Microwave Power ... Journal of Microwave Power [*A publication*]
J Microwave Pwr ... Journal of Microwave Power [*A publication*]
JMP............ Jack Morton Productions, Inc. [*New York, NY*] [*Telecommunications*]   (TSSD)
JMP............ Jump [*Data processing*]
JMPO.......... Journal of Microwave Power [*A publication*]
JMS............ Jump to Subroutine Instruction [*Data processing*]
JMSX.......... Job Memory Switch Matrix   (CAA)
JMX............ Jumbogroup Multiplex [*Bell System*]
JN............... Journal Name [*Online database field identifier*]
JNMR.......... Joint National Media Research [*Database producer*]   (CUAD)
JOCIT .... JOVIAL [*Joule's Own Version of the International Algorithmic Language*] Compiler Implementation Tool [*Data processing*]   (MCD)
JODC .... Japan Oceanographic Data Center [*Information service*]   (EISS)
JOHNNIAC ... John's [*Von Neumann*] Integrator and Automatic Computer [*An early computer*]
JOIS............ Japan Online Information System [*Database*]
JOL .... Job Organization Language [*1979*] [*Data processing*]   (CSR)
JOSS........... JOHNNIAC [*John's Integrator and Automatic Computer*] Open Shop System [*Time-sharing language*] [*Rand Corp.*] [*1962*] [*Data processing*]
JOVIAL .... Joule's Own Version of the International Algebraic [*or Algorithmic*] Language [*1958*] [*Data processing*]
JP................ Job Processor   (CAA)
JP................ Junction Panel [*or Point*] [*Electronics*]
JP................ Jute Protection [*Telecommunications*]   (TEL)
JPA .... Job Pack Area [*Data processing*]   (IBMDP)
JPC .... Just Prior Condition [*Data processing*]
JPCD........... Just Perceptible Color Difference [*Telecommunications*]   (TEL)
JPGS........... Japan Publications Guide Service [*Information service*]   (EISS)
JPL.............. Jet Propulsion Laboratory [*Renamed H. Allen Smith Jet Propulsion Laboratory, 1973, after a retiring congressman. However, name is not expected to be used officially*] [*California Institute of Technology*] [*NASA*] [*Research center*]
Jpn Annu Rev Electron Comput Telecommun ... Japan Annual Reviews in Electronics, Computers, and Telecommunications [*A publication*]
J Pop Film & TV ... Journal of Popular Film and Television [*A publication*]
J Pop Fi TV ... Journal of Popular Film and Television [*A publication*]
J Popular F ... Journal of Popular Film and Television [*A publication*]
JPTDS......... Junior Participating Tactical Data System [*Also known as "Jeep"*]   (MCD)
JPU .... Job Processing Unit   (CAA)
JPW............. Job Processing Word
JRA .... Jam-Resistant Antenna
JRSC........... Jam-Resistant Secure Communications
JRSVC .... Jam-Resistant Secure Voice Communications   (MCD)
JRT .... Jugoslovenska Radio-Televizija [*Radio and television network*] [*Yugoslavia*]
JS................ Jam Strobe   (IEEE)
J/S............... Justified   (CDH)
JSCB........... Job Step Control Block [*Data processing*]   (BUR)
JSCC .... Scott Cable Communications [*NASDAQ symbol*]   (NQ)
JSD .... Justification Service Digit [*Telecommunications*]   (TEL)
JSF.............. Job Services File   (CAA)
JSF.............. Junctor Switch Frame [*Telecommunications*]   (TEL)
JSI............... Journal. American Society for Information Science [*A publication*]
JSL.............. Job Specification Language   (OA)
JSM............. Journal of Systems Management [*A publication*]
JSR .... Jam to Signal Ratio   (MCD)
JSR .... Jump to Subroutine [*Data processing*]   (BUR)
JSSPG .... Job Shop Simulation Program Generator   (KSC)
J Sys Mgmt ... Journal of Systems Management [*A publication*]
J Sys Mgt ... Journal of Systems Management [*A publication*]
J Systems Mgt ... Journal of Systems Management [*A publication*]
J Systems Software ... Journal of Systems and Software [*A publication*]
J Syst Man ... Journal of Systems Management [*A publication*]
J Syst Manage ... Journal of Systems Management [*A publication*]
J Syst Mgt ... Journal of Systems Management [*A publication*]
JTDS........... Joint Track Data Storage
JTEC........... Japan Telecommunications Engineering and Consultancy   (TEL)
J Tech Writ Commun ... Journal of Technical Writing and Communication [*A publication*]
J Telecommun Networks ... Journal of Telecommunication Networks [*A publication*]
JTPS .... Job and Tape Planning System   (CAA)
JTR .... Japan Telecommunications Review [*A publication*]
JTSCC .... Joint Telecommunications Standards Coordinating Committee [*American National Standards Institute*] [*Telecommunications*]
JU................ Joint User [*Telecommunications*]   (TEL)
JUG............. Joint Users Group [*Data processing*]
JUGFET...... Junction Gate Field-Effect Transistor   (TEL)
JULIE .... Joint Utility Locating Information for Excavators [*Telecommunications*]   (TEL)
JUN .... Jump Unconditionally [*Data processing*]
JURG .... Joint Users Requirements Group   (NASA)
JURIS.......... Juristisches Informationssystem [*Judicial Information System*] [*Federal Ministry of Justice*] [*Legal database*] [*West German*]   (EISS)
JURIS.......... Justice Retrieval and Inquiry System [*Department of Justice*] [*Legal databank*] [*Information service*]   (EISS)

K

K	Dielectric Constant
K	Invitation to Transmit [*Communications*] (FAAC)
K	Key
k	Kilo [*A prefix meaning multiplied by 10^3*] [*SI symbol*]
K	Kilobyte [*Data processing*]
K	Thousand
kA	Kiloampere
KAD	Keyboard and Display [*Data processing*]
KAK	Key-Auto-Key [*Data processing*]
KALDAS	Kidsgrove ALGOL [*Algorithmic Language*] Digital Analogue Simulation [*Data processing*] [*British*]
KAM	Keep-Alive Memory [*Data processing*]
KARL	[*A*] programing language (CSR)
KAU	Keystation Adapter Unit [*Data processing*]
KAYP	Kaypro Corp. [*NASDAQ symbol*] (NQ)
KB	Keyboard [*Data processing*]
kb	KiloBIT [*Binary Digit*] [*Data processing*]
KB	Kilobyte [10^3 *bytes*]
KBC	K-Band Circulator
KBE	Keyboard Encoder [*Data processing*]
KBE	Keyboard Entry [*Data processing*]
KBF	K-Band Feed
KBF	Kurzberichte aus der Bauforschung [*Information retrieval*] (ODIN)
KBIM	Keyboard Interface Module (MCD)
KBIT/S	KiloBITS [*Binary Digits*] per Second [*Transmission rate*] [*Data processing*] (TEL)
KBM	Keyboard Monitor [*Data processing*]
KBP	Keyboard Process [*Data processing*]
kbps	KiloBITS [*Binary Digits*] per Second [*Transmission rate*] [*Data processing*]
kbs	KiloBITS [*Binary Digits*] per Second [*Transmission rate*] [*Data processing*]
KBU	Keyboard Unit [*Data processing*] (NASA)
KC	Kilocharacter (BUR)
kc	Kilocycle [*Radio*]
KCB	Keyboard Change Button [*Data processing*]
KCC	Keyboard Common Contact [*Data processing*]
KCC	Koplar Communications Center [*St. Louis, MO*] [*Telecommunications*] (TSSD)
KCMX	Keyset Central Multiplexer (VIT)
KCO	Keep Cost Order [*Telecommunications*] (TEL)
KCR	Key Call Receiver [*Telecommunications*] (TEL)
kcs	Kilocycles per Second
KCS	Thousand Characters per Second
KCU	Keyboard Control Unit (CAA)
KDC	Keyed Display Console
KDD	Kokusai Denshin Denwa Co. Ltd. [*Telegraph & Telephone Corp.*] [*Tokyo, Japan*] [*Telecommunications*]
KDE	Keyboard Data Entry (CAA)
KDE	Klein Diversified Enterprises, Inc. [*Madison, WI*] [*Software manufacturer*] (DASOS)
KDEM	Kurzweil Data Entry Machine [*for optical character recognition*]
KDOS	Key to Disk Operating System (CAA)
KDOS	Key Display Operating System (CAA)
KDP	Key Development Plan [*Telecommunications*] (TEL)
KDP	Keyboard, Display, and Printer (CAA)
KDR	Keyboard Data Recorder [*Data processing*] (CGC)
KDS	Key to Disc System (CAA)
KDS	Key Display System [*Data processing*] (MDG)
KDT	Key Data Terminal (CAA)
KE	Key Equipment [*Telecommunications*] (TEL)
KE	Knowledge Engineer [*Data processing*]
KEAN	Keane, Inc. [*NASDAQ symbol*] (NQ)
KEE	Knowledge Engineering Environment [*An artificial intelligence system*]
KEIS	Kentucky Economic Information System [*Database producer*] [*Information service*]
KEP	Key Entry Processing (CAA)
KEPROM	Keyed-Access, Erasable, Programable Read-Only Memory [*Data processing*]
keV	Kiloelectron Volt
KEYMAT	Keying Material [*Data processing*] (NVT)
KEYPER	Keywords Permuted (DIT)
KF	Key Field (CAA)
KFAS	Keyed File Access System (CAA)
kg	Kilogram [*Also, k*] [*Symbol*] [*SI unit for mass*]
KGM	Key Generator Module (CAA)
Khz	Kilohertz
KIAC	Kerr Industrial Applications Center [*Southeastern Oklahoma State University, Durant, OK*] [*Information service*] (EISS)
KIBIC	Karolinska Institutets Bibliotek och Informationscentral [*Karolinska Institute Library and Information Center*] [*Sweden*] [*Information service*] (EISS)
KICU	Keyboard Interface Control Unit (CAA)
KIDDCOS	Kitchens Design Drawing and Costing [*Kitchens International DMS Electronics Ltd.*] [*Software package*] [*British*] (NCC)
KIL	Keyed Input Language (CAA)
KIM	Keyboard Input Matrix [*Data processing*]
KIOPI	Kienzle Input/Output Peripheral Interface (CAA)
KIP	Knowledge Information Processing [*Data processing*]
KIPI	Knowledge Industry Publications, Incorporated [*White Plains, NY*] [*Telecommunications*] [*Information service*]
KIPO	Keyboard Input Printout [*Data processing*] (IEEE)
KIPS	Kilo-Instructions per Second
KIS	Keyboard Input Simulation [*Data processing*]
KISS	Keep It Short and Sweet [*Radio messages*]
KISS	Keep It Simple, Sir [*Data processing*]
KISS	Keep It Simple Software Corp. [*Coral Gables, FL*] [*Software manufacturer*] (DASOS)
KISS	Keep It Straight and Simple [*Data processing*] (TUT)
KISS	Keyed Indexed Sequential Search (CAA)
KIST	Korean Institute for Science and Technology
KIT	Key Issue Tracking [*Database*] (DEEC)
KKK	Konferenzberichte Kernforschung, Kerntechnik [*Information retrieval*] (ODIN)
KL	Keller's Language [*1977*] [*Data processing*] (CSR)
KL	Key Length [*Data processing*] (BUR)
KLIC	Keyletter-in-Context [*Data processing*]
KLS	Knotted List Structure (BUR)
KLU	Key and Lamp Units [*Telecommunications*] (DEEC)
km	Kilometer
kMc	Kilomegacycle
KMK	Konyvtartudomanyi es Modszertani Kozpont [*Center for Library Science and Methodology*] [*Hungary*] [*Information service*] (EISS)
KMON	Keyboard Monitor [*Digital Equipment Corp.*] (CAA)
KMPS	Kernel Multiple Processing System [*Data processing*]
KMS	Keysort Multiple Selector
KMWS	KMW Systems Corp. [*NASDAQ symbol*] (NQ)
KOBOL	Keystation On-Line Business-Oriented Language [*Data processing*]
KOHM	Kilohm (MCD)
KOM	Kilometric Wavelength [*Radio astronomy*]
KOPS	Thousands of Operations per Second (NASA)
KORE	Kinetic Analysis Using Over-Relaxation [*FORTRAN computer program*] [*Physical chemistry*]
KORSTIC	Korea Scientific and Technological Information Center [*INSPEC operator*]
KP	Key Pulsing
KP	Keyboard Perforator
KP	Keypunch [*Data processing*]
KPA	Key Pulse Adapter [*Telecommunications*] (TEL)
KPC	Keyboard/Printer Control [*Data processing*]
KPC	Keypunch Cabinet [*Data processing*]
KPF	Key Pulse on Front Cord [*Telecommunications*] (TEL)
KPIC	Key Phrase in Context (DEEC)
KPLS	Key Pulsing (MSA)
KPM	Kathode Pulse Modulation
KPO	Keypunch Operator [*Data processing*]
KR	Key Register (CAA)
KR	Keying Relay
KRI	King Research, Incorporated [*Computer consultant*] [*Information service*] (EISS)
KRL	Knowledge Representation Language (CAA)
KRM	Kurzweil Reading Machine

KSA	Kite-Supported Antenna
KSAM	Keyed Sequential Access Method [*Data processing*] (CMD)
KSAM	Keyed Sequential Access Mode [*Data processing*]
KSDS	Key Sequenced Data Set (CMD)
KSH	Key Strokes per Hour (CAA)
KSL	Keyboard Simulated Lateral Telling [*Data processing*]
KSOC	Key Symbol Out of Context [*Data processing*] (DIT)
KSR	Keyboard Send and Receive [*Data processing*]
KSS	Keying Switching Station
KST	Key Station Terminal [*Data processing*]
KSU	Key System Control Unit [*Telecommunications*]
KTA	Key Telephone Adapter [*Telecommunications*] (TEL)
KTC	Kellogg Telecommunications Corporation [*Littleton, CO*] [*Telecommunications*] (TSSD)
KTDS	Key to Disk Software (CAA)
KTI	Kitchen Table International [*David D. Busch's vaporware software company*]
KTM	Key Transport Module (CAA)
KTOS	Kratos, Inc. [*NASDAQ symbol*] (NQ)
KTR	Keyboard Typing Reperforator [*Data processing*]
KTS	Key Telephone System Modules
KTU	Key Telephone Unit
KV	Key Verifier [*Data processing*]
kV	Kilovolt
kVA	Kilovolt Ampere (CBSS)
KW	Key Word [*Online database field identifier*] (OBD)
kW	Kilowatt
KW	Kiloword (BUR)
KWA	Key Word Adapted [*Data processing*]
KWAC	Keyword and Context [*Indexing*] (DIT)
kWh	Kilowatt-Hour
KWIC	Keyword in Context [*Indexing*]
KWIT	Keyword in Title [*Indexing*]
KWOC	Keyword out of Context [*Indexing*]
KWOT	Keyword out of Title [*Indexing*]
KYBD	Keyboard (MSA)

L

L	Inductance [*Symbol*]	
L	Label (MDG)	
L	Lamp	
L	Left [*Direction*]	
L	Length	
L	Link	
L	Load (MDG)	
L	Local	
L	Looper [*Data processing*] (MDG)	
L	Low	
L6	Laboratories Low-Level Linked List Language [*Bell Systems*] (DIT)	
LA	Language [*Online database field identifier*]	
LA	Light Armor [*Telecommunications*] (TEL)	
LA	Line Adapter (CMD)	
LA	Listed Address [*Telecommunications*] (TEL)	
LA	Local Address (CAA)	
LA	Log Analyzer Processor [*Data processing*]	
LA	Logarithmic Amplifier	
LA	Logical Address (CAA)	
LA	Loop Antenna (DEN)	
LA	Los Alamos Scientific Laboratory [*Also, LASL*]	
LAB	Local Area Broadcast	
LABORDOC	International Labour Documentation [*International Labour Office*] [*Geneva, Switzerland*] [*Bibliographic database*] (OBD)	
LABSTAT	Labor Statistics [*Database*] [*Department of Labor*] (FDB)	
LACE	Language for ALGOL [*Algorithmic Language*] Compiler Extension [*Data processing*] (CSR)	
LACE	Local Automatic Circuit Exchange [*Telecommunications*]	
LACE	Luton Analogue Computing Engine [*British*] (DEN)	
LACES	London Airport Cargo Electronic-Data-Processing Scheme	
LACONIQ	Laboratory Computer Online Inquiry	
LAD	Logical Aptitude Device (BUR)	
LADAPT	Lookup Dictionary Adaptor Program (IEEE)	
LADB	Laboratory Animal Data Bank [*Columbus Laboratories*] [*Columbus, OH*] [*Information service*] (EISS)	
LADB	Latin American Data Bank [*University of Florida*] (EISS)	
LADDER	Language Access to Distributed Data with Error Recovery (CAA)	
LADM	Laboratory Automated Data Management	
LADS	Local Area Data Set (CAA)	
LADT	Local Area Data Transport [*AT & T*]	
LAF	Limited Amplifier Filter	
LAFOA	Laser Focus [*A publication*]	
LAG	Load and Go (BUR)	
LAH	Logical Analyzer of Hypothesis (IEEE)	
LAI	Load Address Immediate (BUR)	
LALR	Lookahead Left to Right [*Data processing*]	
LALSD	Language for Automated Logic and System Design [*Data processing*] (CSR)	
LAM	Loop Addition and Modification [*Data processing*]	
LAMA	Local Automatic Message Accounting [*Telecommunications*] (TEL)	
LAMC	Language and Mode Converter [*Data processing*] (TEL)	
LAMSAC	Local Authorities Management Services and Computer Committee [*British*] (OA)	
LAN	Local Area Network [*Computer technology*]	
LAN/RM	Local Area Network Reference Model (CCD)	
LAP	Lesson Assembly Program (IEEE)	
LAP	Line Access Point [*Telecommunications*] (TEL)	
LAP	Link Access Procedure [*Telecommunications*] (TEL)	
LAP	Link Access Protocol (CCD)	
LAP	List Assembly Programing [*Data processing*]	
LAPB	Link Access Procedure Balanced [*Data processing*]	
LAPIS	Legislative Authorization Program Information System [*General Accounting Office*] (EISS)	
LAR	Limit Address Register [*Data processing*]	
LARAM	Line Addressable Random Access Memory [*Data processing*] (MDG)	
LARC	Large Automatic Research Computer	
LARC	Livermore Atomic Research Computer	
LARP	Local and Remote Printing [*Data processing*] (DEEC)	
LARPS	Local and Remote Printing Station [*Data processing*] (CAA)	
LAS	Local Address Space (CAA)	
LAS	Low-Altitude Satellite	
LASCAR	Language for Simulation of Computer Architecture (CSR)	
LASER	Light Amplification by Stimulated Emission of Radiation [*Acronym was coined in 1957 by scientist Gordon Gould*]	
LASERCOM	LASER Communications (MCD)	
Laser Foc	Laser Focus Buyers Guide [*A publication*]	
Laser Focus Fiberoptic Commun	Laser Focus with Fiberoptic Communications [*A publication*]	
Laser Focus Fiberoptic Technol	Laser Focus with Fiberoptic Technology [*A publication*]	
Laser Rep	Laser Report [*A publication*]	
LASL	Los Alamos Scientific Laboratory [*Also, LA*]	
LASP	Local Attached Support Processor (CAA)	
LASS	Logistics Analysis Simulation System (CAA)	
LASSO	Library Acquisition Services System Online [*Suggested name for the Library of Cogress computer system*]	
LAST	Large Aperture Scanning Telescope (TEL)	
LATA	Local Access Transport Area [*Telecommunications*]	
LATIS	Loop Activity Tracking Information System [*Telecommunications*] (TEL)	
LB	Line Buffer [*Data processing*]	
LB	Load Bank [*Data processing*] (KSC)	
LB	Logical Block (CAA)	
LBA	Linear-Bounded Automaton	
LBA	Local Bus Adapter [*Data processing*] (CAA)	
LBB	[*The*] Little Black Book [*Cygnet Technologies, Inc.*] [*Database software*]	
LBC	Liberty Bell Communications, Inc. [*Detroit, MI*] [*Telecommunications*] (TSSD)	
LBC	Local Bus Controller (CAA)	
LBEN	Low-Byte Enable (CAA)	
LBJ	Load Bank and Jump [*Data processing*]	
LBL	Lawrence Berkeley Laboratory [*Later, Lawrence Livermore Laboratory*] [*University of California*] (EISS)	
LBM	Load Buffer Memory [*Data processing*]	
LBM	Logic Bus Monitor [*Data processing*] (CET)	
LBN	Line Balancing Network [*Telecommunications*] (TEL)	
LBO	Line Building Out	
LBP	Lanier Business Products, Inc. [*NYSE symbol*] [*Delisted*]	
LBR	LASER Beam Recorder [*or Recording*]	
LBR	Low BIT [*Binary Digit*] Rate (MCD)	
LBS	Line Buffer System [*Data processing*]	
LBS	Load Balance System [*Telecommunications*] (TEL)	
LBT	L-Band Transmitter	
LBT	Low BIT [*Binary Digit*] Test [*Data processing*] (IEEE)	
LBT CBS	Local-Battery Talking, Common-Battery Signaling [*Telecommunications*] (TEL)	
LBTS	Land-Based Test Site (VIT)	
LBU	Large Base Unit [*Telecommunications*]	
L/C	Inductance/Capacitance	
LC	Language Code [*Online database field identifier*] (OBD)	
LC	Library of Congress [*Online database field identifier*]	
LC	Library of Congress Classification (CAH)	
LC	Line Circuit [*Telecommunications*] (DEEC)	
LC	Line Concentrator (CAA)	
LC	Line Control (CAA)	
LC	Load Computer [*or Controller*] (MCD)	
LC	Loading Coil [*Telecommunications*] (TEL)	
LC	Local Call [*Followed by telephone number*]	
LC	Location Counter [*Data processing*]	
LC	Lowercase [*i.e., small letters*] [*Typography*]	
LCA	Line Control Adapter	
LCA	Local Communications Adapter [*IBM Corp.*] (CAA)	
LCAP	Loop Carrier Analysis Program [*Bell System*]	
LCB	Least Common BIT [*Binary Digit*] (MCD)	
LCB	Line Control Block [*Data processing*]	
LCB	Logic Control Block (CAA)	
LCC	Language for Conversational Computing (MDG)	
LCC	Lead Covered Cable [*Telecommunications*] (TEL)	
LCC	Loading Coil Case [*Telecommunications*] (TEL)	
LCC	Local Communications Complex	
LCC	Local Communications Console	

Computer & Telecommunications Acronyms

LCCR .... Laboratory for Computer and Communications Research [*Simon Fraser University*] [*Canada*] [*Research center*]   (RCD)
LCCS .... Large Capacity Core Storage [*Data processing*]   (MDG)
LCD .... Language for Computer Design   (CSR)
LCD .... Liquid Crystal Display
LCDS .... Low-Cost Development System [*National Semiconductor Corp.*]   (CAA)
LCDTL .... Load-Compensated Diode Transistor Logic [*Data processing*]
LCF .... Language Central Facility [*Data processing*]   (IEEE)
LCF .... Level Control Function [*Data processing*]
LCF .... Logical Channel Fill   (CAA)
LCFS .... Last-Come, First-Served   (CAA)
LCG .... Lead Computing Gyro   (MCD)
LCH .... Logical Channel [*Data processing*]
LCL .... Limited Channel Logout   (CAA)
LCL .... Linkage Control Language [*Data processing*]   (BUR)
LCM .... Large-Core Memory [*Data processing*]
LCM .... Line Concentrator Module   (CAA)
LCM .... Line Control Module [*Telecommunications*]   (TEL)
LC MARC .... Library of Congress Machine Readable Catalog [*Library of Congress*] [*Washington, DC*] [*Bibliographic database*]   (OBD)
LCN .... Local Computer Network   (CCD)
LCOS .... Lead Computing Optical Sight
LCOSS .... Lead Computing Optical Sighting System   (MCD)
LCP .... Language Conversion Program [*Data processing*]   (BUR)
LCP .... Lawyers Co-Operative Publishing Co. [*Rochester, NY*]
LCP .... Local Control Point [*Telecommunications*]   (TEL)
LCPG .... Logic Clock Pulse Generator [*Data processing*]
LCQ .... Logical Channel Queue [*Data processing*]   (BUR)
LCS .... Laboratory for Computer Science [*Massachusetts Institute of Technology*] [*Research center*]   (RCD)
LCS .... Large Capacity [*or Core*] Storage [*Data processing*]   (CIT)
LCS .... LASER Communications System
LCS .... Library Computer System
LCS .... Liquid Crystal Shutter [*Epson*] [*Printer technology*]
LCSN .... Local Circuit Switched Network   (CCD)
LCSR .... Laboratory for Computer Science Research [*Rutgers University*] [*Research center*]   (RCD)
LCSU .... Local Concentrator Switching Unit [*Telecommunications*]   (TEL)
LCT .... Logical Channel Termination   (CAA)
LCU .... Line Control Unit [*Data communications*]   (CAA)
LCU .... Link Control Unit [*Telecommunications*]   (TEL)
LCVD .... Least Coincidence Voltage Detection   (MDG)
LCW .... Line Control Word   (OA)
LD .... Linker Directive [*Telecommunications*]   (TEL)
LD .... Logic Driver [*Data processing*]
LD .... Logical Design   (CAA)
LD .... Long Distance
LD .... Loop Diagram   (VIT)
LD .... Loop-Disconnect [*Telecommunications*]   (TEL)
LD .... Low Density   (CIT)
LDA .... Local Data Administrator   (CAA)
LDA .... Logical Device Address [*Data processing*]   (IBMDP)
LDB .... Launch Data Bus [*Data processing*]   (MCD)
LDB .... Legislative Data Base [*Department of Energy*] [*Information service*]   (EISS)
LDB .... Logical Database   (CAA)
LDC .... Library Development Consultants, Inc. [*Information service*]   (EISS)
LDC .... Local Display Controller   (CAA)
LDC .... Long-Distance Call   (DDI)
LDC .... Long-Distance Communications
LDC .... Low-Speed Data Channel   (CAA)
LDCS .... Long-Distance Control System   (IEEE)
LDD .... Local Data Distribution   (CAA)
LDD .... Logic Design Data [*Telecommunications*]   (TEL)
LDJ .... Load D-Bank and Jump [*Data processing*]
LDL .... Language Description Language [*Data processing*]
LDLA .... Limited Distance Line Adapter   (CAA)
LDM .... Limited-Distance MODEM [*Data processing*]
LDM .... Linear Delta Modulation   (CAA)
LDM .... Local Data Manager   (CAA)
LDM .... Logical Data Management, Inc. [*Covina, CA*] [*Software manufacturer*]   (DASOS)
LDMS .... Laboratory Data Management System [*IBM Corp.*]
LDMX .... Local Digital Message Exchange
LDN .... Listed Directory Number [*Bell System*]
LDO .... Logical Device Order [*Data processing*]   (IBMDP)
LDP .... Language Data Processing   (MSA)
LDP .... Local Data Processor
LDP .... Lomas Data Products [*Marlboro, MA*]
LDR .... Line Driver-Receiver [*Computer communication*]   (TEL)
LDR .... Low Data Register [*Data processing*]
LDS .... Large Disk Storage [*Data processing*]   (IEEE)
LDS .... Local Digital Switch [*Telecommunications*]   (TEL)
LDS .... Local Distribution System [*Cable television*]   (MDG)
LDT .... Language Dependent Translator   (CAA)
LDT .... Local Descriptor Table [*Data processing*]
LDT .... Logic Design Translator [*Data processing*]   (TUT)
LDT .... Long Distance Transmission   (BUR)
LDU .... Line Driver Unit [*Computer communication*]   (MCD)

LD/USA ...... Long Distance/USA, Inc. [*Honolulu, HI*] [*Telecommunications*]   (TSSD)
LDX .... Long-Distance Xerography [*Xerox Corp.*] [*Communications facsimile system*]
LDY .... Lundy Electronics & Systems, Inc. [*American Stock Exchange symbol*]
LE .... Antenna Effective Length for Electric-Field Antennas   (IEEE)
LE .... Laboratory of Electronics [*Rockefeller University*] [*Research center*]   (RCD)
LE .... Line Equipment [*Telecommunications*]   (TEL)
LE .... Local Exchange [*Telecommunications*]   (TEL)
LE .... Logic Element   (OA)
LE .... Loop Extender [*Telecommunications*]   (TEL)
LEA .... Load Effective Address [*Data processing*]
LEAD .... Learn, Execute, and Diagnose   (CAA)
LEADER ...... Lehigh Automatic Device for Efficient Retrieval [*Center for Information Sciences, Lehigh University*] [*Bethlehem, PA*] [*Data processing*]
LEADS .... Law Enforcement Automated Data System   (IEEE)
LEADS .... Library Experimental Automated Demonstration System [*Data processing*]
LEAF .... LISP Extended Algebraic Facility   (CAH)
LEAP .... Language for Expressing Associative Procedures [*Data processing*]
LEAP 5 ...... Linear Elastic Analysis Program [*SIA Computer Services*] [*Software package*] [*British*]   (NCC)
LEAPS .... Local Exchange Area Planning Simulation [*Bell Laboratories*]
LEAS .... Lease Electronic Accounting System   (IEEE)
LEAS .... Lower Echelon Automatic Switchboard
LEASAT ...... Leased Satellite Communications   (NVT)
LEC .... Light Energy Converter [*Telecommunications*]   (TEL)
LECO .... Local Engineering Control Office [*Telecommunications*]   (TEL)
LECS .... Law Enforcement Computer Systems, Inc. [*Sarasota, FL*] [*Software manufacturer*]   (DASOS)
LED .... Light-Emitting Diode [*Display component*]
LED .... Line Embossing Device [*Data processing*]
LEDA .... Landsat Earthnet Data Availability [*ESA-Earthnet Programme Office*] [*Database*]   (CUAD)
LEDA .... Lee Data Corp. [*NASDAQ symbol*]   (NQ)
LEF .... Left-In Telephone [*Telecommunications*]   (TEL)
LEF .... Line Expansion Function   (CAA)
LEGIS .... Legislative Information and Status System [*for House of Representatives*]
LEIN .... Law Enforcement Information Network
LEIS .... LeisureLine [*Footscray, Vic.*] [*Database*] [*Information service*]   (EISS)
LEL .... Link-Edit Language [*Data processing*]
LEM .... Antenna Effective Length for Magnetic-Field Antennas   (IEEE)
LEM .... Logic Enhanced Memory   (CAA)
LEM .... Logical End of Media
LEMS .... Linear Econometric Modeling System   (BUR)
LEN .... Length
LEQ .... Line of Equipment [*Telecommunications*]   (TEL)
LEQ .... Line Equipped [*Telecommunications*]   (TEL)
LERN .... Learning Resources Network [*Formerly, FUN*]
LET .... Letter
LETB .... Local Exchange Test Bed [*Telecommunications*]   (TEL)
LETS .... Law Enforcement Teletype [*or Teletypewriter*] Service [*Phoenix, AZ*]
LEV .... Level   (DDI)
LEV .... Loader/Editor/Verifier [*Telecommunications*]   (TEL)
LEVN .... Levin Computer Corp. [*NASDAQ symbol*]   (NQ)
LEX .... Line Exchange [*Telecommunications*]   (CAA)
LEXD .... Lexidata Corp. [*NASDAQ symbol*]   (NQ)
LEXI .... Lexicon Corp. [*NASDAQ symbol*]   (NQ)
LEXIS .... Legal Research Service   (EISS)
LEXIS .... Lexicography Information Service [*West German*] [*Data processing*]   (DEEC)
LF .... Leapfrog Configuration [*Circuit theory*]   (IEEE)
LF .... Line Feed [*Control character*] [*Data processing*]
LF .... Line Finder [*Teletype*]
LF .... Linear Filter
LF .... Logic Function   (OA)
LF .... Logical File [*Data processing*]   (BUR)
LF .... Low Frequency
LFB .... Limited Frequency Band
LFB .... Low-Frequency Beacon
LFC .... Local Forms Control [*Data processing*]   (CMD)
LFC .... Logic Flow Chart [*Data processing*]
LFD .... Line Fault Detector [*Telecommunications*]   (TEL)
LFD .... Local Frequency Distribution   (CAA)
LFD .... Low-Frequency Disturbance
LFE .... Logarithmic Feedback Element [*Data processing*]
LFFTD .... Laser Focus with Fiberoptic Technology [*A publication*]
LFG .... Lexical Functional Grammar [*Artificial intelligence*]
LFM .... Local File Manager   (CAA)
LFMOP .... Linear Frequency Modulation on Pulse   (MCD)
LFMS .... Laminated Ferrite Memory System
LFN .... Logical File Name   (CAA)
LFPS .... Low-Frequency Phase Shifter [*Telecommunications*]   (OA)
LFRAP .... Long Feeder Route Analysis Program [*Bell System*]
LFS .... Local Format Storage   (CAA)
LFS .... Logic Fault Simulator [*Data processing*]

Computer & Telecommunications Acronyms

Acronym	Expansion
LFSR	Linear Feedback Shift Register (CAA)
LFU	Least Frequently Used [Data processing] (CAA)
LG	Language [Online database field identifier] (OBD)
LG	Large
LG	Line Generator [Data processing] (CGC)
LG	Linear Gate
LGA	Landesgewerbeamt [Nuremburg] [Information retrieval] (ODIN)
LGA	Low-Gain Antenna (CIT)
LGC	Launch Guidance Computer (SKY)
LGCP	Lexical-Graphical Composer Printer [Photocomposition]
LGE	Logic Gate Expander [Data processing]
LGL	Local Graphics Library [Cambridge Computer Graphics Ltd.] [Software package] [British] (NCC)
LGN	Line Gate Number [Data processing]
LGN	Logical Group Number [Data processing] (IBMDP)
LGN	Logicon, Inc. [American Stock Exchange symbol]
LH	Linear Hybrid
L/H	Low-to-High (MDG)
LHF	List Handling Facility (CAA)
LHNCBC	Lister Hill National Center for Biomedical Communications [National Library of Medicine] [Information service] (EISS)
LHTN	Library Hi Tech News [Published a bibliography using machine-readable datastrips]
LI	Left in Place [Telecommunications] (TEL)
LIA	Label Information Area (CMD)
LIA	Loop Interface Address (CAA)
LIBACC	Library Acquisition Program [Computer program] (CIT)
LIBMAS	Library Master File [FORTRAN program]
LIBMRG	Library Merge Program [Computer program] (CIT)
LIBR	Librarian
LIBR	Library (CDH)
LIBRIS	Library Information Service [or System] [The Royal Library] [Sweden] [Database] [Information service] (EISS)
LIBSET	Library Set [Computer program] (CIT)
LIBSYS	Library System [Computer program] (CIT)
LIC	Linear Integrated Circuit
LIC	Load Interface Circuit (MCD)
LID	Labor Information Database [International Labor Office] [Information service] (EISS)
LID	Local Issue Data [Telecommunications] (TEL)
LIDAR	Light Detection and Ranging
LIDB	Logistics Intelligence Data Base
LIDF	Line Intermediate Distributing Frame
LIDS	Laboratory for Information and Decision Systems [Massachusetts Institute of Technology] [Research center] (RCD)
LIEB	Liebert Corp. [NASDAQ symbol] (NQ)
LIFMOP	Linearly Frequency-Modulated Pulse
LIFT	Logically Integrated FORTRAN Translator [UNIVAC]
LIH	Line Interface Handler (CAA)
LIM	Language Interpretation Module (CAA)
LIM	Line Interface Module
LIMA	Logic-in-Memory Array (CAA)
LIMAC	Large Integrated Monolithic Array Computer (MCD)
LIMIT	Lot-Size Inventory Management Interpolation Technique (BUR)
LIMS	Library Information Management System [Computerized library system]
LIMS	Limb-Motion Sensor [System]
LINA	Literaturnachweise [Literature References] [Informationszentrum Raum und Bau der Fraunhofer-Gesellschaft] [Database] (ODIN)
LINC	Laboratory Instrument Computer [Medical analyzer]
LINC	Library & Information Consultants Ltd. [Canada] [Information service] (EISS)
LINCO	Linearly Organized Chemical Code for Use in Computer Systems (DIT)
LINCOMPEX	Linked Compressor and Expander (NATG)
LINCOS	Lingua Cosmica [Artificial language consisting of radio signals of varying lengths and frequencies]
LINCS	Language Information Network and Clearinghouse System [Center for Applied Linguistics] [Washington, DC]
LINGO	[A] programing language [1978] (CSR)
LINUS	Logical Inquiry and Update System (CAA)
LIOC	Lighted Independent of Computer
LIOCS	Logical Input/Output Control System [Data processing]
LIONS	Library Information and On-Line Network Service [New York Public Library] [Information service] (EISS)
LIOP	Life in One Position [Telecommunications] (TEL)
LIPL	Linear Information Processing Language [High-order programing language] [Data processing] (IEEE)
LIPS	Logical Inferences per Second [Data processing]
LIRES	Literature Retrieval System [Data processing]
LIRES-MC	Literature Retrieval System - Multiple Searching, Complete Text [Data processing]
LIRG	Library and Information Research Group [Loughborough University] [British] [Information service] (EISS)
LIRS	Legal Information and Reference Services [General Accounting Office] (EISS)
LIRS	Library Information Retrieval System
LIS	Large Interactive Surface [Automated drafting table that serves as a computer input and output device] (CCD)
LIS	Legislative Information System [National Conference of State Legislatures] [Information service] (EISS)
LIS	Library and Information Science (IDA)
LIS	Library Information Services [Information service] (EISS)
LIS	Licensure Information System [Public Health Service] (EISS)
LIS	Line Information Store [Telecommunications] (TEL)
LIS	Link Information Sciences (BUR)
LIS	Load I-Bank and Jump [Data processing]
LISA	LARC Instruction Assembly
LISA	Library and Information Science Abstracts [Library Association Publishing Ltd.] [Bibliographic database] [A publication] [British]
LISA	Library Systems Analysis
LISA	Linked Indexed Sequential Access (CAA)
LISA	Locally Integrated Software Architecture [Apple microcomputer] [Data processing]
LISC	Library and Information Services Council [British]
LISI	Library Interface Systems, Incorporated [Information service] (EISS)
LISN	Long Island Sports Network [Cable-television system]
LISP	List Processing [Programing language] [Data processing]
LISP	List Processor [Standard programing language] [1958] [Data processing]
LIST	Library Index Search and Transcribe (TUT)
LITA	Library and Information Technology Association [Formerly, ISAD] [American Library Association] [Chicago, IL]
LITTLE	[A] programing language [1970-1973] (CSR)
LIU	Line Interface Unit [Data communications]
LIZARDS	Library Information Search and Retrieval Data System (IEEE)
LJE	Local Job Entry (CAA)
LJSU	Local Junction Switching Unit [Telecommunications] (TEL)
LK	Looking for Party [Telecommunications] (TEL)
LK	Low-Priority Key [Data processing]
LKM	Low-Key Maintenance (CAA)
LL	Land-Line [Telecommunications] (TEL)
LL	Leased Line [Private telephone or Teletype line] [Telecommunications]
LL	Line Leg [Telegraph] [Telecommunications] (TEL)
LL	Link Level [Telecommunications] (CCD)
LL	Liquid Limit (IEEE)
LL	Local Line [Telecommunications] (CAA)
LL	Long Line [Telecommunications] (MCD)
LLA	Leased Line Adapter [Telecommunications] (CAA)
LLBA	Language and Language Behavior Abstracts [Sociological Abstracts, Inc.] [Bibliographic database] [A publication]
LLC	Logical Link Control (CCD)
LLD	Logic Level Driver [Data processing] (MCD)
LLE	Large Local Exchange [Telecommunications] (TEL)
LLE	Long Line Equipment [Telecommunications] (TEL)
LLF	Line Link Frame [Telecommunications] (TEL)
LLG	Logical Line Group [Data processing] (IBMDP)
LLI	Low-Level Interface (CAA)
LLL	Lawrence Livermore Laboratory [Also, LLNL] [University of California]
LLLLLL	Laboratories Low-Level Linked List Language [Bell Systems] (MCD)
LLM	Low-Level Multiplexer (CAA)
LLN	Line Link Network [Bell System]
LLNL	Lawrence Livermore National Laboratory [Also, LLL] [University of California]
LLP	Line Link Pulsing [Telecommunications]
LLSU	Low-Level Signaling Unit [Telecommunications] (TEL)
LM	Large Memory
LM	Leave Message [Word processing]
LM	Leg Multiple [Telegraph] [Telecommunications] (TEL)
L/M	Lines per Minute [Data processing]
LM	Link Manager (CAA)
LM	Load Module (MCD)
LM	Local Memory
LM	Logic Module [Data processing] (MCD)
LM	Loop Multiplexer (CAA)
LMBI	Local Memory Bus Interface [Data processing] (CAA)
LMCC	Land Mobile Communications Council [Washington, DC] (EANO)
LMCP	Laboratory Module Computer Program
LME	L. M. Ericsson [Swedish telecommunications company] (TEL)
LME	Logistics Management Engineering, Inc. [Annapolis, MD] [Telecommunications] (TSSD)
LMF	Language Media Format (CET)
LMG	Laurer Markin Gibbs, Inc. [Toledo, OH] [Telecommunications] (TSSD)
LMI	Local Memory Image (CAA)
LML	Logical Memory Level (CAA)
LMLR	Load Memory Lockout Register
LMMS	Local Message Metering Service [Telecommunications] (TEL)
LMOS	Loop Maintenance Operations System [Formerly, MLR] [Bell System]
LMS	Level Measuring Set [for test signals] [Telecommunications] (TEL)
LMS	List Management System (CAA)
LMS	Local Measured Service [Telecommunications] (TEL)
LMSN	Local Message Switched Network (CCD)
LMT	Logical Mapping Table (CAA)
LMU	Line Monitor Unit
LMX	L-Type Multiplex [Telecommunications] (TEL)
LN	Background Noise Level (CAAL)
LN	Line

By Acronym

Computer & Telecommunications Acronyms

Acronym	Expansion
LNA	Launch Numerical Aperture [*Telecommunications*] (TEL)
LNA	Local Numbering Area [*Telecommunications*] (TEL)
LNA	Low-Noise Amplifier (CIT)
LNA	Low-Noise Antenna
LNB	Local Name Base [*Data processing*] (CAA)
LNB	Low-Noise Block [*Satellite communications*]
LNBF	Low-Noise Block Feed [*Satellite communications*]
LNC	Low-Noise Cable
LNC	Low-Noise Converter [*Satellite communications*]
LND	Local Number Dialed [*Telecommunications*] (TEL)
LNDEL	Lundy Electronics & Systems, Inc. Uts [*NASDAQ symbol*] (NQ)
LNE	Local Network Emulator (CAA)
LNF	Low-Noise Feed [*Satellite communications*]
LNLM	Low-Noise Level Margin
LNR	Low-Noise Receiver
LNSN	Local Non-Switched Network (CCD)
LO	Connect Me to a Perforator Receiver [*Communications*] (FAAC)
LO	Line Occupancy
LO	Local Origination [*Television programing*]
LO	Local Oscillator [*Electronics*]
LO	Lock-Out
LO	Locked Oscillator
LO	Low (KSC)
LOAMP	Logarithmic Amplifier (IEEE)
LOC	Linked Object Code (TEL)
LOC	Local
LOC	Location (AFM)
LOCAL	Load On-Call [*Data processing*] (IDA)
LOCAP	Low Capacitance [*Cable*] [*Bell System*]
LOCATE	Local Area Telecommunications, Inc. [*Digital microwave carrier*] (TSSD)
LOCI	Logarithmic Computing Instrument
LOCIS	Library of Congress Information System [*Information service*] (EISS)
LOCOS	Local Oxidation of Silicon [*Transistor technology*]
LOCS	Logic and Control Simulator [*Data processing*] (BUR)
LOD	Leading Ones Detector [*Data processing*]
LOD	Location Dependent (OA)
LODESMP	Logistics Data Element Standardization and Management Process (IEEE)
LODESTAR	Logically Organized Data Entry, Storage, and Recording
LOF	Local Oscillator Filter [*Electronics*]
LOF	Local Oscillator Frequency [*Electronics*]
LOFAR	Low-Frequency Analysis and Recording
LOG	Logarithm [*Mathematics*]
LOGAL	Logical Algorithmic Language [*Data processing*] (CSR)
LOGALGOL	Logical Algorithmic Language [*Data processing*]
LOGEL	Logic Generating Language [*Data processing*]
LOGFED	Log File Editor Processor [*Data processing*]
LOGICOM	Logical Communications, Inc. [*East Norwalk, CT*] [*Telecommunications*] (TSSD)
LOGIN	Local Government Information Network [*Commercial information service*] [*Control Data Corp.*] [*Database*]
LOGIPAC	Logical Processor and Computer
LOGO	[*A*] programing language [*For schoolchildren*] [*1967*] (CSR)
LOGREC	Log Recording [*Data processing*]
LOGTAB	Logic Tables (IEEE)
LOIS	Library Order Information System [*Computer system*] [*Library of Congress*] [*Obsolete*]
LOLA	Library On-Line Acquisitions [*Washington State University*] [*Data processing system*]
LOLITA	Language for the On-Line Investigation and Transformation of Abstractions [*Data processing*] (TUT)
LOLITA	Library On-Line Information and Text Access [*Oregon State University*] [*Corvallis, OR*] [*Data processing system*]
LOMA	Life Office Management Association [*Atlanta, GA*]
LOMAR	Local Manual Attempt Recording (TEL)
LOMUSS	Lockheed Multiprocessor Simulation System (IEEE)
LONAL	Local Off-Net Access Line [*Telecommunications*] (TEL)
LONO	Low Noise
LOOPS	Local Office Online Payment System [*Unemployment insurance*]
LOP	Last Operation Completed [*Data processing*] (TUT)
LOP	Line-Oriented Protocol (CAA)
LOPAC	Load Optimization and Passenger Acceptance Control [*Airport computer*]
LOPAD	Logarithmic Outline Processing System for Analog Data (IEEE)
LO-QG	Locked Oscillator-Quadrature Grid [*Data processing*]
LOR	Low-Frequency Omnidirectional Radio Range
LOR	Lower Operator Rate [*Telecommunications*] [*British*]
LORADAC	Long-Range Active Detection and Communications System
LORBAS	Large Off-Line Retrieval Text Base Access System
LORD	Licensing Online Retrieval Data
LORDS	Licensing On-Line Retrieval Data System
LOREC	Long-Range Earth Current Communications
LORES	Long-Route Engineering Study [*Bell System*]
LO-RES	Low Resolution [*Data processing*]
LORPGAC	Long-Range Proving Ground Automatic Computer (IEEE)
LORSA	Long-Range Steerable Antenna (MCD)
LOS	Line Out of Service [*Telecommunications*] (TEL)
LOS	Line of Sight
LOS	Loss of Signal
LOSR	Limit of Stack Register (CAA)
LOT	Light Operated Typewriter (CAA)
LOTCIP	Long-Term Communications Improvement Plan (NATG)
LOTIS	Logical Structure: The Timing and the Sequencing of Synchronous/Asynchronous Machines [*Data processing*] (CSR)
LOTS	Lotus Development Corp. [*NASDAQ symbol*] (NQ)
LP	Light Pen (CAA)
LP	Line Printer [*Data processing*] (CGC)
LP	Linear Phase (CIT)
LP	Linear Polarization
LP	Linear Programing [*Data processing*]
LP	List Processor [*Standard programing language*] [*Data processing*] (BUR)
LP	Load Point (BUR)
LP	Lodge-Pole Pine [*Utility pole*] [*Telecommunications*] (TEL)
LP	Log Periodic [*Antenna*] (NATG)
LP	Logic Probe (CAA)
LP	Longitudinal Parity [*Telecommunications*] (TEL)
LP	Low Pass [*Electronics*]
LPA	Light Pulser Array
LPA	Linear Power Amplifier
LPA	Link Pack Area [*Data processing*] (MCD)
LPA	Log Periodic Antenna
LPA	Low-Power Amplifier (CET)
LPAA	Log Periodic Array Antenna
LPB	Lunar and Planetary Bibliography [*Lunar and Planetary Institute*] [*Information service*] (EISS)
LPBBA	Log Periodic Broadband Antenna
LPC	Linear Power Controller
LPC	Linear Predictive Coding [*Digital coding technique*] [*Telecommunications*]
LPC	Loop-Control [*Relay*] (IEEE)
LPCM	Linear Phase Code Modulation (CAA)
LP-CW	Long Pulse - Continuous Wave (NG)
LPD	Language Processing and Debugging [*Data processing*] (BUR)
LPE	Liquid Phase Epitaxy [*Magnetic film*]
LPF	Low-Pass Filter [*Electronics*]
LPG	Langage de Programmation et de Gestion [*French computer language*] (IEEE)
LPGS	Liquified Petroleum Gas Report [*American Petroleum Institute*] [*Database*] (FDB)
LPI	Lines per Inch [*Printing*]
LPI	Longitudinally Applied Paper Insulation [*Telecommunications*] (TEL)
LPID	Logical Page Identifier (BUR)
LPL	Linear Programing Language [*Intertechnique*] [*French*] [*Data processing*] (BUR)
LPL	List Processing Language [*Data processing*] (IEEE)
LPL	Local Processor Link (CAA)
LPM	Linearly Polarized Mode [*Telecommunications*] (TEL)
LPM	Lines per Minute [*Data processing*]
LPN	Logical Page Number (BUR)
LPN	Low-Pass Network [*Electronics*]
LPR	Lanpar Technologies, Inc. [*Toronto Stock Exchange symbol*]
LPR	Line Printer [*Data processing*] (NASA)
LPRB	Loaded Program Request Block [*Data processing*] (BUR)
LPRINT	Lookup Dictionary Print Program (IEEE)
LPS	Laboratory Peripheral System
LPS	Library Processes System [*EDUCOMP*] [*Information service*] (EISS)
LPS	Line Procedure Specifications (CMD)
LPS	Linear Programing System [*Data processing*]
LPS	Lines per Second [*Data processing*]
LPS	Low-Power Schottky [*Electronics*]
LPSN	Local Packet Switched Network (CCD)
LPSS	Line Protection Switching System [*Bell System*]
LPTR	Line Printer [*Data processing*] (MSA)
LPTTL	Low-Power Transistor-Transistor Logic
LPTV	Low-Power Television
LPU	Language Processor Unit (CAA)
LPU	Line Processing Unit (CAA)
LPU	Low-Power Unit (CAAL)
LPUG	Lasers in Publishing Users Group (EANO)
LPUU	Linear Programing under Uncertainty [*Data processing*]
LPV	Log Periodic V [*Antenna*]
LPVT	Large Print Video Terminal (CAA)
LR	Letter [*Online database field identifier*] (OBD)
LR	Limit Register (CAA)
L/R	Local/Remote [*Telecommunications*] (TEL)
LR	Logical Record (CAA)
LRC	Library Research Center [*University of Illinois*] (EISS)
LRC	Linguistics Research Center [*University of Texas at Austin*] [*Research center*] (RCD)
LRC	Longitudinal Redundancy Check [*Data processing*]
LRCC	Longitudinal Redundancy Check Character [*Telecommunications*] (TEL)
LRCE	LASER Relay Communication Equipment
LRCO	Limited Remote Communication Outlet
LRCOM	Long-Range Very-High-Frequency/Ultrahigh-Frequency Communications (FAAC)
LRDC	Learning Research and Development Center [*University of Pittsburgh*] [*Research center*]
LRDD	Limited Rights to Delivered Data
LRECL	Logical Records of Fixed Length (MCD)

Computer & Telecommunications Acronyms

LRF	Long-Range Facility [*Telecommunications*] (TEL)
LRFAX	Low-Resolution Facsimile [*Telecommunications*] (TEL)
LRFS	Long-Range Forecasting System (TEL)
LRI	Legal Resource Index [*Information Access Corp.*] [*Bibliographic database*] [*Information service*] (EISS)
LRIP	Language Research in Progress (DIT)
LRIR	Limb Radiance Inversion Radiometer
LRIR	Low-Resolution Infrared Radiometer
LRIRR	Low-Resolution Infrared Radiometer (MSA)
LRL	Linking Relocating Loader (CAA)
LRL	Logical Record Length (CAA)
LRL	Logical Record Location (CAA)
LRLTRAN	Lawrence Radiation Laboratory FORTRAN [*Programing language*] [*1961*] (CSR)
LRPS	Long-Range Planning Service [*Stanford Research Institute*] [*Assists businesses in investment activities*] (EISS)
LRR	Loop Regenerative Repeater (CAA)
LRRS	Library Reports & Research Service, Inc. [*Denver, CO*] [*Information service*] (EISS)
LRSA	Laboratoire de Recherche en Sciences de l'Administration [*Laval University*] [*Canada*] [*Research center*] (RCD)
LRT	Long-Range Radiotelephone
LRU	Least Recently Used [*Replacement algorithm*] [*Data processing*]
LRU	Line Removable Unit
LRU	Line Replaceable Unit (AFM)
LRU	Link Retraction Unit (KSC)
LS	Language Specification (IEEE)
LS	Least Significant (IEEE)
LS	Least Squares [*Mathematical statistics*]
LS	Line Switch [*Telecommunications*] (TEL)
LS	Loading Splice [*Telecommunications*] (TEL)
LS	Local Store (CAA)
LS	Local Sunset
LS	Low-Power Schottky [*Electronics*]
LS	Low-Speed
LSA	Line-Sharing Adapter (CAA)
LSAP	Link Layer Service Access Point (CCD)
LSB	Least Significant BIT [*Binary Digit*] [*Data compaction*] [*Data processing*]
LSB	Line Segment Block [*Data processing*]
LSB	Lower Sideband [*Data transmission*]
LSBY	Least Significant Byte [*Data processing*]
LSC	Large-Scale Computer
LSC	Least Significant Character (IEEE)
LSC	Limit Signaling Comparator
LSC	Low-Speed Concentrator (CAA)
LSCC	Local Servicing Control Center [*Telecommunications*] (TEL)
LSCG	Law School Computer Group [*Southern Methodist University*] [*Dallas, TX*] (EANO)
LSCP	Low-Speed Card Punch [*Data processing*]
LSCU	Local Servicing Control Unit [*Telecommunications*] (TEL)
LSD	Language for Systems Development (OA)
LSD	Least Significant Digit [*Data compaction*] (MUGU)
LSD	Line-Sharing Device
LSD	Line Signal Detector
LSDR	Local Store Data Register (CAA)
LSDS	Low-Speed Data Service [*RCA Global Communications, Inc.*] [*Telecommunications*] (TSSD)
LSDU	Link Layer Service Data Unit (CCD)
LSE	Lattice Screen Editor [*Program editor*]
LSF	Line Switch Frame [*Telecommunications*] (TEL)
LSFR	Local Storage Function Register (CAA)
LSG	Language Structure Group [*CODASYL*] (CAA)
LSI	Large-Scale Integration [*of circuits*] [*Electronics*]
LSI	Lear-Siegler, Incorporated [*NYSE symbol*]
LSI	Learning Systems Institute [*Florida State University*] [*Research center*] (RCD)
LSIC	Large-Scale Integrated Circuit [*Electronics*] (KSC)
LSID	Local Session Identification [*Data processing*] (IBMDP)
LSL	Ladder Static Logic (OA)
LSL	Link and Selector Language (CAA)
LSL	Logical Shift Left [*Data processing*]
LSM	Line Selection Module [*Telecommunications*] (TEL)
LSMA	Low-Speed Multiplexer Arrangement (CAA)
LSOCE	Linear Stochastic Optimal Control and Estimation [*Computer program*]
LSP	Least Significant Position (CMD)
LSP	Library Software Package
LSP	Linked Systems Project
LSP	Local Store Pointer (CAA)
LSP	Low-Speed Printer
LSPK	Loudspeaker (TEL)
LSPS	Local Service Planning System [*Telecommunications*] (TEL)
LSPTP	Low-Speed Paper Tape Punch [*Telecommunications*]
LSPTR	Low-Speed Paper Tape Reader [*Telecommunications*] (TEL)
LSQA	Local System Queue Area [*Data processing*] (BUR)
LSR	Local Shared Resources [*Data processing*] (IBMDP)
LSR	Logical Shift Right [*Data processing*]
LSR	Low-Speed Reader (CAA)
LSRP	Local Switching Replacement Planning [*Telecommunications*] (TEL)
LSS	Language for Symbolic Simulation (CAA)
LSS	Local Synchronization Subsystem [*Telecommunications*] (TEL)
LSS	Loop Switching System [*Telecommunications*] (DEEC)
LST	Last (BUR)
LSTTL	Low-Power Schottky Transistor-Transistor Logic [*Electronics*]
LSU	Leading Signal Unit [*Telecommunications*] (TEL)
LSU	Line-Sharing Unit (CAA)
LSU	Load Storage Unit [*Data processing*] (CAA)
LSU	Local Storage Unit [*Data processing*] (CAA)
LSU	Local Switching Unit [*Telecommunications*] (TEL)
LSU	Local Synchronization Utility [*Telecommunications*] (TEL)
LSU	Lone Signal Unit [*Telecommunications*] (TEL)
LSV	Line Status Verifier [*Telecommunications*] (TEL)
LT	Language Translation [*Data processing*]
LT	Less Than (IBMDP)
LT	Letter Telegram
L/T	Line Telecommunications
LT	Line Telegraphy
L & T	Line and Terminal [*Telecommunications*] (TEL)
LT	Line Terminator (CAA)
LT	Link Terminal [*Telecommunications*] (TEL)
LT	Linked Term [*Online database field identifier*] (OBD)
LT	Logic Theorist [*or Theory*] [*Data processing*]
LTA	Logical Transient Area (CAA)
LTB	Last Trunk Busy [*Telecommunications*] (TEL)
LTB	Line Term Buffer [*Data processing*]
LTC	Line Time Clock (CAA)
LTC	Line Traffic Coordinator (CET)
LTC	Linear Transmission Channel
LTC	Local Telephone Circuit [*Telecommunications*] (TEL)
LTC	Local Terminal Controller (CAA)
LTD	Line Transfer Device (CAA)
LTD	Local Test Desk (KSC)
LTE	Large Table Electroplotter [*Data processing*]
LTE	Line Termination Equipment [*Telecommunications*] (TEL)
LTE	Linear Threshold Element [*Data processing*]
LTEC	Lincoln Telecommunications [*NASDAQ symbol*] (NQ)
LTFD	Logic and Test Function Drawer [*Data processing*] (MCD)
LT/FM	Long-Term/Frequency Modulation
LTH	Logical Track Header (CAA)
LTM	Line Type Modulation [*Radio*]
LTM	Live Traffic Model [*Telecommunications*] (TEL)
LTM	Long-Term Memory
LTP	Long Term Projections [*Townsend-Greenspan & Co., Inc.*] [*Database*] (CUAD)
LTPL	Long-Term Procedural Language (CAH)
LTR	Letter (AFM)
LTRS	Letters Shift [*Teleprinters*]
LTS	Line Transient Suppression (CAA)
LTS	Long-Term Storage [*Memory*] [*Data processing*]
LTTL	Low-Power Transistor-Transistor Logic (IEEE)
LTU	Line Terminating Unit (CET)
LU	Logical Unit [*Data processing*]
LUB	Logical Unit Block [*Data processing*] (TUT)
LUB	Lubricate
LUCC	Lehigh University Computing Center [*Pennsylvania*] [*Research center*] (RCD)
LUCID	Language Used to Communicate Information System Design
LUCID	Language for Utility Checkout and Instrumentation Development
LUE	Link Utilization Efficiency (CAA)
LUF	Lowest Usable [*or Useful*] Frequency [*Radio*]
LUGL	Lumen & Glare Calculations [*Facet Ltd.*] [*Software package*] [*British*] (NCC)
LUHF	Lowest Usable [*or Useful*] High-Frequency [*Radio*]
LULU	Logical Unit to Logical Unit (CAA)
LUN	Logical Unit Number (CAA)
LUS	Large Ultimate Size [*Telecommunications*] (TEL)
LUT	Line Unit [*Data processing*] (BUR)
LUT	Local User Terminal
LV	LaserVision
LV	Level of Study [*Online database field identifier*] (OBD)
LVA	Local Virtual Address (OA)
LVD	Low-Voltage Drop (CET)
LVDT	Linear Variable Differential Transformer
LVOR	Low-Powered, Very-High-Frequency Omnirange
LVP	Low-Voltage Plate
LVPS	Laboratory Vehicle Procedure Simulator
LVPS	Low-Voltage Power Supply
LVR	Longitudinal Video Recording
LVR	Low-Voltage Rack
LVR	Low-Voltage Relay (DDI)
LV/RVV	Local Vertical/Relative Velocity Vector
LVS	Low-Velocity Scanning
LVST	Longitudinal Velocity Sorting Tube
LVTR	Low-VHF [*Very-High-Frequency*] Transmitter-Receiver
LW	Langwelle [*Long Wave*] [*German*] (MCD)
LW	Leave Word [*Telecommunications*] (TEL)
LW	Long Wave [*Radio*]
LWA	Last Word Address (NITA)
LWA	Long Wire Antenna
LWD	Larger Word [*Data processing*]
LXMAR	Load External Memory Address Register (NITA)
LYA	Lynch, Young & Associates [*Newport Beach, CA*] [*Telecommunications*] (TSSD)

LYpAS .... Logicheskii Yazyk dlia Predstavleniya Algoritmov Sinteza Releinykh Ustroistv [*A Programing Language for Logic and Coding Algorithm*] [*Book title*]
LYRIC .... Language for Your Remote Instruction by Computer [*Data processing*]   (MDG)

M

M	Magnetron (MDG)		MACSS	Medium-Altitude Communications Satellite System
M	Management Assistance, Inc. [NYSE symbol]		MACSYMA	MAC [Massive Algebraic Computation] Symbolic Manipulator [Programing language] [1969] (CSR)
M	Mean Active Maintenance Downtime [Data processing]		MacTEP	Mac [Apple's Mackintosh computer] Terminal Emulation Program
(M)	Median		MACTIS	Marine and Coastal Technology Information Service [United Nations] (EISS)
M	Mega [A prefix meaning multiplied by one million] [Symbol]		MAD	Machine ANSI Data (OA)
M	Megabyte [Data processing] [Data storage capacity]		MAD	Master Accession Document [Data processing] (BUR)
M	Memory		MAD	Master Air Data [Computer]
M	Merge [Data processing] (IBMDP)		MAD	Michigan Algorithmic Decoder [IBM Corp.] [University of Michigan] [Programing language] [1961]
m	Meter [SI unit of length]		MAD	Mixed Analog and Digital [Telecommunications] (TEL)
m	Milli- [A prefix meaning divided by 1000] [SI symbol]		MAD	Multiple Audio Distribution [Communications]
M	Million		MADAM	Moderately Advanced Data Management [Data processing]
M	Mode		MADAM	Multipurpose Automatic Data Analysis Machine
M	Modulation Depth [Broadcasting]		MADAP	Maastricht Automatic Data Processing and Display System [Air traffic control]
M	Monitor (MDG)		MADAR	Malfunction Analysis, Detection, and Recording [Data processing]
M	Mutual Inductance [Symbol] [IUPAC]		MADARS	Maintenance Analysis, Detection, and Reporting System [Data processing] (AFM)
M2	Masterspec 2 [Production Systems for Architects & Engineers, Inc.] [Information service] (EISS)		MADARS	Malfunction Analysis, Detection, and Recording Subsystem [Data processing] (DDI)
3M	Minnesota Mining & Manufacturing Co. [Also, MMM]		MADC	Multiplexer Analog-to-Digital Converter (MCD)
MA	Memory Address [Data processing]		MADDAM	Macromodule and Digital Differential Analyzer Machine [Data processing]
mA	Milliampere		MADE	Magnetic Device Evaluator [Data processing]
MA	Modify Address (IEEE)		MADE	Multichannel Analog-to-Digital Data Encoder
MAACS	Multi Address Asynchronous Communication System (OA)		MADIS	Millivolt Analog-Digital Instrumentation System
MAAP	Maintenance and Administration Panel [Bell System]		MADM	Manchester Automatic Digital Machine [Manchester University] [British] (IEEE)
MAAT	Management of Advanced Automation Technology Center [Worcester Polytechnic Institute] [Research center] (RCD)		MADR	Microprogram Address Register (NITA)
MAB	Macroaddress Bus (NITA)		MADRE	Magnetic Drum Receiving Equipment
MAB	Master Acquisition Bus [Data processing] (MCD)		MADRE	Martin Automatic Data-Reduction Equipment
MAC	Machine-Aided Cognition [Computer project] [Massachusetts Institute of Technology]		MADS	Machine-Aided Drafting System (IEEE)
MAC	Man and Computer (DIT)		MAECAM	Micro Aided Engineering/Computer Aided Manufacturing [Micro Aided Engineering Ltd. and Digital Microsystems Ltd.] [Software package] [British] (NCC)
MAC	Massive Algebraic Computation [Programing language] [1958] [Data processing] (CSR)		MAECON	Mid-America Electronics Conference
MAC	Measurement and Analysis Center [Telecommunications] (TEL)		MAEDOS	Micro Aided Engineering/Drawing Office System [Micro Aided Engineering Ltd.] [Software package] [British] (NCC)
MAC	Mechanical Analog Computer (DEN)		MAESTRO	Machine-Assisted Educational System for Teaching by Remote Operation (IEEE)
MAC	Medium Access Control (CCD)		MAEVIS	Micro Aided Engineering 3D Visualisation [Micro Aided Engineering Ltd. and Micro Aided Engineering Digital Microsystems Ltd.] [Software package] [British] (NCC)
MAC	Memory Access Controller (NITA)			
MAC	Message Authentication Code (NITA)			
MAC	Monthly Availability Charge (BUR)			
MAC	Multiaction Computer		MAF	Multiple Access Facility [Data processing]
MAC	Multiple Access Computer		MAG	Macrogenerator [SEMIS] (NITA)
MAC	Multiple Access Control [Data processing] (DIT)		MAG	Magnetic (AFM)
MAC	Multiplexed Analog Component [Satellite television] [British]		MAGE	Mechanical Aerospace Ground Equipment (TEL)
MACBANK	Machining Data Bank [PERA] [Software package] [British] (NCC)		MAGG	Modular Alphanumeric Graphics Generator (IEEE)
MACC	Madison Academic Computing Center [University of Wisconsin - Madison] [Information service] [Research center]		MAGGS	Modular Advanced Graphics Generation System (IEEE)
MACC	Modular Alter and Compose Console [Data processing]		MAGI	Master Group Information System [AT & T]
MACCS	Molecular Access System [Computer program]		MAGIC	Machine-Aided Graphics for Illustration and Composition [Bell Telephone] (NITA)
MACDAC	Machine Communication with Digital Automatic Computer (OA)		MAGIC	Machine for Automatic Graphics Interface to a Computer
MACE	Machine-Aided Composition and Editing		MAGIC	Market Analysis Guide - Intercity Communications [AT & T]
MACE	Management Applications in a Computer Environment (IEEE)		MAGIC	Marketing and Advertising General Information Centre [Datasolve Ltd.] [Database] (CUAD)
MACH	Machine [or Machinery]		MAGIC	Matrix Algebra General Interpretive Coding (IEEE)
MACHY	Machinery		MAGIC	Michigan Automatic General Integrated Computation (MCD)
MACMIS	Maintenance and Construction Management Information System [Data processing]		MAGIC	Modern Analytical Generator of Improved Circuits [Data processing]
MACON	Matrix Connector Punched Card Programer [Data processing] (IEEE)		MAGIC	Motorola Automatically Generated Integrated Circuits
MACOPT	Machining Optimisation [PERA] [Software package] [British] (NCC)		MAGIC	Multipurpose and Generalized Interface to COBOL [Data processing] (TUT)
MACP	Mission Analysis Computer Program		MAGLOC	Magnetic Logic Computer
MAC-PAC	Manufacturing Planning and Control [Arthur Anderson & Co.] [Software package] [British] (NCC)		MAGPIE	Machine Automatically Generating Production Inventory Evaluation [Data processing] (IEEE)
MACRO	Merge and Correlate Recorded Output [Data processing] (NASA)		MAGPIE	Markov Game Planar Intercept-Evasion Package [Data processing]
MACROL	Macro-Based Display Oriented Language [Raytheon Co.] (NITA)			
MACS	Management & Computer Services, Inc. [Information service] (EISS)			
MACS	McDonnell Automatic Checkout System [McDonnell Douglas Corp.]			
MACS	Medium-Altitude Communications Satellite			
MACS	Microwave Attitude Control Sensor			
MACS	Monitoring and Control Station (NITA)			
MACS	Multiple Application Connector System			
MACS	Multiple-Technique Analytical Computer System			

123

Computer & Telecommunications Acronyms

MAI .... Management Assistance, Incorporated [*Tustin, CA*] [*Software manufacturer*] (DASOS)
MAI .... Multiple Access Interface (NITA)
MAID .... Maintenance Automatic Integration Director [*Data processing*]
MAID .... Market Analysis and Information Database [*Information service*] (EISS)
MAID .... Merger Acquisition Improved Decision [*Data processing*]
MAID .... Monroe Automatic Internal Diagnosis [*Data processing*]
MAIDS .... Machine-Aided Information and Dissemination Systems
MAIDS .... Management Automated Information Display System (KSC)
MAINT .... Maintenance (AFM)
MAIP .... Matrix Algebra Interpretive Program (IEEE)
MAK .... Monopulse Antenna Kit
MAL .... Macroassembly Language [*Data processing*] (BUR)
MAL .... Memory Access Logic (NITA)
MAL .... Meta Assembly Language (NITA)
MAL .... Multiple Address Letter
MALT .... Mnemonic Assembly Language Translator [*Data processing*] (IEEE)
MAM .... Memory Allocation Manager (NITA)
MAM .... Message Access Method [*Honeywell, Inc*] (NITA)
MAM .... Multiapplication Monitor (NITA)
MAM .... Multiple Access to Memory [*Data processing*] (IEEE)
MAMA .... Material Acquisition Management Application [*Suggested name for the Library of Congress computer system*]
MAMI .... Machine-Aided Manufacturing Information [*Data processing*]
MAMI .... Modified Alternate Mark Inversion [*Telecommunications*] (TEL)
MAMS .... Multiple Access to Memory System [*Data processing*] (CIT)
MAN .... Magnetic Automatic Navigation [*System*] (RDA)
MAN .... Manual (KSC)
MAN .... Metropolitan Area Network (CCD)
MANDATE ... Multiline Automatic Network Diagnostic and Transmission Equipment (NITA)
MANIAC ..... Mathematical Analyzer, Numerical Integrator and Computer
MANIAC ..... Mechanical and Numerical Integrator and Computer (IEEE)
MANIP .... Manual Input [*Data processing*]
MANS .... Map Analysis System [*Data processing*]
MAP .... Macro Arithmetic Processors [*Data processing*] (MDG)
MAP .... Macroassembly Program [*Data processing*]
MAP .... Management Analysis Program (TUT)
MAP .... Manufacturing Activity Projection (TUT)
MAP .... Manufacturing Automation Protocol [*General Motors computer compatibility program*]
MAP .... Mathematical Analysis without Programing [*Data processing*]
MAP .... Medical Audit Program [*Computerized system of abstracted medical record information*]
MAP .... Memory Allocation and Protection (NITA)
MAP .... Microcomputer Adaptation Procedures Corp. [*Indianapolis, IN*] [*Software manufacturer*] (DASOS)
MAP .... Microprocessor Application Project [*In manufacturing industry*] [*Department of the Interior*] (DEEC)
MAP .... Microprogramed Array Processor (NITA)
MAP .... Minimum Acceptable Performance [*Telecommunications*] (TEL)
MAP .... Model and Program [*Data processing*] (CGC)
MAP .... Modular Analysis Processor [*Applied Data Research, Inc.*] (NITA)
MAP .... Modular Application System [*Data processing*]
MAP .... Multiple Array Processor
MAPCHE..... Mobile Automatic Programed Checkout Equipment
MAPE........... Microcomputers and Primary Education
MAPG .... Maximum Available Power Gain (MSA)
MAPICS...... Manufacturing, Accounting, and Production Information Control System [*IBM Corp.*]
MAPID .... Machine-Aided Program for Preparation of Instruction Data
MAPP.......... Masking Parameter Printout [*Data processing*]
MAPS.......... Machine Automated Parts System (MCD)
MAPS.......... Maintenance Analysis and Procedures System [*Data processing*]
MAPS.......... Measurement of Air Pollution from Satellites
MAPS.......... Multicolor Automatic Projection System (IEEE)
MAPS.......... Multiple Address Processing System
MAR .... Macroaddress Register (NITA)
MAR .... Memory-Address Register [*Data processing*]
MAR .... Microprogram Address Register (NITA)
MARC .... Machine-Readable Cards
MARC .... Machine-Readable Cataloging [*Library of Congress*]
MARC .... Manufacturing Resource Control System [*Deritend Computer Bureau Ltd.*] [*Software package*] [*British*] (NCC)
MARCOM ... Microwave Airborne Communications Relay (IEEE)
MARC-S ..... Machine Readable Cataloguing - Serials
MARCS....... Melcom All Round Adaptive Consolidated Software [*Japanese*] (NITA)
MARDATA ... Maritime Data Network [*Maritime Data Network Ltd.*] [*Database*] (CUAD)
MARECS .... Maritime Communications Satellite
MARG .... Market Analysis Report Generator [*Data processing*]
MARGEN .... Management Report Generator [*Randolph Data Services, Inc.*] [*Software package*] [*Data processing*] (IEEE)
MARGIE...... Memory Analysis, Response Generation, and Interference in English (NITA)
MARISAT.... Maritime Satellite System [*COMSAT*]
MARPIC...... Marine Pollution Information Centre [*Marine Biological Association of the United Kingdom*] (EISS)
MARQUIS ... Master Remote Query Interface System [*Data processing*]
MARS .... Machine Automated Realty Service
MARS .... Maintenance Activities and Resources Simulation [*Data processing*]
MARS .... Management Analysis Reporting System [*Data processing*]
MARS .... Marconi Automatic Relay System (IEEE)
MARS .... Market Analysis and Reference System [*Vancouver stock exchange computer system*] [*Canada*]
MARS .... Marketing and Advertising Reference Service [*Predicasts, Inc.*] [*Database*] (CUAD)
MARS .... Memory-Address Register Storage [*Data processing*]
MARS .... Multiaperture Reluctance Switch [*Data storage unit*]
MARS .... Multiple Access Retrieval System [*Control Data Corp.*] (NITA)
MARS .... PTS [*Predicasts*] Marketing and Advertising Reference Service [*Cleveland, OH*] [*Information service*] (EISS)
MARSAT..... Maritime Satellite [*COMSAT*]
MARSATS ... Maritime Satellite System [*COMSAT*]
MARSYAS ... Marshall System for Aerospace Simulation [*Programing language*] [1966-68] (CSR)
MARTOS..... Multiaccess Real-Time Operating System [*AEG Telefunken*] [*West German*] (NITA)
MARUNET ... Maruzen Online Network [*Maruzen Co. Ltd.*] [*Tokyo, Japan*] [*Telecommunications*] (TSSD)
MAS............. Macroassembler (NITA)
MAS............. Marine Advisory Service [*National Oceanic and Atmospheric Administration*] [*Information service*] (EISS)
MAS............. Modular Application Systems [*Martin Marietta Data Systems*] (NITA)
MAS............. Monitor and Alarm System (MCD)
MASCO ...... Microprogrammed and Simulated Computer Organization
MASCOT .... Modular Approach to System Construction Operation and Test (MCD)
MASCOT .... Motorola Automatic Sequential Computer Operated Tester
MASER .... Microwave Amplification by Stimulated Emission of Radiation
MASIS .... Maruzen Scientific Information Service Center [*Maruzen Co. Ltd.*] [*Tokyo, Japan*] [*Telecommunications*] (TSSD)
MASK .... Multilevel Amplitude Shift Keying
MASM......... Meta-Assembler Language [*Sperry UNIVAC computer language*]
MASM......... Motorized Antenna Switching Matrix
MAS/MILS ... Minerals Availability System/Minerals Industry Location Subsystem [*Bureau of Mines*] [*Database*] (FDB)
MASMOD .... Mass Model [*Computer program*]
MASS .... Materials Acquisition Sub-System [*Data processing*]
MASS .... Michigan Automatic Scanning System (IEEE)
MASS .... Monitor and Assembly System [*Data processing*] (BUR)
MASS .... Multiple Access Sequential Selection [*Data processing*] (BUR)
MASSBUS ... Memory Bus [*Digital Equipment Corp.*] (NITA)
MASTER..... Matching Available Student Time to Educational Resources [*Data processing*]
MASTER..... Multiple Access Shared Time Executive Routine [*Control Data Corp.*] [*Data processing*]
MASTIR ...... Microfilmed Abstract System for Technical Information Retrieval [*Illinois Institute of Technology*] (EISS)
MAT .... Machine-Assisted Translation
MAT .... Machine Available Time [*Data processing*]
Mat.............. Matrix [*A publication*]
MAT .... Memory Address Test (NITA)
MAT .... Metropolitan Area Trunk [*Telecommunications*] (TEL)
MAT .... Microalloy Transistor
MAT .... Microwave Antenna Tower
MAT .... Multiple Address Telegrams
MATE.......... Microprocessor Automatic Testing [*ASMAP Electronics Ltd.*] [*Software package*] [*British*] (NCC)
MATE.......... Modular Automatic Test Equipment
MATE.......... Multiple-Access Time-Division Experiment (IEEE)
MATELO...... Maritime Air Telecommunications Organization [*NATO*] (NATG)
MATFAP...... Metropolitan Area Transmission Facility Analysis Program [*AT&T*] [*Telecommunications*] (TEL)
MATH.......... Mathematics
MATH.......... Mathematics Abstracts [*Fachinformationszentrum Energie, Physik, Mathematik GmbH*] [*Database*] (CUAD)
Math Comput Simul ... Mathematics and Computers in Simulation [*A publication*]
Math Comput Simulation ... Mathematics and Computers in Simulation [*A publication*]
MATHDI...... Mathematical Didactics [*Fachinformationszentrum Energie, Physik, Mathematik GmbH*] [*Database*] (CUAD)
MATHLAB ... Mathematical Laboratory [*Programing language*] (CSR)
MATLAN..... Matrix Language [*Data processing*] (IEEE)
MATPS........ Machine-Aided Technical Processing System [*Yale University Library*] [*New Haven, CT*] [*Data processing*]
MATR.......... Management Access to Records (NITA)
MATV.......... Master Antenna Television
MAU............ Media Access Unit (CCD)
MAU............ Memory Access Unit
MAU............ Multiple Access Unit (NITA)
MAUG......... MicroNet Apple User's Group [*CompuServe*] [*Database*]
MAVI........... Microwave Automatic Vehicle Identification (MCD)
MAVICA..... Magnetic Video Camera [*Sony Corp.*]
MAVIN .... Machine-Assisted Vendor Information Network (CGC)
MAVIS .... McDonnell Douglas Automated Voice Information System (MCD)
MAX .... Maximum
MAX .... Modular Applications Executive [*Modular Computer Systems*] (NITA)

Computer & Telecommunications Acronyms

MAXCOM	Modular Applications Executive for Communications [*Modular Computer Systems*] (NITA)
MAXIT	Maximum Interference Threshold [*Telecommunications*] (TEL)
MB	Maintenance Busy [*Telecommunications*] (TEL)
MB	MegaBIT [*Binary Digit*] [*Data processing*]
Mb	Megabyte [*Data storage capacity*] [*Data processing*]
MB	Memory Buffer [*Data processing*]
MB	Memory Bus (NITA)
mb	Millibyte [*Data processing*]
MB	Million Bytes [*Data processing*] (BUR)
MB	Module Balance [*Data processing*]
MB	Multiband (DEN)
MBA	Multibeam Antenna
MBC	Master Bus Controller [*Data processing*]
MBC	Memory Bus Controller (NITA)
MBC	Multiple Basic Channel (NITA)
MBCD	Modified Binary-Coded Decimal (NITA)
MBD	Magnetic-Bubble Domain Device [*Data processing*] (IEEE)
MBDS	Modular Building Distribution System [*Telecommunications*] (TEL)
MBE	Mail Boxes Etc. USA [*Carlsbad, CA*] [*Telecommunications*] (TSSD)
MBF	Materials Business File [*American Society for Metals, The Institute for Metals*] [*Information service*] (EISS)
MBI	Memory Bank Interface (NITA)
MBI	Multibus Interface [*Data processing*] (MCD)
MBIO	Microprogramable Block Input/Output (NITA)
MBIS	Master of Business Information Systems
MBIT	MegaBIT [*Binary Digit*] [*Data processing*] (MDG)
MBM	Magnetic Bubble Memory [*Data processing*]
MBPRE	Multitype Branching Process in a Random Environment [*Data processing*]
MBPS	MegaBITS [*Binary Digits*] per Second [*Transmission rate*] [*Data processing*]
MBQ	Modified Biquinary Code [*Data processing*]
MBR	Mechanical Buffer Register [*Data processing*]
MBR	Memory Base Register (NITA)
MBR	Memory Buffer Register [*Data processing*]
MBRA	Multibeam Radiometer Antenna
MBRE	Memory Buffer Register, Even [*Data processing*]
MBRO	Memory Buffer Register, Odd [*Data processing*]
MB/S	MegaBITS [*Binary Digits*] per Second [*Transmission rate*] [*Data processing*]
MBS	Multiblock Synchronization Signal Unit [*Telecommunications*] (TEL)
MBS	Multiple Batch Station [*Data processing*] (OA)
MBS	Mutual Broadcasting System
MBU	Memory Buffer Unit [*Data processing*] (OA)
MC	Magnetic Card [*Word processing*]
MC	Main Channel (OA)
MC	Management Contents [*Information service*] (EISS)
MC	Marginal Check [*Computer*]
MC	Master Control
Mc	Megacycle
MC	Memory Configuration [*Data processing*] (MCD)
MC	Memory Control [*Unit*] [*Data processing*]
MC	Message Composer [*Communications, data processing*]
MC	Minimum Call [*Television studio on standby*]
MC	Modular Computer
MC	Monitor Call [*Data processing*] (IBMDP)
MC	Monitor and Control [*Data processing*] (BUR)
MC	Multichip [*Circuit*] [*Electronics*]
MCA	Master Community Antenna
MCA	Microfilming Corporation of America [*Los Angeles, CA*] [*Information service*] (EISS)
MCA	Microwave Communications Association [*Washington, DC*] [*Telecommunications*] (EANO)
MCA	Multichannel Analyzer
MCA	Multiprocessor Communications Adapter (NITA)
MCALS	Minnesota Computer-Aided Library System [*University of Minnesota*]
MCAR	Machine Check Analysis and Recording (BUR)
MCASP	Multiple Constraint Alternative Selector Program [*Bell System*]
MCAUTO	McDonnell Douglas Automation Co. [*Robotics*]
MCB	Message Control Block (CET)
MCB	Microcomputer Board (NITA)
MCBF	Mean Cycles between Failures [*Quality control*]
MCBS	Micro Computer Business Services
MCC	Main Communications Center
MCC	Maintenance Control Center (AFM)
MCC	Management Control Center [*Data processing*] (BUR)
MCC	Master Control Center (NATG)
MCC	Master Control Console
MCC	Microelectronic and Computer Technology Research [*A research cooperative based in Austin, TX*]
MCC	Multichannel Communications Controller
MCC	Multicomponent Circuits
MCC	Multiple-Chip Carrier [*Computer technology*]
MCC	Multiple Communications Control (BUR)
MCC	Multiple Computer Complex
MCCAA	Mobile Communications Corp. of America Cl A [*NASDAQ symbol*] (NQ)
MCCS	Mechanized Calling Card Service [*Formerly, ABC*] [*Telecommunications*]
MCCU	Multiple Channel Control Unit (NITA)
MCCU	Multiple Communications Control Unit [*Data processing*]
MCD	McDonnell Douglas Corp.
MCD	Multiple Concrete Duct [*Telecommunications*] (TEL)
MCDBSU	Master Control and Data Buffer Storage Unit (NITA)
MCDC	McDonnell Douglas Corporation
MCDP	Microprogramed Communication Data Processor
MCDR	Multichannel DIFAR [*Directional Frequency Analysis and Recording System*] Relay (NVT)
MCDS	Multicommand Data System
MCDS	Multifunction CRT [*Cathode-Ray Tube*] Display System (NASA)
MCDT	Mean Corrective Downtime [*Data processing*]
MCDU	Multifunction CRT [*Cathode-Ray Tube*] Display Unit (NASA)
MCEL	Machine Check Extended Logout (NITA)
MCEWG	Multinational Communication-Electronics Working Group [*Formerly, SGCEC*] [*NATO*] (NATG)
MCF	Multichannel Fixed
MCG	Man Computer Graphics [*Data processing*]
MCH	Machine-Check Handler [*Data processing*] (MCD)
MCHAN	Multichannel
MCI	Machine Check Interruption [*Data processing*] (BUR)
MCI	Malicious Call Identification [*Telecommunications*] (TEL)
MCI	Management Consultants International, Inc. [*Canada*] [*Information service*] (EISS)
MCI	Marketing Concepts, Incorporated [*New York, NY*] [*Telecommunications*] (TSSD)
MCI	Microwave Communications of America, Incorporated
MCIA	Microcomputer Investors Association [*Fredericksburg, VA*] [*Database producer*] (EANO)
MCIC	Machine Check Interruption Code (NITA)
MCIC	MCI Communications Corp. [*NASDAQ symbol*] (NQ)
MCIC	Metals and Ceramics Information Center [*Battelle Columbus Laboratories*] [*Columbus, OH*] [*Information service*] (EISS)
MCIU	Manipulator Controller Interface Unit (NASA)
MCL	Memory Control and Logging [*Hewlett-Packard Co.*] (NITA)
MCL	Message Control Language [*Data processing*]
MCL	Microprogram Control Logic [*Data processing*] (MDG)
MCL	Minimal Computer Load
MCLA	Microcoded Communications Line Adapter (NITA)
MCLK	Master Clock
MCM	Circular Mils, Thousands
MCM	Machines for Coordinated Multiprocessing
MCM	Magnetic Core Memory [*Data processing*]
MCM	Maintenance Control Module [*Telecommunications*] (TEL)
MCM	Manual Communication Module [*Telecommunication device for the deaf*]
MCM	McCarthy, Crisanti & Maffei, Inc. [*New York, NY*] [*Information service*] (EISS)
MCM	Memory Control Module (NITA)
MCM	Monte Carlo Method [*Data processing*]
MCMS	Multichannel Memory System [*Data processing*]
MCN	Museum Computer Network, Inc. [*American Association of Museums*] [*Stony Brook, NY*] [*Research center*] (RCD)
MCNC	Microelectronics Center of North Carolina [*Research Triangle Park, NC*] [*Research center*] (RCD)
MCOM	Mathematics of Computation (IEEE)
MCOM	Medical Communications [*A publication*]
MCOM	Mincomp Corp. [*NASDAQ symbol*] (NQ)
MCON	Moment Connections [*Computer Services Consultants Ltd.*] [*Software package*] [*British*] (NCC)
MCOS	Microprogramable Computer Operating System (NITA)
MCP	Main Call Process [*Telecommunications*] (TEL)
MCP	Master Control Program [*Burroughs Corp.*]
MCP	Memory-Centered Processing [*or Processor*] [*System*] [*Data processing*]
MCP	Message Control Program [*Data processing*]
MCP	Multichannel Communications Program (IEEE)
MCP	Multiple Chip Package
MCP	Multiple Control Program [*Data processing*]
MCPA	Memory Clock Pulse Amplifier
MCPG	Media Conversion Program Generator (NITA)
MCPS	Mini Core Processing Subsystem (TEL)
MCPU	Multiple Central Processing Unit (NITA)
MCR	Magnetic Card Reader [*Data processing*] (NITA)
MCR	Magnetic Character Reader [*Data processing*] (IEEE)
MCR	Magnetic Character Recognition [*Data processing*] (BUR)
MCR	Master Control Register (NITA)
MCR	Master Control Routine
MCR	Memory Control Register (NITA)
MCR	Multichannel Receiver
MCRML	Midcontinental Regional Medical Library Program [*University of Nebraska*] [*Library network*] (EISS)
MCRN	Moscow City Relay Network (OA)
MCRR	Machine Check Recording and Recovery [*Data processing*] (TUT)
MCRS	Maintenance Computing and Recording System
MCRWV	Microwave
MCS	Maintenance Control Section [*DCE*]
MCS	Management Control System (MCD)
MCS	Maneuver Control System [*Data processing*]
MCS	Manufacturing Control System (TUT)

Computer & Telecommunications Acronyms

MCS	Master Control System
MCS	Medical Computer Services (IEEE)
MCS	Message Control System [*Burroughs Corp.*] [*Data processing*] (BUR)
MCS	Microcomputer System (NITA)
MCS	Microwave Carrier Supply
MCS	Microwave Communication System
MCS	Mobile Communications System (MCD)
MCS	Modular Computer System (IEEE)
MCS	Multiple Character Set (CMD)
MCS	Multiple Computer System
MCS	Multiple Console Support [*Fujitsu Ltd.*] [*Data processing*] (MCD)
MCS	Multiprogramed Computer System (IEEE)
MCS	Multipurpose Communications and Signaling
MCS	Music Construction Set [*Computer program designed by Will Harvey and published by Electronic Arts*]
MCSA	Microcomputer Software Association [*Arlington, VA*] (EANO)
MCSP	Maintenance Control and Statistics Process [*Telecommunications*] (TEL)
MCST	Magnetic Card "Selectric" Typewriter [*IBM Corp.*]
MCT	Memory Cycle Time [*Data processing*] (MCD)
MCT	Message Control Task [*Data processing*]
MCT	Mobile Communication Terminal (OA)
MCTR	Message Center (DDI)
MCTRAP	Mechanized Customer Trouble Report Analysis Plan [*Telecommunications*] (TEL)
MCTV	Manhattan Cable TV, Inc. [*New York, NY*] [*Telecommunications*] (TSSD)
MCU	Maintenance Control Unit [*Data processing*] (NITA)
MCU	Master Clock Unit (VIT)
MCU	Master Control Unit (NITA)
MCU	Memory Control Unit (OA)
MCU	Message Construction Unit
MCU	Microcomputer Control Unit (NITA)
MCU	Microprocessor Control Unit
mcU	Microunit
MCU	Multicoupler Unit [*Antenna*] [*Telecommunications*] (TEL)
MCU	Multiplexer Control Unit (OA)
MCU	Multiprocessor Communications Unit (NITA)
MCVF	Multichannel Voice Frequency [*Telecommunications*]
MCVFT	Multichannel Voice Frequency Telegraphy [*Telecommunications*] (TEL)
MCW	Memory Card Writer [*Telecommunications*] (TEL)
MCW	Modulated Continuous Wave [*Radio signal transmission*]
MD	Magnetic Disk [*Data processing*] (BUR)
MD	Message Data
MD	Messages per Day
MD	Microwave Desorber [*Instrumentation*]
M/D	Modulator-Demodulator [*Telecommunications*] (CET)
MD	Monitor Displays [*Data processing*] (BUR)
MD	Multiple Dissemination
MDA	Measurement, Decision, and Actuation [*Data processing*]
MDA	Mechanically Despun Antenna (KSC)
MDA	Mechanized Directory Assistance [*Telecommunications*] (TEL)
MDA	Microprocessor Development Aid
MDA	Multidimensional Access (OA)
MDA	Multidimensional Analysis (IEEE)
MDA	Multidimensional Array (OA)
MDA	Multiple Digit Absorbing [*Telecommunications*] (TEL)
MDAC	Multiplying Digital-to-Analog Converter [*Data processing*] (IEEE)
MDB	Memory-Data Bank
MDB	Metrology Data Bank [*GIDEP*]
MDB	Multiplex Data Bus [*Data processing*] (MCD)
MDBM	MULTICS Data Base Manager
MDC	Machinability Data Center [*Computerized search service*] [*DoD*] (EISS)
MDC	Main Display Console
MDC	Master Data Center, Inc. [*Southfield, MI*] [*Information service*] (EISS)
MDC	McDonnell Douglas Corporation
MDC	Mead Data Central [*Dayton, OH*]
MDC	Memory Disk Controller
MDC	Muller Data Corporation [*Information service*] (EISS)
MDC	Multiple Device Controller (NITA)
MDCU	Magnetic Disk Control Unit (NITA)
MDD	Magnetic Disk Drive (NITA)
MDD	Million Dollar Directory [*Dun's Marketing Services*] [*Database*]
MDDCS	Memorial Dose Distribution Computation Service [*Memorial Sloan-Kettering Cancer Center*] [*Information service*] (EISS)
MDE	Magnetic Decision Element [*Data processing*] (BUR)
MDES	Multiple Data Entry System (NITA)
MDF	Main Distributing Frame [*Bell System*]
MDF	Manual Direction Finder [*Radio*]
MDF	Master Data File
MDF	Master Directory File [*Data processing*]
MDF	Master Document File [*Data processing*]
MDF	Medium-Frequency Direction Finder [*or Finding*]
MDF	Metal Data File [*National Research Council of Canada*] [*Database*]
MDF	Microcomputer Development Facilities (IEEE)
MDF	Multiband Direction Finder
MDF/I	Metals Datafile/I [*American Society for Metals*] [*Database*] (CUAD)
MDG	Multiplier Decoder Gate [*Data processing*]
MDIC	Microwave Dielectric Integrated Circuit (IEEE)
MDIF	Manual Data Input Function [*Data processing*]
MDIS	Manual Data Input Section [*Data processing*]
MDIU	Manual Data Input Unit [*Data processing*]
MDL	Macro Description Language [*Data processing*] (BUR)
MDL	Maintenance Diagnostic Logic [*Data processing*] (BUR)
MDL	Microwave Delay Line
MDL	Modular Design Language [*Data processing*] (CSR)
MDL	Muddle [*A computer language*]
MDLC	Mutliple Data Link Controller (NITA)
MDM	Multiplexer/Demultiplexer (NASA)
MDN	Managed Data Network
MDOS	Motorola Disk Operating System (NITA)
MDOSIS	Management Data Online Status/Inquiry System (MCD)
MDP	Main Data Path (NITA)
MDP	Message Discrimination Process [*Telecommunications*] (TEL)
MDQS	Management Data Query System [*Data processing*]
MDR	Magnetic Drum Recorder
MDR	Mark Document Reader [*Trademark*] [*Bell & Howell*]
MDR	Market Data Retrieval [*Westport, CT*] [*Originator, operator, and databank*] [*Information service*] (EISS)
MDR	Memory-Data Register
MDR	Message Detail Recording [*Later, SMDR*] [*Telecommunications*]
MDR	Microcircuit [*or Microwave*] Device Reliability (MCD)
MDRI	Multipurpose Display Repeater Indicator (MCD)
MDRS	Management Data Reporting System (MCD)
MDRS	Manufacturing Data Retrieval System (NASA)
MDS	Magnetic Drum System
MDS	Maintenance Data System (MCD)
MDS	Maintenance Documentation System [*Bell System*]
MDS	Management Data System (NASA)
MDS	Manufacturers Data Services, Inc. [*Hendersonville, TN*] [*Software manufacturer*] (DASOS)
MDS	Mass Digital Storage
MDS	Master Drum Sender
MDS	Medical Documentation Service [*College of Physicians*] [*Information service*] (EISS)
MDS	Memory Disk System [*Data processing*] (IEEE)
MDS	Meteorological Data System
MDS	Microprocessor Development System [*Motorola, Inc.*]
MDS	Minerals Data System [*Database*] (FDB)
MDS	Minimum Discernible Signal [*Radio*]
MDS	Minimum Discernible System (NASA)
MDS	Modern Data Systems (IEEE)
MDS	Modular Data System (NITA)
MDS	Modulate-Demodulate Subsystem (CIT)
MDS	Mohawk Data Sciences Corp. [*NYSE symbol*]
MDS	Monitor Distribution System [*Television*]
MDS	Multiple Dataset System
MDS	Multipoint Distribution System [*Line-of-sight relay system for electronic signals*]
MDS	Municipal Data Service [*International City Management Association*] [*Information service*] (EISS)
MDSC	Management Data Service Center
MDSC	Modular Digital Scan Converter (MCD)
MDSD	Magnetic Disk Storage Device [*Data processing*]
MDSF	Mass Data Storage Facility (SKY)
MDSI	Manufacturing Data Systems, Incorporated [*Ann Arbor, MI*] [*Software manufacturer*] (DASOS)
MDSIA	MDS [*Multipoint Distribution System*] Industry Association [*Washington, DC*] [*Telecommunications*] (EANO)
MDSPR	Mode Suppressor (KSC)
MDSS	Magnetic Drum Storage System
MDSS	Mass Digital Storage System
MDSS	Meteorological Data Sounding System (IEEE)
MDSS	Microprocessor Development Support System (NITA)
MDSS	Multidimensional Switching System [*Instrumentation*]
MDSS-PCT	Multidimensional Switching System - Packed Column Trap [*Instrumentation*]
MDT	Maintenance Demand Time (MCD)
MDT	Maintenance Downtime (MCD)
MDT	Mean Delay Time (CAAL)
MDT	Mean Detonating Time (NASA)
MDT	Mean Downtime [*Data processing*]
MDT	Mobile Data Terminal (MCD)
MDT	Modular Display Tactical
MDT	Multidimensional Tasking [*Honeywell, Inc.*] (NITA)
MDTA	Modulation, Demodulation, Terminal, and Associated Equipment
MDTS	MegaBIT [*Binary Digit*] Digital Troposcatter Subsystem [*Communications*] (MCD)
MDTS	Mobile Doppler Tracking Station
MDTS	Modular Data Transaction System
MDU	Maintenance Diagnostic Unit (NITA)
MDU	Master Driver Unit (VIT)
MDU	Message Decoder Unit
MDUS	Medium Data Utilization Station [*Australia*] [*Telecommunications*] (TEL)
MDW	Multiple Drop Wire [*Telecommunications*] (TEL)
ME	Main Entry [*Library Science*] [*Online database field identifier*] (OBD)

Computer & Telecommunications Acronyms

ME	Memory Element [*Data processing*] (NITA)
ME	Message Element [*Telecommunications*] (TEL)
MEAL	Media Expenditure Analysis Ltd. [*Database producer*] (CUAD)
MEAN	Microcomputer Education Application Network [*Commercial firm*] [*Educational Turnkey Systems, Inc.*] [*Falls Church, VA*] (EANO)
MEANINGEX	Meaning Extraction [*Programing language*] [*1971*] (CSR)
MEBS	Marketing, Engineering, and Business Services [*Telecommunications*] (TEL)
MECA	Micro Education Corporation of America
MECC	Miller Technology & Communications Corporation [*NASDAQ symbol*] (NQ)
MECC	Minnesota Educational Computing Consortium
MECHSIM	Mechanical Simulation [*of a computer-based directory assistance system*]
MECL	Motorola Emitter-Coupled Logic (IEEE)
MECOM	Middle East Electronic Communications Show and Conference [*Arabian Exhibition Management WLL*] [*Manama, Bahrain*] [*Telecommunications*] (TSSD)
MED	Media
MED	Message Entry Device
MED	Microwave Emission Detector [*Instrumentation*]
MEDAB	Middle East Database [*New York Times Information Service, Inc.*] (EISS)
MEDAC	Medical Electronic Data Aquisition and Control (OA)
MEDAX	Message Data Exchange Terminal (MCD)
MEDC	Moessbauer Effect Data Center [*University of North Carolina*] [*Information service*] (EISS)
Med Commun	Medical Communications [*A publication*]
MEDDARS	Medical Display Analysis and Recording System
MEDDOC	Medical Documentation Systems [*Eli Lilly & Co.*] [*Information service*] (EISS)
MEDEMG	Medical Emergencies [*Computerized management course*]
Media Rpt	Media Report to Women [*A publication*]
MEDICO	Model Experiment in Drug Indexing by Computer [*Rutgers University*]
MEDICOR	Centre for Offshore and Remote Medicine [*Memorial University of Newfoundland*] [*Research center*] (RCD)
MEDITECH	Medical Information Technology, Inc. [*Westwood, MA*] [*Software manufacturer*] (DASOS)
MEDLARS	Medical Literature Analysis and Retrieval System [*National Library of Medicine*] [*Bethesda, MD*] [*Database*]
MEDLINE	MEDLARS [*Medical Literature Analysis and Retrieval System*] On-Line [*National Library of Medicine*] [*Bibliographic database*]
MEDOC	Medical Documents [*Eccles Health Sciences Library - University of Utah*] [*Salt Lake City, UT*] [*Bibliographic database*] (OBD)
MEDOL	Medically Oriented Language
MEDS	Medical Evaluation Data System (IEEE)
MEDSARS	Maintenance Engineering Data Storage and Retrieval System (NG)
MEDSI	Mechanical Engineering Data Services, Incorporated [*St. Louis, MO*] [*Software manufacturer*] (DASOS)
MEDT	Mean Elapsed Downtime [*Data processing*] (MCD)
MEDUSA	Multiple Element Directional Universally Steerable Antenna
MEF	Mideast File [*Tel-Aviv University*] [*Information service*] (EISS)
MEG	Mega [*A prefix meaning multiplied by one million*]
MEG	Megohm
MEG	Message Expediting Group (IEEE)
MEIE	Microcomputer Electronic Information Exchange [*Institute for Computer Science and Technology*]
MELCOM	[*A*] computer series [*Mitsubishi Corp.*] [*Japan*] (NITA)
MELCU	Multiple External Line Control Unit (NITA)
MELEC	Microelectronics (IEEE)
MELEM	Microelement (IEEE)
MELISS	Mitsubishi Electric Corp. Literature and Information Search Service
MEM	Memory (MSA)
MEME	Multiple Entry Multiple Exit (NITA)
MEMOREX	Memory Excellence [*Brand name*]
MENTOR	[*A*] programing language [*1963*] (CSR)
MEOTBF	Mean Engine Operating Time between Failures [*Quality control*]
MEP	Magnetic Energy Product
MEQA	Mechanized Equipment Assignment [*AT & T*]
MER	Monthly Energy Review [*Department of Energy*] [*Database*] (FDB)
MERCON	Universal Transversal Mercator Converter [*Computer program*]
MERES	Matrix of Environmental Residuals for Energy Systems [*Computerized information system*]
MERGE	Mechanized Retrieval for Greater Efficiency [*Data processing*]
MERLIN	Machine Readable Library Information [*British Library*] [*Information service*] (EISS)
MERMUT	Mobile Electronic Robot Manipulator and Underwater Television (IEEE)
MERS	Most Economical Route Selection [*Also, ARS*] [*Bell System*] [*Telecommunications*]
MES	Manual Entry Subsystem (IEEE)
MESC	Master Event Sequence Controller (KSC)
MESFET	Metal-Semiconductor Field-Effect Transistor
MeSH	Medical Subject Heading [*National Library of Medicine*] [*Thesaurus*]
MESH	Museum Exchange for System's Help [*National Museum of Natural History*] (EISS)
MESS	Misalignment Estimation Software System (MCD)
MESS	Monitor Event Simulation System (IEEE)
MET	Motorola Environmental Telemetry (DDI)
MET	Multiemitter Transistor
META	Computer series [*Digital Scientific*] (NITA)
META	Methods of Extracting Text Automatically [*General Electric Co.*] [*Text retrieval language*] (IEEE)
METADEX	Metal Abstracts Index Data Base [*American Society for Metals*] [*Bibliographic database*] [*British*] (EISS)
METAPLAN	Methods-of-Extracting-Text-Auto-Programing Language [*Data processing*] (IEEE)
METASYMBOL	Metalanguage Symbol (CAH)
METREX	Metropolitan Centrex [*Telephone network*]
METRO	Michigan Effectuation, Training, and Research Organization [*Computer-programed simulation game*]
MEU	Memory Expansion Unit (NITA)
MEU	Message Encoder Unit
MEU	Multiplexer Encoder Unit
MEWT	Matrix Electrostatic Writing Technique (NITA)
MEX	MODEM [*Modulator-Demodulator*] Executive [*Data processing*]
M/F	Master File
MF	Measurement Facility [*Data processing*] (IBMDP)
MF	Medium Frequency [*Radio electronics*]
MF	Microfarad
MF	Multifrequency
MFA	Malfunction Alert [*Data processing*] (BUR)
MFA	Master File Activities [*Data processing*]
MFA	Multifunction Antenna
MFA	Multiple Filer Audit Program
MFB	Mixed Functional Block (IEEE)
MFB	Motional Feedback
MFC	Magnetic Film Counter
MFC	Magnetic Tape Field Scan [*Data processing*]
MFC	Manual Frequency Control
MFC	Master File Copy (KSC)
MFC	Microfilm Frame Card
MFC	Microfunctional Circuit
MFC	Multifrequency Signaling, Compelled [*Telecommunications*] (TEL)
MFCA	Master File Change Activity [*Data processing*] (MCD)
MFCA	Mutlifunction Communications Adapter (NITA)
MFCM	Multifunction Card Machine (BUR)
MFCS	Magnetic Field Calibration System
MFCU	Multifunction Card Unit
MFD	Magnetic Frequency Detector
MFD	Main Feed (MCD)
MFD	Master File Directory [*Data processing*]
MFD	Microfarad
MFD	Millifarad (MCD)
MFD	Multifunction Display (MCD)
MF/DF	Medium-Frequency Direction Finder [*or Finding*]
MFDP	Maintenance Float Distribution Point [*Data processing*] (NATG)
MFDSUL	Multifunction Data Set Utility Language (NITA)
MFE	Magnetic Field Energy
MFE	Magnetic Fusion Energy
MFEA	Magnetic Fusion Engineering Act
MFF	Magnetic Flip-Flop [*Data processing*]
MFG	Message Flow Graph (NITA)
MFH	Magnetic Film Handler (CMD)
MFI	Magnetic Field Indicator
MFI	Magnetic Field Intensity
MFID	Multiple-Electrode Flame Ionization Detector
MFIT	Manual Fault Isolation Test
MFJ	Modified Final Judgment [*Telecommunications*]
MFKP	Multifrequency Key Pulsing
MFL	Magnetic Field Line
MFLOPS	Million Floating-Point Operations per Second [*Processing power units*] [*Data processing*]
MFLP	Multifile Linear Programing (NITA)
MFM	Magnetic Forming Machine
MFM	Master File Maintenance
MFM	Micrometer Frequency Meter
MFM	Miniature Fluxgate Magnetometer
MFM	Multistage Frequency Multiplexer (NITA)
M2FM	Modified Modified Frequency Modulation (NITA)
MFMA	Monolithic Ferrite Memory Array
MFMR	Multifrequency Microwave Radiometer (MCD)
MFMT	Microwave Frequency Modulation Transmitter
MFO	Master Frequency Oscillator (NG)
MFP	Magnetic Field Perturbation
MFP	Master File Program [*Data processing*] (CIT)
MFP	Multiform Printer (NITA)
MFP	Multifrequency Pulsing (MSA)
MFP	Multifunction Peripheral
MFPC	Multifunction Protocol Converter (NITA)
MFPG	Mechanical Failures Prevention Group
MFR	Mail File Requirement [*Code*] [*Data processing*]
MFR	Malfunction Rate
MFR	Multifrequency Receiver [*Telecommunications*]
MFR	Multifunctional Receiver (NASA)
MFRS	Master File Replacement System [*Data processing*]

Computer & Telecommunications Acronyms

MFRS	Multifunction Receiver System
MFS	Magnetic Field Strength
MFS	Magnetic Tape Field Search [*Data processing*] (CGC)
MFS	Message Format Service
MFS	Multifunction Sensor (MCD)
MFS	Multiple-Frequency Synthesizer
MFSK	Multiple-Frequency Shift Keying
MFSR	Magnetic Film Strip Recorder
MFT	Magnetic Flow Transmitter
MFT	Mainframe Termination [*Telecommunications*] (TEL)
MFT	Metallic Facility Terminal [*Telecommunications*] (TEL)
MFT	Multiprograming with Fixed Number of Tasks [*Data processing*] (BUR)
MFTRS	Magnetic Flight Test Recording System
MFV	Microfilm Viewer
MFVD	Maximum Forward Voltage Drop
MG	Message Generator
mg	Milligram
MGA	Medium-Gain Antenna
MGA	Meteorological and Geostrophysical Abstracts [*American Meteorological Society*] [*Bibliographic database*] [*A publication*]
M & GA	Meteorological and Geostrophysical Abstracts [*American Meteorological Society*] [*Bibliographic database*] [*A publication*]
MGAA	Medium-Gain Autotrack Antenna
MGAP	Magnetic Attitude Prediction
MGC	Major Gain Control
MGC	Manual Gain Control
MGFS	Media General Financial Services, Inc. [*Information service*] (EISS)
MGG	Memory Gate Generator [*Data processing*]
MGL	Matrix Generator Language [*Data processing*] (BUR)
MGM	Master Group Multiplexer
MGN	Magneto [*Generator*]
MGN	Multigrounded Neutral [*Telecommunications*] (TEL)
MGP	Multiple Goal Programing (NITA)
MGRW	Matrix Generator and Report Writer [*Data processing*]
MGS	Microcomputer Graphic System
MGT	Master-Group Translator [*Telecommunications*] (TEL)
MGT	Mobile [*Truck-Mounted*] Ground Terminal
MGTMTR	Magnetometer
MGV	Miniature Gate Valve
MH	Magnetic Head [*or Heading*]
MH	Manual Hold [*Telecommunications*] (DEEC)
MH	MeSH Heading [*Online database field identifier*] (OBD)
MH	Message Handler [*Data processing*]
mH	Millihenry
MH	Minneapolis-Honeywell [*Minneapolis-Honeywell Regulator Co.*] [*Later, HON*]
M-H	Minneapolis-Honeywell Regulator Co. [*Later, HON*]
MH	Miscellaneous Hardware
MHAC	Man-Hour Accounting Card (DDI)
MHC	MAD [*Magnetic Anomaly Detector*] Hunting Circle
MHD	Magnetohydrodynamics [*Electric power*]
MHD	Metering Head Differential (DDI)
MHD	Minimum Hamming Distance [*Data processing*]
MHD	Moving Head Disk [*Data processing*] (TEL)
MHD	Multihead Disk (NASA)
MHDF	Medium- and High-Frequency Direction-Finding Station
MHDG	Magnetic Heading (FAAC)
MHF	Master History File
MHF	Medium-High Frequency
MHFA	Multiple Conductor, Heat and Flame Resistant, Armor [*Cable*]
MHH	Medizinische Hochschule Hannover [*Information retrieval*] (ODIN)
MHL	Microprocessor Host Loader [*Electronics*]
MHP	McGraw-Hill, Inc. [*NYSE symbol*]
MHP	Message Handling Processor (NITA)
MHS	Magnetic Heading System
MHS	Multiple Host Support (NITA)
MHSC	Manipulator Handset Controller (MCD)
MHSDC	Multiple High-Speed Data Channel (NITA)
MHTL	Motorola High-Threshold Logic
MHVDF	Medium-, High-, and Very-High-Frequency Direction-Finding Station
MHVPS	Manual High-Voltage Power Supply
MHz	Megahertz [*Megacycles per Second*] [*See also MCPS, MCS, MC/S, MH*]
MI	Machine Independent (NITA)
MI	Magazine Index [*Information Access Corp.*] [*Information service*]
MI	Manual Input [*Data processing*]
MI	Market Identifiers [*Dun's Marketing Services*]
M/I	Mechanical Impulse (KSC)
MI	Mellon Institute [*Carnegie-Mellon University*] [*Research center*] (RCD)
MI	Memory Interface (NITA)
MI	Miniaturized Instrumentation (MCD)
M/I	Minimum Impulse (KSC)
MIA	Metal Interface Amplifier
MIA	Multiplex Interface Adapter (NASA)
MIAC	Minimum Automatic Computer (IEEE)
MIACF	Meander Inverted Autocorrelated Function (OA)
MIACS	Manufacturing Information and Control System (OA)
MIADS	Map Information Assembly and Display System
MIAS	Marine Information and Advisory Service [*Institute of Oceanographic Sciences*] [*Databank*] [*British*] (EISS)
MIB	Manual Input Buffer [*Data processing*]
MIB	Medical Information Bureau [*Databank*]
MIB	Microinstruction Bus [*Data processing*] (NITA)
MIB	Minimum Impulse BIT [*Binary Digit*] [*Data processing*] (MCD)
MIB	Mutual Inductance Bridge
MIC	Management Information Center
MIC	Management Information Corporation [*Cherry Hill, NJ*] [*Information service*] (EISS)
MIC	Mellonics Information Center [*Litton Systems, Inc.*] [*Information service*] (EISS)
MIC	Memory Interface Connection [*Data processing*]
MIC	Message Identification Code [*Data processing*] (BUR)
MIC	Michigan Instructional Computer
MIC	Microwave Integrated Circuitry
MIC	Microwave Interference Coordination
MIC	Missing Interruption Checker (MCD)
MIC	Monolithic Integrated Circuit
MIC	Mutual Interference Chart (IEEE)
MICA	Macroinstruction Compiler Assembler [*Data processing*]
MICAH	Micro Applications & Hardware [*Sausalito, CA*] [*Software manufacturer*] (DASOS)
MICC	Micron Corporation [*NASDAQ symbol*] (NQ)
MICMPTR	Microcomputer (MSA)
MICPAK	Modular Integrated Circuit Package
MICR	Magnetic Ink Character Recognition [*Banking*] [*Data processing*]
MICRO	Microcomputer (DEEC)
MICRO	Microelectronics Innovation and Computer Science Research Program [*University of California*] [*Research center*] (RCD)
MICRO	Microprocessor (DEEC)
MICRO	Multiple Indexing and Console Retrieval Options [*Information retrieval*] [*Data processing*]
MICRO-C	[*A*] programing language [*1977*] (CSR)
Microcomput Printout	Microcomputer Printout [*A publication*]
Microelectron Reliab	Microelectronics and Reliability [*A publication*]
Microel Rel	Microelectronics and Reliability [*A publication*]
Micro Jrl	Microwave Journal [*A publication*]
MICROM	Microinstruction Read-Only Memory (NITA)
MICROMIN	Microminiature (IEEE)
MICROPAC	Micromodule Data Processor and Computer (IEEE)
MICROSECS	Microfilm Sequential Coding System [*Bell System*]
Microwave J	Microwave Journal [*A publication*]
Microwave Syst News	Microwave Systems News [*A publication*]
Microw Syst News	Microwave Systems News [*A publication*]
MICRS	Main Instrument Console and Readout Stations (NATG)
MICS	Maintenance Inventory Control System [*Bell System*]
MICS	Management Integrated Control System (VIT)
MICS	Micom Systems, Inc. [*NASDAQ symbol*] (NQ)
MICS	Microprocessor Inertia and Communication System
MICS	Multiplex Interior Communications (NG)
MID	Magnetically Insulated Diode [*Physics*]
MID	Message Input Description (NITA)
MID	Message Input Device
MID	Mid-Continent Telephone Corp. [*NYSE symbol*] [*Delisted*]
MIDAC	Michigan [*University of*] Digital Automatic Computer
MIDAN	Microprocessor Data Analyzer [*Instrumentation*]
MIDAR	Microwave Detection and Ranging
MIDARM	Microdynamic Angle and Rate Monitoring System
MIDAS	Management Integrated Data Accumulating System (VIT)
MIDAS	Measurement Information Data Analytic System (IEEE)
MIDAS	Memory Implemented Data Acquisition Systems (NITA)
MIDAS	Meteorological Integrating Data Acquisition System
MIDAS	Microcomputer-Interfaced Data Acquisition System [*Data processing*]
MIDAS	Microimaged Data Addition System [*CAPS Equipment Ltd.*]
MIDAS	Microprogramable Integrated Data Acquisition System (NITA)
MIDAS	Microprograming Design Aided System [*RCA*] (NITA)
MIDAS	Miniature Data Acquisition System
MIDAS	Modified Integration Digital Analog Simulator [*Data processing*] (MCD)
MIDAS	Modulator Isolation Diagnostic Analysis System (IEEE)
MIDAS	Monopoly Information and Data Analysis System
MIDAS	Multimode International Data Acquisition Service [*Australia*] [*Information service*] (EISS)
MIDAS	Multiple Index Data Access System [*Prime Computer, Inc.*] (NITA)
MIDDLE	Microprogram Design Description Language [*1977*] [*Data processing*] (CSR)
MIDEF	Microprocedure Definition (NITA)
MIDF	Major Item Data File
MIDI	Musical Instrument Digital Interface [*Port*] [*Socket on an electronic synthesizer that permits a direct computer connection*]
MIDIST	Mission Interministerielle de l'Information Scientifique et Technique [*Interministerial Mission for Scientific and Technical Information*] [*France*] [*Information service*] (EISS)
MIDS	Management Information and Data Systems (NVT)
MIDS	Marketing Information Data Systems, Inc. [*Information service*] (EISS)

Computer & Telecommunications Acronyms

MIDS	Miniature Integrated Data System (MCD)
MIDS	Multifunctional Information Distribution System [NATO] (MCD)
MIDS	Multimode Information Distribution System (NITA)
MIDWEEK	Manager Integrated Dictionary Week [Manager Software Products] [Lexington, MA] (EANO)
MIF	Manual Intervention Facility
MIF	Master Index File
MIF	Master Inventory File
MIF	Master Item File (MCD)
MIF	Monopulse Interference Filter
MIFE	Minimum Independent Failure Element
MIFIR	Microwave Instantaneous Frequency Indication Receiver (MCD)
MIFL	Master International Frequency List
MIFR	Master International Frequency Register
MIFR	Multiband Infrared Filter Radiometer
MIFS	Multiplex Interferometric Fourier Spectroscopy
MIH	Missing Interruption Handler [Data processing] (IBMDP)
MIH	Multiplex Interface Handler (NITA)
MIICS	Master Item Identification Control System
MIIS	Miscellaneous Inputs Information Subsystem [Data processing]
MIKER	Microbalance Inverted Knudsen Effusion Recoil
MIL	Magnetic Indicator Loop
MIL	Malfunction Investigation Laboratory
MIL	Microimplementation Language [Burroughs Corp.] (NITA)
MIL	Minnesota Instructional Language [Data processing] (CSR)
MIL	Module Interconnection Language (NITA)
MILCS	Metropolitan Interlibrary Cooperative System [New York Public Library] [Information service]
MILIC	Microwave Insular Line Integrated Circuit (IEEE)
MIM	Magnetic Interaction Mechanism
MIM	Message Input Module [Telecommunications] (TEL)
MIM	MODEM Interface Modules [Data processing] (CGC)
MIMC	Microforms International Marketing Corporation [Pergamon]
MIMD	Multiple Instruction, Multiple Data (MCD)
MIMIC	[A] programing language [1965] (CSR)
MIMO	Man In, Machine Out [Data processing]
MIMOLA	Machine Independent Microprograming Language (NITA)
MIMR	Magnetic Ink Mark Recognition
MIMS	Mitrol Industrial Management System [Mitrol, Inc.] [Information service] (EISS)
MIMS	Modular Isodrive Memory Series
MIMUG	Meetings Industry Microcomputer Users Group [Dallas, TX] [Information clearinghouse] (EANO)
MIMUSA	Matrix Iteration Method of Unfolding Spectra [Data processing]
MIN	Minimum (AFM)
MIN	Minute (AFM)
MINC	Minicomputer
MIND	Magnetic Integrator Neuron Duplicator
MIND	Modular Interactive Network Designer (NITA)
MINDO	Modified Intermediate Neglect of Differential Overlap [Quantum mechanics]
MINEAC	Miniature Electronic Auto-Collimator
MINET	Medical Information Network [GTE Telenet Communications Corp.] [Reston, VA] [Telecommunications]
MINI	Minicomputer Industry National Interchange [An association] (EANO)
Minicomput Rev	Minicomputer Review [A publication]
MINIT	Minimum Interference Threshold [Telecommunications] (TEL)
MINITAB II	[A] programing language [1970] (CSR)
MINITEX	Minnesota Interlibrary Telecommunications Exchange [Library cooperative]
MIN MC	Minimum Material Condition [Data processing] (CDH)
MINOS	Modular Input/Output System (NITA)
MINPRT	Minimum Processing Time per Operation (DDI)
MINSK	[A] Russian digital computer [Moscow University] (CAH)
MINSOP	Minimum Slack Time per Operation (DDI)
MINTS	Mutual Institutions National Transfer System, Inc.
MINY	Miniscribe Corp. [NASDAQ symbol] (NQ)
MIO	Multiple Input/Output (NITA)
MIOP	Multiplexing Input-Output Processor [Data processing] (BUR)
MIOS	Modular Input-Output System [Telecommunications] (TEL)
MIP	Machine Instruction Processor [Data processing] (BUR)
MIP	Manual Input Processing [or Program] [Data processing]
MIP	Matrix Inversion Program [Data processing] (BUR)
MIP	Message Input Processing (DDI)
MIP	Microwave Interference Protection
MIP	Million Instructions per Second
MIP	Missouri Institute of Psychiatry [University of Missouri - Columbia] [Research center] (RCD)
MIP	Mixed Integer Programing [Data processing]
MIPIE	Michigan Products Information Exchange [Menominee, MI] [Information service] (EISS)
MIPRCS	Microprocessor (MSA)
MIPS	Microwave Pulse Storage Subsystem (MCD)
MIPS	Millions of Instructions per Second [Facetiously translated as "Meaningless Indication of Performance"] [Processing power units] [Data processing]
MIR	Magnetic Ink Read
MIR	Memory-Information Register [Data processing]
MIR	Memory Input Register [Data processing]
MIR	Microinstruction Register (NITA)
MIR	Model Incident Report [Telecommunications] (TEL)
MIR	Multiband Infrared Radiometer
MIR	Music Information Retrieval [Data processing]
MIRACL	Management Information Report Access without Computer Languages [Data processing] (IEEE)
MIRACLE	Multidisciplinary Integrated Research Activities in Complex Laboratory Environments [National Science Foundation]
MIRACODE	Microfilm Information Retrieval Access Code
MIRAID	Maintenance Information Retrieval Aid
MIRED	Microreciprocal Degrees
MIRF	Multiple Instantaneous Response File
MIRFAC	Mathematics in Recognizable Form Automatically Compiled [Data processing] (TUT)
MIRIAM	Major Incident Room Index and Action Management [Police computer] [British]
MIRS	Manpower Information Retrieval System (IEEE)
MIS	Management Information Science (TUT)
MIS	Management Information Service
MIS	Management Information Specialist
MIS	Management Information Systems [Corporation for Public Broadcasting] [Information service] (EISS)
MIS	Management Integrated System (TEL)
MIS	Manufacturing Information System [Data processing] (BUR)
MIS	Marketing Information System
MIS	Metal-Insulator-Semiconductor
MIS	Monte-Carlo Inelastic Scattering [Code] [Data processing]
MISAM	Multiple Index Sequential Access Method (NITA)
MISCO	McCall Information Systems Company
MISD	Multiple Instruction, Single Data [Processor configuration] (IEEE)
MISED	Machine Independent Systems Effectiveness Data System (MCD)
MISER	Microwave Space Electronics Relay
MISER	Minimum Size Executive Routines (NITA)
MISFET	Metal-Insulator-Semiconductor Field-Effect Transistor
MIS/IL	Metal-Insulator-Semiconductor Inversion Layer [Photovoltaic energy systems]
MISM	Metal-Insulator-Semiconductor Metal (MCD)
MISMDS	Muliple Instruction Streams Multiple Data Steams (NITA)
MISP	Management Information System Plan
MISP	Manned Interceptor Simulation Program
MISP	Medical Information Systems Program [Data processing] (BUR)
MISRE	Microwave Space Relay [Electronics]
MISS	Medical Information Science Section [National Institutes of Health] [Information service] (EISS)
MISS	Microwave Imager Sensor Study (MCD)
MISS	Minicomputer Interfacing Support System [Data processing]
MISS	Multiband Image Scanning System (SKY)
MISSIL	Management Information System Symbolic Interpretive Language [Data processing]
MIST	Medical Information System via Telephone [University of Alabama]
MIST	Minimum Structure Module
MIST	Multi-Input Standard Tape
MISTIC	Michigan State Integral Computer
MISTRAL	[A] programing language (CSR)
MIT	Machine Interface Terminal D. N. C. [Tangram Computer Aided Engineering] [Software package] [British] (NCC)
MIT	Massachusetts Institute of Technology [Cambridge, MA]
MIT	Master Instruction Tape [Data processing]
MIT	Modular Industrial Terminal (NITA)
MIT	Modular Intelligent Terminal (NITA)
MITA	Microcomputer Industry Trade Association (NITA)
MITC	Microfilm and Information Technology Center
MITE	Magnetic Insulation Test Experiment
MITE	Master Instrumentation Timing Equipment (CET)
MITE	Microelectronic Integrated Test Equipment
MITE	Microelectronics Test and Evaluation [Raytheon Co.]
MITE	Miniaturized Integrated Telephone Equipment
MITE	Multiple Input Terminal Equipment
MITER	Modular Installation of Telecommunications Equipment Racks (TEL)
MITI	Magnetic Information Technology [NASDAQ symbol] (NQ)
MITI	Ministry of International Trade and Industry [Japan]
MITILAC	Massachusetts Institute of Technology Information Laboratory Automatic Coding
MITOL	Machine-Independent Telemetry-Oriented Language [Data processing] (IEEE)
MITRE	Miniature Individual Transmitter-Receiver Equipment (MCD)
MITS	Management Information and Text System (NITA)
MITS	Michigan Information Transfer Source [University of Michigan] (EISS)
MITS	Microfiche Image Transmission System (MCD)
MIU	Message Interface Unit (CAAL)
MIU	Multistation Interface Unit [Data processing]
MIW	Microinstruction Word (NITA)
MJ	Major Subject Descriptor [Online database field identifier] (OBD)
MJD	Modified Julian Date [Telecommunications] (TEL)
MJR	Maintenance Job Request
MJR	Management Job Review [LIMRA]
MJU	Multijunction Unit [Data processing] (BUR)
MK	Manual Clock [Data processing] (MDG)
MK	Mark (KSC)
MK	Microphone (MDG)
MKH	Multiple Key Hashing (NITA)
MKS	Meter-Kilogram-Second [System of units]

Acronym	Definition
MKS	Microwave Keying Switch
MKSS	Microwave Keying Switching Station
MKTI	Morrison-Knudsen Technologies, Incorporated [*Boise, ID*] [*Telecommunications*] (TSSD)
ML	Land Mobile Station [*ITU designation*] (NATG)
ML	Machine Language [*Data processing*]
ML	Main Lobe (IEEE)
ML	Maximum Likelihood [*Statistics*]
ML	Microprograming Language (NITA)
MLA	Manpack Loop Antenna
MLA	Matching Logic and Adder (NITA)
MLA	Microprocessor Language Assembler [*Data processing*]
MLA	Microwave Linear Accelerator
MLA	MLA [*Modern Language Association of America*] International Bibliography of Books and Articles on the Modern Languages and Literature [*Database*] [*A publication*]
MLA	Multilinear Array [*In earth scanning*]
MLA	Multiplex Line Adapter (SKY)
MLAB	Modeling Laboratory [*Programing language*] [*1970*] (CSR)
MLBR	Medium Low-BIT [*Binary Digit*] Rate [*Data processing*] (SKY)
MLC	Machine Level Control [*Data processing*] (TUT)
MLC	Magnetic Ledger Card (CMD)
MLC	Microelectric Logic Circuit
MLC	Microprogram Location Counter (NITA)
MLC	Multilayer Circuit
MLC	Multiline Control (BUR)
MLCB	Multilayer Circuit Board
MLCC	Multilayer Ceramic Capacitor [*Electronics*]
MLCP	Multiline Communications Processor (NITA)
MLD	Machine Language Debugger [*National Computer Sharing Service*] (NITA)
MLE	Maximum Likelihood Estimate [*or Estimator*] [*Statistics*] (CIT)
MLE	Medium Local Exchange [*Telecommunications*] (TEL)
MLE	Microprocessor Language Editor [*Data processing*]
MLES	Multiple-Line Encryption System
M/LF	Medium/Low Frequency (NATG)
MLI	Machine Language Instruction (NITA)
MLIA	Multiplex Loop Interface Adapter (NITA)
MLIM	Matrix Log-In Memory (NITA)
MLIS	Micropolis Corp. [*NASDAQ symbol*] (NQ)
MLIS	Multiple Level Indexing Scheme [*Data processing*] (TUT)
MLISP	Meta LISP [*List Processor*] [*Programing language*] [*Data processing*] (CSR)
MLLE	Medium Large Local Exchange [*Telecommunications*] (TEL)
MLMA	Multilevel Multiaccess (CCD)
MLP	Machine Language Program [*Data processing*]
MLP	Multiple Line Printing (CMD)
MLPA	Modified Link Pack Area (MCD)
MLPC	Multilayer Printed Circuit
MLPCB	Machine Language Printed Circuit Boards [*Data processing*] (IEEE)
MLPP	Multilevel Precedence and Preemption [*Telecommunications*] (TEL)
MLPWB	Multilayer Printed-Wiring Board (IEEE)
MLR	Mechanized Line Records [*Later, LMOS*] [*Bell System*]
MLR	Memory Lockout Register [*Data processing*]
MLS	Machine Literature Searching [*Data processing*] (DIT)
MLS	Microwave Line Stretcher
MLS	Multilanguage System [*Data processing*] (IEEE)
MLSI	Multilevel Large-Scale Integration
MLSO	Mode-Locked Surface-Acoustic Wave Oscillator [*Telecommunications*] (TEL)
MLSP	Multiple-Link Satellite Program (CIT)
MLT	Magnetic Local Time
MLT	Master Library Tape [*Data processing*]
MLT	Mechanized Line Testing [*Telecommunications*] (TEL)
MLT	Mechanized Loop Testing (MCD)
MLT	Microlayer Transistor
MLT	Mitel Corp. [*NYSE symbol*] [*Toronto Stock Exchange symbol*]
MLTA	Multiple Line Terminal Adapter [*Data processing*] (BUR)
MLU	Memory Logic Unit [*Data processing*]
MLU	Multiple Logical Unit (NITA)
MLY	Multiply (MDG)
MM	Main Memory
MM	Mass Memory (NASA)
MM	Memory Module (MCD)
MM	Memory Multiplexer [*Data processing*] (MDG)
mm	Millimeter [*Metric*]
MMA	Management and Marketing Abstracts [*PIRA*] [*Bibliographic database*] [*British*] (OBD)
MMA	Memory-to-Memory Adapter [*Data processing*]
MMA	Multifunction Microwave Aperture
MMA	Multiple Module Access
MMAR	Main Memory Address Register (NITA)
MMC	Man-Machine Communication [*Data processing*]
MMC	Martin Marietta Corporation (KSC)
MMC	Memory Management Controller (IEEE)
MMC	Multiport Memory Controller (NITA)
MMCIAC	Metal Matrix Composites Information Analysis Center [*DoD*] [*Information service*] (EISS)
MMCS	Mass Memory Control Subsystem (TEL)
MMD	Microwave Mixer Diode
MMD	Multimode Display
MMDB	Master Measurement Database (NASA)
MMDS	Martin Marietta Data Systems (NITA)
MMDS	Multichannel Multipoint Distribution Service [*Broadcasting term*]
mmf	Magnetomotive Force
MMI	Man-Machine Interface
MMIRC	Mind-Machine Interaction Research Center [*University of Florida*] [*Research center*] (RCD)
MMIU	Multiport Memory Interface Unit (NITA)
MML	Man-Machine Language [*Data processing*] (TEL)
MMM	Minnesota Mining & Manufacturing Co. [*Also, 3M*] [*NYSE symbol*]
MMMM	Connect to Stations [*Communications*] (FAAC)
MMOD	Micromodule (IEEE)
MMOS	Message Multiplexer Operating System (NITA)
MMP	Maintenance Message Process [*Telecommunications*] (TEL)
MMP	Multiplexed Message Processor
MMPP	Mechanized Market Programing Procedures [*Data processing*] (TEL)
MMPT	Man-Machine Partnership Translation [*Telecommunications*] (IEEE)
MMPU	Memory Manager and Protect Unit (IEEE)
MMR	Main Memory Register (NITA)
MMR	Missed Message Rate (CAAL)
MMR	Multiple Match Resolver (OA)
MMS	Maintenance Management Software
MMS	Man-Machine System (MCD)
MMS	Manufacturing Monitoring System [*Data processing*] (IBMDP)
MMS	Mass Memory Store [*Data processing*] (IEEE)
MMS	Memory Management System (NITA)
MMS	Micro Measurement System [*3D Digital Design & Development Ltd.*] [*Software package*] [*British*] (NCC)
MMS	Microfiche Management System (DEEC)
MMS	Modular Multiband Scanner (MCD)
MMS	Money Market Services, Inc. [*Database producer*] (CUAD)
MMSE	Minimum Mean Squared Error
MMTC	Maritime Mobile Telegraphy Calling
MMTDC	Maritime Mobile Telegraph Distress and Calling
MMU	Main Memory Unit (NITA)
MMU	Memory Management Unit [*Data processing*]
MMU	Metered Message Unit [*Telecommunications*] (TEL)
MMU	Multimessage Unit [*Telecommunications*] (TEL)
MMX	Mastergroup Multiplex [*AT & T*]
MMX	Memory Multiplexer [*Data processing*]
MMYD	Mental Measurements Yearbook Database [*University of Nebraska, Lincoln*] [*Database*]
MN	Main Network [*Telecommunications*] (TEL)
MN	Manual (CDH)
MN	Minor Subject Descriptor [*Online database field identifier*] (OBD)
MNA	Multishare Network Architecture [*Mitsubishi Corp.*] (BUR)
MNC	Microcomputer Numerical Control (MCD)
MNC	Multiplicative Noise Compensator [*Telecommunications*] (TEL)
MNCMPTR	Minicomputer (MSA)
MNCS	Multipoint Network Control System
MNF	Multisystem Networking Facility (NITA)
MNFI	Michigan Natural Features Inventory [*Michigan State Department of Natural Resources*] [*Information service*] (EISS)
MNOS	Metal-Nitride-Oxide Silicon [*or Semiconductor*]
MNRU	Modulated Noise Reference Unit [*Telecommunications*] (TEL)
MNS	MacNeal-Schwendler Corp. [*American Stock Exchange symbol*]
MNS	Microband National System, Inc. [*New York, NY*] [*Telecommunications*] (TSSD)
MNSC	Main Network Switching Center [*Telecommunications*] (TEL)
MNT	Modern Network Theory [*Electrical engineering computer*]
MNTK	Mezhotraslevoi Naucho-Tekhni-Cheskii Kompleks [*Interdisciplinary Scientific-Technological Complex*] [*Russian*]
MNTR	Monitor (MDG)
MO	Master Oscillator [*Radio*]
MO	Memory Output [*Data processing*] (NITA)
MO	Month (AFM)
MOBIDIC	Mobile Digital Computer [*Sylvania Electric Products Co.*]
MOBILESAT	Mobile Satellite Corp. [*King Of Prussia, PA*] [*Telecommunications*] (TSSD)
MOBL	Macro-Oriented Business Language [*Data processing*]
MOBOL	Mohawk Business-Oriented Language [*Mohawk Data Systems*] (NITA)
MOBSSL-UAF	Merritt and Miller's Own Block Structured Simulation Language, Unpronounceable Acronym For [*1969*] [*Data processing*] (CSR)
MOBULA	Model Building Language [*Programing language*] (IEEE)
MOC	Mathematical Operations Computer
MOC	Memory Operating Characteristic [*Data processing*] (IEEE)
MOC	Ministry of Communications
MOD	Message Output Description [*Data processing*] (NITA)
MOD	Model (KSC)
MOD	Modification [*or Modify*] (AFM)
MOD	Modular Observation Device (RDA)
MOD	Modulation [*Telecommunications*] (KSC)
MOD	Modulator (CET)
MOD	Modulator-Demodulator [*Telecommunications*] (MCD)
MOD	Moving Domain Memories [*Data processing*] (MDG)
MODABUND	Mosquito Data Bank of the University of Notre Dame
MODAC	Mountain System Digital Automatic Computer

Acronym	Definition
MODACS	Modular Data Acquisition and Control System [or Subsystem] [Modular Computing Systems, Inc.] (NITA)
MODAL	[A] programing language [1973] (CSR)
MODAP	Multiple Operational Data Acquisition Program [Data processing]
MODAPS	Maintenance and Operational Data Presentation Study
MODAPS	Modal Data Acquisition and Processing System
MODAPTS	Modular Arrangement of Predetermined Time Standards (TUT)
MODCOM	Modular Computer System
MODCOMP	Modular Computer [In company name, MODCOMP Systems, Inc.] [Fort Lauderdale, FL] [Software manufacturer] (DASOS)
MODEM	Modulate/Demodulate [or Modulation/Demodulation or Modulator-Demodulator] [Data processing]
MODI	Modular Optical Digital Interface (NITA)
MODS	Manpower Operations Data System [Employment and Training Administration] [Department of Labor]
MODS	Medically Oriented Data System (MCD)
MODULA	Modular Programing Language (CSR)
MOF	Maximum Observed Frequency [Radio]
MOJ	Material on Job Date [Telecommunications] (TEL)
MOJ	Metering over Junction [Network administration] [Telecommunications] (TEL)
MOL	Machine-Oriented Language [Programing language]
MOLDS	Management On-Line Data System [University of Syracuse]
MOLDS	Multiple Online Debugging System [Data processing] (IEEE)
MOLECOM	Molecularized Digital Computer
MOLLI	Micro Online Library Information
MOM	Message Output Module [Telecommunications] (TEL)
MOM	Micromation Online Microfilmer
MOMS	Multimegabit Operation Multiplexer System
MON	Monitor (DEN)
MoNHI	Missouri Natural Heritage Inventory [Missouri State Department of Conservation] [Information service] (EISS)
MOP	Memory Organization Packet [Artificial intelligence]
MOP	Message Output Processing (DDI)
MOP	Multiple Online Programing [Data processing] (DIT)
MOPA	Master Oscillator Power Amplifier [Radio]
MOPA	Modus Operandi - Personal Appearance [FBI computer procedure]
MOPS	Million Operations per Second [Processing power units] [Data processing]
MOPT	Mean One Way Propagation Time [Telecommunications] (TEL)
MOR	Memory Output Register [Data processing]
MOR	Middle of the Road
MORPHS	Minicomputer-Operated Retrieval (Partially Heuristic) System [Data processing]
MOS	Manufacturing Operating System [IBM Corp.]
MOS	Master Operating System [Sperry UNIVAC] (CAH)
MOS	Memory Operating Software [Data processing]
MOS	Memory-Oriented System (NITA)
MOS	Metal-Oxide Semiconductor
MOS	Microprogram Operating System (NITA)
MOS	Modular Operating System (BUR)
MOS	Multiprograming Operating System (NITA)
MOSAIC	Macro Operation Symbolic Assembler and Information Compiler [Data processing] (IEEE)
MOSAIC	Ministry of Supply Automatic Integrator and Computer [British] (DEN)
MOSFET	Metal-Oxide-Semiconductor Field-Effect Transistor
MOS-LSI	Metal-Oxide-Semiconductor - Large-Scale Integration
MOSS	Modelling Systems [Moss Systems Ltd.] [Software package] [British] (NCC)
MOST	Metal-Oxide-Semiconductor Transistor
MOSTL	Metal-Oxide-Semiconductor Transistor Logic (CET)
MOT	Motorola, Inc. [NYSE symbol]
MOTAR	Modular Thermal Analyzer Routine [Data processing]
MOTNE	Meteorological Operational Telecommunications Network Europe
MOUTH	Modular Output Unit for Talking to Humans (NITA)
Mov Im	Moving Image [A publication]
MOVIMS	Motor Vehicle Information Management System [Bell System]
MOXY	Model X-Y [AEC computer code]
MP	Macroprocessor (NITA)
MP	Maintenance Panel
MP	Maintenance Period
MP	Maintenance Plan
MP	Maintenance Point
MP	Maintenance Prints
MP	Maintenance Procedure (MCD)
MP	Maintenance Program
MP	Manual Pulser
MP	Mathematical Programing [Data processing]
MP	Media Processor [Data processing] (BUR)
MP	Microprint
MP	Microprocessor [Instrumentation]
MP	Microprogram (NITA)
MP	Multiple Processor [Data processing] (BUR)
MP	Multiprocessing [Data processing]
MP	Multipurpose
MPA	Microwave Power Amplifier
MPA	Multiple Peripheral Adapter (NITA)
MPAD	Menlo Park Applications Development [IBM Corp.]
MPAR	Microprogram Address Register (NITA)
MPBDS	Material Properties Bibliographic Data System [Purdue University] [Database] (FDB)
MPC	Machine Punch Card
MPC	Marker Pulse Conversion [Telecommunications] (TEL)
MPC	Message Processing Center
MPC	Microprogram Control (NITA)
MPC	Miniature Protector Connector [Telecommunications] (TEL)
MPC	Modular Peripheral Interface Converter (NITA)
MPC	Multiple-Purpose Communications (NG)
MPC	Multiprocessor Computer
MPC	Multiprogram Control [Data processing]
MPC	Multipurpose Computer (CMD)
MPCABS	Michigan Project for Computer-Assisted Biblical Studies [University of Michigan] [Information service] (EISS)
MPCB	Multilayer Printed Circuit Board
MPCC	Multiprocessor Computer Complex
MPCC	Multiprotocol Communications Controller
MPCD	Manufacturing Process Control Document (KSC)
MPCI	Multiport Programable Communications Interface (NITA)
MPCM	Microprogram Control Memory (NITA)
MPCS	Multiparty Connection Subsystem [Telecommunications] (TEL)
MPCS	Multiprocessing Control System [Data processing]
MPDT	Mean Preventive Downtime [Data processing]
MPE	Memory Parity Error (NITA)
MPE	Multiprograming Executive [Hewlett-Packard Co.] (NITA)
MPECC	Multiprocessor Experimental Computer Complex
MPF	Million Pair Feet [Telecommunications] (TEL)
MPGS	Microprogram Generating System (NITA)
MPI	Micro Peripherals, Incorporated [Salt Lake City, UT] [Hardware manufacturer] (DASO)
MPI	Microprocessor Interface (NITA)
MPIC	Message Processing Interrupt Count
MPL	Message Processing Language [Burroughs Corp.] (NITA)
MPL	Microprocessor [or Motorola's] Programing Language [1975] [Data processing] (CSR)
MPL	Multischedule Private Line
MPLX	Multiplexer
MPM	Magnetic Phase Modulator
MPM	Message Processing Modules (MCD)
MPM	Microprogram Memory (NITA)
MPM	Microwave Power Meter
MPM	Monocycle Position Modulation
MP/M	Multiprocessing Monitor Control Program [Data processing]
MPM	Multiprograming Monitor (NITA)
MPNDS	Material Properties Numerical Data System [Purdue University] [Database] (FDB)
MPO	Memory Printout [Data processing]
MPO	Memory Protect Override (NITA)
MPOS	Multipurpose Optimization System [Data processing]
MPP	Massively Parallel Processor [Image processing]
MPP	Message Processing Program [Data processing] (TUT)
MPPHA	Multiparameter Pulse Height Analyzer
MPPL	Multipurpose Processing Language [Data processing] (IEEE)
MPPL	Multipurpose Programing Language
MPR	Message Processing Region [IBM Corp.] (NITA)
MPR	Multipurpose Recorder (DDI)
MPROM	Mask Programed Read-Only Memory (NITA)
MPS	Mathematical Programing System [Data processing] (CGC)
MPS	Mathematical Programing Society
MPS	MegaBITS [Binary Digits] per Second [Transmission rate] [Data processing] (MCD)
MPS	Memory Processor Switch
MPS	Message Processing System (NVT)
MPS	Microprocessor Series [or System] (MDG)
MPS	Microwave Phase Shifter
MPS	Microwave Pressure Sounder (MCD)
MPS	Microwave Pulse Source
MPS	Modular Power System (MCD)
MPS	Multiprograming System [Data processing] (CGC)
MPSCL	Mathematical Programing System Control Language [1974] [Data processing] (CSR)
MPSG	Marketing Programs and Services Group, Inc. [Gaithersburg, MD] [Information service] [Telecommunications] (TSSD)
MPSK	Multiple Phase Shift Keying [Data processing] (TEL)
MPSN	Microwave Pulse Shaping Network
MPSX	Mathematical Programing System Extended [IBM Corp.] [Data processing]
MPT	Maryland Public Television [Owings Mills] [Information service] [Telecommunications] (TSSD)
MPT	Memory Processing Time (NITA)
MPT	Microprograming Technique
MPT	Ministry of Posts and Telecommunications [British]
MPT	Motional Pickup Transducer (MCD)
MPTWT	Medium Power Traveling Wave Tube
MPU	Memory Protection Unit (NITA)
MPU	Microprocessor Unit [CPU of microcomputer] [Data processing]
MPU	MIDI Processing Unit [Computer technology]
MPU	Monitor Printing Unit [Data processing] (TUT)
MPU	Motorola Processor Unit
MPWB	Multilayer Printed Wiring Board
MPWD	Machine-Prepared Wiring Data [Telecommunications] (TEL)
MPX	Multiplex [or Multiplexer] [Telecommunications]
MPX	Multiprograming Executive [Data processing]

Computer & Telecommunications Acronyms

MPXR......... Multiplexer
MPY .... Multiply   (MDG)
MQ .... Multiplier Quotient [*Data processing*]
MQD........... Monolithic Quad Device
MQE........... Message Queue Element [*Data processing*]   (NITA)
MQR........... Multiplier Quotient Register [*Data processing*]
MQS........... Master of Quantitative Systems
MQU........... Media Quality Unit [*Communications*]
MQU........... Multiplier Quotient Unit [*Data processing*]
MQW.......... Multiple Quantum Well [*Switch for an optical computer*]
MR .... Mask Register   (NITA)
MR .... Master Reset   (MCD)
MR .... Memory Read [*Data processing*]
MR .... Memory Register [*Data processing*]
MR .... Message Register
MR .... Message Repeat
MR .... Microminiature Relay
MR .... Modular Redundancy   (NITA)
MR .... Modulation Response
MR .... Multiple Requesting [*IBM Corp.*]   (NITA)
MR .... Multiplier Register   (NITA)
MR .... Radiolocation Mobile Station [*ITU designation*]
MRA........... Medium-Powered Radio Range (Adcock)
MRAC......... Meter-Reading Access Circuit [*Bell Laboratories*]
MRAD......... Mass Random Access Disk [*Data processing*]
MRADS....... Mass Random Access Data Storage [*Data processing*]
MRB........... Magnetic Recording Boresight [*or Borescope*]
MRB........... Magnetospheric Radio Burst
MRB........... Modification Review Board   (AFM)
MRC........... Machine-Readable Code
MRC........... Manitoba Research Council [*Winnipeg, MB*] [*Research center*]   (RCD)
MRC........... Manufacturing Resource Control [*Kongsberg UK*] [*Software package*] [*British*]   (NCC)
MRC........... Memory Request Controller   (NITA)
MRC........... Metrics Research Corporation [*Information service*]   (EISS)
MRC........... Midwestern Relay Company [*Milwaukee, WI*] [*Telecommunications*]   (TSSD)
MRCF......... Mayo Biotechnology Research Computer Facility [*Mayo Clinic*] [*Research center*]   (RCD)
MRCS......... Multiple Report Creation System   (NITA)
MRD........... Manual Ringdown [*Telecommunications*]   (TEL)
MRD........... Memory Raster Display [*Data processing*]   (TUT)
MRDF......... Machine-Readable Data Files
MRDG......... Manufacturing Research and Design Group [*McMaster University*] [*Canada*] [*Research center*]   (RCD)
MRDOS...... Mapped Real-Time Disk Operating System [*Data processing*]   (MDG)
MRE........... Multiple-Response Enable   (IEEE)
MRF........... Message Refusal [*Telecommunications*]   (TEL)
MRFAC....... Manufacturers' Radio Frequency Advisory Committee   (EANO)
MRFL......... Master Radio Frequency List   (NATG)
MRGX........ Margaux Controls, Inc. [*NASDAQ symbol*]   (NQ)
MRH........... Magnetic Recording Head
MRH........... Mechanical Recording Head
MRH........... Mobile Remote Handler
MRI .... Measurement Requirements and Interface   (MCD)
MRI .... Mediamark Research, Incorporated [*Database producer and database*] [*Information service*]   (EISS)
MRI .... Memory Reference Instruction   (NITA)
MRI .... Monopulse Resolution Improvement
MRIO.......... Multiregional Input-Output
MRIS........... Market Research Information System [*Bell System*]
MRJ............ Microwave Rotary Joint
MRJE.......... Multileaving Remote Job Entry [*IBM Corp.*]
MRKD......... Marked [*Data processing*]   (MDG)
MRL .... Machine Representation Language   (NITA)
MRL .... Medium-Powered Radio Range [*Loop radiators*]
MROM........ Macro Read-Only Memory [*Data processing*]   (NITA)
MROM........ Masked Read-Only Memory [*Data processing*]
MRP .... Manufacturing Resource Planning [*Data processing*]
MRP .... Material Requirements Planning [*Tipdata Ltd.*] [*Software package*] [*British*]   (NCC)
MRP .... Message Routing Process [*Telecommunications*]   (TEL)
MRP .... Multiplex Recording Photography
MRPA......... Modified Random Phase Approximation
MRPS......... Manufacturing & Resource Planning System [*Cincom Systems Ltd.*] [*Software package*] [*British*]   (NCC)
MRR .... Microelectronic Radio Receiver
MRR .... Microfilm Reader Recorder   (TUT)
MRR .... Multiple Response Resolver   (NITA)
MRRS......... Magnetic Reed Rotary Switch
MRS .... Magnetic Reed Switch
MRS .... Microfilm Replacement System [*Data processing*]
MRSA......... Microwave Radiometer, Scatterometer, and Altimeter   (MCD)
MRT .... Machine-Readable Tapes [*Data processing*]   (DDI)
MRT .... Mean Repair Time   (DDI)
MRT .... Miniature Receiver Terminal
MRTE......... Master of Radio and Television Engineering
MRT Eng..... Master of Radio and Television Engineering
MRTS......... Meteorological Real-Time System [*Data processing*]   (KSC)
MRTU......... Multiplex Remote Terminal Unit   (MCD)
MRU........... Machine Records Unit [*Data processing*]

MRU........... Message Retransmission Unit
MRU........... Microfilm Recording Unit
MRU........... Microwave Relay Unit
MRU........... Multifunction Reference Unit   (MCD)
MRWC....... Multiple Read-Write Compute
MRX .... Memorex Corp. [*NYSE symbol*] [*Delisted*]
MS .... Macromodular System [*Data processing*]   (IEEE)
MS .... Magnetic Storage [*Data processing*]
MS .... Main Storage   (NITA)
MS .... Management Science [*Data processing*]   (BUR)
MS .... Mass Storage [*Data processing*]
MS .... Master Scheduler   (CMD)
MS .... Measured Service Pricing [*Telecommunications*]   (TEL)
MS .... Mechanized Scheduling [*Telecommunications*]   (TEL)
MS .... Meeting Series [*Online database field identifier*]   (OBD)
MS .... Memory System
MS .... Mesa [*Type of transistor*]   (MDG)
MS .... Microprogram Storage [*Data processing*]   (MDG)
MS .... Microwave Spectrum
ms .... Millisecond [*Also, msec*]
MS .... Mobile Service [*Telecommunications*]   (TEL)
MS .... Most Significant   (CAH)
MS .... Ship Station [*ITU designation*]   (CET)
MSA........... Management Science America, Inc. [*Atlanta, GA*] [*Software manufacturer*]   (DASOS)
MSA........... Management Science Associates, Inc. [*Information service*]   (EISS)
MSA........... Management System Analysis
MSA........... Mass Storage Adapter   (NITA)
MSA........... Metropolitan Statistical Area [*Census Bureau*]
MSA........... Microcomputer Software Association [*Arlington, VA*]   (EANO)
MSA........... Multichannel Signal Averager [*Data processing*]
MSA........... Multisubsystem Adapter [*Sperry UNIVAC*]   (NITA)
MSAC......... Moore School of Automatic Computers [*University of Pennsylvania*]
MSAI.......... Management Science of America [*NASDAQ symbol*]   (NQ)
MSAM........ Multi-Indexed Sequential Access Method [*Data processing*]
MSB........... Mass Spectrometry Bulletin [*Mass Spectrometry Data Centre*] [*Bibliographic database*] [*British*]   (OBD)
MSB........... Memory Storage Buffer [*Data processing*]   (CAAL)
MSB........... Most Significant BIT [*Binary Digit*] [*Data processing*]
MSBR......... Maximum Storage Bus Rate   (NITA)
MSBVW ...... Magnetostatic Backward Volume Wave [*Telecommunications*]   (TEL)
MSC........... Macro Selection Compiler [*Data processing*]   (BUR)
MSC........... Main Storage Control [*Data processing*]   (BUR)
MSC........... Management Services Contractor [*INTELSAT*]   (CBSS)
MSC........... Mass Storage Control [*Data processing*]   (BUR)
MSC........... Master Sequence Controller   (NASA)
MSC........... Memory Storage Control [*Data processing*]
MSC........... Message Sequence Chart [*Telecommunications*]   (TEL)
MSC........... Message Switching Center [*Telecommunications*]
MSC........... Message Switching Computer [*Telecommunications*]   (TEL)
MSC........... Message Switching Concentration   (NITA)
MSC........... Migent Software [*Vancouver Stock Exchange symbol*]
MSC........... Mile of Standard Cable
MSC........... Mode Selector Controller   (MCD)
MSC........... Moding Sequencing and Control   (MCD)
MSC........... Most Significant Character [*Data processing*]   (MDG)
MSC........... Multiple Scan Correlator
MSC........... Multiple Systems Coupling [*Data processing*]
MSC........... Multistrip Coupler [*Telecommunications*]   (TEL)
MSCA......... Microwave Switch Control Assembly
MSCE......... Main Storage Control Element [*Data processing*]   (IEEE)
MSCH .... Mode Switch Chassis
MSCI .... MacNeal-Schwendler Corporation [*NASDAQ symbol*]   (NQ)
MSCIS .... Master of Science in Computer Information Systems
MSCS .... Management Scheduling and Control System [*Telecommunications*]   (TEL)
MSCS .... Master of Science in Computer Science
MSCS .... Multiservice Communications Systems   (RDA)
MSCU .... Modular Store Control Unit   (NITA)
MSCW .... Marked Stack Control Word   (NITA)
MSD........... Magnetic Storage Drum [*Data processing*]
MSD........... Mass Storage Device [*Data processing*]
MSD........... Master Standard Data
MSD........... MODEM Sharing Device   (NITA)
MSD........... Most Significant Digit [*Data processing*]   (CIT)
MSD........... Multifrequency Signal Detector [*Telecommunications*]
MSD........... Multisensor Display
MSDB......... Main Storage Database   (NITA)
MSDC......... Maintenance Signal Data Converter   (MCD)
MSDC......... Mass Spectrometry Data Centre [*British*]   (EISS)
MSDC......... Microwave Spectra Data Center [*National Bureau of Standards*]
MSDC......... Molten Salts Data Center [*National Bureau of Standards*] [*Rensselaer Polytechnic Institute*] [*Research center*]   (EISS)
MSDG......... Multiple Sensor Display Group   (MCD)
MSDM........ Medium-Speed DynaBIT [*Binary Digit*] Memory [*Data processing*]
MS-DOS..... Microsoft Disk Operating System [*IBM Corp.*] [*Data processing*]
MSDR......... Maintenance Signal Data Recorder   (MCD)
MSDRS....... Maintenance Signal Data Recording Set [*or System*]   (MCD)
MSDS......... Magnetic Storage Drum System [*Data processing*]
MSDS......... Message Switching Data Service   (NITA)

Computer & Telecommunications Acronyms

MSDS	Multispectral Scanner and Data System
MSDT	Meshless Storage Display Tube
MSE	Mass Storage Editor [*Data processing*] (MCD)
MSE	Mean Square Error [*Statistics*]
msec	Millisecond [*Also, ms*]
MSED	Minimum Signal Element Duration [*Telecommunications*] (TEL)
M/SEQ	Master Sequencer (DDI)
MSES	Mobile Status Entry System
MSF	Mass Storage Facility [*Data processing*] (IBMDP)
MSF	Master Source File [*Data processing*] (BUR)
MSF	Medium Standard Frequency (DEN)
MSFVW	Magnetostatic Forward Volume Wave [*Telecommunications*] (TEL)
MSG	Madison Square Garden Network [*Cable-television system*]
MSG	Message (AFM)
MSG	Microwave Signal Generator
MSGG	Message Generator (MSA)
MSG/WTG	Message Waiting (MDG)
MSHP	Maintain System History Program [*IBM Corp.*]
MSI	Maintenance Support Index
MSI	Manned Satellite Inspector
MSI	Medium-Scale Integration [*Circuit packaging*]
MSI	Microwave Services International, Inc. [*Denville, NJ*] [*Telecommunications*] (TSSD)
MSI	MSI Data Corp. [*American Stock Exchange symbol*]
MSID	Medium-Scale Integration Device [*Circuit packaging*]
MSIMD	Multiple Single Instruction, Multiple Data (MCD)
MSIO	Mass Storage Input-Output [*Data processing*] (IEEE)
MSIR	Machine Survey and Installation Report (TUT)
MSIS	Manned Satellite Inspection System
MSIS	Mask Shop Information System [*Bell Laboratories*]
MSIS	Mass Spectral Information System
MSIS	Master of Science in Computer-Based Information Systems
MSIS	Multistate Information System [*Patient records*]
MSK	Manual Select Keyboard [*Data processing*] (KSC)
MSK	Minimum Shift Keying
MSL	Machine Specification Language (NITA)
MSL	Management Systems Laboratories [*Virginia Polytechnic Institute and State University*] [*Research center*] (RCD)
MSL	Microstar Software Limited [*Nepean, ON*] [*Telecommunications*] (TSSD)
MSLOUG	Medium-Sized Libraries/OCLC [*Online Computer Library Center*] Users Group
MSM	Major System Mode (CAAL)
MSM	Memory Storage Module (NITA)
MSM	Micro Surface Mapping [*Software package*] [*British*] (NCC)
MSM	Motorized Switching Matrix
MS/MIS	Master of Science/Management Information Systems
MSMLCS	Mass Service Mainline Cable Systems (OA)
MSN	Message Sequence Number (CAAL)
MSN	Microwave Systems News [*A publication*]
MSN	Mobil Showcase Network [*Television*]
MSN	Modern Satellite Network [*Cable-television system*]
MSNF	Multisystem Networking Facility [*Data processing*]
MSO	Mobile Switching Office [*Bell System*]
MSO	Multiple System Operator [*Cable television*]
MSOC	Marine Systems Operational Compiler
MSOE	Multiband Spectral Observation Equipment
MSORS	Mechanized Sales Office Record System [*Telecommunications*] (TEL)
MSOS	Mass Storage Operating System [*Control Data Corp.*] [*Data processing*] (NVT)
MSP	Mass Storage Processor [*Honeywell, Inc.*] (NITA)
MSP	Modular System Programs [*IBM Corp.*]
MSP	Most Significant Position (CMD)
MSP	Multisensor Processor (CAAL)
MSPLT	Master Source Program Library Tape [*Data processing*] (BUR)
MSPR	Master Spares Positioning Resolver [*Data processing*]
MSR	Magnetic Storage Ring [*Data processing*]
MSR	Mark Sense Reading (NITA)
MSR	Mark Sheet Reader [*Data processing*] (BUR)
MSR	Mass Storage Resident [*Data processing*] (IEEE)
MSR	Mechanized Storage and Retrieval [*Data processing*]
MSR	Message Has Been Misrouted [*Communications*]
MSR	Multijunction Semiconductor Rectifier
MSRF	Microwave Space Research Facility
MSRIS	Molten-Salt Reactor Information System
MSS	Management Statistics Subsystem (TEL)
MSS	Mass Storage System [*Data processing*]
MSS	Master Switching Station (MCD)
MSS	Master System Schedule (MCD)
MSS	Mastergroup Surveillance System [*AT & T*]
MSS	Message Switching Station [*Telecommunications*] (CET)
MSS	Meteorological Satellite Section
MSS	Microwave Switching Station
MSS	Midcourse Surveillance System (MCD)
MSS	Miniature Stepping Switch
MSS	Mode Selection Switch (KSC)
MSS	Modern Satellite Systems, Inc. [*Whitehouse Station, NJ*] [*Telecommunications*] (TSSD)
MSS	Multispectral Scanner [*or Sensor*]
MSSC	Mass Storage System Communicator [*Data processing*] (IBMDP)
MSSC	Mass Storage System Control [*Data processing*] (BUR)
MSSS	Mass Spectral Search System [*National Bureau of Standards, Environmental Protection Agency, and National Institutes of Health*] [*Database*]
MSSSW	Mass Spectral Search System-Wiley [*Cornell University*] [*Database*] (CUAD)
MSSW	Magnetostatic Surface Wave [*Telecommunications*] (TEL)
MST	Maximum Service Telecasters
MST	Microsecond Trip
MST	Monolithic Systems Technology
MSTC	Microwave Sensitivity Time Control [*Circuit*]
MSTG	Mass Storage Task Group [*CODASYL*] (NITA)
MSTR	Master
MSTS	Multisubscriber Time-Sharing Systems [*Computer system*]
MSTV	Master-Scale Television
MSU	Main Storage Unit [*Data processing*]
MSU	Maintenance Signal Unit [*Telecommunications*] (TEL)
MSU	Maintenance and Status Unit [*Telecommunications*] (TEL)
MSU	Management Signal Unit [*Telecommunications*] (TEL)
MSU	Management Systems Unit (TUT)
MSU	Mass Storage Unit [*Data processing*] (NASA)
MSU	Memory Service Unit [*Data processing*]
MSU	Message Switching Unit
MSU	Microwave Sounding Unit [*Telecommunications*] (TEL)
MSU	Multiblock Synchronization Signal Unit [*Telecommunications*] (TEL)
MSU	Multiple Signal Unit [*Telecommunications*] (TEL)
MSUDC	Michigan State University Discrete Computer
MSUS/PALS	Minnesota State Universities System Project for Automated Library Systems [*Information service*]
MSV	Mass Storage Volume (NITA)
MSVC	Mass Storage Volume Control [*Data processing*] (BUR)
MSW	Machine Status Word [*Data processing*]
MSW	Magnetostatic Waves [*Telecommunications*] (TEL)
MSW	Master Switch
MSW	Microswitch (KSC)
MSW	Microwave Spectrometer (TEL)
MSY	Modular Computer Systems, Inc. [*NYSE symbol*]
MSYNC	Master Synchronization [*Telecommunications*] (TEL)
MT	Machine Translation [*Data processing*]
MT	Machine Translation [*A publication*]
MT	Magnetic Tape
MT	Master Timer
MT	Measured Time
MT	Mechanical Translation [*Data processing*]
MT	Mechanical Translation [*A publication*]
MT	Modified Tape Armor [*Telecommunications*] (TEL)
MT	Multitasking (NITA)
MT	MUX [*Multiplex*] Terminal (MCD)
MTA	Magnetic Tape Accessory [*General Electric Co.*] (NITA)
MTA	Multiple-Terminal Access [*Data processing*] (IBMDP)
MTA	Multiterminal Adapter (IEEE)
MTAC	Mathematical Tables and Other Aids to Computation
MTBASIC	Multitasking BASIC [*Data processing*]
MTBD	Mean Time between Degradations [*Quality control*] [*Telecommunications*] (TEL)
MTBE	Mean Time between Errors [*Quality control*] (NITA)
MTBF	Mean Time between Failures [*Quality control*]
MTBI	Mean Time between Interrupts [*Quality control*] (NITA)
MTBM	Mean Time between Maintenance [*Quality control*] (AFM)
MTBO	Mean Time between Outages [*Quality control*] [*Telecommunications*] (TEL)
MTBSF	Mean Time between Software Failures [*Quality control*] (CAAL)
MTBSF	Mean Time between System Failures [*Quality control*]
MTC	Magnetic Tape Cassette [*Data processing*]
MTC	Magnetic Tape Channel [*Data processing*] (NITA)
MTC	Magnetic Tape Control [*Data processing*] (TUT)
MTC	Main Trunk Circuit [*World Meteorological Organization*] [*Telecommunications*] (TEL)
MTC	Manufacturing Technology Centre of New Brunswick [*Fredericton, NB*] [*Research center*] (RCD)
MTC	Master Tape Control
MTC	Memory Test Computer [*SAGE*]
MTC	Message Transmission Controller (NITA)
MTC	Morse Telegraph Club
MTCA	Multiple-Terminal Communication Adapter [*Data processing*]
MTCC	Master Timing and Control Circuit
MTCC	Modular Tactical Communications Center
MTCE	Maintenance [*Telecommunications*] (TEL)
MTCH	Mining Technology Clearing House [*British*] [*Information service*] (EISS)
MTCS	Minimal Terminal Communications System (NVT)
MTCS	Minimum Teleprocessing Commmunications System (NITA)
MTCU	Magnetic Tape Control Unit [*Data processing*]
MTD	Mass Tape Duplicator/Verifier [*Data processing*] (MCD)
MTD	Master Tape Data
MTD	Microwave Target Designator
MTD	Multiple Tile Duct [*Telecommunications*] (TEL)
MTDE	Maritime Tactical Data Exchange (NATG)
MTDS	Manufacturing Test Data System (IEEE)
MTDS	Marine Tactical Data System
MTDS	Marine Toebreak Data System (NG)
MTDS	Metallurgical and Thermochemical Data Service [*British*] [*Information service*] (EISS)

By Acronym

Computer & Telecommunications Acronyms

Acronym	Definition
MTDSK	Magnetic Tape Disk [*Data processing*] (NASA)
MTE	Microwave Test Equipment
MTE	Mobile Telephone Exchange [*Nordic Mobile Telephone*]
MTE	Multiple Terminal Emulator (NITA)
MTEL	MCS Telecommunications [*NASDAQ symbol*] (NQ)
MTF	Mean Time to Failure [*Quality control*]
MTF	Microwave Test Facility (CIT)
MTF	Modulation Transfer Function [*Resolution measure*]
MTF	Multitarget Frequency
MTFA	Modulation Transfer Function Analyzer
MTFD	Minimum Tracking Flux Density
MTG	Main Traffic Group [*Telecommunications*] (TEL)
MTH	Magnetic Tape Handler [*Data processing*]
MTI	Modern Telecommunications, Incorporated [*New York, NY*] (TSSD)
MTIS	MTI Systems Corp. [*NASDAQ symbol*] (NQ)
MTL	Master Tape Loading
MTL	Merged-Transistor Logic
MTLP	Master Tape Loading Program
MTM's	Magnetic Tape Transmissions (CET)
MT/MF	Magnetic Tape to Microfilm
MTOS	Magnetic Tape Operations System [*Data processing*]
MTP	Message Transmission Part [*Telecommunications*] (TEL)
MTPS	Magnetic Tape Programing System [*Data processing*] (IEEE)
MTPT	Minimal Total Processing Time (IEEE)
MTPUG	PASCAL/MT Users Group [*Westmont, IL*] (EANO)
MTR	Magnetic Tape Recorder
MTR	Monitor [*Data processing*] (BUR)
MTR	Monopulse Tracking Receiver
MTRE	Magnetic Tape Recorder End
MTRF	Master Training File [*Data processing*]
MTRS	Magnetic Tape Recorder Start
MTRS	Magnetic Tape Reformatting System [*Hewlett-Packard Co.*]
MTS	Magnetic Tape Station [*Data processing*] (CET)
MTS	Magnetic Tape System [*Data processing*]
MTS	Main Trunk System [*Telecommunications*] (TEL)
MTS	MARS [*Military Affiliate Radio System*] Technical Service (CET)
MTS	Mass Termination System [*Data processing*] (IEEE)
MTS	Message Telecommunications Service
MTS	Message Toll Service [*Communications*]
MTS	Message Transmission Subsystem [*Telecommunications*] (TEL)
MTS	Michigan Terminal System [*Data processing*]
MTS	Microwave Test Set (MCD)
MTS	Mobile Telephone Service
MTS	Mobile Terminal System [*IBM Corp.*]
MTSC	Magnetic Tape "Selectric" Composer [*IBM Corp.*]
MTSC	MTS Systems Corporation [*NASDAQ symbol*] (NQ)
MTSO	Mobile Telephone Switching Office [*Telecommunications*]
MTSR	Mean Time to Service Restoral [*Quality control*] [*Telecommunications*] (TEL)
MTSS	Magnetic Tape Storage System
MTST	Magnetic Tape "Selectric" Typewriter [*IBM Corp.*]
MTSU	Magnetic Tape Search Unit [*Data processing*]
MTT	Magnetic Tape Terminal [*Data processing*]
MTT	Magnetic Tape Transport [*Data processing*] (IEEE)
MTT	Microwave Theory and Technique (MCD)
MTTA	Multi-Tenant Telecommunications Association [*Washington, DC*] (EANO)
MTTD	Mean Time to Diagnosis [*Quality control*] (BUR)
MTTE	Magnetic Tape Terminal Equipment [*Data processing*] (CET)
MTTF	Mean Time to Failure [*Quality control*]
MTTM	Magnetic Tape and Telemetry (MCD)
MTTM	Mean Time to Maintain [*Quality control*] (CMD)
MTTR	Mean Time to Removal [*Quality control*]
MTTR	Mean Time to Repair [*Quality control*] (CAAL)
MTTR	Mean Time to Replacement [*Quality control*]
MTTR	Mean Time to Restore [*Quality control*] (IEEE)
MTTRS	Mean Time to Restore Software [*Quality control*] (CAAL)
MTTS	Multitask Terminal System (NITA)
MTTU	Modular Timing Terminal Unit
MTU	Magnetic Tape Unit [*Data processing*]
MTU	Multiplexer and Terminal Unit
MTU	Multiterminal Unit (TEL)
MTV	Multicultural Television
MTV	Music Television [*Warner Amex Satellite Entertainment Co.*] [*Cable-television system*]
MTVAL	Master Tape Validation
MTWX	Mechanized Teletypewriter Exchange (TEL)
MU	Machine Unit
MU	Memory Unit [*Data processing*] (MCD)
M/U	Monitor Unit [*Telecommunications*] (TEL)
MU	Multiplexing Unit (VIT)
MUC	Multicoupler (DDI)
MUD	Memory Unit Drum [*Data processing*]
MUD	Multi-User Dungeon [*Computer game*]
MUDET	Militarized Universal Digital Element Tester (MCD)
MUDL	Microwave Ultrasonic Delay Line
MUDPAC	Melbourne University Dual-Package Analog Computer [*Australia*]
MUF	Maximum Usable Frequency [*Signal transmission*]
MUG	Maximum Usable Gain [*Bell System*]
MUG	MUMPS [*Massachusetts General Hospital Utility Multiprograming System*] Users' Group [*College Park, MD*] (EANO)
MUI	Machine Utilization Index [*Data processing*]
MUI	Mass Unbalance Input [*Data processing*] (CIT)
MUI	Mode-Independent Unnumbered Information (CCD)
MUIG	Minicomputer Users Interest Group [*Later, Mini/Micro Special Interest Group*] (EANO)
MUL	Multiply (MDG)
MULDEM	Multiplexer/Demultiplexer [*Bell Laboratories*]
MULDEX	Multipoint Cross-Reference Index
MULS	Signed Multiplication [*Data processing*]
MULT	Multi Solutions, Inc. [*NASDAQ symbol*] (NQ)
MULT	Multiple
MULTI	Multiplexer (SKY)
MULTICS	Multiplexed Information and Computing Service [*Honeywell, Inc.*]
MULU	Unsigned Multiplication [*Data processing*]
MUM	Methodology for Unmanned Manufacture [*Robotics project*] [*Japanese*]
MUM	Multiple Unit Message [*Telecommunications*] (IEEE)
MUM	Multiuser Monitor (NITA)
MUMPS	Massachusetts General Hospital Utility Multiprograming System [*Programing language*]
MUMS	Mobile Utility Module System (IEEE)
MUMS	Multiple-Use MARC [*Machine-Readable Cataloging*] System [*Library of Congress*] [*Online retrieval system*] [*Information service*]
MUNE	Multiple Negative [*Circuit*]
MUNG	Mush until No Good [*Describes destruction of computer software*]
MUO	Maximum Undistorted Output
MUPO	Maximum Undistorted Power Output
MUPO	Multiple Positive [*Circuit*]
MUPROF	Multiple Projected Fibonacci [*Microwave circuit*]
MUPS	Mechanized Unit Property System [*Telecommunications*] (TEL)
MUPS	Multiple Utility Peripheral System [*Data processing*]
MUR	Management Update and Retrieval System
MUR	Radio Relay Message Unit [*Telecommunications*] (TEL)
MUS	Multiprograming Utility System [*Regnecentralen*] [*Denmark*] (NITA)
MUS	Multiutility System (MCD)
MUS	Music
MUSA	Multiple Unit Steerable Antenna [*Electronics*]
MUSE	Microcomputer Users in Education
MUSE	Multiple Sub-Nyquist Subsampling Encoding [*Digital recording system introduced 1984*]
MUSIC	McGill University System for Interactive Computing
MUSIL	Multiprograming Utility System Interpretive Language [*Regnecentralen*] [*Denmark*] (NITA)
MUTTS	Multiple Unit Terminal Test Set (MCD)
MUX	Multiplex [*or Multiplexer*] [*Telecommunications*] (CIT)
MUX/DEMUX	Multiplexer and Demultiplexer
MUXER	Multiplexer
MUXES	Multiplexes [*or Multiplexers*] [*Telecommunications*]
MUXMOD	Multiplex Modulation (CIT)
M/V	Magnetic Variation (MCD)
mV	Millivolt
MV	Move [*Telecommunications*] (TEL)
MVA	Machine Vision Association (EANO)
MVCU	Multivariable Control Unit [*Data processing*]
MVDF	Medium- and Very-High-Frequency Direction-Finding Station
MVDS	Modular Video Data System [*Sperry UNIVAC*] (NITA)
MVL	Man-Vehicle Laboratory [*Massachusetts Institute of Technology*] [*Research center*] (RCD)
MVM	Medium-Voltage Mode
MVM	Minimum Virtual Memory (OA)
MVS	Magnetic Voltage Stabilizer
MVS	Mobile Video Services Ltd. [*Washington, DC*] [*Telecommunications*] (TSSD)
MVS	Multiple Virtual Storage [*IBM Corp.*] [*Data processing*]
MVS	Multiple Virtual System [*Data processing*]
MVSSE	Multiple Virtual Storage System Extension (NITA)
MVT	Multiprograming with a Variable Number of Tasks [*IBM Corp.*] [*Control program*] [*Data processing*]
MW	Manual Word
MW	Medium Wave Band
MW	Memory Write [*Data processing*]
MW	Microwave
mW	Milliwatt
MWAVE	Microwave (DDI)
MWB	Multilayer Wiring Board
MWC	Magnetoionic Wave Component
MWC/CS	Mechanized Wire Centering/Cross Section [*AT & T*] [*Telecommunications*] (TEL)
MWCE	Millimeter Wave Communications Experiment
MWCH	Monchik-Weber Corporation [*NASDAQ symbol*] (NQ)
MWCS	Midwest Cable & Satellite, Inc. [*Minneapolis, MN*] [*Telecommunications*] (TSSD)
MWCS	Millimeter Wave Contrast Seeker (MCD)
MWD	Megaword (NITA)
MWD	Millimeter Wave Device
MWE	Millimeter Wave Experiment
MWFM	Microwave Window Failure Mechanism
MWI	Message-Waiting Indicator
mWL	Milliwatt Logic
MWM	Millimeter Wave Mixer
MWO	Millimeter Wavelength Oscillator

MWP	Millimeter Wave Propagation
MWPC	Multiple Wire Proportional Counter
MWPS	Multimeter Wave Power Source
MWS	Management Work Station [*Data processing*] (BUR)
MWS	Microwave Scatterometer [*Telecommunications*] (TEL)
MWS	Microwave Station
MWS	Multiwork Station (NITA)
MWSR	Magnetic Wire Shift Register
MWT	Millimeter Wave Tube
Mwt	Thermal Megawatt [*Also, TMW*]
MWTCS	Modernized Weather Teletypewriter Communication System (FAAC)
MWW	Manual Wire Wrap
MWWF	Manual Wire Wrap Fixture
MX	Matrix (BUR)
Mx	Maxwell [*Unit of magnetic flux*] [*Also, abWb*]
MX	Multiple Address (DDI)
MX	Multiplex [*or Multiplexer*]
MXD	Multiple Transmitter Duplicator
MXDCR	Mode Transducer (MSA)
MXK	Multiple-Frequency X- and K-Band (CIT)
MXU	Multiplexer Unit [*Telecommunications*]
MYCOS	My Compact Operating System [*Toshiba*] (NITA)
MYIM	Mylar Insulation Material

N

N	Magnetic Flux [*Symbol*]
n	Nano [*A prefix meaning divided by one billion*] [*SI symbol*]
n	Negative [*Crystal*]
N	Night [*Broadcasting term*]
N	Noise [*Broadcasting*]
N	North [*or Northern*]
N	Number
N	Numeric
N/A	Name and Address
nA	Nanoampere
NA	Night Alarm [*Telecommunications*] (TEL)
NA	No Access [*Telecommunications*] (TEL)
NA	North Atlantic Industries
NA	Not And [*Logical operator*] [*Data processing*]
NA	Not Assigned
NA	Not Available
NA	Numerical Analysis [*Data processing*] (BUR)
NA	Numerical Aperture [*Microscopy*]
NAACS	National Association of Aircraft and Communications Suppliers (EANO)
NAARS	National Automated Accounting Research System [*American Institute of Certified Public Accountants*] [*Database*] [*Information service*] (EISS)
NAB	National Association of Broadcasters [*Telecommunications*] (TEL)
NABB	National Association for Better Broadcasting [*Formerly, NAFBRAT*]
NABER	National Association of Business and Educational Radio [*Washington, DC*]
NABUG	National Association of Broadcast Unions and Guilds
NAC	National Air Communications [*British*]
NAC	Network Access Controller (NITA)
NACDPA	National Association of County Data Processing Administrators (EANO)
NACHA	National Automated Clearing House Association (EANO)
NACIS	National Credit Information Service [*TRW, Inc.*] [*Long Beach, CA*] [*Credit-information databank*] (EISS)
NACK	Nonacknowledgment Character [*Data processing*]
NACLIS	National Commission on Libraries and Information Science
NACOM	National Communications [*System*]
NACS	National Association of Computer Stores [*Stamford, CT*] (EANO)
NACS	Northern Area Communications System
NACSA	North American Computer Service Association [*Casselberry, FL*] [*Absorbed International Association of Service Companies (1982)*] (EANO)
NACTP	National Association of Computerized Tax Processors [*Annapolis, MD*] (EANO)
NACUBO	National Association of College and University Business Officers [*Washington, DC*]
NAD	Network Access Device (CCD)
NADAR	North American Data Airborne Recorder
NADB	National Aerometric Data Bank [*Environmental Protection Agency*]
NADIN	National Airspace Data Interchange Network (FAAC)
NADIS	National Aerometric Data Information System [*Environmental Protection Agency*]
NADUG	North American Datamanager Users Group (EANO)
NAEB	National Association of Educational Broadcasters [*Formerly, Association of College and University Broadcasting Stations (1934)*] [*Washington, DC*]
NAEC	National Association for Educational Computing (EANO)
NAECON	National Aerospace Electronics Conference [*IEEE*]
NAED	National Association of Electrical Distributors
NAEIC	Nevada Applied Ecology Information Center [*Department of Energy*] (EISS)
NAEKM	National Association of Electronic Keyboard Manufacturers (EANO)
NAEPIRS	National Assessment of Educational Progress Information Retrieval System [*National Institute of Education*] [*Database*] (FDB)
NAF	Name and Address File [*IRS*]
NAF	Network Access Facility (NITA)
NAFAX	National Facsimile Network [*National Weather Service*]
NAFB	National Association of Farm Broadcasters
NAFBRAT	National Association for Better Radio and Television [*Later, NABB*]
NAFMB	National Association of FM [*Frequency Modulation*] Broadcasters [*Later, NRBA*]
NAFMIS	Nonappropriated Funds Management Information System
NAG	Networking Advisory Group [*Library of Congress*]
NAG	Numerical [*formerly, Nottingham*] Algorithms Group
NAGARA	National Association of Government Archives and Records Administrators (EANO)
NAGC	National Association of Government Communicators (EANO)
NAHU	North American Honeywell Users Association [*Formerly, HUG-SMS*] (EANO)
NAI	Nims Associates, Incorporated [*Decatur, IL*] [*Software manufacturer*] (DASOS)
NAI	No-Address Instruction
NAICC	National Association of Independent Computer Companies (NITA)
NAILTE	National Association of Instructional Leaders in Technical Education (EANO)
NAIT	National Association of Industrial Technology (EANO)
NAIT	Northern Alberta Institute of Technology [*Edmonton, AB*]
NAITPD	National Association of Independent Television Producers and Distributors (EANO)
NAK	Negative Acknowledge [*or Acknowledgment*] [*Data communication*]
NAK	Network Acknowledgment
NAKOSTA	Natural Convection in the Stationary Condition [*Computer program*]
NAL	New Assembly Language (NITA)
NALECOM	National Law Enforcement Telecommunications System
NAM	National Account Management [*Bell System*]
NAM	Network Access Machine [*National Bureau of Standards*] [*Data processing*]
NAM	Network Access Method [*Control Data Corp.*] [*Telecommunications*] (TEL)
NAN	Network Application Node (NITA)
NAND	Not And [*Logical operator*] [*Data processing*]
NANWEP	Navy Numerical Weather Prediction [*Computer system*] [*Control Data Corp.*] (CAH)
NAP	Network Access Pricing [*Telecommunications*] (TEL)
NAP	Network Access Protocol (NITA)
NAP	Noise Analysis Program (NITA)
NAPBC	Native American Public Broadcasting Consortium, Inc. [*Lincoln, NE*] [*Telecommunications*] [*An association*] (EANO)
NAPLPS	North American Presentation Level Protocol Syntax [*Computer display system*] [*Pronounced "naplips"*]
NAPS	Nimbus Automatic Programing System (IEEE)
NAPSS	Numerical Analysis Problem Solving System (TUT)
NAPTIC	National Air Pollution Technical Information Center [*of National Air Pollution Control Administration*] [*Also, APTIC*] (DIT)
NAPWPT	National Association of Professional Word Processing Technicians [*Philadelphia, PA*] (EANO)
NAQUADAT	National Water Quality Data Bank [*Canada*] [*Information service*] (EISS)
NAR	Numerical Analysis Research
NAR	Nutrition Abstracts and Reviews [*Database*] (ODIN)
NARC	Nonautomatic Relay Center
NARIC	National Rehabilitation Information Center [*Catholic University of America*] [*Bibliographic database*] (EANO)
NARPV	National Association for Remotely Piloted Vehicles (MCD)
NARS	National Archives and Records Service [*of GSA*] [*Washington, DC*]
NARS	National Association of Radiotelephone Systems [*Later, Telocator Network of America*] (EANO)
NARS	North Atlantic Radio System
NARTE	National Association of Radio and Telecommunications Engineers (EANO)
NARTEL	North Atlantic Radiotelephone
NARUC	National Association of Regulatory Utility Commissioners [*Telecommunications*] [*Information service*]
NAS	National Academy of Sciences [*Washington, DC*]
NAS	Nonlinear Antenna System

Computer & Telecommunications Acronyms

NAS	Normalized Alignment Score
NAS	Numerical Analysis Subroutines [*Data processing*] (BUR)
NASA	National Aeronautics and Space Administration [*Washington, DC*]
NASAGA	North American Simulation and Gaming Association (EANO)
NASA/RECON	National Aeronautics and Space Administration Remote Console
NASD	National Association of Securities Dealers
NASDAQ	National Association of Securities Dealers Automated Quotations [*Over-the-counter stock quotations*] [*Bunker Ramo Corp.*] [*Trumbell, CT*]
NASECODE	Numerical Analysis of Semiconductor Devices and Integrated Circuits [*Data processing*]
NASEM	National Association of Satellite Equipment Manufacturers [*Tulsa, OK*] (EANO)
NASF	Numerical Aerodynamic Simulation Facility
NASIS	National Association for State Information Systems [*Lexington, KY*]
NASTOCK	North American Stock Market [*I. P. Sharp*] [*Database*]
NASWA	North American Shortwave Association (EANO)
NAT	Information Content Natural Unit [*Information theory*]
NATA	North American Telecommunications Association [*Washington, DC*] [*Information service*] (TSSD)
NATA	North American Telephone Association [*Washington, DC*] (EANO)
NATCOM	National Communications Symposium [*IEEE*]
NATCOM	National Conference on Communications (MCD)
NATEL	Nortronics Automatic Test Equipment Language [*Data processing*]
NATL	North Atlantic Industries [*NASDAQ symbol*] (NQ)
Natl Comput Conf	National Computer Conference [*United States*] [*A publication*]
NATOA	National Association of Telecommunications Officers and Advisors [*National League of Cities*] [*Washington, DC*] (EANO)
NATOSAT	North Atlantic Treaty Organization Satellite
NATPE	National Association of Television Program Executives
NATRON	National Cash Register Electronic Data Processing System (MCD)
NATS	National Activity to Test Software
Nat Semi	National Semiconductor Corp.
NAU	Network Address Unit [*Data processing*] (BUR)
NAVJAC	North American Vane Jump Angle Computer
NAWDEX	National Water Data Exchange [*United States Geological Survey*] [*Information service*]
NAWPS	National Association of Word Processing Specialists [*Later, WPS*] (EANO)
NB	Narrow Beam (NATG)
NB	Narrowband
N/B	Noise Power/Bandwidth (CIT)
NBC	Narrowband Conducted (IEEE)
NBC	National Broadcasting Company, Inc. [*New York, NY*]
NBC	Natural Background Clutter
NBC	Noise Balancing Circuit (DEN)
NBC/CSC	NBC Computer Service Corporation [*Lincoln, NE*] [*Software manufacturer*] (DASOS)
NBCD	Natural Binary-Coded Decimal (NITA)
NBCD	Negate BCD [*Binary-Coded Decimal*] Number [*Data processing*]
NBCV	Narrowband Coherent Video (IEEE)
NBD	Narrowband Detector
NBDC	National Blood Data Center [*American Blood Commission*] [*Information service*] (EISS)
NBDF	Narrowband Dicke-Fix [*Electronics*] (CET)
NBDFX	Narrowband Dicke-Fix [*Electronics*] (MSA)
NBER	National Bureau of Economic Research [*Cambridge, MA*]
NBF	Narrowband Filter
NBFM	Narrowband Frequency Modulation [*Radio*]
NBH	Network Busy Hour [*Telecommunications*] (TEL)
NBI	NBI, Inc. [*NYSE symbol*]
NBI	Northern Business Information, Inc. [*New York, NY*] [*Information service*] (TSSD)
NBI	Nothing but Initials [*Initialism is name of commercial word processor firm*]
NBIE	National Burn Information Exchange [*Ann Arbor, MI*] [*Information service*] (EISS)
NBK	Nabu Network Corp. [*Toronto Stock Exchange symbol*]
NBLD	Narrowband Linear Detector (MCD)
NBN	Narrowband Network
NBN	Narrowband Noise
NBN	National Black Network [*A radio network*]
NBN	Nationality Broadcasting Network [*Cable-television system*]
NBO	Network Buildout (IEEE)
NBOC	Network Building Out Capacitor [*Telecommunications*] (TEL)
NBOR	Network Building Out Resistor [*Telecommunications*] (TEL)
NBPM	Narrowband Phase Modulation (MCD)
NBR	Narrowband Radiated (IEEE)
NBR	Number (KSC)
NBRF	National Biomedical Research Foundation [*Georgetown University*] [*Research center*]
NBS	Narrowband Search (MCD)
NBS	National Bureau of Standards [*Department of Commerce*] [*Washington, DC*]
NBS	New British Standard [*Imperial wire gauge*]
NBSCCST	National Bureau of Standards Center for Computer Sciences and Technology (DIT)
NBSFS	National Bureau of Standards Frequency Standard (IEEE)
NBSLD	National Bureau of Standards Load Determination [*Computer program*]
NBST	Narrowband Subscriber Terminal (CET)
NBT	New Brunswick Telephone Co. Ltd. [*Toronto Stock Exchange symbol*]
NBTR	Narrowband Tape Recorder
NBV	Net Book Value [*Telecommunications*] (TEL)
NBW	Noise Bandwidth
NC	Network Congestion [*Telecommunications*] (TEL)
NC	Network Connect
NC	Network Controller
NC	Network Countdown (SKY)
NC	No Charge
NC	No Connection [*Valve pins*] [*Technical drawings*] [*Radio*]
NC	Noise Correlation (MSA)
NC	Noise Criterion
NC	Normally Closed [*Switch*]
NC	Numerical Control [*Data processing*]
NCA	National Communications Association [*New York, NY*] [*Formerly, PCA*] (EANO)
NCA	National Computer Association [*Littleton, CO*] [*Computer users group*] (EANO)
NCA	National Congressional Analysis Corp. (EISS)
NCA	Northwest Computing Association
NCAC	NCA Corporation [*NASDAQ symbol*] (NQ)
NCAIR	National Center for Automated Information Retrieval (EISS)
NCALI	National Clearinghouse for Alcohol Information [*Rockville, MD*] (EISS)
NCAM	Network Communication Access Method (NITA)
NCAP	Nonlinear Circuit Analysis Program (MCD)
NCB	Network Control Block (NITA)
NCBEC	National Center for Business and Economic Communication [*American University*] [*Research center*] (RCD)
NCC	National Computer Center [*IRS*]
NCC	National Computer Conference
NCC	National Computing Centre [*Manchester, England*]
NCC	Network Control Center (DEEC)
NCC	New Computer Center [*Social Security Administration*]
NCCBMI	National Consortium for Computer Based Music Instruction [*University of Delaware*] [*Newark, DE*] [*Research clearinghouse*] (EANO)
NCCCD	National Center for Computer Crime Data [*Formerly, National Computer Crime Data Center (1979)*] [*Los Angeles, CA*] [*Database producer*] (EANO)
NCCDPC	NATO Command, Control, and Information Systems and Automatic Data Processing Committee (NATG)
NCCF	Network Communications Control Facility [*IBM program product*]
NCCI	North Central Computer Institute [*Madison, WI*] [*Research center*] (RCD)
NCD	Negotiated Critical Dates [*Telecommunications*] (TEL)
NCD	Network Cryptographic Device (NITA)
NCDCF	National Civil Defense Computer Facility
NCE	Network Connection Element (NITA)
NCEF	National Calling and Emergency Frequencies (CET)
NCEFT	National Commission on Electronic Fund Transfers
NCF	National Communications Forum [*National Engineering Consortium, Inc.*] [*Chicago, IL*] [*Telecommunications*] (TSSD)
NCFPI	National Clearinghouse for Family Planning Information [*Database*] (FDB)
NCFT	National Council for Families and Television (EANO)
NCGA	National Computer Graphics Association [*Fairfax, VA*] (EANO)
NCGIC	National Cartographic and Geographic Information Center [*Geological Survey*] [*Reston, VA*] [*Database*] (FDB)
NCH	Network Connection Handler (NITA)
NCHGD	National Clearinghouse for Human Genetic Diseases [*Public Health Service*] [*Information service*] (EISS)
NCHRTM	National Clearing House of Rehabilitation Training Materials [*Oklahoma State University*] [*Information service*] (EISS)
NCHS	National Center for Health Statistics [*Health Services and Mental Health Administration*] [*Rockville, MD*] [*Originator and database*]
NCI	National Cancer Institute [*of National Institutes of Health*] [*Database producer*]
NCI	National Captioning Institute [*Falls Church, VA*] [*Telecommunications*] (EANO)
NCI	National Computer Institute (MCD)
NCI	National Computing Industries, Inc. [*Atlanta, GA*] [*Software manufacturer*] (DASOS)
NCI	Noncoded Information [*Data processing*] (IBMDP)
NCIC	National Crime Information Center [*FBI*] [*Washington, DC*]
NCIS	National Chemical Information System (DIT)
NCIS	National Credit Information Service [*TRW, Inc.*] [*Long Beach, CA*] [*Credit-information databank*]
NCJRS	National Criminal Justice Reference Service [*Later, ICJC*] [*Department of Justice*] [*Bibliographic database*]
NCL	Network Control Language (NITA)
NCL	Node Compatibility List [*Telecommunications*] (TEL)
NCLIS	National Commission on Libraries and Information Science [*Washington, DC*]

Computer & Telecommunications Acronyms

Acronym	Definition
NCLS	National Clearinghouse for Legal Services [*Legal Services Corp.*] [*Information service*] (EISS)
NCM	Network Control Module (NITA)
NCMHI	National Clearinghouse for Mental Health Information [*Rockville, MD*] [*Database*] [*HEW*]
NCN	National Christian Network [*Cable-television system*]
NCN	National Computer Network of Chicago, Inc. [*Information service*] (EISS)
NCN	Network Control Node (NITA)
NCN	Nixdorf Communications Network [*Nixdorf*] [*West German*] (NITA)
NCO	Network Control Office [*Telecommunications*] (TEL)
NCO	Number-Controlled Oscillator (CIT)
NCOS	Non-Concurrent Operating System [*Sperry UNIVAC*] (CAH)
NCP	Network Control Program [*IBM Corp.*] [*Telecommunications*] (BUR)
NCPAS	National Computer Program Abstract Service (EISS)
NCR	National Cash Register Co. [*Later, NCR Corp.*] [*Computer manufacturer*]
NCR	NCR Corp. [*Formerly, National Cash Register Co.*] [*NYSE symbol*]
NCR	Network Control Room [*Television*]
NCRCRD	North Central Regional Center for Rural Development [*Iowa State University*] [*Research center*] (RCD)
NCRDS	National Coal Resources Data System [*Geological Survey*] [*Databank*] [*Information service*] (EISS)
NCS	National Communications System [*GSA*]
NCS	National Computer Systems, Inc. (CAH)
NCS	National Crime Survey [*University of Michigan*] [*Database*] (FDB)
NCS	NCR [*NCR Corp.*] Century Software (NITA)
NCS	Net Control Station [*Communications*] [*Amateur radio*]
NCS	Network Control System (NITA)
NCS	No Checking Signal [*Telecommunications*] (TEL)
NCS	Numerical Control Society [*Glenview, IL*]
NCSA	National Center for Supercomputing Applications [*University of Illinois*] [*Research center*] (RCD)
NCSCI	National Center for Standards and Certification Information [*National Bureau of Standards*] [*Database*] (FDB)
NCSI	National Communication System Instructions
NCSS	National Conversational Software Systems, Inc. (NITA)
NCT	Night Closing Trunks [*Telecommunications*] (TEL)
NCTA	National Cable [*formerly, Community*] Television Association
NCTI	National Cable Television Institute (EANO)
NCTR	National Center for Telephone Research [*Commercial firm*] [*Louis Harris and Associates*] [*New York, NY*] (EANO)
NCU	Network Control Unit [*Data processing*]
NCUG	Nevada COBOL [*Common Business-Oriented Language*] Users Group [*Norcross, GA*] (EANO)
ND	I am not able to deliver message addressed to aircraft [*Telecommunications*] (FAAC)
ND	Nondirectional Antenna
ND	Nothing Doing [*Amateur radio slang*]
ND	Number of Document [*Online database field identifier*] (OBD)
NDA	No Data Available [*Data processing*]
NDAB	Numerical Data Advisory Board [*National Research Council*] [*Information service*] (EISS)
NDB	Numeric Data Base [*INPADOC*] [*Data processing*]
NDB(ADF)	Nondirectional Beacon (Automatic Direction Finder)
NDBMS	Network Database Management System (NITA)
NDBO	NOAA [*National Oceanic and Atmospheric Administration*] Data Buoy Office (EISS)
NDC	National Data Communication (OA)
NDC	National Data Corporation
NDC	Network Diagnostic Control (NITA)
NDC	Normalized Device Coordinates [*Data processing*]
NDDEIC	National Digestive Diseases Education and Information Clearinghouse [*Public Health Service*] (EISS)
NDES	Normal Digital Echo Suppressor [*Telecommunications*] (TEL)
NDEX	Newspaper Index [*Bell & Howell Co.*] [*Database*]
NDI	Nuclear Data, Incorporated [*American Stock Exchange symbol*]
NDIC	National Diabetes Information Clearinghouse [*Public Health Service*] (EISS)
NDL	National Diet Library [*Tokyo, Japan*] (DIT)
NDL	Network Definition Language [*Burroughs Corp.*]
NDLC	Network Data Link Control (NITA)
NDMS	Network Design and Management System (NITA)
NDN	National Diffusion Network [*Department of Education*] [*Information service*] (EISS)
NDPS	National Data Processing Service (NITA)
NDR	National Driver Register
NDR	Nondestructive Read [*Data processing*]
NDRO	Nondestructive Readout [*Data processing*]
NDRW	Nondestructive Read/Write [*Data processing*]
NDS	Nonparametric Detection Scheme [*Communication signal*]
NDT	Net Data Throughout
NDTP	Nuclear Data Tape Program
NDTRAN	Notre Dame Translator [*Programing language*] [*1977*] [*Data processing*] (CSR)
NDU	Nuclear Data Unit [*International Atomic Energy Agency*] (DIT)
NE	Northeast
NE	Not Equal [*Relational operator*]
NEAC	Nippon Electric Automatic Computer (IEEE)
NEA-DB	NEA [*Nuclear Energy Agency*] Data Bank [*France*] [*Information service*] (EISS)
NEADS	Network Engineering Administrative Data System [*AT & T*]
NEAT	NCR [*NCR Corp.*] Electronic Autocoding Technique [*Data processing*] (IDA)
NEB	National Enterprise Board [*Later, BTG*] [*British*]
NEB	Noise-Equivalent Bandwidth
NEBULA	Natural Electronic Business User's Language [*International Computers Ltd.*] (CAH)
NEC	National Electrical Code
NEC	National Electronics Conference [*Later, National Engineering Consortium*]
NEC	Nippon Electric Company [*Japan*]
NECA	National Exchange Carriers Association
NECC	National Education Computer Center
NECCTA	National Educational Closed-Circuit Television Association [*British*]
NECS	Nationwide Educational Computer Service (IEEE)
NEDCC	New England Document Conservation Center [*Andover, MA*] [*Information service*] (EISS)
NEDRES	National Environmental Data Referral Service [*Online database*]
NEEDS-IR	NIKKEI [*Nihon Keizai Shimbun, Inc.*] Economic Electronic Databank Service - Information Retrieval [*Japan*] [*Information service*] (EISS)
NEEDS-TS	NIKKEI [*Nihon Keizai Shimbun, Inc.*] Economic Electronic Databank Service - Time Sharing [*Japan*] [*Information service*] (EISS)
NEEMIS	New England Energy Management Information System
NEF	Noise-Equivalent Flux
NEG	Negate a Binary Number [*Data processing*]
NEG	Negative
NEGX	Negate a Binary Number with Extend [*Data processing*]
NEH	I am connecting you to a station which will accept traffic for the station you request [*Telecommunications*] (FAAC)
NEI	Nordic Energy Index [*Nordic Atomic Libraries Joint Secretariat*] [*Denmark*] [*Databank*] [*Information service*] (EISS)
NEIC	National Electronic Information Corporation [*Information service*] (EISS)
NEICA	National Energy Information Center Affiliate [*University of New Mexico*] [*Albuquerque, NM*] (EISS)
NEIS	National Earthquake Information Service [*United States Geological Survey*] (EISS)
NEIS	National Engineering Information System (BUR)
NEISS	National Electronic Injury Surveillance System [*Consumer Product Safety Commission*] [*Washington, DC*] [*Databank*]
NEL	National Engineering Laboratory [*Superseded IAT*] [*National Bureau of Standards*]
NELPAC	National Engineering Laboratory's Thermophysical Properties Package [*British*] [*Information service*] (EISS)
NEMA	National Electrical Manufacturers Association [*Database producer and database*]
NEMO	Never Ever Mention Outside [*Secret computer toy project of Axlon, Inc.*]
NEP	Noise-Equivalent Power
NEPCON	National Electronic Packaging and Production Conference
NEPHIS	Nested Phrase Indexing System [*Automated indexing system*] (NITA)
NERC	Newton-Evans Research Company, Inc. [*Ellicott City, MD*] [*Information service*] (TSSD)
NERComP	New England Regional Computing Program, Inc. [*Boston, MA*]
NERDC	Northeast Regional Data Center [*University of Florida*] [*Research center*] (RCD)
NES	Nonerasable Storage [*Data processing*]
NESC	National Electrical Safety Code
NESC	National Energy Software Center [*Department of Energy*] [*Information service*] (EISS)
NESDIS	National Environmental Satellite, Data, and Information Service [*National Oceanic and Atmospheric Administration*]
NESN	New England Sports Network [*Cable-television system*]
NESS	National Environmental Satellite Service [*National Oceanic and Atmospheric Administration*] [*Telecommunications*] (TEL)
NESS	Northeast Satellite Systems [*Avoca, PA*] [*Telecommunications*] (TSSD)
NET	Network [*Telecommunications*]
NET	New Era Technologies, Inc. [*Washington, DC*] [*Telecommunications*] (TSSD)
NETCON	Network Control (CIT)
NETI	Network Technologies International, Inc. [*Ann Arbor, MI*] [*Telecommunications*] (TSSD)
NETSET	Network Synthesis and Evaluation Technique [*Data processing*] (TUT)
NETTEL	Network Telecommunications [*Denver, CO*] [*Telecommunications*] (TSSD)
NETV	Nebraska ETV [*Educational Television*] Network [*Lincoln, NE*] [*Telecommunications*] (TSSD)
New Inf Syst Serv	New Information Systems and Services [*United States*] [*A publication*]
NEWRIT	Northeast Water Resources Information Terminal (EISS)
NEWW	New World Computer [*NASDAQ symbol*] (NQ)
NEX	National Exchange, Inc. [*Los Angeles, CA*] [*Telecommunications*] (TSSD)
NEXIS	[*A*] newspaper database [*Mead Data Control*] (DEEC)
NEXT	Near-End Crosstalk [*Bell System*]

NF	Noise Factor
NF	Noise Frequency (MSA)
NF	Not Found [Telephone listing] [Telecommunications] (TEL)
NFAIS	National Federation of Abstracting and Information [formerly, Indexing] Services [Pronounced "enface"] [Philadelphia, PA]
NFAM	Network File Access Method (NITA)
NFAP	Network File Access Protocol (NITA)
NFCBRO	National Federation of Citizen Band Radio Operators (EANO)
NFCS	Nuclear Forces Communications Satellite
NFE	Network Front End (NITA)
NFM	Narrowband Frequency Modulation [Radio]
NFPA	National Fire Protection Association [Boston, MA] [Databank originator]
NFPCA	National Fire Prevention and Control Administration [Later, United States Fire Administration] [Department of Commerce]
NFPDB	NATO Force Planning Data Base (NATG)
NFS	National Field Service Corp. [Suffern, NY] [Telecommunications] (TSSD)
NFT	Networks File Transfer (NITA)
NFU	Not for Us [Communications]
NFY	Notify [Telecommunications] (TEL)
NFYD	Notified [Telecommunications] (TEL)
NGA	National Graphical Association [British printers' union]
NGB	Nippon Gijutsu Boeki Co. Ltd. [Japan] [Information service] (EISS)
NGDB	National Geochemical Data Bank [Natural Environment Research Council] [British] [Information service] (EISS)
NGI	Nederlands Genootschap voor Informatica [Netherlands Society for Informatics] [Information service] (EISS)
NGIC	National Geodetic Information Center [National Oceanic and Atmospheric Administration] (EISS)
NGM	Neutron-Gamma Monte Carlo [Data processing]
NGN	National Geographic Names Data Base [Geological Survey] [Database] (FDB)
NGP	Network Graphics Protocol (NITA)
NGSDC	National Geophysical and Solar-Terrestrial Data Center [National Oceanic and Atmospheric Administration] [Boulder, CO] (EISS)
NGSIC	National Geodetic Survey Information Center [National Oceanic and Atmospheric Administration] (EISS)
NHD	Not Heard [Communications]
NHIC	National Health Information Clearinghouse [Public Health Service] (EISS)
NHK	Nippon Hoso Kyokai [Japan National Broadcasting Corporation]
NHP	Network Host Protocol (NITA)
NHPIC	National Health Planning Information Center [Hyattsville, MD] [HEW] [Database] (EISS)
NI	Noise Index
N/I	Noise to Interference Ratio [Telecommunications] (TEL)
NI	Notice of Information [Data processing]
NI	Numerical Index (BUR)
NIA	No Input Acknowledge [Data processing]
NIAC	Nutritional Information and Analysis Center [Illinois Institute of Technology and Institute of Food Technologists] (EISS)
NIB	Negative Impedance Booster [Electronics]
NIB	Network Interface Board (CCD)
NIB	Node Initialization Block [Data processing] (IBMDP)
NIC	Nearly Instantaneous Compounding (MCD)
NIC	Negative Immittance Converter
NIC	Negative Impedance Converter
NIC	Netherlands Information Combine [Information service] (EISS)
NIC	Network Interface Card [Data processing]
NIC	Network Interface Control (NITA)
NIC	Nineteen-Hundred Indexing and Cataloging (DIT)
NI & C	Nippon Information and Communication [Joint venture of IBM Corp. Japan and Nippon Telegraph and Telephone]
NICATELSAT	Nicaraguan Telecommunication by Satellite [Commercial firm]
NICE	National Information Conference and Exposition [Associated Information Managers]
NICE	National Institute for Computers in Engineering [Rockville, MD] (EANO)
NICE	Normal Input-Output Control Executive [Data processing]
NICEM	National Information Centre for Educational Media [Access Innovation database]
NICOL	New Integrated Computer Language (TUT)
NICOL	Nineteen-Hundred Commercial Language (CAH)
NICS	NATO Integrated Communications System (NATG)
NICS	Network Integrity Control System (NITA)
NICSO	NATO Integrated Communications System Organization (NATG)
NID	Network In-Dial [Automatic Voice Network] (CET)
NIDA	Numerically Integrated Differential Analyzer [Data processing]
NIF	Network Information Files [Burroughs Corp.] (NITA)
NIF	Noise Improvement Factor (IEEE)
NIFO	Next In, First Out (NITA)
NIH	National Institutes of Health [Public Health Service] [Bethesda, MD]
NIH	Not Invented Here [Industrial term] [Data processing colloquialism]
NII	Northouse Industries, Incorporated [Milwaukee, WI] [Software manufacturer] (DASOS)
NIKKEI	Nihon Keizai Shimbun, Inc. (EISS)

NIL	I have nothing to send to you [Telecommunications] (FAAC)
NILPT	National Institute for Low Power Television (EANO)
NIM	Network Interface Machine [Datapac] (NITA)
NIM	Network Interface Monitor (NITA)
NIMMS	Nineteen-Hundred Integrated Modular Management System (NITA)
NIMPH	Network Interface Message Processing Host [NERComP]
NIOD	Network In-Out Dial [Automatic Voice Network] (CET)
NIP	Network Input Processor [Data processing] (MCD)
NIP	Network Interface Processor (MCD)
NIP	Nonimpact Printer (NITA)
NIP	Nucleus Initialization Program [Data processing]
NIPNY	NEC Corp. ADR [NASDAQ symbol] (NQ)
NIPOLOS	Nonimpact Off-Line Operating System [Data processing]
NIPS	Nippon Information Processing System [Nippon Shuppan Hanbai, Inc.] [Database] (CUAD)
NIRC	National Information Retrieval Colloquium [Later, Benjamin Franklin Colloquium on Information Science]
NIS	National Information System [Later, GIP] [UNESCO] (BUR)
NIS	Network Information System [AT & T]
NIS	Network Interface System (NITA)
NIS	Noise Information System [Environmental Protection Agency] (EISS)
NISA	Numerically Integrated Elements System A [Harris Systems Ltd.] [Software package] [British] (NCC)
NISARC	National Information Storage and Retrieval Center
NISH	National Information Sources on the Handicapped [Clearinghouse on the Handicapped] [Database] (FDB)
NISTF	National Information Systems Task Force [Society of American Archivists] [Information service] (EISS)
NIT	National Instructional Television [Superseded by AIT] (EANO)
NITR	National Institute for Telecommunications Research [South Africa] (CIT)
NIU	Network Interface Unit [Data processing] (CCD)
NJCC	National Joint Computer Committee [of ACM, AIEE, IRE] [Superseded by AFIPS]
NJCL	Network Job Control Language (NITA)
NJE	Network Job Entry (NITA)
NJI	Network Job Interface (NITA)
NJS	Noise Jammer Simulator [Telecommunications] (TEL)
NJT	National Jewish Television [Cable-television system]
NL	New Line [Data processing]
NL	Non-Labeled [Tape] [Data processing]
NLC	New Line Character [Keyboard] [Data processing] (MDG)
NLCS	National Computer Systems, Inc. [NASDAQ symbol] (NQ)
NLDB	Natural Language Data Base
NLETS	National Law Enforcement Telecommunications System
NLL	National Lending Library for Science and Technology [Later, BLLD] [British Library]
NLLSQ	Nonlinear Least Squares [Computer program]
NLM	National Library of Medicine [Public Health Service] [Bethesda, MD] [Database producer]
NLOS	Natural Language Operating System (NITA)
NLP	Natural Language Processing [Data processing]
NLP	Nonlinear Programing [Algorithm]
NLQ	Near Letter Quality [Computer printer usage]
NLR	Noise Load Ratio
NLS	On-Line System [Stanford Research Institute] [Data processing]
NLSI	National Library of Science and Invention [British] (DIT)
NLSPN	National List of Scientific Plant Names [Department of Agriculture] (EISS)
NLST	Nonlisted Name [Telecommunications] (TEL)
NLT	Night Letter [Telegraphic communications]
NLT	Not Less Than
NM	Neiman-Marcus, Inc.
NM	Network Manager (MCD)
NM	Night Message
NM	Noise Meter (MSA)
NMA	National Management Association [Dayton, OH]
NMA	National Microfilm Association [Later, National Micrographics Association, now AIIM] [Trade association] (CAH)
NMA	National Micrographics Association [Later, AIIM] [Silver Spring, MD] [Trade association]
NMAA	National Machine Accountants Association [Later, DPMA]
NMC	Network Management Center [Data processing]
NMC	Network Measurement Center (NITA)
NMCS	National Military Command System
NMF	New Master File (NITA)
NMF	Nonmaster File [Data processing]
NMI	Nonmasking Interrupt
NMI	Northwest Microfilm, Incorporated [Information service] (EISS)
NMMW	Near Millimeter Wave System [Telecommunications] (TEL)
NMOS	Negative Channel Metal-Oxide Semiconductor
NMOS	Nonvolatile Metal-Oxide Semiconductor (MCD)
NMRA	National Mobile Radio Association (EANO)
NMRLIT	Nuclear Magnetic Resonance Literature Search System [National Institutes of Health] [Database] (FDB)
NMRS	National Mobile Radio System [Later, Telocator Network of America]
NMS	Network Management Services [Ohio Bell Communications, Inc.] [Cleveland, OH] [Telecommunications] (TSSD)
NMS	Network Management Signal [Telecommunications] (TEL)
NMS	Network Measurement System [Computer network]

Computer & Telecommunications Acronyms

Acronym	Definition
NMS	Noise Measuring Set [*Telecommunications*] (TEL)
NMSD	Next Most Significant Digit (OA)
NMT	Nordic Mobile Telephone [*Radio-telephone system for car users*] [*Denmark, Finland, Norway, Sweden*]
NN	Nearest Neighbor [*Mathematics*] [*Computer search term*]
NNA	New Network Architecture (NITA)
NN/CA	National Numerical Control Applications [*Buffalo, NY*] [*Software manufacturer*] (DASOS)
NND	National Network Dialing [*Telecommunications*] (TEL)
NNDC	National Nuclear Data Center [*Department of Energy*] (EISS)
NNECH	National Nutrition Education Clearing House [*Society for Nutrition Education*] (EISS)
NNI	National Newspaper Index [*Information Access Co.*] [*Bibliographic database*] [*Information service*] (EISS)
NNR	National Number Routed [*Telecommunications*] (TEL)
NO	Normally Open [*Switch*]
NO	Not Or [*Logical operator*] [*Data processing*]
NO	Notes [*Online database field identifier*] (OBD)
NO	Number
N-O-A	Not-Or-And [*Data processing*]
NOAA	National Oceanic and Atmospheric Administration [*Pronounced "Noah"*] [*Rockville, MD*] [*Department of Commerce*]
NOALA	Noise-Operated Automatic Level Adjustment
NOC	National Online Circuit [*Santa Barbara Public Library*] [*Santa Barbara, CA*] [*Online user group*] [*An association*] (EANO)
NOC	Network Operation Center [*Bell System*]
NOCF	National Office Computer Facility [*IRS*]
NOCP	Network Operator Control Program (NITA)
NOD	Network Out-Dial [*Automatic Voice Network*] (CET)
NOD	Noise Output Device
NODAL	Network-Oriented Data Acquisition Language (NITA)
NODAN	Noise-Operated Device for Antinoise [*Telecommunications*] (TEL)
NODAP	Nonlinear Distortion Analysis Program [*Bell System*]
NODC	National Oceanographic Data Center [*Washington, DC*] [*National Oceanic and Atmospheric Administration*] [*Databank originator*]
NOF	NCR [*NCR Corp.*] Optical Font (MCD)
NOF	Network Operations Forum [*Exchange Carriers Standards Association*] [*Telecommunications*]
NOGAD	Noise-Operated Gain-Adjusting Device
NOLC	National Obscenity Law Center (EISS)
NOLO	No Live Operator (NG)
NOM	Number of Open Microphones
NOMAD	[*A*] programing language (CSR)
NOMDA	National Office Machine Dealers Association
NONSAP	Nonlinear Structural Analysis Program [*Data processing*]
NOOP	No Operation (NITA)
NOP	No Operation [*Data processing*]
NOR	Not Or [*Logical operator*] [*Data processing*]
NORD	Norsk Data [*Manufacturer and computer series*] [*Norway*] (NITA)
NORDICOM	Nordic Documentation Center for Mass Communication Research [*Finland*] [*Database originator*] [*Information service*] (EISS)
NORDINFO	Nordic Council for Scientific Information and Research Libraries [*Finland*] [*Information service*] (EISS)
NORIANE	Normes et Reglements Informations Automatisees Accessibles en Ligne [*Automated Standards and Regulations Information Online*] [*Association Francaise de Normalisation*] [*Databank*] [*Information service*] [*France*] (EISS)
NORMATERM	Normalisation, Automatisation de la Terminologie [*Standardization and Automation of Terminology*] [*Databank*] [*Information service*] [*France*] (EISS)
NORTEB	Norwegian Telecommunications Users Group [*Oslo*] (TSSD)
NORTR	Nortronics Corp. (DDI)
NOS	Network Operating System (NITA)
NOSBE	Network Operating System/Batch Environment (NITA)
NOSP	Network Operation Support Program [*Data processing*]
NOTAL	Not at All
NOTAL	Not to, nor Needed by, All
NOTES	National Organization of Telecommunications Engineers and Scientists [*Telecommunications*] (TSSD)
NOTIS	Network Operations Trouble Information System [*Telecommunications*] (TEL)
NOTIS	Northwestern On-Line Total Integrated System [*Northwestern University Library*] [*Evanston, IL*] [*Library automation project*] [*Information service*] (EISS)
NOWT	Northwest Telecommunications [*NASDAQ symbol*] (NQ)
NP	Network Planning [*Data processing*] (TUT)
NP	No Parity (NITA)
NP	No Print [*Telecommunications*] (TEL)
NP	Nonpolarized [*Data processing*]
NP	Northern Pine [*Utility pole*] [*Telecommunications*] (TEL)
NPA	National Payphone Association (EANO)
NPA	New Product Announcements [*Database*]
NPA	Numbering Plan Area [*Bell System*] [*Telecommunications*]
NPA	PTS [*Predicasts*] New Product Announcements [*Cleveland, OH*] [*Information service*] (EISS)
NPC	Nonprinting Character [*Data processing*]
NPD	Network Protection Device [*Telecommunications*] (TEL)
NPDA	Network Problem Determination Application [*Data processing*]
NPDC	National Planning Data Corporation [*Information service*] (EISS)
NPF	Network Pulse Forming
NPIRS	National Pesticide Information Retrieval System [*Database*] (FDB)
NPIS	National Physics Information System [*American Institute of Physics*] [*New York, NY*] (DIT)
NPL	New Product Line (CGC)
NPL	New Programing Language [*1974*] [*Later, PL/1*] [*Data processing*] (CGC)
NPM	Narrowband Phase Modulation (DEN)
N-P-N	Negative-Positive-Negative [*Transistor*] (CET)
NPNP	Negative-Positive-Negative-Positive [*Transistor*]
NPP	Network Protocol Processor (NITA)
NPR	National Public Radio [*Washington, DC*] [*Telecommunications*] (TSSD)
NPR	Noise Power Ratio
NPR	Noise Prediction and Reduction
NPRL	Nonprocedural Referencing Language (NITA)
NPS	Network Processing Supervisor [*Honeywell, Inc.*] (NITA)
NPS	Numerical Plotting System
NPSA	New Program Status Area (IEEE)
NPSWL	New Program Status Word Location (NITA)
NPT	Network Planning Technique [*Data processing*] (IEEE)
NPTN	National Pesticide Telecommunications Network (EANO)
NPU	Network Processing Unit (NITA)
NQD	Nonquaded [*Telecommunications*] (TEL)
NQR	Nuclear Quadrupole Resonance [*Frequencies*]
NR	Noise Ratio
NRBA	National Radio Broadcasters Association [*Formerly, FMDA, NAFMB*]
NRC	Nonrecurring Costs (KSC)
NRCd	National Reprographic Centre for Documentation [*Hatfield Polytechnic Institute*] [*Hertfordshire, England*] [*Evaluation and information group*] [*Information service*]
NRC/DME	National Research Council of Canada, Division of Mechanical Engineering [*Ottawa, ON*] [*Research center*] (RCD)
NRCL	National Research Council Library (DIT)
NRFD	Not Ready for Data (NITA)
NRI	National Resource Inventory [*US database on erosion*]
NRI	Net Radio Interface [*Telecommunications*] (TEL)
NRI	Nomura Research Institute [*Database producer*] (CUAD)
NRI	Nonrecurring Installation Charge [*Telecommunications*] (TEL)
NRIC	National Rehabilitation Information Center [*Catholic University of America*] [*Database*] (FDB)
NRIC	Nuclear Research Information Center [*American Nuclear Center*] [*Information service*] (EISS)
NRL	National Research Library [*Canada*] (DIT)
NRL	Network Restructuring Language (NITA)
NRM	Normal Response Mode (NITA)
NRMS	Natural Resource Management System [*Army Corps of Engineers*] [*Database*] (FDB)
NRRI	National Regulatory Research Institute [*Ohio State University*] [*Research center*] (RCD)
NRSCC	National Registry System for Chemical Compounds (DIT)
NRZ	Nonreturn to Zero [*Data transmission*]
NRZ1	Nonreturn to Zero Change on One (BUR)
NRZC	Nonreturn to Zero Change
NRZI	Nonreturn to Zero Inverted [*Recording method*]
NRZL	Nonreturn to Zero Level
NRZM	Nonreturn to Zero Mark
ns	Nanosecond [*100 billionth of a second*] [*Also, nsec*]
N-S	Nassi-Schneiderman [*Data processing*]
NS	New System [*Data processing*] (CGC)
NS	Next System [*Data processing*] (CGC)
NSC	National Semiconductor Corporation (NITA)
NSC	National Society of Computer/Genealogists (EANO)
NSC	Network Switching Center [*Telecommunications*] (TEL)
NSC	Network Systems Corporation [*Brooklyn Park, MN*] [*Telecommunications*] (TSSD)
NSC	Nodal Switching Center (NITA)
NSCA	National Satellite Cable Association (EANO)
NSCA	National Sound and Communications Association (EANO)
NSCEC	National School Curriculum Center for Educational Computing (EANO)
NSCO	Network Systems Corporation [*NASDAQ symbol*] (NQ)
NSCS	North Star Computer Society [*Seattle, WA*] (EANO)
NSD	Next Most Significant Digit [*Data processing*]
NSD	Norsk Samfunnsvitenskapelig Datatjeneste [*Norwegian Social Science Data Services*] [*Information service*] (EISS)
nsec	Nanosecond [*100 billionth of a second*] [*Also, ns*]
NSEI	Norsk Selskap for Elektronisk Informasjonselskap [*Norwegian Computer Society*] [*Oslo, Norway*]
NSF	National Science Foundation [*Washington, DC*] [*Database originator*]
NSF	Norges Standardiseringsforbund [*Norwegian Standards Association*] [*Information service*] (EISS)
NSG	Newspaper Systems Group [*An association*] (EANO)
NSH	Nashua Corp. [*NYSE symbol*]
NSI	Network Strategies, Incorporated [*Burke, VA*] [*Telecommunications*] (TSSD)
NSI	Next Sequential Instruction (NITA)
NSI	Norsk Senter for Informatikk [*Norwegian Center for Informatics*] [*Information broker, host, and database originator*] [*Information service*] (EISS)

NSL............ National Science Library [*Later, Canada Institute for Scientific and Technical Information*] (DIT)
NSL............ Net Switching Loss [*Telecommunications*] (TEL)
NSL............ Nonstandard Label [*Data processing*]
NSM........... National Semiconductor Corp. [*NYSE symbol*]
NSM........... Network Security Module (NITA)
NSN............ National Stock Number (MCD)
NSO............ Noise Suppression Oscillator (MCD)
NSP............ Network Services Protocol [*Digital Equipment Corp.*] [*Telecommunications*] (TEL)
NSP............ Network Signal Processor (NASA)
NSPC.......... National Sound-Program Center [*Telecommunications*] (TEL)
NSPI........... National Society for Performance and Instruction [*Formerly, National Society for Programed Instruction*] [*Washington, DC*]
NSR............ Nuclear Structure References [*Database*] (ODIN)
NSRS.......... National Scholarship Research Service [*Information service*] (EISS)
NSS............ Network Supervisor System (NITA)
NSS............ Network Support System [*Data processing*]
NSS............ Network Synchronization Subsystem [*Telecommunications*] (TEL)
NSS............ Noise Suppressor System (MCD)
NSTAF........ National Solar Technical Audience File [*Solar Energy Research Institute*] [*Database*] (FDB)
NSTDB....... National Strategic Target Data Base
NSTN.......... Nonstandard Telephone Number [*Telecommunications*] (TEL)
NSUR......... Compu-Plan, Inc. [*NASDAQ symbol*] (NQ)
NSV............ Nonautomatic Self-Verification [*Data processing*] (MDG)
NSW........... National Software Works (NITA)
NSY............ National Systems Corp. [*American Stock Exchange symbol*] [*Delisted*]
NT............... No Transmission [*Telecommunications*] (CDH)
NT............... Northern Telecom Ltd. [*NYSE symbol*]
NT............... Note [*Online database field identifier*] (OBD)
NTA............. National Telecommunications Agency (NITA)
NTA............. Norwegian Telecommunications Administration [*Oslo*] (TSSD)
NTC............ National Telecommunications Conference [*IEEE*]
NTC............ National Television Center [*Telecommunications*] (TEL)
NTC............ National Timesharing Council (EANO)
NTCA.......... National Telephone Cooperative Association [*Washington, DC*]
NTCC.......... Neutron Transport Computer Code
NTD............ Neutron Transmutation Doped [*Silicon for semiconductor use*]
NTF............. National Theater File [*Theater Sources, Inc.*] [*Information service*] (EISS)
NTF............. No Trouble Found (NITA)
NTI.............. Noise Transmission Impairment [*Telecommunications*]
NTIA........... National Telecommunications and Information Administration [*Department of Commerce*]
NTIC........... Nondestructive Testing Information Center [*Battelle Memorial Institute*] [*Databank*] [*Information service*] (EISS)
NTIS............ National Technical Information Service [*Department of Commerce*] [*Springfield, VA*] [*Database producer and database*]
NTIS............ NEC [*Nippon Electric Company*]-Toshiba Information Systems, Inc. [*Japan*] (NITA)
NTL............. Night Telegraph Letter
NTL............. Northern Telecom Limited [*Toronto Stock Exchange symbol*] [*Vancouver Stock Exchange symbol*]
NTM........... Night Message (MSA)
NTN............ National Telecommunications Network [*Boca Raton, FL*] (TSSD)
NTNF.......... Norges Teknisk-Naturvitenskapelige Forskningsraad [*Online database*]
NTO............ Network Terminal Option [*Data processing*]
NTOTC....... National Training and Operational Technology Center [*Cincinnati, OH*] [*Environmental Protection Agency*] (EISS)
NTP............. Network Terminal Protocol (NITA)
NTP............. Network Terminating Point [*Telecommunications*] (TEL)
NTP............. Network Termination Processor (NITA)
NTPF.......... Number of Terminals per Failure [*Data processing*]
NTR............ Next Task Register (NITA)
NTR............ Noise Temperature Ratio
NTS............ National Traffic System [*Amateur radio*]
NTS............ Non-Traffic Sensitive [*Costs*] [*Telecommunications*]
NTSC.......... National Television Standard Code [*Video equipment*] (RDA)
NTSC.......... National Television Systems Committee
NTSK.......... Nordiska Tele-Satelit Kommitton [*Norway*] (OA)
NTT............. Nippon Telegraph and Telephone [*Telecommunications and videotex company*] [*Japan*]
NTU............ Network Terminating Unit
NTV............ Nippon Television Network Corp. [*Japan*]
NU.............. Nullified Unpostable [*Data processing*]
NU.............. Number Unobtainable [*Telecommunications*]
NUA............ Network User Address [*Information retrieval*] (ODIN)
NUA............ Network Users Association (EANO)
NUBA.......... National UHF [*Ultrahigh Frequency*] Broadcasting Association (EANO)
NUC............ National University Consortium for Telecommunications in Teaching (EANO)
NUCSEQ..... Nucleotide Sequencing Search System
NUDETS..... Nuclear Detonation Detection and Reporting System
NUFTIC....... Nuclear Fuels Technology Information Center (DIT)

NUG............ Federation of NCR User Groups (EANO)
NUI.............. Network User Identifier [*Password*] (DEEC)
NUL............. Null Character [*Keyboard*] [*Data processing*]
NUM............ Number [*or Numerator, or Numeric*] (CAH)
NUM............ Numeral [*or Numerical*]
NUMERALS... Numerical Analysis System (BUR)
NUT............. Number Unobtainable Tone [*Telecommunications*] (TEL)
NUTN.......... National University Teleconference Network [*Stillwater, OK*] [*Telecommunications*] (TSSD)
NVC............ National Video Clearinghouse, Inc. [*Information service*] (EISS)
NVRAM....... Nonvolatile Random-Access Memory [*Data processing*]
NVS............. Narrowband Voice Security
NVSM.......... Nonvolatile Semiconductor Memory (MCD)
NVT............. Network Virtual Terminal (NITA)
NW.............. Northwest
NWC............ Newcorp, Inc. [*American Stock Exchange symbol*] [*Delisted*]
NWCS......... NATO-Wide Communications System (NATG)
NWD........... Network Wide Directory (NITA)
NWES......... Norwesco, Inc. [*NASDAQ symbol*] (NQ)
NWL............ Natural Wavelength
NWSA......... Northwest Software Associates [*Spokane, WA*] [*Software manufacturer*] (DASOS)
NYAP.......... New York Assembly Program [*Data processing*]
NYET LC..... Not Yet in Library of Congress [*Suggested name for the Library of Congress computer system*]
NYNEX........ New York New England Exchange [*Telecommunications*]
NYPS.......... National Yellow Pages Service
NYRA.......... New York Racing Authority [*Cable-television system*]
NYSE.......... New York Stock Exchange
NYTIS......... New York Times Information Service, Inc. [*Database originator and host*] (EISS)
NZPO.......... New Zealand Post Office [*Telecommunications*] (TEL)
NZT............. Nonzero Transfer (NITA)

O

O	Octal [*Number system with a base of eight*] [*Data processing*] (BUR)		OCC	Octal Correction Cards [*Data processing*]
O	Operation		OCC	Operational Computer Complex (KSC)
O	Operator		OCC	Operations Control Center [*or Console*] (AFM)
O	Output (BUR)		OCC	Operator Control Command (BUR)
O	Overall Rating [*Broadcasting*]		OCC	Other Common Carrier [*Telecommunications*]
OA	Omniantenna		OCCF	Operator Communication and Control Facility [*IBM Corp.*]
OA	Operand Address Register (NITA)		OCCM	Office of Commercial Communications Management (AFM)
OA	Operational Amplifier [*Telecommunications*] (TEL)		OCCP	Outside Communications Cable Plant (CET)
OA	Output Amplitude		OCCULT	Optical Covert Communications Using LASER Transceivers (MCD)
OAAU	Orthogonal Array Arithmetic Unit (NITA)		OCCULT	Ordered Computer Collation of Unprepared Literary Texts
OAC	Office of Academic Computing [*University of California, Los Angeles*] [*Research center*] (RCD)		OCD	Office of Civil Defense
OADMS	Office of Automated Data Management Services [*General Services Administration*]		OCF	Operator Console Facility [*Data processing*] (IBMDP)
			OCG	Optimal Code Generation
OAF	Origin Address Field [*Data processing*] (IBMDP)		OCHC	Operator Call Handling Center [*Telecommunications*] (TEL)
OAG-EE	Official Airline Guide-Electronic Edition [*Official Airline Guides, Inc.*] [*Database*] (CUAD)		OCI	Office of Computer Information [*Department of Commerce*] [*Originator and database*]
OAIDE	Operational Assistance and Instructive Data Equipment		OCI	Optically Coupled Isolator (OA)
OAM	Oscillator Activity Monitor [*Telecommunications*] (TEL)		OCIS	Office of Computing and Information Services [*University of Georgia*] [*Research center*] (RCD)
OAMP	Optical Analog Matrix Processing		OCL	Operator Control Language [*Data processing*] (BUR)
OANAD	Online-ADL-Nachrichten [*A publication*]		OCL	Overall Connection Loss [*Telecommunications*] (TEL)
OAP	Orthogonal Array Processor [*Computer*] (NITA)		OCLC	Online Computer Library Center [*Formerly, Ohio College Library Center. Initialism used in reference to cataloging system it developed*] [*Information service*]
OAPCB	Old-Age-Pensioner CBer [*Experienced citizens band radio operator*]			
OAPM	Optimal Amplitude and Phase Modulation		OCM	Oscillator and Clock Module (NITA)
OAR	Operator Authorization Record [*Data processing*] (IBMDP)		OCMS	Optional Calling Measured Service [*Telecommunications*] (TEL)
OARAC	Office of Air Research Automatic Computer		OCP	Order Code Processor [*International Computers Ltd.*] (NITA)
OARS	On-Line Automated Reference Service [*Library science*]		OCP	Output Control Program (NITA)
OAS	Office Automation System [*Prime Computer Ltd.*] [*Software package*] [*British*] (NCC)		OCP	Overload Control Process [*Telecommunications*] (TEL)
			OCPO	Office of Computer Processing Operations [*Social Security Administration*]
OAS	Organization of American States [*Washington, DC*]		OCR	Optical Character Reader [*Data processing*]
OASC	Office of Advanced Scientific Computing [*National Science Foundation*]		OCR	Optical Character Recognition [*Data processing*]
			OCR	Output Control Register (NITA)
OASD(T)	Office of the Assistant Secretary of Defense (Telecommunications)		OCRA	Optical Character Recognition - ANSI Standard (Font A) (CAH)
OASI	Office Automation Society International (EANO)		OCRB	Optical Character Recognition - ANSI Standard (Font B) (CAH)
OASIS	Operational Automatic Scheduling Information System (MUGU)		OCRE	Optical Character Recognition Equipment [*Data processing*]
OASIS	Outlook and Situation Information System [*Department of Agriculture*] (EISS)		OCRUA	Optical Character Recognition Users Association [*Later, RTUA*] (EANO)
OASYS	Office Automation System (NITA)		OCS	Office of Computing Services [*Georgia Institute of Technology*] [*Research center*] (RCD)
OASYS	Order Allocation System (CGC)			
OB	Octal-to-Binary [*Data processing*] (BUR)		OCS	Operations Control System
OB	Output Buffer [*Data processing*]		OCS	Optical Character Scanner [*Data processing*]
OB	Output Bus (NITA)		OCS	Optical Communicator System (MCD)
OB	Outside Broadcasts		OCS	Output Control Subsystem (OA)
OBC	Ohio Bell Communications, Inc. [*Telecommunications*] (TSSD)		OCS	Overload Control Subsystem [*Telecommunications*] (TEL)
OBC	On-Board Computer (MCD)		OCSP	Office of Cued Speech Programs [*Gallaudet College*] [*Research center*] (RCD)
OBC	One Big Computer [*Proposed model for automation of the New York and American stock exchanges*]		OCT	Octal [*Number system with a base of eight*] [*Data processing*] (CET)
OBH	Office Busy Hour [*Telecommunications*] (TEL)		OCT	Operational Cycle Time (OA)
OBI	Omnibearing Indicator [*Radio*]		OCTL	Open-Circuited Transmission Line
OBN	Office Balancing Network [*Telecommunications*] (TEL)		OCTV	Open-Circuit Television
OBN	Out-of-Band Noise (CBSS)		OCU	Operational Control Unit
OBR	Optical Bar Code		OCV	Open-Circuit Voltage (CIT)
OBR	Outboard Recorder (BUR)		OD	Oceanographic Datastation [*Telecommunications*] (TEL)
OBS	Official Bulletin Station [*Amateur radio*]		OD	Octal-to-Decimal [*Data processing*] (BUR)
OBS	Omnibearing Selector [*Radio*]		OD	Output Data (IEEE)
OBS	On-Line Business Systems, Inc. [*Information service*] (EISS)		OD	Output Disable (NITA)
OBTS	Offender Base Transaction Statistical System [*Department of Justice*] [*Washington, DC*] [*Database*] [*Information service*] (EISS)		OD	Outside Diameter
			OD	Overload Detection [*Telecommunications*] (TEL)
OC	Occurs (MDG)		ODA	Octal Debugging Aid [*Data processing*]
OC	On Call (BUR)		ODA	Omnidirectional Antenna
OC	Operational Computer (IEEE)		ODA	Operational Design and Analysis (IEEE)
OC	Output Computer		ODA	Oscillating Doublet Antenna
OCA	Office of Computing Activities [*Later, DCR*] [*National Science Foundation*]		ODAC	On Demand Analyzer Computer
			ODB	Output Data Buffer (NITA)
OCAL	Online Cryptanalytic Aid Language [*Data processing*] (TUT)		ODB	Output to Display Buffer [*Data processing*]
OCAM	Office, Computing, and Accounting Machinery		ODC	Output Data Control (NITA)
OCAS	Online Cryptanalytic Aid System [*Data processing*] (IEEE)		ODCC	On-Board Digital Computer Control
OCB	Outgoing Calls Barred [*Telecommunications*] (TEL)		ODCP	One-Digit Code Point [*Telecommunications*] (TEL)
OCB	Override Control BITS [*Binary Digits*] [*Data processing*]		ODD	Operator Distance Dialing

Computer & Telecommunications Acronyms

ODD	....	Optical Data Digitizer [*Data processing*]
ODD	....	Optical Digital Data Disc
ODDH	....	On-Board Digital Data Handling
ODESY	....	Online Data Entry System [*Burroughs Corp.*] (NITA)
ODG	....	Offline Data Generator (NITA)
ODIN	....	Online Dokumentations- und Informationsverbund [*Online Documentation and Information Affiliation*] (ODIN)
ODIN	....	Optimal [*or Orbital*] Design Integration [*Computer program*]
ODIS	....	Optical Disk Interface System [*Data processing*]
ODM	....	Optical Display Memory [*Data processing*]
ODM	....	Outboard Data Manager (BUR)
ODP	....	Optical Data Processing
ODR	....	Omnidirectional Range
ODR	....	Operator Data Register [*Telecommunications*] (TEL)
ODR	....	Output Definition Register (NITA)
ODS	....	Output Data Strobe
ODSI	....	Ocean Data Systems, Incorporated [*Rockville, MD*] [*Information service*] (EISS)
ODT	....	Octal Debugging Technique (IEEE)
ODT	....	Omnidirection Transmission
ODT	....	Online Debugging Technique (NITA)
ODTS	....	Optical Data Transmission System
ODU	....	Optical Display Unit [*Data processing*] (MCD)
ODU	....	Output Display Unit [*Data processing*]
OE	....	Original Entry [*Data processing*]
OE	....	Output Enable [*Semiconductor memory*] (IEEE)
OE	....	Own Exchange [*Telecommunications*] (TEL)
OEAP	....	Operational Error Analysis Program (NITA)
OECD	....	Organization for Economic Cooperation and Development [*Databank originator*]
OEDSF	....	On-Board Experimental Data Support Facility
OEIS	....	Office of Energy Information Services [*Department of Energy*] (EISS)
OEM	....	Original Equipment Manufacturer
OEM	....	Other Equipment Manufacturers (CMD)
OEMI	....	Office Equipment Manufacturers Institute [*Later, CBEMA*]
OES	....	Official Experimental Station [*Amateur radio*]
OES	....	Outgoing Echo Suppressor [*Telecommunications*] (TEL)
Oesterr Z Elektrizitaetswirtsch	...	Oesterreichische Zeitschrift fuer Elektrizitaetswirtschaft [*A publication*]
OF	....	One of the Firm [*Telecommunications*] (TEL)
OF	....	Output Factor [*Data processing*] (IEEE)
OF	....	Overflow
OFHC	....	Oxygen-Free, High-Conductivity [*Copper*]
OFNPS	....	Outstate Facility Network Planning System [*Telecommunications*] (TEL)
OFR	....	Off Frequency Rejection [*Radio communications*]
OFT	....	Optical Fiber Tube (NITA)
OFTEL	....	Office of Telecommunications [*Independent government agency*] [*British*]
OG	....	Or Gate [*Data processing*]
O/G	....	Outgoing [*Data processing*]
OGC	....	Oregon Graduate Center for Study and Research [*Beaverton, OR*] [*Research center*] (RCD)
OGDD	....	Outgoing/Delay Dial [*Telecommunications*] (TEL)
OGID	....	Outgoing/Immediate Dial [*Telecommunications*] (TEL)
OGJ	....	Outgoing Junction [*Telecommunications*] (TEL)
OGL	....	Outgoing Line
OGP	....	Outgoing Message Process [*Telecommunications*] (TEL)
OGR	....	Outgoing Repeater
OGT	....	Outgoing Trunk
OGWS	....	Outgoing/Wink Start [*Telecommunications*] (TEL)
O-H	....	Octal-to-Hexadecimal (IEEE)
OH	....	Overhead
OHM	....	Ohmmeter
OHM-TADS	...	Oil and Hazardous Materials Technical Assistance Data System [*Environmental Protection Agency*] [*Databank*] (EISS)
OHS	....	Occupational Health Services, Inc. [*Medical databank originator*] [*Information service*]
OHS	....	Off-Hook Service [*Telecommunications*] (TEL)
OHS MSDS	...	Occupational Health Services Material Safety Data Sheets [*Database*] (CUAD)
OIC	....	Online Instrument and Control Program [*Data processing*]
OID	....	Octal Identifier [*Data processing*] (KSC)
OIDI	....	Optically Isolated Digital Input (NITA)
OIDPS	....	Oversea Intelligence Data Processing System
OIR	....	Organisation Internationale de Radiodiffusion [*International Radio Organization*]
OIRT	....	Organisation Internationale de Radiodiffusion et Television [*International Radio and Television Organization*]
OIS	....	Office of Information Systems [*Social and Rehabilitation Service, HEW*]
OISE	....	Ontario Institute for Studies in Education [*University of Toronto*] [*Research center*] (RCD)
OITT	....	Outpulser, Identifier, Trunk Test
OIU	....	Operator Interface Unit [*Data processing*]
OJ	....	Originating Junctor [*Telecommunications*] (TEL)
OJT	....	On-the-Job Training
OL	....	Online (CAH)
OL	....	Operating Level (IEEE)
OL	....	Other Line [*Telecommunications*] (TEL)
OL	....	Output Latch (NITA)
OLAC	....	Offline Adaptive Computer [*Data processing*]
OLAS	....	On-Line Acquisitions Systems [*Brodart, Inc.*] [*Book acquisition system*] [*Information service*] (EISS)
OLB	....	Open-Loop Bandwidth [*Also, OLBW*]
OLB	....	Outer Lead Bond [*Integrated circuit technology*]
OLBW	....	Open-Loop Bandwidth [*Also, OLB*]
OLC	....	Online Computer [*System*] [*Data processing*]
OLC	....	Outgoing Line Circuit
OLCA	....	Online Circuit Analysis [*System*] [*Data processing*]
OLDB	....	Online Database (NITA)
OLDC	....	Online Data Collection [*Data processing*] (MCD)
OLDS	....	Offshore Lease Data System [*Department of the Interior*] [*Information service*] (EISS)
OLDS	....	Online Display System [*Data processing*]
OLE	....	On-Line Encyclopedia [*Hypergraphics Corp.*]
OLERT	....	Online Executive for Real Time [*Data processing*] (IEEE)
OLHMIS	......	On-Line Hospital Management Information System [*Data processing*]
OLIFLM	....	Online Image Forming Light Modulator (NITA)
OLIP	....	Online Instrument Package [*Data processing*]
OLIS	....	Oregon Legislative Information System [*Information service*]
OLL	....	Output Logic Level
OLLS	....	Online Logical Simulation System [*Data processing*] (KSC)
OLM	....	Online Monitor [*Data processing*]
OLO	....	Online Operation [*Data processing*]
OLOE	....	Online Order Entry (NITA)
OLP	....	Online Processor (TEL)
OLP	....	Online Programing (NITA)
OLPARS	.....	Online Pattern Analysis and Recognition System [*Data processing*] (MCD)
OLPS	....	Online Programing System [*Data processing*]
OLR	....	Objective Loudness Rating [*of telephone connections*] (IEEE)
OLR	....	Offline Recovery [*Telecommunications*] (TEL)
OLR	....	Open-Loop Receiver [*or Response*] (CIT)
OLR	....	Outgoing Long-Wave Radiation [*Satellite sensed*]
OLR	....	Overload Relay
OLRT	....	Online Real Time [*Data processing*]
OLS	....	Online Scan [*Data processing*] (CAAL)
OLS	....	Online System
OL'SAM	......	Online Database Search Assistance Machine [*Franklin Institute*] [*Information service*] (EISS)
OLSC	....	Online Scientific Computer [*Data processing*]
OLSF	....	Online Subsystem Facility [*Data processing*] (MCD)
OLSS	....	Online Software System [*Data processing*] (IEEE)
OLT	....	Online Test [*Data processing*]
OLTEP	....	On-Line Test Executive Program [*IBM Corp.*] [*Data processing*]
OLTS	....	Online Test System [*Data processing*] (BUR)
OLTS	....	Online Time Share [*Data processing*]
OLTT	....	Online Terminal Test [*Data processing*] (IBMDP)
OLUD	....	Online Update (TEL)
OLUM	....	Online Update Control Module (TEL)
OM	....	Old Man [*Communications operators' colloquialism*]
O & M	....	Operation and Maintenance
OM	....	Operations Manager (CIT)
OM	....	Output Module (NITA)
OMA	....	Operations Monitor Alarm (NITA)
OMAC	....	Online Manufacturing, Accounting, and Control System (NITA)
OMAP	....	Object Module Assembly Program (NITA)
OMAR	....	Optical Mark Reader [*Data processing*]
OMB	....	Office of Management and Budget [*Washington, DC*] [*Formerly, Bureau of the Budget*]
OMC	....	Operations Monitoring Computer
OMD	....	Open Macrodefinition (NITA)
OMEF	....	Office Machines and Equipment Federation [*British*] (DIT)
OMF	....	Old Master File (NITA)
OMFS	....	Office Master Frequency Supply [*Telecommunications*] (TEL)
OMI	....	Omnibus Computer Graphics, Inc. [*Toronto Stock Exchange symbol*]
OMIBAC	.....	Ordinal Memory Inspecting Binary Automatic Computer (IEEE)
OMIS	....	Operational Management Information System [*Data processing*]
OML	....	Outgoing Matching Loss [*Telecommunications*] (TEL)
OMM	....	Organisation Meteorologique Mondiale [*World Meteorological Organization - WMO*]
OMM	....	Organizacion Meteorologica Mundial [*World Meteorological Organization - WMO*] [*Spanish*]
OMNI	....	Omnidirectional (SKY)
OMNIRANGE	...	Omnidirectional Radio Range (MSA)
OMNITAB	....	Omnibus Program with Tabular Numerical Functions [*Programing language*] [*1965*] (CSR)
OMNITENNA	...	Omnirange Antenna
OMNRF	....	Omni Resources, Inc. [*NASDAQ symbol*] (NQ)
OMPR	....	Optical Mark Page Reader [*Data processing*]
OMR	....	Optical Mark Reader [*Data processing*]
OMR	....	Optical Mark Recognition [*Data processing*] (MCD)
OMS	....	Output Multiplex Synchronizer
OMS	....	Overnight Message Service [*Diversified Data Processing and Consulting, Inc.*] [*Oak Park, MI*] [*Telecommunications*] (TSSD)
OMTC	....	Ontario Ministry of Transportation and Communications [*Downsview, ON*] [*Telecommunications*] (TSSD)
OMTN	....	Other Military Teletypewriter Network (CET)
ONAL	....	Off-Net Access Line [*Telecommunications*] (TEL)
ONC	....	Ordinary National Certificate [*British*]
ONE	....	Office Network Exchange [*Honeywell, Inc.*]

Computer & Telecommunications Acronyms

ONGA .... Overseas Number Group Analysis [*Telecommunications*]   (TEL)
ONI .... Operator Number Identification [*Bell System*]
ONIX .... Onyx + IMI, Inc. [*NASDAQ symbol*]   (NQ)
ONL .... On-Line Systems, Inc. [*American Stock Exchange symbol*] [*Delisted*]
ONLICATS ... Online Shared Cataloging System [*Data processing*]
Online .... Online Review [*A publication*]
Online Database Rep ... Online Database Report [*A publication*]
Online Rev ... Online Review [*A publication*]
On-Line Rv ... On-Line Review [*A publication*]
ONLY .... Online Yield [*Data processing*]
ON-OFF ...... Oscillatory, Nonoscillatory Flip-Flop [*Data processing*]
ONTAP .... On-Line Training and Practice File [*Lockheed*] [*Data processing*]
OOB .... Out of Band [*Telecommunications*]   (TEL)
OOC .... Over-Ocean Communications
OOD .... Object-Oriented Design [*Data processing*]
OOK .... On-Off Keying [*Data processing*]   (IEEE)
OOL .... Operator-Oriented Language [*Data processing*]
OOLR .... Overall Objective Loudness Rating [*of telephone connections*]   (IEEE)
OOO .... Out of Order [*Telecommunications*]   (TEL)
OOPS .... Off-Line Operating Simulator [*Data processing*]
OOR .... Operator Override [*Telecommunications*]   (TEL)
OOS .... Operational Operating System [*Telecommunications*]   (TEL)
OOT .... Out-of-Town [*Word processing*]
OP .... Operation   (AFM)
OP .... Output
OPA .... Optoelectronic Pulse Amplifier
OPAC .... Online Public Access Catalog
OPAL .... Operational Performance Analysis Language [*Data processing*]
OP AMP ...... Operational Amplifier
OPASTCO ... Organization for the Protection and Advancement of Small Telephone Companies [*Washington, DC*] [*Telecommunications*]   (EANO)
OPC .... Online Plotter Controller [*California Computer Products, Inc.*]   (NITA)
OPC .... Operation Code   (NITA)
OPC .... Operator Position Controller [*Telecommunications*]
OPC .... Optional Calling Plans [*Telecommunications*]   (TEL)
OPCE .... Operator Control Element [*Data processing*]   (IBMDP)
OP-COM ..... Operations-Communications
OPD .... Operational Programing Department [*Telecommunications*]   (TEL)
OPE .... Optimized Processing Element   (NITA)
OPEN .... Open Protocol Enhanced Network [*Northern Telecom communications network*] [*Canada*]
OPERATORS ... Optimization Program for Economical Remote Trunk Arrangement and TSPS [*Traffic Service Positions System*] Operator Arrangements [*Telecommunications*]   (TEL)
OPERG .... Operating   (MDG)
Oper Syst Rev ... Operating Systems Review [*A publication*]
OPIM .... Order Processing and Inventory Monitoring [*Data processing*]
OPM .... Operations per Minute [*Performance measure*]
OPM .... Operator Programing Method [*Data processing*]
OPNS .... Operations
OPOL .... Optimization-Oriented Language   (NITA)
OPP .... Octal Print Punch [*Data processing*]
OPPOSIT .... Optimization of a Production Process by an Ordered Simulation and Iteration Technique   (IEEE)
OPR .... Optical Page Reader [*Data processing*]   (CGC)
OPR .... Optical Pattern Recognition   (DEEC)
OPS .... Off-Premise Station [*Telecommunications*]   (TEL)
OPS .... Official Phone Station [*Amateur radio*]
OPS .... On-Line Process Synthesis [*Data processing*]
OPS .... Operations   (MCD)
OPS .... Operator's Subsystem [*Telecommunications*]   (TEL)
OPSKS .... Optimum Phase Shift Keyed Signals [*Telecommunications*]   (OA)
OPSWL .... Old Program Status Word Location   (NITA)
OPS-X .... Operational Teletype Message   (CIT)
OPSYS .... Operating System   (NITA)
OPT .... Optional
OPTC .... Optelecom, Inc. [*NASDAQ symbol*]   (NQ)
OPTIM .... Order Point Technique for Inventory Management   (BUR)
OPTIMUS.... Office of Public Trustee Information Management User System [*Canada*]
OPTS .... Online Peripheral Test System   (NITA)
OPUR .... Object Program Utility Routine   (NITA)
OPX .... Off-Premise Extension
OQL .... Online Query Language   (NITA)
OR .... Omnidirectional Radio Range
OR .... Operations Research [*Data processing*]
OR .... Optical Reader   (BUR)
ORACLE ..... Oak Ridge Automatic Computer and Logical Engine
ORACLE ..... On-Line Retrieval and Computational Language for Economists [*Data processing*]
ORACLE ..... Optical Reception of Announcements by Coded Line Electronics
ORATE .... Ordered Random Access Talking Equipment
ORBIT .... Oak Ridge Binary Internal-Translator
ORBIT .... On-Line, Real-Time, Branch Information Transmission [*IBM Corp.*] [*Data processing*]
ORBIT .... On-Line Reduced Bandwidth Information Transfer [*Data processing*]
ORBIT .... On-Line Retrieval of Bibliographic Text [*Search system*] [*Data processing*]
ORBIT .... ORACLE Binary Internal Translator [*Algebraic programing system*]
ORC .... On-Line Reactivity Computer [*Data processing*]
ORC .... Operations Research Center [*Massachusetts Institute of Technology*] [*Research center*]   (KSC)
ORC .... Orthogonal Row Computer   (NITA)
ORCHIS ...... Oak Ridge Computerized Hierarchical Information System [*AEC*]   (EISS)
ORCS .... Omnitronics Research Corporation [*NASDAQ symbol*]   (NQ)
ORD .... Order
ORDVAC .... Ordnance Variable Automatic Computer
OREC .... Optimises Rectangles [*AERE Harwell*] [*Software package*] [*British*]   (NCC)
OREO .... Orbiting Radio Emission Observatory [*Satellite*]
ORER .... Official Railway Equipment Register [*National Railway Publication Company*] [*Information service*]   (EISS)
ORG .... Organization
ORG .... Origin   (MDG)
ORIADOC ... Orientation and Access to Information and Documentation Sources in France [*Commission de Coordination de la Documentation Administrative*] [*Database*]   (CUAD)
ORION .... Online Retrieval of Information over a Network   (IDA)
ORIS .... Office of Regulatory Information Systems [*Energy Regulatory Commission*]   (EISS)
ORJETS ...... On-Line Remote Job Entry Terminal System [*Data processing*]
ORLIS .... Orts-, Regional-, und Landesplanung Literaturinformationssystem [*Literature Information System for Town and Regional Planning*] [*1974-1978*] [*Database*]   (ODIN)
ORM .... Overlapping Resolution Mapping [*Data processing*]
OR/MS .... Operations Research or Management Science
ORNLL .... Oak Ridge National Laboratory Library [*AEC*]   (DIT)
ORNLY-NDP ... Oak Ridge National Laboratory Nuclear Data Project [*Database producer*]   (ODIN)
OROS .... Optical Read-Only Storage [*Data processing*]
ORS .... Official Relay Station [*Amateur radio*]
ORS .... Optimal Real Storage   (CMD)
ORSA .... Operations Research Society of America [*Baltimore, MD*]
ORSER .... Office for Remote Sensing of Earth Resources [*Pennsylvania State University*] [*Research center*]
ORT .... Order of Railroad Telegraphers [*Later, Transportation-Communication Employees Union*]
ORTS .... Optional Residential Telephone Service [*Telecommunications*]   (TEL)
ORU .... On-Line Replacement Unit [*Data processing*]   (MCD)
OS .... Office System   (NITA)
OS .... Operating Software   (MCD)
OS .... Operating System [*Data processing*]   (BUR)
OS .... Optical Scanning [*Data processing*]
OS .... Organizational Source [*Online database field identifier*] [*Data processing*]
OSA .... Open Systems Architecture [*Data processing*]
OSA .... Optical Society of America [*Washington, DC*]
OSAM .... Overflow Sequential Access Method [*Data processing*]   (TUT)
OSAR .... Optical Storage and Retrieval [*Data processing*]
OSB .... Operational Status BIT [*Binary Digit*]   (NITA)
OSC .... Complete Operational Software [*Telecommunications*]   (TEL)
OSC .... Operator Services Complex [*Telecommunications*]   (TEL)
OSC .... Oscillate [*or Oscillation, Oscillator, Oscillograph, Oscilloscope*]   (KSC)
OSCAP .... Operating System Communication Application Program [*Data processing*]   (TUT)
OSCAR .... Optically Scanned Character Automatic Reader [*Data processing*]   (DIT)
OSCAR .... Optimum Systems Covariance Analysis Results   (IEEE)
OSCAR .... Orbiting Satellite Carrying Amateur Radio [*Telecommunications*]   (TEL)
OSCAR .... Order Status Control and Reporting [*Telecommunications*]   (TEL)
OSCAR .... Oregon State Conversational Aid to Research [*Data processing*]   (CSR)
OSC-MULT ... Oscillator-Multiplier [*Telecommunications*]   (TEL)
OSCRL .... Operating System Command and Response Language   (NITA)
OSD .... Online System Drivers [*NCR Corp.*]   (NITA)
OSD .... Optical Scanning Device [*Data processing*]
OS/DOS ..... Operating System/Disk Operating System [*Software*]
OSDU .... Output Signal Distribution Unit   (MCD)
OSEOS .... Operational Synchronous Earth Observatory Satellite [*Telecommunications*]   (TEL)
OSG .... Operand Select Gate [*Data processing*]
OSHB .... One-Sided Height Balanced [*Telecommunications*]   (NITA)
OSI .... On-Line Software International, Inc. [*Fort Lee, NJ*] [*Telecommunications*]   (TSSD)
OSI .... Open Standards Interconnection [*International Standards Organisation*]
OSI .... Open System Interconnections [*Networking technique*] [*Data processing*]
OSI .... Operating System Interface   (NITA)
OSIE .... Office of Software Improvement and Engineering [*Social Security Administration*]
OSII .... On-Line Software International [*NASDAQ symbol*]   (NQ)
OSIL .... Operating System Implementation Language   (OA)

Computer & Telecommunications Acronyms

OSIS .... Office of Science Information Service [*National Science Foundation*]
OSL .... Operating System Language   (NITA)
OSM .... Operating System Monitor   (NITA)
OSM .... Opisu Struktur Mikroprogramownych [*Programing language*]   (CSR)
OS/MFT ...... Operating System/Multiprograming with a Fixed Number of Tasks [*IBM Corp.*] [*Data processing*]
OS/MVS ..... Operating System/Multiprograming with Virtual Storage [*Data processing*]
OS/MVT ..... Operating System/Multiprograming with a Variable Number of Tasks [*Data processing*]
OSN .... Output Sequence Number   (NITA)
OSO .... Orbiting Solar Observatory [*A satellite*]
OSO .... Origination Screening Office [*Telecommunications*]   (TEL)
OSP .... Outside Plant [*Telecommunications*]   (TEL)
OSR .... Operand Storage Register   (NITA)
OSR .... Optical Scanning Recognition [*Data processing*]
OSS .... Operating System Software [*Personal computers*]
OSS .... Operating System Supervisor   (NITA)
OSS .... Optimized Systems Software [*San Jose, CA*]
OSSL .... Operating System Simulation Language [*1971*] [*Data processing*]   (CSR)
OSSU .... Operator Services Switching Unit [*Telecommunications*]   (TEL)
OST .... On-Shift Test   (IEEE)
OST .... Originating Station Treatment [*Telecommunications*]   (TEL)
OSTEST ...... Operating System Test [*Telecommunications*]   (TEL)
OSTI .... Office of Scientific and Technical Information [*Later, BLR & DD*] [*British Library*]
OSTL .... Operating System Table Loader [*Telecommunications*]   (TEL)
OSTP .... Office of Science and Technology Policy [*Executive Office of the President*]
OS/VS .... Operating System/Virtual Storage [*Data processing*]   (MDG)
OSWS .... Operating System Workstation [*Data processing*]
OT .... Office of Telecommunications [*US government*]   (NITA)
OT .... Old Timer [*Communications operators' colloquialism*]
OT .... Old Top [*Communications operators' colloquialism*]
OT .... Output Terminal   (NITA)
OTA .... Omnidirectional Transmitter Antenna
OTC .... Operating Telephone Company [*Bell System*]   (TEL)
OTC .... Originating Toll Center [*Telecommunications*]   (TEL)
OTC .... Overseas Telecommunications Commission [*Australia*]   (TEL)
OTCS .... Operational Teletype Communications Subsystem   (CIT)
OTDR .... Optical Time-Domain Reflectometer [*Data processing*]
OTE .... Hellenic Telecommunications Organization [*Greece*]   (TEL)
OTF .... Optical Transfer Function
OTF .... Optimum Traffic Frequency [*Radio*]
OTG .... Option Table Generator   (NITA)
OTI .... Original Title [*Online database field identifier*]   (OBD)
OTL .... Online Task Loader   (NITA)
OTM .... Office of Telecommunications Management [*Later, OTP*] [*FCC*]
OTMA .... Office Technology Management Association [*Milwaukee, WI*] [*Information service*]   (TSSD)
OTN .... Octal Track Number [*Data processing*]
OTN .... Operational Teletype Network
OTP .... Office of Telecommunications Policy [*Terminated, 1978*] [*Executive Office of the President*]
OTRAC .... Oscillogram Trace Reader [*Non-Linear Systems, Inc.*] [*Data processing*]
OTS .... Orbital Test Satellite [*Communications satellite*] [*European Space Agency*]
OTS .... Own Time Switch [*Connection or call*] [*Telecommunications*]   (TEL)
OTSO .... Office of Telecommunications Systems Operations [*Social Security Administration*]
OTSS .... Off-the-Shelf System [*Bell System*]
OTT .... Outgoing Teletype
OTTI .... Ostbayrisches Technologie-Transfer-Institut [*Information retrieval*]   (ODIN)
OTTS .... Outgoing Trunk Testing System [*Telecommunications*]   (TEL)
OTU .... Operational Taxonomic Unit [*Numerical taxonomy*]
OU .... Operation Unit   (NITA)
OUCC .... Ohio University Cartographic Center [*Research center*]   (RCD)
OUCH .... Off-Line Universal Command History [*Data processing*]   (KSC)
OUT .... Organization for Use of the Telephone   (EANO)
OUT .... Output   (NASA)
OUTLIM ...... Output Limiting Facility [*Data processing*]   (MDG)
OUTPUTM ... Output Measures for Public Libraries [*Clarion University of Pennsylvania*] [*Information service*]   (EISS)
OUTRAN ..... Output Translator [*IBM Corp.*]
OUTWATS ... Outgoing Wide-Area Telephone Service [*Telecommunications*]   (TEL)
OUTXLTR ... Output Translator [*IBM Corp.*]   (MSA)
OV .... Overflow   (DEEC)
OVCS .... Operational Voice Communication Subsystem
OVD .... Optical Video Disk   (DEEC)
OVF .... Overflow [*Data processing*]
OVLBI .... Orbital Very-Long Baseline Interferometer [*Communications satellite*] [*Telecommunications*]   (IEEE)
OWD .... On-Line Wholesale Distribution System [*Data processing*]   (BUR)
OWF .... Optimum Working Frequency [*Telecommunications*]
OWL .... Online without Limits   (NITA)
OWP .... One-Way Polar [*Telegraph*]

OZ .... [*A*] programing language [*1975*]   (CSR)

P

P	P-Register [*Data processing*]		PACT	Pay Actual Computer Time
P	Parallel		PACT	Philco Automatic Circuit Tester
P	Parity [*Atomic physics*]		PACT	Program for Automatic Coding Techniques [*Data processing*]
P	Pencil Tube (MDG)		PACT	Programable Asynchronous Clustered Teleprocessing (NITA)
P	Pentachlorophenol [*Also, PCP*] [*Wood preservative*] [*Organic chemistry*] (TEL)		PACT	Programed Analysis Computer Transfer (KSC)
P	Person to Person [*Telecommunications*] (TEL)		PACT	Programed Automatic Circuit Tester
p	Pico [*A prefix meaning divided by one trillion*] [*SI symbol*]		PACT	Project for the Advancement of Coding Techniques
P	Pole		PACX	Private Automatic Computer Exchange
P	Portable (MDG)		PAD	Packet Assembler/Disassembler [*Switching technique*] [*Data processing*]
p	Positive [*Crystal*]		PAD	Personal Articulation Device [*Facetious term for pre-word-processing equipment*]
P	Power [*Symbol*] [*IUPAC*]		PAD	Positioning Arm Disk (NITA)
P	Prefix [*Indicating a private radiotelegram*]		PAD	Program Analysis for Documentation [*Data processing*]
P	Present BIT [*Binary Digit*] [*Data processing*]		PAD	Pulse Averaging Discriminator
P	Print		PADIS	Pan-African Documentation and Information System [*United Nations*] (EISS)
P	Priority [*Telecommunications*] (TEL)		PADL	Part and Assembly Description Language [*Data processing*]
P	Program (KSC)		PADLA	Programable Asynchronous Dual Line Adapter (NITA)
P	Propagation Distribution [*Broadcasting*]		PADRE	Patient Automatic Data Recording Equipment (IEEE)
P	Punch		PADS	Programer Advanced Debugging System [*Data processing*]
PA	Paper Advance (BUR)		PAEM	Program Analysis and Evaluation Model (IEEE)
PA	Permanently Associated [*Telecommunications*] (TEL)		PAF	Page Address Field (NITA)
PA	Photodiode Amplifier		PAF	Peripheral Address Field (NITA)
pA	Picoampere		PAFC	Phase-Locked Automatic Frequency Control [*Telecommunications*] (OA)
PA	Power Amplifier		PAGAN	Pattern Generation Language [*Data processing*]
PA	Preamplifier		PAGE	PERT [*Program Evaluation and Review Technique*] Automated Graphical Extension (KSC)
PA	Predictive Analyzer [*Data processing*] (DIT)		PAGES	Program Affinity Grouping and Evaluation System (NITA)
PA	Process Allocator [*Telecommunications*] (TEL)		PAI	Pacific Aerospace Index (DIT)
PA	Process Automation (CMD)		PAI	Production Adjustment Index [*Word processing*]
PA	Program Access (NITA)		PAI	Programer Appraisal Instrument [*Data processing*] (IEEE)
PA	Program Address		PAI	Public Affairs Information, Inc. [*Sacramento, CA*] [*Database producer*] [*Information service*]
PA	Program Analysis [*Data processing*] (CGC)		PAIC	Public Address Intercom System
PA	Program Application Instructions [*Telecommunications*] (TEL)		PAIS	Public Affairs Information Service [*New York, NY*] [*Bibliographic database*] [*A publication*]
PA	Program Attention Key [*Data processing*]		PAK	Power Amplifier Klystron
PA	Programable Automation		PAK	Program Attention Key [*Data processing*] (BUR)
PA	Public Address [*Amplification equipment*] [*Communications*]		PAL	Paradox Application Language [*ANSA*] [*Data processing*]
PA	Publishers' Association [*London, England*] (DIT)		PAL	Pedagogic Algorithmic Language [*Data processing*] (TUT)
PA	Pulse Amplifier		PAL	Phase Alternation Line [*West German color television system*]
PAA	Phased Array Antenna		PAL	Precision Artwork Language [*Data processing*] (TUT)
PAA	Planar Array Antenna		PAL	Process Assembler Language
PAA	Power Amplifier Assembly		PAL	Programable Algorithm Machine Assembly Language [*Data processing*]
PAAC	Program Analysis Adaptable Control [*Data processing*]		PAL	Programable Array Logic [*Data processing*] (IEEE)
PAAS	Phased Array Antenna System		PAL	Programed Application Library [*IBM Corp.*] (CDH)
PAATI	Phased Array Antenna Technology Investigation		PAL	Programer Assistance and Liaison [*Data processing*]
P(A)BX	Private (Automatic) Branch Exchange [*Telecommunications*] (DEN)		PALAPA	Indonesian satellite
PAC	Packaged Assembly Circuit		PALASM	Programable Array Logic Assembler [*Data processing*] (IEEE)
PAC	Pedagogic Automatic Computer (IEEE)		PAL-D	Phase Alternation Line Delay (IEEE)
PAC	Personal Analog Computer		PALIS	Property and Liability Information System (CGC)
PAC	Pneumatic Analog Computer		PALS	Phase Alternation Line Simple [*TV decoding system*] (DEEC)
PAC	Polled Access Circuit (NITA)		PAM	Partitioned Access Method [*Data processing*]
PAC	Programable Automatic Comparator		PAM	Peripheral Adapter Module
PACCALL	Pacific Fleet Calls [*Radio call signs*]		PAM	Personal Applications Manager [*Hewlett-Packard Co.*]
PACE	Packaged CRAM [*Card Random-Access Memory*] Executive [*NCR Corp.*] [*Data processing*]		PAM	Phase-Amplitude Modulation (CBSS)
PACE	Performing Arts, Culture, and Entertainment [*Proposed cable television system*]		PAM	Phased Array Module
PACE	Phased Array Control Electronics		PAM	Pole Amplitude Modulation (IEEE)
PACE	Planned Action with Constant Evaluation [*Data processing*]		PAM	Primary Access Method [*Sperry UNIVAC*] (NITA)
PACE	Precision Analog Computing Equipment		PAM	Primary Auxiliary Memory [*Unit*] [*Data processing*] (MCD)
PACE	Programed Automatic Communications Equipment		PAM	Process Automation Monitor [*Texas Instruments, Inc.*] (OA)
PACE	Programing Analysis Consulting Education (IEEE)		PAM	Processor and Memory [*Data processing*]
PACER	Process Assembly Case Evaluator Routine [*Data processing*] (TUT)		PAM	Programable Algorithm Machine [*Data processing*]
PACER	Programed Automatic Circuit Evaluator and Recorder		PAM	Pulse-Address MODEM
PACERS	Pacing and Cardiac Electrophysiology Retrieval System [*Intermedics, Inc.*] [*Information service*] (EISS)		PAM	Pulse Amplitude Modulation [*Electronics*]
PACFORNET	Pacific Coast Forest Research Information Network [*Later, WESTFORNET*] [*Forest Service*] (EISS)		PAMA	Pulse-Address Multiple Access [*Satellite communications*]
PACM	Pulse Amplitude Code Modulation [*Electronics*]		PAMD	Process Automation Monitor/Disk Version [*Texas Instruments, Inc.*] (NITA)
PACNET	Plymouth Audioconferencing Network [*Plymouth Polytechnic*] [*Plymouth, England*] [*Telecommunications*] (TSSD)		PAM-FM	Pulse Amplitude Modulation - Frequency Modulation [*Electronics*]
PACS	Patient Accounting, Census, and Statistics (TUT)			
PACS	Process Automation & Computer Systems			

Computer & Telecommunications Acronyms

PAMS.......... Preselected Alternate Master-Slave [*Telecommunications*] (TEL)
PAMS.......... Public Access Message System
PAN............ Performing Artists Network [*Electronic network*]
PAN............ Polled Access Network (NITA)
PAN............ Switchboard Panel [*Telecommunications*] (TEL)
PANAFTEL ... Pan-African Telecommunications Network
PANAMAC ... Pan American World Airways Communications System
PANC.......... Power Amplifier Neutralizing Capacitor (DEN)
PANDA .... Prestel Advanced Network Design Architecture (DEEC)
PANDS........ Print and Search Processor [*Data processing*]
PANS .... Pansophic Systems [*NASDAQ symbol*] (NQ)
PAO .... Pulsed Avalanche Diode Oscillator [*Telecommunications*] (IEEE)
PAP............ Phase Advance Pulse (NITA)
PAPA .... Probabilistic Automatic Pattern Analyzer [*Data processing*]
PAPA .... Programer and Probability Analyzer [*Data processing*] (IEEE)
PAPERCHEM ... Paper Chemistry [*Institute of Paper Chemistry*] [*Appleton, WI*] [*Bibliographic database*] (OBD)
PAR............ Page Address Register (NITA)
PAR............ Parameter (VIT)
PAR............ Peak-to-Average Ratio [*Communications*]
PAR............ Performance Analysis Routine [*Data processing*]
PAR............ Production Automated Riveting
PAR............ Professional Abstracts Registries [*Database Innovations, Inc.*]
PAR............ Program Address Register (NITA)
PAR............ Program-Aid Routine [*Data processing*]
PAR............ Program Appraisal and Review (IEEE)
PARAM .... Parameter (KSC)
PARAMP..... Parametric Amplifier (CIT)
PARASYN .... Parametric Synthesis [*Data processing*]
PaRCL......... Parsec Research Control Language [*Pronounced "parkul"*] [*Robotics*]
PARD .... Precision Annotated Retrieval Display [*System*] [*Data processing*]
PARDAC..... Parallel Digital-to-Analog Converter (VIT)
PAREX........ Programed Accounts Receivable Extra Service [*Data processing*]
PARFAS...... Passive Radio Frequency Acquisition System
PARIS .... Pictorial and Artifact Retrieval and Information System [*Data processing*]
PARIS .... Planning Aid for Retail Information System [*IBM Corp.*]
PARIS .... Pulse Analysis-Recording Information System
PARMA....... Program for Analysis, Reporting, and Maintenance [*Data processing*] (TUT)
PARS .... Passenger Airlines Reservation System (CGC)
PARSEC ..... Parser and Extensible Compiler [*Programing language*] (CSR)
PARSYN ..... Parametric Synthesis [*Data processing*]
PARTNER ... Proof of Analog Results through a Numerical Equivalent Routine [*Data processing*]
PAS............ Program Address Storage (IEEE)
PAS............ Public Address System
PASCAL ..... Philips Automatic Sequence Calculator
PASCAL ..... Program Applique a la Selection et a la Compilation Automatique de la Litterature [*Centre National de la Recherche Scientifique-Informascience*] [*Bibliographic database*] (OBD)
PASCAL ..... [*A*] programing language [*1968*] [*Named after French mathematician Blaise Pascal, 1623-62*] (DEEC)
PASG .... Pulse Amplifier/Symbol Generator
PASG .... Pulse Analyzer Signal Generator
PASLA .... Programable Asynchronous Line Adapter (NITA)
PASS .... Pro-Am Sports Systems [*Cable-television network*]
PASS .... Procurement Automated Source System [*Small Business Administration*] [*Information service*] (EISS)
PASS .... Program Aid Software Systems [*Data processing*] (IEEE)
PASS .... Programed Access/Security System [*Card Key Systems*] (NITA)
PASSION .... Program for Algebraic Sequences Specifically of Input-Output Nature [*Data processing*]
PASSWD .... Password [*Data processing*]
PAST .... Process Accessible Segment Table (NITA)
PAT............ Peripheral Assignment Table (CMD)
PAT............ Personalized Array Translator (IEEE)
PAT............ Production Acceptance Test (KSC)
PAT............ Programer Aptitude Test
PAT............ Pseudoadder Tree [*Data processing*]
PATCA........ Phase Lock Automatic Tuned Circuit Adjustment [*Telecommunications*] (OA)
PATN .... Pattern (MDG)
PATO .... Partial Acceptance and Takeover Date [*Telecommunications*] (TEL)
PATOS........ Patent-Online-System [*Bertelsmann Datenbankdienste GmbH*] [*Database*] (CUAD)
PAT-PTR..... US Patent Data Base - Patent Technology Reports [*Patent and Trademark Office*] [*Database*] (FDB)
PATRIC....... Pattern Recognition and Information Correlations [*Police crime-detection computer*]
PATRIC....... Pattern Recognition Interpretation and Correlation (CET)
PATRICIA ... Practical Algorithm to Receive Information Coded in Alphanumeric [*Information retrieval*] (IDA)
PATROL...... Program for Administrative Traffic Reports On-Line [*Computer program*] [*Bell System*]
PATS .... Payment and Telecommunications Services Corp. [*New York, NY*] [*Telecommunications*] (TSSD)
PATS .... Predicasts Abstract Terminal System [*Data processing*]
PATSEARCH ... Patent Search [*Data processing*]

PATSY .... Parametric Test Synthesis [*Data processing*]
PATSY .... Programer's Automatic Testing System (DEEC)
PATT.......... Partial Automatic Translation Technique
Patt Recog ... Pattern Recognition [*A publication*]
PAU............ Pattern Articulation Unit [*Data processing*]
PAWS .... Programed Automatic Welding System
PAX............ Physical Address Extension (NITA)
PAX............ Private Automatic Exchange [*Telecommunications*]
PB .... Peripheral Buffer
PB .... Physics Briefs [*Database*] [*Information retrieval*] (ODIN)
PB .... Physikalische Berichte [*Physics Briefs*] [*Database*] [*Information retrieval*] (ODIN)
PB .... Pitney-Bowes, Inc.
PB .... Primary Bus [*Data processing*] (CAAL)
P-as-B........ Program as Broadcast [*Radio*] (DEN)
PB .... Proportional Band (NITA)
PB .... Publisher's Name [*Online database field identifier*] (OBD)
PB .... Push Button
PBA............ Pencil Beam Antenna
PBA............ Pill Box Antenna
PBC............ Peripheral Bus Computer [*Bell System*]
PBC............ Program Booking Center [*Telecommunications*] (TEL)
PBDG .... Push-Button Data Generator (IEEE)
PBI .... Pitney-Bowes, Incorporated [*NYSE symbol*]
PBIC.......... Programable Buffer Interface Card [*Data processing*] (NASA)
PBIT .... Parity BIT [*Binary Digit*] [*Data communications*]
PBM .... Probability Based-Matched [*Database search techniques*]
PBN .... Physical Block Number (NITA)
PBN .... Primary Block Number [*Data processing*]
PBR............ Pole Broken [*Telecommunications*] (TEL)
PBS............ Public Broadcasting Service [*Sometimes facetiously translated "Petroleum Broadcasting Service," because of many grants from oil companies*] [*Washington, DC*]
PBT .... Piggyback Tape [*or Twistor*] [*Data processing*]
PBT .... Push-Button Telephone
PBW .... Proportional Bandwidth
PBWF .... Pulse Burst Waveform
PBX............ Private Branch Exchange [*Telecommunications*]
PC .... Path Control [*Data processing*] (IBMDP)
PC .... Peg Count [*Telecommunications*] (TEL)
PC .... Peripheral Control (BUR)
PC .... Personal Computer
PC .... Photoconductor
PC .... Picture (MDG)
PC .... Plant Computer
PC .... Plug Compatible [*Data processing*] (BUR)
PC .... Pocket Computer
PC .... Port Control [*Telecommunications*] (TEL)
PC .... Portable Computer
PC .... Printed Circuit
PC .... Process Computer
PC .... Process Control (DEN)
PC .... Processing Center [*Telecommunications*] (TEL)
PC .... Processor Controller [*Data processing*] (MDG)
PC .... Program Counter
PC .... Project Control (NASA)
PC .... Pulsating Current
PC .... Pulse Comparator
PC .... Pulse Counter [*Data processing*] (MDG)
PC .... Punched Card [*Data processing*]
PCA............ Port Communications Area [*Telecommunications*] (TEL)
PCA............ Printed Circuit Assembly [*Telecommunications*] (TEL)
PCA............ Printer Communications Adapter (NITA)
PCA............ Private Communications Association [*Later, NCA*]
PCA............ Protective Clothing Arrangement [*Telecommunications*] (TEL)
PCA............ Protective Connecting Arrangement [*Telecommunications*] (TEL)
PCA............ Pulse Counter Adapter (NITA)
PCAM .... Partitioned Content Addressable Memory (NITA)
PCAM .... Punched Card Accounting Machine [*Data processing*]
PCAS .... Punch Card Accounting System [*Data processing*]
PCASS....... Parts Control Automated Support System [*Database*] (FDB)
PCB............ Page Control Block [*Data processing*] (IBMDP)
PCB............ Port Check BIT [*Binary Digit*] [*Telecommunications*] (TEL)
PCB............ Power Circuit Breaker (MSA)
PCB............ Printed Circuit Board (MCD)
PCB............ Process Control Block
PCB............ Program Communication Block (NITA)
PCB............ Program Control Block [*Data processing*] (BUR)
PCB............ Public Coin Box [*Telecommunications*] (TEL)
PCBS .... Printed Circuit Board Socket
PCC............ Peripheral Control Computer (OA)
PCC............ Pertec Computer Corporation [*NYSE symbol*] [*Delisted*]
PCC............ Process Control Computer
PCC............ Processor Control Console [*Telecommunications*] (TEL)
PCC............ Program Control Counter (NITA)
PCC............ Program Controlled Computer (DIT)
PCCM .... Private Circuit Control Module [*Telecommunications*] (TEL)
PCCS .... Processor Common Communications System (NITA)
PCCU......... Punched Card Control Unit [*Data processing*]
PCD .... Planned Completion Date [*Telecommunications*] (TEL)
PCD .... Port Control Diagnostic [*Telecommunications*] (TEL)
PCDB .... Poison Control Data Base [*Database*] (FDB)

Computer & Telecommunications Acronyms

PCDDS	Private Circuit Digital Data Service [*Telecommunications*] (TEL)
PCDP	Punched Card Data Processing
PCE	Plug Compatible Ethernet (CCD)
PCE	Punch Card Equipment [*Data processing*] (AFM)
PCF	Program Control Facility (NITA)
PCF	Programed Cryptographic Facility [*Data processing*]
PCG	Programable Character Generator (NITA)
PCH	Punch (KSC)
PCHAR	Printing Character [*Data processing*]
PCHK	Parity Check [*Data communications*] (TEL)
PCI	Packet Communications, Incorporated (NITA)
PCI	Panel Call Indicator
PCI	Pattern Correspondence Index
PCI	Peripheral Controller Interface (NITA)
PCI	Process Control Interface (DEEC)
PCI	Production Control Information [*Sheffield, England*] [*Software supplier*] (NCC)
PCI	Program Check Interruption [*Data processing*] (MDG)
PCI	Program-Controlled Interruption [*Data processing*] (IBMDP)
PCI	Programable Communications Interface (NITA)
PCII	Protocol Computers [*NASDAQ symbol*] (NQ)
PCIOS	Processor Common Input/Output System [*Data processing*]
PCIS	Patient Care Information System [*Datacare, Inc.*] (EISS)
PCK	Printed Circuit Keyboard
PCKB	Printed Circuit Keyboard
PCL	Parallel Communications Link (NITA)
PCL	Print Control Language (NITA)
PCL	Procedural Control Language [*1971*] [*Data processing*] (CSR)
PCLA	Process Control Language [*Texas Instruments, Inc.*] (NITA)
PCLN	Personalcomputer Literaturnachweis [*Datendienst Weiss*] [*Database*] (CUAD)
PCM	Plug Compatible Mainframe [*Data processing*]
PCM	Plug Compatible Manufacturer [*Data processing*]
PCM	Plug Compatible Memory (NITA)
PCM	Port Command Area [*Telecommunications*] (TEL)
PCM	Process Control Module [*Telecommunications*] (TEL)
PCM	Project Cost Model [*Project Software Ltd.*] [*Software package*] [*British*] (NCC)
PCM	Pulse Code Modulation [*Telecommunications*]
PCM	Pulse-Count Modulation
PCM	Punch Card Machine [*Data processing*]
PCMA	Personal Computer Management Association [*Commercial firm*] [*Orange, CA*] [*Information service*] (EANO)
PCMI	Photochromic Microimage [*Microfiche*]
PCMMU	Pulse Code Modulation Master Unit [*Electronics*] (NASA)
PCM/NRZ	Pulse Code Modulation/Nonreturn to Zero (KSC)
PCM-PS	Pulse Code Modulation - Phase-Shift
P Cmp Sc St	Proceedings. Computer Science and Statistics [*A publication*]
PCMR	Patient Computer Medical Record
PCMR	Photochromic Microreproduction (DIT)
PCMS	Pulse Code Modulation Shared (MCD)
PCMS	Punched Card Machine System [*Data processing*]
PCOS	Primary Communications-Oriented System (IEEE)
PCOS	Process Control Operating System (OA)
PCP	Parallel Cascade Processor (IEEE)
PCP	Peripheral Control Program
PCP	Peripheral Control Pulse [*Data processing*]
PCP	Portable Code Processor
PCP	Primary Control Program [*Data processing*]
PCP	Printed Circuit Patchboard
PCP	Programable Communication Processor (OA)
PCP	Prototype Communications Processor (CIT)
PCP	Pulse Comparator
PCP	Punched Card Punch [*Data processing*] (IEEE)
PCPI	Personal Computer Products [*San Diego, CA*] [*NASDAQ symbol*] (NQ)
PCPS	Pulse-Coded Processing System
PCR	Page Control Register (NITA)
PCR	Pass Card Reader [*Telecommunications*] (TEL)
PCR	Peripheral Control Routine (CMD)
PCR	Preventative Cyclic Retransmission [*Telecommunications*] (TEL)
PCR	Print Command Register (NITA)
PCR	Program Control Register
PCR	Punched Card Reader [*Data processing*] (BUR)
PCR	Punched Card Requisition [*Data processing*] (MCD)
PCS	Personal Computing System (DEEC)
PCS	Plant Computer System
PCS	Port Command Store [*Telecommunications*] (TEL)
PCS	Port Control Store [*Telecommunications*] (TEL)
PCS	Port Control System [*Telecommunications*] (TEL)
PCS	Power Conditioning System
PCS	Print Contrast Scale (IEEE)
PCS	Print Contrast Signal [*Data processing*]
PCS	Print Contrast System (BUR)
PCS	Process Computer System
PCS	Production Control System (BUR)
PCS	Programable Communications Subsystem (NITA)
PCS	Project Control Sheet [*Data processing*]
PCS	Project Control System [*Data processing*]
PCS	Proprietary Computer Systems, Inc. [*Information service*] (EISS)
PCS	Punched Card System [*Data processing*]
PCSFSK	Phase Comparison Sinusoidal Frequency Shift Keying (NITA)
PCT	Peripheral Control Terminal (NITA)
PCT	Portable Conference Telephone [*Bell Laboratories*]
PCT	Positron Computed Tomography
PCT	Program Control Table [*Data processing*]
PCT	Project Control Tool (BUR)
PCT	Pulse Count [*Telecommunications*] (TEL)
PCTM	Pulse-Count Modulation (MSA)
PCTR	Program Counter
PCU	Paging Control Unit [*Telecommunications*] (TEL)
PCU	Peripheral Control Unit (CMD)
PCU	Power Control Unit
PCU	Processor Control Unit (NITA)
PCU	Program Control Unit [*Data processing*]
PCU	Punched Card Utility [*Data processing*] (TUT)
PCW	Program Control Word (NITA)
PCW	Pulsed Continuous Wave (IEEE)
PD	Peripheral Device (BUR)
PD	Plane Disagreement [*Telecommunications*] (TEL)
PD	Plasma Display (NITA)
PD	Potential Difference [*Electricity*]
PD	Protective Device (BUR)
PD	Publication Date [*Online database field identifier*] (OBD)
PDA	Patient Data Automation
PDA	Physical Device Address [*Data processing*] (IBMDP)
PDAID	Problem Determination Aid [*Data processing*] (MDG)
PDATE	Production Date [*Data processing*]
PDB	Process Descriptor Base [*Telecommunications*] (TEL)
PDBM	Pulse Delay Binary Modulation (MCD)
PDC	Parallel Data Controller
PDC	Performance Data Computer
PDC	Photo-Data Card [*Trademark*] [*Data processing*]
PDC	Population Documentation Center [*United Nations*] [*Information service*] (EISS)
PDC	Project Data Control (MCD)
PDCS	Parallel Digital Computing System
PDCS	Performance Data Computer System (MCD)
PDD	Post Dialing Delay [*Telecommunications*] (TEL)
PDD	Premodulation Processor - Deep Space - Data
PDD	Program Design Data
PDD	Projected Data Display
PDD	Pulse Delay Device
PDDB	Product Definition Database (MCD)
PDE	Partial Differential Equation
PDED	Partial Double Error Detection (NITA)
PDEL	Partial Differential Equation Language [*Data processing*]
PDELAN	Partial Differential Equation Language [*Data processing*] (CSR)
PDF	Post Detection Filter [*Telecommunications*] (TEL)
PDF	Probability Density Function [*Statistics*]
PDF	Processor Defined Function (NITA)
PDG	Patent Documentation Group (DIT)
PDGS	Product Design Graphics System [*Prime Computer Ltd.*] [*Software package*] [*British*] (NCC)
PDGY	Prodigy Systems, Inc. [*NASDAQ symbol*] (NQ)
PDI	Pilot Direction Indicator [*Electronic communications*]
PDI	Public Demographics, Incorporated [*Information service*] (EISS)
PDIO	Parallel Digital Input/Output (NITA)
PDL	Procedure Definition Language [*Data processing*] (BUR)
PDL	Program Design Language (NASA)
PDL	Programed Digital Logic
PDL	Publishers' Databases Limited [*Publishing consortium*] [*British*]
PDM	Patient Data Management
PDM	Practical Data Manager [*Hitachi Ltd.*] [*Japan*] (NITA)
PDM	Print Down Module
PDM	Processor Data Monitor (NASA)
PDM	Pulse Delta Modulation (IEEE)
PDM	Pulse-Duration Modulation [*Data transmission*]
PDM	Push Down Memory [*Data processing*]
PDMM	Push Down Memory MODEM [*Data processing*]
PDMS	Plant Design and Management System [*Computer Aided Design Centre*] [*Software package*] [*British*] (NCC)
PDMS	Power-Plant and Process Design Management System [*Data processing*]
PDN	Partnerships Data Net [*Washington, DC*] (EANO)
PDN	Public Data Network
PDO	Printer Direction Optimizer (BUR)
PDP	Plasma Display Panel [*Data processing*]
PDP	Procedure Definition Processor [*Data processing*]
PDP	Programed Data Processor
PDP	Programed Digital Processor (CIT)
PDPS	Parts Data Processing System [*Bell Telephone*]
PDPS	Program Data Processing Section
PDQ	Programed Data Quantizer
PDQ	Protocol Data Query [*Database*] [*National Institutes of Health*] (FDB)
PDR	Page Data Register (NITA)
PDR	Price Description Record [*Data processing*] (IBMDP)
PDR	Processing Data Rate (IEEE)
PDR	Program Document Requirement (BUR)
PDS	Parameter Driven Software, Inc. [*Birmingham, MI*] [*Software manufacturer*] (DASOS)
PDS	Partitioned Data Set [*Data processing*] (NASA)
PDS	Penultimate Digit Storage [*Telecommunications*] (TEL)
PDS	Petroleum Data System [*University of Oklahoma*] [*Databank*] (EISS)

Computer & Telecommunications Acronyms

PDS............ Pharma-Dokumentations-Service [*Pharma Documentation Service*] [*West Germany*] [*Information service*]   (EISS)
PDS............ Photo-Digital Store   (NITA)
PDS............ Power Distribution System [*or Subsystem*]
PDS............ Probability Distribution Subprogram [*Data processing*]   (BUR)
PDS............ Problem Descriptor System
PDS............ Program Data Source   (BUR)
PDS............ Program Development System [*Data processing*]
PDSM.......... Powder Diffraction Search-Match System [*International Data Center*]
PDS/MAGEN ... Problem Descriptor System/Matrix Generation [*Programing language*] [*1965*]   (CSR)
PDSS.......... Post-Deployment Software System   (MCD)
PDT............ Plasma Display Terminal [*Data processing*]
PDT............ Pollable Data Terminal [*Bell System*]
PDT............ Programable Data Terminal [*Digital Equipment Corp.*]   (IEEE)
PDTS......... Program Development Tracking System [*Data processing*]
PDU........... Power Distribution Unit
PDU........... Programable Delay Unit   (NITA)
PDU........... Protocol Data Unit   (CCD)
PE .... Parity Error   (NITA)
PE .... Phase Encoding [*Magnetic tape recording*] [*Data processing*]   (MDG)
PE .... Pre-Emption [*Telecommunications*]   (TEL)
PE .... Processing Element [*of central processing unit*]
PE .... Program Element   (AFM)
PE .... Pulse Encoding [*Data processing*]
PEA........... Push-Effective Address [*Data processing*]   (IEEE)
PEARL .... Process and Experiment Automation Real-Time Language [*Data processing*]
PEARL .... Programed Editor and Automated Resources for Learning   (NITA)
PECC......... Product Engineering Control Center [*Telecommunications*]   (TEL)
PECUS....... Personal Engineering Computer User's Society [*Boston, MA*]   (EANO)
PEF........... Prediction Error Filter [*Wave frequency and phase modifier*]
PEG........... Process Evaluation Guide [*Graphic Communications Association*]
PEG........... Protection Engineers Group [*United States Telephone Association*] [*Telecommunications*]
PEGS .... Project Engineering Graphics System [*Computer Aided Design Centre*] [*Software package*] [*British*]   (NCC)
PEK........... Phase-Exchange Keying [*Data processing*]   (IEEE)
PEL........... Picture Element [*Single element of resolution in image processing*]   (IBMDP)
PEM.......... Processing Element Memory [*Data processing*]
PEN........... Program Element Number [*Data processing*]   (KSC)
PEN........... Program Error Note [*Data processing*]
PENCIL...... Pictorial Encoding Language [*Data processing*]   (IEEE)
PENCIL...... Portable Encoder/Illustrator [*Facetious term for pre-word-processing equipment*]
P/E NEWS ... Petroleum/Energy Business News Index [*American Petroleum Institute*] [*New York, NY*] [*Bibliographic database*]   (OBD)
PENNSTAC ... Penn State University Automatic Digital Computer
PEP........... Paperless Entry Processing   (CSR)
PEP........... Partitioned Emulation Program [*Data processing*]   (BUR)
PEP........... Peak Envelope Power [*Telecommunications*]
PEP........... Peripheral Event Processor [*Data processing*]
PEP........... Perkin-Elmer Processor [*Computer*]
PEPC......... Polynomial Error Protection Code [*Data processing*]
PEPE......... Parallel Element Processing Ensemble [*Burroughs Corp.*]   (BUR)
PEPR......... Precision Encoding and Pattern Recognition Device [*Data processing*]
PEPS......... Production Engineering Productivity System [*Camtek Ltd.*] [*Software package*] [*British*]   (NCC)
PER........... Program Event Recording [*Data processing*]   (MDG)
PER........... Program Execution Request   (NITA)
PERC......... Processor Emergency Recovery Circuit [*Bell System*]
PERCOM .... Peripheral Communications   (FAAC)
PERF......... PerfectData, Inc. [*NASDAQ symbol*]   (NQ)
PERGO....... Project Evaluation and Review with Graphic Output   (IEEE)
PERM........ Program Evaluation for Repetitive Manufacture   (IEEE)
Pers Comput World ... Personal Computer World [*A publication*]
PERSON..... Personnel Simulation On-Line [*Department of State*] [*Computer program*]
PERSYST ... Personal Systems Technology, Inc. [*Irvine, CA*] [*Hardware manufacturer*]   (DASO)
PERT......... Program Evaluation Research Task   (IEEE)
PERT......... Program Evaluation and Review Technique [*Data processing*] [*Computer performance management*]
PERTSIM .... Program Evaluation and Review Technique Simulation [*Game*]
PERT/TIME ... Program Evaluation and Review Technique/Time Analyzer [*Sperry UNIVAC*]   (CDH)
PES........... Program Execution System   (NITA)
PEST......... Parameter Entity Symbol Translator [*Elstree Computing Ltd.*] [*Software package*] [*British*]   (NCC)
PEST......... Parameter Estimation by Sequential Testing [*Computer*]
PESTDOC.... Pest Control Literature Documentation [*Derwent Publications Ltd.*] [*Bibliographic database*] [*Information service*]   (EISS)
PET........... Peripheral Equipment Tester [*Data processing*]   (BUR)
PET........... Personal Electronic Transactor [*Computer*] [*Commodore Business Machines*]
PET........... Portable Electronic Telephone
PET........... Program Evaluator and Tester [*Data processing*]
PETS......... Programed Extended Time Sharing [*Data processing*]

PEU........... Port Expander Unit   (NITA)
PEV........... Peak Envelope Voltage [*Telecommunications*]   (TEL)
PEVM......... Personal'naia Elektronnaia Vychislitel'naia Mashina [*Personal Computer*] [*Russian*]
PEVM......... Professional'naia Elektronnaia Vychislitel'naia Mashina [*Professional Computer*] [*Russian*]
PF.............. Page Footing   (BUR)
PF.............. Page Formatter   (MDG)
PF.............. Plane Frame [*Camutek*] [*Software package*] [*British*]   (NCC)
PF.............. Plot Function [*Data processing*]
PF.............. Power Factor [*Radio*]
PF.............. Power Frame [*Telecommunications*]   (TEL)
PF.............. Program Function [*Data processing*]   (IBMDP)
PF.............. Programable Format [*Perforating keyboard*]
PF.............. Punch Off [*Data processing*]   (BUR)
PFA............ Pitch Follow-Up Amplifier
PFA............ Program and File Analysis   (NITA)
PFAM......... Programed Frequency Amplitude Modulation
PFAR.......... Power Fail Automatic Restart [*Data processing*]
PFB............ Provisional Frequency Board [*ITU*]
PFC............ Positive Feedback Circuit
PFD............ Power Flux Density [*Telecommunications*]   (TEL)
PFD............ Pulse-Frequency Diversity [*Electronics*]   (NG)
PFDA.......... Pulse-Frequency Distortion Analyzer
PFEP.......... Programable Front-End Processor [*Data processing*]
PFF............ Primary Focus Feed [*Satellite communications*]
PFK............ Programed Function Keyboard [*Data processing*]
PFN............ Permanent File Name   (NITA)
PFN............ Pulse-Forming Network
PFP............ Program File Processor   (NITA)
PFR............ Power Fail Recovery System [*Data processing*]   (MDG)
PFR............ Power Fail/Restart   (NITA)
PFR............ Programed Film Reader [*System*]
PFR............ Pulse Frequency   (MDG)
PFR............ Punch Feed Read   (CMD)
PFS............ Personal Filing System [*Data-base program*] [*Software Publishing Corp.*]
PFS............ Primary Frequency Supply [*Telecommunications*]   (TEL)
PFT............ Page Frame Table   (BUR)
PG............. Page [*or Pagination*] [*Online database field identifier*]
PG............. Permanent Glow [*Telecommunications*]   (TEL)
PG............. Port Group [*Telecommunications*]   (TEL)
PG............. Program Generic [*Data processing*]   (TEL)
PG............. Programer
PG............. Pulse Generator
PGA........... Power Gain Antenna
PGA........... Programable Gate Array   (NITA)
PGAP......... Professional Group - Antennas and Propagation
PGBTR....... Professional Group - Broadcast and Television Receivers
PGBTS....... Professional Group - Broadcast Transmission Systems
PGC........... Port Group Control [*Telecommunications*]   (TEL)
PGCS......... Professional Group - Communications Systems
PGCT......... Professional Group - Circuit Theory
PGD........... Planar Gas Discharge   (MCD)
PGED......... Professional Group - Electronic Devices
PGF............ Presentation Graphic Feature [*Data processing*]
PGH........... Port Group Highway [*Telecommunications*]   (TEL)
PGHFE....... Professional Group - Human Factors in Electronics
PGHTS....... Port Group Highway Timeslot [*Telecommunications*]   (TEL)
PGI............ Port Group Interface [*Telecommunications*]   (TEL)
PGM.......... Program
PGMTT...... Professional Group - Microwave Theory and Techniques
PGP........... Programable Graphics Processor   (NITA)
PGRFI........ Professional Group - Radio Frequency Interference
PGS........... Program Generation System [*Data processing*]   (MDG)
PGSET....... Professional Group on Space Electronics and Telemetry
PGT........... Page Table [*Data processing*]   (IBMDP)
PH............. Page Heading   (BUR)
PH............. Phantom Circuit [*Telecommunications*]   (TEL)
PH............. Phase   (KSC)
PH............. Phone   (MDG)
PHA........... Pulse Height Analysis [*Spectroscopy*]
PHALSE...... Phreakers, Hackers, and Laundry Service Employees [*East Coast group of computer trespassers raided by the FBI*]
PHD........... Parallel Head Disk   (NITA)
PHDS......... Post-Harvest Documentation Service [*Kansas State University*]   (EISS)
PHHC......... Programable Hand-Held Calculator   (RDA)
PHI............ Philippine Long Distance Telephone Co. [*American Stock Exchange symbol*]
PHIL.......... Programable Algorithm Machine High-Level Language [*Data processing*]
PHILCOM.... Philippine Global Communications, Inc. [*Manila*] [*Telecommunications*]   (TSSD)
PHINet....... Prentice-Hall Information Network [*New York, NY*] [*Information service*]   (EISS)
PHM.......... Phase Modulation [*Radio data transmission*]   (DEN)
PHODEC.... Photometric Determination of Equilibrium Constants [*Data processing*]
PHOSIAC.... Photographically Stored Information Analog Comparator
PHOTAC..... Phototypesetting and Composing [*AT & T*]
PHPL......... Parallel Hardware Processing Language [*1977*] [*Data processing*]   (CSR)

Computer & Telecommunications Acronyms

PHYCOM	Physicians Communication Service [*Database*] (CUAD)
PI	Parallel Input [*Data processing*] (BUR)
PI	Positive Interlace [*Television*]
PI	Priority Interrupt (IEEE)
PI	Processor Interface (NITA)
PI	Program Indicator Code (CMD)
PI	Program Instruction [*Data processing*] (BUR)
PI	Program Interrupt
PI	Programed Information [*Data processing*] (CGC)
PI	Programed Instruction
PI	Programed Introduction (MCD)
PI	Proportional-Plus Integral [*Digital control*]
PIA	Peripheral Interface Adapter [*Data processing*]
PIA	Plug-In Amplifier
PIB	Processor Interface Buffer [*Telecommunications*] (TEL)
PIB	Programable Input Buffer (NITA)
PIC	Peak Identification Computer
PIC	Pershing Instant Comment [*Donaldson, Lufkin & Jenrette*] [*Database*] (CUAD)
PIC	Polyethylene Insulated Conductor [*Telecommunications*]
PIC	Position Independent Code [*Telecommunications*] (TEL)
PIC	Power Integrated Circuit [*Data processing*]
PIC	Printer Interface Cartridge [*Epson America, Inc.*]
PIC	Priority Interrupt Controller (DEEC)
PIC	Process Interface Control (OA)
PIC	Program Identification Code (MUGU)
PIC	Program Instruction, Calibration [*Marine Corps*]
PIC	Program Interrupt Control [*Data processing*]
PIC	Programable Interval Clock (NASA)
PIC	Publishers' Information Card [*Later, IBIS*] [*British*] (DIT)
PICA	Power Industry Computer Applications
PICA	Printing Industry Computer Associates, Inc.
PICA	Project for Integrated Catalogue Automation [*Royal Netherlands Library*] [*Cataloging cooperative*] (EISS)
PICA	Property Services Agency Information on Construction and Architecture [*Property Service Agency Library Service*] [*Database*] (CUAD)
PICA	Public Interest Computer Association [*Washington, DC*] (EANO)
PICAC	Power Industry Computer Applications Conference (MCD)
PICE	Programable Integrated Control Equipment
PICON	Process Intelligent Control [*A data processing system from LISP Machine, Inc.*]
PICP	Program Interface Control Plan (NASA)
PICRS	Program Information Control and Retrieval System (NASA)
PICRS	Program Information Coordination and Review Service (NASA)
PICS	Personnel Information Communication [*or Control*] System [*Data processing*]
PICS	Pharmaceutical Information Control System (DIT)
PICS	Plug-In Inventory Control System [*Bell System*]
PICS	Predefined Input Control Sequence (MCD)
PICS	Production Information and Control System [*IBM Corp.*] [*Software package*]
PICS	Production Inventory Control System (TUT)
PICS	Productivity Improvement and Control System (BUR)
PICS/DCPR	Plug-In Inventory Control System/Detailed Continuing Property Record [*Telecommunications*] (TEL)
PICTUREBALM	[*A*] programing language [*1979*] (CSR)
PICU	Parallel Instruction Control Unit (NITA)
PICU	Priority Interrupt Control Unit [*Data processing*] (MDG)
PID	Pictorial Information Digitizer [*Data processing*] (DIT)
P & ID	Piping & Instrumentation Diagrams [*Calcomp Ltd.*] [*Software package*] [*British*] (NCC)
PID	Port Identification [*Telecommunications*] (TEL)
PID	Proportional-Plus Integral-Plus Derivative [*Digital control algorithm*]
PID	Pseudo Interrupt Device (OA)
PIDCOM	Process Instruments Digital Communication System [*Beckman Industries*] (NITA)
PIE	Pacific Islands Ecosystems [*Springfield, VA*] [*Department of the Interior*] [*Bibliographic database*] (OBD)
PIE	Parallel Instruction Execution [*Data processing*] (BUR)
PIE	Parallel Interface Element (NITA)
PIE	Plug-In Electronics
PIE	Program Interrupt Entry [*Data processing*]
PIE	Pulse Interference Emitting (MCD)
PIERS	Port Import Export Reporting Services [*Journal of Commerce, Inc.*] [*Database*] (CUAD)
PIF	Program Information File
PIGLET	Purchase Information, Gifts, Loans, Exchanges Tracking [*Suggested name for the Library of Congress computer system*]
PIGS	PAFEC Interactive Graphics System [*PAFEC Ltd.*] [*Software package*] [*British*] (NCC)
PIIC	Pergamon International Information Corporation [*Information service*] (EISS)
PIL	Pitt Interpretive Language [*Data processing*] (DIT)
PIL	Processing Information List [*Data processing*]
PILC	Paper-Insulated, Lead-Covered Cable [*Telecommunications*]
PILL	Programed Instruction Language Learning [*Data processing*]
PILOT	Permutation Indexed Literature of Technology (IEEE)
PILOT	Printing Industry Language for Operations of Typesetting
PILP	Parametric Integer Linear Program [*Data processing*]
PIM	Peripheral Interface Module (CCD)
PIM	Processor Interface Module (NITA)
PIM	Pulse Intensity Modulation
PIM	Pulse Interval Modulation
PIMS	Personnel Inventory Management System [*AT & T*]
PIMS	Programable Implantable Medication System
PIN	P-Type Intrinsic N-Type [*or Positive-Intrinsic-Negative*]
PIN	Personal Identification Number [*Banking*]
PIN	Piece Identification Number (IDA)
PIN	Plant Information Network [*Fish and Wildlife Service*] (EISS)
PIN	Product Information Network [*McGraw-Hill Information Systems Co.*] [*Information service*] (EISS)
PINCCA	Price Index Numbers for Current Cost Accounting [*Service in Information and Analysis*] [*Databank*] [*British*] (EISS)
PINO	Positive Input - Negative Output [*Data processing*]
PINS	Political Information System [*Databank of political strategist Richard Wirthlin*]
PIO	Parallel Input/Output (DEEC)
PIO	Precision Interactive Operation [*Data processing*] (CDH)
PIO	Private Input/Output [*Telecommunications*] (TEL)
PIO	Processor Input-Output [*Data processing*] (MDG)
PIO	Programed Input/Output (NITA)
PIOCS	Physical Input-Output Control System [*Data processing*] (BUR)
PIOU	Parallel Input-Output Unit [*Data processing*] (IEEE)
PIP	Path Independent Protocol (NITA)
PIP	Peripheral Interchange Program [*Data processing*]
PIP	Peripheral Interface Programer [*Circuit*] [*Data processing*]
PIP	Personal Identification Project [*Data processing*]
PIP	Photo Interpretive Program (BUR)
PIP	Picture-in-a-Picture [*Multi-Vision Products*] [*Video technology*]
PIP	Population Information Program [*Johns Hopkins University*] [*Information service*] (EISS)
PIP	Primary Indicating Position Data Logger (IEEE)
PIP	Problem Identification Program (MCD)
PIP	Problem Input Preparation [*Data processing*] (BUR)
PIP	Program in Process [*Data processing*] (BUR)
PIP	Programable Integrated Processor (IEEE)
PIP	Project on Information Processing (IEEE)
PIPO	Parallel-In Parallel-Out [*Telecommunications*] (TEL)
PIPS	Pattern Information Processing System (NITA)
PIQ	Parallel Instruction Queue (NITA)
PIR	Program Incident Report (NITA)
PIR	Protein Identification Resource [*National Biomedical Research Foundation*] [*Information service*] (EISS)
PIRS	Personal Information Retrieval System (DEEC)
PISA	Persistent Information Space Architecture [*Data processing*]
PISO	Parallel-In Serial-Out [*Telecommunications*] (TEL)
PIT	Peripheral Input Tape [*Data processing*]
PIT	Program Instruction Tape [*Data processing*] (IEEE)
PIT	Programable Interval Timer (DEEC)
PIT	Programed Instruction Text
PIT	Projected Inactive Time [*Data processing*]
PITE	Project on Information Technology and Education [*Carnegie Corp. of New York*] (EANO)
PIU	Path Information Unit [*Data processing*]
PIU	Plug-In Unit
PIU	Process Input Unit [*Data processing*] (BUR)
PIU	Process Interface Unit (NITA)
PIW	Program Interrupt Word (NITA)
PIXEL	Picture Element [*Single element of resolution in image processing*] (CIT)
PJ	Picojoule [*Logic gate efficiency measure*] (MDG)
PKA	Paul Kagan Associates, Inc. [*Carmel, CA*] [*Information service*] [*Telecommunications*] (EISS)
PKB	Photoelectric Keyboard
PKB	Portable Keyboard
PKC	Position Keeping Computer
PKD	Programable Keyboard and Display [*Data processing*] (NASA)
P & KI	Promisel & Korn, Inc. [*Bethesda, MD*] [*Information service*] (EISS)
PKN	Perkin-Elmer Corp. [*NYSE symbol*]
PKSCAT	Parkes Catalogue of Radio Sources [*Australian National Radio Astronomy Observatory*] [*Information service*] (EISS)
PL	Path Loss [*Communications*] (CBSS)
PL	Private Line
PL	Program Logic [*Data processing*] (TEL)
PL	Programing Language [*Data processing*]
PL	Pulse Length
PL/1	Programing Language, Version One [*Data processing*] (MCD)
PLA	Plain Language Address [*Telecommunications*] (TEL)
PLA	Print Load Analyzer (NITA)
PLA	Programable Line Adapter (NITA)
PLA	Programable Logic Array [*Data processing*]
PLA	Pulsed LASER Annealing [*Semiconductor technology*]
PLACE	Programing Language for Automatic Checkout Equipment
PLAID	Programed Learning Aid
PLAN	Problem Language Analyzer [*Data processing*] (CGC)
PLAN	Program Language Analyzer [*Data processing*] (IEEE)
PLAN	Program for Learning in Accordance with Needs [*Westinghouse Learning Corp.*]
PLAN	Programing Language Nineteen-Hundred [*Data processing*]

Computer & Telecommunications Acronyms

PLAN .... Public Libraries Automation Network [*California State Library*] [*Sacramento, CA*]
PLANCODE ... Planning, Control, and Decision Evaluation System [*IBM Corp.*]
PLANES ...... Programed Language-Based Enquiry System   (NITA)
PLANEX ...... [*The*] Planning Exchange Database [*Pergamon InfoLine*] [*Glasgow, Scotland*] [*Database*] [*Information service*]   (EISS)
PLANIT ...... Programing Language for Interaction and Teaching [*1966*] [*Data processing*]
PLANMAN ... Planned Maintenance [*Contract Data Research*] [*Software package*] [*British*]   (NCC)
PLANNER ... [*A*] programing language   (CSR)
PLANS .... Program Logistics and Network Scheduling System   (IEEE)
PLANS .... Programing Language for Allocation and Network Scheduling [*1975*] [*Data processing*]   (CSR)
PLANT .... Program for Linguistic Analysis of Natural Plants   (IEEE)
PLAS .... Private Line Assured Service [*Telecommunications*]   (TEL)
PLAS .... Program Logical Address Space   (NITA)
PLATO .... Programed Logic for Automatic Teaching [*or Training*] Operations [*University of Illinois*] [*Programing language*]
PLC .... Power Line Communications
PLC .... Primary Location Code [*Data processing*]
PLC .... Program Level Change [*Data processing*]   (IBMDP)
PLC .... Programable Logic Control [*Data processing*]
PLC .... Programing Language Committee [*CODASYL*]   (NITA)
PLCB .... Pseudoline Control Block [*Data processing*]
PL)d .... Path Loss, Downlink [*Communications*]   (CBSS)
PLD .... Pulse-Length Discriminator   (IEEE)
PLDC .... Primary Long-Distance Carrier [*Telephone service*]
PLE .... Phased Loading Entry [*Data processing*]
PLE .... Plesetsk [*Satellite launch complex*] [*USSR*]   (CBSS)
PLEA .... Prototype Language for Economic Analysis [*Data processing*]   (EISS)
PLF .... Page Length Field   (NITA)
PLF .... Private Line Telephone
PLI .... Private Line Interface   (NITA)
PLIANT .... Procedural Language Implementing Analog Techniques [*Data processing*]   (IEEE)
PLINK .... American People/Link [*American Home Network, Inc.*] [*Information service*]   (EISS)
PLIS .... Preclinical Literature Information System [*Data processing*]
PLISP .... [*A*] programing language   (CSR)
PLITTY .... Private Line Teletypewriter Service [*Telecommunications*]   (TEL)
PLM .... Passive Line Monitor [*Datapoint*]   (NITA)
PL/M .... Programing Language/Microcomputers [*Intel Corp.*] [*1973*] [*Data processing*]   (CSR)
PLM .... Programing Logic Manual   (TUT)
PLM .... Pulse-Length Modulation
PLMX .... PL/M Extended [*Programing language*]   (CSR)
PLN .... Program Logic Network   (NASA)
PLO .... Phase-Locked Oscillator
PLOD .... Periodic List of Data [*Data processing*]
PLONEF ...... Plates on Elastic Foundations [*Structures & Computers Ltd.*] [*Software package*] [*British*]   (NCC)
PLP .... Presentation Level Protocol [*AT & T Videotex System*]
PLP .... Procedural Language Processor   (NITA)
PLPA .... Pageable Link-Pack Area   (NITA)
PLR .... Pulse Link Relay [*Telecommunications*]   (TEL)
PLR .... Pulse Link Repeater [*Telecommunications*]   (TEL)
PLS .... Private Line Service
PLS .... Pulsed LASER System
PLS .... Pulsed Light Source
PLT .... Power Line Transient   (IEEE)
PLT .... Private Line Telephone
PLT .... Private Line Teletypewriter
PLT .... Program Library Tape [*Data processing*]   (IEEE)
PL)u .... Path Loss, Uplink [*Communications*]   (CBSS)
PLUS .... Program Library Update System   (TUT)
PLUS .... Programing Language for UNIVAC [*Universal Automatic Computer*] Systems [*Data processing*]   (CSR)
PLUS .... Project Literacy US [*Joint project of American Broadcasting Company and Public Broadcasting Service*]
PLUSF .... Plexus Corp. [*NASDAQ symbol*]   (NQ)
PLX .... Plantronics, Inc. [*NYSE symbol*]
PLY .... Plessey Co. Ltd. [*NYSE symbol*]
PLZ .... Programing Languages for the Zilog [*Data processing*]   (CSR)
PM .... Permanent Magnet [*Loudspeaker*]
PM .... Phase Modulation [*Radio data transmission*]
PM .... Photomultiplier
PM .... Polarization Modulation   (MCD)
PM .... Procedures Manual   (IEEE)
PM .... Processing Module [*Data processing*]
PM .... Program Monitoring   (MUGU)
PM .... Pulse Modulation
PMA .... Physical Memory Address   (NITA)
PMA .... Preamplifier Module Assembly
PMA .... Priority Memory Access   (NITA)
PMA .... Protected Memory Address   (NITA)
PMAC .... Parallel Memory Address Counter [*Data processing*]
PMAR .... Page Map Address Register   (NITA)
PMB .... Print Measurement Bureau [*Print Measurement Bureau*] [*Database*]   (CUAD)
PMB .... PROM [*Programable Read-Only Memory*] Memory Board   (NITA)

PMBX .... Private Manual Branch Exchange [*Communications*]
PMC .... Private Meter Check [*Telecommunications*]   (TEL)
PMC .... Programable Machine Controller
PMC .... Pseudo Machine Code [*Data processing*]   (BUR)
PMCD .... Post Mortem Core Dump [*Data processing*]
PMCS .... Pulse-Modulated Communications System
PMD .... Post Mortem Dump [*Data processing*]
PMD .... Program Module Dictionary   (OA)
PMD .... Program Monitoring and Diagnosis
PME .... Processor Memory Enhancement   (NITA)
PMH .... Production per Man-Hour
PMI .... Peripheral Maintenance, Incorporated [*Fairfield, NJ*] [*Hardware manufacturer*]   (DASO)
PMI .... Precision Methods, Incorporated [*Lorton, VA*] [*Hardware manufacturer*]   (DASO)
PMI .... Processor Monitoring Instrument [*Data processing*]
PMI .... Programable Machine Interface   (MCD)
PMIA .... Parallel Multiplexer Interface Adapter   (MCD)
PMIC .... Parallel Multiple Incremental Computer   (NITA)
PML .... Physical Memory Level   (NITA)
PMLA .... Publications. Modern Language Association of America [*Database*] [*A publication*]
PMLC .... Programed Multiline Controller   (NITA)
PMM .... Pool Maintenance Module [*Telecommunications*]   (TEL)
PMM .... Programable Microcomputer Module   (NITA)
PMM .... Pulse Mode Multiplex
PMMB .... Parallel Memory-to-Memory Bus   (NITA)
PMOS .... Positive-Channel Metal-Oxide Semiconductor [*Telecommunications*]   (TEL)
PMP .... Parallel Microprogramed Processor [*Data processing*]
PMP .... Premodulation Processor
PMP .... Program Management Plan
PMP .... Pulsed Microwave Power
PMR .... Pressure Modulation Radiometer
PMRT .... Program Management Responsibility Transfer   (MCD)
PMS .... People's Message System [*For Apple II computers*] [*Electronic bulletin boards*]
PMS .... Performance Measurement System   (MCD)
PMS .... Picturephone Meeting Service [*AT & T*]
PMS .... Planned Maintenance Systems [*Falls Church, VA*] [*Software manufacturer*]   (DASOS)
PMS .... Processors, Memories, and Switches [*Programing language*]   (CSR)
PMS .... Production Management System [*Safe Computing Ltd.*] [*Software package*] [*British*]   (NCC)
PMS .... Program Management System [*Data processing*]
PMS .... Project Management System [*IBM Corp.*] [*Data processing*]
PMS .... Public Message Service [*Western Union Corp.*]
PMSX .... Processor Memory Switch Matrix   (NITA)
PMT .... Permanent Magnet Twistor [*Memory*] [*Bell Laboratories*]
PMT .... Phase-Modulated Transmission
PMT .... Photomultiplier Tube
PMT .... Portable Magnetic Tape
PMT .... Prepare Master Tape
PMT .... Program Master Tape
PMT .... Programed Math Tutorial [*National Science Foundation*]
PMTD .... Post Mortem Tape Dump [*Data processing*]
PMTT .... Phase-Modulated Telemetry Transmission
PMU .... Performance Monitor Unit [*Communications*]
PMU .... Portable Memory Unit [*Data processing*]
PMUS .... Permanently Mounted User Set [*Data processing*]
PMUX .... Programable Multiplex [*Data processing*]   (TEL)
PMW .... Private Microwave [*System*]
PMX .... Packet Multiplexer
PMX .... Private Manual Exchange
PMX .... Protected Message Exchange   (NITA)
PN .... Perceived Noise
P/N .... Positive/Negative
PN .... Programable Network   (NITA)
PN .... Project Number [*Data processing*] [*Online database field identifier*]
PN .... Pseudonoise
PN .... Pseudorandom Number
PN .... Public Network [*Telecommunications*]
PN .... Publisher's Name [*Online database field identifier*]   (OBD)
PN .... Punch On   (NITA)
PNA .... Processing Terminal Network Architecture [*Data processing*]   (BUR)
PNA .... Project Network Analysis   (DEEC)
PNAF .... Potential Network Access Facility   (NITA)
PNC .... Police National Computer [*British*]
PNCC .... Partial Network Control Center   (NITA)
PNCH .... Punch   (CAH)
PND .... Premodulation Processor - Near Earth Data   (KSC)
PND .... Program Network Diagram [*Telecommunications*]   (TEL)
PNdB .... Perceived Noise Decibels
PNDC .... Parallel Network Digital Computer   (IEEE)
PNF .... Prenex Normal Form [*Logic*]
PNI .... Pharmaceutical News Index [*Data Courier, Inc.*] [*Louisville, KY*] [*Bibliographic database*] [*Information service*]
P-NID .... Precedence Network In-Dialing [*Telecommunications*]   (TEL)
PNL .... Panel   (KSC)
PNL .... Penril Corp. [*American Stock Exchange symbol*]

PNL	Perceived Noise Level
PNLT	Perceived Noise Level, Tone Corrected
PNM	Pulse Number Modulation
PNP	Positive-Negative-Positive [*Transistor*]
PNPN	Positive-Negative-Positive-Negative [*Transistor*] (MUGU)
PNTR	Pinetree Computer Systems [*NASDAQ symbol*] (NQ)
PO	Parallel Output [*Data processing*] (BUR)
PO	Parity Odd (NITA)
PO	Postpay Coin Telephone [*Telecommunications*] (TEL)
PO	Pulse Output (NITA)
PO	Pulsed Carrier without Any Modulation Intended to Carry Information (IEEE)
PO	Radio Positioning Mobile Station [*ITU designation*] [*Telecommunications*] (CET)
POA	Pay-on-Answer [*Telecommunications*] [*British*]
POC	Parallel Optical Computer
POC	Process Operator Console
PODA	Priority-Oriented Demand Assignment (NITA)
PODAF	Post Operation Data Analysis Facility
PODAF	Power Density Exceeding a Specified Level over an Area with an Assigned Frequency Band (IEEE)
PODAPS	Portable Data Processing System (VIT)
PODAS	Portable Data Acquisition System
PODRS	Patent Office [*later, PTO*] Data Retrieval System
POE	Print Out Effect
POETRI	Programme on Exchange and Transfer of Information on Community Water Supply and Sanitation [*World Health Organization*] [*Information service*] (EISS)
POF	Point-of-Failure [*Data processing*] (IBMDP)
POGO	Programer-Oriented Graphics Operation (IEEE)
POIS	Procurement Operations Information System (MCD)
POIS	Prototype On-Line Instrument Systems [*Data processing*]
POL	Problem-Oriented Language [*Data processing*]
POL	Procedure-Oriented Language [*Data processing*]
POL	Process-Oriented Language [*Data processing*] (IEEE)
POL	Public Opinion Laboratory [*Northern Illinois University*] [*Research center*] (RCD)
POLANG	Polarization Angle [*Telecommunications*] (OA)
POLE	Point-of-Last-Environment [*Data processing*] (IBMDP)
POLGEN	Problem-Oriented Language Generator [*Data processing*] (BUR)
POLIS	Parliamentary On-Line Information System [*House of Commons Library*] [*Bibliographic database*] [*Information service*] [*British*] (EISS)
POLLS	Parliamentary On-Line Library Study [*Atomic Energy Authority*] [*British*]
POLLY	[*A*] programing language [*1973*] (CSR)
Polyscope Comput and Elektron	Polyscope. Computer and Elektronik [*A publication*]
POLYTRAN	Polytranslation Analysis and Programing (IEEE)
POLYU	PolyComputers, Inc. Uts [*NASDAQ symbol*] (NQ)
POM	Pool Operational Module [*Telecommunications*] (TEL)
POM	Printer Output Microfilm
POM	Program Operation Mode
POOS	Priority Order Output System [*Japan*] (DIT)
POP	Parallel Output Platform
POP	Power On/Off Protection (CGC)
POP	Printing-Out Paper
POP	Programed Operators and Primitives [*Data processing*] (CGC)
Pop Comput	Popular Computing [*A publication*]
Pop Electr	Popular Electronics [*A publication*]
POPLER	[*A*] programing language (CSR)
POPLINE	Population Information On-Line [*Population Information Program, Johns Hopkins University*] [*Bibliographic database*] (EISS)
POPO	Push-On, Pull-Off [*Data processing*]
POPS	Process Operating System [*Toshiba Corp.*] [*Japan*] (NITA)
POPS	Program for Operator Scheduling [*Bell System computer program*]
POPUS	Post Office Processing Utility Subsystem [*Telecommunications*] (TEL)
POR	Problem-Oriented Routine (IEEE)
PORS	Product Output Reporting System
PORTAL	Process-Oriented Real-Time Algorithmic Language [*1978*] [*Data processing*] (CSR)
POS	Point-of-Sale Terminal [*Data transmission*] (TSSD)
POS	Position (KSC)
POS	Positive (AFM)
POS	Primary Operating System (IEEE)
POSD	Program for Optical System Design
POSH	Permuted on Subject Headings [*Indexing technique*] (DEEC)
POSS	Passive Optical Satellite Surveillance [*System*] (NATG)
POST	Power-On Self Test [*IBM-PC feature*]
POST	Programer Operating Standards Technique
POSTFAX	Post Office Fast Facsimile [*Transmission of documents*] [*British*]
POSTP	Posterior Probability [*Computations*]
POT	Parallel Output (CIT)
POT	Plain Old Telephone [*Bell System's basic model*]
POT	Post Office Telecommunications [*British*]
POT	Potential (AFM)
P O Telecommun J	Post Office Telecommunications Journal [*A publication*]
POTOMAC	Patent Office Techniques of Mechanized Access and Classification [*Automation project, shut down in 1972*]
POTS	Photo-Optical Terrain Simulator (MUGU)
POTS	Plain Old Telephone Service [*Humorous term for Long Lines Department of AT&T*]
POWU	Post Office Work Unit [*Computer performance measure*] [*British Telecom*] (OA)
PP	Page Printer (NVT)
PP	Parallel Processor (OA)
PP	Peak-to-Peak
PP	Peripheral Processor [*Data processing*] (CGC)
P-P	Person to Person [*Word processing*]
PP	Plane Polarized [*Telecommunications*] (TEL)
PP	Plot Points [*Data processing*]
PP	Preprocessor
PP	Print Positions (NITA)
PP	Print-Punch [*Data processing*] (BUR)
PP	Printer Page [*Data processing*]
PP	Program Product [*Data processing*]
P-P	Push-Pull
PPA	Pulsed Power Amplifier
PPB	PROM [*Programable Read-Only Memory*] Programer Board (NITA)
PPC	Peak Power Control [*Telecommunications*] (TEL)
PPC	Personal Portable Computer
PPC	Print Position Counter (NITA)
PPC	Professional Personal Computer
PPCB	Page Printer Control Block [*Data processing*]
PPCS	Person to Person: Collect and Special Instruction [*Telecommunications*] (TEL)
PPD	Pulse-Type Phase Detector (OA)
PPDB	Point-Positioning Data Base [*Cartography*] (RDA)
PPDC	Programing Panels and Decoding Circuits (OA)
PPDS	Physical Property Data Service [*Institution of Chemical Engineers*] [*Rugby, England*] [*Databank*] [*Information service*] (EISS)
PPE	Potomac Pacific Engineering, Inc.
PPE	Problem Program Efficiency (IEEE)
PPE	Problem Program Evaluator (NITA)
PPI	Plan Position Indicator Mode [*Data processing*]
PPI	Programable Peripheral Interface (MCD)
PPI	Pulses per Inch (CMD)
PPIB	Programable Protocol Interface Board (NITA)
PPIU	Programable Peripheral Interface Unit (NITA)
PPL	Polymorphic Programing Language [*1971*] [*Data processing*] (CSR)
PPL	Program Production Library [*Data processing*]
PPM	Periodic Pulse Metering [*Telecommunications*] (TEL)
PPM	Previous Processor Mode (NITA)
PPM	Pulse Position Modulation [*Radio data transmission*]
PPMS	Program Performance Measurement Systems (IEEE)
PPN	Project, Programer Number
PPO	Program Printout (MCD)
PPO	Push-Pull Output (DEN)
PPP	Parallel Pattern Processor (NITA)
PPQA	Pageable Partition Queue Area [*Data processing*] (OA)
PPR	Portable Propagation Recorder [*Bell System*]
PPRF	Pulse Pair Repetition Frequency (MCD)
PPS	Page Printing System [*Honeywell, Inc.*] [*Data processing*]
PPS	Parallel Processing System [*Data processing*] (MDG)
PPS	Parameter Processing System (CAAL)
PPS	Patchboard Programing System
PPS	Personnel/Payroll System (TUT)
PPS	Production Planning System [*TDS Business Systems Ltd.*] [*Software package*] [*British*] (NCC)
PPS	Programable Power Supply
PPS	Programed Processor System (NITA)
PPS	Programing Program Strela [*Data processing*] (CDH)
PPS	Pulses per Second [*Data transmission*]
PPSP	Page Printer Spooling System [*Data processing*]
PPT	Periodic Programs Termination [*Data processing*]
PPT	Process Page Table [*Telecommunications*] (TEL)
PPT	Punched Paper Tape [*Data processing*]
PPTR	Punched Paper Tape Reader [*Data processing*]
PPU	Peripheral Processing Unit [*Data processing*] (CGC)
PPV	Pay-per-View [*Pay-television service*]
PPX	Packet Protocol Extension (NITA)
PPX	Private Packet Exchange (NITA)
PQA	Protected Queue Area [*Data processing*] (BUR)
PQUE	Print Queue Processor [*Data processing*]
PR	Pattern Recognition (BUR)
PR	Prefix [*Indicating a private radiotelegram*] (BUR)
PR	Premature Release [*Telecommunications*] (TEL)
PR	Price [*Online database field identifier*] (OBD)
PR	Principal Register [*Data processing*]
PR	Printed [*or Printer*]
PR	Printing Request
PR	Program Register [*Data processing*] (BUR)
PR	Pulse Ratio (IEEE)
PRA	Print Alphanumerically [*Data processing*] (MDG)
PRA	Probabilistic Risk Assessment [*Computer-based technique for accident prediction*]
PRA	Program Reader Assembly [*Data processing*]
PRACL	Page-Replacement Algorithm and Control Logic [*Data processing*]
Pract Comput	Practical Computing [*A publication*]

Computer & Telecommunications Acronyms

PRAD .... Pitch Ratio Adjust Device (MCD)
PRBS .... Pseudorandom Binary Sequence [*Data processing*]
PRBSG ...... Pseudorandom Binary Sequence Generator [*Data processing*]
PRC .... Planning Research Corp. [*In company name, PRC Realty Systems*] [*McLean, VA*] [*Software manufacturer*] (DASOS)
PRC .... Plant Records Center [*of the American Horticultural Society*] (EISS)
PRC .... Primary Routing Center [*Telecommunications*] (TEL)
PRC .... Procession Register Clock (NITA)
PRCSG ...... Processing (MSA)
PRD .... Polaroid Corp. [*NYSE symbol*]
PRD .... Printer Driver
PRD .... Printer Dump
PRE .... Prefix (NITA)
PRE .... Prepayment Coin Telephone [*Telecommunications*] (TEL)
PRECIS ...... Pre-Coordinate Indexing System (DEEC)
PRE-MED .... Previous to Appearance in MEDLINE [*Latham, NY*] [*Bibliographic database*] (OBD)
PREP .... Productivity Research and Extension Program [*North Carolina State University*] [*Research center*] (RCD)
PRESAC ..... Photographic Reconnaissance System Analysis by Computer
PRF .... Processor Request Flag [*Telecommunications*] (TEL)
PRF .... Publications Reference File [*Government Printing Office*] [*Database*] (MCD)
PRF .... Pulse Rate Frequency (MUGU)
PRF .... Pulse Recurrence Frequency
PRF .... Pulse Repetition Frequency [*Data processing*] (CDH)
PRFD .... Pulse Recurrence Frequency Discrimination [*Telecommunications*] (TEL)
PRFM .... Pseudorandom Frequency Modulated [*Data processing*] (DDI)
PRFU .... Processor Ready for Use [*Telecommunications*] (TEL)
PRGM .... Program (AFM)
PRGMG ...... Programing (MSA)
PRGMR ...... Programer (AFM)
PRI .... Priority (AFM)
PRIA .... Priam Corp. [*NASDAQ symbol*] (NQ)
PRICE .... Pricing Review to Intensify Competitive Environment [*Data processing*]
PRIDE .... Priority Receiving with Inter-Departmental Efficiency [*Data processing*]
PRIM .... Program for Information Managers [*Later, AIM*] [*An association*]
PRIMATE .... Personal Retrieval of Information by Microcomputer and Terminal Ensemble
PRIME .... Planning through Retrieval of Information for Management Extrapolation
PRIMENET ... Prime Network Software Package [*Prime Computer, Inc.*] (NITA)
PRIMER ...... Patient Record Information for Education Requirements [*Data processing*]
PRIMOS ...... Prime Operating System [*Prime Computer, Inc.*] (NITA)
PRINCE .... Programed International Computer Environment [*International relations simulation game*]
PRINT .... Pre-Edited Interpretive System [*Data processing*]
PRISE .... Page Reader Input System with Editing (NVT)
PRISNET ..... Private Switching Network [*Telecoms*]
PRIZE .... Program for Research in Information Systems Engineering [*University of Michigan*] [*Research center*] (RCD)
PRLINK .... Public Relations Society of America Online Information Service (EISS)
PRM .... Prime Computer, Inc. [*NYSE symbol*]
PRM .... Programer Reference Manual [*Data processing*]
PRM .... Pulse Rate Modulation
PRMTR .... Parameter
PRN .... Print Numerically (DEN)
PRN .... Pseudorandom Noise
PRN .... Pseudorandom Number
PRNET .... Packet Radio Network (NITA)
PRNTR .... Printer
PRO .... Professional Resellers Organization (EANO)
PRO .... Programable Remote Operation [*Computer Devices, Inc.*] (NITA)
PROBFOR ... Probability Forecasting [*Computer program*] [*Bell System*]
Probl Control Inf Theor ... Problems of Control and Information Theory [*A publication*]
Probl Control and Inf Theory ... Problems of Control and Information Theory [*A publication*]
Probl Control and Inf Theory (Engl Transl Pap Rus) ... Problems of Control and Information Theory (English Translation of the Papers in Russian) [*A publication*]
Problems Control Inform Theory/Problemy Upravlen Teor Inform ... Problems of Control and Information Theory. Problemy Upravlenija i Teorii Informacii [*Budapest*] [*A publication*]
Problems Inform Transmission ... Problems of Information Transmission [*A publication*]
Probl Inf Transm ... Problems of Information Transmission [*A publication*]
Probl Inf Transm (USSR) ... Problems of Information Transmission (USSR) [*A publication*]
PROC .... Procedure
PROC .... Proceedings
PROC .... Process
PROC .... Processor [*or Processing*] (NITA)
PROC .... Programing Computer [*Data processing*]
Proc Inst Elec Eng Pt E Computers Digital Tech ... Proceedings. Institution of Electrical Engineers. Part E. Computers and Digital Techniques [*A publication*]

Proc Inst Elec Eng Pt F Commun Radar Signal Process ... Proceedings. Institution of Electrical Engineers. Part F. Communications, Radar, and Signal Processing [*A publication*]
PROCOMP ... Process Computer [*Data processing*]
PROCOMP ... Program Compiler [*Data processing*] (IEEE)
PROCSD ...... Processed
PROCTOR ... Priority Routine Organizer for Computer Transfers and Operations of Registers (CDH)
PROD .... Product [*or Production*]
PRODAC ..... Programed Digital Automatic Control [*Data processing*]
PROF .... Pupil Registering and Operational Filing [*Data processing*]
PROFILE ..... [*A*] programing language (CSR)
PROFIT .... Programed Reviewing, Ordering, and Forecasting Inventory Technique
PROFS .... Professional Office System [*IBM Corp.*]
PROG .... Program (KSC)
PROG .... Programer [*or Programming*] (CAH)
PROGMG .... Programing
PROGOFOP ... Program of Operation [*Data processing*]
Prog Quantum Electron ... Progress in Quantum Electronics [*A publication*]
Program Autom Libr Inf Syst ... Program. Automated Library and Information Systems [*England*] [*A publication*]
Program and Comput Software ... Programming and Computer Software [*A publication*]
Program Learn and Educ Technol ... Programmed Learning and Educational Technology [*A publication*]
Programmed Learning ... Programmed Learning and Educational Technology [*A publication*]
Programming and Comput Software ... Programming and Computer Software [*A publication*]
Program News Comput Libr ... Program. News of Computers in Libraries [*A publication*]
PROJ .... Project (AFM)
PROJID .... Project Identification [*Data processing*]
PROLAMAT ... Programing Languages for Machine Tools [*Conference*]
PROLAN ...... Processed Language [*Data processing*]
PROLOG ..... Programing in Logic [*Programing language*] [1970]
PROM .... Pockels Readout Optical Modulator
PROM .... Programable Read-Only Memory [*Data processing*]
PROMIS ...... Problem-Oriented Medical Information System [*Computerized patient-management system*]
PROMIS ...... [*A*] Process Management and Information System [*I. P. Sharp Associates Ltd.*] [*Software package*] [*British*] (NCC)
PROMPT ..... Production, Reviewing, Organizing, and Monitoring of Performance Techniques (BUR)
PROMPT ..... Program Monitoring and Planning Techniques (IEEE)
PROMPT ..... Project Management and Production Team Technique [*Data processing*]
PROMT .... Predicasts Overviews of Marketing and Technology [*Business database*]
PROMUS .... Provincial-Municipal Simulator [*Computer-based urban management system*]
PRONTO ..... Program for Numeric Tool Operation [*Data processing*]
PRONTO ..... Programable Network Telecommunications Operating System (NITA)
PROOF .... Projected Return on Open Office Facilities [*Computer program*]
PROP .... Performance Review for Operating Programs (BUR)
PROSE .... Problem Solution Engineering [*Programing language*] [*Data processing*] (CSR)
PROSIM ...... Production System Simulator [*Data processing*]
PROSPRO ... Process Systems Program (OA)
PROT .... Protect [*or Protection*] (MSA)
PROTECON ... Process and Test Control [*Pendar Technical Association Ltd.*] [*Software package*] [*British*] (NCC)
PROTEUS ... [*A*] programing language (CSR)
PRP .... Program Requirements Package [*Data processing*]
PRP .... Pseudorandom Pulse
PRP .... Pulse Recurrence [*or Repetition*] Period (CET)
PRPQ .... Programing Request for Price Quotation [*Data processing*]
PRR .... Pulse Recurrence [*or Repetition*] Rate (MUGU)
PRRM .... Pulse Repetition Rate Modulation [*Data transmission*] [*Data processing*] (TEL)
PRS .... Pattern Recognition Society [*Georgetown University Medical Center*] [*Washington, DC*]
PRS .... Population Research Service [*Austin, TX*] [*Information service*] (EISS)
PRS .... Pseudorandom Sequence
PRT .... Personal Rapid Transit [*Computer-guided transit system*]
PRT .... Portable Radio Telephone
PRT .... Portable Remote Terminal
PRT .... Printer [*Data processing*] (MDG)
PRT .... Production Run Tape (IDA)
PRT .... Program Reference Table
PRT .... Pulse Recurrence [*or Repetition*] Time (CET)
PRTM .... Printing Response-Time Monitor
PRTOT .... Prototype Real-Time Optical Tracker [*Data processing*]
PRTR .... Printer (DDI)
PRTRNS ..... Programable Transformer Converter (MCD)
PRTS .... Personal Rapid Transit System [*Computer-guided transit system*]
PrtSc .... Print Screen [*Computer keyboard*]
PRTY .... Priority (CAH)
PRU .... Packet Radio Unit (NITA)
PRW .... Paired Wire [*Telecommunications*] (TEL)

Computer & Telecommunications Acronyms

P/S	Parallel to Serial [*Converters*] (MCD)
PS	Pascal Software, Inc. [*Moorhead, MN*] [*Hardware manufacturer*] (DASO)
PS	Permanent Signal [*Telecommunications*] (TEL)
PS	Phase-Shift
ps	Picosecond
PS	Port Store [*Telecommunications*] (TEL)
PS	Port Strobe [*Telecommunications*] (TEL)
PS	Power Supply
PS	Presentation Services [*Data processing*] (IBMDP)
PS	Problem Specification (OA)
PS	Process Subsystem [*Telecommunications*] (TEL)
PS	Processor Status (OA)
PS	Program Start (KSC)
PS	Program Store [*Data processing*] (IEEE)
PS	Program Summary (NG)
PS	Programing System (OA)
PS	Pulses per Second [*Data transmission*] (DEN)
PSA	Parametric Semiconductor Amplifier (OA)
PSA	Path Selection Algorithm [*Telecommunications*] (TEL)
PSA	Port Storage Area [*Telecommunications*] (TEL)
PSA	Presunrise Authority
PSA	Public Service Announcement
PSA	Push Down Stack Automaton [*Data processing*]
PSAD	Prediction, Simulation, Adaptation, Decision [*Data processing*]
PSAL	Programing System Activity Log [*Data processing*] (TUT)
PSAM	Partitioned Sequence Access Method (NITA)
PSAP	Plane Stress Analysis and Plot [*Data processing*]
PSAP	Public Safety Answering Point [*Telecommunications*] (TEL)
PSAR	Programable Synchronous/Asynchronous Receiver (IEEE)
PSAT	Programable Synchronous/Asynchronous Transmitter (IEEE)
PSB	Program Specification Block [*IBM Corp.*]
PSC	Pacific Studies Center [*Mountain View, CA*] [*Research center*] (EANO)
PSC	Phase-Sensitive Converter (VIT)
PSC	Printer Systems Corporation [*Gaithersburg, MD*] [*Hardware manufacturer*] (DASO)
PSC	Program Standards Checker [*Data processing*]
PSC	Program Status Chart [*Data processing*]
PSC	Program Structure Code (AFM)
PSC	Project Systems Control (MCD)
PSC	Public Service Commission [*Usually, of a specific state*]
PSCF	Processor Storage Control Function (NITA)
PSCL	Programed Sequential Control Language (NITA)
PSCM	Process Steering and Control Module [*Telecommunications*] (TEL)
PSCR	Permanent Scratch File [*Data processing*]
PSCR	Photo-Selective Copper Reduction [*For circuit board manufacture*]
PSCS	Program Support Control System
PSD	Packed Switched Data (NITA)
PSD	Permanent Signal Detection [*Telecommunications*] (TEL)
PSD	Phase-Sensitive Demodulator
PSD	Photoconductive, Semiconductive Device
PSD	Post Sending Delay (DEEC)
PSD	Program Status Documents [*Data processing*] (TUT)
PSD	Program Status Doubleword (NITA)
PSD	Pulse Shape Discriminator
PSDA	Partial Source Data Automation (NVT)
PSDDS	Pilot [*or Public*] Switched Digital Data Service [*Telecommunications*] (TEL)
PSDI	Project Software & Development, Incorporated [*Cambridge, MA*] [*Software manufacturer*] (DASOS)
PSDP	Phrase Structure and Dependency Parser (DIT)
PSDS	Packet Switched Data Service [*Telecommunications*] (TEL)
PSE	Packet-Switching Exchange
PSE	Phase-Shifter, Electronic
PSE	Please (MDG)
PSF	Permanent Signal Finder
PSF	Point Spread Function
PSF	Provisional System Feature [*Telecommunications*] (TEL)
PSFAM	Parameter Sensitive Frequency Assignment Method (MCD)
PSG	Planning Systems Generator
PSG	Programable Sound Generator [*Atari, Inc.*]
PSG	Pulse Sequence Generation [*Instrumentation*]
PSI	Pacer Software, Incorporated [*La Jolla, CA*] [*Software manufacturer*] (DASOS)
PSI	Paid Service Indication [*Telecommunications*] (TEL)
PSI	Participation Systems, Incorporated [*Electronics Communications Co.*] [*Winchester, MA*] [*Telecommunications*] (TSSD)
PSI	Permuterm Subject Index [*Institute for Scientific Information*] [*A publication*] (EISS)
PSI	Planned Start Installation [*Telecommunications*] (TEL)
PSI	Preprogramed Self-Instruction [*Data processing*] (IEEE)
PSI	Pressure Sensitive Identification (CAH)
PSI	Program Status Information [*Data processing*] (MCD)
PSIC	Process Signal Interface Controller (NITA)
PSI-LOGO	Listing of Oil and Gas Opportunities [*Online Resource Exchange, Inc.*] [*Database*] (CUAD)
PSK	Phase-Shift Keying [*Data processing*]
PSK	Program Selection Key [*Data processing*] (BUR)
PSK	Pulse Shift Keying (CAAL)
PSKM	Phase-Shift Keying MODEM
PSK-PCM	Phase-Shift Keying - Pulse Code Modulation (DDI)
PSL	Physical Sciences Laboratory [*University of Wisconsin - Madison, New Mexico State University*] [*Research center*]
PSL	Pocket Select Language [*Burroughs Corp.*] (NITA)
PSL	Power and Signal List [*Telecommunications*] (TEL)
PSL	Power Source Logic (CIT)
PS & L	Power Switching and Logic (CIT)
PSL	Problem Specification Language (OA)
PSL	Process Simulation Language [*Data processing*] (TEL)
PSLI	Packet Switch Level Interface (NITA)
PSLI	Penta Systems International [*NASDAQ symbol*] (NQ)
PSL/PSA	Problem Statement Language/Problem Specification Analyzer [*Data processing*]
PSM	Peak Selector Memory [*Data processing*]
PSM	Phase-Sensitive Modulator (MCD)
PSM	Phase-Shifter Module
PSM	Program-Sensitive Malfunction
PSM	Programing Support Monitor [*Texas Instruments, Inc.*] (NITA)
PSMI	Phase-Shift Modal Interference
PSML	Processor System Modeling Language [*1976*] [*Data processing*] (CSR)
PSN	Packet Switching Node (NITA)
PSN	Permanent Sort Number [*Data processing*]
PSN	Private Satellite Network, Inc. [*New York, NY*] [*Telecommunications*] (TSSD)
PSN	Public Switched Network (BUR)
PSNR	Power Signal-to-Noise Ratio (CIT)
PSNS	Programable Sampling Network Switch (OA)
PSOP	Power System Optimization Program [*Data processing*]
PSP	Packet Switching Processor (NITA)
PSP	Peak Sideband Power (DEN)
PSP	Planned Standard Programing [*Data processing*]
PSP	Portable Service Processor (IEEE)
PSP	Programable Signal Processor (MCD)
PSQA	Pageable System Queue Area [*Data processing*] (MCD)
PSR	Phase Sequence Relay
PSR	Physical Sciences Research Program [*North Carolina State University*] [*Research center*] (RCD)
PSR	Program Status Register (NITA)
PSR	Program Support Requirements (KSC)
PSR	Programing Status Report [*Data processing*] (TUT)
PSR	Programing Support Representative [*IBM Corp.*]
PSRM	Processor State Register Main [*Data processing*]
PSRO	Professional Standards Review Organization [*Generic term for groups of physicians who may review the policies and decisions of their colleagues*]
PSRR	Product and Support Requirements Request [*Data processing*] (IBMDP)
PSRU	Processor State Register Utility [*Data processing*]
PSS	Packet Switching Service [*Telecommunications*] [*Information service*] [*British*] (EISS)
PSS	Patent Search System [*Pergamon*] [*Database*] [*Data processing*] [*British*]
PSS	Proprietary Software Systems [*Data processing*] (IEEE)
PSS	Public Services Satellite
PSSC	Public Service Satellite Consortium [*Washington, DC*] [*Telecommunications*] [*Information service*] (EANO)
PSSP	Phone Center Staffing and Sizing Program [*Telecommunications*] (TEL)
PST	Pair Selected Ternary [*Data processing*]
PST	Patentstelle fuer die Deutsche Forschung [*Munich*] [*Information retrieval*] (ODIN)
PST	Periodic Self-Test [*Data processing*]
PST	Priority Selection Table [*Data processing*] (IBMDP)
PST	Program Synchronization Table (CMD)
PSTA	Packaging Science and Technology Abstracts [*International Food Information Service*] [*Database*] (CUAD)
PSTC	Public Switched Telephone Circuits [*Telecommunications*] (TEL)
PST-E	Priority Selection Table Extension [*Data processing*] (IBMDP)
PSTN	Public Switched Telephone Network
PSU	Packet Switching Unit (NITA)
PSU	Path Setup [*Telecommunications*] (TEL)
PSU	Port Storage Utility [*Telecommunications*] (TEL)
PSU	Power Supply Unit (MSA)
PSU	Processor Speed Up [*Computer memory core*]
PSU	Program Storage Unit [*Data processing*] (MDG)
PSVM	Phase-Sensitive Voltmeter
PSW	Politically Simulated World [*Computer-assisted political science game*]
PSW	Processor Status Word (DEEC)
PSW	Program Status Word [*Data processing*]
PsycINFO	Psychological Abstracts Information Services [*American Psychological Association*] (EISS)
PT	Paper Tape
PT	Part [*Online database field identifier*] (OBD)
PT	Pay Tone [*Telecommunications*] (TEL)
PT	Point (CAH)
PT	Port Number [*Telecommunications*] (TEL)
PT	Postal Telegraph Co. [*Terminated*]
P et T	Postes et Telecommunications
PT	Printer Terminal (NITA)
PT	Priority Telegram

Computer & Telecommunications Acronyms

PT .... Processing Time   (NITA)
PT .... Programer and Timer
PT .... Publication Type [*Online database field identifier*]   (OBD)
PT .... Punched Tape [*Data processing*]
PTA .... Phototransistor Amplifier
PTA .... Platinized Titanium Anode
PTA .... Programable Translation Array   (NITA)
PTB .... Physical Transaction Block   (NITA)
PTBR .... Punched Tape Block Reader [*Data processing*]
PTC .... Pacific Telecommunications Council   (EANO)
PTC .... Patent, Trademark, and Copyright Institute [*Franklin Pierce College*]   (EISS)
PTC .... Programable Test Console
PTC .... Programed Transmission Control   (BUR)
PTC .... Programer Training Center
PT/CC .... Problem Tracking and Change Control [*Data processing*]
PTD .... Plant Test Date [*Telecommunications*]   (TEL)
PTD .... Posttuning Drift
PTDOS .... Processor Technology Disk Operating System   (NITA)
PTDTL .... Pumped Tunnel Diode Transistor Logic
PTE .... Page Table Entry   (NITA)
PTETS .... Pioneer Television and Electronic Technicians Society [*Defunct*]
PTF .... Program Temporary Fix [*Data processing*]
PTFP .... Public Telecommunications Facilities Program [*Department of Commerce*]
PTG .... Precise Tone Generator [*Telecommunications*]   (TEL)
PTGAP .... Professional Technical Group on Antennas and Propagation [*of the IEEE*]
PTGC .... Programed Temperature Gas Chromatography
PTGEC .... Professional Technical Group on Electronic Computers [*Later, IEEE Computer Society*]
PTI .... Party Identity [*Telecommunications*]   (TEL)
PTI .... Production Training Indicator [*Data processing*]
PTI .... Program Transfer Interface   (NITA)
PTI .... Programed Test Input   (MCD)
PTI .... Public Technology, Inc. [*Washington, DC*] [*Research center*]   (RCD)
PTIS .... Programed Test Input System   (MCD)
PTL .... Process and Test Language   (OA)
PTLRS .... Publications and Technical Literature Research Section [*Environmental Protection Agency*]   (EISS)
PTM .... Phase Time Modulation
PTM .... Portable Traffic Monitor [*Telecommunications*]   (TEL)
PTM .... Programable Terminal Multiplexer [*Texas Instruments, Inc.*]   (NITA)
PTM .... Programable Timer Module   (NITA)
PTM .... Pulse Time Modulation [*Radio*]
PTM .... Pulse Time Multiplex
PTM .... Pulse Transmission Mode   (MCD)
PTML .... PNP [*Positive-Negative-Positive*] Transistor Magnetic Logic   (IEEE)
PTN .... Plant Test Number [*Telecommunications*]   (TEL)
PTOS .... Paper Tape Oriented Operating System   (NITA)
PTOUT .... Printout   (MSA)
PTP .... Paper Tape Perforator
PTP .... Paper Tape Punch
PTP .... Programable Text Processor [*Programing language*]   (CSR)
PTP .... Programed Turn Phase
PTR .... Paper Tape Reader
PTR .... Perforated Tape Reader
PTR .... Photoelectric Tape Reader
PTR .... Poor Transmission [*Telecommunications*]   (TEL)
PTR .... Power Transformers   (MCD)
PTR .... Precision Transmitter Receiver
PTR .... Pretransmit Receiving
PTR .... Printer   (MSA)
PTR .... Processor Tape Read
PTR .... Punched Tape Reader [*Data processing*]
PTS .... Paper Tape-to-Magnetic Tape Conversion System   (DIT)
PTS .... Paper-Tape Sender
PTS .... Papiertechnische Stiftung [*Database producer*]   (CUAD)
PTS .... Predicasts Terminal Systems [*Predicasts, Inc.*] [*Cleveland, OH*] [*Database*]
PTS .... Private Telecommunications Systems [*Radio-Suisse Ltd.*] [*Berne, Switzerland*] [*Telecommunications*]   (TSSD)
PTS .... Proceed to Select [*Telecommunications*]   (TEL)
PTS .... Proceed to Send [*Telecommunications*]   (TEL)
PTS .... Program Test System [*Data processing*]   (IEEE)
PTS .... Programer Test Station
PTS .... Public Telephone Service [*or System*] [*Telecommunications*]   (TEL)
PTS .... Pure Time Sharing [*Data processing*]   (IEEE)
PTS PROMT ... Predicasts Overview of Markets and Technology [*Predicasts, Inc.*] [*Cleveland, OH*] [*Bibliographic database*]   (OBD)
PTSS .... Princeton Time Sharing Services, Inc.
PTT .... Pacific Telephone & Telegraph Co.   (FAAC)
PTT .... Party Test [*Telecommunications*]   (TEL)
PTT .... Post und Telegraphenverwaltung [*Postal and Telegraph Administration*] [*Vienna, Austria*] [*Telecommunications*]   (TSSD)
PTT .... Post, Telephon und Telegraphenbetriebe [*Berne, Switzerland*] [*Telecommunications*]   (TSSD)
PTT .... Postal, Telegraph, and Telephone Administration   (NATG)

PTT .... Postes, Telegraphes, et Telediffusion [*Post, Telegraph, and Telephone*] [*General Post Office*] [*France*]
PTT .... Program Test Tape [*Data processing*]   (IEEE)
PTT .... Public Telecommunications Trust [*Proposed replacement for Corporation for Public Broadcasting*]
PTT .... Push to Talk
PTTC .... Paper Tape and Transmission Code   (NITA)
PTTI .... Postal, Telegraph, and Telephone International [*See also IPTT*] [*Brussels, Belgium*]
PTU .... Package Transfer Unit   (NITA)
PTV .... Pay Television
PTV .... Public Television
PTV .... Punched Tape Verifier [*Data processing*]
PTW .... Playing to Win   (EANO)
PU .... Peripheral Unit [*Computers*]   (MSA)
PU .... Physical Unit [*Data processing*]   (IBMDP)
PU .... Processing Unit [*Data processing*]
PU .... Processor Utility [*Telecommunications*]   (TEL)
PU .... Publisher [*Online database field identifier*]   (OBD)
PUB .... Physical Unit Block [*Data processing*]   (TUT)
Public TC Review ... Public Telecommunications Review [*A publication*]
PUC .... Processing Unit Cabinet [*Data processing*]
PUC .... Public Utilities Commission [*Data traffic regulator*]
PUDT .... Propellant Utilization Data Translator
PUDVM ...... Pulsed Ultrasound Doppler Velocity Meter
PUFF .... Picofarad   (MDG)
PUFFT .... Purdue University Fast FORTRAN [*Formula Translation*] Translator [*Data processing*]
PUFS .... Programer's Utility Filing System   (DIT)
PUG .... PASCAL Users' Group [*Cleveland, OH*]   (EANO)
PUG .... Penta Users Group [*Glen Burnie, MD*]   (EANO)
PUG .... Prime Users Group [*Natick, MA*]   (EANO)
PUL .... Program Update Library   (NITA)
PUM .... Processor Utility Monitor [*Telecommunications*]   (TEL)
PUN .... Prepare a New Perforated Tape for Message [*Communications*]   (FAAC)
PUNC .... Practical, Unpretentious, Nomographic Computer
PUNC .... Program Unit Counter
PUP .... Peripheral Unit Processor [*Data processing*]
PUP .... Pickup   (FAAC)
PUR .... Patch Unit Radio [*Bell System*]
PUR .... Program Utility Routines [*Data processing*]
PURC .... Public Utility Research Center [*University of Florida*] [*Research center*]   (RCD)
PUS .... Processor Utility Subsystem [*Telecommunications*]   (TEL)
PUSAS .... Proposed United States of America Standard   (CGC)
PUT .... Program Update Tape   (NITA)
PV .... Path Verification   (NITA)
PVC .... Permanent Virtual Circuit   (NITA)
PVC .... Position and Velocity Computer
PVCS .... Portable Voice Communications System
PVI .... Programable Video Interface   (NITA)
PVR .... Precision Voltage Reference   (MDG)
PVR .... Process Variable Record   (NITA)
PVS .... Program Validation Services [*Data processing*]
PVSC .... Professional Video Services Corporation [*Washington, DC*] [*Telecommunications*]   (TSSD)
PVT .... Page View Terminal [*Typography*] [*Videotex terminal*]
PVT .... Par Voie Telegraphique [*By Telegraph*] [*French*]
PVTAP .... Photovoltaic Transient Analysis Computer Program
PWA .... Printed Wire Assembly [*Data processing*]
PWAC .... Present Worth of Annual Charges [*Pronounced "p-wack"*] [*Bell System*]
PWB .... Printed Wiring Board
PWBA .... Printed Wiring Board Assembly   (MCD)
PWC .... Printed Wiring Cards [*Telecommunications*]
PWC .... Pulse-Width Coded
PWE .... Present Worth Expenditures [*Telecommunications*]   (TEL)
PWE .... Pulse-Width Encoder
PWFG .... Primary Waveform Generator [*Telecommunications*]   (TEL)
PWM .... Printed Wiring Master
PWM .... Pulse-Width Modulation [*Electronic instrumentation*]
PWM .... Pulse-Width Multiplier   (IEEE)
PWS .... Programer Work Station   (NITA)
PWS .... Project Work Schedule [*Data processing*]
PWTC .... Powertec, Inc. [*NASDAQ symbol*]   (NQ)
PX .... Private Exchange
PY .... Publication Year [*Online database field identifier*]   (OBD)
PZ .... Produktivitaetszentrale Saar eV [*Saarbruecken*] [*Information retrieval*]   (ODIN)
PZT .... Piezoelectric Translator   (DEEC)

Q

Q	Merit of a Coil or Capacitor [*Electronics*]		QSM	Quasi-Linear Sequential Machine
Q	Quarter Word Designator [*Data processing*]		QSS	Quasi-Stellar Source
Q	Query		QSTX	Questronics, Inc. [*NASDAQ symbol*] (NQ)
Q	Query Language [*1975*] (CSR)		QT	Quebec-Telephone [*Toronto Stock Exchange symbol*]
Q	Queue (DEEC)		QT	Queuing Theory [*Telecommunications*]
QA	Quality Assurance [*Data processing*]		QT	Queuing Time [*Telecommunications*] (TEL)
QA	Query Analyzer (IEEE)		QTAM	Quadrature Amplitude Modulation (MCD)
QA	Quiescent Aerial [*or Antenna*]		QTAM	Queued Telecommunications Access Method [*IBM Corp.*] [*Data processing*] (CGC)
QADS	Quality Assurance Data System		QTAM	Queued Terminal Access Method [*Data processing*] (NITA)
QAM	Quadrature Amplitude Modulation		QTH	Queued Transaction Handling [*Data processing*] (NITA)
QAM	Queued Access Method [*Data processing*]		QU	Query
QAS	Question-Answering System		QUAC	Quadratic Arc Computer
QASAR	Quality Assurance Systems Analysis Review (FAAC)		QUAD	Quadraphonic
QASK	Quadrature Amplitude Shift Keying		QUAD	Quadrex Corp. [*NASDAQ symbol*] (NQ)
QBE	Query by Example [*Data processing search method*]		QUAL	Quality (KSC)
QC	Quality Control [*or Controller*]		QUALTIS	Quality Technology Information Service [*Atomic Energy Authority*] [*British*] (EISS)
QC	Quantek Corporation [*Trademark*]		QUAM	Quadrature Amplitude Modulation (IEEE)
QC	Quantum Counter		QUANTRAS	Question Analysis Transformation and Search [*Data processing*]
QC	Quiesce-Completed [*Data processing*] (IBMDP)		QUARK	Quantizer, Analyzer, and Record Keeper [*Telecommunications*] (TEL)
QCB	Queue Control Block [*Data processing*]		QUEST	Query Evaluation and Search Technique (NITA)
QCD	Quality Control Data		QUESTER	Quick and Effective System to Enhance Retrieval [*Data processing*]
QCM	Quantitative Computer Management (IEEE)		QUICKTRAN	Quick FORTRAN [*Programing language*] [*1979*] (DEEC)
QCPE	Quantum Chemistry Program Exchange		QUIL	Quad in Line [*Electronics*] [*Telecommunications*] (TEL)
QCPSK	Quaternary Coherent Phase-Shift Keying		QUIP	Quad In-Line Package (DEEC)
Q & D	Quick and Dirty [*Data processing*] (CGC)		QUIP	Query Interactive Processor (IEEE)
QDPSK	Quaternary Differential Phase-Shift Keying (TEL)		QUIP	QUOTA [*Query Online Terminal Assistance*] Input Processor [*Data processing*]
QDS	Quality Data System (NASA)		QUOTA	Query Online Terminal Assistance [*Data processing*]
QDXR	Quadriplexer (SKY)		QVLBI	Quasi-Very-Long-Baseline Interferometry
QE	Queue Entry (NITA)		QWIKTRAN	Quick FORTRAN [*Programing language*] [*1979*] (CSR)
QEC	Quiesce-at-End-of-Chain [*Data processing*] (IBMDP)			
QED	Quick Text Editor			
QF	Queue Full (NITA)			
QFE	Query Formulation and Encoding			
QFF	Quadrupole Flip-Flop [*Data processing*]			
QFM	Quantized Frequency Modulation			
QFMR	Quantized Frequency Modulation Repeater			
QIL	Quad In-Line (DEEC)			
QIO	Queue Input/Output (NITA)			
QISAM	Queued Indexed Sequential Access Method [*IBM Corp.*] [*Data processing*] (TUT)			
QL	Query Language [*Data processing*] (DIT)			
QL	Queue Length [*Telecommunications*] (TEL)			
QLISP	[*A*] programing language (CSR)			
QLP	Query Language Processor [*Data processing*]			
QLSA	Queue Line Sharing Adapter [*Data processing*] (NITA)			
QM	Queue Manager [*Data processing*] (CMD)			
QMS	Quadrupole Mass Spectrometer			
QMS	Quality Micro Systems [*Trademark*]			
QN	Query Normalization (NITA)			
QNT	Quantizer (MDG)			
QNTM	Quantum Corp. [*NASDAQ symbol*] (NQ)			
QOS	Quality of Service [*Telecommunications*] (TEL)			
QP	Quadratic Programing [*Data processing*] (BUR)			
QPM	Quantized Pulse Modulation			
QPRS	Quadrature Partial-Response System [*Telecommunications*] (TEL)			
QPSK	Quad-Phase Shift Key			
Q-Q	Quantile-Quantile [*Data processing*]			
QR	Quotation Request			
Q & RA	Quality and Reliability Assurance			
QRL	Quick Relocate and Link (NITA)			
QRM	Artificial Interference to Transmission or Reception [*Broadcasting*] (DDI)			
QRP	Query and Reporting Processor (NITA)			
QRR	Quadrupole Resonance Response			
QRT	Queue Run-Time [*Data processing*] (NITA)			
QS	Query System [*Data processing*] (NITA)			
QS	Queue Select [*Data processing*] (NITA)			
QSA	Quad Synchronous Adapter [*Perkin-Elmer*] (NITA)			
QSAM	Quadrature Sideband Amplitude Modulation			
QSAM	Queued Sequential Access Method [*IBM Corp.*] [*Data processing*] (TUT)			
QSL	Queue Search Limit [*Data processing*] (NITA)			

R

R	R-Register [Data processing]		RADS	Raw Data System (DDI)
R	Radiotelegram		RADTT	Radio Teletypewriter (CET)
R	Rational Number (MDG)		RAE	Radiodifusion Argentina al Exterior [Broadcasting organization]
R	Read		RAEN	Radio Amateur Emergency Network (IEEE)
R	Real		RAES	Remote Access Editing System [Data processing] (IEEE)
R	Receiver		RAFA	Rank Annihilation Factor Analysis [Data processing]
R	Remote [Telecommunications] (TEL)		RAFT	Recomp Algebraic Formula Translator [Data processing]
R	Repetitive [Electronics]		RAG	ROM [Read-Only Memory] Address Gate [Data processing] (NITA)
R	Reset (MDG)		RAGN	Ragen Corp. [NASDAQ symbol] (NQ)
R	Resistance [Symbol] [IUPAC]		RAI	Radiotelevisione Italiana [Italian government-controlled radio and television company]
R	Resistor		RAI	Random Access and Inquiry [Data processing]
R	Right [Direction]		RAIAM	Random Access Indestructive Advanced Memory [Data processing] (MSA)
R	Ring Lead [Telecommunications] (TEL)		RAID	Remote Access Interactive Debugger [Data processing] (IEEE)
3R	Request, Retrieve, and Report [Data processing] (TUT)		RAIN	Relational Algebraic Interpreter (NITA)
RA	Random Access [Data processing]		RAIR	Random Access Information Retrieval [Data processing] (IEEE)
RA	Ready-Access [Telecommunications] (TEL)		RAIR	Recordak Automated Information Retrieval [System]
R/A	Recorded Announcement [Telecommunications] (TEL)		RAIR	Remote Access Immediate Response [Data processing] (TUT)
RA	Relocation Address (NITA)		RAIS	Range Automated Information System (KSC)
R/A	Repeat Attempt [Telecommunications] (TEL)		RAITV	Radiotelevisione Italiana [Italian government-controlled radio and television company]
RA	Replacement Algorithm (OA)		RAK	Read Access Key (NITA)
RA	Return Address (NITA)		RAK	Regeln fuer die Alphabetische Katalogisierung [Rules for Alphabetical Cataloging] [Information retrieval] (ODIN)
RA	Ripple Adder (NITA)		RAK	Remote Access Key (NITA)
RAAR	RAM Address Register (OA)		RAL	Robotics & Automation Research Laboratory [University of Toronto] [Research center] (RCD)
RAC	Read Address Counter		RALF	Relocatable Assembly Language Floating Point (NITA)
RAC	Rectified Alternating Current [Radio]		RALU	Register and Arithmetic/Logic Unit [Data processing]
RAC	Reflect Array Pulse Compressor (RDA)		RAM	Radio Attenuation Measurement [Spacecraft for testing communications]
RACE	Random Access Computer Equipment		RAM	Random Access Measurement [System] [Data processing]
RACE	Random Access Control Equipment (IEEE)		RAM	Random Access Memory [Data processing]
RACE	Rapid Automatic Checkout Equipment		RAM	Random Angle Modulation
RACE	Research in Advanced Communications in Europe [European Commission]		RAM	Raytheon Airborne Microwave (MCD)
RACE	Research on Automatic Computation Electronics		RAM	Resident Access Methods (MCD)
RACEP	Random Access and Correlation for Extended Performance		RAMAC	Random Access Method of Accounting and Control [Data processing]
RACF	Resource Access Control Facility [IBM Corp.]		RAMB	Random Access Memory Buffer [Data processing]
RACS	Random Access Communications System		RAMBO	Real-Time Acquisitions Management and Bibliographic Order System [Suggested name for the Library of Congress computer system]
RACS	Remote Access Computing System [Data processing]		RAMD	Random Access Memory Device [Data processing]
RACS	Remote Automatic Control System (KSC)		RAMIS	Rapid Access Management Information System [Data processing] (CGC)
RACT	Remote Access Computer Technique [Data processing] (IEEE)		RAMM	Random Access Memory Module [Data processing]
RAD	Radio		RAMP	Radio Attenuation Measurement Project
RAD	Random Access Data (BUR)		RAMP	Raytheon Airborne Microwave Platform [Sky station]
RAD	Random Access Device		RAMP	Reliability and Maintainability Program (NITA)
RAD	Random Access Disc (MCD)		RAMS	Random Access Measurement System [Data processing]
RAD	Rapid Access Data [Xerox Corp.] (NITA)		RAMS	Random Access Memory Store [Data processing] (TEL)
RAD	Rapid Access Device (NITA)		RAMS	Reduced-Size Antenna Monopulse System
RAD	Rapid Access Disk		RAMS	Remotely Accessible Management Systems [Data processing]
RAD	Rapid Access Drive (BUR)		RAMSH	Reliability, Availability, Maintainability, Safety, and Human Factors [Telecommunications] (TEL)
RAD	Records Arrival Date [Bell System] (TEL)		RANCID	Real and Not Corrected Input Data [Data processing]
RAD	Research and Advanced Development		RANCOM	Random Communication Satellite
RADAC	Rapid Digital Automatic Computing		RANDAM	Random Access Nondestructive Advanced Memory [Data processing]
RADAC	Raytheon Automatic Drafting Artwork Compiler		RANDID	Rapid Alphanumeric Digital Indicating Device
RADAR	Repertoire Analytique d'Articles de Revues de Quebec [Database] [A publication]		RANT	Reentry Antenna Test
RADAS	Random Access Discrete Address System		RAO	Regional Accounting Office [Telecommunications] (TEL)
RADB	Radiometric Age Data Bank [Geological Survey] (EISS)		RAP	Random Access Program [Data processing]
RADC	Rome Air Development Center [ESD]		RAP	Random Access Projector
RADEM	Random Access Delta Modulation		RAP	Relational Associative Processor (IEEE)
RADIAC	Radiation Detection, Indication, and Computation [Radiological measuring instruments]		RAP	Requirements Analysis Package [Data processing]
RADIC	Redifon Analog-Digital Computer [British]		RAP	Resident Assembler Program (NITA)
Radio-Electr	Radio-Electronics [A publication]		RAP	Resource Allocation Processor (CMD)
Radio Electron	Radio Electronica [Netherlands] [A publication]		RAP	Response Analysis Program [Data processing] (IBMDP)
Radio-Electron	Radio-Electronics [A publication]		RAP	Ring-Around Programing (CAAL)
Radio Electron Commun Syst	Radio Electronics and Communications Systems [A publication]		RAPCOE	Random Access Programing and Checkout Equipment
Radio Eng Electron Phys	Radio Engineering and Electronic Physics [A publication]			
Radio Eng Electron (USSR)	Radio Engineering and Electronic Physics (USSR) [A publication]			
Radio Engrg Electron Phys	Radio Engineering and Electronic Physics [A publication]			
Radio Sci	Radio Science [A publication]			
RADIR	Random Access Document Indexing and Retrieval			
RADIT	Radio Teletype (IEEE)			

Computer & Telecommunications Acronyms

RAPIC .... Remedial Action Program Information Center [*Department of Energy*] [*Information service*]   (EISS)
RAPID .... Random Access Personnel Information Dissemination   (IDA)
RAPID .... Reactor and Plant Integrated Dynamics [*Data processing*]   (KSC)
RAPID .... Relative Address Programing Implementation Device [*Data processing*]
RAPID .... Remote Access Planning for Institutional Development [*Data processing*]
RAPID .... Research in Automatic Photocomposition and Information Dissemination
RAPID .... Retrieval through Automated Publication and Information Digest [*Data processing*]   (DIT)
RAPID .... Retrieval and Processing Information for Display   (DDI)
RAPID .... Rocketdyne Automatic Processing of Integrated Data [*Data processing*]
RAPS .... Retrieval Analysis and Presentation System [*Data processing*]   (TUT)
RAPTAP ...... Random Access Parallel Tape
RAPTN .... Rapra Trade Names [*Rapra Technology Ltd.*] [*Information service*]   (EISS)
RAPUD .... Revenue Analysis from Parametric Usage Descriptions [*Telecommunications*]   (TEL)
RAR .... Radio Acoustic Ranging
RAR .... Rapid Access Recording   (IEEE)
RAR .... Return Address Register   (NITA)
RAR .... ROM [*Read-Only Memory*] Address Register   (NITA)
RARP .... Radio Affiliate Replacement Plan [*Canadian Broadcasting Corporation*]
RARU .... Radio Range Station Reported Unreliable [*Message abbreviation*]
RAS .... Radio Science [*A publication*]
RAS .... Records and Analysis Subsystem   (TEL)
RAS .... Reflector Antenna System
RAS .... Reliability, Availability, and Serviceability [*IBM Corp. slogan*]   (MCD)
RAS .... Route Accounting Subsystem [*Telecommunications*]   (TEL)
RAS .... Row-Address Strobe   (IEEE)
RASCA .... Radio Science [*A publication*]
RASCAL ...... Random Access Secure Communications Antijam Link
RASD MARS ... RASD [*Reference and Adult Services Division*] Machine-Assisted Reference Section
RASM .... Remote Analog Submultiplexer   (MCD)
RASP .... Remote Access Switching and Patching   (NITA)
RASP .... Retrieval and Sort Processor [*Data processing*]
RASS .... Rock Analysis Storage System [*United States Geological Survey*]   (EISS)
RASTAC ..... Random Access Storage and Control [*Data processing*]
RASTAD ..... Random Access Storage and Display [*Data processing*]
RATAC .... Raytheon Acoustic Telemetry and Control
RATC .... Rate-Aided Tracking Computer
RATE .... Remote Automatic Telemetry Equipment
RATEL .... Radiotelephone
RATEL .... Raytheon Automatic Test Equipment Language [*Data processing*]   (CSR)
RATELO ...... Radiotelephone Operator
RATES .... Rapid Access Tariff Expediting Service [*Journal of Commerce, Inc.*] [*Database*]   (CUAD)
RATFOR ...... Rational FORTRAN [*Data processing*]
RATG .... Radiotelegraph
RATIO .... Radio Telescope in Orbit   (IEEE)
RATT .... Radioteletype
RATTC .... Radio and Teletype Control Center   (DDI)
RAVE .... Random Access Video Editing [*Computerized film editing*]
RAW .... Read after Write   (NITA)
RAW .... Read and Write [*Data processing*]
RAX .... Remote Access [*Data processing*] [*Telecommunications*]
RAYCI .... Raytheon Controlled Inventory [*Data processing*]
RAY-COM .... Raytheon Communications Equipment [*Citizens band radio*]
RAYDAC ..... Raytheon Digital Automatic Computer   (MUGU)
RAYSISTOR ... Raytheon Resistor [*Electro-optical control device*]
RAYSPAN ... Raytheon Spectrum Analyzer
RAY-TEL ..... Raytheon Telephone [*Citizens band radio*]
R/B .... Radio Beacon
RB .... Radio Bearing   (DEN)
RB .... Radio Brenner [*Radio network*] [*West Germany*]
RB .... Read Back [*Communications*]   (FAAC)
RB .... Read Buffer
RB .... Relay Block   (MSA)
RB .... Repeated Back [*Communications*]   (FAAC)
RB .... Request Block   (NITA)
RB .... Reverse Blocked
RB .... Rollback [*Telecommunications*]   (TEL)
RBA .... Relative Byte Address [*Data processing*]   (MCD)
RBA .... Rotary Beam Antenna
RBA .... Rotor Blade Antenna
RBBS .... Remote Bulletin Board System [*For IBM computers*]
RBC .... Radio Beam Communications
RBC .... Reactive Bias Circuit   (MCD)
RBCS .... Radio Beam Communications Set
RBD .... Reliable Block Diagram   (MCD)
RBE .... Remote Batch Entry   (CMD)
RBF .... Remote Batch Facility   (NITA)
RBHA .... Rotor Blade Homing Antenna
RBI .... Radio Berlin International
RBI .... Ripple-Blanking Input   (IEEE)
RBL .... Rebroadcast Link [*Aerial*]
RBM .... Real-Time Batch Monitor [*Xerox Corp.*]   (NITA)
RBM .... Remote Batch Module   (NITA)
RBMT .... Retrospective Bibliographies on Magnetic Tape   (NASA)
RBN .... PTS [*Predicasts*] Regional Business News [*Cleveland, OH*] [*Database*] [*Information service*]   (EISS)
RBN .... Random Block Number [*Data processing*]
RBO .... Ripple-Blanking Output   (IEEE)
RBOT .... Robotics Information [*Cincinnati Milacron Industries, Inc.*] [*Database*]
RBP .... Registered Business Programer [*Offered earlier by Data Processing Management Association, now discontinued*]   (IEEE)
RBS .... Remote Batch System   (NITA)
RBT .... Remote Batch Terminal
RBT .... Ringback Tone [*Telecommunications*]   (TEL)
RBV .... Return Beam Vidicon [*Satellite camera*]
RBVC .... Return Beam Vidicon Camera
RC .... Circular Radio Beacon
RC .... Nondirectional Radio Beacon [*ITU designation*]   (CET)
RC .... Radio Code Aptitude Area
R/C .... Radio Command [*or Control*]   (KSC)
RC .... Radio Compass
RC .... Rate Center [*Telecommunications*]   (TEL)
RC .... Read and Compute
RC .... Real Circuit   (NITA)
RC .... Record Count [*Data processing*]
RC .... Recording Completing [*Trunk*] [*Telecommunications*]   (TEL)
RC .... Reference Clock [*Telecommunications*]   (TEL)
RC .... Relay Computer   (BUR)
RC .... Remote Computer   (NITA)
RC .... Remote Concentrator   (NITA)
RC .... Remote Control
RC .... Resistance Capacitance
RC .... Resistance Coupled   (CIT)
R-C .... Resistor-Capacitor
RCA .... Radio Club of America
RCA .... Radio Collectors of America   (EANO)
RCA .... RCA Corp. [*Formerly, Radio Corporation of America*] [*NYSE symbol*]
RCA .... Remote Control Amplifier   (MCD)
RCAC .... Radio Corporation of America Communications   (MCD)
RCAC .... Remote Computer Access Communications Service
RCAG .... Remote-Controlled Air-Ground Communication Site   (MCD)
RCAN .... Recorded Announcement [*Telecommunications*]   (TEL)
RCAT .... Radio Code Aptitude Test
RCAT .... Radio-Controlled Aerial Target
RCB .... Region Control Block [*Data processing*]   (BUR)
RCB .... Reinforced Concrete Design [*Camutek*] [*Software package*] [*British*]   (NCC)
RCB .... Remote Circuit Breaker   (MCD)
RCB .... Remote Control Bandwidth
RCB .... Resource Control Block [*Data processing*]   (IBMDP)
RCC .... Radio Common Carrier
RCC .... Radio Common Channels
RCC .... Radio Communications Center
RCC .... Rag Chewers' Club [*Amateur radio*]
RCC .... RCA Corporation Communications
RCC .... Read Channel Continue
RCC .... Real-Time Computer Complex
R & CC .... Recorder and Communications Control   (NASA)
RCC .... Rectangular Concrete Columns [*Jacys Computing Services*] [*Software package*] [*British*]   (NCC)
RCC .... Remote Communications Central
RCC .... Remote Communications Complex
RCC .... Remote Communications Concentrator   (NITA)
RCC .... Remote Communications Console
RCC .... Research Computing Center [*University of New Hampshire*] [*Research center*]   (RCD)
RCC .... Reset Control Circuit
RCC .... Resistor Color Code   (DEN)
RCCA .... Record Carrier Competition Act [*1981*]
RCCB .... Remote Control Circuit Breaker   (NASA)
RCCOL .... Reinforced Concrete Column [*Camutek*] [*Software package*] [*British*]   (NCC)
RCCP .... Recorder and Communications Control Panel   (NASA)
RCD .... Receiver-Carrier Detector
RCD .... Record
RCD .... Route Control Digit [*Telecommunications*]   (TEL)
RCE .... Radio Communications Equipment
RCE .... Remote Control Equipment   (DIT)
RCEEA .... Radio Communications and Electronic Engineers Association
RCF .... Reader's Comment Form   (IBMDP)
RCF .... Remote Call Forwarding [*Bell System*]
RCF .... Retail Computer Facilities
RCG .... Radio Command Guidance
RCI .... Radio Canada International
RCI .... Radio Communications Instruction   (MUGU)
RCI .... Read Channel Initialize
RCI .... Remote Control Indicator   (CAAL)
RCI .... Remote Control Interface   (NITA)

Computer & Telecommunications Acronyms

RCI	Rochester Commercial and Industrial [*Electronic service*]
RCI	Routing Control Indicator [*Telecommunications*] (TEL)
RCIU	Remote Computer Interface Unit (NITA)
RCL	Radio Command Linkage
RCL	Recall (MSA)
RCL	Remote Control Location
RCL	Research Computation Laboratory [*University of Houston*] [*Research center*] (RCD)
RCLR	Radio Communications Link Repeater (FAAC)
RCLT	Radio Communications Link Terminal (FAAC)
RCM	Reliability Corporate Memory (IEEE)
RCMA	Radio Communications Monitoring Association (EANO)
RCN	Record Number [*Online database field identifier*] (OBD)
RCN	Recovery Communications Network (SKY)
RCO	Radio Control Operator
RCO	Receiver Cuts Out [*Telecommunications*] (TEL)
RCO	Remote Communication Outlet [*ATCS*]
RCOA	Radio Club of America
RC/OC	Reverse Current/Overcurrent (KSC)
RCP	Receive Clock Pulse (NITA)
RCP	Recognition and Control Processor [*Data processing*] (IBMDP)
RCP	Remote Control Panel
RCP	Restoration Control Point [*Telecommunications*] (TEL)
RCS	Radio Command System
RCS	Radio Communications Set
RCS	Rearward Communications System (MDG)
RCS	Reloadable Control Storage [*Data processing*]
RCS	Remote Computing Service
RCS	Remote Computing Supplies [*Downers Grove, IL*] [*Hardware manufacturer*] (DASO)
RC(S)	Remote Control (System) (DEN)
RCS	Remote Control System
RCSS	Random Communication Satellite System
RCT	Radiobeacon Calibration Transmitter
RCT	Region Control Task [*Data processing*] (BUR)
RCTL	Resistance-Coupled Transistor Logic (DDI)
RCTL	Resistor-Capacitor Transistor Logic
RCTSR	Radio Code Test, Speed of Response
RCTV	RCA Cable and Rockefeller Center Cable Pay-TV Program Service
RCU	Remote Control Unit
RCV	Receive (AFM)
RCV	Remote-Controlled Vehicle (MCD)
RCVR	Receiver
RCW	Record Control Word [*Data processing*]
RCW	Return Control Word (NITA)
RD	Directional Radio Beacon [*ITU designation*] (CET)
RD	Read
RD	Read Data (NITA)
RD	Read Direct (OA)
RD	Readiness Data
RD	Received Data (IEEE)
RD	Record Description [*Data processing*]
RD	Recording Demand (DEN)
R & D	Research and Development
RD	Ringdown [*Telecommunications*] (TEL)
RDA	Real-Time Debugging Aid (NITA)
RDA	Regional Data Associates [*Information service*] (EISS)
RDA	Remote Data Access (NASA)
RDAL	Representation Dependent Accessing Language (NITA)
RDAT	Rotary Digital Audio Tape
RDAU	Remote Data Acquisition Unit
RDB	Rare Disease Database [*National Organization for Rare Disorders*] [*Information service*] (EISS)
RDB	Relational Database (NITA)
RDBL	Readable (CDH)
RDC	Read Data Check (CMD)
RDC	Regional Data Center
RDC	Reliability Data Center (KSC)
RDC	Remote Data Collection (MCD)
RDC	Remote Data Concentrator
RDCM	Reduced Delta Code Modulation [*Digital memory*]
RDCP	Remote Display Control Panel (MCD)
RDD	Random Digit Dialing [*Telecommunications*]
RDD	Requisition Due Date (TEL)
RDDMI	Radio Digital Distance Magnetic Indicator (MCD)
RDE	Reliability Data Extractor (MCD)
RDE	Rotating Disc Electrode
RDF	Radio Direction Finder [*or Finding*]
RDF	Record Definition Field [*Data processing*] (BUR)
RDFSTA	Radio Direction Finder Station
RDI	Radio Doppler Inertial
RDI	Route Digit Indicator [*Telecommunications*] (TEL)
RDIS	Research and Development Information System [*Later, EPD/RDIS*] [*Electric Power Research Institute*] [*Information service*] (EISS)
RDIU	Remote Device Interface Unit (NITA)
RDL	Remote Display Link
RDL	Resistor Diode Logic (NITA)
RDM	Real-Time Data Manager (MCD)
RDM	Remote Digital Multiplexer (MCD)
RDO	Radio
RDO	Radio Readout
RDOS	Real-Time Disk-Operating System [*Data processing*]
RDOUT	Readout
RDP	Range Data Processor (MCD)
RDP	Receiver and Data Processor (MCD)
RDP	Remote Data Processor
RDR	Raw Data Recorder (NASA)
RDR	Reader (MSA)
RDR	Receive Data Register [*Data processing*] (MDG)
RDR	Remote Digital Readout
RDRD	Remote Digital Readout
RDS	RADAUS [*Radio-Austria AG*] Data-Service [*Vienna*] [*Telecommunications*] (TSSD)
RDS	Radio Digital System [*Telecommunications*] (TEL)
RDS	Raytheon Data Systems Co.
RDS	Request for Data Services
RDSM	Remote Digital Submultiplexer (KSC)
RDT	Radio Digital Terminal [*Bell System*]
RDT	Remote Data Transmitter
RDT	Resource Definition Table [*Data processing*] (IBMDP)
RDTL	Resistor Diode Transistor Logic (IEEE)
RDUC	Receiver Data from Unit Control (MCD)
RDW	Response Data Word (MCD)
RDW	Return Data Word (MCD)
RDY	Ready
RE	Radio Electrician
RE	Radio Exposure
RE	Receiver/Exciter (CIT)
RE	Reference [*Online database field identifier*] (OBD)
RE	Reference Equivalent [*Telecommunications*] (TEL)
RE	Reset (MDG)
R2E	Realisations et Etudes Electronique [*French computer manufacturer*] (NITA)
REAC	Reeves Electronic Analog Computer
REACCS	Reaction Access System [*Computer program*]
REACT	Radio Emergency Associated Citizens Teams [*Acronym alone is now used as official association name*] (EANO)
REACT	Register Enforced Automated Control Technique [*Cash register-computing system*]
REACTS	Reader Action Service [*ZIP code computer*]
READ	Real-Time Electronic Access and Display [*System*] [*Data processing*]
READ	Remote Electronic Alphanumeric Display [*Data processing*] (IEEE)
REALCOM	Real-Time Communications [*RCA*]
REAP	Remote Entry Acquisition Package (CGC)
REASTAN	Renton Electrical Analog for Solution of Thermal Analogous Networks
REBA	Relativistic Electron Beam Accelerator
REBAT	Restricted Bandwidth Techniques (NG)
REBK	Repertoire des Banques de Donnees en Conversationnel [*Database*] (CUAD)
REBUD	Rehabilitation Budgeting Program [*Telecommunications*] (TEL)
REBUS	Routine for Executing Biological Unit Simulations [*Computer program*]
REC	Receiver
REC	Recognition Equipment, Inc. [*NYSE symbol*]
REC	Record
REC	Recover [*or Recovery*]
REC	Rehabilitation Engineering Center for the Hearing Impaired [*Gallaudet College*] [*Research center*] (RCD)
RECIPE	Recomp Computer Interpretive Program Expediter [*Data processing*]
RECMF	Radio and Electronic Component Manufacturers' Federation
RECODEX	Report Collection Index [*Studsvik Energiteknik AB*] [*Database*] (CUAD)
RECOL	Retrieval Command Language [*Computer search language*] (DEEC)
RECOMP	Recomplement (CDH)
RECOMP	Redstone Computer
RECOMP	Retrieval and Composition (DIT)
RECON	Reliability and Configuration Accountability System
RECOV	Recovery (KSC)
RECOVER	Remote Continual Verification [*Telephonic monitoring system*]
RECR	Receiver
RECSTA	Receiving Station
RECSYS	Recreation Systems Analysis [*Data processing*]
RED	Radiation Experience Data [*Food and Drug Administration*] [*Database*] (FDB)
RED	Reduce [*or Reduction*]
REDAC	Real-Time Data Acquisition (NITA)
REDAP	Reentrant Data Processing
REDI	Real Estate Data, Incorporated [*Information service*] (EISS)
REDUCE	Reduction of Electrical Demand Using Computer Equipment [*Energy Management System*]
REEP	Range Estimating and Evaluation Procedure [*Data processing*]
REF	Reference [*Online database field identifier*] (NATG)
REFLES	Reference Librarian Enhancement System [*University of California*] [*Online microcomputer system*]
REFTEL	Reference Telegram
REFTS	Resonant Frequency Tracking System
REG	Range Extender with Gain [*Bell System*]
REG	Register
REGIS	Register

REGIS .... Relational General Information System (NITA)
REIN .... Raymond Engineering [*NASDAQ symbol*] (NQ)
REIN .... Real Estate Information Network [*Electronic service*]
REIS .... Research and Engineering Information Services [*Exxon Research & Engineering Co.*] (EISS)
REJ .... Reject (MSA)
REL .... Rapidly Extensible Language System [*Data processing*] (CSR)
REL .... Relative
REL .... Release
REL .... Relocatable [*Data processing*]
RELE .... Radio Electrician
RELI .... Religion Index [*American Theological Library Association*] [*Chicago, IL*] [*Bibliographic database*] (OBD)
RELMS .... Relational Memory Systems [*San Jose, CA*] [*Hardware manufacturer*] (DASO)
RELQ .... Release-Quiesce [*Data processing*]
REM .... Recognition Memory [*Semionics Associates*] [*Data processing*]
REMAP .... Record Extraction, Manipulation, and Print (DEEC)
REMARC ...... Retrospective Machine Readable Catalog [*Carrollton Press, Inc.*] [*Arlington, VA*] [*Bibliographic database*] [*Online version of the US Library of Congress Shelflist*] (OBD)
REMC .... Radio and Electronics Measurements Committee [*London, England*] (DEN)
REMIS .... Real Estate Management Information System (BUR)
REMOS .... Real-Time Event Monitor [*Data processing*] (IEEE)
REMP .... Research and Evaluation Methods Program [*University of Massachusetts*] [*Research center*] (RCD)
REMR .... Remington Rand Corp. [*NASDAQ symbol*] (NQ)
REM-RAND ... Remington Rand Corp. [*Later, a division of Sperry-Rand*]
REMSTA ...... Remote Electronic Microfilm Storage Transmission and Retrieval (NITA)
REN .... Remote Enable (IEEE)
RENM .... Request for Next Message (OA)
REP .... Re-Entrant Processor (NITA)
REP .... Replication [*Telecommunications*] (TEL)
Rep Comput Centre Univ Tokyo ... Report. Computer Centre. University of Tokyo [*A publication*]
REPERF .... Reperforator [*Telecommunications*] (TEL)
REPLAB .... Responsive Environment Programed Laboratory (IFFF)
REP-OP .... Repetitive Operation [*Data processing*] (MDG)
REPROM ..... Reprogramable Programable Read-Only Memory [*Data processing*] (TEL)
REPROM ..... Reprogramable Read-Only Memory [*Data processing*] (KSC)
REPROTOX ... Reproductive Toxicology [*Database*]
REPTWX ..... Reply by TWX [*Teletypewriter communications*] (FAAC)
REQ .... Request
REQD .... Required
REQS .... Requires
REQT .... Requirement
RER .... Residual Error Rate (DEEC)
RERAD .... Reference Radio
RES .... Record Element Specification [*Data processing*]
RES .... Remote Entry Services (MCD)
RES .... Restore (NITA)
RESCAN ...... Reflecting Satellite Communication Antenna
RESCU .... Radio Emergency Search Communications Unit
RESORS ..... Remote Sensing On-Line Retrieval System [*Canada Centre for Remote Sensing*] [*Database*] [*Information service*] (EISS)
REST .... Range Endurance Speed and Time [*Computer*]
RETA .... Retrieval of Enriched Textual Abstracts [*Information retrieval program*]
RETAIN .... Remote Technical Assistance and Information Network [*Data processing*]
RETD .... Red Especial de Transmision de Datos [*Spanish telephone co.*] (TEL)
RETMA .... Radio-Electronics-Television Manufacturers Association [*Later, Electronic Industries Association*]
RETP .... Retape
RETR .... Retention Register [*Data processing*]
RETR .... Retrieve (KSC)
RETRV .... Retrieve (MCD)
REU .... Rectifier Enclosure Unit [*Power supply*] [*Telecommunications*] (TEL)
REV .... Reverse
REV .... Revolution
REVOP .... Random Evolutionary Operation
REVS .... Requirements Engineering and Validation System (NITA)
Rev Telecommun ... Revue des Telecommunications [*France*] [*A publication*]
Rev Telecomun (Madrid) ... Revista de Telecomunicacion (Madrid) [*A publication*]
REW .... Rewind (MDG)
REWDAC ..... Retrieval by Title Words, Descriptors, and Classification (DIT)
REX .... Real-Time Executive Routine [*Data processing*]
REX .... Rechtswissenschaftliche Experten und Gutachter [*NOMOS Datapool*] [*Database*] (CUAD)
REX .... Run Executive [*Data processing*]
REYNA .... Reynolds & Reynolds [*NASDAQ symbol*] (NQ)
RF .... Radio Frequency [*Transmission*]
RF .... Read Forward
RF .... Reference [*Online database field identifier*] (OBD)
RF .... Register File (NITA)
RF .... Reporting File (NITA)
RFA .... Radio Frequency Amplifier

RFA .... Recurrent Fault Analysis [*Telecommunications*] (TEL)
RFA .... Remote File Access (NITA)
RFB .... Reason for Backlog [*Telecommunications*] (TEL)
RFC .... Radio Facility Charts
RFC .... Radio Frequency Chart
RFC .... Radio Frequency Choke
RFC .... Radio Frequency Compatibility
RFC .... Radio Frequency Crystal
RFD .... Ready for Data (IEEE)
RFDU .... Reconfiguration and Fault Detection Unit (OA)
RFE .... Radio Free Europe
RFE/RL .... Radio Free Europe/Radio Liberty
RFG .... Report Format Generator (NITA)
RFHT .... Radio Frequency Horn Technique
RFI .... Radio Frequency Indicator
RFI .... Radio Frequency Interchange (MDG)
RFI .... Radio Frequency Interference
RFI .... Ready for Installation (MCD)
RFI .... Request for Information
RFIM .... Radio Frequency Interference Meter
RFIP .... Radio Frequency Impedance Probe
RFIT .... Radio Frequency Interference Tests (KSC)
RFJ .... Radio Frequency Joint
RFMS .... Remote File Management System
RFN .... Radio Frequency Noise
RFNM .... Ready for Next Message (NITA)
RFO .... Radio Frequency Oscillator
RFO .... Reason for Outage (FAAC)
RFP .... Request for Programing [*Data orocessing*] (CIT)
RFP .... Request for Proposal
RFQ .... Request for Quotation
RFS .... Radio Frequency Seal
RFS .... Radio-Frequency Shift (IEEE)
RFS .... Random Filing System (NITA)
RFS .... Range Frequency Synthesizer
RFS .... Ready for Service (DDI)
RFS .... Regional Frequency Supplies [*Telecommunications*] (TEL)
RG .... Release Guard [*Telecommunications*] (TEL)
RG .... Report Generator (CMD)
RG .... Ringing Generator [*Telecommunications*] (TEL)
RGB .... Red Green Blue [*Video monitor*]
RGBI .... Red Green Blue Intensity [*Video monitor*]
RGE .... Range [*Maps and charts*] (MDG)
RGICC .... Region Internal Computer Code [*Data processing*]
RGL .... Report Generator Language [*Data processing*] (IEEE)
RGP .... Remote Graphics Processor
RGT .... Resonant Gate Transistor [*Data processing*]
RH .... Random House, Inc. [*NYSE symbol*] [*Delisted*]
RH .... Receive Hub [*Telegraph*] [*Telecommunications*] (TEL)
RH .... Report Heading (BUR)
RH .... Request-Response Header [*Data processing*] (BUR)
RH .... Research Highlights [*A publication*] (DIT)
RHEL .... Rutherford High Energy Laboratory (MCD)
RHL .... Reverse Half-Line [*Feed*]
RHR .... Receiver Holding Register (NITA)
RHS .... Right-Hand Side
RHTM .... Regional Highway Traffic Model [*Database*] [*No longer available online*] (CUAD)
RHW .... Reversible Half-Wave
RHW .... Right Half Word
RHWAC .... Reversible Half-Wave Alternating Current
RHWACDC ... Reversible Half-Wave Alternating Current - Direct Current
RHWDC .... Reversible Half-Wave Direct Current
RI .... Radio Inertial (MCD)
RI .... Radio Influence
RI .... Radio Inspector
RI .... Radio Interference (MCD)
RI .... Read-In (DEN)
RI .... Reliability Index
RI .... Repeat Indication [*Telecommunications*] (TEL)
RI .... Rockwell International Corp. (MCD)
RI .... Routing Identifier [*or Indicator*] (AFM)
RIA .... Research Institute of America [*New York, NY*] [*Information service*] (EISS)
RIA .... Robotic Industries Association (EANO)
RIAA .... Recording Industry Association of America [*Formerly, Record Industry Association of America*] [*New York, NY*]
RIACS .... Research Institute for Advanced Computer Science [*University Space Research Association*] [*Research center*] (RCD)
RIC .... Read-In Counter (NITA)
RIC .... Rockwell International Corporation (NASA)
RICAL .... Research Information Center and Library [*Foster Wheeler Corp.*] [*Information service*] (EISS)
RICC .... Remote Intercomputer Communications Interface (MCD)
RICE .... Resources in Computer Education [*Northwest Regional Educational Laboratory Microcomputer Software and Information for Teachers*] [*Database*]
RID .... Records Issue Date [*Bell System*] (TEL)
RID .... Retrofit Installation Data (MCD)
RIDC .... Ryerson International Development Centre [*Ryerson Polytechnical Institute*] [*Canada*] [*Research center*] (RCD)
RIDF .... Random Input Describing Function [*Data processing*]
RIDS .... Range Information Display System (MCD)

Computer & Telecommunications Acronyms

RIDS............ Receiving Inspection Data Status [*Report*]
RIDS............ Regional Operations Control Centre Information Display System [*NORAD*]
RIE .... Reactive Ion Etching [*Semiconductor technology*]
RIE .... Resources in Education [*Formerly, Research in Education*] [*National Institute of Education*] [*Database*]
RIF .... Radio-Influence Field   (IEEE)
RIF .... Rate Input Form   (NVT)
RIF .... Reliability Improvement Factor
RIGFET .... Resistive Insulated-Gate Field Effect Transistor   (NITA)
RIISE........... Research Institute for Information Science and Engineering, Inc. [*Information service*]   (EISS)
RILM .... RILM [*Repertoire International de la Litterature Musicale*] Abstracts of Music Literature [*City University of New York*] [*Database*] [*A publication*]
RIM .... Read Interrupt Mask [*Data processing*]
RIM .... Receiver Intermodulation [*Telecommunications*]   (TEL)
RIM .... Recreation Information Management [*Department of Agriculture*] [*Database*]   (FDB)
RIM .... Resource Interface Module [*Datapoint*]   (NITA)
RIMS........... Remote Information Management System   (NITA)
RIN .... Reference Indication Number
RINS........... Rand Information Systems [*NASDAQ symbol*]   (NQ)
RIO............. Relocatable Input/Output   (NITA)
RIOT........... RAM Input/Output Timer   (NITA)
RIOT........... Real-Time Input-Output Transducer [*or Translator*] [*Data processing*]
RIOT........... Remote Input/Output Terminal [*Data processing*]
RIOT........... Resolution of Initial Operational Techniques
RIOT........... Retrieval of Information by On-Line Terminal [*Atomic Energy Authority*] [*Data processing*] [*British*]
RIP .... Random Input Sampling [*Data processing*]   (TUT)
RIP .... Raster Image Processor [*Printer technology*]
RIP .... Retired in Place [*Telecommunications*]   (TEL)
RIP .... Routing Information Process [*Telecommunications*]   (TEL)
RIPFCOMTF ... Rapid Item Processor to Facilitate Complex Operations on Magnetic Tape Files [*Data processing*]
RIPL............ Representation-Independent Programing Language   (NITA)
RIQS .... Remote Information Query System [*Information retrieval service*] [*Data processing*]
RIR .... ROM [*Read-Only Memory*] Instruction Register   (NITA)
RIRMS........ Remote Information Retrieval and Management System [*Data processing*]   (BUR)
RIRO .... Roll-In/Roll-Out [*Storage allocation*] [*Data processing*]   (NITA)
RIS .... Recorded Information Service [*Telecommunications*]   (TEL)
RIS .... Regulatory Information Service [*Congressional Information Service, Inc.*] [*Bethesda, MD*] [*Telecommunications*]
RIS .... Remote Information System   (NITA)
RIS .... Research Information Service [*John Crerar Library*] [*Information service*]   (EISS)
RIS .... Research Information System [*Rehabilitation Services Administration*]   (EISS)
RIS .... Retail Information System   (BUR)
RIS .... Retransmission Identity Signal [*Telecommunications*]   (TEL)
RISC .... Reduced Instruction Set Computer
RISE........... Register for International Service in Education [*Information service*]   (EISS)
RI/SME....... Robotics International   (EANO)
RISS........... Range Instrumentation and Support Systems
RISS........... Refractive Index Sounding System
RIT .... Radio Network for Inter-American Telecommunications
RIT .... Rate of Information Throughput [*Data processing*]   (BUR)
RIT .... Receiver Incremental Tuning
RITA........... Rand Intelligent Terminal Agent   (DEEC)
RITE........... Rapidata Interactive Text Editor   (IEEE)
RJ11 .... Standard modular telephone jack for a single line instrument   (TSSD)
RJE .... Remote Job Entry [*Data processing*]
RJETS......... Remote Job Entry Terminal System [*Data processing*]   (MCD)
RJO .... Remote Job Output [*Data processing*]   (NITA)
RJP .... Remote Job Processing [*Data processing*]
RJS .... Remote Job System [*Data processing*]   (MCD)
RJT .... Rejection Message [*Communications*]   (FAAC)
RKNFSYS ... Rock Information System [*National Science Foundation*] [*Washington, DC*] [*Databank*]   (EISS)
RL .... Radio Liberty
RL .... Radiolocation
RL .... Random Logic
RL .... Receive Leg [*Telecommunications*]   (TEL)
RL .... Record Length   (NITA)
RL .... Reel
RL .... Reflection Loss [*Telecommunications*]   (TEL)
RL .... Relay Logic
R/L .... Remote/Local   (NASA)
RL .... Resistor Logic   (IEEE)
RL .... Return Loss
RL .... Right to Left   (CAH)
RL .... Ring Level   (BUR)
RLA .... Relay   (FAAC)
RLA .... Remote Line Adaptor   (NITA)
RLA .... Rui Lopes Associates, Inc. [*Sunnyvale, CA*] [*Telecommunications*]   (TSSD)
RLC .... ROM [*Read-Only Memory*] Location Counter   (NITA)

RLC .... Run Length Coding
RLCU .... Reference Link Control Unit [*Telecommunications*]   (TEL)
RLD .... Relocation Dictionary   (DEEC)
RLE .... Request Loading Entry [*Data processing*]
RLE .... Research Laboratory of Electronics [*MIT*] [*Research center*]
RLG .... Release Guard [*Telecommunications*]   (TEL)
RLG .... [*The*] Research Libraries Group, Inc. [*Database producer*]
RLIB .... Relocatable Library [*Data processing*]
RLIN .... Research Libraries Information Network [*Pronounced "arlen"*] [*Formerly, BALLOTS*] [*Library network*] [*Information service*]
RLL .... Relocating Linking Loader   (NITA)
RLL .... Representation-Language Language [*Data processing*]
RLL .... Run-Length-Limited [*Data processing*]
RLR .... Record Length Register   (NITA)
RLS .... Remote Line Switch [*Telecommunications*]   (TEL)
RLSD .... Received Line Signal Detector
RLST........... Release Timer [*Telecommunications*]   (TEL)
RLU .... Remote Line Unit [*Telecommunications*]
RLY .... Relay
R/M .... Read/Mostly [*Data processing*]   (TEL)
RM .... Readout Matrix
RM .... Receiver, Mobile
RM .... Receiving Memo
RM .... Record Mark   (BUR)
RM .... Register Memory   (NITA)
RM .... Remote Multiplexer [*Data processing*]   (CAAL)
RM .... Resource Manager   (NITA)
RM .... Rollback Module [*Telecommunications*]   (TEL)
RM .... Rolm Corp. [*NYSE symbol*] [*Delisted*]
RMA .... Random Multiple Access   (NITA)
RMA .... Reactive Modulation Amplifier   (OA)
RMA .... Reliability, Maintainability, and Availability [*Standards*]   (DDI)
RMATS-1.... Remote Maintenance, Administration, and Traffic System-1 [*Telecommunications*]   (TEL)
RMAX.......... Range, Maximum
RMC .... Resource Management Consultants [*Salem, NH*] [*Telecommunications*]   (TSSD)
RMC .... Rod Memory Computer [*NCR Corp.*]
RMCS .... Remote Monitoring and Control System [*Telecommunications*]
RME .... Request Monitor Entry [*Data processing*]
RMF .... Residual Master File [*Data processing*]
RMF .... Resource Measurement Facility [*Data processing*]
RMI .... Route Monitoring Information [*Telecommunications*]   (TEL)
RML .... Relational Machine Language   (NITA)
RML .... Remote Maintenance Line [*Bell Laboratories*]
RMM .... Read-Mostly Memory [*Data processing*]
RMM .... Read-Mostly Mode [*Data processing*]
RMM .... Remote Maintenance Monitor [*Data processing*]   (MCD)
RMMU......... Removable Media Memory Units
RMON .... Resident Monitor   (NITA)
RMOS .... Refractory Metal-Oxide Semiconductor   (IEEE)
RMPI........... Remote Memory Port Interface   (NITA)
RMS .... Random Mass Storage [*Data processing*]   (TUT)
RMS .... Record Management System   (NITA)
RMS .... Recovery Management Support [*Data processing*]
RMS .... Remote Maintenance System
RMS .... Reports Management System [*Office of Management and Budget*] [*Database*]   (FDB)
RMS .... Root Mean Square [*of transmission waves*]
RMSE.......... Root Mean Square Error
RMT .... Remote [*Telecommunications*]   (MSA)
RMTB.......... Reconfiguration Maximum Theoretical Bandwidth   (NITA)
RMU .... Radio Maintenance Unit   (DEN)
RMU .... Remote Multiplexer Unit [*Data processing*]   (KSC)
R/M/W........ Read/Modify/Write   (OA)
RN .... Radio Navigation
RN .... Reception Nil [*Radio logs*]
RN .... Reception Node   (NITA)
RN .... Record Number [*Online database field identifier*]   (OBD)
RNA .... Radio Navigational Aids [*NATO*]   (NATG)
RNAC .... Remote Network Access Controller   (NITA)
RNBM .... Radio Noise Burst Monitor   (MCD)
RNC .... Radio Noncontingent
RNC .... Rainbow Network Communications [*Floral Park, NY*] [*Telecommunications*]   (TSSD)
RNC .... Request Next Character   (NITA)
RNE............. Radio Nacional de Espana [*Radio network*] [*Spanish Sahara*]
RNF............. Radio Noise Figure   (CET)
RNF............. Receiver Noise Figure
RNG .... Radio Range
RNIT........... Radio Noise Interference Test
RNK .... Radiodiffusion Nationale Khmere [*Radio network*] [*Khmer Republic*]
RNM .... Radio-Navigation Mobile
RNP............. Remote Network Processor
RNR............. Receive Not Ready [*Data processing*]   (IEEE)
RNTWPA..... Radio-Newsreel-Television Working Press Association
RNV............. Radio Noise Voltage
RO .... Radio Operator
RO .... Read Only [*Data processing*]   (IBMDP)
RO .... Receive Only
RO .... Register Output   (NITA)

Computer & Telecommunications Acronyms

RO	Relocatable Output [Data processing]
ROADS	Roadway Analysis and Design System [Data processing]
ROAR	Royal Optimizing Assembly Routing [Royal McBee Corp.] [Data processing]
ROBIN	Remote On-Line Business Information Network [Data processing] (IEEE)
ROBINS	Roberts Information Services, Inc. [Fairfax, VA] [Information service] (EISS)
Robotics T	Robotics Today [A publication]
R/OC	Receive-Only Center (FAAC)
ROC	Remote Operator's Console
ROCC	Regional Operations Control Center [AT & T]
ROCR	Remote Optical Character Recognition [Data processing]
RODATA	Registered Organization Data Bank
RODIAC	Rotary Dual Input for Analog Computation
ROF	Remote Operator Facility [Honeywell, Inc.] (NITA)
ROFR	Repair of Repairables (MCD)
R-O-H	Receiver Off the Hook
ROI	Radio, Optical, Inertial
ROIS	Radio Operational Intercom System (KSC)
ROJ	Range of Jamming
ROK	Rockwell International Corp. [NYSE symbol] [Toronto Stock Exchange symbol]
ROL	Rotate Left [Data processing]
ROLR	Receiving Objective Loudness Rating [Telephones] (IEEE)
ROM	Read-Only Memory [Computer memory] [Data processing]
ROM	Readout Memory (IEEE)
ROMAD	Radio Operator/Maintenance Driver
ROMM	Read-Only Memory Module [Data processing]
ROMON	Receiving-Only Monitor
RONCO	Rock-Oldies-News-Commercials Operation [Formula radio]
RONLY	Receiver Only [Radio]
ROO	Radio Optical Observatory
ROP	Receive-Only Printer [Data processing]
ROPES	Remote Online Print Executive System (NITA)
ROPP	Receive-Only Page Printer
ROR	Rotate Right [Data processing]
RORIS	Remote Operated Radiographic Inspection System
ROS	Read-Only Storage [Data processing]
ROS	Resident Operating System (NITA)
ROSAR	Read-Only Storage Address Register (NITA)
ROSAT	Roentgen Satellite [Space research]
ROSCOPS	Report of Observation/Samples Collected by Oceanographic Programs [Bureau National des Donnees Oceaniques] [Database] (CUAD)
ROSDR	Read-Only Storage Data Register (NITA)
ROSE	Retrieval by Online Search [Data processing]
ROT	Rotate
ROTCC	Receiver-Off-Hook Tone Connecting Circuit
ROTH	Read-Only Tape Handler (NITA)
ROTL	Remote Office Test Line [Bell Laboratories]
ROTR	Receive-Only Typing Reperforator
ROTR-S/P	Receive-Only Typing Reperforator - Series to Parallel
ROTS	Rotary Out Trunk Switch [Telecommunications] (TEL)
ROTSAL	Rotate and Scale [Data processing]
ROTT	Reorder Tone Trunks [Telecommunications] (TEL)
ROTWX	Reference Our TWX [Teletypewriter communications] (FAAC)
ROXL	Rotate through X Left [Data processing]
ROXR	Rotate through X Right [Data processing]
RP	Reader Printer
RP	Reader Punch (OA)
RP	Receive Processor (NITA)
RP	Reception Poor [Radio logs]
RP	Remote Pickup
RP	Remote Printer (BUR)
RP	Repeater (CDH)
RP	Reply Paid
RP	Restoration Priority (CET)
RP	Rollback Process [Telecommunications] (TEL)
RPA	Re-Entrant Process Allocator [Telecommunications] (TEL)
RPA	Resident Programer Analyst [Data processing]
RPAA	Rotating Phase Array Antenna
RPC	Registered Protective Circuit
RPC	Remote Position Control
RPC	Remote Power Controller
RPC	Row Parity Check (IEEE)
RPE	Remote Peripheral Equipment (IEEE)
RPF	Radio Proximity Fuze
RPG	Report Program Generator [Programing language] [1962]
RPI	Read, Punch, and Interpret (NITA)
RPL	Remote Program Load (NITA)
RPL	Request Parameter List [Data processing] (BUR)
RPL	Running Program Language [Data processing]
RPM	Read Program Memory [Data processing] (MDG)
RPM	Revolutions per Minute [e.g., in reference to phonograph records]
RPMO	Radio Projects Management Office
RPN	Reverse Polish Notation [Arithmetic evaluation] [Data processing] (IEEE)
RPQ	Request for Price Quotation
RPS	Real-Time Programing System [Data processing] (IEEE)
RPS	Records per Sector [Data processing] (NITA)
RPS	Relative Performance Score [Telecommunications] (TEL)
RPS	Remote Printing System (NITA)
RPS	Remote Processing Service (BUR)
RPS	Requirements Planning System [Data processing] (TUT)
RPS	Revolutions per Second (AFM)
RPS	Rotational Position Sensing [Data processing]
RPT	Repeat
RPT	Reply Paid Telegram
RPT	Request Programs Termination [Data processing]
RPU	Receiver Processor Unit [Electronics]
RPU	Regional Processing Unit (NITA)
R/Q	Resolver/Quantizer (IEEE)
RQA	Recursive Queue Analyzer (IEEE)
RQUS	Remote Query Update System [Data processing] (DDI)
RR	Radio Range
RR	Radio Recognition
RR	Radio Regulations
RR	Radio Relay
RR	Radio Research
RR	Readout and Relay
RR	Receive Ready [Data processing] (IEEE)
R/R	Record/Retransmit (IEEE)
RR	Reference Register [Data processing]
RR	Register to Register (MCD)
RR	Relay Rack [Telecommunications] (TEL)
RR	Reroute [Telecommunications] (TEL)
RR	Return Rate (IEEE)
RR	Return Register (NITA)
RRA	Remote Record Address (NITA)
RRAR	ROM Return Address Register (NITA)
RRB	Radio Research Board (DEN)
RRC	Radio Receptor Company
RRC	Radio Relay Center (NATG)
RRC	Radio Research Company
RRC	Recreation Resources Center [University of Wisconsin] [Research center] (RCD)
RRCVR	Remote Receiver (FAAC)
RRD	Requisition Received Date [Bell System] (TEL)
RRD	Route/Route Destination [Telecommunications] (TEL)
RRDE	Radio Research and Development Establishment (MCD)
RRDS	Relative Record Data Set (NITA)
RRE	Receive Reference Equivalent [Telecommunications] (TEL)
RRFS	Range Rate Frequency Synthesizer
RRG	Resource Request Generator (NITA)
RRI	Reroute Inhibit [Telecommunications] (TEL)
RRL	Radio Relay Link (NATG)
RRL	Radio Research Laboratory
RRN	Relative Record Number [Data processing]
RRO	Responsible Reporting Office [Telecommunications] (TEL)
RROS	Resistive Read-Only Storage (NITA)
RRP	Radio Relay Pod
RRR	Range and Range Rate
RRRS	Route Relief Requirements System [Telecommunications] (TEL)
RRS	Radio Receiver Set
RRS	Radio Recording Spectrophotometer
RRS	Radio Relay Station
RRS	Radio Relay System
RRS	Radio Remote Set (CAAL)
RRS	Research Referral Service [International Federation for Documentation] [Information service] (EISS)
RRS	Retransmission Request Signal [Telecommunications] (TEL)
RRT	Relative Retention Time
RRT	Ring-Ring Trip [Telecommunications] (TEL)
RRTD	Rural Rehabilitation Technologies Database [University of North Dakota] [Information service] (EISS)
RRX	Railroad Crossing [Telecommunications] (TEL)
RS	Radio Duties - Special
RS	Radio Simulator
RS	Radio Switchboard (CAAL)
RS	Random Splice [Telecommunications] (TEL)
RS	Reader Stop [Data processing] (BUR)
RS	Real Storage (NITA)
RS	Receiver Station
RS	Receiving Ship [or Station]
RS	Reception Station
RS	Recommended Standard [Telecommunications] (TEL)
RS	Reconnaissance Satellite
RS	Record Separator [Control character] [Data processing]
RS	Reel Sequence [Data processing]
RS	Register Select (NITA)
RS	Register and Storage (MCD)
R/S	Relay Set [Telecommunications] (TEL)
RS	Request to Send (NITA)
RS	Reset-Set [Data processing] (CIT)
RS	Route Switching [Telecommunications] (TEL)
RSA	Remote Station Alarm
RSA	Remote Storage Activities
RSA	Repair Sevice Attendant [Telecommunications] (TEL)
RSA	Requirements Statement Analyzer (NITA)
RSAC	Radiological Safety Analysis Computer (MCD)
RSB	Repair Service Bureau [Telecommunications] (TEL)
RSC	Remote Store Controller (NITA)
RSCAA	Radio Shack Computer Alumni Association (EANO)
RSCG	Radio Set Control Group

Computer & Telecommunications Acronyms

RSCS	Remote Spooling Communications Subsystem [*IBM Corp.*] [*Data processing*] (IBMDP)
RSDC	Radiation Subprogramme Data Center
RSE	Request Select Entry [*Data processing*]
RSEU	Remote Scanner-Encoder Unit [*Bell Laboratories*]
RSF	Remote Support Facility (NITA)
RSG	Relay Switch Group
RSI	Register Sender Inward [*Telecommunications*] (TEL)
RSI	Remote Sensing Institute [*South Dakota State University*] [*Research center*] (RCD)
RSIC	RSI [*Resource Services, Inc.*] Corporation [*NASDAQ symbol*] (NQ)
RSID	Resource Identification Table [*Data processing*]
RSITA	Reglement du Service International des Telecommunications de l'Aeronautique
RSL	Radio Standards Laboratory [*National Bureau of Standards*]
RSL	Received Signal Level [*Telecommunications*] (TEL)
RSL	Requirements Statement Language
RSL	Research Services Ltd. [*Database producer*] (CUAD)
RSM	Radio Squadron Mobile (MUGU)
RSM	Real Storage Management [*Data processing*] (IBMDP)
RSM	Reed Switching Matrix
RSMS	Radio Spectrum Measurement System [*National Telecommunications and Information Administration*]
RSN	Reject Sequence Number [*Data processing*]
RSO	Register Sender Outward [*Telecommunications*] (TEL)
RSP	Radio Switch Panel
RSP	Reader/Sorter Processor (NITA)
RSP	Record Select Program [*Data processing*] (TUT)
RSP	Replication Synchronization Process [*Telecommunications*] (TEL)
RSP	Restoration Priority [*Telecommunications*] (TEL)
RSP	Robotic Sample Processor [*Automation*]
RSP	Rural Satellite Program [*US Agency for International Development*] [*Washington, DC*] [*Telecommunications*] (TSSD)
RSPP	Radio Simulation Patch Panel (CET)
RSPT	Real Storage Page Table [*Data processing*] (BUR)
RSRE	Royal Signals and Radar Establishment [*Malvern, England*] [*Computer chip designer*]
RSS	Radio Subsystem (CIT)
RSS	Real-Time Switching System (SKY)
RSS	Remote Safing Switch (VIT)
RSS	Remote Sensing Society (EANO)
RSS	Remote Switching System [*Telecommunications*]
RST	Reset [*Telecommunications*] (TEL)
RST	Reset-Set Trigger
R Sta	Radio Telegraph Station
RSTN	Radio Solar Telescope Network (MCD)
RSTS	Resource-Sharing Time-Sharing System (NITA)
RSU	Recorder Switch Unit
RSU	Register Storage Unit (NITA)
RSU	Relay Storage Unit
RSU	Remote Service Unit (NASA)
RSU	Remote Switching Unit [*Telecommunications*]
RSVC	Resident Supervisor Call (BUR)
RSVP	Rapid Serial Visual Presentation [*Data processing*]
RSVP	Remote System Verification Program (NITA)
RSVP	Response Segmentation and Validation Program [*Donnelley Marketing Information Services*] [*Information service*] (EISS)
RSWB	Raumordnung, Stadtebau, Wohnungswesen, Bauwesen [*Regional Policy, Urban Development, Housing and Civil Engineering*] [*Database*] (ODIN)
RT	Radio Telegraphy
RT	Radio Telephone (MSA)
RT	Radio/Television Repair Program [*Association of Independent Colleges and Schools specialization code*]
RT	Radio Tracking (KSC)
RT	Radio Transmitter
RT	Radiotelegraphy
RT	Radiotelephone
R/T	Radiotelephony
RT	Ratio Transformer [*Unit*] (CDH)
RT	Readout Technique
RT	Real Time [*Computer*]
RT	Receive-Transmit [*Radio*]
RT	Received Text
R/T	Receiver/Transmitter [*Radio*] (KSC)
RT	Receiving Tube
RT	Register Traffic [*Telecommunications*] (TEL)
RT	Register Transfer [*Data processing*]
R/T	Register Translator [*Telecommunications*] (TEL)
RT	Regression Testing [*Data processing*] (IEEE)
RT	Relay Tester (VIT)
RT	Relay Transmitter (DDI)
RT	Remote Terminal [*Data processing*]
R/T	Reperforator/Transmitter [*Teletypewriter*] [*Data processing*]
RT	Resistor Transistor
RT	Response Time [*Data processing*]
RT	Retention Time [*Data processing*]
RT	Ring Trip [*Telecommunications*] (TEL)
RT	Ringing Tone [*Telecommunications*] (TEL)
RT	RISC [*Reduced-Instruction Set Computer*] Technology [*IBM Corp.*]
RT	Route Treatment [*Telecommunications*] (TEL)
RTA	Radically Tapered Antenna
RTA	Real-Time Analyzer [*Electronics*]
RTA	Reliable Test Analyzer [*Data processing*]
RTA	Remote Test Access [*Telecommunications*] (TEL)
RTA	Remote Trunk Arrangement [*Telecommunications*] (TEL)
RTAC	Real-Time Adaptive Control (NITA)
RTAM	Remote Telecommunications Access Method [*Data processing*]
RTAM	Remote Terminal Access Method [*Data processing*] (BUR)
RTAM	Resident Terminal Access Method [*Data processing*]
RTAPS	Real-Time Terminal Application Program System [*Data processing*]
RTB	Radiodiffusion-Television Belge [*Radio and television network*] [*Belgium*]
RTB	Read Tape Binary [*Data processing*] (IEEE)
RTB	Response/Throughput Bias [*Data processing*] (BUR)
RTBM	Real-Time BIT [*Binary Digit*] Mapping (DEEC)
RTC	Radio Transmission Control (NATG)
RTC	Radio Tuned Circuit (DEN)
RTC	Reader Tape Contact
RTC	Real-Time Clock [*Data processing*] (MCD)
RTC	Real-Time Command [*Data processing*]
RTC	Real-Time Computer (CIT)
RTC	Real-Time Control [*Data processing*] (MCD)
RTC	Real-Time Counter [*Data processing*] (SKY)
RTC	Relative Time Clock [*Data processing*] (MDG)
RTC	Remote Terminal Controller (NITA)
RTCA	Radio Technical Commission for Aeronautics [*Washington, DC*]
RTCC	Real-Time Computer Complex
RTCDS	Real-Time Cinetheodolite Data System
RTCF	Real-Time Computer Facility (CIT)
RTCM	Radio Technical Commission for Maritime Services (EANO)
RTCMS	Radio Technical Commission for Marine Services [*Later, RTCM*]
RTCP	Radio Transmission Control Panel (NATG)
RTCP	Real-Time Communications Processor (NASA)
RTCS	Real-Time Communication System (NITA)
RTCS	Real-Time Computer Science Corp. [*Camarillo, CA*] [*Software manufacturer*] (DASOS)
RTCS	Real-Time Computer System
RTD	Real-Time Display
RTD	Resistance Temperature Detector
RTDC	Real-Time Data Channel (IEEE)
RTDD	Real-Time Data Distribution
RTDD	Remote Timing and Data Distribution
RTDDC	Real-Time Digital Data Correction (MUGU)
RTDHS	Real-Time Data Handling System
RTDR	Reliability Test Data Report
RTDS	Real-Time Data System
RTDT	Real-Time Data Translator (CIT)
RTE	Radio Telefis Eireann [*Radio and television network*] [*Ireland*]
RTE	Radio Trans-Europe
RTE	Radio Trunk Extension (NATG)
RTE	Real-Time Executive [*Data processing*] (TUT)
RTE	Remote Terminal Emulator [*For teleprocessing validation*]
RTE	Return from Exception [*Data processing*]
RTE-B	Real-Time Basic [*Data processing*] (MDG)
RTECS	Registry of Toxic Effects of Chemical Substances [*NIOSH*] [*Database*]
RTel	Radio Telemetry
RTEL	Radio Telephony (MSA)
RTES	Real-Time Executive System [*SEMIS*] (NITA)
RTF	Radio Transmission Facility
RTF	Radiodiffusion-Television Francaise [*Radio and television network*] [*France*]
RTF	Radiotelephone
RTF	Real-Time FORTRAN [*Data processing*] (CIT)
RTFMS	Radio Transmission Frequency Measuring System (DDI)
RTG	Radiotelegraph
RTG	Reglement Telegraphique [*Telegraph Regulations*] [*French*]
RTGD	Real-Time Graphic Display
RTH	Regional Telecommunications Hub [*Telecommunications*] (TEL)
RTI	Radiodiffusion Television Ivoirienne [*Radio and television network*] [*Ivory Coast*]
RTI	Referred-to-Input (CIT)
RTIO	Remote Terminal Input/Output (NITA)
RTI/OC	Real-Time Input/Output Controller [*Data processing*] (IEEE)
RTIP	Remote Terminal Interactive Processor (MCD)
RTIP	Remote Terminal Interface Package (NITA)
RTIRS	Real-Time Information Retrieval System
RTL	Radio-Tele-Luxembourg
RTL	Real-Time Language [*Data processing*] (IEEE)
RTL	Register Transfer Language [*Data processing*] (CSR)
RTL	Register Transfer Level (NITA)
RTL	Register-Transistor Logic [*Data processing*]
RTL	Resistor-Transistor Logic [*Data processing*] (BUR)
RTL	Run-Time Library [*Interdata*] (NITA)
RTLG	Radio Telegraph (MSA)
RTLP	Reference Transmission Level Point [*Telecommunications*] (CBSS)
RTM	Real-Time Monitor [*Systems Engineering Labs*]
RTM	Receiver-Transmitter-Modulator

Acronym	Expansion
RTM	Recovery Termination Management [*Data processing*]
RTM	Register Transfer Module [*Data processing*] (MDG)
RTM	Response Time Module (OA)
RTMD	Real-Time Multiplexer Display
RTMOS	Real-Time Multiprograming Operating System [*Data processing*] (IEEE)
RTMS	Real-Time Memory System (NITA)
RTMS	Real-Time Multiprograming System (NITA)
RTN	Radio Telescope Network
RTN	Remote Terminal Network
RTNR	Ringtone No Reply [*Telecommunications*] (TEL)
RTO	Radiotelephone Operator
RTO	Referred-to-Output (CIT)
RTOS	Real-Time Operating System [*Control Data Corp.*] (CIT)
RTP	Radiotelevisao Portuguesa [*Radio and television network*] [*Portugal*]
RTP	Real-Time Peripheral (IEEE)
RTP	Real-Time Profiler [*Instrumentation*]
RTP	Reference Telephonic Power (DEN)
RTPL	Real-Time Procedural Language [*Data processing*] (MDG)
RTPM	Real-Time Program Management (CIT)
RTQC	Real-Time Quality Control
R TR	Radio Tower
RTR	Real-Time Readout
RTR	Response Time Reporting (NITA)
RTR	Return and Restore Status Register [*Data processing*]
RTRC	Radio and Television Research Council
RTRC	Radiotelemetry and Remote Control (MCD)
RTRCDS	Real-Time Reconnaissance Cockpit Display System [*or Subsystem*]
RTRO	Real-Time Readout
RTRS	Real-Time Rescheduling Subsystem
RTS	Radiodiffusion Television du Senegal [*Radio and television network*] [*Senegal*]
RTS	Radiotelemetry Subsystem (CIT)
RTS	Radioteletypewriter Set
RTS	Rapid Transmission and Storage [*Goldmark Corp.*] [*TV system*]
RTS	Reactive Terminal Service [*International Telephone & Telegraph computer*]
RTS	Real-Time Subroutines (OA)
RTS	Real-Time System
RTS	Remote Terminal Supervisor (CMD)
RTS	Remote Test System [*Bell System*]
RTS	Request to Send
RTS	Return from Subroutine [*Data processing*]
RTS	Rosner Television Systems, Inc. [*New York, NY*] [*Telecommunications*] (TSSD)
RTSA	Radio Tracking System Analyst (MUGU)
RTSDS	Real-Time Scheduling Display System (CIT)
RTSF	Real-Time Simulation Facility (MCD)
RTSP	Real-Time Signal Processor (NVT)
RTT	Radiotelemetric Theodolite
RTT	Radioteletypewriter
RTT	Receiver Threshold Test (CET)
RTT	Remote Tuning Technique
RTTAA	Railway Telegraph and Telephone Appliance Association
RTTD	Real-Time Telemetry Data
RTTDS	Real-Time Telemetry Data System
RTTS	Real-Time Telemetry System (CIT)
RTTV	Real-Time Television
RTTY	Radioteletypewriter
RTU	Railroad Telegraphers Union
RTU	Receiver/Transmitter Unit
RTU	Remote Terminal Unit
RTU	Right to Use [*Telecommunications*] (TEL)
RTUA	Recognition Technologies Users Association (EANO)
RTV	Radiodiffusion Television (Upper Volta) [*Radio and television network*]
RTV	Real-Time Video
RTVP	Real-Time Video Processing
RTX	Real-Time Executive (OA)
RTZ	Return-to-Zero [*Recording scheme*]
RU	Are You? [*Communication*]
RU	Request/Response Unit [*Data processing*]
RUC	Reporting Unit Code [*Data processing*]
RUF	Resource Utilization Factor (NITA)
RUFE	Zeitschrift fuer Rundfunk und Fernsehen [*NOMOS Datapool*] [*Database*] (CUAD)
RUG	Recomp Users Group [*Data processing*]
RUG	Regional User Group [*Data processing*]
RUG	Roscoe User Group [*Princeton, NJ*]
RUM	Resource Utilization Monitor (NITA)
RUMP	Radio-Controlled Ultraviolet Measurement Program (MUGU)
RUN	Rewind and Unload (OA)
RUN	Runstream [*Data processing*]
RUNCIBLE	Revised Unified New Compiler with Its Basic Language Extended [*Data processing*]
RUNID	Run Identification [*Data processing*]
RURAX	Rural Automatic Exchange [*Telecommunications*] (TEL)
RUSH	Remote User Shared Hardware [*Data processing*] (DDI)
RUT	Remote User Terminal [*Data processing*] (CAAL)
RUT	Standard Regional Route Transmitting Frequencies [*Communications*] (FAAC)
Rutgers Comput and Technol Law J	Rutgers Computer and Technology Law Journal [*A publication*]
Rutgers J Computers & Law	Rutgers Journal of Computers and the Law [*A publication*]
Rutgers J Comput & Law	Rutgers Journal of Computers and the Law [*A publication*]
Rutgers J Comput Technol and Law	Rutgers Journal of Computers, Technology, and the Law [*A publication*]
RUTOP	Rutowski Optimization [*Computer program*]
RUTWX	Reference Your TWX [*Teletypewriter Communications*] (FAAC)
RV	Radio Vehicle (DEN)
RVA	Recorded Voice Announcement [*Telecommunications*] (IBMDP)
RVA	Relative Virtual Address (NITA)
RVC	Relative Velocity Computer
RVC	Rotary Voice Coil [*Computer technology*]
RVI	Reverse Interrupt Character [*Keyboard*] (NITA)
RVT	Reliability Verification Tests (NITA)
RVT	Resource Vector Table [*Data processing*] (IBMDP)
R-W	Read-Write [*Data processing*] (MSA)
R/W	Report Writer [*Data processing*]
RWC	Read, Write, and Compute
RWC	Read-Write-Continue [*Data processing*]
RWD	Rewind (DEEC)
RWED	Read/Write Extend Delete (NITA)
RWG	Rigid Waveguide
RWI	Read-Write-Initialize [*Data processing*]
RWM	Read-Write Memory [*Data processing*] (MCD)
RWM	Rectangular Wave Modulation (IEEE)
RWND	Rewind (MSA)
RWP	Radio Wave Propagation
RWR	Read/Write Register (NITA)
RWT	Read-Write Tape [*Data processing*]
RWV	Read-Write-Verify [*Data processing*]
RX	Receiver [*or Reception*] [*Radio*] (NATG)
RX	Register and Indexed Storage (MCD)
RX	Remote Exchange [*Telecommunications*] (TEL)
RX	Rush [*on teletype messages*]
RYBF	Royal Business Group [*NASDAQ symbol*] (NQ)
RZ	Return-to-Zero Recording [*Data processing*]
RZ(NP)	Nonpolarized Return-to-Zero Recording [*Data processing*] (IBMDP)
RZ(P)	Polarized Return-to-Zero Recording [*Data processing*] (IBMDP)

S

S	Scalar [*Mathematics*]		SADIC	Solid-State Analog-to-Digital Computer
S	Second [*or Secondary*]		SADIE	Scanning Analog-to-Digital Input Equipment [*National Bureau of Standards*]
S	Sent [*Communications*] (FAAC)		SADIE	Secure Automatic Data Information Exchange [*System*]
S	Set		SADIE	Sterling and Decimal Invoicing Electronically (IEEE)
S	Short Circuit		SADP	Structured Analysis, Design, and Programing [*Data processing*]
S	Signal [*Telecommunications*] (TEL)		SADP	Synthetic Array Data Processor
S	Signal Strength [*Broadcasting*]		SADP	System Architecture Design Package (NITA)
S	Simultaneous Transmission of Range Signals and Voice		SADPO	Systems Analysis and Data Processing Office
S	Single		SADSAC	Sampled Data Simulator and Computer
S	Sixth Word Designator [*Data processing*]		SADSAC	Seiler ALGOL Digitally Simulated Analog Computer
S	Slewed [*Antenna*]		SADT	Structured Analysis and Design Technique [*Programing language*] [1978]
S	Source		SAF	Segment Address Field (NITA)
S	Static		SAFE	Store and Forward Element [*Telecommunications*] (TEL)
S	Stereo Broadcast [*Radio*] [*British*]		SAFF	Store and Forward Facsimile (NITA)
S	Storage (NITA)		SAFFI	Special Assembly for Fast Installations [*Telecommunications*] (TEL)
S	Switch		SAFRAS	Self-Adaptive Flexible Format Retrieval and Storage System [*Data processing*] (EISS)
S	Switchboard [*Telecommunications*] (TEL)		SAG	Standard Address Generator (IEEE)
S3	Signal Selection Switchboard (CAAL)		SAGA	Software AG Systems Group [*NASDAQ symbol*] (NQ)
S3	Systems and Software Simulator		SAGM	Separate Absorption, Grading, and Multiplication Layers [*Semiconductor technology*]
SA	Sausage Aerial [*Radio*]		SAGMOS	Self-Aligning Gate Metal Oxide Semiconductor (IEEE)
SA	Service Assistant [*Telecommunications*] (TEL)		SAHYB	Simulation of Analog and Hybrid Computers
SA	Ship Abstracts [*Helsinki University of Technology*] [*Bibliographic database*] (OBD)		SAI	Subarchitectural Interface (NITA)
SA	Single Armor [*Telecommunications*] (TEL)		SAIL	Simple Analytical Interactive Language [*Data processing*]
SA	Source Address (CCD)		SAIL	Stanford Artificial Intelligence Laboratory [*Stanford University*]
SA	Station Address [*Data processing*] (BUR)		SAINT	Satellite Array for International and National Telecommunications (MCD)
SA	Storage Allocator [*Telecommunications*] (TEL)		SAINT	Symbolic Automatic Integrator (CAH)
SA	Structured Analysis [*Programing language*] [1977] (CSR)		SAK	Stop Acknowledge (CMD)
SA	Symbolic Assembler (IEEE)		SAL	Saperstein & Associates Limited [*Vancouver, BC*] [*Telecommunications*] (TSSD)
SA	Systems Analyst (NITA)		SAL	Structured Assembly Language (NITA)
SAA	Sanders Associates, Inc. [*NYSE symbol*]		SAL	Symbolic Assembly Language [*Data processing*] (DIT)
SAA	Satellite Attitude Acquisition		SAL	Systems Assembly Language [*Data processing*] (IEEE)
SAA	Slot Array Antenna		SALC	SAL Cable Communications [*NASDAQ symbol*] (NQ)
SAA	Step Adjustable Antenna		SALE	Simple Algebraic Language for Engineers [*Data processing*]
SAARDT	Syndicat Autonome des Agents de la Radiodiffusion du Togo [*Autonomous Union of Radiobroadcasting Workers of Togo*]		SALT	Society for Applied Learning Technology [*Warrenton, VA*] (EANO)
SAB	Stack Access Block (NITA)		SALT	Subscribers' Apparatus Line Tester [*Telecommunications*] (TEL)
SABBA	System Analysis-Building Block Approach [*Ge Cae International and Gen-Red Ltd.*] [*Software package*] [*British*] (NCC)		SALT	Symbolic Algebraic Language Translator [*Data processing*]
SABH	Simultaneous Automatic Broadcast Homer (FAAC)		SAM	Sample and Analysis Management System [*Data processing*]
SABIR	Semiautomatic Bibliographic Information Retrieval		SAM	Script Applier Mechanism [*Programing language*] [1975] (CSR)
SABIRS	Semiautomatic Bibliographic Information Retrieval System (DIT)		SAM	Semiautomatic Mathematics (IEEE)
SABM	Set Asynchronous Balanced Mode (CCD)		SAM	Sequential Access Memory [*Data processing*] (IEEE)
SABR	Symbolic Assembler for Binary Relocatable Programs (NITA)		SAM	Sequential Access Method [*IBM Corp.*] [*Data processing*] (TUT)
SABRE	Sales and Business Reservations Done Electronically (CGC)		SAM	Serial Access Memory [*Data processing*] (DEEC)
SABRE	Store Access Bus Recording Equipment [*Telecommunications*] (TEL)		SAM	Service Attitude Measurement [*Bell System*]
SAC	Security Access Control [*Data processing*]		SAM	Simulation of Analog Methods [*Data processing*]
SAC	Semiautomatic Coding		SAM	Squarewave Amplitude Modulation
SAC	Serving Area Concept [*Bell System*]		SAM	Strachey and McIlroy [*in SAM/76, a programing language named after its authors and developed in 1976*] (CSR)
SAC	Servo Adapter Coupler		SAM	Subsequent Address Message [*Telecommunications*] (TEL)
SAC	Single Address Code		SAM	Symbolic and Algebraic Manipulation (IEEE)
SAC	Special Area Code [*Bell System*]		SAM	System Activity Monitor [*Data processing*] (CGC)
SAC	Specific Acoustic Capacitance		SAM	Systems Adapter Module (NITA)
SAC	Storage Access Channel (CMD)		SAM	Systems Analysis Module (IEEE)
SAC	Storage Access Control [*Data processing*] (NITA)		SAMA	Scientific Apparatus Makers Association
SAC	Store and Clear Accumulator [*Data processing*] (CDH)		SAMANTHA	System for the Automated Management of Text from a Hierarchical Arrangement
SAC	Systems Auditability and Control [*Data processing*]		SAMI	Selling Areas-Marketing, Incorporated [*Originator and database*] [*Information service*] (EISS)
SACMAP	Selective Automatic Computational Matching and Positioning (MCD)		SAMMIE	System for Aiding Man-Machine Interaction [*Prime Computer (UK) Ltd. and Prime Computers CAD/CAM Ltd.*] [*Software package*] [*British*] (NCC)
SACMAPS	Selective Automatic Computational Matching and Positioning System		SAMOS	Silicon and Aluminum Metal-Oxide Semiconductor
SACNET	Secure Automatic Communications Network		SAMPLE	Single Assignment Mathematical Programing Language [1971] [*Data processing*] (CSR)
SACS	Scheduling Activity Control System [*PA Computers & Telecommunications Ltd.*] [*Software package*] [*British*] (NCC)		SAMS	Sampling Analog Memory System
SACS	Synchronous Altitude Communications Satellite		SAMS	Satellite Automatic Monitoring System [*Programing language*]
SAD	Sentence Appraiser and Diagrammer			
SAD	Space Antennae Diversity [*Telecommunications*] (TEL)			
SAD	Store Address Director (NITA)			
SADAP	Simplified Automatic Data Plotter			
SADAR	Satellite Data Reduction [*Processor system*]			
SADC	Sequential Analog-Digital Computer (DIT)			

Computer & Telecommunications Acronyms

SAMSARS ... Satellite-Based Maritime Search and Rescue System [*Telecommunications*] (TEL)
SAMSON .... Strategic Automatic Message-Switching Operational Network [*Canada*] (MCD)
SAND .... Sorting and Assembly of New Data
SANSS .... Substructure and Nomenclature Searching System [*Chemical Information Systems, Inc.*] [*Database*] (CUAD)
SAP .... Service Access Point (CCD)
SAP .... Share Assembly Program [*Data processing*]
SAP .... Structural Analysis Program (MCD)
SAP .... Symbolic Assembly Program [*Data processing*]
SAP .... Systems Assurance Program [*IBM Corp.*]
SAPIS .... State Alcoholism Profile Information System [*Public Health Service*] (EISS)
SAR .... Segment Address Register [*Telecommunications*] (NITA)
SAR .... Service Analysis Report [*Telecommunications*] (TEL)
SAR .... Service Analysis Request [*Telecommunications*] (TEL)
SAR .... Source Address Register [*Telecommunications*] (NITA)
SAR .... Storage Address Register [*Telecommunications*]
SAR .... Street Address Record [*Telecommunications*] (TEL)
SAR .... Successive Approximation Register [*Data processing*]
SARA .... Sequential Automatic Recorder and Annunciator
SARA .... Systems Analysis and Resource Accounting [*Data processing system*]
SARM .... Set Asynchronous Response Mode (NITA)
SARS .... Sensor Analog Relay System
SARTS .... Switched Access Remote Test System [*Bell System*]
SAS .... Small Applications Satellite (KSC)
SAS .... Small Astronomy Satellite
SAS .... Spacecraft Antenna System
SAS .... Statistical Analysis System [*Programing language*] [1966]
SAS .... Switched Access System [*Telecommunications*] (TEL)
SASI .... System Application Software [*Data processing*] (BUR)
SASI .... System Automation Software, Incorporated
SASRS .... Satellite-Aided Search and Rescue System [*Telecommunications*]
SASTU .... Signal Amplitude Sampler and Totalizing Unit (IEEE)
SAT .... Satellite
SAT .... System Access Technique [*Sperry UNIVAC*] (NITA)
SATAN .... Satellite Automatic Tracking Antenna
SATANAS .. Semiautomatic Analog Setting (IEEE)
SATCOMA ... Satellite Communications Agency [*AEC/DCA*]
SATDAT ..... Satellite Data (MCD)
SATELCO ... Satellite Telecommunications Company [*Japanese-American firm*]
SATELDATA ... Satellite Databank [*European Space Agency*] [*Database*] (CUAD)
Satell Commun ... Satellite Communications [*A publication*]
Satellite ...... Satellite Communications [*A publication*]
Satel News ... Satellite News [*A publication*]
SATF .... Shortest Access Time First (NITA)
SATL .... Satellite
SATNET ..... Satellite Data Broadcast Networks, Inc. [*New York, NY*] [*Telecommunications*] (TSSD)
SATPATT ... Satellite Paper Tape Transfer
SATS .... Small Applications Technology Satellite (MCD)
SATSERV ... Service by Satellite
SATT .... Strowger Automatic Toll Ticketing [*Telecommunications*]
SATURN ..... Simulation and Assignment of Traffic to Urban Road Networks [*Kins Developments Ltd.*] [*Software package*] [*British*] (NCC)
SAU .... Smallest Addressable Unit (NITA)
SAU .... System [*or Subsystem*] Availability Unit (NITA)
SAUCB ...... Soviet Automatic Control [*English Translation*] [*A publication*]
SAV .... Service Availability [*AT & T*]
SAVE .... System for Automatic Value Exchange [*Data processing*]
SAVITAR .... Sanders Associates Video Input/Output Terminal Access Resource [*Data processing*] (IEEE)
SAVOR ...... Single-Actuated Voice Recorder
SAVT .... Save Area Table [*Data processing*] (IBMDP)
SAVT .... Secondary Address Vector Table [*Data processing*] (IBMDP)
SAW .... Surface Acoustic Wave [*Microwave system*]
SAWO .... Surface Acoustic Wave Oscillator [*Telecommunications*] (TEL)
SAX .... Small Automatic Exchange [*Telecommunications*] (TEL)
SAXA .... Slotted Array X-Band Antenna
SB .... International Standard Book Number [*Online database field identifier*] (OBD)
SB .... Sideband [*Radio frequency*]
SB .... Simultaneous Broadcast
SB .... Special Billing [*Telecommunications*] (TEL)
SBA .... Satellite Broadcasters Association (EANO)
SBA .... Shared Batch Area [*Data processing*] (IBMDP)
SBA .... Systems Builders Association (EANO)
SBAS .... S-Band Antenna Switch (MCD)
SBC .... Service Bureau Corporation
SBC .... Single Board Computer (DEEC)
SBC .... Small Business Computer (BUR)
SBC .... Spaceborne Computer
SBC .... Standard Buried Collector [*Circuit*]
SBC .... Swiss Broadcasting Corporation
SBCA .... Sensor-Based Control Adapter (OA)
SBCD .... Subtract BCD [*Binary Coded Decimal*] Number [*Data processing*]
SBCU .... Sensor-Based Control Unit [*Data processing*]

S-BD .... S-Band (NASA)
SBD .... Steel Beam Design [*Modray Ltd.*] [*Software package*] [*British*] (NCC)
SBE .... S-Band Exciter [*System*] [*Also, SBES*]
SBE .... Society of Broadcast Engineers (EANO)
SBE .... Sub BIT [*Binary Digit*] Encoder (MCD)
SBED .... Serial BIT [*Binary Digit*] Error Detector
SBEI .... SBE, Incorporated [*NASDAQ symbol*] (NQ)
SBES .... S-Band Exciter System [*Also, SBE*]
SBF .... Short Backfire [*Antenna*]
SBFM .... Silver-Band Frequency Modulation (IEEE)
SBH .... Strip-Buried Heterostructure [*Telecommunications*] (TEL)
SBH .... Switch Busy Hour [*Telecommunications*] (IEEE)
SBI .... Single Byte Interleaved (NITA)
SBIR .... Storage Bus in Register (NITA)
SBM .... System Balance Measure (BUR)
SBMDL ...... Submodel
SBP .... Spaceborne Programer
SBPK .... Staatsbibliothek Preussischer Kulturbesitz [*Berlin*] [*Information retrieval*] (ODIN)
SBR .... Segment Base Register (BUR)
SBR .... Storage Buffer Register (NITA)
SBS .... Satellite Business Systems [*McLean, VA*] [*Telecommunications*] (MCD)
SBS .... Semiconductor Bilateral Switch (MSA)
SBS .... Sensor Based System (BUR)
SBS .... Silicon Bilateral Switch
SBS .... Straight Binary Second
SBSG .... Small Business Systems Group [*Westford, MA*] [*Telecommunications*] (TSSD)
SBSS .... Spare Band Surveillance System (MCD)
SBT .... Simultaneous Baseband Transmission [*of information*]
SBT .... Six BIT [*Binary Digit*] Transcode (CMD)
SBT .... Surface Barrier Transistor
SBTT .... Southern Bell Telephone & Telegraph Co. (KSC)
SBU .... Small Base Unit [*Telecommunications*]
SBU .... Station Buffer Unit [*Data processing*] (OA)
SBURCS .... Six-BIT [*Binary Digit*] Universal Random Character Set [*Data processing*]
SBUV .... Solar and Backscatter Ultraviolet Spectrometer (MCD)
SBUV/TOMS ... Solar and Backscattered Ultraviolet and Total Ozone Mapping System
SBW .... Spectral Bandwidth
SBX .... S-Band Transponder
SC .... Satellite Computer (NITA)
SC .... Search Control (IEEE)
SC .... Semiconductor
SC .... Sending Complete [*Telecommunications*] (TEL)
SC .... Sequence Controller (NITA)
SC .... Service Code [*Telecommunications*] (TEL)
SC .... Session Control [*Data processing*] (IBMDP)
SC .... Set/Clear [*Flip-flop*] [*Data processing*]
SC .... Set Clock
SC .... Shift Control Counter [*Data processing*] (MDG)
SC .... Short Circuit
SC .... Signal Comparator (VIT)
SC .... Single Circuit [*Electricity*]
SC .... Single Contact [*Switch*]
SC .... Solid-State Circuit (MCD)
SC .... Source Code
SC .... Special Circuit
SC .... Start Computer (VIT)
SC .... Start Conversion [*Data processing*]
SC .... Status Statement [*Online database field identifier*] (OBD)
SC .... Storage Capacity
S/C .... Subcable (KSC)
SC .... Superimposed Coding [*Data processing*] (DIT)
SC .... Supplementary Information [*Telecommunications*] (TEL)
SC .... Suppressed Carrier (IEEE)
SCA .... Single Channel Analyzer
SCA .... Sterba Curtain Antenna
SCA .... Subcarrier Authorization (MSA)
SCA .... Subcarrier Channel [*Telecommunications*]
SCA .... Subchannel Adapter
SCA .... Subsidiary Communications Authorization [*Facilities used to transmit background music to subscribing customers*]
SCA .... Surface Coatings Abstracts [*Paint Research Association of Great Britain*] [*Bibliographic database*] (OBD)
SCA .... Switch Control Assembly
SCA .... Synchronous Communications Adapter (NITA)
SCA .... System Comparison Analysis [*Bell System*]
SCA .... System Control Area (NITA)
SCAD .... Scan Converter and Display [*Systems*]
SCADA .... Supervisory Control and Data Acquisition (IEEE)
SCADC .... Standard Central Air Data Computer
SCADS .... Simulation of Combined Analog Digital Systems [*Data processing*] (IEEE)
SCAEPA ..... Society for Computer Applications in Engineering, Planning, and Architecture [*Formerly, CEPA*] (EANO)
SCAL .... STAR [*Self Testing and Reporting*] Computer Assembly Language (CIT)
SCALD .... Structural Computer-Aided Logic Design (NITA)
SCALE .... Statutes and Cases Automated Legal Enquiry

Computer & Telecommunications Acronyms

SCAM	Soil Classification and Mapping Branch [*Department of Agriculture*] (EISS)
SCAM	Synchronous Communications Access Method (NITA)
SCAMC	Symposium on Computer Applications in Medical Care [*Baltimore, MD*]
SCAMP	Signal Conditioning Amplifier
SCAMP	Single Channel Amplitude Monopulse Processing
SCAMPS	Small Computer Analytical and Mathematical Programing System (IEEE)
SCAN	Satellite Cable Audio Networks [*Cable-television service*]
SCAN	Savings Comparative Analysis [*Federal Home Loan Bank Board*] [*Database*] (CUAD)
SCAN	Scanner Association of North America (EANO)
SCAN	Seismic Computerized Alert Network [*For warning of an earthquake*]
SCAN	Short Current Abstracts and Notes (DIT)
SCAN	Stock Control and Analysis (BUR)
SCAN	Stock Market Computer Answering Network [*British*]
SCAN	Student Career Automated Network (IEEE)
SCANP	Scandinavian Periodicals Index in Economics and Business [*Database*] [*Swedish*] (CUAD)
SCANS	Scheduling and Control by Automated Network System
SCANS	System Checkout Automatic Network Simulator
SCARF	System Control Audit Review File [*Data processing*]
SCARS	Software Configuration Accounting and Reporting System (OA)
SCAS	Subsystem Computer Application Software (MCD)
SCAT	Schottky Cell Array Technology (NITA)
SCAT	Space Communications and Tracking
SCAT	Special Advisory Committee on Telecommunications
SCAT	State Change Algorithm Translator
SCATHA	Spacecraft Charging at High Altitudes [*Satellite*]
SCATS	Sequentially Controlled Automatic Transmitter Start
SCATT	Scientific Communication and Technology Transfer [*System*] [*University of Pennsylvania*]
SCATT	Shared Catalog Accessed Through Terminals [*Data processing system*]
SCB	Segment Control BIT [*Binary Digit*] (OA)
SCB	Session Control Block [*Data processing*] (BUR)
SCB	Stack Control Block (NITA)
SCB	Station Control Block [*Data processing*] (IBMDP)
SCC	Satellite Communication Concentrator (NITA)
SCC	Satellite Communications Controller
SCC	Satellite Control Center
SCC	Satellite-Controlled Clock
SCC	Sequential Control Counter [*Data processing*] (BUR)
SCC	Set Conditionally [*Data processing*]
SCC	Short-Circuit Current
SCC	Signaling Conversion Circuit [*Telecommunications*] (TEL)
SCC	Simplified Computer Code
SCC	Single Conductor Cable (MSA)
SCC	Single Cotton-Covered [*Wire insulation*]
SCC	Specialized Common Carrier [*Telecommunications*]
SCC	Storage Connecting Circuit [*Teletype*]
SCC	Switching Control Center [*Bell System*]
SCC	Synchronous Communications Controller (NITA)
SCC	Systems Control Center
SCCAC	Society for Conceptual and Content Analysis by Computer [*Bowling Green University*] [*Bowling Green, OH*] [*Association for Computers and the Humanities special interest group*] (EANO)
SCCB	Software Configuration Control Board (KSC)
SCCC	Satellite Communications Control Centre [*British*]
SCCE	Satellite Configuration Control Element (MCD)
SCCF	Satellite Communication Control Facility
SCCPG	Satellite Communications Contingency Planning Group (NATG)
SCCS	Source Code Control System [*Data processing*]
SCCS	Switching Control Center System [*Telecommunications*] (TEL)
SCCU	Single Channel Control Unit (NITA)
SCD	Science Communication Division [*George Washington University Medical Center*] [*Information service*] (EISS)
SCD	Screwed (MDG)
SCD	Software Conceptual Design [*Data processing*]
SCDP	Society of Certified Data Processors (EANO)
SCDR	Subsystem Controller Definition Record [*Data processing*] (IBMDP)
SCDS	Scan Converter Display System (MCD)
SCDS	Sensor Communication and Display System (MCD)
SCDSB	Suppressed-Carrier Double Sideband
SCE	Scan Conversion Equipment [*Television*]
SCE	Signal Conversion Electronics [*Telecommunications*] (TEL)
SCEA	Society of Communications Engineers and Analysts
SCEC	Spaceborne Computer Engineering Conference (MCD)
SCEKS	Spectrum Clear Except Known Signals (MUGU)
SCELBAL	Scientific Elementary Basic Language [*1963*] [*Data processing*] (CSR)
SCEPTRE	System Computerized for Economical Performance, Tracking, Recording and Evaluation [*North Central Airlines*]
SCERT	Systems and Computers Evaluation and Review Technique [*Data processing*]
SCETV	South Carolina Educational Television [*Columbia*] [*Telecommunications*] (TSSD)
SCEU	Selector Channel Emulation Unit (NITA)
SCF	Scientific Computing Facility (CIT)
SCFD	Standard Cubic Feet per Day [*Of gasoline*] [*Telecommunications*] (TEL)
SCFEL	Standard COMSEC [*Communications Security*] Facility Equipment List
SCFM	Subcarrier Frequency Modulation [*Telecommunications*] (TEL)
SCG	Scientific Computing Group [*University of Toronto*] [*Research center*] (RCD)
SCGA	Synergistic Communications [*NASDAQ symbol*] (NQ)
SCH	Schedule
SCH	Seizures per Circuit per Hour [*Telecommunications*] (TEL)
SCHM	Schematic
SCHOLAR	Schering-Oriented Literature Analysis and Retrieval System [*Schering-Plough Corp.*] [*Information service*] (EISS)
SCI	Scientific Computers, Incorporated (MCD)
SCI	Seminar Clearinghouse International, Inc. [*Information service*] (EISS)
SCI	Short Circuit
SCI	Simulation Councils, Incorporated
SCI	Storer Communications, Incorporated [*NYSE symbol*]
SCI	System Consultants, Incorporated [*Mason, MI*] [*Software manufacturer*] (DASOS)
SCI	System Control Interface (NITA)
SCIC	Semiconductor Integrated Circuit
SCICC	Service Center Internal Computer Code [*Data processing*]
SCICLOPS	Systems Control, Incorporated Computerized Library Operations [*Information service*] (EISS)
SCIE	Scientific Computers [*NASDAQ symbol*] (NQ)
SCIL	Small Computers in Libraries [*A publication*]
SCIP	Stanford Center for Information Processing [*Stanford University*] [*Database*]
SCIPIO	Sales Catalog Index Project Input On-Line [*Art Institute of Chicago, Cleveland Museum of Art, Metropolitan Museum of Art*] [*Information service*] (EISS)
SCISEARCH	Science Citation Index Search [*Institute for Scientific Information*] [*Philadelphia, PA*] [*Bibliographic database*] (OBD)
SCISRS	Sigma Center Information Storage and Retrieval System
Sci Tech Inf Process	Scientific and Technical Information Processing [*A publication*]
Sci Tech Inf Process (Engl Transl)	Scientific and Technical Information Processing (English Translation) [*A publication*]
Sci Tech Inf Process (Eng Transl Nauchno-Tekh Inf Ser I)	Scientific and Technical Information Processing (English Translation of Nauchno-Tekhnicheskaya Informatsiya Seriya I) [*A publication*]
SCL	Sequential Control Logic (NITA)
SCL	Software Career Link [*Database provider*]
SCL	String Control Language [*Data processing*]
SCL	System Command Language [*Data processing*]
SCL	Systems Control Language [*Data processing*] (NITA)
SCLOG	Security Log [*Telecommunications*] (TEL)
SCM	Selective Complement Accumulator
SCM	Single-Channel MODEM [*Telecommunications*] (TEL)
SCM	Small-Core Memory [*Data processing*]
SCM	Society for Computer Medicine [*Later, AAMSI*] (EANO)
SCM	Software Configuration Management [*Data processing*] (IEEE)
SCM	Streamline Curvature Method [*Computer program*]
SCM	Subscribers' Concentration Module [*Telecommunications*] (TEL)
SCM	Supervision Control Module [*Telecommunications*] (TEL)
SCMO	Subsidiary Communications Multiplex Operation [*FM radio frequency unused portion*]
SCN	Satellite Communications Network, Inc. [*Edison, NJ*] [*Telecommunications*] (TSSD)
SCN	Schematic Change Notice
SCN	Self-Compensating Network [*Telecommunications*] (TEL)
SCN	Shortest Connected Network (OA)
SCNA	Sudden Cosmic-Noise Absorption
SCNN	Scan-Tron Corp. [*NASDAQ symbol*] (NQ)
SCNR	Sequence Control Number Register [*Data processing*]
SCOBOL	Structured COBOL (NITA)
SCOM	Site Cutover Manager [*Telecommunications*] (TEL)
SCOM	Spacecraft Communicator (SKY)
SCOOP	Scientific Computation of Optimal Programs (IEEE)
SCOP	Single Copy Order Plan [*Later, STOP*] [*Bookselling*]
SCOPE	Supervisory Control of Program Execution (MCD)
SCOPE	System to Coordinate the Operation of Peripheral Equipment
SCORAN	Scorer and Analyzer [*Computerized educational testing*]
SCORE	System for Computerized Olympic Results and Events [*Texas Instruments, Inc.*]
SCORPIO	Subject-Content-Oriented Retriever for Processing Information On-Line [*Congressional Research Service*]
SCOT	Satellite Communications Overseas Transmission
SCOTICE	Scotland to Iceland Submarine Cable System [*Telecommunications*] (TEL)
SCOTS	Surveillance and Control of Transmission Systems [*Bell Laboratories*]
SCOTS	System Checkout Test Set (MCD)
SCOTT	Synchronous Continuous Orbital Three-Dimensional Tracking
SCP	Station Communications Processor (CIT)
SCP	Stromberg-Carlson Practices [*Telecommunications*] (TEL)
SCP	Supervisory Control Program [*Burroughs Corp.*] (NITA)
SCP	Symbolic Conversion Program (BUR)
SCP	System Communication Pamphlet (IEEE)

Acronym	Definition
SCP	System Control Processor [*Honeywell, Inc.*] (NITA)
SCP	System Control Programing [*Data processing*]
SCPC	Single-Channel-per-Carrier [*Telecommunications*]
SCPE	Scope, Inc. [*NASDAQ symbol*] (NQ)
SCPI	Small Computer Program Index [*Allm Books*] [*Information service*] [*A publication*] [*British*] (EISS)
SCPR	Semiconductor Parameter Retrieval [*Information Handling Services*] [*Database*] (CUAD)
SCP(S)	Subscribers' Call Processing (Subsystem) [*Telecommunications*] (TEL)
SCR	Scanning Control Register
SCR	Selective Chopper Radiometer
SCR	Selenium Control Rectifier
SCR	Semiconductor
SCR	Semiconductor-Controlled Rectifier
SCR	Signal Conversion Relay [*Telecommunications*] (TEL)
SCR	Single Character Recognition (NITA)
SCR	Software Correction Report (CAAL)
SCR	System Change Request
SCRAP	Series Computation of Reliability and Probability [*Data processing*]
SCRATCHPAD	[*A*] programing language (CSR)
SCRI	Southern Center for Research and Innovation, Inc. [*University of Southern Mississippi*] [*Research center*] (RCD)
SCRI	Supercomputer Computations Research Institute [*Florida State University*] [*Research center*] (RCD)
SCRIPT	System Controlling Research Image Processing Tasks (MCD)
SCRLC	South Central Research Library Council [*Ithaca, NY*] [*Library network*] (EISS)
SCROLL	String and Character Recording Oriented Logogrammatic Language [*1970*] [*Data processing*] (CSR)
SCRS	Service Center Replacement System [*Data processing*]
SCRT	Sealed Cathode Ray Tube
SCRT	Subscribers' Circuit Routine Tester [*Telecommunications*] (TEL)
SCS	Satellite Control Satellite [*Telecommunications*] (TEL)
SCS	Scan Converter [*or Counter*] System
SCS	Scientific Control Systems (DIT)
SCS	Single Channel Simplex
SCS	Single Control Support (BUR)
SCS	Small Computer System (NITA)
SCS	Society for Computer Simulation [*La Jolla, CA*]
SCSBM	Society for Computer Science in Biology and Medicine
SCSC	Summer Computer Simulation Conference
SCSI	Small Computer System Interface
SCSN	Standard Computer Software Number
SCSO	Space Communications Station Operation
SCT	Sample Control Tape [*Data processing*]
SCT	Schottky Clamped Transistor
SCT	Semiconductor Curve Tracer
SCT	Sequence Checking Tape
SCT	Special Characters Table [*Data processing*] (IBMDP)
SCT	Step Control Table (CMD)
SCT	Subroutine Call Table [*Data processing*] (CDH)
SCT	Subscriber Carrier Terminal [*Telecommunications*] (TEL)
SCT	System Circuit Test (VIT)
SCT	System Compatibility Tests
SCTC	Systems & Computer Technology Corporation [*NASDAQ symbol*] (NQ)
SCTP	Straight Channel Tape Print [*Data processing*] (KSC)
SCTPP	Straight Channel Tape Print Program [*Data processing*] (KSC)
SCU	Sequence Control Unit (KSC)
SCU	Servicing Control Unit [*Telecommunications*] (TEL)
SCU	Station Control Unit (OA)
SCU	Storage Control Unit
SCU	Subscribers' Concentrator Unit [*Telecommunications*] (TEL)
SCU	System Control Unit
SCUL	Simulation of the Columbia University Libraries [*Data processing research*]
SCULL	Serial Communication Unit for Long Links (NITA)
SCUP	School Computer Use Plan (IEEE)
SD	Sample Data (NG)
SD	Schematic Diagram
SD	Send Digits [*Telecommunications*] (TEL)
SD	Serializer/Deserializer (NITA)
SD	Sort File Description [*Data processing*] (DDI)
SD	Source Document [*Data processing*]
SD	Standardization Data
SD	Systems Development (MCD)
SDA	Software Design Associates, Inc. [*New York, NY*] [*Software manufacturer*] (DASOS)
SDA	Source Data Acquisition (BUR)
SDA	Source Data Automation
SDA	Supporting Data Analysis
SDA	Symbolic Device Address (OA)
SDA	Symbolic Disk Address (AFM)
SDA	Symbols-Digits-Alphabetics
SDA	Systems Data Analysis (CIT)
SDAA	Stacked Dipole Aerial Array
SDADS	Satellite Digital and Display System
SDAE	Source Data Automation Equipment
SDAL	Switched Data Access Line (NITA)
SDAS	Scientific Data Automation System (IEEE)
SDAS	Source Data Automation System
SDAS	Systems Data Analysis Section
SDAT	Stationery Digital Audio Tape
SDAU	SDA [*Software Design Associates*] Users' Group
SDB	Securities Data Base System [*Capital Market Systems, Inc.*] [*Information service*] (EISS)
SDB	Segment Descriptor Block (NITA)
SDB	Shakespeare Data Bank, Inc. [*Evanston, IL*] [*Information service*] (EISS)
SDB	Storage Data Bus (NITA)
SDC	Scientific Data Center (MCD)
SDC	Seismological Data Center [*Environmental Science Services Administration*]
SDC	Signal Data Converter
SDC	Stabilization Data Computer
SDC	System for Data Calculation [*Information retrieval*] (ODIN)
SDC	System Development Corporation [*Information service*]
SDCR	Source Data Communication Retrieval (OA)
SDCS	Sample Data Control System (MCD)
SDD	Signal Data Demodulator
SDD	Software Design Description [*Data processing*] (IEEE)
SDD	Stored Data Description (NITA)
SDDL	Stored Data Definition Language
SDDS	Secondary Data Display System (MCD)
SDDS	Signal Data Demodulator Set [*or System*] (CIT)
SD/DS	Synchro-Digital/Digital-Synchro (CAAL)
SDDTTG	Stored Data Definition and Translation Task Group (OA)
SDE	Society of Data Educators [*Memphis, TN*]
SDE	Source Data Entry (NITA)
SDE	Students for Data Education (IEEE)
SDF	Satellite Distribution Frame [*Telecommunications*] (TEL)
SDF	Screen Definition Facility [*Data processing*]
SDF	Standard Distribution Format [*Data processing*]
SDF	Standard Drug File [*Derwent Publications Ltd.*] [*Database*] (CUAD)
SDF	Supergroup Distribution Frame [*Telecommunications*] (TEL)
SDF	System Data Format [*Data processing*]
SDFL	Schottky Diode FET [*Field Effect Transistor*] Logic
SDFS	Standard Disk Filing System (NITA)
SDG	Scan Display Generator
SDG	Simulated Data Generator
SDG	Situation Display Generator
SDGA	Single Degaussing Cable
SDH	Structured Document Handbook [*Data processing*]
SDHE	Spacecraft Data Handling Equipment
SDI	Selective Dissemination of Information [*System*] [*Data processing*]
SDI	Source Data Information
SDI	Standard Data Interface [*Data processing*]
SD & I	System Development and Integration (MCD)
SDILINE	Selective Dissemination of Information Online [*National Library of Medicine*] [*Bethesda, MD*] [*Bibliographic database*] (OBD)
SDIM	System of Documentation and Information for Metallurgy [*Commission of the European Communities*] [*Database*] [*Information service*] (EISS)
SDIM1	System fuer Dokumentation und Information der Metallurgie [*System for Documentation and Information in Metallurgy*] [*Fachinformationszentrum Werkstoffe*] [*Database*] [*German*] (ODIN)
SDIM1	Systeme de Documentation et d'Information en Metallurgie [*System for Documentation and Information in Metallurgy*] [*Database*] [*French*] (ODIN)
SDIO	Serial Digit Input/Output [*Data processing*] (NITA)
SDK	System Design Kit (NITA)
SDL	Software Design Language (NITA)
SDL	Software Development Language [*Burroughs Corp.*] (NITA)
SDL	Specification and Description Language [*Telecommunications*] (TEL)
SDL	System Descriptive Language [*Data processing*] (IEEE)
SDL	System Design Language (NITA)
SDL	System Development Language [*1971*] [*Data processing*] (CSR)
SDL	System Directory List [*Data processing*] (BUR)
SDL	Systematic Design Language [*Data processing*]
SDLC	Synchronous Data-Link Control [*Data processing*]
SDLC	System Data Link Control
SDM	Semiconductor Disk Memory (NITA)
SDM	Sequency-Division Multiplexing (IEEE)
SDM	Space Division Multiplexing [*Physics*]
SDM	Spares Determination Method [*Bell System*]
SDM	STARAN Debug Module (OA)
SDM	Subsystem Design Manual (MCD)
SDM	Synchronous Digital Machine (NITA)
SDMA	Shared Direct Memory Access [*Sperry UNIVAC*] (NITA)
SDMA	Space Division Multiple Access (CBSS)
SDME	Synchronous Data Modem Equipment
SDMIS	Standardization Data Management Information System (DDI)
SDMIX	South Dakota Medical Information Exchange [*University of South Dakota*] [*Sioux Falls*] [*Telecommunications*] (TSSD)
SDMS	Shipboard Data Multiplex System (MCD)
SDN	Separation Designation Number
SDN	Service Dealer's Newsletter [*Abington, PA*] [*A publication*] [*Information service*] (EISS)
SDN	Subscriber's Directory Number [*Telecommunications*] (TEL)
SDN	Synchronized Digital Network [*Telecommunications*] (TEL)

Computer & Telecommunications Acronyms

SDN & SU ... Step-Down and Step-Up (MSA)
SDO .... Source Data Operation (MDG)
SDP .... Signal Data Processor
SDP .... Signal Dispatch Point [*Telecommunications*] (TEL)
SDP .... Silicon Diode Pellet
SDP .... Site Data Processors
SDP .... Source Data Processing (NITA)
SDP .... Station Data Processing (CIT)
SDP .... Survey Data Processing
SDPL .... Servomechanisms and Data Processing Laboratory [*Massachusetts Institute of Technology*]
SDPS .... Signal Data Processing System
SDR .... Search Decision Rule [*Data processing*]
SDR .... Sensor Data Record [*For spacecraft*]
SDR .... Software Design Review (MCD)
SDR .... Statistical Data Recorder [*Data processing*] (MDG)
SDR .... Storage Data Register (MCD)
SDR .... Survey of Doctorate Recipients [*National Research Council*] [*Database*] (FDB)
SDR .... System Data Record (CIT)
SDR .... System for Data Retrieval [*Information retrieval*] (ODIN)
SDR .... System Definition Record [*Data processing*] (IBMDP)
SDR .... System Definition Requirements
SDR .... System Design Report [*NATO*] (NATG)
SDR .... System Discrepancy Report
SDRP .... Simulated Data Reduction Program
SDRS .... Signal Data Recording Set (MCD)
SDS .... Safety Data Sheet (KSC)
SDS .... Scientific Data System [*Later, XDS*]
SDS .... Simulating Digital Systems (CAH)
SDS .... Simulation Data Subsystem (KSC)
SDS .... Software Development System
SDS .... Space Division Switching [*Telecommunications*]
SDS .... Spectrometer Digital System
SDS .... Status Display Support (MCD)
SDS .... Steering Damping System (MCD)
SDS .... System Data Synthesizer (KSC)
SDS .... System Design Specification
SDS .... Systematic Design Language [*Data processing*] (TUT)
SDSD .... Satellite Data Services Division [*National Oceanic and Atmospheric Administration*] [*Information service*] (EISS)
SDSD .... Single Disk Storage Device [*Data processing*] (BUR)
SDSI .... Shared Data Set Integrity (NITA)
SDS & RU ... Soil Data Storage and Retrieval Unit [*Department of Agriculture*] (EISS)
SDSW .... Sense Device Status Word (OA)
SDT .... Serial Data Transmission
SDT .... Simulated Data Tape
SDT .... Start-Data-Traffic [*Data processing*] (IBMDP)
SDT .... Surveillance Data Transmission
SDTI .... Selective Dissemination of Technical Information [*Data processing*]
SDTP .... Startover Data Transfer and Processing [*Program*]
SDTR .... Serial Data Transmitter/Receiver [*Telecommunications*] (TEL)
SDTS .... Satellite Data Transmission System (DIT)
SDU .... Signal Distribution Unit
SDU .... Source Data Utility (NITA)
SDU .... Station Display Unit (NITA)
SDW .... Segment Descriptor Word (NITA)
SDX .... Satellite Data Exchange (NITA)
SE .... Series Statement [*Online database field identifier*] (OBD)
SE .... Set (CDH)
SE .... Software Engineering (MCD)
SE .... Southeast
SE .... Systems Engineer [*or Engineering*] [*Data processing*]
SEA .... Spherical Electrostatic Analyzer
SEA .... Static Error Analysis (NITA)
SEA .... Systems Effectiveness Analyzer (IEEE)
SEAC .... Standards Eastern [*or Electronic*] Automatic Computer [*National Bureau of Standards*]
SEAL .... Standard Electronic Accounting Language [*Data processing*] (BUR)
SEALF .... Semiempirical Absorption Loss Formula [*Radio*]
SEAM .... Software Engineering and Management (NITA)
SEAMINFO ... Surface Mining and Environment Information System [*University of Arizona*] (EISS)
SEAMUS ..... Society for Electro-Acoustic Music in the United States (EANO)
SEARCH ..... System for Electronic Analysis and Retrieval of Criminal Histories [*Project succeeded by National Crime Information Center*] [*Department of Justice*]
SEARCH ..... System for Exploring Alternative Resource Commitments in Higher Education [*Data processing*]
SEATELCOM ... Southeast Asia Telecommunications System
SEATS .... Shubert Entertainment and Arts Ticketing System [*National computerized theatre-ticket selling system*]
SEBD .... Software Engineering Bibliographic Data Base [*Data and Analysis Center for Software*] [*Database*] (FDB)
SEC .... Second (AFM)
SEC .... Sector
SEC .... Simple Electronic Computer [*Birkbeck College*] [*London, England*] (DEN)
SEC .... Single Error Correcting (NITA)
SEC .... Switching Equipment Congestion [*Telecommunications*] (TEL)

SECA .... Southern Educational Communications Authority [*Television network*]
SECAD .... Services Engineering Computer-Aided Design [*Pierce Management Services*] [*Software package*] [*British*] (NCC)
SECAM ...... Sequence Electronique Couleur avec Memoire [*Color Sequence with Memory*] [*French color television system*]
SECC .... Scientific and Engineering Computing Council (MCD)
SECDED ..... Single-BIT [*Binary Digit*] Error Correction and Double-BIT [*Binary Digit*] Error Detection (NITA)
SECIR .... Semiautomatic Encoding of Chemistry for Information Retrieval (DIT)
SECO .... Sequential Coding
SECO .... Sequential Control [*Teletype*] [*Data processing*]
SECO .... Station Engineering Control Office [*Telecommunications*] (TEL)
SECOBI ...... Servicio de Consulta a Bancos de Informacion [*Data Base Consultation Service*] [*Mexico*] [*Information service*] (EISS)
SECORD .... Secure Voice Cord Board [*Telecommunications*] (TEL)
SECS .... Simulation and Evaluation of Chemical Synthesis [*Data processing*]
SECU .... Slave Emulator Control Unit (NITA)
SED .... Software Engineering Data [*Data Analysis Center for Software*] [*Database*] (FDB)
SED .... Status Entry Device [*Telecommunications*] (TEL)
SEDA .... Structured Exploratory Data Analysis
SEDIC .... Sociedad Espanola de Documentacion e Informacion Cientifica [*Spanish Society for Documentation and Information Sciences*] [*Information service*] (EISS)
SEDIT .... Sophisticated String Editor (IEEE)
SEDM .... Status Entry Device Multiplexer [*Telecommunications*] (TEL)
SEDPC .... Scientific and Engineering Data Processing Center
SEDR .... System Effective Data Rate (BUR)
SEDS .... State Energy Data System [*Department of Energy*] [*Database*] (FDB)
SEE .... Systems Equipment Engineer [*Telecommunications*] (TEL)
SEEA .... Software Error Effects Analysis (NITA)
SEEDIS ...... Socio-Economic Demographic Information System [*Lawrence Berkeley Laboratory*] [*Database*] (FDB)
SEEK .... Systems Evaluation and Exchange of Knowledge [*Data processing*] (CGC)
SEER .... System for Electronic Evaluation and Retrieval [*Data processing*]
SEF .... Software Engineering Facility (NITA)
SEF .... Standard External File (NITA)
SEG .... Segment
SEI .... Software Engineering Institute [*DoD*]
SEIC .... SEI Corporation [*NASDAQ symbol*] (NQ)
SEIDB .... Solar Energy Information Data Bank [*Department of Energy*]
SEIMC .... Special Education Instructional Materials Centers [*Office of Education*] [*Albany, NY*] [*Database producer*] (EISS)
SEIRS .... Suppliers and Equipment Information Retrieval System [*International Civil Aviation Organization*] [*Databank*] [*Information service*] (EISS)
SEIS .... Solar Energy Information Services (EISS)
SEL .... Selector (DEN)
SEL .... Space Environment Laboratory [*National Oceanic and Atmospheric Administration*]
SEL .... Stanford Electronics Laboratory [*Stanford University*] [*Research center*]
SEL .... System Engineering Laboratories (MCD)
SELCAL ..... Selective Calling [*Radio*]
SELDADS ... Space Environment Laboratory Data Acquisition and Display System [*National Oceanic and Atmospheric Administration*]
SELGEM ..... Self-Generating Master [*Information management system*] [*Data processing*]
SELL .... Sales Environment Learning Laboratory [*Computer-based marketing game*]
SEM .... Standard Electronic Module (CAAL)
SEM .... Standard Estimating Module (IEEE)
SEM .... Station Engineering Manual [*Telecommunications*] (TEL)
SEM .... Subarray Electronics Module [*Data processing*]
SEMI .... Semiconductor Equipment and Materials Institute
Semicond Insul ... Semiconductors and Insulators [*A publication*]
Semicond and Insul ... Semiconductors and Insulators [*A publication*]
Semicond Semimet ... Semiconductors and Semimetals [*A publication*]
SEMP .... Standard Electronics Module Program (MCD)
SEMS .... Severe Environment Memory Series [*or System*] [*Data processing*]
SEN .... Software Error Notification [*Data processing*]
SEN .... System Error Notification [*Data processing*]
SENTOS ..... Sentinel Operating System (IEEE)
SEP .... Separation Parameter
SEP .... Serial Entry Printer
SEPOL .... Settlement Problem-Oriented Language [*Data processing*] (IEEE)
SEPOL .... Soil Engineering Problem-Oriented Language [*Data processing*] (TUT)
SEPTEL ...... Separate Telegram
SEQ .... Sequence
SEQP .... Supreme Equipment & Systems [*NASDAQ symbol*] (NQ)
SEQS .... Simultaneous Equation Solver [*Computer program*]
SEQUEL ..... Structured English Query Language [*1974*] [*Data processing*] (CSR)
SEQUIN ..... Sequential Quadrature Inband [*Television system*] (DEN)
SER .... Sequential Events Recorder

Computer & Telecommunications Acronyms

SER............ Serial (AFM)
SER............ System Environment Recording (BUR)
SERDES..... Serializer, Deserializer
SEREP........ System Environment Recording, Editing, and Printing [Data processing] (TUT)
SEREP........ System Error Record Editing Program [Data processing]
SERIX........ Swedish Environmental Research Index [Swedish National Environmental Protection Board] [Database] (EISS)
SERLINE..... Serials On-Line [National Library of Medicine] [Bethesda, MD] [Database]
SERMLP..... Southeastern Regional Medical Library Program [Emory University] [Atlanta, GA] [Library network] (EISS)
SERP.......... Software Engineering Research Projects [Data Analysis Center for Software] [Database] (FDB)
SERUG....... SII [Systems Integrators, Incorporated] Eastern Regional Users Group [Scranton, PA] (EANO)
SES............ Service Evaluation System [Telecommunications] (TEL)
SES............ Special Exchange Service [Telecommunications] (TEL)
SES............ System External Storage (NITA)
SESAME..... Service, Sort and Merge [Data processing]
SE/SE......... Single Entry/Single Exit (NITA)
SESLP........ Sequential Explicit Stochastic Linear Programing [Data processing]
SESOME..... Service, Sort, and Merge [Data processing] (IEEE)
SET............ Self-Extending Translator (IEEE)
SET............ Software Engineering Technology
SET............ Software Engineering Terminology [Data processing] (IEEE)
SET............ Stepped Electrode Transistor (NITA)
SETAB....... Sets Tabular Material [Phototypesetting computer]
SETAD....... Secure Transmission of Acoustic Data (NVT)
SETB.......... Set Theoretic Language - BALM [1973] [Data processing] (CSR)
SETF.......... STARAN Evaluation and Training Facility (OA)
SETI........... Societe Europeenne pour le Traitement de l'Information [European Society for the Processing of Information] (CAH)
SETL.......... Set Theoretic Language [1971] [Data processing] (CSR)
SETM......... Societe d'Etudes et de Travaux Mecanographiques (OA)
SETS.......... Set Equation Transformation System [1970] [Data processing] (CSR)
SEW........... Surface Electromagnetic Wave
SF.............. Scale Factor
SF.............. Select Frequency (NITA)
SF.............. Short Format (NITA)
SF.............. Side Frequency (DEN)
SF.............. Signal Frequency
SF.............. Skip Flag [Data processing] (MDG)
S/F............. Store-and-Forward [Data communications]
SFA............ Scientific-Atlanta, Inc. [NYSE symbol]
SFA............ Segment Frequency Algorithm (NITA)
SFAR.......... System Failure Analysis Report (IEEE)
SFB............ Semiconductor Functional Block (IEEE)
SFC............ S-Band Frequency Converter
SFC............ Sectored File Controller (NITA)
SFC............ Selector File Channel (NITA)
SFCW......... Sweep Frequency, Continuous Wave
SFD............ System Function Description (IEEE)
SFE............ Smart Front End (NITA)
SFERT........ Systeme Fundamental Europeen de Reference pour la Transmission Telephonique [European master telephone reference system] (DEN)
SFJ............ Swept Frequency Jamming
SFK............ Special Function Key [Calculators]
SFL............ Substrate Fed Logic (NITA)
SFM........... Switching Mode Frequency Multipliers (OA)
SFMR......... Stepped-Frequency Microwave Radiometer [For measuring rain rate and wind speed]
SFOLDS..... Ship Form Online Design System [British Ship Research Association] [Software package] [British] (NCC)
SFP............ Security Filter Processor (NITA)
SFP............ Slack Frame Program (OA)
SFRS.......... Swept Frequency Radiometer System
SFS............ S-Band Feed System
SFS............ Sektion fuer Systementwicklung [GID] [Information retrieval] (ODIN)
SFS............ Software Facilities and Standards [Data processing] (TEL)
SFS............ Symbolic File Support
SFTS.......... Standard Frequency and Time Signals (IEEE)
SFTWR...... Software [Data processing] (MCD)
SFU............ Special Function Unit (NITA)
SFU............ Status Fill-In Unit [Telecommunications] (TEL)
SG............. Signal Generator
SG............. Signal Ground (BUR)
SG............. Sort Generator
SG............. Super Group (NATG)
SG............. System Gain (NITA)
SGB........... Safeguard Business Systems, Inc. [NYSE symbol]
SGC........... Stabilizer Gyro Circuit
SGC........... Supergroup Connector [Telecommunications] (TEL)
SGD........... Self-Generating Dictionary (NITA)
SGD........... Signaling Ground [Telecommunications] (TEL)
SGDF......... Supergroup Distribution Frame [Telecommunications] (TEL)
SGDI.......... Switched Ground Discrete Input (MCD)
SGDO......... Switched Ground Discrete Output (MCD)
SGJP.......... Satellite Graphic Job Processor [Data processing]

SGLS.......... Satellite Grand Link System (NATG)
SGML........ Standard Generalized Markup Language [Electronic manuscript preparation and production]
SGNMOS.... Screen-Grid N-Channel Metal Oxide Semiconductor
SGS........... Stream Generation Statement [Data processing]
SGS........... Symbol Generation and Storage [Data processing]
SGSR......... Society for General Systems Research [Washington, DC]
SGT............ Satellite Ground Terminal
SGT............ Segment Table [Data processing] (IBMDP)
SGTS.......... Satellite Ground Terminal System
SGX........... Selector Group Matrix [Telecommunications] (TEL)
S/H............ Sample and Hold (IEEE)
SH............. Section Heading Code [Online database field identifier] (OBD)
SH............. Send Hub [Telegraphy] (TEL)
SH............. Session Handler (NITA)
SH............. Shunt [Electricity]
SH............. Source Handshake (NITA)
SH............. Specified Hours of Operation [Broadcasting term]
SH............. Super-High-Frequency [Radio wave] (NG)
SH............. Switch Handler [Telecommunications] (TEL)
SHADRAC... Shelter Housed Automatic Digital Random Access [Data processing]
SHAL......... Subject Heading Authority List [Data processing]
SHARE....... Society to Help Avoid Redundant Effort [in data processing]
SHAS......... Shared Hospital Accounting System [Data processing]
SHCRT....... Short Circuit
SHELF....... Super-Hard Extremely-Low Frequency (MCD)
SHF........... Shift (MSA)
SHF........... Super-High-Frequency [Radio wave]
SHIEF........ Shared Information Elicitation Facility [Data processing]
SHIELD...... Sylvania High-Intelligence Electronic Defense
SHIOER...... Statistical Historical Input/Output Error Rate Utility [Sperry UNIVAC] (NITA)
SHIP........... Standard Hardware Interface Program
SHIRTDIF... Storage, Handling, and Retrieval of Technical Data in Image Formation [Data processing] (IEEE)
SHOC......... Software/Hardware Operational Control (NITA)
SHR........... Share [Business and trade]
SHRI.......... Sciences and Humanities Research Institute [Iowa State University] [Research center] (RCD)
SHRTWV.... Short Wave (FAAC)
SI.............. Sample Interval
SI.............. Serial Input (DEEC)
SI.............. Service Indicator [Telecommunications] (TEL)
SI.............. Shift-In Character [Keyboard] [Data processing]
SI.............. Signal Interface
S/I............. Signal-to-Interference
SI.............. Society of Indexers [British] (DIT)
SI.............. Special Instruction
SI.............. Speech Interpolation [Telecommunications] (TEL)
SI.............. Storage Immediate (CAH)
SI.............. Superimpose (MDG)
SI.............. Symbolic Input [Data processing]
SI.............. Systeme International d'Unites [International System of Units] [Also, SIU]
SIA............ Semiconductor Industry Association (EANO)
SIA............ Serial Input Adapter (SKY)
SIA............ Service in Information and Analysis [Host] [British] (BUR)
SIA............ Software Institute of America [Andover, MA] [Telecommunications] (TSSD)
SIA............ Standard Interface Adapter (NITA)
SIA............ Storage Instantaneous Audimeter [Measures television viewing]
SIA............ Subminiature Integrated Antenna
SIAC.......... Securities Industry Automation Corporation [NYSE/ASE]
SIAF.......... Service Indicator Associated Field [Telecommunications] (TEL)
SIAM.......... Separate Index Access Method [Data processing] (BUR)
SIAM.......... Signal Information and Monitoring Service [American radio monitoring service]
SIAM.......... Society for Industrial and Applied Mathematics [Philadelphia, PA]
SIAM J Comput ... SIAM [Society for Industrial and Applied Mathematics] Journal on Computing [A publication]
SIB............ Serial Interface Board (NITA)
SIB............ Systems Information Bulletin [Data processing]
SIBIL.......... Systeme Integre pour les Bibliotheques Universitaires de Lausanne [Integrated System for the University of Lausanne Libraries] [Switzerland] [Information service] (EISS)
SIC............ Semiconductor Integrated Circuit
SIC............ Serial Interface Chip
SIC............ Silicon Integrated Circuit
SIC............ SONAR Information Center (NVT)
SIC............ Special Interest Committee (CGC)
SIC............ Specific Inductive Capacity
SIC............ Standard Industrial Classification [File indexing code]
SIC............ States Information Center [Council of State Governments] (EISS)
SIC............ Systeme Informatique pour la Conjoncture [Information System for the Economy] [France] [Information service] [Databank] (EISS)
SICDOC...... Special Interest Committee on Program Documentation [Association for Computing Machinery]
SICOB........ Salon International de l'Informatique, de la Communication, et de l'Organisation du Bureau [Business equipment exhibition] (NITA)

Computer & Telecommunications Acronyms

SICOM	Securities Industry Communication [*Western Union Corp.*] [*Information service*]
SICS	Ships Integrated Communications System (MCD)
SID	Scheduled Issue Date [*Telecommunications*] (TEL)
SID	Sequence Information Data (DDI)
SID	Serial Input Data [*Data processing*]
SID	Sketch-In-Depth [*Parthorn*] [*Software package*] [*British*] (NCC)
SID	Society for Information Display [*Playa Del Rey, CA*]
SID	Sound Interface Device [*Computer chip*]
SID	Sudden Ionospheric Disturbance [*Telecommunications*]
SID	SWIFT [*Society for Worldwide Interbank Financial Telecommunications*] Interface Device (NITA)
SID	Syntax Improving Device (IEEE)
SID	Systems Integration and Deployment [*Program*] [*Department of Transportation*]
SIDAR	Selective Information Dissemination and Retrieval [*Data processing*] (DIT)
SIDASE	Significant Data Selection
SIDES	Source Input Data Edit System (NITA)
SIDF	Sinusoidal Input Describing Function [*Data processing*]
SIDS	Spares Integrated Data System
SIDS	Support Integrated Data System (MCD)
SIDY	Science Dynamics Corp. [*NASDAQ symbol*] (NQ)
SIE	Science Information Exchange [*Later, SSIE*] [*Smithsonian Institution*]
SIE	Select Information Exchange [*Information service*] (EISS)
SIEA	Sensor Interface Electronics Assembly (MCD)
SIEC	Suicide Information and Education Centre [*Canadian Mental Health Association*] [*Information service*] (EISS)
SIF	Signaling Information Field [*Telecommunications*] (TEL)
SIF	Storage Interface Facility (NITA)
SIFCS	Sideband Intermediate Frequency Communications System
SIFR	Sun-Improved Frequency Response
SIFT	Share Internal FORTRAN Translator [*Data processing*] (IEEE)
SIFT	Simplified Input for Toss [*Data processing*]
SIG	Signal
SIG	Special Interest Group
SIGACC	Special Interest Group on Academic and Associated Computing [*Formerly, SIGUCC*] [*Association for Computing Machinery*]
SIGACT	Special Interest Group on Automata and Computability Theory [*Association for Computing Machinery*]
SIGADA	Special Interest Group on Ada [*Association for Computing Machinery*] [*New York, NY*] (EANO)
SIG/ALP	Special Interest Group/Automated Language Processing [*American Society for Information Science*]
SIGAPL	Special Interest Group on APL Programing Language [*Association for Computing Machinery*] [*New York, NY*] (EANO)
SIGARCH	Special Interest Group for Architecture of Computer Systems [*Association for Computing Machinery*] [*New York, NY*] (CSR)
SIGART	Special Interest Group on Artificial Intelligence [*Association for Computing Machinery*] [*New York, NY*] (EANO)
SIGBDP	Special Interest Group on Business Data Processing and Management [*Association for Computing Machinery*] [*New York, NY*] (MCD)
SIGBIO	Special Interest Group on Biomedical Computing [*Association for Computing Machinery*] (EANO)
SIGCAPH	Special Interest Group for Computers and the Physically Handicapped [*Association for Computing Machinery*] [*New York, NY*]
SIGCAS	Special Interest Group on Computers and Society [*Association for Computing Machinery*] [*New York, NY*] (CSR)
SIGCHI	Special Interest Group on Computer and Human Interaction [*Association for Computing Machinery*] [*Northwestern University*] [*Evanston, IL*] (EANO)
SIGCOMM	Special Interest Group on Data Communication [*Association for Computing Machinery*]
SIGCOSIM	Special Interest Group on Computer Systems, Installation Management [*Association for Computing Machinery*]
SIGCPR	Special Interest Group on Computer Personnel Research [*Association for Computing Machinery*] [*Indiana University*] [*Bloomington, IN*]
SIGCS	Special Interest Group for Computers and Society [*Association for Computing Machinery*] (EANO)
SIG/CSE	Special Interest Group for Computer Science Education [*Association for Computing Machinery*] [*New York, NY*]
SIGCUE	Special Interest Group for Computer Uses in Education [*Association for Computing Machinery*] [*New York, NY*]
SIGDA	Special Interest Group for Design Automation [*Association for Computing Machinery*] [*New York, NY*]
SIGDOC	Special Interest Group on Documentation [*Association for Computing Machinery*]
SIGFIDET	Special Interest Group on File Description and Translation [*Association for Computing Machinery*] [*Later, Special Interest Group on the Management of Data*]
SIGGEN	Signal Generator (IEEE)
SIGGRAPH	Special Interest Group on Computer Graphics [*Association for Computing Machinery*] [*New York, NY*]
Sight & S	Sight and Sound [*A publication*]
SIGI	System for Interactive Guidance Information [*Computerized career-counseling service offered by the Educational Testing Service*]
SIGIR	Special Interest Group on Information Retrieval [*Association for Computing Machinery*] [*New York, NY*]
SIGLASH	Special Interest Group on Language Analysis and Studies in the Humanities [*Association for Computing Machinery*]
SIGLE	System for Information on Grey Literature in Europe [*European Association for Grey Literature Exploitation*] [*Database*] (EISS)
SIGLINT	Signal Intelligence [*US surveillance satellite*]
SIGMAP	Special Interest Group for Mathematical Programing [*Association for Computing Machinery*] [*Washington, DC*]
SIGMETRICS	Special Interest Group on Measurement and Evaluation [*Association for Computing Machinery*] (CSR)
SIGMICRO	Special Interest Group on Microprograming [*Association for Computing Machinery*] [*New York, NY*]
SIGMINI	Special Interest Group on Minicomputers [*Later, SIGSMALL*] [*Association for Computing Machinery*]
SIGMOD	Special Interest Group on Management of Data [*Association for Computing Machinery*]
SIGNUM	Special Interest Group for Numerical Mathematics [*Association for Computing Machinery*] (CSR)
SIGOA	Special Interest Group on Office Automation [*Association for Computing Machinery*]
SIGOPS	Special Interest Group on Operating Systems [*Association for Computing Machinery*]
SIGPC	Special Interest Group on Personal Computing [*Association for Computing Machinery*]
SIGPLAN	Special Interest Group on Programing Languages [*Association for Computing Machinery*] [*New York, NY*]
SIGREAL	Special Interest Group on Real Time Processing [*Association for Computing Machinery*]
SIGSAC	Special Interest Group on Security, Audit, and Control [*Association for Computing Machinery*] [*New York, NY*]
SIGSAM	Special Interest Group for Symbolic and Algebraic Manipulation [*Association for Computing Machinery*]
SIGSCSA	Special Interest Group on Small Computing Systems and Applications [*Later, SIGSMALL*] [*Association for Computing Machinery*] [*New York, NY*] (EANO)
SIG/SDI	Special Interest Group/Selective Dissemination of Information [*American Society for Information Science*]
SIGSIM	Special Interest Group on Simulation [*Association for Computing Machinery*] [*New York, NY*]
SIGSMALL	Special Interest Group on Small Computing Systems and Applications [*Formerly, SIGSCSA*] [*Association for Computing Machinery*] (EANO)
SIGSOC	Special Interest Group on Social and Behavioral Science Computing [*Association for Computing Machinery*]
SIGSOFT	Special Interest Group on Software Engineering [*Association for Computing Machinery*] [*New York, NY*]
SIGSOP	Signals Operator
SIGSPAC	Special Interest Group on Urban Data Systems, Planning, Architecture, and Civil Engineering [*Association for Computing Machinery*]
SIGUCCS	Special Interest Group for University and College Computing Services [*Association for Computing Machinery*] [*Later, Special Interest Group on Academic and Associated Computing*] [*Drake University*] [*Des Moines, IA*]
SIIRS	Smithsonian Institution Information Retrieval System (DIT)
SIL	Scanner Input Language (NITA)
SIL	Schedule Interface Log
SIL	SNOBOL Implementation Language Reimplemented [*1974*] [*Data processing*] (CSR)
SIL	Speech Interference Level
SIL	Store Interface Link (NITA)
SILICA	System for International Literature Information on Ceramics and Glass [*Fachinformationszentrum Werkstoffe*] [*Database*] (CUAD)
SILS	Shipboard Impact Locator System
SILT	Stored Information Loss Tree (NITA)
SILTE	Sindacato Italiano Lavoratori Telecomunicazioni [*Italian Union of Telecommunications Workers*]
SILTS	Sindacato Italiano Lavoratori Telefoni di Stato [*Italian Union of Government Telephone Workers*]
SILULAP	Sindacato Italiano Lavoratori Uffici Locali ed Agenzie Postelegrafonici [*Italian Union of Local Post and Telegraph Office Workers*]
SIM	Service Instructions Message [*Telecommunications*] (TEL)
SIM	Set Interrupt Mask [*Data processing*]
SIM	Synchronous Interface Module (NITA)
SIMBAD	Simulation as a Basis for Social Agents' Decisions [*Data processing*]
SIMC	Silicon Integrated Monolithic Circuit
SIMCOM	Simulation and Computer [*Data processing*]
SIMCOM	Simulator Compiler [*Computer*]
SIMD	Single Instruction, Multiple Data (IEEE)
SIMILE	Simulator of Immediate Memory in Learning Experiments
SIMM	Single In-Line Memory Module [*Data processing*]
SIMP	Satellite Information Message Protocol
SIMPAC	Simplified Programing for Acquisition and Control (IEEE)
SIMPAC	Simulation Package [*Data processing*]
SIMPL	Simulation Implementation Machine Programing Languages (KSC)
SIMPL/1	Simulation Language Based on Programing Language, Version One

Computer & Telecommunications Acronyms

SIMPLAN .... Simple Modeling and Planning [*SIMPLAN Users Group*] [*New York, NY*]
SIMPLAN .... Simplified Modeling and Planning [*Programing language*] [*1973*]
SIMPLE .... Simulation of Industrial Management Problems [*Program*] [*1958*] [*Data processing*]   (CSR)
SIMPLE .... System for Integrated Maintenance and Program Language Extension   (NITA)
SIMS .... Sedna Information Management System [*Sedna Corp.*] [*Information service*]   (EISS)
SIMSCRIPT ... [*A*] simulation programing language [*1963*] [*Data processing*]   (CAH)
SIMSYS ...... Simulated System   (CAAL)
SIMUL .... Simultaneous
SIMULA ...... Simulation Language [*1964*] [*Data processing*]   (TUT)
SIMUPOL .... Simulative Procedure Oriented Language   (MCD)
SIN .... Spanish International Network [*Cable-television system*]
SIN .... Symbolic Integrator   (NITA)
SINAD .... Signal Plus Noise and Distortion
SINAP .... Satellite Input to Numerical Analysis and Prediction [*National Weather Service*]
SINCGARS ... Single Channel Ground and Airborne Radio System   (MCD)
SINCGARS-V ... Single-Channel Ground and Airborne Radio System, Very High Frequency
SIND .... Satellite Inertial Navigation Determination   (MCD)
SINFDOK .... Statens Rad for Vetenskaplig Information och Dokumentation [*Swedish Council for Scientific Information and Documentation*]   (EISS)
SINGAN ...... Singularity Analyzer [*Data processing*]
SINT .... System Integrators [*NASDAQ symbol*]   (NQ)
SIO .... Start Input/Output   (NITA)
SIOA .... System Input/Output Adapter   (CAAL)
SIOC .... Serial Input/Output Channel   (NITA)
SIOP .... Selector Input/Output Processor [*Data processing*]   (IEEE)
SIOUX .... Sequential and Iterative Operation Unit X   (IEEE)
SIP .... Satellite Information Processor
SIP .... Satellite Inspector Program
SIP .... Scientific Information [*or Instruction*] Processor [*Honeywell, Inc.*]   (NITA)
SIP .... Short Irregular Pulses
SIP .... Simulated Input Processor [*Data processing*]
SIP .... Single In-Line Package [*Data processing*]
SIP .... Software Instrumentation Package [*Sperry UNIVAC*] [*Data processing*]
SIP .... Software in Print [*Technique Learning*] [*Information service*]   (EISS)
SIP .... Symbolic Input Program [*Data processing*]   (BUR)
SIPO .... Serial-In, Parallel-Out [*Telecommunications*]   (TEL)
SIPOP .... Satellite Information Processor Operational Program   (AFM)
SIPP .... System Information Processing Program   (MCD)
SIPPS .... System of Information Processing for Professional Societies
SIPROS ...... Simultaneous Processing Operation System [*Control Data Corp.*] [*Data processing*]
SIPS .... Simulated Input Preparation System   (IEEE)
SIPS .... Statistical Interactive Programing System   (NITA)
SIR .... Scientific Information Retrieval, Inc. [*Database management system*] [*Information service*]   (EISS)
SIR .... Segment Identification Register   (NITA)
SIR .... Selective Information Retrieval [*Data processing*]
SIR .... Semantic Information Retrieval [*Massachusetts Institute of Technology*] [*Data processing*]   (DIT)
SIR .... Signal-to-Interference Ratio
SIR .... Special Information Retrieval
SIR .... Specification Information Retrieval System [*Data processing*]   (MCD)
SIR .... Stratified Indexing and Retrieval [*Japan*] [*Data processing*]   (DIT)
SIR .... Symbolic Input Routine [*Data processing*]   (DIT)
SIRC .... Sport Information Resource Centre [*Coaching Association of Canada*] [*Database*]   (EISS)
SIRE .... Satellite Infrared Experiment   (MCD)
SIRF .... System Information Reports Formatting   (MCD)
SIRS .... Salary Information Retrieval System   (IEEE)
SIRS .... System Integration Receiver System   (MCD)
SIRSA .... Special Industrial Radio Service Association [*Land Mobile Communications Council*] [*Rosslyn, VA*]
SIS .... Satellite Interceptor System   (AFM)
SIS .... Savage Information Services   (EISS)
SIS .... Scientific Instruction Set   (NITA)
SIS .... Semiconductor-Insulator-Semiconductor
SIS .... Shared Information Service   (CMD)
SIS .... Signaling Interworking Subsystem [*Telecommunications*]   (TEL)
SIS .... Simulation Interface Subsystem   (KSC)
SIS .... Stage Interface Substitute
SIS .... Standard Instruction Set   (MSA)
SIS .... Standards Information Service [*National Bureau of Standards*]   (EISS)
SIS .... Station Identification Store [*Bell Laboratories*]
SIS .... Superconductor-Insulator-Superconductor [*Transistor technology*]
SIS .... System Interrupt Supervisor   (NITA)
SISB .... SIS Corp. [*NASDAQ symbol*]   (NQ)
SISD .... Scientific Information Systems Department [*Merrell Dow Pharmaceuticals, Inc.*] [*Information service*]   (EISS)
SISD .... Single Instruction, Single Data   (IEEE)
SISO .... Science Information Services Organization [*Franklin Institute*]   (EISS)
Si & So .... Sight and Sound [*A publication*]
SISO .... Single-Input, Single-Output [*Process engineering*]
SISS .... Semiconductor-Insulator-Semiconductor System
SISS .... Synchronous Identification System Study
SISTRAN .... System for Information Storage and Retrieval and Analysis
SIT .... Simulation Input Tape
SIT .... Static Induction Transistor [*Telecommunications*]   (TEL)
SIT .... Systems Interface Test   (NVT)
SITA .... Societe Internationale des Telecommunications Aeronautiques [*International Society of Aeronautical Telecommunications*] [*London, England*]
SITC .... Satellite International Television Center [*Telecommunications*]   (TEL)
SITC .... Standard Industrial Trade Classification [*United Nations*]
SITC .... Standard International Trade Classification
SITE .... Satellite Instructional Television Experiment [*NASA/Indian Space Research Organization, 1974*]
SITI .... Swiss Institute for Technical Information [*Information service*]   (EISS)
SIU .... Sequence Initiate Update   (SKY)
SIU .... Signal Interface Unit   (MCD)
SIU .... Slide-In Unit [*Telecommunications*]   (TEL)
SIU .... System [*or Subsystem*] Interface Unit
SIU .... Systeme International d'Unites [*International System of Units*] [*See also SI*]
SJ .... Source Jamming   (DDI)
SJCC .... Spring Joint Computer Conference [*American Federation of Information Processing Societies*]
SJF .... Shortest Job First [*Data processing*]
SJP .... Serialized Job Processor   (NITA)
SJS .... Search Jam System
SKB .... Skew Buffer   (NITA)
SKDU .... Ship's Keyboard Display Unit
SKED .... Sort Key Edit [*Library of Congress*]
SKIL .... Scanner Keyed Input Language   (NITA)
SKILL .... Satellite Kill
SKIPI .... Super Knowledge Information Processing Intelligence [*Data processing*]
SKM .... Sine-Kosine Multiplier
SKP .... Skip   (BUR)
SKR .... Saturn Kilometer-Wave Radiation [*Planetary science*]
SKU .... Stores Keeping Unit
SL .... Send Leg [*Telegraphy*]   (TEL)
SL .... Simulation Language [*Data processing*]   (BUR)
SL .... Source Language [*Data processing*]   (BUR)
SL .... Standard Label [*Data processing*]
SL .... Studio Location
SL .... Subscriber's Loop [*Telecommunications*]   (TEL)
SL .... Synchronous Line Medium Speed   (BUR)
SL .... System Language   (NITA)
S & L .... System and Logistics
SLA .... Shared Line Adapter   (NITA)
SLA .... Square Loop Antenna
SLA .... Stored Logic Array   (NITA)
SLA .... Synchronous Line Adapter   (NITA)
SLAD .... System Logic and Algorithm Development
SLAM .... Short LOFAR [*Low-Frequency Acquisition and Ranging*] Alerting Message   (NVT)
SLAM .... Simulation Language for Alternative Modeling [*Data processing*]   (CSR)
SLAM .... Symbolic Language Adapted for Microcomputers   (NITA)
SLAMS ...... Simplified Language for Abstract Mathematical Structures [*Data processing*]   (IEEE)
SLANG .... Systems Language
SLAP .... Symbolic Language Assembly Program [*Data processing*]   (KSC)
SLAPS .... Subscriber Loop Analysis Program System [*Bell System*]
SLAR .... Select ADC [*Analog-to-Digital Converter*] Register [*Data processing*]   (MDG)
SLAR .... Steerable LASER Radiometer   (MCD)
SLASH .... Seiler Laboratory ALGOL Simulated Hybrid [*Data processing*]
SLATE .... Stimulated Learning by Automated Typewriter Environment
SLB .... Schlumberger Ltd. [*NYSE symbol*]
SLC .... Selector Channel   (NITA)
SLC .... Set Location Counter   (CMD)
SLC .... Shift Left and Count Instructions [*Data processing*]   (MDG)
SLC .... Simulated Linguistic Computer
SLC .... Single Line Control   (BUR)
SLC .... Small Library Computing, Inc. [*Holbrook, NY*] [*Information service*]   (EISS)
SLC .... Subscriber Loop Carrier [*Telecommunications*]   (TEL)
SLC .... Synchro Loop Closure   (VIT)
SLC .... Synchronous Line Medium Speed with Clock   (BUR)
SLC .... System Life Cycle
SLCM .... Software Life Cycle Management   (NITA)
SLCU .... Synchronous Line Control Unit   (NITA)
SLD .... Solid Logic Dense   (BUR)
SLD .... Source Language Debug [*Data processing*]   (IEEE)
SLD .... Straight Line Depreciation [*Telecommunications*]   (TEL)
SLD .... Synchronous Line Driver   (NITA)

Computer & Telecommunications Acronyms

SLDD .... Scientific Library and Documentation Division [*National Science and Technology Authority*] [*Philippines*] [*Information service*] (EISS)
SLDTSS ...... Single Language Dedicated Time-Sharing System (NITA)
SLE .... Small Local Exchange [*Telecommunications*] (TEL)
SLED .... Special Learning Education [*In company name, SLED Software*] [*Minneapolis, MN*] [*Software manufacturer*] (DASOS)
SLEUTH ...... UNIVAC 1108 Assembly Language (CAH)
SLF .... Straight-Line Frequency
SLF .... System Library File [*Data processing*] (BUR)
SLG .... Synchronous Line Group (BUR)
SLI .... Suppress Length Indication (BUR)
SLI .... Synchronous Line Interface (NITA)
SLIB .... Subsystem Library [*Data processing*] (IBMDP)
SLIC .... Selective Letters [*or Listing*] in Combination
SLIC .... Subscriber's Line Interface Circuit [*Telecommunications*] (TEL)
SLICE .... System Life Cycle Estimation (NITA)
SLIDE .... [*A*] programing language (CSR)
SLIH .... Second Level Interrupt Handler (CMD)
SLIMS .... Supply Line Inventory Management System [*Bell System*]
SLIP .... Symbolic List Processor (NITA)
SLIP .... Symmetric List Interpretive Program [*Data processing*] (TUT)
SLIP .... Symmetric List Processor [*FORTRAN extension*]
SLIPR .... Source Language Input Program (NITA)
SLIS .... Shared Laboratory Information System
SLLL .... Synchronous Line, Low, Load (BUR)
SLM .... Subscriber Loop Multiplex [*Bell System*]
SLM .... Synchronous Line Module (NITA)
SLN .... Service Link Network [*Bell Laboratories*]
SLO .... Segment Limits Origin (NITA)
SLOCOP ..... Specific Linear Optimal Control Program [*Hydrofoil*] [*Grumman Aerospace Corp.*]
SLO/SRI ..... Shift Left Out/Shift Right In (NITA)
SLOTH .... Suppressing Line Operands and Translating to Hexadecimal [*Telecommunications*] (TEL)
SLP .... Segmented Level Programing [*Data processing*] (IEEE)
SLP .... Source Language Processor [*Data processing*] (BUR)
SLPM .... Silicon Light Pulser Matrix
SLR .... Service Level Reporter [*IBM Corp.*]
SLR .... Simple Left to Right [*Data processing*]
SLR .... Storage Limits Register
SLS .... Signaling Link Selection [*Telecommunications*] (TEL)
SLS .... Source Library System (NITA)
SLSI .... Super Large-Scale Integration (DEEC)
SLSMS .... Spacelab Support Module Simulator (MCD)
SLSS .... Systems Library Subscription Service [*Data processing*] (IBMDP)
SLT .... Self-Loading Tape (AFM)
SLT .... Ship Letter Telegram
SLT .... Solid Logic Technique [*Data processing*] (IEEE)
SLT .... Solid Logic Technology (DEEC)
SLT .... Switchman's Local Test [*Telecommunications*] (TEL)
SLTF .... Shortest Latency Time First
SLU .... Serial Line Unit (NITA)
SLU .... Source Library Update (NITA)
SLU .... Subscriber Line Use [*Telecommunications*]
SLU .... Switching Logic Unit (CAAL)
SLUC .... Standard Level User Charges
SLUS .... Subscriber's Line Use System [*AT & T*] [*Telecommunications*] (TEL)
SLW .... Store Logical Word
SLW .... Straight-Line Wavelength
SLWL .... Straight-Line Wavelength (MSA)
SLZ .... Suppress Leading Zero [*Data processing*]
SM .... Secondary Memory [*Data processing*] (BUR)
SM .... Semiconductor Memory (NITA)
SM .... Service Monitoring [*Telecommunications*] (TEL)
SM .... Set Mode (BUR)
SM .... Shared Memory [*Data processing*] (BUR)
SM .... Signaling Module [*Telecommunications*] (TEL)
SM .... Structure Memory (NITA)
SM .... Synchronous MODEM (NITA)
SM .... Systems Memory [*Data processing*] (BUR)
SMAC .... Science and Mathematics Analysis Center [*ERIC*]
SMAC .... Scientific Machine Automation Corporation
SMAC .... Serial Memory Address Counter [*Computer*]
SMAC .... Simulation, Manual and Computerized
SMACS .... Simulated Message Analysis and Conversion Subsystem
SMAG .... Systems Management Analysis Group (MCD)
SMAIL .... Source Mail [*Electronic mail*]
SMAL .... Single Mode Alignment (CAAL)
SMAL .... Structural Macroassembly Language (NITA)
SMALGOL ... Small Computer Algorithmic Language
Small Bus Comput ... Small Business Computers [*A publication*]
Small Bus Comput News ... Small Business Computer News [*A publication*]
Small Sys ... Small Systems World [*A publication*]
Small Sys Soft ... Small Systems Software [*A publication*]
Small Syst Software ... Small Systems Software [*A publication*]
Small Syst World ... Small Systems World [*A publication*]
SMALLTALK ... [*A*] programing language (CSR)
SMART .... Salton's Magical Automatic Retriever of Texts [*Data processing*]
SMART .... Socony Mobil Automatic Real Time (DIT)
SMART .... Sort Merge and Reduction Tapes (CAAL)
SMART .... Space Management and Retail Tracking System [*Information Resources, Inc.*]
SMART .... System for Management and Allocation of Resources Technique [*Data processing*]
SMART .... System for the Mechanical Analysis and Retrieval of Text (DEEC)
SMARTS ..... Selective Multiple Addresses Radio and Television Service [*A program delivery service introduced by RCA*]
SMARTS ..... Status Memory and Real Time System [*AT & T*]
SMAS .... Switched Maintenance Access System [*Bell System*]
SMASH ...... Step-by-Step Monitor and Selector Hold [*Telecommunications*] (TEL)
SMATV .... Satellite Master Antenna Television
SMB .... Sunbeam Corp. [*NYSE symbol*] [*Delisted*]
SMB .... System Monitor Board (NITA)
SMBL .... Symbol Technologies [*NASDAQ symbol*] (NQ)
SMC .... Sequential Machine Controller [*Programing language*] [*1977-78*] (CSR)
SMC .... Storage Module Controller (NITA)
SMC .... Switch Maintenance Center [*Telecommunications*] (TEL)
SMC .... System Monitor Console (CAAL)
SMD .... Silicon Multiplier Detector
SMD .... Storage Module Drive (NITA)
SMD .... Synchronous Modulator-Demodulator (MCD)
SMD .... Systems Manufacturing Division [*IBM Corp.*]
SMDL .... Subminiature Microwave Delay Line
SMDO .... Special Microwave Devices Operation [*Raytheon Co.*]
SMDR .... Station Message Detail Recording [*Formerly, MDR*] [*Telecommunications*]
SMDT .... Shore Mode Data Transmitter (MCD)
SME .... Society of Manufacturing Engineers
SMED .... Shared Medical Systems [*NASDAQ symbol*] (NQ)
SMEK .... Summary Message Enable Keyboard
SMETDS ..... Standard Message Trunk Design System [*Telecommunications*] (TEL)
SMF .... S-Band Multifrequency (CIT)
SMF .... Senior Management Forum [*Information Industry Association*]
SMF .... Societe Mathematique de France (NITA)
SMF .... Software Maintenance Function [*Data processing*] (TEL)
SMF .... System Management Facility [*IBM Corp.*]
SMF .... System Measurement Facility [*Data processing*] (IEEE)
SMFA .... Simplified Modular Frame Assignment System [*Telecommunications*] (TEL)
SMFAS .... Simplified Modular Frame Assignment System [*Bell System*]
SMG .... Science Management Corp. [*American Stock Exchange symbol*]
SMG .... Software Message Generator [*Telecommunications*] (TEL)
SMI .... Simulation of Machine Indexing
SMI .... Static Memory Interface [*Data processing*] (MDG)
SMI .... System Memory Interface [*Data processing*] (NITA)
SMI .... Systems Management, Incorporated [*Rosemont, IL*] [*Software manufacturer*] (DASOS)
SMI .... Systems Measurement Instrument [*Data processing*]
SMID .... Semiconductor Memory Integrated Device (MCD)
SMIIS .... Solar Microwave Interferometer Imaging System
SMILE .... Significant Milestone Integration Lateral Evaluation [*Data processing*]
SMIP .... Structure Memory Information Processor (NITA)
SMIRE .... Senior Member of the Institution of Radio Engineers
SMIRS .... School Management Information Retrieval Service [*University of Oregon*] [*Eugene, OR*]
SMIS .... Society for Management Information Systems [*Chicago, IL*] (EANO)
SMIS .... Survey Methodology Information System [*Inter-University Consortium for Political & Social Research*] [*Database*] (FDB)
SMIS .... Symbolic Matrix Interpretation System (NITA)
SMIS INC .... Societe de Microelectronique Industrielle de Sherbrooke, Inc. [*University of Sherbrooke*] [*Canada*] [*Research center*] (RCD)
SML .... Search Mode Logic
SML .... Small (FAAC)
SML .... Software Master Library [*Data processing*] (TEL)
SML .... Spool Multileaving [*Data processing*] (IBMDP)
SML .... Standard Markup Language [*Data processing*]
SML .... Symbolic Machine Language [*Data processing*]
SMLE .... Small-Medium Local Exchange [*Telecommunications*] (TEL)
SMLM .... Simple-Minded Learning Machine (IEEE)
SMM .... Semiconductor Memory Module (NITA)
SMM .... Shared Multiport Memory (NITA)
SMM .... Spectral Matrix Method (KSC)
SMM .... Start of Manual Message (BUR)
SMM .... Systems Maintenance Management [*Data processing*]
SMMB .... Stores Management Multiplex Bus [*Data processing*] (MCD)
SMMR .... Scanning Multichannel [*or Multifrequency or Multispectral*] Microwave Radiometer
SMOC .... Simulation Mission Operation Computer (MCD)
SMOC .... Submodule and Operator Controller [*For sequence of telephonic operations*]
SMOG .... Special Monitor Output Generator (IEEE)
SMP .... Software Management Plan (MCD)
SMP .... Symmetric Multiprocessing (NITA)
SMP .... System Modification Program [*Data processing*]
SMPS .... Simplified Message Processing Simulation (IEEE)

Computer & Telecommunications Acronyms

Acronym	Definition
SMPTE	Society of Motion Picture and Television Engineers [*Formerly, Society of Motion Picture Engineers*] [*Scarsdale, NY*]
SMR	Series Mode Rejection (NITA)
SMR	Specialized Mobile Radio
SMR	Switching Mode Regulator
SMRB	Simmons Market Research Bureau, Inc. [*Database producer*] (CUAD)
SMRT	Single Message Rate Timing
SMS	Screen Management System [*Computer technology*]
SMS	Semiconductor-Metal-Semiconductor
SMS	Shared Mass Storage (NITA)
SMS	Signal Messenger Service (NATG)
SMS	Standard Modular System
SMS	Stores Management System (MCD)
SMS	Switching and Maintenance Set
SMSA	Standard Metropolitan Statistical Area [*Later, MSA*] [*Census Bureau*]
SMSC	Standard Modular System Card [*Data processing*] (BUR)
SMSS	School of Management and Strategic Studies [*Founded 1982 by Richard Farson, offers a two-year management program through GTE Telenet*]
SMT	S-Band Megawatt Transmit (CIT)
SMU	Secondary Multiplexing Unit (OA)
SMU	Store Monitor Unit (NITA)
SMU	Super-Module Unit [*Telecommunications*] (TEL)
SMU	System Maintenance Unit [*Data processing*]
SMU	System Monitoring Unit (NITA)
SMX	Semi-Micro Xerography (DEEC)
SMX	Submultiplexer Unit
SN	Semiconductor Network (IEEE)
S/N	Sequence Number (CIT)
SN	Signal Node (NITA)
S/N	Signal to Noise Ratio [*Unweighted*] (CMD)
S/N	Speech/Noise [*Ratio*] [*Electronics*]
SN	Sponsoring Agency [*Online database field identifier*] (OBD)
SNA	Satellite Networking Associates, Inc. [*New York, NY*] [*Telecommunications*] (TSSD)
SNA	Systems Network Architecture [*IBM Corp.*] [*Data processing*]
SNACS	Share News on Automatic Coding Systems [*Data processing*]
SNAP	Simplified Needs Assessment Profile System [*Developed by Texas Instruments, Inc.*]
SNAP	Simplified Numerical Automatic Programer [*Data processing*]
SNAP	Single Number Access Plan [*Telecommunications*] (TEL)
SNAP	Six Node Averaging Program [*Data processing*]
SNAP	Standard Network Access Protocol [*Data processing*]
SNAP	Steerable Null Antenna Processor (RDA)
SNAP	Switching Network Analysis Program [*Bell System*]
SNAP	System Network Activity Program [*Sperry UNIVAC*] (NITA)
SNAPS	Standard Notes and Parts Selection (TEL)
SNAPS	Switching Node and Processing Sites [*ITT*] (TEL)
SNASOR	Static Nonlinear Analysis of Shells of Revolution [*Computer program*]
SNBU	Switched Network Backup [*Data processing*] (IBMDP)
SNC	Satellite News Channel [*Cable-television system*] [*Went off the air October, 1983*]
SNC	Standard Navigation Computer
SNCC	System Network Computer Center [*Louisiana State University*] [*Research center*] (RCD)
SND	Society of Newspaper Design (EANO)
SNE	Sony Corp. [*NYSE symbol*] [*Toronto Stock Exchange symbol*] [*Vancouver Stock Exchange symbol*]
SNG	Southern New England Telephone Co. [*NYSE symbol*]
SNGL	Single
SNI	Selective Notification of Information (NITA)
SNI	Signal-to-Noise Improvement [*Data transmission*] (IEEE)
SNI	Sistema Nacional de Informacion [*National Information System*] [*Colombia*] (EISS)
SNI	Standard Network Interconnection [*Telecommunications*]
SNIR	Signal-to-Noise Plus Interference Ratio
SNL	Selected Nodes List [*Telecommunications*] (TEL)
SNO	Serial Number (MDG)
SNOBOL	String-Oriented Symbolic Language [*1963*] [*Data processing*]
SNOOPI	System Network Online Operations Information [*Suggested name for the Library of Congress computer system*]
SNORE	Signal-to-Noise Ratio Estimator (CIT)
SNP	Statistical Network Processor (NITA)
SNP	Synchronous Network Processor (NITA)
SNP	System Network Processor
SNR	Signal-to-Noise Ratio
SNS	Skyline Network Service [*Satellite Business Systems*] [*McLean, VA*] [*Telecommunications*] (TSSD)
SNTCC	Simplified Neutron Transport Computer Code
SNTE	Santec Corp. [*NASDAQ symbol*] (NQ)
SNY	Sydney Development Corp. [*Toronto Stock Exchange symbol*]
SO	Send Only
SO	Serial Output (NITA)
SO	Shift-Out Character [*Keyboard*] [*Data processing*]
SO	Slow Operate [*Relay*]
SO	Source [*Online database field identifier*] (OBD)
SO	Symbolic Output [*Data processing*]
SO	System Override
SOA	Start of Address (NITA)
SOAP	Simplify Obscure ALGOL [*Algorithmic Language*] Programs (MCD)
SOAP	Symbolic Optimum Assembly Programing [*IBM Corp.*] [*Data processing*]
SOB	Service Observance Bureau [*A telephone-monitoring section of the Bell System*]
SOB	Start of Block (NITA)
SOBLIN	Self-Organizing Binary Logical Network [*OTS*]
SOC	Set Overrides Clear (IEEE)
SOC	Simulated Operational Computer (KSC)
SOC	Simulation Operation Computer (MCD)
SOC	Single Orbit Computation
SOCCER	SMART's Own Concordance Constructor, Extremely Rapid [*Cornell University*] [*Data processing*]
SOCCS	Summary of Component Control Status
SOCIAL SCISEARCH	Social Science Citation Index Search [*Database*] (ODIN)
SOCOM	Solar Communications
SOCR	Scan-Optics, Inc. [*NASDAQ symbol*] (NQ)
SOCR	Synchronous Orbit Communication Relay (MCD)
SOD	Serial Output Data [*Data processing*]
SOD	Systems Operational Description [*or Design*]
SODAS	Structure-Oriented Description and Simulation (IEEE)
SODEX	Social Data Exchange Association [*Council for Community Services*] [*Information service*] (EISS)
SODRS	Synchronous Orbit Data Relay Satellite
SOE	Start of Entry [*Data processing*]
SOEEA	Soviet Electrical Engineering [*English Translation*] [*A publication*]
SOF	Satisfactory Operation Factor [*Telecommunications*] (TEL)
SOF	Start of Frame (NITA)
S/OFF	Sign Off [*Data processing*] (MDG)
SOFIE	Sources de Financement des Entreprises [*CCMC Informatique de Gestion*] [*Database*] (CUAD)
SOFRECOM	Societe Francaise d'Etudes et de Realisations d'Equipements de Telecommunications [*French communications engineering company*] [*Telecommunications*] (TEL)
SOFT	Simple Output Format Translator (IEEE)
SOFT	SofTech, Inc. [*NASDAQ symbol*] (NQ)
Soft Eng	IEEE. Transactions on Software Engineering [*A publication*]
Software	Software: Practice and Experience [*A publication*]
Software Pract Exper	Software: Practice and Experience [*A publication*]
Software Pract and Exper	Software: Practice and Experience [*A publication*]
Software Rev	Software Review [*A publication*]
Software Tools Commun	Software Tools Communications [*A publication*]
Softw Newsl	Software Newsletter [*A publication*]
Soft World	Software World [*A publication*]
SOG	Same Output Gate [*Data processing*]
SOGESCI	Societe Belge pour l'Application des Methodes Scientifiques de Gestion [*Brussels, Belgium*]
SOH	Start of Heading [*Transmission control character*] [*Data processing*]
SOL	Simulation Oriented Language [*Data processing*]
SOL	System Oriented Language
SOLAR	Serialized On-Line Automatic Recording [*Data processing*] (IEEE)
SOLB	Start of Line Block (CET)
SOLD	Simulation of Logic Design
SOLID	Self-Organizing Large Information Dissemination System (IEEE)
Solid Stat	Solid State Technology [*A publication*]
Solid State Commun	Solid State Communications [*A publication*]
Solid State Technol	Solid State Technology [*A publication*]
Solid St Commun	Solid State Communications [*A publication*]
SOLIS	Social Sciences Literature Information System [*Informationszentrum Sozialwissenschaften*] [*Database*] (CUAD)
SOLIS	Symbionics On-Line Information System [*Data processing*] (TUT)
SOLO	Supply On-Line Option [*IMS America Ltd.*] [*Database*] (CUAD)
SOLO	System for Ordinary Life Operations [*Insurance*]
SOLOMON	Simultaneous Operation Linked Ordinal Modular Network
SOLR	Sidetone Objective Loudness Rating [*of telephone connections*] (IEEE)
Sol St Comm	Solid State Communications [*A publication*]
Sol St Tech	Solid State Technology [*A publication*]
SOM	Securities Order Matching [*Data processing*]
SOM	Self-Organizing Machine
SOM	Start-of-Message
SOMADA	Self-Organizing Multiple-Access Discrete Address [*Data processing*] (IEEE)
SOM-H	Start-of-Message - High Precedence (CET)
SOM-L	Start-of-Message - Low Precedence (CET)
SOM-P	Start-of-Message - Priority
SOMS	Service Order Mechanization [*or Mechanized*] System [*AT & T*]
SOMS	Synchronous, Operational Meteorological Satellite
SOMTS	Division of Ship Operations and Marine Technical Support [*University of California, San Diego*] [*Research center*] (RCD)
S/ON	Sign On [*Data processing*] (MDG)
SONAD	Speech-Operated Noise Adjusting Device [*Telecommunications*] (TEL)
SONIC	System-Wide On-Line Network for Information Control [*Data processing*]

SOP............ Seat of the Pants   (CGC)
SOP............ Simulated Output Program [*Data processing*]
SOP............ Standard [*or Standing*] Operating Procedure
SOP............ Study Organization Plan   (BUR)
SOPAD........ Summary of Proceedings and Debate [*of House of Representatives*]
SOPODA...... Social Planning, Policy & Development Abstracts [*Sociological Abstracts, Inc.*] [*Database*]   (CUAD)
SORD.......... Southwestern Order Retrieval and Distribution [*Southwest Bell Telephone Co.*]
SORDC....... Southwest Ohio Regional Data Center [*University of Cincinnati*] [*Research center*]   (RCD)
SORM......... Set-Oriented Retrieval Module   (NITA)
SORT.......... Structures for Orbiting Radio Telescope
SOS............ Satellite Observation System   (DDI)
SOS............ Service Order System [*Telecommunications*]   (TEL)
SOS............ Share Operating System [*Data processing*]
SOS............ Silicon-on-Sapphire [*Integrated circuit*]
SOS............ Sophisticated Operating System [*Apple III microcomputer*] [*Data processing*]
SOS............ Speed of Service [*Telecommunications*]   (TEL)
SOS............ Start of Significance [*Data processing*]   (BUR)
SOS............ Symbolic Operating System [*Data processing*]   (CGC)
SOSE.......... Silicon-on-Something-Else [*Telecommunications*]   (TEL)
SOSI........... Shift In, Shift Out   (IEEE)
SOST.......... Special Operator Service Traffic [*Telecommunications*]   (TEL)
SOSTEL....... Solid-State Electric Logic   (NG)
SOT............ Start of Text   (NITA)
SOT............ State of Termination [*Telecommunications*]   (TEL)
SOT............ Subscriber Originating Trunk [*Telecommunications*]   (TEL)
SOT............ Syntax-Oriented Translator   (IEEE)
SOTA.......... State of the Art
SOTUS........ Sequentially Operated Teletypewriter Universal Selector
SOUTC....... Satellite Operators and Users Technical Committee [*McLean, VA*]   (EANO)
SOUTHFORNET ... Southern Forestry Information Network [*Forest Service*]   (EISS)
Sov Automat Contr ... Soviet Automatic Control [*A publication*]
Sov Autom Control ... Soviet Automatic Control [*A publication*]
Sov Elec Eng ... Soviet Electrical Engineering [*A publication*]
Sov Electr Eng ... Soviet Electrical Engineering [*English Translation of Elektrotekhnika*] [*A publication*]
Soviet Automat Control ... Soviet Automatic Control [*A publication*]
Sov Power Eng ... Soviet Power Engineering [*A publication*]
Sov Power Eng (Engl Transl) ... Soviet Power Engineering (English Translation of Elektricheskie Stantsii) [*A publication*]
SOW........... Start of Word
SOW........... Statement of Work   (MCD)
SOWP......... Society of Wireless Pioneers [*Santa Rosa, CA*]   (EANO)
SP.............. Satellite Processor [*Data transmission*]
SP.............. Scientific Processor   (BUR)
SP.............. Semipublic [*Telecommunications*]   (TEL)
SP.............. Send Processor   (NITA)
SP.............. Sensor Processor   (BUR)
SP.............. Sequence Programer [*Data processing*]
SP.............. Sequential Processor   (NITA)
S/P............. Serial to Parallel   (KSC)
SP.............. Sewer Pipe [*Telecommunications*]   (TEL)
S/P............. Signal Processor   (NASA)
SP.............. Singing Point [*Telecommunications*]   (TEL)
SP.............. Single-Pole [*Switch*]
SP.............. Single Programer
SP.............. Southern Pine [*Utility pole*] [*Telecommunications*]   (TEL)
SP.............. Space Character [*Keyboard*]
SP.............. Stack Pointer [*Data processing*]
S & P.......... Standard & Poor's Corp.
SP.............. Standard Program [*Data processing*]   (BUR)
SP.............. Static Pointer
SP.............. Structured Programing [*Data processing*]   (BUR)
SP.............. Supervisory Process [*Telecommunications*]   (TEL)
SP.............. Switch Panel
SP.............. Symbol Programer   (MUGU)
SP.............. System Processor   (IEEE)
SPA............ S-Band Power Amplifier
SPA............ Scatter Propagation Antenna
SPA............ Self-Phasing Array
SPA............ Semipermanently Associated [*Telecommunications*]   (TEL)
SPA............ Silicon Pulser Array
SPA............ Software Publishers Association [*Washington, DC*]   (EANO)
SPA............ Systems and Procedures Association [*Later, ASM*]
SPAC.......... Spatial Computer
SPACE........ Sales Profitability and Contribution Evaluator [*Data processing*]
SPACE........ Self-Programing Automatic Circuit Evaluator
SPACE........ Sequential Position and Covariance Estimation   (IEEE)
SPACE........ Society for Private and Commercial Earth Stations [*Washington, DC*] [*Telecommunications*] [*Information service*]   (EANO)
SPACE........ Support Package for Aerospace Computer Emulation   (MCD)
SPACE........ Symbolic Programing Anyone Can Enjoy
SPACECOM ... Space Communications
SPAD.......... Satellite Position Prediction and Display
SPAD.......... Scratch Pad Memory [*Data processing*]

SPADE........ Single-Channel-per-Carrier, Pulse-Code-Modulation, Multiple-Access, Demand-Assignment Equipment [*Telecommunications*]
SPADE........ Sparta Acquisition Digital Equipment
SPADE........ Sperry Air Data Equipment
SPAID......... Sheffield Package Analysis and Identification of Data [*Commercial & Industrial Development Bureau*] [*Software package*] [*British*]   (NCC)
SPAM.......... Satellite Processor Access Method   (OA)
SPAM.......... Soil-Plant-Atmosphere [*Computer simulation model*]
SPAN.......... Space Communications Network
SPAN.......... Statistical Processing and Analysis [*Data processing*]
SPAN.......... Storage Planning and Allocation [*Data processing*]
SPAR.......... Symbolic Program Assembly Routine [*Data processing*]
SPARC........ Space Air Relay Communications   (MCD)
SPARC........ Standards Planning and Requirements Committee [*ANSI*]
SPARMIS.... Standard Police Automated Resource Management Information System
SPARTA...... Sequential Programed Automatic Recording Transistor Analyzer
SPASM....... System Performance and Activity Software Monitor [*Data processing*]   (IEEE)
SPB............ Stored Program Buffer   (NITA)
SPC............ IEEE. Spectrum [*A publication*]
SPC............ Site Programer Course
SPC............ Small Peripheral Controller   (NITA)
SPC............ Southern Pacific Communications Corp.   (NITA)
SPC............ Stored Program Command [*or Control*] [*Data processing*]
SPCA.......... Special-Purpose Cable Assembly
SPCC.......... Southern Pacific Communications Corporation   (CBSS)
SPCC.......... Stored Program CAMAC [*Computer-Aided Measurement and Control*] Channel [*Data processing*]
SPCC.......... Strength Power and Communications Cable
SPCCS....... Spill Prevention Control and Countermeasure System [*Environmental Protection Agency*] [*Information service*]   (EISS)
SPCN.......... Stored Program Controlled Network [*Telecommunications*]
SPCS.......... Selective Paging Communications System
SPCS.......... Storage and Processing Control System   (NITA)
SPD............ S-Band Polarization Diversity   (CIT)
SPD............ Speech Processing Device
SPD............ Synchronous Phase Demodulator
SPDM......... Subprocessor with Dynamic Microprograming   (NITA)
SPDP......... Stored Program Data Processor   (KSC)
SPDT......... Single-Pole, Double-Throw [*Switch*]
SPDTDB..... Single-Pole, Double-Throw, Double-Break [*Switch*]   (VIT)
SPDTNCDB ... Single-Pole, Double-Throw, Normally-Closed, Double-Break [*Switch*]   (VIT)
SPDTNO..... Single-Pole, Double-Throw, Normally-Open [*Switch*]   (VIT)
SPDTNODB ... Single-Pole, Double-Throw, Normally-Open, Double-Break [*Switch*]   (VIT)
SPDTSW..... Single-Pole, Double-Throw Switch   (VIT)
SPEAKEASY ... [*An*] information retrieval system   (CAH)
SPEAL........ Special-Purpose Engineering Analysis Language   (MCD)
SPEARS..... Satellite Photoelectric Analog Rectification System
SPEC.......... Specification   (AFM)
SPEC.......... Speech Predictive Encoded Communications [*Telephone channels*]
SPEC.......... Stored Program Educational Computer
SPECD....... Specification Data Base
SPECOL..... Special Customer-Oriented Language   (IDA)
SPECOMALT ... Special Communications Alteration   (DDI)
SPECT....... Single Photon Emission Computed Tomography
SPECVER... Specification Verification [*Data processing*]   (IEEE)
SPEDAC..... Solid-State, Parallel, Expandable, Differential Analyzer Computer
SPEDE....... System for Processing Educational Data Electronically
SPEDTAC... Stored Program Educational Transistorized Automatic Computer
SPEED....... Self-Programed Electronic Equation Delineator
SPEED....... Systematic Plotting and Evaluation of Enumerated Data [*National Bureau of Standards*] [*Data processing*]
SPES.......... Stored Program Element System [*Data processing*]   (IEEE)
SPESS....... Stored Program Electronic Switching System [*Telecommunications*]   (TEL)
SPF............ Standard Pesticide File [*Derwent Publications Ltd.*] [*Database*]   (CUAD)
SPF............ Structured Programing Facility [*Data processing*]
SPF............ Subscriber Plant Factor [*Telecommunications*]
SPF............ System Performance Factor [*Telecommunications*]   (TEL)
SPF............ System Productivity Facility [*Data processing*]
SPFW......... Single-Phase Full Wave
SPG........... Sort Program Generator [*Data processing*]   (BUR)
SPHERE..... Scientific Parameters for Health and the Environment, Retrieval and Estimation [*Environmental Protection Agency*] [*Database*]   (CUAD)
SPHW........ Single-Phase Half Wave
SPI............ Shared Peripheral Interface   (NITA)
SPI............ Single Processor Interface   (NITA)
SPI............ Single Program Initiation [*Data processing*]   (TUT)
SPI............ Station Program Identification [*Telecommunications*]   (TEL)
SPI............ Synthetic Phase Isolation [*Telemetry*]
SPIC.......... Ship Position Interpolation Computer   (VIT)
SPIC.......... Summary Punch IBM [*International Business Machines*] Collector   (VIT)
SPIDAC..... Specimen Input to Digital Automatic Computer   (OA)

Computer & Telecommunications Acronyms

SPIE .... Self-Programed Individualized Education   (IEEE)
SPIE .... Society of Photo-Optical Instrumentation Engineers [*Bellingham, WA*]
SPIF .... School Practices Information File [*Educational testing service*] [*Database*]
SPIN .... School Practices Information Network [*Bibliographic Retrieval Services*] [*Information service*]   (EISS)
SPIN .... Searchable Physics Information Notices [*American Institute of Physics*] [*New York, NY*] [*Bibliographic database*]
SPINDEX ..... Subject Profile Index [*Computer-based*]
SPINES .... Science and Technology Policies Information Exchange System [*UNESCO*] [*Paris, France*] [*Bibliographic database*]   (EISS)
SPINSTRE ... Spencer Information Storage and Retrieval System   (DIT)
SPIR .... Search Program for Infrared Spectra [*Canadian Scientific Numeric Database Service*] [*Database*]   (CUAD)
SPIRES .... Stanford Public Information Retrieval System [*Stanford University Libraries*] [*Stanford, CA*] [*Bibliographic database management system*] [*Information service*]
SPIRIT .... Sales Processing Interactive Real-Time Inventory Technique [*NCR Corp. trademark*]
SPIRIT .... Sensible Policy in Information Resources and Information Technology   (EANO)
SPIT .... Selective Printing of Items from Tape [*Data processing*]
SPL .... Service Priority List   (BUR)
SPL .... Signal Processing Language [*Data processing*]   (CSR)
SPL .... Simple Phrase Language [*Data processing*]
SPL .... Simple Programing Language [*Data processing*]
SPL .... Simulation Programing Language [*Data processing*]   (NITA)
SPL .... Software Parts List [*Data processing*]   (TEL)
SPL .... Software Programing Language [*Data processing*]   (IEEE)
SPL .... Source Program Library   (NITA)
SPL .... Space Programing Language [*Data processing*]
SPL .... Special-Purpose Language [*Data processing*]
SPL .... Splice [*Telecommunications*]   (TEL)
SPL .... System Program Loader   (NITA)
SPL .... System Programing Language [*Data processing*]   (NASA)
SPLAT .... Simplified Programing Language for Artists [*1978*] [*Data processing*]   (CSR)
SPLC .... Standard Point Location Code [*American Trucking Association and Association of American Railroads*]
SPLIT .... Space Program Language Implementation Tool   (KSC)
SPLIT .... Sundstrand Processing Language Internally Translated
SPLM .... Space Programing Language Machine
SPM .... Scratch Pad Memory [*Data processing*]   (BUR)
SPM .... Sequential Processing Machine   (DIT)
SPM .... Solar Proton Monitor
SPM .... Source Program Maintenance [*IBM Corp.*]
SPM .... Subscriber's Private Meter [*Telecommunications*]   (TEL)
SPM .... Symbol Processing Machine   (IEEE)
SPMC .... Society of Professional Management Consultants, Inc. [*New York, NY*]
SPMOL .... Source Program Maintenance Online   (NITA)
SPMP .... Special-Purpose Multiprocessor [*Data processing*]
SPN .... Satellite Programming Network [*Cable-television system*]
SPNS .... Switched Private Network Service [*ITT service mark*]
SPO .... Separate Partition Option   (NITA)
SPOC .... Single-Point Orbit Calculator
SPOOF .... Structure and Parity Observing Output Function   (NITA)
SPOOK .... Supervisor Program Over Other Kinds [*Data processing*]
SPOOL .... Simultaneous Peripheral Operation Online [*Data processing*]   (MCD)
SPOT .... Satellite Positioning and Tracking
SPP .... Signal Processing Peripheral   (NITA)
SPP .... Special Purpose Processor   (NITA)
SPP .... System Package Plan [*or Program*]
SPPAY .... Semipost-Pay, Pay-Station [*Telecommunications*]   (TEL)
SPPO .... Scheduled Program Printout   (NATG)
SPPS.......... Semipost-Pay, Pay-Station [*Telecommunications*]   (TEL)
SPPS.......... Subsystem Program Preparation Support [*Programing language*] [*Data processing*]
SPR .... Satellite Parametric Reduction
SPR .... Send Priority and Route Digit [*Telecommunications*]   (TEL)
SPR .... Spare [*Telecommunications*]   (TEL)
SPR .... Storage Protection Register   (NITA)
SPR .... System Parameter Record [*Data processing*]   (IBMDP)
SPR .... System Performance Rating
SPR .... System Program Review
SPREAD ..... Supercomputer Project Research Experiment in Advanced Development [*Lawrence Livermore Laboratory, Los Alamos National Laboratory, and SRI*]
SPREC .... Specular Reflection Computer Program   (MCD)
SPRINT ...... Selective Printing [*Data processing*]
SPRINT ...... Southern Pacific Communications' Switched Long Distance Service [*Telecommunications*]   (TEL)
SPRINT ...... Special Police Radio Inquiry Network [*New York City*]
S-P/ROM ... Slave Programable Read-Only Memory   (NITA)
SPROM ...... Switched Programable Read-Only Memory   (NITA)
SPROPS ..... Section Properties [*Camutek*] [*Software package*] [*British*]   (NCC)
SPS .... Samples per Second
SPS .... Satellite and Production Services [*Tallahassee, FL*] [*Telecommunications*]   (TSSD)
SPS .... Signal Processing System   (KSC)
SPS .... Space Planning System [*Applied Research of Cambridge Ltd.*] [*Software package*] [*British*]   (NCC)
SPS .... String Processing System [*Word processing software*]   (DEEC)
SPS .... Symbolic Programing System [*Data processing*]
SPS .... Symbols per Second [*Data processing*]
SPS .... System Performance Score [*Telecommunications*]   (TEL)
SPSS .... Statistical Package for the Social Sciences [*Programing language*] [*1970*]
SPST .... Single-Pole, Single-Throw [*Switch*]
SPSTNC ..... Single-Pole, Single-Throw, Normally-Closed [*Switch*]   (VIT)
SPSTNO ..... Single-Pole, Single-Throw, Normally-Open [*Switch*]   (VIT)
SPSTNODM ... Single-Pole, Single-Throw, Normally-Open, Double-Make [*Switch*]
SPT .... Sectors per Track   (NITA)
SPT .... Structural Programing Technique   (NITA)
SPT .... Symbolic Program Tape [*Data processing*]   (IEEE)
SPT .... Symbolic Program Translator [*Data processing*]   (IEEE)
SPT .... System Page Table [*Telecommunications*]   (TEL)
SPT .... System Parameter Table [*Data processing*]   (IBMDP)
SPTD .... Signal Processor Techniques Department
SPTF .... Signal Processing Test Facility
SPTP .... Special-Purpose Test Program   (MCD)
SPU .... Signal Processing Unit
SPU .... Slave Processing Unit   (NITA)
SPU .... System Partitioning Unit [*Data processing*]
SPUR .... Single Precision Unpacked Rounded [*floating-point package*] [*Computer program system*] [*Sperry Rand Corp.*]
SPUR .... Source Program Utility Routine   (NITA)
SPV .... Storage Protect Violation   (CMD)
SPWM .... Single-Sided Pulse Width Modulation [*Telecommunications*]   (OA)
SPX .... Simplex Circuit
SQ .... Square
SQA .... Software Quality Assurance [*Data processing*]   (IEEE)
SQA .... System Queue Area [*Data processing*]   (BUR)
SQD .... Signal Quality Detector
SQL/DS ...... Structured Query Language/Data System [*IBM Corp.*]
SQR .... Square Root [*Data processing*]
SQUARE ..... Specifying Queries as Relational Expressions [*Programing language*] [*1973*] [*Data processing*]   (CSR)
SQUID .... Sperry Quick Updating of Internal Documentation   (IEEE)
SQUID .... Superconducting Quantum Interference Detector [*or Device*] [*For studying changes in the Earth's magnetic field*]
SQW .... Squarewave   (MSA)
SQWV .... Squarewave   (DDI)
SR .... Scanning Radiometer
SR .... Send and Receive
SR- .... Series Number [*Online database field identifier*]   (OBD)
S-R .... Set-Reset [*Flip-Flop*] [*Data processing*]
SR .... Settlement Register [*Data processing*]
SR .... Shift Register
SR .... Sorter Reader   (OA)
SR .... Special Register   (NITA)
SR .... Speech Recognition   (NITA)
SR .... Status Register   (NITA)
SR .... Storage Register   (NITA)
S & R .... Storage and Retrieval [*Data processing*]   (DDI)
SR .... Subroutine [*Data processing*]
SR .... Supervisor   (TEL)
SR .... Switch Register   (NITA)
SRA .... Science Research Associates, Inc. [*Chicago, IL*] [*Software manufacturer*]   (DASOS)
SRA .... System Reaction Analysis [*Bell System*]
SRAEN .... Systeme de Reference pour la Determination de l'Affaiblissement Equivalent pour la Nettete [*Master telephone transmission reference system*]   (DEN)
SRAM .... Semirandom Access Memory   (NITA)
SRAM .... Some Remarks on Abstract Machines [*Data processing*]
SRAM .... Static Random Access Memory [*Data processing*]
SRATS .... Solar Radiation and Thermospheric Structure [*Japanese satellite*]
SRB .... Service Request Block [*Data processing*]   (BUR)
SRB .... Sorter Reader Buffer   (OA)
SRC .... Science Research Council [*Later, SERC*] [*British*]
SRC .... Send Register Control [*Data processing*]
SRC .... Source Range Channel   (IEEE)
SRC .... Survey Research Center [*University of Kentucky*] [*Research center*]   (RCD)
SRC .... Synchronous Remote Control   (NITA)
SRCC .... Sensor Referenced and Computer Controlled [*For remote manipulators*]
SRCC .... Simplex Remote Communications Central
SRCD .... Set-Reset Clocked Data [*Data processing*]
SRCI .... Survey Research Consultants International [*Information service*]   (EISS)
SRCNET ..... Science and Engineering Research Council Network [*Later, SERCNET*]   (DEEC)
SRCR .... System Run Control Record   (NITA)
SRD .... Software Requirements Document [*Data processing*]   (CIT)
SRDAS .... Service Recording and Data Analysis System   (IEEE)
SRDG .... Software Research and Development Group [*University of Calgary*] [*Research center*]   (RCD)
SRDI .... Safety-Related Display Instrumentation
SRDM .... Subrate Data Multiplexer [*Telecommunications*]   (TEL)

Computer & Telecommunications Acronyms

SRDS .... Standard Reference Data System   (DIT)
SRE .... Signaling Range Extender [*Telecommunications*]   (TEL)
SRE .... Single Region Execution   (NITA)
SRE .... Site Resident Engineer [*Telecommunications*]   (TEL)
SRE .... Society of Reliability Engineers   (EANO)
SREM .... Software Requirements Engineering Methodology
SRF .... Software Recording Facility   (NITA)
SRF .... Software Recovery Facility [*Data processing*]   (IBMDP)
SRF .... Sorter Reader Flow   (OA)
SRF .... Surface Roughness Factor [*Telecommunications*]   (TEL)
SRFF .... Set-Reset Flip-Flop [*Data processing*]
SRG .... Surge   (MSA)
SRI .... Signal Routing and Interface   (MCD)
SRI .... Spectrum Resources, Incorporated [*St. Charles, MO*] [*Telecommunications*]   (TSSD)
SRI .... Stanford Research Institute [*Later, SRI International*] [*Databank originator*]
SRIS .... Safety Recommendation Information System [*Database*]   (FDB)
SRIS .... Safety Research Information Service [*National Safety Council*] [*Chicago, IL*]   (EISS)
SRL .... Schema Representation Language
SRL .... Singing Return Loss [*Telecommunications*]   (TEL)
SRL .... Stability Return Loss [*Telecommunications*]   (TEL)
SRL .... Standard Reference Library   (TUT)
SRL .... Structural Return Loss [*Telecommunications*]   (TEL)
SRM .... Shift Register Memory
SRM .... Short Range MODEM   (NITA)
SRM .... Square Root Mode [*Data processing*]
SRM .... System Resource Manager [*IBM Corp.*]   (BUR)
SRMS .... Scheduling and Resource Management System [*Tymshare UK*] [*Software package*] [*British*]   (NCC)
SRNFC .... Source Range Neutron Flux Channel   (IEEE)
SRP .... Source Record Punch
SRR .... Shift Register Recognizer   (IEEE)
SRR .... Systems Requirement Review
SRS .... Slave Register Set   (NITA)
SRS .... Speech Reinforcement System
SRS .... Student Response System [*Automated group instruction*]   (CGC)
SRS .... Subscriber-Response System [*Study of cable television*] [*Hughes Aircraft Co.*]
SRS .... Synchronous Relay Satellite [*Telecommunications*]   (TEL)
SRT .... Single Requesting Terminal [*Data processing*]   (IBMDP)
SRTC .... Special Real-Time Command   (KSC)
SRTC .... Stored Program Real-Time Commands   (MCD)
SRTF .... Shortest Remaining Time First [*Data processing*]
SRZ .... Satz Rechen Zentrum [*Computer Composition Center*] [*West German*] [*Information service*]   (EISS)
SS .... Satellite-Switched
SS .... Schwab Safe Co. [*American Stock Exchange symbol*]
SS .... Select Standby   (NITA)
SS .... Semifinal Splice [*Telecommunications*]   (TEL)
SS .... Sight and Sound [*A publication*]
S & S .... Sight and Sound [*A publication*]
SS .... Signal Strength [*Broadcasting*]   (KSC)
SS .... Signaling System [*Telecommunications*]   (TEL)
SS .... Solid State
S/S .... Source/Sink [*Data processing*]   (IBMDP)
SS .... Space Switch [*Telecommunications*]   (TEL)
SS .... Spread Spectrum   (CET)
SS .... Stack Segment [*Data processing*]
S/S .... Start/Stop   (NITA)
S to S .... Station to Station
SS .... Storage to Storage   (MCD)
SS .... Subscriber Switching [*Telecommunications*]   (TEL)
ss .... Substructure [*Data processing*]
SS .... System Software   (MCD)
SS .... System Supervisor   (NITA)
SSA .... Segment Search Argument [*Data processing*]   (BUR)
SSA .... Social Security Administration [*of HEW*]
SSADARS ... Social Security Administration Data Acquisition and Response System
SSAN .... Social Security Account Number
SSAP .... Source Service Access Point   (CCD)
SSAS .... Station Signaling and Announcement Subsystem [*Telecommunications*]   (TEL)
SSB .... Single Sideband
SSB .... Subscriber Busy [*Telecommunications*]   (TEL)
SSBAM .... Single Sideband Amplitude Modulation   (KSC)
SSBFM .... Single Sideband Frequency Modulation   (IEEE)
SSBSC .... Single Sideband Suppressed Carrier
SSBSCOM ... Single Sideband Suppressed Carrier Optical Modulator
SSC .... Satellite Systems Corporation [*Virginia Beach, VA*] [*Telecommunications*]   (TSSD)
SSC .... Sector Switching Center [*Telecommunications*]   (TEL)
SSC .... Secure Systems Corporation [*Manassas, VA*] [*Telecommunications*]   (TSSD)
SSC .... Serial Shift Counter [*Data processing*]
SSC .... Signaling and Supervisory Control   (NITA)
SSC .... Single Silk-Covered [*Wire insulation*]
SSC .... Special Service Center [*Bell System*]
SSC .... Standards Steering Committee [*ANSI*]
SSC .... Station Selection Code   (BUR)
SSC .... Subsystem Computer   (MCD)

SSC .... Systems Support Center   (BUR)
SSCC .... Common Channel Signaling System [*Telecommunications*]   (TEL)
SSCD .... Start Sample Command Delayed
SS/CF .... Signal Strength, Center Frequency [*Broadcasting*]
SSCI .... Social Sciences Citation Index [*Institute for Scientific Information*] [*Database*] [*A publication*]
SSCP .... System Services Control Point [*Data processing*]
SSCS .... Shipboard Satellite Communications System
SSCS .... Steep-Spectrum Compact Sources [*of galactic radio waves*]
SSD .... Software System Design [*Data processing*]   (CIT)
SSD .... Solid-State Storage Device [*Data processing*]
SSD .... Squared Successive Differences [*Data processing*]
SS & D .... Synchronization Separator and Digitizer
SSD .... System Status Display   (SKY)
SSD .... System Summary Display   (MCD)
SSDA .... Social Science Data Archives [*University of California, Los Angeles*] [*Information service*]   (EISS)
SSDA .... Synchronous Serial Data Adapter   (NITA)
SSDC .... Signal Source Distribution Center
SSDC .... Social Science Data Center [*University of Connecticut*] [*Research center*]   (EISS)
SSDC .... Social Science Documentation Centre [*UNESCO*]   (EISS)
SSDD .... Single-Sided, Double-Density Disk [*Magnetic disk*] [*Data processing*]
SSDD .... Software System Design Document   (MCD)
SSDL .... Social Science Data Center [*Hunter College of City University of New York*] [*Research center*]   (RCD)
SSDP .... Standard Source Data Package
SSDPS .... Solar System Data Processing System   (CIT)
SSDR .... Steady State Determining Routine   (OA)
SSDR .... Supermarket Subsystem Definition Record [*Data processing*]   (IBMDP)
SSE .... Satellite Systems Engineering, Inc. [*Bethesda, MD*] [*Information service*]   (TSSD)
SSE .... Single Silk Covering over Enamel Insulation [*Telecommunications*]   (TEL)
SSEC .... Selective Sequence Electronic Calculator [*Data processing*]
SSF .... Single Sideband Filter
SSF .... Single Sided Frame [*Telecommunications*]   (TEL)
SSF .... Symmetrical Switching Function   (NITA)
SSFC .... Sequential Single Frequency Code System [*Telecommunications*]   (TEL)
SSFS .... Special Services Forecasting System [*Telecommunications*]   (TEL)
SSFT .... Scientific Software [*NASDAQ symbol*]   (NQ)
SSG .... State Services Group [*Information service*]   (EISS)
SSG .... Symbolic Stream Generator [*Data processing*]
SSI .... Satellite Services, Incorporated [*Houston, TX*] [*Telecommunications*]   (TSSD)
SSI .... Scientific Software-Intercomp, Inc. [*Denver, CO*] [*Software manufacturer*]   (DASOS)
SSI .... Sector Scan Indicator
SSI .... Service Software, Incorporated [*Cherry Hill, NJ*] [*Software manufacturer*]   (DASOS)
SSI .... Small-Scale Integration
SSI .... Start Signal Indicator [*Telecommunications*]   (TEL)
SSI .... Storage-to-Storage Instruction   (IEEE)
SSI .... Survey Sampling, Incorporated [*Information service*]   (EISS)
SSI .... Synchronous Systems Interface   (NITA)
SSI .... System Status Indicator [*Bell System*]
SSIE .... Smithsonian Science Information Exchange [*Smithsonian Institution*] [*Washington, DC*] [*Database*]
SSIP .... Systems Software Interface Processing   (MCD)
SSL .... Scientific Subroutine Library   (NITA)
SSL .... Shift and Select [*Data processing*]   (MDG)
SSL .... Software Sciences Limited [*British*]   (OA)
SSL .... Software Slave Library [*Data processing*]   (TEL)
SSL .... Software Specification Language   (NITA)
SSL .... Source Statement Library [*Data processing*]
SSL .... Storage Structure Language   (NITA)
SSL .... System Specification Language   (NITA)
SSLC .... Synchronous Single-Line Controller   (NITA)
SSLT .... Solid-State Logic Timer
SSM .... Semiconductor Storage Module   (NITA)
SSM .... Signal Strength Monitor [*Broadcasting*]
SSM .... Single Sideband Modulation
SSM .... Single Sideband Signal Multiplier [*Telecommunications*]   (OA)
SSM .... Small Semiconductor Memory   (NITA)
SSM .... Special Safeguarding Measures [*Telecommunications*]   (TEL)
SSM .... Spread Spectrum Modulation   (NATG)
SSMA .... Solid-State Microwave Amplifier
SSMA .... Spread-Spectrum Multiple Access [*Satellite communications*]
SSMB .... Special Services Management Bureau [*Telecommunications*]   (TEL)
SSMD .... Silicon Stud-Mounted Diode
SSME .... Satellite System Monitoring Equipment
SSMF .... Symbol Sink - Matched Filter   (CIT)
SSMG .... Satellite Systems Monitoring Group [*INTELSAT*]   (CBSS)
SSN .... Segment Stack Number   (NITA)
SSN .... Social Security Number
SSN .... Standard Serial Numbers   (DIT)
SSN .... Switched Service Network [*Telecommunications*]
SSOA .... Software Services of America [*NASDAQ symbol*]   (NQ)

By Acronym

Computer & Telecommunications Acronyms

SSOC......... Switching Service Operations Center [*Telecommunications*]
SSOG......... Satellite Systems Operations Guide [*INTELSAT*]   (CBSS)
SSORD....... Software Review [*A publication*]
SSOU1....... System Output Unit 1 [*IBM Corp.*]   (MDG)
SSP............ Scientific Subroutine Package [*Data processing*]
SSP............ Society of Satellite Professionals [*Washington, DC*] [*Telecommunications*] [*Information service*] [*An association*]   (EANO)
SSP............ Special Services Protection [*Telecommunications*]   (TEL)
SSP............ Subsatellite Point [*Telecommunications*]   (TEL)
SSP............ System Status Panel   (NITA)
SSP............ System Support Program   (AFM)
SSPS.......... Solar-Based Solar Power Satellite
SSR............ Satellite Situation Report
SSR............ Static Squelch Range
SSR............ Synchronous Stable Relaying   (IEEE)
SSR............ System Status Report   (NITA)
SSRA......... Spread Spectrum Random Access System [*Telecommunications*]   (TEL)
SSRFC....... Social Science Research Facilities Center [*University of Minnesota*] [*Research center*]   (RCD)
SSRI.......... Social Science Research Institute [*of CRESS*] [*University of Hawaii at Manoa*] [*Research center*]   (RDA)
SSS............ Satellite Syndicated Systems [*Douglasville, GA*] [*Cable TV programing service*] [*Telecommunications*]
SSS............ Scientific Subroutine System [*Data processing*]   (BUR)
S/SS.......... Sector/Subsector
SSS............ Single Signal Superheterodyne [*Radio*]
SSS............ Software Staging Section [*Social Security Administration*]
SSS............ Solid-State System
SSS............ Southern Satellite Systems, Inc. [*Tulsa, OK*] [*Telecommunications*]   (TSSD)
SSS............ Subscribers' Switching Subsystem [*Telecommunications*]   (TEL)
SSS............ Subsystem Support Service   (BUR)
SSSD......... Single-Sided, Single-Density Disk [*Magnetic disk*] [*Data processing*]
SSSP......... Station to Station Send Paid [*Telecommunications*]   (TEL)
SSSV......... Scientific Systems Services, Inc. [*NASDAQ symbol*]   (NQ)
SST............ Single Sideband Transmission [*Telecommunications*]   (TEL)
SST............ Subscriber Transferred [*Telecommunications*]   (TEL)
SST............ Synchronous System Trap   (NITA)
SST............ System Segment Table   (NITA)
SSTC......... Single-Sideband Transmitted Carrier   (IEEE)
SST-DMA... Satellite Switched Time Division Multiple Access   (NITA)
SSTF.......... Shortest Seek Time First   (NITA)
SSTV......... Slow-Scan Television
SSU............ Semiconductor Storage Unit [*Data processing*]   (TUT)
SSU............ Single Signaling Unit [*Telecommunications*]   (TEL)
SSU............ Stratospheric Sounding Unit [*Telecommunications*]   (TEL)
SSU............ Subscriber Switching Unit [*Telecommunications*]   (TEL)
SSU............ Subsequent Signal Unit [*Group of BITS*] [*Telecommunications*]   (TEL)
SSVM........ Self-Scaling Variable Metric [*Algorithms*] [*Data processing*]
SSW.......... Space Switch [*Telecommunications*]   (TEL)
SSWO....... Special Service Work Order [*Telecommunications*]   (TEL)
ST.............. Self-Test
ST.............. Shares Time with [*Broadcasting term*]
ST.............. Sidetone [*Telecommunications*]   (TEL)
ST.............. Status
ST.............. Supplementary Term [*Online database field identifier*]   (OBD)
ST.............. System Test
STA............ Station [*Telecommunications*]
STA............ Status [*Online database field identifier*]
STA............ Swedish Telecommunications Administration [*Farsta*] [*Telecommunications*]   (TSSD)
STAC......... Software Timing and Control   (NITA)
STAD......... Start Address [*Telecommunications*]   (TEL)
STAE......... Specify Task Asynchronous Exit [*Data processing*]
STAI.......... Subtask ABEND [*Abnormal End*] Intercept [*Data processing*]   (BUR)
STAIRS...... Storage and Information Retrieval System [*IBM Corp.*]
STAIRS/VS... Storage and Information Retrieval System/Virtual Storage [*IBM Corp.*]
STALPETH... Steel, Aluminum, Polyethylene [*Components of a type of telecommunications cable*]
STAM........ Shared Tape Allocation Manager   (NITA)
STAMP...... Satellite Telecommunications Analysis and Modeling Program
STAMP...... Systems Tape Addition and Maintenance Program [*Data processing*]   (IEEE)
STAPL....... SIGPLAN Technical Committee on APL [*A Programming Language*] [*Association for Computing Machinery*]
STAPP....... Simulation Tape Print Program
STAR......... Self-Test Automatic Readout
STAR......... Self-Testing and Repairing [*Computer self-repair*]
STAR......... Standard Telecommunications Automatic Recognizer [*Data processing*]
STAR......... Statistical Table Assembly and Retrieval System [*Proposed for Social Security Administration*]
STAR......... Sting Array [*Computer system*]   (MCD)
STAR......... Stock Technical Analysis Reports [*Innovest Systems, Inc.*] [*Database*]   (CUAD)
STAR......... String Array Processor   (NITA)

STAR......... System for Telephone Administrative Response [*Data processing*]
STARAN..... Stellar Attitude Reference and Navigation
STARFIRE... System to Accumulate and Retrieve Financial Information with Random Extraction [*Data processing*]
STARS........ Satellite Transmission and Reception Specialists [*Houston, TX*] [*Telecommunications*]   (TSSD)
STARS........ Software Technology for Adaptable, Reliable Systems [*Data processing*]
STAT......... Status   (MSA)
STATCAT... Statistical Context-Aided Testing [*North-Holland Publishing Co.*] [*Software package*] [*British*]   (NCC)
STATIC...... Student Taskforce Against Telecommunication Information Concealment [*Student legal action organization*]
STATLIB.... Statistical Computing Library [*Bell System*]
STATPAC... Statistics Package [*Computer program*]   (IEEE)
STB............ Segment Tag BITS [*Binary Digits*]   (OA)
STBA.......... Selective Top-to-Bottom Algorithm   (DIT)
STC............ Satellite Television Corporation [*Washington, DC*] [*Telecommunications*]   (TSSD)
STC............ Serving Test Center [*Bell System*]
STC............ Simulation Tape Conversion
STC............ Society of Telecommunications Consultants [*New York, NY*] [*Telecommunications*] [*Information service*] [*An association*]   (EANO)
STC............ Source Telecomputing Corporation [*McLean, VA*] [*Telecommunications*]   (TSSD)
STC............ Standard Telephone and Cable [*IT & T affiliate*] [*British*]
STC............ Standard Transmission Code [*Data processing*]
STC............ Station Technical Control [*Telecommunications*]   (TEL)
STC............ Stern Telecommunications Corporation [*New York, NY*] [*Telecommunications*]   (TSSD)
STC............ Storage Technology Corporation [*In company name, STC Systems, Inc.*] [*Waldwick, NJ*] [*Software manufacturer*]   (DASOS)
STCB......... Subtask Control Block [*Data processing*]   (IBMDP)
STCC......... Spacecraft Technical Control Center   (MDG)
STCDHS..... Spacecraft Telemetry Command Data Handling System   (CIT)
STCDS....... System Test Complex Data System   (CIT)
STCE......... System Test Complex Equipment   (CIT)
STCI.......... Siebert Telecommunications Consulting, Incorporated [*Cincinnati, OH*] [*Telecommunications*]   (TSSD)
STCOL....... Steel Column [*Camutek*] [*Software package*] [*British*]   (NCC)
STD............ Standard   (AFM)
STD............ Subscriber Trunk Dialing [*Telephone communications*]
STDM........ Statistical Time-Division Multiplexer [*or Multiplexing*]   (NITA)
STDM........ Synchronous Time-Division Multiplexing [*Data processing*]   (MDG)
STE............ Segment Table Entry [*Data processing*]   (MDG)
STE............ Span Terminating Equipment [*Telecommunications*]   (TEL)
STEEP....... Shock Two-Dimensional Eulerian Elastic Plastic [*Computer code*]
STEP.......... Simple Transition to Economical Processing   (IEEE)
STEP.......... Simple Transition to Electronic Processing
STEP.......... Standard Tape Executive Package [*or Program*] [*NCR Corp.*]   (CGC)
STEP.......... Standard Terminal Program [*Data processing*]   (IEEE)
STEP.......... Supervisory Tape Executive Program [*Data processing*]
STET......... Specialized Technique for Efficient Typesetting
STF............ Supervisory Time Frame   (NITA)
STF............ Systems Technology Forum [*Burke, VA*] [*Telecommunications*]   (TSSD)
STGE......... Storage
STIC.......... Science and Technology Information Center [*China*]   (EISS)
STICAP...... Stiff Circuit Analysis Program [*Data processing*]
STII............ Stanford Telecommunications [*NASDAQ symbol*]   (NQ)
STIL........... Statistical Interpretive Language [*Data processing*]   (MDG)
STIS........... Scientific & Technical Information Services, Inc. [*Information service*]   (EISS)
STIS........... Sumika Technical Information Service, Inc. [*Osaka, Japan*] [*Information service*]   (EISS)
STK............ Stack   (MSA)
STK............ Standard Test Key [*Data processing*]
STK............ Storage Technology Corp. [*NYSE symbol*]
STL............ Satellite   (CBSS)
STL............ Schottky Transistor Logic   (IEEE)
STL............ Simulated Tape Load
STL............ Standard Telegraph Level [*Telecommunications*]   (TEL)
STL............ Synchronous Transistor Logic   (MDG)
STL............ System Test Loop   (IEEE)
STLT.......... Satellite   (FAAC)
STLT.......... Small Transportable Link Terminal
STM........... Satellite Technology Management, Inc. [*Torrance, CA*] [*Telecommunications*]   (TSSD)
STM........... Send Test Message
STM........... Short-Term Memory
STM........... Statistical Multiplexing [*Telecommunications*]
STMIS....... System Test Manufacturing Information System   (IEEE)
STMT........ Statement   (AFM)
STN............ Satellite Television Network [*Washington, DC*] [*Telecommunications*]   (TSSD)
STN............ Scientific and Technical Information Network
STN............ Station
STN............ Switched Telecommunications Network   (NITA)

Computer & Telecommunications Acronyms

STO	Segment Table Origin (NITA)
STO	System Test Objectives
STOC	Systems for Test Output Consolidation [*Data processing*]
STOL	Systems Test and Operation Language (NITA)
STOP	Single Title Order Plan [*Bookselling*]
STOQ	Storage Queue (NITA)
STOR	Segment Table Origin Register [*Data processing*] (BUR)
STOR	Storage (AFM)
STORAD	Stored Address [*Data processing*]
STORE	Storage Technology for Operational Readiness
STORES	Syntactic Tracer Organized Retrospective Enquiry System [*Instituut voor Wiskunde, Informatiewerk, en Statistiek*] [*Data processing*] [*Dutch*]
STORET	Storage and Retrieval [*Data processing*]
STORET	Storage and Retrieval for Water Quality Data [*Environmental Protection Agency*] [*Databank*]
STORM	Statistically Oriented Matrix Program (IEEE)
STP	Selective Tape Print
STP	Self-Test Program (MCD)
STP	Short Term Projections [*Townsend-Greenspan & Co., Inc.*] [*Database*] (CUAD)
STP	Signal Transfer Point [*Telecommunications*] (TEL)
STP	Solar-Terrestrial Physics (EISS)
STP	Standardized Test Program (DDI)
STPL	Sidetone Path Loss [*Telecommunications*] (TEL)
STPST	Stop-Start [*Telecommunications*] (TEL)
STR	Questar Corp. [*NYSE symbol*]
STR	Segment Table Register (NITA)
STR	Sidetone Reduction [*Telecommunications*] (TEL)
STR	Speed Tolerant Recording [*Electronic Processors, Inc.*] (NITA)
STR	Store (CDH)
STR	Synchronous Transmitter Receiver [*Data processing*]
STRA	Stratus Computer, Inc. [*NASDAQ symbol*] (NQ)
STRACS	Small Transportable Communications Stations
STRAD	Signal Transmission Reception and Distribution (IEEE)
STRAIN	Structural Analytical Interpreter (NITA)
STRAM	Synchronous Transmit Receive Access Method (CMD)
STRAW	Simultaneous Tape Read and Write
STRD	Stored
STRESS	Structural Engineering Systems Solver [*Programing language*] [*1962*]
STRETCH	[*An*] early large computer [*IBM 7030*] (CAH)
STRIP	String Processing Language [*Data processing*] (DIT)
STROBES	Shared-Time Repair of Big Electronic Systems [*Data processing*]
STRUBAL	Structured Basic Language [*Data processing*] (CSR)
STRUC	Structure
STRUDL	Structural Design Language [*Data processing*]
STRUFO	Structural Formula [*Data processing*] [*Chemistry*]
STRX	Syntrex, Inc. [*NASDAQ symbol*] (NQ)
STS	Satellite Transmissions Systems, Inc. [*Hauppauge, NY*] [*Telecommunications*] (TSSD)
STS	Simulator Test Set (CAAL)
STS	Skaggs Telecommunications Service [*Salt Lake City, UT*] [*Telecommunications*] (TSSD)
STS	Sonic Telex System [*Sonicair*] [*Phoenix, AZ*] [*Telecommunications*] (TSSD)
STS	Space-Time-Space [*Digital switching structure*] [*Telecommunications*] (TEL)
STS	Spacecraft Telecommunications System (CIT)
STS	Survey Tabulation Services, Inc. [*Information service*] (EISS)
STS	System Test Software (CAAL)
STSC	Scientific Time Sharing Corporation [*Host*] [*Information service*] (EISS)
STSK	Scandinavian Committee for Satellite Communications [*Telecommunications*] (TEL)
STSN	Set-and-Test-Sequence-Number [*Data processing*] (IBMDP)
STT	Seek Time per Track (NITA)
STT	Syndicat des Travailleurs en Telecommunications [*Telecommunications Workers Union - TWU*] [*Canada*]
S/TTL	Schottky Transistor-Transistor Logic (DEEC)
STU	Secure Telephone Unit [*Data processing*]
STU	Signal Transfer Unit
STU	Space-Time Unit [*Computer*]
STU	Subscribers' Trunk Unit [*Telecommunications*] (TEL)
STU	System Transition Unit [*Data processing*]
STUB	Stadt- und Universitaetsbibliothek Frankfurt [*Database producer*] (ODIN)
STV	Subscription Television
STV	Surveillance Television (AFM)
STVD	Spacecraft Television Video Data (CIT)
STX	Start of Text Character [*Keyboard*] [*Data processing*]
SU	Selectable Unit (BUR)
SU	Signaling Unit
SU	Storage Unit [*Data processing*]
SU	Subject [*Online database field identifier*] (OBD)
SU	Suppressor [*Electronics*] (MDG)
SU	Switching Unit (VIT)
SUA	Satellite Unfurlable Antenna
SUA	Standard Unit of Accounting [*Data processing*]
SUAR	Start Unload Address Register (SKY)
SUB	Subroutine (NITA)
Sub	Subscriber
SUB	Substitute Character [*Keyboard*] (AFM)
SUB	Subtract Binary Number [*Data processing*]
SUCC	State University Computation Center [*Iowa State University*] [*Research center*] (RCD)
SUDOSAT	Sudanian Satellite (CBSS)
SUDS	Satellite Undetected Duds
SUGI	SAS [*Statistical Analysis System*] Users Group International (EANO)
SUHL	Sylvania Ultrahigh-Level Logic (IEEE)
SUI	Standard Universal Identifying Number (NITA)
SUL	Simplified User Logistics
SUL	Standard User Labels [*Data processing*]
SUM	Set-Up [*Control*] Module [*Telecommunications*] (TEL)
SUM	System Utilization Monitor [*Data processing*] (TUT)
SUMC	Space Ultrareliable Modular Computer
SUMEX	Stanford University Medical Experimental Computer Project [*Stanford University*] [*Research center*] (RCD)
SUMIT	Standard Utility Means for Information Transformation [*Data processing*] (TUT)
SUMMIT	Sperry UNIVAC Minicomputer Management of Interactive Terminals (NITA)
SUMMIT	Supervisor of Multiprograming, Multiprocessing, Interactive Time Sharing [*Data processing*] (IEEE)
SUMS	Sperry UNIVAC Material System
SUN	Spanish Universal Network [*Cable-television system*]
SUN	Sun Co., Inc. [*NYSE symbol*]
SUN	Switching Unit
SUNIST	Serveur Universitaire National de l'Information Scientifique et Technique [*Online service*] (CUAD)
SUNSAT	Sun-Energy Collecting Satellite
SUNY	State University of New York [*Computer retrieval and control projects*] [*Albany, NY*]
SUNY/OCLC	State University of New York Online Computer Library Center [*Library network*]
SUP	Standard Unit of Processing [*Data processing*]
SUP	Statistical Utility Program
SUPCUR	Superimposed Current
SUPE	Superior Electric Co. [*NASDAQ symbol*] (NQ)
SUPERNOVA	[*A*] NOVA Computer [*Data General Corp.*] (CAH)
SURCAL	Surveillance Calibration Satellite
SURE	Symbolic Utilities Revenue Environment [*IBM Corp.*]
SUREJ	Surface Ship Electromagnetic Jammer (DDI)
SURF	Support of User Records and Files [*Data processing*]
SURGE	SEASAT Users Group of Europe
SURGE	Sorting, Updating, Report Generating, Etc. [*IBM Corp.*] [*Data processing*]
SURSAT	Satellite Surveillance Program [*Canadian*]
SURVSA	Survivable Satellite Communications System (MCD)
SURVSATCOM	Survivable Satellite Communications System (CBSS)
SURWAC	Surface Water Automatic Computer
SUS	Semiconductor Unilateral Switch (MSA)
SUS	Silicon Unilateral Switch
SUS	Small Ultimate Size [*Telecommunications*] (TEL)
SUS	Speech Understanding System (NITA)
SUSIE	Stock Updating Sales Invoicing Electronically (IEEE)
SUSIS	Sport und Sportwissenschaftliche Informationssystem [*Sport and Sports-Scientific Information System*] [*West Germany*] (EISS)
SUT	Satellite Under Test
SUT	System under Test
SV	Simulated Video (MCD)
SV	Single Value (NITA)
SV	Single Vibrations [*Half cycles*]
SV	Status Valid (NITA)
SVA	Sectionalized Vertical Antenna
SVA	Shared Virtual Area [*Data processing*]
SVC	Supervisor Call (NASA)
SVC	Switched Virtual Circuit
SVD	Simultaneous Voice/Data
SVDF	Segmented Virtual Display File (NITA)
SVI	Service Interception [*Telecommunications*] (TEL)
SVIPA	Swiss Viewdata Information Providers Association [*Zurich*] [*Telecommunications*] (TSSD)
SVLOG	Servicing Log [*Telecommunications*] (TEL)
SVM	Silicon Video Memory (OA)
SVOR	Schweizerische Vereinigung fuer Operations Research [*Bern, Switzerland*]
SVP	Service Processor (BUR)
SVR	Super Video Recorder (DEEC)
SVRB	Supervisor Request Block [*Data processing*] (BUR)
SVRD	Silicon Voltage Reference Diode
SVS	Secure Voice Switch
SVS	Secure Voice System [*Telecommunications*]
SVS	Single Virtual Storage [*IBM Corp.*] [*Data processing*]
SVS	Still-Camera Video System [*Canon, Inc.*]
SVSS	Sprague Voltage-Sensitive Switch
SVT	Solar Vacuum Telescope
SVT	System Validation Testing (NITA)
SW	Shortwave [*Electronics*]
SW	Software [*Data processing*] (CIT)
SW	Southwest
SW	Switch
SW	Switchband Wound [*Relay*]
SWA	Scheduler Work Area [*Data processing*] (IBMDP)

By Acronym

SWA............	Single Wire Armored [*Cables*]
SWA............	Standing Wave Apparatus
SWA............	Straight Wire Antenna
SWA............	System Work Area (NITA)
SWAC.........	Standards Western Automatic Computer [*National Bureau of Standards*]
SWADS.......	Scheduler Work Area Data Set [*IBM Corp.*] (MCD)
SWALC.......	Southwest Academic Library Consortium [*Library network*] (EISS)
SWAM.........	Sine Wave Amplitude Modulation
SWAMI........	Software-Aided Multiform Input [*Software*] [*Data processing*]
SWAMI........	Standing Wave Area Monitor Indicator (MUGU)
SWAP.........	Society for Wang Applications and Programs (CSR)
SWAP.........	Standard Wafer Array Programing (DEEC)
SWAP.........	Stress Wave Analyzing Program
SWAT.........	Stress Wave Analysis Technique
SWBD.........	Switchboard
SWC............	Shortwave Converter
SWCENT....	Switching Central [*Telecommunications*]
SWCH.........	Switch (MCD)
SWD............	Self-Wiring Data [*Telecommunications*] (TFI)
SWD............	Single Word Dump (SKY)
SWD............	Standing Wave Detector
SWD............	Surface Wave Dielectrometer
SWD............	Synchronous Wave Device
SWDC.........	Shock Wave Data Center [*Lawrence Radiation Laboratory*]
SWDL..........	Surface Wave Delay Line
SWDS.........	Software Development System (MCD)
SWE............	Spherical Wave Expansion [*Telecommunications*] (TEL)
SWE............	Status Word Enable (NITA)
SWE............	Stress Wave Emission
SWEDIS......	Swedish Drug Information System [*Swedish National Board of Health and Welfare*] [*Databank*] [*Sweden*] (EISS)
SWEDTEL...	Swedish Telecoms International AB [*Stockholm*] [*Telecommunications*] (TSSD)
SWEEP.......	Structures with Error Expurgation Program
SWF............	Shortwave Fadeouts
SWFG.........	Secondary Waveform Generator [*Telecommunications*] (TEL)
SWFR..........	Slow Write, Fast Read [*Data processing*] (IEEE)
SWG............	Sine Wave Generator
SWG............	Slotted Waveguide
SWG............	Squarewave Generator
SWG............	Standard Wire Gauge [*Telecommunications*]
SWI.............	Sine Wave Inverter
SWI.............	Software Interrupt [*Data processing*]
SWI.............	Special World Intervals
SWIDOC.....	Sociaal-Wetenschappelijk Informatie-en Documentatiecentrum [*Social Science Information and Documentation Center*] [*Netherlands*] [*Information service*] (EISS)
SWIFT.........	Significant Word in the Full Title [*Data processing*] (DIT)
SWIFT.........	Society for Worldwide Interbank Financial Telecommunication [*La Hulpe, Belgium*] [*Banking network*]
SWIFT.........	Software Implemented Friden Translator [*Data processing*]
SWIFT.........	System Workshops in Forecasting Techniques [*Bell System*]
SWIFT LASS ...	Signal Word Index of Field and Title - Literature Abstract Specialized Search (DIT)
SWIFT SIR ...	Signal Word Index of Field and Title - Scientific Information Retrieval (DIT)
SWIR...........	Shortwave Infrared
SWL............	Short Wavelength Limit
SWL............	Shortwave Listener [*Radio*]
SWM............	Surface Wave Mode
SWOC.........	Subject Word out of Context [*Data processing*] (DIT)
SWOP.........	Specifications for Web Offset Publications [*Printing technology*]
SWP............	Surface Wave Phenomena
SWR............	Shortwave Ratio (DEN)
SWR............	Special Warning Receiver (MCD)
SWRA.........	Selected Water Resources Abstracts [*Service of WRSIC*] [*Database*]
SWROM......	Standing Wave Read-Only Memory [*Data processing*]
SWRP.........	Satellite Wildlife Research Project
SWS............	Shift Word, Substituting
SWT............	Shortwave Transmitter
SWTL..........	Surface Wave Transmission Line
SX...............	Simplex [*Transmission direction*] (CET)
SXA.............	Stored Index to Address
SXN.............	Section (MDG)
SxS.............	Step-by-Step Switching System [*Telecommunications*]
SY...............	Sperry Corp. [*NYSE symbol*]
SY...............	Synchronized (MDG)
SYCLOPS...	SYFA Concurrent Logic Operating System (NITA)
SYCOM.......	Synchronous Communications [*Satellite*] [*GSFC*]
SYCP...........	Syncom Corporation [*NASDAQ symbol*] (NQ)
SYDIA.........	System Developer Interface Activity [*Data processing*]
SYFA..........	System for Application [*Data processing*]
SYKE..........	Sykes Datatronics [*NASDAQ symbol*] (NQ)
SYM............	Symbol [*or Symbolic*]
SYM............	System (MDG)
SYMAN.......	Symbol Manipulation [*Data processing*]
SYMAP.......	Synagraphic Mapping System [*Computer-made maps*]
SYMBAL.....	Symbolic Algebraic Language [*Data processing*] (TUT)
SYMBOLANG ...	Symbolic Manipulation Language [*Data processing*] (CSR)
SYMDEB.....	Symbolic Debugger [*Data processing*]
SYMP.........	Symposium (MSA)
SYMPAC.....	Symbolic Program for Automatic Control
SYMRO.......	System Management Research Operation (DIT)
SYN.............	Synchronous
SYN.............	Synchronous Idle [*Transmission control character*] [*Data processing*]
SYNC...........	Synchromechanism (DDI)
SYNC...........	Synchronize
SYNCD........	Synchronized
SYNCG........	Synchronizing
SYNCH........	Synchronize (CBSS)
SYNCH........	Synchronous Transmission [*Data processing*] (TSSD)
SYNCR........	Synchronizer
SYNCS........	Synchronous
SYNSEM.....	Syntax and Semantics (IEEE)
SYNTOL......	Syntagmatic Organization Language [*Data processing*]
SYNTRAN...	Syntax Translation [*Data processing*] (DIT)
SYS.............	System (AFM)
SYSAD........	Systems Adviser (CIT)
SYSCAP.....	System of Circuit Analysis Program
SYSCOM.....	System Communications (CIT)
SYSCON.....	Systems Control
SYSEC........	System Synthesizer and Evaluation Center
SYSGEN.....	Systems Generator [*or Generation*] [*Data processing*] (CGC)
SYSIN.........	System Input [*Data processing*] (MDG)
SYSLIB.......	System Library [*Data processing*] (MDG)
SYSLOG.....	System Log [*Data processing*]
SYSM..........	System Industries [*NASDAQ symbol*] (NQ)
SYSOP........	System Operator [*Computer networking*]
SYSOUT.....	System Output [*Data processing*] (IBMDP)
SYSPOP.....	System Programed Operators [*Data processing*] (MDG)
SYSRES.....	System Residence [*Data processing*] (TUT)
SYST...........	System
SYST...........	Systematics, Inc. [*NASDAQ symbol*] (NQ)
Syst-Comput-Controls ...	Systems-Computers-Controls [*A publication*]
SYSTRAN...	Systems Analysis Translator [*Data processing*]
SYSVER......	System Specification Verification (IEEE)
SZ...............	Seizure [*Telecommunications*] (TEL)
SZ...............	Size (MDG)
SZP.............	Synchro Zeroing Procedure

T

T	American Telephone & Telegraph Co. [*NYSE symbol*] [*Wall Street slang name: "Telephone"*]		TADS	Teletypewriter Automatic Dispatch System
T	Technical [*or Technician*]		TADS	Thermal Analysis Data Station
T	Telegram		TADSS	Tactical Automatic Digital Switching System
T	Telegraph		TAF	Transaction Facility (NITA)
T	Telephone		Taffie	Technologically Advanced Family
T	Telephone Trunk Call [*British*]		TAG	[*The*] Acronym Generator [*An RCA computer program*]
T	Teletype		TAG	Telecomputer Applications Group
T	Temperature		TAG	Telemetry System Analysis Group (CIT)
T	Tera [*A prefix meaning multiplied by 10^{12}*] [*SI symbol*]		TAG	Time Automated Grid (NITA)
T	Teracycle (BUR)		TAGS	Text and Graphic System [*Savoy Software Science Ltd.*] [*Software package*] [*British*] (NCC)
T	Terminal		TAHA	Tapered Aperture Horn Antenna
T	Terrain		TAI	Temps Atomique International [*International Atomic Time*] [*Telecommunications*] (TEL)
T	Test (MSA)		TAI	Traditionally Administered Instruction (BUR)
T	Third Word Designator [*Data processing*]		TAI	Turnaround Index [*Data processing*]
T	Time		TAKIS	Tutmonda Asocio pri Kibernetiko, Informatiko, kaj Sistemiko [*World Association of Cybernetics, Computer Science, and System Theory*] (EANO)
T	Tip [*Switchboard plug*] [*Telecommunications*] (TEL)		TAL	Terminal Application Language (NITA)
T	Transmit [*or Transmitting*]		TALBE	Talk and Listen Beacon [*Radio*]
T	Transmitter		TALMIS	Technology-Assisted Learning Market Information Services [*Educational Programming Systems, Inc.*]
T-1	Carrier which identifies the all-digital communications links (TSSD)		TALTC	Test Access Line Termination Circuit [*Telecommunications*] (TEL)
3T	Triple Throw [*Switch*]		TAM	Telecommunications Access Method (NITA)
TA	Tape Armored [*Telecommunications*] (TEL)		TAM	Telephone Answering Machine (IEEE)
TA	Telegraphic Address		TAM	Terminal Access Method (OA)
TA	Test Access [*Telecommunications*] (TEL)		TAM	Test Access Multiplexer [*Telecommunications*] (TEL)
TA	Transmission Authenticator [*Telecommunications*] (TEL)		TAMIS	Telemetric Automated Microbial Identification System
TAA	Telephone Artifacts Association (EANO)		TAMOS	Terminal Automatic Monitoring System (NITA)
TAA	Television Appliance Association		TAN	Tandy Corp. [*NYSE symbol*]
TAAP	Three-Axis Antenna Positioner		TAN	Teletype Alert Network (NVT)
TAB	Tabular Language [*Data processing*] (IEEE)		TANO	Tano Corp. [*NASDAQ symbol*] (NQ)
TAB	Tape Automated Bonding [*Integrated circuit technology*]		TAP	Telemetry Acceptance Pattern (KSC)
TAB	Telecommunications Advisory Board		TAP	Telemetry Antenna Pedestal
TABS	Telephone Area Billing System		TAP	Terminal Access Processor (NITA)
TABS	Terminal Access to Batch Service [*Data processing*] (BUR)		TAP	Terminal Applications Package (IEEE)
TABS	Time Analysis and Billing System (BUR)		TAP	Test Assistance Program [*Sperry UNIVAC*] (NITA)
TABS	Total Automatic Banking System [*Trademark of Diebold, Inc.*]		TAP	Time-Sharing Assembly Program [*Data processing*] (DIT)
TABSIM	Tabulator Simulator		TAP	Transaction Application Program [*Data processing*]
TABSOL	Tabular Systems-Oriented Language [*General Electric Co.*] [*British*]		TAP	Transponder Access Program [*Satellite Business Systems*] [*McLean, VA*] [*Telecommunications*] (TSSD)
TAC	Technical Assistance Center [*Telecommunications*]		TAP	Trend Analysis Program [*American Council of Life Insurance*] [*Information service*] (EISS)
TAC	Teleconference Association of Canada [*Toronto, ON*] [*Information service*] (TSSD)		TAPAC	Tape Automatic Positioning and Control
TAC	TELENET Access Controller (NITA)		TAPAK	Tape-Pack
TAC	Terminal Access Controller [*Advanced Research Projects Agency Network*] [*DoD*] (CCD)		TAPAT	Tape Programed Automatic Tester
TAC	Test Access Control [*Telecommunications*] (TEL)		TAPE	Totally Automated Programing Equipment (CIT)
TAC	TRANSAC [*Transistorized Automatic Computer*] Assembler Compiler		TAPS	Terminal Application Program System [*Data processing*]
TAC	Transformer Analog Computer		TAPS	Time Analysis of Program Status (DDI)
TAC	Transistor-Assisted Circuit		TAR	Terminal Address Register (NITA)
TAC	Transistorized Automatic Control		TAR	Threat Avoidance Receiver (MCD)
TAC	Translator, Assembler, Compiler		TAR	Track Address Register
TAC	True Airspeed Computer		TARE	Telegraphic Automatic Relay [*or Routing*] Equipment (NG)
TACA	Telecoms Authorities Cryptographic Algorithm [*Bell Telephone encryption chip*]		TARE	Telemetry Automatic Reduction Equipment
TACADS	Tactical Automated Data Processing System		TARE	Transistor Analysis Recording Equipment
TACI	Test Access Control Interface [*Telecommunications*] (TEL)		TARIF	Telegraphic Automatic Routing in the Field (MCD)
TACOL	Thinned Aperture Computed Lens (IEEE)		TARP	Test and Repair Processor [*Data processing*]
TACOS	Tool for Automatic Conversion of Operational Software (NITA)		TARPAC	Television and Radio Political Action Committee [*National Association of Broadcasters*]
TACOS	Travel Agents Computer Society (EANO)		TARS	Turnaround Ranging Station [*Telecommunications*] (TEL)
TACPOL	Tactical Procedure Oriented Language [*Data processing*] (CSR)		TAS	Tactical Automatic Switch
TACPOL	Tactile Procedure-Oriented Language (CSR)		TAS	Telecommunications Authority Singapore (TEL)
TACT	Terminal Activated Channel Test (NITA)		TAS	Telemetry Antenna Subsystem (NASA)
TACT	Transistor and Component Tester		TAS	Telephone Answering Service [*or System*]
TAD	Telemetry Analog to Digital [*Information converter*] (CDH)		TAS	Terminal Address Selector
TAD	Telephone Answering Device		TAS	Test Access Selector [*Telecommunications*] (TEL)
TAD	Terminal Address Designator (NITA)		TAS	Test and Set [*Data processing*]
TAD	Traitement Automatique des Donnees [*Automatic Data Processing*] [*French*]		TAS	Tracking Antenna System
TAD	Transaction Application Drive [*Computer Technology, Inc.*] (NITA)		TASC	Telecommunication Alarm Surveillance and Control [*AT & T*]
TADIC	Telemetry Analog-Digital Information Converter		TASC	True Airspeed Computer
TADS	Tactical Automatic Digital Switch			

183

TASCC	Test Access Signaling Conversion Circuit [*Telecommunications*] (TEL)
TASCON	Television Automatic Sequence Control
TASI	Time Assignment Speech Interpolation [*Timesharing technique*] [*Telecommunications*]
TASK	Temporary Assigned Skeleton [*Data processing*] (TUT)
TASO	Television Allocations Study Organization [*Defunct*]
TASP	Toll Alternatives Studies Program [*Telecommunications*] (TEL)
TAS-PAC	Total Analysis System for Production, Accounting, and Control [*Data processing*]
TASS	Trouble Analysis System or Subsystem [*Telecommunications*] (TEL)
TAT	Transatlantic Telephone [*Cable*]
TATC	Transatlantic Telephone Cable (IEEE)
TATE	Tank Arrangement Thermal Efficiency [*Computer program*] (KSC)
TATG	Tuned Anode Tuned Grid (DEN)
TAU	Test Access Unit [*Telecommunications*] (TEL)
TAU	Trunk Access Unit (NITA)
TAXIR	Taxonomic Information Retrieval [*Data processing*] (DIT)
TB	Telegraph Bureau
Tb	TeraBIT [*Binary Digit*] [10^{12} BITs]
TB	Terabyte [10^{12} bytes]
TB	Time-Bandwidth
TB	Tone Burst (NITA)
TBA	Towed Buoy Antenna
TBAM	Tone Burst Amplitude Modulation
TBC	Television Briefing Console
TBC	Time Base Corrector [*Videotape recording element*] [*Early processing device*]
TBC	Token Bus Controller [*Motorola, Inc.*]
TBC	Trunk Block Connector
TBDF	Transborder Data Flows [*Also, TDF*] [*Telecommunications*]
TBE	Transmitter Buffer Empty [*Data processing*]
TBEM	Terminal-Based Electronic Mail (NITA)
TBF	Time between Failures [*Quality control*]
TBL	Trouble [*Telecommunications*] (TEL)
TBM	TeraBIT [*Binary Digit*] Memory [*Data processing*]
TBM	Tone Burst Modulation (NITA)
TBMT	Transmitter Buffer Empty [*Data processing*]
TBN	Trinity Broadcasting Network [*Cable-television system*]
TBP	Tab Products Co. [*American Stock Exchange symbol*]
TBR	Arbeitsgemeinschaft Technologieberatung Ruhr [*Information retrieval*] (ODIN)
TBR	T-Bar, Inc. [*American Stock Exchange symbol*]
TBR	Table Base Register (NITA)
TBS	Talk-between-Ships [*which are tactically maneuvering; also, the VHF radio equipment used for this purpose*]
TBS	Tape and Buffer System [*Data processing*]
TBS	Tokyo Broadcasting System
TBS	Translator Bail Switch
TBS	Turner Broadcasting System [*Cable-television system*]
TBTI	Telebyte Technology [*NASDAQ symbol*] (NQ)
TBU	Terminal Buffer Unit [*Telecommunications*] (TEL)
TBW	Total Bandwidth
TBWO	Tuned Backward Wave Oscillator
TC	T-Carrier [*Telecommunications*] (TEL)
TC	Tactile Communicator [*Device which aids the deaf by translating certain sounds into coded vibrations*]
TC	Tape Command (OA)
TC	Technical Committee
TC	Technical Communication
TC	Technicolor (KSC)
TC	Telecommunications
TC	Telex Corporation [*NYSE symbol*]
TC	Terminal Computer (BUR)
TC	Terminal Concentrator (NITA)
TC	Terminal Congestion [*Telecommunications*] (TEL)
TC	Terminal Controller
TC	Test Collection [*Educational Testing Service*] [*Information service*] (EISS)
TC	Tidal Constants Data Base
T & C	Time and Charges [*Telecommunications*] (TEL)
TC	Time Clock (NITA)
TC	Time to Computation
TC	Toll Center [*Telecommunications*]
TC	Toll Completing [*Telecommunications*]
TC	Translation Controller (SKY)
TC	Transmission Controller
T/C	True or Complement (OA)
TC	Trunk Control (NITA)
TCA	TEAC Corporation of America [*Montebello, CA*] [*Hardware manufacturer*] (DASO)
TCA	Teach Cable Assembly [*Robot technology*]
TCA	Tele-Communications Association [*Santa Ana, CA*] (EANO)
TCA	Telemetering Control Assembly
TCA	Telephone Consultants of America [*Bergenfield, NJ*] [*Telecommunications*] (TSSD)
TCA	Terminal Communication Adapter (NITA)
TCA	Typographic Communications Association [*Commercial firm*] (EANO)
TCAI	Tutorial Computer-Assisted Instruction (IEEE)
TCAM	Telecommunications Access Method [*IBM Corp.*] [*Data processing*]
TCAS	T-Carrier Administration System [*Minicomputer*] [*Bell System*]
TCAT	Tape-Controlled Automatic Testing
TCB	[*The*] College Board [*Information service*] (EISS)
TCB	Task Control Block [*Data processing*]
TCB	Task Force for Community Broadcasting (EANO)
TCB	Transfer Control Block (NITA)
TCC	[*The*] Computer Company, Inc. [*Information service*] (EISS)
TCC	New Mexico Institute of Mining and Technology Computer Center [*Socorro, NM*] [*Research center*] (RCD)
TCC	Task Control Character (CMD)
TCC	Technical Computing Center (IEEE)
TCC	Technical Control Center
TCC	Telecommunications Center (CET)
TCC	Telecommunications Consumer Coalition (EANO)
TCC	Telecommunications Coordinating Committee [*Department of State*]
TCC	Teleconcepts in Communications, Inc. [*New York, NY*] [*Telecommunications*] (TSSD)
TCC	Television Control Center
TCC	Temperature Control Circuit (CIT)
TCC	Through-Connected Circuit [*Telecommunications*] (TEL)
TCC	Tracking Computer Controls (MCD)
TCC	Transcontinental Corps [*Amateur radio*]
TCC	Transfer Channel Control (IEEE)
TCC	Transmission Control Character [*Telecommunications*] (TEL)
TCC	Transmit Carry and Clear
TCCO	Technical Communications [*NASDAQ symbol*] (NQ)
TCCS	Technical Committee on Communications Satellites (DDI)
TCD	Telemetry and Command Data (KSC)
TCDMS	Telecommunication/Data Management System
TCE	Telemetry Checkout Equipment (KSC)
TCE	Telephone Company Engineered [*Telecommunications*] (TEL)
TCF	Technical Control Facility [*or Function*]
TCF	Tunable Control Frequency
TCG	[*The*] Crimson Group [*Cambridge, MA*] [*Telecommunications*] (TSSD)
TCG	Telecommunications Consulting Group, Inc. [*Washington, DC*] (TSSD)
TCG	Test Call Generator [*Telecommunications*] (TEL)
TCGS	Terak Corporation [*NASDAQ symbol*] (NQ)
TCI	Technology Communications, Incorporated
TCI	Technology Concepts, Incorporated [*Sudbury, MA*] [*Telecommunications*] (TSSD)
TCI	Tele-Communications, Incorporated [*Brookpark, OH*] (TSSD)
TCI	Teleconferencing Systems International, Inc. [*Elk Grove Village, IL*] [*Telecommunications*] (TSSD)
TCI	Telemetry Components Information (KSC)
TCID	Terminal Computer Identification (KSC)
TCII	Technology for Communications International [*NASDAQ symbol*] (NQ)
TCIS	TELEX Computer Inquiry Service (NITA)
TCK	TEC, Inc. [*American Stock Exchange symbol*]
TCL	Telecommunication Laboratories [*Taiwan*]
TCL	Terminal Command Language [*Applied Digital Data Systems*] (NITA)
TCL	Terminal Control Language (NITA)
TCL	Toll Circuit Layout [*Telecommunications*] (TEL)
TCL	Transistor Contact Land
TCL	Transistor Coupled Logic
TCL	Troposcatter Communications Link
TCL	Tulane Computer Laboratory [*Tulane University*] [*Research center*] (RCD)
TCLR	Toll Circuit Layout Record [*Telecommunications*] (TEL)
TCM	Telecommunications Monitor (NITA)
TCM	Telemetry Code Modulation
TC & M	Telemetry Control and Monitoring (CIT)
TCM	Telephone Channel Monitor
TCM	Terminal-to-Computer Multiplexer
TCM	Test Call Module [*Telecommunications*] (TEL)
TCMF	Touch Calling Multifrequency (IEEE)
TCMS	Toll Centering and Metropolitan Sectoring [*AT & T*] [*Telecommunications*] (TEL)
TCN	Telecommunications Cooperative Network (EANO)
TCN	Teleconference Network [*University of Nebraska Medical Center*] [*Omaha, NE*] [*Telecommunications*] (TSSD)
TCOM	Terminal Communications (FAAC)
TCOM	Tethered Communications, Inc. [*Westinghouse subsidiary*]
TCOMA	Tele-Communications, Inc. Cl A [*NASDAQ symbol*] (NQ)
TCOMB	Tele-Communications, Inc. Cl B [*NASDAQ symbol*] (NQ)
TCOMP	Tape Compare Processor [*Data processing*]
TCOMW	Tele-Communications, Inc. Wts [*NASDAQ symbol*] (NQ)
TCOR	Tandon Corporation [*NASDAQ symbol*] (NQ)
TCOS	Trunk Class of Service [*Telecommunications*] (TEL)
TCP	Tape Conversion Program [*Data processing*] (MDG)
TCP	Task Control Program (NITA)
TCP	Terminal Control Program (NITA)
TCP	Transmission Control Program (DEEC)
TCP	Transmission Control Protocol [*Advanced Research Projects Agency Network*] [*DoD*] (CCD)
TCR	Tape Cassette Recorder (NITA)
TCR	Telemetry Compression Routine

Computer & Telecommunications Acronyms

Acronym	Definition
TCR	Transceiver
TCR	Transmittal Control Record [*Data processing*]
TCR	Two-Color Radiometer
TCS	[*The*] Computer Store [*NASDAQ symbol*] (NQ)
TCS	Telecommunications Control System [*Toshiba Corp.*] [*Data processing*]
TCS	Telecommunications System (NITA)
TCS	Teleconference System [*Memorial University of Newfoundland*] [*St. John's, NF*] [*Telecommunications*] (TSSD)
TCS	Telephone Conference Summary
TCS	Terminal Communications Subsystem (OA)
TCS	Terminal Computer System (BUR)
TCS	Terminal Control System [*Hewlett-Packard Co.*] (SKY)
TCS	Traffic Control Satellite
TCS	Transaction Control System [*Hitachi Ltd.*] (NITA)
TCS	Transmission Controlled Spark (MCD)
TCS	Transportable Communications System
TCS	Transportation and Communications Service [*of GSA*] [*Abolished, 1972*]
TCS	Transportation Concepts & Services [*Metuchen, NJ*] [*Software manufacturer*] (DASOS)
TCS	Troposcatter Communications System
TCSC	Trainer Control and Simulation Computer
TCSP	Tandem Cross-Section Program [*Bell System*]
TCT	Telemetry-Computer Translator [*Bell Laboratories*]
TCT	Toll Connecting Trunk [*Telecommunications*] (TEL)
TCT	Translator and Code Treatment Frame (IEEE)
TCTS	Trans-Canada Telephone System (MCD)
TCTV	Telemedia Communication Television [*Cable-television system*]
TCU	Tape Control Unit
TCU	Teletype Communications Unit (NVT)
TCU	Teletypewriter Control Unit (CET)
TCU	Terminal Control Unit (MCD)
TCU	Test Computer Unit (VIT)
TCU	Timing Control Unit (NITA)
TCU	Transmission Control Unit
TCUCC	Texas Christian University Computer Center [*Fort Worth, TX*] [*Research center*] (RCD)
TCVR	Transceiver (CET)
TCW	Track Confirmation Word [*Data processing*] (TUT)
TCWG	Telecommunication Working Group
TCXO	Temperature-Compensated Crystal Oscillator
TD	Tabular Data (BUR)
TD	Telegraph Department
TD	Telephone Department
TD	Telephone Directory
TD	Terminal Digit [*Telecommunications*] (TEL)
TD	Terminal Display (BUR)
TD	Test Distributor [*Telecommunications*] (TEL)
TD	Top Down (NITA)
T & D	Transmission and Distribution
TD	Transmit Data (IEEE)
T-D	Transmitter-Distributor (CIT)
TD	Tunnel Diode
TDA	Telecommunications Dealers Association [*Formerly, Telephone Retailers Association*] [*Cincinnati, OH*] (EANO)
TDA	Telemetric Data Analyzer
TDA	Toll Dial Assistance [*Telecommunications*] (TEL)
T & DA	Tracking and Data Acquisition (CET)
TDA	Tracking and Data Acquisition
TDA	Tracking Data Analysis (CIT)
TDA	Tunnel-Diode Amplifier
TDA/AE	Tracking and Data Acquisition/Advanced Engineering (CIT)
TDAS	Tracking and Data Acquisition System
TDAS	Traffic Data Administration System [*Bell System*]
TDB	Toxicology Data Bank [*Department of Energy*] [*Oak Ridge, TN*] [*Database*] (EISS)
TDC	Temperature Density Computer
TDC	Total Distributed Control [*Data processing*]
TDCC	Transportation Data Coordinating Committee [*Washington, DC*]
TDCS	Tape Data Control Sheet [*Data processing*]
TDCS	Time Division Circuit Switching [*Telecommunications*] (NITA)
TDD	Telecommunications Device for the Deaf
TDD	Telemetry Data Digitizer
TDD	Telephone Device for the Deaf
TDDL	Time-Division Data Link [*Radio*]
TDDO	Time Delay Dropout [*Relay*]
TDE	Total Data Entry (NITA)
TDF	Transborder Data Flows [*Also, TBDF*] [*Telecommunications*]
TDF	Trunk Distribution Frame (DEN)
TDFCHB	Telemetry Data Format Control Handbook (KSC)
TDFS	Terminal Digit Fitting System
TDG	Telemetry Data Generation (SKY)
TDG	Test Data Generator (BUR)
TDHS	Tape Data Handling System
TDI	Telecommunications Data Interface
TDI	Tymnet DTS, Incorporated [*San Jose, CA*] [*Telecommunications*] (TSSD)
TDIO	Timing Data Input-Output
TDIS	Terminal Data Input System (MCD)
TDK	TDK Corp. ADS [*NYSE symbol*]
TDL	Transaction Definition Language (NITA)
TDL	Transformation Definition Language [*Data processing*] (IBMDP)
TDL	Translation Definition Language
TDL	Tunnel-Diode Logic
TDM	Telecommunications Data-Link Monitor (CET)
TDM	Telemetric Data Monitor
TDM	Template Descriptor Memory (NITA)
TDM	Time-Division Multiplexing [*Communications*]
TDM	Tunnel-Diode Mixer
TDMA	Tape Direct Memory Access (NITA)
TDMA	Time-Division [*or Time-Domain*] Multiple Access [*Computer control system*]
TDMC	Technical Data Management Center [*Department of Energy*] [*Information service*] (EISS)
TDMD	Time-Division Multiplex Device [*Radio*]
TDMG	Telegraph and Data Message Generator (MCD)
TDMS	Telegraph Distortion Measuring System
TDMS	Telemetry Data Monitor Set
TDMS	Time-Shared Data Management System (TUT)
TDMS	Transmission Distortion Measuring Set
TDM-VDMA	Time-Division Multiplex - Variable Destination Multiple Access [*Telecommunications*] (TEL)
TDNS	Total Data Network System (TEL)
TDO	Telegraph Delivery Order
TDOS	Tape Disk Operating System [*Data processing*] (TUT)
TDP	Technical Data Package
TDP	Teledata Processing
TDP	Tracking Data Processor
TDP	Tracking and Display Processor (CAAL)
TDP	Traffic Data Processing
TDPL	Top-Down Parsing Language (NITA)
TDPP	Traffic Data Processing Program (MCD)
TDPSK	Time Differential Phase-Shift Keying
TDPU	Telemetry Data Processing Unit (CAAL)
TDR	Tape Data Register (NITA)
TDR	Technical Data Relay (IEEE)
TDR	Temporarily Disconnected at Subscriber's Request [*Telecommunications*] (TEL)
TDR	Terminal Digit Requested [*Telecommunications*] (TEL)
TDR	Time Delay Relay
TDR	Time-Domain Reflectometry
TDR	Tone Dial Receiver (NITA)
TDR	Transistorized Digital Readout
TDR	Transmit Data Register [*Data processing*] (MDG)
TDRE	Tracking and Data Relay Experiment [*Telecommunications*] (TEL)
TDRM	Time-Domain Reflectometry Microcomputer
TDRS	Telemetering Data Recording Set (CAAL)
TDRS	Traffic Data Recording System [*Bell System*]
TDS	Tape Data Selector
TDS	Technical Database Services, Inc. [*New York, NY*] [*Information service*] (EISS)
TDS	Track Data Simulator
TDS	Track Data Storage
TDS	Transaction Distribution System (NITA)
TDS	Transaction Driven System [*Honeywell, Inc.*] (NITA)
TDS	Transistor Display and Data-Handling System [*Data processing*] (MDG)
TDS	Trusco Data Systems [*Atlanta, GA*] [*Software manufacturer*] (DASOS)
TDSA	Telegraph and Data Signals Analyzer (MCD)
TD & SA	Telephone, Data, and Special Audio (NASA)
TDSC	Tesdata Systems Corporation [*NASDAQ symbol*] (NQ)
TDSCC	Tidbinbilla Deep Space Communications Complex (CIT)
TDSIC	Theatre/Drama, and Speech Information Center (EISS)
TDT	Tunnel-Diode Transducer
TDTL	Tunnel-Diode Transistor Logic
TDU	Time Display Unit (NASA)
TDUM	Tape Dump and Utility Monitor [*Data processing*]
TDX	Time Division Exchange (OA)
TDX	Torque-Differential Transmitter (MUGU)
TE	Telegram
TE	Test Equipment
TE	Text Editor [*Data processing*]
TE	Trailing Edge
TE	Transverse Electric [*or Electrostatic*] [*Wave propagation mode*]
TEAM	Teleterminals Expandable Added Memory (NITA)
TEAM	Terminology Evaluation and Acquisition Method (DEEC)
TEAMS	Technical Evaluation & Management Systems, Inc. [*Dallas, TX*] [*Software manufacturer*] (DASOS)
TEARS	[*The*] Exeter Abstract Reference System [*Exeter University*] [*Information service*] (EISS)
TEBOL	Terminal Business-Oriented Language (NITA)
TEC	[*The*] Entertainment Channel [*Pay-television network*] [*Obsolete*]
TEC	Tele-Engineering Corporation [*Framingham, MA*] [*Telecommunications*] (TSSD)
TEC	Telephone Engineering Center [*Telecommunications*] (TEL)
TEC	Triple Erasure Correction (NITA)
TECE	Teleprinter Error Correction Equipment
TECH	Technical
TECH	Technology
TECH	Techtran Industries, Inc. [*NASDAQ symbol*] (NQ)
TECHSAT	Technology Satellite
TECN	Technalysis Corp. [*NASDAQ symbol*] (NQ)
TECS	Television Confirming Sensor (MCD)

Computer & Telecommunications Acronyms

Acronym	Definition
TECS	Treasury Enforcement Communications System [*Customs Service*]
TECTRA	Technology Transfer Data Bank [*California State University*] [*Information service*] (EISS)
TeD	Telefunken-Decca [*Video disk system*]
TED	Tenders Electronic Daily [*Office for Official Publications of the European Communities*] [*Database*] (CUAD)
TED	Terminal Editor
TED	Translation Error Detector (DIT)
TED	Trunk Encryption Device [*Telecommunications*] (TEL)
TEDAR	Telemetered Data Reduction
TEDES	Telemetry Data Evaluation System
TEDL	Transferred-Electron-Device Logic (MSA)
TEDPAS	Technical Data Package Automated System
TEDS	Teleteach Expanded Delivery System [*US Air Force*] [*Wright-Patterson AFB, OH*] [*Telecommunications*] (TSSD)
TEE	Tape Editing Equipment
TEE	Telecommunications Engineering Establishment [*British*]
TEGAS	Test Generation and Simulation (NITA)
TEGAS	Time Generation and Simulation [*Telecommunications*] (TEL)
TEI	Telecommunications Engineering, Incorporated [*Dallas, TX*] (TSSD)
TEK	Tektronix, Inc. [*NYSE symbol*]
TEL	Task Execution Language (NITA)
TEL	TelAutograph Corp. [*NYSE symbol*] [*Delisted*]
TEL	TeleCom Corp. [*NYSE symbol*]
TEL	Telecommunications (FAAC)
TEL	Telegram
TEL	Telegraph
TEL	Telemetry (KSC)
TEL	Telephone
TEL	Teletypewriter [*Telecommunications*]
TELCO	Telephone Operating Company [*Also, TELOP*]
TELCOM	Telecommunications (NASA)
Telcom Rep	Telcom Report [*A publication*]
TELCON	Telephone Conference [*or Conversation*]
TELE	Telegram
TELE	Telegraph
TELE	Telephone
TELECAMRA	Television Camera (MDG)
TELECAR	Telemetry Carrier Acquisition and Recovery (MCD)
TELECAST	Television Broadcasting (CET)
TELECOM	Telecommunications (AFM)
Telecom	Telecommunications [*A publication*]
Telecom Aust Res Q	Telecom Australia Research Quarterly [*A publication*]
Telecom J	Telecommunication Journal of Australia [*A publication*]
Telecom J Aust	Telecommunication Journal of Australia [*A publication*]
Telecomm	Telecommunications [*A publication*]
Telecomm J	Telecommunication Journal [*A publication*]
Telecomm J Aust	Telecommunication Journal of Australia [*A publication*]
Telecomms	Telecommunications [*International Edition*] [*A publication*]
Telecommun J	Telecommunication Journal [*A publication*]
Telecommun J Aust	Telecommunication Journal of Australia [*A publication*]
Telecommun J (Engl Ed)	Telecommunication Journal (English Edition) [*A publication*]
Telecommun Radio Eng	Telecommunications and Radio Engineering [*A publication*]
Telecommun Radio Eng (USSR) Part 2	Telecommunications and Radio Engineering (USSR). Part 2. Radio Engineering [*A publication*]
TELECON	Telephone [*or Teletype*] Conference [*or Conversation*] (AFM)
TELECONV	Telephone Conversation
TELEDAC	Telemetric Data Converter
TELEDIS	Teletypewriter Distribution (NATG)
TELEG	Telegram
TELEG	Telegraph
Telem Ant	Telemetry Antenna
TELENET	TELENET Communications Corp. [*GTE*] (TEL)
TELEPAK	Telemetering Package
TELEPH	Telephone
Teleph Eng & Manage	Telephone Engineer and Management [*A publication*]
Telephone	Telephone Engineer and Management [*A publication*]
TELESAT	Telecommunications Satellite
TELESUN	Telecommunications Software User's Network [*Telesun Corp.*] [*Salt Lake City, UT*] (TSSD)
TELETECH	National Telecommunications & Technology Fund, Inc. [*New York, NY*] (TSSD)
TELETYPE	Teletypewriter [*Telecommunications*]
TELEX	Automatic Teletypewriter Exchange Service [*of Western Union*]
TELG	Telegram
TELIDON	[*A*] television terminal-based interactive information retrieval system (NITA)
TELINT	Telemetry Intelligence
TELL-A-GRAF	[*A*] programing language [*1978*] (CSR)
TELM	Telegram
TELNET	Georgia Telecommunications Network [*Georgia Hospital Association*] [*Atlanta, GA*] [*Telecommunications*] (TSSD)
Tel Off	Telegraph Office
TELOP	Telephone Operating Co. [*Also, TELCO*]
TELOPS	Telemetry Online Processing System [*Data processing*]
TELPAK	Telephone Package
TELR	Teleram Communications [*NASDAQ symbol*] (NQ)
Tel Rad E R	Telecommunications and Radio Engineering (USSR) [*A publication*]
TELRY	Telegraph Reply (FAAC)
TELSAM	Telephone Service Attitude Measurement [*Telephone interviews*] [*AT&T*]
TELSCOM	Telemetry-Surveillance-Communications
TEL-SYS	Telephone System
TELUQ	Tele-Universite (University of Quebec) [*Quebec, PQ*] [*Telecommunications*] (TSSD)
TELUS	Telemetric Universal Sensor
TELV	TeleVideo Systems [*NASDAQ symbol*] (NQ)
TE & M	Telephone Engineer & Management [*Harcourt Brace Jovanovich Publications, Inc.*] [*Geneva, IL*] [*Information service*] [*A publication*]
TEM	Transmission Electron Microscope [*or Microscopy*]
TEM	Transverse Electromagnetic [*Wave*] [*Radio*]
TEMA	Telecommunication Engineering and Manufacturing Association [*British*] (NITA)
TEMAC	Turbine Engine Monitoring and Control [*ASMAP Electronics Ltd.*] [*Software package*] [*British*] (NCC)
TEMP	Technique for Econometric Modeling Program (BUR)
TEMP	Temperature
TEMP	Temporary
TEMPER	Technological, Economic, Military, and Political Evaluation Routine [*Computer-based simulation model*]
TEMPO	Technique for Extreme Point Optimization (BUR)
TEMPOS	Timed Environment Multipartitioned Operating System (NITA)
TEO	Telephone Equipment Order [*Telecommunications*] (TEL)
TEP	Table Editing Process
TEP	Tape Edit Processor [*Data processing*]
TEP	Terminal Error Program (NITA)
TEP	Transmitter Experiment Package
TEPIGEN	Television Picture Generator (MCD)
TEPOS	Test Program Operating System (NITA)
TER	Test Effectiveness Ratio [*Data processing*]
TER	Transmission Equivalent Resistance (IEEE)
TERC	Technical Education Research Centers, Inc. [*Cambridge, MA*] [*Research center*]
TERM	Terminal
TERM	Terminal Data Corp. [*NASDAQ symbol*] (NQ)
TERMINOQ	Banque de Terminologie de Quebec [*Terminology Bank of Quebec*] [*Information service*]
TERP	Terminal Equipment Replacement Program [*Electronic communications system*] [*Department of State*]
TERPS	Terminal Enquiry/Response Programing System [*British*] (DIT)
TERPS	Terminal Instrument Procedures
TES	Telemetry Evaluation Station
TES	Text Editing System (NITA)
TES	Time Encoded Speech [*Telecommunications*] (TEL)
TEST	Transamerica Electronic Scoring Technique [*Credit risk evaluation*]
TESTRAN	Test Translator [*Data processing*]
TET	Tetrode [*Electronics*]
TETRA	Terminal Tracking Telescope
TETRAC	Tension Truss Antenna Concept
TEU	Telemetry Equipment Unit
TEX	Automatic Teleprinter Exchange Service [*of Western Union Corp.*]
TEX	TELEX (CAH)
TEXTIR	Text Indexing and Retrieval [*Data processing*]
TF	Tape Feed (NITA)
TF	Telegram for Delivery by Telephone
TF	Telegraph Form
TF	Telephone (NATG)
TF	Test Frame [*Telecommunications*] (TEL)
TF	Transmitter Frequency
TF	Triple Frequency (DDI)
TF	Trunk Frame [*Telecommunications*] (TEL)
TFA	Transistor Feedback Amplifier
TFC	Transfer Function Computer
TFC	Transmission Fault Control [*Telecommunications*] (TEL)
TFC	Trigonometric Function Computer
TFCC	Tank Fire Combat Computer
TFG	Test File Generator [*Data processing*]
TFL	Telemetry Format Load (MCD)
TFLX	Termiflex Corp. [*NASDAQ symbol*] (NQ)
TFM	Tape File Management (NITA)
TFM	Transmit Frame Memory
TFM	Transmitter Frequency Multiplier
TFMS	Text and File Management System (NITA)
TFMS	Trunk and Facilities Maintenance System [*Telecommunications*] (TEL)
TFO	Telemedicine for Ontario [*Toronto, ON*] [*Telecommunications*] (TSSD)
TFPECTS	Thin-Film Personal Communications and Telemetry System (MCD)
TFR	Tape-to-File Recorder (DDI)
TFR	Television Film Recorder
TFR	Theoretical Final Route [*Telecommunications*] (TEL)
TFR	Transaction Formatting Routines (NITA)
TFR	Tunable Frequency Range (CIT)
TFS	Tape File Supervisor (NITA)
TFS	Telemetry Format Selection (NASA)

Computer & Telecommunications Acronyms

TFS	Traffic Flow Security [*Telecommunications*] (TEL)
TFS	Traffic Forecasting System [*Telecommunications*] (TEL)
TFS	Trunk Forecasting System [*Telecommunications*] (TEL)
TFT	Thin-Film Field-Effect Transistor
TFT	Thin-Film Transistor
TFTP	Television Facility Test Position [*Telecommunications*] (TEL)
TFU	Telecommunications Flying Unit [*British*]
TG	Task Group
TG	Telegram
TG	Telegraph
TG	Terminator Group (NITA)
TG	Tracking and Guidance
TGARQ	Telegraphic Approval Requested
TGC	Transmit Gain Control (MSA)
TGCS	Transportable Ground Communications Station
TGEEP	Terminal Guidance Environmental Effects Program (MCD)
TGF	Through Group Filter [*Telecommunications*] (TEL)
TGID	Trunk Group Identification [*Telecommunications*] (TEL)
TGL	Toggle
TGM	Telegram
TGM	Trunk Group Multiplexer [*Telecommunications*] (TEL)
TGN	Trunk Group Number [*Telecommunications*] (TEL)
TGS	Telemetry Ground Station
TGS	Telemetry Ground System (NASA)
TGS	Translator Generator System (IEEE)
TGURG	Telegraphic Authority Requested
TH	Transmission Header [*Data processing*] (IBMDP)
THAT	Twenty-Four-Hour Automatic Teller [*Trademark for self-service banking display panel*]
THD	Total Harmonic Distortion [*Electronics*]
Theor Comput Sci	Theoretical Computer Science [*A publication*]
Theoret Comput Sci	Theoretical Computer Science [*A publication*]
THF	Tremendously High Frequency [*Telecommunications*] (TEL)
THFR	Three-Conductor, Heat and Flame Resistant, Radio Cable
THH	Tierärztliche Hochschule Hannover [*Information retrieval*] (ODIN)
THI	Telehop, Incorporated [*Fresno, CA*] [*Telecommunications*] (TSSD)
THIR	Temperature-Humidity Infrared Radiometer
THL	Transhybrid Loss [*Telecommunications*] (TEL)
THOPS	Tape Handling Operational System [*Data processing*] (IEEE)
THOR	Tape-Handling Optional Routines [*Honeywell, Inc.*]
THOR	Thought Organizer [*Computer program produced by Fastware, Inc.*]
THOR	Transistorized High-Speed Operations Recorder
THP	Terminal Handling Processor (NITA)
THR	Transmittal Header Record [*Data processing*]
THR	Transmitter Holding Register (NITA)
THRU	I am connecting you to another switchboard [*Telecommunications*] (FAAC)
THUDD	Thermal Uplink Data Display [*Data processing*]
THz	Terahertz
TI	Terminal Interface (NITA)
TI	Texas Instruments, Inc.
TI	Title [*Online database field identifier*] [*Data processing*]
TI	Trade and Industry Index [*Information Access Corp.*] [*Information service*] (EISS)
TIAC	Texas Instruments Automatic Computer
TIC	Tape Identification Card
TIC	Tape Intersystem Connection [*Data processing*]
TIC	Technicon Integrator/Calculator
TIC	Technology and Innovation Council [*Information Industry Association*]
TIC	Telemetry Instruction Conference (KSC)
TIC	Telemetry Instrumentation Controller (SKY)
TIC	Terminal Identification Code (NITA)
TIC	Transfer-In Channel (CMD)
TIC	Tuned Integrated Circuit
TICCIT	Time-Shared Interactive Computer-Controlled Information Television [*System*] [*Mitre Corp.*] [*Brigham Young University*] [*1971*]
TICOM	Texas Institute for Computational Mechanics [*University of Texas at Austin*] [*Research center*] (RCD)
TICS	Teacher Interactive Computer System (IEEE)
TICS	Telecommunication Information Control System (NITA)
TICTAC	Time Compression Tactical Communications
TID	Technical Information Division [*Romar Consultants, Inc.*] [*Information service*] (EISS)
TID	Technology Information Division [*Canada Centre for Mineral and Energy Technology*] [*Information service*] (EISS)
TIDAR	Texas Instruments Digital Analog Readout
TIDDAC	Time in Deadband Digital Attitude Control
TIDES	Time-Division Electronics Switching System (KSC)
TIDF	Trunk Intermediate Distribution Frame [*Telecommunications*] (TEL)
TIDMA	Tape Interface Direct Memory Access (NITA)
TIDOS	Table and Item Documentation System
TIDY	Teletypewriter Integrated Display
TIE	Technology Information Exchange [*of Public Technology, Inc.*]
TIE	Terminal Interface Equipment (NITA)
TIE	Tie Communications [*American Stock Exchange symbol*]
TIE	Time Interval Error [*Telecommunications*] (TEL)
TIES	Total Information for Educational Systems [*Saint Paul, MN*] (BUR)
TIES	Total Integrated Engineering System
TIF	Tape Inventory File (IEEE)
TIF	Telephone Interference Factor (DEN)
TIF	Terminal Independent Format (NITA)
TIG	Telegram Identification Group [*Telecommunications*] (TEL)
TIG	Teletype Input Generator
TIGER	Total Information Gathering and Executive Reporting [*International Computers Ltd.*] (NITA)
TIGS	Terminal Independent Graphics System (NITA)
TIH	Trunk Interface Handler (NITA)
TII	Texas Instruments, Incorporated
TIIPS	Technically Improved Interference Prediction System (IEEE)
TIM	Table Input to Memory (NITA)
TIM	Technical Information on Microfilm [*British*] (DIT)
TIM	Topic Indexing Matrix
TIM	Transient Intermodulation [*Distortion*]
TIM	Transistor Information Microfile
TIM	Trigger Inverter Module (VIT)
TI-MIX	Texas Instruments Mini/Microcomputer Information Exchange [*Austin, TX*] (EANO)
TIMM	Thermionic Integrated Micromodule
TIMS	[*The*] Institute of Management Sciences
TIMS	Transmission Impairment Measuring Set [*Telecommunications*] (TEL)
TIN	Temperature Independent [*Ferrite computer memory core*]
TINDX	Texas Instruments, Inc. Index Access Method (NITA)
TI-NET	Transparent Intelligent Network (NITA)
TINET	Travel Industry Network, Inc. [*Winter Springs, FL*] [*Telecommunications*] (TSSD)
TINKER	Timber Information Keyword Retrieval [*Timber Research and Development Association*] [*Information service*] (EISS)
TIO	Test Input/Output [*Data processing*] (NITA)
TIOC	Terminal Input/Output Coordinator [*Data processing*] (IBMDP)
TIOM	Terminal Input/Output Module [*Data processing*] (TUT)
TIOT	Task Input/Output Table [*Data processing*] (BUR)
TIOWQ	Terminal Input/Output Wait Queue [*Data processing*] (NITA)
TIP	Technical Information Processing (IEEE)
TIP	TELENET Interface Processor (NITA)
TIP	Teletype Input Processing
TIP	Terminal Impact Prediction (SKY)
TIP	Terminal Interface Package [*Data processing*]
TIP	Total Information Processing (BUR)
TIP	Tracking Impact Prediction [*of satellites*]
TIP	Transaction Interface Package [*Sperry UNIVAC*] [*Data processing*]
TIP	Transaction Interface Processor (NITA)
TIP	Transit Improvement Program [*Satellite*] (MCD)
TIP	Transponder Interrogator Processor
TIPACS	Texas Instruments Planning and Control System
TIPE	Transponder, Interrogator, Pinger, and Echo Sounder
TIPI	Transportable Automated Intelligence Processing and Interpretation System (MCD)
TIPL	Teach Information Processing Language
TIPMG	[*The*] International Project Management Group, Inc. [*Glyndon, MD*] [*Telecommunications*] (TSSD)
TIPS	Technical Information Processing System [*Rockwell International Corp.*] (AFM)
TIPS	Technical Information for Product Safety [*Consumer Product Safety Commission*] (EISS)
TIPS	Text Information Processing System (NITA)
TIPTOP	Tape Input - Tape Output [*Honeywell, Inc.*] [*Data processing*]
TIQ	Task Input Queue [*Data processing*] (IBMDP)
TIR	Target Instruction Register (NITA)
TIRAS	Technical Information Retrieval and Analysis System (CAAL)
TIRKS	Trunks Integrated Record Keeping System [*Bell System*]
TIS	Taft Information System [*Provides information on private foundations*] (EISS)
TIS	Technical Information Service (EISS)
TIS	Technical Information Services [*Acurex Corp.*] (EISS)
TIS	Technology Information System [*Lawrence Livermore National Laboratory*] (EISS)
TIS	Telemetry Input System (CIT)
TIS	Terminal Interface Subsystem [*Telecommunications*] (TEL)
TIS	Test Interface Summary (MCD)
TIS	Total Information System [*Data processing*] (CGC)
TISAP	Totalized Interface Subroutine and Post Processor [*Data processing*] (BUR)
TISL	Telecommunications and Information Systems Laboratory [*University of Kansas*] [*Research center*] (RCD)
TIT	Test Item Taker (NITA)
TITUS	Textile Information Treatment Users' Service [*French Textile Institute*] [*Bibliographic database*] [*Information service*] (EISS)
TIU	Telecommunications International Union [*Hamden, CT*] [*Independent labor union*] (EANO)
TIU	Terminal Interface Unit [*Bell System*]
TJ	Telephone Jack (DEN)
TJB	Time-Sharing Job Control Block [*Data processing*] (IBMDP)
TJID	Terminal Job Identification (BUR)
TJR	Trunk and Junction Routing [*Telecommunications*] (TEL)
TJS	Terminal Junction System (DDI)

Computer & Telecommunications Acronyms

TK	Track (DDI)
TK	Trunk Equipment [*Telecommunications*] (TEL)
TKO	Trunk Offer [*Telecommunications*] (TEL)
T/L	Talk/Listen (NASA)
TL	Tape Library (BUR)
TL	Tie Line [*Communication channel*]
TL	Transaction Language (NITA)
TL	Transmission Level [*or Line*]
TL	Transmitter Location
T²L	Transistor-Transistor Logic [*Also, TTL*]
TLA	Transmission Line Adapter [*or Assembly*]
TLAB	Tellabs [*NASDAQ symbol*] (NQ)
TLAB	Translation Lookaside Buffer [*Data processing*] (CMD)
TLB	Translation Lookaside Buffer [*Data processing*] (BUR)
TLC	[*The*] Learning Channel [*Cable-television system*]
TLC	Tangent Latitude Computer
TLC	Task Level Controller (NITA)
TLC	Telecommand (NASA)
TLC	Touch and Learn Computer
TLCA	Tangent Latitude Computer Amplifier
TLCC	Thin-Line Communications Connectivity
TLCT	Total Life Cycle Time (NITA)
TLEICS	Treasury Law Enforcement Information and Communications System
TLF	Trunk Link Frame [*Telecommunications*] (TEL)
TLG	Telegraph
TLI	Telephone Line Interface (IEEE)
TLK	Talking [*Telecommunications*] (TEL)
TLL	Television LASER Link
TLM	Telemeter [*or Telemetry*]
TLMB	Telemetry Data Buffer (CIT)
TLMG	Telemetering
TLMS	Tape Library Management System (NITA)
TLMY	Telemetry (MSA)
TLN	Transmittal Locator Number [*Data processing*]
TLN	Trunk Line Network (NITA)
TLP	Telegraph Line Pair (BUR)
TLP	Telephone Line Patch (NITA)
TLP	Total Language Processor [*Data processing*] (IEEE)
TLP	Transmission Level Point [*Telecommunications*]
0TLP	Zero Transmission Level Point (IEEE)
TLR	Toll Line Release
TLS	Tape Librarian System (NITA)
TLS	Technical Library Service (EISS)
TLS	Telemetry Listing Submodule
TLS	Total Logic Solution
TLSA	Transparent Line Sharing Adapter (NITA)
TLT	Teleprinter Load Tables (KSC)
TLTK	Teletek, Inc. [*NASDAQ symbol*] (NQ)
TLTP	Trunk Line Test Panel [*Telecommunications*] (TEL)
TLU	Table Look Up [*Data processing*]
TLU	Terminal Logic Unit [*Telecommunications*] (TEL)
TLU	Threshold Logic Unit
TLX	TELEX [*Automated Teletypewriter Exchange Service*] [*Western Union Corp.*]
TLX	Trans-Lux Corp. [*American Stock Exchange symbol*]
TLXN	Telxon Corp. [*NASDAQ symbol*] (NQ)
TM	Tape Mark [*Data processing*] (BUR)
TM	Telegramme Multiple [*Telegram with Multiple Addresses*] [*French*]
TM	Telemetry
TM	Test Mode (NITA)
TM	Thematic Mapper [*Satellite technology*]
T & M	Time and Materials
TM	Time Modulation
TM	Transmission Matrix (IEEE)
TM	Transverse Magnetic
TM	Travelwriter Marketletter [*New York, NY*] [*Information service*] (EISS)
TMA	Telecommunications Managers Association [*Orpington, England*] (TSSD)
TMA	Time-Modulated Antenna
TMAB	Telecommunications Managers Association - Belgium [*Brussels*] (TSSD)
TMA BITS	TMA [*Tobacco Merchants Association*] Bibliographic Index to the Tobacco Scene [*Database*] (CUAD)
TMAC	Telecommunication Management and Control [*AT & T*]
TMAX	Maximum Time [*Telecommunications*] (TEL)
TMC	[*The*] Movie Channel [*Cable-television system*]
TMC	Tape Management Catalog (NITA)
TMC	Telamarketing Communications, Inc. [*Louisville, KY*] [*Telecommunications*] (TSSD)
TMC	Telecommunications Management Corporation [*Dedham, MA*] (TSSD)
TMC	Telecommunications Marketing Corporation [*Bay Shore, NY*] (TSSD)
TMC	Transmission Maintenance Center [*Telecommunications*] (TEL)
TMCC	Time-Multiplexer Communications Channels
TMCI	Telemetering Control Indicator (VIT)
TMCOMP	Telemetry Computation
TMCS	Toshiba Minicomputer Complex System (NITA)
TMD	Telemetered Data
TMDT	Total Mean Downtime
TME	Test Maintenance Equipment [*Data processing*]
TMF	Telemetry Module Facility
TMF	Trunk Maintenance Files [*Telecommunications*] (TEL)
TMI	[*The*] Mortgage Index, Inc. [*Remote Computing Corp.*] [*Information service*] (EISS)
TMI	Telecommunications Management, Incorporated [*Oakbrook, IL*] [*Telecommunications*] (TSSD)
TMI	Transaction Management, Incorporated [*Lexington, MA*] [*Hardware manufacturer*] (DASO)
TMIC	Toxic Materials Information Center [*Oak Ridge National Laboratory*] (EISS)
TMIN	Minimum Time [*Telecommunications*] (TEL)
TML	Tandem Matching Loss [*Telecommunications*] (TEL)
TML	Terminal
TML	Terrestrial Microwave Link
TMM	Test Message Monitor
TMO	Telegraph Money Order
TMP	Teleprinter Message Pool (SKY)
TMP	Temperature (BUR)
TMP	Terminal Monitor Program [*Data processing*] (BUR)
TMP	Terminal Panel (NASA)
TMP	Test Maintenance Panel [*Data processing*]
TMPRLY	Temporarily (MDG)
TMPROC	Telemetry Processing
TMPS	Test Maintenance Panel Subassembly [*Data processing*]
TMR	Telemanagement Resources, Inc. [*Charlotte, NC*] [*Telecommunications*] (TSSD)
TMR	Triple Modular Redundancy [*Data processing*]
TMRAO	Table Mountain Radio Astronomy Observatory (CIT)
TMRS	Traffic Measuring and Recording System [*Telecommunications*] (TEL)
TMS	[*The*] Manufacturing System [*Burroughs Machines Ltd.*] [*Software package*] [*British*] (NCC)
TMS	Tape Management System (MCD)
TMS	Telecommunications Message Switcher
TMS	Telemetry Modulation System
TMS	Telemetry Multiplex System (SKY)
TMS	Time Multiplexed Switching [*Telecommunications*]
TMS	Time-Shared Monitor System [*Data processing*] (IEEE)
TMS	Transaction Management System (BUR)
TMS	Transmission Measuring Set [*Bell Laboratories*]
TMS	Transportation Management Services [*Salt Lake City, UT*] [*Software manufacturer*] (DASOS)
TMSA	Technical Marketing Society of America (EANO)
TMT	Temperature (MDG)
TMT	Terminal Monitor Program [*Data processing*] (MDG)
TMT	Testing Methods and Techniques [*Telecommunications*] (TEL)
TMTC	Thru-Mode [*or Tri-Mode*] Tape Converter
TMTD	Transmitted (FAAC)
TMTG	Transmitting (FAAC)
TMTN	Transmission (FAAC)
TMTNO	No Transmitting Capability (FAAC)
TMTR	Transmitter
TMTS	Transmits (FAAC)
TMU	Test Maintenance Unit [*Data processing*]
TMU	Transmission Message Unit
TMUS	Temporarily Mounted User Set [*Data processing*]
TMVS	Times Mirror Videotex Services, Inc. [*Information service*] (EISS)
TMW	Thermal Megawatt [*Also, Mwt*]
TMW	Transverse Magnetic Wave [*Radio*]
TMX	Telemeter Transmitter
TN	Telephone (NATG)
TN	Telephone Number
TN	Terminal Node (NITA)
TN	Twisted Nematic [*Telecommunications*] (TEL)
TNA	Telocator Network of America [*Formerly,, National Mobile Radio System (1977)*] [*Washington, DC*] [*Telecommunications*] [*An association*] (TSSD)
TNC	Terminal Network Controller (NITA)
TNC	Track Navigation Computer
TNC	Transport Network Controller (NITA)
TNDC	Thai National Documentation Center (EISS)
TNDM	Tandem Computers [*NASDAQ symbol*] (NQ)
TNDS	Total Network Data System [*Bell System*]
TNF	Third Normal Form [*Databases*] (NITA)
TNI	[*The*] Networking Institute [*Commercial firm*] (EANO)
TNL	Technical Newsletter (TUT)
TNL	Terminal Net Loss
TNN	[*The*] Nashville Network [*Cable-television system*]
TNOP	Total Network Operations Plan [*Telecommunications*] (TEL)
TNS	[*The*] National Switchboard [*Phoenix, AZ*] [*Telecommunications*] (TSSD)
TNS	Transaction Network Service [*AT & T*]
TNT	Teleconference Network of Texas [*University of Texas*] [*San Antonio*] [*Telecommunications*] (TSSD)
TNTDL	Tabulated Numerical Technical Data List
TNX	Thanks [*Communications operator's procedural remark*]
TO	Telegraph Office
TO	Telephone Office
TO	Time-Out
TO	Transmitter Oscillator
TOADS	Terminal-Oriented Administrative Data System (NITA)
TOB	Telemetry Output Buffer [*Data processing*]

Computer & Telecommunications Acronyms

TOC	Table of Coincidences [*Telecommunications*] (TEL)
TOC	Task-Oriented Costing [*Telecommunications*] (TEL)
TOC	Television Operating Center
TOC	To Be Continued, Circuit Time Permitting (FAAC)
TOC	Turn-On Command (KSC)
TOCAP	Terminal Oriented Control Applications Program
TOCC	Technical and Operations Control Center [*INTELSAT*] (CBSS)
TOCED	Table of Contents Editor Processor [*Data processing*]
TOCM	Tocom, Inc. [*NASDAQ symbol*] (NQ)
TOCS	Terminal-Oriented Computer System (NITA)
TOCS	Textile Operational Control System [*Data processing*]
TOD	Time of Day
TODARS	Terminal Oriented Data Analysis and Retrieval System [*National Bureau of Standards*]
TODAS	Typewriter-Oriented Documentation-Aid System
TODS	Test-Oriented Disk System (IEEE)
TODS	Transactions on Database Systems
TOF	Tone Off [*Telecommunications*] (TEL)
TOG	Toggle
TOJ	Track on Jamming
TOL	Test-Oriented Language [*Data processing*]
TOLAR	Terminal On-Line Availability Reporting (NITA)
TOLD	Telecoms On-Line Data System [*Telecommunications*] (TEL)
TOLIP	Trajectory Optimization and Linearized Pitch [*Computer program*]
TOLR	Toll Restricted [*Telecommunications*] (TEL)
TOLR	Transmitting Objective Loudness Rating [*of telephone connections*] (IEEE)
TOLTEP	Teleprocessing On-Line Test Executive Program [*IBM Corp.*] (NITA)
TOLTS	Total On-Line Testing System [*Honeywell, Inc.*] (NITA)
TOMCAT	Telemetry On-Line Monitoring Compression and Transmission
TOMS	Transactions on Mathematical Software
TON	Tone On [*Telecommunications*] (TEL)
TONLAR	Tone-Operated Net Loss Adjuster Receiving
TOO	Time of Origin [*Communications*]
TOOL	Test-Oriented Operated Language [*Programing language*] [*Data processing*]
TOP	Technical and Office Protocol [*Boeing, MAP*]
TOPES	Telephone Office Planning and Engineering System [*Telecommunications*] (TEL)
TOPICS	Total On-Line Program and Information Control System [*Japan*]
TOPLAS	Transactions on Programing Languages and Systems (MCD)
TOPP	Terminal-Operated Production Program (BUR)
TOPS	Telemetry On-Line Processing System [*Data processing*]
TOPS	Telephone Order Processing System (OA)
TOPS	Teleregister Omni Processing and Switching [*Data processing*]
TOPS	Teletype Optical Projection System (IEEE)
TOPS	Testing and Operating System (CAH)
TOPS	Time-Sharing Operating System (NITA)
TOPS	Total Operations Processing System [*Data processing*] (CGC)
TOPS	Traffic Operator Position System [*Telecommunications*] (TEL)
TOPS	Transcendental Network [*Centram Systems West, Inc.*] [*Berkeley, CA*] [*Telecommunications*] (TSSD)
TOPTS	Test-Oriented Paper-Tape System [*Data processing*] (IEEE)
TOR	Telegraph on Radio [*Telecommunications*] (TEL)
TORC	Traffic Overload Reroute Control
TORS	Trade Opportunity Referral Service [*Department of Agriculture*] [*Information service*] (EISS)
TOS	Taken Out of Service [*Telecommunications*] (TEL)
TOS	Tape Operating System [*IBM Corp.*] [*Data processing*] (CGC)
TOS	Temporarily Out of Service (DEN)
TOS	Terminal-Oriented Software [*Data processing*] (IEEE)
TOS	Terminal-Oriented System [*Data processing*] (IEEE)
TOS	Time-Ordered System (MCD)
TOS	Top of Stack [*Data processing*] (NITA)
TOS	Tramiel Operating System
TOSBAC	Toshiba Scientific and Business Automatic Computer [*Toshiba Corp.*]
TOSCA	Total On-Line Searching and Cataloging Activities [*Information service*]
TOSD	Telephone Operations and Standards Division [*Rural Electrification Administration*] [*Telecommunications*] (TEL)
TOSHIBA	Tokyo Shibaura Electric Co. [*Computer manufacturer*] [*Japanese*] (CAH)
TOSL	Terminal-Oriented Service Language (NITA)
TOSS	Television Ordnance Scoring System (MCD)
TOSS	Terminal-Oriented Support System (NITA)
TOSSA	Transient or Steady-State Analysis [*Data processing*]
TOT	Total
TOT	Transfer of Technology [*Telecommunications*] (TEL)
TOTE	Teleprocessing On-Line Test Executive [*Data processing*] (IBMDP)
TOTRAD	Tape Output Test Rack Autonetics Diode
TOTS	Total Operating Traffic System [*Bell System*]
TOV	Telemetering Oscillator Voltage (VIT)
TOXBACK	TOXLINE Back-File [*Information retrieval*] (ODIN)
TOXICON	Toxicology Information Conversational On-Line Network [*National Library of Medicine*] [*Later, TOXLINE*]
TOXLINE	Toxicology On-Line [*National Library of Medicine*] [*Bethesda, MD*] [*Bibliographic database*]
TOYCOM	[*A*] programing language [*1971*] (CSR)
TP	Tape (BUR)
TP	Telemetry Processor
TP	Telephone (CET)
TP	Teleprinter
TP	Teleprocessing [*Data processing*] (MCD)
TP	Terminal Pole [*Telecommunications*] (TEL)
TP	Terminal Processor (NITA)
TP	Test Position
TP	Text Processor (NITA)
TP	Time Pulse
TP	Toll Point [*Telecommunications*] (TEL)
TP	Toll Prefix [*Telecommunications*] (TEL)
TP	Transaction Processing (NITA)
TP	Triple Pole [*Switch*]
TPA	Telephone Pioneers of America [*New York, NY*]
TPA	Toll Pulse Accepter [*Telecommunications*] (TEL)
TPA	Transient Program Area (DEEC)
TPAM	Teleprocessing Access Method (NITA)
TPAT	Test Point Algorithm Technique (MCD)
TPB	Tape Playback BIT [*Binary Digit*] [*Data processing*]
TPB	Tape Block (CIT)
TPC	Telecommunications Planning Committee [*Civil Defense*]
TPC	Telephone Pickup Coil
TPC	Transistor Photo Control
TPC	Twisted Pair Cable
TPCB	[*The*] Personal Computer Book
TPCO	Teleprinter Coordinator (SKY)
TPD	Terminal Protective Device (MSA)
TPD	Thermoplastic Photoconductor Device (NITA)
TPDT	Triple-Pole, Double-Throw [*Switch*]
TPESP	Technical Panel on the Earth Satellite Program
TPF	Temporary Program File [*Data processing*]
TPF	Time Prism Filter [*Telecommunications*] (TEL)
TPFI	Terminal Pin Fault Insertion (NITA)
TPFW	Three-Phase Full Wave
TPG	Telecommunication Program Generator (NITA)
TPG	Teletype Preamble Generator (CIT)
TPHO	Telephotograph
TPHW	Three-Phase Half Wave
TPI	Tracks per Inch [*Magnetic storage devices*] [*Data processing*] (TUT)
TPI	Transmission Performance Index [*Telecommunications*] (TEL)
TPL	Table Producing Language [*1971*] [*Data processing*] (EISS)
TPL	Terminal per Line [*Telecommunications*]
TPL	Terminal Processing Language (NITA)
TPL	Test Point Logic
TPL	Toll Pole Line [*Telecommunications*] (TEL)
TPM	Tape Processing Machine
TPM	Technical Performance Measurement
TPM	Telemetry Processor Module
TPMM	Teleprocessing Multiplexer Module (NITA)
TP & N	Triple Pole and Neutral [*Switch*]
TPNS	Teleprocessing Network Simulator
TPP	Telephony Preprocessor [*Telecommunications*] (TEL)
TPP	Teletype Page Printer
TPPS	Tape Post-Processing System (SKY)
TPR	Tape Programed Row [*Data scanner*]
TPR	Teleprinter
TPR	Transmitter Power Rating
TPS	Tape Processing System (CMD)
TPS	Telecommunications Programing System (OA)
TPS	Telemation Program Services
TPS	Terminal Polling System (NITA)
TPS	Terminals per Station [*Telecommunications*]
TPS	Transaction Processing System (NITA)
TPSC	Test Planning and Status Checker [*Data processing*]
TPSF	Telephonie sans Fil [*Wireless telephony*]
TPST	Triple-Pole, Single-Throw [*Switch*]
TPT	Teleprinter Planning Table (SKY)
TPTG	Tuned Plate Tuned Grid [*Electronic tube*]
TPU	Task Processing Unit (NITA)
TPU	Telecommunications Processing Unit (NITA)
TPU	Trunk Processing Unit [*Bell System*]
TPUC	Telephone Pickup Coil
TPUG	Toronto PET Users Group [*Canada*]
TQC	Technical Quality Control [*Telecommunications*] (TEL)
TQE	Timer Queue Element (NITA)
TQP	Transistor Qualification Program
TQT	Transistor Qualification Test
TQTP	Transistor Qualification Test Program
TR	Tape Register
TR	Tape Resident (NITA)
TR	Telegraphe Restant [*Telegram to Be Called for at a Telegraph Office*] [*French*]
TR	Test Run
T & R	Testing and Regulating Department [*Especially, in a wire communications maintenance division*]
TR	Track
TR	Traffic Route [*Telecommunications*] (TEL)
T/R	Transceiver
TR	Translation Register (NITA)
TR	Transmission Report [*Telecommunications*] (TEL)
T-R	Transmit-Receive (CIT)
TR	Transmitter (CDH)

TR .... Trouble Report
TRAC .... Telecommunications Research and Action Center [*Washington, DC*] [*Information service*] [*Telecommunications*]   (TSSD)
TRAC .... Text Reckoning and Compiling [*Data processing*]
TRACAP ..... Transient Circuit Analysis Program [*Data processing*]
TRACE .... Teleprocessing Recording for Analysis by the Customer   (IEEE)
TRACE .... Time-Shared Routines for Analysis, Classification, and Evaluation   (DIT)
TRACE .... Tolls Recording and Computing Equipment   (IEEE)
TRACE .... Toronto Region Aggregation of Computer Enthusiasts [*Canada*]
TRAF .... Traffic
TRAMP .... Test Retrieval and Memory Print [*Data processing*]
TRAMP .... Time-Shared Relational Associative Memory Program [*Data processing*]   (IEEE)
TRAMPS ..... Traffic Measure and Path Search [*Telecommunications*]   (TEL)
TRAN .... Transmit
TRANS .... Transistor
TRANSAC ... Transistorized Automatic Computer
Trans Am Inst Electr Eng Part 1 ... Transactions. American Institute of Electrical Engineers. Part 1. Communication and Electronics [*A publication*]
TRANSCOM ... Transportable Communications
TRANSEC ... Transmission Security [*Communications*]
TRANSFAX ... Facsimile Transmission [*Telecommunications*]
TRANSIM ..... Transit Simplified Receiver [*Satellite navigation system*]
Trans Inst Electron & Commun Eng Jap A ... Transactions. Institute of Electronics and Communication Engineers of Japan. Part A [*A publication*]
Trans Inst Electron Commun Eng Jap Sect J Part D ... Transactions. Institute of Electronics and Communication Engineers of Japan. Section J [*Japanese*] Part D [*A publication*]
Trans Inst Electron Commun Eng Jpn Part B ... Transactions. Institute of Electronics and Communication Engineers of Japan. Part B [*A publication*]
Trans Inst Electron and Commun Eng Jpn Part B ... Transactions. Institute of Electronics and Communication Engineers of Japan. Part B [*A publication*]
Trans Inst Electron and Commun Eng Jpn Part C ... Transactions. Institute of Electronics and Communication Engineers of Japan. Part C [*A publication*]
TRANSIS ..... Transportation Safety Information System [*Department of Transportation*]   (EISS)
TRANSLANG ... Translator Language [*Data processing*]
TRANSMON ... Transmission
TRANSMTG ... Transmitting
TRANSPLAN ... Transaction Network Service Planning Model [*Telecommunications*]   (TEL)
TRAPATT ..... Trapped Plasma Avalanche Triggered Transit [*Bell Laboratories*]
TRAPV .... Trap on Overflow BIT [*Binary Digit*] Set [*Data processing*]
TRAVIS .... Traffic Retrieval Analysis Validation and Information System [*Telecommunications*]   (TEL)
TRB .... Technical Reference Branch [*Department of Transportation*]   (EISS)
TRC .... Tape Record Coordinator [*Data processing*]   (CGC)
TRC .... Telemetry and Remote Control   (IEEE)
TRC .... Transmit/Receive Control Unit   (NITA)
TRC .... Transverse Redundancy Check [*Data processing*]   (IBMDP)
TRC-AS ...... Transmit/Receive Control Unit-Asynchronous Start/Stop   (NITA)
TRCC .... T-Carrier Restoration Control Center [*Bell System*]
TRC-SC ...... Transmit/Receive Control Unit-Synchronous Character   (NITA)
TRC-SF .... Transmit/Receive Control Unit-Synchronous Framing   (NITA)
TRCVR .... Transceiver   (CET)
TRDC .... Tourism Reference and Data Centre [*Canada*] [*Information service*]   (EISS)
TRE .... Telecommunications Research Establishment [*British*]
TRECOMS ... Treasury Computer Systems
TREET .... [A] programing language   (CSR)
TREM .... Tape Reader Emulator Module   (NITA)
TRESNET ... Trent Resource Sharing Network [*Ontario Library Service Trent*] [*Richmond Hill, ON*] [*Telecommunications*]   (TSSD)
TRF .... Tuned Radio Frequency
TRG .... Telecommunications Research Group [*Culver City, CA*] [*Telecommunications*]   (TSSD)
T/R & G .... Transmit, Receive, and Guard   (MSA)
TRI .... Telecomputer Research, Incorporated [*Bala Cynwyd, PA*] [*Information service*] [*Telecommunications*]   (TSSD)
TRI .... Transponder Receiver Isolation
TRIA .... Telemetry Range Instrumentation Aircraft
TRIAL.......... Technique to Retrieve Information from Abstracts of Literature [*Data processing*]
TRIB .... Transfer Rate of Information BITS [*Binary Digits*] [*Dial telephone network*] [*American National Standards Institute*]
TRIDAC ...... Three-Dimensional Analog Computer [*British*]   (MCD)
TRIM .... Tailored Retrieval and Information Management   (NITA)
TRIMMS...... Telecom Canada Remote Interface Monitoring and Management System
TRIP .... Transformation and Identification Program [*Commercial & Industrial Development Bureau*] [*Software package*] [*British*]   (NCC)
TRIPS.......... Transportation Planning Suite [*MVA Systematica*] [*Software package*] [*British*]   (NCC)
TRIS .... Transportation Research Information Services [*Transportation Research Board*] [*Bibliographic database*]

TRK .... Track
TRL .... Transistor Resistor Logic
TRL .... Trunk Register Link [*Telecommunications*]   (TEL)
TRM .... Terminal Response Monitor   (NITA)
TRM .... Test Request Message [*Data processing*]
TRML .... Terminal   (AFM)
TRMS .... Technical Requirements Management System
TRN .... Transmit   (BUR)
TRNSMT .... Transmitter
TRO............. Tropical [*Broadcasting antenna*]
TROL .... Tapeless Rotorless On-Line Cryptographic Equipment   (NATG)
TROLL .... [A] programing language [*1966*]   (CSR)
TROO.......... Transponder On-Off
TROPAG ..... Tropical Agriculture [*Royal Tropical Institute*] [*Bibliographic database*] [*Dutch*]   (OBD)
TROS .... Tape Resident Operating System [*Data processing*]   (IEEE)
TROS .... Transformer Read Only Storage   (NITA)
TRP .... Television Remote Pickup
TRQ .... Task Ready Queue   (NITA)
TRR.............. Tape Read Register   (NITA)
TRS .... Terrestrial Radio System
TRS .... Tetrahedral Research Satellite
TRS .... Ticket Reservation Systems, Inc.
TRS .... Toll Room Switch [*Telecommunications*]   (TEL)
TRSC .... Triad Systems Corporation [*NASDAQ symbol*]   (NQ)
TRT .... Traffic Route Testing [*Telecommunications*]   (TEL)
TRT .... Tuned Receiver Tuner
TRTL .... Transistor-Resistor-Transistor Logic   (IEEE)
TRU .... Transformer-Rectifier Unit   (MCD)
TRU .... Transmit-Receive Unit
TRUMP .... Teller Register Unit Monitoring Program   (IEEE)
TRVM .... Transistorized Voltmeter
TRW .... TRW, Inc. [*Formerly, Thompson Ramo Wooldridge, Inc.*] [*NYSE symbol*]
TRX .... Triplex
TS .... Telecommunications System   (SKY)
TS .... Telegraph System   (MSA)
TS .... Television, Sound Channel
TS .... Time Sharing [*Data processing*]   (CGC)
TS .... Time Slot [*Telecommunications*]   (TEL)
TS .... Time Switch   (MSA)
TS .... Timing Selector
TS .... Timing System   (MCD)
TS .... Toll Switching [*Trunk*] [*Telecommunications*]   (TEL)
TS .... Transmission Set
TS .... Transmitter Station
TSA............. Telegraph System Analyzer
TSA............. Time Slot Access   (NITA)
TSA............. Transition State Analog
TSA............. Two-Step Antenna
TSAC........... Time Slot Assignment Circuit [*Telecommunications*]   (TEL)
TSAM .... Time Series Analysis and Modeling [*Software*]   (NITA)
TSAR .... Telemetry System Application Requirements   (VIT)
TSAU .... Time Slot Access Unit [*Telecommunications*]   (TEL)
TSB............. Terminal Status Block [*Data processing*]   (IBMDP)
TSB............. Twin Sideband
TSC............. Telephone Software Connection, Inc.
TSC............. TeleSciences, Inc. [*American Stock Exchange symbol*]
TSC............. Television Scan Converter
TSC............. Test Set Computer
TSC............. Three-State Control [*Data processing*]
TSC............. Time Sharing Control Task [*Data processing*]   (BUR)
TSC............. Totally Self-Checking   (NITA)
TSC............. Transit Switching Center [*Telecommunications*]   (TEL)
TSC............. Transmitter Start Code [*Bell System*]
TSCAPP ..... Toxic Substances Control Act Plant and Production Data [*Environmental Protection Agency*] [*Database*]   (FDB)
TSCATS ..... Toxic Substances Control Act Test Submissions [*Environmental Protection Agency*] [*Database*]   (CUAD)
TSCC........... Telemetry Standards Coordination Committee
TSCLT .... Transportable Satellite Communications Link Terminal
TSCOM .... TS Communications [*Springfield, IL*] [*Telecommunications*]   (TSSD)
TSCT .... Transportable Satellite Communications Terminal
TSDM.......... Time-Shared Data Management [*System*] [*Data processing*]   (IEEE)
TSDOS........ Time-Shared Disk Operating System [*Data processing*]   (IEEE)
TSE .... Terminal Source Editor   (NITA)
TSES........... Transportable Satellite Earth Station
TSF .... Telegraphie sans Fil [*Wireless Telegraphy*] [*French*]
TSF .... Telephone Service Fitting
TSF .... Ten-Statement FORTRAN [*Data processing*]   (IEEE)
TSF .... Thin Solid Films   (IEEE)
TSFS........... Trunk Servicing Forecasting System [*Telecommunications*]   (TEL)
TSG............. Timeslot Generator [*Telecommunications*]   (TEL)
TSI .... Threshold Signal-to-Interference Ratio   (IEEE)
TSI .... Timeslot Interchange [*Telecommunications*]   (TEL)
TSID........... Track Sector Identification   (NITA)
TSII............. TSI, Incorporated [*NASDAQ symbol*]   (NQ)
TSIMS......... Telemetry Simulation Submodule
TSIU............ Telephone System Interface Unit   (NITA)

Computer & Telecommunications Acronyms

Acronym	Expansion
TSK	Time Shift Keying
TSL	Test Set Logic
TSL	Test Source Library (NITA)
TSL	Total Service Life [*Telecommunications*] (TEL)
TSL	Tristate Logic [*Electronics*]
TSLD	Troubleshooting Logic Diagram (NASA)
TSM	Terminal Support Module (NITA)
TSM	Time-Shared Monitor System [*Data processing*] (IEEE)
TSMO	TACSATCOM [*Tactical Satellite Communications*] Management Office
TSMOK	Transmitting Capability Returned to Service (FAAC)
TSMT	Transmit (CDH)
TSN	[*The*] Sports Network [*Huntingdon Valley, PA*] [*Cable-television system*] [*Information service*] (EISS)
TSN	Tape Serial Number [*Data processing*]
TSN	Temporary Sort Number [*Data processing*]
TSO	Telecommunications Service Order [*Telecommunications*] (TEL)
TSO	Telephone Service Observation [*Telecommunications*] (TEL)
TSO	Time-Sharing Option [*Data processing*]
TSODB	Time Series Oriented Database (NITA)
TSORT	Transmission System Optimum Relief Tool [*Telecommunications*] (TEL)
TSOS	Time-Sharing Operating System [*Data processing*] (IEEE)
TSP	Telemetry Simulation Program (CIT)
TSP	Total Systems Performance [*MODCOMP*] (NITA)
TSP	Traffic Service Position [*Telephone*]
TSPAK	Time Series Package [*Bell System*]
TSPS	Time-Sharing Programing System [*Data processing*] (IEEE)
TSPS	Traffic Service Position System [*Telecommunications*]
TSPSCAP	Traffic Service Position System Real-Time Capacity Program [*Telecommunications*] (TEL)
TSR	Telecommunications Service Request (CET)
TSR	Temporary Storage Register (NITA)
TSR	Time Sharing Resources, Inc. [*Information service*] (EISS)
TSR	Time Status Register
TSR	Tokyo Shoko Research Ltd. [*Database producer*] (CUAD)
TSRP	Toll Service Results Plan [*Bell System*]
TSS	Telecommunication Switching System
TSS	Teletype Switching System [*or Subsystem*] (CIT)
TSS	Terminal Security System [*Data processing*]
TSS	Terminal Send Side (NITA)
TSS	Time-Sharing System [*Data processing*]
TSS	Toll Switching System [*Telecommunications*] (TEL)
TSS	Transmission Surveillance System [*Bell System*]
TSS	Trunk Servicing System [*Bell System*]
TSSA	Telemetry Subcarrier Spectrum Analyzer
TSSA	Test Scorer and Statistical Analyzer [*Data processing*]
TSS-C	Transmission Surveillance System - Cable [*Telecommunications*] (TEL)
TSSD	Telecommunications Systems and Services Directory [*A publication*]
TSSST	Time-Space-Space-Space-Time [*Telecommunications*] (TEL)
TST	Telemetry Simulation Terminal (CIT)
TST	Television Signal Tracer (DEN)
TST	Test
TST	Time-Sharing Terminals, Inc.
TST	Time-Space-Time [*Digital switching*] [*Telecommunications*] (TEL)
TST	Total Surface Tested (TUT)
TST	Transaction Step Task (NITA)
TSTA	Transmission, Signaling, and Test Access
TSTPAC	Transmission and Signaling Test Plan and Analysis Concept [*Telecommunications*] (TEL)
TSTR	Transistor
TSTRZ	Transistorized (MSA)
TSU	Tandem Signal Unit [*Telecommunications*] (TEL)
TSU	Tape Search Unit (CET)
TSU	Telecommunications Study Unit [*American Topical Association*] [*Milwaukee, WI*] [*Telecommunications*] [*Information service*] [*An association*] (EANO)
TSU	Telephone Signal Unit [*Telecommunications*] (TEL)
TSU	Test Signal Unit [*Telecommunications*] (TEL)
TSVS	Time Sharing - Virtual System [*Data processing*] (MCD)
TSW	Test Software (MCD)
TSW	Test Switch
TSW	Time Switch [*Telecommunications*] (TEL)
TSW	Transfer Switch
TSW	Transmitting Slide Wire
TSX	Telephone Satellite, Experimental
TSX	Time-Sharing Executive [*Modular Computer Systems*] [*Data processing*]
TT	Telegraphic Transfer [*of funds*] [*Banking*]
TT	Teletype
TT	Teletypewriter [*Telecommunications*]
TT	Temporarily Transferred [*Telecommunications*] (TEL)
T/T	Timing and Telemetry
TT	Total Time (MSA)
TT	Traffic Tester [*Telecommunications*] (TEL)
TT	Transaction Terminal (BUR)
TTA	Traffic Trunk Administration [*Telecommunications*] (TEL)
TTB	Teletypewriter Buffer (CET)
TTB	Toll Testboard [*Telecommunications*] (TEL)
TTC	Telecommunication Training Centre [*Suva, Fiji*] [*Telecommunications*] (TSSD)
TTC	Telephone Terminal Cables (KSC)
TTC	Terminating Toll Center (DEN)
TT & C	Tracking, Telemetry, and Command
TTC	Tracking, Telemetry, and Command (MCD)
TT & C	Tracking, Telemetry, and Control
TTC & M	Telemetry, Tracking, Command, and Monitoring (CBSS)
TTCU	Teletypewriter Control Unit
TTCV	Tracking, Telemetry, Command, and Voice
TTD	Temporary Text Delay (NITA)
TTD	Transponder Transmitter Detector
TTDR	Tracking Telemetry Data Receiver
TTE	Telephone Terminal Equipment
TTEC	Teletypewriter Technician
TTF	Tone Telegraph Filter
TTI	Technology Transfer Institute [*Santa Monica, CA*] [*Telecommunications*] (TSSD)
TTI	Teletype Test Instruction (KSC)
TTIPS	Ticker Tape Information Processing System [*Quote service*]
TTK	Two-Tone Keying
TTL	Teletype Telling
TTL	Title [*Online database field identifier*] (OBD)
TTL	Transistor-Transistor Logic [*Also, T²L*] (VIT)
TTL-S	Transistor-Transistor Logic - Schottky (NITA)
TTM	Temperature Test Model (CIT)
T/TM	Test and Training Monitor
TTM	Transit Time Modulation (DEN)
TTM	Two-Tone Modulation
TTMF	Touch-Tone Multifrequency (CET)
TT/N	Test Tone to Noise Ratio [*Telecommunications*] (TEL)
TTO	Traffic Trunk Order [*Telecommunications*] (TEL)
TTO	Transmitter Turn-Off
TTP	Tape-to-Print
TTR	Tab-Tronic Recorder (DIT)
TTR	Tape-Reading Tripping Relay
TTR	Teletypewriter Translator (CET)
TTRSA	Twisted Telephone Radio, Shielded, Armored (VIT)
TTS	Tele-Tech Services [*Franklin, NJ*] [*Information service*] [*Telecommunications*] (TSSD)
TTS	Telecommunications Terminal Systems
TTS	Telegraphic Transfers [*of funds*] [*Banking*]
TTS	Telemetry Transmission System
TTS	Teletype Switching Facilities (FAAC)
TTS	Teletypesetter
TTS	Teletypewriter System (CIT)
TTS	Transistor-Transistor Logic Schottky Barrier (IEEE)
TTS	Transmission Test Set (IEEE)
TTS	Transportable Telemetry Set
TTSPN	Two Terminal Series Parallel Networks (NITA)
TTTA	Teletypewriter Terminal Assembly (CIT)
TTY	Teletype (CAAL)
TTY	Teletypewriter [*Telecommunications*]
TTYA	Teletypewriter Assembly (CIT)
TTYD	Tele-Typewriters for the Deaf [*An association*]
TTYQ/RSS	Teletypewriter Query-Reply Subsystem (CET)
TU	Tape Unit
TU	Taxicrinic Unit [*Data processing*]
TU	Terminal Unit
TU	Thank You [*Communications operator's procedural remark*]
TU	Timing Unit
TU	Traffic Unit
TU	Transfer Unit
TU	Transmission Unit
TU	Transport Unit (MCD)
TUC	Telecommunications Users Coalition (EANO)
TUCC	Triangle Universities Computation Center [*Durham, NC*]
TUDRIP	Tube Plate Drilling Program [*Kongsberg UK*] [*Software package*] [*British*] (NCC)
TUF	Transmitter Underflow (NITA)
TUFF-TUG	Tape Update of Formatted Files-Format Table Tape Updater and Generator [*Data processing*]
TUG	Tape Unit Group [*Telecommunications*] (TEL)
TUG	Teleram Users Group (EANO)
TUG	TRANSAC [*Transistorized Automatic Computer*] Users Group
TULE	Transistorized Universal Logic Elements
TUM	Technische Universitaet Muenchen [*Technical University of Munich*] [*Information retrieval*] (ODIN)
TUM	Tuning Unit Member (IEEE)
TUN	Tuning
TUNA	Tunable Attribute Display Subsystem (CAAL)
TUP	Telephony User Part [*Telecommunications*] (TEL)
TUPS	Technical User Performance Specifications [*US Independent Telephone Association*] [*Telecommunications*] (TEL)
TUR	Traffic Usage Recorder
TURS	Terminal Usage Reporting System [*Data processing*]
TUT	Transistor under Test (IEEE)
TUT	Travailleurs Unis du Telegraphe [*United Telegraph Workers - UTW*] [*Canada*]
TUTOR	[*A*] programing language (CSR)
TV	Television
T & V	Test and Verify Programs [*Data processing*] (MDG)
TV	Transfer Vector (NITA)

TVA	Tennessee Valley Authority [*Knoxville, TN*] [*Databank originator*]
TVC	Televideo Consultants, Inc. [*Evanston, IL*] [*Telecommunications*] (TSSD)
TVCS	Television Communications Subsystem (CIT)
TVDR	Tag Vector Display Register (OA)
TVF	Tape Velocity Fluctuation (OA)
TVG	Time Variation of Gain
TVI	Television Interference [*Communications*]
TVIC	Television Input Converter
TVIG	Television and Inertial Guidance
TVIS	Time Video Information Services, Inc. (EISS)
TVIST	Television Information Storage Tube
TVLF	Transportable Very-Low-Frequency [*Transmitter*]
TVOR	Terminal VHF [*Very-High Frequency*] Omnirange [*Radio*]
TVRM	Television Receiver/Monitor
TVRO	Television Receive Only [*Telecommunications*]
TVS	Telemetry Video Spectrum
TVS	Telephone Video System [*NEC America, Inc.*] [*Elk Grove Village, IL*] [*Telecommunications*] (TSSD)
TVS	Television Subsystem [*Spacecraft*] (CIT)
TVS	Transient Voltage Suppressor
TVSG	Television Signal Generator
TVSM	Television System Monitor (SKY)
TVSO	Television Space Observatory
TVSS	Television Systems Section
TVT	Television Terminal (CMD)
TVT	Television Typewriter (DEEC)
TW	Transit Working [*Telecommunications*] (TEL)
TW	Typewriter
TWA	Trailing Wire Antenna [*on aircraft*]
TWA	Transaction Work Area (NITA)
TWA	Traveling-Wave Amplifier
TWAT	Traveling-Wave Amplifier Tube
TWB	Typewriter Buffer (OA)
TWCRT	Traveling-Wave Cathode-Ray Tube (IEEE)
TWDD	Two-Way/Delay Dial [*Telecommunications*] (TEL)
TWEB	Transcribed Weather Broadcast
TWERL	Tropical Wind, Energy Conversion, and Reference Level [*National Science Foundation*]
TWERLE	Tropical Wind, Energy Conversion, and Reference Level Experiment [*National Science Foundation*]
TWG	Telemetry Working Group
TWID	Two-Way/Immediate Dial [*Telecommunications*] (TEL)
TWIX	Teletypewriter Message (DDI)
TWP	Twisted Wire Pair (NITA)
TWPL	Teletypewriter, Private Line
TWPS	Traveling-Wave Phase Sifter
TWR	Tape Write Register (NITA)
TWR	Trans-World Radio
TWR	Traveling-Wave Resonator
TWS	Track-while-Scan [*Communications*]
TWT	Traveling-Wave Tube [*Radio*]
TWTA	Traveling-Wave Tube Amplifier [*Radio*]
TWWS	Two-Way/Wink Start [*Telecommunications*] (TEL)
TWX	Telegraphic Message (MSA)
TWX	Teletypewriter Exchange Service [*Western Union*] [*Term also used generically for teletypewriter message*]
TWX	Time Wire Transmission
TX	TELEX (DEEC)
TX	Terminating Toll Operator [*Telecommunications*] (TEL)
TX	Time to Equipment Reset [*Data processing*] (MDG)
TX	Torque Transmitter
TX	Transmitter
TXD	Telephone Exchange (Digital) [*Telecommunications*] (TEL)
TXE	Telephone Exchange (Electronics) [*Telecommunications*] (IEEE)
TXK	Telephone Exchange (Crossbar) [*Telecommunications*] (TEL)
TXN	Texas Instruments, Inc. [*NYSE symbol*]
TXRX	Transmitter-Receiver
TXS	Telephone Exchange (Strowger) [*Telecommunications*] (TEL)
TXT	Text
TYC	Teach Yourself by Computer [*In company name, TYC Software*] [*Pittsford, NY*] [*Software manufacturer*] (DASOS)
TYDAC	Typical Digital Automatic Computer
TYM	Tymshare, Inc. [*NYSE symbol*] [*Delisted*]
TYMNET	Timeshare, Inc. Network [*Telecommunications*] (TEL)
TYP	Typical
TYPNO	Teletypewriter Communications Interrupted (FAAC)
TYPOK	Teletypewriter Communications Resumed (FAAC)
TYPWRTR	Typewriter
TZ	Transmitter Zone [*Telecommunications*] (TEL)

U

U	Unit	
U	Unlimited Time [*Broadcasting term*]	
U	You [*Communications*]	(FAAC)
UA	Unnumbered Acknowledge [*or Acknowledgment*] [*Telecommunications*]	(IEEE)
UA	User Area [*Information storage*]	(DEEC)
UAC	Uninterrupted Automatic Control	(NITA)
UACN	Unified Automated Communication Network	(NITA)
UACN	University of Alaska Computer Network [*Fairbanks, AK*] [*Research center*]	(RCD)
UACTE	Universal Automatic Control and Test Equipment	
UADC	Universal Air Data Computer	
UADP	Uniform Automated [*or Automatic*] Data Processing	(VIT)
UADPS	Uniform Automated [*or Automatic*] Data Processing System	
UADPS/INAS	Uniform Automated [*or Automatic*] Data Processing System/Industrial Naval Air Station	
UADS	User Attribute Data Set [*Data processing*]	(MDG)
UAIDE	Users of Automatic Information Display Equipment	
UAIMS	United Aircraft Information Management System	(DEEC)
UAL	User Adaptive Language	
UAMPT	Union Africaine et Malagache des Postes et Telecommunications	
UAP	User Area Profile	(NITA)
UAR	Unit Address Register	(NITA)
UARCO	UARCO, Inc. [*Formerly, United Autographic Register Company*]	
UART	Universal Asynchronous Receiver/Transmitter	
UAX	Unit Automatic Exchange	
UB	Universitaetsbibliothek [*University Library*] [*German*] [*Information retrieval*]	
UBA	Umweltbundesamt [*Berlin*] [*Information retrieval*]	(ODIN)
UBA	Unblocking Acknowledge [*Telecommunications*]	(TEL)
UBC	United Business Communications, Inc. [*Atlanta, GA*] [*Telecommunications*]	(TSSD)
UBC	Universal Block Channel	(DEEC)
UBD	Utility Binary Dump [*Data processing*]	
UBHR	User Block Handling Routine [*Data processing*]	(IBMDP)
UBKA	Universitaetsbibliothek Karlsruhe [*Karlsruhe University Library*] [*Information retrieval*]	(ODIN)
UBL	Unblocking [*Telecommunications*]	(TEL)
UBM	Universitaetsbibliothek Muenchen [*Munich University Library*] [*Information retrieval*]	(ODIN)
UBN	United Business Network [*United Business Communications, Inc.*] [*Atlanta, GA*] [*Telecommunications*]	(TSSD)
UC	Unichannel	(NITA)
UC	Up Converter	(NITA)
UC	Uppercase [*i.e., capital letters*] [*Typography*]	
UCA	Under Color Addition [*Printing technology*]	
UCA	Units Consistency Analyzer [*Data processing*]	
UCB	Unit Control Block	(MCD)
UCB	Universal Character Buffer	(NITA)
UCBLL	Language Laboratory [*University of California, Berkeley*] [*Research center*]	(RCD)
UCBT	Universal Circuit Board Tester	
UCC	Computing Center [*University of Rochester*] [*Research center*]	(RCD)
UCC	Universal Copyright Convention	
UCC	University College Computer [*London, England*]	(DEN)
UCC	University Computer Center [*North Dakota State University*] [*Research center*]	(RCD)
UCC	University Computer Center [*New Mexico State University*] [*Research center*]	(RCD)
UCC	University Computer Center [*Oklahoma State University*] [*Research center*]	(RCD)
UCC	University Computer Center [*San Diego State University*] [*Research center*]	(RCD)
UCC	University Computer Center [*University of Minnesota*] [*Research center*]	(RCD)
UCC	University Computing Company [*International computer bureau*]	(OA)
UCCC	Computing Center [*University of Cincinnati*] [*Research center*]	(RCD)
UCD	Uniform Call Distribution [*Telephone system*]	
UCDP	Uncorrected Data Processor	
UCF	Utility Control Facility	(NITA)
UCGF	Undergraduate Computer Graphics Facility [*Stevens Institute of Technology*] [*Research center*]	(RCD)
UCIMT	University Center for Instructional Media and Technology [*University of Connecticut*] [*Research center*]	(RCD)
UCIS	University Center for International Studies [*University of Pittsburgh*] [*Research center*]	(EISS)
UCIS	University Computing and Information Services [*Villanova University*] [*Research center*]	(RCD)
UCIS	Uprange Computer Input System	
UCLA	University of California, Los Angeles [*Databank originator*]	
UCM	Universal Communications Monitor	(NITA)
UCO	Utility Compiler	
UCOS	Uprange Computer Output System	
UCP	Uninterruptable Computer Power	(NITA)
UCP	Update Control Process [*Telecommunications*]	(TEL)
UCS	Unbalanced Current Sensing	(MCD)
UCS	Underwater Cable System	
UCS	Underwater Communications System	
UCS	Uniform Communications System	
UCS	United Computing Systems, Inc.	
UCS	Universal Call Sequence	(NITA)
UCS	Universal Card Scanner [*Data processing*]	(DIT)
UCS	Universal Character Set [*Data processing*]	(CGC)
UCS	Universal Classification System	
UCS	Universal Clothing System [*Software package*] [*British*]	(NCC)
UCS	University Computer Services [*Ball State University*] [*Research center*]	(RCD)
UCS	University Computing Services [*State University of New York at Buffalo*] [*Research center*]	(RCD)
UCS	University Computing Services [*University of Southern California*] [*Research center*]	(RCD)
UCS	User Control Store	(DEEC)
UCSD	Universal Communications Switching Device	
UCSTR	Universal Code Synchronous Transmitter Receiver	(NITA)
UCW	Unit Control Word [*Data processing*]	(BUR)
UD	Update [*Data processing*]	(NASA)
UDAC	User Digital Analog Controller	(NITA)
UDAM	Universal Digital Avionics Module	(MCD)
UDAP	Universal Digital Autopilot	
UDAR	Universal Digital Adaptive Recognizer	(IEEE)
UDAS	Unified Direct Access System	(BUR)
UDAS	Universal Data Acquisition System	
UDAT	Unidata Systems, Inc. [*NASDAQ symbol*]	(NQ)
UDB	Unified Data Base	
UDB	Up-Data Buffer [*Data processing*]	
UDC	Universal Decimal Classification [*Online database field identifier*]	
UDC	Universal Digital Control	(NITA)
UDE	Universal Data Entry	(NITA)
UDEC	Unitized Digital Electronic Calculator	(MCD)
UDF	UHF [*Ultrahigh Frequency*] Direction Finder	(FAAC)
UDF	Utility and Data Flow	(NASA)
UDI	Utility Data Institute [*Information service*]	(EISS)
UDID	Unique Data Item Description	(MCD)
UDL	Uniform Data Language	(NITA)
UDL	Universal Development Laboratory [*Computer bug hunter*] [*Orion Instruments*]	
UDL	Up-Data Link [*Data processing*]	
UDOP	UHF [*Ultrahigh Frequency*] Doppler System	
UDP	United Data Processing	(BUR)
UDR	Universal Digital Readout	
UDR	Universal Document Reader	(BUR)
UDR	Urgent Data Request [*GIDEP*]	
UDR	Usage Data Report	
UDRC	Utility Data Retrieval Control	
UDRO	Utility Data Retrieval Output	
UDS	Unified Data System [*Data processing*]	(TUT)
UDS	Universal Data Set	(CMD)
UDS	Universal Digital Switch	(MCD)
UDS	Universal Distributed System [*UNIVAC*]	(NITA)
UDS	Urban Data Service [*International City Management Association*]	(EISS)
UDT	User Display Terminal	(CIT)
UDTC	User-Dependent-Type Code	(CIT)

UDTI	Universal Digital Transducer Indicator
UDTS	Universal Data Transfer Service [ITT World Communications, Inc.] [Secaucus, NJ] [Telecommunications] (TSSD)
UDTS	Universal Data Transmission System [For international access]
UE	Unit Exception (CMD)
UE	User Equipment (NITA)
UEC	USS Engineers & Consultants, Inc. [Information service] (EISS)
UEP	Unusual End of Program [Data processing]
UET	Universal Emulating Terminal (NITA)
UF	Ultrasonic Frequency (MSA)
UF	Utility File (NITA)
UFAM	Universal File Access Method (NITA)
UFC	Universal Flight Computer
UFC	Universal Frequency Counter (NITA)
UFD	User File Directory (NASA)
UFDC	Universal Flight Director Computer
UF-F	Universal Flip-Flop [Data processing] (CIT)
UFI	Usage Frequency Indicator (NITA)
UFI	User Friendly Interface (NITA)
UFIRS	Uniform Fire Incident Reporting System [National Fire Protection Association]
UFM	User to File Manager (NITA)
UFP	Utility Facilities Program [Data processing] (IBMDP)
UFT	Ultrasonic Frequency Transformer [or Translator]
UG	Underground [Technical drawings]
UGB	Unity Gain Bandwidth
UGBW	Unity Gain Bandwidth
UGC	Ultrasonic Grating Constant
UGLI	Universal Gate for Logic Implementation [Data processing] (MCD)
UGLIAC	United Gas Laboratories Internally Programmed Automatic Computer
UGR	Universal Graphic Recorder [Raytheon Co.]
UGT	Upgraded Third-Generation Enroute Software Program [Data processing] (MCD)
UHELP	[A] programing language (CSR)
UHF	Ultrahigh-Frequency [Electricity of radio waves]
UHFDF	Ultrahigh-Frequency Direction Finder
UHFF	Ultrahigh-Frequency Filter
UHFG	Ultrahigh-Frequency Generator
UHF/HF	Ultrahigh-Frequency/High-Frequency (MCD)
UHFJ	Ultrahigh-Frequency Jammer
UHFO	Ultrahigh-Frequency Oscillator
UHFR	Ultrahigh-Frequency Receiver
UHL	User Header Label (CMD)
UI	USE, Incorporated [Acronym is now used as organization name]
UI	User Interface (CIT)
UIC	User Identification Code (NITA)
UIG	User Instruction Group (NITA)
UIII	Urban Information Interpreters, Incorporated (EISS)
UIL	UNIVAC Interactive Language [Data processing] (IEEE)
UIM	Ultra-Intelligent Machine
UIOD	User Input/Output Devices [Data processing] (RDA)
UIR	User Instruction Register (NITA)
UIS	United Information Services, Inc. (EISS)
UIT	Union Internationale des Telecommunications [International Telecommunications Union]
UJCL	Universal Job Control Language (NITA)
UJL	Uninet Japan Limited [Telecommunications]
UJS	Universal Jamming System
UJT	Unijunction Transistor
UKAC	United Kingdom Automation Council [London, England]
UKAEA	United Kingdom Atomic Energy Authority [London, England] [Databank originator and operator]
UKB	Universal Keyboard [Data processing]
UKCIS	United Kingdom Chemical Information Service [University of Nottingham] [Nottingham, England] [Information broker, databank originator, and host]
UKITO	United Kingdom Information Technology Organization (DEEC)
UK MARC	UK [British Library] Machine Readable Catalogue [Bibliographic database] (OBD)
UKOLUG	United Kingdom On-Line User Group [Information service] (EISS)
UKPO	United Kingdom Post Office [Telecommunications] (TEL)
UKWE	Ultrakurzwellenempfaenger [Very-High-Frequency Receiver] [German]
UL	Underwriters Laboratories, Inc. [Also, ULI]
UL	Up Link [Data processing]
UL	Upper Limit
UL	User Language [Data processing] (DIT)
UL	Utility Lead [Telecommunications] (TEL)
ULA	Uncommitted Logic Array [Semiconductor technology]
ULAIDS	Universal Locator Airborne Integrated Data System (MCD)
ULANG	User Language [Data processing]
ULB	Universal Logic Block (IEEE)
ULC	Uniform Loop Clock (NITA)
ULC	Unit Ledger Card [Data processing]
ULC	Universal Logic Circuit
U & LC	Uppercase and Lowercase [i.e., capital and small letters] [Typography]
ULCS	Unit Level Circuit Switch (CAAL)
ULF	Ultralow Frequency
ULF	Upper Limiting Frequency
ULFJ	Ultralow-Frequency Jammer
ULFO	Ultralow-Frequency Oscillator
ULI	Underwriters Laboratories, Incorporated [Also, UL]
ULI	Universal Logic Implementer
ULM	Universal Line Multiplexer (NITA)
ULM	Universal Logic Module
ULP	Utilitaire Logique Processor [Programing language] [Data processing] (CSR)
ULSI	Ultralarge-Scale Integration [of circuits] [Semiconductor technology]
ULT	Ultimate Corp. [American Stock Exchange symbol]
ULTRACOM	Ultraviolet Communications
UMASS	Unlimited Machine Access from Scattered Sites [Data processing]
UMC	Unibus Microchannel (NITA)
UMD	Unitized Microwave Devices
UMI	University Microfilms International [Commercial firm] [Ann Arbor, MI] [Microfilm and database producer]
UMIST	University of Manchester Institute of Science and Technology [British] [Databank originator and research institute]
UMLC	Universal Multiline Controller (NITA)
UMPLIS	Informations- und Dokumentationssystem Umwelt [Berlin] [Information retrieval] (ODIN)
UMS	Universal Memory System [Intel Corp.] (NITA)
UMS	Universal Micro Systems [San Rafael, CA] [Software manufacturer] (DASOS)
UMS	Unmanned Multifunction Satellite
UMSSS	UDAM [Universal Digital Avionics Module] Microprocessor Software Support System (MCD)
UMTRIS	Urban Mass Transportation Research Information Service [Department of Transportation] [Database]
UMW	Ultramicrowaves
UN	Unassigned [Telecommunications] (TEL)
UN	Unknown [Telecommunications] (TEL)
UNA	Universal Night Answering [Telecommunications] (TEL)
UNADS	UNIVAC Automated Documentation System [Data processing]
UNALC	User Network Access Link Control (NITA)
UNBAL	Unbalanced [Telecommunications] (TEL)
UNBIS	United Nations Bibliographic Information System [New York, NY] (EISS)
UNC	Universal Navigation Computer
UNCERT	Uncertainty [Standard deviation] [Data processing]
UNCHS	United Nations Center for Human Settlements [Information broker] [Kenya]
UNCM	User Network Control Machine (NITA)
UNCOL	Universal Computer Oriented Language [Programing language] [Data processing]
UNDEF	Undefined
UNDF	Underfrequency
UNEP	United Nations Environmental Program [Nairobi, Kenya] [Database originator]
UNESCO	United Nations Educational, Scientific, and Cultural Organization [Paris, France] [Database originator and operator]
UNGR	Ungermann-Bass, Inc. [NASDAQ symbol] (NQ)
UNHCC	University of New Haven Computer Center [West Haven, CT] [Research center] (RCD)
UNIBID	UNISIST International Centre for Bibliographic Descriptions [UNESCO] [Information service] (EISS)
UNIBUS	Universal Bus [Digital Equipment Corp.] (NITA)
UNICCAP	Universal Cable Circuit Analysis Program [Bell System]
UNICOM	Underwater Integration Communication (VIT)
UNICOM	Unidad Informativa Computable [Computerized Information Unit] [Mexico] [Information service] (EISS)
UNICOM	Unified Communications [Radio station]
UNICOMP	Universal Compiler (IEEE)
UNIPEDE	Union Internationale de Producteurs et Distributeurs d'Energie Electrique [International Union of Producers and Distributors of Electrical Energy]
UNIPOL	Universal Problem-Oriented Language [Data processing] (MCD)
UNIPOL	Universal Procedure-Oriented Language
UNIPRO	Universal Processor [Data processing]
UNIQUE	Uniform Inquiry Update Element (NITA)
UNIRAR	Universal Radio Relay
UNISAP	UNIVAC Share Assembly Program [Sperry UNIVAC] [Data processing] (IEEE)
UNISTAR	UNIVAC Storage and Retrieval System [Sperry UNIVAC] [Data processing]
UNISTAR	User Network for Information Storage, Transfer Acquisition, and Retrieval (MCD)
UNISTAT	University Science Statistics Project [Moshman Associates, Inc.] [Information service] (EISS)
UNIT	Universal Numerical Interchange Terminal
UNITEL	Universal Teleservice [Satellite information service]
UNITRAC	Universal Trajector Compiler (IEEE)
UNIVAC	Universal Automatic Computer [Remington Rand Corp.] [Early computer]
UNP	Unpostable [Data processing]
UNSCC	United Nations Standards Co-Ordinating Committee
UNSCC	University of Nevada System Computing Center [Research center] (RCD)
UOC	Universal Output Computer
UODDL	User-Oriented Data Display Language [Data processing]
UOI	User On-Line Interaction [Data processing]

Computer & Telecommunications Acronyms

Acronym	Definition
UOL	Utility Octal Load
UOL	Utility-Oriented Language (MCD)
UOMS	Unmanned Orbital Multifunction Satellite
UOS	Unmanned Orbital Satellite
UP	Uniprocessor (NITA)
UP	Unpostable [*Data processing*]
UP	Update [*Online database field identifier*] [*Data processing*]
UPACS	Universal Performance Assessment and Control System (NITA)
UPC	Unit of Processing Capacity (NITA)
UPC	Universal Peripheral Controller (NITA)
UPC	Universal Product Code [*Grocery industry*]
UPC	Unpostable Code [*Data processing*]
UPDATE	Unlimited Potential Data through Automation Technology in Education (IEEE)
UPI	United Press International
UPL	Universal Programing Language [*Data processing*] (BUR)
UPL	User Programing Language [*Burroughs Corp.*] [*Data processing*] (IEEE)
UPM	Universal Permissive Module (IEEE)
UPOS	Utility Program Operating System (IEEE)
UPP	Universal PROM Programer (NITA)
UPS	Uninterruptible Power Supply [*or System*]
UPS	Universal Processing System (NITA)
UPSI	User Program Sense Indicator (NITA)
UPSI	User Program Switch Indicator [*Data processing*] (TUT)
UPSIS	United States Political Science Information Service [*University of Pittsburgh*] (EISS)
UPT	Urgent Postal Telegram
UPT	User Process Table (NITA)
UQT	User Queue Table (NITA)
UR	Unit Record [*Data processing*] (CGC)
UR	Unit Register (NITA)
URA	User Requirements Analysis (NITA)
URC	UARCO, Inc. [*NYSE symbol*] [*Delisted*]
URC	Unit Record Card
URC	Unit Record Control (NITA)
URC	Utility Radio Communication
URG	Universal Radio Group
URISA	Urban and Regional Information Systems Association [*McLean, VA*]
URL	User Requirements Language [*Data processing*]
URM	Unlimited Register Machine
URN	Uniform Random Numerator [*Data processing*]
URN	Unique Record Number [*Data processing*]
URP	Unit Record Processor (NITA)
URR	Ultra-Rapid Reader [*Data processing*]
URS	Update Report System (TEL)
URSI	Union Radio Scientifique Internationale [*International Union of Radio Science*] [*Also, ISRU*] [*Brussels, Belgium*]
URT	Utility Radio Transmitter
URTNA	Union des Radio-Televisions Nationales Africaines [*Union of African National Radio and Television Stations*]
US	Unit Separator [*Control character*] [*Data processing*]
US	Update State [*Online database field identifier*] (OBD)
U3S	United Software Systems & Services Corp. [*Los Angeles, CA*] [*Software manufacturer*] (DASOS)
USA	Unix Systems Association (EANO)
USAM	Unique Sequential Access Method (NITA)
USART	Universal Synchronous/Asynchronous Receiver and Transmitter [*Data processing*]
USAS	United States of America Standard (IEEE)
USASCII	United States of America Standard Code for Information Interchange
USASCOCR	United States of America Standard Character Set for Optical Character Recognition [*Data processing*]
USASCSOCR	United States of America Standard Character Set for Optical Character Recognition [*Data processing*]
USASI	United States of America Standards Institute [*Formerly, ASA*] [*Later, ANSI*]
USATCO	Universal Satellite Corporation [*New York, NY*] [*Telecommunications*] (TSSD)
USB	Upper Sideband
USC	United Satellite Communications [*Cable TV programing service*]
USC	University Statistics Center [*New Mexico State University*] [*Research center*] (RCD)
USCC	United States Cellular Corporation [*Park Ridge, IL*] [*Telecommunications*] (TSSD)
USDA	United States Department of Agriculture [*Washington, DC*] [*Database originator*]
USDC	US Design Corporation [*NASDAQ symbol*] (NQ)
USE	UNIVAC Scientific Exchange [*Later, UI, USE, Inc.*]
USEC	United System of Electronic Computers (IEEE)
USEC	United System of Electronic Services (MCD)
USEEM	United States Establishment and Enterprise Microdata Base [*Brookings Institution*]
USEMA	[*The*] United States Electronic Mail Association
USERID	User Identification [*Data processing*]
USGRA	United States Government Report Announcements (EISS)
USGS	United States Geological Survey [*Reston, VA*] [*Databank originator*]
USI	Universal Software Interface [*MRI Systems Corp.*] (NITA)
USI	User/System Interface (OA)
USIA	United States Information Agency
USICA	United States International Communication Agency [*Also, ICA*] [*Formerly called BECA and USIA, it later became known again as USIA*]
USIO	Unlimited Sequential Input/Output (NITA)
USISL	United States Information Service Library (DIT)
USITA	United States Independent Telephone Association [*Washington, DC*]
USL	United Satellites Limited [*London, England*] [*Telecommunications*] (TSSD)
USMI	Universal Software Market Identifier [*Technique Learning*] [*Information service*] (EISS)
USNARS	United States National Archives and Records Service (DIT)
USNC	United States National Committee [*IEC*]
USO	Universal Service Order [*Bell System*] (TEL)
USOA	Uniform System of Accounts [*Telecommunications*] (TEL)
USOC	Uniform Service Order Code [*Bell System*] (TEL)
USP	Universal Signal Processor
USP	Usage Sensitive Pricing [*Telecommunications*]
USPA	US Patents Alert [*Derwent, Inc.*] [*Database*]
USPS	United States Postal Service
USPSD	United States Political Science Documents [*University of Pittsburgh*] [*Bibliographic database*] [*Information service*] (EISS)
USR	User Service Routine [*Digital Equipment Corp.*] (NITA)
USRO	Ultrasmall Structures Research Office [*University of Michigan*] [*Research center*] (RCD)
USRS	United States Robotics Society (CSR)
USRT	Universal Synchronous Receiver/Transmitter
USS	Unified S-Band System [*Radio*]
USS	Usage Sensitive Service [*Telecommunications*]
USSB	United States Satellite Broadcasting Co., Inc. [*Minneapolis, MN*] [*Telecommunications*] (TSSD)
USSS	Unmanned Sensing Satellite System
USTA	United States Telephone Association [*Washington, DC*] (EANO)
US TEL	US Telephone, Inc. [*Dallas, TX*] [*Telecommunications*] (TSSD)
USTSA	US Telecommunications Suppliers Association [*Chicago, IL*] [*Telecommunications*] (EANO)
USTTI	US Telecommunications Training Institute [*Washington, DC*] [*Telecommunications*] (TSSD)
UT	Uncontrolled Term [*Online database field identifier*] (OBD)
UT	United Telecommunications, Inc. [*NYSE symbol*]
UT	Universal Time [*Astronomy*]
UT	Up Time (CAH)
UT	User's Terminal (MCD)
UT	Utility (BUR)
UTA	Upper Terminal Area (NATG)
UTA	User Transfer Address (NITA)
UTC	Unit Time Coding
UTC	Universal Test Console (KSC)
UTC	Universal Time Code (CIT)
UTC	Universal Time Coordinated [*The Universal Time emitted by coordinated radio stations*]
UTC	Utilities Telecommunications Council (EANO)
UTCC	University of Tennessee at Knoxville Computer Center [*Research center*] (RCD)
UTCLK	Universal Transmitter Clock
UTCPTT	Union Internationale des Organismes Touristiques et Culturels des Postes et des Telecommunications [*International Union of Tourist and Cultural Associations in the Postal and Telecommunications Services*]
UTCS	Urban Traffic Control System
UTD	Universal Transfer Device (NITA)
UTEC	Universal Test Equipment Compiler (KSC)
UTI	International Universal Time [*Telecommunications*] (TEL)
UTI	Union Telegraphique Internationale
UTIL	Utility [*or Utilization*] (AFM)
UTIPS	Upgraded Tactical Information Processing System [*Data processing*]
UTL	Unit Transmission Loss
UTL	Up Telecommunications Switch (SKY)
UTL	User Trailer Label (CMD)
UTLY	Utility (BUR)
UTO	United Telephone Organizations
UTOL	Universal Translator Oriented Language (NITA)
UTP	Universal Tape Processor
UTP	Upper Turning Point
UTP	Utility Tape Processor
UTR	Unprogramed Transfer Register
UTS	Ultimate Tensile Strength [*or Stress*]
UTS	Unified Transfer System [*Computer to translate Russian to English*]
UTS	Universal Terminal System [*Sperry UNIVAC*] [*Data processing*]
UTS	Universal Time Sharing [*Data processing*] (IEEE)
UTS	Unmanned Teleoperator Spacecraft (MCD)
UTS	Update Transaction System (TEL)
UTTC	Universal Tape-to-Tape Converter
UTV	Uncompensated Temperature Variation (TEL)
UTW	United Telegraph Workers (EANO)
UTX	United Technologies Corp. [*NYSE symbol*]
UU	Ultimate User
UUA	UNIVAC Users Association [*Later, AUUA*]
UV	Ultraviolet [*Electromagnetic spectrum range*]
UVC	Ultraviolet Communications System

UV-EPROMS ... Ultraviolet-Erasable Programable Read-Only Memories [*Data processing*]
UVLI .... Ustav Vedeckych Lekarskych Informaci [*Institute for Medical Information*] [*Czechoslovakia*] [*Database operator*] [*Information service*]   (EISS)
UVP .... Ultra-Violet Products, Inc. [*San Gabriel, CA*] [*Hardware manufacturer*]   (DASO)
UVPROM ..... Ultraviolet Programable Read Only Memory   (NITA)
UVTEI .... Ustredi Vedeckych, Technickych, a Ekonomickych Informaci [*Central Office of Scientific, Technical, and Economic Information*] [*Prague, Czechoslovakia*] [*Information service*]   (EISS)
UWA .... User Working Area   (NITA)
UWAT .... User Written Application Test [*Data processing*]

V

V	Variable		VCG	Verification Condition Generator (NITA)
V	Vector [*Mathematics*]		VCH	Video Concert Hall
V	Volt [*Symbol*] [*SI unit of electric potential difference*]		VCM	Vertical Current Meter
V	Voltage (CAH)		VCO	Verbit & Company, Consultants to Management [*Bala Cynwyd, PA*] [*Telecommunications*] (TSSD)
V	Voltmeter		VCO	Voice Controlled Oscillator [*Telecommunications*] (TEL)
V	Volts (SKY)		VCO	Voltage-Controlled Oscillator
VA	End of Work [*Morse telephony*] (FAAC)		VCP	Video Cassette Player
VA	Virtual Address (NITA)		VCR	Video Cassette Recorder
V-A	Volt-Ampere		VCS	Validation Control System (NITA)
VAA	Voice Access Arrangement (NITA)		VCS	Video Clutter Suppression (CAAL)
VAB	Voice Answer Back		VCS	Video Communications System
VAC	Value-Added Carrier [*Telecommunications*]		VCS	Video Computer System [*Atari, Inc.*]
VAC	Vector Analog Computer		VCS	Video Contrast Seeker
VAC	Victor Analog Computer [*Data processing*] (CDH)		VCS	Visual Call Sign [*Communications*]
VACC	Value-Added Common Carrier [*Telecommunications*]		VCT	Voice Code Translation (BUR)
VAD	Vapor Axial Deposition [*Optical fiber technology*]		VCTCA	Virtual Channel to Channel Adapter (NITA)
VAD	Voltmeter Analog-to-Digital Converter		VCTR	Vector Graphic, Inc. [*NASDAQ symbol*] (NQ)
VADAC	Voice Analyzer Data Converter (NITA)		VCVS	Voltage-Controlled Voltage Source
VADC	Video Analog to Digital Converter (NITA)		VD	Video Disk (BUR)
VADE	Versatile Automatic Data Exchange (MCD)		VD	Virtual Data (NITA)
VADIS	Voice and Data Integrated System [*Telecommunications*] (TEL)		V/D	Voice/Data (BUR)
VADS	Value Added and Data Services		VDA/D	Video Display Adapter with Digital Enhancement [*AT & T*]
VADS	Vendor Automated Data System (MCD)		VDAM	Virtual Data Access Method (IEEE)
VADS	Visual-Aural Digit Span Test		VDB	Vector Data Buffer (NITA)
VAEP	Variable, Attributes, Error Propagation (IEEE)		VDB	Video Display Board (NITA)
VAI	Video-Assisted Instruction (TUT)		VDC	Variable Diode Circuit
VAL	Value		VDC	Venture Development Corporation [*Natick, MA*] [*Telecommunications*] (TSSD)
VAL	Vicarm Arm Language		VDC	Voltage to Digital Converter
VALOR	Veterans Administration Libraries Online Resources		VDC	Voltage Doubler Circuit
VALSAS	Variable Length Word Symbolic Assembly System (IEEE)		VDC	Volts Direct Current
VAM	Virtual Access Method (OA)		VDCP	Video Data Collection Program
VAMP	Vector Arithmetic Multiprocessor [*Data processing*] (IEEE)		VDCU	Videograph Display Control Unit
VAN	Value-Added Network [*Data processing*] [*Telecommunications*]		VDD	Version Description Document (KSC)
VANS	Value Added Network Service [*Data processing*] [*Telecommunications*]		VDD	Video Detector Diode
VAOR	VHF [*Very-High-Frequency*] Aural Omnirange		VDD	Visual Display Data
VAR	Variable (AFM)		VDD	Voice Digital Display
VAR	Variation		VDDP	Video Digital Data Processing
VAR	Video-Audio Range [*Radio*]		VDE	Verband Deutsche Elektrotechniker [*German*] [*Telecommunications*] (TEL)
VAR	Visual-Aural Range [*Radio*]		VDETS	Voice Data Entry Terminal System (NITA)
VARC	Variable Axis Rotor Control System [*Telecommunications*] (TEL)		VDF	Very-High-Frequency Direction-Finding
VARGUS	Variable Generator of Unfamiliar Stimuli [*Computer program*]		VDF	Video Frequency
VARR	Visual-Aural Radio Range (MSA)		VDFG	Variable Diode Function Generator
VAS	Value Added Service [*Telecommunications*] (TEL)		VDG	Video Display Generator (NITA)
VAS	Vector Addition System (NITA)		VDG-DOK	Verein Deutscher Giessereifachleute eV - Dokumentationsstelle und Bibliothek [*Dusseldorf*] [*Information retrieval*] (ODIN)
VASCAR	Visual Average Speed Computer and Recorder [*Speed trap*]		VDI	Video Display Input (DEEC)
VAT	Virtual Address Translation		VDI	Video Display Interface (NITA)
VAT	Voice-Activated Typewriter		VDI	Virtual Device Interface [*Computer technology*]
VATE	Versatile Automatic Test Equipment [*Computers*]		VDI	Visual Display Input (DEEC)
V-ATE	Vertical Anisotropic Etch [*Raytheon Co.*]		VDI	Voluntary Data Inquiry
VAU	Vertical Arithmetic Unit (NITA)		VDI-N	VDI-Nachrichten [*VDI-Verlag GmbH*] [*Database*] (CUAD)
VAX	Virtual Address Extension [*Data processing*]		VDL	Video Data Link (NVT)
VB	Voice Band [*Telecommunications*] (NITA)		VDL	Vienna Definition Language [*1960*] [*Data processing*] (CSR)
VB	Voice Bank [*Telecommunications*] (TEL)		VDL	Voice Direct Line
VBI	Vertical Blanking Interval [*Telecommunications*]		VDM	Varian Data Machines (NITA)
VBI	Vital Bus Inverter [*Data processing*] (IEEE)		VDM	Video Delta Modulation
VBOMP	Virtual Base Organization and Maintenance Processor (NITA)		VDP	Vertical Data Processing
VBP	Virtual Block Processor (NITA)		VDP	Video Data Processor (NITA)
VBW	Video Bandwidth		VDPS	Voice Data Processor System
VC	Verification Condition (NITA)		VDR	Voice & Data Resources, Inc. [*New York, NY*] [*Information service*] [*Telecommunications*] (TSSD)
VC	Virtual Circuit		VDR	Voice Digitization Rate (NITA)
VCA	Valve Control Amplifier (MDG)		VDS	Video Display System
VCA	Viewdata Corporation of America, Inc. [*Miami Beach, FL*] [*Telecommunications*] (TSSD)		VDS	Voice Data Switch (NITA)
VCA	Virtual City Associates Ltd. [*London, England*] [*Telecommunications*] (TSSD)		VDT	Video Data Terminal [*Data processing*]
VCA	Voice Connecting Arrangement [*Telecommunications*] (TEL)		VDT	Video [*or Visual*] Display Terminal [*Data processing*]
VCA	Voltage Control of Amplification		VDT	Visual Display Terminal (DEEC)
VCC	Video Compact Cassette [*Video recorder*] [*Philips*] (DEEC)		VDU	Video Display Unit [*Data processing*]
VCC	Vogelback Computing Center [*Northwestern University*] [*Research center*] (RCD)		VDU	Visual Display Unit (IDA)
VCCS	Voltage-Controlled Current Source [*Electronics*]		VE	Value Engineering
VCF	Voltage Controlled Filter (NITA)			

Acronym	Definition
VEAMCOP	Viking Error Analysis Monte Carlo Program [*Data processing*]
VECTRAN	[*A*] programing language (CSR)
VENUS	Valuable and Effective Network Utility Services (BUR)
VER	Verify (AFM)
VERT	Venture Evaluation and Review Technique
VERT	Vertical Polarization (AFM)
VET	Video Editing Terminal [*Data processing*]
VETDOC	Veterinary Literature Documentation [*Derwent Publications Ltd.*] [*Bibliographic database*] (OBD)
VF	Voice Frequency [*Communications*]
V/F	Voltage to Frequency [*Converter*] [*Data processing*]
VFB	Vertical Format Buffer (NITA)
VFC	Variable File Channel (NITA)
VFC	Vertical Format Control (NITA)
VFC	Video Frequency Carrier [*or Channel*] (CET)
VFC	Voice Frequency Carrier [*or Channel*]
VFC	Voltage to Frequency Converter
VFCT	Voice Frequency Carrier [*or Channel*] Telegraph [*or Teletype*]
VFCTT	Voice Frequency Carrier Teletype (MSA)
VFFT	Voice Frequency Facility Terminal [*Telecommunications*] (TEL)
VFL	Variable Field Length (MCD)
VFL	Voice Frequency Line [*Telecommunications*] (TEL)
VFMED	Variable Format Message Entry Device [*Data processing*] (MCD)
VFO	Variable Frequency Oscillator
VFSS	Voice Frequency Signaling System
VFT	Voice Frequency Telegraphy (NATG)
VFT	Voice Frequency Terminal
VFTG	Voice Frequency Telegraphy
VFU	Vertical Format Unit (BUR)
VFU	Vocabulary File Utility (NITA)
VG	Voice Grade [*Telecommunications*] (TEL)
VGAM	Vector Graphics Access Method (NITA)
VGCA	Voice Gate Circuit Adaptors [*Data processing*] (MCD)
VH-1	Video Hits One [*Cable-television system*]
VHA	Van Houten Associates [*Information service*] (EISS)
VHA	Voluntary Hospitals of America [*Cable-television system*]
VHF	Very-High-Frequency [*Electronics*]
VHF/AM	Very-High-Frequency, Amplitude Modulated (NASA)
VHF/DF	Very-High-Frequency Direction-Finding
VHFF	Very-High-Frequency Filter
VHF-FM	Very-High-Frequency, Frequency Modulated
VHFG	Very-High-Frequency Generator
VHFI	Very-High-Frequency Indeed [*Ultrahigh frequency*] [*British*]
VHFJ	Very-High-Frequency Jammer
VHFO	Very-High-Frequency Oscillator
VHFOR	Very-High-Frequency Omnirange (AFM)
VHFR	Very-High-Frequency Receiver
VHFT	Very-High-Frequency Termination
VHM	Virtual Hardware Monitor [*Data processing*] (IEEE)
VHOL	Very-High-Order Language (NITA)
VHR	Video-to-Hardcopy Recorder
VHS	Video Home System
VHSI	Very-High-Speed Integrated [*Electronics*]
VHSIC	Very-High-Speed Integrated Circuit [*Electronics*]
VHST	Very-High-Speed Transit
VHTR	Very-High-Temperature Reactor
VI	Volume Indicator [*Radio equipment*]
VIA	Videotex Industry Association [*Rosslyn, VA*] [*Telecommunications*] [*Information service*] (EANO)
VIBRA	Vehicle Inelastic Bending Response Analysis [*Computer program*]
VIBROT	Vibrational-Rotational [*Spectra*] [*Data processing*]
VIC	Variable Instruction Computer
VIC	Virtual Interaction Controller (NITA)
VICAM	Virtual Integrated Communications Access Method [*Sperry UNIVAC*] (NITA)
VICAR	Video Image Communication and Retrieval (NITA)
VICOED	Visual Communications Education
VICR	Victor Technologies [*NASDAQ symbol*] (NQ)
VID	Video
VIDAC	Visual Information Display and Control
VIDAP	Vibration Data Accuracy Program
VIDEO	Visual Data Entry On-Line [*Data processing*]
VIDF	Vertical Side of Intermediate Distribution Frame [*Telecommunications*] (TEL)
VIDF	Video Frequency (IEEE)
VIDPI	Visually Impaired Data Processors International [*Washington, DC*] (EANO)
VIL	Vertical Injection Logic [*Data processing*]
VIM	CDC 6000 Series users organization [*Abbreviation is derived from the Roman numerals for 6 and thousand*] (CAH)
VIM	Voice Input Module [*Cascade Graphics Development Ltd.*] [*Software package*] [*British*] (NCC)
VIMTPG	Virtual Interactive Machine Test Program Generator (NITA)
VIN	Voltage Input (TEL)
VINITI	Vsesoyuznyy Institut Nauchnoy i Tekhnicheskoy Informatsii [*All-Union Institute of Scientific and Technical Information*] [*USSR*]
VIO	Heavy [*Used to qualify interference or static reports*] [*Telecommunications*] (FAAC)
VIO	Video Input/Output (NITA)
VIO	Virtual Input/Output [*Data processing*] (IBMDP)
VIOC	Variable Input-Output Code
VIP	Variable Information Processing [*Naval Ordnance Laboratory*] [*Information retrieval*]
VIP	Variable Input Phototypesetter
VIP	Vector Instruction Processor (NITA)
VIP	Vermont Information Processes, Inc. [*Middlebury, VT*] [*Information service*] (EISS)
VIP	Versatile Information Processor [*Data processing*]
VIP	Video Integrator and Processor
VIP	Vision Information Program (EISS)
VIP	Visual Image Projection
VIP	Visual Information Projection (CGC)
VIP	Visual Input [*System*] [*AT & T*]
VIP	Voice Integrated Presentations [*Telecommunications*] (RDA)
VIPER	Video Processing and Electronic Reduction (IEEE)
VIPP	Variable Information Processing Package
VIPS	Variable Item Processing System (NITA)
VIPS	Video Image Processing System (SKY)
VIPS	Voice Interruption Priority System
VIR	Vertical Interval Reference [*Automatic color adjustment*] [*Television*]
VIR	Virco Manufacturing Corp. [*American Stock Exchange symbol*]
VIS	Minority Vendor Information Service [*National Minority Supplier Development Council, Inc.*] (EISS)
VIS	Vector Instruction Set [*Data processing*]
VIS	Virtual Information Storage (BUR)
VIS	Visual
VIS	VNR [*Van Nostrand Reinhold*] Information Services [*New York, NY*] (EISS)
VISC	Video Disc (DEEC)
VISPAC	Videotex Information Service Providers Association of Canada (EISS)
VISTA	Variable Interlace System for Television Applications
VISTA	Verbal Information Storage and Text Analysis [*in FORTRAN computer language*]
VISTA	Viewing Instantly Security Transactions Automatically [*Wall Street*]
VISTA	Visual Information for Satellite Telemetry Analysis
VITA	VMEbus International Trade Association (EANO)
VITA	Volunteers in Technical Assistance [*Arlington, VA*] [*Telecommunications*]
VITAL	Variably Initialized Translator for Algorithmic Languages [*Data processing*]
VITAL	VAST [*Versatile Avionics Shop Test*] Interface Test Application Language (OA)
VITS	Vertical Interval Test Signal (IEEE)
VIU	Video Interface Unit (MCD)
VIU	Voice Intercommunications Unit
VIU	Voice Interface Unit [*Telecommunications*] (TEL)
VIURAM	Video Interface Unit Random Access Memory (NITA)
VL	Video Logic (IEEE)
VLA	Video Logarithmic Amplifier
VLAM	Variable Level Access Method [*Data processing*] (TUT)
VLBA	Very Long Baseline Array
VLBI	Very Long Baseline Interferometer [*or Interferometry*]
VLCE	Visible LASER Communication Experiment
VLCS	Voltage-Logic-Current-Switching [*Electronics*]
VLF	Variable Length Field (CAH)
VLF	Very-Low-Frequency [*Electronics*]
VLFJ	Very-Low-Frequency Jammer [*Electronics*]
VLFR	Very-Low-Frequency Receiver [*Electronics*]
VLID	Valid Logic Systems [*NASDAQ symbol*] (NQ)
VLON	Verwaltungslexikon [*NOMOS Datapool*] [*Database*] (CUAD)
VLP	Video Long Player [*Video disk system*] [*Philips/MCA*] (DEEC)
VLS	Virtual Linkage System [*or Subsystem*] (NITA)
VLS	Volume Loadability Speed (IEEE)
VLSI	VLSI Technology, Inc. [*NASDAQ symbol*] (NQ)
VLSIC	Very-Large-Scale Integrated Circuit [*Electronics*]
VLSW	Virtual Line Switch (NITA)
VLT	Video Layout Terminal [*Data processing*]
VLU	Video Logic Unit (MCD)
VLVS	Voltage-Logic-Voltage-Switching [*Electronics*]
VM	Virtual Machine [*Data processing*]
VM	Virtual Memory [*Data processing*] (MCD)
VM	Voice Modulation
VMA	Valid Memory Address [*Data processing*]
VMA	Virtual Machine Assist [*IBM Corp.*] (NITA)
VMA	Virtual Memory Allocation (OA)
VMAPS	Virtual Memory Array Processing System (NITA)
VMBLOK	Virtual Machine Control Block [*Data processing*] (IBMDP)
VMC	Variable Message Cycle
VMC	Variable Mica Capacitor
VMCB	Virtual Machine Control Block (OA)
VMCF	Virtual Machine Communication Facility (NITA)
VM/CMS	Virtual Machine/Conversational Monitor System [*Data processing*]
VMDF	Vertical Side of Main Distribution Frame [*Telecommunications*] (TEL)
VMDP	Veterinary Medical Data Program [*Association of Veterinary Medical Data Program Participants*] [*Information service*] (EISS)
VME	Virtual Machine Environment [*International Computers Ltd.*] (NITA)
VMG	Video Mapping Group

Computer & Telecommunications Acronyms

VMG	Video Mixer Group
VMI	Voicemail International, Incorporated [*Santa Clara, CA*] [*Telecommunications*] (TSSD)
VMID	Virtual Machine Identifier (OA)
VMIRL	VMI Research Laboratories [*Virginia Military Institute*] [*Research center*] (RCD)
VMM	Virtual Machine Monitor [*Data processing*] (IEEE)
VMOS	V-Groove Metal-Oxide Semiconductor (MCD)
VMOS	Virtual Memory Operating System [*Sperry UNIVAC*] [*Data processing*] (IEEE)
VMR	Violation Monitor and Remover [*Bell System*]
VMS	Videofile Microwave System
VMS	Virtual Memory Operating System [*Data processing*]
VMS	Voice Messaging System [*Telecommunications*]
VMT	Variable Microcycle Timing (NITA)
VMT	Velocity Modulated Transistor [*Solid-state physics*]
VMT	Video Matrix Terminal (OA)
VMT	Virtual Memory Technique [*Data processing*] (MDG)
VMTSS	Virtual Machine Time-Sharing System [*Data processing*] (IEEE)
VN	Verify Number If No Answer [*Telecommunications*] (TEL)
VNC	Voice Numerical Control (NITA)
VNHP	Vermont Natural Heritage Program [*Montpelier, VT*] [*Information service*] (EISS)
VNL	Via Net Loss [*Telecommunications*]
VNLF	Via Net Loss Factor (TEL)
VNN	Vacant National Number [*Telecommunications*] (TEL)
VOA	Voice of America
VOBANC	Voice Band Compression (CET)
VOC	Voice Order Circuit (CET)
VOCA	Voice Output Communications Aid
VOCAB	Vocabulary
VOCODER	Voice Coder
VOCOM	Voice Communications
VOCS	Voice Operated Computer Systems [*St. Louis Park, MN*] [*Software manufacturer*] (DASOS)
VODACOM	Voice Data Communications
VODAS	Voice-Operated Device Antising (CET)
VODAT	Voice-Operated Device for Automatic Transmission
VODER	Voice Coder
VODER	Voice-Operated Demonstrator
VOF	Variable Operating Frequency (NATG)
VOI	Video Output Impedance
VOL	Volume
VOLCAS	Voice-Operated Loss Control and Suppressor
VOM	Volt-Ohm Meter (NITA)
VOM	Volt-Ohm-Milliammeter
VOPR	Voice-Operated Relay
VOR	Voice-Operated Relay
VORDAC	VHF [*Very-High-Frequency*] Omnidirectional Range/Distance-Measuring for Air Coverage
VORDME	VHF [*Very-High-Frequency*] Omnirange - Distance-Measuring Equipment (CET)
VORLOC	VHF [*Very-High-Frequency*] Omnirange Localizer (CET)
VOS	Vehicle Origin Survey [*R. L. Polk & Co.*] [*Information service*] (EISS)
VOS	Virtual Operating System (NITA)
VOS	Voice-Operated Switch
VOSC	VAST [*Versatile Avionics Shop Test*] Operating System Code (OA)
VOT	Voice Onset Time
VOT	VOR [*Very-High-Frequency Omnidirectional Range*] Test Signal (CET)
VOTC	Volume Table of Contents [*Data processing*]
VOV	Video Output Voltage
VOX	Voice-Operated Keying [*Data processing*]
VOX	Voice-Operated Transmission
VP	Vector Processor (NITA)
VP	Verifying Punch (CMD)
VP	Video Processor
VP	Virtual Processor (OA)
VPAM	Virtual Partitioned Access Method (OA)
VPBA	Varipolarization Beacon Antenna
VPC	Video Processor Control (MCD)
VPC	Visual Punch Card
VPN	Virtual Page Number (NITA)
VPRF	Variable Pulse Repetition Frequency (IEEE)
VPSS	Vector Processing Subsystem
VPSW	Virtual Program Status Word (OA)
VPT	Voice plus Telegraph [*Telecommunications*] (TEL)
VPZ	Virtual Processing Zero (NITA)
VQT	Viewers for Quality Television (EANO)
VR	Validation and Recovery (NITA)
VRAM	Variable Random Access Memory [*Data processing*]
VRAM	Variable Rate Adaptive Multiplexing [*Telecommunications*] (TEL)
VRAM	Video Random Access Memory (DEEC)
VRB	Verbatim Corp. [*American Stock Exchange symbol*]
VRC	Vertical Redundancy Check (BUR)
VRC	Virtual Redundancy Check [*Data processing*]
VRC	Visual Record Computer
VRE	Vermont Research Corp. [*American Stock Exchange symbol*]
VRH	Vertical Receiving Hydrophone
VRI	Varistor [*Telecommunications*] (TEL)
VROM	Vocabulary Read-Only Memory [*Data processing*]
VRP	Visual Record Printer (NITA)
VRR	Visual Radio Range
VRRC	Vehicle Radio Remote Control
VRS	Vehicular RADIAC [*Radioactivity Detection, Indication, and Computation*] System
VRS	Video Reception System
VRS	Video Relay System
VRU	Voice Response Unit
VRX	Virtual Resource Executive [*NCR Corp.*] (NITA)
VS	Single Vibrations [*Half cycles*]
VS	Virtual Storage [*Data processing*]
VS	Virtual System (DEEC)
VS	Visual Storage [*Data processing*]
VS	Vocal Synthesis (NITA)
VSA	Velocity Sensor Antenna (CIT)
VSA	Videocom Satellite Associates [*Dedham, MA*] [*Telecommunications*] (TSSD)
VSAL	Visual Technology [*NASDAQ symbol*] (NQ)
VSAM	Virtual Sequential Access Method (NITA)
VSAM	Virtual Storage Access Method [*Data processing*]
VSAM	Virtual System Access Method (NITA)
VSB	Vestigial Sideband [*Radio*]
VSBF	Vestigial Sideband Filter
VSBS	Very Small Business System (NITA)
VSC	Variable Speech Control [*Device that permits distortion-free rapid playback of speech recorded on tape*]
VSC	Virtual Subscriber Computer (NITA)
VSD	Variable Slope Delta
VSD	Variable Speed Drive
VSDA	Video Software Dealers Association (EANO)
VSDM	Variable Slope Delta Modulation (NITA)
VSE	Virtual Storage Extension [*IBM Corp.*] [*Data processing*]
VSF	Vestigial Sideband Filter
VSI	Video Simulation Interface (NASA)
VSI	Video Sweep Integrator
VSL	Variable Specification List (NITA)
VSLE	Very Small Local Exchange [*Telecommunications*] (TEL)
VSM	Video Switching Matrix (KSC)
VSM	Virtual Storage Manager (BUR)
VSM	Virtual Storage Memory [*Data processing*] (MCD)
VSMF	Visual Search Microfilm File [*Trademark*] [*Data processing*]
VSMS	Video Switching Matrix System
VSN	Video Switching Network (MCD)
VSP	Vehicle Scheduling Program [*Data processing*]
VSP	Virtual Switching Point [*Telecommunications*] (TEL)
VSPC	Virtual Storage Personal Computing [*IBM Corp.*] [*Data processing*]
VSPX	Vehicle Scheduling Program Extended [*Data processing*]
VSR	Validation Summary Report (NITA)
VSS	Video Select Switch (MCD)
VSS	Video Signal Simulator (NATG)
VSS	Video Storage System [*or Subsystem*]
VSS	Virtual Storage System [*SEMIS*] (NITA)
VSS	Vocabulary Switching System [*Data processing*]
VSS	Voltage to Substrate and Sources [*Microelectronics*] (DEEC)
VST	Video Scroller Terminal [*Data processing*]
VST	Volume Sensitive Tariff [*Telecommunications*] (TEL)
VSW	Voltage Standing Wave
VSWR	Voltage Standing-Wave Ratio
VSYNC	Vertical Synchronous (DEEC)
VT	Variable Transmission
VT	Vertical Tabulation [*Data processing*]
VT	Vertical Tail
VTAC	Video Timing and Control (NITA)
VTAM	Virtual Telecommunications [*or Teleprocessing*] Access Method [*IBM Corp.*] [*Data processing*]
VTAM	Virtual Terminal Access Method (NITA)
VTAM	VORTEX [*Varian Omnitask Real-Time Executive*] Telecommunications Access Method (DEEC)
VTAME	Virtual Telecommunications Access Method Entry
V-TAS	Vericom Test Application System [*Vericom Ltd.*] [*Software package*] [*British*] (NCC)
VtB	Verkehrswasserbaubibliothek [*Bundesanstalt fuer Wasserbau*] [*Database*] (CUAD)
VTDI	Variable Threshold Digital Input (NITA)
VTF	Vertical Test Fixture
VTF	Vertical Tracking Force [*of a phonograph cartridge*]
VTI	Vermont Telecommunications, Incorporated [*Burlington, VT*] [*Telecommunications*] (TSSD)
VTI	Video Terminal Interface (NITA)
VTLS	Virginia Technical Library System [*Virginia Polytechnic Institute and State University Center for Library Automation*] [*Information service*]
VTOC	Volume Table of Contents [*Data processing*]
VTP	VIEWDATA Terminal Program (NITA)
VTP	Virtual Terminal Protocol (NITA)
VTPR	Vertical Temperature Profile [*or Profiling*] Radiometer
VTR	Videotape Recorder [*or Recording*]
VTR	Voltage Transformation Ratio [*Physics*]
V + TU	Voice plus Teleprinter Unit
VT(V)	Vacuum-Tube (Voltmeter) (DEN)
VTVM	Vacuum-Tube Voltmeter
VU	Voice Unit [*Signal amplitude measurement*]

VU	Volume Unit [*Signal amplitude measurement*]
VUA	Virtual Unit Address (BUR)
VUCC	Computer Center [*Vanderbilt University*] [*Research center*] (RCD)
VULCAN	[*A*] programing language (CSR)
V/V	Validation/Verification (CAAL)
V & V	Verification and Validation [*Data processing*]
VWOA	Veteran Wireless Operators Association [*Clifton, NJ*]
VWS	Variable Word Size (NITA)

W

W	Watt [Broadcasting term]
W	West [or Western]
W	Whole Word Designator [Data processing]
W	Width
W	Word
W	Write (NITA)
4W	Four-Wire
WA	Wire Assembly (MSA)
WA	Wohl Associates [Bala Cynwyd, PA] [Telecommunications] (TSSD)
WA	Word After [Message handling]
WAA	World Aluminum Abstracts [American Society for Metals] [Metals Park, OH] [Database] [A publication] (EISS)
WACK	Wait before Transmitting Positive Acknowledgment (DEEC)
WADEX	Words and Authors Index [Computer-produced index]
WADS	Wide-Angle Display System
WADS	Wide-Area Data Service [Data transmission service]
WAIT	Western Australia Institute of Technology [Database originator and operator]
WAK	Wait Acknowledge (NITA)
WAK	Write Access Key (NITA)
WAM	Words a Minute
WAN	Wang Laboratories, Inc. [American Stock Exchange symbol]
WAN	Wide Area Network (CCD)
WAP	Work Analysis Program [Data processing] (BUR)
WAP	Work Assignment Procedure
WARC	World Administrative Radio Conference [Takes place every 20 years] [Held in 1979 in Geneva, Switzerland] [International Telecommunications Union]
WARC-MAR	World Administrative Radio Conference for Maritime Mobile Telecommunications
WARC-ST	World Administrative Radio Conference for Space Telecommunications
WAS	Wideband Antenna System
WASAR	Wide Application System Adapter (NITA)
WASSP	Wallingford Storm Sewer Package [Hydraulics Research] [Software package] [British] (NCC)
WATDOC	Water Resources Document Reference Centre [Canadian Department of Fisheries and the Environment] [Ottawa, ON] [Database] (EISS)
WATFOR	Waterloo FORTRAN [University of Waterloo] [Canada]
WAVES	Weight and Value Engineering System [Data processing]
WB	Wave-Band
WB	Wideband [Radio transmission]
WBAI	Wesley Bull & Associates, Incorporated [Seattle, WA] [Telecommunications] (TSSD)
WBC	Westinghouse Broadcasting Company
WBCO	Waveguide below Cutoff (IEEE)
WBCS	Wideband Communications Subsystem (CIT)
WBCV	Wideband Coherent Video (IEEE)
WBFM	Wideband Frequency Modulation (CIT)
WBL	Wideband Limiting (IEEE)
WBRS	Wideband Remote Switch (IEEE)
WBS	Work Breakdown Structure [Data processing]
WBT	Wideband Transformer [or Transmitter]
WC	Western Cedar [Utility pole] [Telecommunications] (TEL)
WC	Wire Chief [Test clerk] [Telecommunications] (TEL)
WC	Word Count [Data processing]
WC	World Coordinate (CCD)
WCAM	Wisconsin Center for Applied Microelectronics [University of Wisconsin - Madison] [Research center] (RCD)
WCAT	Wicat Systems, Inc. [NASDAQ symbol] (NQ)
WCB	Way Control Block (NITA)
WCB	Weekly Criminal Bulletin [Canada Law Book] [Database]
WCC	Gerard P. Weeg Computing Center [University of Iowa] [Research center] (RCD)
WCC	Wallace Communications Consultants [Tampa, FL] [Telecommunications] (TSSD)
WCC	Waters Computing Center [Rose-Hulman Institute of Technology] [Research center] (RCD)
WCCC	Wisconsin Clinical Cancer Center [University of Wisconsin] [Research center] (RCD)
WCF	Workload Control File (NITA)
WCGA	World Computer Graphics Association [Washington, DC] (EANO)
WCGM	Writable Character Generation Module [Data processing] (BUR)
WCI	Warner Communications, Inc. [NYSE symbol]
WCIS	Wisconsin Career Information System [Information service]
WCIU	Workshop Computer Interface Unit (MCD)
WCL	Word Control Logic (NITA)
WCLP	Women's Computer Literacy Project [Commercial firm] [San Francisco, CA] (EANO)
WCM	Writable Control Memory [Data processing] (BUR)
WCR	Word Count Register (NITA)
WCS	Wallace Computer Services [NYSE symbol]
WCS	Wang Computer System (NITA)
WCS	Writable Control Storage [Data processing]
WCTP	Wire Chief Test Panel [Telecommunications] (TEL)
WD	Word
WD	Write Data (NITA)
WD	Write Direct (OA)
WDC	Western Digital Corporation [American Stock Exchange symbol]
WDC	World Data Center [National Academy of Sciences] [Data collection and exchange center]
WDC	Write Data Check (CMD)
WDCL	Western Digital Corporation [NASDAQ symbol] (NQ)
WDCS	Writable Diagnostic Control Store (NITA)
WDM	Wavelength Division Multiplex
WDP	Women in Data Processing [San Diego, CA] (EANO)
WDPC	Western Data Processing Center [University of California, Los Angeles]
WDT	Watch Dog Timer (CIT)
WE	Western Electric Co.
W/e	Width-to-Length [Ratio] (MDG)
WE	Write Enable (IEEE)
WEA	Warner-Eddison Associates, Inc. [Information service] (EISS)
WEC	Westinghouse Electric Corporation
WECO	Western Electric Company
WECO	Westinghouse Electric Corporation
WEDAC	Westinghouse Digital Airborne Computer
WEFAX	Weather Facsimile Experiment [Environmental Science Services Administration]
WEMA	Western Electronic Manufacturers Association [Later, AEA]
WENDS	World Energy Data System [Department of Energy] [Information service] (EISS)
WES	Wind Electric System [Telecommunications] (TEL)
WESCON	Western Electronics Show and Convention [IEEE]
WEST	Western Educational Society for Telecommunications [Arizona State University] [Tempe, AZ] (EANO)
WESTAR 6	Communications satellite
WESTFORNET	Western Forest Research Information Network
West Union Tech Rev	Western Union Technical Review [A publication]
WETAC	Westinghouse Electronic Tubeless Analog Computer
WETARFAC	Work Element Timer and Recorder for Automatic Computing
WFD	Waveform Distortion [Telecommunications] (TEL)
WFF	Well-Formed Formula [Logic]
WFG	Waveform Generator
WFL	Work Flow Language [Data processing] (BUR)
WG	Working Group (FAAC)
WGBC	Waveguide Operating below Cutoff (IEEE)
WH	Watt-Hour
WH	We Have, Ready with Called Party [Telecommunications] (TEL)
WH	Western Hemlock [Utility pole] [Telecommunications] (TEL)
WHAI	Walter Hinchman Associates, Incorporated [Chevy Chase, MD] [Telecommunications] (TSSD)
WHCLIS	White House Conference on Library and Information Services [Washington, DC, 1979]
WHCS	Well History Control System [Petroleum Information Corp.] [Information service] (EISS)
WHO	World Health Organization [The pronunciation "who" is not acceptable] [United Nations affiliate] [Geneva, Switzerland] [Databank originator]
WI	Welding Institute [Cambridge, England] [Database originator and operator] (EANO)
WICHE	Western Interstate Commission of Higher Education
WID	Width

Acronym	Definition
WIDETRACK	Wideband Transmission Relay Acoustic Communications (MCD)
WIDJET	Waterloo Interactive Direct Job Entry Terminal System [*IBM Corp.*]
WIDOWAC	Wing Design Optimization with Aerolastic Constraints [*Computer program*]
WIMIS	Walk-In Management Information System [*Data processing*]
WIMS	Works Information and Management System [*M & E White Consultants Ltd.*] [*Software package*] [*British*] (NCC)
WIN	Well Information Network [*Database*] (CUAD)
WIN	Wiswesser Line Notation [*Information retrieval*] (ODIN)
WINC	Worldwide Integrated Communications [*Mohawk Data Sciences Corp.*] [*Parsippany, NJ*] [*Telecommunications*] (TSSD)
WIP	Women in Information Processing (EANO)
WIP	Work in Progress (AFM)
WIPO	World Intellectual Property Organization [*Geneva, Switzerland*]
WIPS	Word Image Processing System [*Datacopy*]
WISCOM	Wisconsin Information Science and Communications Consortium [*University of Wisconsin - Madison*] [*Research center*] (RCD)
WISE	Wang Intersystem Exchange (NITA)
WISE	World Information Systems Exchange [*Defunct*] (EANO)
WISER	Western Information System for Energy Resources [*Dataline, Inc.*] [*Database*] (CUAD)
WIT	Women in Telecommunications [*San Francisco, CA*] (EANO)
WITS	Washington Interagency Telecommunications System [*GSA*]
WJCC	Western Joint Computer Conference
WKQDR	Work Queue Directory (OA)
WL	Wavelength [*Electronics*]
WL	Western Larch [*Utility pole*] [*Telecommunications*] (TEL)
WL	Word Line (NITA)
WLN	Washington Library Network [*Washington State Library*] [*Olympia, WA*] [*Library network*]
WLN	Western Library Network [*Library of Congress*] [*Database*] (CUAD)
WL/PD	Warner-Lambert/Parke-Davis [*Computer files of chemical and biological data*]
WLR	Wrong Length Record [*Data processing*] (TUT)
WLSP	World List of Scientific Periodicals [*A publication*] (DIT)
WM	Word Mark (BUR)
WMI	World Metal Index [*Sheffield City Libraries*] [*British*] [*Information service*] (EISS)
WMIB	Waste Management Information Bureau [*Atomic Energy Authority*] [*British*] [*Information service*] (EISS)
WMO	World Meteorological Organization [*See also OMM*] [*Geneva, Switzerland*] (EANO)
WMR	Wideband Multichannel Receiver
WN	Wrong Number [*Telecommunications*] (TEL)
WNIC	With No Identification Columns [*Intelligent assistant communication*]
WNO	Wrong Number [*Telecommunications*] (TEL)
WNTL	Winterhalter, Inc. [*NASDAQ symbol*] (NQ)
WO	Without (AFM)
WO	Write Only
WOGSC	World Organization of General Systems and Cybernetics [*Blackburn, England*]
WOM	Write-Only Memory [*Data processing*] (TUT)
WOM	Write Optional Memory (IEEE)
WOP	World Oil Project [*National Science Foundation*] (EISS)
WOPC	World Oceanographic Data Processing and Services Center
WOPR	War Operation Plan Response [*Pronounced "whopper"*] [*Name of NORAD computer in film "WarGames"*]
WORAM	Word-Oriented Random Access Memory [*Data processing*] (MCD)
Word and Inf Process	Word and Information Processing [*A publication*]
Word Process Now	Word Processing Now [*A publication*]
WORM	Write Once, Read Mostly [*Data processing*]
WOROM	Write-Only Read-Only Memory [*Data processing*] (MDG)
WOSUS	Wang Office Systems User Society (CSR)
WP	Wespercorp [*American Stock Exchange symbol*]
WP	Western Pine [*Utility pole*] [*Telecommunications*] (TEL)
WP	Word Processing [*Movement to improve secretarial/clerical function through a managed system of people, procedures, and modern office equipment*]
WP	Word Processor
WP	Write Protect (NITA)
WP/AS	Word Processing/Administrative Support [*Extension of Word Processing*]
WPATC	Western Pennsylvania Advanced Technology Center [*University of Pittsburgh, Carnegie-Mellon University*] [*Research center*] (RCD)
WPC	Watts per Candle [*Electricity*]
WPC	Weldable Printed Circuit
WPC	Wired Program Computer
WPC	Word Processing Center
WP + C	Work Planning and Control [*Data processing*]
WPDA	Writing Pushdown Acceptor (NITA)
WPI	World Patents Index [*Derwent Publications Ltd.*] [*Database*]
WPL	Wave Propagation Laboratory [*University of Houston*] [*National Oceanic and Atmospheric Administration*] [*Research center*]
WPM	Words per Minute
WPM	Write Program Memory [*Data processing*]
WPM	Write Protect Memory (NITA)
WPN	Write Punch [*Data processing*] (MCD)
WPS	International Association of Word Processing Specialists [*Formerly, NAWPS*] (EANO)
WPS	Word Processing System (BUR)
WPS	Words per Second
WPSI	Word Processing Society, Incorporated (EANO)
WR	Working Register (NITA)
WR	Write (CAH)
WRA	Water Resources Abstracts [*Database*] [*A publication*]
WRAIS	Wide Range Analog Input Subsystem (NITA)
WRG	Wrong [*Telecommunications*] (TEL)
WRI	Waterloo Research Institute [*University of Waterloo*] [*Research center*] (RCD)
WRIU	Write Interface Unit (NITA)
WRQ	Westinghouse Resolver/Quantizer (IEEE)
WRRS	Wire Relay Radio System
WRS	Washington Representative Services, Inc. [*Information service*] (EISS)
WRS	Working Transmission Reference System [*Telecommunications*] (TEL)
WRSIC	Water Resources Scientific Information Center [*Department of the Interior*] [*Washington, DC*] [*Database originator*]
WRTC	Working Reference Telephone Circuit [*Telecommunications*] (TEL)
WRU	Who Are You? [*Communication*]
WS	Weak Signals [*Radio*]
WS	Wire Send [*Telecommunications*] (TEL)
WS	Working Space (NITA)
WS	Working Storage [*Data processing*] (MDG)
WSAA	Waveguide Slot Array Antenna
WSC	Wideband Signal Conditioner (MCD)
WSCA	World Surface Coatings Abstracts [*Paint Research Association*] [*Database*] [*A publication*]
WSD	World Systems Division [*of Communications Satellite Corp.*] [*Telecommunications*] (TEL)
WSDB	World Studies Data Bank (EISS)
WSF	Work Station Facility (NITA)
WSG	Wired Shelf Group [*Telecommunications*] (TEL)
WSI	Wafer-Scale Integration [*Microelectronics*]
WSI	Weather Services International Corp. [*Information service*] (EISS)
WSP	Wideband Signal Processor
WSR	Weak Signal Reception
WSVA	Wang Software Vendors' Association [*Defunct*] (EANO)
WT	Will Talk [*Telecommunications*] (TEL)
WT	Wireless Telegraphy [*or Telephony*]
WT	Word Terminal (NITA)
WTA	World Teleport Association [*New York, NY*] [*Telecommunications*] (TSSD)
WTA	World Textile Abstracts [*Shirley Institute*] [*Database*] [*British*]
WTC	Western Telecommunications Consulting Co. [*Los Angeles, CA*] [*Telecommunications*] (TSSD)
WTCI	Western Telecommunications, Incorporated [*Englewood, CO*] [*Telecommunications*] (CBSS)
WTEL	Walker Telecommunications Corp. [*NASDAQ symbol*] (NQ)
WTI	World Transindex [*International Translations Centre*] [*Bibliographic database*] [*Dutch*] (OBD)
WTO	Write-to-Operator [*Data processing*] (IBMDP)
WTOR	Write-to-Operator with Reply [*Data processing*] (IBMDP)
WTS	Word Terminal Synchronous
4WTS	Four-Wire Terminating Set [*Telecommunications*] (TEL)
WU	Western Union Corp. [*Upper Saddle River, NJ*] [*NYSE symbol*]
WUC	Western Union Corporation (NITA)
WUEMI	Western Union Electronic Mail, Incorporated [*McLean, VA*] [*Telecommunications*] (TSSD)
WUI	Western Union International [*Division of WUI, Inc.*]
WUIS	Water Use Information System [*Westinghouse Hanford Co.*] (EISS)
WULDS	Western Union Long Distance Service [*Western Union Telegraph Co.*] [*Upper Saddle River, NJ*] [*Telecommunications*] (TSSD)
WUT	Western Union Telegraph Co. [*Upper Saddle River, NJ*] [*NYSE symbol*]
WUTC	Western Union Telegraph Company [*Upper Saddle River, NJ*] (NITA)
WUTELCO	Western Union Telegraph Company [*Upper Saddle River, NJ*]
WUX	Western Union Exchange [*Teleprinter*]
WV	Working Voltage (MSA)
WVAC	Working Voltage, Alternating Current (DEN)
WVDC	Working Voltage, Direct Current
WVNET	West Virginia Network for Educational Telecomputing [*Morgantown, WV*] [*Research center*] (RCD)
WW	Wire Way [*Technical drawings*]
WW	Wire-Wound
WWCC	Western Wisconsin Communications Cooperative [*Independence, WI*] [*Telecommunications*] (TSSD)
WWRF	Who's Who Resource File [*Minority Business Development Agency*] [*Database*] (FDB)
WWW	World Weather Watch [*World Meteorological Office*] [*Databank*]
WX	Westinghouse Electric Corp. [*NYSE symbol*] [*Wall Street slang name: "Wex"*]
WXTRN	Weak External Reference [*Data processing*] (BUR)

WYSIWYG ... What You See Is What You Get [*Pronounced "whizziwig"*]
[*Indicates that video display on word processor bears a high-quality resemblance to printed page that will result*]

X-Y-Z

X	Transmit	
XA	Extended Architecture [*Data processing*]	
XA	Transmission Adapter	(MDG)
XACT	X Automatic Code Translation	(IEEE)
XAFH	X-Band Antenna Feed Horn	
XAS	X-Band Antenna System	
XB	Crossbar [*Bell System*]	
XBASIC	Extension of BASIC [*Data processing*]	
XBC	External Block Controller	(NITA)
XBIOS	Extended BIOS	
XBL	Extension Bell [*Telecommunications*]	(TEL)
XBM	Extended BASIC Mode [*International Computers Ltd.*]	(NITA)
XBT	Crossbar Tandem [*Telecommunications*]	(TEL)
Xc	Capacitive Reactance	
XCS	Ten Call Seconds [*Telecommunications*]	(TEL)
XCS	Xerox Computer Services [*Xerox Corp.*]	(NITA)
XCT	X-Band Communications Transponder	
XCVR	Transceiver	
XD	Crossed [*Telecommunications*]	(TEL)
XD	Ex-Directory [*Telecommunications*]	(TEL)
XDA	X-Band Drive Amplifier	
XDS	Xerox Data Systems [*Formerly, SDS*]	
XDUP	Extended Disk Utilities Program	(NITA)
XEBEC	XEBEC [*NASDAQ symbol*]	(NQ)
XEC	Execute	(DEEC)
XEQ	Execute	(SKY)
XFC	Extended Function Code	(NITA)
XFC	Transfer Charge [*Telecommunications*]	(TEL)
XFER	Transfer	
XFRMR	Transformer	
XGP	Xerox Graphic Printer [*Xerox Corp.*]	
XH	Sign-Filled Half-Word Designator [*Data processing*]	
XHF	Extra-High Frequency	
XIC	Transmission Interface Converter	
XICS	Xerox Integrated Composition System [*Xerox Corp.*] [*Computer typesetting system*]	
XID	Exchange Identification	(CCD)
XI/O	Execute Input/Output	(DEN)
XIS	X*PRESS Information Services [*Golden, CO*]	(EISS)
XIT	Extra Input Terminal	(NITA)
XL	Execution Language	(NITA)
XLISP	Extension of LISP [*List Processor*] 1.5 [*Programing language*]	(CSR)
XM	Expanded Memory	(NITA)
XMIT	Transmit [*or Transmitter*]	
XMS	Xerox Memory System	(NITA)
XMSN	Transmission	
XMT	Transmit	(MSA)
XMT	X-Band Microwave Transmitter	
XMTD	Transmitted	(MCD)
XMTG	Transmitting	
XMTL	Transmittal	(IEEE)
XMTR	Transmitter	
XMT-REC	Transmit-Receive	
XMTR-REC	Transmitter-Receiver	
XNOS	Experimental Network Operating System	(NITA)
XO	Crystal Oscillator	(IEEE)
XOC	Experimental On-Line Capabilities [*Data processing*]	
XOFF	Transmitter Off	(BUR)
XON	Cross-Office Highway [*Telecommunications*]	(TEL)
XON	Transmitter On	(BUR)
XOP	Extended Operation	(NITA)
XOR	Exclusive Or [*Gates*] [*Data processing*]	
XOS	Cross-Office Slot [*Telecommunications*]	(TEL)
XOS	Xerox Operating System	(CAH)
XOW	Express Order Wire [*Telecommunications*]	(TEL)
XPA	X-Band Parametric Amplifier	
XPA	X-Band Passive Array	
XPA	X-Band Planar Array	
XPA	X-Band Power Amplifier	
XPAA	X-Band Planar Array Antenna	
XPD	Cross-Polarization Discrimination	
XPI	Cross-Polarization Interference [*in radio transmission*]	(DEEC)
XPLOR	Xerox 9700 Users' Association	(EANO)
XPM	Xerox Planning Model [*A computerized representation of the Xerox Corp.'s operations*]	
XPPA	X-Band Pseudopassive Array	
XPPA	X-Band Pulsed Power Amplifier	
XPS	X-Band Phase Shifter	
XPSW	External Processor Status Word	(NITA)
XPT	Crosspoint [*Switching element*]	(MSA)
XPT	Express Paid Telegraph	
XPT	External Page Table [*Data processing*]	(BUR)
XPT	X-Band Pulse Transmitter	
XR	Index Register	(NITA)
X-REF	Cross Reference	(NG)
XRF	Experimental Reproduction Film	(DIT)
XRM	External Relational Memory	(NITA)
XRX	Xerox Corp. [*NYSE symbol*]	
XS3	Excess Three [*Code*]	(CAH)
XSA	X-Band Satellite Antenna	
XSTA	X-Band Satellite Tracking Antenna	
XSTD	X-Band Stripline Tunnel Diode	
XSTDA	X-Band Stripline Tunnel Diode Amplifier	
XSTR	Transistor	
XT	Cross Talk	(IEEE)
XTA	X-Band Tracking Antenna	
XTALK	Crosstalk [*Telecommunications*]	(MSA)
XTC	External Transmit Clock	
XTEL	Cross Tell	(IEEE)
XTEN	Xerox Telecommunications Network [*Proposed*]	(TSSD)
XTPA	X-Band Tunable Parametric Amplifier	
XTS	Cross-Tell Simulator	(IEEE)
XTWA	X-Band Traveling Wave Amplifier	
XTWM	X-Band Traveling Wave MASER	
XTX	X-Band Transmitter	(CIT)
XUG	Xyvision Users Group [*Richmond, VA*]	(EANO)
XVR	Exchange Voltage Regulator [*Telecommunications*]	(TEL)
XXC	Xerox Canada, Inc. [*Toronto Stock Exchange symbol*]	
YAP	Yield Analysis Pattern [*Data processing*]	
YCC	Computer Center [*Yale University*] [*Research center*]	(RCD)
YDC	Yaw Damper Computer	
YEC	Youngest Empty Cell	(NITA)
YG	Yankee Group [*Boston, MA*] [*Information service*] [*Telecommunications*]	(TSSD)
YIG	Yttrium Iron Garnet	
YN	Yes-No [*Response prompt*]	
YPD	Yellow Pages Datasystem [*National Planning Data Corp.*] [*Database*]	(CUAD)
YPS	Yellow Pages Service [*Telecommunications*]	(TEL)
YR	Year [*Online database field identifier*]	
YRAP	Yellow Page Rate Base Analysis Plan [*Bell System*]	
YTD	Year to Date	(MCD)
Z	Impedance [*Symbol*] [*IUPAC*]	
Z	Zero	
ZADI	Zentralstelle fuer Agrardokumentation und -Information [*Center for Agricultural Documentation and Information*] [*Databank originator*] [*Information service*] [*West German*]	(EISS)
ZAED	Zentralstelle fuer Atomkernenergie-Dokumentation beim Gmelin-Institut [*Central Agency for Atomic Energy Documentation of the Gmelin Institute*] [*Germany*] [*Database originator*] [*Also, AED*]	
ZAS	Zero Access Storage	
ZBB	Zero-Base Budgeting	
ZBMED	Zentralbibliothek der Medizin [*Cologne*] [*Information retrieval*] [*West German*]	(ODIN)
ZCR	Zero Crossing Rate	(NITA)
ZDE	Zentralstelle Dokumentation Elektrotechnik [*Electrical Engineering Documentation Center*] [*Offenbach, WG*] [*Originator and database*] [*Information service*]	(EISS)
ZDM	Zentralblatt fuer Didaktik der Mathematik [*Information retrieval*]	(ODIN)
ZED	Zero Express Dialing	
ZEGL	Ziegler Co., Inc. [*NASDAQ symbol*]	(NQ)
ZENT	Zentec Corp. [*NASDAQ symbol*]	(NQ)

ZFM .... Zentralblatt fuer Mathematik und Ihre Grenzgebiete [*Information retrieval*]   (ODIN)
ZFP .... Dokumentation Zerstorungsfreie Pruefung [*Nondestructive Testing Documentation*] [*West Germany*] [*Information service*]   (EISS)
Z/I .... Zoom In [*Cinematography and Video*]
ZIID .... Zentralinstitut fuer Information und Dokumentation [*Central Institute for Information and Documentation*] [*East Germany*] [*Information service*]   (EISS)
ZIL .... Zork Interactive Language [*Computer science*]
ZLISP .... Zilog List Processor [*Programing language*] [*1979*]   (CSR)
ZMMD ...... Zurich, Mainz, Munich, Darmstadt [*A joint European university effort on ALGOL processors*]
ZN .... Zone   (OA)
ZPID .... Zentralstelle fuer Psychologische Information und Dokumentation [*Center for Psychological Information and Documentation*] [*West Germany*] [*Database operator*] [*Information service*]   (EISS)
ZRC .... Zenith Radio Corporation
ZUM .... Zeitschrift fuer Urheber und Medienrecht [*NOMOS Datapool*] [*Database*]   (CUAD)
ZWC .... Zone Wind Computer
ZYT .... Zytec Computers [*Vancouver Stock Exchange symbol*]

Computer & Telecommunications Acronyms
By Meaning

A

A. M. Best Electronic Retrieval Services [*A. M. Best Co.*]
  [*Database*]   (CUAD) .... AMBERS
Abandon Call and Retry [*Telecommunications*] .... ACR
Abbreviated COBOL Preprocessor [*Data processing*]   (IEEE) .... ACOPP
Abbreviated Test Language for All Systems [*Data processing*] .... ATLAS
Abbreviated Test Language for Avionics Systems   (CAA) .... ATLAS
Abnormal End [*Data processing*] .... ABEND
Abridged Index Medicus Accessed by Teletypewriter Exchange
  Service [*National Library of Medicine*] .... AIM-TWX
Abrupt Junction Varactor Doubler .... AJVD
Abrupt Space Charge Edge [*Algorithm*] .... ASCE
Absolute [*Flowchart*] .... ABS
Absolute Address .... AA
Absolute Assembly Language [*Programing language*]   (BUR) .... AAL
Absolute Output [*Data processing*] .... AO
Absolute Value   (BUR) .... ABV
Absolute Value BIT [*Binary Digit*] **Synchronizer**   (CIT) .... AVBS
Absolute Virtual Address [*Data processing*]   (CAA) .... AVA
Absorption Limiting Frequency   (DEN) .... ALF
Abstract [*Online database field identifier*] .... AB
Abstract Family of Languages [*Data processing*] .... AFL
Abstract Information Digest Service [*Forest Products Research
  Society*] [*Madison, WI*] [*Information service*]   (EISS) .... AIDS
Abstract Machine Description Language [*1977*] [*Data processing*]
    (CSR) .... AMDL
Abstracted Business Information [*Data Courier, Inc.*] .... ABI
Abstracting Board [*International Council of Scientific Unions*]
  [*Information service*]   (EISS) .... AB
Abstracts of Computer Literature [*A publication*] .... Abstr Comput Lit
**Abstracts of Instructional Materials/Abstracts of Research
  Materials** .... AIM/ARM
Academic Computation Center [*Georgetown University*] [*Research
  center*]   (RCD) .... ACC
Academic Computer Center [*University of Washington*] [*Research
  center*]   (RCD) .... ACC
Academic Computer Facility [*Roosevelt University*] [*Research
  center*]   (RCD) .... ACF
Academic Computer Service [*Miami University*] [*Research center*]
    (RCD) .... ACS
Academic Computer Services [*Northeastern University*] [*Research
  center*]   (RCD) .... ACS
Academic Computer Services [*University of Calgary*] [*Research
  center*]   (RCD) .... ACS
Academic Computer Services [*Michigan Technological University*]
  [*Research center*]   (RCD) .... ACS
Academic Computer Services Division [*Milwaukee School of
  Engineering*] [*Research center*]   (RCD) .... ACSD
Academic Computing Center [*University of Vermont*] [*Research
  center*]   (RCD) .... ACC
Academic Computing Center [*University of California, Riverside*]
  [*Research center*]   (RCD) .... ACC
Academic Computing Group .... ACCOMP
Academic Computing Services [*Syracuse University*] [*Research
  center*]   (RCD) .... ACS
Academic Computing Services [*University of Colorado - Boulder*]
  [*Research center*]   (RCD) .... ACS
Academic Computing Services [*University of Wisconsin - Eau
  Claire*] [*Research center*]   (RCD) .... ACS
Academy for Educational Development [*Washington, DC*]
  [*Telecommunications*] .... AED
Accelerated Learning of Logic .... ALL
**Accelerated Project to Automate Critical Hardware Hardcore
  Systems** .... APACHE
Accent on Information [*Data bank for the handicapped and
  rehabilitation professionals sponsored by association of the
  same name*] [*Bloomington, IL*]   (EISS) .... AOI
Acceptable Quality Level [*Quality control*] .... AQL
Acceptable Reliability Level [*Quality control*] .... ARL
Acceptance Data Package   (KSC) .... ADP
Acceptance and Takeover Date [*Telecommunications*]   (TEL) .... ATD
Acceptance Test Plan [*or Procedure*] .... ATP
Access [*Telecommunications*]   (TEL) .... AC
Access [*Telecommunications*]   (MSA) .... ACS
Access Block Diagram .... ABD
Access Control Facility .... ACF
Access and Control Point [*Telecommunications*]   (TEL) .... A & CP
Access Control Register   (CAA) .... ACR
Access Method [*Data processing*] .... AM
Access Method Control Block [*Data processing*]   (BUR) .... ACB
**Access Method for Indexed Data Generalized for Operating
  System** [*Data processing*]   (TUT) .... AMIGOS
Access Method Service [*Data processing*]   (BUR) .... AMS
Access Point [*Telecommunications*]   (TEL) .... AP
Access Refusal and Barrier Interface Terminal [*Hardware-based
  security device from Computer Security Systems*] .... ARBITER
Access Type BITS [*Data processing*]   (OA) .... ATB
Accessed BIT [*Binary Digit*] [*Data processing*] .... A
Accession Number [*Online database field identifier*]   (OBD) .... ACN
Accession Number [*Online database field identifier*]   (OBD) .... AN
Accessory Drive System   (NG) .... ADS
Accident Information Retrieval System   (RDA) .... AIRS
Account [*or Accountant*]   (AFM) .... ACCT
Account Identification and Description Services [*Dun &
  Bradstreet*]   (EISS) .... AIDS
Account Identifier [*Data processing*] .... ACCTID
Account Manager Code   (TEL) .... AMC
Accountability Data Package   (MCD) .... ADP
Accountants Computer Users Technical Exchange [*Indianapolis,
  IN*] .... ACUTE
Accounting Computer System [*Burroughs Corp.*]   (CAA) .... ACSYS
Accounting Control System   (TUT) .... ACS
Accounting Control Table   (CMD) .... ACT
Accounting and Data Processing Abstracts [*A publication*] .... ADPA
Accounting Data System   (TUT) .... ADS
Accounting Incomplete Records System [*Software package*]
  [*British*]   (NCC) .... AIRS
Accounting Information System   (BUR) .... AIS
Accounting Line Number .... ALN
Accounting Processing Code .... APC
Accounts Register [*Data processing*] .... AR
Accumulation Distribution Unit [*Data processing*] .... ADU
Accumulator [*Data processing*]   (MDG) .... A
Accumulator [*Data processing*] .... AC
Accumulator [*Flowchart*]   (MSA) .... ACC
Accumulator High [*Data processing*] .... AH
Accumulator Low [*Data processing*] .... AL
Accumulator Register   (CAA) .... AR
Accumulator Register [*Data processing*] .... AX
Accumulator Switch [*Data processing*] .... ACS
Accumulators Shift Right [*Data processing*]   (BUR) .... ASR
Accurately Defined System [*Data processing*] .... ADS
Accuray Corp. [*NASDAQ symbol*]   (NQ) .... ACRA
Acknowledge Receipt Of [*Telecommunications*]   (TEL) .... AKRO
Acknowledgement Signal Unit [*Telecommunications*]   (TEL) .... ASU
Acknowledgement Unit [*Telecommunications*]   (TEL) .... ACU
Acknowledgment Character [*Keyboard*] [*Data processing*] .... ACK
Acknowledgment of Receipt [*Message handling*]
  [*Telecommunications*] .... AR
ACM [*Association for Computing Machinery*] **Accreditation
  Committee**   (CAH) .... ACMAC
ACM [*Association for Computing Machinery*] **National Conference
  Proceedings** [*A publication*] .... ACM Proc
ACM [*Association for Computing Machinery*] **Standards
  Committee**   (CAH) .... ACMSC
ACM [*Association for Computing Machinery*] **Transactions on
  Database Systems** [*A publication*] .... ACM Trans Database Syst
ACM [*Association for Computing Machinery*] **Transactions on
  Database Systems** [*A publication*] .... ACM Trans Database Systems
ACM [*Association for Computing Machinery*] **Transactions on
  Mathematical Software** [*A publication*] .... ACM Trans Math Softw
ACM [*Association for Computing Machinery*] **Transactions on
  Mathematical Software** [*A publication*] .... ACM Trans Math Software
ACM [*Association for Computing Machinery*] **Transactions on
  Office Information Systems** [*A publication*] .... ACM Trans Off Inf Syst
ACM [*Association for Computing Machinery*] **Transactions on
  Programming Languages and Systems** [*A publication*] .... ATPSD

Acorn RISC [Reduced Instruction Set Computer] ... ARM
Acoustic Control and Telemetry System ... ACTS
Acoustic Coupler [*Computer MODEM*] ... AC
Acoustic Data Analysis Center ... ADAC
Acoustic Data Capsule ... ACODAC
Acoustic Data Processor (MCD) ... ADP
Acoustic Data Reduction Program (CAAL) ... ADRP
Acoustic Deception Device (CAAL) ... ADD
Acoustic Detection Device (MCD) ... ADD
Acoustic Digital Memory ... ADM
Acoustic Intelligence Gathering System (CAAL) ... AIGS
Acoustic Telemetry Subsystem (MCD) ... ATS
Acoustic Transmission System ... ATS
Acoustic Wave Analysis ... AWA
Acoustic Wave Analysis System ... AWAS
Acoustical Society of America [*New York, NY*] ... ASA
Acquisition Bus Monitor [*Data processing*] (MCD) ... ABM
Acquisition and Control Query Executive [*Programing language*] (DDI) ... ACQE
Acquisition Data Input Equipment ... ADIE
Acronym Data Base ... ACRODABA
[*The*] **Acronym Generator** [*An RCA computer program*] ... TAG
Acronym May Be Ignored Totally [*Data processing*] (CSR) ... AMBIT/L
Acta Polytechnica Scandinavica. Mathematics and Computer Science Series [*A publication*] ... Acta Polytech Scand Math Comput Sci Ser
Acta Polytechnica Scandinavica. Mathematics and Computing Machinery Series [*Finland*] [*A publication*] ... Acta Polytech Scand Math Comput Mach Ser
Acta Polytechnica Scandinavica. Mathematics and Computing Machinery Series [*A publication*] ... Acta Polytech Scand Math and Comput Mach Ser
Action Data Automation [*British*] (NATG) ... ADA
Action Information Display System ... AIDS
Action Surveys, Incorporated [*Silver Spring, MD*] [*Information service*] (EISS) ... ASI
Active Business Records [*Bell & Howell Co.*] ... ABR
Active Certificate Information Program [*for stock certificates*] [*Data processing*] ... ACIP
Active Disk Table [*Data processing*] (IBMDP) ... ADT
Active File Table [*Data processing*] (IBMDP) ... AFT
Active Maintenance Downtime ... AMDT
Active Microwave Workshop ... AMW
Active Satellite Attitude Control ... ASAC
Active Status Register (CAA) ... ASR
Active Television System (MCD) ... ATS
Active Time List [*Data processing*] ... ATL
Actively Shared Knowledge [*Data processing system*] ... ASK
Activity Data Method (IEEE) ... ADM
Activity Data Sheet (IEEE) ... ADS
Actron Microprocessor Softwear Support System (MCD) ... AMSSS
Actual Block Processor [*IBM Corp.*] [*Data processing*] (BUR) ... ABP
Actual Measured Loss [*Telecommunications*] (TEL) ... AML
Actual Work Time [*Bell System*] ... AWT
Actuarial Data Base [*I. P. Sharp Associates*] [*Database*] (CUAD) ... ACT
Ada Joint Program Office [*Data processing*] (RDA) ... AJPO
Ada Programing Support Environments [*Data processing*] (RDA) ... APSE
Adage, Inc. [*NASDAQ symbol*] (NQ) ... ADGE
Adaptable Board Computer [*Signetics*] (CAA) ... ABC
Adaptable Data Base System [*Database management system*] ... ADABAS
Adaptable Data Manager [*Hitachi Ltd.*] [*Japan*] (CAA) ... ADM
Adaptable Surface Interface Terminal (MCD) ... ASIT
Adaptation Mathematical Processor ... AMP
Adapter Control Block [*Data processing*] (IBMDP) ... ACB
Adaption Binary Load [*Program*] (CET) ... ABL
Adaptive Arithmetical Method ... ADAM
Adaptive Computer Technologies ... ACT
Adaptive Control System ... ACS
Adaptive Control of Thought [*Computer simulation program*] ... ACT
Adaptive Differential Pulse Code Modulation (MCD) ... ADPCM
Adaptive Intercommunication Requirement (NASA) ... AIR
Adaptive Interference Cancellation System (CAAL) ... AICS
Adaptive Learning Network [*Data processing*] ... ALN
Adaptive Line Canceller and Enhancer (CAAL) ... ALICE
Adaptive Linear Predictive Coding (TEL) ... ALPC
Adaptive Logic Circuit (OA) ... ALC
Adaptive Man-Machine Nonarithmetic Information Processing [*Documentation*] ... AMNIP
Adaptive Mission-Oriented Software System (MCD) ... AMOSS
Adaptive Mode Planning System [*Computer program*] (CIT) ... AMPS
Adaptive Mode Planning System Input [*Computer program*] (CIT) ... AMPSIN
Adaptive Multiplexer (CAAL) ... AM
Adaptive Narrowband FM [*Frequency Modulation*] **MODEM** [*Telecommunications*] (TEL) ... ANBFM
Adaptive Null Antenna ... ANA
Adaptive Pattern Perceiving Electronic Computer System ... APPECS
Adaptive Predictive Coding [*Telecommunications*] (TEL) ... APC
Adaptive Programing Technology ... APT
Adaptive Pulse Code Modulation [*Telecommunications*] (TEL) ... APCM
Add BCD [*Binary Coded Decimal*] **Number with Extend** [*Data processing*] ... ABCD
Add One to Memory [*Data processing*] ... AOM
Add Packed [*Data processing*] ... AP
Added Entry [*Online database field identifier*] ... AE
Addendum (KSC) ... ADD
Adder [*Computer device*] ... ADDR
Adder [*Computer device*] (MDG) ... ADR
Adder, Logical, and Transfer Unit [*Computer*] ... ALTU
Addison Wesley Publishers [*NASDAQ symbol*] (NQ) ... ADSNB
Addison-Wesley Series in Computer Science and Information Processing [*A publication*] ... Addison-Wesley Ser Comput Sci Inform Process
Addition ... ADD
Additional (KSC) ... ADDL
Additional Listing [*Telecommunications*] (TEL) ... AL
Additional Memory Module (CAA) ... AMM
Additional Reference Carrier Transmission [*Telecommunications*] (TEL) ... ART
Additive Color Viewer Printer ... ACVP
Additive White Gaussian Noise [*Telecommunications*] (TEL) ... AWGN
Addmaster Corporation [*NASDAQ symbol*] (NQ) ... ADDC
Address [*Computer character*] [*Data processing*] ... A
Address [*Computer character*] [*Data processing*] ... ADDR
Address [*Computer character*] [*Data processing*] ... ADR
Address [*Computer character*] [*Data processing*] (AFM) ... ADRS
Address [*Message handling*] ... ADS
Address Arithmetic Unit [*Data processing*] (CAA) ... AAU
Address Bus [*Data processing*] ... AB
Address Coding Guide ... ACG
Address Complete, Charge [*Telecommunications*] (TEL) ... ADC
Address Complete, Coin-Box [*Telecommunications*] (TEL) ... ADX
Address Complete, No-Charge [*Telecommunications*] (TEL) ... ADN
Address Complete, Subscriber Free, Coin-Box [*Telecommunications*] (TEL) ... AFX
Address Complete, Subscriber Free, No-Charge [*Telecommunications*] (TEL) ... AFN
Address Constant [*Data processing*] ... ADCON
Address Control Unit [*Data processing*] (MDG) ... ACU
Address Incomplete [*Telecommunications*] (TEL) ... ADI
Address Incomplete [*Telecommunications*] (TEL) ... AI
Address Indicating Group [*Data processing*] [*NATO*] ... AIG
Address Key Register (CAA) ... AKR
Address Latch Enable [*Data processing*] ... ALE
Address Locator Logic [*Data processing*] ... ALL
Address Mark [*Microprocessors*] ... AM
Address Mode [*Data processing*] (CAA) ... AM
Address Modifier (CAA) ... AM
Address Recognition Unit (CAA) ... ARU
Address Register (BUR) ... ADR
Address Register (CMD) ... AR
Address-Selective [*British*] (MCD) ... ADSEL
Address Space Identifier (BUR) ... ASID
Address Translation Chip ... ATC
Address Translator [*Data processing*] (CAA) ... AT
Address Unit [*Data processing*] ... AU
Addressable Remote Multiplexer Unit (MCD) ... ARMU
Addressograph-Multigraph Copier Duplicator ... AMCD
Adelson-Velskii and Landis Trees [*Data processing*] ... AVL
Adjacent Channel Interference ... ACI
Adjacent Charging Group [*Telecommunications*] (TEL) ... ACG
Adjoint Gamma-Ray Moments [*Computer code*] ... ADJMOM
Adjust Mode [*Data processing*] ... ADMD
Adjusted Output [*Data processing*] ... AO
Adjutant General Management Information System ... AGMIS
Administration [*or Administrator*] ... ADMIN
Administration of Designed Services (TEL) ... ADS
Administrative Computing Service (CIT) ... ACS
Administrative Control System [*Telecommunications*] (TEL) ... ACS
Administrative Data Processing (KSC) ... ADP
Administrative Data Systems ... ADS
Administrative Data Systems - Teleprocessing (IEEE) ... ADS-TP
Administrative Engineering Information Management System ... AEIMS
Administrative Information Data System (AFM) ... AIDS
Administrative Telecommunications Agency [*Canada*] ... ATA
Administrative Terminal System [*IBM Corp.*] ... ATS
Adoption of Automatically Programed Tools [*Data processing*] (IEEE) ... ADAPT
ADP [*Automatic Data Processing*] **Systems Resources Analysis** ... ASRA
ADPE [*Automatic Data Processing Equipment*] **Resources Management System** (AFM) ... ARMS
Adult and Vocational Educational Electronic Mail Network [*National Center for Research in Vocational Education*] [*Columbus, OH*] [*Telecommunications*] (TSSD) ... ADVOCNET
Advance [*Flowchart*] (AFM) ... ADV
Advance Circuit Order and Layout Information [*Telecommunications*] (TEL) ... ACOLI
Advance Count Switch ... ACS
Advance Payment [*Telecommunications*] (TEL) ... AP
Advance Programing and Proposal Operations (MCD) ... AP & PO
Advanced Accounting System (TUT) ... AAS
Advanced Analytical [*In company name, AA Computer Systems*] [*Tarzana, CA*] [*Software manufacturer*] (DASOS) ... AA
Advanced Banking On-Line System (BUR) ... ABOS
Advanced Business Communications, Incorporated [*McLean, VA*] [*Telecommunications*] (TSSD) ... ABCI

Advanced Business Processor [*Datapoint Corp.*] (CAA) ... ABP
Advanced Circuit Module ... ACM
Advanced Color Technology, Inc. [*Chelmsford, MA*] [*Printer manufacturer*] ... ACT
Advanced Command Data System (NG) ... ACDS
Advanced Communications Control System (CAAL) ... ACCS
Advanced Communications Equipment Depot (NATG) ... ACED
Advanced Communications Function [*IBM Corp.*] [*Data processing*] ... ACF
Advanced Communications Service [*Later, AIS*] [*AT & T*] ... ACS
Advanced Communications Technology [*Tymshare, Inc.*] (CAA) ... ACT
Advanced Compilation Equipment (MCD) ... ACE
Advanced Computational Processor ... ACP
Advanced Computer for Array Processing ... ACAP
Advanced Computer Communications [*Santa Barbara, CA*] [*Hardware manufacturer*] (DASO) ... ACC
Advanced Computer Environmental Systems Support, Inc. [*Silver Spring, MD*] [*Hardware manufacturer*] (DASO) ... ACESS
Advanced Computer for Medical Research [*Stanford University*] ... ACME
Advanced Computer Oriented System (BUR) ... ACOS
Advanced Computer Services [*Honeywell Information Systems*] (IEEE) ... ACS
Advanced Computer System [*IBM Corp.*] (IEEE) ... ACS
Advanced Computer Techniques Corp. [*NASDAQ symbol*] (NQ) ... ACTP
Advanced Computer Techniques Project (KSC) ... ACTP
Advanced Continuous Simulation Language [*Pronounced "axle"*] [*Data processing*] (CSR) ... ACSL
Advanced Data Communications Control Procedure [*American National Standards Institute*] ... ADCCP
Advanced Data Entry (CAA) ... ADE
Advanced Data Link Control [*Data processing*] (CAA) ... ADLC
Advanced Data Management [*Kingston, NJ*] ... ADAM
Advanced Data Scalar (CIT) ... ADS
Advanced Database System (CAA) ... ADBS
Advanced Debugging System (CAA) ... ADS
Advanced Design Methods Laboratory [*Ohio State University*] [*Research center*] (RCD) ... ADML
Advanced Digital Signal Processor ... ADSP
Advanced Diskette Operating System (CAA) ... ADOS
Advanced Display System ... ADS
Advanced Electronic Design ... AED
Advanced Fault Tree Analysis Program [*SIA Computer Services*] [*Software package*] [*British*] (NCC) ... AFTP
Advanced File Organization (CAA) ... AFO
Advanced Hybrid Computer System ... AHCS
Advanced Image Management Software [*Data processing*] ... AIMS
Advanced Information Manager [*Fujitsu Ltd.*] [*Japan*] (CAA) ... AIM
Advanced Information System/Net 1 Service [*Formerly, ACS*] [*American Bell, Inc.*] ... AIS
Advanced Instructional System (MCD) ... AIS
Advanced Instrumentation and Data Analysis System ... AIDAS
Advanced Integrated Data System (AFM) ... AIDS
Advanced Integrated Diagnostics (BUR) ... AID
Advanced Integrated Magnetic Anomaly Detection System (MCD) ... AIMS
Advanced Integrated Modular Instrumentation System (MCD) ... AIMIS
Advanced Integrated Safety and Optimizing Computer ... ADVISOR
Advanced Interactive Debugging System (CAA) ... AIDS
Advanced Interactive Draughting [*McGrane Computer Systems Ltd.*] [*Software package*] [*British*] (NCC) ... AID
Advanced Interactive Presentation System ... AIPS
Advanced Interior Communication System ... AICS
Advanced Library Concepts, Inc. [*Honolulu, HI*] [*Information service*] (EISS) ... ALC
Advanced Library Systems, Inc. [*Andover, MA*] [*Information service*] (EISS) ... ALS
Advanced Life Information System [*Data processing*] ... ALIS
Advanced Linear Programing System [*Operational research technique*] ... ALPS
Advanced Memory Systems, Inc. (IEEE) ... AMS
Advanced Micro Devices, Inc. [*Computer manufacturer*] [*NYSE symbol*] ... AMD
Advanced Microprocessor Programing Language [*Texas Instruments, Inc.*] (CAA) ... AMPL
Advanced Microprocessor Prototyping Laboratory [*Texas Instruments, Inc.*] (CAA) ... AMPL
Advanced Microprogramable Processors (MCD) ... AMPP
Advanced Minuteman Computer ... AMC
Advanced Mobile Phone Service [*Bell System*] ... AMPS
Advanced Mobile Telephone System (MCD) ... AMTS
Advanced Model Builder Shell [*Programing language*] [*1970*] (CSR) ... AMBUSH
Advanced Narrowband Digital Voice Terminal (MCD) ... ANDVT
Advanced Network System Architecture (BUR) ... ANSA
Advanced On-Board Processor [*Computer*] ... AOP
Advanced Operating Facility [*Computer Technology, Inc.*] (CAA) ... AOF
Advanced Operating System [*Data General Corp.*] (CAA) ... AOS
Advanced Optical Character Reader ... AOCR
Advanced Patent Technique (TUT) ... APT
Advanced Performance Computer ... APC
Advanced Personnel Data System (MCD) ... APDS
Advanced Programing Course [*Data processing*] ... APC
Advanced Programing Language [*Data processing*] ... APL
Advanced Programing Language Statistical Package (MCD) ... APLSTATPACK
Advanced Real-Time Executive (BUR) ... ARE
Advanced Reconfigurable Computer System ... ARCS
Advanced Reconnaissance Satellite ... ARS
Advanced Research Projects Agency ... ARPA
Advanced Research and Technology (MUGU) ... AR & T
Advanced Research and Technology ... ART
Advanced Scientific Computer [*Texas Instruments, Inc.*] ... ASC
Advanced Scientific Instruments Symbolic Translator [*Assembly program*] (DEN) ... ASIST
Advanced Shipboard Communications ... ADSCOM
Advanced Signal Processor [*Data processing*] ... ASP
Advanced Simulation Technology (IEEE) ... AST
Advanced Software Products, Inc. [*Delray Beach, FL*] [*Software manufacturer*] (DASOS) ... ASP
Advanced Solid Logic Technology [*Data processing*] ... ASLT
Advanced Statistical Analysis Program [*Data processing*] (MCD) ... ASTAP
Advanced System [*NAS*] (CAA) ... AS
Advanced System for Communications and Education in National Development (MCD) ... ASCEND
Advanced System Concept (MCD) ... ASC
Advanced System Data Processing Simulation ... ASDPSIM
Advanced Systems Division [*IBM Corp.*] ... ASD
Advanced Systems Engineering (DDI) ... ASE
Advanced Systems Technology (IEEE) ... ASTEC
Advanced Technology [*In PC AT, model name of a computer*] [*IBM Corp.*] ... AT
Advanced Technology/Libraries [*Information service*] ... AT/L
Advanced Technology Microelectronic Array Computer (MCD) ... ATMAC
Advanced Technology Satellite ... ATS
Advanced Technology Systems, Inc. [*Arlington, VA*] [*Telecommunications*] (TSSD) ... ATS
Advanced Television Seeker (MCD) ... ATVS
Advanced Text Management System [*IBM Corp.*] ... ATMS
Advanced Time-Division Multiple Access (IEEE) ... ATDMA
Advanced TV Systems Committee (EANO) ... ATVSC
Advanced Universal Jamming System ... AUJS
Advanced Very-Large-Scale Integration [*Electronics*] ... AVLSI
Advanced Vidicon Camera System ... AVCS
Advanced Visual Information Display ... AVID
Advances in Electronics and Electron Physics [*A publication*] ... Advan Electron and Electron Phys
Advances in Electronics and Electron Physics [*A publication*] ... Adv Electron Electron Phys
Advances in Electronics and Electron Physics. Supplement [*A publication*] ... Adv Electron Electron Phys Suppl
Advances in Engineering Software [*A publication*] ... Adv Engng Software
Advances in Engineering Software [*A publication*] ... Adv Eng Software
Adventist Radio Television Services [*Canada*] ... ARTS
Advertised Computer Technologies [*Data Courier, Inc.*] [*Database*] [*Information service*] (EISS) ... ACT
Advertising and Marketing Intelligence Service [*Mead Data Central*] [*Database*] (EISS) ... AMI
Advice of Charge [*Telecommunications*] (TEL) ... AC
Advise Duration and Charge [*British telephone term*] ... AD and C
Adviser Business Oriented Language [*Programing language*] (CAA) ... ABOL
Advisory Committee for the Co-Ordination of Information Systems [*Database producer*] (CUAD) ... ACCIS
Advisory Committee on Information Dissemination in Science and Technology ... CIDST
Advisory Committee for Scientific and Technical Information [*British*] (DIT) ... ACSTI
Advisory Group for Aerospace Research and Development [*Paris, France*] ... AGARD
Advisory Unit for Computer Based Education [*Hatfield, England*] [*Information service*] [*Telecommunications*] (TSSD) ... AUCBE
Aerial Distribution Wire [*Telecommunications*] (TEL) ... ADW
Aerial Tape Armor [*Telecommunications*] (TEL) ... AT
Aero/Acoustic Rotor (RDA) ... A/AR
Aerodynamic Data Analysis and Integration System [*Data processing*] ... ADAIS
Aeronautical Communications Satellite System [*Proposed*] ... AEROSAT
Aeronautical Fixed Telecommunications Network ... AFTN
Aeronautical Fixed Telecommunications Service ... AFTS
Aeronautical Radio, Incorporated [*Annapolis, MD*] [*Telecommunications*] ... ARINC
Aeronautical Radionavigation Land Station [*ITU designation*] ... AL
Aeronautical Radionavigation Mobile Station [*ITU designation*] ... AM
Aeronautical Telecommunications Operator ... ATO
Aeronomy Satellite - Neutral Atmosphere Temperature Experiment ... AEROS-NATE
Aerospace Business Environment Simulator [*Computer-programed management game*] ... ABES
Aerospace Communications ... AEROSPACECOM
Aerospace Data Systems (MCD) ... ADS
Aerospace and Environmental Medicine Information System (EISS) ... AEMIS
Aerospace Intelligence Data System [*IBM Corp.*] (DIT) ... AIDS
Aerospace Research Satellite ... ARS
Aetna Telecommunications Consultants [*Centerville, MA*] [*Telecommunications*] (TSSD) ... ATC

Affiliate ... AFFIL
Affiliated Computer Systems [*Dallas, TX*] [*Telecommunications*] (TSSD) ... ACS
Affiliation of Author [*Online database field identifier*] (OBD) ... AF
AFIPS [*American Federation of Information Processing Societies*] **National Computer Conference and Exposition. Conference Proceedings** [*A publication*] ... AFIPS Nat Comput Conf Expo Conf Proc
After Date of Award of Contract [*Telecommunications*] (TEL) ... ADA
After Receipt of Order ... ARO
AFTN [*Aeronautical Fixed Telecommunications Network*] **Communications Center** [*FAA*] (FAAC) ... AFCOM
Again [*Telecommunications*] (TEL) ... AG
Agence des Telecommunications Administratives [*Administrative Telecommunications Agency*] [*Canada*] ... ATA
Agence des Telecommunications Gouvernementales [*Government Telecommunications Agency*] [*Canada*] ... ATG
Agence Transequatoriale des Communications [*Trans-Equatorial Communications Agency*] [*or CCEAE*] ... ATEC
Agency of Industrial Science and Technology [*Japanese*] (NASA) ... AIST
Agency for Instructional Television ... AIT
Agri-Markets Data Service [*Capitol Publications, Inc.*] [*Database*] (FDB) ... AMDS
Agricultural Computer Association [*Elk Grove, CA*] (EANO) ... ACA
Agricultural, Ecological, and Geographical Information System (CAA) ... AEGIS
Agricultural Information Bank for Asia [*Southeast Asian Regional Center for Graduate Study and Research in Agriculture*] [*Laguna, Philippines*] [*Information service*] (EISS) ... AIBA
Agricultural Information and Documentation Section [*Royal Tropical Institute*] [*Amsterdam, Netherlands*] [*Information service*] (EISS) ... AIDS
Agricultural Network Serving Extension and Research [*University of Kentucky*] [*Information service*] [*Research center*] (EISS) ... ANSER
Agricultural On-Line Access [*Formerly, CAIN*] [*National Agricultural Library, Information Systems Division*] [*Beltsville, MD*] [*Bibliographic database*] [*Information service*] (EISS) ... AGRICOLA
Agricultural Research Information Centre [*New Delhi, India*] (EISS) ... ARIC
Agricultural Research Information System [*United Nations*] ... AGRIS
AGS Computers, Inc. [*NYSE symbol*] ... AGS
AGS Computers, Inc. [*NASDAQ symbol*] (NQ) ... AGSC
Aiken Dahlgren Electronic Calculator ... ADEC
Air Communications Network ... AIRCOMNET
Air Data Computer Static Pressure Compensator (MCD) ... ADCSPC
Air Data Computers [*or Computing*] (MCD) ... ADC
Air Data Computing System ... ADCS
Air Data Converter ... ADC
Air Data Package ... ADP
Air Data Probe (MCD) ... ADP
Air Data Sensor (MCD) ... ADS
Air Data Subsystem (RDA) ... ADS
Air Data Transducer (MCD) ... ADT
Air Data Transducer Assembly (NASA) ... ADTA
Air Density/Injun [*Explorer satellite*] ... AD/I
Air Flow Actuated Switch ... AFAS
Air-Ground-Air Communications System ... AGACS
Air-Ground Communications Channel ... AGCC
Air Isolated Monolithic [*Circuit*] ... AIM
Air Lines of Communication ... AIRLOC
Air Monitoring Analysis and Prediction [*System*] ... AIRMAP
Air Navigation Radio Aids ... ANRA
Air Pollution Information and Computation System ... APICS
Air Pollution Technical Information Center [*Also, NAPTIC*] [*Environmental Protection Agency*] [*Bibliographic database*] ... APTIC
Air Pressure Analysis Program [*Bell System*] ... AIRPAP
Air Traffic Data Processor ... ATDP
Air Transportable Acoustic Communications (CAAL) ... ATAC
Air Transportable Communications Complex ... ATRAX
Airline Group of International Federation of Operational Research Societies [*Lyngby, Denmark*] ... AGIFORS
Airport Business Center, Incorporated [*Minneapolis, MN*] [*Telecommunications*] (TSSD) ... ABCI
Aktiebolaget Atomenergi Computer-Based User-Oriented Service ... ABACUS
Al Lee & Associates, Inc. [*Dallas, TX*] [*Software manufacturer*] (DASOS) ... ALA
Alarm [*Telecommunications*] (TEL) ... AL
Alarm Communications and Display Segment (MCD) ... ACADS
Alarm Communications and Display System (MCD) ... ACAD
Alarm Control Module [*Telecommunications*] (TEL) ... ACM
Alarm and Control System [*Telecommunications*] (TEL) ... ACS
Alarm Control Unit [*Bell System*] [*Telecommunications*] ... ACU
Alarm Display and Control Unit [*Telecommunications*] (TEL) ... ADCU
Alarm Indication Signal [*Telecommunications*] (TEL) ... AIS
Alarm Inhibit Signal [*Telecommunications*] (TEL) ... AIS
Alarm Interface Unit [*Telecommunications*] (TEL) ... AIU
Alarm Monitor Computer ... AMC
Alarm Monitor Unit [*Telecommunications*] (TEL) ... AMU
Alarm Receiving and Reporting Equipment [*Telecommunications*] (TEL) ... ARRE
Alarm Reporting Telephone [*Telecommunications*] (TEL) ... ART
Alarm Termination Subsystem [*Telecommunications*] (TEL) ... ATS
Alaskan Integrated Communications Exchange ... ALICE
Albanian Telegraph Agency ... ATA
Alberta Microelectronic Centre [*University of Alberta*] [*Research center*] (RCD) ... AMC
Alberta Statistical Information System [*Alberta Treasury, Bureau of Statistics*] [*Database*] (CUAD) ... ASIST
Album Oriented Rock ... AOR
Alcatel Thomson Gigadisc [*Optical disk*] ... ATG
Alcatel-Thomson Gigadisk ... AGA
Alerting Search Service from Kinokuniya [*Kinokuniya Co. Ltd.*] [*Tokyo, Japan*] [*Information service*] (EISS) ... ASK
Alexander & Alexander Services, Inc. [*NYSE symbol*] ... AAL
Algebra Package [*Data processing*] ... ALPAK
Algebraic Compiler [*Data processing*] ... ALCOM
Algebraic Compiler and Translator [*Data processing*] ... ACT
Algebraic Interpretive Dialogue [*Data processing*] (BUR) ... AID
Algebraic Manipulation by Identity Translation (TUT) ... AMBIT
Algebraic Operating System [*Texas Instruments, Inc.*] [*Data processing*] ... AOS
Algebraic Technological Function [*Data processing*] ... ATF
Algebraic Translator [*Programing language*] [*1969*] ... ALTRAN
Algebraic Translator and Compiler [*Data processing*] (MCD) ... ALTAC
ALGOL Compiler [*Data processing*] (DIT) ... ALCOM
ALGOL Extended for Design [*1967*] [*Data processing*] ... AED
ALGOL-to-FORTRAN Translator [*Data processing*] (MCD) ... ALFTRAN
Algonquin Radio Observatory [*Herzberg Institute of Astrophysics, National Research Council of Canada*] [*Research center*] (RCD) ... ARO
Algorithm (MSA) ... ALGO
Algorithmic and Business Oriented Language [*Data processing*] ... ALABOL
Algorithmic Language [*1958*] [*Formerly, IAL*] [*Data processing*] ... ALGOL
Algorithmic Language for Economic Calculations [*Data processing*] ... ALGEC
Algorithmic Remote Manipulation [*Programing language*] ... ARM
All-Band Intercept Receiver ... ABIR
All [*Text*] **Before** [*Specified Point*] [*Message handling*] ... AB
All Busy Low [*AT & T*] ... ABL
All-Canada Weekly Summaries [*Canada Law Book Ltd.*] [*Database*] ... ACWS
All-Digital Data Tape (KSC) ... ADDT
All-Digital Phase-Locked Loop (KSC) ... ADPLL
All-Digital Simulator ... ADS
All Figure Number [*Telecommunications*] (TEL) ... AFN
All Numbers Calling [*Telephone*] ... ANC
All Points Addressable [*Data processing*] ... APA
All-Purpose Communications System ... ALPURCOMS
All-Purpose Electronic Computer (IEEE) ... APEC
All Purpose Electronic x Computer [*Early computer*] [*Birkbeck College*] [*British*] (CAH) ... APExC
All-Purpose Terminal [*Computer technology*] ... APT
All Routes Busy [*Telecommunications*] (TEL) ... ARB
All Tariffs Computerized [*Project*] ... ATAC
All Trunks Busy [*Telecommunications*] ... ATB
All Type Equipment Leasing, Inc. [*San Francisco, CA*] [*Software manufacturer*] (DASOS) ... ATEL
All Wave Antenna ... AWA
All-Weather Yaw Damper Computer ... AWYDC
Allarcom Pay Television Ltd. [*Canada*] ... APT
ALLC [*Association for Literary and Linguistic Computing*] **Bulletin** [*A publication*] ... ALLCB
ALLC [*Association for Literary and Linguistic Computing*] **Journal** [*A publication*] ... ALLC J
Allegheny International, Inc. [*NYSE symbol*] ... AG
Alliance of Independent Telephone Unions [*Later, TIU*] ... AITU
Alliance of Independent Telephone Unions [*Later, TIU*] ... ATU
Alliance of Information and Referral Systems [*Indianapolis, IN*] (EANO) ... AIRS
Allied Corporation [*Initialism is trademark*] ... A-C
Allied Corporation [*Toronto Stock Exchange symbol*] ... ACD
Allocate [*or Allocation*] (AFM) ... ALLOC
Allstates-Programming & Systems, Incorporated ... APSI
[*The*] **Almanac of American Politics** [*National Journal Inc.*] [*Database*] [*A publication*] (CUAD) ... AMPOL
Almost Differential Quasiternary Code [*Telecommunications*] (TEL) ... ADQ
Alpha Block Control Number [*Data processing*] ... ABC
Alpha-Comp Simulation Package [*Alpha-Comp Ltd.*] [*Software package*] [*British*] (NCC) ... ASIM
Alpha Microsystems [*NASDAQ symbol*] (NQ) ... ALMI
Alpha Microsystems Operating System (CAA) ... AMOS
Alpha Omega Computer System (IEEE) ... AOCS
ALPHA [*AMC Logistics Program - Hardcore Automated*] **Remote Terminal Interactive System** ... ARTIS
Alpha Repertory Television Service [*Cable-television system*] ... ARTS
Alphabetic ... A
Alphabetical [*Flowchart*] ... ALPHA
Alphanumeric ... AN
Alphanumeric Impact Printer (CAA) ... AIP
Alphanumeric Photocomposer System (IEEE) ... APS
Alterable Control Memory (CAA) ... ACM
Alterable Read-Only Memory [*Data processing*] ... AROM
Alterable Read-Only Operating System (CAA) ... AROS
Alternate ... ALT
Alternate Call Listing [*Telecommunications*] (TEL) ... AC
Alternate CPU [*Central Processing Unit*] **Recovery** [*IBM Corp.*] [*Data processing*] (BUR) ... ACR
Alternate Joint Communications Center ... AJCC
Alternate Mark Inversion [*Telecommunications*] (IEEE) ... AMI

Computer & Telecommunications Acronyms

Alternate Media Center [*New York University*] [*Telecommunications*]	AMC
Alternate Mode (CAAL)	AM
Alternate Path Reentry [*Fujitsu Ltd.*] [*Data processing*] (MCD)	APR
Alternate Route [*Telecommunications*] (TEL)	A/R
Alternate Voice Data	AVD
Alternating Continuous Waves [*Radio*]	ACW
Alternating Current	AC
Alternating Current Circuit	ACC
Alternating Current/Direct Current	A-C/D-C
Alternating Current Dump	ACD
Alternating Direction Implicit [*Algorithm*]	ADI
Alternative Fuel Data Bank [*Bartlesville Energy Technology Center*] [*Database*] (FDB)	AFDB
Alternative Information Network (EANO)	AIN
Altimeter/Velocity Sensor Antenna (CIT)	A/VSA
Altitude Indication System	AIS
Altos Computer Systems [*NASDAQ symbol*] (NQ)	ALTO
Aluminum Cable Steel Reinforced	ACSR
Aluminum Conductor Steel Reinforced	ACSR
Aluminum, Nickel, Cobalt [*Alloy*]	ALNICO
Aluminum and Polyethylene [*Components of a type of telecommunications cable*]	ALPETH
AM International, Inc. [*Formerly, Addressograph-Multigraph Corp.*] [*American Stock Exchange symbol*]	AM
Amalgamated Software of North America, Inc. [*Malibu, CA*] [*Software manufacturer*] (DASOS)	ASNA
Amateur Radio Emergency Service	ARES
Amateur Radio Monitor	ARM
Amateur Radio Public Service Corps	ARPSC
Amateur (Radio) Station [*ITU designation*] (CET)	AR
Amateur Station [*ITU designation*]	AT
Ambiguity Eliminator [*Electronics*]	AMBEL
Amdahl Corp. [*American Stock Exchange symbol*]	AMH
Amdahl Diagnostics Assistance Center (CAA)	AMDAC
Amdahl Internally Developed Software (CAA)	AIDS
Amdahl Users Group (EANO)	AUG
America: History and Life [*ABC-Clio Information Services*] [*Database*]	AHL
American Academy of Arts and Sciences [*Boston, MA*]	AAAS
American Agricultural Economics Documentation Center [*Department of Agriculture*] [*Washington, DC*] (EISS)	AAEDC
American Association for the Advancement of Science [*Washington, DC*]	AAAS
American Association for Artificial Intelligence (EANO)	AAAI
American Association of Computer Professionals [*Stockbridge, GA*] (EANO)	AACP
American Association of Health Data Systems [*Ann Arbor, MI*] (EANO)	AAHDS
American Association for Medical Systems and Informatics [*Bethesda, MD*] (EANO)	AAMSI
American Association of Microcomputer Investors (EANO)	AAMI
American Association of Microprocessor Engineers (CAA)	AAME
American Association of Public Welfare Information Systems Management (EANO)	AAPWISM
American Automatic Control Council [*Wickliffe, OH*]	AACC
American Bell, Incorporated	ABI
American Broadcasting Companies, Inc. [*New York, NY*] [*NYSE symbol*]	ABC
American Business Network [*US Chamber of Commerce*] [*Washington, DC*] [*Cable-television system*] [*Telecommunications*] (TSSD)	BIZNET
American Cable & Radio Corp.	AC & R
American Cable Supply Corp. [*Fort Lauderdale, FL*] [*Hardware manufacturer*] (DASO)	ACS
American Christian Television [*Cable-television system*]	ACTS
American Communication Services [*Evanston, IL*] [*Telecommunications*] (TSSD)	ACS
American Communications Association	ACA
American Communications & TV [*NASDAQ symbol*] (NQ)	ASTV
American Council for Competitive Telecommunications [*Formerly, Ad Hoc Committee for Competitive Telecommunications*] [*Washington, DC*] (EANO)	ACCT
American Council for Private International Communications, Inc. [*Proposed corporation to replace Radio Free Europe*]	ACPIC
American Documentation Institute [*Later, American Society for Information Science*]	ADI
American Electronics Association [*Formerly, WEMA*]	AEA
American Express Co.	AMEX
American Express Company	AMEXCO
American Express Co. [*NYSE symbol*] [*Toronto Stock Exchange symbol*]	AXP
American Federation of Information Processing [*Formerly, AFIPS*] (CAH)	AFIP
American Federation of Information Processing Societies [*Reston, VA*]	AFIPS
American Federation of Information Processing Societies. Conference Proceedings. Fall Joint Computer Conference [*A publication*]	AFIPS Conf Proc Fall Jt Comput Conf
American Federation of Information Processing Societies. Conference Proceedings. Fall and Spring Joint Computer Conferences [*A publication*]	AFIPS Conf Proc Fall Spring Jt Comput Conf
American Federation of Information Processing Societies. Conference Proceedings. Spring Joint Computer Conference [*A publication*]	AFIPS Conf Proc Spring Jt Comput Conf
American Federation of Information Processing Societies. National Computer Conference and Exposition. Conference Proceedings [*A publication*]	AFIPS Natl Comp Conf Expo Conf Proc
American Fiber Optics [*NASDAQ symbol*] (NQ)	FIBR
American Health Consultants [*Atlanta, GA*] [*Information service*] (EISS)	AHC
American Hospital Video Network [*Satellite television system*]	AHVN
American Information Technologies [*Telecommunications*]	AMERITECH
American Institute of Aeronautics and Astronautics [*New York, NY*]	AIAA
American Institute of Certified Public Accountants [*New York, NY*]	AICPA
American Institute for Decision Sciences (EANO)	AIDS
American Institute of Electrical Engineers [*Later, IEEE*]	AIEE
American Institute of Industrial Engineers [*Later, IIE*]	AIIE
American Interactive Media, Inc. [*Software manufacturer*]	AIM
American International Communications Corp.	AIC
American Library Association [*Chicago, IL*]	ALA
American Library Association's Electronic Information Service	ALANET
American Library Directory [*Online database*]	ALD
American Low Power Television Association (EANO)	ALPTA
American Management Associations [*New York, NY*]	AMA
American Management Systems [*NASDAQ symbol*] (NQ)	AMSY
American Management Systems, Inc. [*Arlington, VA*] [*Information service*] (EISS)	AMS
American Mathematical Society [*Providence, RI*]	AMS
American Medical Association [*Chicago, IL*]	AMA
American Men and Women of Science [*R. R. Bowker Co., 1979*] [*New York, NY*] [*A publication*] (EISS)	AMWS
American Meteorological Society [*Boston, MA*]	AMS
American Microcomputer Dealers Association [*Tustin, CA*] (EANO)	AMDA
American Microsystems, Incorporated (MCD)	AMI
American National Dictionary for Information Processing [*A publication*] (IEEE)	ANDIP
American National Dictionary for Information Processing Systems [*A publication*]	ANDIPS
American National Standard [*ANSI*] (MCD)	ANS
American National Standard Code for Information Interchange (MCD)	ANSCII
American National Standard Labels (BUR)	ANL
American National Standard Vocabulary for Information Processing	ANSVIP
American National Standards Institute [*New York, NY*]	ANSI
American National Standards (Institute) Committee	ANSC
American Osteopathic Network [*Chicago, IL*] [*Information service*] (EISS)	AONET
American People/Link [*American Home Network, Inc.*] [*Information service*] (EISS)	PLINK
American Private Line Services, Inc. [*Newton, MA*] [*Telecommunications*] (TSSD)	APLS
American Production and Inventory Control Society, Inc. [*Washington, DC*]	APICS
American Programmers Guild	APG
[*The*] American Psycho/Info Exchange [*New York, NY*] [*Information service*] (EISS)	APIE
American Psychological Association [*Database producer*]	APA
American Radio Relay League [*Newington, CT*]	ARRL
American Rheumatism Association Medical Information System [*Palo Alto, CA*] [*Database producer*] (EISS)	ARAMIS
American Satellite Company [*Rockville, MD*] [*Telecommunications*] (TSSD)	ASC
American Shortwave Listeners Club	ASWLC
American SMR [*Special Mobile Radio*] Network Association (EANO)	ASNA
American Society of Civil Engineers [*New York, NY*]	ASCE
American Society of Computer Dealers [*Dallas, TX*] (EANO)	ASCD
American Society for Cybernetics	ASC
American Society for Engineering Education [*Washington, DC*]	ASEE
American Society for Engineering Education. Computers in Education Division. Transactions [*A publication*]	Am Soc Eng Educ COED Trans
American Society for Engineering Education. Computers in Education Division. Transactions [*A publication*]	Am Soc Eng Educ Comput Educ Div Trans
American Society for Industrial Security	ASIS
American Society for Information Science [*Washington, DC*]	ASIS
American Society of Mechanical Engineers [*New York, NY*]	ASME
American Society for Quality Control [*Milwaukee, WI*]	ASQC
American Society for Testing and Materials [*Philadelphia, PA*] [*Research center*]	ASTM
American Software CI A [*NASDAQ symbol*] (NQ)	AMSWA
American Software Users Group [*Franklin Park, IL*] (EANO)	ASUG
American Standard Code for Information Interchange [*Pronounced "ask-ee"*] [*American National Standards Institute*] [*Data processing*]	ASCII
American Standard Vocabulary for Information Processing (BUR)	ASVIP
American Standards Association [*Later, USASI, ANSI*]	ASA
American Statistical Association [*Washington, DC*]	ASA
American Statistics Index [*Congressional Information Service, Inc.*] [*Bibliographic database*] [*A publication*]	ASI

By Meaning

Computer & Telecommunications Acronyms

American Telecommunications Corp. [*Vancouver Stock Exchange symbol*] .... AMT
American Telemarketing Association [*Glenview, IL*] (EANO) .... ATA
American Telephone & Telegraph Co. [*New York, NY*] .... AT & T
American Telephone & Telegraph Co. [*New York, NY*] .... ATT
American Telephone & Telegraph Co. [*NYSE symbol*] [*Wall Street slang name: "Telephone"*] .... T
American Video Channels, Inc. [*New York, NY*] [*Telecommunications*] (TSSD) .... AVC
American Video Teleconferencing Corporation [*Oceanside, NY*] [*Telecommunications*] .... AVTC
American Videotext Services, Inc. [*Peekskill, NY*] [*Telecommunications*] (TSSD) .... AVS
Americas UNIVAC [*Universal Automatic Computer*] Users Association [*Formerly, UUA*] [*Winston-Salem, NC*] (EANO) .... AUUA
Ameritech Mobile Communications, Incorporated [*Schaumburg, IL*] [*Telecommunications*] (TSSD) .... AMCI
AMEX [*American Stock Exchange*] Communications [*Network*] .... AMCOM
AMEX [*American Stock Exchange*] Computerized Order Display and Execution System .... AMCODE
Ammeter (MDG) .... A
Ammeter (DDI) .... AMTR
Ammeter Switch (MSA) .... AS
AMP, Inc. [*NYSE symbol*] .... AMP
Ampere [*Unit of electric current*] [*SI symbol*] .... A
Ampere [*Unit of electric current*] (AFM) .... AMP
Ampere Hour .... A h
Ampere-Hour (MDG) .... AMP-HR
Ampere Second .... As
Ampere-Turn per Meter (MCD) .... AT/M
Amperes (KSC) .... AMPS
Amperes per Meter .... A/M
Amperes per Square Foot .... ASF
Ampex Corp. [*NYSE symbol*] [*Delisted*] .... APX
Amplifier (KSC) .... AMP
Amplifier .... AMPL
Amplifier-Control Intercommunications (MCD) .... ACI
Amplifier Oscillator, Radiofrequency (DDI) .... AORF
Amplifier Output [*Data processing*] .... AO
Amplifier Output Stage .... AOS
Amplifier Power Supply .... APS
Amplifier Subsystem (NASA) .... AMS
Amplifier and Switch Assembly (MCD) .... ASA
Amplitude [*Physics*] .... A
Amplitude .... AMP
Amplitude Companded Single Sideband [*Electronics*] .... ACSB
Amplitude-Frequency Distortion .... AFD
Amplitude Keyed .... AK
Amplitude and Latency Measuring Instrument with Digital Output .... ALMIDO
Amplitude Modulated Link [*Electronics*] .... AML
Amplitude-Modulated Transmitter [*Electronics*] .... AMT
Amplitude Modulation [*Electronics*] .... AM
Amplitude Modulation, Double Sideband [*Electronics*] .... AMDSB
Amplitude Modulation, Double Sideband, Suppressed Carrier [*Electronics*] (CET) .... AMDSB/SC
Amplitude Modulation Equivalent [*Telecommunications*] (TEL) .... AME
Amplitude Modulation Link Program .... AMLP
Amplitude Modulation, Single Sideband [*Electronics*] .... AMSSB
Amplitude Modulation, Single Sideband, Suppressed Carrier [*Electronics*] (CET) .... AMSSB/SC
Amplitude Phase Shift Keying (MCD) .... APK
Amplitude Probability Distribution [*Telecommunications*] .... APD
Amplitude and Rise Time Compensation (IEEE) .... ARC
Amplitude Shift Keying .... ASK
Amron Information Services [*Union, NJ*] (EISS) .... AIS
Amtel, Inc. [*NYSE symbol*] [*Delisted*] .... ATI
Anacomp, Inc. [*NYSE symbol*] .... AAC
Anaconda Co. [*NASDAQ symbol*] [*Delisted*] .... A
Analog (NASA) .... ANL
Analog (MSA) .... ANLG
Analog Alarm Section .... AAS
Analog Antenna Positioner .... AAP
Analog Computer .... AC
Analog Computer .... ANACOM
Analog Computer Facility (CIT) .... ACF
Analog Computer Subsystem .... ACSS
Analog Computer System .... ACS
Analog Computer Translator .... ACTRAN
Analog Conditioning and Test System (CIT) .... ACTS
Analog Data Acquisition Module .... ADAM
Analog Data Digitizer .... ADD
Analog Data Distributor and Control [*Data processing*] (KSC) .... ADDAC
Analog Data Handling System .... ADHS
Analog Data Recorder Transcriber .... ADRT
Analog Data Reduction System (CAAL) .... ADAR
Analog Delay Unit .... ADU
Analog-to-Digital [*Converter*] [*Data processing*] .... A-to-D
Analog-to-Digital [*Converter*] [*Data processing*] (AFM) .... AD
Analog-Digital Automatic Program Tester [*Data processing*] .... ADAPT
Analog-to-Digital Conversion System [*Data processing*] .... ADIC
Analog-to-Digital Converter [*Data processing*] (MUGU) .... ADC
Analog-to-Digital Converter [*Data processing*] .... ADCON

Analog-to-Digital Data Recording System [*Data processing*] (IEEE) .... ADRS
Analog-to-Digital Data Reduction System for Oceanographic Research .... ADDRESOR
Analog-Digital-Designer [*Trademark*] .... ADD
Analog Digital/Digital Analog (RDA) .... AD/DA
Analog-Digital Input/Output System [*Data processing*] (CAA) .... ADIOS
Analog-Digital Integrating Translator [*Data processing*] .... ADIT
Analog and Digital Monitoring System [*Data processing*] (MCD) .... ADMS
Analog-Digital Recorder [*Data processing*] .... ADR
Analog Display Unit .... ADU
Analog Electronic Computer .... AEC
Analog Event Distribution System [*Data processing*] (MCD) .... AEDS
Analog Event System [*Data processing*] (MCD) .... AES
Analog Facility Terminal [*Data processing*] (TEL) .... AFT
Analog Factor Calibration Network .... AFCAN
Analog Filter Assembly (MCD) .... AFA
Analog to Frequency Converter .... AFC
Analog Function Generator .... AFG
Analog Ground Bus (VIT) .... AGBUS
Analog Input Module [*Data processing*] (CIT) .... AIM
Analog Input/Output Package [*Data processing*] .... AIOP
Analog Input System (CAA) .... AIS
Analog Instrumentation Subsystem (CIT) .... AIS
Analog Junction (TEL) .... AJ
Analog Junction Module (TEL) .... AJM
Analog Line Driver [*Data processing*] (BUR) .... ALD
Analog Line Termination Subsystem [*Telecommunications*] (TEL) .... ALTS
Analog Link [*Telecommunications*] (TEL) .... AL
Analog Loop-Back [*Telecommunications*] (TEL) .... AL
Analog Major Alarm (MCD) .... AMA
Analog Matched Filter .... AMF
Analog Module [*Telecommunications*] (TEL) .... AM
Analog Monitor Module [*Data processing*] (CAA) .... AMM
Analog Multiplexer Quantizer [*Data processing*] (KSC) .... AMQ
Analog Output [*Data processing*] (NASA) .... AO
Analog Output Differential [*Data processing*] (MCD) .... AOD
Analog Panel Meter (IEEE) .... APM
Analog to Pressure Converter .... APC
Analog Pressure Transducer .... APT
Analog Program Tape [*Data processing*] .... APT
Analog Programing and Checking [*Data processing*] .... APACHE
Analog-to-Pulse Duration .... APD
Analog-to-Pulse Width Converter (CIT) .... A/PW
Analog Recording Dynamic Analyzer [*Data processing*] .... ARDA
Analog Recording System (CIT) .... ARS
Analog Remote Unit .... ARU
Analog Response Conditioner (MCD) .... ARC
Analog Response Unit (SKY) .... ARU
Analog Rotation Speed Control .... ARSC
Analog Schematic Translator to Algebraic Language [*Data processing*] (IEEE) .... ASTRAL
Analog Select Keyboard [*Data processing*] (KSC) .... ASK
Analog Self-Checking Automatic Tester .... ASCAT
Analog Shift Register [*Data processing*] .... ASR
Analog Signal Converter (DDI) .... ASC
Analog Signal Correlator .... ASC
Analog Simulation System .... ASS
Analog Stimulus Unit (SKY) .... ASU
Analog Strip Chart .... ASC
Analog Strip Chart Recorder .... ASCR
Analog System Assembly Pack .... ASAP
Analog Tape Recorder .... ATR
Analog Technology Company (CIT) .... ATC
Analog Threshold Logic .... ATL
Analog to Time to Digital [*Data processing*] .... ATD
Analog Translator [*Data processing*] (CGC) .... ANATRAN
Analog Tree-Organized Multiplexer .... ATOM
Analog Video Bandwidth .... AVB
Analogic Corp. [*NASDAQ symbol*] (NQ) .... ALOG
Analogue Simulation of Competitive Operational Tactics [*Game*] .... ASCOT
Analysis of Automatic Line Insulation Test [*Bell System*] .... ANALIT
Analysis Computer System (CIT) .... ACS
Analysis of Digitized Seismic Signals [*Data processing*] .... ADSS
Analysis of Internal Management Systems .... AIMS
Analysis Program Linear Active Circuits (NASA) .... APLAC
Analysis of Random Data [*System documentation*] [*Oregon State University*] .... ARAND
Analysis of Variance [*Also, ANOVA*] .... ANOV
Analysis of Variance [*Also, ANOV*] .... ANOVA
Analyst Intelligence Display and Exploitation System .... AIDES
Analysts International Corporation [*Minneapolis, MN*] [*Software manufacturer*] (DASOS) .... AIC
Analysts International Corp. [*NASDAQ symbol*] (NQ) .... ANLY
Analytic Language Manipulation System .... ALMS
Analytic Processing Unit (CCD) .... APU
Analytical Computer Program .... ACP
Analytical Electron Microscopy .... AEM
Analytical Quality Control Laboratory (EISS) .... AQCL
Analyzer-Recorder-Controller .... ARC
Ancillary Control Processor (CAA) .... ACP
And Gate [*Logic element*] [*Data processing*] .... AG
Anderson Jacobson, Inc. [*Terminal manufacturer*] [*American Stock Exchange symbol*] .... AJ

Computer & Telecommunications Acronyms

Andrew R. Jennings Computing Center [*Case Western Reserve University*] [*Research center*] (RCD) .... ARJCC
Andrew Sipos Associates [*New York, NY*] [*Software manufacturer*] (DASOS) .... ASA
Andrus Gerontological Information Center [*University of Southern California*] [*Los Angeles, CA*] (EISS) .... AGIC
Angle Data Recorder .... ADR
Angle Data Subsystem (CIT) .... ADS
Angle Deception Jamming .... ADJ
Angle Deception Jamming System .... ADJS
Angle Jamming System .... AJS
Angle, Time, Range [*Data processing*] .... ATR
Angle Versus Length [*Data processing*] .... AVL
Anglo-American Code [*Cataloging*] (DIT) .... AAC
Angstrom [*Also, AU*] .... A
Angstrom Unit [*Also, A*] .... AU
Angular Distribution Data Tape .... ADDT
Angular Mapping Transformation [*Data processing*] .... AMT
Angus Telemanagement Group, Inc. [*Toronto, ON*] [*Information service*] [*Telecommunications*] (TSSD) .... ATMG
Animated Computer Education (CGC) .... ACE
Animated Film Language (BUR) .... AFL
Animated Movie Language (BUR) .... AML
Anisotropically Conductive Silicone [*Rubber*] .... ACS
Annoyance Call Bureau [*Telephone-pest control*] .... ACB
Annual Review in Automatic Programming [*A publication*] .... Annu Rev Autom Program
Annual Review of Information Science and Technology [*Encyclopedia Britannica*] [*A publication*] .... Annu Rev Inf Sci Technol
Annunciator [*Electronically controlled signal board*] (KSC) .... ANN
Annunciator Display Unit (MCD) .... ADU
Anodal Opening .... AO
Anode [*Technical drawings*] .... A
Anode Voltage Drop .... AVD
Anomalous Propagation [*Telecommunications*] (TEL) .... AP
Answer (AFM) .... ANS
Answer-Back Code [*Telecommunications*] (TEL) .... ABC
Answer Complete [*Telecommunications*] (TEL) .... AC
Answer, No-Charge [*Telecommunications*] (TEL) .... ANN
Answering Machine Owner .... AMO
Answering, Recording, and Dialing (CAA) .... ARD
Answering Time Recorder [*Telecommunications*] (TEL) .... ATR
Antarctic Meteorite Bibliography [*Lunar and Planetary Institute*] [*Database*] (FDB) .... AMB
Antenna (AFM) .... ANT
Antenna for Communications .... AFC
Antenna Contour Measuring Equipment .... ACME
Antenna Control Console .... ACC
Antenna Control Display .... ACD
Antenna Control and Display Panel (MCD) .... ACDP
Antenna Control Unit .... ACU
Antenna Coupler Receiver (MCD) .... ACR
Antenna Coupling Regulator (IEEE) .... ACR
Antenna Cross Talk .... ACT
Antenna Dish Control .... ADC
Antenna Dummy Load .... ADL
Antenna Effective Length for Electric-Field Antennas (IEEE) .... LE
Antenna Effective Length for Magnetic-Field Antennas (IEEE) .... LEM
Antenna Feed System .... AFS
Antenna Field Gain .... AFG
Antenna Homing System .... AHS
Antenna Impedance .... AI
Antenna Input Resistance .... AIR
Antenna Interface Subsystem (CAAL) .... AIS
Antenna Laboratory (MCD) .... AL
Antenna Loading Coil .... ALC
Antenna Lobe for Variable Ionospheric Nimbus (IEEE) .... ALVIN
Antenna Matching Unit .... AMU
Antenna Ohmic Resistance .... AOR
Antenna Pattern Analyzer .... APA
Antenna Pattern Correction [*for spacecraft data*] .... APC
Antenna Pattern Error Analysis .... APEA
Antenna Pointing Angle Change (CIT) .... APAC
Antenna Pointing Subsystem (CIT) .... APS
Antenna Position Indicator .... API
Antenna Position Recorder .... APR
Antenna Positioning Device .... ANPOD
Antenna Positioning Mechanism .... APM
Antenna Power Gain .... APG
Antenna Radiation Pattern .... ARP
Antenna Radiation Resistance .... ARR
Antenna Range Equipment (CIT) .... ARE
Antenna Rotation Rate .... ARR
Antenna Select Logic Unit (NASA) .... ASLU
Antenna Solar Panel Positioner (CIT) .... ASPP
Antenna Steering Group .... ASG
Antenna Switching Matrix .... ASM
Antenna System Readiness Monitor (MCD) .... ASRM
Antenna Test Facility .... ATF
Antenna Test Model (CIT) .... ATM
Antenna and Transmitter Improvement Study .... ATIS
Antenna Tuning Unit (MSA) .... ATU
Antennas and Propagation .... A/P
Anti-Digit Dialing League .... ADDL
Anti-Transmit-Receive .... ATR
Anti-Transmit-Receive Tube .... ATRT
Antijam Display .... AJD
Antijam Equipment .... AJE
Antijam Frequency .... AJF
Antijam Frequency Hopper .... AJFH
Antijam Hopper .... AJH
Antijam Operator (CET) .... AJO
Antijam Synthesizer .... AJS
Antijam Technique .... AJT
Antijamming/Anti-Interference (CET) .... AJ/AI
Antijamming Blackout .... AJBO
Antijamming Improvements .... AJI
Antilogarithm .... ANTILOG
Antilogarithmic Function .... ANLG
Antisidetone [*Telecommunications*] (TEL) .... AST
Any Tape Search [*Computer program*] (KSC) .... ANTS
APCHE [*Automatic Program Checkout Equipment*] Relay Box .... ARB
API [*American Petroleum Institute*] Literature [*New York, NY*] [*Bibliographic database*] (OBD) .... APILIT
Apollo Computer, Incorporated [*NASDAQ symbol*] (NQ) .... APCI
Appalachian Community Service Network [*Cable-television system*] .... ACSN
Apparatus Repair - Strategy Evaluation Guidelines [*Telecommunications*] .... AREG
Apparel Business Control [*System*] [*Data processing*] .... ABC
Apple Bulletin Board System [*Pronounced "abbies"*] .... ABBS
Apple Computer, Inc. [*NASDAQ symbol*] (NQ) .... AAPL
Appliance, Range, Adjust [*Data processing*] .... ARGA
Application of Computer Methods in the Mineral Industry. Proceedings of the International Symposium [*A publication*] .... ACMIC
Application Control Language [*Data processing*] (BUR) .... ACL
Application Date [*Bell System*] (TEL) .... APP
Application Design Service [*IBM Corp.*] .... ADS
Application Development Facility [*IBM Corp.*] [*Data processing*] .... ADF
Application Development Systems [*Data processing*] .... ADS
Application Functions Module [*Data processing*] .... AFM
Application Library File [*Data processing*] (CAA) .... ALF
Application Module Library [*IBM Corp.*] .... AML
Application Oriented Language [*Data processing*] (BUR) .... AOL
Application Process [*or Program*] (Structure) [*Telecommunications*] (TEL) .... AP(S)
Application Process Subsystem [*Telecommunications*] (TEL) .... APS
Application Program [*Data processing*] (BUR) .... AP
Application Program Generator [*Data processing*] .... APG
Application Program Interface [*Data processing*] (BUR) .... API
Application of Space Techniques Relating to Aviation [*International Civil Aviation Organization*] .... ASTRA
Application Specific Integrated Circuit [*National Semiconductor Corp.*] .... ASIC
Application Terminal Unit [*Telecommunications*] (TEL) .... ATU
Application Transfer Teams [*IBM Corp.*] .... ATT
Applications Environment System .... AES
Applications Vertical Test Program [*Communication Satellite program*] .... AVT
Applicative Language Idealized Computing Engine .... ALICE
Applied Business Technology Corp. .... ABT
Applied Business Telecommunications [*San Ramon, CA*] [*Information service*] [*Telecommunications*] (TSSD) .... ABC
Applied Circuit Technology [*Anaheim, CA*] [*Hardware manufacturer*] (DASO) .... ACRT
Applied Color Systems, Inc. [*Princeton, NJ*] [*Software manufacturer*] (DASOS) .... ACS
Applied Communication Research, Inc. [*Information service*] (EISS) .... ACR
Applied Communications Systems Center [*AT & T*] .... ACSC
Applied Computer Research [*Phoenix, AZ*] [*Information service*] (EISS) .... ACR
Applied Data Communications [*NASDAQ symbol*] (NQ) .... ADCC
Applied Data Research, Inc. [*Software supplier*] [*American Stock Exchange symbol*] .... ADR
Applied Decision Systems [*Lexington, MA*] [*Information service*] (EISS) .... ADS
Applied Digital Data Systems, Inc. [*NASDAQ symbol*] .... ADDS
Applied Digital Data Systems, Inc. [*NYSE symbol*] [*Delisted*] .... ADS
Applied Economic Research & Information Center [*Canada*] (CUAD) .... AERIC
Applied Information and Data Management Systems Section [*Battelle Memorial Institute*] [*Information service*] (EISS) .... AIDMS
Applied Information Development, Inc. [*Oak Brook, IL*] [*Software manufacturer*] (DASOS) .... AID
Applied Information Management Sciences, Inc. [*Monroe, LA*] [*Software manufacturer*] (DASOS) .... AIMS
Applied Information Management System [*Data processing*] (DIT) .... AIMS
Applied Information Technologies Research Center [*Columbus, OH*] [*Information service*] (EISS) .... AITRC
Applied Parallel Programing Language Experiment [*Data processing*] (MCD) .... APPLE
Applied Research Corporation .... ARC
Applied Research and Design Center [*California State University, Sacramento*] [*Research center*] (RCD) .... ARDC
Applied Systems and Personnel (BUR) .... ASAP
Applied Urbanetics, Incorporated [*Information service*] (EISS) .... AUI

Approach by Concept [*Information retrieval*] ABC
Approach and Landing Procedures Simulator (MCD) ALPS
Approach and Landing Simulator ALS
Approved Data Element (AFM) ADE
Approximately APPROX
Aptitude Assessment Battery Programing [*Data processing*] (IEEE) AABP
Aquatic Information Retrieval Database [*Database*] [*Environmental Protection Agency*] (FDB) AQUIRE
Aquatic Sciences and Fisheries Abstracts [*Information Retrieval Ltd.*] [*Bibliographic database*] [*A publication*] ASFA
Aquatic Sciences and Fisheries Information System [*Rome, Italy*] [*United Nations*] (EISS) ASFIS
Arab Satellite Communications Organization [*Riyadh, Saudi Arabia*] [*Telecommunications*] (TSSD) ARABSAT
Arabian Communication Satellite (CBSS) ARCOMSAT
Arbeitsgemeinschaft der Berufsvertretungen Deutscher Apotheker [*Information retrieval*] (ODIN) ABDA
Arbeitsgemeinschaft fuer Daten Verarbeintung [*Data Processing Association of Austria*] [*Vienna, Austria*] ADV
Arbeitsgemeinschaft Information Meeresforschung und Meerestechnik eV [*Hannover*] [*Information retrieval*] (ODIN) AIM
Arbeitsgemeinschaft Technologieberatung Ruhr [*Information retrieval*] (ODIN) TBR
Arbeitsschutzinformationssystem [*Information System for Occupational Safety and Health*] [*West Germany*] (EISS) ASIS
Arbitrary Function Generator (MUGU) AFG
Arc-Plasma Spraying [*Magnetic film*] APS
Architects Job Costing [*ICS*] [*Software package*] [*British*] (NCC) ARCOS
Architectural Block Diagram Language (CAA) ABL
Architectural Periodicals Index [*Royal Institute of British Architects*] [*London, England*] [*Information service*] (EISS) API
Architecture Description Language [*Data processing*] (CSR) ADL
Architecture Technology Corporation [*Minneapolis, MN*] [*Information service*] [*Telecommunications*] (TSSD) ATC
Archive Corp. [*NASDAQ symbol*] (NQ) ACHV
Archive of Italian Data of Geology [*Center for Stratigraphy and Petrology of the Central Alps*] [*Database*] (CUAD) ADIGE
Archivio Dati e Programmi per le Scienze Sociali [*Data and Program Archive for the Social Sciences*] [*University of Milan*] [*Milan, Italy*] [*Information service*] (EISS) ADPSS
Arctic Environmental Information and Data Center [*University of Alaska*] [*Research center*] (EISS) AEIDC
Arctic Science and Technology Information System [*Arctic Institute of North America*] [*University of Calgary*] [*Calgary, AB, Canada*] (EISS) ASTIS
Are You? [*Communication*] RU
Area A
Area Communications Operations Center [*Telecommunications*] (TEL) ACOC
Area Computing Facilities (CET) ACF
Area of Dominant Influence [*Telecommunications*] ADI
Area Frequency Coordinator (MUGU) AFC
Area Multiplexer (CAAL) AM
Area Resource File [*Public Health Service*] [*Rockville, MD*] [*Information service*] (EISS) ARF
Argonne Code Center [*Department of Energy*] (EISS) ACC
Argonne Computer-Aided Diffraction Equipment ARCADE
Argonne Microprocessor AMP
Argonne National Laboratory [*Argonne, IL*] ANL
Argonne Reactor Computation (IEEE) ARC
Argument ARG
Argument Programing (MSA) AP
Argus Corp. Ltd. [*Toronto Stock Exchange symbol*] AR
Arid Lands Information System [*University of Arizona*] [*Tucson, AZ*] (EISS) ALIS
ARINC Communication Addressing Reporting System (IEEE) ACARS
Arithmetic ARITH
Arithmetic Assignment Statement AAS
Arithmetic Building Element [*Data processing*] (CAA) ABE
Arithmetic Computer (VIT) ACU
Arithmetic and Control Processor (CAA) ACP
Arithmetic and Control Unit (BUR) ACU
Arithmetic Element (BUR) AE
Arithmetic Expression (IEEE) AE
Arithmetic Factor Register [*Data processing*] (CDH) D
Arithmetic Logic and Control Unit [*Data processing*] (CAA) ALCU
Arithmetic Logic Processor (CAA) ALP
Arithmetic Logic Section [*Data processing*] (CAA) ALS
Arithmetic and Logic Unit [*Data processing*] A & LU
Arithmetic and Logic Unit [*Data processing*] ALU
Arithmetic Output Control Unit (CAA) AOCU
Arithmetic Output Data [*Data processing*] (CAA) AOD
Arithmetic Output Unit (CAA) AOU
Arithmetic Processing Unit [*Data processing*] APU
Arithmetic Processor (CAA) AP
Arithmetic Proficiency Training Program [*Computer-assisted training program*] APTP
Arithmetic Progression AP
Arithmetic Register (OA) AR
Arithmetic Shift Left [*Data processing*] ASL
Arithmetic Shift Right [*Data processing*] ASR
Arithmetic Unit [*Data processing*] AU
Arizona Statistical Repetitive Analog Computer ASTRAC
Arlen Communications, Incorporated [*Bethesda, MD*] [*Information service*] [*Telecommunications*] (TSSD) ACI
Armed Forces Radio-Television [*Cable-television system*] AFRTS
ARMS/FIRMS Users Association [*Toledo, OH*] (EANO) AFUA
Army Institute for Research in Management Information and Computer Science (IEEE) AIRMICS
ARPA [*Advanced Research Projects Agency*] **Network Terminal System** (CAA) ANTS
Array Interconnection Logic [*Data processing*] (CAA) AIL
Array Interface Unit [*Data processing*] (CAAL) AIU
Array Machine Language [*Data processing*] (CAA) AML
Array Processing Instruction Set [*Data processing*] (MSA) APIS
[*An*] **Array Processing Language** [*Programing language*] (CAA) AAPL
Array Processor [*Data processing*] (BUR) AP
Array Processor Access Method [*Data processing*] (BUR) APAM
Array Processor Assembly Language [*Data processing*] (CAA) APAL
Array Processor Software [*Data processing*] (IEEE) APS
Array Processor Subroutine Package [*Data processing*] (BUR) APSP
Arrow Electronics, Inc. [*NYSE symbol*] ARW
Artel Communications [*NASDAQ symbol*] (NQ) AXXX
Arthur D. Little, Inc. [*Cambridge, MA*] [*Research code symbol*] ADL
Article Procurement with Online Local Ordering [*Document delivery system*] [*Telecommunications*] APOLLO
Articulated Computing Hierarchy [*British*] ARCH
Articulation Score [*Percentage of words correctly understood over a radio channel perturbed by interference*] [*Telecommunications*] AS
Artificial [*Telecommunications*] (TEL) ART
Artificial Earth Research and Orbiting Satellite (NATG) AEROS
Artificial Intelligence AI
Artificial Intelligence Laboratory [*Massachusetts Institute of Technology*] [*Research center*] (RCD) AIL
Artificial Intelligence in Medicine AIM
Artificial Interference to Transmission or Reception [*Broadcasting*] (DDI) QRM
Artificial Satellite AS
Artificial Satellite Time and Radio Orbit (MCD) ASTRO
Artikkel-Indeks Database [*Norwegian Center for Informatics*] [*Database*] (CUAD) AID
Artikkel-Indeks Tidsskrifter [*Norwegian Center for Informatics*] [*Database*] (CUAD) AITI
Arts & Entertainment Network [*Cable-television system*] A & E
ASCII COBOL [*Data processing*] ACOB
ASCII COBOL Data Manipulation Language-Preprocessor [*Data processing*] ADMLP
Asia Pacific Broadcasting Union [*Kuala Lumpur, Malaysia*] [*Telecommunications*] (EANO) ABU
Asia-Pacific Telecommunity [*Bangkok, Thailand*] [*Telecommunications*] (TSSD) APT
Asian Information Center for Geotechnical Engineering [*Asian Institute of Technology*] [*Bangkok, Thailand*] (EISS) AGE
Ask Computer Systems [*NASDAQ symbol*] (NQ) ASKI
Assemble/Load [*Data processing*] (VIT) A/L
Assembler [*Sperry UNIVAC*] [*Data processing*] ASM
Assembler Language [*Data processing*] (CMD) ASS
Assembler Language for MULTICS (CAA) ALM
Assembly Control System [*IBM Corp.*] (BUR) ACS
Assembly Instruction Mnemonics [*Data processing*] AIM
Assembly Language [*Data processing*] (CGC) AL
Assembly Language Coding [*Data processing*] ALC
Assembly Language Preprocessor [*Data processing*] (IEEE) ALP
Assembly Language Program [*Data processing*] (CGC) ALP
Assembly Language Translator [*Xerox Corp.*] (CAH) ALTRAN
Assembly Management Operating System (MCD) AMOS
Assembly of Parties [*INTELSAT*] (CBSS) AP
Assembly Programing Language [*Data processing*] APL
Assembly Programing System [*Data processing*] (IEEE) APS
Assembly System for Central Processor [*Data processing*] ASCENT
Assembly System for the Peripheral Processors [*Data processing*] ASPER
Asset Control Techniques ACT
Assigned Night Answer [*Telecommunications*] (TEL) ANA
Assignment Date [*Telecommunications*] (TEL) AD
Assistant Data Recording System Analyst (MUGU) ADRSA
Assistant Secretary of Defense (Telecommunications) ASD (T)
Assistive Device Center [*California State University, Sacramento*] [*Research center*] (RCD) ADC
Associate Client Program [*Business International Corp.*] [*Information service*] (EISS) ACP
Associated Broadcast News [*Cable-television system*] ABN
Associated Information Managers [*Formerly, PRIM*] [*Rockville, MD*] (EANO) AIM
Associated Logic Parallel System (BUR) ALPS
Associated Long-Distance Interstate Message [*Telecommunications*] (TEL) ALDI
Associated Maintenance Module [*Telecommunications*] (TEL) AMM
Associated Minicomputer Dealers of America (EANO) AMDA
Associated Press [*Online news wire service*] AP
Associated Press Network AP
Associated Telemanagement, Incorporated [*Boston, MA*] [*Telecommunications*] (TSSD) ATI
Associated Telephone Answering Exchanges [*Formerly, ATE*] [*Alexandria, VA*] ATAE
Associated Telephone Exchanges [*Later, ATAE*] ATE

Computer & Telecommunications Acronyms

Association	ASSN
Association of Agricultural Computer Companies (EANO)	AACC
Association of Atlantic Universities/Blackwell North America [Project] [Lake Oswego, OR] [Information service] (EISS)	AAU/BNA
Association for Automatic Language Processing	ATALA
Association pour l'Avancement de la Micro-Informatique [Association for the Advancement of Micro-Information] [Canada]	AMIQ
Association of Better Computer Dealers [Lexington, KY] (EANO)	ABCD
Association Canadienne des Entreprises de Telecommunications [Canadian Association of Telecommunication Businesses]	ACET
Association Canadienne de l'Informatique [Canadian Information Processing Society - CIPS]	ACI
Association of College and University Telecommunications Administrators [Madison, WI] (EANO)	ACUTA
Association of Compact Disk Publishers (EANO)	ACDP
Association for Computational Linguistics [Bell Communications Research] [Morristown, NJ]	ACL
Association for Computer Art and Design Education (EANO)	ACADE
Association of Computer Professionals [New York, NY] (EANO)	ACP
Association of Computer Programmers and Analysts [Kensington, MD] (EANO)	ACPA
Association of Computer Retailers (EANO)	ACR
Association of Computer Time-Sharing Users (CAA)	ACTSU
Association of Computer Users [Formerly, ATSU, ASCU] [Boulder, CO] (EANO)	ACU
Association for Computers and the Humanities [University of Minnesota] [Minneapolis, MN] (EANO)	ACH
Association for Computing Machinery [New York, NY]	ACM
Association for Computing Machinery - German Association for Applied Mathematics and Mechanics [Frankfurt/Main, Germany]	ACM-GAMM
Association for Computing Machinery. Journal [A publication]	Assn Comp Mach J
Association of Data Communications Users [Bloomington, MN] [Telecommunications] (EANO)	ADCU
Association of Data Processing Service Organizations [Also, ADPSO] [Includes American and Canadian companies] [Arlington, VA]	ADAPSO
Association of Data Processing Service Organizations [Also, ADAPSO] [Includes American and Canadian companies] [Arlington, VA]	ADPSO
Association of Data Terminal Distributors (CAA)	ADTD
Association of Database Producers [Oxford, England] (EISS)	ADP
Association for Development of Computer-Based Instructional Systems [Formerly, ADIS] [Western Washington State College] [Bellingham, WA] (EANO)	ADCIS
Association for Development of Instructional Systems [Later, ADCIS] [Western Washington University] [Bellingham, WA] (BUR)	ADIS
Association for Educational Communications and Technology [Washington, DC]	AECT
Association for Educational Data Processing (CAH)	AEDP
Association for Educational Data Systems [Washington, DC]	AEDS
Association of Electronic Cottagers [Sierra Madre, CA] (EANO)	AEC
Association of Entertainment Industry Computer Professionals [Los Angeles, CA] (EANO)	AEICP
Association pour les Etudes sur la Radio-Television Canadienne [Asscciation for the Study of Canadian Radio and Television - ASCRT]	AERTC
Association of Federal Communications Consulting Engineers [Bloomfield Hills, MI]	AFCCE
Association for Federal Information Resources Management (EANO)	AFFIRM
Association Francaise de Calcul [French computing association] (OA)	AFCAL
Association Francaise pour la Cybernetique Economique et Technique [Paris, France]	AFCET
Association Francaise des Informaticiens [Paris, France]	AFIN
Association Francaise de Normalisation [French Standardization Association] [Paris, France] [Database producer]	AFNOR
Association of Hospital Television Networks [Pittsburgh, PA] [Telecommunications] (EANO)	AHTN
Association of Independent Microdealers (EANO)	AIM
Association of Independent Software Companies [Later, ADAPSO] (EANO)	AISC
Association of Independent Television Stations (EANO)	INTV
Association of Information and Dissemination Centers [Athens, GA]	ASIDIC
Association for Information and Image Management [Silver Spring, MD] (EANO)	AIIM
Association of Information Managers for Financial Institutions (EANO)	AIM
Association of Information Systems Professionals [Willow Grove, PA] (EANO)	AISP
Association of Information Systems Professionals [Canada]	AISP
Association pour l'Informatique de Gestion [Paris, France]	AIG
Association of the Institute for Certification of Computer Professionals [Des Plaines, IL] (EANO)	AICCP
Association for Integrated Manufacturing Technology (EANO)	AIMT
Association Internationale pour le Calcul Analogique [International Association for Analogue Computation] [Later, IMACS]	AICA
Association Internationale de Cybernetique [International Association for Cybernetics - IAC]	AIC
Association Internationale des Etudes et Recherches sur l'Information [International Association of Mass Communications Research]	AIERI
Association for Literary and Linguistic Computing (EANO)	ALLC
Association of Long Distance Telephone Companies [Washington, DC] (EANO)	ALTEL
Association for Machine Translation and Computational Linguistics [Later, Association for Computational Linguistics]	AMTCL
Association for Media-Based Continuing Education for Engineers [Atlanta, GA] [Telecommunications] (EANO)	AMCEE
Association of Minicomputer Users [Framingham, MA] (EANO)	AMU
Association Nationale pour l'Infographie [National Computer Graphics Association of Canada]	ANI
Association Nationale de la Recherche Technique [Database producer] (CUAD)	ANRT
Association Package Sequence Number (MCD)	APSN
Association of Programmed Learning [London, England] (MCD)	APL
Association for Programmed Learning and Educational Technology	APLET
Association of Public Data Users [Princeton University] [Princeton, NJ] (EANO)	APDU
Association of Radio and Television Employees of Canada	ARTEC
Association of Records Managers and Administrators, Inc. [Prairie Village, KS]	ARMA
Association of Rehabilitation Programs in Data Processing (EANO)	ARPDP
Association of Scientific, Technical, and Managerial Staffs [British]	ASTMS
Association of Small Computer Users [Later, ACU] (EANO)	ASCU
Association of Small Computer Users [Later, ACU] (EANO)	ASCUE
Association for Software Protection [Computer software developers and vendors] (EANO)	ASP
Association-Storing Processor [Data processing]	ASP
Association of System 2000 Users for Technical Exchange	ASTUTE
Association for Systems Management [Formerly, SPA] [Cleveland, OH] (TUT)	ASM
Association of Telephone Answering Services [New York, NY]	ATAS
Association of Time-Sharing Users [Later, ACU] (EANO)	ATSU
Association for Women in Computing [Silver Spring, MD] (EANO)	AWC
Associative Array Processor (MCD)	AAP
Associative Communication Multiplexer (OA)	ACM
Associative Computer Device	ACD
Associative Content Retrieval Network [A. D. Little, Inc.] [Information service] (IDA)	ACORN
Associative Index Method (CAA)	AIM
Associative Interactive Dictionary [for databases] [National Library of Medicine]	AID
Associative Linear Array Processor [Data processing] (CAA)	ALAP
Associative Memory [Data processing]	AM
Associative Memory Address [Data processing] (CAA)	AMA
Associative Memory Array [Data processing] (CAA)	AMA
Associative Memory Computer [Data processing]	AMC
Associative Memory Device [Data processing] (DIT)	AMD
Associative Memory Processor [Data processing] (BUR)	AMP
Associative Output Control Unit (CAA)	AOCU
Associative Output Unit [Data processing] (CAA)	AOU
Associative Parallel Processor [Data processing]	APP
Associative Processor [Data processing] (BUR)	AP
Associative Processor Computer System (IDA)	APCS
Associative Processor Control [Data processing] (CAA)	APC
Associative Processor Programing Language Evaluation (OA)	APPLE
Associative Programing Language [Data processing] (BUR)	APL
Associative Register [Data processing]	AR
Associative Registers for Generalized User Switching [Computer typesetting system]	ARGUS
Associative Structure Computer (BUR)	ASC
Associative Structures Package (BUR)	ASP
Associazione Italiana per il Calcolo Automatico [Italian Association for Automatic Data Processing]	AICA
Associazione Nazionale Italiana per l'Automazione [Milan, Italy]	ANIPLA
Associometrics Data Management System (IEEE)	ADAM
Associometrics Remote Terminal Inquiry Control System (IEEE)	ARTIC
Astro Guidance Digital Computer (IEEE)	AGDIC
Astrocom Corp. [NASDAQ symbol] (NQ)	ACOM
Astronomical Image Processing System	AIPS
Astronomical Unit [Equal to average distance from earth to sun]	AU
Astronomisches Recheninstitut [Information retrieval] (ODIN)	ARI
Astronuclear Laboratory [Westinghouse Electric Corp.] (MCD)	AL
Asymmetric Data Exchange (CAA)	ADX
Asymmetric Multiprocessing System [IBM Corp.] (CAA)	AMS
Asymmetric Stress Analysis of Axisymmetric Solids [Computer program]	ASAAS
Asymptote [Mathematics]	ASYMP
Asynchronous (MSA)	ASYN
Asynchronous	ASYNC
Asynchronous	ASYNCH
Asynchronous Address Communications Systems (OA)	AACS
Asynchronous Balanced Mode (CCD)	ABM
Asynchronous Communication Procedure (BUR)	ASC
Asynchronous Communications Control (CAA)	ACC
Asynchronous Communications Control Attachment (OA)	ACCA

Asynchronous Communications Interface Adapter [*Data processing*] (MDG) .... ACIA
Asynchronous Data Communications Channel (CAA) .... ADCC
Asynchronous Data Multiplexer Synchronizer .... ADMS
Asynchronous Data Transceiver (CAA) .... ADT
Asynchronous Disconnected Mode (CCD) .... ADM
Asynchronous Line Control Unit [*Telecommunications*] (CAA) .... ALCU
Asynchronous Line Driver [*Prentice Corp.*] (CAA) .... ALD
Asynchronous Line Interface [*Telecommunications*] (CAA) .... ALI
Asynchronous Line Module (CAA) .... ALM
Asynchronous Line Multiplexer [*Telecommunications*] (CAA) .... ALM
Asynchronous Line Unit [*Telecommunications*] (CAA) .... ALU
Asynchronous Look-Ahead Simulator (IEEE) .... ALAS
Asynchronous MODEM (CAA) .... AM
Asynchronous Multiline Controller [*Telecommunications*] (CAA) .... AMLC
Asynchronous Response Mode [*Data processing*] (CAA) .... ARM
Asynchronous State Machine (IEEE) .... ASM
Asynchronous Synchronous Programable Interface [*Data processing*] (CAA) .... ASPI
Asynchronous Terminal Adapter [*Telecommunications*] (CAA) .... ATA
Asynchronous Time-Division Multiplexing [*Data processing*] .... ATDM
AT & T [*American Telephone & Telegraph Co.*] **Communications** [*Bedminster, NJ*] [*Telecommunications*] (TSSD) .... ATTCOM
AT & T [*American Telephone & Telegraph Co.*] **Information Systems** .... ATIS
ATACC [*Alberta Teachers' Association, Computer Council*] **Journal** [*A publication*] .... ATACC J
Atanasoff-Berry Computer [*Early computer*] .... ABC
Atari Hard-Disk Controller .... AHDC
Atari Message and Information System [*Computer-based bulletin board system*] .... AMIS
Atari-Version American Standard Code for Information Interchange [*Character code*] .... ATASCII
Atkins Stress Analysis System [*Atkins Research & Development*] [*Software package*] [*British*] (NCC) .... ASAS
Atlantic Ocean Region [*INTELSAT*] (CBSS) .... AOR
Atlantic Ocean Ship [*INTELSAT*] (CBSS) .... AOS
Atlantic Research Corporation .... ARC
Atlantic Research Corporation [*NASDAQ symbol*] (NQ) .... ATRC
Atlantic Satellite Network [*Cable-television system*] .... ASN
Atlas Basic Language [*Data processing*] (CGC) .... ABL
Atlas Commercial Language [*Data processing*] (BUR) .... ACL
Atlas General Survey Program (IEEE) .... AGSP
Atmospheric Monitor System (IEEE) .... AMS
Atmospheric and Oceanographic Information Processing System [*Satellite image enhancing system*] (MCD) .... AOIPS
Atomic and Molecular Physical Data Program [*American Society for Testing and Materials*] (EISS) .... AMD
Atomics International Evaluated Nuclear Data Files (KSC) .... AIENDF
ATR: Australian Telecommunication Research [*A publication*] .... ATR Aust Telecommun Res
Attached Applications Processor (CAA) .... AAP
Attached FORTRAN Processor [*Burroughs Corp.*] [*Data processing*] (BUR) .... AFP
Attached Processor [*Data processing*] (BUR) .... AP
Attached Support Processor [*Data processing*] (CGC) .... ASP
Attachment [*Telecommunications*] (TEL) .... ATT
Attack/Decay/Sustain/Release [*Audio programming parameters*] .... ADSR
Attempts per Circuit per Hour [*Telecommunications*] (TEL) .... ACH
Attendant [*Telecommunications*] (TEL) .... AD
Attended Public Telephone [*Telecommunications*] (TEL) .... ATT
Attention (AFM) .... ATTN
Attention Display [*Communications device*] .... AD
Attitude Command System (IEEE) .... ACS
Attitude Control System [*Telecommunications*] (TEL) .... ACS
Attitude Display System (MCD) .... ADS
Attitude Heading Reference System (NG) .... AHRS
Attitudinal Information Data System (NVT) .... AIDS
Atto [*A prefix meaning divided by 10 to the 18th power*] [*SI symbol*] .... a
Audible Doppler Enhancer [*Telecommunications*] (TEL) .... ADE
Audio Cassette Recorder (RDA) .... ACR
Audio Center - Receiver (KSC) .... ACRV
Audio Center - Transmitter (KSC) .... ACTM
Audio Commercial Message Repeating Unit [*Device delivering a recorded commercial from cigarette vending machines*] .... ACMRU
Audio Communications System .... ACS
Audio Frequency [*Data transmission*] .... AF
Audio Frequency Amplifier .... AFA
Audio Frequency Apparatus .... AFA
Audio Frequency Change .... AFC
Audio Frequency Choke .... AFC
Audio Frequency Coder .... AFC
Audio Frequency Shift (IEEE) .... AFS
Audio Frequency Shift Key .... AFSK
Audio Frequency Transformer .... AFT
Audio Input Frequency Tolerance .... AIFT
Audio Peak Clipping Amplifier .... APCA
Audio Reply (IEEE) .... AUDREY
Audio Response [*International Harvester Co. computer*] .... AUDRE
Audio Response Control (BUR) .... ARC
Audio Response System (CAA) .... ARS
Audio Response Unit .... ARU
Audio Visual Communications [*A publication*] .... Audiov Commun
Audio Wave Analyzer .... AWA
Audiographic Teleconference (CAA) .... AGT
Audiolingual Language Programing [*Data processing*] .... ALLP
Audiometer Telephone Interface [*for the hearing-impaired*] .... ATI
Audiovisual .... AV
Audiovisual, Computer, and Communication Office Automation .... AVCCOA
Audiovisuals On-Line [*National Library of Medicine*] [*Rockville Pike, MD*] [*Database*] .... AVLINE
Audit Bureau of Circulations [*Database producer*] .... ABI
Audit Command Language (IDA) .... ACL
Audit Entry (BUR) .... AE
Audit Entry Language [*Burroughs Corp.*] (CAA) .... AEL
Audit Trail (OA) .... AT
Auditory Information Display .... AID
Auditory Input Task [*Data processing*] .... AUDIT
Auerbach Data Base Management [*A publication*] .... Auerbach Data Base Manage
Auerbach Data Base Management [*A publication*] .... DBMAD
Auerbach Reporter [*A publication*] .... Auerbach Rep
Augmented Content-Addressed Memory (CAA) .... ACAM
Augmented Human Intellect (KSC) .... AHI
Augmented Logistics Support (MCD) .... ALS
Augmented Predictive Analyzer [*Data processing*] (DIT) .... APA
Augmented Programing Training [*Data processing*] (IEEE) .... APT
Augmented Transition Network [*Language analysis*] .... ATN
Aural .... AUR
Australasian Software Report [*A publication*] .... ASR
Australian Bibliographic Network [*National Library of Australia*] [*Canberra, Australia*] [*Information service*] (EISS) .... ABN
Australian Business [*Australian Consolidated Press*] [*Database*] (CUAD) .... AUSB
Australian Business Computer [*A publication*] .... ABC
Australian Clearing House for Publications in Recreation Sport and Tourism [*Information service*] (EISS) .... ACHPIRST
Australian Computer Bulletin [*A publication*] .... ACB
Australian Computer Bulletin [*A publication*] .... Aust Comput Bull
Australian Computer Journal [*A publication*] .... Aust Comput J
Australian Computer Science Communications [*A publication*] .... Aust Comput Sci Commun
Australian Computer Society (CAA) .... ACS
Australian Education Index [*Australian Council for Educational Research*] [*Information service*] (EISS) .... AEI
Australian Personal Computer [*A publication*] .... APC
Australian Political Register [*Australian Consolidated Press*] [*Database*] (CUAD) .... APOL
Australian Telecommunication Research [*A publication*] .... ATR
Australian Telecommunication Research [*A publication*] .... Aust Telecomm Res
Australian Telecommunication Research [*A publication*] .... Aust Telecomm Research
Australian Telecommunication Research [*A publication*] .... Aust Telecommun Res
Australian Telecommunications Development Association. Annual Report [*A publication*] .... Aust Telecommun Dev Assoc
Australian Telecommunications Users Group [*Sydney, Australia*] (TSSD) .... ATUG
Author [*Online database field identifier*] [*Data processing*] .... AU
Author [*Online database field identifier*] [*Data processing*] (OBD) .... AUT
Author and Keyword in Context (DEEC) .... AKWIC
Authorized Item Identification Data Collaborator Code .... AIIDC
Authorized Item Identification Data Receiver Code .... AIIDR
Authorized Item Identification Data Submitter Code .... AIIDS
Authorized Program Analysis Report [*Data processing*] (IBMDP) .... APAR
Authorized Program Facility [*Data processing*] (BUR) .... APF
Auto-Initiate Manual-Confirm (CAAL) .... AIMC
Auto-Interactive Design [*Combines operator-executed and automatic features*] [*Data processing*] (CCD) .... AID
Auto-Lock Channel Tuning [*Television technology*] .... ACT
Auto/Manual (MDG) .... A/M
Auto-Manual Bridge Control [*Telecommunications*] (TEL) .... AMB
Auto-Manual Center [*Telecommunications*] (TEL) .... AMC
Auto Tracking Scan System [*for television video quality*] [*Sony Corp.*] .... ATSS
Auto-Trol Technology [*NASDAQ symbol*] (NQ) .... ATTC
Autocoder to COBOL Conversion Aid Program [*IBM Corp.*] [*Data processing*] .... ACCAP
Autocoder-to-COBOL Translating Service [*Data processing*] (IEEE) .... ACTRAN
AUTODIN/AUTOVON Interface (CET) .... AAI
AUTODIN Coordination Station (CET) .... ADCS
AUTODIN Digital Subscriber Terminal .... ADST
AUTODIN Multimedia Terminal (NVT) .... AMT
AUTODIN Station Maintenance Console .... ASMC
AUTODIN Switch Upgrade Project (MCD) .... ASUP
AUTODIN Switching Center .... ASC
Automatech Graphics Corporation [*New York, NY*] [*Information service*] (EISS) .... AGC
Automated Accounting System (BUR) .... AAS
Automated Auger Microprobe .... A^2M
Automated Batch Mixing [*Data processing*] .... ABM
Automated Bibliography (DEEC) .... AB
Automated Budget System .... AUTOBUS
Automated Chemistry Program [*Data processing*] .... ACP
Automated Circuit Card Etching Layout [*Data processing*] .... ACCEL

Automated Circulation Control System [*Library management*] .... ACCS
Automated Circulation System [*Data processing*] .... ACS
Automated Clearinghouse [*Banking*] .... ACH
Automated Code Evaluation System (CAA) .... ACES
Automated Coder of Report Narrative [*Data processing*] (DIT) .... ACORN
Automated Combustor [*Computer code*] .... AUTOCOM
Automated Communications Publications .... ACP
Automated Communications Set (BUR) .... ACS
Automated Computer Controlled Editing Sound System .... ACCESS
Automated Computer Science Education .... ACSED
Automated Computer Science Education System (IDA) .... ACSES
Automated Contingency Translator [*Data processing*] .... ACT
Automated Control and Checking of Electrical Systems Support (MCD) .... ACCESS
Automated Control of a Document Management System [*Data processing*] (DIT) .... ACDMS
Automated Cross-Section Analysis Program [*Data processing*] .... ACSAP
Automated Custom Terminal System .... ACTS
Automated Data Acquisition System [*GCA Corp.*] .... ADAS
Automated Data Analysis and Presentation Techniques (MCD) .... ADAPT
Automated Data Exchange [*Berkeley, CA*] [*Software manufacturer*] (DASOS) .... ADE
Automated Data Management Information System .... ADMIS
Automated Data Preparation by Electronic Photocomposition (MCD) .... ADPEP
Automated Data Preparation Evaluation Program (MCD) .... ADPEP
Automated Data Reports Submission System .... ADRSS
Automated Data Subsystem .... ADSS
Automated Data System Analysis Technique .... AUTOSATE
Automated Data and Telecommunications Service [*Later, Office of Information and Resources Management*] .... ADTS
Automated Data Unit Movement .... ADUM
Automated Data Wiring .... ADW
Automated Debugging Environment [*Applied Data Research, Inc.*] (CAA) .... ADE
Automated Design Engineering [*Telecommunications*] (TEL) .... ADE
Automated Design System (MCD) .... ADS
Automated Dialer and Recorded Message Player (IEEE) .... ADRMP
Automated Digital Design System [*Raytheon Co.*] .... ADDS
Automated Direct Entry Packaging Technique (OA) .... ADEPT
Automated Document Control System [*Data processing*] (MCD) .... ADCS
Automated Documentation Systems [*Data processing*] .... ADS
Automated Drafting and Digitizing Machine [*Data processing*] (RDA) .... ADDM
Automated Drafting System .... ADS
Automated Educational Services On-Line Processing (MCD) .... AESOP
Automated Engineering Design [*Programing language*] [*1960*] [*Data processing*] .... AED
Automated Engineering Design Circuit Analysis Program .... AEDCAP
Automated Environmental Prediction (CAAL) .... AEP
Automated Environmental Prediction System (MCD) .... AEPS
Automated Fare Collection .... AFC
Automated Frequency Assignment System [*Telecommunications*] .... AFAS
Automated Guided Vehicle [*Robotics*] .... AGV
Automated Hospital Information System [*Washington, DC*] [*Veterans Administration*] (EISS) .... AHIS
Automated Image Data Extraction System (MCD) .... AIDES
Automated Image Device Evaluator [*Electronics*] .... AIDE
Automated Implementation Plan .... AIP
Automated Industrial Management System .... AIMS
Automated Information Data System .... AIDS
Automated Information Management (NASA) .... AIM
Automated Information and Management System (BUR) .... AIMS
Automated Information and Management Systems (MCD) .... AIMES
Automated Information and Reservation Computer Operated Network .... AIRCON
Automated Information System .... AIS
Automated Information Transfer System [*Department of Commerce*] [*Database*] (FDB) .... AITS
Automated Inspection of Data .... AIDA
Automated Instructional Materials Services [*Developed by the System Development Corp.*] (EISS) .... AIMS
Automated Instrumentation System .... AIS
Automated Insurance Rating Services, Inc. [*Naperville, IL*] [*Software manufacturer*] (DASOS) .... AIRS
Automated Insurance Service .... AIS
Automated Intelligence Processing System (MCD) .... AIPS
Automated Intelligent Microscope .... AIM
Automated Inventory Management Evaluation System (IEEE) .... AIMES
Automated Language Processing Systems [*Provo, UT*] [*Software manufacturer*] (DASOS) .... ALPS
Automated Layout Design Program [*IBM Corp.*] .... ALDEP
Automated Learning Process .... ALP
Automated Library Acquisitions System [*Suggested name for the Library of Congress computer system*] .... ALAS
Automated Library Information System [*Dataphase Systems, Inc.*] [*Shawnee Mission, KS*] (EISS) .... ALIS
Automated Library Issue Document (NVT) .... ALID
Automated Library Processing Services [*System Development Corp.*] (EISS) .... ALPS
Automated Library Program [*Data processing*] (DIT) .... ALP
Automated Library System [*Foundation for Library Research, Inc.*] [*Information service*] (EISS) .... ALS
Automated Library Technical Services [*Program*] [*Los Angeles Public Library*] .... ALTS
Automated Line Record Update [*Telecommunications*] (TEL) .... ALRU
Automated Linguistic Extraction and Retrieval Technique .... ALERT
Automated Linguistic Fieldworker [*Data processing*] (DIT) .... AUTOLING
Automated Literature Alerting System [*Data processing*] (DIT) .... ALAS
Automated Local Evaluations in Real Time [*National Oceanic and Atmospheric Administration*] .... ALERT
Automated Location of Isolation and Continuity Error [*Module*] [*Raytheon Co.*] .... ALICE
Automated Logic Diagram [*Data processing*] (IBMDP) .... ALD
Automated Logic Implementation [*Data processing*] (IEEE) .... ALI
Automated Logistics Data Processing System .... ALDPS
Automated Management Information System (DIT) .... AMIS
Automated Management Reports (BUR) .... AMR
Automated Material Processing System [*Data processing*] (TUT) .... AMPS
Automated Materials Handling System [*Data processing*] (DDI) .... AMHS
Automated Message Handling System .... AMHS
Automated Minerals Information System [*Bureau of Mines*] [*Database*] (FDB) .... AMIS
Automated Modification Analyzer [*Data processing*] .... AMA
Automated Network Schedule with Evaluation of Resources (MCD) .... ANSWER
Automated Packaging Code (MCD) .... APC
Automated Packaging Planning System (MCD) .... APPS
Automated Procedures for Engineering Consultants, Inc. .... APEC
Automated Process Information File [*Library of Congress*] .... APIF
Automated Procurement Planning, Execution, and Control .... APEX
Automated Professional Systems [*NASDAQ symbol*] (NQ) .... APSI
Automated Program Support System [*Data processing*] .... APSS
Automated Programable Assembly System [*Data processing*] .... APAS
Automated Project Management Information System [*Data processing*] .... APMIS
Automated Projective Drawing [*GMW Computers Ltd.*] [*Software package*] [*British*] (NCC) .... AUTOPROD
Automated Quill, Incorporated [*Englewood, CO*] [*Software manufacturer*] (DASOS) .... AQI
Automated Reliability Estimation Program [*Data processing*] .... ARIES
Automated Rent Collections (TUT) .... ARC
Automated Repair Service Bureau (TEL) .... ARSB
Automated Requirements Allocation Data (MCD) .... ARAD
Automated Responsive Environment (BUR) .... ARE
Automated Route Management (DEN) .... ARM
Automated Ship Data Library (IEEE) .... ASDL
Automated Software Evaluation System (CAA) .... ASES
Automated Specifications [*Data processing*] (DIT) .... AUTOSPEC
Automated Spooling Priority [*Data processing*] (CGC) .... ASP
Automated Statistical Analysis Program .... ASAP
Automated Storage/Retrieval Systems .... AS/RS
Automated Switched Communications Network (MCD) .... ASCON
Automated System for Composing, Revising, Illustrating, and Phototypesetting .... AUTOSCRIPT
Automated Tape Label Assignment System .... ATLAS
Automated Tape Library .... ATL
Automated Technical Control [*System*] [*Honeywell, Inc.*] .... ATEC
Automated Teller .... AT
Automated [*or Automatic*] **Teller Machine** [*Banking*] .... ATM
Automated Terminal Weather Dissemination Display System (MCD) .... ATWDDS
Automated Test-Case Guidance [*Data processing*] .... ATG
Automated Test Data Generator [*Data processing*] .... ATDG
Automated Test Plan (BUR) .... ATP
Automated Testing Analyzer [*Data processing*] .... ATA
Automated Trading System [*NYSE computer*] .... ATS
Automated Travel Agents Reservation (CGC) .... ATAR
Automated Verification System [*Data processing*] (MCD) .... AVS
Automated Vocabulary Control [*Subsystem of PLIS*] [*Data processing*] .... AVOCON
Automated Want and Warrant System [*Data processing system used in police work*] .... AWWS
Automatic Address Recognition System [*or Subsystem*] [*Data processing*] (CAA) .... AARS
Automatic Addressing System [*Data processing*] .... AAS
Automatic Air Traffic Control [*System*] (IEEE) .... AATC
Automatic Alternate Voice/Data [*Data processing*] .... AAVD
Automatic Amplitude Control (CET) .... AAC
Automatic Announcement Subsystem [*Telecommunications*] (TEL) .... AAS
Automatic Answer [*Telecommunications*] (TEL) .... AA
Automatic Antenna Timer .... AAT
Automatic Band Rate (IEEE) .... ABR
Automatic Bandwidth Control (MSA) .... ABWC
Automatic Bass Compensation [*Radio*] .... ABC
Automatic Bass Compensation [*Radio*] (MSA) .... ABSC
Automatic Bass Control .... ABC
Automatic Bill Calling [*Later, MCCS*] [*Telecommunications*] .... ABC
Automatic Binary Computer .... ABC
Automatic Binary Data Link [*Data processing*] (CET) .... ABDL
Automatic BIT [*Binary Digit*] **Error Rate Test** [*Data processing*] (MCD) .... ABERT
Automatic Bootstrap Loader [*Data processing*] (CAA) .... ABL
Automatic Brightness Control [*Telecommunications*] (TEL) .... ABC
Automatic Broadcast (FAAC) .... ABCST
Automatic Broadcasting Control System [*Japan*] .... ABCS

Automatic Bulk Tape Degausser ... ABTD
Automatic Cable Tester ... ACT
Automatic Call Distribution [*Switching system*] [*Telecommunications*] ... ACD
Automatic Call Distributor - Electronic Switching System [*Telecommunications*] (TEL) ... ACD-ESS
Automatic Call Origination [*Telecommunications*] (CAA) ... ACO
Automatic Call Recording [*Telecommunications*] (CMD) ... ACR
Automatic Calling Equipment [*Telecommunications*] (BUR) ... ACE
Automatic Calling Unit [*Telecommunications*] (TEL) ... ACU
Automatic Calling Unit Interface [*Telecommunications*] (IEEE) ... ACUI
Automatic Card Control Entrance Security System [*Data processing*] (TUT) ... ACCESS
Automatic Carrier Control [*Telecommunications*] (TEL) ... ACC
Automatic Channel and Time [*Toshiba Corp.*] [*Programable television set*] ... ACT
Automatic Checkout (BUR) ... AC
Automatic Checkout and Control System ... ACCS
Automatic Checkout Equipment ... ACE
Automatic Checkout Equipment ... ACOE
Automatic Checkout Equipment Sequencer (NASA) ... ACES
Automatic Checkout and Readiness Equipment ... ACRE
Automatic Checkout and Recording Equipment ... ACORN
Automatic Checkout Set ... ACOS
Automatic Checkout System ... ACHS
Automatic Checkout Test Equipment ... ACTE
Automatic Circuit Analysis Program ... ACAP
Automatic Circuit Analyzer ... ACA
Automatic Circuit Assurance Feature (CET) ... ACAF
Automatic Circuit Board Card Tester ... ACBCT
Automatic Circuit Board Tester ... ACBT
Automatic Circuit Exchange ... ACE
Automatic Circuit Exchange (MSA) ... ACKTX
Automatic Circuit Tester ... ACT
Automatic Classification and Interpretation of Data (BUR) ... ACID
Automatic Code Generator (CAA) ... ACG
Automatic Code Translation [*Data processing*] ... ACT
Automatic Coding Machine [*Data processing*] (CET) ... ACOM
Automatic Coin Telephone Service ... ACTS
Automatic Color-Scanned Device (MCD) ... ACSD
Automatic Comprehensive Display System [*Data processing*] ... ACDS
Automatic Computer ... AC
Automatic Computer-Controlled Electronic Scanning System [*National Bureau of Standards*] ... ACCESS
Automatic Computer Evaluation (BUR) ... ACE
Automatic Computer, Ministry of Supply [*British*] (DEN) ... AMOS
Automatic Computer Telex Services ... ACTS
Automatic Computerized Transverse Axial [*Computer X-ray system*] ... ACTA
Automatic Computing Engine [*Early computer*] [*National Physical Laboratory*] ... ACE
Automatic Computing Transfer Oscillator (IEEE) ... ACTO
Automatic Conference Arranger (CET) ... ACA
Automatic Continuous Function Generation [*Data processing*] ... ACFG
Automatic Contour Digitizer ... ACD
Automatic Control of Air Transmissions (NATG) ... AUTOCAT
Automatic Control and Computer Sciences [*A publication*] ... Automat Control and Computer Sci
Automatic Control and Computer Sciences [*A publication*] ... Automat Control Comput Sci
Automatic Control and Computer Sciences [*A publication*] ... Autom Control Comput Sci
Automatic Control and Computer Sciences [*A publication*] ... Autom Control and Comput Sci
Automatic Control Console (NASA) ... ACC
Automatic Control System ... ACS
Automatic Control Theory and Applications [*A publication*] ... Automat Control Theory Appl
Automatic Control Theory and Applications [*A publication*] ... Automatic Control Theory Appl
Automatic Control Theory and Applications [*A publication*] ... Autom Control Theory & Appl
Automatic Counter System ... ACS
Automatic Data Accumulation and Transfer ... ADAT
Automatic Data Acquisition ... ADA
Automatic Data Collection System (RDA) ... ADCS
Automatic Data Descriptor ... ADD
Automatic Data Entry Unit ... ADEU
Automatic Data Equalized Modem ... ADEM
Automatic Data Evaluation ... ADE
Automatic Data Exchange ... ADX
Automatic Data Extraction Routine (CAAL) ... ADER
Automatic Data Extractor and Plotting Table ... ADEPT
Automatic Data Handling [*Data processing*] ... ADH
Automatic Data Interchange System [*International Civil Aviation Organization*] ... ADIS
Automatic Data Link [*Data processing*] ... ADL
Automatic Data Plotter ... ADP
Automatic Data Processing ... ADP
Automatic Data Processing Budget Control Totals (DDI) ... ADPBCT
Automatic Data Processing Center ... ADPC
Automatic Data Processing Engineering (DDI) ... ADPE
Automatic Data Processing Equipment ... ADPE
Automatic Data Processing by Equipment Systems ... ADPES
Automatic Data Processing Field Branch [*BUPERS*] (DDI) ... ADPFB
Automatic Data Processing, Inc. [*Trademark for data processing services*] ... ADP
Automatic Data Processing, Inc. [*NYSE symbol*] ... AUD
Automatic Data Processing Information Bulletin [*A publication*] ... Automat Data Process Inform B
Automatic Data Processing Information Bulletin [*A publication*] ... Autom Data Process Inf Bull
Automatic Data Processing Machine ... ADPM
Automatic Data Processing Management Information System ... ADPMIS
Automatic Data Processing Modification Order ... ADPMO
Automatic Data Processing Programs (FAAC) ... ADPP
Automatic Data Processing Resource Estimating Procedure ... ADREP
Automatic Data Processing Resource Estimating Procedures ... ADPREP
Automatic Data Processing System [*or Subsystem*] ... ADPS
Automatic Data Rate Changer ... ADRC
Automatic Data Reporting System (NATG) ... ADRS
Automatic Data Routing Group ... ADRG
Automatic Data and Select Program (KSC) ... ADASP
Automatic Data Service Center ... ADSC
Automatic Data Switching System [*Deep Space Network*] (CIT) ... ADSS
Automatic Data System [*Data processing*] ... ADS
Automatic Data System Uniform Practices ... ADSUP
Automatic Data Test System [*Bell System*] ... ADTS
Automatic Data Translator [*or Transmitter*] ... ADT
Automatic Data Unit (CAA) ... ADU
Automatic Debit Transfer [*Banking*] ... ADT
Automatic Depositor [*Banking*] (BUR) ... AD
Automatic Detection and Tracking (MCD) ... ADT
Automatic Development System (MCD) ... ADS
Automatic Diagnostic Input/Output System [*Data processing*] (CAA) ... ADIOS
Automatic Diagnostic Maintenance Information Retrieval [*Data processing*] (MCD) ... ADMIRE
Automatic Dialing Unit [*Telecommunications*] ... ADU
Automatic Digit Recognition ... AUDREY
Automatic Digital Assembly Test Equipment (MCD) ... ADATE
Automatic Digital Calculator [*Data processing*] ... ADC
Automatic Digital Data Acquisition and Recording [*Data processing*] ... ADDAR
Automatic Digital Data Assembly System [*Data processing*] (DDI) ... ADDAS
Automatic Digital-Data-Error Recorder [*Data processing*] ... ADDER
Automatic Digital Encoding System [*Data processing*] ... ADES
Automatic Digital Information Network ... AUTODIN
Automatic Digital Input/Output System [*Data processing*] ... ADIOS
Automatic Digital Message Switching ... ADMS
Automatic Digital Message Switching Center [*AUTODIN*] ... ADMSC
Automatic Digital Network [*DoD*] ... AUTODIN
Automatic Digital On-Line Instrumentation System ... ADONIS
Automatic Digital Recording and Control ... ADRAC
Automatic Digital Switch ... ADS
Automatic Digital Test Unit ... ADTU
Automatic Digital Tracking Analyzer Computer [*Data processing*] (FAAC) ... ADTAC
Automatic Direct Access to Information with the On-Line UDC [*Universal Decimal Classification*] **System** [*American Institute of Physics*] [*Information retrieval*] ... AUDACIOUS
Automatic Direct Analog Computer (BUR) ... ADAC
Automatic Direct-Distance Dialing System [*Telecommunications*] (IEEE) ... ADDDS
Automatic Direction Finding System ... ADFS
Automatic Display [*Data processing*] ... AD
Automatic Display Finder [*Data processing*] (NASA) ... ADF
Automatic Display Mode [*Data processing*] (BUR) ... ADM
Automatic Display and Plotting System (BUR) ... ADAPS
Automatic Display Switching Oscilloscope ... ADSO
Automatic Distribution of Microfiche ... ADM
Automatic Document Analysis (DIT) ... ADA
Automatic Document Request Service [*or System*] (DEEC) ... ADRS
Automatic Document Storage and Retrieval [*Data processing*] ... ADSTAR
Automatic Drafting Machine (DIT) ... ADMA
Automatic Drawing Device (DIT) ... ADD
Automatic Dynamic Evaluation by Programed Test ... ADEPT
Automatic and Dynamic Monitor with Immediate Relocation, Allocation, and Loading (IEEE) ... ADMIRAL
Automatic Electronic Switching Center ... AESC
Automatic Electronic Voice Switch (RDA) ... AEVS
Automatic Environment Monitoring (BUR) ... AEM
Automatic Equalization/Analyzation System ... AEAS
Automatic Error Analysis ... AEA
Automatic Fault Isolation ... AFI
Automatic Field Analog Computer ... AFAC
Automatic Film Data Collection System (MCD) ... AFDCS
Automatic Fine Tuning ... AFT
Automatic Fingerprint Verification Computer System ... AFVCS
Automatic Flexible Test Station ... AFTS
Automatic Flight Control ... AFC
Automatic Format Recognition [*Data processing*] ... AFR
Automatic Frequency Assignment Model [*Telecommunications*] ... AFAM
Automatic Frequency Control [*Electronics*] ... AFC
Automatic Frequency/Phase-Controlled [*Loop*] (IEEE) ... AF/PC
Automatic Frequency Tone Shift ... AFTS

Computer & Telecommunications Acronyms

Automatic Frequency Tuner	AFT
Automatic Funds Transfer	AFT
Automatic Gain Adjusting Amplifier [*Telecommunications*] (TEL)	AGAMP
Automatic Gain Control [*Electronics*]	AGC
Automatic Generation of Requests [*Data processing*] (DIT)	AUTOQEST
Automatic Ground-to-Air Communications System	AGACS
Automatic Ground Checkout System (KSC)	AGCS
Automatic Ground Computer System (KSC)	AGCS
Automatic Ground Control Station (KSC)	AGCS
Automatic Ground Control System Computer (KSC)	AGCSC
Automatic Guidance Electronics	AGE
Automatic Guidance Programing (NATG)	AGP
Automatic Guided Flight (MUGU)	AGF
Automatic Guided Vehicle Systems (EANO)	AGVS
Automatic Heading Reference System (DDI)	AHRS
Automatic Identified Outward Dialing	AIOD
Automatic Illustrated Documentation System [*Information International, Inc.*]	AIDS
Automatic Image Retrieval System (MCD)	AIRS
Automatic Imagery Interpretation	AII
Automatic Indexing and Proofreading System	AIPS
Automatic Information Retrieval System [*Data processing*] (BUR)	AIRS
Automatic Information Station [*or System*] (BUR)	AIST
Automatic Initiation Circuit (IEEE)	AIC
Automatic Inlet Control System (NG)	AICS
Automatic Input [*Data processing*] (BUR)	AI
Automatic Integrated Circuit Tester	AICT
Automatic Integrated Debugging System [*Data processing*] (BUR)	AIDS
Automatic Integrating Fluctuation Meter	AIFM
Automatic Interaction Detection [*or Detector*] [*Data processing*]	AID
Automatic Intercept Bureau [*Telecommunications*] (TEL)	AIB
Automatic Intercept Center [*Bell System*]	AIC
Automatic Intercept System [*Bell System*]	AIS
Automatic Intercom Switching System	AISS
Automatic Intermediate Station (MCD)	AIS
Automatic Interplanetary Station [*USSR*]	AIS
Automatic Jamming Avoidance Circuitry	AJAC
Automatic Language Data Processing	ALDP
Automatic Language Processing Advisory Committee [*National Research Council*]	ALPAC
Automatic LASER Encoder	ALE
Automatic Lead Former	ALF
Automatic Letter Facer	ALF
Automatic Level Recorder	ALR
Automatic Level Setting	ALS
Automatic License Plate Scanning	ALPS
Automatic Life Testing and Recording of Electronic Components [*Canada*] (CDH)	ALTREC
Automatic Light Aircraft Readiness Monitor	ALARM
Automatic Lightning Detection System [*To aid in the prevention of forest fires*]	ALDS
Automatic Line Buildout [*Bell Laboratories*]	ALBO
Automatic Line Feed [*Telecommunications*] (CAA)	ALF
Automatic Line Insulation Test [*or Tester*] [*Bell System*]	ALIT
Automatic Line Integration (NVT)	ALI
Automatic Line Test Set [*Telecommunications*] (TEL)	ALTS
Automatic Line Tracer and Programing Equipment	ALTAPE
Automatic Linear Positioning System (DDI)	ALPS
Automatic Linear Temperature Programer	ALTP
Automatic List Classification and Profile Production	ALCAPP
Automatic Literature Processing, Handling, and Analysis	ALPHA
Automatic Load Control	ALC
Automatic Load Regulator	ALR
Automatic Local Frequency Control	ALFC
Automatic Location Identification [*Street crime locator*]	ALI
Automatic Lock-On (MCD)	ALO
Automatic Logging Electronic Reporting and Telemetering System [*Maintains surveillance over petroleum wells and pipelines*]	ALERT
Automatic Logic Testing and Recording Equipment	ALTARE
Automatic Logical Equipment Readiness Tester	ALERT
Automatic Logical Translation and Information Retrieval [*Data processing*] (DIT)	ALTAIR
Automatic Low Date Rate Input	ALDRI
Automatic Low-Frequency Gain-Limiting Circuit (RDA)	ALFGL
Automatic Machining Program	AUTOMAP
Automatic Magnetic Guidance	AMG
Automatic Magnetic Tape Dissemination [*Defense Documentation Center*] (CIT)	AMTD
Automatic Map Display	AMD
Automatic Mathematical Analysis and Symbolic Translation [*Data processing*]	AUTOMAST
Automatic Mathematical Translator [*Programing language*] [*1970*]	AMTRAN
Automatic Measuring Computing and Sorting	AMECOS
Automatic Memory Allocation [*Data processing*] (BUR)	AMA
Automatic Message Accounting [*Bell Laboratories*] [*Telecommunications*]	AMA
Automatic Message Accounting Recording System [*Bell System*]	AMARS
Automatic Message Accounting System (MCD)	AMAS
Automatic Message Address Routing System	AMARS
Automatic Message Counting	AMC
Automatic Message Distribution System (CET)	AMDS
Automatic Message Entry System [*Data processing*] (MCD)	AMES
Automatic Message Exchange	AMX
Automatic Message Exchange Service (CAA)	AUTOMEX
Automatic Message Processing Center	AMPC
Automatic Message Recording	AMR
Automatic Message Registering	AMR
Automatic Message Routing (BUR)	AMR
Automatic Meteorological Data Acquisition and Processing System (MCD)	AMDAPS
Automatic Meteorological Observation [*or Observing*] Station [*or System*]	AMOS
Automatic Meter Reading	AMR
Automatic Microfiche Editor (IDA)	AME
Automatic Microfilm Information System	AMFIS
Automatic Modal Tuning and Analysis System (NASA)	AMTAS
Automatic Mode Status (CAAL)	AMS
Automatic Module for Industrial Control Analysis	AMICA
Automatic Monitoring (CET)	AM
Automatic Multimode Mass Spectrometry	AMMS
Automatic Navigation and Data Acquisition System	ANDAS
Automatic Nesting Program [*Kongsberg UK*] [*Software package*] [*British*] (NCC)	AUTONEST
Automatic Network Analyzer	ANA
Automatic Network Dialing [*Telecommunications*] (TEL)	AND
Automatic Network Display (CGC)	AUTONET
Automatic Noise Limiter [*Electronics*]	ANL
Automatic Number Announcer [*Telecommunications*] (TEL)	ANA
Automatic Number Identification [*Telecommunications*]	ANI
Automatic Number Identification Failure [*Telecommunications*] (TEL)	ANF
Automatic Operating and Scheduling Program [*Data processing*]	AOSP
Automatic Operating System [*IBM Corp.*]	AUTOPSY
Automatic Operation Control	AOC
Automatic Outgoing Message Processor System (NVT)	AOMPS
Automatic Outgoing Trunk Test [*Bell System*]	AOTT
Automatic Output Control	AOC
Automatic Overload Circuit	AOC
Automatic Overload Circuit (MSA)	AOVC
Automatic Overload Control (IEEE)	AOC
Automatic Passbook Reader (BUR)	APR
Automatic Patching System (IEEE)	APS
Automatic Pattern Recognition	APR
Automatic Performance Analysis System	APAS
Automatic Personal Identification Code [*IBM Corp.*]	AUTOPIC
Automatic Phase and Amplitude Data System (MCD)	APADAS
Automatic Phase Control [*Telecommunications*] (TEL)	APC
Automatic Picture Taking (IEEE)	APT
Automatic Plate Processor	APP
Automatic Point Marking, Measuring, and Recording Instrument	APMMRI
Automatic Position Telemetering	APT
Automatic Positioning Telemetering Antenna	APOTA
Automatic Power Input Controller	APIC
Automatic Priority Group [*Fujitsu Ltd.*] [*Japanese*] (MCD)	APG
Automatic Priority Interrupt [*Data processing*]	API
Automatic Processing of Jezebel [*Sonobuoy System*] Information (DDI)	APOJI
Automatic Program Analysis Report [*Data processing*] (BUR)	APAR
Automatic Program Finding [*Electronics*]	APF
Automatic Program Loading Unit [*Data processing*]	APLU
Automatic Program System [*Data processing*] (DDI)	APS
Automatic Program Unit High-Speed [*Component of ADIS*]	APUHS
Automatic Program Unit Low-Speed [*Component of ADIS*]	APULS
Automatic Programed Checkout Equipment	APCHE
Automatic Programing [*Data processing*]	AP
Automatic Programing Information Centre [*British*]	APIC
Automatic Programing Instruction [*Data processing*]	API
Automatic Programing Language [*Data processing*] (CMD)	APL
Automatic Programing Machine [*Data processing*]	APM
Automatic Programing of Machine Tools [*IBM Corp.*]	AUTOPROMT
Automatic Programing and Recording [*Data processing*]	APAR
Automatic Programing and Recording [*Data processing*] (MCD)	APR
Automatic Radio Information [*System which relays traffic information through car radios*]	ARI
Automatic Ram Control (CAAL)	ARC
Automatic Random Access Transport	ARAT
Automatic Record Analysis Language [*Data processing*]	ARAL
Automatic Record Evaluation	ARE
Automatic Recording Infrared Spectrometer	ARIS
Automatic Relay Calculator [*Early computer*] [*Birkbeck College*] [*British*] (MCD)	ARC
Automatic Repeat Request [*Data processing*] (MCD)	ARQ
Automatic Reporting Feature (MCD)	ARF
Automatic Reporting Telephone [*Telecommunications*] (TEL)	ART
Automatic Request for Repetition [*Data transmission*] (CMD)	ARQ
Automatic Rerouting [*Telecommunications*] (TEL)	ARR
Automatic Retrieval of Text from Europe's Multinational Information Service	ARTEMIS
Automatic Route Control System [*Truck-delivery computer system*]	ARCS
Automatic Route Selection [*Also, MERS*] [*Bell System*] [*Telecommunications*]	ARS
Automatic Routine Generating and Updating System [*Compiler*] [*Data processing*]	ARGUS
Automatic Scan Counter	ASC

Automatic Scan Counter System ... ASCS
Automatic Scheduling and Operating Program (BUR) ... ASOP
Automatic Scheduling with Time-Integrated Resource Allocation ... ASTRA
Automatic Secure Voice Communications (CAAL) ... ASVC
Automatic Secure Voice Communications ... AUTOSEVOCOM
Automatic Selection of Digital Electronic Computers ... ASDEC
Automatic Self-Verification ... ASV
Automatic Send/Receive Teletypewriter [*Communications equipment*] ... AS/R
Automatic Sensitivity Control ... ASC
Automatic Sequence Controlled Calculator [*First all-automatic calculating machine*] ... ASCC
Automatic Shaft-Position Data Encoder ... ASPDE
Automatic Sheet Feeder (CAA) ... ASF
Automatic Signature Verification System (CAA) ... ASVS
Automatic Space Management ... ASM
Automatic Spectrum Display and Signal Recognition System (IEEE) ... ASDSRS
Automatic Speech Recognition ... ASR
Automatic Steerable Null Antenna Processor ... ASNAP
Automatic Steering Antenna ... ASA
Automatic Stellar Tracking, Recognition, and Orientation Computer ... ASTROC
Automatic Subject Citation Alert [*A publication*] ... ASCA
Automatic Switching Center ... ASC
Automatic Switching Panel ... ASP
Automatic Switching Unit [*Telecommunications*] (OA) ... ASU
Automatic System Checkout Program (CAA) ... ASCP
Automatic Systems Analysis (KSC) ... ASA
Automatic Tabulating, Listing, and Sorting System [*Software*] (DEEC) ... ATLAS
Automatic Tape Load Audit System ... ATLAS
Automatic Telecommunications Switching System (CAA) ... ATSS
Automatic Telegram Transmission with Computers [*Telecommunications*] (TEL) ... ATECO
Automatic Telemetry Decommutation System ... ATDS
Automatic Telemetry System ... ATS
Automatic Telemetry Tracking Receiving Antenna ... ATTRA
Automatic Telemetry Tracking System ... ATTS
Automatic Telephone Set ... ATS
Automatic Teleprinter Exchange Service [*of Western Union Corp.*] ... TEX
Automatic Teletypewriter Exchange Service [*of Western Union*] ... TELEX
Automatic TELEX Exchange [*Telecommunications*] (TEL) ... ATX
Automatic Terminal System (NASA) ... ATS
Automatic Test Break and Access [*Telecommunications*] (TEL) ... ATBA
Automatic Test Equipment ... ATE
Automatic Test System ... ATS
Automatic Text Formatter (CAA) ... ATF
Automatic Toll Ticketing (TEL) ... ATT
Automatic Tracking Antenna System ... ATAS
Automatic Traffic Usage Recording System (TEL) ... ATURS
Automatic Transmission of Mail [*Early electronic mail system*] (CAA) ... ATOM
Automatic Transmission Measuring Equipment [*Telecommunications*] (TEL) ... ATME
Automatic Transmission Measuring System ... ATMS
Automatic Transmission Test and Control [*Telecommunications*] (TEL) ... ATTC
Automatic Transmitter Identification System [*Citizens band radio*] ... ATIS
Automatic Trouble Analysis (TEL) ... ATA
Automatic Trunk Measuring System [*Bell System*] ... ATMS
Automatic Trunk Routiner (MCD) ... ATR
Automatic Trunk Synchronizer [*Telecommunications*] (TEL) ... ATS
Automatic Unattended Detection Inspection Transmitter [*Raytheon Co.*] ... AUDIT
Automatic Voice Data (MCD) ... AVD
Automatic Voice Network [*DoD*] ... AUTOVON
Automatic Volume Control [*Radio*] ... AVC
Automatic Volume Recognition (MCD) ... AVR
Automatica [*United States*] [*A publication*] ... ATCAA
Automatically Directed Outgoing Intertoll Trunk [*Bell System*] ... ADOIT
Automatically Directed Outgoing Trunk [*Bell System*] ... ADOT
Automatically Programed Remote Indication Logged ... APRIL
Automatically Programed Tools [*Computer software*] [*Data processing*] (TUT) ... APT
Automatically Reconfigurable Modular Multiprocessor [*or Multiprocessing*] **System** [*Data processing*] ... ARMMS
Automatico Associazione Italiana per il Calcolo [*Italian computing association*] (CAH) ... AICA
Automation of Bibliography through Computerization [*ABC-Clio Press*] ... ABC
Automation of Field Operations and Services [*National Weather Service*] ... AFOS
Automation Industries Research Laboratory (KSC) ... AIRL
Automation Instrument Data Service [*Computer-based industrial information system*] [*Indata Ltd.*] [*British*] ... AIDS
Automation and Remote Control [*A publication*] ... AURCA
Automation and Remote Control [*USSR*] [*A publication*] ... Automat Remote Contr
Automation and Remote Control [*A publication*] ... Automat Remote Control
Automation and Remote Control [*USSR*] [*A publication*] ... Autom & Remote Control
Automation and Remote Control [*USSR*] [*A publication*] ... Autom Remote Control
Automation and Remote Control (USSR) [*A publication*] ... Aut Remot R
Automation for Storage and Retrieval of Information (IDA) ... AFSARI
Automix Keyboards, Incorporated ... AKI
Automized Medical Anamnesis Dialog Assistant [*Computer*] ... AMANDA
Automotive Competitive Assessment Data Bank [*Ward's Research*] [*Database*] (CUAD) ... COMPASS
Automotive Information Test ... AIT
Automotive Manufacturers EDP [*Electronic Data Processing*] **Council** [*Teaneck, NJ*] (EANO) ... AMEDPC
Autonome Transfer Unit [*Data processing*] (DIT) ... ATU
Autonomous Data Transfer (CAA) ... ADT
Autonomous Line Scanning Unit (MCD) ... ALSU
Autonomous Multiplexer Channel (CAA) ... AMC
Autopilot Ground Control Unit ... AGCU
AutoPrep 5000 Users Group [*South Windsor, CT*] (EANO) ... APUG
Autoregressive Moving Average [*Statistics*] ... ARMA
AUTOVON Centralized Alarm System ... ACAS
Auxiliary (AFM) ... AUX
Auxiliary Computer Input Multiplexer (SKY) ... ACIM
Auxiliary Computer Power Unit ... ACPU
Auxiliary Core Memory [*Data processing*] (MCD) ... ACM
Auxiliary Core Storage [*Data processing*] (BUR) ... ACS
Auxiliary Data Annotation Set [*or System*] ... ADAS
Auxiliary Data Processing Equipment ... ADPE
Auxiliary Data Translator Unit ... ADTU
Auxiliary Display Request Keyboard (SKY) ... ADRK
Auxiliary Encoder System ... AES
Auxiliary Engineering Signal Processor ... AESP
Auxiliary Functional Unit [*Data link*] (NG) ... AFU
Auxiliary Marker [*Telecommunications*] (TEL) ... AM
Auxiliary Memory ... AM
Auxiliary Memory Drum ... AMD
Auxiliary Memory Set (MCD) ... AMS
Auxiliary Memory Unit ... AMU
Auxiliary Processing Unit ... APU
Auxiliary Program Storage [*Data processing*] (BUR) ... APS
Auxiliary Recording Control [*Circuit*] [*Bell System*] ... AUXRC
Auxiliary Storage [*Data processing*] (CAA) ... AS
Auxiliary Storage Manager [*Data processing*] ... ASM
Auxiliary System for Interactive Statistics [*Sweden*] [*Information service*] (EISS) ... AXIS
Auxiliary Tape Memory [*Spacecraft guidance*] ... ATM
Auxiliary Video Switching Matrix (SKY) ... AVSM
Auxton Computer Enterprises [*NASDAQ symbol*] (NQ) ... AUXT
Availability Factor [*Generating time ratio*] (IEEE) ... AF
Availability, Reliability, and Maintainability [*Computer performance*] (CAA) ... ARM
Available [*or Availability*] [*Online database field identifier*] [*Data processing*] ... AV
Available [*or Availability*] (KSC) ... AVAIL
Available Database Management System (OA) ... ADBMS
Available Space List [*Data processing*] ... ASL
Avalanche-Induced Migration (MCD) ... AIM
Avalanche Photodiode Detector ... APD
Avalanching Junction Light Output ... AJLO
Avant-Garde Computing [*NASDAQ symbol*] (NQ) ... AVGA
Average ... AV
Average ... AVE
Average (AFM) ... AVG
Average Blank Data [*Data processing*] ... AVEBD
Average Business Day [*Bell System*] ... ABD
Average Busy Season Busy Hour [*Telecommunications*] (TEL) ... ABSBH
Average Instruction Execution Time [*Computer parameter*] (OA) ... AIET
Average Instructions per Second [*Data processing*] ... AIP
Average Operating Cost (KSC) ... AOC
Average Picture Level ... APL
Average Power Control [*Telecommunications*] (TEL) ... APC
Average Response Amplitude ... ARA
Average Response Amplitude Data ... ARAD
Average Response Computer ... ARC
Average Transfer Rate of Information BITS [*Binary Digits*] [*Data processing*] (IEEE) ... ATRIB
Average Turnaround [*Data processing*] ... ATA
Aviation Data Service, Inc. [*Information service*] (EISS) ... ADS
Aviation Electronic Equipment Information Exchange System (MCD) ... AVEXS
Aviation Information Services Limited [*Hounslow, Middlesex, England*] (EISS) ... AISL
Avionic Integration Support Facility (MCD) ... AISF
Avionics, Control, and Information Systems (MCD) ... ACIS
Avionics Interface Unit (MCD) ... AIU
Avionics Multiplex ... AMUX
Avionics Processing System ... APS
AVM Corporation [*NASDAQ symbol*] (NQ) ... AVMC
Awaiting Connection [*Telecommunications*] (TEL) ... AC
Awaiting Disconnection [*Telecommunications*] (TEL) ... AD
Awaiting Forward Release [*Telecommunications*] (TEL) ... AFR
Awaiting Incoming Continuity [*Telecommunications*] (TEL) ... AIC
Awaiting Incoming Message [*Telecommunications*] (TEL) ... AIM
Awaiting Number Received [*Telecommunications*] (TEL) ... ANR
Awaiting Outgoing Continuity [*Telecommunications*] (TEL) ... AOC

Awaiting Reply [*Telecommunications*]   (TEL) .... AR
Axisymmetric Forging [*Leeds University*] [*Software package*]
   [*British*]   (NCC) AXFOR1
Aydin Corp. [*NYSE symbol*] .... AYD
Ayer Information Center [*N. W. Ayer, Inc.*] [*Information service*]
   (EISS) .... AIC

B

B-Mode Receiving Station [*Telecommunications*] (TEL)	BRS
Bachelor of Telecommunications Engineering	BTelE
Back End (MSA)	BE
Back-End Processor [*Computer*] (TSSD)	BEP
Back Tape Reader (CCD)	BTR
Back Up Register (CAA)	BUR
Backboard [*Telecommunications*] (TEL)	BB
Background [*Low-priority processing*]	BG
Background Equivalent Concentration [*Data processing*]	BEC
Background Noise Level (CAAL)	LN
Background Operating System (IEEE)	BOS
Backscatter Electron	BSE
Backscatter Ultraviolet [*Spectrometry*]	BUV
Backspace Character [*Keyboard*] [*Data processing*] (BUR)	BKSP
Backspace Character [*Keyboard*] [*Data processing*]	BS
Backspace File (BUR)	BSF
Backspace Recorder	BSR
Backup (KSC)	BKUP
Backup Air Data Sensor Assembly (MCD)	BADSA
Backup Bus Controller [*Data processing*]	BBC
Backup Digital Computer	BDC
Backup Digital Computer	BUDC
Backup Digital System	BUDS
Backup Emergency Communications	BUEC
Backus Naur [*or Normal*] Form [*ALGOL*] [*Data processing*] (BUR)	BNF
Backward [*Telecommunications*] (TEL)	BWD
Backward Indicator [*Telecommunications*] (TEL)	BI
Backward Indicator BIT [*Binary Digit*] [*Telecommunications*] (TEL)	BIB
Backward Interworking Telephony Event [*Telecommunications*] (TEL)	BITE
Backward Sequence Number [*Telecommunications*] (TEL)	BSN
Backward Signaling [*Telecommunications*] (TEL)	BS
Backward Volume Wave [*Telecommunications*] (TEL)	BVW
Backward Wave Oscillator	BWO
Bad Data Lister (CIT)	BDL
Bahrain Telecommunications Company [*Manama, Bahrain*] (TSSD)	BATELCO
Baker & Taylor Electronic Book Ordering Service [*Baker & Taylor Companies*] [*Trademark*]	BaTaSYSTEMS
Baker and Taylor's Automated Buying System [*Teleordering system*] [*Baker & Taylor Companies*] [*Information service*] (EISS)	BATAB
Balance Return Loss [*Telecommunications*] (TEL)	BRL
Balanced-to-Unbalanced Line Transformer [*Telecommunications*] (TEL)	BALUN
Banctec, Inc. [*NASDAQ symbol*] (NQ)	BTEC
Band Amplitude Product	BAP
Band Elimination	BE
Band Elimination Filter	BEF
Band Filter Cutoff (MSA)	BFCO
Band-Limited Signal	BLS
Bandpass	BP
Bandpass Crystal Filter	BCF
Bandpass Filter	BF
Bandpass Filter	BPF
Bandpass Network	BPN
Bandpass Transformer	BPT
Bandwidth [*Frequency range*]	B
Bandwidth [*Frequency range*]	BW
Bandwidth Ratio	BWR
Bangladesh National Scientific and Technical Documentation Centre [*Information service*] (EISS)	BANSDOC
Bank Administration Institute [*Formerly, National Association for Bank Audit, Control, and Operation*] [*Arlington Heights, IL*]	BAI
Bank Automated Service Information System (BUR)	BASIS
Bank Descriptor Index [*Data processing*]	BDI
Bank Descriptor Registers [*Data processing*]	BDR
Bank Descriptor Word [*Data processing*]	BDW
Bank Draft Number (TEL)	BDN
Bank Information System Network (CAA)	BISNET
Bank Management Information System (CAA)	BMIS
Bank-Switching [*Computer technology*]	BS
Bankers' Automated Clearing Service [*British*] (CAA)	BACS
Bankers Trust Information Service [*Database producer*] (CUAD)	BTIS
Banking Information Processing System (BUR)	BIPS
Banking On-Line Package System (BUR)	BOPS
Banking Systems Information Exchange (CAA)	BSIE
Banque de Donnees Macroeconomiques [*Institut National de la Statistique et des Etudes Economiques*] [*Database*] (CUAD)	BDM
Banque d'Information Robert Debre [*Centre International de l'Enfance*] [*Database*] (CUAD)	BIRD
Banque d'Informations Politiques et d'Actualites [*Political and Current Events Information Bank*] [*Database*] [*Telesystems - Questel*] [*Paris, France*] [*Information service*] (EISS)	BIPA
Banque de Terminologie du Quebec [*Terminology Bank of Quebec*] [*French Language Board*] [*Information service*] (EISS)	BTQ
Banque de Terminologie de Quebec [*Terminology Bank of Quebec*] [*Information service*]	TERMINOQ
Baptist Telecommunications Network [*Cable-television system*]	BTN
Bartlesville Energy Technology Center [*Later, NIPER*] [*Department of Energy*] [*Information service*]	BETC
Bartok Archives Z-Symbol Rhythm Extraction [*Data processing*]	BARZREX
Baruch Retrieval of Automated Information for Negotiations [*City University of New York*] [*Information service*] (EISS)	BRAIN
Base	B
Base Address Register [*Data processing*] (BUR)	BAR
Base de Datos Geomagneticos [*Instituto Geografico Nacional*] [*Database*] (CUAD)	BASEMAG
Base de Donnees des Obligations Francaises [*DAFSA*] [*Database*] (CUAD)	BDO
Base File (CAH)	BF
Base Organization and Maintenance Processor (IEEE)	BOMP
Base Pointer [*Data processing*]	BP
Base Rate Area [*Telecommunications*] (TEL)	BRA
Base Rate Boundary [*Telecommunications*] (TEL)	BRB
Base Register (CMD)	BR
Base Register [*Data processing*]	BX
Base for Uniform Language Definition [*Data processing*] (IEEE)	BUILD
Base and User [*A publication*]	BUSED
BASIC-52 Computer/Controller	BCC-52
Basic Access Method [*Data processing*]	BAM
Basic Adaptive Hardware	BAH
Basic Additional Teleprocessing Support [*Data processing*] (BUR)	BATS
Basic Algebraic Symbolic Interpretive Compiler (IEEE)	BASIC
Basic Assembler Program [*Data processing*]	BAP
Basic Assembly Language [*Programing language*] [*Sperry UNIVAC*] [*Data processing*]	BAL
Basic Automatic Checkout Equipment	BACE
Basic Automatic Stored Instruction Computer (BUR)	BASIC
Basic Business Language [*Data processing*] (IEEE)	BBL
Basic Combined Programing Language	BCPL
Basic Computer Unit (SKY)	BCU
Basic Control [*Mode*] [*Data processing*]	BC
Basic Control Frequency	BCF
Basic Control Monitor (BUR)	BCM
Basic Control System [*For satellites*] (MDG)	BCS
Basic Device Unit [*Data processing*] (IBMDP)	BDU
Basic Direct Access Method [*IBM Corp.*] [*Data processing*] (BUR)	BDAM
Basic Disk Operating System	BDOS
Basic Display Unit [*Data processing*] (CGC)	BDU
Basic Education Assistance Material Service [*National Multimedia Center for Adult Basic Education*] (EISS)	BEAMS
Basic Encoding Unit (OA)	BEU
Basic Encyclopedic Redundancy Media (IEEE)	BERM
Basic Error Control System (CAA)	BECS
Basic Exchange Rate Planning Model [*Telecommunications*] (TEL)	BERPM
Basic Executive System [*Honeywell, Inc.*] (CAA)	BES
Basic File Access System (CAA)	BFAS
Basic Floppy Disk (CAA)	BFD
Basic Impulse Insulation Level [*Electronics*]	BIL
Basic Indexed Sequential Access Method [*IBM Corp.*] [*Data processing*]	BISAM
Basic Indexing and Retrieval System [*Data processing*] (DIT)	BIRS
Basic Information Unit (BUR)	BIU

Basic Input-Output System [*IBM Corp.*] .... BIOS
BASIC Interpreter Package (CAA) .... BIP
Basic Language for the Implementation of System Software [*Data processing*] .... BLISS
Basic Language Machine [*Computer*] (BUR) .... BLM
BASIC Language Translator [*Data processing*] (MCD) .... BLT
Basic Level Automation of Data through Electronics .... BLADE
Basic Library Inquiry Subsystem [*Data processing*] .... BLISS
Basic Link Unit [*Data processing*] (BUR) .... BLU
Basic Literal Automatic Coding .... BALITAC
Basic Logic Unit (IEEE) .... BLU
Basic Main Frame (NATG) .... BMF
Basic Mapping Support [*Data processing*] .... BMS
Basic Message Switching Center [*Data processing*] (CGC) .... BSC
Basic Operating Consumer-Oriented Language [*Data processing*] (CGC) .... BOCOL
Basic Operating Monitor (TUT) .... BOM
Basic Operating System [*IBM Corp.*] [*Data processing*] .... BOS
Basic Operating System Software [*Toshiba Corp.*] [*Japan*] (CAA) .... BOSS
Basic Partitioned Access Method [*IBM Corp.*] [*Data processing*] (TUT) .... BPAM
Basic Peripheral Channel (CAA) .... BPC
Basic Processing Unit (CET) .... BPU
BASIC [*Beginner's All-Purpose Symbolic Instruction Code*] **Processor and Computer** (CDH) .... BASICPAC
Basic Programing Knowledge Test (MCD) .... BPKT
Basic Programing Support [*IBM Corp.*] (BUR) .... BPS
Basic Programing System (TUT) .... BPS
Basic Query Language [*Data processing*] (BUR) .... BQL
Basic Semantic Element [*Data processing*] (DIT) .... BASE
Basic Sequential Access Method [*IBM Corp.*] [*Data processing*] (TUT) .... BSAM
Basic Sounding Unit [*Telecommunications*] (TEL) .... BSU
Basic System (IEEE) .... BASYS
Basic System Memory [*Data processing*] (BUR) .... BSM
Basic Tape Access Method [*Data processing*] (CAA) .... BTAM
Basic Telecommunications Access Method [*IBM Corp.*] [*Data processing*] (CGC) .... BTAM
Basic Teleprocessing Access Method [*IBM Corp.*] (CAH) .... BTAM
Basic Terminal Access Method [*Data processing*] (IDA) .... BTAM
Basic Time-Sharing System (BUR) .... BTSS
Basic Transient Diode Logic [*Data processing*] (BUR) .... BTDL
Basic Transmission Header [*Data processing*] (IBMDP) .... BTH
Basic Transmission Unit [*Data processing*] .... BTU
Batch Data Transmission System .... BDTS
Batch Disk Operating System (CAA) .... BDOS
Batch Job Foreground [*Data processing*] (CAH) .... BJF
Batch Operating Software System (CAA) .... BOSS
Batch Operating System [*Data processing*] (CAA) .... BOS
Batch Processing (CAA) .... BP
Batch Processing Monitor [*Xerox Corp.*] [*Data processing*] (MCD) .... BPM
Batch Processing System (OA) .... BPS
Batch Query Language [*Programing language*] (CAA) .... BQL
Batch Terminal Simulator [*Data processing*] .... BTS
Batch Time-Sharing Monitor [*Xerox Corp.*] [*Data processing*] (MCD) .... BTM
Batch Transfer Program (DEEC) .... BTP
Bathythermograph Report [*Radio message*] .... BATHY
Battelle Automated Search Information System [*Database management system*] [*Battelle Memorial Institute*] [*Information service*] .... BASIS
Battelle Institute Learning Automation [*Battelle Memorial Institute*] (IEEE) .... BILA
Battelle Monte Carlo [*Data processing*] .... BMC
Battelle's Educational Computer User's Network [*Battelle Memorial Institute*] [*Columbus, OH*] [*Information service*] (EISS) .... BECUN
Battery (AFM) .... BTRY
Battery Cutoff [*Telecommunications*] (TEL) .... BCO
Battery Information Index [*Battelle Memorial Institute*] (EISS) .... BII
Baud [*Unit of data transmission speed*] (MCD) .... B
Baud [*Unit of data transmission*] (CET) .... Bd
Baud Rate [*Data transmission speed*] [*Data processing*] .... BDRT
Baud Rate Generator (CAA) .... BRG
Baudot Code (DEEC) .... BAUD
Bauforschungsprojekte [*Research Projects in Civil Engineering*] [*Information Center for Regional Planning and Building Construction of the Fraunhofer Society*] [*Database*] (ODIN) .... BAUFO
Bauobjektdokumentation [*Information Centre for Regional Planning and Building Construction of the Fraunhofer-Society*] [*Database*] (CUAD) .... BODO
Bayerische Staatsbibliothek [*Information retrieval*] (ODIN) .... BSB
Bayerisches Landwirtschaftliches Informationssystem [*Bavarian Agricultural Information System*] [*Databank*] [*West Germany*] (EISS) .... BALIS
Bayesian Analysis Modified by Inspection [*Data processing*] .... BAMBI
Bayesian Reliability Demonstration Test [*Data processing*] .... BRDT
Baylor Computing Center [*Baylor College of Medicine*] [*Research center*] (RCD) .... BCC
BCS [*Boeing Computer Services*] **Interactive Graphics** .... BIG
Beacon Antenna Equipment .... BAE
Beam Addressed Metal Oxide Semiconductor [*Memory technology*] (CAA) .... BEAMOS
Beam Communications Set .... BCS
Beam-Heated Cathode .... BHC
Beam Splitter [*Instrumentation*] .... BS
Beat-Frequency Oscillator .... BFO
Bechtel Information Services [*Gaithersburg, MD*] (EISS) .... BIS
Becker & Hayes, Inc. [*Santa Monica, CA*] [*Information service*] (EISS) .... B & H
Beckman Translation [*Programing language*] [*Beckman Instruments, Inc.*] .... BECKTRAN
Bedford Systems Users Group [*Salt Lake City, UT*] (EANO) .... BSUG
Beehive International [*American Stock Exchange symbol*] [*Delisted*] .... BHI
Before Computer .... BC
Before Video .... BV
Begin Bracket [*Indicator*] [*Data processing*] (IBMDP) .... BB
Beginner's All-Purpose Symbolic Instruction Code [*Programing language invented by T. E. Kurtz and J. G. Kemeny at Dartmouth College in 1963-64*] .... BASIC
Beginning of File (NASA) .... BOF
Beginning of Information Marker [*Data processing*] .... BIM
Beginning of Magnetic Tape [*Data processing*] (MDG) .... BMT
Beginning, Negative, Positive, Finish [*ASCII subset*] (DEEC) .... BNPF
Beginning of Tape [*Data processing*] (CGC) .... BOT
Beginning Tape Label [*Data processing*] (BUR) .... BTL
Behavioral Science Programing Language [*Data processing*] .... BSPL
Bel [*Ten decibels*] .... B
Belady Optimum Replacement [*Algorithm*] [*Data processing*] .... BOR
Belgian Archives for the Social Sciences [*Information service*] (EISS) .... BASS
Belgian Centre for Information Processing (CAH) .... BCIP
Belgian Information and Dissemination Service [*European host database system*] [*Brussels, Belgium*] (EISS) .... BELINDIS
Bell (IEEE) .... BL
Bell Administrative Network Communication System [*Telecommunications*] (TEL) .... BANCS
Bell Audit Relate System [*Bell Laboratories*] .... BARS
Bell Audit System [*Bell Laboratories*] .... BAS
Bell Canada International, Inc. [*Ottawa, ON*] [*Telecommunications*] (TSSD) .... BCI
Bell Character [*Keyboard*] .... BEL
Bell Data Network [*Telecommunications*] .... BDN
Bell Doesn't Ring [*Telecommunications*] (TEL) .... BDR
Bell FLICKS [*Programing language*] [*1973*] (CSR) .... BEFLIX
Bell & Howell Co. .... BH
Bell & Howell Co. [*NYSE symbol*] .... BHW
Bell-Independent Relations [*Telecommunications*] (TEL) .... B-IR
Bell Information Network .... BIN
Bell Laboratories Automatic Design System [*Computer program*] .... BLADES
Bell Laboratories Automatic Design System [*Computer program*] .... BLADS
Bell Laboratories Automatic Device .... BLADE
Bell Laboratories FORTRAN Assembly Program [*Data processing*] (IEEE) .... BEFAP
Bell Laboratories Interpretive System [*Computer program*] .... BLIS
Bell Laboratories Machine-Aided Technical Information Center (DIT) .... BELLMATIC
Bell Laboratories Record [*A publication*] .... Bell Lab Re
Bell Laboratories Record [*A publication*] .... Bell Lab Rec
Bell Laboratories Record [*A publication*] .... BELR
Bell Laboratories Record [*A publication*] .... BLRCA
Bell Little Electrodata Symbolic System for the Electrodata [*Symbolic assembly program*] .... BLESSED
Bell Log System .... BLS
Bell-Northern Research [*Telecommunications*] (TEL) .... BNR
Bell Number Screening [*Telecommunications*] (TEL) .... BNS
Bell Operating Company [*Also, BSOC*] [*Post-divestiture division of American Telephone & Telegraph Co.*] .... BOC
Bell Operating System [*Telecommunications*] (TEL) .... BOS
Bell Owned and Maintained [*Telecommunications*] (TEL) .... BOAM
Bell Rings Faintly [*Telecommunications*] (TEL) .... BRF
Bell System Center for Technical Education .... BSCTE
Bell System Common Language [*Telecommunications*] (TEL) .... BSCL
Bell System Operating Company [*Also, BOC*] [*Post-divestiture division of American Telephone & Telegraph Co.*] .... BSOC
Bell System Practices .... BSP
Bell System Reference Frequency Standard [*Telecommunications*] (TEL) .... BSRFS
Bell System Repair Specification [*Telecommunications*] (TEL) .... BSRS
Bell System Technical Journal [*A publication*] .... Bell System Tech J
Bell System Technical Journal [*A publication*] .... Bell Syst T
Bell System Technical Journal [*A publication*] .... Bell Syst Tech J
Bell System Technical Journal [*A publication*] .... BSTJ
Bell System Technical Journal [*A publication*] .... BSTJA
Bell Telephone .... BELLTEL
Bell Telephone Laboratories, Inc. [*Murray Hill, NJ*] .... BTL
Bell Telephone Magazine [*A publication*] .... Bell Telephone Mag
Bell Telephone System. Technical Publications. Monographs [*A publication*] .... Bell Teleph Syst Tech Publ Monogr
Benchmark [*Computer system evaluation*] .... BM
Benchmark Monitor Display System [*Sperry UNIVAC*] (CAA) .... BMD
Bendix Optimum Configuration Satellite (IEEE) .... BOCS
Berks Community Television [*Reading, PA*] [*Telecommunications*] (TSSD) .... BCTV
Best Alternative Equally Effective Data System .... BAEDS
Best Execution Analysis Tabulation [*Data processing*] .... BEAT
Between (KSC) .... BET

Between Commands Testing [*Data processing*] (CAA) ... BCT
Between Job Monitor [*Data processing*] (CAH) ... BJM
BGS Systems, Inc. [*NASDAQ symbol*] (NQ) ... BGSS
Bi-Duplexed Redundancy [*Telecommunications*] (CAA) ... BDR
BI, Inc. [*NASDAQ symbol*] (NQ) ... BIAC
Bias [*Telecommunications*] (CDH) ... B
Bible Research Systems [*Austin, TX*] [*Information service*] (EISS) ... BRS
Biblio Service Informatique [*Informatics Biblio Service*] [*France*] [*Information service*] (EISS) ... BSI
Bibliographia Huntiana [*Computer-based bibliography*] ... BH
Bibliographic Automation of Large Library Operations Using a Time-Sharing System [*Later, RLIN*] [*Stanford University*] ... BALLOTS
Bibliographic Data Processing Program [*For keyword indexing*] [*Information retrieval software*] ... BIDAP
Bibliographic Index of Library Documents [*Helsinki School of Economics*] [*Database*] (CUAD) ... BILD
Bibliographic Information on Southeast Asia [*Database*] [*Australia*] [*Information service*] (EISS) ... BISA
Bibliographic and Library Information Search Service ... BLISS
Bibliographic Network [*OCLC retrieval system*] [*Data processing*] ... BIBNET
Bibliographic On-Line Display [*Document storage and retrieval system*] [*Data processing*] ... BOLD
Bibliographic On-Line Organized Knowledge [*Data processing*] (KSC) ... BOOK
Bibliographic Retrieval Services, Inc. [*Database host system*] [*Scotia, NY*] ... BRS
Bibliographic Systems Center [*Case Western Reserve University*] (EISS) ... BSC
Bibliographical Center for Research, Inc., Rocky Mountain Region [*Denver, CO*] [*Research center*] (RCD) ... BCR
Bibliographie Linguistischer Literatur [*Bibliography of Linguistic Literature*] [*Database*] [*Information retrieval*] (ODIN) ... BLL
Bibliographie zur Offentlichen Unternehmung und Verwaltung [*NOMOS Datapool*] [*Database*] (CUAD) ... BOWI
Bibliography of Linguistic Literature [*Database*] [*Information retrieval*] (ODIN) ... BLL
Biblioteca Nacional de Agricultura [*National Library of Agriculture*] [*Brazil*] [*Information service*] (EISS) ... BINAGRI
Bibliothekar-Lehrinstitut [*Information retrieval*] (ODIN) ... BLI
Bibliotheks- und Informationssystem [*Library and Information System*] [*German*] (ODIN) ... BIS
Bidirectional Reference Array, Internally Derived [*Data processing*] (DIT) ... BRAID
Bidirectional Transceiver Element [*Telecommunications*] (CAA) ... BTE
Big Machine on Campus [*Computer*] ... BMOC
Bildschirmtext [*Viewdata system*] [*Federal Ministry of Posts and Telecommunications*] [*Bonn, WG*] (TSSD) ... BTX
Bilingual Education Bibliographic Abstracts [*National Clearinghouse for Bilingual Education*] [*Rosslyn, VA*] [*Database*] ... BEBA
Bilingual Education Telecommunications Network [*National Clearinghouse for Bilingual Education*] [*Rosslyn, VA*] (TSSD) ... BETNET
Bill in Care Of [*Telecommunications*] (TEL) ... BCO
Bill of Material Processor ... BOMP
Bill of Materials [*Digital Dynamics Ltd.*] [*Software package*] ... BOM
Bill of Quantities [*Contract Data Research*] [*Software package*] [*British*] (NCC) ... BQ2
Billboard Information Network [*Billboard Publications, Inc.*] [*New York, NY*] [*Information service*] (EISS) ... BIN
Billing, Accounts Receivable, Sales Analysis (IBMDP) ... BARSA
Billing Cease Date (TEL) ... BC
Billing-Collecting-Remitting (TEL) ... BCR
Billing Group [*Telecommunications*] (TEL) ... BG
Billing Instructions [*Telecommunications*] (TEL) ... BI
Billing, Inventory Control, Accounts Receivable, Sales Analysis (IBMDP) ... BICARSA
Billing and Ordering Forum [*Exchange Carriers Standards Association*] [*Telecommunications*] ... BOF
Billing Telephone Number [*Telecommunications*] (TEL) ... BTN
Billings Corp. [*NASDAQ symbol*] (NQ) ... BIEN
Billion Conductor Feet [*Telecommunications*] (TEL) ... BCF
Billion Electron Volts ... BeV
Billion Floating-Point Operations per Second [*Data processing*] ... BFLOPS
Billion Instructions per Second [*Computing power measurement*] [*Data processing*] ... BIPS
Binary (BUR) ... B
Binary (AFM) ... BIN
Binary Add [*Data processing*] ... BA
Binary-Analog Conversion [*Data processing*] (DIT) ... BAC
Binary Asymmetric Channel ... BAC
Binary Asymmetric Dependent Channel ... BADC
Binary Asymmetric Independent Channel ... BAIC
Binary Automatic Computer [*Eckert-Maudely Computer Corp.*] ... BINAC
Binary Automatic Data Annotation System ... BADAS
Binary Code ... BC
Binary Code Frequency Shift Keying [*SAGE*] ... BCFSK
Binary-Coded Data [*or Decimal*] [*Data processing*] ... BCD
Binary-Coded Decimal/Binary (DEN) ... BCD/B
Binary-Coded Decimal Counter ... BCDC
Binary-Coded Decimal Interchange Code (IEEE) ... BCDIC
Binary-Coded Decimal Interchange Code (CAH) ... BDIC
Binary-Coded Decimal/Quaternary (DEN) ... BCD/Q
Binary-Coded Information ... BCI
Binary Coded Matrix [*Telecommunications*] (TEL) ... BCM
Binary-Coded Octal [*Data processing*] ... BCO
Binary Counting Unit (IEEE) ... BCU
Binary to Decimal [*Data processing*] ... B/D
Binary to Decimal [*Data processing*] (BUR) ... BTD
Binary-to-Decimal Converter [*Data processing*] ... BIDEC
Binary Decimal Counter [*Data processing*] ... BDC
Binary-to-Decimal Decoder [*Data processing*] ... BDD
Binary Deck-to-Tape [*Data processing*] ... BDT
Binary Decode Scaler [*Data processing*] ... BDS
Binary Decoder [*Data processing*] ... BD
Binary Delta Modulation ... BDM
Binary Differential Phase-Shift Keying [*Telecommunications*] (TEL) ... BDPSK
Binary Digit [*Data processing*] ... BIT
Binary Digital Data [*Data processing*] ... BDD
Binary Digital Multiplier [*Data processing*] ... BDM
Binary Digits [*Data processing*] ... BITS
Binary Dump Routine (CAA) ... BDR
Binary Error Erasure Channel (IEEE) ... BEEC
Binary Floating-Point Digital Differential Analyzer (IEEE) ... BFPDDA
Binary Frequency Generator (IEEE) ... BFG
Binary to Hexadecimal (BUR) ... BH
Binary Image Processor [*Data processing*] (OA) ... BIP
Binary Intersystem Transmission Standard ... BITS
Binary Logic Element [*Data processing*] (BUR) ... BLE
Binary Logical Association (CAA) ... BLA
Binary Number [*Data processing*] ... BN
Binary Number System [*Data processing*] (CGC) ... BNS
Binary to Octal [*Data processing*] (BUR) ... BO
Binary Order of Magnitude [*Data processing*] ... BOM
Binary Output Program ... BOP
Binary Phase-Shift Keying [*Data processing*] (IEEE) ... BPSK
Binary Program Loader (CAA) ... BPL
Binary Rate Divider (OA) ... BRD
Binary Run Tape [*Data processing*] (BUR) ... BRT
Binary to Seven Segment [*Data processing*] ... BINSS
Binary Symmetric Channel [*Data processing*] ... BSC
Binary Symmetric Dependent Channel [*Data processing*] ... BSDC
Binary Symmetric Independent Channel [*Data processing*] (CGC) ... BSIC
Binary Synchronous Communication [*IBM Corp.*] [*Data processing*] ... BSC
Binary Synchronous Communications Adapter [*Data processing*] ... BSCA
Binary Synchronous Communications Macro (CAA) ... BSCM
Binary Synchronous Communications/Start-Stop (CAA) ... BSC/SS
Binary Synchronous Transmission [*Data processing*] ... BISYNC
Binding Post (KSC) ... BP
Binding Post Chamber [*Telecommunications*] (TEL) ... BPC
Biochemical Modeling [*Data processing*] ... BIOMOD
Bioethics Online [*Database*] ... BIOETHICSLINE
Biography Master Index [*Bibliographic database*] [*Gale Research Co.*] [*A publication*] (EISS) ... BMI
Biological Information Processing Organization [*Later, SIGBIO*] ... BIO
Biological Records Centre [*British*] [*Information service*] (EISS) ... BRC
Biomedical ... BMD
Biomedical Communications Network [*Proposed*] [*National Library of Medicine*] ... BCN
Biomedical Computing Society [*Later, SIGBIO*] (BUR) ... BCS
Biomedical Computing Technology Information Center [*Oak Ridge National Laboratory*] [*Department of Energy*] (EISS) ... BCTIC
Biomedical Engineering Current Awareness Notification [*England*] [*A publication*] (EISS) ... BECAN
Biomedical Engineering Unit [*McGill University*] [*Canada*] [*Research center*] (RCD) ... BMEU
Biomedical Experiment Scientific Satellite (NASA) ... BESS
Biomedical Studies Section [*Oak Ridge National Laboratory*] (EISS) ... BMS
Biometric Computer Service, Incorporated (OA) ... BCSI
BioScience Information Service [*Database producer*] [*Philadelphia, PA*] ... BIOSIS
BIOSIS Previews [*Information retrieval*] (ODIN) ... BP
Biosystematic Code [*Online database field identifier*] (OBD) ... BS
Bipolar Junction Transistor [*Electronics*] ... BJT
Bipolar Metal-Oxide Semiconductor (IEEE) ... BiMOS
Birkbeck College Computation Laboratory [*British*] (CAH) ... BCCL
Birmingham Wire Gauge ... BWG
Birth Defects Information System [*Tufts University*] [*Boston, MA*] [*Information service*] (EISS) ... BDIS
Bistable Magnetic Core [*Data processing*] (CGC) ... BIMAC
Bistable Magnetic Core (OA) ... BIMAG
BIT [*Binary Digit*] [*Data transmission speed*] [*Data processing*] (DIT) ... B
BIT [*Binary Digit*] **Buffer Unit** [*Data processing*] (CET) ... BBU
BIT [*Binary Digit*]**/Byte Conversion** [*Telecommunications*] (TEL) ... BB
BIT [*Binary Digit*] **Control Block** [*Data processing*] (IBMDP) ... BCB
BIT [*Binary Digit*] **Control Panel** [*Data processing*] (MCD) ... BCP
BIT [*Binary Digit*] **Count Integrity** [*Telecommunications*] (TEL) ... BCI
BIT [*Binary Digit*] **Density** [*Data processing*] ... BD
BIT [*Binary Digit*] **Effectiveness Report** (CAAL) ... BER
BIT [*Binary Digit*] **Error Probability** [*Data processing*] (KSC) ... BEP
BIT [*Binary Digit*] **Error Rate** [*Data processing*] ... BER
BIT [*Binary Digit*] **Error Rate Monitor** (CAA) ... BERM
BIT [*Binary Digit*] **Error-Rate-Test** [*Set*] [*Data processing*] ... BERT
BIT [*Binary Digit*] **Image Memory** [*Data processing*] ... BIM
BIT [*Binary Digit*]**-Oriented Message** (RDA) ... BOM
BIT-Oriented Protocol (DEEC) ... BOP
BIT [*Binary Digit*]**-Plane Encoding** [*Data processing*] ... BPE

BIT [*Binary Digit*] **Rate** [*Data transmission speed*] [*Data processing*] (MCD) ... BR
BIT [*Binary Digit*] **Scan** [*Data processing*] (BUR) ... BSCN
BIT [*Binary Digit*] **Scan Command** [*Data processing*] ... BSC
BIT [*Binary Digit*] **Serial Link** (CAA) ... BSL
BIT [*Binary Digit*] **Slippage Rate** [*Data processing*] ... BSR
BIT [*Binary Digit*] **Storage Density** [*Data processing*] ... BSD
BIT [*Binary Digit*] **Sync** [*Data processing*] (CIT) ... BS
BIT [*Binary Digit*] **Sync Acquisition** [*Data processing*] ... BSA
BIT [*Binary Digit*] **Sync Generator** [*Data processing*] (CIT) ... BSG
BIT [*Binary Digit*] **Sync Matched Filter** [*Data processing*] (CIT) ... BSMF
BIT [*Binary Digit*] **Test** [*Data processing*] ... BTST
BIT [*Binary Digit*] **Time Counter** [*Data processing*] ... BTC
BITS [*Binary Digits*] **per Inch** [*Data density measurement*] [*Data processing*] ... BPI
BITS [*Binary Digits*] **per Millimeter** (CAA) ... BPMM
BITS [*Binary Digits*] **per Minute** [*Data processing*] (SKY) ... BPM
BITS [*Binary Digits*] **per Second** [*Data processing*] (OA) ... BITS
BITS [*Binary Digits*] **per Second** [*Data transmission speed*] [*Data processing*] ... BPS
BITS [*Binary Digits*] **per Second** [*Data transmission speed*] [*Data processing*] (CET) ... B/S
BITS per Square Inch (CAA) ... BPSI
Black Data Processing Associates [*Philadelphia, PA*] (EANO) ... BDPA
Black Data Processing Associates (EANO) ... DPA
Black Entertainment Television [*Cable-television system*] ... BET
Black Resources Information Coordinating Services [*Information service*] (EISS) ... BRICS
Blank (BUR) ... B
Blank Line [*Data processing*] ... BL
Blanking (DEN) ... BL
Blanking Input (IEEE) ... BI
Blinking Light Monitor ... BLM
Blip/Frame (CET) ... B/F
Block (BUR) ... BLCK
Block [*Unit of data*] ... BLK
Block Access Method [*Data processing*] (CAA) ... BAM
Block Automation System [*NYSE trading computer*] ... BAS
Block out of Balance [*Data processing*] ... BOOB
Block Check Character [*Data processing*] ... BCC
Block Control Header [*Data processing*] (IBMDP) ... BCH
Block Control Sheet [*Data processing*] ... BCS
Block Control Signal [*Telecommunications*] (TEL) ... BCS
Block Control Unit [*Data processing*] (IBMDP) ... BCU
Block Count [*Data processing*] ... BC
Block Diagram Compiler ... BLODI
Block Diagram Compiler B (IEEE) ... BLODIB
Block Downconverter [*Satellite communications*] ... BDC
Block Error Rate Test (CAA) ... BLERT
Block Handler [*Data processing*] ... BH
Block Handler Routine [*Data processing*] (BUR) ... BHR
Block Header Record [*Data processing*] ... BHR
Block Input Length [*Data processing*] (BUR) ... BIL
Block Length (CAA) ... BL
Block and List Manipulator [*Data processing*] (CSR) ... BALM
Block Mode Terminal Interface [*Data processing*] (CAA) ... BMTI
Block Multiplexer Channel (CAA) ... BMC
Block-Oriented Computer ... BOC
Block-Oriented Random-Access Memory [*Data processing*] ... BORAM
Block Parity [*Error checking method*] [*Telecommunications*] (TEL) ... BP
Block Proof List [*Data processing*] ... BPL
Block Proof Record [*Data processing*] ... BPR
Block Received Signal [*Telecommunications*] (TEL) ... BRS
Block Structured Assembly Language (CAA) ... BSAL
Block Transfer Controller [*Data processing*] (CAA) ... BTC
Block Type Manipulation Facility (OA) ... BTMF
Blocking [*Telecommunications*] (TEL) ... BLO
Blocking Acknowledgment [*Telecommunications*] (TEL) ... BLA
Blocking Factor (CMD) ... BKF
Blood Information Service [*Information service*] (EISS) ... BLDIS
Bloomington Academic Computer Services [*Indiana University*] [*Research center*] (RCD) ... BACS
Board ... BD
Board of Broadcast Governors [*Later, Canadian Radio-Television Commission*] ... BBG
Board of Standards Review [*American National Standards Institute*] ... BSR
Boating Accident Data Base [*Coast Guard*] [*Database*] (FDB) ... BADB
Boating Accident Reports System [*Washington, DC*] [*Coast Guard*] [*Information service*] (EISS) ... BARS
Bob White Computing & Software, Inc. [*Oak Brook, IL*] [*Software manufacturer*] (DASOS) ... BWCS
Boeing Airplane Company [*later, Boeing Co.*] **Algebraic Interpretive Computing System** ... BACAIC
Boeing Computer Services Co. [*Vienna, VA*] ... BCS
Boeing Electronic Analog Computer (CDH) ... BEAC
Boeing Engineering Analog Computer (IEEE) ... BEAC
Bogart-Brociner Associates, Inc. [*Annapolis, MD*] [*Information service*] (EISS) ... BBA
Bolt, Beranek & Newman, Inc. [*NYSE symbol*] ... BBN
Bolt-On Intelligence [*Proposed use for the biochip*] ... BOI
Book Indexing with Context and Entry Points from Text [*Indexing method*] [*Data processing*] (DIT) ... BICEPT
Book Order and Selection [*Data processing*] ... BOS
Book Review Editors File [*University Press of New England*] [*Information service*] (EISS) ... BREF
Books in Print [*Bibliographic database*] [*R. R. Bowker Co.*] [*A publication*] ... BIP
Boolean Normal Form [*Mathematics*] ... BNF
Booth Library On-Line Circulation [*Data processing system*] [*Eastern Illinois University*] [*Charleston, IL*] ... BLOC
Bootstrap Combined Programing Language [*Data processing*] (CSR) ... BCPL
Bored Insitu Piles [*Camutek*] [*Software package*] [*British*] (NCC) ... BPILE
Bose-Chaudhuri-Hocquenghem [*Cyclic codes*] [*Telecommunications*] ... BCH
Boston Computer Exchange ... BCE
Boston Educational Computing, Inc. [*Boston, MA*] [*Software manufacturer*] (DASOS) ... BEC
Both Sideband ... BSB
Bottom Up (CAA) ... BU
Bottom-Up Modular Programing (CAA) ... BUMP
Boundary ... BDRY
Boundary Element Analysis System [*Computational Mechanics Ltd.*] [*Software package*] [*British*] (NCC) ... BEASY
Boundary Element Tape [*Computational Mechanics Ltd.*] [*Software package*] [*British*] (NCC) ... BET
Box-Office Computer System ... BOCS
BPI Systems, Incorporated [*NASDAQ symbol*] (NQ) ... BPII
Bradford National Corp. [*American Stock Exchange symbol*] [*Delisted*] ... BDR
Braille Time-Sharing System (CAA) ... BTSS
Branch Always [*Data processing*] ... BRA
Branch Back and Load [*Data processing*] ... BBL
Branch-Bound Mixed Integer Programing [*Data processing*] ... BBMIP
Branch Conditional (OA) ... BRC
Branch Conditionally [*Data processing*] ... BCC
Branch Exchange [*Telecommunications*] (CAA) ... BX
Branch If Multiplexer (OA) ... BIM
Branch No Group [*Data processing*] (MDG) ... BNG
Branch Output Interrupt [*Data processing*] (MDG) ... BOI
Branch and Store Instruction [*Data processing*] (MDG) ... BSI
Branch to Subroutine [*Data processing*] ... BSR
Branching Filter [*Telecommunications*] (TEL) ... BF
Brassboard Fault Tolerant Spaceborne Computer (MCD) ... BFTSC
Brazilian Association of Tele-Education ... ABT
Break [*Electronics*] ... B
Break-In [*Telecommunications*] (TEL) ... BKI
Break Request [*Data processing*] (MDG) ... BR
Break Request Signal [*Data processing*] (CGC) ... BRS
Break Signal [*Used to interrupt a transmission in progress*] [*Communications*] (FAAC) ... BK
Break Transmission (NVT) ... BT
Breakdown Maintenance ... BM
Breakdown Voltage [*Telecommunications*] (TEL) ... BDV
Breakpoint [*Telecommunications*] (TEL) ... BP
Bridge [*Interconnects computer networks*] ... BR
Bridge [*or Bridging*] [*Telecommunications*] (TEL) ... BRG
Bridged Frequency Ringing [*Telecommunications*] (TEL) ... BFR
Bridging Key [*on Dial Assistance Switchboard*] (CET) ... BR
Bright Cathode-Ray Tube (DEN) ... BCRT
Bright Display Equipment ... BDE
Brightness Contrast Value ... BCV
British Approvals Board for Telecommunications ... BABT
British Association of Viewdata Information Providers (DEEC) ... BAVIP
British Communications and Electronics [*England*] [*A publication*] ... Br Commun Electron
British Computer Society ... BCS
British Library Automated Information Service [*European host database system*] [*London*] (EISS) ... BLAISE
British Micro Manufacturer Group ... BMMG
British Overseas Airways [*later, British Airways*] **Digital Information Computer for Electronic Automation** ... BOADICEA
British Post Office ... BPO
British Standard Data Code (BUR) ... BSDC
British Standard Gauge [*Telecommunications*] (TEL) ... BSG
British Standards Institution [*Promulgates manufacturing standards and specifications*] [*London*] ... BSI
British Telecom [*or Telecommunications*] [*Common carrier*] ... BT
British Telecom Journal [*A publication*] ... Br Telecom J
British Telecom Phonecards [*Prepaid cards for use in noncoin pay telephones*] ... BTP
British Telecommunications [*Toronto Stock Exchange symbol*] ... BTY
British Telecommunications International (TSSD) ... BTI
British Telecommunications Systems Ltd. (TEL) ... BTS
British Thermal Unit [*Also, BTHU*] ... BTU
British Universities Film & Video Council [*Database producer*] (CUAD) ... BUFVC
Broadband [*Communications channel description*] (IEEE) ... BB
Broadband Acoustic Array Section ... BAAS
Broadband Active Analyzer ... BAA
Broadband Antenna Kit ... BAK
Broadband Communication Network (BUR) ... BCN
Broadband Conducted (IEEE) ... BBC
Broadband Exchange [*Western Union communication system*] ... BEX
Broadband Radiated (IEEE) ... BBR
Broadband Subsystem (CIT) ... BRD
Broadcast [*Information transmission*] (AFM) ... BCST

Broadcast Band	BCB
Broadcast Bureau [of FCC]	BB
Broadcast Communications System	BCS
Broadcast Control Center	BCC
Broadcast Keying Station (NVT)	BKS
Broadcast Net (NATG)	BRN
Broadcast Requested (FAAC)	BCREQ
Broadcast Satellite [Japan] (CBSS)	BS
Broadcast Station (FAAC)	BCSTN
Broadcast and Television Receivers (MCD)	BTR
Broadcast Transmission Systems (MCD)	BTS
Broadcaster	BCSTR
Broadcasting	B
Broadcasting	B
Broadcasting [A publication]	BC
Broadcasting (MCD)	BCSTG
Broadcasting Amplitude Modulation	BAM
Broadcasting Satellite Experimental [Japan] (MCD)	BSE
Broadcasting Station	BS
Broadcasting Station, Television [ITU designation]	BT
Broker Services, Incorporated [Englewood, CO] [Information service] (EISS)	BSI
Brokerage Accounting System Elements [IBM computer program]	BASE
Brookings Economics and Statistical Translator [Data processing] (TUT)	BEAST
Brought into Service [Telecommunications] (TEL)	BIS
Brown	BR
Brown [Telecommunications] (TEL)	BWN
Brown University Display for Working Set References (OA)	BUDWSR
Brown University Graphic System (OA)	BUGS
Brown University Interpreter [Data processing] (TUT)	BRUIN
Browne, Bortz & Coddington, Inc. [Denver, CO] [Telecommunications] (TSSD)	BBC
Browsing On-Line with Selective Retrieval (DEEC)	BROWSER
BTI Computer Systems [Formerly, Basic Timesharing, Inc.] (CAA)	BTI
Bubble Memory [Data storage device] [Data processing] (BUR)	BM
Bubble Memory [Data storage device] [Data processing] (MSA)	BUBMEM
Bubble Memory Controller (CAA)	BMC
Bubble Memory Device (CAA)	BMD
Bucket-Brigade Device [Electronics]	BBD
Bucknell Computer Services [Bucknell University] [Research center] (RCD)	BCS
Budget Accounting Information System [IBM Corp.]	BACIS
Buffer [Data storage device] (MSA)	BFR
Buffer (CAH)	BUF
Buffer Access Card [Data processing] (NASA)	BAC
Buffer Address Register [Data processing]	BAR
Buffer Amplifier [Data processing]	BA
Buffer Control Junction Switch [Data processing]	BCJS
Buffer Control Unit [Data processing] (CET)	BCU
Buffer Control Word [Data processing] (CGC)	BCW
Buffer Index [Data processing]	BI
Buffer Input-Output Memory [Data processing]	BIOM
Buffer Interface Unit [Data processing] (NASA)	BIU
Buffer Map [Data processing] (NASA)	BMAP
Buffer Module [Data processing]	BM
Buffer/Multiplexer [Data processing] (CET)	B/M
Buffer Register [Data processing]	BR
Buffer Word Counter [Data processing] (CAA)	BWC
Buffered Data and Control Bus (CAA)	BDCB
Buffered Data Transmission Simulator (CAA)	BDTS
Buffered Flip-Flop [Data processing]	BFF
Buffered Printing (CAA)	BP
Buffered Selector Channel (CAH)	BSELCH
Buffered Send/Receive (CAA)	BSR
Build Out Capacitor [Telecommunications] (TEL)	BOC
Build Out Lattice [Telecommunications] (TEL)	BOL
Building Design System [Applied Research of Cambridge Ltd.] [Software package] [British] (NCC)	BDS
Building Industry Consulting Service [Telecommunications] (TEL)	BICS
Building Industry Consulting Service International [Telecommunications]	BICSI
Building Optimization Program [Data processing]	BOP
Building Services Calculations [Amazon Computers] [Software package] [British] (NCC)	BSC
Building Services Estimating [Tipdata Ltd.] [Software package] [British] (NCC)	BSE
Building Services Programs [Amazon Computers] [Software package] [British] (NCC)	BSP
Built-In Test [or Testing] [Data processing]	BIT
Built-In Test Equipment	BITE
Bulk-Channel Charge-Coupled Device [Electronics] (TEL)	BCCD
Bulk Data Switching (CAA)	BDS
Bulk Data Transfer Subsystem [Telecommunications] (TEL)	BDTS
Bulk Media Conversion (CAA)	BMC
Bulk Storage Device (IEEE)	BSD
Bulk Storage System (CAA)	BSS
Bulk Store Memory Device (MCD)	BSMD
Bulk Transfer Facility (CAA)	BTF
Bulletin. American Society for Information Science [A publication]	Am Soc Info Science Bul
Bulletin. American Society for Information Science [A publication]	BASIC
Bulletin. American Society for Information Science [A publication]	BASIS
Bulletin. American Society for Information Science [A publication]	Bull Am Soc Inform Sci
Bulletin. American Society for Information Science [A publication]	Bull Am Soc Inf Sci
Bulletin Articles Information Subsystem [Data processing]	BAIS
Bulletin Board [Computer online message system]	BB
Bulletin Board Systems [Personal computer message network system]	BBS
Bulletin Officiel des Annonces des Marches Publics [Direction des Journaux Officiels] [Database] (CUAD)	BOAMP
Bunching Block (MSA)	BB
Bundesanstalt fuer Geowissenschaften und Rohstoffe [Hannover] [Information retrieval] (ODIN)	BGR
Bundesanstalt fuer Materialpruefung [Database producer] [Information retrieval] (ODIN)	BAM
Bundesforschungsanstalt fuer Ernaehrung [Karlsruhe] [Information retrieval] (ODIN)	BFE
Bundesforschungsanstalt fuer Fischerei [Database producer] (ODIN)	BFF
Bundesforschungsanstalt fuer Forst- und Holzwirtschaft [Hamburg] [Information retrieval] (ODIN)	BFH
Bundesgesundheitsamt [Database producer] (ODIN)	BGA
Bundesinstitut fuer Sportwissenschaft [Cologne, West Germany] [Information retrieval] (ODIN)	BISP
Bundesstelle fuer Aussenhandelsinformation [Foreign Trade Information Office] [West Germany] [Information service] (EISS)	BfA
Bundesstelle fuer Aussenhandelsinformation [Foreign Trade Information Office] [West Germany] [Information service] (EISS)	BFAI
Bureau of Applied Social Research [Columbia University] (EISS)	BASR
Bureau of Business Research [University of Texas, Austin] [Information service]	BBR
Bureau of Economic Analysis [Department of Commerce] (EISS)	BEA
Bureau of Educational Research and Service [Memphis State University] [Research center] (RCD)	BERS
Bureau of Hygiene and Tropical Diseases [Database producer] (CUAD)	BHTD
Bureau International des Poids et Mesures [International Bureau of Weights and Measures]	BIPM
Bureau of Justice Statistics [Department of Justice] [Information service] (EISS)	BJS
Bureau National des Donnees Oceaniques [National Bureau for Ocean Data] [European host database system] [France] [Information service] (EISS)	BNDO
Bureau National de l'Information Scientifique et Technique [National Scientific and Technical Information Bureau] [France] [Information service] (EISS)	BNIST
Bureau of Educational and Cultural Affairs [Later Known as USIA, then as ICA or USICA, then again as USIA]	BECA
Buried	BUR
Buried Distribution Wire [Telecommunications] (TEL)	BDW
Buried Tape Armor [Telecommunications] (TEL)	BT
Buried Wire [Telecommunications] (TEL)	BW
Burr-Brown Corporation [NASDAQ symbol] (NQ)	BBRC
Burroughs Advanced Statistical Inquiry System [Data processing] (BUR)	BASIS
Burroughs Algebraic Compiler (IEEE)	BALGOL
Burroughs Common Language [Data processing] (BUR)	BCL
Burroughs Computer Output to Microfilm (IEEE)	BCOM
Burroughs Corporation	BC
Burroughs Corp. [NYSE symbol]	BGH
Burroughs Corporation	BRC
Burroughs Current Mode Logic (CAA)	BCML
Burroughs Data Link Control [Data processing] (BUR)	BDLC
Burroughs Distribution Scheduling System [Data processing] (BUR)	BURDS
Burrough's Electrographic Printer-Plotter for Ordnance Computing	BEPOC
Burroughs Electronic Accounting Machine (BUR)	BEAM
Burroughs Hospital Administrative System [Data processing] (BUR)	BHAS
Burroughs Inventory Control System [Data processing] (BUR)	BICS
Burroughs Inventory Planning Analysis and Simulation System [Data processing] (BUR)	BIPASS
Burroughs Optical Lens Docking System (MCD)	BOLDS
Burroughs Scientific Processor [Data processing] (BUR)	BSP
Burroughs, UNIVAC, NCR, Control Data, Honeywell [IBM competitors in computer manufacture]	BUNCH
Burst Multiplexer Channel [Telecommunications] (CAA)	BMC
Bus Acknowledgement [Data processing] (TEL)	BUSAK
Bus Available [Data processing]	BA
Bus-Bar Layout Drawing [Data processing] (TEL)	BB
Bus Control Electronics (MCD)	BCE
Bus Control Interface Unit (MCD)	BCIU
Bus Coupler [Data processing] (MCD)	BC
Bus Direction [Data processing] (TEL)	BDIR
Bus Interface [Data processing]	B/I
Bus Interface Circuit [Data processing] (MDG)	BIC
Bus Interface Module (CAA)	BIM
Bus Interface Unit [Data processing]	BIU
Bus Out Register [Data processing] (CAA)	BOR
Bus Request [Data processing] (TEL)	BUSRQ
Bus Selector [Data processing]	BSLR
Bus Tie Breaker	BTB

Bus Unit [*Data processing*] .... BU
Business Application Language (CAA) .... BAL
Business Communications Company, Inc. [*Stamford, CT*]
  [*Information service*] [*Telecommunications*] (TSSD) .... BCC
Business Communications Service [*British Telecommunications International*] [*London*] (TSSD) .... BCS
Business Communications Systems [*Telecommunications*] (TEL) .... BCS
Business Computer Network [*San Antonio, TX*]
  [*Telecommunications*] (TSSD) .... BCN
Business Customer Services [*Telecommunications*] (TEL) .... BCS
Business Data Processing (CIT) .... BDP
Business Development Report System [*Department of Commerce*]
  [*Database*] (FDB) .... BDRS
Business EDP [*Electronic Data Processing*] **Systems Technique**
  [*NCR Corp.*] .... BEST
Business Electronics Computer [*Used in training*] .... BEC
Business and Engineering Enriched FORTRAN [*Programing language*] [*Sperry UNIVAC*] .... BEEF
Business Equipment Manufacturers Association [*Later, CBEMA*] .... BEMA
Business Equipment Software Techniques [*Data processing*] .... BEST
Business Equipment & Supply Company [*Columbus, MS*]
  [*Software manufacturer*] (DASOS) .... BESCO
Business Equipment Trade Association [*London, England*] .... BETA
Business Forms Management Association, Inc. .... BFMA
Business Information Analysis and Integration Technique [*Data processing*] .... BIAT
Business Information Network [*Telecommunications*] (TEL) .... BIN
Business Information Service [*Financial Times Business Information Ltd.*] [*British*] (EISS) .... BIS
Business Information System/Trunks and Special Services
  [*Telecommunications*] (TEL) .... BISTSS
Business Information Systems [*Bell System*] .... BIS
Business Information Systems Analysis and Design [*Bell System*]
  (DIT) .... BISAD
Business Information Systems Communications [*Bell System*] .... BISCOM
Business Information Systems Customer Service [*Bell System*] .... BISCUS
Business Information Systems Customer Service/Facilities Assignment and Control System [*Bell System*] (MCD) ...... BISCUS/FACS
Business Input/Output Rerun [*UNIVAC compiling system*] .... BIOR
Business Intelligence Program [*SRI International*] [*Menlo Park, CA*] [*Information service*] (EISS) .... B-I-P
Business Lead Identification System [*Timeplace, Inc.*] [*Database*]
  (CUAD) .... BLIS
Business Machine Computer (TUT) .... BISMAC
Business Machines Group [*Burroughs Corp.*] (CAA) .... BMG
Business Management System (BUR) .... BMS
Business Office Supervisor [*Telecommunications*] (TEL) .... BOS
Business-Oriented Software System [*Digital Equipment Corp.*]
  [*Data processing*] (BUR) .... BOSS
Business Products Standards Association (CAA) .... BPSA
Business Service Unit [*Telecommunications*] (TEL) .... BSU
Business Systems Planning .... BSP
Business Systems Technology, Inc. (CAA) .... BST
Business and Technology Center [*Control Data Corp.*] [*British*]
  (CAA) .... BTC
Business Telecommunications Corporation [*Chicago, IL*] (TSSD) .... BTC
Business Telecommunications Equipment [*Canada*] .... BTE
Business Terminal Equipment [*Telecommunications*] (TEL) .... BTE
Business User Groups [*Data processing*] .... BUG'S
Busy [*Telecommunications*] (TEL) .... BY
Busy Hour Call [*Telecommunications*] (TEL) .... BHC
Busy Hour Call Attempts [*Telecommunications*] .... BHCA
Busy Hour Load [*Telecommunications*] (TEL) .... BHL
Busy Hour Model [*Data processing*] .... BHM
Busy Lamp Field [*Phone console*] [*Bell System*] .... BLF
Busy Tone [*Telecommunications*] (TEL) .... BT
Busy Tone Trunks [*Telecommunications*] (TEL) .... BOTTS
Busy Verification [*Telecommunications*] (TEL) .... BV
Bypass (KSC) .... BYP
Bypass Label Processing [*Data processing*] .... BLP
Byte [*Usually 8 BITS*] [*Data processing*] .... B
Byte Information Exchange [*Electronic conferencing system provided by McGraw-Hill's Byte magazine*] .... BIX
Byte Input Control [*Data processing*] .... BIC
Byte-Multiplexer Channel (CAA) .... BYMUX
Byte Output Control [*Data processing*] .... BOC
Bytes per Inch [*Data processing*] (CGC) .... BPI
Bytes per Second [*Data processing*] (BUR) .... BPS

C

C-Band Communications Transponder ... CCT
C-Band Frequency Converter ... CFC
C-Band Transponder [Radio] ... CBX
C-Band Transponder Antenna [Radio]   (CET) ... CBA
C. Itoh Electronics [In company name, CIE Systems, Inc.] [Irvine, CA] [Software manufacturer]   (DASOS) ... CIE
"C" Message Weighting [Telecommunications]   (TEL) ... CMSG
C & W [Cable & Wireless North America, Inc.] Network Services [Dallas, TX] [Telecommunications]   (TSSD) ... CWNS
Cable ... C
Cable   (MSA) ... CA
Cable Access Cover ... CAC
Cable Activity System [Telecommunications]   (TEL) ... CAS
Cable Communications Resource Center   (EANO) ... CRC
Cable Interconnection Diagram   (KSC) ... CID
Cable Maintenance Center [Telecommunications]   (TEL) ... CMC
Cable Network Engineering Program [Bell System] ... CNEP
Cable News Network [Cable-television system] ... CNN
Cable On-Line Data Exchange [A. C. Nielson Co.] [Database]   (CUAD) ... CODE
Cable Pair Identification [Telecommunications]   (TEL) ... CPI
Cable Pressure Monitoring System [Bell System] ... CPMS
Cable Relay Service [or Station] [Television transmission] ... CARS
Cable Report [A publication] ... Cable Rpt
Cable Satellite Public Affairs Network [Cable-television system] ... C-SPAN
Cable Splicing Kit ... CSK
Cable Telemetry System ... CTS
Cable Television [Later, CTV] ... CATV
Cable Television [Formerly, CATV] ... CTV
Cable Television Administration and Marketing Society   (EANO) ... CTAM
Cable Television Engineering [A publication] ... Cable Telev Eng
Cable Television Information Center ... CTIC
Cable Terminal Section [Telecommunications]   (TEL) ... CTS
Cable Termination Equipment   (CET) ... CTE
Cable Termination Network ... CTN
Cable Transfer [of funds] ... C/T
Cable Trouble Ticket [Telecommunications]   (TEL) ... CTT
Cable Turning Section [Telecommunications]   (TEL) ... CTS
Cable and Wireless Ltd. [Telecommunications]   (TEL) ... C & W
Cablecasting, Cable TV Engineering [A publication] ... Cablecast Cable TV Eng
Cables and Transmission [A publication] ... Cables & Transm
Cables and Transmission [A publication] ... Cables Transm
Cableshare, Inc. [Toronto Stock Exchange symbol] ... CSH
Cabletelevision Advertising Bureau   (EANO) ... CAB
Cabling Interface Drawing   (MCD) ... CID
CACI, Inc. [NASDAQ symbol]   (NQ) ... CACI
CAD/CAM [Computer-Aided Design/Computer-Aided Manufacturing] Technology [A publication] ... CAD/CAM Tech
CAGE [Computerized Aerospace Ground Equipment] Test Language [Data processing]   (KSC) ... CTL
Calculated ... CALC
Calculation of Indirect Resources and Conversion to Unit Staff [Data processing] ... CIRCUS
Calculations of Patient and Hospital Education Resources [Data processing] ... CIPHER
Calculator   (MDG) ... CC
Calendar Process [Telecommunications]   (TEL) ... CP
Calendar Year   (TEL) ... CY
Calgary Public Library Government Documents [Calgary, AB] [Information service]   (EISS) ... CALDOC
Cali Computer Systems [NASDAQ symbol]   (NQ) ... CCSS
Calibrate   (CET) ... CAL
Calibrating, Amplitude-Variation, and Level-Correcting Analog-Digital Equipment   (DEN) ... CAVALCADE
California Computer Products, Inc.   (CAH) ... CALCOMP
California Computer Products, Incorporated [American Stock Exchange symbol] [Delisted] ... CPI
California Educational Data Processing Association   (CAH) ... CEDPA
California Law Enforcement Telecommunications System ... CLETS
California Microwave, Inc. [NASDAQ symbol]   (NQ) ... CMIC
California Natural Diversity Data Base [California State Department of Fish and Game] [Information service]   (EISS) ... CNDDB

California Union List of Periodicals [Cooperative Library Agency for Systems and Services] [Database]   (CUAD) ... CULP
Call Accounting Reconciliation Process [Telecommunications]   (TEL) ... CARP
Call Accounting System [or Subsystem] [Telecommunications] ... CAS
Call Attempts per Second [Telecommunications]   (TEL) ... CAPS
Call Back [Word processing] ... CB
Call Box Discrimination [Telecommunications]   (TEL) ... CBD
Call Box Station   (MSA) ... CBS
Call Control Processing [Telecommunications]   (TEL) ... CCP
Call Control Systems [San Clemente, CA] [Telecommunications]   (TSSD) ... CCS
Call Detail Recording [Telecommunications]   (TEL) ... CDR
Call Directing Code ... CDC
Call Failed [or Failure] [Telecommunications]   (TEL) ... CFL
Call Finder [Telecommunications] ... CF
Call Hold and Trace [Telecommunications]   (TEL) ... CHT
Call Holding Time [Telecommunications]   (TEL) ... CHT
Call Indicator [Data processing]   (CGC) ... CI
Call Key [Telecommunications] ... CK
Call Number [Online database field identifier]   (OBD) ... CN
Call Paid [Telecommunications] ... CP
Call Progress Indicator [Telecommunications]   (TEL) ... CPI
Call Protocol Message [Telecommunications]   (TEL) ... CPM
Call Request [Telecommunications]   (TEL) ... CRQ
Call Sign [or Signal] [Radio] ... CS
Call Store [Telecommunications]   (TEL) ... CS
Call Supervision Module [Telecommunications]   (TEL) ... CSM
Call Waiting Indication [Telecommunications]   (TEL) ... CWI
Called Subscriber Answer [Telecommunications]   (TEL) ... CSA
Called Subscriber Held [Telecommunications]   (TEL) ... CSH
Calling Card Service [Bell System] ... CCS
Calling Device [Telecommunications] ... CD
Calling Line Identification [or Identity] [Telecommunications]   (TEL) ... CLI
Calling Party Cannot Hear [Telecommunications]   (TEL) ... CPCH
Calling Party Forced Release [Telecommunications]   (TEL) ... CPFR
Calling Party's Category [Telecommunications]   (TEL) ... CPC
Calling Processing Subsystem [Telecommunications]   (TEL) ... CPS
Calls per Second [Telecommunications]   (TEL) ... CS
Calls for Service Signal [Telecommunications]   (TEL) ... CFS
Calls Waiting [Telephone communication] ... CW
Calspan On-Line Information Service [Calspan Corp.] [Information service]   (EISS) ... COINS
Cam-Net Communications Network, Inc. [Vancouver Stock Exchange symbol] ... CWK
CAMAC [Computer-Aided Measurement and Control] Input-Output Processor [Computer] ... CIOP
Cambridge Algebraic System [Programing language] [1975]   (CSR) ... CAMAL
Cambridge Analog Simulator for Predicting Atomic Reactions [British]   (DIT) ... CASPAR
Cambridge Automatic Digital Computer   (IEEE) ... CADC
Cambridge Computer Science Texts [A publication] ... Cambridge Comput Sci Texts
Cambridge Crystallographic Data File [Database]   (ODIN) ... CCDF
Cambridge Memories, Incorporated   (CAA) ... CMI
Cambridge Monitor System ... CMS
Cambridge Scientific Abstracts [Bethesda, MD] [Information service]   (EISS) ... CSA
Camp-On [Telecommunications]   (TEL) ... CMP
Campus Conference Network [Services by Satellite, Inc.] [Washington, DC] [Telecommunications]   (TSSD) ... CCN
Canada Geographic Information System [Ottawa, ON]   (EISS) ... CGIS
Canada Institute for Scientific and Technical Information [Ottawa, ON]   (EISS) ... CISTI
Canada Systems Group [Database producer] [Information service] ... CSG
Canadian Advisory Committee on Programming Languages ... CAC/PL
Canadian Association for Information Science [Ottawa, ON] ... CAIS
Canadian Association for Information Science/Association Canadienne des Sciences de l'Information [Ottawa, ON]   (EISS) ... CAIS/ACSI
Canadian Book Exchange Centre [Ottawa, ON]   (EISS) ... CBEC
Canadian Broadcasting Corporation [Telecommunications] ... CBC

231

Canadian Business Index [*Micromedia Ltd.*] [*Database*] [*A publication*] ..... CBI
Canadian Clearinghouse for Ongoing Research in Nursing [*University of Alberta*] [*Edmonton, AB*] (EISS) ..... CORN
Canadian Communication Association ..... CCA
Canadian Communications and Power Conference. Proceedings [*A publication*] ..... Can Commun Power Conf Proc
Canadian Computer-Based Reference Service [*National Library of Canada*] [*Information service*] (EISS) ..... CAN/CRS
Canadian Computer Show (CAA) ..... CCS
Canadian Consortium for Social Research (EISS) ..... CCSR
Canadian Criminal Cases [*Database*] CCC
Canadian Datasystems [*A publication*] ..... Can Datasyst
Canadian Datasystems [*A publication*] ..... Cdn Data
Canadian Electrical Engineering Journal [*A publication*] ..... Can Electr Eng J
Canadian Electrical Manufacturers' Association ..... CEMA
Canadian Electronics Engineering [*A publication*] ..... CAEEA
Canadian Electronics Engineering [*A publication*] ..... Can Electron Eng
Canadian Electronics Engineering [*A publication*] ..... Cdn Elec E
Canadian Engineering Standards Association [*Later, Canadian Standards Association*] ..... CESA
Canadian Financial Database [*Toronto, ON*] [*Information service*] (EISS) ..... CFD
Canadian Information Industry Association [*Ottawa, ON*] (EISS) ..... CIIA
Canadian Information Processing Society [*Toronto, ON*] (CGC) ..... CIPS
Canadian Institute of Metalworking [*McMaster University*] [*Research center*] (RCD) ..... CIM
Canadian Inventory of Historic Building [*Ottawa, ON*] [*Information service*] (EISS) ..... CIHB
Canadian Journal of Information Science [*A publication*] ..... Can J Info Science
Canadian Law Information Council [*Ottawa, ON*] (EISS) CLIC
Canadian Magazine Index [*Micromedia, Ltd.*] [*Information service*] (EISS) ..... CMI
Canadian Man-Computer Communications Society ..... CMCS
Canadian Mineral Occurrence Index [*Ottawa, ON*] [*Information service*] (EISS) ..... CANMINDEX
Canadian National Telecommunications ..... CNT
Canadian News Index [*Micromedia Ltd.*] [*Database*] [*A publication*] ..... CNI
Canadian On-Line Record Database ..... CORD
Canadian Operational Research Society ..... CORS
Canadian Overseas Telecommunications Corporation ..... COTC
Canadian Periodical Index [*Canadian Library Association*] [*Ottawa, ON*] [*Information service*] (EISS) ..... CPI
Canadian Radio and Telecommunications Commission [*Conseil de la Radiodiffusion et des Telecommunications Canadiennes*] [*Ottawa, ON*] [*Telecommunications*] ..... CRTC
Canadian Restricted [*Broadcasting term*] ..... CR
Canadian Satellite Communications, Inc. [*Mississauga, ON*] [*Telecommunications*] (TSSD) ..... CANCOM
Canadian Society for Electrical Engineers (MCD) ..... CSEE
Canadian Socio-Economic Information Management System [*Statistics Canada*] [*Database*] (EISS) ..... CANSIM
Canadian Standards Association ..... CSA
Canadian Technology Satellite (CAA) ..... CTS
Canadian Telecommunications Carriers Association ..... CTCA
Canadian Teleconference Network, Inc. [*Toronto, ON*] [*Telecommunications*] (TSSD) ..... CTN
Canadian Transatlantic Telephone Cable [*Between Canada and England*] ..... CANTAT
Cancel (FAAC) ..... CNCL
Cancel Character [*Keyboard*] [*Data processing*] ..... CAN
Canceled ..... CANC
Canceled Transmission (CET) ..... CANTRAN
Cancer Information Clearinghouse [*National Cancer Institute*] [*Database*] (FDB) CIC
Cancer Literature [*National Library of Medicine*] [*Database*] ..... CANCERLIT
Cancer Research Projects [*National Library of Medicine*] [*Database*] ..... CANCERPROJ
Can't Add, Doesn't Even Try [*Data processing*] ..... CADET
Can't Be Called [*Telecommunications*] (TEL) ..... CBC
Can't Be Heard [*Telecommunications*] (TEL) ..... CBH
Can't Break Dial Tone [*Telecommunications*] (TEL) ..... CBDT
Can't Call - No Dial Tone [*Telecommunications*] (TEL) ..... CC-NDT
Can't Hear [*Telecommunications*] (TEL) ..... CH
Capability Password Level [*Telecommunications*] (TEL) ..... CPL
Capacitance Electronic Disk ..... CED
Capacitive Reactance Xc
Capacitive Read-Only Memory [*Data processing*] (IEEE) ..... CROM
Capacitor (CET) C
Capacitor-Diode Logic (MSA) ..... CDL
Capacitor Read-Only Storage [*Data processing*] (CAA) ..... CROS
Capacity (AFM) ..... CAP
Capacity Planning and Operations Sequencing System [*IBM Corp.*] ..... CAPOSS
Capacity Planning and Operations Sequencing System - Extended [*IBM Corp.*] ..... CAPOSS-E
Capital Cities Communications, Incorporated CCCI
Capital Equipment Corporation [*Burlington, MA*] ..... CEC
Capital PC [*Personal Computer*] **User Group** [*Gaithersburg, MD*] (EANO) ..... CPCUG
Capital Planning Information Ltd. [*British*] [*Information service*] (EISS) ..... CPI
Capital Systems Group, Inc. [*Kensington, MD*] [*Information service*] (EISS) ..... CSG
Capitol Services, Incorporated [*Bethesda, MD*] [*Database producer*] [*Information service*] (EISS) ..... CSI
Captive Installation Function [*Telecommunications*] (TEL) ..... CIF
Car Information and Navigation System [*Compact disc technology*] ..... CARIN
Carbon-13 Nuclear Magnetic Resonance Search System [*Netherlands Information Combine*] [*Database*] (CUAD) ..... CNMR
Carbon-Carbon Data Base [*Battelle Columbus Laboratories*] [*Database*] (FDB) ..... CCDB
Carbon Dioxide Information Center [*Oak Ridge National Laboratory*] [*Database*] (FDB) ..... CDIC
Carcinogenesis Bioassay Data System [*National Cancer Institute*] (EISS) ..... CBDS
Card (MSA) ..... CD
Card-Automated Reproduction and Distribution System [*Library of Congress*] ..... CARDS
Card Automatic Code System [*IBM Corp.*] (IEEE) ..... CARDCODER
Card Capacitor Read-Only Storage [*Data processing*] (IEEE) ..... CCROS
Card Computer Interface [*Data processing*] (EISS) CCI
Card Count [*Data processing*] (TUT) CC
Card Image Correction [*Data processing*] ..... CIMCO
Card Input [*Data processing*] (BUR) CI
Card-to-Magnetic Tape Conversion System [*Data processing*] (DIT) ..... CTS
Card and Printer Remote Interface (CAA) ..... CAPRI
Card Programed Calculator [*Early IBM machine - late 1940's*] [*Data processing*] ..... CPC
Card Programing System (CMD) ..... CPS
Card Punch [*Data processing*] (BUR) ..... CP
Card Punch and Reader [*Data processing*] (CAA) ..... CP/R
Card Punching Printer [*Computer output device*] [*Data processing*] (BUR) ..... CPP
Card Random-Access Memory [*NCR Corp.*] [*Data processing*] ..... CRAM
Card Reader [*Data processing*] (NVT) ..... CR
Card Reader [*Data processing*] (OA) ..... CRD
Card Reader/Punch [*Data processing*] (CAA) ..... CRP
Card Reader Unit [*Data processing*] (CAA) ..... CRU
Card Station [*Data processing*] (BUR) ..... CS
Card-to-Tape Tape [*Data processing*] ..... CTT
Cardboard Illustrative Aid to Computation [*Bell Telephone Co.*] [*Data processing*] ..... CARDIAC
Cards per Day [*Data processing*] (BUR) ..... CPD
Cards per Hour [*Data processing*] ..... CPH
Cards per Minute (CAH) ..... CM
Cards per Minute [*Data processing*] ..... CPM
Cards per Second [*Data processing*] ..... CPS
Career Placement Registry, Inc. [*Database producer*] [*Alexandria, VA*] [*Information service*] (EISS) ..... CPR
Caribbean Super Station ..... CSS
Carnegie Multi-Mini Processor ..... CMMP
Carolina Library Services, Inc. (EISS) ..... CLS
Carolina Population Center [*University of North Carolina*] [*Research center*] (EISS) ..... CPC
Carriage Control Character [*Data processing*] (TUT) CCC
Carriage, Insurance, and Freight (CDH) ..... CIF
Carriage Return [*Keyboard*] ..... CR
Carriage Return/Line Feed ..... CR/LF
Carrier [*Telecommunications*] (AFM) ..... CARR
Carrier [*Telecommunications*] ..... CXR
Carrier Detector (BUR) ..... CD
Carrier Frequency Alarm [*Telecommunications*] (TEL) ..... CFA
Carrier Frequency Telephone Repeater [*Telecommunications*] (CDH) ..... CRF
Carrier Group Alarm [*Telephone communications*] ..... CGA
Carrier-to-Interference Ratio [*Data processing*] (CGC) ..... C/I
Carrier-to-Noise [*Ratio*] (CIT) ..... C/N
Carrier-to-Noise Density (CBSS) ..... C/No
Carrier-to-Noise Density, Downlink (CBSS) ..... C/No)d
Carrier-to-Noise Density, Intermodulation (CBSS) ..... C/No)im
Carrier-to-Noise Density, Total (CBSS) ..... C/No)t
Carrier-to-Noise Density, Uplink (CBSS) ..... C/No)u
Carrier-to-Noise, Downlink (CBSS) ..... C/N)d
Carrier-to-Noise, Intermodulation (CBSS) ..... C/N)im
Carrier-to-Noise Ratio ..... CNR
Carrier-to-Noise Temperature, Downlink (CBSS) ..... C/T)d
Carrier-to-Noise Temperature, Intermodulation (CBSS) ..... C/T)im
Carrier-to-Noise Temperature, Total (CBSS) ..... C/T)t
Carrier-to-Noise Temperature, Uplink (CBSS) ..... C/T)u
Carrier-to-Noise, Total (CBSS) ..... C/N)t
Carrier-to-Noise, Uplink (CBSS) ..... C/N)u
Carrier-Operated Device, Antinoise [*Radio*] ..... CODAN
Carrier-Operated Noise Suppression ..... CONS
Carrier Power Supply, Transistorized [*Telecommunications*] (TEL) ..... CST
Carrier Sense Multiple Access (DEEC) ..... CSMA
Carrier Sense Multiple Access with Collision Detection [*Data processing*] ..... CSMA/CD
Carrier Telegraph Receiver ..... CTR
Carrier Telephone Channel ..... CT
Carrier Transmission Maintenance System [*Bell System*] ..... CTMS
Carrier Virtual Circuit [*Telecommunications*] (CAA) CVC
Carrier Wave [*A form of radio transmission in code*] (KSC) ..... CRW
Carrier Wave [*A form of radio transmission in code*] ..... CW
Carry ..... CY

Computer & Telecommunications Acronyms

Carry Propagate Adder [*Computer*]	CPA
Cartridge Direct Memory Access (CAA)	CDMA
Cartridge Tape Unit [*Telecommunications*] (TEL)	CTU
Cascade Charge Coupled Device [*Electronics*]	C3D
Cascade-Failure Analysis (IEEE)	CFA
Case Copy [*Data processing*] (CDH)	CY
Cash Dispenser (BUR)	CD
Cashiers' Automatic Processing System (DIT)	CAPS
Cassette Magnetic Tape (CAA)	CMT
Cassette-Operated System (MSA)	COS
Cassette Operating Monitor (CAA)	COM
Cassette Programing System [*Digital Equipment Corp.*] (IDA)	CAPS
Cassette Tape (CAA)	CT
Cassette Tape Loader (CAA)	CTL
Cassette Tape Operating System (IEEE)	CTOS
Cassette User Tape System (DEEC)	CUTS
Cast Iron [*Telecommunications*] (TEL)	CI
CAST [*Computerized Automatic System Tester*] Programing Language (OA)	CPL
Cataclysmic Binary [*Data processing*]	CB
Catalog (BUR)	CATLG
Catalog Access System [*Project for automated library systems*]	CATS
Catalog of the New York Public Library	CATNYP
Catalog On-Line [*National Library of Medicine*] [*Bibliographic database*]	CATLINE
Catalog of Programs (OA)	CAPR
Catalog Recovery Area [*Data processing*]	CRA
Cataloging and Indexing Number [*Later, AGRICOLA*] [*National Agricultural Library*] [*Database*]	CAIN
Cataloging Support Service [*UTLAS International*]	CATSS
Catalyst Resources for Women [*New York, NY*] [*Bibliographic database*]	CRFW
Category Code [*Online database field identifier*] (OBD)	C
Cathode	CA
Cathode	CA
Cathode-Ray Oscilloscope [*or Oscillograph*]	CRO
Cathode-Ray Tube	CRT
Cathode-Ray Tube Automatic Direction Finding (IEEE)	CADF
Cathode-Ray Tube Controller (CAA)	CRTC
Cathode-Ray Typesetting	CRT
Catholic Telecommunications Network of America [*New York, NY*] (TSSD)	CTNA
Catholic Television Network [*Cable-television system*]	CTN
Cause-Effect Graph Language [*Data processing*] (IBMDP)	CEGL
Cause of Failure [*Telecommunications*] (TEL)	COF
Cawkell Information & Technology Services, Ltd. [*Uxbridge, England*] [*Telecommunications*] (EISS)	CITECH
CB Radio Patrol (EANO)	CBRP
CCI Corp. [*NYSE symbol*] [*Delisted*]	CCI
CCITT [*Consultative Committee on International Telegraphy and Telephony*] High-Level Language [*Telecommunications*] (TEL)	CHILL
CD [*Compact Disc*] Data Report [*McClean, VA*] [*A publication*] (EISS)	CDDR
CDC 6000 Series users organization [*Abbreviation is derived from the Roman numerals for 6 and thousand*] (CAH)	VIM
Cell Simulation [*Programing language*] [*1973*] (CSR)	CELLSIM
Cellular Communications Industry Association [*Washington, DC*] [*Telecommunications*] (EANO)	CCIA
Cellular General Purpose Computer (CAA)	CGPC
Cellular Logic Image Processor [*Telecommunications*] (TEL)	CLIP
Cellular Ventures, Inc. [*Atlanta, GA*] [*Telecommunications*] (TSSD)	CV
Cement Conduit [*Telecommunications*] (TEL)	CEM
Center for Academic & Administrative Computing [*George Washington University*] [*Research center*] (RCD)	CAAC
Center for Advanced Visual Studies [*Massachusetts Institute of Technology*] [*Research center*] (RCD)	CAVS
Center for Applied Research in the Language Arts [*Texas Tech University*] [*Research center*] (RCD)	CARLA
Center for Architecture and Urban Planning Research [*University of Wisconsin - Milwaukee*] [*Research center*] (RCD)	CAUPR
Center for Automation and Intelligent Systems Research [*Case Western Reserve University*] [*Research center*] (RCD)	CAISR
Center for Automation Research [*University of Maryland*] [*Research center*] (RCD)	CfAR
Center for Business & Economics Research [*University of Nevada - Las Vegas*] [*Research center*] (RCD)	CBER
Center for Business Information [*Information service*] (EISS)	CBI
Center for Climatic and Environmental Assessment [*National Oceanic and Atmospheric Administration*] (EISS)	CCEA
Center for Composite Materials [*University of Delaware*] [*Research center*] (RCD)	CCM
Center for Computer Aided Design [*University of Iowa*] [*Research center*] (RCD)	CCAD
Center for Computer-Assisted Legal Instruction [*Minneapolis, MN*] (EANO)	CCALI
Center for Computer-Based Behavioral Studies [*University of California, Los Angeles*] [*Research center*] (RCD)	CCBS
Center for Computer/Law [*Manhattan Beach, CA*] (EANO)	CCL
Center for Computer Research in Music and Acoustics [*Pronounced "karma"*] [*Stanford University*]	CCRMA
Center for Computer Sciences and Technology [*Later, ICST*] [*National Bureau of Standards*]	CCST
Center for Computer Systems Design [*Washington University*] [*Research center*] (RCD)	CCSD
Center for Curriculum Design [*Information service*] [*Defunct*] (EISS)	CCD
Center for Cybernetic Studies [*University of Texas at Austin*] [*Research center*] (RCD)	CCS
Center for Data Systems and Analysis [*Montana State University*] [*Research center*] (RCD)	CDSA
Center for Econometrics and Decision Sciences [*University of Florida*] [*Research center*] (RCD)	CEDS
Center for Educational Experimentation, Development, and Evaluation [*University of Iowa*] [*Research center*] (RCD)	CEEDE
Center for Engineering Development and Research [*University of South Florida*] [*Research center*] (RCD)	CEDAR
Center for Engineering Systems Advanced Research [*Oak Ridge National Laboratory*]	CESAR
Center for Environmental Assessment Services [*National Oceanic and Atmospheric Administration*] [*Rochester, NY*] [*Information service*] (EISS)	CEAS
Center for Information and Numerical Data Analysis and Synthesis [*Purdue*] [*National Bureau of Standards*] [*Research center*] (MCD)	CINDAS
Center for Information Research [*Drexel University, University of Florida*] [*Research center*] (EISS)	CIR
Center for Information Technology [*Stanford University*] [*Stanford, CA*]	CIT
Center for Instructional and Research Computing Activities [*University of Florida*] [*Research center*] (RCD)	CIRCA
Center for Instructional Services [*Purdue University*] [*Research center*] (RCD)	CIS
Center for Instructional Services and Research [*Memphis State University*] [*Research center*] (RCD)	CISR
Center for Integrated Electronics [*Rensselaer Polytechnic Institute*] [*Research center*] (RCD)	CIE
Center for Integrated Systems [*Stanford University*] [*Research center*] (RCD)	CIS
Center for Intelligent Machines and Robotics [*University of Florida*] [*Research center*] (RCD)	CIMAR
Center for Interactive Computer Graphics [*Rensselaer Polytechnic Institute*] [*Research center*] (RCD)	CICG
Center for Interactive Programs [*University of Wisconsin-Extension*] [*Madison*] [*Information service*] [*Telecommunications*] (TSSD)	CIP
Center for Interdisciplinary Research in Computer-Based Learning [*University of Delaware*] [*Research center*] (RCD)	CIRCL
Center for International Financial Analysis and Research, Inc. [*Princeton, NJ*] [*Information service*] (EISS)	CIFAR
Center for Machine Intelligence [*University of Michigan, Electronic Data Systems*] [*Research center*] (RCD)	CMI
Center for Manufacturing Productivity and Technology Transfer [*Rensselaer Polytechnic Institute*] [*Research center*] (RCD)	CMP
Center for Mass Communication [*Columbia University*]	CMC
Center for Migration Studies [*City University of New York*] (EISS)	CMS
Center for Nuclear Studies [*Memphis State University*] [*Research center*] (RCD)	CNS
Center for Process Analytical Chemistry [*University of Washington*] [*Research center*] (RCD)	CPAC
Center of Programed Instruction (DIT)	CPI
Center for Research in Computing Technology [*Harvard University*] [*Research center*] (RCD)	CRCT
Center for Research [*formerly, Robotics*] in Integrated Manufacturing [*University of Michigan*] [*Research center*] (RCD)	CRIM
Center for Research on Learning and Teaching [*University of Michigan*] [*Research center*] (RCD)	CRLT
Center for Research in Scientific Communication [*Johns Hopkins University*] (EISS)	CRSC
Center for Research in Security Prices [*University of Chicago*] [*Information service*] (EISS)	CRSP
Center for Robotic Systems in Microelectronics [*University of California, Santa Barbara*] [*Research center*] (RCD)	CRSM
Center for Social Science Research and Documentation for the Arab Region [*UNESCO*] [*Information service*] (EISS)	ARCSS
Center for the Social Sciences [*Columbia University*] [*Research center*] (RCD)	CSS
Center for Solid State Electronics [*Arizona State University*] [*Research center*] (RCD)	CSSER
Center for Space Policy, Inc. [*Cambridge, MA*] [*Telecommunications*] (TSSD)	CSP
Center for Space Research [*Massachusetts Institute of Technology*] [*Research center*] (RCD)	CSR
Center for Space Research and Applications [*University of Texas at Austin*] [*Research center*] (RCD)	CSR
Center for State Employment Security Automated Systems	CSESAS
Center for the Study of Data Processing [*Washington University*] [*Research center*] (RCD)	CSDP
Center for the Study of Information and Education [*Syracuse University*] (EISS)	CSIE
Center for the Study of Language & Information [*Stanford University*] [*Research center*] (RCD)	CSLI
Center for Teaching Effectiveness [*University of Texas at Austin*] [*Research center*] (RCD)	CTE
Center for Technology and Administration [*American University*] [*Research center*] (RCD)	CTA

Computer & Telecommunications Acronyms

Center for Telecommunications Studies [*Formerly, Broadcast Research Center*] [*Ohio University*] [*Research center*] (RCD) .... CTS
Center for Telephone Information [*Laguna Hills, CA*] [*Telecommunications*] (TSSD) .... CTI
Center for UFO [*Unidentified Flying Object*] Studies [*Lima, OH*] [*Information service*] (EISS) .... CUFOS
Centi [*A prefix meaning divided by 100*] [*SI symbol*] c
Centibels [*Telecommunications*] (CDH) .... Cb
Centimeter .... cm
Centimeter-Gram-Second [*System of units*] .... CGS
Centimeters per Second [*Telecommunications*] (TEL) .... CM/SEC
Central Abstracting and Indexing Service [*American Petroleum Institute*] [*New York, NY*] [*Information service*] (EISS) .... CAIS
Central Address Memory [*Data processing*] (CGC) .... CAM
Central Air Data Computer .... CADC
Central Analog Data Distributing and Computing System (KSC) .... CADDAC
Central Battery Telephone [*Telecommunications*] .... CBT
Central Battery Telephone Apparatus [*Telecommunications*] .... CBTA
Central Battery Telephone Set [*Telecommunications*] .... CBTS
Central Bureau for Astronomical Telegrams (EANO) .... CBAT
Central Bureau of Statistics [*Netherlands*] [*Information service*] (EISS) .... CBS
Central Communications Controller (CAA) CCC
Central Computational Computer (OA) CCC
Central Computer CC
Central Computer Accounting .... CCA
Central Computer Accounting Corporation .... CCAC
Central Computer Center .... CCMPTC
Central Computer Complex CCC
Central Computer Station (OA) .... CCS
Central Computer and Telecommunications Agency [*British*] .... CCTA
Central Computer Unit .... CCU
Central Control (KSC) CC
Central Control Computer System .... CCCS
Central Control and Display Console .... CCDC
Central Control and Monitoring System [*for managing buildings' heating, ventilation, and security needs*] .... CCMS
Central Control Unit .... CCU
Central Data Bank .... CDB
Central Data Buffer [*Data processing*] (MCD) .... CDB
Central Data Collection System (AFM) .... CDCS
Central Data-Conversion Equipment .... CDCE
Central Data Display .... CDD
Central Data Management .... CDM
Central Data Processing Computer .... CDPC
Central Data Station .... CDS
Central Data Subsystem (NASA) .... CDS
Central Digital Computer .... CDC
Central Display Unit .... CDU
Central Eastern Personnel Organization [*Computerized scouting combine for professional football teams*] .... CEPO
Central Exchange .... CENTREX
Central Files .... CF
Central Information Dispatch [*Genesis Electronics Corp.*] [*Folsom, CA*] [*Telecommunications*] (TSSD) .... CINDI
Central Information File .... CIF
Central Information, Library, and Editorial Section [*CSIRO*] [*Information service*] (EISS) .... CILES
Central Information Processor (MCD) .... CIP
Central Input-Output Multiplexer [*Data processing*] (CGC) .... CIO
Central Logic Bus [*Data processing*] (CAA) .... CLB
Central Logic Control [*Data processing*] (OA) CLC
Central Logic Rack [*Telecommunications*] (TEL) .... CLR
Central Logic Unit .... CLU
Central Magnetic Tape Exchange [*Data processing*] .... CEMTEX
Central Memory [*Data processing*] (BUR) .... CM
Central Memory Access Priority [*Data processing*] (CAA) .... CMAP
Central Memory Extension [*Data processing*] (CAA) .... CME
Central Office to Central Office [*Bell System*] .... CO-CO
Central Office Equipment Estimation System [*Bell System*] .... COEES
Central Office Maintenance Management System [*Telecommunications*] (TEL) .... COMMS
Central Office Maintenance Management System - Preventive Maintenance [*Telecommunications*] (TEL) .... COMMS-PM
Central Office Signaling Panel [*Telecommunications*] (TEL) .... COSP
Central Office Terminal [*Telecommunications*] (TEL) .... COT
Central Path Method [*Data processing*] .... CPM
Central Processing Element [*Data processing*] .... CPE
Central Processing Modules [*Data processing*] (MCD) .... CPM
Central Processing Point [*Data processing*] .... CPP
Central Processing Subsystem [*Data processing*] .... CPSS
Central Processing System [*Data processing*] .... CPS
Central Processing Unit [*Data processing*] .... CPU
Central Processor [*Data processing*] (CGC) .... CP
Central Processor Memory Address (CAA) .... CPMA
Central Processor Subunit [*Data processing*] .... CPSU
Central Processor Test Console [*Data processing*] .... CPTC
Central Programer and Evaluator .... CPE
Central Pulse Distributor [*Telecommunications*] (TEL) .... CPD
Central Radio Office [*Telecommunications*] (TEL) .... CRO
Central Signal Processor .... CSP
Central Switching Center [*Telecommunications*] (TEL) .... CSC
Central Switching Facility .... CSF
Central Switching Unit .... CSU
Central Telegraph Office [*British*] .... CTO
Central Telephone Operator [*British*] .... CTO
Central Telephone Pfd [*NASDAQ symbol*] (NQ) .... CTELP
Central Telephone & Utilities Corp. [*NYSE symbol*] [*Delisted*] .... CTU
Central Terminal Signaling Interface [*Telecommunications*] (TEL) .... CTSI
Central Terminal Unit [*Telecommunications*] .... CTU
Central Traffic Control .... CTC
Central Trunk Terminals .... CTT
Central Unit-Memory .... CUM
Central Unit-Memory Programer (MCD) .... CUMP
Centralized Alarm and Control System [*Telecommunications*] (TEL) .... CACS
Centralized Attendants Service [*Bell System*] .... CAS
Centralized Automatic Loop Reporting System [*Telecommunications*] (TEL) .... CALRS
Centralized Automatic Message Accounting [*Bell System*] .... CAMA
Centralized Automatic Message Accounting - Computerized [*Bell System*] (TEL) .... CAMA-C
Centralized Automatic Message Accounting - Operator Number Identification [*Telecommunications*] (TEL) .... CAMA-ONI
Centralized Automatic Recording on Trunks [*Bell System*] .... CAROT
Centralized Automatic Toll Ticketing [*Telecommunications*] (TEL) .... CATT
Centralized Automatic Trouble-Locating and Analysis System [*AT & T*] (TEL) .... CATLAS
Centralized Branch Exchange [*Telecommunications*] (TEL) .... CBE
Centralized Data Processing (IEEE) .... CDP
Centralized Intercept Bureau [*Bell System*] .... CIB
Centralized Mail Remittance [*Telecommunications*] (TEL) .... CMR
Centralized Maintenance System [*Telecommunications*] .... CMS
Centralized Message Data System [*Bell System*] .... CMDS
Centralized Personnel Record System [*Telecommunications*] (TEL) .... CPRS
Centralized Records Business Office [*Telecommunications*] (TEL) .... CRBO
Centralized Repair Service Attendants [*Telecommunications*] (TEL) .... CRSA
Centralized Results System [*Telecommunications*] (TEL) .... CRS
Centralized Service Observation [*Telecommunications*] (TEL) .... CSO
Centralized Status, Alarm, and Control System [*Bell System*] .... CSACS
Centralized Supervisory and Control (BUR) .... CSC
Centralized Ticket Investigation [*Telecommunications*] .... CTI
Centralized Translation System [*Communications*] .... CTS
Centre d'Assistance Technique et de Documentation [*Center for Technical Assistance and Documentation*] [*Database producer*] [*France*] [*Information service*] (EISS) .... CATED
Centre Commun d'Etudes de Television et de Telecommunications [*Videotex research center*] [*French*] (DEEC) .... CCETT
Centre de Compilation de Donnees Neutroniques [*Neutron Data Compilation Center*] [*France*] [*Information service*] (EISS) .... CCDN
Centre de Documentation Internationale des Industries Utilisatrices de Produits Agricoles [*International Documentation Center for Industries Using Agricultural Products*] [*France*] [*Database producer*] [*Information service*] (EISS) .... CDIUPA
Centre de Documentation de la Mecanique [*Documentation Center for Mechanics*] [*France*] [*Information service*] (EISS) .... CDM
Centre de Documentation Sciences Humaines [*Documentation Center for Human Sciences*] [*France*] [*Information service*] (EISS) .... CDSH
Centre de Donnees Stellaires [*Stellar Data Center*] [*France*] [*Information service*] (EISS) .... CDS
Centre d'Etude des Supports Publicitaires [*Database producer*] (CUAD) .... CESP
Centre d'Etudes Prospectives et d'Informations Internationales [*Database producer*] (CUAD) .... CEPII
Centre Francais de la Couleur [*Online service*] (CUAD) .... CFC
Centre for Industrial Control [*Concordia University*] [*Canada*] [*Research center*] (RCD) CIC
Centre d'Information Spectroscopique et Physico-Chimique d'Analyse [*Information Center for Spectroscopic and Physicochemical Analysis*] [*France*] [*Information service*] (EISS) .... CIS
Centre d'Information en Temps Reel pour l'Europe [*European Center for Information in Real Time*] [*France*] [*Information service*] (EISS) .... CITERE
Centre d'Informatique et Documentation Automatique [*Center for Automated Information and Documentation*] [*France*] [*Information service*] (EISS) .... CIDA
Centre International de Documentation Parlementaire [*International Center for Parliamentary Documentation*] [*Switzerland*] [*Information service*] (EISS) .... CIDP
Centre International d'Informations de Securite et d'Hygiene du Travail [*International Occupational Safety and Health Information Center*] (EISS) .... CIS
Centre for Library and Information Management [*Loughborough University of Technology*] [*British*] [*Information service*] (EISS) .... CLAIM
Centre National de Documentation [*National Documentation Center*] [*Morocco*] [*Information service*] (EISS) .... CND
Centre National de Documentation Scientifique et Technique [*National Scientific and Technical Documentation Center*] [*Senegal*] [*Information service*] (EISS) .... CNDST

Computer & Telecommunications Acronyms

Centre National de l'Information Chimique de France [*National Center for Chemical Information of France*] [*Information service*] (EISS) .... CNIC
Centre National de Prevention et de Traitement des Intoxications [*National Poison Control Center*] [*Information service*] (EISS) .... CNPTI
Centre National de la Recherche Scientifique [*Database producer*] (CUAD) .... CNRS
Centre for Offshore and Remote Medicine [*Memorial University of Newfoundland*] [*Research center*] (RCD) .... MEDICOR
Centre de Preparation Documentaire a la Traduction [*Center for Translation Documentation*] [*France*] [*Information service*] (EISS) .... CPDT
Centre de Recherches sur les Communications [*Sherbrooke University*] [*Canada*] [*Research center*] (RCD) .... CRCS
Centre de Recherches et de Documentation des Institutions Chretiennes [*Christian Institutions Research and Documentation Center*] [*France*] [*Information service*] (EISS) ...... CERDIC
Centre for Research in Librarianship [*University of Toronto*] [*Research center*] (RCD) .... CRL
Centre Technique des Industries de la Fonderie [*Database producer*] (CUAD) .... CTIF
Centre Technique des Industries Mecaniques [*Database producer*] (CUAD) .... CETIM
Centrex [*Bell System*] .... CTX
Centrex Central Office [*Telecommunications*] (TEL) .... CTXCO
Centrex Customer [*Telecommunications*] (TEL) .... CTXCU
Centrex System Number [*Telecommunications*] (TEL) .... CTX
Centro Argentino de Informacion Cientifica y Tecnologica [*Argentine Center for Scientific and Technological Information*] [*Information service*] (EISS) .... CAICYT
Centro de Calculo Electronico Universidad Nacional Autonoma de Mexico [*National Autonomous University of Mexico, Data Processing Center*] [*Villa Obregon, Mexico*] .... CCE
Centro de Documentacao Cientifica e Tecnica [*Scientific and Technical Documentation Center*] [*Portugal*] [*Information service*] (EISS) .... CDCT
Centro de Informacion Cientifica/Humanistica [*Center for Scientific and Humanistic Information*] [*Mexico*] [*Information service*] (EISS) .... CICH
Centro de Informacoes Nucleares [*Center for Nuclear Information*] [*Brazil*] [*Information service*] (EISS) .... CIN
Centro Latinoamericano de Documentacion Economica y Social [*Latin American Center for Economic and Social Documentation*] [*United Nations*] [*Information service*] (EISS) .... CLADES
Centro Nacional de Desenvolvimento Micrografico [*National Center for Micrographic Development*] [*Brazil*] [*Information service*] (EISS) .... CENADEM
Centro Nacional de Informacion y Documentacion en Salud [*National Center for Health Information and Documentation*] [*Mexico*] [*Information service*] (EISS) .... CENIDS
Centro di Riferimento Italiano DIANE [*Italian Reference Center for EURONET DIANE*] [*Information service*] (EISS) .... CRID
Centronics Data Computer Corp. [*NYSE symbol*] .... CEN
Centrum voor Informatie Beleid [*Netherlands Center for Information Policy*] [*Information service*] (EISS) .... CIB
Century Analysis, Incorporated [*Pacheco, CA*] [*Software manufacturer*] (DASOS) .... CAI
Ceramic-Based Microcircuit .... CBM
Ceramic Dual In-Line Package (DEEC) .... CER-DIP
Cermetek Microelectronics [*NASDAQ symbol*] (NQ) .... CRMK
Certificate in Computer Programing [*Designation awarded by Institute for the Certification of Computer Professionals*] .... CCP
Certificate in Data Education (BUR) .... CDE
Certificate in Data Processing [*Designation awarded by Institute for Certification of Computer Professionals*] .... CDP
Certron Corp. [*American Stock Exchange symbol*] [*Delisted*] .... CT
CGA Computer Association [*NASDAQ symbol*] (NQ) .... CGAC
Chained File Management System [*IBM Corp.*] .... CFMS
Chalk River Nuclear Laboratories [*Atomic Energy of Canada Ltd.*] [*Information service*] [*Research center*] (EISS) .... CRNL
Chameleon Micro Implementation Language [*1978*] [*Data processing*] (CSR) .... CHAMIL
Chancellor Computer [*NASDAQ symbol*] (NQ) .... CHCC
Change .... CH
Change [*Telecommunications*] (TEL) .... CHN
Change [*or Changing*] to Frequency [*Followed by number*] [*Communications*] (FAAC) .... CF
Change Management/Tracking [*IBM Corp.*] .... CM/T
Change of Subscribers [*Telecommunications*] (TEL) .... COS
Changed Number Interception [*Telecommunications*] (TEL) .... CNI
Chanin Consulting Services, Inc. [*New York, NY*] [*Software manufacturer*] (DASOS) .... CCS
Channel .... CH
Channel [*Data processing*] .... CHAN
Channel [*Electrical transmission*] (AFM) .... CHNL
Channel Adapter [*Data processing*] (IBMDP) .... CA
Channel Address Register [*Data processing*] (CGC) .... CAR
Channel Address Word [*Data processing*] (CGC) .... CAW
Channel Allocation and Routing Data (IEEE) .... CARD
Channel to Channel (CAA) .... CTC
Channel-to-Channel Adapter (CAA) .... CCA
Channel-to-Channel Adapter [*Data processing*] (IBMDP) .... CTCA
Channel-Check Handler [*Japanese*] (MCD) .... CCH
Channel Command [*or Control*] Word [*Data processing*] (CGC) .... CCW
Channel Continuity Check Transmission [*Communications*] (FAAC) .... CHC
Channel Control (BUR) .... CHC
Channel Control Unit (CMD) .... CCU
Channel Control Unit (CAA) .... CHCU
Channel Data Check (OA) .... CDK
Channel End (BUR) .... CHE
Channel Evaluation and Call (IEEE) .... CHEC
Channel Extension Unit (CAA) .... CEU
Channel Flow Control (CAA) .... CFC
Channel Indirect Data Addressing (IBMDP) .... CIDA
Channel Interface (CAA) .... CHIF
Channel and Isolation Supervision [*Telecommunications*] (TEL) .... CIS
Channel Multiplier Array .... CMA
Channel Processor (CAA) .... CHP
Channel Program Block [*Data processing*] .... CPB
Channel Program Commands (OA) .... CPC
Channel Service Unit [*Telecommunications*] (TEL) .... CSU
Channel Status Indicator [*Data processing*] (MDG) .... CST
Channel Status Word [*Data processing*] (BUR) .... CSW
Channel Synchronizer Unit [*Data processing*] (TUT) .... CSU
Channel Translating Equipment [*Telecommunications*] (TEL) .... CTE
Channel Verification Signal Generator .... CVSG
Character (BUR) C
Character [*Data processing*] (BUR) .... CH
Character (KSC) .... CHAR
Character (BUR) .... CHR
Character Assemble/Disassemble (CAA) .... CAD
Character Control Block [*Data processing*] (IBMDP) .... CCB
Character Error Rate Test (CAA) .... CERT
Character Generator [*Telecommunications*] .... CG
Character Instruction Set (IEEE) .... CIS
Character Manipulation Procedures (CAH) .... CHAMP
Character Mode Communications Adapter (CAA) .... CMCA
Character Multiplexer [*Telecommunications*] (CAA) .... CMX
Character and Pattern Telephone Access Information Network [*Viewdata system*] [*Japan*] [*Telecommunications*] (TEL) .... CAPTAIN
Character Printer [*Data processing*] .... CP
Character Scan or Alternate [*Data processing*] (CIT) .... CSA
Character Scan Command [*Data processing*] .... CSCN
Character Scan or Fail [*Data processing*] (CIT) .... CSF
Character Set Computer Development .... CSCD
Character Start-Stop (CAA) .... CSS
Character String Scanner [*Computer program*] .... CSS
Characteristic Distortion Compensation [*Telecommunications*] (TEL) .... CDC
Characteristic Independence (CGC) CI
Characters per Hour [*Data processing*] .... CPH
Characters per Inch [*Data processing*] (CMD) .... CHPI
Characters per Inch [*Typesetting*] .... CPI
Characters per Minute [*Data processing*] .... CPM
Characters per Second [*Data processing*] (CMD) .... CHPS
Characters per Second [*Data processing*] (CGC) .... CPS
Charge-Coupled Device [*Data storage device*] .... CCD
Charge-Injection Device [*Electronics*] .... CID
Charge Priming Device .... CPD
Charge-Transfer Device [*Electronics*] .... CTD
Charge Transforming Operator (IEEE) .... CTO
Charge Transforming Parameter (IEEE) .... CTP
Charles Babbage Institute for the History of Information Processing [*University of Minnesota*] [*Research center*] (EANO) .... CBI
Charles River Associates, Inc. [*Boston, MA*] [*Telecommunications*] (TSSD) .... CRA
Chart Maker [*Computer Design*] [*Software package*] [*British*] (NCC) .... CM
Chase Econometrics Associates, Incorporated [*Cynwyd, PA*] [*Information service*] (EISS) .... CEAI
Chase Econometrics/Interactive Data Corporation .... CE/IDC
Chase World Information Corporation [*Information service*] (EISS) .... CWIC
Check (KSC) .... CHK
Check Authorization Record (IBMDP) .... CAR
Check Digit Verification (CMD) .... CDV
Check Not OK [*Telecommunications*] (TEL) .... CN
Check OK [*Telecommunications*] (TEL) .... CO
Check Operator (DEN) .... CKO
Check Processing Control System [*IBM Corp.*] (BUR) .... CPCS
Check Register Against Bounds [*Data processing*] .... CHK
Check Signal Unit [*Telecommunications*] (TEL) .... CSU
Checkout-Oriented Language [*Data processing*] (IEEE) .... COOL
Checkout Test Language [*Data processing*] (TUT) .... CTL
Checkpoint [*Data processing*] (BUR) .... CHKPT
CHEM Singly Indexed Substances [*DIALOG Information Services, Inc.*] [*Database*] (CUAD) .... CHEMSIS
Chemical Abstracts [*Chemical Abstracts Service*] [*Database*] [*A publication*] .... CA
Chemical Abstracts Condensates [*A publication*] (EISS) .... CAC
Chemical Abstracts Condensates [*Database*] (CAA) .... CACON
Chemical Abstracts Integrated Subject File [*Chemical Abstracts Service*] [*Database*] [*A publication*] (EISS) .... CAISF
Chemical Abstracts Service [*Database producer*] .... CAS
Chemical Abstracts Service Source Index [*Online database*] .... CASSI
Chemical Abstracts Subject Index Alert [*Database*] [*A publication*] ...... CASIA

Chemical Age Project File [*Pergamon InfoLine Inc.*] [*Database*] (CUAD) ... CAPF
Chemical Automated Search Terminal [*Computer Corp. of America*] [*Information service*] (EISS) ... CAST
Chemical-Biological Computer System ... CBCS
Chemical Business NewsBase [*Database*] ... CBNB
Chemical Carcinogenous Research Information System [*SRI International*] [*Database*] (FDB) ... CCRIS
Chemical Data Center, Inc. [*Columbus, OH*] [*Information service*] (EISS) ... CDC
Chemical Dictionary On-Line [*National Library of Medicine*] [*Bethesda, MD*] [*Database*] ... CHEMLINE
Chemical Economics Handbook [*SRI International*] [*Database*] ... CEH
Chemical Effects Information Center [*Oak Ridge, TN*] [*Department of Energy*] (EISS) ... CEIC
Chemical Engineering Abstracts [*Royal Society of Chemistry*] [*Bibliographic database*] [*British*] (OBD) ... CEA
Chemical Engineering Investigation of Reaction Paths [*Data processing*] ... CHIRP
Chemical Evaluation Search and Retrieval System [*Database*] [*Michigan Department of Natural Resources*] (FDB) ... CESARS
Chemical Index [*Database*] (CAA) ... CHEMDEX
Chemical Industry Notes [*Chemical Abstracts Service*] [*Bibliographic database*] [*A publication*] ... CIN
Chemical Information Management, Incorporated [*Information service*] (EISS) ... CIMI
Chemical Information Services [*Stanford Research Institute*] (EISS) ... CIS
Chemical Information System [*Computer Sciences Corp.*] [*Falls Church, VA*] ... CIS
Chemical Information Systems Operators [*Later, EUSIDIC*] (IDA) ... CHEOPS
Chemical Modeling Laboratory ... CHEMLAB
Chemical Monograph Referral Center [*Consumer Product Safety Commission*] [*Information service*] (EISS) ... CHEMRIC
Chemical Name Dictionary [*Dialog Information Services, Inc.*] [*Database*] ... CHEMNAME
Chemical On-Line Data Analyzer [*Interactive Elements, Inc.*] ... CODA
Chemical Reactions Documentation Service [*Derwent Publications Ltd.*] [*Bibliographic database*] [*England*] (EISS) ... CRDS
Chemical Regulations and Guidelines System [*CRC Systems, Inc.*] [*Fairfax, VA*] [*Information service*] (EISS) ... CRGS
Chemical Substances Information Network [*Federal Interagency Toxic Substances Data Committee*] [*Information service*] ... CSIN
Chemistry Records and Grading System [*Data processing*] ... CRAGS
Cherry Electronic Products Corp. [*NASDAQ symbol*] (NQ) ... CHER
Chesapeake Information Retrieval Service [*Edgewater, MD*] (EISS) ... CIRS
Chicago Area Computer Hobbyist Exchange ... CACHE
Chief Testboard Man [*Telecommunications*] (TEL) ... CTBM
Chinese Linguistics Bibliography on Computer [*Cambridge University Press*] [*England*] ... CLIBOC
Chip Enable [*Input*] [*Data processing*] ... CE
Chip Enable Output [*Data processing*] ... CEO
Chip Hermeticity in Plastic [*Electronics*] (MDG) ... CHIP
Chip Select [*Input*] [*Data processing*] ... CS
Chopp Computer Corp. [*Vancouver Stock Exchange symbol*] ... CRP
Christian Broadcasting Network [*Cable-television system*] ... CBN
Christian Computer Users [*Christian Ministries Management Association*] [*Diamond Bur, CA*] (EANO) ... CCU
Christiane Fabre de Morlhon [*In information service name CFM Documentazione*] [*Information service*] (EISS) ... CFM
Chromatogram Automatic Soaking Scanning and Digital Recording Apparatus ... CASSANDRA
Chromatography Laboratory Automatic Software ... CLAS
Chrysler Improved Numerical Differencing Analyzer [*Data processing*] ... CINDA
Chrysler Improved Numerical Differencing Analyzer for Third-Generation Computers [*Data processing*] ... CINDA-3G
Cincinnati Uplink, Incorporated [*Cincinnati, OH*] [*Telecommunications*] (TSSD) ... CUI
Cinema Television Digest ... CTVD
Cipher Data Products [*NASDAQ symbol*] (NQ) ... CIFR
Cipher Feedback (CAA) ... CFB
Cipher Text Auto Key [*Data processing*] ... CTAK
Ciprico, Incorporated [*NASDAQ symbol*] (NQ) ... CPCI
CIPS [*Canadian Information Processing Society*] **Review** [*A publication*] ... CIPS Rev
CIRC [*Central Information Reference and Control*] **Online Experiment** ... COLEX
Circuit ... CKT
Circuit ... CT
Circuit Access Point [*Telecommunications*] (TEL) ... CAP
Circuit Analysis [*Data processing*] ... CIRCAL
Circuit Board Card Tester ... CBCT
Circuit Board Extractor ... CBE
Circuit Board Holder ... CBH
Circuit Closing ... CC
Circuit Concentration Bay (IEEE) ... CCB
Circuit Control ... C/C
Circuit Control Office [*Automatic Digital Information Network*] (CET) ... CCO
Circuit Description (MSA) ... CD
Circuit Design, Fabrication, and Test Data Systems (NASA) ... CDF & TDS
Circuit Group [*Telecommunications*] (TEL) ... CGRP
Circuit Group Congestion [*Telecommunications*] (TEL) ... CGC
Circuit Identification [*Telecommunications*] (TEL) ... CKT-ID
Circuit Layout [*AT & T*] ... CL
Circuit Layout Record Card [*Telecommunications*] (TEL) ... CLRC
Circuit Maintenance System [*AT & T*] ... CMS
Circuit Modeller [*Seasim Engineering Software Ltd.*] [*Software package*] [*British*] (NCC) ... CM
Circuit Modeller Plus [*Seasim Engineering Software Ltd.*] [*Software package*] [*British*] (NCC) ... CMP
Circuit Order Layout Record [*Telecommunications*] (TEL) ... COLR
Circuit Order Preparation [*or Processing*] **System** [*AT & T*] ... COPS
Circuit Provision System [*AT & T*] ... CPS
Circuit Quality Monitoring System ... CQMS
Circuit Switched Data (CAA) ... CSD
Circuit Switched Digital Capability [*AT & T*] ... CSDC
Circuit Switched Voice [*Telecommunications*] (CAA) ... CSV
Circuit Switching Center [*Telecommunications*] (TEL) ... CSC
Circuit Switching Network ... CSN
Circuit Switching Station (CET) ... CSS
Circuit Switching Unit (CET) ... CSU
Circuit Terminating Arrangement ... CTA
Circuit under Test (IEEE) ... CUT
Circuit Test Set ... CTS
Circuits Manufacturing [*A publication*] ... Circuits Manuf
Circuits Manufacturing [*A publication*] ... Circuits Mfg
Circuits, Systems, and Signal Processing [*A publication*] ... CSSP
Circular Mils, Thousands ... MCM
Circular Radio Beacon ... RC
Circular Sequential Access Memory (CAA) ... CSAM
Circulation Input Recording Center [*Data processing system*] ... CIRC
Circulation Library Automated System for Inventory Control [*Cincinnati Electronics Corp.*] [*Information service*] (EISS) ... CLASSIC
Cited Reference [*Online database field identifier*] (OBD) ... CR
Citibank Economic Database [*Citibank, NA*] [*New York, NY*] [*Information service*] (EISS) ... CITIBASE
Citizens Band [*A radio frequency band for limited-range, two-way voice communications by persons without technical training or standard operator licenses*] ... CB
Citizens Band Operating Area ... CBOA
Civic Information & Techniques Exchange [*Citizens Forum on Self-Government/National Municipal League*] [*New York, NY*] [*Information service*] (EISS) ... CIVITEX
CL & CL. Computational Linguistics and Computer Languages [*Budapest*] [*A publication*] ... CL & CL Comput Linguist Comput Lang
Claritas Corporation [*Alexandria, VA*] [*Information service*] (EISS) ... CLC
Class Marks [*Telecommunications*] (TEL) ... CM
Class-Oriented Ring-Associative Language [*Data processing*] ... CORAL
Class of Service [*Telecommunications*] (TEL) ... COS
Class of Service [*Telecommunications*] (TEL) ... CS
Classification Code [*IRS*] [*Online database field identifier*] ... CC
Classification and Search Support Information System [*Patent and Trademark Office*] [*Information service*] ... CASSIS
Classroom-Aided Dynamic Educational Time-Sharing System (IEEE) ... CADETS
Clear [*Calculators*] ... C
Clear (KSC) ... CLR
Clear Back [*Telecommunications*] (TEL) ... CB
Clear Both [*Data processing*] ... CLB
Clear Forward [*Telecommunications*] (TEL) ... CLF
Clear Language for Expressing Orders [*Data processing*] (IEEE) ... CLEO
Clear Record [*Telecommunications*] (TEL) ... CR
Clear to Send ... CTS
Clear to Send/Request to Send (OA) ... CTSRTS
Clear and Subtract (IEEE) ... CLS
Clear and Subtract ... CS
Clear to Zero [*Data processing*] ... CLR
Clearance (FAAC) ... CLR
Clearing House Accession Number [*Online database field identifier*] (OBD) ... CHAN
Clearing House Interbank Payment System (BUR) ... CHIPS
Clearinghouse for Occupational Safety and Health Information [*Cincinnati, OH*] [*HEW*] (EISS) ... COSHI
Clerk (AFM) ... CLK
Client-Oriented Data Acquisition Process [*FDA*] ... CODAP
Climate Assessment Data Base [*National Meteorological Center*] [*Database*] (FDB) ... CADB
Clinical Cancer Protocols [*National Library of Medicine*] [*Database*] ... CLINPROT
Clinical Laboratory Data Acquisition System [*Data processing*] ... CLDAS
Clinical Laboratory Management System [*Data processing*] ... CLMS
Clinical Toxicology of Commercial Products [*Dartmouth Medical School; University of Rochester*] [*Database*] [*A publication*] ... CTCP
Clock ... CLK
Clock Pulse ... CP
Clock Pulse Generator ... CPG
Clock Pulsed Control ... CPC
Clockwise ... CW
Close [*Data processing*] (BUR) ... CLS
Close Type Control Circuit Contact (MSA) ... CTCCC
Closed Captioning ... CC
Closed-Circuit Radio (DDI) ... CCR
Closed-Circuit Television ... CCTV
Closed Flux Memory [*Data processing*] ... CFM
Closed Loop Accounting for Stores Sales (IEEE) ... CLASS

Computer & Telecommunications Acronyms

Closed-Loop Bandwidth .... CLBW
Closed-Loop Television   (VIT) .... CLTV
Closed User Group [Communications] .... CUG
Cloud Nine [Manufacturer of remote control devices for home
 electronics] [Company founded by Stephen Wozniak] CL9
Cluster [Programing language] [1973]   (CSR) .... CLU
CMC International [NASDAQ symbol]   (NQ) .... CMCI
Coal Research Projects [IEA Coal Research] [Database]   (CUAD) .... COALPRO
Coalition Opposed to Signal Theft   (EANO) .... COST
Coarse-Fine/Pulse Code Modulator   (DDI) .... C F/PCM
Coastal Harbor [Telecommunications]   (TEL) .... CH
Coastal Telegraph Station [ITU designation]   (CET) .... CT
Coastal Zone Color Scanner .... CZCS
Coaxial .... CA
Coaxial .... COAX
Coaxial Adapter Waveguide .... CAWG
Coaxial Single-Pole Relay .... CSR
Cobalt Information Center [Battelle Memorial Institute]
 [Information service]   (EISS) CIC
COBOL [Common Business-Oriented Language] Automatic
 Language Modifier [Data processing]   (TUT) .... CALM
COBOL-to-COBOL Translator   (IEEE) .... COTRAN
COBOL [Common Business-Oriented Language] Compiler
 Validation System [Data processing] .... CCVS
COBOL [Common Business-Oriented Language] Conversion [Data
 processing]   (MCD) .... COCO
COBOL [Common Business-Oriented Language] Element Subtype
 [Data processing] .... COB
COBOL [Common Business-Oriented Language] Instrumentation
 Package [Data processing] .... CIP
COBOL [Common Business-Oriented Language] Library [Data
 processing]   (MCD) .... COBLIB
COBOL Shared Access Method [Pertec]   (CAA) .... COSAM
COBOL Virtual Machine   (CAA) .... CVM
Cockpit Television Sensor   (MCD) .... CTV
CODAP [Control Data Assembly Program] Language Block-
 Oriented Compiler   (MCD) .... COBLOC
CODATA [Committee on Data for Science and Technology] Bulletin
 [A publication] .... CODATA Bull
CODATA [Committee on Data for Science and Technology]
 Newsletter [France] [A publication] .... CODATA Newsl
Code Actuated Random Load Apparatus   (MCD) .... CARLA
Code Control   (AFM) CC
Code Directing Character [Data processing] .... CDC
Code Division Multiple Access .... CDMA
Code to Handle Angular Data   (IEEE) .... CHAD
Code for Magnetic Characters   (IEEE) .... CMC
Code Mark Inversion [Telecommunications]   (TEL) .... CMI
Code of Practice [Telecommunications]   (TEL) .... COP
Code Segment [Data processing] .... CS
Code Segment:Instruction Pointer [Data processing] ...... CS:IP
Code Segment Table   (CAA) .... CST
Code Selection Language [Data processing]   (BUR) ...... CSL
Code Table Buffer   (CAA) .... CTB
Code Telegram .... CT
Code Universel de Produit [Universal Product Code] [Canada] ...... CUP
Code and Visual Entry Authorization Technique [Closed-circuit
 TV]   (MCD) .... CAVEAT
Coded Address Private Radio Intercommunications .... CAPRI
Coded Automatic Reading Device .... CARD
Coded Division Multiplex .... CDM
Coded Optical Character [Data processing]   (BUR) .... COC
Coden [Online database field identifier]   (OBD) .... CD
Coden [Online database field identifier]   (OBD) .... CO
Codenoll Technology [NASDAQ symbol]   (NQ) .... CODN
Coder-Decoder   (MCD) .... CODEC
Coder and Random Access Switch .... CRAS
Coder Sequential Pulse .... CSP
Coding Specification   (CAH) .... CS
Cognitive Science Society   (EANO) .... CSS
Coherent Frequency Shift Keying .... CFSK
Coherent Microwave Memory .... CMM
Coherent Phase Shift Keyed [System] [Data processing] .. CPSK
Coherent Processing Interval [Data processing] .... CPI
Coherent Signal Processor .... CSP
Coin Box [Telecommunications]   (TEL) .... CB
Coin Box Telephone [Telecommunications] .... CBT
Coin Collect [Telecommunications]   (TEL) CC
Coin Collecting Box, Pay Station [Telecommunications]   (TEL) .. CX
Coin Completing [Telecommunications]   (TEL) CC
Coin and Fee Checking [Telecommunications]   (TEL) .... CFC
Coin Level Indicator [Telephone communications] CLI
Coin Phone Operational and Information Network System
 [Telecommunications]   (TEL) .... COIN
Coin Trunk [Telecommunications]   (TEL) .... CN
Coinbox Line [Telecommunications]   (TEL) .... CO
Coinbox Set [Telecommunications]   (TEL) CX
Cold Start Entry [Data processing] .... CSE
Collation [Online database field identifier]   (OBD) .... CLLT
Collation [Online database field identifier]   (OBD) .... CO
Collator .... COLL
Collect Call [Telecommunications]   (TEL) CC

Collected Algorithm for Learning Machines [Data processing] .. CALM
Collective Call Sign [Radio] .... CCS
Collector [Electronics] C
College Applicant Status Report [Honeywell, Inc.] [Data
 processing]   (CDH) .... CASTOR
[The] College Board [Information service]   (EISS) .... TCB
College Selection Service [Peterson's Guides] [Princeton, NJ]
 [Information service]   (EISS) .... CSS
College and University Machine Records Conference   (EANO) .. CUMREC
College and University Systems Exchange [Acronym is now used
 as name of association] .... CAUSE
Color Computer .... COCO
Color Data Display .... CDD
Color Difference Computer   (MUGU) .... CODIC
Color Electronic Prepress Systems [Printing technology] .. CEPS
Color/Graphics Monitor Adapter [Computer technology] .. CGA
Color Graphics Printer   (CAA) .... CGP
Color Infrared [Image] .... CIR
Color Television   (DEN) .... CTV
Colorado Technical Reference Center [University of Colorado -
 Boulder] [Information service]   (EISS) .... CTRC
Colorado Video, Incorporated CVI
Colorant Mixture Computer [Du Pont trademark] .... COMIC
Columbia Broadcasting System [Later, CBS, Inc.] .... CBS
Column .... COL
Column-Address Strobe   (IEEE) .... CAS
Column-Digit Binary Network .... CDBN
Comac Condition Base Monitor Module [Comac Systems PLC.]
 [Software package] [British]   (NCC) .... CCBMM
Combined Amplitude Phase Shift Keying   (MCD) .... CAPSK
Combined Analog-Digital Systems Simulator [Data processing]
 (CGC) .... CADSS
Combined Antenna System   (CAAL) .... CAS
Combined Engineering Plant Exchange Record
 [Telecommunications]   (TEL) .... CEPER
Combined File Search [IBM program] [Data processing] .. CFS
Combined File Search Strategy [Data processing] .... CFSS
Combined Line and Recording [Telecommunications]   (TEL) .. CLR
Combined Master File [Data processing] .... CMF
Combined Programing Language [Data processing] ...... CPL
Combined Receiving and Transmitting Unit .... CRTU
Combined Retrospective Index Sets [Carrollton Press, Inc.]
 [Information service]   (EISS) .... CRIS
Combined System Test Stand   (IEEE) .... CSTS
Combined VHF [Very-High-Frequency]-Band .... CVB
Comite Consultatif International des Radiocommunications
 [International Radio Consultative Committee] [Switzerland] .. CCIR
Comite Consultatif International Telegraphique et Telephonique
 [Consultative Committee on International Telegraphy and
 Telephony] [Geneva, Switzerland] .... CCITT
Comite Consultatif International Telephonique des Frequences
 [International Telephone Consultative Committee]   (NATG) .. CCIF
Comite de Coordination des Telecommunications [Coordinating
 Committee for Communications] [NATO]   (NATG) ...... CCT
Comite Europeen de Coordination des Normes [European
 Committee for Coordination of Standards] .... CEN
Comite Europeen de Coordination des Normes Electriques
 [European Electrical Standards Coordinating Committee] .. CENEL
Comite International Radio Maritime [International Maritime Radio
 Committee] .... CIRM
Comite International Special des Perturbations Radioelectriques
 [International Special Committee on Radio Interference] .. CISPR
Comite International des Telecommunications de Presse
 [International Press Telecommunications - IPTC] .... CIPT
Comite des Normes Gouvernementales en Informatique
 [Government Electronic Data Processing Standards
 Committee] [Canada] .... CNGI
Comite des Travaux Historiques et Scientifiques [Ministere de
 l'Education Nationale] [Database]   (CUAD) .... CTHS
Command .... CMD
Command   (IBMDP) .... CMND
Command Access Keys   (OA) .... CAK
Command Acknowledge   (BUR) .... CAK
Command Analysis [Telecommunications]   (TEL) .... CANAL
Command Arithmetic Unit .... CAU
Command Automated Procurement System   (MCD) ...... CAPS
Command Communications Service Designator   (CET) .. CCSD
Command Computer CC
Command Computer Console   (CIT) .... CMDCC
Command Computer Input Multiplexer   (MCD) .... CCIM
Command and Control [Pronounced "see-squared"] ...... C^2
Command and Control   (CGC) .... C & C
Command Control Block [Data processing]   (BUR) .... CCB
Command, Control, and Communications [Pronounced "see-cubed"] .. C^3
Command, Control, Communications, and Computer Systems   (NVT) .. C^4
Command, Control, Communications, Computing/Information
 and Intelligence .... C^4I^2
Command, Control, Communications, and Intelligence
 [Telecommunications]   (TEL) CCCI
Command, Control, and Subordinate Systems
 [Telecommunications]   (TEL) .... CCS^2
Command Data Acquisition   (MSA) .... CDA
Command and Data Handling   (DEN) .... CDH

Computer & Telecommunications Acronyms

Command and Data-Handling Console (CIT) .... CDC
Command and Data-Handling Console (KSC) .... CDHC
Command Data Management Routine [Data processing] .... CDMR
Command Data Management System (NASA) .... CDMS
Command Data Processing Interface Equipment .... CDPIE
Command Data Processor (CIT) .... CDP
Command and Decision Sensor Interface Data System (MCD) .... CDSIDS
Command Decoder Coaxial (MCD) .... CDC
Command Display and Control Processor .... CDCP
Command Display Indicator (MCD) .... CDI
Command and Edit Program [Burroughs Corp.] [Data processing] (BUR) .... CANDE
Command Guidance Computer (NASA) .... CGC
Command Input Block [Data processing] .... CIB
Command Input Buffer [Data processing] (IBMDP) .... CIB
Command Interface Test (KSC) .... CIT
Command Language (CAA) CL
Command Language Interpreter [Data processing] (OA) CLI
Command Language for Interrogating Computers [Royal Radar Establishment] [British] CLIC
Command Language Processor .... CLP
Command Line Interface [For Amiga computers] CLI
Command Load Acceptance Message (SKY) .... CLAM
Command Load Controller (SKY) CLC
Command Logic Unit (MCD) .... CLU
Command Manpower Data System .... CMDS
Command Output .... CO
Command Processor [Data processing] (BUR) .... CP
Command Read Pulse (KSC) .... CRP
Command Register .... CR
Command Retrieval Information System .... CRIS
Command Scheduling Control Block [Data processing] (BUR) ..... CSCB
Command String Interpreter [Digital Equipment Corp.] (CAA) ... CSI
Command and Telemetry Data Handling (IEEE) .... CTDH
Command Translator and Programer .... CTP
Command Transmitter (KSC) .... C/T
Command Word [Data processing] (MCD) .... CW
Commerce Business Daily [Department of Commerce] [Database] [A publication] .... CBD
Commerce Clearing House [NASDAQ symbol] (NQ) .... CCLR
Commercial BASIC (CAA) .... C-BASIC
Commercial Communications Satellite [Japan] (CBSS) ..... CCS
Commercial Data Processing Center (IEEE) .... CDPC
Commercial Instruction Processor [Honeywell, Inc.] (CAA) ..... CIP
Commercial Instruction Set (CAA) .... CIS
Commercial Satellite Communications System .... COMSATCOM
Commercial Satellite Systems [Berkeley, CA] [Telecommunications] (TSSD) .... CSS
Commercial Service Authorization [Telecommunications] (TEL) ...... CSA
Commercial Subroutine Package [IBM Corp.] (BUR) .... CSP
Commercial Synchronous Communication Satellite (NASA) .... CSCSAT
Commercial System [Data General Corp.] (CAA) .... CS
Commercial Telegraphers' Union [Later, UTW] .... CTU
Commercial Television .... CTV
Commercial Translator (IEEE) .... CT
Commercial Wire Center Forecast Program [Telecommunications] (TEL) .... COMFOR
Commercially Available Organic Chemicals Index [Chemical Notation Association] [Databank] [British] .... CAOCI
Commissie voor Bibliografie en Documentatie [Netherlands Bibliographical and Documentary Committee] [Information service] (EISS) .... COBIDOC
Commission Electrotechnique Internationale [International Electrotechnical Commission] [See also IEC] .... CEI
Commission Mixte Internationale pour les Experiences Relatives a la Protection des Lignes de Telecommunication et des Canalisations Souterraines .... CMI
Commission on Software Issues in the 80s (EANO) .... COSIE
Committee on Data Interchange and Data Centers .... CDIDC
Committee of Inquiry into Technological Change in Australia (CAA) .... CITCA
Committee on Office Systems and Technology [Stanford University] [Stanford, CA] .... COST
Committee on Scientific and Technical Information [Defunct] [Federal Council for Science and Technology] .... COSATI
Committee on Scientific and Technical Information [Defunct] [Federal Council for Science and Technology] (IEEE) ..... CSTI
Committee on Statistics of Drilling [American Association of Petroleum Geologists] (EISS) .... CSD
Committee on Storage, Automatic Processing, and Retrieval of Geological Data [International Union of Geological Sciences] [Information service] (EISS) .... COGEODATA
Commodities Data Information Service [MJK Associates] [Information service] (EISS) .... CDIS
Commodities Research Unit Ltd. [Originator and Databank] [Information service] [British] (EISS) .... CRU
Commodity Data Information System [MJK Associates] [Database] (CUAD) .... CDIS
Commodity Information Services Company (EISS) .... CISCO
Commodity News Services, Inc. [Information service] (EISS) .... CNS
Commodity Options [I. P. Sharp Associates] [Database] (CUAD) .... COMPTIONS
Commodity-Oriented Digital Label Input System .... CODILS

Commodity Systems, Incorporated [Information service] (EISS) .... CSI
Commodore Corporation [American Stock Exchange symbol] .... CCT
Commodore Information Network [Commodore Business Machines] [West Chester, PA] [Telecommunications] (TSSD) ..... CIN
Common Access Security Terminal .... CAST
Common Aerial Working [Telecommunications] (TEL) ..... CAW
Common Base [Data processing] (MSA) .... CB
Common Battery [Electronics; technical drawings] ...... CB
Common Battery Signaling [Telecommunications] (TEL) ... CBS
Common Business-Oriented Language [1959] [Data processing] ...... COBOL
Common Carrier CC
Common Carrier Bureau [of FCC] .... CCB
Common Carrier Special Application (CAH) .... CCSA
Common Channel Interoffice Signaling [System] [Bell System] ..... CCIS
Common Channel Signaling [Telecommunications] (TEL) .... CCS
Common Channel Signaling System [Telecommunications] (TEL) ...... SSCC
Common Communication Adapter [Data processing] ..... CCA
Common Control [Telecommunications] (TEL) CC
Common Control Echo Suppressor [Telecommunications] (TEL) ..... CCES
Common Control Switching Arrangement [AT & T] [Telecommunications] .... CCSA
Common Data Bus [Data processing] .... CDB
Common Data Translation Language (CAA) .... CDTL
Common Database [Data processing] (CAAL) .... CDB
Common Display Logic [Data processing] (CGC) .... CDL
Common Field Effect Transistor [Data processing] ..... CFET
Common File System [Data processing] .... CFS
Common Ground [A publication] .... CG
Common High-Order Language (DEEC) .... CHOL
Common Input Processor .... CIP
Common Language System [Data processing] (BUR) ..... CLS
Common Machine Language [Data processing] .... CML
Common Mode Input Resistance .... CMIR
Common Mode Logic (CAA) .... CML
Common Mode Operation [Telecommunications] (TEL) ... CMO
Common Mode Rejection .... CMR
Common Mode Rejection Ratio .... CMRR
Common On-Line Package [Fujitsu Ltd.] [Japan] (CAA) ... COP
Common Operating System Control Language (CAA) ..... COSCL
Common Process [Telecommunications] (TEL) .... CP
Common Program Language [Data processing] .... CPL
Common Program Support System (CGC) .... CPSS
Common Service Area [Data processing] (BUR) .... CSA
Common Services Network [Telecommunications] (TEL) ... CSN
Common Services Rack [Telecommunications] (TEL) ..... CSR
Common Services Subsystem [Telecommunications] (TEL) ... CSS
Common Services Unit [Telecommunications] (TEL) ..... CSU
Common Signaling Channel (IEEE) .... CSC
Common Systems Main Interconnecting [Frame system] [Bell System] .... COSMIC
Common Test Subroutine [Data processing] (OA) ...... CTS
Common Usage Radio Frequency Checkout Equipment (KSC) .... CURFCOE
Common User Data [Telecommunications] (TEL) .... CUDAT
Common User Data Network .... CUDN
Common User Digital Information Exchange [Satellite communication] (NVT) ...... CUDIX
Common User Digital Information Exchange System [or Subsystem] [Satellite communication] (MCD) ...... CUDIXS
Common User Radio Transmission Sounding System (MCD) ...... CURTS
Common User System [Telecommunications] (TEL) ..... CUS
Commonly Used System Programs [Digital Equipment Corp.] (CAA) .... CUSP
Commonwealth Agricultural Bureaux [Buchs, England] [Database producer] (EANO) .... CAB
Commonwealth Regional Renewable Energy Resources Information System (EISS) .... CRRERIS
Commonwealth Telecommunications Board [British] (DEN) ..... CTB
Commonwealth Telecommunications Organization (CBSS) ..... CTO
Commonwealth Telephone Enterprises, Inc. [NASDAQ symbol] (NQ) .... CWTE
Communicate (MDG) .... CMCT
Communicate [or Communications] .... COM
Communicating Magnetic Card Typewriter .... CMCT
Communicating Word Processing System .... CWPS
Communicating Word Processor (DEEC) .... CWP
Communication (AFM) .... COMM
Communication .... COMN
Communication Advisors, Incorporated [Southfield, MI] [Telecommunications] (TSSD) .... CAI
Communication Automatic Processing Equipment ...... CAPE
Communication and Broadcasting [A publication] ...... COBRD
Communication and Broadcasting [England] [A publication] .... Commun Broadcast
Communication Center Console (CIT) CCC
Communication Computer Programing Center (AFM) ..... CCPC
Communication Control Program (BUR) .... CCP
Communication Control System .... CCS
Communication Control Unit .... CCU
Communication Countermeasures .... COMCM
Communication Desk (BUR) .... CDK
Communication Education [A publication] .... Comm Educ
Communication Electronic Instructions .... CEI

Computer & Telecommunications Acronyms

Communication Engineering [*A publication*] .... Commun Eng
Communication Identifier [*Data processing*] (IBMDP) .... CID
Communication Industrial Services .... CIS
Communication Information System (IEEE) .... CIS
Communication Interface Monitor (CAA) .... CIM
Communication Interrupt Control Program [*Data processing*]
  (IBMDP) .... CICP
Communication Jamming Processor (IEEE) .... CJP
Communication Line Adapters .... CLA
Communication Line Adapters for Teletype .... CLAT
Communication Line Processor (CAA) .... CLP
Communication Line Terminal [*Data processing*] (CGC) .... CLT
Communication Line Terminator [*IBM Corp.*] .... COLT
Communication Link Analyzer (IEEE) .... CLA
Communication Link Subsystem .... CLSS
Communication Management System [*Data processing*] .... CMS
Communication Managers Association .... CMA
Communication Monographs [*A publication*] .... Com M
Communication Monographs [*A publication*] .... Comm Monogr
Communication Output Printer (CAA) .... COP
Communication Planning Corporation [*Jacksonville, FL*]
  [*Telecommunications*] (TSSD) .... CPC
Communication Quarterly [*A publication*] .... Comm Q
Communication Quarterly [*A publication*] .... Commun Quart
Communication Radio and Teletype (Secure) System .... CRATTZ
Communication, Range, and Azimuth Unit [*Data processing*] .... COMRAZ
Communication Representative .... CR
Communication Research [*A publication*] .... Comm Res
Communication Research Center [*Florida State University*]
  [*Research center*] (RCD) .... CRC
Communication Research Center [*University of Florida*] [*Research center*] (RCD) .... CRC
Communication Research Center [*Boston University*] [*Research center*] (RCD) .... CRC
Communication Research Trends [*A publication*] .... Comm Res Trends
Communication Resources [*Haddonfield, NJ*]
  [*Telecommunications*] (TSSD) .... CR
Communication Satellite Planning Center [*Stanford University*]
  [*Research center*] (RCD) .... CSPC
Communication Scanner Base (IBMDP) .... CSB
Communication Sciences Laboratory [*University of Florida*] .... CSL
Communication Services Limited [*Hong Kong*]
  [*Telecommunications*] (TSSD) .... CSL
Communication Signal Distribution System .... CSDS
Communication Station .... CS
Communication System Control Element [*of TCCF*] (MCD) .... CSCE
Communication System Simulation Language [*Data processing*]
  (IEEE) .... COMSL
Communication Systems Ltd. [*London, England*]
  [*Telecommunications*] (TSSD) .... COMSYS
Communication Technical Evaluation Console (KSC) .... CTEC
Communication Training Consultants, Inc. [*New York, NY*]
  [*Telecommunications*] (TSSD) .... CTC
Communication Vector Table (BUR) .... CVT
Communications C
Communications .... COMMS
Communications .... COMMUN
Communications Access Device (CET) .... CAD
Communications. ACM [*Association for Computing Machinery*] [*A publication*] .... CACM
Communications. ACM [*Association for Computing Machinery*] [*A publication*] .... Comm ACM
Communications. ACM [*Association for Computing Machinery*] [*A publication*] .... Commun ACM
Communications Adapter (CAA) .... CA
Communications Advisory Committee .... COMAC
Communications Analysis Corporation [*Framingham, MA*]
  [*Telecommunications*] (TSSD) .... CAC
Communications Antenna Sleeve .... CAS
Communications Buffer [*Data processing*] (CAA) .... CB
Communications Buffer Memory [*Data processing*] .... CBM
Communications and Cable [*NASDAQ symbol*] (NQ) .... CCAB
Communications Carrier, Incorporated [*Austin, TX*]
  [*Telecommunications*] (TSSD) CCI
Communications Center .... COMMCEN
Communications Center of Clarksburg [*Clarksburg, MD*]
  [*Telecommunications*] (TSSD) CCC
Communications Concentrator Software Package [*Data processing*] .... CCSP
Communications Concepts, Incorporated [*Newport Beach, CA*]
  [*Telecommunications*] (TSSD) CCI
Communications and Configuration Console (MCD) .... CACC
Communications Consultants, Incorporated [*Asbury, NJ*]
  [*Telecommunications*] (TSSD) CCI
Communications Control (MCD) CC
Communications Control Applications Program (CGC) .... CCAP
Communications Control Block [*Data processing*] (CAA) .... CCB
Communications Control Center (FAAC) CCC
Communications Control Equipment (MCD) .... CCE
Communications Control Field .... CCF
Communications Control Language CCL
Communications Control Module [*Telecommunications*] (TEL) .... CCM
Communications Control Processor (CAA) .... CCP

Communications and Control Systems Laboratory .... CCSL
Communications Controller Multichannel [*Data processing*] .... CCM
Communications Coupling Unit (CET) .... CCU
Communications and Data .... C & D
Communications Data Base [*Canada*] [*Information service*] (EISS) .... COMBASE
Communications-Data Field .... CDF
Communications and Data Link (KSC) .... CADL
Communications and Data Processing Operation .... CADPO
Communications Data Processing System (NVT) .... CDPS
Communications Data Processor [*Electronics*] .... CDP
Communications and Data Systems Integration (NASA) .... CADSI
Communications, Electronic, Technical, and Salaried Workers of Canada .... CWC
Communications and Electronics .... C & E
Communications-Electronics .... C-E
Communications-Electronics .... COMMEL
Communications and Electronics [*England*] [*A publication*] .... Commun Electron
Communications-Electronics Consolidated Mobilization Reserve List .... CECMRL
Communications-Electronics Coordinating Section [*NATO*] .... CECS
Communications-Electronics Facility Inoperative for Parts (MCD) .... CEFIP
Communications-Electronics-Meteorological [*Equipment*] .... CEM
Communications-Electronics Operating Instruction .... CEOI
Communications-Electronics Standing Instruction .... CESI
Communications Equipment .... CE
Communications Equipment and Systems Design [*A publication*] .... Commun Equip & Syst Des
Communications Errors Statistics (CMD) .... CES
Communications Expansion Unit (OA) .... CEU
Communications-Failure Detecting and Switching Equipment (MDG) .... COMMSWITCH
Communications Fraud Control Association (EANO) .... CFCA
Communications Group, Incorporated [*Concord, MA*]
  [*Telecommunications*] (TSSD) .... CGI
Communications Handler for Automatic Multiple Programs (CAA) .... CHAMP
Communications Industries Association of Japan [*Tokyo*]
  [*Telecommunications*] (TSSD) .... CIAJ
Communications and Information Handling Equipment and Services .... CO IN HES
Communications and Information Processing Group [*Rensselaer Polytechnic Institute*] [*Research center*] (RCD) .... CIPG
Communications Input and Output Control System (BUR) .... CIOCS
Communications Input/Output Multiplexer .... CIOM
Communications Intelligence Channel (OA) CIC
Communications Interface (CAA) CI
Communications Interface Assembly [*Data processing*] (CIT) .... CIA
Communications Interface Modules [*Data processing*] (CGC) .... CIM
Communications Interface System (MCD) .... CIS
Communications Interface Unit (CAA) .... CIU
Communications Interrupt Analysis [*Sperry UNIVAC*] (IEEE) .... CIA
Communications Interrupt Program (CAA) .... CIP
Communications Line Control (CAA) CLC
Communications Line Expander [*Electrodata, Inc.*]
  [*Telecommunications*] (CAA) .... CLE
Communications Line Multiplexer (CAA) .... CLM
Communications Line Switch (CAA) .... CLS
Communications Link Analyzer System .... CLAS
Communications Link Characterization Experiment
  [*Communications Technology Satellite*] (MCD) .... CLCE
Communications Link Controller [*International Computers Ltd.*]
  [*Telecommunications*] (CAA) CLC
Communications Logistics Network (IEEE) .... COMLOGNET
Communications Maintenance and Storage (NASA) .... CM & S
Communications Market Association (EANO) .... CMA
Communications Mode Control .... CMC
Communications Monitoring and Control Subsystem (NVT) .... CMCS
Communications Multiplexer [*Data processing*] .... CM
Communications Multiplexer Module (CAA) .... CMM
Communications Need .... COMNEED
Communications Network (CAA) .... CN
Communications Network (AFM) .... COMNET
Communications Network Architecture (CAA) .... CNA
Communications Network Control Element (MCD) .... CNCE
Communications Network Design Program .... CNDP
Communications Network Emulator (CAA) .... CNE
Communications Network Management Interface (CAA) .... CNMI
Communications Network Processor (CAA) .... CNP
Communications Network Service [*Satellite Business Systems*]
  [*McLean, VA*] [*Telecommunications*] (TSSD) .... CNS
Communications, Networks, and Information Processing Theory Group [*MIT*] .... CNIPTG
Communications News [*A publication*] .... Comms N
Communications News [*A publication*] .... Commun News
Communications Office Building (NASA) .... COB
Communications Operating System (CAA) .... COS
Communications-Oriented Automatic Test (MCD) .... COATS
Communications-Oriented Language (CAA) .... COL
Communications-Oriented Processing Equipment .... COPE
Communications-Oriented Production Information and Control System [*IBM Corp.*] .... COPICS

Computer & Telecommunications Acronyms

Communications-Oriented Real-Time Executive (OA)	CORTEX
Communications Oriented Software (CAA)	COS
Communications-Oriented User Programing Language (CAA)	COUPLE
Communications Procedure-Oriented Language [Data processing]	CPOL
Communications Processing Center (CET)	CPC
Communications Processing System (CIT)	CPS
Communications Processing Unit (CET)	CPU
Communications Processor	COM
Communications Processor	CP
Communications Processor Conversion Center (CIT)	CPCC
Communications Processor Utility [Telecommunications] (TEL)	CPU
Communications Publishing Group, Inc. [Boston, MA] [Information service] [Telecommunications] (TSSD)	CPG
Communications Register (OA)	CR
Communications Regulatory Commission (CAA)	CRC
Communications Requirements Systems Configuration and Equipment List (NVT)	CORESCEL
Communications Research Advisory Board [Canada]	CRAB
Communications Research Center [University of Tennessee at Knoxville] [Research center] (RCD)	CRC
Communications Research Centre [Defunct] [Canada]	CRC
Communications Research Establishment (NATG)	CRE
Communications Research Institute (MCD)	CRI
Communications Research Laboratory [McMaster University] [Canada] [Research center] (RCD)	CRL
Communications/Research/Machines, Inc. [Publisher]	CRM
Communications Routing Indicator	COMRI
Communications. Royal Society of Edinburgh. Physical Science [A publication]	Comm Roy Soc Edinburgh Phys Sci
Communications Sales Results Measurement Plan [Telecommunications] (TEL)	CSRMP
Communications Satellite (MUGU)	COMMUNICAT
Communications Satellite [Japan] (CBSS)	CS
Communications satellite	WESTAR 6
Communications Satellite Advanced Research [AFSC]	CSAR
Communications Satellite Corp. [Assignee of operational and developmental responsibilities for Telstar and other international communications space devices] [Washington, DC]	COMSAT
Communications Satellite Corporation [See also COMSAT]	COMSATCORP
Communications Satellite Corp. [See also COMSAT] [NYSE symbol]	CQ
Communications Satellite Corp. [See also COMSAT]	CSC
Communications Satellite for Experimental Purposes [Japanese] [Telecommunications] (TEL)	CSE
Communications Satellite Project Office	CSPO
Communications Satellite Relay (NG)	CSR
Communications Security Association (EANO)	COMSEC
Communications Security Education Program (AFM)	CSEP
Communications Security Equipment Engineering Bulletin (MCD)	CSEEB
Communications Security Publication	CSP
Communications Security System (MCD)	CSS
Communications Simulator [Sperry UNIVAC] (CAA)	CS
Communications Solutions, Incorporated [San Jose, CA] [Information service] [Telecommunications] (TSSD)	CSI
Communications Storage Unit (DEEC)	COMM-STOR
Comparison Subsystem	CSS
Communications Surveillance Transistor	CST
Communications Switch Operating System (MCD)	CSOS
Communications Switchboard Console	CSC
Communications Switcher (CIT)	CS
Communications Switching Unit (CAAL)	CSU
Communications/Symbiont Processor [Sperry UNIVAC] (CAA)	C/SP
Communications System	CS
Communications System Control Console (SKY)	CSCC
Communications System Status Display (KSC)	CSSD
Compensator Systems [NASDAQ symbol] (NQ)	CSII
Communications Systems Center	CSC
Communications Systems Engineer (KSC)	CSE
Communications Systems, Incorporated	CSI
Communications Systems Management Association (MCD)	CSMA
Communications Task Group [CODASYL] (CAA)	CTG
Communications Technology Impact [A publication]	Communication Tech Impact
Communications Technology Management, Inc. [McLean, VA] [Telecommunications] (TSSD)	CTM
Communications Technology Satellite	CTS
Communications and Telemetry	CMTM
Communications Terminal [Data processing]	CT
Communications Terminal Module [Data processing] (CGC)	CTM
Communications Terminal Module Controller [Data processing] (CGC)	CTMC
Communications Terminal, Synchronous [Data processing]	CTS
Communications Timing Procedure (NASA)	CTP
Communications and Tracking System [or Subsystem]	CATS
Communications and Tracking System [or Subsystem]	CTS
Communications Union Canada	CUC
Communications Unit Executor	CUE
Communications Unlimited [Charlotte, NC] [Telecommunications] (TSSD)	CU
Communications User Program [Sperry UNIVAC]	CUP
Communications Validating Office (CET)	CVO
Communications Workers of America [Formerly, NFTW]	CWA
Communications Zone (MUGU)	COMMZ
Communications Zone (MCD)	CZ
Communitatis Europeae Lex [European Community Law] [Information service] (EISS)	CELEX
Community Antenna Relay [Service] [FCC]	CAR
Community Antenna Relay Service [FCC] [Telecommunications]	CARS
Community Antenna Television [Later, CTV]	CATV
Community Automatic Exchange [Telephone] (BUR)	CAEX
Community Automatic Exchange [Telephone]	CAX
Community Dial Office [Small switching system] [Telecommunications]	CDO
Community Electronic Teller System	COMETS
Community Health Computing	CHC
Community Information Utility (BUR)	CIU
Community of Interest [Telecommunications] (TEL)	CI
Community On-Line Intelligence Network System [Computer network] [National Science Administration and Central Intelligence Agency]	COINS
Community Telecommunications Development Foundation [Washington, DC] (TSSD)	CTDF
Commutation et Electronique [A publication]	CELCA
Comp-U-Card International [NASDAQ symbol] (NQ)	CUCD
Comp-U-Check, Inc. [NASDAQ symbol] (NQ)	CMUC
Compact Automatic Retrieval Device [Massachusetts Institute of Technology] [Data processing]	CARD
Compact Automatic Retrieval Display [Data processing] (EISS)	CARD
Compact Data Disk Association [Philadelphia, PA] (EANO)	CDDA
Compact Disc Group [New York, NY] (EANO)	CDG
Compact Disc - Interactive	CD-I
Compact Disk [Audio/video technology] [Philips]	CD
Compact Disk Read-Only Memory [Data processing]	CD-ROM
Compagnie Generale d'Electricite [General Electric Company] [French]	CGE
Compagnie Industrielle de Telecommunication [Computer manufacturer] [French] (CAH)	CIT
Compagnie Internationale pour l'Informatique Honeywell-Bull [Computer manufacturer] [French] (CAA)	CIIHB
Compagnie Internationale de Services en Informatique [International Information Services Co.] [French] [Information service] (EISS)	CISI
Companded Delta Modulation [Telecommunications] (TEL)	CDM
Companding and Frequency Modulation [Telecommunications] (TEL)	CFM
Compania Telefonica Nacional de Espana [National Telephone Company of Spain] [Madrid] [Telecommunications] (TSSD)	CTNE
Compaq Computer Corp. [NASDAQ symbol] (NQ)	CMPQ
Compaq Telecommunications Corporation [Dallas, TX]	CTC
Comparably Efficient Interconnection [Telecommunications]	CEI
Comparator (CET)	COMP
Comparator [Data processing]	COMPTR
Comparator Buffer [Data processing] (MUGU)	CB
Compare [Data processing]	CMP
Compare Numeric Equal (OA)	CNE
Compare Numeric Unequal (OA)	CNU
Compare Zone Equal [Data processing] (OA)	CZE
Compare Zone Unequal [Data processing] (OA)	CZU
Comparison of Recognition Algorithms [US Postal Service]	CORAL
Compass Integrated System Compiler [IEEE]	CISCO
Compatibility Operating System [Data processing] (CGC)	COS
Compatible	COMP
Compatible Algebraic Compiler and Translator	COMPACT
Compatible High-Density Bipolar Code [Telecommunications] (TEL)	CHDB
Compatible Independent Peripherals (IEEE)	CIP
Compatible Time-Sharing System [Massachusetts Institute of Technology] [Data processing]	CTSS
Compensator Design [Data processing]	COMPDES
Competitive Telecommunications Association [Washington, DC] [Telecommunications] (TSSD)	COMPTEL
Compile, Load, and Go [Data processing] (BUR)	CLG
Compile Online and Go [Data processing]	COLINGO
Compile and Test (BUR)	CAT
Compiler	COMP
Compiler-Assembler	COMPASS
Compiler and Assembler by General Electric	CAGE
Compiler for Automatic Machine Programing (BUR)	CAMP
Compiler for Automatic Teaching Operation (IEEE)	CATO
Compiler and Generalized Translator [Argonne National Laboratory] [List processor] (IEEE)	COGENT
Compiler Language (DIT)	CL
Compiler Language for Information Processing [System Development Corp.] [Programing language]	CLIP
Compiler/Massachusetts Institute of Technology (IEEE)	COMIT
Compiler Monitor System (BUR)	CMS
Compiler Object Code [Telecommunications] (TEL)	COC
Compiler Oriented for Multiprogramming and Multiprocessing Environments (IEEE)	COMMEN
Compiler System	COSY
Complementary Bipolar Integrated Circuit [Telecommunications] (TEL)	CBIC
Complementary Constant Current Logic [Data processing] (BUR)	CCCL
Complementary Constant Current Logic (MCD)	C^3L

Computer & Telecommunications Acronyms

Complementary High-Performance Metal-Oxide Semiconductor	CHMOS
Complementary Magnetic Oxide on Silicone [Data processing]	CMOS
Complementary Metal-Oxide Semiconductor [Transistor] [Electronics]	CMOS
Complementary Metal-Oxide Semiconductor/Silicon-on-Sapphire [Electronics]	CMOS/SOS
Complementary Metal-Oxide Semiconductor Transistor [Electronics]	CMOST
Complementary Symmetry/Metal Oxide Semiconductor	COS/MOS
Complementary Transistor Logic [Data processing]	CTL
Complementary Transistor-Transistor Logic	CTTL
Complementary Unijunction Transistor (IEEE)	CUJT
Complete ADR [Applied Data Research, Inc.] Environment (EANO)	CADRE
Complete Automatic Reliable Testing (CDH)	CART
Complete Calls To [Telecommunications] (TEL)	CCT
[A] Complete Computerized Examination System [Anatomy and physiology]	ACCESS
Complete Management Systems	CMS
Complete Operating Information [Data processing]	COIN
Complete Operational Software [Telecommunications] (TEL)	OSC
Complete with Related Order [Telecommunications] (TEL)	CRO
Complete Translation [Telecommunications] (TEL)	CT
Complete Treatment Module [Telecommunications] (TEL)	CTM
Completely Automatic Operational System [UNIVAC]	CAOS
Complex (DDI)	CMPX
Complex Utility Routine	CUR
Component Failure Impact Analysis [IBM Corp.]	CFIA
Component Manufacturer [Foundry Business Systems] [Software package] [British] (NCC)	CM
Composite Analog Video (CIT)	CAV
Composite External Symbol Dictionary (BUR)	CESD
Composite Mechanized Information and Document Retrieval System	COMEINDORS
Composite Signaling [Telecommunications] (TEL)	CX
Compound Batch Identification [Data processing] (CGC)	CBI
Comprehensive Assembler System [Programing language] [1964] [Control Data Corp.] (CGC)	COMPASS
Comprehensive Display System	CDS
Comprehensive Dissertation Index [University Microfilms International] [Ann Arbor, MI] [Bibliographic database] [A publication]	CDI
Comprehensive Information System and Database	CIS & DB
Comprehensive Self-Check [Computer]	CSC
Compressed Data Storage	CDS
Compressed Data Storage System	CDSS
Compressed Data Tape	CDT
Compressed Index Sequential Access Method (CAA)	CISAM
Compressed Symbolic [Programing language] [Control Data Corp.]	COSY
Compression Labs, Incorporated [San Jose, CA] [Telecommunications] (TSSD)	CLI
Compressor Expander [Telecommunications] (IEEE)	COMPANDER
Comptamation Electronics Designer System [COMPUTAMION] [Software package] [British] (NCC)	CEDS
Comptek Research, Inc. [NASDAQ symbol] (NQ)	CMTK
Compu-Plan, Inc. [NASDAQ symbol] (NQ)	NSUR
Compucare, Inc. [NASDAQ symbol] (NQ)	CMPC
Compucats' Computer Club [Aberdeen, MD] (EANO)	CCC
Compucom Development [NASDAQ symbol] (NQ)	CMDC
Compucorp [NASDAQ symbol] (NQ)	CCUP
Compugraphic Corp. [NYSE symbol]	CPU
Compugraphics Users Association [Bend, OR] (EANO)	CUA
CompuServe Information Service [CompuServe, Inc.] (EISS)	CIS
CompuServe Network Services [CompuServe, Inc.] [Columbus, OH] [Telecommunications] (TSSD)	CNS
CompuShop, Inc. [NASDAQ symbol] (NQ)	CSHP
Computation (AFM)	COMP
Computation Center-Advanced Graphics Laboratory [University of Texas at Austin] [Research center] (RCD)	AGL
Computation and Communication Trade-Off Study [ARPA]	CACTOS
Computation and Data Processing Center (DIT)	CDPC
Computational (MDG)	CMP
Computational Arithmetic Program	CAP
Computational Linguistics (IEEE)	CL
Computational Linguistics [A publication]	Comput L
Computational Linguistics and Computer Languages [A publication]	CLCL
Computational Statistics and Data Analysis [A publication]	Comput Stat and Data Anal
Compute [or Computer] (MDG)	C
Compute [or Computer]	CMPT
Compute Air-Trans Systems, Inc.	CATS
Compute Parallel (IEEE)	COMPEL
Computed	CMPTD
Computer (MUGU)	CMP
Computer (KSC)	CMPTR
Computer (AFM)	COMP
Computer [A publication]	Comput
Computer Abstracts [A publication]	ComAb
Computer Abstracts [A publication]	Comput Abstr
Computer Access Device	CAD
Computer Access Device Input (CET)	CADI
Computer Access Device Output (CET)	CADO
Computer-Accessed [or-Aided] Telemetry System (CIT)	CATS
Computer Accounting System [Boole & Babbage, Inc.] (IDA)	CAS
Computer Achievement Monitoring (MCD)	CAM
Computer Address Matrix	CAM
Computer Address Panel (CAAL)	CAP
Computer-Administered Instruction (RDA)	CAI
Computer-Administered Instructional System	CAIS
Computer Administrative Instruction	CADMINI
Computer-Aided Alerting Subsystem (CAAL)	CAAS
Computer-Aided Analysis and Information Recovery Systems (MCD)	CAIRS
Computer-Aided Batch Scheduling (CAA)	CABS
Computer-Aided Chartroom	COACH
Computer-Aided Circuit Design	CACD
Computer-Aided Classification (CAA)	CAC
Computer-Aided [or -Assisted] Communication System (CAA)	CACS
Computer-Aided Design	CAD
Computer-Aided Design [A publication]	Comput Aided Des
Computer-Aided Design and Analysis	CADA
Computer-Aided Design, Analysis, and Reliability (IEEE)	CADAR
Computer-Aided Design/Computer-Aided Manufacturing	CAD/CAM
Computer-Aided Design and Design Automation	CADDA
Computer-Aided Design Development	CADD
Computer-Aided Design and Drafting [Software package] (MCD)	CADD
Computer-Aided Design and Electrical Test	CADET
Computer-Aided Design of Electronic Circuits [Elsevier Book Series] [A publication]	CADEC
Computer-Aided Design of Electronic Products (IEEE)	CADEP
Computer-Aided Design Engineering (RDA)	CADE
Computer-Aided Design Environment [Software system] (IEEE)	COMRADE
Computer-Aided Design and Evaluation (MCD)	CADE
Computer-Aided Design Experiment Translator	CADET
Computer Aided Design of Fire Escapes [Micro Core Ltd.] [Software package] [British] (NCC)	CAFE
Computer Aided Design and Graphics Laboratory [Purdue University] [Research center] (RCD)	CADLAB
Computer-Aided Design of Integrated Circuits	CADIC
Computer-Aided Design Laboratory [Pennsylvania State University] [Research center] (RCD)	CAD-LAB
Computer-Aided Design, Manufacture, and Test (DEEC)	CADMAT
Computer-Aided Design/Numerical Control	CD/NC
Computer-Aided Design and Numerical Control Effort	CADANCE
Computer Aided Design of Optical Systems [Energy Soft Computer Systems Ltd.] [Software package] [British] (NCC)	CADOS
Computer-Aided Design and Test [System]	CADAT
Computer-Aided Detection	CAD
Computer-Aided Drafting	CAD
Computer-Aided Education (BUR)	CAE
Computer-Aided Engineering	CAE
Computer-Aided Engineering Center [University of Wisconsin - Madison] [Research center] (RCD)	CAE
Computer-Aided Engineering Laboratory [Lawrence Institute of Technology] [Research center] (RCD)	CAE LAB
Computer-Aided Film Editor (TUT)	CAFE
Computer-Aided [or -Assisted] Instruction	CAI
Computer-Aided Instruction (IEEE)	CAIS
Computer-Aided Instruction System [Programing language] [1971] (CSR)	CAISYS
Computer-Aided [or -Assisted] Learning (BUR)	CAL
Computer-Aided Line Balance	CALB
Computer-Aided Makeup [Graphic arts]	CAM
Computer-Aided Manufacturing	CAM
Computer Aided Manufacturing International [Arlington, TX] [An association] (EANO)	CAM-I
Computer-Aided Mechanical Drafting	CAMD
Computer-Aided Patient Management	CAPM
Computer-Aided Pattern Evaluation and Recognition (KSC)	CAPER
Computer-Aided Pipe Sketching [System] [Du Pont]	CAPS
Computer-Aided Piping Design and Construction (MCD)	CAPDAC
Computer-Aided Planning (CCD)	CAP
Computer Aided Planning and Estimating [Marlow Microplan National Engineering Laboratory] [Software package] [British] (NCC)	CAPE
Computer Aided Planning and Estimating [Inbucon Productivity Services Ltd.] [Software package] [British] (NCC)	CAPES
Computer-Aided Process Design (MCD)	CAPD
Computer-Aided Process Planning (MCD)	CAPP
Computer-Aided Processing and Terminal Access Information Network [Rutgers University] [New Brunswick, NJ] [Library computer network]	CAPTAIN
Computer-Aided [or Assisted] Production	CAP
Computer Aided Production Planning and Control [John Yates & Associates] [Software package] [British] (NCC)	CAPPAC
Computer-Aided Programing (CAA)	CAP
Computer-Aided Programing System	CAPS
Computer-Aided Quality Assurance	CAQA
Computer-Aided Railway Engineering System (MCD)	CARES
Computer-Aided Reference Service [Information service]	CARS
Computer-Aided Reliability Data Systems [Bell System]	CARDS
Computer-Aided Reliability Estimation	CARE
Computer-Aided Reorder Trap Analysis [Bell Laboratories]	CARTA
Computer-Aided Requirements Definition Software	CARDS

By Meaning

Computer-Aided Research into Stock Market Applications .... CARISMA
Computer-Aided Routing System (CGC) .... CARS
Computer-Aided Software Engineering (CAA) .... CASE
Computer-Aided Structural Design (MCD) .... CASD
Computer-Aided Structural Technology (MCD) .... CAST
Computer-Aided System Design [*Programing language*] (BUR) .... CASD
Computer-Aided System Evaluation (TUT) .... CASE
Computer-Aided Tactical Information System (IEEE) .... CATIS
Computer-Aided Teaching (CGC) .... CAT
Computer-Aided Teaching System (IEEE) .... CATS
Computer-Aided Technology (MCD) .... CAT
Computer-Aided Test [*Telecommunications*] (TEL) .... CAT
Computer-Aided Test Equipment (MSA) .... CATE
Computer Aided Testing [*Hoskyns Group Ltd.*] [*Software package*] [*British*] (NCC) .... CAT
Computer-Aided Translation (IEEE) .... CAT
Computer-Aided Troubleshooting .... CATS
Computer-Aided Typesetting Process .... CATP
Computer-Aided Work Sampling .... CAWS
Computer Amplifier Alarm .... CAA
Computer Analog Input/Output (CGC) .... CAIOP
Computer Analysis of Thermochemical Data Tables [*University of Sussex*] [*Sussex, England*] .... CATCH
Computer Analysts & Programmers Ltd. [*British*] (CAH) .... CAP
Computer Analyzed Newspaper Data On-Line [*Newspaper Advertising Bureau, Inc.*] [*Information service*] (EISS) .... CAN DO
Computer Animation Language (TUT) .... CAL
Computer Annunciation Matrix (MCD) .... CAM
Computer Application Services, Incorporated [*Los Alamitos, CA*] [*Telecommunications*] (TSSD) .... CASI
Computer Applications [*A publication*] .... Comput Appl
Computer Applications in Archaeology [*A publication*] .... Comput Appl Archaeol
Computer Applications Digest [*A publication*] .... CAD
Computer Applications of Military Problems [*Computer users' group*] .... CAMP
Computer Applications in the Natural and Social Sciences [*A publication*] .... Comput Appl Nat and Soc Sci
Computer Applications Service [*A publication*] .... Comput Appl Serv
Computer Applications in Shipping and Shipbuilding [*Elsevier Book Series*] [*A publication*] .... CASS
Computer Applications Unlimited, Inc. [*Portchester, NY*] [*Software manufacturer*] (DASOS) .... CAU
Computer Architecture News [*A publication*] .... Comput Archit News
Computer Architecture Research Unit [*York University*] [*Canada*] [*Research center*] (RCD) .... CARU
Computer Architecture Specification Language (CSR) .... CASL
Computer Arts Society (EANO) .... CAS
Computer-Assisted Accounting (BUR) .... CAA
Computer-Assisted Acquisition System [*for libraries*] (DEEC) .... CAAS
Computer-Assisted Action Information System [*NATO*] .... CAIS
Computer-Assisted Classification and Assignment System (IEEE) .... COMPASS
Computer-Assisted Design .... CAD
Computer-Assisted Development Aids .... CADA
Computer-Assisted Diagnosis .... CAD
Computer-Assisted Dialog .... CAD
Computer-Assisted Dispatching System [*IBM Corp.*] .... CADS
Computer-Assisted Disposal Simulation [*Game*] .... CADISIM
Computer-Assisted Distribution and Assignment (NVT) .... CADA
Computer-Assisted Enrollment [*IBM Corp.*] (IEEE) .... CAE
Computer-Assisted Entry (CIT) .... CAE
Computer-Assisted Estimating .... CAE
Computer-Assisted Indexing and Categorizing [*or Classification*] (IDA) .... CAIC
Computer-Assisted Information Retrieval System (DEEC) .... CAIRS
Computer-Assisted Instruction Center (DDI) .... CAIC
Computer-Assisted Instruction Study Management System (MCD) .... CAISMS
Computer-Assisted Interactive Resources Scheduling System .... CAIRS
Computer-Assisted Learning Network .... CALN
Computer-Assisted Library Mechanization (CGC) .... CALM
Computer-Assisted Maintenance .... CAM
Computer-Assisted Maintenance Planning and Control System .... CAMCOS
Computer-Assisted Makeup [*Graphic arts*] .... CAM
Computer-Assisted/Managed Instructional Language (CSR) .... CAMIL
Computer-Assisted Management of Portfolios (CGC) .... CAMP
Computer-Assisted Mapping and Records Activities System (IEEE) .... CAMRAS
Computer-Assisted Mathematics Program [*Scott, Foresman, 1968-1969*] [*Textbook series*] (BUR) .... CAMP
Computer-Assisted Menu Planning .... CAMP
Computer-Assisted Method Assembly [*Analytical method writing*] .... CAMA
Computer-Assisted Movie Production (IEEE) .... CAMP
Computer-Assisted Network Scheduling System (IEEE) .... CANS
Computer-Assisted Placement Service [*British*] .... CAPS
Computer-Assisted Printing .... CAP
Computer-Assisted Prisoner Transportation Index Service [*National Sheriffs' Association*] .... CAPTIS
Computer-Assisted Problem Solving (IEEE) .... CAPS
Computer-Assisted Prosthesis Selection [*Orthopedic surgery*] .... CAPS
Computer-Assisted Reliability and Maintainability Simulation [*Game*] .... CARMSIM
Computer-Assisted Repair Simulation [*Game*] .... CARESIM
Computer-Assisted Research (BUR) .... CAR
Computer-Assisted Retrieval .... CAR
Computer-Assisted Scanning Techniques .... CAST
Computer-Assisted Search (CAAL) .... CAS
Computer-Assisted Search Planning (MCD) .... CASP
Computer-Assisted Simulation of Supply and Related Systems .... CASSARS
Computer-Assisted Surveillance Subsystem (MCD) .... COMPASS
Computer-Assisted Technique for Numerical Indexing Purposes .... CATNIP
Computer-Assisted Telephone Interviewing .... CATI
Computer-Assisted Test Shop .... CATS
Computer-Assisted Testing (BUR) .... CAT
Computer-Assisted Tomography .... CAT
Computer-Assisted Trading System .... CATS
Computer-Assisted Training (IEEE) .... COMAT
Computer-Assisted Training System [*IRS*] .... CATS
Computer-Associated [*or -Assisted*] **Device** (SKY) .... CAD
Computer-Associated Diagnostic and Evaluation Tests (CAAL) .... CADET
Computer-Associated Self-Assessment [*British*] .... CASA
Computer Associates International [*NASDAQ symbol*] (NQ) .... CASI
Computer Audio Research Laboratory [*University of California, San Diego*] [*Research center*] (RCD) .... CARL
Computer Audit Retrieval System [*Trade name for Sage Systems, Inc., computer software product*] .... CARS
Computer Audit Specialist [*IRS*] .... CAS
Computer Augmented Learning (CMD) .... CAL
Computer-Augmented Loft Lines [*Graphic arts*] (MCD) .... CALL
Computer-Automated Measurement and Control (MSA) .... CAMAC
Computer-Automated Real-Time Betting Information Network (IEEE) .... CARBINE
Computer-Automated Social Simulation .... CASS
Computer-Automated Support Equipment .... CASE
Computer and Automated Systems Association [*Later, CASA/SME*] [*Dearborn, MI*] .... CASA
Computer and Automated Systems Association of Society of Manufacturing Engineers [*Formerly, CASA*] [*Dearborn, MI*] (EANO) .... CASA/SME
Computer-Automated Test System [*AT & T*] .... CATS
Computer-Automated Transit Systems .... CATS
Computer Automatic Scheduling System .... CASS
Computer Automation [*NASDAQ symbol*] (NQ) .... CAUT
Computer Automation, Inc. [*Richardson, TX*] (TSSD) .... CA
Computer Automation, Incorporated (CAH) .... CAI
Computer of Average Transients .... CAT
Computer-Based Behavioral Studies (MCD) .... CBBS
Computer-Based Bibliographic Search Service .... CBBS
Computer-Based Case Tracing [*Medicine*] .... COMTRAC
Computer-Based Education [*Project*] .... C-BE
Computer-Based Education Research Laboratory [*University of Illinois*] [*Research center*] .... CERL
Computer-Based Estimating Technique for Contractors .... COBESTCO
Computer-Based Financial Management System [*Harper & Shuman, Inc.*] [*Information service*] (EISS) .... CFMS
Computer-Based Instruction [*Education*] .... CBI
Computer-Based Instruction System (IEEE) .... COBIS
Computer-Based Instructional System (IEEE) .... CBIS
Computer-Based Laboratory for Automated School Systems [*System Development Corp. project*] .... CLASS
Computer-Based Learning .... CBL
Computer-Based Message System [*Electronic mail*] .... CBMS
Computer-Based Optimization Routines and Techniques for Effective X (DIT) .... CORTEX
Computer-Based Reference Service [*Information service*] .... CBRS
Computer-Based Resource Units [*Education*] .... CBRU
Computer-Based Terminal .... CBT
Computer-Based Training .... CBT
Computer Bulletin [*A publication*] .... Comp Bul
Computer Bulletin [*A publication*] .... Comput Bull
Computer Bulletin Board System .... CBBS
Computer Burst Order .... CBO
Computer and Business Equipment Manufacturers Association [*Washington, DC*] (EANO) .... CBEMA
Computer Business News [*A publication*] .... Comput Busn
Computer Business News [*A publication*] .... Comput Bus News
Computer Business Systems [*Youngstown, OH*] [*Software manufacturer*] (DASOS) .... CBS
Computer Calculator CC
Computer Campaign Services [*Data processing firm in field of politics*] .... CCS
Computer Center [*Telecommunications*] (TEL) CC
Computer Center (DDI) .... CMPCTR
Computer Center [*Haverford College*] [*Research center*] (RCD) .... HCCC
Computer Center [*Vanderbilt University*] [*Research center*] (RCD) .... VUCC
Computer Center [*Yale University*] [*Research center*] (RCD) .... YCC
Computer Central Processing [*Telecommunications*] (TEL) .... CCP
Computer Character Recognition .... CCR
Computer Command Control [*General Motors Corp.*] CCC
Computer Command Engineer (MCD) .... CCE
Computer & Commercial Technology [*NASDAQ symbol*] (NQ) .... CCTC
Computer Communications [*A publication*] .... COC
Computer Communications [*A publication*] .... Comp Comm
Computer Communications [*A publication*] .... Comput Commun

Computer Communications Console (AFM) ... CCC
Computer Communications Converter (MCD) ... CCC
Computer Communications Group [*Canada*] ... CCG
Computer Communications, Incorporated (CAA) ... CCI
Computer and Communications Industry Association [*Arlington, VA*] (EANO) ... CCIA
Computer Communications Networks Group [*University of Waterloo*] [*Canada*] [*Information service*] [*Research center*] (EISS) ... CCNG
Computer Community (IEEE) ... CC
[*The*] **Computer Company, Inc.** [*Information service*] (EISS) ... TCC
Computer-Compatible Tape ... CCT
Computer Complex (VIT) ... CC
Computer Components and System Group ... CCSG
Computer Composition Corporation [*Madison Heights, MI*] ... CCC
Computer-to-Computer (NASA) ... C-to-C
Computer Conference ... COMPCON
Computer Conferencing ... CC
Computer Consoles, Inc. [*American Stock Exchange symbol*] ... CCS
Computer Consulting Service (BUR) ... CCS
Computer Contributions [*A publication*] ... Comput Contrib
Computer and Control Abstracts [*IEE*] [*A publication*] ... CCA
Computer and Control Abstracts [*IEE*] [*A publication*] ... Comput & Contr Abstr
Computer and Control Abstracts [*IEE*] [*A publication*] ... Comput Control Abstr
Computer and Control Abstracts [*IEE*] [*A publication*] ... Comput Control Abstracts
Computer Control Communication (BUR) ... CCC
Computer Control Complex (OA) ... CCC
Computer Control Corporation (CIT) ... CCC
Computer Control Indicator (CAAL) ... CCI
Computer Control Loading ... CCL
Computer Control Panel (SKY) ... CCP
Computer Control Unit ... CCU
Computer-Controlled Area Sterilization Multisensor System ... CASMS
Computer-Controlled Automatic Test Equipment (DDI) ... CATE
Computer-Controlled Coil Ignition ... C^{3}I
Computer-Controlled Display (CGC) ... CCD
Computer-Controlled Interconnect System (MCD) ... CCIS
Computer-Controlled Microfilm Search System (MCD) ... CCMSS
Computer Controller Multiplexer Unit (SKY) ... CCMU
Computer Core Segment (NASA) ... CCS
Computer Corporation of America [*Cambridge, MA*] ... CCA
Computer Craft, Inc. [*NASDAQ symbol*] (NQ) ... CRFT
Computer Cross Select Unit ... CCSU
Computer Data [*A publication*] ... Comp Data
Computer Data Entry Keyboard ... CDEK
Computer Data Recording System (KSC) ... CDRS
Computer Data Switchboard ... CDS
Computer Data System (CIT) ... CDS
Computer Data Systems, Incorporated [*Information service*] (EISS) ... CDSI
Computer Data Systems, Inc. [*NASDAQ symbol*] (NQ) ... CPTD
Computer Data Word (CET) ... CDW
Computer Dealer Exposition ... COMDEX
Computer Dealers Association (CAA) ... CDA
Computer Dealers and Lessors Association [*Washington, DC*] (EANO) ... CDLA
Computer Decisions [*A publication*] ... Comp Dec
Computer Decisions [*A publication*] ... Comp Decisions
Computer Decisions [*A publication*] ... Comput Decis
Computer Description Language (BUR) ... CDL
Computer Design [*A publication*] ... CD
Computer Design [*A publication*] ... Comp Des
Computer Design [*A publication*] ... Comput Des
Computer Design and Architecture Series [*Elsevier Book Series*] [*A publication*] ... CDAS
Computer Design and Education System (OA) ... CODES
Computer Design and Evaluation System (IEEE) ... CODES
Computer Design Language (CSR) ... CDL
Computer Designed Systems [*NASDAQ symbol*] (NQ) ... CDSI
Computer-Developed Instruction ... CDI
Computer Development Center (KSC) ... CDC
Computer Development Center (KSC) ... CDEVC
Computer Development Laboratory [*Fujitsu Ltd., Hitachi Ltd., and Mitsubishi Corp.*] [*Japan*] (CAA) ... CDL
Computer Developments Limited Automatic Coding System (IEEE) ... CODEL
Computer Devices, Incorporated (CAA) ... CDI
Computer Direct to Telegraph ... CODIT
Computer-Directed Communications ... CODIC
Computer-Directed Drawing ... CDD
Computer-Directed Drawing Instrument ... CDDI
Computer-Directed Instrument ... CDI
Computer-Directed Training Lesson Building System ... CDTLBS
Computer-Directed Training System ... CDTS
Computer Directions Advisors, Inc. [*Information service*] (EISS) ... CDA
Computer Directions Corporation ... CDC
Computer Display Channel ... CDC
Computer Display Unit (MCD) ... CDU
Computer-Driven Simulation Environment [*FAA*] ... CDSE
Computer Duplex System (BUR) ... CDS
Computer Education Conference [*A publication*] ... Computer Ed
Computer Education for Management (OA) ... CEM
Computer Election Systems, Inc. ... CES
Computer Electrical System [*Davy Computing Ltd.*] [*Software package*] [*British*] (NCC) ... COMPELS
Computer Electronics Telecommunications Instruments Automation ... CETIA
Computer Elements and Systems [*A publication*] ... Comput Elem Syst
Computer Engineer (CGC) ... CE
Computer Engineering Series [*A publication*] ... Computer Engrg Ser
Computer Engineering Service ... CES
Computer Enhanced Spectroscopy [*A publication*] ... CES
Computer Enhanced Spectroscopy [*A publication*] ... Comput Enhanc Spectrosc
Computer Entry Keyboard (SKY) ... CEK
Computer Entry Punch ... CEP
Computer Entry and Readout Equipment (KSC) ... CERE
Computer Entry Systems [*NASDAQ symbol*] (NQ) ... CESC
Computer Evaluation of Scanning Electron Microscope Image ... CESEMI
Computer Execute Function (KSC) ... CEF
Computer-Extended Instruction (IEEE) ... CEI
Computer Facilities Management (MCD) ... CFM
Computer Factory, Inc. [*American Stock Exchange symbol*] ... CFA
Computer Family Architecture (CAA) ... CFA
Computer Format Control Buffer ... CFCB
Computer Fraud and Security Bulletin [*A publication*] ... Comput Fraud and Secur Bull
Computer-Generated Hologram ... CGH
Computer-Generated Imagery ... CGI
Computer Generated Letter (CAA) ... CGL
Computer-Generated Purchase Request ... CGPR
Computer Graphics (MCD) ... CG
Computer Graphics Aided 3D Interactive [*IBM UK Ltd.*] [*Software package*] [*British*] (NCC) ... CATIA
Computer Graphics and Art [*A publication*] ... Comput Graphics and Art
Computer-Graphics Augmented Design and Manufacturing [*Software package*] [*British*] (NCC) ... CADAM
Computer Graphics Forum [*A publication*] ... CGF
Computer Graphics and Image Processing [*A publication*] ... Comput Graphics Image Process
Computer Graphics and Image Processing [*A publication*] ... Comput Graphics and Image Process
Computer Graphics Research Group [*Ohio State University*] [*Research center*] (RCD) ... CGRG
Computer Graphics Structural Analysis ... CGSA
Computer Graphics World [*A publication*] ... Comput Graphics World
Computer Guidance Corporation (CGC) ... CGC
Computer Hardware Description Language ... CHDL
Computer and Human-Assisted Organization of a Technical Information Center [*National Bureau of Standards*] ... CHAOTIC
Computer-Human Interaction (BUR) ... CHI
Computer Identics Corp. [*NASDAQ symbol*] (NQ) ... CIDN
Computer Image Generator (MCD) ... CIG
Computer Index of Neutron Data [*Atomic Energy Authority*] [*Databank*] [*British*] ... CIND
Computer Index of Neutron Data [*Atomic Energy Authority*] [*Databank*] [*British*] ... CINDA
Computer Indicator (AFM) ... CI
Computer Industry Association (CAH) ... CIA
Computer Information [*A publication*] ... Comput Inf
Computer Information Center (MCD) ... COPIC
Computer/Information/Library Sciences [*Abstracts*] ... C/I/L
Computer and Information Sciences ... COINS
Computer and Information Sciences Research Laboratory [*University of Alabama in Birmingham*] [*Research center*] (RCD) ... CIS
Computer and Information Services [*Corporation for Public Broadcasting*] (EISS) ... CIS
Computer and Information Systems [*A publication*] ... CIS
Computer and Information Systems [*A publication*] ... Comput & Info Sys
Computer-Informationsdienst Graz [*Graz Computer-Information Service*] [*Austria*] (EISS) ... CIG
Computer Innovations Distribution, Inc. [*Toronto Stock Exchange symbol*] ... CIC
Computer Input Matrix (KSC) ... CIM
Computer Input Microfilming ... CIM
Computer Input Multiplexer (KSC) ... CIM
Computer Inquiries ... CI
Computer Instruction and Training Assistance for the Blind ... CITAB
Computer Instruments Corporation ... CIC
Computer Instruments Corp. [*American Stock Exchange symbol*] [*Delisted*] ... CUI
Computer Integrated Draughting [*Terminal Display Systems Ltd.*] [*Software package*] [*British*] (NCC) ... CID
Computer-Integrated Factory ... CIF
Computer-Integrated Instruction (NVT) ... CII
Computer-Integrated Manufacturing ... CIM
Computer-Integrated Test Equipment ... CITE
Computer Interface Adapter (CGC) ... CIA
Computer Interface Conditioning Unit (MCD) ... CICU
Computer Interface Control [*Part of digital television computer*] (CIT) ... CIC
Computer Interface Device (NASA) ... CID
Computer Interface Technology (IEEE) ... CIT
Computer Interface for Television (MCD) ... CINTEL
Computer Interface Terminal (CET) ... CIT

Computer Interface Unit .... CIU
Computer Investors Group, Inc. [American Stock Exchange
  symbol] [Delisted] .... CIG
Computer Journal [British] [A publication] .... CJ
Computer Journal [A publication] .... Comp J
Computer Journal [A publication] .... Computer J
Computer Journal [A publication] .... Comput J
Computer Laboratory of Harvard University .... CLHU
Computer Laboratory for Instruction in Psychological Research
  [University of Colorado - Boulder] [Research center] (RCD) .... CLIPR
Computer Language to Aid and Stimulate Scientific,
  Mathematical, and Technical Education .... CLASSMATE
Computer Language Recorder .... CLR
Computer Language Research (IEEE) .... CLR
Computer Language Research, Incorporated [NASDAQ symbol]
  (NQ) .... CLRI
Computer Language Translator .... CLT
Computer Languages [A publication] .... CLAND
Computer Languages [A publication] .... Comput Lang
Computer/LASER Access Systems for Information Exchange .... CLASIX
Computer Law Association [Falls Church, VA] (EANO) .... CLA
Computer Law Service Reporter .... CLSR
Computer Law and Tax Report [A publication] .... Comp Law
Computer Lessors Association [Later, CDLA] (EANO) .... CLA
Computer Library Services, Incorporated [Wellesley Hills, MA] .... CLSI
Computer Listing Service, Inc. [Round Rock, TX] [Information
  service] (EISS) .... CLS
Computer Listings of Employment Opportunities [The Copley
  Press, Inc.] [Database] (CUAD) .... CLEO
Computer Load and Resource Analysis (MCD) .... CLARA
Computer Lock-On .... CLO
Computer Logic Demonstrator .... CLD
Computer Logic Unit Tester (MCD) .... CLUT
Computer Main Memory [Telecommunications] (TEL) .... CMM
Computer Maintenance & Leasing Corp. [Minneapolis, MN]
  [Hardware manufacturer] (DASO) .... CMLC
Computer Maintenance Test Set .... CMTS
Computer-Managed Instruction .... CMI
Computer-Managed Laboratory .... CML
Computer Management [British] [A publication] (CAH) .... CM
Computer Management [A publication] .... Comp Mgmt
Computer Management [A publication] .... Comput Manage
Computer Management [A publication] .... Comput Mgmt
Computer Management Association (CAA) .... CMA
Computer Management System [Burroughs Corp.] (BUR) ...... CMS
Computer-Marked Assignment [Education] [British] .... CMA
Computer Marketing [Standard & Poor's] .... COMPMARK
Computer Marketing Services [Anaheim, CA] [Information service]
  (EISS) .... CMS
Computer Measurement and Evaluation (CAA) .... CME
Computer Memories [NASDAQ symbol] (NQ) .... CMIN
Computer Memory Element .... CME
Computer Memory Tester .... CMT
Computer Memory Unit (OA) .... CMU
Computer Message Transmission (CAA) .... COMET
Computer Method of Sequencing Operations for Assembly Lines
  (MCD) .... COMSOAL
Computer Methods in Applied Mechanics and Engineering [A
  publication] .... Comp Methods Appl Mech Eng
Computer Methods in Applied Mechanics and Engineering [A
  publication] .... Comput Methods Appl Mech Eng
Computer Methods in Applied Mechanics and Engineering [A
  publication] .... Comput Methods Appl Mech & Eng
Computer Methods in Applied Mechanics and Engineering [A
  publication] .... Comput Methods Appl Mech & Engng
Computer Methods in Applied Mechanics and Engineering [A
  publication] .... Comput Methods Appl Mech Engrg
Computer Microfilm Corp. [NASDAQ symbol] (NQ) .... COMI
Computer Microfilm International Corporation [Information
  service] (EISS) .... CMIC
Computer Micrographics Technology [An association] (EANO) ..... CMT
Computer Micrographics Technology [An association]
  [Northbrook, IL] (EANO) .... COMTEC
Computer Modelling Group [Calgary, AB] [Research center] (RCD) .... CMG
Computer Modelling System [Computer Modelling International
  Ltd.] [Software package] [British] (NCC) .... CMS
Computer Module .... CM
Computer Monitor Adapter (CAA) .... CMA
Computer Monitor and Control Console (CAAL) .... CMCC
Computer Multiple Listing Service [Fairfax, VA] [Information
  service] (EISS) .... CMLS
Computer Music Journal [A publication] .... Computer Mus J
Computer Music Journal [A publication] .... Comput Mus
Computer Music Journal [A publication] .... Comput Music J
Computer Negotiations Report [A publication] .... C N Report
Computer Network Corp. [NASDAQ symbol] (NQ) .... CNET
Computer Network Corp. [Information service] (EISS) ..... COMNET
Computer Networks [A publication] .... Comp Net
Computer Networks [A publication] .... Comput Networks
Computer Numerical Control [Data processing] .... CNC
Computer On-Line Real-Time Applications Language [Data
  processing] (IEEE) .... CORAL

Computer with On-Line Remote Devices [National Bureau of
  Standards] .... CORD
Computer-Operated [or -Oriented] Electronic Display .... COED
Computer-Operated Multifunction Electronic Test System
  (MCD) .... COMETS
Computer-Operated Universal Test .... COUNT
Computer Operations Facility .... COF
Computer Operations Group .... COG
Computer Operations Management Association (CAH) .... COMA
Computer Operator Handbook .... COH
Computer Operators' Course .... COC
Computer Optimization Package [or Program] [General Electric Co.] ...... COP
Computer Optimized Fabrication [Sheet metal] [Raytheon Co.] .... COF
Computer Optimized Sheetmetal Technology [Raytheon Co.] .... COST
Computer Oriented Classicists (EANO) .... COC
Computer-Oriented Design of Electronic Devices .... CODED
Computer-Oriented Language [Programing language] [Data
  processing] .... COL
Computer-Oriented Language Translator (IEEE) .... COLT
Computer-Oriented Mechanical Design (MCD) ..... COMMEND
Computer-Oriented Modal Control and Appraisal System ..... COMCAS
Computer-Oriented Partial Sum (NVT) .... COPS
Computer-Oriented Programed Instruction (IEEE) ...... COPI
Computer-Oriented Reference System for Automatic Information
  Retrieval [Forsvarets Forskningsamsalt] [Swedish] .... CORSAIR
Computer-Oriented Reporting Efficiency (AFM) .... CORE
Computer-Oriented Retrieval of Auto Larcenists .... CORRAL
Computer-Oriented System for Management Order Synthesis
  [IBM Corp.] (BUR) .... COSMOS
Computer-Oriented System - Newly Organized Storage-to-
  Retrieval Apparatus (KSC) .... COSNOSTRA
Computer Output Microfilm [or Microfiche or Microform] (BUR) .... COM
Computer Output Microfilm Equipment .... COME
Computer Output Microfilm Package (DEEC) .... COMPAC
Computer Output Microform Catalog .... COMCAT
Computer Packages (MCD) .... COMPAC
Computer Paragraph .... CP
Computer Payroll (BUR) .... COMPAY
Computer Performance [A publication] .... Comput Performance
Computer Performance Analysis [Boole & Babbage, Inc.] (CAA) .... CPA
Computer Performance Evaluation .... CPE
Computer Performance Evaluation Users Group [National Bureau
  of Standards] [Gaithersburg, MD] .... CPEUG
Computer Performance Management (CAA) .... CPM
Computer Peripheral Equipment (KSC) .... CPE
Computer Peripheral Manufacturers Association .... CPMA
Computer Peripheral Products [NASDAQ symbol] (NQ) .... CPPI
Computer Peripheral Unit (IEEE) .... CPU
Computer Peripherals Review [A publication] ...... Comput Peripherals Rev
Computer Personnel [A publication] .... Comp Pers
Computer Personnel [A publication] .... Comput Pers
Computer Personnel Research Group [Later, Special Interest
  Group for Computer Personnel Research] .... CPRG
Computer Personnel Research Proceedings [A publication] .... CPR Proc
Computer and Photographic Assisted Learning .... CAPAL
Computer Physics Communications [A publication] ...... Comp Phys Comm
Computer Physics Communications [A publication] ..... Computer Ph
Computer Physics Communications [A publication] ..... Comput Phys Comm
Computer Physics Communications [A publication] ......
  .... Comput Phys Commun
Computer Physics Reports [A publication] .... Comput Phys Rep
Computer-Planning and Aircraft-Weighing Scales .... CPAWS
Computer Planning and Control Technique (BUR) ..... COMPACT
Computer Pneumatic Input Panel .... CPIP
Computer Power Center (DEEC) .... CPC
Computer Power Supply .... CPS
Computer Power Support System (CAA) .... CPSS
Computer Praxis [A publication] .... Comput Prax
Computer-Prescribed Instruction (IEEE) .... CPI
Computer Press Association [Homewood, IL] (EANO) ..... CPA
Computer Print Console .... CPC
Computer Printer Unit (MCD) .... CPU
Computer Process Control .... CPC
Computer Process Utility, Inc. [Muskegon, MI] [Software
  manufacturer] (DASOS) .... CPU
Computer Processor Unit (OA) .... CPU
Computer Products [NASDAQ symbol] (NQ) .... CPRD
Computer Professionals for Social Responsibility (EANO) ...... CPSR
Computer Program (IEEE) .... COMPROG
Computer Program Abstracts [A publication] ...... Comput Program Abstr
Computer Program Associated Contractor .... CPAC
Computer Program for Automatic Control .... COMPAC
Computer Program Book .... CPB
Computer Program Change Request (NASA) .... CPCR
Computer Program Components (MCD) .... CPC
Computer Program Configured Item (MCD) .... CPCI
Computer Program Contract End Item .... CPCEI
Computer Program Development and Management System
  (CAA) .... CPDAMS
Computer Program End Item (NASA) .... CPEI
Computer Program Identification Number (MCD) ..... CPIN
Computer Program Implementation Process .... CPIP
Computer Program Integration Contractor .... CPIC

Computer Program Library (BUR) ... CPL
Computer Program Module (NASA) ... CPM
Computer Program Package (CAAL) ... CPP
Computer Program Specification (AFM) ... CPS
Computer Program Tapes (MCD) ... CPT
Computer Program Test and Evaluation (CAA) ... CPT & E
Computer Program Test Plan (CAAL) ... CPTPL
Computer Program Test Procedures (CAAL) ... CPTPR
Computer Program Update (TUT) ... CPU
Computer Program Users Manual CSIRO [*Commonwealth Scientific and Industrial Research Organisation. Division of Applied Geomechanics*] [*A publication*] ... CSIRO Div Appl Geomech Prog Circ
Computer-Programed Automatic Checkout and Test System ... COMPACT
Computer Programing Concepts (BUR) ... CPC
Computer Programing Performance Specification (MCD) ... CPPS
Computer Programing Service ... CPS
Computer Programing and Testing Activity (IEEE) ... CPTA
Computer Programs in Biomedicine [*A publication*] ... Computer Pr
Computer Programs in Biomedicine [*A publication*] ... Comput Programs Biomed
Computer Programs for Chemistry [*A publication*] ... Comput Programs Chem
Computer Projects, Incorporated [*Greensboro, NC*] [*Telecommunications*] (TSSD) ... CPI
Computer Projects Limited (OA) ... CPL
Computer Report. Department of Architectural Science. University of Sydney [*A publication*] ... Comput Rep Dep Archit Sci Syd Univ
Computer Research [*NASDAQ symbol*] (NQ) ... CORE
Computer Research, Systems, and Software (IEEE) ... COMPRESS
Computer Reset Pulse (KSC) ... CRP
Computer Resource Unit (CGC) ... CRU
Computer Resources [*NASDAQ symbol*] (NQ) ... CRII
Computer Response Corporation ... CRC
Computer Retrieval Editor [*Used to manage CORKIPER file family*] ... COREDITOR
Computer Retrieval of Information on Scientific Projects (EISS) ... CRISP
Computer Retrieval of Kinetic Parameters of Electrode Reactions ... CORKIPER
Computer Retrieval of Organic Structures Based on Wiswesser ... CROSSBOW
Computer Review and Orientation Course ... CROC
Computer Run Report (NASA) ... CRR
Computer Science (BUR) ... CS
Computer Science and Applied Mathematics [*A publication*] ... Comput Sci Appl Math
Computer Science Center [*North Carolina A & T State University*] [*Research center*] (RCD) ... CSC
Computer Science Center [*University of Maryland*] [*Research center*] (RCD) ... CSC
Computer Science Division (CAH) ... CSD
Computer Science and Engineering ... CSE
Computer Science Monographs (Tokyo) [*A publication*] ... Comput Sci Monographs (Tokyo)
Computer Sciences Corporation [*El, Segunda, CA*] [*Database originator*] [*NYSE symbol*] ... CSC
Computer Search Center [*Illinois Institute of Technology Research Center*] [*Chicago, IL*] ... CSC
Computer Search International Corp. [*Database producer*] (CUAD) ... CSI
Computer Search Services ... CSS
Computer Security (MSA) ... CMPSCTY
Computer Security Evaluation Center ... CSEC
Computer Security Institute [*Northboro, MA*] (EANO) ... CSI
Computer Sensitive Language [*Programing language*] ... CSL
Computer Sequence Number ... CSN
[*A*] **Computer Series** [*Nippon Electric Company*] [*Japan*] (CAA) ... ACOS
Computer series [*Digital Scientific*] (NITA) ... META
Computer Service and Bureaux Association [*British*] (OA) ... COSBA
Computer Service Center ... CSC
Computer Service Corp. ADR [*NASDAQ symbol*] (NQ) ... CSKKY
Computer Services Association [*British*] ... CSA
Computer Services Division [*University of South Carolina at Columbia*] [*Research center*] (RCD) ... CSD
Computer Services - Long Beach (MCD) ... CSLB
Computer Set Control (CAAL) ... CSC
Computer Sharing Services, Inc. [*Information service*] (EISS) ... CSS
Computer Simulation (RDA) ... CS
Computer Simulation Language (BUR) ... CSL
Computer Simulation Program ... CSP
Computer Society of Canada (CAH) ... CSC
Computer Software and Applications Conference (CAA) ... COMPSAC
Computer Software Data Tapes (MCD) ... CSDT
Computer & Software Enterprises, Inc. [*San Luis Obispo, CA*] [*Software manufacturer*] (DASOS) ... CASE
Computer Software Management and Information Center [*University of Georgia*] [*NASA*] [*Research center*] (RCD) ... COSMIC
Computer Software and Peripheral Show (IEEE) ... COMPSO
Computer for Special Small Tactical Application ... COSSTA
Computer Sports World [*Boulder City, NV*] [*Information service*] (EISS) ... CSW
Computer Status Lights (MCD) ... CSL
Computer Status Matrix (MCD) ... CSM
Computer Stock Inventory Control (MCD) ... CSIC
Computer Stock Timing and Analysis Technique ... COM-STAT
[*The*] **Computer Store** [*NASDAQ symbol*] (NQ) ... TCS
Computer-Stored Ambulatory Record (MCD) ... COSTAR
Computer Structure Language [*1974*] [*Data processing*] (CSR) ... CSL
Computer Studies in the Humanities and Verbal Behavior [*A publication*] ... Comput Stud Hum & Verbal Behav
Computer Studies in the Humanities and Verbal Behavior [*A publication*] ... CSHVB
Computer Subsystem (NASA) ... CSS
Computer Subsystem Controller ... CSC
Computer Support Base ... CSB
Computer Support Equipment (MCD) ... CSE
Computer Survey [*A publication*] ... Comput Surv
Computer System Analyst (BUR) ... CSA
Computer System Interface Circuits (IEEE) ... CSIC
Computer System Language ... CSL
Computer System for Main Frame Operations [*Bell System*] ... COSMOS
Computer System Manual ... CSM
Computer System for Medical Information Services (DIT) ... COSMIS
Computer System Science Training [*IBM Corp.*] ... CSST
Computer System Simulator [*Programing language*] [*1969*] ... CSS
Computer Systems Association (CAH) ... CSA
Computer Systems Development Ltd. [*London, England*] [*Software supplier*] (NCC) ... CSD
Computer Systems Director (KSC) ... CSD
Computer Systems and Electronics Requirements Board [*British*] (CAA) ... CSERB
Computer Systems Integration Review (NASA) ... CSIR
Computer Systems International (OA) ... CSI
Computer Systems Research Institute [*University of Toronto*] [*Research center*] (RCD) ... CSRI
Computer Systems Support and Evaluation Command ... CSSEC
Computer Talk [*A publication*] ... Comput Talk
Computer Tape Recorder ... CTR
Computer Task Group [*NASDAQ symbol*] (NQ) ... CTSK
Computer Technology (IEEE) ... CT
Computer Technology Center ... CTC
Computer Telewriter Systems (MCD) ... CTS
Computer TELEX Exchange [*RCA Corp.*] (CAA) ... CTE
Computer Terminal Systems [*NASDAQ symbol*] (NQ) ... CTML
Computer Terminals Review [*A publication*] ... Comput Terminals Rev
Computer Test Set (VIT) ... CTS
Computer Time Bookers (OA) ... CTB
Computer Times with Computacards [*A publication*] ... Comput Times with Computacards
Computer Training System ... CTS
Computer Transceiver [*NASDAQ symbol*] (NQ) ... CTRC
Computer Transceiver Systems, Incorporated (CAA) ... CTSI
Computer Translation, Incorporated [*Information service*] (EISS) ... CTI
Computer Transponder (MCD) ... CT
Computer Typing System ... CTS
Computer Unit [*American Topical Association*] [*Rockville, MD*] (EANO) ... CU
Computer Update Equipment ... CUE
Computer Usage Co. [*NASDAQ symbol*] (NQ) ... CUSE
Computer Usage Control (NASA) ... CUC
Computer Usage List Processor (IEEE) ... CULP
Computer Usage's Business-Oriented Language [*Data processing*] (TUT) ... CUBOL
Computer Use in the Health Service [*British*] ... CUHS
Computer Use in Social Services Network [*University of Texas at Arlington*] (EANO) ... CUSSN
Computer User Education [*An association*] ... CUE
Computer Users Association (CAA) ... CUA
Computer Using Educators of BC [*British Columbia*] **Journal** [*Canada*] [*A publication*] ... CUE J
Computer Utility Educational System (MCD) ... CUES
Computer Utilization Accounting System (IEEE) ... CUAS
Computer Utilization Reporting System (IEEE) ... CURES
Computer Vision. Graphics and Image Processing [*A publication*] ... Comput Vision Graphics and Image Process
Computer Vision Laboratory [*University of Maryland*] [*Research center*] (RCD) ... CVL
Computer Voice Response (CAA) ... CVR
Computer Week [*A publication*] ... Comput Week
Computer Weekly [*A publication*] ... Computer Wkly
Computer Weekly [*A publication*] ... Comput Wkly
Computer Weekly [*A publication*] ... Comp Wkly
Computer Weekly International [*A publication*] ... Comput Wkly Int
Computer World [*A publication*] ... Comput World
Computer World Trade Group [*British*] (OA) ... CWTG
Computerised Information from National Criminological Holdings [*Australian Institute of Criminology Library*] [*Database*] [*Information service*] (EISS) ... CINCH
Computerised Instrumented Residential Audit [*Energy auditing*] ... CIRA
Computerised Library of Analysed Igneous Rocks [*Australia*] [*Information service*] (EISS) ... CLAIR
[*A*] **Computerised London Information Service** [*Greater London Council Research Library*] [*British*] (DEEC) ... ACOMPLIS
[*A*] **Computerised London Information System Online** [*Greater London Council Research Library*] [*Bibliographic database*] [*British*] (OBD) ... ACOMPLINE

Computerization of World Facts [*Stanford Research Institute*] [*Databank*] ... COMPACT
Computerized Acquisitions Systems Series [*A publication*] ... Comput Acquis Syst Ser
Computerized Agricultural Research Information System [*United Nations Food and Agricultural organization information system*] ... CARIS
Computerized AIDS [*Acquired Immune Deficiency Syndrome*] **Information Network** [*Los Angeles Gay and Lesbian Community Services Center*] [*Database*] (CUAD) ... CAIN
Computerized Annotated Bibliography System [*Alberta University*] [*Canada*] ... CABS
Computerized Area Pricing [*Telecommunications*] (TEL) ... CAPRI
Computerized, Automated, Bus Spacing and Dispatching System ... CABSADS
Computerized Automatic Inertial Test Set (MCD) ... CAITS
Computerized Automatic Rating Technique (DEN) ... CART
Computerized Automatic Systems Tester (MCD) ... CAST
Computerized Automotive Replacement Scheduling [*Bell System*] ... CARS
Computerized Automotive Reporting Service (BUR) ... CARS
Computerized Axial Tomography Scanner [*Roentgenography*] ... CATscan
Computerized Boolean Reliability Analysis [*Boeing*] ... COBRA
Computerized Bulletin Board ... CBB
Computerized Cable Upkeep Administrative Program [*Bell System*] ... CCUAP
Computerized Cataloging Systems Series [*A publication*] ... Comput Cat Syst Ser
Computerized Circulation Systems Series [*A publication*] ... Comput Circ Syst Ser
Computerized Clinical Information System [*Micromedex, Inc.*] [*Database*] ... CCIS
Computerized Conferencing and Communications Center [*New Jersey Institute of Technology*] [*Research center*] (RCD) ... CCCC
Computerized Criminal History [*FBI*] ... CCH
Computerized Deployment Execution System ... CODES
Computerized Dispersive Spectroscopy ... CDS
Computerized Distribution and Control of Microfilm [*American Motors Corp.*] ... CODICOM
Computerized Documentation System [*UNESCO*] (EISS) ... CDS
Computerized Documentation System/Integrated Set of Information Systems [*UNESCO*] (EISS) ... CDS/ISIS
Computerized Drawing Electrical Information (NG) ... CODEIN
Computerized Engineering Index [*Engineering Index, Inc.*] [*New York, NY*] [*Bibliographic database*] ... COMPENDEX
Computerized Freight Remittance System [*Pronounced "coffers"*] ... COFRS
Computerized Hierarchy and Relationship Table ... CHART
Computerized Hospital Information System (MCD) ... CHICS
Computerized Interactive Graphics (MCD) ... CIG
Computerized Library Acquisitions System [*Lukac Data Systems*] [*Lewis and Clark College*] [*Information service*] (EISS) ... CLAS
Computerized Link Analysis System ... CLANS
Computerized Literature Access Search Service ... CLASS
Computerized Literature Searching Service ... CLSS
Computerized Lubrication Control [*Sun Oil Co.*] ... CLC
Computerized Maintenance and Administration Support III [*Telecommunications*] (TEL) ... COMASIII
Computerized Management Network [*For Agricultural Cooperative Extension Service Education*] [*Virginia Polytechnic Institute*] [*Database*] (FDB) ... CMN
Computerized Medical Information Support System [*Veterans Administration*] ... COMISS
Computerized National Range Documentation ... CONRAD
Computerized Online Testing ... COLT
Computerized Operating Room Information System ... CORIS
Computerized Operational Audit Routine ... COPAR
Computerized Optimization of Elastic Booster Autopilot ... COEBRA
Computerized Outside Plant Records [*Telecommunications*] (TEL) ... COPR
Computerized Performance and Analysis Response Evaluator (IEEE) ... COMPARE
Computerized Performance Rating [*of a horse*] ... CPR
Computerized Private Branch Exchange [*Telecommunications*] ... CBX
Computerized Private Branch Exchange [*Telecommunications*] ... CPBX
Computerized Reader Enquiry Service System (IEEE) ... CRESS
Computerized Rearrangements of Special Subjects [*or Subject Specialties*] ... CROSS
Computerized Recall Identification System [*Automobile industry*] ... CRIS
Computerized Register of Voice Research [*Southern Illinois University at Carbondale*] [*Information service*] (EISS) ... CRVR
Computerized Relationship Layout Planning ... CORELAP
Computerized Relative Allocation of Facilities Technique [*IBM Corp.*] ... CRAFT
Computerized Reliability Analysis Method ... CRAM
Computerized Reliability Organization System ... CROS
Computerized Resources Information Bank [*United States Geological Survey*] (EISS) ... CRIB
Computerized Retrieval Service ... CRS
Computerized Scientific Management Planning System ... CSMPS
Computerized Serials Systems Series [*A publication*] ... Comput Ser Syst Ser
Computerized Spot Television Evaluation and Processing [*Advertising*] ... COM-STEP
Computerized Tomography [*A publication*] ... Comput Tomogr
Computerized Tomography [*A publication*] ... CTOMD
Computerized Tomography Society (EANO) ... CTS
Computerized Travel Aid [*Mobility device for the blind*] ... CTA
Computerized Vocational Information System [*Guidance program*] ... CVIS
Computerizing Medical Examination [*IBM Corp.*] ... CME
Computermarkt [*A publication*] ... COP
Computers and Applied Chemistry (China) [*A publication*] ... Comput Appl Chem (China)
Computers and Automation (BUR) ... CA
Computers and Automation [*Later, Computers and People*] [*A publication*] ... Comp & Automation
Computers and Automation [*Later, Computers and People*] [*A publication*] ... Comput Autom
Computers and Automation and People [*A publication*] ... Comput and Autom and People
Computers and Automation Universal Mailing List (IEEE) ... CAUML
Computers in Biology and Medicine [*A publication*] ... Comput Biol Med
Computers in Biology and Medicine [*A publication*] ... Comput Biol and Med
Computers and Biomedical Research [*A publication*] ... Comput Biom
Computers and Biomedical Research [*A publication*] ... Comput Biomed Res
Computers and Biomedical Research [*A publication*] ... Comput and Biomed Res
Computers in Cardiology [*A publication*] ... Comput Cardiol
Computers in Chemical and Biochemical Research [*A publication*] ... Comput Chem Biochem Res
Computers and Chemical Engineering [*A publication*] ... Comput & Chem Eng
Computers and Chemical Engineering [*A publication*] ... Comput Chem Eng
Computers and Chemistry [*A publication*] ... Comp Chem
Computers and Chemistry [*A publication*] ... Comput Chem
Computers in Chemistry and Instrumentation [*A publication*] ... Comput Chem Instrum
Computers and Communications ... C & C
Computers and Communications (DEEC) ... COMPUNICATIONS
Computers and Computing Information Resources Directory [*In preparation*] [*A publication*] ... CCIRD
Computers, Control, and Information Theory [*A publication*] ... Comput Control Inf Theory
Computers and Education [*A publication*] ... Comp & Educ
Computers and Electrical Engineering [*A publication*] ... Comput & Electr Eng
Computers and Electrical Engineering [*A publication*] ... Comput Electr Eng
Computers and Electrical Engineering [*A publication*] ... Comput Electr Engrg
Computers, Environment, and Urban Systems [*England*] [*A publication*] ... Comput Environ Urban Syst
Computers and Fluids [*A publication*] ... Comp Fluids
Computers and Fluids [*A publication*] ... Comput & Fluids
Computers and Fluids [*A publication*] ... Comput Fluids
Computers and Fluids [*A publication*] ... Comput and Fluids
Computers and Geosciences [*A publication*] ... Computers Geosci
Computers and Geosciences [*A publication*] ... Comput & Geosci
Computers and Geosciences [*A publication*] ... Comput Geosci
Computers and Graphics [*A publication*] ... Comput Graphics
Computers and Graphics [*A publication*] ... Comput & Graphics
Computers and the Humanities [*Database*] [*A publication*] ... CHum
Computers and the Humanities [*Database*] [*A publication*] ... Computer Hu
Computers and the Humanities [*Database*] [*A publication*] ... Comput Hum
Computers and the Humanities [*Database*] [*A publication*] ... Comput & Humanities
Computers and the Humanities [*Database*] [*A publication*] ... CPHCC
Computers and Industrial Engineering [*A publication*] ... Comput Ind Eng
Computers in Industry [*A publication*] ... CINUD
Computers in Industry [*Netherlands*] [*A publication*] ... Comput Ind
Computers, Information Processing, and Office Machines ... CIPOM
Computers Lawyers Association (EANO) ... CLA
Computers and Mathematics with Applications [*A publication*] ... Comput Math Appl
Computers and Mathematics with Applications [*A publication*] ... Comput & Math with Appl
Computers and Medicine [*A publication*] ... Comp & Med
Computers and Medicine [*A publication*] ... Comput Med
Computers and Operations Research [*A publication*] ... CMO
Computers and Operations Research [*A publication*] ... CMORA
Computers and Operations Research [*A publication*] ... Comp Oper Res
Computers and Operations Research [*A publication*] ... Comput Oper Res
Computers and Operations Research [*A publication*] ... Comput & Oper Res
Computers at Oregon State University, North Carolina Educational Computing Service, Dartmouth College, and the Universities of Iowa and Texas at Austin [*An educational consortium*] ... CONDUIT
Computers and People [*A publication*] ... CAP
Computers and People [*A publication*] ... Comp & People
Computers and People [*A publication*] ... Computer Pe
Computers and People [*A publication*] ... Comput and People
Computers and Security [*A publication*] ... Comput and Secur
Computers and Society [*A publication*] ... Comput and Soc
Computers and Standards [*A publication*] ... CS
Computers and Structures [*A publication*] ... Comput Struct
Computers and Structures [*A publication*] ... Comput and Struct
Computers and Structures [*A publication*] ... Comput and Structures
Computers and Systems (MCD) ... CS
Computers and Systems (IEEE) ... C & S
Computers and Their Applications [*A publication*] ... Comput Appl

Computers Users' Committee [*United Nations Development Program*] ... CUC
ComputerTown, USA! [*San Ramon, CA*] [*An association*] (EANO) ... CTUSA
Computervision Corp. [*NYSE symbol*] ... CVN
Computerworld [*A publication*] ... Computwrld
Computerworld [*A publication*] ... CW
Computing ... CMPTG
Computing Across America [*From book title, "Computing Across America: The Bicycle Odyssey of a High-Tech Nomad" by Steven K. Roberts*] ... CAA
Computing. Archiv fuer Elektronisches Rechnen [*A publication*] ... Comput Arch Elektron Rechn
Computing. Archiv fuer Informatik und Numerik [*A publication*] ... Comput Arch Inf Num
Computing Assistance Program [*Taylor University*] [*Information service*] (EISS) ... CAP
Computing Center [*Emory University*] [*Research center*] (RCD) ... EUCC
Computing Center [*University of Rochester*] [*Research center*] (RCD) ... UCC
Computing Center [*University of Cincinnati*] [*Research center*] (RCD) ... UCCC
Computing and Data Processing Services [*University of Maine*] [*Research center*] (RCD) ... CAPS
Computing & Information Systems [*East Carolina University*] [*Research center*] (RCD) ... CIS
Computing Journal Abstracts [*A publication*] ... Computing J Abs
Computing Media ... CM
Computing Newsletter for Schools of Business [*A publication*] ... Comput Newsl Schools Bus
Computing Research Laboratory [*New Mexico State University*] [*Research center*] (RCD) ... CRL
Computing Reviews [*A publication*] ... Comp Rev
Computing Reviews [*A publication*] ... Comput Rev
Computing Reviews [*A publication*] ... ComRev
Computing Reviews [*A publication*] ... CR
Computing Services Center [*Texas A & M University*] [*Research center*] (RCD) ... CSC
Computing Services Division [*Seton Hall University*] [*Research center*] (RCD) ... CSD
Computing & Software, Inc. [*NYSE symbol*] [*Delisted*] ... CSW
Computing South Africa [*A publication*] ... Comput S Afr
Computing. Supplementum [*Vienna*] [*A publication*] ... Comput Suppl
Computing Support Services [*California Institute of Technology*] [*Research center*] (RCD) ... CSS
Computing Surveys [*A publication*] ... Comp Surv
Computing Surveys [*A publication*] ... Comput Surv
Computing Surveys [*A publication*] ... Comput Survey
Computing Today [*A publication*] ... Comput Today
Computone Systems [*NASDAQ symbol*] (NQ) ... CTON
Computrac, Inc. [*NASDAQ symbol*] (NQ) ... CTTX
Computrac Instruments [*NASDAQ symbol*] (NQ) ... CTII
Computrex Centres [*Vancouver Stock Exchange symbol*] ... CXC
COMRADE [*Computer-Aided Design Environment*] **Data Management System** (OA) ... CDMS
COMRADE [*Computer-Aided Design Environment*] **Data Storage Facility** (OA) ... CDSF
COMRADE [*Computer-Aided Design Environment*] **Permanent File Management System** (OA) ... CPFMS
COMSAT [*Communications Satellite Corp.*] **Maritime Communications Satellite** (MCD) ... CMCS
COMSAT [*Communications Satellite Corp.*] **Nonreflecting** [*Solar cell*] ... CNR
COMSAT [*Communications Satellite Corp.*] **Technical Review** [*A publication*] ... COMSAT Tech Rev
COMSAT [*Communications Satellite Corp.*] **Technical Review** [*A publication*] ... CSTRC
COMSAT [*Communications Satellite Corp.*] **Technical Review** [*A publication*] ... CTR
Comserv Corp. [*NASDAQ symbol*] (NQ) ... CMSV
Comshare, Inc. [*NASDAQ symbol*] (NQ) ... CSRE
Comtech Group International Ltd. [*Toronto Stock Exchange symbol*] ... CTG
Comtech, Inc. [*Toronto Stock Exchange symbol*] ... CMT
Comtech Telecommunications [*NASDAQ symbol*] (NQ) ... CMTL
Concentrated Range Extension with Gain [*Telecommunications*] (TEL) ... CREG
Concentrateur Exploitant les Temps d'Inactivite des Circuits [*French*] [*Telecommunications*] (TEL) ... CELTIC
Concentration Module Extension [*Telecommunications*] (TEL) ... CMX
Concentration Module Main [*Telecommunications*] (TEL) ... CMM
Concentrator Isolation Working Subsystem [*Telecommunications*] (TEL) ... CIWS
Concentrator Terminal Buffer [*Data processing*] (IBMDP) ... CTB
Concept Learning System [*Data processing*] (BUR) ... CLS
Concerned Broadcasters Using Inter-City Video Transmission Facilities (EANO) ... CBUIVTF
Concerned Broadcasters Using Inter-City Video Transmission Facilities (EANO) ... CON-VID
Concurrent Algorithmic Programing Language [*Data processing*] (CSR) ... CAP
Concurrent Concession (MDG) ... CC
Concurrent Operating System [*Sperry UNIVAC*] [*Data processing*] (IEEE) ... COS
Concurrent Peripheral Operations (BUR) ... CPO
Condition (MDG) ... CND
Condition (AFM) ... COND
Condition BIT [*Binary Digit*] [*Data processing*] ... CB
Condition Code ... CC
Condition Code Register (CAA) ... CCR
Conditional Transfer of Control (CAH) ... CTC
Conditional Variable Incremental Computer (IEEE) ... CVIC
Conditioned Reflex [*Machine*] (IEEE) ... CONFLEX
Conditioned Reflex Analog (IEEE) ... CORA
Conducted Emission (IEEE) ... CE
Conducted Susceptibility (IEEE) ... CS
Conduction Band [*Electronics*] ... CB
Conductive Plastic Potentiometer ... CPP
Conductivity Modulated Bipolar [*Data processing*] ... CMB
Conductor (KSC) ... COND
Confederation of Information Communication Industries [*British*] ... CICI
Conference (AFM) ... CONF
Conference on Computers in Undergraduate Science Education ... COMUSE
Conference on Data Systems Languages [*Washington, DC*] ... CODASYL
Conference Europeenne des Administrations des Postes et des Telecommunications [*Conference of European Postal and Telecommunications Administrations*] [*Berne, Switzerland*] [*Telecommunications*] (EANO) ... CEPT
Conference on Inter-American Telecommunications [*Organization of American States*] [*Telecommunications*] (TSSD) ... CITEL
Conference on Interlibrary Communications and Information Networks [*September 28 - October 2, 1970*] ... CICIN
Conference on Self-Operating Systems [*Data processing*] ... COSOS
Configuration Block Diagram [*Telecommunications*] (TEL) ... CBD
Configuration Control Function [*Telecommunications*] (TEL) ... CCF
Configuration Data Control ... CDC
Configuration Item ... CI
Configuration Management ... CM
Configuration Process [*Telecommunications*] (TEL) ... CONFG
Configuration and Tuning Module [*Data processing*] ... CTM
Configuration Utilization Efficiency (BUR) ... CUE
Confirming Design Layout Report Date [*Bell System*] (TEL) ... CDLRD
Confirming Engineering Information Report Date [*Bell System*] (TEL) ... CEIRD
Confirming Informal Order [*Telecommunications*] (TEL) ... CIO
Confirming Telephone [*or message*] **Authority Of** ... COTA
Congestion [*Telecommunications*] (TEL) ... CONG
Congressional Information Service [*Washington, DC*] [*Database producer*] [*Information service*] ... CIS
Congressional Record On-Line [*Capitol Services, Inc.*] [*Washington, DC*] [*Bibliographic database*] ... CRECORD
Congressional Session [*Online database field identifier*] (OBD) ... CS
Conical Monopole Antenna ... CMA
Conical Scan Antenna ... CSA
Connect (FAAC) ... CNCT
Connecticut On-Line Law-Enforcement Communications and Teleprocessing [*Computer law-enforcement system*] ... COLLECT
Connecting Block [*Telecommunications*] (TEL) ... CB
Connection Pending [*Telecommunications*] (TEL) ... CP
Connection Point [*Data processing*] (IBMDP) ... CP
Connectionless Acknowledged Information (CCD) ... CAI
Connections per Circuit per Hour [*Telecommunications*] (TEL) ... CCH
Connectivity Table [*Data processing*] ... CT
Connector for Networked Information Transfer [*Massachusetts Institute of Technology*] [*Information service*] (EISS) ... CONIT
Connectorized Exchange Cable Splicing [*Telecommunications*] (TEL) ... CONECS
Conrac Corp. [*NYSE symbol*] ... CAX
CONRAIL [*Consolidated Rail Corp.*] **Analysis Model** [*Data processing*] ... CRAM
Consco Enterprises [*NASDAQ symbol*] (NQ) ... CNSO
Conseil International des Telecommunications de Press [*International Press Telecommunications Council*] ... CITP
Conservation and Renewable Energy Inquiry and Referral Service [*Database*] (FDB) ... CEIRS
Console [*Data processing*] ... CONS
Console Command Processor [*Digital Research*] (DEEC) ... CCP
Console to Computer Buffer (MUGU) ... CCB
Console Computer Interface Adapter ... CCIA
Console Control Circuit ... CCC
Console Control Package (OA) ... CCP
Console Digital Display Programer (MUGU) ... CDDP
Console Input/Output (CAA) ... CONIO
Console Message Processor [*Data processing*] ... CMP
Console Operator Proficiency Examination [*Computer Usage Co.*] (CDH) ... COPE
Console-Oriented Model Building [*Data processing*] ... COMB
Console-Oriented Statistical Matrix Operator System [*Data processing*] ... COSMOS
Console Processor (NASA) ... CP
Console Reply Queuing (CAA) ... CRQ
Console Simulator [*Data processing*] ... CONSIM
Consolidate Time Rate ... CTR
Consolidated Computer and Control Center ... CCCC
Consolidated Function Ordinary [*IBM Corp.*] ... CFO
Consolidated Telecommunications Program ... CTP
Consortium Communications International, Inc. [*New York, NY*] [*Telecommunications*] (TSSD) ... CCI

Consorzio Interuniversitario Lombardo per l'Elaborazione Automatica [*Lombard Interuniversity Consortium for Data Processing*] [*Italy*] [*Information service*] (EISS) ... CILEA
Constant ... C
Constant ... CONST
Constant Bandwidth (MCD) ... CB
Constant Bandwidth ... CBW
Constant BIT [*Binary Digit*] **Density** [*Control feature of magnetic tape recorders*] [*Data processing*] ... CBD
Constant Net Loss [*Telecommunications*] (TEL) ... CNL
Constant-Output Amplifier (MUGU) ... COA
Constant-Output Level Adapter ... COLA
Constant Voltage and Constant Frequency (BUR) ... CVCF
Constant Voltage Transformer ... CVT
Constrado Structural Analysis System [*Structures & Computers Ltd.*] [*Software package*] [*British*] (NCC) ... CONSAS
Constrained Optimal Design [*Data processing*] (RDA) ... COD
Construction Design Criteria [*Telecommunications*] (TEL) ... CDC
Construction Dollar Control System [*AT & T*] ... CDCS
Construction Dollar Spreading [*System*] [*AT & T*] ... CDS
Construction Permit [*Broadcasting term*] ... CP
Construction Program Administration System [*Telecommunications*] (TEL) ... CPAS
Construction Scheduling and Coordination [*AT & T*] ... CSC
Construction Unit [*Data processing*] ... CU
Consultative Committee on International Telegraphy and Telephony [*ITU*] ... CCITT
Consultative Committee on International Telephony [*Later, CCITT*] [*ITU*] ... CCIT
Consultative Panel on Public Information [*United Nations*] [*Telecommunications*] (TEL) ... CPPI
Consultec Canada Limited [*Vancouver, BC*] [*Telecommunications*] (TSSD) ... CCL
Consumer Demographics, Incorporated [*Information service*] (EISS) ... CDI
Consumer Drug Information [*American Society of Hospital Pharmacists*] [*Database*] [*Information service*] (EISS) ... CDIF
Consumer Drug Information on Disk [*American Society of Hospital Pharmacists*] [*Database*] ... CDID
Consumer Electronics Show [*Computer industry*] ... CES
Consumer Goods System [*Data processing*] ... COGS
Consumer Price Index [*Department of Labor*] [*Database*] ... CPI
Consumer and Producer Price Indexes [*Department of Labor*] [*Database*] (CUAD) ... CPI/PPI
Contact [*A publication*] ... CNTA
Contact [*A publication*] ... Con
Contact Resistance Variation [*Telecommunications*] (TEL) ... CRV
Contemporary Digital Services, Incorporated [*New Rochelle, NY*] [*Telecommunications*] (TSSD) ... CDSI
Content Addressable Computing System (CAA) ... CACS
Content-Addressable File Store [*Data processing*] (IEEE) ... CAFS
Content-Addressable Memory [*Data processing*] ... CAM
Content-Addressable Parallel Processor [*Data processing*] ... CAPP
Content Dependent Information Language (CAA) ... CODIL
Contention Priority-Oriented Demand Assignment [*Protocol*] [*Data processing*] ... CPODA
Context Addressed Segment Sequential Memory (CAA) ... CASSM
Context Free (BUR) ... CF
Context Free Language ... CFL
Context, Input, Process, Product [*Data processing*] ... CIPP
ContiCurrency Foreign Exchange and Money Market Database [*No longer available online*] (CUAD) ... CCFX
Continental Health Care [*NASDAQ symbol*] (NQ) ... CHSI
Continental Telecom [*Formerly, Continental Telephone Corporation*] [*NYSE symbol*] ... CTC
Continue-Any [*Mode*] [*Data processing*] (IBMDP) ... CA
Continue Calling Until (FAAC) ... CONCA
Continue-Specific [*Mode*] [*Data processing*] (IBMDP) ... CS
Continuity [*Telecommunications*] (TEL) ... COT
Continuity Message [*Telecommunications*] (TEL) ... CM
Continuity Tone Detector [*Telecommunications*] (TEL) ... CTD
Continuity Transceiver [*Telecommunications*] (TEL) ... CT
Continuity Transceiver Module [*Telecommunications*] (TEL) ... CTM
Continuous Alarm Reporting Service [*Telecommunications*] (TEL) ... CARS
Continuous Audit Program [*Data processing*] (IEEE) ... CAP
Continuous Automated Placement Survey [*Department of Labor*] ... CAPS
Continuous Automatic Line Monitoring System ... CALMS
Continuous Beam [*Camutek*] [*Software package*] [*British*] (NCC) ... CONTB
Continuous-Beam Analysis [*Jacys Computing Services*] [*Software package*] [*British*] (NCC) ... CBA
Continuous Color Sequence [*Telecommunications*] ... CCS
Continuous Correlation Processing ... CCP
Continuous Expression Processor, Inc. [*Medfield, MA*] [*Hardware manufacturer*] (DASO) ... CEP
Continuous Multibay Frames [*Jacys Computing Services*] [*Software package*] [*British*] (NCC) ... CMF
Continuous Multiple Access Collator [*Proposed by Mortimer Taube, 1957*] [*Data processing*] ... COMAC
Continuous Operation during Hours Shown [*Broadcasting*] ... C
Continuous Operation Production Allocation and Control [*Data processing*] ... COPAC
Continuous Operation Program [*Data processing*] (MDG) ... COP
Continuous Phase Frequency Shift Keying (CAA) ... CPFSK
Continuous Process Control [*Design Software Ltd.*] [*Software package*] [*British*] (NCC) ... CPC
Continuous Progress Indicator [*Telecommunications*] (TEL) ... CPR
Continuous Receiver On [*Electronic device*] ... CRO
Continuous Ring Tone [*Telecommunications*] (TEL) ... CRT
Continuous Sheet Memory [*Data processing*] (BUR) ... CSM
Continuous Slope Delta Modulation [*Telecommunications*] (CAA) ... CSDM
Continuous System Modeling Program [*Data processing*] ... CSMP
Continuous System Simulation Language [*Data processing*] ... CSSL
Continuous Update Memory Display ... CUMD
Continuous Variable Slope Delta [*Modulation*] ... CVSD
Continuous Wave [*A form of radio transmission*] ... CW
Continuous Wave Frequency-Modulated (MSA) ... CWFM
Continuous Wave Transmitter (CAAL) ... CWX
Continuous Wave Video ... CWV
Continuously Updated Dynamic Optimizing Systems (IEEE) ... CUDOS
Continuously Variable Slope Delta Modulation [*Telecommunications*] (TEL) ... CVSDM
[*The*] **Continuum Company** [*NASDAQ symbol*] (NQ) ... CTUC
Contract Completion Date [*Telecommunications*] (TEL) ... CCD
Contract Configuration Process [*Telecommunications*] (TEL) ... CCP
Contract Number [*Data processing*] ... CN
Contracting Officer's Representative [*Telecommunications*] (TEL) ... COR
Contralateral Routing of Signal [*Audiometry*] ... CROS
Contrast Transfer Function ... CTF
Control ... C
Control (KSC) ... CNTL
Control ... CNTRL
Control (MSA) ... CONT
Control ... CTL
Control Access Manager (BUR) ... CAM
Control Assembly Program (BUR) ... CAP
Control Automation System [*IBM Corp.*] (CAA) ... CAS
Control Card Listing [*Data processing*] ... CCL
Control Character [*Keyboard*] ... CTRL
Control Computer (KSC) ... CC
Control Contactor (IEEE) ... CCR
Control Data Assembly Program [*Control Data Corp.*] ... CODAP
Control Data Communications Control Procedure [*Telecommunications*] (TEL) ... CDCCP
Control Data Corp. [*NYSE symbol*] ... CDA
Control Data Corporation ... CDC
Control Data Corp. [*Toronto Stock Exchange symbol*] ... CTD
Control Data Education Institutes ... CDEI
Control Data Institute (DDI) ... CDI
Control Data Panel (VIT) ... CDP
Control Data System (NASA) ... CDS
Control Data Terminal ... CDT
Control Data Unit ... CDU
Control and Diagnostic Unit [*Data processing*] ... CDU
Control Diagram Language [*Data processing*] (IEEE) ... CODIL
Control Differential Transmitter ... CDX
Control and Display Panel (MCD) ... CDP
Control Display Unit ... CDU
Control Footing (CAH) ... CF
Control Functional Unit [*Data link*] (NG) ... CFU
Control Heading (BUR) ... CH
Control Hole (BUR) ... CH
Control in Information Systems ... COINS
Control Interval Definition Field [*Data processing*] (BUR) ... CIDF
Control Language [*Data processing*] (BUR) ... CL
Control Language Translator (IEEE) ... COLT
Control Leader [*Data processing*] ... CL
Control Logic ... CL
Control Logic Array ... CLA
Control Logic and Drive Assembly ... CLDA
Control Maintenance Unit (CAA) ... CMU
Control Mark (DEN) ... CM
Control Memory [*Telecommunications*] (TEL) ... CM
Control Memory Address Register [*Data processing*] (CAA) ... CMAR
Control Monitor (MCD) ... CM
Control-Oriented Language [*Data processing*] (IEEE) ... COOL
Control Processing Unit (MCD) ... CPU
Control Processor (IEEE) ... CP
Control Program [*Data processing*] ... CP
Control Program Assist [*IBM Corp.*] (CAA) ... CPA
Control Program Facility (MCD) ... CPF
Control Program-Five [*Operating system*] [*Xerox Corp.*] (CAA) ... CP-V
Control Program for Microcomputers [*Operating system*] ... CP/M
Control Program/Monitor [*Data processing*] ... CP/M
Control Program - Real-Time [*Xerox Corp.*] (CAA) ... CP-R
Control Programs Support (IEEE) ... CPS
Control and Protection of Transoceanic Air Lanes of Communication ... CAPTALC
Control Read-Only Memory [*Data processing*] ... CROM
Control and Reproducibility Monitor (IEEE) ... CRM
Control ROM [*Read-Only Memory*] **Address Register** [*Data processing*] (CAA) ... CRAR
Control Routine (OA) ... CR
Control Signal Processor [*for spacecraft*] ... CSP
Control Signaling Subsystem [*Telecommunications*] (TEL) ... CSS
Control and Simulation Language [*Data processing*] ... CSL
Control and Status Logic (KSC) ... CSL

Control Status Register (CAA) ... CSR
Control Store (CAA) ... CS
Control Store Address Register (CAA) ... CSAR
Control Store Data Register (CAA) ... CSDR
Control Subroutine Language [*Data processing*] (IEEE) ... CONSUL
Control Switching Point (BUR) ... CSP
Control and Timing Unit [*Data processing*] ... CTU
Control Track Direction Computer ... CTDC
Control Translator [*Honeywell, Inc.*] [*Data processing*] ... CONTRAN
Control Transmitter (MUGU) ... CX
Control Unit [*Data processing*] ... CU
Control Unit Busy (CMD) ... CUB
Control Unit End (CMD) ... CUE
Control Unit Tester [*Sperry UNIVAC*] (BUR) ... CUT
Control Word ... CW
Control Word Address (CAA) ... CWA
Controlled Avalanche Transit Time [*Electronics*] ... CATT
Controlled Communications Systems [*Chicago, IL*] [*Telecommunications*] (TSSD) ... CCS
Controlled Digital Simulator ... CODIS
Controlled Element Computer ... CEC
Controlled Term [*Online database field identifier*] (OBD) ... CT
Controller (KSC) ... CONT
Controller Checkout Console (NASA) ... CCC
Controller/Director Information File (AFM) ... CDIF
Controller Input Test Equipment ... CITE
Controller Interface Unit (MCD) ... CIU
Controls and Monitoring Processor (IEEE) ... CAMP
Convergent Technology [*NASDAQ symbol*] (NQ) ... CVGT
Conversation Factor [*Data processing*] (CDH) ... CF
Conversational Algebraic Language [*Adaptation of JOSS language*] [*Data processing*] ... CAL
Conversational Communication Access Method (CAA) ... CCAM
Conversational Compiling System [*Xerox Corp.*] (IEEE) ... CCS
Conversational Extensible Language [*Data processing*] (CSR) ... CEL
Conversational File Information Retrieval and Management System [*Data processing*] (MCD) ... CONFIRM
Conversational Interactive Digital/Analog Simulator [*IBM Corp.*] (IEEE) ... CIDAS
Conversational Language for Input/Output [*Data processing*] (CAA) ... CLIO
Conversational Language for Interactive Computing (CAA) ... CLIC
Conversational Mode Terminal [*Friden, Inc.*] (IEEE) ... CMT
Conversational Modeling Language [*Data processing*] ... CML
Conversational Monitor System [*IBM Corp.*] [*Data processing*] ... CMS
Conversational Parts Programing Language [*Data processing*] (IEEE) ... CAPT
Conversational Program Module [*Fujitsu Ltd.*] [*Japan*] (CAA) ... CPM
Conversational Programing Language [*High-level language*] [*Digital Equipment Corp.*] [*Data processing*] ... CPL
Conversational Programing System [*Data processing*] ... CPS
Conversational Remote Batch Entry [*Data processing*] ... CRBE
Conversational Remote Job Entry [*Data processing*] ... CRJE
Conversational Software System [*National CSS, Inc.*] (CAA) ... CSS
Conversational System with On-Line Remote Terminals [*Data processing*] (IEEE) ... CONSORT
Conversational Terminal System [*Data processing*] (BUR) ... CTS
Conversational Time-Sharing [*Data processing*] (IEEE) ... CTS
Conversion ... CONV
Conversion Computer Unit (VIT) ... CCU
Conversion, Memory, and Fault Indication [*Telecommunications*] (TEL) ... C/MFI
Convert Gray to Binary ... CGB
Converter (KSC) ... CONV
Converter Amplifier Unit (MCD) ... CAU
Converter/Programer (MCD) ... C/P
Converter Simulator Signal Unit (MCD) ... CSSU
Conveyorized Automatic Tube Tester [*Data processing*] (CGC) ... CATT
Cooley Electronics Laboratory [*University of Michigan*] [*Research center*] (RCD) ... CEL
Cooperating Users of Burroughs Equipment [*Detroit, MI*] [*Data processing*] ... CUBE
Cooperative Communicators Association (EANO) ... CCA
Cooperative Computing System [*Echo detection*] ... CCS
Cooperative Documents Network Project [*University of Guelph Library*] [*Database*] ... CODOC
Cooperative Library Agency for Systems and Services [*San Jose, CA*] [*Telecommunications*] (TSSD) ... CLASS
Cooperative Machine-Readable Cataloging Program [*Library of Congress*] ... COMARC
Cooperative National Plant Pest Survey and Detection Program [*Database*] (FDB) ... CNPPSDP
Cooperative Users of Equimatics Financial Systems (CSR) ... CUEFS
Cooperative Users of FICS and MARS [*Atlanta, GA*] ... CUFAM
Coopers & Lybrand USA [*New York, NY*] [*Telecommunications*] (TSSD) ... C & L
Coordinate Conversion Computer (MCD) ... CCC
Coordinate Data Set (CDH) ... CORDAT
Coordinate Rotation Digital Computer ... CORDIC
Coordinated Commentary Programing [*Data processing*] ... CCP
Coordinated Geometry [*Programing language*] [*1957*] (CSR) ... COGO
Coordinated Occupational Information Network [*Bell & Howell Co.*] (EISS) ... COIN
Coordinated Science Laboratory [*University of Illinois*] [*Research center*] ... CSL
Coordinates Computed (MUGU) ... CC
Coordinating Council for Computers in Construction [*New York, NY*] (EANO) ... CCCC
Coordination of Operating Data by Automatic Computer ... CODAC
Coordination of Record and Data Base System [*Telecommunications*] (TEL) ... CORDS
Coordinative Retrieval of Selectively Sorted Permuted Analogue-Title Entries [*Data processing*] ... CROSSPATE
Coplanar Waveguide ... CPW
Copolar Attenuation [*Telecommunications*] (TEL) ... CPA
Copper Weld Steel [*Telecommunications*] (TEL) ... CWS
Copy (BUR) ... CPY
Copyright (TEL) ... COPR
Cordatum, Inc. [*NASDAQ symbol*] (NQ) ... CDAT
Core Diode Logic ... CDL
Core File (IEEE) ... COFIL
Core Image Converter [*Data processing*] (TUT) ... CIC
Core Image Library (CMD) ... CIL
Core Load Overlay Builder [*General Automation, Inc.*] (CAA) ... CLOB
Core Memory ... CM
Core Memory Unit (MCD) ... CMU
Core and Random Access Manager [*General Automation, Inc.*] (CAA) ... CRAM
Core Storage Terminal Table [*Data processing*] ... CSTT
Core Transistor Logic [*Data processing*] ... CTL
Cornell Computing Language [*Data processing*] ... CORC
Cornell Hotel Administration Simulation Exercise [*Computer-programed management game*] ... CHASE
Cornell List Processor [*Data processing*] (TUT) ... CLP
Cornell Manufacturing Engineering and Productivity Program [*Cornell University*] [*Research center*] (RCD) ... COMEPP
Coronary Care Unit [*University of Southern California*] [*Research center*] (RCD) ... CCU
Corporate Committee of Telecommunications Users (EANO) ... CCTU
Corporate Communications System [*Bell-Northern Research Ltd.*] [*Data processing*] ... COCOS
Corporate Consolidated Data Network [*IBM Corp.*] [*Telecommunications*] ... CCDN
Corporate Conversions [*Dobbs Ferry, NY*] [*Information service*] (EISS) ... CC
Corporate Database [*Data processing*] (TUT) ... CDB
Corporate and Industry Research Reports [*JA Micropublishing, Inc.*] [*Database*] (CUAD) ... CIRR
Corporate Information Officer ... CIO
Corporate Research Information Service [*Frederick Research*] ... CRIS
Corporate Source [*Online database field identifier*] (OBD) ... COR
Corporate Source [*Online database field identifier*] ... CS
Correct [*British*] (CDH) ... CQT
Correctable Gate [*Data processing*] (MDG) ... CORREGATE
Correcting Computer (MCD) ... CORCOM
Correction System (OA) ... COSY
Corrections to Applied Research Laboratories Ion-Sputtering Mass Analyzers [*Data processing*] ... CARISMA
Correlated Data Processor ... CDP
Correlation Data Analyzer Recorder (CAAL) ... CODAR
Correlation Display Analyzing and Recording ... CODAR
Correlation of the Recognition of Degradation with Intelligibility Measurements [*Telecommunications*] (TEL) ... CORODIM
Corrosion Protection [*Telecommunications*] (TEL) ... CP
Corrugated-Laminated Coaxial [*Cable*] ... CLOAX
Corvus Systems, Inc. [*NASDAQ symbol*] (NQ) ... CRVS
Cosine, Hyperbolic ... COSH
Cosite Analysis Model [*Data processing*] ... COSAM
Cosmic Ray Satellite [*Japan*] ... CORSA
Cost per Instruction [*Data processing*] ... CPI
Council on Advanced Programing ... CAP
Council for Computerized Library Networks (EISS) ... CCLN
Council for Educational Technology [*London, England*] [*Telecommunications*] (TSSD) ... CET
Council of Institute of Telecommunication Engineers ... CITE
Council on Science and Technology for Development (EANO) ... CSTD
Council for UHF [*Ultrahigh Frequency*] **Broadcasting** (EANO) ... CUB
Count (CAH) ... CNT
Count Back Order and Sample Select [*Data processing*] (CAA) ... CBOSS
Count Forward [*Data processing*] (CGC) ... CF
Count Register [*Data processing*] ... CX
Count Reverse [*Data processing*] ... CR
Count Routine Applied to Zero Input [*Computer program*] ... CRAZI
Count/Time Data System (IEEE) ... C/TDS
Counter (MDG) ... CNT
Counter (MSA) ... CNTR
Counter (CDH) ... CT
Counter (KSC) ... CTR
Counter Electromotive Force (MCD) ... CEMF
Counter Flip-Flop [*Data processing*] (VIT) ... CFF
Counter, n Stages [*Electronics*] (DEN) ... CT/N
Counter/Timer Circuit [*Data processing*] (CAA) ... CTC
Counter-Timer Controller ... CTC
Country [*Online database field identifier*] (OBD) ... CY
Country Music Television [*Cable-television system*] ... CMTV
Country and Western ... C & W
Coupled Channel [*Electronics*] ... CC

Coupler Cut-Through ... CCT
Coupling Data Unit ... CDU
Courant Alternatif [*Alternating Current*] [*French*] ... CA
Courant Institute of Mathematical Sciences [*New York University*] [*Research center*] (RCD) ... CIMS
Course Author Language [*Data processing*] (CGC) ... CAL
Course Generator (TUT) ... CG
Coursewriter [*IBM Corp. programing language*] ... CW
Court of Customs and Patent Appeals ... CCPA
Courtauld's All-Purpose Simulator (IEEE) ... CAPS
Courtauld's Rapid Extract, Sort, and Tabulate System (IEEE) ... CRESTS
Covered Radio Teletype (NVT) ... CRATT
Covert Submarine Transmitter and Receiver (MCD) ... CO-STAR
Cox Cable Communications, Inc. [*of Cox Broadcasting Corp.*] [*American Stock Exchange symbol*] [*Delisted*] ... CXC
CP National Network Services [*Concord, CA*] [*Telecommunications*] (TSSD) ... CPNS
CPI Corporation [*NASDAQ symbol*] (NQ) ... CPIC
CPT Corporation [*NASDAQ symbol*] (NQ) ... CPTC
CPU Power Calibration Instrument (CAA) ... CPCI
CR [*Christian Rovsing*] **Computer Systems, Inc.** [*Los Angeles, CA*] [*Telecommunications*] (TSSD) ... CRCS
Cray Research [*NYSE symbol*] ... CYR
Cray Research, Incorporated (CAA) ... CRI
Creation Facilities Program [*Data processing*] (IBMDP) ... CFP
Creative Computer Applications [*NASDAQ symbol*] (NQ) ... CCAI
Creative Computing [*A publication*] ... Creatv Comp
Creative Industries of Detroit, Inc. [*Warren, MI*] [*Telecommunications*] (TSSD) ... CID
Credit Authorization Terminal ... CAT
Creosote [*Telecommunications*] (TEL) ... C
Creosoted Wood Duct [*Telecommunications*] (TEL) ... CWD
Crescomm Transmission Services, Inc. [*Fairfield, NJ*] [*Telecommunications*] (TSSD) ... CTS
Crew Module Computer (MCD) ... CMC
Crew Software Interface (MCD) ... CSI
Crew Software Training Aid (MCD) ... CSTA
Criminal Justice Information System ... CJIS
Criminal Justice Periodical Index [*University Microfilms International*] [*Bibliographic database*] [*A publication*] ... CJPI
Criminalistic Laboratory Information Systems [*FBI*] ... CLIS
[*The*] **Crimson Group** [*Cambridge, MA*] [*Telecommunications*] (TSSD) ... TCG
Crisis-Oriented Program (TUT) ... COP
Critical [*Telecommunications*] (TEL) ... CRIT
Critical Bandwidth [*of noise*] ... CBW
Critical Design Review (AFM) ... CDR
Critical Flashover [*Voltage*] (IEEE) ... CFO
Critical Hours [*Broadcasting term*] ... CH
Critical Path Method [*Graph theory*] [*Telecommunications*] (TEL) ... CPM
Critical Path Scheduling Method [*Management*] (OA) ... CPSM
Cromemco Local Area Network [*Cromemco, Inc.*] [*Mountain View, CA*] [*Telecommunications*] (TSSD) ... C-NET
Cross Connection Point [*Telecommunications*] (TEL) ... CCP
Cross Information Company [*Boulder, CO*] [*Telecommunications*] (TSSD) ... CIC
Cross-Interleaved Reed-Solomon Code [*Data processing*] ... CIRC
Cross-Office Highway [*Telecommunications*] (TEL) ... XON
Cross-Office Slot [*Telecommunications*] (TEL) ... XOS
Cross-Polarization Discrimination ... XPD
Cross-Polarization Interference [*in radio transmission*] (DEEC) ... XPI
Cross Program Auditor [*Applied Data Research, Inc.*] (CAA) ... CPA
Cross Reference (AFM) ... CREF
Cross Reference (NG) ... X-REF
Cross Reference Utility [*Data processing*] ... CULL
Cross Talk (IEEE) ... XT
Cross-Talk Unit ... CU
Cross Tell (IEEE) ... XTEL
Cross-Tell Simulator (IEEE) ... XTS
Crossbar [*Bell System*] ... XB
Crossbar Tandem [*Telecommunications*] (TEL) ... XBT
Crossed [*Telecommunications*] (TEL) ... XD
Crosspoint [*Switching element*] (MSA) ... XPT
Crosstalk [*Telecommunications*] (MSA) ... XTALK
CRT [*Cathode-Ray Tube*] **Display Unit** (MCD) ... CDU
Crude Oil Analysis Data Bank [*Department of Energy*] [*Database*] (FDB) ... COA
Cryogenic Continuous Film Memory [*Data processing*] (DIT) ... CCFM
Cryotron Associative Processor (IEEE) ... CAP
Crypto-Communication Network (MDG) ... CRYPTONET
Crystal Oscillator ... CO
Crystal Oscillator (IEEE) ... XO
Crystallographic Computing Network [*AEC*] (EISS) ... CRYSNET
CSIRO [*Commonwealth Scientific and Industrial Research Organisation*] **Computing Research Section. Memorandum** [*A publication*] ... CSIRO Computing Res Sect Memo
CT. Journal of Computed Tomography [*A publication*] ... CT J Comput Tomography
CTI. Communication Technology Impact [*A publication*] ... CTI Commun Technol Impact
CTS Corp. [*NYSE symbol*] ... CTS
Cubic ... CU
Cubic Feet per Hour ... CFH
Cubic Feet per Minute ... CFM
Cumulative Abbreviated Trouble File [*Telecommunications*] (TEL) ... CAT
Cumulative Audience [*Telecommunications*] ... CUME
Cumulative Computer Abstracts [*A publication*] ... Cum Comput Abstr
CUNY [*City University of New York*] **Data Service** [*Information service*] (EISS) ... CDS
Currency Sign [*Telecommunications*] (TEL) ... CS
Current ... CUR
Current [*Electronics*] (CDH) ... I
Current Abstracts of Chemistry [*Institute for Scientific Information*] [*Database*] [*A publication*] ... CAC
Current Agricultural Research Information System [*United Nations*] [*Information service*] (EISS) ... CARIS
Current Awareness and Document Retrieval for Engineers (DIT) ... CADRE
Current BIT [*Binary Digit*] **Monitor Unit** [*Data processing*] ... CBMU
Current Cancer Research Project Analysis Center [*Database producer*] ... CCRESPAC
Current-Controlled Oscillator (IEEE) ... CCO
Current Data BIT [*Binary Digit*] [*Data processing*] ... CDB
Current Fault File [*Telecommunications*] (TEL) ... CFF
Current Hogging Injection Logic [*Electronics*] (IEEE) ... CHIL
Current-Hogging Logic [*Electronics*] ... CHL
Current Information Selection [*IBM Technical Information Retrieval Center*] [*White Plains, NY*] ... CIS
Current Injection Logic [*Data processing*] (CAA) ... CIL
Current Instruction Register ... CIR
Current Line Pointer [*Data processing*] (IBMDP) ... CLP
Current Literature Awareness Search Service [*BIOSIS*] [*Database*] ... CLASS
Current Mode Complementary Transistor Logic (IEEE) ... CMCTL
Current-Mode Digital-to-Analog Converter [*Data processing*] ... CMDAC
Current-Mode Logic [*Data processing*] ... CML
Current-Mode Switching [*Data processing*] (MSA) ... CMS
Current Operational Data System (DDI) ... CODAS
Current Operator - Next Operator [*Data processing*] (MDG) ... CO/NO
Current Papers on Computers and Control [*A publication*] ... CPC
Current Processor Mode (CAA) ... CPM
Current Research File [*NIOSH*] [*Database*] (FDB) ... CRF
Current Research Information System [*Department of Agriculture*] [*Washington, DC*] [*Database*] ... CRIS
Current Switch Logic (IEEE) ... CSL
Current Transfer Ratio [*Bell System*] ... CTR
Current Transformer ... CT
Current Word Pointer (CAA) ... CWP
Cursor Control [*Data processing*] (BUR) ... CC
Custom Chip [*Personal computers*] ... CC
Custom Computer System (IEEE) ... CCS
Custom Electronics, Inc. [*Chicopee, MA*] [*Software manufacturer*] (DASOS) ... CE
Custom Input/Output Unit [*Data processing*] (IEEE) ... CIOU
Custom Packages for Automation [*3D Digital Design & Development Ltd.*] [*Software package*] [*British*] (NCC) ... CPFA
Custom Work Order [*Telecommunications*] (TEL) ... CWO
Customer Acquisition Unit (NASA) ... CAU
Customer-Bank Communication Terminal [*Computerized banking*] ... CBCT
Customer Code [*Telecommunications*] (TEL) ... CUS
Customer Communications Exchange [*Bell System*] ... CCX
Customer Dial Pulse Receiver [*Telecommunications*] (TEL) ... CDPR
Customer Engineer [*Data processing*] ... CE
Customer Information Control System [*Pronounced "kicks"*] [*IBM Corp.*] ... CICS
Customer Information Control System Virtual Storage [*IBM Corp.*] [*Data processing*] ... CICS/VS
Customer Information File [*Data processing*] (BUR) ... CIF
Customer Information System [*IBM Corp.*] ... CIS
Customer Network Control Center [*Telecommunications*] (TEL) ... CNCC
Customer-Operated Terminal [*Data processing*] ... COT
Customer Order Processing (BUR) ... COP
Customer Order Processing System (TUT) ... COPS
Customer-Oriented Data System (DIT) ... CODAS
Customer-Oriented Terminal [*Data processing*] (CAA) ... COT
Customer-Orienting Program (TUT) ... COP
Customer-Owned and Maintained [*Equipment*] ... COAM
Customer Owned and Telephone Company Maintained [*Telecommunications*] (TEL) ... COTM
Customer Premises Equipment [*Telecommunications*] ... CPE
Customer-Premises Facility Terminal [*Telecommunications*] (TEL) ... CPFT
Customer Premises System [*Bell System*] ... CPS
Customer Provided Equipment [*Telecommunications*] ... CPE
Customer Records and Billing [*Bell System*] ... CRB
Customer Satisfaction Research Institute [*Lenexa, KS*] [*Telecommunications*] (TSSD) ... CSRI
Customer Service (BUR) ... CS
Customer Service Administration Control Center System [*Telecommunications*] (TEL) ... CSACCS
Customer Service Representative ... CSR
Customer Set-Up [*Data processing*] ... CSU
Customer Support (BUR) ... CS
Customer Support Unit ... CSU
Customer Switching System [*Telecommunications*] (TEL) ... CSS
Customer Trouble Report Analysis Plan [*Telecommunications*] (TEL) ... CTRAP
Customer's Other Service [*Telecommunications*] (TEL) ... COS

Customer's Report [*Telecommunications*]   (TEL) .... CR
Customized Processor [*IBM Corp.*]   (IEEE) .... CP
Customs Optical Reader Passport Systems [*A scanning device capable of reading the latest US passports*] .... CORPS
Cutoff [*Telecommunications*]   (TEL) .... CTO
Cutter Location File   (CCD) CL
Cybernetics and Systems [*A publication*] .... Cybernet Systems
Cycle Program Control   (MCD) .... CPC
Cycle Program Counter   (IEEE) .... CPC
Cycles per Second [*See also Hz*] .... CPS
Cyclic Check Character [*Data processing*]   (TUT) CCC
Cyclic Code   (BUR) CC
Cyclic Data Management Routine [*Data processing*]............................. CDMR
Cyclic Redundancy Check [*Data processing*] .... CRC
Cyclic Redundancy Check Character [*Data processing*]   (IEEE)............. CRCC
Cylinder.. CYL
Cylinder-Cylinder-Head-Sector [*Data processing*]   (IBMDP).................. CCHS
Cymomotive Force [*Telecommunications*]   (TEL)...................................... CMF
Cyphernetics Text Processing Language [*1970*] [*Data processing*]   (CSR) .... CYPHERTEXT

D

Dacron Braid Lacquered (MDG)	DL
Daily Automatic Rescheduling Technique [*Data processing*]	DART
Daily Transaction Register File [*Data processing*]	DTRF
Daily Transaction Registering [*or Reporting*] [*Data processing*]	DTR
Daisy Wheel [*Printer*] (CAA)	DW
Dallas Fort Worth Teleport Ltd. [*Irving, TX*] [*Telecommunications*] (TSSD)	DFWT
Damage Assessment Routines (MDG)	DAR
Danish Federation for Information Processing and Management [*Copenhagen, Denmark*]	DANFIP
Danish Veterinary and Agricultural Library Catalogue [*Database*] (CUAD)	DVJB
Danmarks Tekniske Bibliotek [*National Technological Library of Denmark*] [*Information service*] (EISS)	DTB
Dansk Databehandlinsforening [*Danish Data Processing Association*] [*Copenhagen, Denmark*]	DBF
Dartmouth Time-Sharing System [*Data processing*]	DTSS
DASD [*Direct Access Storage Device*] **Dump Restore** [*Data processing*] (IBMDP)	DDR
Data Access Arrangement [*Telecommunications*] [*Obsolete*]	DAA
Data Access Line	DAL
Data Access Protocol [*Digital Equipment Corp.*]	DAP
Data Access Register [*Data processing*] (MDG)	DAR
Data Access Security (CAA)	DAS
Data Access System Language (CAA)	DASL
Data Access Systems, Inc. [*American Stock Exchange symbol*] [*Delisted*]	DAC
Data Accession List (NASA)	DAL
Data Accountability System (CIT)	DAS
Data Accumulating and Reporting Sheet	DARS
Data Accumulation and Transfer Sheet	DATS
Data Acquisition (MDG)	DA
Data Acquisition Camera	DAC
Data Acquisition Center (KSC)	DAQC
Data Acquisition Chassis	DAC
Data Acquisition Computer	DAC
Data Acquisition and Control (NASA)	DAC
Data Acquisition and Control	DAX
Data Acquisition Control and Buffer (MCD)	DACB
Data Acquisition and Control Buffer Unit (NASA)	DACBU
Data Acquisition and Control Executive [*Hewlett-Packard Co.*] (CAH)	DACE
Data Acquisition, Control, and Simulation Centre [*University of Alberta*] [*Research center*] (RCD)	DACS
Data Acquisition Control System (IEEE)	DACS
Data Acquisition and Control Unit (TUT)	DACU
Data Acquisition Controller	DAC
Data Acquisition and Decommutation Equipment	DADE
Data Acquisition and Digital Signal Processing	DADiSP
Data Acquisition Display Subsystem (OA)	DADS
Data Acquisition and Display System	DADS
Data Acquisition Facility [*of STADAN*]	DAF
Data Acquisition and Interpretation System	DAISY
Data Acquisition Language [*Data processing*] (CSR)	DAL
Data Acquisition List (MCD)	DAL
Data Acquisition Logging System (DDI)	DALS
Data Acquisition and Monitoring Equipment [*Electronics*]	DAME
Data Acquisition Multiprogramming System [*IBM Corp.*] [*Data processing*]	DAMPS
Data Acquisition Plan (MCD)	DAP
Data Acquisition and Processing (SKY)	DA & P
Data Acquisition and Processing in Biology and Medicine [*A publication*]	Data Acquis Process Biol Med
Data Acquisition and Processing in Biology and Medicine. Proceedings of the Rochester Conference [*A publication*]	Data Acquis Process Biol Med Proc Rochester Conf
Data Acquisition and Processing System	DAPS
Data Acquisition Recording System	DARS
Data Acquisition and Reduction System	DARS
Data Acquisition Requirements Document (KSC)	DARD
Data Acquisition Station (DDI)	DAS
Data Acquisition Statistical Recorder	DASR
Data Acquisition Subsystem Group	DASG
Data Acquisition Support Document (KSC)	DASD
Data Acquisition System	DAS
Data Acquisition Test [*Later, DST*]	DAT
Data Acquisition and Transmission System (MCD)	DATS
Data Acquisition Unit	DAU
Data Adapter (MCD)	DA
Data Adapter Unit	DAU
Data Address Line (CAA)	DAL
Data Addressed Memory [*Data processing*]	DAM
Data Administration Center Equipment [*Telecommunications*] (TEL)	DACE
Data Administration Section	DAS
Data Administrator (CAA)	DA
Data Aids for Training, Operations, and Maintenance (VIT)	DATOM
Data Amplification Sheet (KSC)	DAS
Data Analog Computer	DATAC
Data Analysing Robot Youth Lifeform [*From the movie entitled "D.A.R.Y.L."*]	DARYL
Data Analysis (AFM)	DA
Data Analysis (IEEE)	DATAN
Data and Analysis Center for Software [*Illinois Institute of Technology*] [*Information service*] (EISS)	DACS
Data Analysis Computer (AFM)	DAC
Data Analysis Console (AFM)	DAC
Data Analysis Control (MCD)	DAC
Data Analysis Database (OA)	DADB
Data Analysis Facility (CIT)	DAF
Data Analysis Laboratory [*Temple University*] [*Research center*] (CIT)	DAL
Data Analysis [*Program*] **of Massachusetts Institute of Technology**	DAMIT
Data Analysis and Processing Facility (DDI)	DAPF
Data Analysis Program (VIT)	DAP
Data Analysis Recording Tape	DART
Data Analysis and Reduction System	DARES
Data Analysis Software [*Telecommunications*] (TEL)	DAS
Data Analysis Station (NASA)	DAS
Data Analysis System	DASY
Data Analysis and Technique Development Center [*Alexandria, VA*] (CDH)	DATICO
Data Architects, Inc. [*NASDAQ symbol*] (NQ)	DRCH
Data Area Initializer and Verifier [*Telecommunications*] (TEL)	DAIV
Data Assembler	DA
Data Association Message	DAM
Data Automatic Reduction Equipment (CET)	DARE
Data Automation (AFM)	DA
Data Automation Activity (AFM)	DAA
Data Automation Digest [*A publication*]	DAD
Data Automation Proposal (AFM)	DAP
Data Automation Research and Experimentation (CET)	DARE
Data Auxiliary Set [*Telecommunications*] (TEL)	DAS
Data Available	DA
Data Bank	DB
Data Bank	DBK
Data Bank	DBNK
Data Bank Release Notice (NASA)	DBRN
Data Base Directory Service [*Formerly, Data Base User Service*] [*Knowledge Industry Publications, Inc.*] [*Database*] (CUAD)	DBDS
Data Base Index	DBI
Data Base and Transaction Management System [*IBM Corp.*]	DTMS
Data Bibliography Card	DBC
Data Buffer Module (IEEE)	DBM
Data Bus [*Data processing*] (MCD)	DB
Data Bus Control [*Data processing*] (MCD)	DBC
Data Bus Control Unit [*Data processing*] (KSC)	DBCU
Data Bus Coupler [*Data processing*] (MCD)	DBC
Data Bus Enable [*Data processing*]	DBE
Data Bus Generation and Maintenance Package [*Data processing*] (MCD)	DBGMP
Data Bus Group [*Data processing*] (MCD)	DBG
Data Bus In [*Data processing*]	DBIN
Data Bus Interface Adapter [*Data processing*] (MCD)	DBIA
Data Bus Interface Unit [*Data processing*] (MCD)	DBIU
Data Bus Interface Unit-Launch [*Data processing*] (MCD)	DBI

Computer & Telecommunications Acronyms

Data Bus Isolation Amplifier [*Data processing*] (MCD)	DBIA
Data Bus Monitor [*Data processing*]	DBM
Data Bus Network [*Data processing*] (MCD)	DBN
Data Business [*A publication*]	Data Bus
Data Call	DC
Data Camera	DC
Data Card Corp. [*NASDAQ symbol*] (NQ)	DATC
Data Carrier Detect [*or Detector*] [*Data communication signal*] [*Telecommunications*] (TEL)	DCD
Data Cartridge (CAA)	DC
Data Cell [*Data processing*] (TUT)	DC
Data Center (KSC)	DC
Data Channel [*Data processing*] (TUT)	DC
Data Channel Filter [*Data processing*]	DCF
Data Channels [*A publication*]	Data Chan
Data Check (BUR)	DC
Data Circuit Concentration (CAA)	DCC
Data Circuit Equipment	DCE
Data Circuit-Terminating Equipment [*Data processing*] (BUR)	DCE
Data Classifier (IEEE)	DC
Data Code	DC
Data Collection	DATACOL
Data Collection	DC
Data Collection Access Method (CAA)	DCAM
Data Collection and Data Relay [*Telecommunications*] (TEL)	DCDR
Data Collection and Evaluation System (NVT)	DCES
Data Collection Module, High Speed	DCMH
Data Collection Module, Low Speed	DCML
Data Collection Operating System (CAA)	DCOS
Data Collection Platform [*National Weather Service*] [*Weather satellite system*]	DCP
Data Collection and Reduction System	DCRS
Data Collection/Relay (MCD)	DC/R
Data Collection System [*or Subsystem*] [*Data processing*] (TUT)	DCS
Data Collection Unit	DCU
Data Command Unit	DCU
Data Communication [*Data processing*] (BUR)	DC
Data Communication Control Character (IEEE)	DCCC
Data Communication to Disk Control (CAA)	DC/DC
Data Communication Equipment	DCE
Data Communication Input Buffer	DCIB
Data Communication Network Architecture (BUR)	DCNA
Data Communication Operating System (CAA)	DACOS
Data Communication Output Selector (KSC)	DCOS
Data Communication Preprocessor	DCPP
Data Communication Processing System	DCPS
Data Communication Processor [*Data processing*] (BUR)	DCP
Data Communication System	DCS
Data Communications [*A publication*]	Data C
Data Communications	DATACOM
Data Communications [*A publication*]	Data Comm
Data Communications [*A publication*]	Data Commun
Data Communications Administrator (CAA)	DCA
Data Communications Channel	DCC
Data Communications Control Unit (DEN)	DCCU
Data Communications Controller [*Data processing*] (CAA)	DCC
Data Communications Corporation [*Information service*] (EISS)	DCC
Data Communications Equipment Monitoring and Switching (MCD)	DACEMS
Data Communications, Inc. [*Information service*] (EISS)	Da-Com
Data Communications Multiplexer (CAA)	DCM
Data Communications Terminal (CIT)	DCT
Data Communications Unit (CAA)	DCU
Data Communications Utility [*Social Security Administration*]	DCU
Data Computation Subsystem Group	DCSG
Data Concentrator [*Data processing*] (BUR)	DC
Data Condition Code	DCC
Data Control (AFM)	DC
Data Control Block [*Data processing*]	DCB
Data Control Characters (CMD)	DCC
Data Control Multiplex System	DCMS
Data Control Panel Submodule	DCPS
Data Control Services (BUR)	DCS
Data Control System [*Burroughs Corp.*]	DCS
Data Control Unit	DCU
Data Control Word (CMD)	DCW
Data Controller	DACON
Data Conversion [*Data processing*] (KSC)	D/C
Data Conversion Equipment [*Data processing*]	DCE
Data Conversion Receiver [*Data processing*]	DCR
Data Conversion System [*Data processing*]	DCS
Data Conversion Transmitter [*Data processing*]	DCT
Data Coordinator (MCD)	DC
Data Coordinator and Retriever [*Data processing*] (CGC)	DCR
Data Correction [*IBM Corp.*]	DACOR
Data Correction Amplifier	DCA
Data Correction Indicator Panel (MUGU)	DCIP
Data Correlation Control Unit (DDI)	DCCU
Data Correlation Facility	DCF
Data Correlation and Transfer System (DDI)	DATACORTS
Data Correlator	DACOR
Data Count Printout [*Data processing*]	DACPO
Data Courier, Inc. [*Louisville, KY*] (EISS)	DCI
Data Definition [*Data processing*] (BUR)	DD
Data Definition Control System (CAA)	DDCS
Data Definition Language	DDL
Data Demand (IDA)	DD
Data Demand Module (IEEE)	DDM
Data Description (MCD)	DD
Data Description Language [*Data processing*]	DAD
Data Description Language	DDL
Data Description Language Committee [*CODASYL*] (CAA)	DDLC
Data Description Table (BUR)	DDT
Data-Design Laboratories [*NASDAQ symbol*] (NQ)	DDES
Data-Design Laboratories [*NYSE symbol*]	DDL
Data Dialog System (MCD)	DDS
Data Dictionary [*Data processing*]	DD
Data Dictionary/Directory	DD/D
Data Dictionary/Directory System	DD/DS
Data Dictionary System (CAA)	DDS
Data Directed Programing System [*British*] (DIT)	DDPS
Data Direction Register [*Microcomputer*]	DDR
Data Display	DDIS
Data Display Board	DDB
Data Display Buffer	DDB
Data Display Central	DDC
Data Display Generator	DDG
Data Display Indicator	DDI
Data Display Module (MCD)	DDM
Data Display Set (MCD)	DDS
Data Display System	DDS
Data Display Unit (NASA)	DDU
Data Distribution Center	DDC
Data Distribution List	DDL
Data Distribution Panel (KSC)	DDP
Data Distribution System [*or Subsystem*]	DDS
Data Documentation Costs	DDC
Data Down Link [*Data processing*] (MCD)	DDL
Data Drawing List	DDL
Data Dynamics [*A publication*]	Data Dyn
Data Education [*A publication*]	Data Ed
Data Element [*Data processing*]	DE
Data Element Description List [*Data processing*]	DEDL
Data Element Management Accounting/Reporting	DELMAR
Data Element Management Accounting and Reporting (MCD)	DEMAR
Data Element Number (MCD)	DEN
Data Encoder (CIT)	DE
Data Encoder Unit (SKY)	DEU
Data Encoder Unit Transmitter (SKY)	DEUT
Data Encryption Algorithm (CAA)	DEA
Data Encryption Standard [*National Bureau of Standards*]	DES
Data Encryption Unit (CAA)	DEU
Data Engineering Section	DES
Data Entry (CAA)	DE
Data Entry Application Language (CAA)	DEAL
Data Entry Control System (CAA)	DECS
Data Entry and Display Panel (MCD)	DEDP
Data Entry and Display Subsystem	DEDS
Data Entry Facility (CAA)	DEF
Data Entry Keyboard [*Data processing*] (MCD)	DEK
Data Entry Language (CAA)	DEL
Data Entry Management Association [*Stamford, CT*] (EANO)	DEMA
Data Entry Panel (MCD)	DEP
Data Entry Reporting System (CAA)	DERS
Data Entry/Separation (MCD)	DE/S
Data Entry System (CAA)	DES
Data Entry System Controller (CAA)	DESC
Data Entry Unit (OA)	DEU
Data Event Control Block [*Data processing*] (BUR)	DECB
Data Exception Error Protection (CAA)	DEEP
Data Exchange (CCD)	DAX
Data Exchange	DEX
Data Exchange Agreement	DEA
Data Exchange Annex	DEA
Data Exchange Auxiliary Console (CAAL)	DEAC
Data Exchange Auxiliary Consoles (MCD)	DEACS
Data Exchange Control	DXC
Data Exchange Control Unit (NASA)	DECU
Data Exchange Program	DEP
Data Exchange System (NASA)	DES
Data Exchange System [*Texas Instruments, Inc.*] (CAA)	DXS
Data Exchange System Statement Translator [*Texas Instruments, Inc.*] (CAA)	DXSST
Data Exchange Unit	DEU
Data Extent Block (MCD)	DEB
Data Extraction (CAAL)	DX
Data Extraction and Analysis Group	DEAG
Data Facility Data Set Services	DFDSS
Data Facility Extended	DFE
Data Facility Product	DFP
Data File/Media Management System	DFMMS
Data File Number (CAA)	DFN
Data File Utility [*Data processing*] (IBMDP)	DFU
Data Flow Control (IBMDP)	DFC
Data Flow Diagram	DFD
Data Flow Engineer (MCD)	DFE

Computer & Telecommunications Acronyms

Data Flow Programing Language (CAA)	DFPL
Data Folder	DF
Data Format Converter (VIT)	DFC
Data Function Information Book (VIT)	DFIB
Data Gathering Monitoring [System]	DGM
Data Gathering System (MCD)	DGS
Data General Corp. [Computer manufacturer] (CAA)	DG
Data General Corporation [Computer manufacturer] (CAH)	DGC
Data General Corp. [NYSE symbol]	DGN
Data General Corp., Westboro, MA [OCLC symbol]	DAT
Data General's System Programing Language (CAA)	DG/L
Data Generating Program	DGP
Data Generation (SKY)	DGEN
Data Graphics Corporation	DGC
Data Handling and Display Subsystem	DHDS
Data Handling Equipment	DHE
Data Handling Subsystem (NATG)	DHSS
Data Handling System	DHS
Data Identification (CIT)	DID
Data Identification Number (AFM)	DIN
Data Identification Table (MCD)	DIT
Data Immediate Access Diagram (CCD)	DIAD
Data Independent Analysis Library (CAAL)	DIAL
Data Independent Architecture Model (OA)	DIAM
Data Information Test Material Checkout (VIT)	DITMCO
Data Input [Data processing] (IEEE)	DI
Data Input Bus [Data processing] (MDG)	DIB
Data Input Clerk [Data processing]	DIC
Data Input Consoles [Data processing]	DIC
Data Input/Data Output [Data processing]	DI/DO
Data Input Display [Data processing]	DID
Data Input Display Console [Data processing]	DIDC
Data Input/Output (CAA)	DIO
Data Input Processor [Data processing] (SKY)	DIP
Data Input Register (CAA)	DIR
Data Input System [Data processing] (CIT)	DIS
Data Input Voice Output Telephone System	DIVOTS
Data Inquiry Terminal	DIT
Data Inserter	DATIN
Data Insertion Converter	DIC
Data Inspection Board [Europe] (CAA)	DIB
Data Inspection Station (VIT)	DIS
Data Integrator (MCD)	DI
Data Interchange Format	DIF
Data Interface	DI
Data Interface Unit	DIU
Data Interfile Transfer, Testing, and Operations Utility [IBM program product]	DITTO
Data Interpretation Module (CAA)	DIM
Data Item	DI
Data Item Category	DIC
Data Item Description	DID
Data Key Idle (OA)	DKI
Data Language	DL
Data Language Version 1 [Data processing] (MCD)	DL/1
Data-Line Concentration System [Bell System]	DLCS
Data Line Flight Direction Unit (MCD)	DLFDU
Data Line Monitor (CAA)	DLM
Data Line Unit (OA)	DLU
Data Link	DL
Data Link (KSC)	DLK
Data Link Adapter (CAA)	DLA
Data Link Address	DLA
Data Link Control [Data processing] (BUR)	DLC
Data Link Control Field [Data processing]	DLCF
Data Link Control Panel [Data processing] (MCD)	DLCP
Data Link Decoder (MCD)	DLD
Data Link Equipment	DLE
Data Link Escape Character [Keyboard] (CMD)	DLE
Data Link Processor [Burroughs Corp.] [Data processing] (BUR)	DLP
Data Link Programs (MCD)	DLP
Data Link Receiver [Data processing] (MCD)	DLR
Data Link Reference Point	DLRP
Data Link Set	DLS
Data Link Simulator	DLS
Data Link Summary Message (MCD)	DLSM
Data Link Terminal	DLT
Data Link Terminal Repeater (NASA)	DLTR
Data Link Test Message	DLTM
Data Link Test Set	DALTS
Data Link Translator	DLT
Data Link Transmission Repeater (NASA)	DLTR
Data Listing Programs (IEEE)	DLP
Data Logging System	DLS
Data Logging and Transmission System (MCD)	DALATS
Data Loop Transceiver [Data processing]	DLT
Data Maintenance Diagnostic Program	DMDP
Data Management [A publication]	Data Manage
Data Management [A publication]	Data Mgmt
Data Management [A publication]	Data Mgt
Data Management (KSC)	DM
Data Management [A publication]	DMG
Data Management (MSA)	DMGT
Data Management Analysis	DMA
Data Management Block (CAA)	DMB
Data Management Center (CAAL)	DMC
Data Management Channel	DMC
Data Management Computer (KSC)	DMC
Data Management Facility (CAA)	DMF
Data Management Group (MCD)	DMG
Data Management Information System [DoD]	DMIS
Data Management Language [Digital Equipment Corp.] (CAA)	DML
Data Management Operating System (CAA)	DMOS
Data Management Routine	DMR
Data Management Service (IEEE)	DMS
Data Management Summary Processor (KSC)	DMSP
Data Management System [Data processing] (MCD)	DATAMAN
Data Management System [Data processing]	DMS
Data Management System/Computer Subsystem [Data processing]	DMS/CS
Data Management Systems, Inc. [Portland, OR] [Software manufacturer] (DASOS)	DAMAS
Data Management Unit [Data processing]	DMU
Data Management Utility System (CAA)	DMUS
Data Manager (CAH)	DM
Data Manager (KSC)	DMAN
Data Manipulation Language [Digital Equipment Corp.] [Data processing]	DML
Data Manipulation Mode (OA)	DMM
Data Master	DM
Data Measuring System	DMS
Data Memory (CAA)	DM
Data Monitoring System	DMS
Data Multiplex [Computer]	DMX
Data Multiplex Subsystem [Data processing]	DMSS
Data Multiplex System [Data processing]	DMS
Data Name	DN
Data-Net [Data-Net, Inc.] [Rochester, NY] [Telecommunications] (TSSD)	DNET
Data Network (CET)	DATANET
Data Network Access Method (CAA)	DNAM
Data Network Identification Code [Telecommunications] (TEL)	DNIC
Data Network Modified Emulator Program [Telecommunications] (TEL)	DMEP
Data Number (CIT)	DN
Data Observing Testing Console	DOTC
Data, Operations, and Control	DOC
Data Optimizing Computer	DOC
Data Output [Data processing] (IEEE)	DO
Data Output Bus (CAA)	DOB
Data Output Channel (MSA)	DOC
Data Output Multiplexer [Data processing] (KSC)	DOM
Data Output Register (CAA)	DOR
Data Package Set (CAAL)	DPS
Data Packaging Corp. [NASDAQ symbol] (NQ)	DPKG
Data Packet (Subsystem) [Telecommunications] (TEL)	DP(S)
Data-Phone Digital Service [Trademark of the American Telephone & Telegraph Co.]	DDS
Data [or Digital] Phone Line Formatter (CIT)	DPLF
Data Plotting Board	DPB
Data Pointer (CAA)	DP
Data Preparation and Maintenance (CAAL)	DPM
Data Present Signal	DPS
Data Printer	DP
Data Printout Program	DROP
Data Process Work Request	DPWR
Data Processing [A publication]	Data Proc
Data Processing [A publication]	Data Proces
Data Processing	DP
Data Processing Activities	DPA
Data Processing Agency (VIT)	DPA
Data Processing Algorithm	DPA
Data Processing Area (CIT)	DPA
Data Processing Assembly (MCD)	DPA
Data Processing Automatic Publication Service (TUT)	DAPS
Data Processing Automatic Record Standardization	DPARS
Data Processing Branch (IEEE)	DPB
Data Processing Center	DPC
Data Processing Central	DPC
Data Processing Computer (CAAL)	DPC
Data Processing and/or Computer Programing Programs [Association of Independent Colleges and Schools specialization code]	DP
Data Processing Control (AFM)	DPC
Data Processing Customer Engineering	DPCE
Data Processing Department	DPD
Data Processing Design, Inc. [Anaheim, CA] [Software manufacturer] (DASOS)	DPD
Data Processing Detachment	DPD
Data Processing Digest [A publication]	Data Process
Data Processing Division [IBM Corp.] (CDH)	DPD
Data Processing for Education [North American Publishing Co.] [A publication]	Data Process Educ
Data Processing Equipment	DPE
Data Processing Facility	DPF
Data Processing and Information Retrieval (DIT)	DPIR

By Meaning

Computer & Telecommunications Acronyms

Data Processing and Information Science Contents	DISC
Data Processing Installation	DPI
Data Processing Language (CAA)	DPL
Data Processing Machine	DPM
Data Processing Magazine [A publication]	Data Process Mag
Data Processing Magazine [A publication]	DPMAA
Data Processing Management Association [Formerly, NMAA] [Park Ridge, IL]	DPMA
Data Processing Manager (CAH)	DPM
Data Processing in Medicine [A publication]	Data Process Med
Data Processing Operation	DPO
Data Processing Practitioner [A publication]	Data Process Pract
Data Processing Products Contract	DPPC
Data Processing Project Engineer (CIT)	DPPE
Data Processing Request	DPR
Data Processing Service Center (DDI)	DPSC
Data Processing Service Request (NVT)	DPSR
Data Processing and Software (NASA)	DP & S
Data Processing and Software (NASA)	DPS
Data Processing Subsystem	DPSS
Data Processing Supplies Association [Later, IOSA]	DPSA
Data Processing System	DPS
Data Processing System Simulator (IEEE)	DPSS
Data Processing Unit	DPU
Data Processor and Computer Test Equipment	DPCTE
Data Project Management System (IEEE)	DPMS
Data Project Plan	DPP
Data Protection Agency [British] (CAA)	DPA
Data Protection Committee [British]	DPC
Data Publishing International [Netherlands] [Information service] (EISS)	DPI
Data Quality Control	DQC
Data Quality Control Monitor	DQCM
Data Quality Monitors (MDG)	DQM
Data Rate [Telecommunications] (TEL)	DR
Data Rate Changer	DRC
Data Rate Indicator (NASA)	DRI
Data Rate Selector	DRS
Data Reaction System	DRS
Data Ready Queue [IBM Corp.] (IBMDP)	DRQ
Data Receiver [or Recorder]	DR
Data Receiving Station (KSC)	DRS
Data Reception Process [Telecommunications] (TEL)	DRP
Data Reckoning Tracer (MSA)	DRT
Data Record Number (MCD)	DRN
Data Recorder/Reproducer (MCD)	DRR
Data Recording (CET)	DATREC
Data Recording (MSA)	DRCDG
Data Recording Camera	DRC
Data Recording Controller [Data processing] (BUR)	DRC
Data Recording Device [Data processing] (BUR)	DRD
Data Recording Interface (MCD)	DRI
Data Recording and Processing Equipment	DRAPE
Data Recording Set	DRS
Data Recording System (MUGU)	DRS
Data Recording System Analyst (MUGU)	DRSA
Data Records Management (MCD)	DRM
Data Recovery Vehicle	DRV
Data Reduction (KSC)	DR
Data Reduction (MSA)	DRDCN
Data Reduction	DRON
Data Reduction and Analysis	DR & A
Data Reduction and Analysis System	DRANS
Data Reduction Center [or Complex]	DRC
Data Reduction Compiler (MCD)	DRC
Data Reduction Equipment	DRE
Data Reduction Input Program [Data processing]	DRIP
Data Reduction Interpreter	DRI
Data Reduction Laboratory	DRL
Data Reduction Procedure [or Program]	DRP
Data Reduction System [Data processing]	DRS
Data Reduction Translator	DART
Data Reduction Working Group (MUGU)	DRWG
Data Redundancy Removal (KSC)	DRR
Data Reference Number	DRN
Data Reference Unit (CAA)	DRU
Data Reformatter Assembly (SKY)	DRA
Data Register (CAA)	DR
Data Regulations (KSC)	DREG
Data Relay Station (NASA)	DRS
Data Relay System (CAAL)	DRS
Data Reorganization Utility [Data processing]	DRU
Data Report	DR
Data Reporting and Accounting (AFM)	DR & A
Data Reporting Form	DRF
Data Request	DRQ
Data Request Keyboard (CIT)	DRK
Data Requirement Form (KSC)	DRF
Data Requirement List (KSC)	DRL
Data Requirements and Analysis (MCD)	DR & A
Data Requirements Language (CAA)	DRL
Data Requirements Specification (KSC)	DRS
Data Resource Administrator (CAA)	DRA
Data Resources Directory Publications Subsystem [Department of Energy] [Database] (FDB)	DRD
Data Resources, Incorporated [Lexington, MA] [Database originator and operator] [Information service] (EISS)	DRI
Data Resources Management System	DRMS
Data Retrieval, Entry, and Management (CAA)	DREAM
Data Retrieval Language [National Bureau of Standards]	DRL
Data Retrieval Program (CAAL)	DRP
Data Retrieval System [Data processing] (BUR)	DRS
Data Return Capsule [or Container]	DRC
Data Review Technician	DRT
Data Routing and Error Detecting	DRED
Data Routing Indicator	DRI
Data Sampling Automatic Receiver	DSAR
Data Scanning (BUR)	DS
Data Scanning and Formatting	DSF
Data Scanning and Routing	DSR
Data Segment	DS
Data Self-Test Program	DSTP
Data Service Unit [Telecommunications]	DSU
Data Services Center [International City Management Association] [Information service] (EISS)	DSC
Data Services Operations [Informatics, Inc.] (EISS)	DSO
Data Services Planning Form	DSPF
Data Set [Data processing]	DS
Data Set Adapter [Data processing] (DEEC)	DSA
Data Set Block (CAA)	DSB
Data Set Control Block [Data processing]	DSCB
Data Set Controller (CAA)	DSC
Data Set Definition (IBMDP)	DSD
Data Set Extension [IBM Corp.] [Data processing] (BUR)	DSE
Data Set Identification (IBMDP)	DSID
Data Set Identifier	DSI
Data Set Label [Data processing]	DSL
Data Set Name	DSN
Data Set Optimizer [Boole & Babbage, Inc.] (CAA)	DSO
Data Set Ready [Model signal]	DSR
Data Sheet (NATG)	DS
Data Smoothing Network [Telecommunications]	DSN
Data Source Panel (MCD)	DSP
Data Source Terminal (MCD)	DST
Data Specification Request	DSR
Data Status Display (CIT)	DSD
Data Status Messages (KSC)	DSM
Data Status Word	DSW
Data Storage [Data processing] (NASA)	DS
Data Storage Description Language (CAA)	DSDL
Data Storage Device	DSD
Data Storage Distribution Unit (MCD)	DSDU
Data Storage Equipment	DSE
Data Storage Memory (CIT)	DSM
Data Storage and Retrieval (MCD)	DSR
Data Storage and Retrieval (MSA)	DS & R
Data Storage System	DSS
Data Storage Unit (DDI)	DSU
Data and Structure Definition Language [Data processing] (BUR)	DASDL
Data Structure Diagram	DSD
Data Structures Language [Data processing] (BUR)	DSL
Data Submitted Information (KSC)	DSI
Data Summary Sheets (MCD)	DSS
Data Survey Report	DSR
Data Switch Corp. [NASDAQ symbol] (NQ)	DASW
Data Switch Operating System (CAA)	DSOS
Data Switching and Data Handling (AFM)	DS & DH
Data Switching Exchange [Telecommunications]	DSE
Data Switching System (CAA)	DSS
Data Synchronization (DEN)	DS
Data Synchronization [or Synchronizer] Unit	DSU
Data Synchronizer Channel	DSC
Data System	DS
Data System Console (CAAL)	DSC
Data System Development Plan (CIT)	DSDP
Data Systems [A publication]	Data Sys
Data Systems [A publication]	Data Syst
Data Systems Administration	DSA
Data Systems and Analysis Directorate (MCD)	DSAD
Data Systems Application Division [Agricultural Research Service]	DSAD
Data Systems Authorization Directory	DSAD
Data Systems Designator (AFM)	DSD
Data Systems Engineering	DSE
Data Systems Environment Functions and Application Design [Course] [Data processing]	DSE/FAD
Data Systems Inquiry	DSI
Data Systems and Mathematics Staff [Bureau of Radiological Health] (EISS)	DSMS
Data Systems Modernization	DSM
Data Systems News [A publication]	Data Systems N
Data Systems Office	DSO
Data Systems Specification	DSS
Data Systems and Statistics (AFM)	DS & S
Data Systems Supervisor (MCD)	DSS
Data Systems Support Office (MCD)	DASSO
Data Systems Test [Formerly, DAT]	DST

Computer & Telecommunications Acronyms

Data Technical Support Group [*Telecommunications*] (TEL) ..... DATEC
Data Telecommunications [*RCA Global Communications Data Transmission Service over Telephone Circuits*] [*Telecommunications*] (TEL) ..... DATEL
Data Telemetering Register ..... DTR
Data Telemetry Exploitation Aid (MCD) ..... DTEA
Data Terminal (CAA) ..... DT
Data Terminal Equipment [*Data processing*] ..... DTE
Data Terminal Reader ..... DTR
Data Terminal Ready ..... DTR
Data Terminal Set (NVT) ..... DTS
Data Terminal Systems, Inc. [*NYSE symbol*] [*Delisted*] ..... DTS
Data Terminal Unit [*Telecommunications*] ..... DTU
Data Terminals & Communications, Inc. (CAA) ..... DTC
Data Terminating Unit (TEL) ..... DTU
Data Test Center [*Telecommunications*] (TEL) ..... DTC
Data Test Station ..... DTS
Data Transcriber ..... DT
Data Transfer and Certification Record (KSC) ..... DTCR
Data Transfer Command Word (NASA) ..... DTCW
Data Transfer Done (OA) ..... DTD
Data Transfer Protocol (CAA) ..... DTP
Data Transfer Rate ..... DTR
Data Transfer Register (CAA) ..... DTR
Data Transfer Timing (VIT) ..... DTT
Data Transfer Unit (DDI) ..... DTU
Data Transition Tracking (CAA) ..... DTT
Data-Transition Tracking Loop (CIT) ..... DTTL
Data Translator (IEEE) ..... DT
Data Transmission ..... DT
Data Transmission Center (KSC) ..... DTC
Data Transmission Channel (CMD) ..... DTC
Data Transmission Co. [*Defunct*] ..... DATRAN
Data Transmission and Control System ..... DTCS
Data Transmission Control Unit [*Burroughs Corp.*] (OA) ..... DTCU
Data Transmission Factor ..... DTF
Data Transmission Feature ..... DTF
Data Transmission Function ..... DTF
Data Transmission Generator (MCD) ..... DTG
Data Transmission and Processing (NATG) ..... DATAP
Data Transmission/Recording Subsystem ..... DT/RSS
Data Transmission and Switching ..... DTAS
Data Transmission System ..... DATS
Data Transmission Terminal Unit [*Burroughs Corp.*] (OA) ..... DTTU
Data Transmission Unit (CIT) ..... DTU
Data Transmittal Form (MCD) ..... DTF
Data Transmittal and Routing Form ..... DTRF
Data Transmitting Equipment ..... DTE
Data Transmitting Equipment (MSA) ..... DXE
Data Transporting Network (CAA) ..... DTN
Data Under Voice [*Bell System*] ..... DUV
Data Universal Numbering System (CGC) ..... DUNS
Data Update Edit Language [*Data processing*] ..... DUEL
Data Use and Access Laboratories [*Information service*] (EANO) ..... DUALABS
Data Use Identifier (AFM) ..... DUI
Data Utilization Station ..... DUS
Data Valid (IEEE) ..... DAV
Data Vetting ..... DV
Data above Voice [*Telecommunications*] (TEL) ..... DAV
Data over Voice [*Telecommunications*] (TEL) ..... DOV
Data/Voice Data (MCD) ..... D/VD
Data Word Buffer [*Data processing*] (MDG) ..... DW
Databank of Program Evaluations [*University of California, Los Angeles*] (EISS) ..... DOPE
Databank Update Request (NASA) ..... DBUR
Database [*Data processing*] (TUT) ..... DB
Database [*United States*] [*A publication*] ..... DTBSD
Database [*A publication*] ..... DTE
Database Access Facility (CAA) ..... DBAF
Database Access Method (IDA) ..... DBAM
Database Acquisition for Student Health ..... DASH
Database Administration [*or Administrator*] [*Data processing*] (BUR) ..... DBA
Database Administration Working Group [*CODASYL*] (CAA) ..... DBAWG
Database Administrator Control System (CAA) ..... DBACS
Database Command Language (CAA) ..... DBCL
Database Computer (MCD) ..... DBC
Database Control Block (CAA) ..... DBCB
Database Control System (CAA) ..... DBCS
Database/Data Communications [*IBM Corp.*] ..... DB/DC
Database Definition Language (CAA) ..... DBDL
Database Description [*Data processing*] (BUR) ..... DBD
Database Design Aid [*Data processing*] (BUR) ..... DBDA
Database File Numbers (MCD) ..... DBFN
Database Generation [*Data processing*] (TUT) ..... DBGEN
Database Generator (CAA) ..... DBG
Database Guide to German Host Operators [*Database*] (ODIN) ..... INFOHOST
Database Handling System (DDI) ..... DBHS
Database Information Science and Practice [*Database*] (ODIN) ..... INFODATA
Database Information System ..... DIS
Database Input Languages [*Data processing*] ..... DBIL
Database Input/Output Control (CAA) ..... DBIOC
Database Journal [*A publication*] ..... Database J
Database Journal [*A publication*] ..... Database Jrnl
Database Language Task Group [*CODASYL*] (CAA) ..... DBLTG
Database List ..... DBL
Database Load [*Data processing*] ..... DBL
Database Management [*or Manager*] [*Data processing*] (NVT) ..... DBM
Database Management Software ..... DBMS
Database Management System [*Data processing*] (BUR) ..... DBMS
Database Management System ..... DMS
Database Management System Problem Specification Model (OA) ..... DBMSPSM
Database of Off-Site Waste Management [*Public Data Access, Inc.*] [*Database*] (CUAD) ..... DOWM
Database Organization and Maintenance Processor ..... DBOMP
Database Oriented Interrogation Technique [*Comserv Corp.*] (CAA) ..... DOIT
Database Processor (CAA) ..... DBP
Database Program Conversion Task Group [*CODASYL*] (CAA) ..... DPCTG
Database Retrieval (CAA) ..... DBR
Database System (MCD) ..... DBS
Database Task Group [*CODASYL*] ..... DBTG
Database Update Time ..... DBUT
Datacopy Corp. [*NASDAQ symbol*] (NQ) ..... DCPY
Dataflex Corp. [*NASDAQ symbol*] (NQ) ..... DFLX
Dataflow Systems, Inc. [*Bethesda, MD*] [*Information service*] (EISS) ..... DfS
Datamation [*A publication*] ..... DAU
Datamation [*A publication*] ..... DTMNA
Datamation Industry Directory (MCD) ..... DID
Dataphone Switched Digital Service [*AT & T*] ..... DSDS
Datapoint Corp. [*NYSE symbol*] ..... DPT
Datapro Reports on Data Communications [*A publication*] ..... Datapro Rep Data Commun
Datapro Reports on Minicomputers [*A publication*] ..... Datapro Rep Minicomput
Datapro Reports on Office Systems [*A publication*] ..... Datapro Rep Office Syst
Dataproducts Corporation [*American Stock Exchange symbol*] ..... DPC
Dataram Corp. [*American Stock Exchange symbol*] ..... DTM
Dataroute Serving Area [*TransCanada Telephone System/Computer Communications Group*] (CAA) ..... DSA
Datascope Computer Output Microfilmer [*Eastman Kodak Co.*] ..... DACOM
Datasouth Computer [*NASDAQ symbol*] (NQ) ..... DSCC
Datasystem Interactive Communications Access Method [*Digital Equipment Corp.*] (CAA) ..... DICAM
Datatech Systems Ltd. [*Toronto Stock Exchange symbol*] [*Vancouver Stock Exchange symbol*] ..... DTK
Datatron Assembly System [*Burroughs Corp.*] ..... DAS
Datatron Users' Organization ..... DUO
Date [*Online database field identifier*] (OBD) ..... DA
Date to Follow [*Telecommunications*] (TEL) ..... DTF
Date Material Required ..... DMR
Date Number ..... DN
Date of Publication [*Online database field identifier*] (OBD) ..... DP
Date-Time Group [*Group of figures at head of radio or Teletype message indicating filing time*] ..... DTG
Datenbank ueber Gifte und Vergiftungen [*Databank for Poisons and Poisoning*] [*German*] (ODIN) ..... GIFTPOOL
Datenbank Informationswissenschaft und -Praxis [*Database Information Science and Practice*] [*Database*] [*Information retrieval*] (ODIN) ..... INFODATA
Datenbank fuer Schulung von GRIPS/DIRS3-Anwendern [*Database for Training of GRIPS/DIRS3 Users*] [*Database*] [*Information retrieval*] (ODIN) ..... DIRSLEARN
Datenbank fuer Wassergefaehrdende Stoffe [*Databank on Substances Harmful to Water*] [*West German*] [*Information service*] (EISS) ..... DABAWS
Datricon Corp. [*NASDAQ symbol*] (NQ) ..... DATN
Datron Corp. [*NASDAQ symbol*] (NQ) ..... DATR
Datum, Inc. [*NASDAQ symbol*] (NQ) ..... DATM
Datum Point ..... DP
Davis Computer Systems, Inc. ..... DCS
Day [*Broadcasting term*] ..... D
Day Letter [*Telegraphy*] ..... DL
Day Night Switching Equipment [*Telecommunications*] ..... DNSW
Dayco Corp. [*NYSE symbol*] ..... DAY
Daystrom Analog-to-Digital Integrating Translator ..... DADIT
Dead Reckoning Automatic Computer [*Obsolete*] (DDI) ..... DRACO
Dead Time ..... DT
Dead Time Log ..... DTL
Deaf Communicating Terminal [*Telephone for the deaf*] ..... DCT
Debug Syntax Analysis [*Telecommunications*] (TEL) ..... DSAN
Debugging Mode ..... DM
Debugging System (CAA) ..... DS
Decentralized Data Entry (IEEE) ..... DDE
Decentralized Data Processing Network System (BUR) ..... DNS
Decentralized Open Network Architecture (BUR) ..... DONA
Decentralized Toll Office [*Telecommunications*] (TEL) ..... DTO
DECHEMA [*Deutsche Gesellschaft fuer Chemisches Apparatewesen, Chemische Technik, und Biotechnologie eV*]
    Data Calculation System [*Information retrieval*] (ODIN) ..... DECALC
DECHEMA [*Deutsche Gesellschaft fuer Chemisches Apparatewesen, Chemische Technik, und Biotechnologie eV*]
    Data Retrieval System [*Information retrieval*] (ODIN) ..... DEDARS

DECHEMA [*Deutsche Gesellschaft fuer Chemisches Apparatewesen, Chemische Technik, und Biotechnologie eV*] **Environmental Technology Equipment Databank** [*Frankfurt am Main*] [*Information service*] [*West German*] (EISS) .... DETEQ
DECHEMA [*Deutsche Gesellschaft fuer Chemisches Apparatewesen Chemische Technik und Biotechnologie eV*] **Equipment Suppliers Databank** [*Database*] (CUAD) .... DEQUIP
DECHEMA [*Deutsche Gesellschaft fuer Chemisches Appartewesen, Chemische Technik, und Biotechnologie eV*] **Stoffdaten Dienst** [*DECHEMA Data Service*] [*Information service*] [*West German*] (EISS) .... DSD
DECHEMA [*Deutsche Gesellschaft fuer Chemisches Apparatewesen, Chemische Technik, und Biotechnologie eV*] **Thermophysical Property Data Bank - Data Evaluation System** [*Database*] (ODIN) .... DETHERM-SDC
DECHEMA [*Deutsche Gesellschaft fuer Chemisches Apparatewesen, Chemische Technik, und Biotechnologie eV*] **Thermophysical Property Data Bank - Data Retrieval System** [*Database*] (ODIN) .... DETHERM-SDR
Deci [*A prefix meaning divided by ten*] [*SI symbol*] .... d
Decibel [*Symbol*] [*SI unit of sound level*] .... dB
Decibel Meter (KSC) .... DBM
Decibels, Adjusted .... dBA
Decibels above One Milliwatt .... dBM
Decibels above Reference Noise .... dBRN
Decimal (BUR) .... D
Decimal (KSC) .... DEC
Decimal-to-Analog (CET) .... DA
Decimal to Binary [*Data processing*] (KSC) .... D/B
Decimal to Binary [*Data processing*] (BUR) .... DTB
Decimal Code Binaire [*Binary Coded Decimal*] [*Data processing*] .... DCB
Decimal Code Translator .... DCT
Decimal Counting Unit .... DCU
Decimal Digit (DIT) .... DECIT
Decimal Digital Differential Analyzer .... DDDA
Decimal Display (IDA) .... DD
Decimal Fraction (MDG) .... DF
Decimal to Hexadecimal (IEEE) .... D-H
Decimal Keyboard [*Data processing*] .... DKB
Decimal Number System .... DNS
Decimal to Octal [*Data processing*] (IEEE) .... D-O
Decimal to Octal Conversion .... DOC
Decimal Register Binary .... DRB
Decimal Voltage Output .... DVO
Decision Acknowledge (BUR) .... DAK
Decision Aiding Information System .... DAISY
Decision Data Computer Corporation [*Horsham, PA*] [*NASDAQ symbol*] (NQ) .... DDCC
Decision, Design, and the Computer [*Symposium*] .... DDC
Decision Element .... DE
Decision Evaluation and Logic .... DEAL
Decision Information Distribution System .... DIDS
Decision Information Services Ltd. [*Information service*] (EISS) .... DIS
Decision Logic Translator (CAA) .... DLT
Decision/Making/Information [*Information service*] (EISS) .... D/M/I
Decision Mapping via Optimum Go-No Networks .... DEMON
Decision-Oriented Evaluation System .... DOES
Decision Outstanding [*Data processing*] (BUR) .... DOS
Decision Sciences Corporation (EISS) .... DSC
Decision Support System .... DSS
Decision Systems, Inc. [*NASDAQ symbol*] (NQ) .... DCSNC
Decision Table [*Data processing*] .... DETAB
Decision Table [*Data processing*] .... DT
Decision Table to COBOL [*Common Business-Oriented Language*] **Processor** [*Data processing*] (CGC) .... DETOC
Decision Table Experimental [*Data processing*] .... DETAB-X
Decision Table Processor [*IBM Corp.*] (CGC) .... DETAP
Decision Table Processor [*IBM Corp.*] .... DTABL
Decision Table Translator [*Data processing*] (CGC) .... DETRAN
Decoder Read-Only Memory (CAA) .... DROM
Decoding Memory Drive [*Data processing*] (MDG) .... DE-ME-DRIVE
Decommutation and Readout System [*Data processing*] .... DARS
Decommutator Distribution Unit (MCD) .... DDU
Decomposition .... DECOMP
Decomposition Mathematical Programing System .... DECOMP
Decrease Feedback .... Dec-FB
Decrement (MDG) .... DECR
Decrement, Test, Branch if Condition True [*Data processing*] .... DBCC
Dedicated Computer Message Switching (CAA) .... DCMS
Dedicated Display and Control Subsystem (NASA) .... DD & CS
Dedicated Planning Terminal (CAAL) .... DPT
Dedicated Total Buried Plant [*Telecommunications*] (TEL) .... DTBP
Deductive Communicator (IEEE) .... DEDUCOM
Deep Level Transient Spectroscopy .... DLTS
Deep Ocean Untended Digital Data Acquisition System .... DOUDDAS
Defective (MSA) .... DEF
Defective Equipment Repair Program [*Telephone company*] .... DERP
Defence Scientific Information Service [*Canada*] [*Information service*] (EISS) .... DSIS
Defense Communications Agency [*DoD*] [*Washington, DC*] [*Telecommunications*] .... DCA
Defense Communications Satellite System [*Telecommunications*] (TEL) .... DCSS
Defense Computer Institute .... DCI
Defense Electronics Supply Center [*DSA*] .... DESC
Defense Information Automated Locator System .... DIALS
Defense Integrated Secure Communications Network [*Australia*] [*Telecommunications*] (TEL) .... DISCON
Defense Mapping Agency Hydrographic/Topographic Center [*Database*] (FDB) .... DMAHTC
Defense Markets & Technology [*Predicasts, Inc.*] [*Database*] .... DM & T
Defense Pest Management Information Analysis Center [*Database*] (FDB) .... DPMIAC
Defense Telephone Service [*DoD*] .... DTS
Defense Telephone Service - Washington [*DoD*] .... DTS-W
Deferred Execution (OA) .... DEX
Define Area .... DA
Define Constant (MDG) .... DC
Define the File [*Data processing*] (BUR) .... DTF
Define File Processor [*Data processing*] .... DFP
Define Storage (CAH) .... DS
Definite-Time [*Relay*] .... DEFT
Definite-Time Relay (MSA) .... DTR
Definition .... DEF
Deflection Factor (IEEE) .... DF
Deformation of Aligned Phase (MCD) .... DAP
Deformographic Storage Display Tube [*IBM Corp.*] .... DSDT
Degaussing Computer (VIT) .... DCMPTR
Degree (AFM) .... DEG
Delay [*Electronics*] .... D
Delay (DDI) .... DEL
Delay (KSC) .... DLY
Delay Line Memory .... DLM
Delay Message [*Aviation code*] (FAAC) .... DEL
Delay Message [*Aviation code*] .... DLA
Delay Timer Multiplier (IEEE) .... DTM
Delay Unit [*Telecommunications*] (TEL) .... D/U
Delayed Automatic Gain Control (MSA) .... DAGC
Delayed Automatic Volume Control .... DAVC
Delayed Broadcast [*Television*] .... DB
Delayed Call Limited [*Telecommunications*] (TEL) .... DCL
Delayed Dialing Tone [*Telecommunications*] (TEL) .... DDT
Delayed Order Notice [*Telecommunications*] (TEL) .... DON
Delayed Output [*Data processing*] .... DLO
Delayed Printer Simulator .... DPS
Delayed Time/Telemetry (KSC) .... DT/TM
Delete Character [*Keyboard*] (CMD) .... DEL
Deliver by Telephone [*Message handling*] .... DELPHO
Delta Modulation [*Telecommunications*] (TEL) .... DEM
Delta Modulation .... DM
Deltak Corp. [*NASDAQ symbol*] (NQ) .... DLTK
Demand Assignment [*Telecommunications*] (TEL) .... DA
Demand Assignment Controller (CAA) .... DAC
Demand-Assignment Multiple Access (CBSS) .... DAMA
Demand-Assignment Signaling and Switching Unit .... DASS
Demand Deposit Accounting [*Banking*] (MDG) .... DDA
Demand Forecasting Program (BUR) .... DFP
Demand Meter .... DM
Demodulator [*Telecommunications*] (KSC) .... DEM
Demodulator [*Telecommunications*] .... DEMOD
Demographic Data Retrieval System [*Census Bureau*] [*Information service*] (EISS) .... DDRS
Demographic Online Retrieval Information System [*CACI, Inc.*] .... DORIS
Demographic Research Company [*Information service*] (EISS) .... DRC
Demographics Laboratory [*Information service*] (EISS) .... DEM/LAB
Demonstration Reliability Acceptance Test .... DRAT
Demultiplexer [*Data processing*] (CIT) .... DEMUX
Demultiplexer [*Data processing*] .... DMUX
Demultiplexing/Mixing/Remultiplexing [*Device*] [*Telecommunications*] (TEL) .... DMR
Denied Usage Channel Evaluator [*Telecommunications*] (TEL) .... DUCE
Density .... D
Density Altitude [*Computer*] .... DENALT
Deny All Knowledge [*Telecommunications*] (TEL) .... DAK
Department of Commerce Library (EISS) .... DOCL
Department of Communications [*Canada*] .... DOC
Department of Computer Science [*University of Illinois*] [*Research center*] (RCD) .... DCS
Department of Computing Service [*University of Waterloo*] [*Research center*] (RCD) .... DCS
Department of Defense Computer Institute .... DODCI
Department of Energy [*Washington, DC*] [*Database producer*] .... DOE
Department of Energy Technical Information Center [*Database producer*] (ODIN) .... DOE-TIC
Department of Energy's Remote Console Information System [*Department of Energy*] [*Database*] (FDB) .... DOE/RECON
Department of Housing and Urban Development .... HUD
Department of Scientific and Industrial Research [*of the Privy Council for Scientific and Industrial Research*] [*Later, SRC*] [*British*] .... DSIR
Department of University Computer Systems [*University of Connecticut*] [*Research center*] (RCD) .... DUCS
Departmental Data Processing Center [*Department of Labor*] .... DDPC
[*A*] **Departmental Reporting System** [*IBM Corp.*] .... ADRS
Dependent Charge Group [*Telecommunications*] (TEL) .... DCG
Depletion-Layer Transistor (IEEE) .... DLT

Computer & Telecommunications Acronyms

Depletion Metal-Oxide Semiconductor (BUR)	DMOS
Deployment Data File	DEPDA
Deposit Ticket/Debit Voucher [*Data processing*]	DT/DV
Depth	D
Derivation & Tabulation Associates, Inc. [*Information service*] (EISS)	DATA
Descriptive Language Implemented by Macroprocessors (IDA)	DLIMP
Descriptor [*Online database field identifier*]	DE
Descriptor Attribute Matrix	DAM
Descriptor Database System (CAA)	DDBS
Design of Aircraft Wing Structures [*Computer program*]	DAWNS
Design, Architecture, Software, and Testing (MCD)	DAST
Design Augmented by Computer [*General Motors Corp.*]	DAC
Design Automation (BUR)	DA
Design Change Package (IEEE)	DCP
Design Change Request	DCR
Design Criteria Plan (IEEE)	DCP
Design Data Book	DDB
Design Data Package	DDP
Design Data Transmittal	DDT
Design and Drafting Management Council (EANO)	DDMC
Design Evaluation Inspection Simulator (NASA)	DEIS
Design Implementation Guide [*Telecommunications*] (TEL)	DIG
Design Interface Meeting (NASA)	DIM
[*A*] Design Language for Indicating Behavior [*1967*] [*Data processing*] (CSR)	ADLIB
Design Layout Report Date [*Telecommunications*] (TEL)	DLRD
Design Objective (IEEE)	DO
Design Professions Technical Specialty Index [*National Society of Professional Engineers*] [*Information service*] (EISS)	DPTSI
Design Quality Assurance [*Telecommunications*] (TEL)	DQA
Design Research Center [*Carnegie-Mellon University*] [*Research center*] (RCD)	DRC
Design Simulator	DESSIM
Design Verification Test	DVT
Designate Command Line [*Data processing*]	DCL
Designated Market Area	DMA
Designator Register [*Data processing*]	DR
Designed, Verified, and Assigned Date [*Telecommunications*] (TEL)	DVA
Designer Choice Logic	DCL
Designers & Builders of Information Systems, Inc. [*New Rochelle, NY*] [*Software manufacturer*] (DASOS)	DBIS
Designers' Workbench (TEL)	DWB
Designs Coordination Group [*Telecommunications*] (TEL)	DCG
Desk Side Computer System [*General Electric Co.*]	DSCS
Desk Side Time Shared [*Data processing*] [*General Electric Co.*]	DSTS
Desktop Page Composition System [*Vision Research*]	DPCS
Destination	DEST
Destination Address (CAA)	DA
Destination Address Field [*Data processing*] (IBMDP)	DAF
Destination Field (CAA)	DF
Destination Index [*Data processing*]	DI
Destination Point Code [*Telecommunications*] (TEL)	DPC
Destination Queues [*Data processing*] (MDG)	DQ
Destination Service Access Point (CCD)	DSAP
Destination Warning Marker (DEEC)	DWM
Destination Word Marker (CMD)	DWM
Destructive Readout	DRO
Detail Condition (MDG)	DC
Detail Program Interrelationships (NASA)	DPI
Detailed Data Display	DDD
Detailed Experimental Computer-Assisted Language	DECAL
Detailed Performance Analysis [*Bell System*]	DPA
Detailed Test Specification (VIT)	DTS
Detailed Traffic Analysis [*Telecommunications*] (TEL)	DTA
Detailed Type Specification (MCD)	DTS
Detected Pulse Interference (CET)	DPI
Detection Scheme with Fixed Thresholds [*Communication signal*]	DSFT
Detection Scheme with Learning of Thresholds [*Communication signal*]	DSLT
Detection Threshold Computer [*Telecommunications*] (TEL)	DTC
Detection and Tracking of Satellites	DATOS
Detection of Unauthorized Equipment [*Bell Laboratories*]	DUE
Detector Electronics [*NASDAQ symbol*] (NQ)	DETX
Determination Effective Levels of Task Automation [*Data processing*]	DELTA
Detroit Suburban Network [*Radio*]	DSN
Deutsche Arbeitsgemeinschaft fuer Rechen-Anlagen [*German Working Committee for Computing Machines*] [*German*] (CDH)	DARA
Deutsche Bibliothek [*Database producer*] (ODIN)	DB
Deutsche Biologische Literatur [*German Biological Literature*] [*Database*] (ODIN)	DT BIOL
Deutsche Gesellschaft fuer Chemisches Apparatewesen, Chemische Technik, und Biotechnologie eV [*Database producer*] (EISS)	DECHEMA
Deutsche Gesellschaft fuer Dokumentation [*German Society for Documentation*] [*Information service*] (EISS)	DGD
Deutsche Gesellschaft fuer Kybernetik [*German Society for Cybernetics*] [*Uber Starnberg, Germany*]	DGK
Deutsche Gesellschaft fuer Metallkunde [*Information retrieval*] (ODIN)	DGM
Deutsche Gesellschaft fuer Operations Research [*German Society for Operational Research*] [*Frankfurt, Germany*]	DGOR
Deutsche Telecom EV [*Cologne, WG*] [*Telecommunications*] (TSSD)	DTEV
Deutscher Normenausschuss [*German Standards Committee*] [*Later, DIN*]	DNA
Deutsches Institut fuer Medizinische Dokumentation und Information [*German Institute for Medical Documentation and Information*] [*Information service*] (EISS)	DIMDI
Deutsches Institut fuer Normung [*German Standards Institute*] [*Formerly, DNA*] [*Berlin, WG*]	DIN
Deutsches Institut fuer Urbanistik [*Vereins fuer Kommunalwissenschaften eV*] [*Database producer*] (ODIN)	DIFU
Deutsches Institut fuer Wirtschaftsforschung [*Data Resources, Inc.*] [*Database*] (CUAD)	DIW
Deutsches Krankenhausinstitut [*Dusseldorf*] [*Information retrieval*] (ODIN)	DKI
Deutsches Krebsforschungszentrum [*Heidelberg*] [*Information retrieval*] (ODIN)	DKFZ
Deutsches Kunststoffinstitut [*Database producer*] (ODIN)	DKI
Deutsches Patentamt [*Information retrieval*] (ODIN)	DPA
Develcon Electronics Ltd. [*Toronto Stock Exchange symbol*]	DLC
Development Management System [*IBM Corp.*]	DMS
Development of Minicomputers in an Environment of Scientific and Technological Information Centers [*Data processing*]	DOMESTIC
Development Reference Service [*Society for International Development*] (EISS)	DRS
Development Sciences Information System [*Information service*] [*Canada*] (EISS)	DEVSIS
Device (KSC)	DEV
Device (MSA)	DVC
Device for Automatic Word Identification and Discrimination [*Data processing*]	DAWID
Device Base Control Block [*Data processing*] (IBMDP)	DVB
Device Characteristics Table [*Data processing*] (IBMDP)	DCT
Device Control	DC
Device Control Character (IEEE)	DCC
Device Control Character (CMD)	DCX
Device Control Unit (OA)	DCU
Device Coordinate (CCD)	DC
Device Dependent Routine (CAA)	DDR
Device End (CAH)	DE
Device Handler (CAA)	DH
Device Identifier (CAA)	DID
Device Independence (CAA)	DI
Device Independent Display Operator Console Support (BUR)	DIDOCS
Device Input Format (CAA)	DIF
Device Interface Module (OA)	DIM
Device Media Control Language [*CODASYL/Honeywell, Inc.*] (DEEC)	DMCL
Device Multiplexing Nonsynchronized Inputs [*Data processing*]	DMNI
Device Multiplexing Nonsynchronized Outputs [*Data processing*] (CET)	DMNO
Device Output Format (CAA)	DOF
Device Reference Table (CAA)	DRT
Device Rise Time [*Photomultipliers for scintillation counting*] (IEEE)	DRT
Device Status Byte [*Data processing*] (BUR)	DSB
Device Status Word (CMD)	DSW
Device under Test	DUT
Dewey Decimal Classification [*Also, DDC*]	DC
Dewey Decimal Classification [*Also, DC*]	DDC
Dewey Decimal Number [*Online database field identifier*] (OBD)	DD
Di-Binary Digit [*Two consecutive binary digits*] (TEL)	DIBIT
Diabetes Research and Training Center [*Yeshiva University*] [*Research center*] (RCD)	DRTC
Diagnostic Control Store (CAA)	DCS
Diagnostic Controlled MODEM [*Data processing*] (BUR)	DCM
Diagnostic Decision Logic Table [*Data processing*]	DDLT
Diagnostic Decision Table [*Data processing*] (TUT)	DDT
Diagnostic Display Unit (MCD)	DDU
Diagnostic Flow Chart [*Data processing*] (IEEE)	DFC
Diagnostic FORTRAN [*Data processing*] (IEEE)	DITRAN
Diagnostic Function Test [*Data processing*]	DFT
Diagnostic Machine Aid Digital [*Programing language*] (CSR)	DMAD
Diagnostic Monitor [*Data processing*] (CIT)	DIAMON
Diagnostic Monitor Executive [*Data processing*] (TUT)	DME
Diagnostic Products Corporation [*NASDAQ symbol*] (NQ)	DPCZ
Diagnostic Utility System (CAA)	DUS
Diagram (KSC)	DIAG
Dial Access Information Retrieval System [*Shippensburg State College, Shippensburg, PA*]	DAIRS
Dial Assist Operator (CET)	DAO
Dial Assistance Switchboard (CET)	DAS
Dial Line Service Observing [*Telecommunications*] (TEL)	DLSO
Dial Long Line [*Bell System*]	DLL
Dial Pulse [*Telecommunications*]	DP
Dial Pulse Access [*Telecommunications*] (TEL)	DPA
Dial Pulse Originating [*Telecommunications*] (TEL)	DPO
Dial Pulse Originating Incoming Register [*Telecommunications*]	DPOIR
Dial Pulse Terminating [*Telecommunications*] (TEL)	DPT
Dial Service Analysis [*Telecommunications*] (TEL)	DSA
Dial Service Assistance (CET)	DSA
Dial Service Assistance Switchboard (CET)	DSAS
Dial a Teacher Assistance [*Telephone service*]	DATA
Dial Teletypewriter Exchange	DTWX

Dial Terminal Unit (CAAL) ... DTU
Dial Tone [*Telecommunications*] (TEL) ... DT
Dial Tone First [*Telecommunications*] (TEL) ... DTF
Dialect of Algorithmic Language ... DIALGOL
Dialed Digit Receiver [*Telecommunications*] (TEL) ... DDR
Dialing Code Information [*Telecommunications*] [*British*] ... DCI
Diameter ... DIA
Diameter ... DIAM
DIBOL Debugging Technique [*Digital Equipment Corp.*] (CAA) ... DDT
Dicomed Corp. [*NASDAQ symbol*] (NQ) ... DCOM
Dictionary of Computer and Control Systems Abbreviations, Signs, and Symbols [*New York: Odyssey Press, 1965*] [*A publication*] ... DCCSA
Diebold, Inc. [*NYSE symbol*] ... DBD
Dielectric Constant ... K
Diesel Engine Monitoring and Control [*ASMAP Electronics Ltd.*] [*Software package*] [*British*] (NCC) ... DEMAC
Difference (KSC) ... DIFF
Difference in Depth of Modulation (IEEE) ... DDM
Different Premises Address [*Telecommunications*] (TEL) ... DPA
Different Premises Information [*Telecommunications*] (TEL) ... DPI
Different Premises Subscriber [*Telecommunications*] (TEL) ... DPS
Different Premises Telephone Number [*Telecommunications*] (TEL) ... DPT
Differential Amplifier (MSA) ... DIFA
Differential Analyzer (IEEE) ... DA
Differential Analyzer Replacement [*Programing language*] [*1967*] (CSR) ... DARE
Differential Coherent Phase Shift Keyed [*System*] [*Data processing*] ... DCPSK
Differential Computing Potentiometer ... DCP
Differential Encoding Phase Shift Keying (MCD) ... DEPSK
Differential Gain ... DG
Differential Long-Baseline Interferometer [*Radio interferometry*] ... DLBI
Differential Phase [*Telecommunications*] ... DP
Differential Phase Exchange Keying (IEEE) ... DPEK
Differential Phase Shift Keying ... DPSK
Differential Pressure Feedback (KSC) ... DPF
Differential Pulse Code Modulation [*Transmission technique*] ... DPCM
Differential Time (IEEE) ... DT
Differential Time Relay (IEEE) ... DIFFTR
Differentially Coherent Pulse Code Modulation (CAA) ... DCPCM
Differentially Encoded Coherent Phase Shift Keying [*Telecommunications*] (TEL) ... DECPSK
Diffusion under [*Epitaxial*] **Film** (IEEE) ... DUF
Diffusion Metal-Oxide Semiconductor [*Telecommunications*] (TEL) ... DMOS
Diffusion in Metals and Alloys Data Center [*National Bureau of Standards*] (EISS) ... DMDC
Diffusion Self-Aligned Metal-Oxide Semiconductor (BUR) ... DSAMOS
Diffusion Transfer Processing System ... DTPS
Digilog, Inc. [*NASDAQ symbol*] (NQ) ... DILO
Digit [*or Digital*] (MDG) ... D
Digit Plane Driver [*Data processing*] (IEEE) ... DPD
Digit Present ... DP
Digit/Record Mark (MDG) ... DIGRM
Digit/Record Mark Group/Mark (MDG) ... DIGRMGM
Digit Select (BUR) ... DS
Digit Storage Relay ... DSR
Digit Tube (IEEE) ... DT
Digital Access and Crossconnect System [*Telecommunications*] (TEL) ... DACS
Digital Acoustic Simulation System (MCD) ... DASS
Digital Acquisition and Documentation Equipment (KSC) ... DADE
Digital Address System (MCD) ... DAS
Digital Advance Production Order [*Telecommunications*] (TEL) ... DAPO
Digital Air Data Computer ... DADC
Digital Air Data Computer Status ... DADCOK
Digital Air Data Computer Test Set ... DADCTS
Digital Air Data System ... DADS
Digital Airborne Computer (IEEE) ... DIGITAR
Digital Aircraft Simulator (MCD) ... DAS
Digital Alternate Representation of Musical Symbols (OA) ... DARMS
Digital Altimeter Scanner ... DAS
Digital-to-Analog [*Converter*] [*Data processing*] ... D-to-A
Digital-to-Analog [*Converter*] [*Data processing*] (CIT) ... D-A
Digital Analog [*Data processing*] (IEEE) ... DIAN
Digital-to-Analog Converter [*Data processing*] ... DAC
Digital-to-Analog Converter [*Data processing*] ... DACON
Digital-to-Analog Converter Unit [*Data processing*] (SKY) ... DACU
Digital Analog Data System (CAAL) ... DADS
Digital-to-Analog Function Table [*Packard Bell Computer Corp.*] ... DAFT
Digital-to-Analog Interface Unit [*Data processing*] ... DAIU
Digital-to-Analog Multiplier (IEEE) ... DAM
Digital Analog Simulator [*Data processing*] ... DAS
Digital Analysis Library [*Computer Design*] [*Software package*] [*British*] (NCC) ... DAL
Digital Angle Data Recorder ... DADR
Digital Angular Torquing Equipment ... DATE
Digital Animated Control System ... DACS
Digital Arithmetic Center ... DAC
Digital Assembly Program (MCD) ... DAP
Digital Attenuator System ... DAS
Digital Audio Tape ... DAT
Digital Audio for Television [*System to improve sound*] [*Public Broadcasting Service*] ... DATE
Digital Automanual Switching Unit [*Telecommunications*] (TEL) ... DAMSU
Digital Automatic Acquisition (MCD) ... DAA
Digital Automatic Gain Control (MCD) ... DAGC
Digital Automatic Pattern Recognition (IEEE) ... DAPR
Digital Automatic Tape Intelligence Checkout ... DATICO
Digital Automatic Weather Network ... DAWN
Digital Autotransducer and Recorder (IEEE) ... DATAR
Digital Auxiliary Information Code [*Data processing*] ... DAXI
Digital Avionics Control ... DIGAC
Digital Avionics System (MCD) ... DAS
Digital-to-Binary Converter [*Data processing*] ... DBC
Digital Block [*Data processing*] ... DB
Digital Block And-Or Gate [*Data processing*] (IEEE) ... DBAO
Digital Block Clock Oscillator [*Data processing*] ... DBCO
Digital Block Flip-Flop [*Data processing*] ... DBFF
Digital Block Inverter Amplifier [*Data processing*] ... DBIA
Digital Block Multivibrator [*Data processing*] ... DBMV
Digital Block Noninverting Amplifier [*Data processing*] ... DBNA
Digital Block Schmitt Trigger [*Data processing*] ... DBST
Digital Block Slave Clock [*Data processing*] ... DBSC
Digital Buffer Unit (OA) ... DBU
Digital Card And-Or Gate [*Data processing*] ... DCAO
Digital Card Clock Oscillator [*Data processing*] ... DCCO
Digital Card Flip-Flop [*Data processing*] ... DCFF
Digital Card Inverting Amplifier [*Data processing*] ... DCIA
Digital Card Multivibrator [*Data processing*] ... DCMV
Digital Card Noninverting Amplifier [*Data processing*] ... DCNA
Digital Card Schmitt Trigger [*Data processing*] ... DCST
Digital Card Slave Clock [*Data processing*] ... DCSC
Digital Cassette Recorder (CAA) ... DCR
Digital Central Office [*Trademark of the Stromberg-Carlson Corp.*] [*Telecommunications*] ... DCO
Digital Channel Link ... DCL
Digital Circuit Module [*Data processing*] ... DCM
Digital Circuit Quality Monitor [*Data processing*] ... DCQM
Digital Coefficient Unit [*Data processing*] (RDA) ... DCU
Digital Color Television ... DCTV
Digital Command Communications System ... DCCS
Digital Command System [*or Subsystem*] ... DCS
Digital Communication through Orbiting Needles ... DICON
Digital Communication System [*Data processing*] (CGC) ... DCS
Digital Communications ... DIGICOM
Digital Communications Associates, Inc. [*Norcross, GA*] [*Software manufacturer*] [*Telecommunications*] (TSSD) ... DCA
Digital Communications Associates, Incorporated [*NASDAQ symbol*] (NQ) ... DCAI
Digital Communications and Control Unit (MCD) ... DCCU
Digital Communications System Evaluator ... DICOSE
Digital Compact Disk ... DCD
Digital Comparator ... DC
Digital Computer ... DC
Digital Computer (IEEE) ... DIGCOM
Digital Computer Association (MUGU) ... DCA
Digital Computer Control Panel ... DCCP
Digital Computer Laboratory [*Massachusetts Institute of Technology*] ... DCL
Digital Computer Processor (IEEE) ... DCP
Digital Computer Programing [*Data processing*] (BUR) ... DCP
Digital Computer Switching Unit (MCD) ... DCSU
Digital Concentration Readout [*Data processing*] ... DCR
Digital Consulting Associates, Incorporated [*Andover, MA*] [*Telecommunications*] (TSSD) ... DCAI
Digital Control Computer ... DCC
Digital Control Design Language [*1968*] [*Data processing*] (CSR) ... DCDL
Digital Control Design System (IEEE) ... DCDS
Digital Control and Interface Unit (MCD) ... DCIU
Digital Control Signal Processor (NASA) ... DCSP
Digital Control Station [*Data processing*] ... DCS
Digital Control System ... DCS
Digital Control Unit (KSC) ... DCU
Digital Coordinate Transformation System ... DCTS
Digital Correlation Demonstrator ... DICODE
Digital Countdown Display [*Data processing*] ... DCD
Digital Countdown Display System [*Data processing*] ... DCDS
Digital Countdown System [*Data processing*] ... DCS
Digital Counting Unit ... DCU
Digital Cross Current (OA) ... DCC
Digital Daily System Operability Test (VIT) ... DDSOT
Digital Data (CET) ... DD
Digital Data Acquisition and Processing System ... DDAPS
Digital Data Acquisition System ... DDAS
Digital Data Archives System ... DDAS
Digital Data Buffer ... DDB
Digital Data Calibration System (KSC) ... DDCS
Digital Data Communications Message Protocol [*Digital Equipment Corp.*] ... DDCMP
Digital Data Communications System (MCD) ... DIDACS
Digital Data Computer ... DIDAC
Digital Data Conversion Equipment ... DDCE
Digital Data Converter ... DDC
Digital Data Display (CGC) ... DIDAD
Digital Data Distributor (CET) ... DDD

Computer & Telecommunications Acronyms

Digital Data Down Link [Data processing] (MCD)	DDDL
Digital Data Exchange [Telecommunications] (TEL)	DDX
Digital Data Generator (IEEE)	DDG
Digital Data Group	DDG
Digital Data Handling	DDH
Digital Data Handling and Display System	DDH & DS
Digital Data Link	DDL
Digital Data Link	DDL
Digital Data Logger	DDL
Digital Data Measuring System	DDMS
Digital Data Network	DDN
Digital Data Output Conversion Equipment	DDOCE
Digital Data Processing Center [or Complex] (MCD)	DDPC
Digital Data Processing Equipment	DDPE
Digital Data Processing System	DDPS
Digital Data Processing Unit (IEEE)	DDPU
Digital Data Processor	DDP
Digital Data Processor	DIDAP
Digital Data Receiver	DDR
Digital Data Recording Head	DDRH
Digital Data Recording System	DDRS
Digital Data Satellite Service [Communications Satellite Corp.]	DIGISAT
Digital Data Servo	DDS
Digital Data Storage Unit	DDSU
Digital Data Switching Group (CAAL)	DDSG
Digital Data Switching Matrix	DDSM
Digital Data System	DDS
Digital Data Terminal (MCD)	DDT
Digital Data Terminal Equipment	DDTE
Digital Data Terminal Equipment Service Module	DDTESM
Digital Data Transceiver (CDH)	DDT
Digital Data Transmission System (KSC)	DDTS
Digital Data Transmitter	DDT
Digital Data Unit (MUGU)	DDU
Digital Datacom, Incorporated [NASDAQ symbol] (NQ)	DDII
Digital Debugging Tape	DDT
Digital Decoder Driver Unit (MCD)	DDDU
Digital Demodulation Technique (CIT)	DDT
Digital Differencing Junction (CIT)	DDJ
Digital Differential Analyzer	DDA
Digital-to-Digital	D-to-D
Digital Display	DD
Digital Display Alarm (IDA)	DDA
Digital Display Converter (BUR)	DDC
Digital Display Driver (KSC)	DDD
Digital Display Generator	DDG
Digital Display Generator Element	DDGE
Digital Display Indicator (MCD)	DDI
Digital Display Machine	DDM
Digital Display Makeup	DDM
Digital Display Processor (CMD)	DDP
Digital Display Scope	DDS
Digital Display Unit	DDU
Digital Distributing Unit	DDU
Digital Distribution Frame [Telecommunications] (TEL)	DDF
Digital Doppler System (MCD)	DIGIDOPS
Digital Drafting System	DDS
Digital Dynamics Simulator (IEEE)	DDS
Digital Electric Monitor	DEMON
Digital Electron Beam Scanner	DEBS
Digital Electronic Countermeasures Analyzer (MCD)	DECA
Digital Electronic Engine Control (MCD)	DEEC
Digital Electronic Message Systems	DEMS
Digital Electronic Universal Calculating Engine	DEUCE
Digital Electrophysiological Data Acquisition and Analysis System [Neurometrics]	DEDAAS
Digital Element (IEEE)	DE
Digital Element Test Set	DETS
Digital Elevation Database (RDA)	DEDB
Digital Encoder (MSA)	DE
Digital Encoder Handbook	DEH
Digital Encoder Handbook	DEHB
Digital End Office [Telecommunications]	DEO
Digital Equation-Solving Computer (IEEE)	DESC
Digital Equipment Company Laboratory (OA)	DECLAB
Digital Equipment Computer Users Society [Marlboro, MA]	DECUS
Digital Equipment Corporation [Maynard, MA] [NYSE symbol]	DEC
Digital Equipment Corp. [Maynard, MA] [FAA designator] (FAAC)	DGT
Digital Equipment Corporation Author Language [Data processing] (CSR)	DECAL
Digital Equipment Corporation Telecommunications Network	DECNET
Digital Equipment's Business-Oriented Language [Data processing] (TUT)	DIBOL
Digital Error Detection Subsystem [Data processing]	DEDS
Digital Error Monitoring System (MCD)	DEMS
Digital European Backbone [System] (MCD)	DEB
Digital Evaluation Computer (VIT)	DEC
Digital Evaluation Equipment	DEE
Digital Evaluation Unit (VIT)	DEU
Digital Event Timer (KSC)	DET
Digital Events Evaluator (MCD)	DEE
Digital Expansion System	DES
Digital Experimental Airborne Navigator	DEXAN
Digital Facility Terminal [Telecommunications] (TEL)	DFT
Digital Facsimile Interface System	DFIS
Digital Fault Analysis	DFA
Digital Ferrite Phase Shifter	DFPS
Digital Field System	DFS
Digital Flight Control and Landing System	DFCLS
Digital Flight Control System	DFCS
Digital Flight Controller	DFC
Digital Flight Data Recorder (MCD)	DFDR
Digital Flight Display	DFD
Digital Flight Guidance System (IEEE)	DFGS
Digital Frequency Analyzer	DFA
Digital Frequency Display	DFD
Digital Frequency Meter [or Monitor]	DFM
Digital Frequency Synthesizer	DFS
Digital Function Generator	DFG
Digital Gas Turbine Engine Control (MCD)	DIGATEC
Digital Ground Bus (VIT)	DGBUS
Digital Ground System	DGS
Digital Guidance and Control Computer	DIGACC
Digital Hardware Voter Monitor (MCD)	DHVM
Digital High-Definition Display (KSC)	DHDD
Digital High-Speed Standard Eastern Automatic Computer	DYSEAC
Digital Ignorant Mechanism [Pocket calculator facetiously described by T. R. Reid in his book, "The Chip"]	DIM
Digital Image Analysis and Display System [Data processing]	DIADS
Digital Image Analysis Laboratory [University of Arizona] [Research center] (RCD)	DIAL
Digital-Image-Generated [Data processing] (IEEE)	DIG
Digital Image Manipulation and Enhancement Systems	DIMES
Digital Incremental Plotter	DIP
Digital Information Display [Data processing]	DID
Digital Information Display System [Data processing]	DIDS
Digital Information Systems Corporation [Sacramento, CA] [Software manufacturer] (DASOS)	DISC
Digital Information Transfer Set (CAAL)	DITS
Digital Input [Data processing] (CGC)	DI
Digital Input [Data processing] (KSC)	DIN
Digital Input [or Integrating] Computer [Data processing]	DIC
Digital Input/Digital Output [Data processing] (CAA)	DIDO
Digital Input Gate (OA)	DIG
Digital Input Module [Data processing]	DIM
Digital Input Multiplexer (CAAL)	DIM
Digital Input/Output Buffer [Data processing]	DIOB
Digital Input/Output Control (CAA)	DIOC
Digital Input/Output Display Equipment (IDA)	DIODE
Digital Input/Output Interface [Data processing] (KSC)	DIOI
Digital Input/Output Package [Data processing]	DIOP
Digital Input Simulator [Data processing] (VIT)	DISIM
Digital Input Unit [Data processing]	DIU
Digital Inquiry - Voice Answerback [Touch-tone] [Bell System] [Telecommunications]	DIVA
Digital Insertion Unit [Data processing]	DIU
Digital Instrumentation Programer (VIT)	DIP
Digital Instrumentation Subsystem (CIT)	DIS
Digital Integrated Business System [Digital Equipment Corp.] (CAA)	DIBS
Digital Integrated Circuit [Data processing]	DIC
Digital Integrated Circuit Element [Data processing]	DICE
Digital Integrated Design Language [Data processing] (CSR)	DIDL
Digital Integration System (IEEE)	DIS
Digital Intercontinental Conversion Equipment (MCD)	DICE
Digital Interface Adapter [Data processing] (MCD)	DIA
Digital Interface Code Converter [Data processing]	DICC
Digital Interface and Control Unit (SKY)	DICU
Digital Interface Switching System (OA)	DISS
Digital Interface Test Unit [Data processing] (KSC)	DITU
Digital Interface Unit [Data processing] (KSC)	DIU
Digital International Switching Center [Telecommunications] (TEL)	DISC
Digital International Switching Unit [Telecommunications] (TEL)	DISU
Digital Isolation Amplifier (CIT)	DIA
Digital Junction [Telecommunications] (TEL)	DJ
Digital Line Engineering Program [Telecommunications] (TEL)	DILEP
Digital Line System [Telecommunications] (TEL)	DLS
Digital Line Termination [Telecommunications] (TEL)	DLT
Digital Logic Circuit	DLC
Digital Logic Module	DLM
Digital Logic System	DLS
Digital Magnetic Tape Controller (CAAL)	DMTC
Digital Magnetic Tape Plotting System	DMTPS
Digital Magnetic Tape System (CAAL)	DMTS
Digital Magnetic Tape Unit (MCD)	DMTU
Digital Major Alarm (MCD)	DMA
Digital Management Unit (MCD)	DMU
Digital Message Entry Device [Data processing]	DMED
Digital Message Entry System	DMES
Digital Message Terminal (MCD)	DMT
Digital Message Terminal Computer (IEEE)	DMTC
Digital Message Unit (MCD)	DMU
Digital Microcircuit	DMC
Digital Microsystems [Digital Microsystems Ltd.] [Software package] [British] (NCC)	DMS
Digital Milliwatt [Telecommunications] (TEL)	DMW
Digital Module [Telecommunications] (TEL)	DM

Computer & Telecommunications Acronyms

Digital Module Automatic Tester	DMAT
Digital Module Test Set	DMTS
Digital Monitor Computer (VIT)	DMC
Digital Monitor Unit (VIT)	DMU
Digital Motor Electronics	DME
Digital Multibeam Steering	DIMUS
Digital Multibeam Steering System	DMSS
Digital Multimeter	DMM
Digital Multiplex Equipment [Telecommunications] (DEEC)	DME
Digital Multiplex Switch	DMS
Digital Multiplexing and Formatting [Data processing] (MCD)	DMF
Digital Multiplexing Synchronizer [Data processing]	DMS
Digital Network Analyzer	DINA
Digital Network Architecture [Digital Equipment Corp.] [Data processing]	DNA
Digital Network-Defense Special Security Communications System [National Security Agency]	DIN/DCSS
Digital Network Simulation System (MCD)	DIGINESS
Digital Network Terminator (CAA)	DNT
Digital Noise Reduction [Television]	DNR
Digital Nonsecure Voice Terminal	DNVT
Digital Oceanographic Data Acquisition System (MCD)	DODAS
Digital Offline Automatic Recording System	DOLARS
Digital Ohmmeter	DOM
Digital Operation System (IEEE)	DOS
Digital Optical Projection System (IEEE)	DOPS
Digital Optical Technology System [3-D television system]	DOTS
Digital Output [Data processing]	DO
Digital Output Adapter (CAA)	DOA
Digital Output Control (CAA)	DOC
Digital Output/Input Translator [Data processing]	DO/IT
Digital Output Multiplexer (CAAL)	DOM
Digital Output Relay (OA)	DOR
Digital Output Timer [Data processing]	DOT
Digital Panel Meter [Data processing]	DPM
Digital Parallel Processing Array	DIPPA
Digital Parallel Processor (CAA)	DPP
Digital Patch Unit (CAA)	DPU
Digital Pattern Generator	DPG
Digital Phase Comparator	DPC
Digital Phase Difference	DPD
Digital Phase Shifter	DPS
Digital Plotter (CAA)	DP
Digital Plotter System	DPS
Digital Power Supply (VIT)	DPS
Digital Pressure Converter	DPC
Digital Pressure Transducer	DPT
Digital Process Controller	DPC
Digital Process Instrument [Data processing] (IEEE)	DPI
Digital Processing and Control Unit	DPCU
Digital Processing Oscilloscope (MCD)	DPO
Digital Processing Unit	DPU
Digital Projection Readout (CAAL)	DPRO
Digital Pseudorandom Inspection (IEEE)	DPI
Digital Quadrature Detection [Instrumentation]	DQD
Digital Quality Monitor	DQM
Digital Radio and Multiplexer Acquisition (MCD)	DRAMA
Digital Radiometer (CDH)	DRM
Digital Range Machine	DRM
Digital Range Safety (NASA)	DRS
Digital Range Unit	DRU
Digital Rate-Integrating Gyro (MCD)	DRIG
Digital Ray and Intensity Projector	DRIP
Digital Read-In Assembly [Data processing] (VIT)	DRA
Digital Read-In Subsystem [Data processing]	DRISS
Digital Readout [Data processing]	DIGRO
Digital Readout [Data processing] (DDI)	DRO
Digital Readout Head [Data processing]	DRH
Digital Readout Light [Data processing]	DRL
Digital Readout Oscilloscope [Data processing]	DRO
Digital Readout Oscilloscope [Data processing]	DROO
Digital Readout System [Data processing]	DRS
Digital Readout Timer [Data processing]	DRT
Digital Receiver Station [Data processing]	DRS
Digital Recorder Analyzer [Data processing]	DRA
Digital Recorder Signal Generator [Data processing]	DRSG
Digital Recording and Measuring System	DRAMS
Digital Recording and Playback Equipment (MCD)	DRAPE
Digital Recording Process	DRP
Digital Recording System (CIT)	DRS
Digital Register Unit (VIT)	DRU
Digital Remote Unit [Data processing]	DRU
Digital Remote Unit Buffer [Data processing]	DRUB
Digital Research, Incorporated	DRI
Digital Rotary Transducer	DRT
Digital Scan Converter (MCD)	DSC
Digital Scan Converter Group (MCD)	DSCG
Digital Scene Matching Area Correlator (MCD)	DIGISMAC
Digital Secure Voice Telephone [Telecommunications] (TEL)	DSVT
Digital Select Matrix (SKY)	DSM
Digital Select Module (KSC)	DSM
Digital Selective Communications	DISCOM
Digital Service Planning Analysis [Telecommunications] (TEL)	DISPLAY
Digital Service Unit [Signal converting device] [Telecommunications] (TSSD)	DSU
Digital Serving Area [Telecommunications] (TEL)	DSA
Digital Shaft Encoder	DSE
Digital Shift Register	DSR
Digital Signal (OA)	DS
Digital Signal Analyzer (IEEE)	DSA
Digital Signal Conditioner (MCD)	DSC
Digital Signal Generator	DSG
Digital Signal Processing System	DSPS
Digital Signal Synchronizer	DSS
Digital Simulated Analog Computer	DYSAC
Digital Simulation Language [Data processing] (CSR)	DSL
Digital Simulation Model (KSC)	DSM
Digital Simulator and Computer (IEEE)	DISAC
Digital Simulator System	DSS
Digital Spectrum Analyzer (NVT)	DSA
Digital Speech Interpolation [Telephone channels]	DSI
Digital Stabilization Console (DDI)	DSC
Digital Stepping Recorder	DSR
Digital Storage System	DSS
Digital Storage Unit (DIT)	DSU
Digital Strain Indicator	DSI
Digital Subscriber Terminal	DST
Digital Subscriber Terminal Equipment (AFM)	DSTE
Digital Subset [or Subsystem]	DSS
Digital Sum Variation [Telecommunications] (DEEC)	DSV
Digital Switching System [Telecommunications] (TEL)	DSS
Digital Synchro Data Source (VIT)	DSDS
Digital System Design (IEEE)	DSD
Digital System Diagram (CAA)	DSD
Digital Tactical Automatic Control (IEEE)	DIGITAC
Digital Tandem Switch	DTS
Digital Tape Conversion	DTC
Digital Tape Recorder (CIT)	DTR
Digital Tape Unit (IEEE)	DTU
Digital Technique	DT
Digital Telemetering Register	DTR
Digital Telemetry Analog Recording (VIT)	DITAR
Digital Telemetry System	DTS
Digital Telemetry Unit	DTU
Digital-to-Teletype (SKY)	DTTY
Digital Television Camera (MCD)	DITEC
Digital Television Camera	DTC
Digital Television Display System	DTDS
Digital Television Encoder	DTE
Digital Television Encoding (CBSS)	DITEC
Digital Television Equipment (KSC)	DTE
Digital Television Monitor	DTM
Digital Television Spectrometer (NG)	DITS
Digital Termination Systems [Telecommunications]	DTS
Digital Test Measurement [or Monitor] System	DTMS
Digital Testing Oscilloscope (IEEE)	DTO
Digital Titration System	DTS
Digital to Tone Converter	DTC
Digital Tracker (CIT)	DT
Digital Tracking System [or Subsystem] (CIT)	DTS
Digital Transmission System (DDI)	DTSY
Digital Transmission Unit (IEEE)	DTU
Digital Transmission and Verification Converter (KSC)	DTVC
Digital Transmitting and Routing System (IEEE)	DTARS
Digital Unit	DU
Digital Universal Test Equipment (MCD)	DUTE
Digital Uplink Assembly	DUA
Digital Variable-Frequency Oscillator (IEEE)	DVFO
Digital Variable Increment Computer	DIVIC
Digital Vascular Imaging [Roentgenology]	DVI
Digital Velocity Meter (CIT)	DVM
Digital Video Bandwidth	DVB
Digital Video Display System	DVDS
Digital Video Generator [Data processing]	DVG
Digital Video Integrator and Processor (MCD)	DVIP
Digital Voice Communications	DVC
Digital Voice Exchange [Telecommunications] (TEL)	DVX
Digital Voice System (MCD)	DVS
Digital-to-Voice Translator	DIVOT
Digital Volt-Ohmmeter	DVOM
Digital Voltmeter	DVM
Digital Waveform Generator (MCD)	DWG
Digitalized Electronics MARC [Machine-Readable Cataloging] and Non-MARC [Machine-Readable Cataloging] Display [Library of Congress]	DEMAND
Digitally Controlled Power Source (IEEE)	DCPS
Digitally Directed Analog (MSA)	DDA
Digitally Directed Control (MSA)	DDC
Digitally Implemented Communications Experiment (MCD)	DICE
Digitally Scanned Image Display (MCD)	DIGISPLAY
Digitech, Inc. [NASDAQ symbol] (NQ)	DGTC
Digitized Moving Target Indicator (CET)	DMTI
Digitizer Logic Unit	DLU
Digitizing and Control Unit (OA)	DACU
Digitronics Equipment Users Association (CAH)	DEUA
Digitronics Users Association [Later, IUA] (EANO)	DUA

Computer & Telecommunications Acronyms

Digroup Terminal [*Telecommunications*] (TEL) .... DT
Dimensioning Unit [*Telecommunications*] (TEL) .... DU
Diminishing Error Method of Optimization for Networks [*Data processing*] (RDA) .... DEMON
 .... D
Diode (MDG) ....
Diode-Transistor Logic .... DTL
Diplex [*Electronics*] (MSA) .... DIPX
Diplexer [*Electronics*] .... DIPLXR
Diploma in Computer Science .... DipCompSc
Diploma in Information Processing .... DipInfmProcessing
Diploma in Numerical Analysis and Automatic Computing .... DipNA & AC
Diploma in Technology (Information Processing) .... DipTech(InfProc)
Diplomatic Telecommunications Service (FAAC) .... DTS
Dipole (DEN) .... DP
Dipole Antenna System .... DAS
Direct Access (BUR) .... DA
Direct Access Arrangement [*Telecommunications*] (CAA) .... DAA
Direct Access Beacon System (MCD) .... DABS
Direct Access Computing (MCD) .... DAC
Direct Access Device Space Management (MCD) .... DADSM
Direct Access File Manager (CAA) .... DAFM
Direct Access Management System (CAA) .... DAMS
Direct Access Memory [*Data processing*] (BUR) .... DAM
Direct Access Method [*Sperry UNIVAC*] [*Data processing*] (TUT) .... DAM
Direct Access Programing System [*Data processing*] .... DAPS
Direct Access to Reference Information [*Xerox Corp.*] .... DATRIX
Direct Access to Remote Data Bases Overseas [*Rome, Italy*] [*Telecommunications*] (TSSD) .... DARDO
Direct Access Storage Device [*Pronounced "daz-dee"*] [*Data processing*] (CGC) .... DASD
Direct Access Storage Dump Restore (CAA) .... DASDR
Direct Access Storage Facility [*Data processing*] (TUT) .... DASF
Direct Access Storage Handler [*Telecommunications*] (TEL) .... DASH
Direct Access Terminal Application [*Data processing*] (BUR) .... DATA
Direct Branch Mode (CAA) .... DBM
Direct Broadcast Satellite [*Television transmission system in which signals are transmitted by satellite directly to individual locations*] .... DBS
Direct Broadcast Satellite Corporation [*Bethesda, MD*] [*Telecommunications*] (TSSD) .... DBSC
Direct Channel Interface (CAA) .... DCI
Direct Channel Interface Option (CAA) .... DCIO
Direct Communications Link [*US/USSR*] .... DCL
Direct Computer Control (OA) .... DCC
Direct Computer Input (MCD) .... DCI
Direct Computer Input Load Module (MCD) .... DCILM
Direct Connection Module [*Data processing*] .... DCM
Direct Control Channel (CAA) .... DCC
Direct Control Feature (CMD) .... DCF
Direct Couple Operating System (CIT) .... DCOS
Direct Couple System .... DCS
Direct-Coupled FET [*Field Effect Transistor*] Logic [*Integrated circuitry*] .... DCFL
Direct Coupled Loop Network [*Data processing*] .... DCLN
Direct-Coupled Transistor Logic .... DCTL
Direct-Coupled Unipolar Transistor Logic .... DCUTL
Direct-Coupling Transistor Logic Circuit .... DCTLC
Direct Current .... DC
Direct-Current Analog Input (MCD) .... DCAI
Direct-Current Circuit Analysis Program [*Data processing*] .... DICAP
Direct Current to Direct Current [*Telecommunications*] .... DC/DC
Direct-Current Dump .... DCD
Direct-Current Key Pulsing (IEEE) .... DCKP
Direct Data Attachment (CAA) .... DDA
Direct Data Channel (CIT) .... DDC
Direct Data Entry [*Data processing*] (BUR) .... DDE
Direct Data Entry Replacement System .... DDERS
Direct Data Entry System .... DDES
Direct Dial In (BUR) .... DDI
Direct Dial Telephone System .... DDTS
Direct Dialing [*or Dialed*] [*Telecommunications*] (TEL) .... DD
Direct Digital Control .... DDC
Direct Digital Control System .... DDCS
Direct Digital Encoder .... DDE
Direct Digital Interface (CBSS) .... DDI
Direct Digital Interface Equipment [*Telecommunications*] (TEL) .... DDIE
Direct Digital Numerical Controller .... DDNC
Direct Disk Attachment (CAA) .... DDA
Direct Distance Dialing [*of telephone numbers for toll calls*] .... DDD
Direct Distance Service .... DDS
Direct Drive .... DDR
Direct Electronic Fourier Transform [*Camera*] .... DEFT
Direct English Access and Control [*Data processing*] .... DEACON
Direct Exchange Line [*Telecommunications*] (DEEC) .... DEL
Direct Formed Supergroup [*Telecommunications*] (TEL) .... DFSG
Direct High-Level Language Processor (IDA) .... DHLLP
Direct to Home [*Satellite broadcast mode*] [*Canada*] .... DTH
Direct Imaging Mass Analyzer .... DIMA
Direct Information Access Network for Europe [*Commission of the European Communities*] [*Information service*] (EISS) .... DIANE
Direct Input/Output [*Telecommunications*] (TEL) .... DIO
Direct Interface Adapter (CAA) .... DIA
Direct Inward Dialing [*Telecommunications*] .... DID
Direct Line [*Followed by telephone number*] .... DL

Direct Machine Environment (CAA) .... DME
Direct Memory Access [*Computing method*] .... DMA
Direct Memory Access Communications Processor (CAA) .... DMACP
Direct Memory Access Control [*Data processing*] .... DMAC
Direct Memory Access Interface (CAA) .... DMAI
Direct Memory Address [*Data processing*] (CDH) .... DMA
Direct Memory Channel .... DMC
Direct Memory Exchange (CAA) .... DMX
Direct Memory Interface (CAA) .... DMI
Direct Memory Processor (CAA) .... DMP
Direct Memory Queue [*Data processing*] (CAA) .... DMQ
Direct Memory Transfer [*Data processing*] (CAA) .... DMT
Direct Multiplexed Control (OA) .... DMC
Direct Multiplexor Channel .... DMC
Direct Numerical Control [*Automation method*] [*Data processing*] .... DNC
Direct Order Recording and Invoicing System [*A computer-based system of British petroleum companies*] .... DORIS
Direct Outward Dialing [*Telecommunications*] .... DOD
Direct Program Control (BUR) .... DPC
Direct Read after Write [*Data processing*] .... DRAW
Direct Read-and-Write [*Data processing*] .... DRAW
Direct Reading Encoder .... DRE
Direct Reading Receiver .... DRR
Direct Reading Totalizer .... DRT
Direct Readout Equatorial Weather Satellite .... DREWS
Direct Readout Ground Station .... DRGS
Direct Readout Image Dissector [*Camera system*] .... DRID
Direct Readout Infrared Radiometer .... DRIR
Direct Readout Miss Distance Indicator .... DROMDI
Direct Readout Satellite .... DROS
Direct Readout Weather Satellite .... DROWS
Direct Satellite Communications .... DSC
Direct Sequence [*Telecommunications*] (TEL) .... DS
Direct Signal Monitoring [*Telecommunications*] (TEL) .... DSM
Direct Storage Access (CAA) .... DSA
Direct Support Unit/General Support Unit [*Computer system*] .... DSU/GSU
Direct System Output [*Data processing*] (MCD) .... DSO
Direct-View Storage Tube [*Princeton Electronic Products*] .... DVST
Direct Voice Line (CET) .... DVL
Directed Format Option [*Rapid access management information system*] (CAA) .... DFO
Direction Cycle (MDG) .... DC
Direction Finder [*or Finding*] [*Radio aid to navigation*] .... DF
Direction Generale des Telecommunications [*General Management of Telecommunications*] [*Paris, France*] [*Telecommunications*] (TSSD) .... DGT
Directional Antenna .... DA
Directional Antenna with Changing Patterns, Day and Night [*Broadcasting term*] DA-2
Directional Antenna with Changing Patterns, Day and Night with Additional Pattern Change [*Broadcasting term*] DA-3
Directional Antenna Day and Night [*Broadcasting term*] DA-1
Directional Antenna Daytime Only [*Broadcasting term*] .... DA-D
Directional Antenna Nighttime Only [*Broadcasting term*] .... DA-N
Directional Antenna Phasing Network .... DAPN
Directional Coupler .... DC
Directional Frequency Analysis and Recording System .... DIFAR
Directional Radiated Power [*Telecommunications*] (TEL) .... DRP
Directional Radio Beacon [*ITU designation*] (CET) .... RD
Directional Reservation Equipment [*Telecommunications*] (TEL) .... DRE
Directly Executable Representation (CAA) .... DER
Directly Executable Test-Oriented Language [*1968*] [*Data processing*] (CSR) .... DETOL
Directly Operable Input/Output (CAA) .... DOIO
Director of Corporate Information .... DCI
Director Deputy of Communications-Electronics .... DC
Director/Telecommunications and Command and Control System (MCD) .... DTACCS
Director's Instant Reversible Talkback [*Device enabling contact between director in control room and crew in studio*] .... DIRT
Directory .... DIR
Directory Assistance [*Telecommunications*] (TEL) .... DA
Directory Assistance System [*Telecommunications*] (TEL) .... DAS
Directory Assistance System/Microfilm [*Bell System*] .... DAS/M
Directory of Associations in Canada [*Micromedia, Ltd.*] [*A publication*] [*Information service*] (EISS) .... DAC
Directory of Automated Information Systems (MCD) .... DAIS
Directory of Automated Library and Information Systems in Australia [*A publication*] .... DALIS
Directory of Computerized Information in Science and Technology [*Leonard Cohen, ed., New York: Science Associates International, 1968*] [*A publication*] .... DCIST
Directory on Disk [*Los Gatos, CA*] [*Information service*] (EISS) .... DOD
Directory Enquiry Service [*Telecommunications*] (TEL) .... DQ
Directory of Information Sources Online [*National Library of Medicine*] [*Database*] .... DIRLINE
Directory of Online Databases [*United States*] [*A publication*] .... Dir Online Databases
Directory Scope Analysis Program [*Bell System*] .... DSAP
Directory of United Nations Databases and Information Systems [*United Nations*] [*Database*] (CUAD) .... DUNDIS
Directory Verification Processor [*Data processing*] .... DIRVIR
Directory Yellow Pages [*Telecommunications*] (TEL) .... DYP

Computer & Telecommunications Acronyms

Disc and Drum Input/Output Routines [Honeywell, Inc.] (CDH)	DIPDOP
Discone Antenna	DSC
Disconnect (KSC)	DISC
Disconnect, End of Transmission (CAA)	DEOT
Disconnect and Make Busy [Telecommunications] (TEL)	DMB
Disconnected Mode (CCD)	DM
Disconnection Pending [Telecommunications] (TEL)	DP
Discontinue (BUR)	DS
Discount Long Distance [Larose, LA] [Telecommunications] (TSSD)	DLD
Discrete Address	DA
Discrete Address Communications System	DACS
Discrete Data Input (MCD)	DDI
Discrete Data Output (MCD)	DDO
Discrete Differential Dynamic Programing [Data processing]	DDDP
Discrete Digital Input (NASA)	DDI
Discrete Elastic System	DES
Discrete Event Evaluator (KSC)	DEE
Discrete Fourier Transform	DFT
Discrete Frequency Generator	DFG
Discrete Hilbert Transform (IEEE)	DHT
Discrete Horizon Sensor (MCD)	DHS
Discrete Input [Data processing] (KSC)	DI
Discrete Input High (MCD)	DIH
Discrete Input Low (MCD)	DIL
Discrete Memoryless Channel [Data processing]	DMC
Discrete Network Simulation	DNS
Discrete Network Simulation	DNWS
Discrete Ordinate Transport	DOT
Discrete Orthonormal Sequence	DOS
Discrete Output [Data processing] (KSC)	DO
Discrete Output High (MCD)	DOH
Discrete Rate Command (MCD)	DRC
Discrete Recovery Area (KSC)	DRA
Discrete Register (MCD)	DR
Discrete Sample Analyzer	DSA
Discrete Space and Discrete Time	DSDT
Discrete System Concept	DSC
Discretionary Capital Expenditure System [Bell System]	DCES
Discriminating Digit [Telecommunications] (TEL)	DD
Discriminating Selector Repeater (DEN)	DSR
Discrimination and Control Computer (MUGU)	DCC
Discrimination Data Processing System	DDPS
Disintegrations per Hour	DPH
Disintegrations per Minute	DPM
Disintegrations per Minute/Second (DEN)	DPM/S
Disintegrations per Second	DPS
Disintegrations per Second	D/S
Disk Allocation Table [Data processing] (IBMDP)	DAT
Disk-Based Operating System (IEEE)	DBOS
Disk Buffer Area Access Method (CAA)	DBAAM
Disk Cartridge Initialization Program (CMD)	DCIP
Disk Communications Area (CMD)	DCOM
Disk Controller [Data processing] (IEEE)	DC
Disk Controller/Formatter (CAA)	DCF
Disk Copy Restore and Backup System (CAA)	DCRABS
Disk Core Image (CMD)	DCI
Disk Data File Conversion Program [IBM Corp.] (CAA)	DFCNV
Disk Data Unit	DDU
Disk Direct Memory Access (CAA)	DDMA
Disk File [Data processing] (BUR)	DF
Disk File Check (OA)	DFC
Disk File Control [Data processing]	DFC
Disk File Control Unit (OA)	DFCU
Disk File Descriptor Control [Data processing]	DFDC
Disk File Electronics Unit (CAA)	DFEU
Disk File Interrogate (OA)	DFI
Disk File Optimizer [Data processing] (BUR)	DFO
Disk File Storage Unit (OA)	DFSU
Disk-Insulated Quad [Telecommunications] (TEL)	DIQD
Disk Management Facility (CAA)	DMF
Disk Memory Controller [Data processing]	DMC
Disk Monitor System [Data processing]	DMS
Disk Operating Monitor (CAA)	DOM
Disk Operating System [IBM Corp.] [Data processing] (EISS)	DOS
Disk Operating System - Large Volumes	DOS-LV
Disk Operating System - Small Volumes	DOS-SV
Disk Operating System/Virtual Storage [IBM Corp.] [Data processing] (MCD)	DOS/VS
Disk-Oriented Computer System (IEEE)	DOCS
Disk-Oriented Engineering System [Data processing]	DOES
Disk Pack [Data processing] (IEEE)	DP
Disk Pack Unit (CAA)	DPU
Disk Preparation Processor [Data processing]	DPREP
Disk Programing System [IBM Corp.] (IEEE)	DPS
Disk Real-Time Monitor (CAA)	DRTM
Disk Real-Time and Programing System (CAA)	DRPS
Disk Recorder (DEN)	DR
Disk Resident Operating System [Data processing] (IEEE)	DROS
Disk Space Management (CAA)	DSM
Disk Storage [Data processing] (NASA)	DS
Disk Storage Controller (CMD)	DSC
Disk Storage Device	DSD
Disk Storage Facility (CAA)	DSF
Disk Storage Unit [Data processing] (MSA)	DSU
Disk System (CAA)	DS
Disk Tape [Data processing] (IEEE)	D/T
Disk Turbine Assembly	DTA
Disk Utility Program [IBM Corp.] [Data processing] (TUT)	DUP
Display (MDG)	D
Display (KSC)	DIS
Display (KSC)	DISP
Display	DSPL
Display Adapter (CAA)	DA
Display/AGAP [Attitude Gyro Accelerometer Package] Electronic Control Assembly (KSC)	DECA
Display Analysis Console	DAC
Display Assignment BITS [Binary Digits] (IDA)	DAB
Display Attention BITS [Binary Digits] [Data processing]	DAB
Display Automated Telemetry Analyzer (MCD)	DATA
Display Buffer [Data processing]	DB
Display of Chromosome Statistics System (OA)	DOCSYS
Display Code (CAH)	DC
Display Computer	DC
Display Computer Control Unit (MCD)	DCCU
Display Console (KSC)	DC
Display Control Console (KSC)	DCC
Display and Control Module (MCD)	DCM
Display Control Panel	DCP
Display and Control Unit (CET)	DCU
Display and Debug Unit [Data processing] (MDG)	DDU
Display Decoder Drive (MCD)	DDD
Display Driver Unit (NASA)	DDU
Display Electronics Unit (NASA)	DEU
Display Element (CAH)	DE
Display Equipment (CAH)	DE
Display Evaluation Flight Testing (MCD)	DEFT
Display Format Facility (CAA)	DFF
Display Format Generator (MCD)	DFG
Display Formatting Language (CIT)	DFL
Display Formatting System (SKY)	DFS
Display Integrated Software System and Plotting Language [Data processing]	DISSPLA
Display Interactive Assembly Language [Data processing] (IEEE)	DIAL
Display Interface Device [Telecommunications] (TEL)	DID
Display Interface Processing (MCD)	DIP
Display/Keyboard (MCD)	DK
Display and Keyboard [Data processing]	DSKY
Display Logic Unit	DLU
Display Management System [IBM Corp.]	DMS
Display Octal Debugging Technique (CAA)	DODT
Display, Oral, Printed, and Electronic [Media] (DDI)	DOPE
Display-Oriented Computer Usage System	DOCUS
Display-Oriented Language [Data processing] (IEEE)	DOL
Display Package	DP
Display Panel	DP
Display Power Control	DPC
Display Processor Code (OA)	DPC
Display Request Keyboard (KSC)	DRK
Display Simulation Program	DSP
Display and Storage (MSA)	D & S
Display Storage Tube (CET)	DST
Display Switching Oscilloscope	DSO
Display System Computer Input Multiplexer (MCD)	DCIM
Display Terminal Interchange (CAA)	DTI
Display Terminal Unit (CMD)	DTU
Display Timing Control (CIT)	DTC
Display Transmission Generator	DTG
Display Unit (NASA)	DU
Display Unit Test Assembly (MCD)	DUTA
Display, Upper (VIT)	DU
Displayed Impact Line (MCD)	DIL
Displayed under Program Control	DUPC
Disposable Tape Reel [Data processing] (OA)	DTR
DISSPLA and TELL-A-GRAF User Community [Argonne National Laboratory] [Argonne, IL]	DISSCO
Distance [Radio term] (EANO)	DX
Distance Measuring Equipment [Navigation]	DME
Distance Measuring Equipment TACAN (NG)	DMET
Distance Measuring Equipment Terminal (CET)	DMET
Distant Element (MDG)	DE
Distant End Disconnect [Telecommunications] (TEL)	DED
Distant Station Connected [Data processing] (BUR)	DSC
Distortion Transmission Impairment [Telecommunications] (TEL)	DTI
Distress Radio Call System [Telecommunications] (TEL)	DRCS
Distributed Application Processing System (CAA)	DAPS
Distributed Array Processor [Sperry UNIVAC] [Telecommunications]	DAP
Distributed Communications Architecture (BUR)	DCA
Distributed Communications Processor [Sperry UNIVAC] (CAA)	DCP
Distributed Computer Network	DCN
Distributed Computer Systems (MDG)	DCS
Distributed Computer Systems [NASDAQ symbol] (NQ)	DCSI
Distributed Control Programing Language [Data processing] (CSR)	DCPL
Distributed Data Entry (CAA)	DDE
Distributed Data Processing	DDP
Distributed Database (CAA)	DDB

Computer & Telecommunications Acronyms

Distributed Digital Control [*Data processing*] ... DDC
Distributed Electronic Test and Analysis (CAA) ... DELTA
Distributed Energy Release [*Computer program*] ... DER
Distributed Feedback ... DFB
Distributed File System (CAA) ... DFS
Distributed Function Architecture (CAA) ... DFA
Distributed Information Processing (CAA) ... DIP
Distributed Information Processing Network Architecture (CAA) ... DINA
Distributed Information System [*Data processing*] ... DIS
Distributed Input/Output System (CAA) ... DIOS
Distributed Intelligence Microcomputer System (DEEC) ... DIMS
Distributed Interactive Secure Telecommunications Area Network (MCD) ... DISTAN
Distributed Lab (MDG) ... DL
Distributed Logic Corp. [*NASDAQ symbol*] (NQ) ... DLOG
Distributed Loop Message Communication Protocol (CAA) ... DLMCP
Distributed Loop Operating System (CAA) ... DLOS
Distributed Microprocessor Unit (CAA) ... DMU
Distributed Network Control System (CAA) ... DNCS
Distributed Network System (CAA) ... DNS
Distributed Operating Multi-Access Interactive Network [*Apollo Computer, Inc.*] [*Chelmsford, MA*] [*Telecommunications*] (TSSD) ... DOMAIN
Distributed Operating System Kernel [*Data processing*] ... DOSK
Distributed Presentation Services [*IBM Corp.*] ... DPS
Distributed Processing Communications Module (CAA) ... DPCM
Distributed Processing Control Executive [*IBM Corp.*] ... DPCX
Distributed Processing Environment (CAA) ... DPE
Distributed Processing Executive Program (CAA) ... DPEX
Distributed Processing Newsletter [*A publication*] ... Dist Proc
Distributed Processing Programing Executive Base [*IBM Corp.*] ... DPPX
Distributed Processing System [*Honeywell, Inc.*] (IDA) ... DPS
Distributed Program Design Language (CAA) ... DPDL
Distributed Read Address Counter ... DRAC
Distributed System (CAA) ... DS
Distributed System Program [*Data processing*] ... DSP
Distributed Systems Environment [*Honeywell, Inc.*] (BUR) ... DSE
Distributed Systems Executive [*IBM Corp.*] ... DSX
Distributed Systems Licensing Option [*IBM Corp.*] (CAA) ... DSLO
Distributed Systems Network [*Hewlett-Packard Co.*] (CAA) ... DSN
Distributed Time (KSC) ... DIST
Distributed Write Address Counter ... DWAC
Distributing Terminal Assembly [*Electronics*] ... DTA
Distribution [*or Distributor*] (AFM) ... DISTR
Distribution Automation and Control (MCD) ... DAC
Distribution Common Point [*Telecommunications*] (TEL) ... DCP
Distribution Frame (KSC) ... DF
Distribution Management Accounting System (IEEE) ... DMAS
Distribution Point ... DP
Distribution Tape Reel [*Data processing*] ... DTR
Distribution Unit (KSC) ... DU
Distributor (KSC) ... DIST
Distributor-to-Printer Electronics ... DPE
District Switching Center [*Telecommunications*] (DEEC) ... DSC
Dittberner Associates, Incorporated [*Bethesda, MD*] [*Information service*] [*Telecommunications*] (TSSD) ... DAI
Diver Equipment Information Center [*Battelle Memorial Institute*] [*Information service*] (EISS) ... DEIC
Diversified Technology Management [*NASDAQ symbol*] (NQ) ... DTMI
Diversity Reception Receiver ... DRR
Divided Access Line Circuit ... DALC
Division of Applied Sciences [*Harvard University*] [*Research center*] (RCD) ... DAS
Division of Computer Research [*Formerly, OCA*] [*National Science Foundation*] ... DCR
Division of Computer Research and Technology [*National Institutes of Health*] ... DCRT
Division of Educational Research Services [*University of Alberta*] [*Research center*] (RCD) ... DERS
Division of Engineering Research [*Michigan State University*] [*Research center*] (RCD) ... DER
Division Entry (BUR) ... DE
Division of Foreign Labor Conditions [*Department of Labor*] ... DFLC
Division of Research and Evaluation in Medical Education [*Ohio State University*] [*Research center*] (RCD) ... DREME
Division of Science Information (EISS) ... DSI
Division of Ship Operations and Marine Technical Support [*University of California, San Diego*] [*Research center*] (RCD) ... SOMTS
Do the Right Thing [*Also, DWIM*] [*In data processing context, translates as "Guess at the meaning of poorly worded instructions"*] ... DTRT
Do What I Mean [*Also, DTRT*] [*In data processing context, translates as "Guess at the meaning of poorly worded instructions"*] ... DWIM
[*The*] DocketSearch Network, Incorporated [*Chicago, IL*] [*Information service*] (EISS) ... DSNI
Dr. Dobb's Journal [*A publication*] ... Dr Dobb's J
Dr. Dobb's Journal of Computer Calisthenics and Orthodontia [*A publication*] ... Dr Dobb's J Comput Calisthenics and Orthod
Dr. Dvorkovitz & Associates [*Information service*] (EISS) ... DDA
Document [*or Documentation*] (AFM) ... DOC
Document Abstract Retrieval Equipment (IEEE) ... DARE
Document Code [*Data processing*] ... DC

Document Composition Facility [*IBM Corp.*] ... DCF
Document Content Architecture [*IBM Corp.*] ... DCA
Document Control (VIT) ... DC
Document Control System [*Data processing*] (TUT) ... DCS
Document Data Indexing Set ... DDIS
Document Delivery [*Information service*] ... DOCDEL
Document Generator ... DOCGEN
Document Handler Processor (CAA) ... DHP
Document Handler Unit (CAA) ... DHU
Document Handling and Information Services Facility [*General Accounting Office*] (EISS) ... DHISF
Document Identification and Description Macros [*IBM Corp.*] (CAA) ... DIDM
Document Information Directory System [*NIOSH*] [*Database*] (FDB) ... DIDS
Document Interchange Format ... DIF
Document Library Facility [*Data processing*] ... DLF
Document Locator Number [*Data processing*] ... DLN
Document Organization and Control System [*Telecommunications*] (TEL) ... DOCS
Document Processing System [*IBM Corp.*] [*Data processing*] ... DPS
Document Read and Format Translator (CAA) ... DRAFT
Document Read, Information Verify, and Edit (CAA) ... DRIVE
Document Retrieval Index (CAA) ... DRI
Document Retrieval System ... DRS
Document Type [*Online database field identifier*] (OBD) ... DT
Documentation Associates Information Services, Inc. (EISS) ... DA
Documentation Informatisee pour les Comptables [*CEDIC*] [*Database*] (CUAD) ... DICOMTA
Documentation of Programs in Core [*Data processing*] (IEEE) ... DOPIC
Documents Information Accessing (BUR) ... DIA
Documents per Minute [*Data processing*] (BUR) ... DPM
Docutel/Olivetti Corp. [*NASDAQ symbol*] (NQ) ... DCTL
Does Everything but Eat [*Superseded by DITTO*] [*Data processing*] ... DEBE
Does Not Answer [*Telephone operator's designation*] ... DNA
Doesn't Answer ... DA
Dokumentation Kraftfahrwesen eV [*Database producer and database*] [*Information retrieval*] (ODIN) ... DKF
Dokumentation Maschinenbau [*FIZ Technik*] [*Database producer*] (ODIN) ... DOMA
Dokumentation Schweisstechnik [*Welding Documentation*] [*Germany*] [*Information service*] (ODIN) ... DS
Dokumentation Zerstorungsfreie Pruefung [*Nondestructive Testing Documentation*] [*West Germany*] [*Information service*] (EISS) ... ZFP
Dokumentations - und Informationsgesellschaft fuer Wirtschaft und Touristik mbH [*Database producer*] (CUAD) ... DIWT
Dokumentationsring Elektrotechnik [*Database*] (ODIN) ... DRE
Dokumentationsstelle fuer Veterinaermedizin [*Information retrieval*] (ODIN) ... DFV
Dokumentationszentrale Feinwerktechnik [*Precision Technology Documentation Center*] [*Originator, operator, and database*] [*Information service*] [*West German*] (EISS) ... DZF
Dokumentationszentrale Feinwerktechnik im Fachinformationszentrum Technik [*Database*] (ODIN) ... DZF
Domain-Originated Functional Integrated Circuit (IEEE) ... DOFIC
Domain Tip Propagation Logic (MCD) ... DTPL
Domestic Information Display System [*Computer graphics*] ... DIDS
Domestic Library Automation Functions [*Data processing*] ... DOMLIB
DOMESTIC [*Development of Microcomputers in an Environment of Scientific and Technological Information Centers*] **Print Generator** [*Data processing*] ... DOMPRINT
Domestic Public Land Mobile [*Telecommunications*] (TEL) ... DPLM
Domestic Satellite [*Communications satellite*] [*Australia*] ... DOMSAT
Domestic Transmission System [*ITT*] [*Telecommunications*] (TEL) ... DTS
Dominion Law Reports [*Canada Book Ltd.*] [*Database*] ... DLR
Don King Sports and Entertainment Network [*Cable-television system*] ... DKSEN
Donnelley Marketing Information Services [*Stamford, CT*] (EISS) ... DMIS
Don't Answer ... DA
Don't Want [*Telecommunications*] (TEL) ... DW
Doppler Data Translator ... DDT
Doppler Filter Mixer-Oscillator [*Electronics*] ... DFMO
Doppler Range and Navigation [*Electronics*] ... DORAN
Dortmund Data Bank [*Universitaet Dortmund*] [*Chemical databank*] [*Information service*] [*West German*] ... DDB
DOS [*Disk Operating System*] under OS [*Operating System*] (CAA) ... DUO
Double Armor [*Telecommunications*] (TEL) ... DA
Double Byte Interleaved (CAA) ... DBI
Double Cotton Covered [*Wire insulation*] ... DCC
Double Current Cable Code [*Telecommunications*] ... DCCC
Double Dacron Braid Lacquered (MDG) ... DD
Double Deflection Tube (BUR) ... DDT
Double Density (CAA) ... DD
Double Density Modular Core Memory (MCD) ... DMCM
Double-Diffused Metal-Oxide Semiconductor [*Microelectronics*] (MCD) ... DMOS
Double Error Detection (CAA) ... DED
Double Frequency (DEEC) ... DF
Double Frequency Shift Keying [*Radio*] ... DFSK
Double In-Line Package [*Data processing*] ... DIP
Double Mark Blank Column (BUR) ... DMBC
Double Pole [*Switch*] ... DP
Double Pole, Double Throw [*Switch*] ... DPDT

Computer & Telecommunications Acronyms

Double-Pole, Double-Throw Switch	DPDTSW
Double Pole, Single Throw [*Switch*]	DPST
Double Pulse Duration Modulation (KSC)	DPDM
Double Pulse Operation	DPO
Double Pulse Ranging (NG)	DPR
Double Sideband	DSB
Double-Sideband Amplitude Modulation [*Telecommunications*] (TEL)	DSBAM
Double-Sideband Amplitude Modulation Reduced Carrier (IEEE)	DSBAMRC
Double-Sideband Emitted Carrier [*Telecommunications*] (TEL)	DSBEC
Double-Sideband Reduced Carrier [*Telecommunications*] (TEL)	DSBRC
Double-Sideband Suppressed Carrier	DSBSC
Double-Sideband Suppressed Carrier [*Modulation*] (IEEE)	DSSC
Double-Sideband Transmitted Carrier	DSBTC
Double-Sided, Double-Density Disk [*Data processing*]	DSDD
Double-Sided Pulse-Width Modulation [*Telecommunications*] (OA)	DPWM
Double-Sided Quad-Density [*Scottsdale Systems*] [*Data processing*]	DSQD
Double Silk Covered [*Wire insulation*]	DSC
Double Tape Armored [*Heavy-duty telephone buried cable*]	DTA
Double Word [*Data processing*] (CAA)	DW
Doubly Resonant Oscillator (IEEE)	DRO
Douglas Fir (MSA)	DF
Dow Jones Cable News [*Cable-television system*]	DJCN
Dow Jones News/Retrieval [*Princeton, NJ*] [*Bibliographic database*] [*Information service*] (OBD)	DJNR
Down Link [*Data processing*]	DL
Down-Link Television Terminal	DLTT
Downconverter [*Satellite communications*]	DC
Downrange Computer Input System (MUGU)	DCIS
Downrange Computer Output System (MUGU)	DCOS
Downtime [*Data processing*] [*Telecommunications*]	DNT
Downtime [*Data processing*] [*Telecommunications*]	DT
Downtime Ratio [*Data processing*] [*Telecommunications*] (TEL)	DTR
Downtown Copy Center [*Washington, DC*] [*Telecommunications*] (TSSD)	DCC
Draft International Standard [*International Standards Organization*]	DIS
Dranetz Technologies [*NASDAQ symbol*] (NQ)	DRAN
Draughting Software System [*Gould Electronics Ltd. Computer Systems*] [*Software package*] [*British*] (NCC)	DSS
Drawing Office Graphics System [*Deltacam Systems Ltd.*] [*Software package*] [*British*] (NCC)	DOGS
Drilling Information Service Company [*Houston, TX*] [*Telecommunications*] (TSSD)	DISC
Drive Unit	DRU
Driver Aid, Information, and Routing [*Data processing*]	DAIR
Driver Augmented Readout [*Data processing*]	DAR
Driver Control Area (BUR)	DCA
Driver Control Area Region Extension (BUR)	DCARE
Driver-Harris Co. [*American Stock Exchange symbol*]	DRH
Drop and Block Wire [*Telecommunications*] (TEL)	DW
Drop Build-Out Capacitor [*Telecommunications*] (TEL)	DBO
Drug Abuse Epidemiology Data Center [*Texas Christian University*] (EISS)	DAEDAC
Drug Abuse Prevention Resource Unit [*National Institute on Drug Abuse*] [*Databank*]	DAPRU
Drug Effects on Laboratory Tests: Attention [*Worldwide Medical Information Ltd.*] [*Database*] (CUAD)	DELTABANK
Drug Information Fulltext [*American Society of Hospital Pharmacists*] [*Database*]	DIF
Drug Information Services [*University of Minnesota*] (EISS)	DIS
Drug Product Information File [*American Society of Hospital Pharmacists*] [*Information service*] (EISS)	DPIF
Drum (MDG)	D
Drum Input to Digital Automatic Computer (OA)	DRIDAC
Drum Interrogation, Alteration, and Loading System [*Honeywell, Inc.*] (IEEE)	DIAL
Drum Memory Assembly [*Data processing*]	DMA
Drum Memory System [*Data processing*]	DMS
Drum Processor [*Data processing*] (IEEE)	DP
Drum-Programed Automatic Tester	D-PAT
Drum-Read Amplifier [*Data processing*] (CET)	DRA
Drum-Read Driver [*Data processing*]	DRD
Drum Storage [*Data processing*] (IEEE)	DS
Drum Storage System	DSS
Drum Storage Unit	DSU
Drum Write [*Data processing*]	DW
Drum Write Driver [*Data processing*]	DWD
Drums and Displays [*Data processing*]	DAD
DSS [*Deep Space Station*] Communications Equipment Subsystem (CIT)	DCES
DSS [*Deep Space Station*] Communications Terminal Subsystem (CIT)	DCT
Dual Access Storage Handling (CAA)	DASH
Dual Emitter Transistor [*Electronics*]	DUET
Dual-Expanded Plastic-Insulated Conductor [*Telecommunications*] (TEL)	DEPIC
Dual Facility	DF
Dual-Feed Coupler	DFC
Dual-Frequency Method (CIT)	DFM
Dual-Frequency Receiver	DFR
Dual In-Line [*Electronic components*]	DIL
Dual In-Line Package [*Data processing*]	DILP
Dual In-Line Pin	DIP
Dual Input Describing Function [*Data processing*]	DIDF
Dual Input Null Network	DINN
Dual Input Transponder	DIT
Dual Interface Adapter (CAA)	DIA
Dual Language (CAA)	DL
Dual Modular Magnetic Tape Unit (CAAL)	DMTU
Dual Port Memory Control (CAA)	DPMC
Dual Program Feature (CAA)	DPF
Dual Radio Magnetic Indicator (MCD)	DRMI
Dual-Speed Magnetic Transducer	DSMT
Dual-Tone Multifrequency [*Telecommunications*]	DTMF
Duck Book Communications Ltd. [*Vancouver Stock Exchange symbol*]	DBC
Ductwork Services [*Focus Software Consultants*] [*Software package*] [*British*] (NCC)	DUCTS
Dump Telemetry (SKY)	DT
Dun & Bradstreet, Inc.	D & B
Dun & Bradstreet, Inc. [*NYSE symbol*]	DNB
Dun's Financial Records [*Dun's Marketing Services*] [*Information service*] (EISS)	DFR
DUNS [*Data Universal Numbering System*] Industrial Affiliations Service [*Dun & Bradstreet, Inc.*] (EISS)	DIAS
Dun's Market Identifier [*Dun & Bradstreet, Inc.*] [*Database*] (EISS)	DMI
Dun's Marketing Services [*Dun & Bradstreet, Inc.*] [*Parsippany, NJ*] [*Information service*] (EISS)	DMS
Duo-Mode Electric Transport System, Inc.	DUETS
Duplex (MSA)	DX
Duplex Line Control (BUR)	DLC
Duplexed Display Distributor	DDD
Duplicate (AFM)	DUP
Dvorak Simplified Keyboard [*Typewriter keyboard developed by August Dvorak in the 1920's*]	DSK
Dyatron Corp. [*NASDAQ symbol*] (NQ)	DYTR
Dynamic Acoustic Response Trigger (IEEE)	DART
Dynamic Active Index Matrix (BUR)	DAIM
Dynamic Address Translation [*Data processing*]	DAT
Dynamic Allocation Interface Routine [*Data processing*] (BUR)	DAIR
Dynamic Analog Differential Equation Equalizer	DADEE
Dynamic Analyzer	DYANA
Dynamic Arm Programer [*Data processing*]	DYNARM
Dynamic Assertion Processor [*Data processing*]	DAP
Dynamic Automatic Monitoring (CET)	DYNAMO
Dynamic Computer Display (IEEE)	DCD
Dynamic Console for Operations Planners	DYCOP
Dynamic Control	DYCON
Dynamic Debugging Technique (DEN)	DDT
Dynamic Device Reconfiguration [*IBM Corp.*] [*Data processing*] (MDG)	DDR
Dynamic Electromagnetic Environment Simulator	DEES
Dynamic Error-Free Transmission	DEFT
Dynamic File Allocation System (CAA)	DFAST
Dynamic Flight Simulator	DFS
Dynamic Instrumentation Data Automobile System [*Telemetering system for auto test tracks*]	DIDAS
Dynamic Instrumentation Digital Analyzer	DIDA
Dynamic Integrated Data Display	DIDD
Dynamic Integrated Data Display System	DIDDS
Dynamic Interface Systems Corporation [*Los Angeles, CA*] [*Software manufacturer*] (DASOS)	DISC
Dynamic Inventory Analysis System [*Data processing*]	DIAS
Dynamic Load Characteristic (MDG)	DL
Dynamic Mapping System [*Hewlett-Packard Co.*]	DMS
Dynamic Model Continuous Time Simulation (BUR)	DYNAMO
Dynamic Octal Load	DOL
Dynamic Overload Controls	DOC
Dynamic Phase Error (CIT)	DPE
Dynamic Pressure Feedback	DPF
Dynamic Processor Overload Control [*Telephone technology*]	DPOC
Dynamic Programing [*Data processing*]	DP
Dynamic Quality Control	DQC
Dynamic Random Access Mechanization	DRAM
Dynamic Random Access Memory [*Data processing*]	d-RAM
Dynamic Real-Time Information Processing System (MCD)	DRIPS
Dynamic Scattering Mode (IEEE)	DSM
Dynamic Shift Register	DSR
Dynamic Sideband Regulator	DSR
Dynamic Signal Analyzer	DSA
Dynamic Simulation System (MCD)	DSS
Dynamic Standby Computer (KSC)	DSC
Dynamic Storage Allocation Language [*in FORTRAN*] [*Data processing*]	DYSTAL
Dynamic Storage Analog Computer (IEEE)	DYSAC
Dynamic Storage Analog Computer	DYSTAC
Dynamic Storage Area (CMD)	DSA
Dynamic Subscription Promotion	DSP
Dynamic Support Program [*Data processing*]	DSP
Dynamic Support System (MCD)	DSS
Dynamic System Electronics	DSE
Dynamic Translation Buffer (CAA)	DTB
Dynamic Universal Assembly Language [*Data processing*] (TUT)	DUAL

Dynamics Differential Analyzer (IEEE) .... DDA
Dynatech Corporation [*NASDAQ symbol*] (NQ) .... DYTC
Dysan Corp. [*NASDAQ symbol*] (NQ)... DYSN

E

EADAS [*Engineering and Administrative Data Acquisition System*]
   Traffic Data Center [*Bell System*] .... ETDC
Eagle Computer, Inc. [*NASDAQ symbol*] (NQ) .... EGLC
Early-Break-Make [*Data processing*] .... EBM
Early Failure Detection .... EFD
Early-Make-Break [*Data processing*] .... EMB
Early Programing Language [*Data processing*] (CGC) .... EPL
Earth-Based Radio Guidance (CIT) .... EBRG
Earth Coverage Horn [*Satellite communications*] .... ECH
Earth-Pointing Instrument Carrier [*A satellite*] .... EPIC
Earth Potential Compensation [*Telecommunications*] (TEL) .... EPC
Earth Resource Survey Operational System (TEL) .... ERSOS
Earth Resources Satellite System (IEEE) .... ERSS
East-West Institute of Culture and Communication [*Research center*] (RCD) .... EW-CLI
Eastern Cedar [*Utility pole*] [*Telecommunications*] (TEL) .... EC
Eastern Educational Network [*Television*] .... EEN
Eastern Joint Computer Conference .... EJCC
Eastern Telecommunications Philippines, Incorporated [*Manila*] (TSSD) .... ETPI
Eastman Kodak Co. [*NYSE symbol*] .... EK
Eastman Kodak Company .... EKC
Easy to Reach [*Telecommunications*] (TEL) .... ER
Eaton Corp. [*NYSE symbol*] .... ETN
EBU [*European Broadcasting Union*] Review [*A publication*] .... EBU Rev
EBU [*European Broadcasting Union*] Review. Part A [*A publication*] .... EBU Rev A
Eccles-Jordan Circuit [*Electronics*] .... EJC
Eccles-Jordan Trigger [*Electronics*] .... EJT
Echo Control Equipment [*Telecommunications*] (TEL) .... ECE
Echo Control Factor [*Telecommunications*] (TEL) .... ECF
Echo Control Subsystem [*Telecommunications*] (TEL) .... ECS
Echo Controller [*Telecommunications*] (TEL) .... EC
Echo-Ranging Masked Acoustic Communications (DDI) .... ERMAC
Echo Return Loss [*Telecommunications*] .... ERL
Echo Suppression Subsystem [*Telecommunications*] (TEL) .... ESS
Echo Suppressor [*Telecommunications*] (TEL) .... ES
Echo Suppressor Control [*Telecommunications*] (TEL) .... ESC
Echo Suppressor, Originating End [*Telecommunications*] (TEL) ... ESO
Echo Suppressor, Terminating End [*Telecommunications*] (TEL) .. EST
Echo Suppressor Testing System [*Telecommunications*] (TEL) ..... ESTS
Ecology of Knowledge Network (EANO) .... EKN
Economic Analysis Division [*Federal Emergency Management Agency*] [*Information service*] (EISS) .... EAD
Economic Commission for Latin America [*Database originator*] [*United Nations*] .... ECLA
Economic Data Retrieval and Application System (BUR) .... EDRAS
Economic Feeder Administration and Relief [*Telecommunications*] (TEL) .... EFAR
Economic Hundred Call Seconds [*Telecommunications*] (TEL) ..... ECCS
Economic Information Systems, Inc. [*Database originator*] (NG) . EIS
Economic Load Dispatching (BUR) .... ELD
Economic and Social Data System [*Agency for International Development*] [*Database*] (FDB) .... ESDS
Economical Storage and Access System [*Data processing*] .... ECSTASY
Economische Voorlichtingsdienst [*Economic Information Service*] [*Netherlands*] [*Information service*] (EISS) .... EVD
Edison Responsive Environment [*Automated learning system*] ..... ERE
Edit Program Generator (TUT) .... EPG
Editorial Data Systems .... EDS
Editorial Processing Center (CAA) .... EPC
EDP [*Electronic Data Processing*] Analyzer [*A publication*] .... EDPAA
EDP [*Electronic Data Processing*] Analyzer [*A publication*] .... EDP Anal
EDP [*Electronic Data Processing*] Audit, Control, and Security Newsletter [*A publication*] .... EDP A C S
EDP [*Electronic Data Processing*] Auditor [*A publication*] .... EDP Aud
EDP [*Electronic Data Processing*] Auditors Association [*Carol Stream, IL*] (EANO) .... EDPAA
EDP [*Electronic Data Processing*] Europa Report [*A publication*] .... EDP Europa
EDP [*Electronic Data Processing*] In-Depth Reports [*A publication*] .... EDP In-Depth Rep
EDP [*Electronic Data Processing*] Industry Report [*A publication*] .... EDP

EDP [*Electronic Data Processing*] Industry Report [*A publication*] .... EDP Indus Rep
EDP [*Electronic Data Processing*] Performance Review [*A publication*] .... EDP Performance Rev
EDP [*Electronic Data Processing*] Performance Review [*A publication*] .... EDP Perf Rev
Education Network [*EDUCOM*] (CAA) .... EDUNET
Education Service Group [*Bibliographic Retrieval Services*] [*Information service*] (EISS) .... ESG
Educational Analog Simulator .... EAS
Educational Assessment Center [*University of Washington*] [*Research center*] (RCD) .... EAC
Educational Communication and Technology Journal [*A publication*] .... Educ Comm & Tech J
Educational Communications [*Inter-University Communications Council*] .... EDUCOM
Educational Computer Corporation [*NASDAQ symbol*] (NQ) .... EDCC
Educational Computing [*A publication*] .... Educ Comput
Educational Data Bank (IEEE) .... EDB
[*Center for*] Educational Diffusion and Social Application of Satellite Telecommunications [*University of Wisconsin*] ...... EDSAT
Educational Document Management and Retrieval System [*Japanese*] [*Database*] (CUAD) .... EDMARS
Educational Information Network [*Princeton, NJ*] .... EIN
Educational Programs That Work [*Department of Education*] [*Information service*] (EISS) .... EPTW
Educational Research Center [*New Mexico State University*] [*Research center*] (RCD) .... ERC
Educational Resources [*formerly, Research*] Information Center [*Office of Education*] [*Bibliographic database*] [*Washington, DC*] .... ERIC
Educational Satellite (KSC) .... EDUSAT
Educational Technology Center [*Harvard University*] [*Research center*] (RCD) .... ETC
Educational Telecommunications Network .... ETN
Educational Teleconference System [*University of Missouri - Columbia*] [*Telecommunications*] (TSSD) .... ETS
Educational Television .... ETV
Educational Testing Service .... ETS
Educational Testing Service Test Collection (EISS) .... ETSTC
Educational Travel Connection [*Oracle Corp.*] [*Information service*] (EISS) .... ETC
EECO, Inc. [*American Stock Exchange symbol*] .... EEC
Effective Address [*Data processing*] (MDG) .... EA
Effective Bandwidth .... EBW
Effective Billing Date (TEL) .... EBD
Effective Mass Approximation .... EMA
Effective Monopole-Radiated Power (TEL) .... EMRP
Effective Radiated Power [*Radio transmitting*] .... ERP
Effective Testing Loss [*Telecommunications*] (TEL) .... ETL
Efficient Assembly System [*Honeywell, Inc.*] [*Assembler language*] ... EASY
Efficient Growth [*Computer program*] (NASA) .... EFFGRO
EG & G, Inc. [*NYSE symbol*] .... EGG
Eidgenossische Technische Hochschule Zurich [*Swiss Federal Institute of Technology*] .... ETH
Eighteenth Century Short Title Catalogue [*Bibliographic database*] (OBD) .... ESTC
Elapsed Time Multiprograming Factor (CAA) .... ETMF
Elastic Diaphragm Switch Technology [*IBM Corp.*] (MCD) .... EDST
Elastic Frame Analysis Program [*Structures & Computers Ltd.*] [*Software package*] [*British*] (NCC) .... EFAP
Elastic Structural Analysis System - Two Dimensional [*Structures & Computers Ltd.*] [*Software package*] [*British*] (NCC) ESAS-2
Electra Data Management System .... EDMS
Electric Accounting Machine [*or Methods*] .... EAM
Electric Accounting Machine and Electronic Data Processing Machine (VIT) .... EAMEDPM
Electric Accounting Machine Unit .... EAMU
Electric Beam Exposure System [*Integrated circuit*] [*Bell Laboratories*] .... EBES
Electric [*or Electronic*] Cipher [*or Coding*] Machine .... ECM
Electric Control Drive .... ECD

Computer & Telecommunications Acronyms

Electric Power Database [*Research and Development Information System*] [*Electric Power Research Institute*] [*Information service*] (EISS) ... EPD/RDIS
Electric Power Industry Abstracts [*Edison Electric Institute*] [*Washington, DC*] [*Bibliographic database*] (OBD) ... EPIA
Electric Power Research Laboratory [*Arizona State University*] [*Research center*] (RCD) ... EPRL
Electrical Accounting for the Security Industry [*IBM Corp.*] (IEEE) ... EASI
Electrical [*or Electronic*] Circuit Analysis Program (CIT) ... ECAP
Electrical and Electronic Abstracts [*United Kingdom*] [*A publication*] ... EEA
Electrical and Electronic Abstracts [*A publication*] ... Elec & Electron Abstr
Electrical and Electronic Measurement and Test Instrumentation Conference (MCD) ... EEMTIC
Electrical and Electronics Standards Board [*American National Standards Institute*] [*Telecommunications*] ... EESB
Electrical Engineering and Electronics [*A publication*] ... Elec Engrg Electron
Electrical Multiplex ... EMUX
Electrical Objective Loudness Rating (IEEE) ... EOLR
Electrical Reproduction Method of Accounting ... ERMA
Electrical Terminal Distributor (KSC) ... ETD
Electrical Typewriter (CMD) ... ET
Electrically Alterable Device (NASA) ... EAD
Electrically Alterable Memory [*Data processing*] ... EAM
Electrically Alterable Programable Read-Only Memory [*Data processing*] ... EAPROM
Electrically Alterable Read-Only Memory [*Data processing*] (TUT) ... EAROM
Electrically Alterable Read-Only Store [*Data processing*] ... EAROS
Electrically Controlled Birefringence [*Telecommunications*] (TEL) ... ECB
Electrically Erasable, Programable, Read-Only Memory [*Data processing*] ... EEPROM
Electrically Erasable Read-Only Memory [*Data processing*] (MDG) ... EEROM
Electrically Polarized [*Relay*] ... EP
Electrically Programable Read-Only Memory [*Data processing*] ... EPROM
Electrically Steerable Antenna Feed Techniques (NG) ... ESAFT
Electrically Transmitted Message ... ETM
Electricite de France [*Bibliographic database*] [*French*] (OBD) ... EDF-DOC
Electro-Optic Digital Deflector (IEEE) ... EODD
Electro-Optic Direction Sensor ... EODS
Electro-Optic Display ... EOD
Electro-Optic Display Test Chamber ... EODTC
Electro-Optic Phase Change (IEEE) ... EOPC
Electro-Optical Alignment Unit ... EOAU
Electro-Optical Imaging System (IEEE) ... EOIS
Electro-Optical Modulator ... EOM
Electro-Optical Systems, Inc. [*Subsidiary of Xerox Corp.*] ... EOS
Electroacoustic Systems Laboratory ... EASL
Electroacoustic Transmission Measuring System [*Telecommunications*] (TEL) ... EATMS
Electrodynamic (DEN) ... ED
Electromagnetic Compatibility ... EMC
Electromagnetic Compatibility Figure of Merit [*Telecommunications*] (TEL) ... EMCFOM
Electromagnetic Compatibility Standardization [*Program*] [*Telecommunications*] (IEEE) ... EMCS
Electromagnetic Control ... EMC
Electromagnetic Control Compatibility ... EMCC
Electromagnetic Effects Capability (NASA) ... EMEC
Electromagnetic Environment Generator ... EMEG
Electromagnetic Environment Recorder (MCD) ... EMER
Electromagnetic Intelligence (MSA) ... EMINT
Electromagnetic Intelligence Collection System ... EICS
Electromagnetic Interference ... EMI
Electromagnetic Interference and Compatibility ... EMIC
Electromagnetic Interference Testing ... EIT
Electromagnetic Pulse ... EMP
Electromagnetic Pulse Simulator (MCD) ... EMPS
Electromagnetic Simulation Unit (MCD) ... EMSU
Electromagnetic Storage ... ES
Electromagnetic Test Environment (MCD) ... ETE
Electromagnetic Test Environment Data System (MCD) ... EMTEDS
Electromagnetic Unit ... EMU
Electromagnetics [*A publication*] ... ETRMD
Electromechanical Relay [*Power switchgear*] (IEEE) ... EMR
Electromechanical Research (IEEE) ... EMR
Electromyosignal [*Data processing*] ... EMS
Electron Beam Readout ... EBR
Electron Beam Recorder [*or Recording*] ... EBR
Electron Beam Regulator ... EBR
Electron Beam Semiconductor ... EBS
Electron Beam System ... EBS
Electron-Bombarded Semiconductor ... EBS
Electron-Bombardment-Induced Conductivity ... EBIC
Electron-Bombardment-Induced Conductivity ... EBICON
Electron-Bombardment Silicon (KSC) ... EBS
Electron-Capture Detection [*Instrumentation*] ... ECD
Electron Coupled (DEN) ... EC
Electron-Coupled Oscillator ... ECO
Electron Device (MCD) ... ED
Electron Devices Society (EANO) ... EDS
Electron Microprobe ... EMP
Electron Microprobe X-Ray Analyzer ... EMX

Electron Microprobe X-Ray Analyzer ... EMXA
Electron Microprobe X-Ray Fluorescence ... EMXRF
Electron Multiplex Switch ... EMS
Electron Paramagnetic ... EP
Electron Readout Measurement (MCD) ... EROM
Electronic Accounting Machine [*Processes punched cards*] ... EAM
Electronic Analog Simulating Equipment [*Data processing*] ... EASE
Electronic Asset Control Center (AFM) ... EACC
Electronic Associates, Inc. [*NYSE symbol*] ... EA
Electronic Associates, Incorporated ... EAI
Electronic Audio Recognition ... EAR
Electronic Automatic Exchange [*See also ESS*] [*General Telephone & Electronics*] [*Telecommunications*] ... EAX
Electronic Automatic Machinery (CIT) ... EAM
Electronic Batch Control ... EBC
Electronic Bearing-Time Recorder ... EBTR
Electronic Business [*A publication*] ... EBI
Electronic Business [*A publication*] ... Elec Busns
Electronic Business [*A publication*] ... Electron Bus
Electronic Business Communications System ... EBCS
Electronic Cabling Unit ... ECU
Electronic Calculating Punch ... ECP
Electronic Calculator (BUR) ... EC
Electronic Calibration (DDI) ... EC
Electronic Calibration and Normalization (KSC) ... ECAN
Electronic Cash Register ... ECR
Electronic Central Office [*Within network*] [*Telecommunications*] (TEL) ... ECO
Electronic Centralized Aircraft Monitoring System ... ECAM
Electronic and Chaff Jamming (IEEE) ... JAFF
Electronic Checkout ... ECO
Electronic Circuit-Making Equipment [*Data processing*] ... ECME
Electronic Circuit Plug-In Unit (VIT) ... ECPIU
Electronic Circuit Protector ... ECP
Electronic Coding (DDI) ... EC
Electronic Command Signal Programer (MCD) ... ECSP
Electronic Common Control [*Telecommunications*] (TEL) ... ECC
Electronic Communicator [*A publication*] ... Electron Commun
Electronic Community Deal Office [*Telecommunications*] (TEL) ... ECDO
Electronic Comparator (VIT) ... EC
Electronic Components Code (NATG) ... ECC
Electronic Components Conference (CAH) ... ECC
Electronic Composing System ... ECS
Electronic Computer (MCD) ... EC
Electronic Computer-Originated Mail [*Postal Service*] ... E-COM
Electronic Computer Programming Institute [*Ceased operation, 1976*] ... ECPI
Electronic Computing ... ELECOM
Electronic Computing, Hospital-Oriented (IEEE) ... ECHO
Electronic Conductivity ... EC
Electronic Confusion Area ... ECA
Electronic Consumer Advertising Network [*Data Corp. of America*] ... ECAN
Electronic Control Amplifier (MCD) ... ECA
Electronic Control Instrumentation ... ECI
Electronic Control Module [*Instrumentation*] ... ECM
Electronic Control Relay (IEEE) ... ECR
Electronic Control Sensor (MCD) ... ECS
Electronic Control Switch (IEEE) ... ECS
Electronic Control Unit ... ECU
Electronic Coordinatograph and Readout System ... ECARS
Electronic Counter ... EC
Electronic Data Communications (DDI) ... EDC
Electronic Data Display ... EDD
Electronic Data Gathering, Analysis, and Retrieval [*Securities and Exchange Commission pilot project*] (EISS) ... EDGAR
Electronic Data Gathering Equipment ... EDGE
Electronic Data Information Technical Service (DIT) ... EDITS
Electronic Data Interchange ... EDI
Electronic Data Local Communications Central ... EDLCC
Electronic Data Processing ... EDP
Electronic Data Processing Center ... EDPC
Electronic Data Processing Equipment ... EDPE
Electronic Data Processing/Industry Report (CAH) ... EDP/IR
Electronic Data Processing Machine [*Also translated by some users of such equipment as "Every Damn Problem Multiplied"*] ... EDPM
Electronic Data Processing Magnetic [*Tape*] (DDI) ... EDPM
Electronic Data Processing System ... EDAPS
Electronic Data Processing System ... EDPS
Electronic Data Processing Test (AFM) ... EDPT
Electronic Data Remote Communications Complex ... EDRCC
Electronic Data Switching System [*Data processing*] (TEL) ... EDS
Electronic Data System (IEEE) ... EDS
Electronic Data Systems Corp. [*NYSE symbol*] [*Delisted*] ... EDS
Electronic Data Systems Federal Corporation ... EDS
Electronic Data Systems Federal Corporation ... EDSFC
Electronic Data Traffic Control Center ... EDTCC
Electronic Data Transmission ... EDT
Electronic Data Transmission Communications Central ... EDTCC
Electronic Delay Storage Automatic Calculator [*or Computer*] [*1949*] ... EDSAC
Electronic Design [*A publication*] ... Elec Des
Electronic Design [*A publication*] ... Elec Desgn
Electronic Design [*A publication*] ... Electron Des

Electronic Design [*A publication*] ... ELODA
Electronic Desk Calculator (IEEE) ... EDC
Electronic Devices Quality Assurance ... EDQA
Electronic Dial Tone Speed Register [*Bell System*] ... EDTSR
Electronic Differential [*Analyzer*] (CDH) ... ED
Electronic Differential Analyzer ... EDA
Electronic Differential Analyzer (MSA) ... EDFA
Electronic Digital [*Analyzer*] (CDH) ... ED
Electronic Digital Analyzer (MCD) ... EDA
Electronic Digital Computer ... EDC
Electronic Digital Tracking and Ranging ... EDITAR
Electronic Discrete Sequential Automatic Computer [*University of Manchester, 1949*] [*British*] (IEEE) ... EDSAC
Electronic Display ... ED
Electronic Display Assembly (NASA) ... EDA
Electronic Display Panel ... EDP
Electronic Display Unit ... EDU
Electronic Distance Measuring ... EDM
Electronic Distance Measuring Equipment (MCD) ... EDME
Electronic Editing [*Telecommunications*] ... EE
Electronic Education [*A publication*] ... Elec Ed
Electronic Egg Exchange [*Computer program*] ... EEX
Electronic Emission Control (MCD) ... EMCON
Electronic Engine Control Module ... EECM
Electronic Engineering Association [*British*] (CAH) ... EEA
Electronic Engineering Times [*A publication*] ... Elec Eng T
Electronic Equipment Engineering [*A publication*] ... EEQEA
Electronic Equipment Modification ... EEM
Electronic Failure Report ... EFR
Electronic Failure Report Only (DDI) ... EFRO
Electronic Flight Control System ... EFCS
Electronic Flight Data Accumulation Service ... EFDAS
Electronic Flight Data and Recording System (MCD) ... EFDARS
Electronic Frequency Control ... EFC
Electronic Frequency Selection (IEEE) ... EFS
Electronic Funds Transfer [*Banking*] ... EFT
Electronic Funds Transfer at Point-of-Sale ... EFTPOS
Electronic Funds Transfer System [*Banking*] [*National Science Foundation*] ... EFTS
Electronic Governor Module (IEEE) ... EGM
Electronic Governor Regulator (IEEE) ... EGR
Electronic Guidance ... EG
Electronic Image Generator ... EIG
Electronic Industries Association [*Washington, DC*] [*Telecommunications*] ... EIA
Electronic Industries Foundation (EANO) ... EIF
Electronic Information Exchange System [*Pronounced "eyes"*] [*New Jersey Institute of Technology*] [*Computer network*] [*Telecommunications*] ... EIES
Electronic Installation Plan (NG) ... EIP
Electronic Intelligence [*or Intercept*] [*Meaning of ELINT determined by reference to before (Intercept) and after (Intelligence) analysis of reconnaissance mission results*] ... ELINT
Electronic Intelligence Analysis Processing Subsystem (MCD) ... EAPSS
Electronic Interface (MCD) ... EI
Electronic Interface Unit ... EIU
Electronic Intrusion Detection ... EID
Electronic Jamming ... EJ
Electronic Journalism ... EJ
Electronic Key Telephone System ... EKTS
Electronic Keyboard ... EKB
Electronic Keyboard System ... EKBS
Electronic Keyboard System ... EKS
Electronic Keyboarding, Incorporated [*Information service*] (EISS) ... EKI
Electronic Knowledge Bank ... EKB
Electronic Legislative Search System [*Commerce Clearing House*] [*Database*] [*Information service*] ... ELSS
Electronic Letter Sorting and Indicator Equipment ... ELSIE
Electronic Lie Detector ... ELD
Electronic Line Indicator [*Tennis*] ... ELI
Electronic Lover ... EL
Electronic Mail [*Telecommunications*] ... E (Mail)
Electronic Mail [*Telecommunications*] ... EM
Electronic Mail Association [*Washington, DC*] [*Telecommunications*] (EANO) ... EMA
Electronic Mail Corporation of America [*NASDAQ symbol*] (NQ) ... EMCA
Electronic Mail Courier ... EMC
Electronic Mail Facility [*Postal Service*] ... EMF
Electronic Mail Handling ... EMH
Electronic Mail and Message Systems (DEEC) ... EMMS
Electronic Mail Service [*Telecommunications*] ... EMS
Electronic Mail System [*Postal Service*] ... EMS
Electronic Maintenance Engineering Association ... EMEA
Electronic Maintenance Proficiency Test ... EMPT
Electronic Management System ... EMS
Electronic Map Display ... EMD
Electronic Market-Research Terminal ... EMRT
Electronic Market Trends [*A publication*] ... Elec Mkt T
Electronic Markets and Information [*McGraw-Hill Publications Co.*] [*Database*] (CUAD) ... EMIS
Electronic Material Change ... EMC
Electronic Material Data Service (MUGU) ... EMDS
Electronic Materials Information Service [*Institution of Electrical Engineers*] [*Database*] (EISS) ... EMIS
Electronic Meeting Services [*Clinton, MD*] [*Telecommunications*] (TSSD) ... EMS
Electronic Memories & Magnetics Corp. [*NYSE symbol*] ... EMM
Electronic Memory Systems Organization [*Burroughs Corp.*] ... EMSO
Electronic Message Service System [*Telecommunications*] (TEL) ... EMSS
Electronic Message System (DEEC) ... EMS
Electronic Moisture Recorder ... EMR
Electronic Multiplying Punches (DEN) ... EMP
Electronic Networking Association [*Philadelphia, PA*] [*Information service*] (EISS) ... ENA
Electronic News [*A publication*] ... Elec News
Electronic News [*A publication*] ... Electronic N
Electronic News [*A publication*] ... EN
Electronic News Gathering [*Television news coverage*] ... ENG
Electronic Numerical Integrator and Calculator [*Early computer, 1946*] ... ENIAC
Electronic Office Centers of America, Inc. [*Schaumburg, IL*] [*Telecommunications*] (TSSD) ... EOCA
Electronic Original Equipment Market ... EOEM
Electronic Packaging and Production [*A publication*] ... Electron Packag Prod
Electronic Packaging and Production [*A publication*] ... ELPPA
Electronic Personnel Information Network [*Data Corp. of America*] ... EPIN
Electronic Point-of-Sale [*Data processing*] ... EPOS
Electronic Position Indicator ... EPI
Electronic Press Kit ... EPK
Electronic Private Automatic Branch Exchange [*Telecommunications*] (MCD) ... EPABX
Electronic Private Branch Exchange [*Telecommunications*] ... EPBX
Electronic Products Magazine [*A publication*] ... Electron Prod
Electronic Products Magazine [*A publication*] ... Electr Prod
Electronic Products & Technology [*Canada*] [*A publication*] ... EP & T
Electronic Program Control ... EPC
Electronic Program Guide [*Cable-television system*] ... EPG
Electronic Programed Procurement Information (NG) ... EPPI
Electronic Progress [*A publication*] ... Elec Prog
Electronic Progress [*A publication*] ... Electron Prog
Electronic Progress [*A publication*] ... ELTPA
Electronic Publishing Abstracts [*The Research Association for the Paper and Board, Printing and Packaging Industries*] [*Database*] (CUAD) ... EPA
Electronic Publishing Review [*A publication*] ... Electron Publishing Rev
Electronic Publishing Review [*A publication*] ... EPR
Electronic Publishing System [*ITT Dialcom*] [*Database*] ... EPUB
Electronic Purchasing Agent Network [*Service of Data Corp. of America*] ... EPAN
Electronic Random Number and Indicating Equipment [*Used for selecting winning premium bond numbers*] [*British*] ... ERNIE
Electronic Reading Automation [*Information retrieval*] ... ERA
Electronic Recording Beam (MDG) ... ERB
Electronic Recording Machine Accounting ... ERMA
Electronic Register-Sender [*Telecommunications*] (TEL) ... ERS
Electronic Remote Switching (MCD) ... ERS
Electronic Representatives Association ... ERA
Electronic Retina Computing Reader ... ERCR
Electronic Scanning and Stabilizing Antenna ... ESSA
Electronic Security Surveillance ... ESS
Electronic Security System ... ESS
Electronic Selective Archives [*Swiss News Agency*] [*Information service*] (EISS) ... ELSA
Electronic Send/Receive (CAA) ... ESR
Electronic Sequence Switching ... ESS
Electronic Signaling and Indicating Equipment (IEEE) ... ELSIE
Electronic Surveillance System ... ESS
Electronic Switching [*Telecommunications*] ... ES
Electronic Switching Programing Language (CAA) ... ESPL
Electronic Switching System [*See also EAX*] [*Telecommunications*] ... ESS
Electronic Switching System Control [*Telecommunications*] (TEL) ... EL-SSC
Electronic Switching Unit [*Telecommunications*] (MCD) ... ESU
Electronic System for Control of Receipt Transactions (MCD) ... ESCORT
Electronic System Integration (KSC) ... ESI
Electronic Systems ... ES
Electronic Systems Assistance Center [*Telecommunications*] (TEL) ... ESAC
Electronic Tandem Switching [*Telecommunications*] (TEL) ... ETS
Electronic Telecommunication Switching System (MCD) ... ETSS
Electronic Teleprinter Cryptographic Regenerative Repeater Mixer (NATG) ... ETCRRM
Electronic Terms for Space Age Language ... ETSAL
Electronic Test Block ... ETB
Electronic Text and Graphics Transfer System (CAA) ... ETGTS
Electronic Toll Center [*AT & T*] ... ETC
Electronic Translator System [*Bell System*] ... ETS
Electronic Translator Unit [*Telecommunications*] ... ETU
Electronic Typewriter ... ET
Electronic Unit ... EU
Electronic Unit Design Section ... EUDS
Electronic Video Recording [*CBS Laboratories' brand name for tape cartridges of TV programs*] ... EVR
Electronic Visual Display Subsystem (CAA) ... EVDS

Electronic Voice Exchange [*Commterm, Inc.*] [*Billerica, MA*] [*Telecommunications*] (TSSD) ... EVX
Electronically Controlled Automatic-Switching System (DEN) ... ECASS
Electronically Controlled Telephone Exchange (DEN) ... ECX
Electronics [*A publication*] ... ELECA
Electronics (KSC) ... ELECTRO
Electronics [*A publication*] ... Electron
Electronics and Communications Abstracts Journal [*A publication*] ... Electron & Communic Abstr J
Electronics and Communications in Japan [*A publication*] ... Electr Co J
Electronics and Communications in Japan [*A publication*] ... Electron Comm Japan
Electronics and Communications in Japan [*A publication*] ... Electron Commun Japan
Electronics and Communications in Japan [*A publication*] ... Electron Commun Jpn
Electronics and Computers [*Cambridge Scientific Abstracts*] [*Bethesda, MD*] [*Bibliographic database*] (OBD) ... ELCOM
Electronics Control Assembly ... ECA
Electronics Control System ... ECS
Electronics Research Laboratory [*Montana State University*] [*Research center*] (RCD) ... ERI
Electronics Research Laboratory [*University of California, Berkeley*] [*Research center*] (RCD) ... ERL
Electronics Services Unlimited [*New York, NY*] [*Telecommunications*] (TSSD) ... ESU
Electronics Test [*A publication*] ... Electron Test
Electronics Today International [*A publication*] ... Elec T Intnl
Electronics Today International [*A publication*] ... Elec Tod
Electronics Today International [*A publication*] ... Electronics Today
Electronics Today International [*A publication*] ... Electron Today Int
Electronics Today International [*A publication*] ... ETI
Electronics Weekly [*A publication*] ... Electron Wkly
Electronics Weekly [*A publication*] ... Elec Week
Electronics Weekly [*A publication*] ... ELWYA
Electroscience Laboratory [*Ohio State University*] [*Research center*] (RCD) ... ESL
Elektrische Nachrichten Technik [*A publication*] ... Elektr Nachr Tech
Elektro-Information Berlin [*Information retrieval*] (ODIN) ... EIB
Elektronische Datenverarbeitung [*Electronic Data Processing*] [*German*] ... EDV
Elektrotechniek. Technisch-Economisch Tijdschrift [*A publication*] ... ETN
Element (MSA) ... ELEM
Element ... ELT
Element Characteristics Equation ... ECE
Element Code (MCD) ... ELECD
Element Load Model ... ELM
Element Number [*Data processing*] ... EN
Elementary Perceiver and Memorizer [*University of California*] [*Learning theory*] [*Computer device*] ... EPAM
Elementary Potential Digital Computing Component ... EPDCC
Elements of Data (MSA) ... EOD
Elephant Memory System [*Data processing*] ... EMS
Elevation Data Edit Terminals (RDA) ... EDET
Eliminate and Count [*Coding*] [*Data processing*] ... ELCO
ELINT [*Electronic Intelligence*] **- Ocean Reconnaissance Satellite** (MCD) ... EORSAT
ELINT [*Electronic Intelligence*] **Receiver Test System** (MCD) ... ERTS
Elliptical Error Probability (CAAL) ... EEP
Ellis Horwood Series. Computers and Their Applications [*A publication*] ... Ellis Horwood Ser Comput Appl
Embar Information Consultants [*Wheaton, IL*] [*Information service*] (EISS) ... EIC
Embedded Computer Resources (MCD) ... ECR
Embedded Computer Systems ... ECS
EMCLASS Terms [*Online database field identifier*] (OBD) ... ET
Emergency Bed Request System [*Data processing*] ... EMBERS
Emergency Call System [*AT & T*] ... ECS
Emergency Communication Network [*Highway*] [*Telecommunications*] (TEL) ... ECN
Emergency Digital Computer ... EDC
Emergency Locator Transmitter ... ELT
Emergency Locator Transmitter Receiver ... ELTR
Emergency Maintenance (BUR) ... EM
Emergency Medicine and Crisis Care [*Database*] (FDB) ... EMCC
Emergency Message Initiation Terminal (MCD) ... EMIT
Emergency Position-Indicating Radio Beacon (MCD) ... EPIRB
Emergency Positive Control Communications System ... EPCCS
Emergency Power Off (SKY) ... EPO
Emergency Power Switching Logic (IEEE) ... EPSL
Emergency Power Unit ... EPU
Emergency Programs Information Center [*Database*] (FDB) ... EPIC
Emergency Reporting System [*Telecommunications*] (TEL) ... ERS
Emergency Safeguards System Activation (IEEE) ... ESSA
Emergency Satellite Communications System (CAA) ... ESCS
Emergency Signal (BUR) ... EMS
Emerson Electric Company ... EEC
Emerson Electric Co. [*NYSE symbol*] ... EMR
Emerson Programer-Evaluator-Controller [*Data processing*] (CDH) ... EPEC
EMF Corporation [*NASDAQ symbol*] (NQ) ... EMFC
EMI [*formerly, Electric & Musical Industries Ltd.*] **Data Electronic Computer** [*Made by EMI Industries - Great Britain*] ... EMIDEC
Emirates Telecommunications Corp. (TEL) ... EMIRTEL
Emitter-Coupled Current-Steered Logic (MSA) ... ECCSL
Emitter-Coupled Logic ... ECL
Emitter-Coupled Logic Operator ... ECLO
Emitter-Coupled Transistor Logic ... ECTL
Emitter Dip Effect (IEEE) ... EDE
Emitter-Emitter Coupled Logic (IEEE) ... EECL
Emitter Follower (MCD) ... EF
Emitter Follower Logic ... EFL
Emitter Identification Guide (NG) ... EIG
Emitter Isolated Difference Amplifier Paralleling [*Bell System*] ... EIDAP
Empire Telecommunications [*British*] [*World War II*] ... ETS
Employment Security Automation Project [*Department of Labor*] ... ESAP
Employment Service Online Placement System [*Data processing*] ... ESOPS
Employment and Training Automated Information and Retrieval System [*Department of Labor*] [*Database*] (FDB) ... ETAIRS
Empresa Brasileira de Telecomunicacoes [*Brazilian Telecommunications Enterprises*] [*Rio De Janeiro*] (TSSD) ... EMBRATEL
Empty Signal Unit [*Telecommunications*] (TEL) ... ESU
Emulation Program [*IBM Corp.*] (BUR) ... EP
Emulex Corp. [*NASDAQ symbol*] (NQ) ... EMLX
En Route Computer Identification (KSC) ... ECID
Enable (MSA) ... ENBL
Encode (MSA) ... ENCD
Encoded Item Identifier (CAAL) ... EII
Encoder (MSA) ... ENCDR
Encoder Address Translator ... EAT
Encoder Coupler (NASA) ... E/C
Encoder Power Supply ... EPS
Encoder Programing Language [*Data processing*] (CAA) ... EPL
End of Address [*Data processing*] ... EOA
End of Block [*Data processing*] ... EOB
End of Card [*Data processing*] (CMD) ... EOC
End of Conversion ... EOC
End of Data [*Data processing*] ... EOD
End of Data Block [*Data processing*] (CET) ... EDB
End of Dialing [*Telecommunications*] (TEL) ... EOD
End Effector Electronics Unit (MCD) ... EEEU
End of Extent [*Data processing*] (IBMDP) ... EOE
End of File [*Data processing*] ... EOF
End of Input [*Data processing*] ... EOI
End of Inquiry [*Data processing*] (CAA) ... EOI
End Interruption Sequence [*Data processing*] ... EIS
End Item Delivery ... EID
End Item Description ... EID
End Item Designators ... EID
End Item Documentation (MCD) ... EID
End Item Maintenance Form ... EIMF
End Item Maintenance Sheets ... EIMS
End Item Maintenance Transmittal Sheet ... EIMTS
End Item Manager ... EIM
End Item Parameter ... EIP
End Item Requirement ... EIR
End Item Specification ... EIS
End Item Test Plan (MCD) ... EITP
End of Job [*Data processing*] ... EOJ
End of Line [*Telecommunications*] (FAAC) ... EOL
End of Line Block [*Data processing*] (CET) ... EOLB
End of Logical Tape [*Data processing*] ... EOLT
End of Magnetic Tape [*Data processing*] (MDG) ... EMT
End of Medium [*Data processing*] ... EM
End of Medium [*Data processing*] (BUR) ... EOM
End of Message [*Data processing*] ... EOM
End of Message Sequence [*Data processing*] (CET) ... EOMS
End Office [*Telecommunications*] (TEL) ... EO
End Output [*Data processing*] (IEEE) ... EOP
End of Program [*Data processing*] (CGC) ... EOP
End of Program [*Data processing*] ... EP
End of Record [*Data processing*] (TUT) ... EOR
End of Recorded Information [*Data processing*] ... ERI
End of Reel ... EOR
End of Run [*Telecommunications*] (TEL) ... EOR
End of Tape [*Data processing*] ... EOT
End of Tape [*Data processing*] (CET) ... ET
End of Tape Test [*Data processing*] ... ETT
End of Tape Warning [*Data processing*] (CET) ... ETW
End of Task [*Data processing*] (TUT) ... EOT
End of Test [*Data processing*] (CIT) ... EOT
End of Text [*Data processing*] ... EOT
End of Text [*Data processing*] (CAA) ... ET
End of Text [*Data processing*] ... ETX
End of Transmission [*Data processing*] ... EOT
End of Transmission Block [*Data processing*] ... ETB
End Use Check ... EUC
End User Facility (CAA) ... EUF
End of Volume [*Data processing*] (TUT) ... EOV
End Warning Area [*Data processing*] (BUR) ... EWA
End of Word [*Data processing*] ... EOW
End of Work [*Morse telephony*] (FAAC) ... VA
Endata, Inc. [*NASDAQ symbol*] (NQ) ... DATA
Ending Sequence Done (OA) ... ESD
Ending Tape Label [*Data processing*] (BUR) ... ETL

Energy Bibliography and Index [*Center for Energy and Mineral Resources - Texas A & M University*] [*College Station, TX*] [*Bibliographic database*] (OBD) .... EBIB
Energy Data System [*Environmental Protection Agency*] [*Databank*] (EISS) .... EDS
Energy and Economics Data Bank [*Fachinformationszentrum Energie, Physik, Mathematik GmbH*] [*Database*] (CUAD) .... ENEC
Energy Enterprises [*Denver, CO*] [*Information service*] (EISS) .... EE
Energy and Environment Data Base [*Oak Ridge National Laboratory*] [*Database*] (FDB) .... EEDB
Energy Industry Information System (IEEE) .... EIIS
Energy Information Administration [*Department of Energy*] (EISS) .... EIA
Energy Information Center [*Battelle Memorial Institute*] (EISS) .... EIC
Energy Information Database [*Department of Energy*] [*Database*] (ODIN) .... EDB
Energy Methods Corp. [*NASDAQ symbol*] (NQ) .... EMTH
Energy and Mineral Resources Research Institute [*Iowa State University*] [*Research center*] (RCD) .... EMRRI
Energy Sciences Corporation [*NASDAQ symbol*] (NQ) .... ESCG
Energy Soft Computer Aided Design [*Energy Soft Computer Systems Ltd.*] [*Software package*] [*British*] (NCC) .... ESCAD
Energy Telecommunications and Electrical Association [*Formerly, PIEA*] (EANO) .... ENTELEC
Enertec Corp. [*Toronto Stock Exchange symbol*] .... ENR
Engaged Tone [*Telecommunications*] (TEL) .... ET
Engine Monitor Computer .... EMC
Engineer .... ENGR
Engineering .... ENGRG
Engineering and Administrative Data Acquisition System [*Bell System*] .... EADAS
Engineering Administrative Data Systems (MCD) .... EADS
Engineering Analysis and Simulation Language [*Data processing*] .... EASL
Engineering Bulletin Board System .... EBBS
Engineering Center for Automated Manufacturing Technology [*Clemson University*] [*Research center*] (RCD) .... CAM
Engineering Change (MCD) .... EC
Engineering Change Announcement (TUT) .... ECA
Engineering Change Order .... ECO
Engineering Computer Laboratory [*University of Southern California*] [*Research center*] (RCD) .... ECL
Engineering Computers [*A publication*] .... Eng Comput
Engineering Control Office [*Telecommunications*] (TEL) .... ECO
Engineering Control System (TUT) .... ECS
Engineering Cybernetics [*English Translation*] [*A publication*] .... ENCYA
Engineering Cybernetics [*A publication*] .... Eng Cybern
Engineering Data Bank [*GIDEP*] .... EDB
Engineering Data Control .... EDC
Engineering Data Information System (IEEE) .... EDIS
Engineering Data Management .... EDM
Engineering Data Plotting [*Data processing*] (CIT) .... EDPLOT
Engineering Design and Simulation System [*Graphic Data Ltd.*] [*Software package*] [*British*] (NCC) .... EDAS
Engineering Drafting Software [*Calcomp Ltd.*] [*Software package*] [*British*] (NCC) .... EDS
Engineering Experiment Station [*University of Missouri - Columbia*] [*Research center*] (RCD) .... EES
Engineering Experiment Station [*University of Arkansas, University of Alaska, Fairbanks*] [*Research center*] .... EES
Engineering Information Report [*Telecommunications*] (TEL) .... EIR
Engineering Information Report Date [*Telecommunications*] (TEL) .... EIRD
Engineering Letter [*Telecommunications*] (TEL) .... EL
Engineering Logic Diagram .... ELD
Engineering, Planning, and Analysis Systems [*Telecommunications*] (TEL) .... EPLANS
Engineering Records Organisation System [*Applied Research of Cambridge Ltd.*] [*Software package*] [*British*] (NCC) .... EROS
Engineering Research Center [*New Mexico State University*] [*Research center*] (RCD) .... ERC
Engineering Route [*Telecommunications*] (TEL) .... ER
Engineering Technology (MCD) .... ET
Engineering Test Satellite .... ETS
Engineers' Language for Automatic Test Equipment .... ELATE
English Title [*Online database field identifier*] (OBD) .... ET
Enhanced Character Set/All Purpose Interface [*Xerox Corp.*] .... ECS/API
Enhanced Expanded Memory Specifications [*AST, Quadram*] .... EEMS
Enhanced Graphics Adapter [*Computer technology*] .... EGA
Enhanced Graphics Monitor [*Computer technology*] .... EGM
Enhanced Master Terminal Unit .... EMTU
Enhanced Network Administration System [*Telecommunications*] (TEL) .... ENADS
Enhanced Private Switched Communications Service [*Pronounced "ep-sis"*] [*AT & T*] .... EPSCS
Enhanced Telephone Unit .... ETU
Enhanced Timing Module (IEEE) .... ETM
Enhancement Metal-Oxide Semiconductor (BUR) .... EMOS
Enquiries [*Telecommunications*] (TEL) .... EQ
Enquiry [*Transmission control character*] .... ENQ
Enquiry Terminal System [*International Computers Ltd.*] (CAA) .... ETS
Enter Exponent [*Data processing*] .... EE
Enterprise Technology [*NASDAQ symbol*] (NQ) .... ENTR
[*The*] **Entertainment Channel** [*Pay-television network*] [*Obsolete*] .... TEC
Entertainment Satellite [*Proposed*] (MCD) .... ENT/SAT
Entertainment and Sports Programing Network, Inc. [*Cable-television system*] .... ESPN
Entity Module [*Data processing*] .... EM
Entre' Computer Centers [*NASDAQ symbol*] (NQ) .... ETRE
Entry Code [*Data processing*] .... EC
Entry Computer (VIT) .... ECU
Entry Data Subsystem (CIT) .... EDS
Entry Interface Time (MCD) .... EIT
Entry Level Interactive Applications Systems [*Data processing*] .... ELIAS
Entry Point (BUR) .... EP
Entry Query Control Console [*Data processing*] .... EQCC
Entry and Recovery Simulation (MCD) .... ERS
Entry Time-Sharing System [*Data processing*] [*IBM Corp.*] .... ETSS
Environment Information Center, Inc. .... EIC
Environment Libraries Automated System [*Environment Canada*] [*Database*] [*Information service*] (EISS) .... ELIAS
Environmental Analog Recording System .... EARS
Environmental Bibliography [*Environmental Studies Institute*] [*Santa Barbara, CA*] [*Bibliographic database*] (OBD) .... ENVIROBIB
Environmental Chemicals Data and Information Network [*Commission of the European Communities*] [*Chemical databank*] [*Italy*] (EISS) .... ECDIN
Environmental Communications Network [*Proposed environmental information exchange network*] .... ECN
Environmental Data Base Directory [*National Oceanographic Data Center*] [*Database*] .... EDBD
Environmental Information Analysis Center [*Battelle Memorial Institute*] (EISS) .... EIAC
Environmental Information Retrieval On-Line [*Environmental Protection Agency*] .... ENVIRON
Environmental Periodicals Bibliography [*Environmental Studies Institute, International Academy at Santa Barbara*] [*Bibliographic Database*] .... EPB
Environmental Protection Agency Chemical Activities Status Report [*Environmental Protection Agency*] [*Database*] (FDB) .... EPACASR
Environmental Protection Data Base [*Environmental Protection Agency*] .... EPDB
Environmental Recording, Editing, and Printing Program (BUR) .... EREP
Environmental Resources Technology Satellite .... ERTS
Environmental Response and Referral Service [*Oak Ridge National Laboratory*] (EISS) .... ERRS
Environmental Sketches in Perspective [*Computer program*] .... ESP
Environmental Survey Satellite (TEL) .... ESSA
Environmental Teratology Information Center [*Department of Energy*] (EISS) .... ETIC
Epitaxial Planar [*Electronics*] .... EP
Equal .... EQ
Equal (MSA) .... EQL
Equal Zero (MDG) .... E/Z
Equalization [*Electronics*] .... EQ
Equate (MDG) .... EQU
Equation Cruncher [*Data processing*] .... EC
Equatorial Communications [*NASDAQ symbol*] (NQ) .... EQUA
Equatorial Communications Company [*Mountain View, CA*] [*Telecommunications*] (TSSD) .... ECC
Equilibrium Mode Simulator (TEL) .... EMS
Equilibrium Problem Solver (IEEE) .... EPS
Equipment (BUR) .... EQ
Equipment (MDG) .... EQPMT
Equipment .... EQPT
Equipment .... EQUIP
Equipment Blockages and Failures [*Telecommunications*] (TEL) .... EB & F
Equipment Controller (CET) .... EC
Equipment Conversion Package [*Telecommunications*] (TEL) .... ECP
Equipment Engaged Tone [*Telecommunications*] (TEL) .... EET
Equipment Group Interface (OA) .... EGIF
Equipment Installation Procedure [*Telecommunications*] (TEL) .... EIP
Equipment Inventory Update [*Telecommunications*] (TEL) .... EIU
Equipment Practice [*Telecommunications*] (TEL) .... EP
Equipment Recall Data System (MCD) .... ERDS
Equipment Replacement and Enhancement Program [*Data processing*] .... EREP
Equipment Replacement Program [*Data processing*] .... ERP
Equipment Supervisory Rack [*Telecommunications*] (TEL) .... ESR
Equitable Life Interpreter [*Computer*] .... ELI
Equivalent Binary Digit .... EBD
Equivalent Full Power Hour [*FCC*] .... EFPH
Equivalent Isotropically Radiated Power [*Microwave transmission*] .... EIRP
Equivalent Logic Element (OA) .... ELE
Equivalent Noise Sideband (DDI) .... ENSB
Equivalent Noise Sideband Input (MCD) .... ENSI
Equivalent Noise Temperature .... ENT
Equivalent Series Resistance .... ESR
Erasable Memory [*Data processing*] (KSC) .... EM
Erasable Memory Octal Dump [*Data processing*] (SKY) .... EMOD
Erasable Memory Program [*Data processing*] .... EMP
Erasable Programable Read-Only Memory [*Data processing*] (MCD) .... EPROM
Erasable Read-Only Memory [*Data processing*] .... EROM
Erase Gap [*Data processing*] (TUT) .... ERG
Erection Computer (VIT) .... EC
Erection Digital Assembly (VIT) .... EDA

Erlang [*Unit*] [*Statistics*] [*Telecommunications*] ... E
Erlanger Rechner-Entwurfs-Sprache [*Programing language*] [*1974*] (CSR) ... ERES
Ernaehrungswissenschaften Giessen [*Nutrition Sciences - Giessen University*] [*Database*] (ODIN) ... EWG
Ernahrungs-, Land- und Forstwissenschaftliches Informations-system [*Zentralstelle fuer Agrardokumentation und -information*] [*Database*] (CUAD) ... ELFIS
Error [*Data processing*] (BUR) ... E
Error (MCD) ... ERR
Error Adaptive Control Computer (IEEE) ... EACC
Error Checking and Correction [*Data processing*] ... ECC
Error Checking and Correction (CAA) ... ERCC
Error Code [*Data processing*] ... EC
Error Control Device (TEL) ... ECD
Error Control Receiver (IEEE) ... ECR
Error Control Translator ... ECT
Error Control Transmitter ... ECT
Error Correcting [*or Correction*] [*Data processing*] ... E/C
Error-Correcting Circuitry [*Data processing*] (MCD) ... ECC
Error-Correcting Tree Automation [*Data processing*] ... ECTA
Error Correction ... ERRC
Error Correction Code (CIT) ... ECC
Error Deletion by Iterative Transmission ... EDIT
Error Demodulator [*or Determination*] **Output** (MCD) ... EDO
Error Detecting [*or Detection*] [*Data processing*] ... ED
Error Detecting Code ... EDC
Error Detection Code Generator ... EDCG
Error Detection and Correction ... EDAC
Error Detection and Correction (NATG) ... EDC
Error Detection and Decision Feedback ... EDDF
Error Detector Assembly ... EDA
Error and Dispersion Analysis (MCD) ... EDA
Error Factor (IEEE) ... EF
Error Free Seconds (TEL) ... EFS
Error Function ... ERF
Error Function, Inverse ... ERFI
Error Likely Situation (IEEE) ... ELS
Error Logging Device ... ELD
Error Mean Square ... EMS
Error Monitor Register (KSC) ... EMR
Error Multiplier ... EM
Error Pattern Register (CAA) ... EPR
Error Rate [*Statistics*] ... ER
Error Rate Test Set (TEL) ... ERTS
Error Recorder (VIT) ... ER
Error Recording Device ... ERD
Error Recovery (BUR) ... ER
Error-Recovery Package [*Data processing*] (MDG) ... ERP
Error-Recovery Procedure [*Data processing*] (TUT) ... ERP
Error Sequence Number [*Data processing*] ... ESN
Error Statistics by Tape Volume [*Data processing*] (IBMDP) ... ESTV
Error Statistics by Volume [*Data processing*] (BUR) ... ESV
Error Status Word [*Data processing*] (BUR) ... ESW
Error Time Word (KSC) ... ETW
Error Unavoidable ... EU
Error Vector Computer (NG) ... EVC
Error Volume Analysis [*Data processing*] (IBMDP) ... EVA
Escape Character [*Keyboard*] (KSC) ... ESC
Especialidades Farmaceuticas Espanolas Data Bank [*Spanish Pharmaceutical Specialities Data Bank*] [*Information service*] (EISS) ... ESPES
Esprit Systems [*American Stock Exchange symbol*] ... ETI
Essential/Nonessential/Update [*Telecommunications*] (TEL) ... ENU
Essential Service Line [*Telecommunications*] (TEL) ... ESL
Essential Service Value [*Telecommunications*] (IEEE) ... ESV
Estimate ... EST
Estimate of Properties for Industrial Chemistry [*Universite de Liege*] [*Database*] (CUAD) ... EPIC
Estimated Consumption [*of gasoline*] [*Computer model*] ... ESCON
Estimated Junction Frequency [*Telecommunications*] (TEL) ... EJF
Estimated Project Duration Time (OA) ... EPDT
Estimated Repair Time [*Telecommunications*] (TEL) ... ERT
Estimated Turnaround Point ... ETP
Eternal Word Television Network [*Cable-television system*] ... EWTN
Euro-Abstracts [*Commission of the European Communities*] [*Luxembourg*] [*Bibliographic database*] (OBD) ... EABS
Europaeische Atomgemeinschaft [*European Atomic Energy Community*] [*German*] [*Information retrieval*] (ODIN) ... EURATOM
Europaeische Gemeinschaften [*European Community*] [*German*] [*Information retrieval*] (ODIN) ... EG
European Academic Research Network [*A computer network*] ... EARN
European Article Number [*Equivalent of Universal Product Code*] ... EAN
European Association for Grey Literature Exploitation [*Database producer*] (CUAD) ... EAGLE
European Association of Manufacturers of Business Machines and Data Processing Equipment (EANO) ... EUROBIT
European Association of Scientific Information Dissemination Studies ... EUSIDIC
European Automated Dictionary (DEEC) ... EURODICAUTOM
European Broadcasting Union [*Geneva, Switzerland*] ... EBU
European Coal Data Bank [*Frankfurt am Main, FRG*] [*Information service*] (EISS) ... COALDATA
European Commission Host Organization [*Commission of the European Communities*] [*Information service*] [*Host system*] [*Luxembourg*] (EISS) ... ECHO
European Communication Satellite ... ECS
European Computer Manufacturers Association [*Geneva, Switzerland*] ... ECMA
European Computer Manufacturers Association Algorithmic Language ... ECMALGOL
European Computer Measurement Association (CAA) ... ECOMA
European Computing Congress (IEEE) ... EUROCOMP
European Computing Services Association (CAA) ... ECSA
European Conference on Telecommunications by Satellite ... ECTS
European Consortium for Political Research (EISS) ... ECPR
European Control Data Users [*Brussels, Belgium*] ... ECODU
European Datamanager Users Group [*London, England*] ... EDUG
European Documentation and Information System for Education [*Council of Europe*] [*Database*] (EISS) ... EUDISED
European Electronics [*A publication*] ... ELE
European Host Network [*Data processing*] ... EHN
European Information Network [*Telecommunications*] (TEL) ... EIN
European Kompass Online [*Reed Publishing Ltd.*] [*Database*] (CUAD) ... EKOL
European Letter Telegram ... ELT
European Nuclear Energy Agency [*Paris, France*] ... ENEA
European On-Line Information Network [*Commission of the European Communities*] [*Information service*] (EISS) ... EURONET
European Petrochemical Association [*Database producer*] (CUAD) ... EPCA
European Petrochemical Industry Computerized System [*Parpinelli Tecnon*] [*Italy*] [*Information service*] (EISS) ... EPICS
European Satellite Consulting Organization [*Montrouge, France*] [*Telecommunications*] (TSSD) ... ESCO
European Scientific Information Referral [*EUSIDIC*] [*Information service*] (EISS) ... EUSIREF
European Shielding Information Service [*EURATOM*] [*Databank*] (EISS) ... ESIS
European Silicon Structures ... ES²
European Space Agency Information Retrieval Service [*Frascati, Italy*] ... ESA-IRS
European Space Tracking and Telemetry Network (MCD) ... ESTRACK
European Telecommunications Satellite Organization [*Paris, France*] [*Telecommunications*] (TSSD) ... EUTELSAT
European Wideband Transmission Media Improvement Program (IEEE) ... EWTMI
Evaluated Nuclear Data File [*AEC*] [*Databank*] ... ENDF
Evaluated Nuclear Structure Data File [*Brookhaven National Laboratory*] [*Database*] (ODIN) ... ENSDF
Evaluation & Planning Systems, Inc. [*Windham, NH*] [*Software manufacturer*] (DASOS) ... EPS
Evanescent Access Method [*Sperry UNIVAC*] (CAA) ... EAM
Evans Economics, Incorporated [*Database producer*] [*Information service*] (EISS) ... EEI
Evans Newton, Incorporated [*Scottsdale, AZ*] [*Software manufacturer*] (DASOS) ... ENI
Evans & Sutherland Computer Corporation [*NASDAQ symbol*] (NQ) ... ESCC
Even Parity Select (CAA) ... EPS
Even Positive Acknowledgment [*Data processing*] (IBMDP) ... ACK0
Event-Based Language [*1979*] [*Data processing*] (CSR) ... EBL
Event Control Block [*Data processing*] (BUR) ... ECB
Event Driven Executive [*IBM Corp.*] (CAA) ... EDX
Event-by-Event Recording and Sorting [*Electronics*] ... EBERAS
Event Queue Element [*Data processing*] (MCD) ... EQE
Event Scheduling System (CAA) ... ESS
Event Sequence Override (SKY) ... ESO
Event Time Digitizer ... ETD
Events Controller (MCD) ... EC
Events Recorder Console (MCD) ... ERC
Events Select Logic and Rates (MCD) ... ESLR
[*An*] **Evolutionary System for On-Line Processing** [*Data processing*] (TUT) ... AESOP
Ex-Directory [*Telecommunications*] (TEL) ... XD
Exceptional Child Education Resources [*Council for Exceptional Children*] [*Bibliographic database*] (OBD) ... ECER
Excerpta Medica Database [*Trademark*] [*Elsevier*] [*Bibliographic database*] ... EMBASE
Excerpta Medica Foundation [*Database producer*] (ODIN) ... EM
Excess Three [*Code*] (CAH) ... XS3
Exchange [*Telecommunications*] (AFM) ... EXCH
Exchange Carrier Association (EANO) ... ECA
Exchange Carriers Standards Association [*Parisippany, NJ*] [*Telecommunications*] (EANO) ... ECSA
Exchange Control Logic (KSC) ... ECL
Exchange Feeder Route Analysis Program [*Bell System*] ... EFRAP
Exchange Identification (CCD) ... XID
Exchange Key [*Word processing*] ... EXC
Exchange Line [*Telecommunications*] (TEL) ... EL
Exchange Line Multiplexing Analysis Program (TEL) ... ELMAP
Exchange Network Facilities for Interstate Access [*Telecommunications*] ... ENFIA
Exchange Parameter Definitions [*Telecommunications*] (TEL) ... EPD
Exchange Price Indicators [*Database*] [*British*] (DEEC) ... EPIC
Exchange Reference File ... ERF
Exchange Servicing Center [*Telecommunications*] (TEL) ... ESC

Computer & Telecommunications Acronyms

Exchange Software Generator (TEL) ..... ESG
Exchange Two Registers [*Data processing*] ..... EXG
Exchange Users Association (EANO) ..... EUA
Exchange Voltage Regulator [*Telecommunications*] (TEL) ..... XVR
Exchange Work List [*Telecommunications*] (TEL) ..... EWL
Exchangeable Disk Storage [*Data processing*] ..... EDS
Exclusive (MDG) ..... EXCLU
Exclusive Exchange Line [*Telecommunications*] (DEEC) ..... EEL
Exclusive Or [*Gates*] [*Data processing*] ..... EO
Exclusive Or [*Data processing*] ..... EOR
Exclusive Or [*Data processing*] (CAA) ..... EXOR
Exclusive Or [*Gates*] [*Data processing*] ..... XOR
Execute (CAH) ..... EX
Execute (MSA) ..... EXEC
Execute (DEEC) ..... XEC
Execute (SKY) ..... XEQ
Execute Channel Program [*Data processing*] ..... EXCP
Execute Input/Output (DEN) ..... XI/O
Execute and Repeat (OA) ..... EXR
Execution Language (NITA) XL
Execution Unit [*Data processing*] ..... EU
Executive Control Language [*Data processing*] ..... ECL
Executive Information Services [*Data processing system*] ..... EIS
Executive Processing Unit (CAA) ..... EPU
Executive Request [*Data processing*] ..... ER
Executive Right of Way [*Telecommunications*] (TEL) ..... EROW
Executive System Problem-Oriented Language [*Burroughs Corp.*] [*Data processing*] (BUR) ..... ESPOL
Executone, Inc. [*American Stock Exchange symbol*] [*Delisted*] ..... EXU
[*The*] Exeter Abstract Reference System [*Exeter University*] [*Information service*] (EISS) ..... TEARS
[*An*] Existing Generalized Information System [*Data processing*] ..... AEGIS
Exit List [*Data processing*] ..... EXLST
Expandable Computerized Automatic Test System (MCD) ..... ECATS
Expanded Calculator Link Processing System [*Data processing*] ..... ECLIPS
Expanded Community Calling [*Telecommunications*] (TEL) ..... ECC
Expanded with Computers and Information Technology ..... EXCITE
Expanded Direct Distance Dialing [*Telecommunications*] ..... EDDD
Expanded Display ..... ED
Expanded Inband Signaling [*Telecommunications*] (TEL) ..... EIS
Expanded Memory (NITA) ..... XM
Expanded Memory Specification [*Data processing*] ..... EMS
Expansion Symbolic Compiling Assembly Program for Engineers ..... ESCAPE
Expected Measured Loss [*Telecommunications*] (TEL) ..... EML
Expected Output ..... EO
Expected Run-Time (CAA) ..... ERT
Expected Time of Response (CAA) ..... ETR
Expected Turnaround [*Data processing*] ..... ETA
Expenditure Analysis Plan (TEL) ..... EAP
Experiment Computer (MCD) ..... EC
Experiment Computer Application Software (MCD) ..... ECAS
Experiment Computer Operating System (MCD) ..... ECOS
Experiment Interface Definition Document (MCD) ..... EIDD
Experimental Computer Complex ..... ECC
Experimental Data Communications Network (MCD) ..... EDCN
Experimental Data Handling Equipment ..... EDHE
Experimental Digital Television System ..... EDITS
Experimental Display Generator ..... EDGE
Experimental Memory - Address Register ..... EMAR
Experimental Monitoring Satellite ..... EMS
Experimental Network Operating System (NITA) ..... XNOS
Experimental On-Line Capabilities [*Data processing*] ..... XOC
Experimental Packet Switching System [*Telecommunications*] ..... EPSS
Experimental Reproduction Film (DIT) ..... XRF
Experimental Solid-State Exchange [*Communication system*] (MCD) ..... ESSEX
Experimental Space Communication Earth Station [*Telecommunications*] (TEL) ..... ESCES
Experimental Use Computer, London Integrated Display ..... EUCLID
Explicit 2-D Patterns Local Operations and Randomness [*Programing language*] [*1975*] (CSR) ..... EXPLOR
Explosive-to-Electric Transducer ..... EET
Express Order Wire [*Telecommunications*] (TEL) ..... XOW
Express Paid Telegraph ..... XPT
Expression-Oriented Language [*Data processing*] (TUT) ..... EOL
Extendable Computer System Simulator [*Programing language*] [*1973*] ..... ECSS
Extendable Debugging and Monitoring System [*Data processing*] ..... EXDAMS
Extended Architecture [*Data processing*] ..... XA
Extended Area Service [*Telecommunications*] ..... EAS
Extended Arithmetic Element ..... EAE
Extended BASIC Mode [*International Computers Ltd.*] (NITA) ..... XBM
Extended Binary-Coded Decimal [*Data processing*] (CIT) ..... EBCD
Extended Binary-Coded Decimal Interchange Code [*Data processing*] ..... EBCDIC
Extended BIOS ..... XBIOS
Extended Branch Mode (CAA) ..... EBM
Extended Control [*Mode*] [*Data processing*] ..... EC
Extended Control Program Support [*IBM Corp.*] (CAA) ..... ECPS
Extended Core Memory [*Data processing*] (MCD) ..... ECM
Extended Core Memory Unit [*Data processing*] (NVT) ..... ECMU

Extended Core Storage [*Data processing*] (CGC) ..... ECS
Extended Data Flow Graph ..... EDFG
Extended Data Management Facility ..... EDMF
Extended Data Management System [*Xerox Corp.*] (CAA) ..... EDMS
Extended Direct Memory Access (CAA) ..... EDMA
Extended Disk Operating System (BUR) ..... EDOS
Extended Disk Utilities Program (NITA) ..... XDUP
Extended Facility [*IBM Corp.*] (CAA) ..... EF
Extended Function Code (NITA) ..... XFC
Extended General Purpose Simulator [*National Electronics Conference*] (IEEE) ..... EGPS
Extended Group Coded Recording [*Data processing*] (IBMDP) ..... E/GCR
Extended Instruction Set [*Honeywell, Inc.*] (CAA) ..... EIS
Extended Memory Unit (NASA) ..... EMU
Extended Operation (NITA) ..... XOP
Extended-Range Floating Point Interpretive System ..... ERFPI
Extended Range Phase-Locked Demodulator (IEEE) ..... ERPLD
Extended-Range and Space Communication (MCD) ..... ERSC
Extended Remote Job Entry (CAA) ..... ERJE
Extended Tape Operating System (BUR) ..... ETOS
Extended Telecommunications Modules ..... EXTM
Extended Term Plan (BUR) ..... ETP
Extended Text Compositor [*Applied Data Research, Inc.*] (CAA) ..... ETC
Extended Virtual Machine (CAA) ..... EVM
Extensible Language Facility [*Data processing*] (IEEE) ..... ELF
Extensible Language I [*Data processing*] ..... ELI
Extensible Programing System [*Data processing*] (CSR) ..... EPS
Extensible Structure Processing Language [*1969-71*] [*Data processing*] (CSR) ..... ESPL
Extensible Video Interactive Language (CAA) ..... EVIL
Extension (MDG) ..... EXTSN
Extension of BASIC [*Data processing*] ..... XBASIC
Extension Bell [*Telecommunications*] (TEL) ..... XBL
Extension of LISP [*List Processor*] 1.5 [*Programing language*] (CSR) ..... XLISP
External Block Controller (NITA) ..... XBC
External Branch Condition Address [*Telecommunications*] (TEL) ..... EBCA
External Branch Condition Input [*Telecommunications*] (TEL) ..... EBCI
External Channels Ratio ..... ECR
External Delay Factor [*Data processing*] ..... EDF
External Device [*Data processing*] ..... ED
External Device [*Data processing*] ..... EXD
External-Device Code [*Data processing*] (MDG) ..... EDC
External-Device Control Word [*Data processing*] ..... EDCW
External Disk/Drum Channel (CAA) ..... EDC
External Entity (CCD) ..... EE
External Event Detection Module [*Data processing*] (MDG) ..... EEDM
External Field Emission ..... EFE
External Finished Reports Information Subsystem [*Data processing*] ..... EFRIS
External Page Storage (BUR) ..... EPS
External Page Table [*Data processing*] (BUR) ..... XPT
External Polarization Modulation (IEEE) ..... EPM
External Processor Status Word (NITA) ..... XPSW
External Reference (BUR) ..... EXTRN
External Relational Memory (NITA) ..... XRM
External Store (CAA) ..... ES
External Symbol Dictionary [*A publication*] ..... ESD
External Transmit Clock ..... XTC
Externally Specified Address (CAAL) ..... ESA
Externally Specified Index ..... ESI
Extra Control [*Wire*] [*Telecommunications*] (TEL) ..... EC
Extra-High Frequency ..... XHF
Extra-High Strength [*Steel*] [*Telecommunications*] (TEL) ..... EHS
Extra-High Tension ..... EHT
Extra Input Terminal (NITA) ..... XIT
Extra-Large-Scale Integration [*Data processing*] (TEL) ..... ELSI
Extra Segment [*Data processing*] ..... ES
Extra Segment:Destination Index [*Data processing*] ..... ES:DI
Extra-Theoretical [*Telecommunications*] (TEL) ..... EXTHEO
Extraordinary Administrative Radio Conference [*ITU*] ..... EARC
Extreme Close-Up [*Television*] ..... ECU
Extremely High Frequency [*Electronics, radio wave*] ..... EHF
Extremely Low Frequency [*Electronics, radio wave*] ..... ELF

F

Faceplate (IEEE)	FP
Fachinformationszentrum [Information retrieval] (ODIN)	FIZ
Facilities Administration Consolidated Tape System (MCD)	FACTS
Facilities Analysis Model [Data processing]	FAM
Facilities Control Console	FCC
Facilities Management (TUT)	FM
Facility for the Analysis of Chemical Thermodynamics [Thermfact Ltd.] [Database] [Information service] (EISS)	FACT
Facility Analysis Plan [Telecommunications] (TEL)	FAP
Facility for Automatic Sorting and Testing	FAST
Facility Interface Unit [Telecommunications]	FIU
Facsimile	FAC
Facsimile (AFM)	FAX
Facsimile Communications System [Telecommunications]	FCS
Facsimile Packet [ITT] [Telecommunications] (TEL)	FAXPAK
Facsimile Switching Unit (CAA)	FSU
Facsimile Transmission [Telecommunications] (MCD)	FAX
Facsimile Transmission [Telecommunications]	TRANSFAX
Facsimile Transmission over AUTODIN	FAXDIN
Factor of Merit [Telecommunications] (TEL)	FOM
Factory Automation, Control, and Test Facility (IDA)	FACT
Factory Automation Systems Technology [British]	FAST
Factory Layout Analysis [PERA] [Software package] [British] (NCC)	FLAN
Factory Management & Control [Computer Automation Ltd.] [Software package] [British] (NCC)	FM & C
Facts Location and Summarized History [General Motors Corp.] [Data processing]	FLASH
Fading Safety Factor [Telecommunications] (TEL)	FSF
Failure	F
Failure Analysis Program (IDA)	FAP
Failure Analysis Report Summary [Bell System]	FARS
Failure Analysis by Statistical Techniques [Data processing code]	FAST
Failure Experience Data Bank [GIDEP]	FEDB
Failure Indication Modules	FIM
Failure Mode Analysis	FMA
Failure Mode and Effects Analysis	FMEA
Failure Mode, Effects, and Criticality Analyses	FMECA
Failure Mode Indicator (MUGU)	FMI
Failure Rate Data (KSC)	FRD
Failure in Time [Telecommunications] (TEL)	FIT
Failure and Usage Data Report (IEEE)	FUDR
Failures per Million Hours [Telecommunications] (TEL)	FPMH
Failures per Year [Telecommunications] (TEL)	FPY
Fall Joint Computer Conference [Replaced by National Computer Conference - NCC]	FJCC
False Removal Rate (CAAL)	FRR
Family Planning Evaluation Branch [Public Health Service] (EISS)	FPEB
Family Planning Evaluation Division [HEW] (EISS)	FPED
Family Resource and Referral Center [National Council on Family Relations] [Information service] (EISS)	FR & RC
Fantasy Unrestricted Network [Cable-television system]	FUN
Far-End Crosstalk [Bell System]	FEXT
Farad [Symbol] [Unit of electric capacitance]	F
Faraday Disc Machine	FDM
Farm Audience Readership Measurement Service [Starch INRA Hooper, Inc.] [Information service] (EISS)	FARMS
Farm Market Infodata Service [Department of Agriculture] [Database] (FDB)	FMIS
Fashion Integrated Merchandising Planning and Control System (BUR)	FIMPACS
Fashion Television [Video sales technique in the apparel industry]	FTV
Fast Access to Computerized Technical Sources [Mill Valley, CA] [Information service] (EISS)	FACTS
Fast Access Current Text (DEEC)	FACT
Fast Access Information Retrieval	FAIR
Fast Access to Systems Technical Information	FASTI
Fast Analysis of Tape and Recovery (IDA)	FATAR
Fast Automatic Transfer	FAT
Fast Auxiliary Memory (IEEE)	FAM
Fast Digital Processor [Data processing]	FDP
Fast Discrete Cosine Transform (MCD)	FDCT
Fast Economic Language [Data processing] (BUR)	FASTEL
Fast Eigensolution Extraction Routine [Computer program]	FEER
Fast Field Program (KSC)	FFP
Fast Fourier Analyzer (MCD)	FFA
Fast Fourier Transform	FFT
Fast Frequency Shift Keying (MCD)	FFSK
Fast Interactive Retrieval System Technology (DEEC)	FIRST
Fast Interline Nonactivate Automatic Control [AT & T]	FINAC
Fast Library Maintenance (CAA)	FLIM
Fast Multitasking Operating System [MVT Microcomputer Systems, Inc.] (CAA)	FAMOS
Fast Processor [Instrumentation]	FP
Fast Pulse Electron Gun (MCD)	FPEG
Fast Queuing System [Data processing] (CAA)	FAQS
Fast Realistic Editor [Word processing program]	FRED
Fast-Response Solar Array Simulator	FRSAS
Fast Retrieval Storage [Data processing]	FRS
Fast Store [Data processing] (TEL)	FS
Fast Time Analyzer System	FTAS
Fast Transient Loader (CAA)	FTL
Fault Analysis Process (TEL)	FAP
Fault Control Module (TEL)	FCM
Fault Detect Verification (OA)	FDV
Fault Detection, Isolation, Identification, and Recompensation (NASA)	FDIIR
Fault Isolation Checkout System	FICS
Fault Isolation Code	FIC
Fault Isolation Module (CAAL)	FIM
Fault Isolation Software (CAAL)	FIS
Fault Location through Interpretive Testing [Data processing]	FLIT
Fault-Location Oscillator [Bell System]	FLO
Fault Location Word (MCD)	FLW
Fault Logic Diagram (VIT)	FLD
Fault Monitor (TEL)	FM
Fault Repair Service [Telecommunications] [British]	FRS
Fault Report Point (TEL)	FRP
Fault Reporting Module (TEL)	FRM
Fault Servicing Process (TEL)	FSP
Fault Simulation Comparator	FSC
Fault-Tolerant Computing	FTC
Fault Tolerant Multiprocessor System [Data processing]	FTMP
Fault Tolerant Spaceborne Computer	FTSC
Fault Tree Analysis (NASA)	FTA
Fear, Uncertainty, and Doubt [Factors hindering sales of lesser-known computers]	FUD
Feature Count [Data processing]	FC
Feature Recognition Processor (DDI)	FRP
Federal ADP [Automatic Data Processing] Users Group	FADPUG
Federal Automated Career System	FACS
Federal Aviation Information Retrieval System (IDA)	FAIRS
Federal COBOL [Common Business-Oriented Language] Compiler Testing Service [National Bureau of Standards]	FCCTS
Federal Communications Bar Association [Washington, DC] [Telecommunications]	FCBA
Federal Communications Bar Journal [Later, Federal Communications Law Journal] [A publication]	Fed Com B J
Federal Communications Commission [Independent government agency]	FCC
Federal Communications Systems (MCD)	FCS
Federal Computer Performance Evaluation and Simulation Center [General Services Administration]	FEDSIM
Federal Data Processing Centers	FDPC
Federal Deposit Insurance Corporation [Independent government agency] [Database]	FDIC
Federal Document Retrievals, Inc. [Information service] (EISS)	FDR
Federal Index [Capitol Services, Inc.] [Washington, DC] [Bibliographic database] (OBD)	FEDEX
Federal Information Network (CAA)	FEDNET
Federal Information Processing Standards [National Bureau of Standards]	FIPS
Federal Information Processing Standards Coordinating and Advisory Committee [National Bureau of Standards]	FIPSCAC
Federal Information Processing Standards Publication [National Bureau of Standards]	FIPS-PUB
Federal Procurement Data Center [Database] (FDB)	FPDC

Computer & Telecommunications Acronyms

Federal Radio Commission [*Functions transferred to FCC, 1934*] .... FRC
Federal Radio Education Committee .... FREC
Federal Register Abstracts [*Capitol Services, Inc.*] [*Washington, DC*] [*Database*] .... FEDREG
Federal Register Search System [*National Institutes of Health and Environmental Protection Agency*] [*Database*] (FDB) .... FRSS
Federal Regulatory Search System [*Database*] [*Environmental Protection Agency*] (FDB) .... FRSS
Federal Software Exchange Center (CAA) .... FSEC
Federal Software Exchange Center .... FSWEC
Federal Telecommunications Records Center .... FTRC
Federal Telecommunications Standards Committee .... FTSC
Federal Telecommunications System [*of GSA*] .... FTS
Federal Telephone and Radio .... FTR
Federal Telephone System (KSC) .... FTS
Federation Against Software Theft .... FAST
Federation of Automated Coding Technologies (EANO) .... FACT
Federation of Government Information Processing Councils, Incorporated [*Fair Oaks, CA*] (EANO) .... FGIPCI
Federation of Information Users [*Pittsburgh, PA*] (EANO) .... FIU
Federation des Ingenieurs des Telecommunications de la Communaute Europeenne [*Federation of Telecommunications Engineers in the European Community*] .... FITCE
Federation Internationale de Documentation [*International Federation for Documentation - IFD*] .... FID
Federation of NCR [*NCR Corp.*] User Groups [*Dayton, OH*] (EANO) .... FNUG
Federation of NCR User Groups (EANO) .... NUG
Federation of Telephone Workers .... FTW
Feed Drive Analysis [*Machine Tool Industry Research Association*] [*Software package*] [*British*] (NCC) FEDRAN-2
Feedback Control Loop [*Data processing*] (BUR) .... FCL
Feedback Control System .... FCS
Feedback Frequency Modulation .... FBFM
Feedback Mechanism .... FM
Feedback, Multiple Loop .... FML
Feedback Network .... FBN
Feedback Node Set .... FNS
Feedback Positive [*Data processing*] .... FP
Feedback Potentiometer .... FP
Feedback Potentiometer (MSA) .... FPOT
Feedback Resistance (IEEE) .... FBR
Feedback Shift Register .... FSR
Feedback Signal .... FBS
Feedback, Stabilized .... FS
Feedback Summing Junction [*Data processing*] .... FSJ
Feedback System .... FBS
Feeder .... FDR
Feeder Distribution Interface [*Bell System*] .... FDI
Fellow of the British Computer Society .... FBCS
Feminist Radio Network [*Defunct*] (EANO) .... FRN
Femto [*A prefix meaning divided by 10 to the 15th power*] [*SI symbol*] .... f
Femtovolt (MDG) .... FV
Fernschreiben [*Teletype message*] or Fernschreiber [*Teletype*] [*German military - World War II*] .... FS
Ferrite Memory Core .... FMC
Ferrite-Rod Antenna (IEEE) .... FERROD
Ferromagnetic Object Recognition Matrix .... FORM
Ferrox Cube [*Telecommunications*] (TEL) .... FXC
Fetch/Load [*Data processing*] (MDG) .... F/L
Fetch and Send [*Telecommunications*] (TEL) .... F/S
Fiber Duct [*Telecommunications*] (TEL) .... FD
Fiber and Integrated Optics [*A publication*] .... Fiber Integr Opt
Fiber Laser News [*A publication*] .... Fiber Laser
Fiber Optic Communications for Aerospace Systems (MCD) .... FOCAS
Fiber Optic Coordinating Committee [*American National Standards Institute*] [*Telecommunications*] .... FOCC
Fiber Optic MODEM [*Modulator-Demodulator*] (CAA) .... FOM
Fiber-Optic Rate Sensors [*Instrumentation*] .... FORS
Fiber Optic Transmission System [*Consists of modulated light signals sent through glass fibers and demodulated by photo-diodes*] [*Data transmission*] (CCD) .... FOTS
Fiber Optics [*Data transmission*] (TEL) .... FO
Fiber Optics Board (MCD) .... FOB
Fiber Optics Borescope .... FOBS
Fiber Optics Communications [*Data transmission*] (TEL) .... FOC
Fiber Optics Guidance Demonstration (RDA) .... FOGD
Fiber Optics LASER .... FOL
Fiber Optics LASER Gyros (MCD) .... FOLG
Fiber Optics Light .... FOL
Fiber Optics Photo Pickup .... FOPP
Fiber Optics Photo Transfer .... FOPT
Fiber Optics Probe .... FOP
Fiberoptics Report [*A publication*] .... Fiberoptcs
Fibronics International [*NASDAQ symbol*] (NQ) .... FBRX
Fichier de Recherches Automatisees sur les Nouvautes, la Communication et l'Information en Sciences Sociales et Humaines [*French Retrieval Automated Network for Current Information in Social and Human Sciences*] [*Database*] .... FRANCIS
Fiduciary Activity Simulation Training [*Investment banking simulation game*] .... FAST
Field [*Data processing*] (AFM) .... FLD
Field Address (CAA) .... FA
Field to Advise [*Telecommunications*] (TEL) .... FTA

Field Alterable Control Element (MDG) .... FACE
Field Automated Intelligence File (AFM) .... FAIF
Field Data Applications, Systems, and Techniques [*Data processing*] .... FAST
Field Data Computer .... FDC
Field Data Processing .... FDP
Field Descriptor Block (CAA) .... FDB
Field Developed Programs [*Data processing*] .... FDPS
Field Effect Device .... FED
Field Effect Transistor .... FET
Field Engineering Theory of Operations (TUT) .... FETO
Field Function [*Telecommunications*] (TEL) .... FF
Field Information System [*Data processing*] .... FIS
Field Intelligence Simulation Test (NATG) .... FIST
Field Intensity .... FI
Field Length (CAA) .... FL
Field Online Data Acquisition and Analysis System .... FODAAS
Field Programable Gate Array [*Data processing*] (CAA) .... FPGA
Field-Programable Logic Array [*Data processing*] .... FPLA
Field Programable Logic Family (TEL) .... FPLF
Field-Programable Read-Only Memory [*Data processing*] (MCD) .... F-PROM
Field Replaceable Unit [*IBM Corp.*] .... FRU
Field Select Command Register (CAA) .... FSCR
Field Select Unit (OA) .... FSU
Field Separator .... FS
Field Strength Meter .... FSM
Fiendishly Rapid Electronic Device .... FRED
Fifty Upward Network [*Cleveland, OH*] (EANO) .... FUN
Figure (AFM) .... FIG
Figure Reading Electronic Device [*Information retrieval*] .... FRED
Figures Shift [*Teleprinters*] .... FIGS
Filament .... F
Filament (KSC) .... FIL
File Access Channel (CAA) .... FAC
File Access Listener (CAA) .... FAL
File Access Manager (CAA) .... FAM
File Access Subsystem [*Data processing*] (TEL) .... FAS
File Address Register (CAA) .... FAR
File Analysis and Selection Technique [*Data processing*] (TUT) .... FAST
File Block (CAA) .... FB
File Code [*Data processing*] (IEEE) .... FC
File Control .... FC
File Control Block [*Data processing*] (BUR) .... FCB
File Control Processor [*Data processing*] (BUR) .... FCP
File Control Program (CAA) .... FCP
File Control Services [*Digital Equipment Corp.*] (CAA) .... FCS
File Control Unit (CAA) .... FCU
File Conversion [*Data processing*] (BUR) .... FC
File Data Block .... FDB
File Data Register (CAA) .... FDR
File Definition [*Data processing*] .... FD
File Description (CAH) .... FD
File Directory (OA) .... FD
File Exchange (CAA) .... FILEX
File Extended Control Block [*Data processing*] (BUR) .... FECB
File Gap [*Data processing*] (BUR) .... FG
File Indirect Register (CAA) .... FIR
File of Industrial Data [*Data processing*] .... FIND
File Information Block .... FIB
File Information Language Executive Routine [*Data processing*] .... FILER
File Information Table [*Data processing*] .... FIT
File Inquiry Technique .... FIT
File Interrogation of Nineteen-Hundred Data [*Data processing*] (DIT) .... FIND
File Interrogation and Reporting System [*Data processing*] (TUT) .... FIRS
File List Processor [*Data processing*] .... FLIST
File Location Code [*Data processing*] .... FLC
File Maintenance [*Data processing*] (BUR) .... FM
File Management (CAA) .... FM
File Management Loading Facility (CAA) .... FMLF
File Management Supervisor [*Honeywell, Inc.*] (CAA) .... FMS
File Management System .... FMS
File Management Transaction Processor .... FMTP
File Manipulation Language (CAA) .... FML
File Next Register (CAA) .... FNR
File Organization Evaluation Model (CAA) .... FOREM
File Organization Generator (CAA) .... FORGE
File Organization System (DIT) .... FOS
File Organization Technique (BUR) .... FORTE
File-Oriented Interpretive Language [*1969*] [*Data processing*] (TUT) .... FOIL
File Processor [*Data processing*] (BUR) .... FP
File Protect .... FP
File Protect Memory [*Data processing*] (BUR) .... FPM
File Register (CAA) .... FR
File and Report Information Processing Generator [*Data processing*] .... FRINGE
File Separator [*Data processing*] .... FS
File Source [*Data processing*] .... FS
File Status Table [*Data processing*] (IBMDP) .... FST
File Storage Region [*Digital Equipment Corp.*] (CAA) .... FSR
File System Control [*Data processing*] .... FSC
File System Control Block [*Data processing*] (IBMDP) .... FSCB
File Transfer Protocol (DEEC) .... FTP

File Utility Routines [*Data processing*] .... FUR
File Utility Routines, Program Utility Routines [*Data processing*] .... FURPUR
File Verification Utility (CAA) .... FVU
Files Management Unit [*Data processing*] .... FMU
Filing Time [*Time a message is presented for transmission*] .... FLT
Filing Time [*Time a message is presented for transmission*] .... FT
Fill Exit Entry [*Data processing*] .... FEE
Fill Start Entry [*Data processing*] .... FSE
Film Input to Digital Automatic Computer .... FIDAC
Film Input to Digital Automatic Computer System .... FIDACSYS
Film Library Instantaneous Presentation [*Data processing*] .... FLIP
Film Optical Sensing Device for Input to Computers [*National Bureau of Standards*] .... FOSDIC
Film Reading Machine .... FRM
Filter Address Correction .... FAC
Filtered Detection Only Processor (CAAL) .... FDOP
Final [*Telecommunications*] (TEL) .... F
Final Address Message [*Telecommunications*] (TEL) .... FAM
Final Address Register [*Data processing*] (MDG) .... FA
Final Estimation of Data [*Data processing*] .... FED
Final Routing Center [*Telecommunications*] (TEL) .... FRC
Final Selector [*Telecommunications*] (DEEC) .... FS
Final Signal Unit [*Telecommunications*] (TEL) .... FSU
Final Station [*Data processing*] .... FINST
Finance Image Processor [*Data processing*] (IBMDP) .... FIP
Financial Analysis Language [*Data processing*] .... FINAL
Financial Analysis Program [*IBM Corp.*] .... FAP
Financial Business Package [*Data processing*] (TUT) .... FBP
Financial Evaluation Program [*IBM Corp.*] .... FEP
Financial Information Control System .... FICS
Financial Information Reporting System [*Data processing*] (CGC) .... FIRST
Financial Institutions Resource Management [*Computer service*] .... FIRM
Financial Network Manager (BUR) .... FNM
Financial News Network [*Cable-television system*] .... FNN
Financial Planning System [*IBM Corp.*] .... FPS
Financial Post Information Centre [*MacLean-Hunter Ltd.*] [*Information service*] (EISS) .... FPIC
Financial Services Terminals Support [*IBM Corp.*] .... FSTS
Financial Software, Incorporated [*Norcross, GA*] [*Software manufacturer*] (DASOS) .... FSI
Financial Times Company Information Database [*Financial Times Business Information Ltd. and Predicasts*] [*Bibliographic database*] [*British*] (OBD) .... FINTEL
Find Called [*or Calling*] **Party** [*Telecommunications*] (TEL) .... FC
Fingerprint Automatic Classification Technique [*Data processing*] .... FACT
Finished Dialing [*Telecommunications*] (TEL) .... FD
Finite Automation Language [*Data processing*] .... FAL
Finite Element Analysis System [*IBM UK Ltd.*] [*Software package*] [*British*] (NCC) .... FEAS
Finite Element Data Generation [*Data processing*] (CIT) .... FEDGE
Finite Element Mesh Generation Program [*Fegs Ltd.*] [*Software package*] [*British*] (NCC) .... FEMGEN
Finite Element Mesh & Result Viewing [*Fegs Ltd.*] [*Software package*] [*British*] (NCC) .... FEMVIEW
Finite Element Method .... FEM
Finite Element Modeling Optimization .... FEMO
Finite Element Structures Analysis Program [*Data processing*] .... FESAP
Finite Fourier Transform .... FFT
Finite State Machine .... FSM
Finnish Periodicals Index in Economics and Business [*Helsinki School of Economics*] [*Database*] (CUAD) .... FINP
Finnish Radio Industries Association .... FRIA
Fire Control Computer .... FCC
Fire Control Data Converter (MCD) .... FCDC
Fire Control Simulator Unit (VIT) .... FCSU
Fire Operational Characteristics Using Simulation [*System for comparing organizations for wildland fire protection services in cost-effective terms*] [*Department of Agriculture, Forest Services*] .... FOCUS
Firmware Control Memory (CAA) .... FCM
First Come, First Served [*Data processing*] (DDI) .... FCFS
First Computer Interface Tester (MCD) .... FIT
First Customer Shipment [*IBM Corp.*] [*Data processing*] .... FCS
First-Ended First-Out [*Data processing*] .... FEFO
First Financial Language [*Data processing*] .... FFL
First Fix Not Converted .... FFNC
First In, First Out [*Queuing technique*] .... FIFO
First Level Adaptive Program .... FLAP
First Market Intelligence Ltd. [*London, England*] [*Information service*] (EISS) .... FMI
First Osborne Group [*Daly City, CA*] [*Computer users*] (EANO) .... FOG
First Word (CAA) .... FW
First Word Address [*Data processing*] .... FWA
Fiscal Management Information System (OA) .... FMIS
Fischer & Porter Co. [*American Stock Exchange symbol*] .... FP
Fish and Wildlife Reference Service [*Database*] .... FWRS
Five International Associations Coordinating Committee [*Budapest, Hungary*] .... FIACC
Fixed Area [*of magnetic disk*] (DEEC) .... FX
Fixed Asset Accounting Package [*Data processing*] (TUT) .... FAAP
Fixed Block (CAA) .... FB
Fixed Block Architecture (CAA) .... FBA
Fixed Ceramic Disk Capacitor .... FCDC
Fixed Code Processor .... FCP
Fixed Control Storage (CAA) .... FCS
Fixed Delay Line .... FDL
Fixed/Exchangeable Disk Store (CAA) .... FEDS
Fixed Format Display (MCD) .... FFD
Fixed-Head Disk [*Data processing*] .... FHD
Fixed-Head Storage Facility [*Data processing*] (CAA) .... FHSF
Fixed-Length Field [*Data processing*] (BUR) .... FLF
Fixed Message Cycle [*Telecommunications*] (TEL) .... FMC
Fixed Path of Operation .... FPO
Fixed Point Calculation .... FPC
Fixed Point Operation .... FPO
Fixed Portion Queue Area [*Data processing*] (OA) .... FPQA
Fixed Position Keyboard .... FPK
Fixed Program Computer .... FPC
Fixed Radio Communication .... FRC
Fixed Radio Transmission Facility .... FRTF
Fixed Sequence Format .... FSF
Fixed Station [*ITU designation*] (CET) .... FX
Fixed Word Length [*Data processing*] .... FWL
Flag [*Data processing*] (MDG) .... FLG
Flag Register Processing .... FRP
Flag Tactical Data System (MUGU) .... FTDS
Flash [*Precedence*] [*Telecommunications*] (TEL) .... F
Flash Override [*Telecommunications*] (TEL) .... FO
Flash/Wink Signal [*Telecommunications*] (TEL) .... FLINK
Flat [*Telecommunications*] (TEL) .... F
Flat-Plate Array Antenna .... FPAA
Flat-Plate Radiometer .... FPR
Flat Response Audio Pickup .... FRAP
Flatter, Squarer Tube [*Television picture tube*] .... FST
Fleet Management System [*Arrencross Ltd.*] [*Software package*] [*British*] (NCC) .... FMS
Fleet-Sizing Analysis and Sensitivity Technique [*Bell System*] .... FAST
Flex Multiplexer/Demultiplexer (MCD) .... FMDM
Flexible Accounting Control System [*Data processing*] (BUR) .... FACS
Flexible Algebraic Scientific Translator [*NCR Corp.*] .... FAST
Flexible Automatic Circuit Tester .... FACT
Flexible Digital Receiving Terminal .... FDRT
Flexible Disk (CAA) .... FD
Flexible Disk Drive (CAA) .... FDD
Flexible Disk System (CAA) .... FDS
Flexible Guidance Software System (MCD) .... FGSS
Flexible Monte Carlo [*Data processing*] .... FMC
Flexible Multipipeline Processor (CAA) .... FMPP
Flexible Reconfigurable Interconnected Multiprocessor (CAA) .... FRIMP
Flexible Waveguide .... FWG
Flexowriter Equipment .... FLEX
Flexowriter Interrogation Tape (CAH) .... FLIT
Flight Control Computer (KSC) .... FCC
Flight Control Console (VIT) .... FCC
Flight Control Data Bus (MCD) .... FCDB
Flight Control Interface Module (MCD) .... FCIM
Flight Control Operational Software (MCD) .... FCOS
Flight Data Acquisition System .... FDAS
Flight Data Acquisition Unit .... FDAU
Flight Data Center (FAAC) .... FDC
Flight Data Distribution System .... FDDS
Flight Data Processing (KSC) .... FDP
Flight Data Recorder .... FDR
Flight Data Recording System .... FDRS
Flight Data Storage Unit .... FDSU
Flight Director Computer (MCD) .... FDC
Flight Display Research System .... FDRS
Flight Displays and Interface System (NVT) .... FDIS
Flight Management Computer System .... FMCS
Flight Programer Computer .... FPC
Flight Radio Subsystem (CIT) .... FRS
Flight Range and Endurance Data Indicator .... FREDI
Flight Service Communications System .... FSCS
Flight Simulation Test Data .... FSTD
Flight Software (MCD) .... FSW
Flight Systems Software Requirement (MCD) .... FSSR
Flight Test Data Recorder (MCD) .... FTDR
Flip-Flop [*Data processing*] (CIT) .... F-F
Flip-Flop [*Data processing*] (DEN) .... FLF
Flip-Flop Circuit [*Data processing*] (DEEC) .... JK
Flip-Flop Complementary [*Data processing*] (MSA) .... FFC
Flip-Flop Latch [*Data processing*] (MSA) .... FFL
Flip-Flop - National Module [*Data processing*] .... FF-NM
Flip-Flop Position Indicator [*Data processing*] (CIT) .... FFPI
Flip-Flop Relay Driver [*Data processing*] .... FFRD
Floating Accumulator (CAA) .... FAC
Floating Add [*Data processing*] (IEEE) .... FAD
Floating Decimal Abstract Coding System .... FACS
Floating Digital Drive .... FDD
Floating Divide or Halt .... FDH
Floating Error Code [*Digital Equipment Corp.*] (CAA) .... FEC
Floating-Gate Avalanche-Injection Metal-Oxide Semiconductor [*Data processing*] .... FAMOS
Floating Indexed Point Arithmetic [*Data processing*] .... FLIP
Floating Input - Floating Output [*Data processing*] .... FIFO
Floating Input to Ground Output .... FITGO

Floating Interpretive Language [*Princeton University*] ... FLINT
Floating Octal Point [*IBM Corp.*] ... FLOP
Floating Point [*Data processing*] ... FLP
Floating Point [*Data processing*] (BUR) ... FP
Floating-Point Arithmetic ... FPA
Floating-Point Arithmetic Package [*Data processing*] ... FAP
Floating Point Arithmetic Unit (CAA) ... FLPAU
Floating-Point Array Processor [*Data processing*] ... FPAP
Floating-Point Binary [*Data processing*] ... FLBIN
Floating-Point Calculation ... FPC
Floating-Point Decimal [*Data processing*] ... FLDEC
Floating Point Hardware [*Data processing*] (OA) ... FPH
Floating-Point Instruction Set [*Data processing*] (MSA) ... FIS
Floating-Point Interpretive Program [*Data processing*] ... FLIP
Floating-Point Operations per Second [*Data processing*] ... FLOPS
Floating-Point Processor [*Data processing*] ... FPP
Floating-Point Register (CAA) ... FPR
Floating-Point Root Isolation [*Data processing*] (MDG) ... FRTISO
Floating-Point Routine ... FPR
Floating-Point System, Inc. ... FPS
Floating Point Systems, Inc. [*NYSE symbol*] ... FLP
Floating-Point Unit [*Data processing*] (MCD) ... FPU
Floppy Disk [*Data processing*] (BUR) ... FD
Floppy Disk Controller [*Data processing*] (MDG) ... FDC
Floppy Disk Drive [*Data processing*] ... FDD
Floppy Disk Operating System [*Data processing*] (IEEE) ... FDOS
Floppy Disk Send/Receive (CAA) ... FDSR
Floppy Disk System (CAA) ... FDS
Flores Assembly Program [*Data processing*] ... FLAP
Florian's Own Statistically Oriented Language [*Data processing*] (CSR) ... FOSOL
Flow Analysis Program [*Data processing*] ... FLAP
Flow Indicator ... FI
Flow Recorder ... FR
Flow Recorder Controller ... FRC
Flow Recording Transmitter ... FRT
Flowcharting FORTRAN [*Data processing*] (IEEE) ... FLOTRAN
Floyd Satellite Communications Terminal ... FSCT
Fluid Digital Computer ... FDC
Fluid-Operated Digital Automatic Computer [*Sperry UNIVAC*] ... FLODAC
Fluidic Logic Module ... FLM
Fluidic Output Device ... FOD
Fluke [*John*] **Manufacturing Co., Inc.** [*American Stock Exchange symbol*] ... FKM
Flutter and Matrix Algebra System [*Data processing*] ... FAMAS
Flux Changes per Inch (CAA) ... FCI
Flux Changes per Inch [*Data processing*] ... FCPI
Flux Current Loop ... FCL
Flux Logic Element Array ... FLEA
Flux Transitions per Inch (CAA) ... FTPI
Fly Around Saturated Sectors and Terminals [*Recorded phone message tells callers where air traffic delays are occurring*] [*National Business Aircraft Association*] ... FASST
Flying Spot Scanner [*Optical character recognition*] ... FSS
FM Broadcasting Station [*ITU designation*] (CET) ... BCF
Follow-the-Leader Feedback [*Circuit theory*] (IEEE) ... FLF
Follow Sender [*Telecommunications*] (TEL) ... FS
Follow-Up Output (NASA) ... FUO
Following Transmitted as Received (FAAC) ... FTAR
Font Change [*Data processing*] (BUR) ... FC
Food Science and Technology Abstracts [*International Food Information Service*] [*Bibliographic database*] [*A publication*] ... FSTA
Force Administration Data System [*Bell System*] ... FADS
Force Out of Service [*Telecommunications*] (TEL) ... FOOS
Force Release [*Telecommunications*] (TEL) ... FR
Forced Fault Entry [*Data processing*] ... FFE
Ford Aerospace Satellite Services Corporation [*Washington, DC*] [*Telecommunications*] (TSSD) ... FASSC
Ford Satellite Plan [*Telecommunications*] ... FSP
Forecast Center Station [*Telecommunications*] (TEL) ... FC
Forecasting Information Retrieval of Management System (IEEE) ... FIRMS
Forecasting International Ltd. [*Information service*] (EISS) ... FI
Forecasting and Modeling System [*Data processing*] (BUR) ... FAMS
Foreground and Background Monitor (CAA) ... FBM
Foreground Initiated Batch [*Data processing*] ... FIB
Foreign Area Consumer Dialing [*Telecommunications*] ... FACD
Foreign Area Toll [*Telecommunications*] (TEL) ... FAT
Foreign Area Translation [*Telecommunications*] (TEL) ... FAT
Foreign Directory Name [*Telecommunications*] (TEL) ... FDN
Foreign Disclosure Automated Data [*System*] ... FORDAD
Foreign Electromotive Force (TEL) ... FEMF
Foreign Exchange [*Telecommunications*] (TEL) ... FEX
Foreign Exchange [*ADP Data Services*] [*Database*] (CUAD) ... FX
Foreign Exchange Rate Service [*ContiCurrency*] [*Information service*] (EISS) ... FX
Foreign Listing [*Telecommunications*] (TEL) ... FL
Foreign Numbering Plan Area [*AT & T*] [*Telecommunications*] (TEL) ... FNPA
Foreign Traders Index [*Department of Commerce*] [*Information service*] (EISS) ... FTI
Form of Control Users System ... FOCUS
Form Feed [*Data processing*] ... FF
Form Retrieval and Manipulation Language ... FOREMAN
Formal Auto-Indexing of Scientific Texts [*Data processing*] (IEEE) ... FAST
Formal Semantic Language [*Data processing*] ... FSL
Formal Training Data System (NVT) ... FTDS
Format Code [*Data processing*] ... F/C
Format Control Buffer ... FCB
Format Control Language (CAA) ... FCL
Format Effector [*Data processing*] ... FE
Format Identification [*Data processing*] (IBMDP) ... FID
Formatted Data Entry Program [*Mohawk Data Systems*] (CAA) ... FDEP
Formatted Data Tapes (OA) ... FDT
Formatted File System [*Data processing*] (TUT) ... FFS
Formatted File System Commercial Users' Group [*Data processing*] (TUT) ... FFSCUG
Formatted Teletypewriter (CET) ... FORTEL
Forms Control Buffer [*Data processing*] (IBMDP) ... FCB
Forms Entry System (CAA) ... FES
Formula Algebraic Processor [*Data processing*] (CSR) ... FLAP
Formula Assembler Translator [*Data processing*] (BUR) ... FAT
Formula Assembler Translator [*Data processing*] ... FORAST
Formula Calculator [*Digital Equipment Corp.*] (CSR) ... FOCAL
Formula Coder [*Data processing*] ... FORC
Formula Manipulation Compiler [*Programing language*] [*1962*] [*Data processing*] ... FORMAC
Formula Manipulation Language [*1970*] [*Data processing*] (MDG) ... FORMAL
Formula for Optimizing through Real-Time Utilization of Multiprograming ... FORUM
Formula and Statement Translator [*Data processing*] (MCD) ... FAST
Formula Translating System [*Programing language*] [*1953-54*] (CSR) ... FORTRAN
Formularorientiertes Interaktives Datenbanksystem [*Forms-Oriented Interactive Database System*] [*West German*] (CAA) ... FIDAS
Forschungsgesellschaft fuer Agrarpolitik und Agrarsoziologie [*Information retrieval*] (ODIN) ... FAA
Forschungsinformationssystem Sozialwissenschaften [*Informationszentrum Sozialwissenschaften*] [*Database*] (CUAD) ... FORIS
Forschungsprojekte Raumordnung, Staedtebau, Wohnungswesen [*Research Projects on Regional Policy, Urban Development and Housing*] [*Database*] (ODIN) ... FORS
FORTH Interest Group [*San Jose, CA*] (EANO) ... FIG
FORTRAN-to-ALGOL Translator [*Data processing*] (IEEE) ... FALTRAN
FORTRAN Analytical Cross Reference Tabulation System [*Data processing*] (TUT) ... FACTS
FORTRAN Assembly Program [*Data processing*] ... FAP
FORTRAN Automatic Debugging System (CAA) ... FADS
FORTRAN Automatic Timing System [*Data processing*] (TUT) ... FATS
FORTRAN Compiled Block-Oriented Simulation Language [*Data processing*] (IEEE) ... FORBLOC
FORTRAN Compiler Validation System (CAA) ... FCVS
FORTRAN Conversational Environment (CAH) ... FORCE
FORTRAN Debugging Aid Program (CAA) ... FORDAP
FORTRAN Extended Graph Algorithmic Language [*1972*] [*Data processing*] (CSR) ... FGRAAL
FORTRAN Information Bulletin [*Data processing*] (IEEE) ... FIB
FORTRAN Input-Output Package [*Data processing*] (IEEE) ... FIOP
FORTRAN Interactive Subroutine Library [*Data processing*] ... FISLIB
FORTRAN and Internal Translator System [*Data processing*] (IEEE) ... FORTRANSIT
FORTRAN List Processing Language [*Data processing*] (IEEE) ... FLPL
FORTRAN Load and Go [*Xerox Corp.*] (CAA) ... FLAG
FORTRAN Load and Go System [*University of Wisconsin*] [*Data processing*] (IEEE) ... FORGO
FORTRAN Logical Information Retrieval Technique [*Data processing*] (TUT) ... FLIRT
FORTRAN Mathematical Programing System [*Data processing*] (IEEE) ... FMPS
FORTRAN Matrix Abstraction Technique [*Data processing*] (MCD) ... FORMAT
FORTRAN Matrix Abstraction Technique-FORTRAN [*Data processing*] (CSR) ... FORMAT-FORTRAN
FORTRAN Matrix Analysis [*Data processing*] ... FORMA
FORTRAN Monitor System [*Data processing*] ... FMS
FORTRAN Operating System [*Data processing*] (TUT) ... FOS
FORTRAN-Oriented Information Management System (CAA) ... FORIMS
FORTRAN Rules Used as a General Applications Language [*Data processing*] ... FRUGAL
FORTRAN Style Runcible [*Data processing*] ... FORTRUNCIBLE
FORTRAN Utility System (CAA) ... FUS
Fortune Systems Corp. [*NASDAQ symbol*] (NQ) ... FSYS
Forty Automatic Report Generating Operation (MCD) ... FARGO
Forum of Control Data Users [*Later, VIM, Inc.*] (TUT) ... FOCUS
Forward (AFM) ... FWD
Forward Error Correction [*Computer code*] ... FEC
Forward Error Detection and Correction ... FEDAC
Forward Events Controller (MCD) ... FEC
Forward Gate ... FG
Forward Half-Line [*Feed*] ... FHL
Forward Indicator BIT [*Binary Digit*] (TEL) ... FIB
Forward Interworking Telephony Event [*Telecommunications*] (TEL) ... FITE
Forward Load Control (MCD) ... FLC
Forward Load Control Assembly (MCD) ... FLCA

Computer & Telecommunications Acronyms

Forward Propagation by Ionospheric Scatter [*Radio communications technique*] .... FPIS
Forward Propagation by Tropospheric Scatter [*Radio communications technique*] .... FPTS
Forward Ready Signal [*Telecommunications*] (TEL) .... FRS
Forward Sequence Number [*Telecommunications*] (TEL) .... FSN
Forward Space Block (CMD) .... FSB
Forward Space File (CMD) .... FSF
Forward Space Record (OA) .... FSR
Forward Transfer [*Telecommunications*] (TEL) .... FOT
Forward Transfer [*Telecommunications*] (TEL) .... FT
Forward Volume Wave [*Telecommunications*] (TEL) .... FVW
Forward Wave Amplifier .... FWA
Forward Wave Tube .... FWT
Foundation for Advanced Computer Technology (CAH) .... FACT
Foundry Business System [*Foundry Business Systems*] [*Software package*] [*British*] (NCC) .... FBS
Four-Address to SOAP [*Self-Optimizing Automatic Pilot*] Translator [*Data processing*] (IEEE) .... FAST
Four-BIT [*Binary Digit*] Interface Logic Unit (CAA) .... FILU
Four-Phase Systems, Inc. [*NYSE symbol*] [*Delisted*] .... FPS
Four-Wire 4W
Four-Wire Terminating Set [*Telecommunications*] (TEL) 4WTS
Fox Programing Language (OA) .... FPL
Foxon-Maddocks Associates [*Reston, VA*] (EISS) .... FMA
Fractional Doppler Gate .... FDG
Fractionally Rapid Electronic Device (OA) .... FRED
Fractionator Reflux Analog Computer .... FRAC
Fragmented Network (MCD) .... FRAGNET
Frame Alignment Signal [*Telecommunications*] (TEL) .... FAS
Frame Analysis System [*IBM UK Ltd.*] [*Software package*] [*British*] (NCC) .... FAS
Frame Check Sequence [*Data processing*] (IBMDP) .... FCS
Frame and Grillage Analysis [*Modray Ltd.*] [*Software package*] [*British*] (NCC) .... F & GA
Frame Ground [*Data processing*] (BUR) .... FG
Frame Pointer .... FP
Frame Reject (CCD) .... FRMR
Frame Representation Language [*Data processing*] .... FRL
Frame Reset [*Telecommunications*] (TEL) .... FR
Frame Scan (DEN) .... FS
Frame Storage System [*Television*] .... FSS
Frame Table Entry [*Data processing*] (IBMDP) .... FTE
Frames per Inch [*Data processing*] .... FPI
Frames per Second [*Data processing*] .... FPS
France Cables & Radio Co. [*Paris, France*] [*Telecommunications*] (TSSD) .... FCR
FRANCIS: Documentation Automatisee en Gestion des Entreprises [*Database*] (CUAD) .... FRANCIS: DOGE
FRANCIS: Reseau Documentaire en Sciences Humaines de la Sante [*French*] [*Database*] (CUAD) .... FRANCIS: RESHUS
Fraunhofer-Institut fuer Lebensmitteltechnologie und Verpackung [*Munich*] [*Information retrieval*] (ODIN) ILV
Free Energy Minimization Procedure [*Data processing*] .... FEMP
Free-Flying Teleoperator [*Program*] [*Electronics*] .... FFTO
Free Line Signal [*Telecommunications*] (TEL) .... FLS
Free Running Frequency .... FRF
Free Space Microwave Interferometer .... FSMWI
Free-Standing Operating System [*General Automation, Inc.*] (CAA) .... FSOS
Free University Network [*Later, LERN*] (EANO) .... FUN
Freie Universitaet Berlin [*Information retrieval*] (ODIN) .... FU
Freight and Equipment Reporting System for Transportation [*IBM Corp.*] .... FERST
Freight and Equipment Reporting System for Transportation/Virtual Storage [*IBM Corp.*] .... FERST/VS
French Computing Association .... FCA
French Title [*Online database field identifier*] (OBD) .... FT
Frequency .... F
Frequency [*Online database field identifier*] (OBD) .... FQ
Frequency .... FRE
Frequency [*or Frequent*] (AFM) .... FREQ
Frequency Coded System (MCD) .... FCS
Frequency Compressive Feedback .... FCF
Frequency Control and Analysis .... FCA
Frequency Control Analysis Facility .... FCAF
Frequency Control Analysis Subsystem (MCD) .... FCAS
Frequency Converter .... FC
Frequency Converter (MCD) .... FREQCONV
Frequency Converter Unit .... FCU
Frequency Data Multiplexer (NASA) .... FDM
Frequency Demodulator (OA) .... FD
Frequency Dependent Rejection [*Telecommunications*] (TEL) .... FDR
Frequency Deviation Meter .... FDM
Frequency-Differential/Phase-Shift Keyed System [*Data processing*] (TEL) .... FD/PSK
Frequency Distance [*Telecommunications*] (TEL) .... FD
Frequency Diversity .... FD
Frequency Divider (MCD) .... FREQDIV
Frequency Division .... FD
Frequency-Division Data Link [*Radio*] .... FDDL
Frequency-Division Multiple Access .... FDMA
Frequency-Division Multiplex [*Telecommunications*] .... FDM
Frequency Division Multiplex/Frequency Modulation [*Telecommunications*] (TEL) .... FDM/FM
Frequency-Division Multiplex Voice Communication .... FDMVC
Frequency-Division Multiplexing System [*Radio*] .... FDMS
Frequency Division Separator [*Multiplexing*] (OA) .... FDS
Frequency Division Switching [*Radio and television broadcasting*] .... FDS
Frequency Domain Coding .... FDC
Frequency Domain Coding Technique .... FDCT
Frequency-Emphasizing Network (IEEE) .... FEN
Frequency of Every Allowable Term [*Data processing*] .... FEAT
Frequency Exchange Keying .... FEK
Frequency Hopping [*Modulation*] .... FH
Frequency Jumper Identification .... FREJID
Frequency and Load Control Box (MCD) .... FLCB
Frequency and Load Controller .... FLC
Frequency Meter .... FM
Frequency Meter .... FREQM
Frequency Meter .... FRM
Frequency Mixer Stage .... FMS
Frequency-Modulated Ranging (MCD) .... FMR
Frequency-Modulated Receiver .... FMR
Frequency-Modulated Transmitter .... FMT
Frequency-Modulated Transmitter (KSC) .... FMX
Frequency Modulation [*Radio*] .... FM
Frequency Modulation Deviation Meter .... FMDM
Frequency Modulation with Feedback .... FMFB
Frequency Modulation Feedback Discriminator (CIT) .... FMFD
Frequency Modulation - Frequency Modulation .... FM-FM
Frequency Modulation on the Pulse (NG) .... FMOP
Frequency Modulation Signal Processor (NASA) .... FMSP
Frequency Monitoring and Interference Control [*Radio*] .... FMIC
Frequency Multiplex .... FM
Frequency-Multiplexed Subcarrier (CIT) .... FMS
Frequency Multiplier (KSC) .... FREQMULT
Frequency Multiplier (KSC) .... FRQMULT
Frequency Multiplier Storer .... FMS
Frequency Network Analyzer .... FNA
Frequency Optimum Traffic .... FOT
Frequency Phase Lock .... FPL
Frequency and Phase Shift Keying (OA) .... FPSK
Frequency Position Modulation [*Telecommunications*] (IEEE) .... FPM
Frequency Programer (IEEE) .... FQPR
Frequency Range .... FR
Frequency Reference Protection .... FRP
Frequency Regulation and Network Keying (IEEE) .... FRANK
Frequency Response .... FR
Frequency Response Function [*Statistics*] .... FRF
Frequency Response Plotter .... FRP
Frequency Response Survey (CET) .... FRS
Frequency Select Control Unit (MCD) .... FSCU
Frequency Selective Receiver System (MCD) .... FSRS
Frequency Selective Voltmeter .... FSV
Frequency Shift (BUR) .... FS
Frequency Shift Communications System .... FSCS
Frequency Shift Converter .... FSC
Frequency Shift Keying [*Telecommunications*] .... FSK
Frequency Shift Keying Low-Frequency [*Converter*] (NATG) .... FSKLF
Frequency Shift Modulation [*Radio*] .... FSM
Frequency Shift Pulsing .... FSP
Frequency Shift Receiver .... FSR
Frequency Shift Reflector .... FSR
Frequency Shift Transmission .... FST
Frequency Stability .... FS
Frequency Stability Analyzer .... FSA
Frequency Standard (DDI) .... FS
Frequency Standard, Primary .... FSP
Frequency Sweep Oscillator .... FSO
Frequency Threshold Curve .... FTC
Frequency Time Base (DEN) .... FTB
Frequency Time Control .... FTC
Frequency and Time-Division Data Link .... FATDL
Frequency and Time Measurement Counter .... FTMC
Frequency Time Modulation (DEN) .... FTM
Frequency Time Schedule (NVT) .... FTS
Frequency Time Standard .... FTS
Frequency Tolerance .... FT
Frequency Tracker (MSA) .... FT
Frequency Transfer Unit .... FTU
Frequency Translation Distortion .... FTD
Frequency Translator (DDI) .... FRELATOR
Frequency Translator/Recursive Filter (CAAL) .... FT/RF
Frequency to Voltage (IEEE) .... F/V
Frequently-Called-Numbers List [*Bell System*] .... FCNL
Frey Associates, Inc. [*NASDAQ symbol*] (NQ) .... FRYA
Friendly Robot Educational Device [*Androbot, Inc.*] .... FRED
Front [*Telecommunications*] (TEL) .... FRT
Front End Communications Processor (CAA) .... FECP
Front End for Databases [*GTE usage*] .... FRED
Front-End Network Processor .... FNP
Front-End Processor [*Computer*] (NASA) .... FEP
Frost & Sullivan, Inc. [*Information service*] (EISS) .... F & S
Fruits Agro-Industrie Regions Chaudes [*Institut de Recherches sur les Fruits et Agrumes*] [*Database*] (CUAD) .... FAIREC

Computer & Telecommunications Acronyms

Fuel Control Computer .... FCC
Fuel Management Computer   (NG) .... FMC
Fuel Monitoring System [*Cheshire County Council*] [*Software package*] [*British*]   (NCC) .... FMS
Fuel Oil Route Delivery and Control System [*Computer-based system*] .... FORDACS
Fugitive Information Data Organizer [*Database*] .... FIDO
Fuji Photo Film ADR [*NASDAQ symbol*]   (NQ) .... FUJIY
Fujitsu Network Architecture [*Fujitsu Ltd.*] [*Japan*]   (CAA) .... FNA
Full Adder [*Data processing*] .... FA
Full Analog Video   (CIT) .... FAV
Full Authority Digital Engine Control .... FADEC
Full Business Day   (TEL) .... FBD
Full-Coverage Area [*Radio and TV*] .... FCA
Full Cycling File Organization   (CAA) .... FCFO
Full Duplex [*Telecommunications*] .... FD
Full Duplex [*Telecommunications*] .... FDX
Full Duplex Teletype .... FDT
Full Normal Plot [*Data processing*] .... FUNOP
Full-Page Composition System [*Data processing*] .... FPCS
Full Scale [*Analog computers*] .... FS
Full-Scale Output .... FSO
Full-Time Equivalent .... FTE
Full Time Equivalent Terminals [*Data processing*]   (DEEC) .... FTET
Full Wave .... FW
Full-Wave Amplifier .... FWA
Full-Wave Bridge Rectifier .... FWBR
Full-Wave Direct Current .... FWDC
Fully Automated Accounting Computer System   (MCD) .... FAACS
Fully Automatic Compiler [*or Computer*]-Translator .... FACT
Fully Automatic Compiling System .... FACS
Fully Automatic Compiling Technique [*Data processing*] .... FACT
Fully Automatic High-Quality Machine Translation [*Data processing*]   (DIT) .... FAHQMT
Fully Automatic High-Quality Translation [*Data processing*] ..... FAHQT
Fully Automatic Reperforator Transmitter Distributor [*Telecommunications*]   (TEL) .... FRXD
Fully Buffered Channel .... FBC
Function .... F
Function   (DDI) .... FCT
Function   (MDG) .... FUN
Function .... FUNC
Function Button [*Data processing*] .... FB
Function Control Block [*Data processing*]   (IBMDP) .... FCB
Function Control Package [*Data processing*] .... FCP
Function Designator Database   (MCD) .... FDDB
Function Generator [*Data processing*]   (IEEE) .... FG
Function Language One   (CAH) FL1
Function Management Data   (IBMDP) .... FMD
Function Return .... FRETURN
Functional Block Diagram [*Telecommunications*]   (TEL) .... FBD
Functional Data Coordinator   (MCD) .... FDC
Functional Description .... FD
Functional Description Block [*Telecommunications*]   (TEL) .... FDB
Functional Description Table   (CAA) .... FDT
Functional Electronic Blocks .... FEB's
Functional Entity [*Telecommunications*]   (TEL) .... FE
Functional Interface Specification [*Telecommunications*]   (TEL) .... FIS
Functional Machine Representation Language [*Data processing*]   (CSR) .... FMRL
Functional Mathematical Programing System [*Data processing*]   (CGC) .... FMPS
Functional Network   (CAA) .... FN
Functional Operational Design   (CAA) .... FOD
Functional Progression Chart [*Telecommunications*]   (TEL) .... FPC
Functional Query Language [*1978*] [*Data processing*]   (CSR) .... FQL
Functional Recovery Routine [*Data processing*]   (BUR) .... FRR
Functional Sequence Diagram [*Data processing*] .... FSD
Functional Simulator   (NASA) .... FSIM
Functional Simulator and Translator [*Data processing*]   (CSR) ..... FST
Functional Specification [*Telecommunications*]   (TEL) .... FS
Functional Specification Block [*Telecommunications*]   (TEL) .... FSB
Functional Specification Package [*Data processing*] .... FSP
Functional Subsystem Software Requirements   (NASA) .... FSSR
Functional Test [*Data processing*] .... FT
Functional Test Requirement   (IEEE) .... FTR
Functionally Distributed Computing System   (CAA) .... FDCS
Fundacion para el Fomento de la Informacion Automatizada [*Foundation for the Automated Information Industry*] [*Madrid, Spain*] [*Information service*]   (EISS) .... FUINCA
Fundamentally Analyzable Simplified English [*Data processing*] ..... FASE
Fundamentals of Application and System Training [*Course*] [*Data processing*] .... FAST
Funeral Telegraph Service .... FTS
Funkstelle [*Radio Station*] [*German military - World War II*] ..... FST
Fusable Read-Only Memory [*Data processing*]   (MDG) .... FROM
Fuse Alarm   (TEL) .... FA
Fuse Chamber   (TEL) .... FC
Future Language Information Processing System   (BUR) ..... FLIPS
Future System [*IBM Corp.*] [*Data processing*] .... FS
Futures Information Retrieval System [*Congressional Research Service*] .... FIRST
Futures Information Service [*Institute for Futures Studies*] [*Database*]   (CUAD) .... FUTU

G

Gadolinium, Gallium, Garnet (DEEC) G3
Gadolinium Gallium Garnet [*Substrate for magnetic film*] .... GGG
Gain (CBSS) .... G
Gain of Antenna (IEEE) .... GA
Gain Bandwidth (DEN) .... GB
Gain-Bandwidth Product .... GBP
Gain Factor [*Data processing*] .... GF
[*Antenna*] **Gain-to-Noise Temperature Ratio** (CBSS) .... G/T
Galactic Radio Wave .... GRW
Galileo Electro-Optics [*NASDAQ symbol*] (NQ) .... GAEO
Gallaudet Information Retrieval Service .... GIRS
Gallium Arsenide [*Semiconductor*] .... GaAs
Galloping Pattern Memory (DEEC) .... GALPAT
Galvanized Steel [*Telecommunications*] .... GS
Galvanized Steel Strand [*Telecommunications*] (TEL) .... GSS
Game on Urban Transport System [*Kins Developments Ltd.*] [*Software package*] [*British*] (NCC) .... GUTS
Gandalf Technologies [*NASDAQ symbol*] (NQ) .... GANDF
Gandalf Technologies, Inc. [*Toronto Stock Exchange symbol*] .... GAN
Gang Punch [*Data processing*] (TUT) .... GP
Garbage Collection [*Slang*] [*Data processing*] .... GC
Garbage In, Garbage Out [*Data processing*] .... GIGO
Gate [*Electronics*] .... G
Gate Turn Off [*Data processing*] .... GTO
Gated Attenuation [*Data processing*] .... GA
Gateway Exchange [*Telecommunications*] (DEEC) .... GE
Gathers Alarms, Reports, Displays, and Evaluates [*General Electric Co.*] (CDH) .... GARADE
Gating Half-Cycle [*Data processing*] .... GHC
Gay News Information and Communication Network [*Woodbury, NY*] [*Information service*] (EISS) .... GNIC
Gaylord Circulation Control System [*Gaylord Bros., Inc.*] [*Information service*] (EISS) .... GLS
Gaz-Physique-Orsay [*Universite Paris-Sud*] [*Database*] (CUAD) .... GAPHYOR
GBC Closed Circuit TV [*NASDAQ symbol*] (NQ) .... GBCC
Geac Computer Corporation Ltd. [*Toronto Stock Exchange symbol*] .... GAC
GEC [*General Electric Company*] **Telecommunications** [*A publication*] .... GEC Telecommun
GenCorp, Inc. [*NYSE symbol*] .... GY
Genealogical Information and Name Tabulating System [*Data processing*] (IEEE) .... GIANT
General Acceptance Test Software (CAA) .... GATS
General Activity Simulation Language [*Data processing*] .... GASL
General Activity Simulation Program [*Programing language*] [*1970*] [*Data processing*] (BUR) .... GASP
General Address Reading Devices [*Data processing*] (DDI) .... GARD
General Agreement on Tariffs and Trade [*Danish Standards Association*] [*Database*] (CUAD) .... GATT
General All-Purpose Simulation Package [*McDonnell Douglas Automation Co.*] (MCD) .... GASP
General Alpha-Numeric Direct Access Library Facility [*Search system*] .... GANDALF
General Analytical Model for Process Analysis (IEEE) .... GRAMPA
General Antenna Package [*COMSAT*] .... GAP
General Assembly Program [*Data processing*] .... GAP
General Assessment Tridimensional Analog Computer (IEEE) .... GATAC
General Asymptotic Composition Program [*Data processing*] .... GEASCOP
General Automation, Inc. .... GA
General Automation, Inc. [*NASDAQ symbol*] (NQ) .... GENA
General Automation Users Group Exchange [*Defunct*] (EANO) .... GAUGE
General Circulation Model [*Data processing*] .... GCM
General Communication, Incorporated [*Anchorage, AK*] [*Telecommunications*] (TSSD) .... GCI
General Communication Subsystem [*Data processing*] .... GCS
General Comprehensive Operating Supervisor [*Data processing*] .... GCOS
General Comprehensive Operating Supervisor [*Data processing*] .... GECOS
General Comprehensive Operating System .... GECOS
General Computer Systems, Inc. (CAA) .... GCS
General Data Acquisition Unit (MCD) .... GDAU
General Database Technology [*NASDAQ symbol*] (NQ) .... GDTI
General DataComm Industries, Inc. [*NYSE symbol*] .... GDC
General [*Purpose*] **Digital Computer** .... GDC
General Drafting System [*Applied Research of Cambridge Ltd.*] [*Software package*] [*British*] (NCC) .... GDS
General Dynamics/Telecommunications .... GD/T
General Education Management System [*Data processing*] (IEEE) .... GEMS
General Electric Co. [*NYSE symbol*] .... GE
General Electric Company Ltd. .... GEC
General Electric Electronic Processor .... GEEP
General Electric Electronic System Evaluator .... GEESE
General Electric General Purpose (CDH) .... GEPURS
General Electric Information Services (OA) .... GEIS
General Electric Information Services Company [*Rockville, MD*] [*Software manufacturer*] [*Information service*] [*Telecommunications*] (EISS) .... GEISCO
General Electric Macro Assembly Language (NASA) .... GMAL
General Electric Manufacturing Simulator (IEEE) .... GEMS
General Electric Network [*Data processing*] .... GEN
General Electric Network for Information Exchange [*Rockville, MD*] [*Online Information Service*] (EISS) .... GEnie
General Electric Process Automation Computer .... GEPAC
General Electric Programable Automatic Comparator (CDH) .... GEPAC
General Electric Remote Terminal Supervisor (CAH) .... GERTS
General Electric Remote Terminal System (IEEE) .... GERTS
General Electric Six Hundred Users' Association [*Later, HLSUA*] [*Data processing*] (TUT) .... GESHUA
General Electric Telemetering and Control (IEEE) .... GE/TAC
General Electric Test Engineering Language [*Data processing*] (IEEE) .... GETEL
General Electric Training Operational Logic [*Data processing*] (IEEE) .... GETOL
General Electric Variable Increment Computer .... GEVIC
General Emulation Language (CAA) .... GEL
General Engineering System .... GENESYS
General File/Record Control [*Honeywell, Inc.*] (CAH) .... GEFRC
General Forecasting Program (BUR) .... GFP
General Information and Analysis Tool (TUT) .... GIANT
General Information Extractor (CAA) .... GENIE
General Information Retrieval System Simulation .... GIRSS
General Input/Output Channel (CAA) .... GIC
General Instrument Corp. [*NYSE symbol*] .... GRL
General Instruments .... GI
General Internal FORTRAN Translator [*Data processing*] (IEEE) .... GIFT
General Kinetics, Incorporated .... GKI
General Machine Test [*Data processing*] (BUR) .... GMT
General Macroassembly Program [*Honeywell, Inc.*] (CAH) .... GMAP
General Maintenance System [*Data processing*] (BUR) .... GMS
General Modular Redundancy (CAA) .... GMR
General Monte Carlo Code [*Data processing*] .... GMC
General Non-Linear Frame Analysis Program [*Structures & Computers Ltd.*] [*Software package*] [*British*] (NCC) .... GENFAP
General Nonlinear Analysis of Two-Dimensional Structures [*Computer program*] .... GNATS
General Numerical Analysis of Transport [*Computer program*] .... GNAT
General Operating Language [*Data processing*] (IEEE) .... GOL
General Operator-Computer Interaction (IEEE) .... GOCI
General Organizational Environment [*Data processing*] (BUR) .... GEORGE
General Peripheral Controller (CAA) .... GPC
General and Practical Energy Information Data Base (MCD) .... GAP
General Problem Solver [*Data processing*] .... GPS
General [*or Generic*] **Problem Statement Simulator** (IDA) .... GPSS
General Process Simulation Studies (VIT) .... GPSS
General Processing Subsystem (MCD) .... GPS
General Processor (IDA) .... GP
General Product (BUR) .... GP
General-Purpose Amplifier .... GPA
General-Purpose Analog Computer (DEN) .... GPAC
General-Purpose Analysis (IEEE) .... GPA
General-Purpose Array (CAA) .... GPA
General-Purpose Buffer Interface Module [*Data processing*] (MCD) .... GPBIM
General-Purpose Communications Adapter (CAA) .... GPCA
General-Purpose Computer .... GPC
General-Purpose Contouring Program (CAH) .... GPCP
General-Purpose Digital Computer .... GPDC

General-Purpose Discipline [*IBM Corp.*] ... GPD
General-Purpose Graphic Language [*Data processing*] (IEEE) ... GPGL
General-Purpose Input/Output [*Data processing*] ... GPIO
General Purpose Input/Output Processor (CAA) ... GIOP
General-Purpose Intercomputer [*Test*] (NVT) ... GPIC
General-Purpose Interface ... GPI
General-Purpose Interface Adapter (IEEE) ... GPIA
General-Purpose Interface Bus [*Data processing*] ... GPIB
General-Purpose Keyboard and Display Control [*Data processing*] (MDG) ... GPKD
General-Purpose Language [*Data processing*] (CSR) ... GPL
General-Purpose Linear Programing [*Data processing*] (IEEE) ... GPLP
General-Purpose Macrogenerator [*Data processing*] (IEEE) ... GPM
General-Purpose Microprogram Simulator [*Data processing*] (IEEE) ... GPMS
General Purpose Operating System ... GPOS
General-Purpose Programing [*Data processing*] ... GPP
General-Purpose Radio Receiver ... GPRR
General-Purpose Radio Transmitter ... GPRT
General-Purpose Register [*Data processing*] (MDG) ... GPR
General-Purpose Satellite Communication System (MCD) ... GPSCS
General-Purpose Simulation Environment [*Data processing*] ... GPSE
General-Purpose Simulation System [*formerly, Systems Simulator*] [*IBM Corp.*] [*1961*] [*Data processing*] ... GPSS
General-Purpose Software Program [*Data processing*] (CIT) ... GPSP
General-Purpose Terminal Interchanges [*Airline communication system*] [*Raytheon Co.*] ... GPTI
General Register Set/Stack [*Data processing*] ... GRS
General Remote Terminal Supervisor (CAA) ... GRTS
General Reporting System (CAA) ... GRS
General Retrieval and Information Processor for Humanities Oriented Studies ... GRIPHOS
General Retrieval of Information Program [*Data processing*] ... GRIP
General Robotics and Active Sensory Processing Laboratory [*University of Pennsylvania*] [*Research center*] (RCD) ... GRASP Lab
General Services Administration ... GSA
General Simulation Program [*Programing language*] (IEEE) ... GSP
General Syntactic Processor (OA) ... GSP
General Syntax Analyzer [*Sperry UNIVAC*] (CAA) ... GSA
General Systems Division [*IBM Corp.*] ... GSD
General Telephone of California [*NASDAQ symbol*] (NQ) ... GTELN
General Telephone Call Processing ... GTCP
General Telephone Co. of Florida [*NYSE symbol*] ... GLF
General Telephone & Electronics Corp. ... GENTEL
General Telephone & Electronics Corp. ... GT & E
General Telephone and Electronics Practice [*Telecommunications*] (TEL) ... GTEP
General Time Sharing System [*Data processing*] ... GTSS
General Transpose [*Data processing*] (CDH) ... GTRP
General Unary Hypothesis Automation (IEEE) ... GUHA
General Utility Library Program [*Data processing*] ... GULP
General Videotex Corporation ... GVC
Generalized Academic Simulation Program [*Data processing*] (IEEE) ... GASP
Generalized Algebraic Translator [*Data processing*] ... GAT
Generalized Algebraic Translator Extended [*Data processing*] ... GATE
Generalized Assembly System [*Data processing*] (IEEE) ... GASS
Generalized Audit Software [*Data processing*] ... GAS
Generalized Burst Trapping (CAA) ... GBT
Generalized Circuit Analysis Program (IEEE) ... GCAP
Generalized Communication Interface (CAA) ... GCI
Generalized Compiler [*Data processing*] ... GECOM
Generalized Computer Program ... GCP
Generalized Data Entry ... GDE
Generalized Data Management System [*Data processing*] (BUR) ... GDMS
Generalized Data Reduction, Manipulation, Evaluation ... GENDARME
Generalized Database Planning System (CAH) ... GPLAN
Generalized Database System (NASA) ... GDBS
Generalized Distributor Program [*Data processing*] (TUT) ... GDP
Generalized Drawing Primitive (CCD) ... GDP
Generalized File Processor (CAA) ... GFP
Generalized Information Management [*Language*] (CGC) ... GIM
Generalized Information Processing System ... GIPSY
Generalized Information Retrieval Language [*US Defense Nuclear Agency*] (IDA) ... GIRL
Generalized Information Retrieval and Listing System ... GIRLS
Generalized Information System [*IBM Corp.*] ... GIS
Generalized Input/Output Controller [*Data processing*] (IEEE) ... GIOC
Generalized Inquiry System [*Data processing*] (TUT) ... GIS
Generalized Macroprocessor (CAA) ... GMAP
Generalized Mainline Framework [*Data processing*] ... GMF
Generalized Management Information System (CAA) ... GMIS
Generalized Markup Language [*Data processing*] ... GML
Generalized Message Control System (BUR) ... GEMCOS
Generalized Multitasking (CAA) ... GMT
Generalized Process Control Programing [*Data processing*] (IEEE) ... GPCP
Generalized Programing [*Data processing*] ... GP
Generalized Programing Extended [*Livermore Atomic Research Computer*] [*Sperry UNIVAC*] ... GPX
Generalized Programing Language [*Data processing*] (TUT) ... GPL
Generalized Queue Entry [*Data processing*] (OA) ... GQE
Generalized Random Extract Device [*Data processing*] ... GRED
Generalized Read and Simulate Program (CAA) ... GRASP
Generalized Remote Access Database (TUT) ... GRAD
Generalized Remote Access Database (IEEE) ... GRADB
Generalized Remote Access Database System (IEEE) ... GRADS
Generalized Remote Acquisition and Sensor Processing (CAA) ... GRASP
Generalized Report Module Program [*Data processing*] ... GRM
Generalized Retrieval and Storage Program [*Data processing*] ... GRASP
Generalized Retrieval System [*Data processing*] (TUT) ... GRS
Generalized Sequential Access Method [*Data processing*] ... GSAM
Generalized Sequential Machine [*Data processing*] ... GSM
Generalized Simulation Language [*Data processing*] (MDG) ... GSL
Generalized Sort/Merge [*Data processing*] ... GSM
Generalized Supervisor Calls [*Data processing*] (IBMDP) ... GSVC
Generalized Top-Down Parsing Language (CAA) ... GTDPL
Generalized Trace Facility [*Data processing*] (MCD) ... GTF
Generalized Upper Bounding [*Data processing*] ... GUB
Generate (CAH) ... GEN
Generated Data File [*Data processing*] ... GEND
Generated Output (CAA) ... GO
Generated Real-Time Output Operations on Voltage-Controlled Equipment [*Data processing*] ... GROOVE
Generating and Analyzing Networks [*Data processing*] (TUT) ... GAN
Generation (MSA) ... GEN
Generation Control Function [*Telecommunications*] (TEL) ... GCF
Generation Data Group [*Data processing*] (BUR) ... GDG
Generation Gather Group [*Data processing*] ... GNG
Generation, Reduction, and Training Input System (IEEE) ... GRATIS
Generation Strategy Language [*Data processing*] (IEEE) ... GSL
Generator [*Data processing*] ... GEN
Generic Control Language [*Data processing*] (TEL) ... GCL
Generic Identifier [*Telecommunications*] (TEL) ... GI
Generic Macro Expander [*Telecommunications*] (TEL) ... GME
Generic Processing System [*Data processing*] (TEL) ... GPS
Generic Structure Diagram [*Telecommunications*] (TEL) ... GSD
Generic Unit (TEL) ... GU
Generic User System [*Data processing*] ... GUS
Genetic Sequence Databank [*Bolt, Beranek & Newman, Inc.*] [*Database*] [*Information service*] (EISS) ... GENBANK
Geneva Consultants Registry [*Alpha Systems Resource*] [*Database*] (CUAD) ... GCR
Genisco Technology Corp. [*American Stock Exchange symbol*] ... GES
GenRad, Inc. [*NYSE symbol*] ... GEN
Geoanomaly Interactive Data Analysis System (MCD) ... GIDAS
Geodetic Data Reduction ... GDR
Geographic Data File [*List Processing Co.*] [*Information service*] (EISS) ... GDF
Geographic Data Technology, Inc. [*Information service*] (EISS) ... GDT
Geographic Distribution of Federal Funds Information System [*Comptroller General of the United States*] ... GDFF
Geographic Information Retrieval and Analysis System [*Department of the Interior*] ... GIRAS
Geographic Information Systems [*United States Geological Survey*] (EISS) ... GIS
Geographic Systems, Incorporated [*Information service*] (EISS) ... GSI
Geographically Referenced Data Storage and Retrieval System [*Canada*] ... GRDSR
Geological Data Center [*Scripps Institution of Oceanography*] (EISS) ... GDC
Geological Reference File [*American Geological Institute*] [*Bibliographic database*] [*Information service*] (EISS) ... GEOREF
Geomechanics Abstracts [*Rock Mechanics Information Service*] [*Bibliographic database*] [*British*] (OBD) ... GMA
Geometric Modeller [*GE CAE International*] [*Software package*] [*British*] (NCC) ... GEOMOD
Geometric and Technical Draughting [*British Olivetti Ltd.*] [*Software package*] [*British*] (NCC) ... GTD
Geometric and Technical Language [*British Olivetti Ltd.*] [*Software package*] [*British*] (NCC) ... GTL
Geopotential Decameter [*Telecommunications*] (TEL) ... GPDM
George M. Low Center for Industrial Innovation [*Rensselaer Polytechnic Institute*] [*Research center*] (RCD) ... CII
Georgetown Automatic Translator [*Data processing*] ... GAT
Georgia Tech Language [*Data processing*] (CSR) ... GTL
Georgia Tech Research Institute [*Georgia Institute of Technology*] [*Research center*] (RCD) ... GTRI
Georgia Telecommunications Network [*Georgia Hospital Association*] [*Atlanta, GA*] [*Telecommunications*] (TSSD) ... TELNET
GEOS [*Geodetic Earth-Orbiting Satellite*] **Data Adjustment Program** ... GDAP
Geostationary Communications Satellite [*WARC*] ... GCS
Geostationary Meteorological Satellite [*Japan*] ... GMS
Geostationary Operational [*or Orbit*] **Environmental Satellite** [*National Oceanic and Atmospheric Administration*] ... GOES
Geostationary Operational Environmental Satellite Data Collection Platform ... GOES/DCP
Geostationary Technology Satellite ... GTS
Gerard P. Weeg Computing Center [*University of Iowa*] [*Research center*] (RCD) ... WCC
Gerber Systems Technology [*NASDAQ symbol*] (NQ) ... GSTI
German Telecommunications Statistics Agency ... GTSA
Gesamthochschule [*General High School*] [*Information retrieval*] [*German*] (ODIN) ... GHS
Gesellschaft fuer Angewandte Mathematik und Mechanik [*German Association for Applied Mathematics and Mechanics*] ... GAMM
Gesellschaft fuer Betriebswirtschaftliche Information mbH [*Online service*] (CUAD) ... GBI

Computer & Telecommunications Acronyms

Gesellschaft fuer Information und Dokumentation mbH [Society for Information and Documentation] [West Germany] [Information service] (EISS) .... GID
Gesellschaft fuer Mathematik und Datenverarbeitung [Society for Mathematics and Data Processing] [West Germany] [Information service] (EISS) .... GMD
Get Quick Answer [Communications] .... GQA
Giga [A prefix meaning multiplied by 10^9] [SI symbol] .... G
GigaBIT [Binary Digit] [10^9 BITs] .... Gb
GigaBITS [Binary Digits] per Second [Transmission rate] [Data processing] (TSSD) .... GBPS
GigaBITS [Binary Digits] per Second [Transmission rate] [Data processing] .... GPS
Gigabyte (10^9 bytes) .... GB
Gigacharacters (CAA) .... GCH
Gigacycle [Measurement] .... Gc
Gigahertz [1,000 megahertz] .... GHz
Gilbert Associates, Incorporated .... GAI
Gilbert Associates, Inc. Cl A [NASDAQ symbol] (NQ) .... GILBA
Give Better Address [Communications] .... GBA
Give Better Reference [Communications] .... GBR
Give Quick Answer [Communications] .... GQA
Global Address (CAA) .... GA
Global Communications Satellite System .... GCSS
Global Data Manager (CAA) .... GDM
Global Data Processing System [World Meteorological Organization] .... GDPS
Global Database (CAA) .... GDB
Global Descriptor Table [Data processing] .... GDT
Global Electronic Mail Service [Electronic Mail Corp. of America] [Old Greenwich, CT] [Telecommunications] (TSSD) .... GEMSERVICE
Global Electronic Markets Company [Joint venture of Citicorp and McGraw-Hill, Inc. to provide computerized buying, selling, shipping, and insuring services for commodities traders] .... GEMCO
Global Information Services, Inc. [Flushing, NY] [Telecommunications] (TSSD) .... GIS
Global Lending and Overseas Banking Evaluator [Chase Econometrics] [Database] (CUAD) .... GLOBE
Global Lightweight Airborne Navigation Computer Equipment .... GLANCE
Global Low-Orbiting Message Relay [Satellite] .... GLOMR
Global Positioning Satellite .... GPS
Global Shared Resources [Data processing] (IBMDP) .... GSR
Global Telecommunication System [World Meteorological Organization] (EISS) .... GTS
Globe Mackay Cable and Radio Corp. [Manila, Philippines] [Telecommunications] (TSSD) .... GMCR
Gnostic Concepts, Incorporated [San Mateo, CA] [Database producer] [Information service] [Telecommunications] (TSSD) .... GCI
Go Ahead [or resume sending] [Communications] .... GA
Goal-Directed Programing (CAA) .... GDP
GOAL [Ground Operations Aerospace Language] Language Processor (MCD) .... GLP
Goal-Oriented Language (CAA) .... GOL
GOAL [Ground Operations Aerospace Language] Processing Language (MCD) .... GPL
Goblin Loose in the Computer Hut [Data processing] .... GLITCH
Golden Common LISP [Artificial intelligence language] .... GC LISP
Golden Gate Productions [San Francisco, CA] [Telecommunications] (TSSD) .... GGP
Golden West Subscription Television [Cable TV programing service] .... GWSTV
Good-By [Amateur radio] .... GB
Good Evening [Amateur radio] .... GE
Good Morning [Amateur radio] .... GM
Good Night [Amateur radio] .... GN
Good Will In, Good Will Out [Data processing] .... GWIGWO
Goodyear Associative Processor [Data processing] .... GAP
Gopher Tape Armor [Telecommunications] (TEL) .... GT
Gould, Inc. [NYSE symbol] .... GLD
Government Communications (TEL) .... GC
Government Computer News [A publication] .... GCNED
Government Data Systems [United States] [A publication] .... Gov Data Syst
Government Data Systems [A publication] .... Govt Data Sys
Government Data Systems [A publication] .... GVDSB
Government EDP [Electronic Data Processing] Standards Committee [Canada] .... GESC
Government-Furnished Equipment .... GFE
Government-Furnished Software (NASA) .... GFS
Government-Industry Data Exchange Program [Later, IDEP] [Department of the Navy] [Database] [Information service] .... GIDEP
Government Microcircuit Applications Conference .... GOMAC
Government Owned and Maintained [Telecommunications] (TEL) .... GOAM
Government Reports Announcements [Department of Commerce] [Database producer] .... GRA
Government Research Corporation [Information service] (EISS) .... GRC
Government Securities Trading [Computer] .... GST
Government Telecommunications Agency [Canada] .... GTA
GR Gordetsky Telecommunications and General Management Consulting [San Diego, CA] [Telecommunications] (TSSD) .... GRG
Grade of Service [Telecommunications] .... GOS
Graduate Resume Accumulation and Distribution [Data processing] .... GRAD
Gram .... g
Grammatical Nonalgorithmic Data Description (CAA) .... GRANADA
Grand Scale Integration (BUR) .... GSI
Grandmet Information Processing [British] (OA) .... GRIP
Grant Information System [Oryx Press] (EISS) .... GIS
Graph Algorithmic Language [Data processing] .... GRAAL
Graph Information Retrieval Language [1970] [Data processing] (CSR) .... GIRL
Graphic Adapter Board (CAA) .... GAB
Graphic Addition to FORTRAN [Data processing] .... GRAF
Graphic Analysis of Three-Dimensional Data .... GATD
Graphic Applications Subroutine Package [Data processing] (BUR) .... GASP
Graphic Communications Computer Association [Printing Industries of America] [Later, GCA] .... GCCA
Graphic Communications International Union [Washington, DC] (EANO) .... GCIU
Graphic Communications International Union [Canada] .... GCIU
Graphic Compatibility System (CAA) .... GCS
Graphic Data Entry Unit [Data processing] (CDH) .... GRAPDEN
Graphic Data Output Area (CMD) .... GDOA
Graphic Data System .... GDS
Graphic Design System (CAA) .... GDS
Graphic Display (CAA) .... GD
Graphic Display Library .... GDL
Graphic Display Processor .... GDP
Graphic Display Terminal .... GDT
Graphic Display Unit .... GDU
Graphic Drawing Library [Graphic Data Ltd.] [Software package] [British] (NCC) GDL1
Graphic Environment Operating System .... GEOS
Graphic Imaging Specification Language [Printing technology] .... GISL
Graphic Interactive Display (IEEE) .... GRID
Graphic Interface for Finite Elements [Graphics data processing] .... GIRAFFE
Graphic Job Processor (MCD) .... GJP
Graphic Machine Language (CAA) .... GML
Graphic Numerical Control [Deltacam Systems Ltd.] [Software package] [British] (MCD) .... GNC
Graphic Online Language [Data processing] (IEEE) .... GOLD
Graphic Programing Services [Data processing] (IBMDP) .... GPS
Graphic Reproduction by Integrated Design .... GRID
Graphic Retrieval and Information Display (NASA) .... GRID
Graphic Service Program (IEEE) .... GRASP
Graphic Structure Input (DEEC) .... GSI
Graphic Subroutine Package [Data processing] .... GSP
Graphic Support Software (CAA) .... GSS
Graphic Surface Kinetics [Computer program] (KSC) .... GASKET
Graphic Tablet Display [Data processing] (IEEE) .... GTD
Graphical Aid [Data processing] .... GRAID
Graphical Analysis of Program Execution [Data processing] .... GRAPE
Graphical Automatically Programed Tools [Data processing] .... GAPT
Graphical Data Definition Language (CAA) .... GDDL
Graphical Data Display Manager [Data processing] .... GDDM
Graphical Data Entry [Data processing] (MUGU) .... GRAPHDEN
Graphical Display System [Station control and data acquisition] (IEEE) .... GDS
Graphical Evaluation and Review Technique .... GERT
Graphical Input [Language] [Data processing] .... GRIN
Graphical Input/Output (CAA) .... GINO
Graphical Input and Output in FORTRAN [GST Computer Systems Ltd.] [Software package] [Data processing] [British] .... GINO-F
Graphical Interaction [Language] [Data processing] GRIN-2
Graphical Interactive Network Designer (CAA) .... GRINDER
Graphical Modeling and Simulation System (CAA) .... GMSS
Graphical Natural Inference System (CAA) .... GRANIS
Graphical PERT [Program Evaluation and Review Technique] Analog [Data processing] (IEEE) .... GPA
Graphical Rewriting Grammar (CAA) .... GRG
Graphical Robot Applications Simulation [BYG Systems Ltd.] [Software package] [British] (NCC) .... GRASP
Graphically Oriented Design and Analysis System [Data processing] .... GODAS
Graphics Access Method (BUR) .... GAM
Graphics Application Program (CAA) .... GAP
Graphics-Assisted Management Application [Data processing] (BUR) .... GAMA
Graphics-Augmented Structural Post-Processing [Module] .... GRASP
Graphics Communications Terminal (CAA) .... GCT
Graphics Device Interface .... GDI
Graphics Display List [Graphic Data Ltd.] [Software package] [British] (NCC) .... GDL 2
Graphics Environment Manager [Data processing] .... GEM
Graphics Environment Manager/Disk Operating System .... GEMDOS
Graphics Flutter Analysis Methods [Data processing] .... GFAM
Graphics Interaction with Proteins [Computer graphics] .... GRIP
Graphics Interactive Programing (CAA) .... GRIP
Graphics for the Multipicture System [Computer graphics] .... GRAMPS
Graphics Network Architecture (CCD) .... GNA
Graphics Operating System [Tektronix] (CAA) .... GOS
Graphics-Oriented Relational Algebraic Interpreter (CAA) .... GRAIN
Graphics Processor (CAA) .... GP
Graphics System Module (CAA) .... GSM
Graphics Terminal (CAA) .... GT
Graphics Text Organizer [Data processing] .... GTO

Computer & Telecommunications Acronyms

Graphite Oxidation from Reactor Excursion [*Engineering computer code*]..GORX
Gravis Computer Peripherals, Inc. [*Vancouver Stock Exchange symbol*]..GVP
Gray Communications Systems [*NASDAQ symbol*]   (NQ) ....GCOM
Great Northern Telegraph Co. [*Denmark*] [*Telecommunications*]   (TEL)..GNT
Greater than or Equal To [*FORTRAN*]..GE
Greater Than [*FORTRAN*]..GT
Greatest Common Divisor..GCD
Greatest Overall Coefficient   (TEL)..GOC
Greatest Upper Bound [*Data processing*]   (CIT)................................GUB
Green Thumbs [*National Weather Service and Department of Agriculture Extension Service telecommunication system*].............GT
Greenwich Mean Time..GMT
Greeting Letter Telegram...GLT
Grid [*Electronics*]..G
Griffin Technology [*NASDAQ symbol*]   (NQ) ....GRIF
Grosspeicherorientierte Listenorganisierte Ermittlungsmethode [*Information retrieval*]   (ODIN)..GOLEM
Ground..G
Ground..GND
Ground-to-Air Communications   (MCD)...G/A COMM
Ground-to-Air Transmitter Terminal...GATT
Ground-to-Air Transmitting-Receiving [*Station*].............................GATR
Ground-Based Computer..GBC
Ground-Based Electronic Omnidirectional Satellite Communications Antenna..GEOSCAN
Ground-Based Software   (MCD)..GBS
Ground Communications Controller   (SKY)....................................GCC
Ground Communications System..GCS
Ground Computer Controller   (SKY)..GCC
Ground-Control Computer Center   (MCD)......................................GCCC
Ground-Control Interface Logic   (MCD)...GCIL
Ground-Control Interface Logic Controller   (MCD).......................GCILC
Ground-Control Interface Logic Unit   (MCD).................................GCILU
Ground Data Acquisition System..GDAS
Ground Data Equipment [*Electronics*]..GDE
Ground Data Terminal..GDT
Ground-to-Ground [*Communications, weapons, etc.*]   (MSA).........G-G
Ground-to-Ground [*Communications, weapons, etc.*].....................GTG
Ground Line of Communications   (AFM)...GLOC
Ground Position Indicator [*Dead-reckoning computer*]...................GPI
Ground Standard Interface Unit   (MCD)...GSIU
Ground Transport Express [*Airport baggage computer*]..................GTX
Group [*Data processing*]..G
Group Busy Hour [*Telecommunications*]   (TEL)..............................GBH
Group Coded Recording [*Data processing*]   (BUR).........................GCR
Group Distributing Frames...GDF
Group Mark [*Data processing*]..GM
Group Operational Access Tester System [*AT & T*].......................GOATS
Group Processing Logic   (TEL)...GPL
Group Reference Pilot [*Telecommunications*]   (TEL)......................GRP
Group Selector [*Telecommunications*]   (TEL)..................................GS
Group Separator [*Data processing*]..GS
Group Switching Center [*British*] [*Telecommunications*]   (TEL).....GSC
Group Translating Equipment   (CBSS)..GTE
Group Visionary Productions, Inc. [*Studio City, CA*] [*Telecommunications*]   (TSSD)..GVP
Groupe des Communications Informatiques [*Computer Communications Group*] [*Canada*]..GCI
Groupe de Recherche sur l'Efficacite Organisationnelle [*University of Quebec at Hull*] [*Research center*]   (RCD)..........................GREFICOR
Groupement Francais des Producteurs de Bases et Banques de Donnees [*French Federation of Data Base Producers*] [*Information service*]   (EISS)..GFPBBD
Groupement Technique de Assureurs du Canada [*Government Telecommunications Agency*] [*Canada*]....................................GTA
Groups [*of code transmitted*] per Minute [*or Message*] [*Telecommunications*]...GPM
Growth Analysis and Review   (BUR)..GAR
Grumman Aerospace Engineering Language for Instructional Checkout   (OA)...GAELIC
Grumman Corp. [*NYSE symbol*]..GQ
GTE [*General Telephone and Electronics Corp.*] Automatic Electric Technical Journal [*A publication*]...GTE Auto
GTE [*General Telephone and Electronics Corp.*] Automatic Electric World-Wide Communications Journal [*A publication*]...............GTE Autom Electr World-Wide Commun J
GTE Corp. [*Formerly, General Telephone & Electronics Corp.*] [*NYSE symbol*]...GTE
GTI Corp. [*American Stock Exchange symbol*]................................GTI
Guard Ring Isolated Monolithic Integrated Circuit   (CAA).............GIMIC
Guest-Host/Liquid Crystal Display [*Telecommunications*]   (TEL)...GH/LCD
Guidance Checkout Computer..GCC
Guidance Computer..GC
Guidance Computer Control Subsystem   (VIT)..............................GUCCO
Guidance Computer Test   (VIT)...GCT
Guidance Computer Test Equipment   (VIT)...................................GCTE
Guidance and Control Computer   (CIT)..GCC
Guidance Control and Sequencing Computer   (CIT).....................GCSC
Guidance Information System [*Time Share Corp.*] [*Information service*]   (EISS)..GIS

Guidance for Users of Integrated Data Processing Equipment.............GUIDE
Guided Fault Isolation   (CAA)...GFI
Guidelines and Rules for Data Systems Management   (TEL)...............GUARDSMAN
Gulf It to FORTRAN [*Translator*] [*Data processing*]......................GIF
Gulf States Information Documentation Center [*Baghdad, Iraq*] [*Information service*]   (EISS)..GSIDC
Gulton Industries, Inc. [*NYSE symbol*]..GUL

H

Hale Systems, Inc. [*NASDAQ symbol*]   (NQ) .... HSYS
Half Adder [*Circuitry*]   (MSA) .... HA
Half Amplitude Duration [*Telecommunications*]   (TEL) .... HAD
Half Duplex Transmission [*Data communication*]   (CET) .... HD
Half Duplex Transmission [*Data communication*] .... HDX
Half-Power Beamwidth   (IEEE) .... HPBW
Half Subtractor [*Circuitry*] .... HS
Half-Word Designator [*Data processing*] .... H
Halt [*Data processing*]   (MDG) .... H
Halt [*Data processing*]   (MDG) .... HLT
Halt Acknowledge [*Data processing*] .... HLTA
Halt and Jump [*Data processing*]   (BUR) .... HJ
Hand or Computer Universal Simulation [*PE Computer Services
   Ltd.*] [*Software package*] [*British*] .... HOCUS
Hand-Held Information Processor   (DDI) .... HHIP
Hand Over Transmitter .... HOT
Handbuch fuer Rundfunk und Fernsehen [*NOMOS Datapool*]
   [*Database*]   (CUAD) .... HARU
Handheld Computer .... HHC
Handicapped Education Learner's Planning System [*Battelle
   Memorial Institute*] [*Information service*]   (EISS) .... HELPS
Handset .... HNDST
Handset .... HS
Handset, Wall Model   (TEL) .... HW
Handshake [*Computers*]   (MSA) .... HDSHK
Handy Dandy Orbital Computer   (IEEE) .... HDOC
Hanging Handset [*Telecommunications*]   (TEL) .... HH
Hangup [*Telecommunications*]   (TEL) .... HU
Harbor Bay Telecommunications [*Alameda, CA*]   (TSSD) .... HBT
Hard Copy [*Data processing*] .... HC
Hard Copy Printer [*Data processing*] .... HCP
Hard Disk Operating System   (CAA) .... HDOS
Hard Tube Modulator [*Electronics*] .... HTM
Hardened Voice Channel   (MSA) .... HVCH
Hardened Voice Circuit   (CET) .... HVC
Hardware [*Data processing*]   (MDG) .... H
Hardware [*Data processing*]   (KSC) .... HDW
Hardware [*Data processing*]   (NASA) .... HW
Hardware-Assisted Software Queue   (CAA) .... HASQ
Hardware Associative Memory [*Data processing*]   (DIT) .... HAM
Hardware Character Generator   (OA) .... HCG
Hardware Check Routine   (CAA) .... HCR
Hardware Description Language [*Data processing*] .... HDL
Hardware Error Recovery System [*Sperry UNIVAC*]   (CAA) .... HERS
Hardware Implemented Fault Tolerance   (CAA) .... HIFT
Hardware Interpreter   (CAA) .... HWI
Hardware Logic Simulator [*Data processing*]   (IEEE) .... HALSIM
Hardware in the Loop Simulation [*Data processing*]   (MCD) .... HITLS
Hardware Message Generator [*Telecommunications*]   (TEL) ..... HMG
Hardware Microcode Optimizer   (CAA) .... HMO
Hardware Monitor Interface   (CAA) .... HMI
Hardware Multiply Module .... HMM
[*A*] Hardware Programing Language [*1971*] [*Data processing*]
   (CSR) .... AHPL
Hardware Read-In Mode   (CAA) .... HRM
Hardware-Software Configuration [*Data processing*] .... HSC
Hardware/Software Integration Review   (MCD) .... H/SIR
Hardware Vector to Raster   (CAA) .... HVR
Hardware Virtualizer [*Data processing*]   (IEEE) .... HV
Hardwell FORTRAN [*Data processing*]   (IEEE) .... HARTRAN
Harris Corp. [*NYSE symbol*] .... HRS
Harte-Hanks Communications, Inc. [*NYSE symbol*] .... HHN
Harvard Business Review [*John Wiley & Sons, Inc.*] [*Bibliographic
   database*] [*A publication*] .... HBR
Harvard University Character Recognizer [*Data processing*] ... HUCR
Harwell Automated Loans [*Library circulation system*]   (DEEC) ... HAL
Hash Algorithm Information Table   (CAA) .... HAIT
Hash Algorithm Library   (CAA) .... HAL
Hastech Users Group   (EANO) .... HUG
Hawaiian Telephone Co. [*NYSE symbol*] [*Delisted*] .... HT
Hayden Analysis and Reporting Tool [*Data processing*]   (TUT) ... HART
Hayes Verification Protocol [*Data processing*] .... HVP
Head Disk Assembly   (CAA) .... HDA

Head Set [*Telecommunications*]   (TEL) .... HDS
Head per Track   (BUR) .... HPT
Head per Track   (CAA) .... H/T
Head, Track, and Selector   (CAA) .... HTS
Header [*Data processing*] .... HDR
Health Audiovisual On-Line Catalog [*Northeastern Ohio
   Universities College of Medicine*] [*Database*] .... HAVC
Health Care Literature Information Network [*Technische
   Universitaet Berlin*] [*West Germany*] [*Database*] [*Information
   service*]   (EISS) .... HECLINET
Health Care Support [*System*] [*IBM Corp.*] .... HCS
Health Communications Network [*Medical University of South
   Carolina*] [*Charleston*] [*Telecommunications*]   (TSSD) .... HCN
Health Environment Long-Range Planning Support [*A computer
   model*] .... HELPS
Health Information Systems [*NASDAQ symbol*]   (NQ) .... HISI
Health Planning and Administration [*National Library of Medicine*]
   [*Database*] .... HEALTHLINE
Health and Safety Executive Online [*Health and Safety Executive*]
   [*Bibliographic database*] [*British*]   (OBD) .... HSELINE
Health Sciences Computing Facility [*UCLA*]   (CIT) .... HSCF
Heating and Ventilation Estimating [*Tipdata Ltd.*] [*Software
   package*] [*British*]   (NCC) .... HAVE
Heavy [*Used to qualify interference or static reports*]
   [*Telecommunications*]   (FAAC) .... VIO
Heavy Fuel Oils [*Database*] [*Department of Energy*]   (FDB) ..... HFO
Heavy Oil/Enhanced Recovery Index [*Alberta Oil Sands
   Information Centre*] [*Database*]   (CUAD) .... HERI
Hecto [*A prefix meaning multiplied by 10^2*] [*SI symbol*] .... h
HEI Corporation [*NASDAQ symbol*]   (NQ) .... HEIC
HEI, Incorporated [*NASDAQ symbol*]   (NQ) .... HEII
Height .... H
Height Above Average Terrain .... HAAT
Height-Position Indicator   (DEN) .... HPI
Heliax Coaxial Cable .... HCC
Helicopter Performance Computer   (NG) .... HPC
Hellenic Telecommunications Organization [*Greece*]   (TEL) .... OTE
Hemispherical Reflective Antenna .... HRA
Henry [*Symbol*] [*SI unit of inductance*] .... H
Hertz [*Symbol*] [*SI unit of frequency*] .... Hz
Hessische Bibliographie [*Hessian Bibliography*] [*Database*]
   [*Information retrieval*]   (ODIN) .... HEBIS-BIB
Hessische Landes- und Hochschulbibliothek [*Darmstadt*]
   [*Information retrieval*]   (ODIN) .... HLHB
Hessische Landesbibliographie - Versuchsversion [*Hessische
   Bibliographie*] [*Information retrieval*]   (ODIN) .... HLBV
Heterodyne Look-Thru [*Telecommunications*]   (TEL) .... HLT
Heterogeneous Element Processor [*Data processing*]   (RDA) ... HEP
Hetra Computer Commercial [*NASDAQ symbol*]   (NQ) .... HETC
Heuristic Concepts   (IEEE) .... HC
Heuristic Paper Trimming System   (BUR) .... HUPATS
Heuristic Path Algorithm   (CAA) .... HPA
Heuristically-Programed Algorithmic [*Name of computer in film,
   "2001: A Space Odyssey." Acronym is also considered to have
   been formed by combining the letters preceding IBM in the
   alphabet*] .... HAL
Hewlett-Packard Co.   (CIT) .... HP
Hewlett-Packard Co. [*NYSE symbol*] .... HWP
Hewlett-Packard Interface Bus [*Instrumentation*] .... HP-IB
Hexadecimal   (BUR) .... H
Hexadecimal [*System*] .... HEX
Hexadecimal-to-Binary [*Data processing*]   (IEEE) .... H-B
Hexadecimal to Binary   (CAA) .... HTB
Hexadecimal-to-Decimal [*Data processing*]   (IEEE) .... H-D
Hexagon .... HEX
HF [*High-Frequency*] Recovery Antenna   (SKY) .... HRA
Hi-G, Incorporated [*American Stock Exchange symbol*] [*Delisted*] ... HGI
Hierarchical Access Method   (CAA) .... HAM
Hierarchical Direct .... HD
Hierarchical Direct Access Method [*Data processing*]   (MCD) ... HDAM
Hierarchical Distributed Control [*Data processing*] .... HDC
Hierarchical Indexed Direct Access Method [*Data processing*]
   (BUR) .... HIDAM

Hierarchical Indexed Sequential Access Method [*Data processing*] (BUR) .... HISAM
Hierarchical Indexed Sequential Direct Access Method [*Data processing*] (CAA) .... HISDAM
Hierarchical Information Control System [*Japanese*] (CAA) .... HICS
Hierarchical Memory Storage [*Data processing*] .... HMS
Hierarchical Network Architecture (CAA) .... HNA
Hierarchical Sequential Access Method [*Data processing*] .... HSAM
Hierarchical Storage Manager .... HSM
Hierarchy plus Input-Process-Output [*Data processing*] .... HIPO
Hierarchy Service System [*Toshiba Corp.*] (CAA) .... HSS
High [*Data processing*] .... HI
High-Accuracy Data Transmission System (MUGU) .... HADTS
High-Altitude Transmitter .... HAT
High-Band Warning Antenna (MCD) .... HBWA
High-Band Warning Receiver (MCD) .... HBWR
High BIT [*Binary Digit*] **Rate** (KSC) .... HBR
High Byte Enable (CAA) .... HBEN
High-Capacity Communication System .... HICAPCOM
High-Capacity Mobile Telecommunications System (TEL) .... HCMTS
High-Definition Television [*Broadcasting term*] .... HDTV
High Density .... HD
High-Density Binary (TEL) .... HDB
High-Density Binary Three Level Signal (TEL) HDB3
High-Density Bipolar Code [*Telecommunications*] (TEL) .... HDB
High-Density Data System [*Data processing*] .... HDDS
High-Density Digital Recording .... HDDR
High-Density Flexible (CAA) .... HDF
High-Density/Low-Density Tariff .... HiD/LoD
High-Density Multitrack Recording (MCD) .... HDMR
High Electron Mobility Transistor [*Data processing*] .... HEMT
High-Fidelity Amplitude Modulation (DEN) .... HIFAM
High Frequency [*Electronics*] .... HF
High-Frequency Accelerometer (NASA) .... HFA
High-Frequency Airborne Antenna .... HFAA
High-Frequency Antenna System (KSC) .... HFAS
High-Frequency Correction .... HFC
High-Frequency Current .... HFC
High-Frequency Phase Shifter [*Telecommunications*] (OA) .... HFPS
High-Frequency Radio Transmitter .... HFRT
High-Frequency Recovery Antenna (KSC) .... HFA
High-Frequency Recovery Antenna (KSC) .... HFRA
High-Frequency Single Sideband [*Telecommunications*] .... HFSSB
High-Frequency Transceiver [*or Transducer*] .... HFX
High-Frequency Wave Analyzer .... HFWA
High Gain Antenna .... HGA
High Gain Antenna Controller (CIT) .... HGAC
High Gain Antenna System (IEEE) .... HGAS
High Gain Link .... HGL
High Incidence Target [*Crime computer*] .... HIT
High Information Delta Modulation [*Data processing*] (BUR) .... HIDM
High-Intensity Noise Generator .... HING
High-Level Arithmetic Function (CAA) .... HLAF
High-Level Automatic Scheduling Program (BUR) .... HASP
High-Level Data Link Control [*International Standards Organization*] [*Data communication*] .... HDLC
High-Level Language [*Data processing*] .... HLL
High-Level Microprograming Language (CAA) .... HLML
High-Level Programing Interface (CAA) .... HLPI
High-Level Query Language (CAA) .... HLQL
High-Level Representation (CAA) .... HLR
High-Level Transistor Logic .... HLTL
High-Level Transistor Translator Logic .... HLTTL
High-Noise-Immunity Logic .... HNIL
High Noise-Level Margin .... HNLM
High-Order Articulated Language [*Data processing*] (MCD) .... HAL
High-Order Assembly Language [*Data processing*] (NASA) .... HAL
High- [*or Higher-*] **Order Language** [*Data processing*] .... HOL
High- [*or Higher-*] **Order Language Working Group** [*Data processing*] (RDA) .... HOLWG
High-Order Software [*Data processing*] (NASA) .... HOS
High Pass [*Electronics*] .... HP
High Pass Filter .... HPF
High-Performance Communications Adapter (CAA) .... HPCA
High Position (MDG) .... H/P
High-Positive (MDG) .... HP
High-Power Amplifier .... HPA
High-Power Transistor-Transistor Logic (IEEE) .... HTTL
High Pressure Data Center [*National Bureau of Standards*] [*Information service*] (EISS) .... HPDC
High-Probability-of-Intercept Receiver [*Telecommunications*] (IEEE) .... HPIR
High Quality [*Home video systems*] .... HQ
High Resolution [*Data processing*] .... HI-RES
High-Resolution Facsimile [*Telecommunications*] (TEL) .... HRFAX
High-Resolution Hemispherical Reflector Antenna Technique .... HIHAT
High-Resolution Tracker .... HRT
High-Speed Analog Computer (DEN) .... HSAC
High-Speed Arithmetic Processing Unit Board (CAA) .... HAPUB
High-Speed Autoradiography .... HARG
High-Speed Buffer (CAA) .... HSB
High-Speed Bus [*Data processing*] .... HSB
High-Speed Card Punch [*Data processing*] .... HSCP
High-Speed Card Reader [*Data processing*] .... HSCR
High-Speed Card Teletypewriter Terminal [*Data processing*] (CET) .... HSCTT
High-Speed Compound Terminal [*Data processing*] (MCD) .... HSCT
High-Speed Concentrator (CAA) .... HSC
High-Speed Data Acquisition [*Data processing*] .... HSDA
High-Speed Data Buffer (CAA) .... HSDB
High-Speed Data Line (CIT) .... HSDL
High-Speed Displacement (IEEE) .... HSD
High-Speed Memory [*Data processing*] (TUT) .... HSM
High-Speed Metal-Oxide Semiconductor [*ROM*] (DEEC) .... HMOS
High-Speed Modular Interface Message Processor .... HSMIMP
High-Speed Nonimpact Printer [*Acronym pronounced "hisnip"*] [*Data processing*] .... HSNP
High-Speed Paper Tape Absolute Loader [*Data processing*] (MDG) .... HSPTAL
High-Speed Paper Tape Punch [*Data processing*] .... HSPTP
High-Speed Paper Tape Reader [*Data processing*] (CET) .... HSPTR
High-Speed Printer [*Data processing*] .... HSP
High-Speed Reader [*Data processing*] .... HSR
High-Speed Selector Channel (CAA) .... HSEL
High-Speed Storage [*Data processing*] (IEEE) .... HSS
High-Speed Transistor-Transistor Logic .... HSTTL
High Technology [*United States*] [*A publication*] .... High Technol
High Tension .... HT
High-Test Recorder and Simulator System (IEEE) .... HYTRESS
High Threshold Logic .... HTL
High-Usage [*Telecommunications*] .... Hi-U
High Usage [*Telecommunications*] (TEL) .... HU
High Voltage .... HV
High-Voltage Generator (OA) .... HVG
High-Voltage Integrated Circuit [*Data processing*] .... HVIC
High-Volume Time Sharing (CAA) .... HVTS
Higher Education Learning Programmes Information Service [*British Universities Film & Video Council*] [*Database*] (CUAD) .... HELPIS
Higher-Order Language Machine [*Data processing*] (KSC) .... HOLM
Highest Possible Frequency [*Electronics*] .... HPF
Highly Automated Logic [*Data processing*] (TUT) .... HAL
Highly Eccentric [*or Elliptical*] **Orbit Satellite** .... HEOS
Highly Extendable Language Processor [*Data processing*] (TUT) .... HELP
Highway .... HWY
Highway Engineering Exchange Program [*Users group*] .... HEEP
History of Medicine On-Line [*National Library of Medicine*] [*Bibliographic database*] (EISS) .... HISTLINE
History of Programing Languages .... HOPL
Hit Ratio (CAA) .... HR
Hitachi Arithmetic Processor [*Data processing*] (IEEE) .... HARP
Hitachi Computer (DIT) .... HITAC
Hitachi Network Architecture (CAA) .... HNA
Hitachi Parametron Automatic Computer .... HIPAC
HN Engineering, Inc. [*Burnaby, BC, Canada*] [*Telecommunications*] (TSSD) .... HNE
[*The*] **Hoberman-Castello Company** [*Reading, PA*] [*Software manufacturer*] (DASOS) .... HCC
Hogan Systems, Inc. [*NASDAQ symbol*] (NQ) .... HOGN
Hold Acknowledge [*Data processing*] .... HLDA
Holding Register (CAA) .... HR
Holding Time [*Telecommunications*] (TEL) .... HT
Hollerith Electronic Computer .... HEC
Home Address .... HA
Home Address Block (CAA) .... HAB
Home Address Register (CAA) .... HAR
Home Amateur [*Radio*] .... HAM
Home Area Toll [*Telecommunications*] (TEL) .... HAT
Home Box Office [*Cable-television system*] .... HBO
Home Entertainment Network [*Cable-television system*] .... HEN
Home Numbering Plan Area [*AT & T*] .... HNPA
Home Radio Beacon - High Power (FAAC) .... HH
Home Sports Entertainment [*Cable-television system*] .... HSE
Home Team Sports [*Cable-television system*] .... HTS
Home Theatre Network [*In network name "HTN Plus"*] [*Cable-television system*] .... HTN
Home User Groups [*Data processing*] .... HUG's
Home View Network [*Cable-television system*] .... HVN
Homing and Warning Computer (MCD) .... HAWC
Homogeneous Computer System .... HCS
Homogeneous Information Sets (CAA) .... HIS
Hon Industries, Inc. [*NASDAQ symbol*] (NQ) .... HONI
Honeywell Associative Parallel Processing Ensemble (CAA) .... HAPPE
Honeywell-Bull .... HB
Honeywell Business Computer .... HBC
Honeywell Equipment Lease Plan .... HELP
Honeywell Error Analysis and Logging System (CAA) .... HEALS
Honeywell File Access System (CAA) .... HFAS
Honeywell, Incorporated (NASA) .... HI
Honeywell, Inc. [*Formerly, MH, M-H*] [*NYSE symbol*] .... HON
Honeywell Information Systems, Inc. (IEEE) .... HIS
Honeywell Information Systems, Incorporated (CAA) .... HISI
Honeywell Institute for Information Science (IEEE) .... HIIS
Honeywell Large Systems Users Association .... HLSUA
Honeywell Time-Sharing System [*Data processing*] (IEEE) .... HTSS
Honeywell Users Group (CAA) .... HUG

Computer & Telecommunications Acronyms

Honeywell Users Group - Small and Medium Systems [Later, NAHU] .... HUG-SMS
Honeywell Verification Simulation Facility (NASA) .... HVSF
Honeywells Distributed Manufacturing [Honeywell Information Systems Ltd.] [Software package] [British] (NCC) .... HDMS
Honeywells Manufacturing System [Honeywell Information Systems Ltd.] [Software package] [British] (NCC) .... HMS
Horizontal .... H
Horizontal .... HOR
Horizontal Arithmetic Unit (CAA) .... HAU
Horizontal Data Processing .... HDP
Horizontal Distributing Frame .... HDF
Horizontal Motion Index [Printer technology] .... HMI
Horizontal Polarization .... HORIZ
Horizontal Side of an Intermediate Distribution Frame [Telecommunications] (TEL) .... HIDF
Horizontal Side of Main Distribution Frame (TEL) .... HMDF
Horizontal Tabulation [Data processing] .... HT
Horsepower .... HP
Hospital Computer Sharing System (IEEE) .... HCSS
Hospital Data Center [American Hospital Association] [Information service] (EISS) .... HDC
Hospital Information System [Data processing] .... HIS
Hospital Information Systems Sharing Group [Reston, VA] (EANO) .... HISSG
Hospital Operating System - Structured Programing Language [Data processing] (CSR) .... HOS-STPL
Hospital Satellite Network [Los Angeles, CA] [Cable-television system] .... HSN
Host Command Facility (CAA) .... HCF
Host Communications Processor (CAA) .... HCP
Host Computer (CAA) .... HC
Host Computer Interface (CAA) .... HCI
Host Language (CAA) .... HL
Host Language Interface (CAA) .... HLI
Host to Network [Data processing] .... HN
Host Processor (CAA) .... HP
Host Remote Node Entry System (CAA) .... HRNES
Host Resident Software (OA) .... HRS
Host Resident Software System (CAA) .... HRSS
Host-to-Satellite (CAA) .... HTS
Hot-Carrier Diode (IEEE) .... HCD
Hot Line [Alert system] .... HL
Hotel (TEL) .... HO
Hotel Billing Information System [Telecommunications] (TEL) .... HOBIS
Hotel Call, Time, and Charges Mandatory [Telecommunications] (TEL) .... HTL
Hour [Also, h] .... H
Hour .... HR
Hour Angle-Declination [Type of antenna mounting] (CIT) .... HA-DEC
Hourly Noise Level .... HNL
House Cable [Telecommunications] (TEL) .... HC
House Information Systems [US House of Representatives] .... HIS
House Logic Unit (OA) .... HLU
House Operating Tape [Telecommunications] (TEL) .... HOP
House of Representatives Information System (CAA) .... HRIS
Households Using Television [Television ratings] .... HUT
Housekeeping Data Acquisition (MCD) .... HDA
Housekeeping Element (TEL) .... HE
Houston Area League of PC [Personal Computer] Users .... HAL-PC
Houston Automatic Priority Spooling [Data processing] .... HAPS
Houston Automatic Spooling Priority System (CAH) .... HASP
Houston International Teleport [Houston, TX] [Telecommunications] (TSSD) .... HIT
Howler [Communications; electronics] .... HW
Hughes Communications International [Hughes Aircraft Co.] .... HCI
Hughes Satellite Communications Terminal .... HSCT
Hughes Television Network [New York, NY] [Cable-television system] .... HTN
Human-Aided Machine Translation (DEEC) .... HAMT
Human-Interface Equipment Catalog Item (TEL) .... HECI
Human Materials Resources Information System (DIT) .... HUMARIS
Human Read/Machine Read [Microfilm memory system] .... HRMR
Hybrid (MSA) .... HYB
Hybrid Analog Logic Language (MCD) .... HYBALL
Hybrid Arithmetic Unit (CAA) .... HAU
Hybrid Assigned Nematic/Liquid Crystal Display (TEL) .... HAN/LCD
Hybrid Computer [for processing both analog and digital data] (NASA) .... HC
Hybrid Computer Link .... HYCOL
Hybrid Computer Translator .... HYCOTRAN
Hybrid Data Acquisition System (CAA) .... HDAS
Hybrid Development System (CAA) .... HDS
Hybrid Digital-Analog Computing [System] [Satellite] .... HYDAC
Hybrid Digital-Analog and Pulse Time .... HYDAPT
Hybrid Electromagnetic Antenna Coupler .... HEMAC
Hybrid Integrated Circuit .... HIC
Hybrid Integrated Network [Bell System] [Telecommunications] .... HIN
Hybrid Modular Redundancy (CAA) .... HMR
Hybrid Operating Program [Data processing] (IEEE) .... HOP
Hybrid Programming Language [Data processing] .... HPL
Hybrid Technology Computer (CAA) .... HTC
Hydrofoil Analysis and Design [Data processing] .... HANDE
Hydrographic Data Acquisition System .... HDAS

Hydrological Operational Multipurpose Subprogramme [World Meteorological Organization] [Information service] (EISS) .... HOMS
Hyper-High-Frequency (DEN) .... HHF
Hypothetical Reference Circuit [Telecommunications] (TEL) .... HRC
I Buy Money [Humorous translation of the letters in IBM Corp., and referring to the appeal of investing in its stocks] .... IBM
IAL Consultancy Services [Southall, England] [Telecommunications] (TSSD) .... IACS
IBM [International Business Machines Corp.] Journal of Research and Development [A publication] .... IBM J
IBM [International Business Machines Corp.] Journal of Research and Development [A publication] .... IBM J R D
IBM [International Business Machines Corp.] Journal of Research and Development [A publication] .... IBM J Res
IBM [International Business Machines Corp.] Journal of Research and Development [A publication] .... IBM J Res Dev
IBM [International Business Machines Corp.] Journal of Research and Development [A publication] .... IBM J Res and Dev
IBM [International Business Machines Corp.] Journal of Research and Development [A publication] .... IBM J Res Develop
IBM Recruitment Information System .... IRIS
IBM [International Business Machines Corp.] System User [A publication] .... IBM User
IBM [International Business Machines Corp.] Systems Journal [A publication] .... IBM Systems J
IBM [International Business Machines Corp.] Systems Journal [A publication] .... IBM Syst J
IBM [International Business Machines Corp.] Systems Journal [A publication] .... ISY
IBM [International Business Machines Corp.] Technical Disclosure Bulletin [A publication] .... IBM Tech Discl Bull
IBM [International Business Machines Corp.] Technical Disclosure Bulletin [A publication] .... IBM Tech Disclosure Bull
IBM Technical Information Retrieval Center .... ITIRC
ICAM [Integrated Computer-Aided Manufacturing] Decision Support System (IEEE) .... IDSS
Iceland-Canada Submarine Cable System [Telecommunications] (TEL) .... ICECAN
ICES [Integrated Civil Engineering System] Users Group [Cranston, RI] (EANO) .... IUG
ICL [International Computers Limited] Technical Journal [A publication] .... ICL Tech J
ICOT Corp. [NASDAQ symbol] (NQ) .... ICOT
ICP [International Computer Programs, Inc.] Interface Administrative and Accounting [A publication] .... ICP Admin
ICP [International Computer Programs, Inc.] Interface Banking Industry [A publication] .... ICP Bank Indus
ICP [International Computer Programs, Inc.] Interface Data Processing Management [A publication] .... ICP DP Mgmt
Ideal Current Negative Immittance Converter .... INIC
Ideas, Resources, Exchange [Computer] [British] .... IREX
Ideassociates, Inc. [Billerica, MA] [Telecommunications] (TSSD) .... IDEA
Identification [Data processing] .... ID
Identification (AFM) .... IDENT
Identification Code (CAA) IC
Identification Record [Data processing] (MCD) .... IDR
Identified Outward Dialing [Telecommunications] (TEL) .... IOD
Identifier [Online database field identifier] .... ID
Identifier Block (CAA) .... IB
Idle (BUR) IL
IDP [Information and Data Base Publishing] Report [United States] [A publication] .... IDP Rep
IEE [Institution of Electrical Engineers] Journal on Computers and Digital Techniques [A publication] .... IEE J Comput Digital Tech
IEE [Institution of Electrical Engineers] Journal on Computers and Digital Techniques [A publication] .... IEE J Comput and Digital Tech
IEE [Institution of Electrical Engineers] Proceedings. Part E. Computers and Digital Techniques [A publication] .... IEE Proc E
IEE [Institution of Electrical Engineers] Proceedings. Part E. Computers and Digital Techniques [England] [A publication] .... IEE Proc Part E
IEEE. Communications Magazine [A publication] .... IEEE Commun Mag
IEEE. Communications Society Magazine [A publication] .... IEEE Commun Soc Mag
IEEE. Computer Graphics and Applications [A publication] .... ICGAD
IEEE. Computer Graphics and Applications [A publication] .... IEEE Comput Graphics and Appl
IEEE. Computer Group News [A publication] .... IEEE Comput Group News
IEEE. Journal of Quantum Electronics [A publication] .... IEEE J Q El
IEEE. Journal of Quantum Electronics [A publication] .... IEEE J Quantum Electron
IEEE. Journal on Selected Areas in Communications [A publication] .... IEEE J Sel Areas Commun
IEEE. Journal of Solid-State Circuits [A publication] .... IEEE J Soli
IEEE. Journal of Solid-State Circuits [A publication] .... IEEE J Solid-State Circuits
IEEE. Spectrum [A publication] .... IEEE S
IEEE. Spectrum [A publication] .... IEEE Spectr
IEEE. Spectrum [A publication] .... IEEE Spectrum
IEEE. Spectrum [A publication] .... SPC
IEEE. Transactions on Acoustics, Speech, and Signal Processing [A publication] .... IEEE Acoust

IEEE. Transactions on Acoustics, Speech, and Signal Processing [*A publication*] ... IEEE Trans Acoust Speech Signal Process
IEEE. Transactions on Acoustics, Speech, and Signal Processing [*A publication*] ... IEEE Trans ASSP
IEEE. Transactions on Acoustics, Speech, and Signal Processing [*A publication*] ... IETAB
IEEE. Transactions on Antennas and Propagation [*A publication*] ... IEEE Antenn
IEEE. Transactions on Antennas and Propagation [*A publication*] ... IEEE Trans Antennas Propag
IEEE. Transactions on Antennas and Propagation [*A publication*] ... IEEE Trans Antennas Propagat
IEEE. Transactions on Antennas and Propagation [*A publication*] ... IEEE Trans Antennas and Propagation
IEEE. Transactions on Circuits and Systems [*A publication*] ... IEEE Circ S
IEEE. Transactions on Circuits and Systems [*A publication*] ... IEEE Trans CAS
IEEE. Transactions on Circuits and Systems [*A publication*] ... IEEE Trans Circuits & Syst
IEEE. Transactions on Circuits and Systems [*A publication*] ... IEEE Trans Circuits and Syst
IEEE. Transactions on Circuits and Systems [*A publication*] ... IEEE Trans Circuits and Systems
IEEE. Transactions on Communication and Electronics [*A publication*] ... IEEE Trans Commun Electron
IEEE. Transactions on Communication Technology [*Later, IEEE Transactions on Communications*] [*A publication*] ... IEEE Trans Commun Technol
IEEE. Transactions on Communication Technology [*Later, IEEE Transactions on Communications*] [*A publication*] ... IEEE Trans Com Tech
IEEE. Transactions on Communications [*A publication*] ... IECMB
IEEE. Transactions on Communications [*A publication*] ... IEEE Commun
IEEE. Transactions on Communications [*A publication*] ... IEEE Trans Com
IEEE. Transactions on Communications [*A publication*] ... IEEE Trans Comm
IEEE. Transactions on Communications Systems [*A publication*] ... IEEE Trans Commun Syst
IEEE. Transactions on Components, Hybrids, and Manufacturing Technology [*A publication*] ... IEEE Trans Components Hybrids Manuf Technol
IEEE. Transactions on Components, Hybrids, and Manufacturing Technology [*A publication*] ... IEEE Trans Components Hybrids and Manuf Technol
IEEE. Transactions on Computers [*A publication*] ... IEEE Comput
IEEE. Transactions on Computers [*A publication*] ... IEEE Trans
IEEE. Transactions on Computers [*A publication*] ... IEEE Trans Comput
IEEE. Transactions on Computers [*A publication*] ... IEEE Trans Computers
IEEE. Transactions on Electromagnetic Compatibility [*A publication*] ... IEEE Elmagn
IEEE. Transactions on Electromagnetic Compatibility [*A publication*] ... IEEE Trans Electromagn Compat
IEEE. Transactions on Electron Devices [*A publication*] ... IEEE Device
IEEE. Transactions on Electron Devices [*A publication*] ... IEEE T El Dev
IEEE. Transactions on Electron Devices [*A publication*] ... IEEE Trans Electron Devices
IEEE. Transactions on Electronic Computers [*United States*] [*A publication*] ... IEEE Trans Electron Comput
IEEE. Transactions on Information Theory [*A publication*] ... IEEE Info T
IEEE. Transactions on Information Theory [*A publication*] ... IEEE Trans Information Theory
IEEE. Transactions on Information Theory [*A publication*] ... IEEE Trans Inf Theory
IEEE. Transactions on Instrumentation and Measurement [*A publication*] ... IEEE Instr
IEEE. Transactions on Instrumentation and Measurement [*A publication*] ... IEEE Trans Instrum Meas
IEEE. Transactions on Instrumentation and Measurement [*A publication*] ... IEEE Trans Instrum and Meas
IEEE. Transactions on Magnetics [*A publication*] ... IEEE Magnet
IEEE. Transactions on Magnetics [*A publication*] ... IEEE Trans Magn
IEEE. Transactions on Microwave Theory and Techniques [*A publication*] ... IEEE Micr T
IEEE. Transactions on Microwave Theory and Techniques [*A publication*] ... IEEE Trans Microwave Theory Tech
IEEE. Transactions on Microwave Theory and Techniques [*A publication*] ... IEEE Trans Microwave Theory and Tech
IEEE. Transactions on Professional Communications [*A publication*] ... IEEE Prof C
IEEE. Transactions on Professional Communications [*A publication*] ... IEEE Trans Prof Commun
IEEE. Transactions on Reliability [*A publication*] ... IEEE Reliab
IEEE. Transactions on Reliability [*A publication*] ... IEEE Trans Rel
IEEE. Transactions on Reliability [*A publication*] ... IEEE Trans Reliab
IEEE. Transactions on Software Engineering [*A publication*] ... IEEE Trans SE
IEEE. Transactions on Software Engineering [*A publication*] ... IEEE Trans Software Eng
IEEE. Transactions on Software Engineering [*A publication*] ... IEEE Trans Software Engrg
IEEE. Transactions on Software Engineering [*A publication*] ... Soft Eng
IEEE. Transactions on Systems, Man, and Cybernetics [*A publication*] ... IEEE Syst M
IEEE. Transactions on Systems, Man, and Cybernetics [*A publication*] ... IEEE Trans Syst Man Cybern
IEEE. Transactions on Systems, Man, and Cybernetics [*A publication*] ... IEEE Trans Syst Man and Cybern
IIT Research Institute [*Illinois Institute of Technology*] [*Research center*] (RCD) ... IITRI
ILA [*Instruction Look Ahead*] **Associative Memory** [*Data processing*] ... IAM
ILA [*Instruction Look Ahead*] **Interrupt Address** [*Data processing*] ... IIA
Illinois Institute for Advanced Computing ... ILLIAC
Illinois Integrator and Automatic Computer [*University of Illinois*] (BUR) ... ILLIAC
Illuminating Engineering Society ... IES
Image ... IMG
Image Analysing Computers, Inc. ... IMANCO
Image Array Processor (CAA) ... IAP
Image Data Processing System ... IDAPS
Image Data Processor ... IDP
Image Description File (CAA) ... IDF
Image Digitizer [*Data processing*] ... ID
Image Display System ... IDS
Image Dissector Camera ... IDC
Image Dissector Camera System ... IDCS
Image Input to Automatic Computers ... IMITAC
Image Processing Center [*Drexel University*] [*Research center*] (RCD) ... IPC
Image Processing Laboratory [*University of Houston*] [*Research center*] (RCD) ... IPL
Image Processing Program [*Computer program*] (CIT) ... IMP
Image Processing System (MCD) ... IPS
Image Resources, Incorporated [*Winter Park, FL*] [*Telecommunications*] (TSSD) ... IRI
Image Storage Retrieval (OA) ... ISR
Image Storage Translation and Reproduction ... ISTAR
Image Store Management System (CAA) ... ISMS
Image Store Processor [*Data processing*] ... ISP
Imagerie, Industrie, Systeme [*Machine vision manufacturer*] [*Bordeaux, France*] ... I2S
IMBLMS [*Integrated Medical Behavioral Measurement System*] **Digital Computer** (MCD) ... IDC
Imbricated Program for Information Transfer [*Data processing*] ... IMPRINT
IMC [*International Information Management Congress*] **Journal** [*A publication*] ... IMC Jrnl
Imero Fiorentino Associates, Inc. [*New York, NY*] [*Telecommunications*] (TSSD) ... IFA
Immediate (DDI) ... IMM
Immediate Constituent Analyzer [*Data processing*] (DIT) ... ICA
Impact Ionization Avalanche Transit Time [*Solid state diodes*] [*Transistor technology*] ... IMPATT
Impact Printer [*Data processing*] (CAA) ... IP
Impedance [*Symbol*] [*IUPAC*] ... Z
Implementation/Installation Plan [*Telecommunications*] (TEL) ... IIP
Implementation Language [*Edinburgh multiaccess system*] (CSR) ... IMP
Implementation Planning and Control Technique [*Data processing*] ... IMPACT
Impregnated (TEL) ... IMPREG
Imprint [*Online database field identifier*] (OBD) ... IMPR
Improved Data Display System ... IDDS
Improved Data Interchange ... IDI
Improved Emergency Message Automatic Transmission System (MCD) ... IEMATS
Improved Mobile Telephone Service ... IMTS
Improved Processing System ... IPS
Improved Programer Test Station (IEEE) ... IMPTS
Improved Programing Technologies (BUR) ... IPT
Improved TIROS [*Television Infrared Observation Satellite*] **Operational Satellite** [*National Oceanic and Atmospheric Administration*] ... ITOS
Impulse Bandwidth (MCD) ... IBW
Impulse Noise ... IPN
Impulse Transfer Function (KSC) ... ITF
Impulses per Minute [*Telecommunications*] ... IPM
Impulses per Second [*Telecommunications*] (TEL) ... IPS
IMS International [*NASDAQ symbol*] (NQ) ... IMSI
In-Circuit Emulator ... ICE
In-Line Integrated Circuit ... ILIC
In-Line Printer ... ILP
In and Out Processing [*Data processing*] (AFM) ... I & OP
In-Process Self Test (MCD) ... IPST
In Pulse to Register [*Telecommunications*] (TEL) ... IPR
In Pulse to Sender [*Telecommunications*] (TEL) ... IPS
In Service [*Telecommunications*] (TEL) ... IS
Inch ... IN
Inches per Hour [*Telecommunications*] (TEL) ... IPH
Inches per Minute ... IPM
Inches per Second ... IPS
Inclusive ... INCL
Incoming [*Telecommunications*] (TEL) ... I/C
Incoming [*Telecommunications*] (KSC) ... INC
Incoming Call Barred [*Telecommunications*] (TEL) ... ICB
Incoming Echo Suppressor [*Telecommunications*] (TEL) ... IES
Incoming Junction [*Telecommunications*] (TEL) ... ICJ
Incoming Matching Loss [*Telecommunications*] (TEL) ... IML
Incoming [*Message*] **Process** [*Telecommunications*] (TEL) ... ICP
Incoming Teletype ... ITT

Computer & Telecommunications Acronyms

Incoming Trunk [*Telecommunications*] (BUR) ... ICT
Incoming Trunk [*Telecommunications*] (TEL) ... INC
Incomplete Translation [*Telecommunications*] (TEL) ... IT
INCOTERM [*International Commerce Term*] **Transaction Entry Management System** (CAA) ... ITEMS
Increased Readiness Information System ... IRIS
Increment ... INC
Increment (AFM) ... INCR
Increment Memory Unit (CAA) ... IMU
Increment and Skip on Zero [*Data processing*] ... ISZ
Incremental Digital Recorder ... IDR
Incremental System Programing Language [*Data processing*] ... ISPL
Incunable Short Title Catalogue [*British Library*] [*Information service*] (EISS) ... ISTC
Indefeasible Right of User [*Telecommunications*] (TEL) ... IRU
Indefinite Admittance Matrix [*Network analysis*] (IEEE) ... IAM
Independent Broadcasting Authority [*Formerly, ITA*] [*British*] ... IBA
Independent Business Systems, Inc. [*Livermore, CA*] [*Hardware manufacturer*] (DASO) ... IBS
Independent Component Release [*Data processing*] (IBMDP) ... ICR
Independent Computer Consultants Association [*Database producer*] (EANO) ... ICCA
Independent Data Communications Manufacturers Association ... IDCMA
Independent Investors Forum [*Penn Yan, NY*] [*Information service*] (EISS) ... IIF
Independent Network News [*Television*] ... INN
Independent Research and Development ... IR & D
Independent Sideband ... ISB
Independent Signal Unit [*Telecommunications*] (TEL) ... ISU
Independent Software Vendor [*Data processing*] ... ISV
Independent Telecommunications Analysts [*Boulder, CO*] (TSSD) ... ITA
Independent Telephone Pioneer Association ... ITPA
Independent Television ... ITV
Independent Television Authority [*Later, IBA*] [*British*] ... ITA
Independent Validation and Verification (CAAL) ... IV & V
Index [*Data processing*] (BUR) ... IX
Index for Design Engineering Applications [*Data retrieval service*] [*Product engineering*] ... IDEA
Index Preparation System [*Foxon-Maddocks Associates*] [*Information service*] (EISS) ... IPS
Index Register (NITA) ... XR
Index to Religious Periodical Literature [*Database*] ... IRPL
Index to Scientific and Technical Proceedings and Books [*Institute for Scientific Information*] ... ISTP & B
Index Term [*Data processing*] ... IT
Index Word [*Online database field identifier*] (OA) ... IW
Indexed Direct Access Method (CAA) ... IDAM
Indexed References to Biomedical Engineering Literature [*A publication*] (EISS) ... IRBEL
Indexed Sequential [*Data processing*] (DEEC) ... IS
Indexed Sequential Access Method [*Pronounced "i-sam"*] [*Data processing*] (CIT) ... ISAM
Indexed Sequential File Management System [*Data processing*] (BUR) ... ISFMS
Indexed Sequential File Manager [*Data processing*] (CAA) ... ISFM
Indexed Sequential Processor (CAA) ... ISP
Indexed Sequential Table Retrieval (CAA) ... ISTR
Indian National Oceanographic Data Centre [*Information service*] (EISS) ... INODC
Indian National Satellite System [*Bangalore, India*] [*Telecommunications*] ... INSAT
Indian Remote-Sensing Satellite ... IRS
Indiana Higher Education Telecommunication System [*Indianapolis*] [*Telecommunications*] (TSSD) ... IHETS
Indianapolis Center for Advanced Research [*Indiana University - Purdue University at Indianapolis*] [*Research center*] (RCD) ... ICFAR
Indicate [*or Indicator*] (KSC) ... IND
Indicating Device (CDH) ... ID
Indirect Control Register [*Data processing*] (CAA) ... ICR
Indirect Reference Word (BUR) ... IRW
Indirect Tag Memory (CAA) ... ITM
Individual Case Basis (TEL) ... ICB
Individual Circuit Analysis [*Telecommunications*] (TEL) ... ICAN
Individual Circuit Usage and Peg Count [*Telecommunications*] (TEL) ... ICUP
Individual Field of View ... IFOV
Individual Load Operation (CAA) ... ILO
Individual Store and Forward (CAA) ... ISF
Indonesian satellite ... PALAPA
Inductance [*Symbol*] ... L
Inductance/Capacitance ... L/C
Induction (MSA) ... IND
Induction Communications System ... ICS
Induction Loop Communications System ... ILCS
Inductive Data Exploration and Analysis [*Data processing*] ... IDEA
Inductive Potentiometer (MDG) ... IPOT
Inductive Recording Head ... IRH
Industrial Aerodynamics Information Service [*British*] (EISS) ... IAIS
Industrial Control System ... ICS
Industrial Data Bank Department [*Gulf Organization for Industrial Consulting*] [*Information service*] (EISS) ... IDB
Industrial Data Processing ... IDP

Industrial Documentation and Information Department [*Industrial Development Center for Arab States*] [*Information service*] (EISS) ... IDID
Industrial Electronics and Control Instrumentation (MCD) ... IECI
Industrial Information's Record Management System [*Data processing*] (TUT) ... IIRMS
Industrial Process Control [*by computers*] ... IPC
Industrial Relations Research Institute [*University of Wisconsin - Madison*] [*Research center*] (RCD) ... IRRI
Industrial Research Institute [*Canada*] [*Research center*] (RCD) ... IRI
Industrial Robot [*A publication*] ... Ind Robot
Industrial Technical Information Service [*Singapore*] (EISS) ... ITIS
Industrial and Technological Information Bank [*UNIDO*] (EISS) ... INTIB
Industrial Technology Institute [*Ann Arbor, MI*] [*Research center*] (RCD) ... ITI
Industrial Television ... ITV
Industrial Transistor Value Automatic Computer ... ITVAC
Industrievereinigung fuer Lebensmitteltechnologie und Verpackung [*Information retrieval*] (ODIN) ... IVLV
Industry Advisory Conference [*Underwriters Laboratories*] [*Telecommunications*] ... IAC
Industry Advisory Group [*Underwriters Laboratories*] [*Telecommunications*] ... IAG
Industry Application Program [*Data processing*] (IBMDP) ... IAP
Industry Media Publishing System [*Omni Industry Corp.*] [*Information service*] (EISS) ... IMPS
Industry Telephone Maintenance [*FCC*] (IEEE) ... IT
Inertial Navigation Computer (MCD) ... INC
Inertialess Steerable Communications Antenna ... ISCAN
Infodata Systems, Incorporated [*Information service*] (EISS) ... ISI
Informatics General Corp. [*NYSE symbol*] ... IG
Informatik-Spektrum [*A publication*] ... Inf-Spektrum
Information [*Data processing*] (MDG) ... IFN
Information [*Data processing*] ... INF
Information [*Data processing*] (AFM) ... INFO
Information Access Corporation [*Information service*] (EISS) ... IAC
Information Age [*A publication*] ... Info Age
Information Associates of Ithaca [*Information service*] (EISS) ... IAI
[*The*] Information Bank [*Computer Sciences of Australia Pty. Ltd.*] [*Database*] ... INFOBANK
Information Bureau [*Telecommunications*] (TEL) ... IB
Information Centers Service [*United States Information Agency*] (EISS) ... ICS
Information Concepts, Incorporated ... ICI
Information Consultants, Incorporated [*Information service*] (EISS) ... ICI
Information Content Natural Unit [*Information theory*] ... NAT
Information and Control [*A publication*] ... IFCNA
Information and Control [*A publication*] ... Inf C
Information and Control [*A publication*] ... Inf Contr
Information and Control [*A publication*] ... Inf Control
Information and Control [*A publication*] ... Inf and Control
Information and Control [*A publication*] ... Inform Contr
Information Data Handling System (DDI) ... IDHS
Information Data Processing (VIT) ... IDP
Information Data Search, Inc. [*Information service*] (EISS) ... IDS
Information on Demand [*Information service*] (EISS) ... IOD
Information Description Language (CAA) ... IDL
Information Display [*A publication*] ... Inf Disp
Information Display [*A publication*] ... Inf Display
Information Display System (CAA) ... IDS
Information Displays [*NASDAQ symbol*] (NQ) ... IDPY
Information Displays Automatic Drafting System (IEEE) ... IDAS
Information Displays, Incorporated, Input-Output Machine ... IDIIOM
Information/Documentation [*Information service*] (EISS) ... INFO/DOC
Information und Dokumentation [*Information and Documentation*] [*German*] [*Information retrieval*] (ODIN) ... IUD
Information Dynamics Corporation ... IDC
Information Gained per Unit Cost [*Data processing*] ... IGUC
Information Gatekeepers, Incorporated [*Boston, MA*] [*Telecommunications*] [*Information service*] (EISS) ... IGI
Information General, Incorporated [*Needham, MA*] [*Information service*] (EISS) ... IGI
Information Group Separator (CAA) ... IGS
Information Grouping Logic [*Data processing*] ... IGL
Information Handling Project (DIT) ... IHP
Information Hotline [*A publication*] ... IH
Information Hotline [*United States*] [*A publication*] ... Inf Hotline
Information Industry Association [*Washington, DC*] [*Affiliated with AIM*] [*Database producer*] ... IIA
Information Industry Bulletin [*Digital Information Group*] [*Information service*] (EISS) ... IIB
Information Intelligence, Incorporated [*Information service*] (EISS) ... III
Information Intelligence Online Newsletter [*A publication*] ... Inf Intell Online Newsl
Information International, Incorporated [*Phoenix, AZ*] [*Information broker*] ... III
Information International, Inc. [*NASDAQ symbol*] (NQ) ... IINT
Information & Library Services [*Information service*] (EISS) ... ILS
Information Logic Machine (IEEE) ... ILM
Information Management and Processing Association [*Lansing, MI*] (EANO) ... IMPA
Information Management, Retrieval, and Dissemination System (DIT) ... IMRADS
Information Management Specialists [*Information service*] (EISS) ... IMS

Information Management System [*IBM Corp.*] [*Data processing*] (CGC) ... IMS
Information Management System Interface (CAA) ... IMSI
Information Manipulation Language (CAA) ... IML
Information Marketing Achievement Award [*Information Industry Association*] ... IMMY
Information Network [*British*] [*Telecommunications*] (TEL) ... INFONET
Information Network and File Organization [*Data processing*] (BUR) ... INFO
Information Network for Freight Overhead Billing, Rating, and Message Switching ... INFORM
Information Network for Operations [*Data processing*] ... INFO
Information Network System [*Japanese*] ... INS
Information Oriented Language [*Information retrieval*] ... INFOL
Information Process Analysis (BUR) ... IPA
Information Processing (BUR) ... IP
Information Processing Association [*Israel*] (CAH) ... IPA
Information Processing Code (DIT) ... IPC
Information Processing Language [*Data processing*] ... IPL
Information Processing Language Five (CAH) ... IPLV
Information Processing and Management [*A publication*] ... Inf Pr Man
Information Processing and Management [*A publication*] ... Inf Processing & Mgt
Information Processing and Management [*A publication*] ... Inf Process Manage
Information Processing and Management [*A publication*] ... Inf Process and Manage
Information Processing and Management [*A publication*] ... Inf Proc Man
Information Processing and Management [*A publication*] ... ISR
Information Processing Society of Canada (CAH) ... IPSOC
Information Processing Society of Japan [*Information service*] (EISS) ... IPSJ
Information Processing Standards for Computers ... IPSC
Information Processing System ... IPS
Information Processing Systems Standards Board [*Later, Board of Standards Review of ANSI*] [*American Standards Association*] ... IPSSB
Information Processing Techniques Corp. [*Palo Alto, CA*] [*Software manufacturer*] (DASOS) ... IPT
Information Products Systems, Inc. [*Houston, TX*] [*Hardware manufacturer*] (DASO) ... IPS
Information and Records Management ... IRM
Information Recovery [*or Retrieval*] **System** [*or Subsystem*] ... IRS
Information Referral System for Technical Cooperation among Developing Countries [*United Nations*] [*Information service*] (EISS) ... INRES/TCDC
Information Relayed Instantly from the Source [*Project*] ... IRIS
Information Requirements of the Social Sciences [*British*] (DIT) ... INFROSS
Information Research Center (DIT) ... IRC
Information Researchers, Incorporated [*Information service*] (EISS) ... IRI
Information Resource Administration (CAA) ... IRA
Information Resource Management [*Data processing*] ... IRM
Information Resources [*NASDAQ symbol*] (NQ) ... IRIC
Information Resources Information System [*Library of Congress*] ... IRIS
Information Resources Specialists [*San Francisco, CA*] [*Information service*] (EISS) ... IRS
Information Retrieval [*Data processing*] ... IR
Information Retrieval Automatic Language [*Data processing*] ... INFRAL
Information Retrieval Center [*BBDO International*] [*Information service*] (EISS) ... IRC
Information Retrieval Center on the Disadvantaged [*ERIC*] ... IRCD
Information Retrieval Databank (IEEE) ... IRDB
Information Retrieval and Display Language [*Data processing*] ... IRDL
Information Retrieval Language [*Data processing*] ... IRL
Information Retrieval Limited [*Database originator*] [*British*] [*Information service*] ... IRL
Information Retrieval Service [*European Space Agency*] [*Host*] (EISS) ... IRS
Information Retrieval Technique ... IRT
Information Returns Processing [*Data processing*] ... IRP
Information Science (IEEE) ... IS
Information Science and Automation Division [*Later, LITA*] [*American Library Association*] ... ISAD
Information Science, Inc. [*Information service*] (EISS) ... InSci
Information Science and Technology (BUR) ... IST
Information Search Language ... ISL
Information Separator [*Control character*] [*Data processing*] ... IS
Information Service ... IS
Information Service Computer System (DIT) ... ISCS
Information Service in Mechanical Engineering [*Cambridge Scientific Abstracts*] [*IEE*] [*British*] [*Bibliographic database*] (EISS) ... ISMEC
Information Service on Toxicity and Biodegradability [*Water Pollution Research Laboratory*] [*British*] (EISS) ... INSTAB
Information Services to Education [*American Society for Information Science*] ... ISE
Information Solutions [*NASDAQ symbol*] (NQ) ... ISOL
Information Sort and Predict ... ISAP
Information Sources [*Virginia Beach, VA*] [*Information service*] (EISS) ... INFOSOR
Information Storage, Incorporated ... ISI
Information Storage and Retrieval [*A publication*] ... IFSRA
Information Storage and Retrieval [*A publication*] ... Inf Storage
Information Storage and Retrieval [*A publication*] ... Inf Storage & Retr
Information Storage and Retrieval [*A publication*] ... Inf Storage Retr
Information Storage and Retrieval [*A publication*] ... Inf Stor Retr
Information Storage and Retrieval [*Data processing*] (DIT) ... ISAR
Information Storage and Retrieval [*Data processing*] ... IS & R
Information Storage and Retrieval [*Data processing*] ... ISR
Information Storage and Retrieval System [*Data processing*] ... INSTARS
Information Storage, Selection, and Retrieval [*Data processing*] ... ISSR
Information Storage System (IEEE) ... ISS
Information Structure Design (CAA) ... ISD
Information System (CAA) ... IS
Information System Access Lines [*Data processing*] (TUT) ... ISAL
Information System Base Language (CAA) ... ISBL
Information System Development [*Telecommunications*] (TEL) ... ISD
Information System Indexing System [*Federal Judicial Center*] [*Database*] (FDB) ... ISIS
Information System Karlsruhe - Conference [*Database*] (ODIN) ... INKA-CONF
Information System Karlsruhe - Corporates in Energy [*Database*] (ODIN) ... INKA-CORP
Information System Karlsruhe - Data Compilations in Energy and Physics [*Database*] (ODIN) ... INKA-DATACOMP
Information System Karlsruhe - Mathematical Education [*Database*] (ODIN) ... INKA-MATHDI
Information System Karlsruhe - Mathematics [*Database*] (ODIN) ... INKA-MATH
Information System Karlsruhe - Nuclear Database Part: Conference Papers: Nuclear Research, Nuclear Technology [*Database*] (ODIN) ... INKA-NUCLEAR PART KKK
Information System Karlsruhe - Nuclear Database Part: International Nuclear Information System [*Database*] (ODIN) ... INKA-NUCLEAR PART INIS
Information System Karlsruhe - Nuclear Database Part: Nuclear Science Abstracts [*Database*] (ODIN) ... INKA-NUCLEAR PART NSA
Information System Karlsruhe - Physics [*Database*] (ODIN) ... INKA-PHYS
Information System Language [*Data processing*] (IEEE) ... ISL
Information System Manager (NATG) ... ISM
Information System Plan (MCD) ... ISP
Information System Software Update Environment (CAA) ... ISSUE
Information Systems [*A publication*] ... Information Syst
Information Systems [*Elmsford, NY*] [*A publication*] ... Info Systems
Information Systems [*A publication*] ... Inf Syst
Information Systems [*Subdivision*] (MCD) ... ISS
Information Systems Architecture [*AT & T*] ... ISA
Information Systems Consultants, Incorporated [*Information service*] (EISS) ... ISCI
Information Systems Design Optimization System ... ISDOS
Information Systems for Management (IEEE) ... ISM
Information Systems Marketing, Inc. [*Information service*] (EISS) ... ISM
Information Systems News [*A publication*] ... Info Sys New
Information Systems Office [*Library of Congress*] ... ISO
Information Systems Program [*National Science Foundation*] ... ISP
Information Systems Resource Manager (CAA) ... ISRM
Information Systems Security ... ISS
Information Systems Security Association (EANO) ... ISSA
Information Systems Services [*Brigham Young University*] [*Research center*] (RCD) ... ISS
Information Systems and Services Division [*Department of Commerce*] (EISS) ... ISSD
Information Systems Standards Board [*American National Standards Institute*] [*Telecommunications*] ... ISSB
Information Systems Standards Management Board ... ISSMB
Information Technology ... IT
Information Technology Acquisition and Marketing Association (EANO) ... ITAMA
Information Technology Electronics and Computers [*A publication*] ... ITEC
Information Technology and Libraries [*A publication*] ... Inf Technol and Libr
Information Technology Research [*Framingham, MA*] [*Telecommunications*] (TSSD) ... ITR
Information Technology Services [*California State University, Long Beach*] [*Research center*] (RCD) ... ITS
Information Technology Systems ... ITS
Information and Technology Transfer Database [*International Research and Evaluation*] ... ITTD
Information Technology Users Group [*Exxon Corp.*] ... ITUG
Information Technology Users' Standards Association ... ITUSA
Information Technology Year [*1982*] ... ITY
Information via Telex [*Telecommunications*] (TEL) ... INFOTEX
Information Transfer Experiment [*Massachusetts Institute of Technology*] (DIT) ... INTREX
Information Transfer Satellite (KSC) ... ITS
Information Transfer [*or Transmission*] **System** ... ITS
Information Transform [*Information service*] (EISS) ... IT
Information Unit (CAA) ... IU
Information Unit Separator [*Data processing*] (CAA) ... IUS
Information Unlimited [*Berkeley, CA*] [*Information service*] (EISS) ... IU
Information World Review [*Oxford, England*] [*A publication*] [*Information service*] (EISS) ... IWR
Informations- und Dokumentationssystem Umwelt [*Berlin*] [*Information retrieval*] (ODIN) ... UMPLIS
Informationssystem Karlsruhe [*Karlsruhe Information System*] [*Information service*] [*West German*] ... INKA
Informationsvermittelungsstelle [*Information retrieval*] (ODIN) ... IVS

Computer & Telecommunications Acronyms

Informationszentrum [*Information Center*] [*German*] [*Information retrieval*] (ODIN) ... IZ
Informationszentrum und Bibliotheken [*Information retrieval*] (ODIN) ... INF
Informationszentrum fuer Biologie [*Forschungsinstitut Senckenberg*] [*Frankfurt*] [*Information retrieval*] (ODIN) ... IZB
Informationszentrum Raum und Bau [*Fraunhofer-Gesellschaft*] [*Information Center for Building and Space Planning*] [*West Germany*] [*Database producer*] [*Information service*] (EISS) ... IRB
Informationszentrum fuer Schnittwertemachning [*Information Center for Machining*] [*Germany*] [*Rheinische-Westfalische Hochschule*] [*Database*] (EISS) ... INFOS
Infosystems [*Wheaton, IL*] [*A publication*] ... Infosys
Infosystems Technology, Incorporated [*Greenbelt, MD*] [*Software manufacturer*] (DASOS) ... ITI
Infotron Systems Corp. [*NASDAQ symbol*] (NQ) ... INFN
Infra-Audible [*Sound*] ... IA
Infra Low-Frequency [*Telecommunications*] (TEL) ... ILF
Infrared ... IR
Infrared Communications System ... ICS
Infrared Communications System ... IRCS
Infrared Fault Isolation Test System (CAA) ... IRFITS
Infrared Information Exchange ... IRIE
Infrared Information System [*Sadtler Research Laboratories, Inc.*] [*Philadelphia, PA*] [*Database*] (FDB) ... IRIS
Infrared Pointer Package ... IPP
Infrared Search System [*Environmental Protection Agency*] [*Database*] (CUAD) ... IRSS
Infrasonic Frequency ... ISF
Inhibit Halt Flip-Flop [*Data processing*] ... IHF
Inhibit Halt Flip-Flop [*Data processing*] (MSA) ... IHFF
Initial Address Designator (CAA) ... IAD
Initial Address Information [*Telecommunications*] (TEL) ... IAI
Initial Address Message (TEL) ... IAM
Initial Condition Word [*Data processing*] (CAA) ... ICW
Initial Connection Protocol (CAA) ... ICP
Initial Defense Communications Satellite (MCD) ... IDCS
Initial Defense Satellite Communications Project [*Telecommunications*] (TEL) ... IDSCP
Initial File Generation Language (CAH) ... IFGL
Initial-Final Address Message [*Telecommunications*] (TEL) ... IFAM
Initial Load Block (CAA) ... ILB
Initial Machine Load [*Data processing*] (IBMDP) ... IML
Initial Memory Protection (MCD) ... IMP
Initial Microprogram Load [*Also, IMPL*] [*Data processing*] (IBMDP) ... IML
Initial Microprogram Load [*Also, IML*] [*Data processing*] ... IMPL
Initial Operating Production (MCD) ... IOP
Initial Phase (IEEE) ... IP
Initial Program Load [*Data processing*] ... INP
Initial Program Load [*Data processing*] (CGC) ... IPL
Initial Satellite Communications Control Center (MCD) ... ISACCC
Initial Selection Done (OA) ... ISD
Initial Signal Unit [*Telecommunications*] (TEL) ... ISU
Initial Software Configuration Map (MCD) ... ISC
Initial System Loading ... ISL
Initial Virtual Memory (OA) ... IVM
Initial Voice Switched Network [*NATO integrated communications system*] (NATG) ... IVSN
Inland Computer Service (IEEE) ... ICS
Inner Lead Bond [*Integrated circuit technology*] ... ILB
Innovative Programming Associates, Inc. [*Princeton, NJ*] [*Software manufacturer*] (DASOS) ... IPA
Innovative Software [*NASDAQ symbol*] (NQ) ... INSO
INPADOC Patent Gazette [*Information retrieval*] (ODIN) ... IPG
Input ... I
Input (MDG) ... IN
Input (MSA) ... INP
Input [*Data processing*] ... I/P
Input Blocking Factor [*Data processing*] (IBMDP) ... BI
Input Buffer [*Telecommunications*] (TEL) ... IB
Input Bus [*Data processing*] (CAA) ... IB
Input Control Register [*Data processing*] (CAA) ... ICR
Input Control Subsystem (OA) ... ICS
Input Control Word [*Data processing*] (MCD) ... ICW
Input Current Offset [*Data processing*] ... ICO
Input Data Assembler ... IDA
Input Data Buffer (CAA) ... IDB
Input Data Processor (CET) ... IDP
Input Data Request ... IDR
Input Data Strobe ... IDS
Input Data Word (MCD) ... IDWD
Input Destination Message Handler (CAA) ... IDMH
Input Display Console [*Data processing*] ... IDC
Input Frequency Tolerance [*Data processing*] ... IFT
Input Interface Unit [*Data processing*] ... IIU
Input Logic Level ... ILL
Input Memory Buffer [*Data processing*] ... IMB
Input Message Acknowledgment [*Data processing*] (CAA) ... IMA
Input Message Processor ... IMP
Input/Output ... I/O
Input/Output Access Unit [*Data processing*] ... IOAU
Input-Output Adapter [*Data processing*] (NASA) ... IOA
Input-Output Address [*Data processing*] (KSC) ... IOA
Input-Output Assembly [*Data processing*] (MCD) ... IOA

Input/Output Block [*Data processing*] (CMD) ... IOB
Input-Output Box [*Data processing*] (MCD) ... IOB
Input-Output Box and Peripheral Simulator [*Data processing*] (MCD) ... IOBPS
Input-Output Buffer [*Data processing*] ... IOB
Input/Output Buffering System [*Data processing*] (OA) ... IOBS
Input-Output Channel [*Data processing*] (DIT) ... IOC
Input-Output Comparator [*Data processing*] ... IOC
Input/Output Console [*Data processing*] (CAAL) ... I/OC
Input-Output Control Center [*or Command*] [*Data processing*] ... IOCC
Input-Output Control Console [*Data processing*] (CAAL) ... I/OCC
Input-Output Control System [*Data processing*] ... IOCS
Input-Output Control Unit [*Data processing*] ... IOCU
Input-Output Controller [*Data processing*] ... IOC
Input-Output Converter [*Data processing*] ... IOC
Input-Output Data Channel [*Data processing*] ... IODC
Input-Output Data Document [*Data processing*] (MCD) ... IODD
Input-Output Delay Counter [*Data processing*] ... IODC
Input/Output Device [*Telecommunications*] (TEL) ... IOD
Input/Output Error Log Table [*Data processing*] (MCD) ... IOE
Input/Output Front End [*Data processing*] (CAA) ... IOF
Input-Output Gate [*Data processing*] ... IOG
Input/Output Interrupt Handler [*Data processing*] (CAA) ... IOIH
Input/Output Link Adapter [*Data processing*] (CAA) ... IOLA
Input/Output Link Control [*Data processing*] (CAA) ... IOLC
Input-Output Module [*Data processing*] (MCD) ... IOM
Input/Output Multiplexer [*Data processing*] ... I/OM
Input-Output Operation [*Data processing*] ... IOOP
Input-Output Package [*IBM Corp.*] [*Data processing*] ... IOP
Input/Output Package [*IBM Corp.*] [*Data processing*] (CAH) ... IOPKG
Input-Output Port [*Data processing*] (MCD) ... IOP
Input-Output Processor [*Data processing*] ... IOP
Input-Output Programing System [*Data processing*] ... IOPS
Input-Output Pulse [*Data processing*] ... IOP
Input-Output Queue [*Data processing*] (IBMDP) ... IOQ
Input-Output Queue Element [*Data processing*] (MCD) ... IOQE
Input/Output Record Block [*Data processing*] ... IORB
Input/Output Request [*Data processing*] (OA) ... IOREQ
Input-Output Selector [*Data processing*] (IEEE) ... IOS
Input-Output Sense [*Data processing*] (KSC) ... IOS
Input/Output Skip [*Data processing*] ... IOS
Input/Output Subsystem [*NCR Corp.*] (CAA) ... IOSS
Input-Output Supervision [*Data processing*] (NASA) ... IOS
Input-Output Switch [*Data processing*] ... IOS
Input/Output System [*General Automation*] [*Data processing*] (CAA) ... IOS
Input/Output Systems Association (EANO) ... IOSA
Input/Output Task Group [*CODASYL*] (CAA) ... IOTG
Input-Output Termination [*Data processing*] ... IOT
Input-Output Transfer [*Data processing*] ... IOT
Input-Output Unit [*Data processing*] ... IOU
Input-Output Utility [*Data processing*] (CIT) ... IOU
Input Power [*Data processing*] ... IP
Input Processor [*Data processing*] (CIT) ... IP
Input Processor Programs (CIT) ... IPP
Input Queue Message Handler [*Data processing*] (CAA) ... IQMH
Input Read Submodule ... IRS
Input Reference Axis (IEEE) ... IRA
Input Register Full (CAA) ... IRF
Input Revision Typewriter ... IRT
Input Secondary [*Electronics*] ... IS
Input Source Message Handler (CAA) ... ISMH
Input Terminal (CAA) ... IT
Input Translator [*IBM Corp.*] [*Data processing*] ... INTRAN
Input Translator [*IBM Corp.*] [*Data processing*] (MSA) ... INXLTR
Input Translator [*IBM Corp.*] [*Data processing*] ... IT
Input Translator Program [*Data processing*] ... ITP
Input Unit (CAA) ... IU
Inquiry Message Exchange (CAA) ... IMX
Inquiry and Reporting System ... IRS
Inserted Connection Losses [*Telecommunications*] ... ICL
Insertion Loss (CIT) ... IL
Insertion Test Signal [*Telecommunications*] (TEL) ... ITS
Inside Diameter ... ID
Inside Wire [*Telecommunications*] (TEL) ... IW
Inside Wiring Cable [*Telecommunications*] (TEL) ... IWCA
Installation ... INSTAL
Installation Enhancement Release [*Data processing*] ... IER
Installation Performance Specification [*Data processing*] (IBMDP) ... IPS
Installation Productivity Option [*IBM Corp.*] ... IPO
Installation Productivity Option/Extended [*IBM Corp.*] ... IPO/E
Installation Start [*Telecommunications*] (TEL) ... IS
Installation Verification Procedure (MCD) ... IVP
Installed User Program [*Data processing*] ... IUP
Instant Data Access Control [*National Design Center, Inc.*] [*Information service*] (EISS) ... IDAC
Instant Language [*Trademark*] [*Data processing*] ... INLAN
Instant Private Network ... IPN
Instant Response Information System (IEEE) ... IRIS
Instant Response Ordering System [*Brodart, Inc.*] [*Teleordering system*] [*Information service*] (EISS) ... IROS
Instant Update [*Professional Farmers of America*] [*Cedar Falls, IA*] [*Telecommunications*] (TSSD) ... IU
Instantaneous ... I

Computer & Telecommunications Acronyms

Instantaneous Automatic Video Control (IEEE) .... IAVC
Instantaneous Automatic Volume Control [Electronics] .... IAVC
Instantaneous Compressor Performance Analysis Computer .... ICPAC
Instantaneous Field of View .... IFOV
Instantaneous Frequency Discriminator (IEEE) .... IFD
Instantaneous Frequency [Indicating] Receivers (IEEE) .... IFR
Institut fuer Bauforschung [Information retrieval] (ODIN) .... IFB
Institut fuer Dokumentation und Information ueber Sozialmedizin und Offentliches Gesundheitswesen [Information retrieval] (ODIN) .. IDIS
Institut fuer Dokumentation, Information, und Statistik [Institute for Documentation, Information, and Statistics] [Information service on cancer research] [Germany] (EISS) .... IDIS
Institut fuer Dokumentationswesen [West German] (OA) .... IDW
Institut fuer Krankenhausbau der TU [Technische Universitaet] Berlin [Information retrieval] (ODIN) .... IFK
Institut fuer Landes- und Stadtentwicklungsforschung [Dortmund] [Information retrieval] (ODIN) .... ILS
Institut fuer Medizinische Statistik, Dokumentation, und Datenverarbeitung der Universitaet Bonn [Information retrieval] (ODIN) .... IMSDD
Institut National de la Propriete Industrielle .... INPI
Institut National de Recherche en Informatique et en Automatique [National Institute for Research in Informatics and Automation] [France] [Research center and database originator] [Information service] (EISS) .... INRIA
Institut National des Techniques de la Documentation [National Institute for Documentation Techniques] [France] [Information service] (EISS) .... INTD
Institut fuer Nationale und Internationale Fleischwirtschaft [Heidelberg] [Information retrieval] (ODIN) .... IFW
Institut Quebecois de la Recherche sur la Culture [Database producer] (CUAD) .... IQRC
Institut de Radio-Telediffusion pour Enfants [Children's Broadcast Institute] [Canada] .... IRTE
Institut de Recherche d'Informatique et d'Automatique [French] [Research center] .... IRIA
Institut de Recherches sur les Fruits et Agrumes [Database producer] (CUAD) .... IRFA
Institute for Advanced Technology [Control Data Corp.] [Rockville, MD] [Telecommunications] .... IAT
Institute of Applied Economic Research [Concordia University] [Canada] [Research center] (RCD) .... IAER
Institute for Behavioral Research [York University] [Canada] [Research center] (EISS) .... IBR
Institute for Certification of Computer Professionals [Des Plaines, IL] (EANO) .... ICCP
Institute for Cognitive Science [University of California, San Diego] [Research center] (RCD) .... ICS
Institute of Cognitive Science [University of Colorado - Boulder] [Research center] (RCD) .... ICS
Institute for Communications Research [Texas Tech University] [Research center] (RCD) .... ICR
Institute for Computational Mathematics and Applications [University of Pittsburgh] [Research center] (RCD) .... ICMA
Institute for Computer Applications in Science and Engineering [Universities Space Research Association] [Research center] (RCD) .... ICASE
Institute for Computer Research [University of Waterloo] [Canada] [Research center] (RCD) .... ICR
Institute for Computer Research in the Humanities [New York University] .... ICRH
Institute [formerly, Center] for Computer Sciences and Technology [National Bureau of Standards] .... ICST
Institute of Computer Technology .... ICT
Institute for Computers in Jewish Life [Chicago, IL] (EANO) .... ICJL
Institute for Computing Science and Computer Applications [University of Texas at Austin] [Research center] (RCD) .... ICSCA
Institute for Continuing Studies in Design, Management and Communication [University of Cincinnati] [Research center] (RCD) .... ICS/DMC
Institute of Data Processing [London, England] .... IDP
Institute of Data Processing Management [British] (DEEC) .... IDPM
Institute of Electrical and Electronics Engineers [New York, NY] [Document publisher] .... IEEE
Institute of Electrical and Electronics Engineers - Computer Society .... IEEE-CS
Institute of Electronics and Radio Engineers [British] (TEL) .... IERE
Institute for Environmental Studies [University of Washington] [Research center] (RCD) .... IES
Institute for the Future [Menlo Park, CA] [Research center] [Telecommunications] (RCD) .... IFTF
Institute for Graphic Communication, Inc. [Boston, MA] [Telecommunications] .... IGC
Institute of Information Scientists [British] (DIT) .... IIS
Institute for Information Storage Technology [University of Santa Clara] [Research center] (RCD) .... IIST
Institute for Land Information [Washington, DC] [Research center] [Information service] (RCD) ILI
Institute of Library Research [University of California] (DIT) .... ILR
[The] Institute of Management Sciences .... TIMS
Institute for Mathematical Studies in the Social Sciences [Stanford University] [Research center] (RCD) .... IMSSS
Institute of Mathematics and Its Applications [South-End-On-Sea, England] .... IMA
Institute of Non-Numerical Information Processing [Switzerland] [Information service] (EISS) .... INIP
Institute for Personal Computing [Miami, FL] (EANO) .... IPC
Institute of Radio Engineers [Later, IEEE] .... IRE
Institute of Science and Technology [University of Michigan] [Research center] (RCD) .... IST
Institute for Scientific Information [Database producer] .... ISI
Institute for Simulation and Training [University of Central Florida] [Research center] (RCD) .... IST
Institute for Software Engineering [Sunnyvale, CA] (EANO) .... ISE
Institute for Systems Design and Optimization .... ISDO
Institute for Telecommunication Sciences [Formerly, ITSA] [Department of Commerce] .... ITS
Institute for Telecommunication Sciences and Aeronomy [Later, ITS] [National Oceanic and Atmospheric Administration] .... ITSA
Institute for Telecommunications and Aeronomy [ESSA] (MCD) .... ITA
Institute of Telecommunications Engineers (CAH) .... ITE
Institute of Telecommunications Services .... ITS
Institution [Online database field identifier] (OBD) .... IN
Institution of Computer Sciences [British] (DIT) .... ICS
Institution of Electrical Engineers [London, England] [Database producer] .... IEE
Institutional Brokers Estimate System [Lynch, Jones & Ryan] [Database] [Information service] (EISS) .... IBES
Institutional Space Inventory Technique [Data processing] .... INSITE
Institutionenverzeichnis Auslaendischer Gesellschaften [Nomos Verlagsgesellschaft] [Database] (CUAD) .... IVAG
Instituto Brasileiro de Informacao em Ciencia e Tecnologia [Brazilian Institute for Information in Science and Technology] [Information service] (EISS) .... IBICT
Instituto de Informacion y Documentacion en Ciencia y Tecnologia [Institute for Information and Documentation in Science and Technology] [Spain] [Database originator and host] [Information service] (EISS) .... ICYT
Instron Corp. [American Stock Exchange symbol] [Delisted] .... ISN
Instruction (CAA) I
Instruction [or Instructor] (AFM) .... INST
Instruction [Data processing] (TEL) .... INSTN
Instruction (CAH) .... INSTR
Instruction Address Register [Data processing] (MDG) .... IAR
Instruction Address Register (CAA) .... INSAR
Instruction Bank [Data processing] .... I (Bank)
Instruction Bank [Data processing] .... IB
Instruction Bus [Data processing] (CAA) .... IB
Instruction Cell (CAA) IC
Instruction Control Memory (CAA) .... ICM
Instruction Control Unit .... ICU
Instruction Counter [Data processing] IC
Instruction/Data (IEEE) .... I/D
Instruction Definition Language (CAA) .... IDL
Instruction Fetch Unit [Data processing] (CAA) .... IFU
Instruction Field (CAA) .... IF
Instruction Input Unit (CAA) .... IIU
Instruction Length Code [Data processing] (BUR) ILC
Instruction List (CAA) IL
Instruction Location Counter (CAA) ILC
Instruction Look-Ahead [Unit] [Data processing] .... ILA
Instruction Memory (CAA) .... IM
Instruction Memory Unit (CAA) .... IMU
Instruction Pointer [Data processing] (CAA) .... IP
Instruction Preprocessing Function (CAA) .... IPPF
Instruction Processing Unit (BUR) .... IPU
Instruction Processor [Data processing] .... IP
Instruction Register [Data processing] .... IR
Instruction and Research Computer Center [Ohio State University] [Research center] (RCD) .... IRCC
Instruction Set Processor [1971] [Data processing] .... ISP
Instruction Set Processor Language [Data processing] .... ISPL
Instruction Set Processor Specification [1977] [Data processing] (CSR) .... ISPS
Instruction Space Key (CAA) .... ISK
Instruction Storage Unit (CAA) .... ISU
Instruction Unit [Data processing] .... IU
Instructional Resources Information System [EPA Instructional Resources Center] [Bibliographic database] (OBD) .... IRIS
Instructional System Package (MCD) .... ISP
Instructional Systems Language [Data processing] (IEEE) .... ISL
Instructional Telecommunications Consortium [Washington, DC] (EANO) .... ITC
Instructional Television .... ITV
Instructional Television Fixed Service [Educational TV] .... ITFS
Instructions per Second [Data processing] .... IPS
Instrument Data Processing System .... IDPS
Instrument Society of America [Pittsburgh, PA] .... ISA
Instrumentation (MDG) .... IM
Instrumentation (MUGU) .... INSTN
Instrumentation and Communication (MCD) .... INST/COMM
Instrumentation Communication Equipment (NASA) .... ICE
Instrumentation and Communication (System) (SKY) .... I & C(S)
Instrumentation and Communications [Cable system] (KSC) .... I & C
Instrumentation and Communications Monitor .... ICM

Instrumentation/Data Collection System ... IDCS
Instrumentation Data Distribution System (MUGU) ... IDDS
Instrumentation Digital On-Line Transcriber [*Data processing*] ... IDIOT
Instrumented Architectural Level Emulation (CAA) ... IALE
Instytut Informacji Naukowej, Technicznej, i Ekonomicznej [*Institute of Scientific, Technical, and Economic Information*] [*Poland*] [*Information service*] (EISS) ... IINTE
Insulate (DDI) ... INS
Insulated-Gate Field-Effect Transistor [*Electronics*] ... IGFET
Insulation/Circuits [*A publication*] ... Insul/Circuits
Insulation Displacement (DEEC) ... ID
Insurance Communication Service [*IBM Information Network*] [*Tampa, FL*] [*Telecommunications*] (TSSD) ... ICS
Insurance Periodicals Index [*NILS Publishing Co.*] [*Information service*] (EISS) ... IPI
IntㄹCom, Inc. [*NASDAQ symbol*] (NQ) ... INCM
Integer (CAH) ... INT
Integral Pulse Frequency Modulation (IEEE) ... IPFM
Integral Systems Experimental Requirements ... ISER
Integral Terminal Block ... ITB
Integrate and Dump Detection [*Telecommunications*] (TEL) ... I & D
Integrated Acoustic Communication System (NVT) ... IACS
Integrated Adapter (CAA) ... IA
Integrated Business Computers [*Chatsworth, CA*] [*Software manufacturer*] (DASOS) ... IBC
Integrated Chip Circuit ... ICC
Integrated Circuit [*Electronics*] ... IC
Integrated Circuit Analysis [*Data processing*] ... ICAN
Integrated Circuit Array ... ICA
Integrated Circuit Description Language (CAA) ... ICDL
Integrated Circuit Keyset Central Multiplexer (CAAL) ... ICKCMX
Integrated Circuit Logic ... ICL
Integrated Circuit Mask ... ICM
Integrated Circuit and Message Switch ... ICMS
Integrated Circuit Parameter Retrieval [*Information Handling Services*] [*Database*] (CUAD) ... ICPR
Integrated Civil Engineering System [*Programing language*] [*Data processing*] ... ICES
Integrated Communication Control Panel (MCD) ... ICCP
Integrated Communication Systems, Inc. [*Atlanta, GA*] [*Telecommunications*] (IEEE) ... ICS
Integrated Communications Access Method [*Data processing*] ... ICAM
Integrated Communications Adapter (MCD) ... ICA
Integrated Communications Adapter Extended (BUR) ... ICAE
Integrated Communications Control (MCD) ... ICC
Integrated Computer-Aided Manufacturing (IEEE) ... ICAM
Integrated Computer Network (CAA) ... ICN
Integrated Computer Telemetry ... ICT
Integrated Control and Display ... ICAD
Integrated Control Facility [*Sperry UNIVAC*] (CAA) ... ICF
Integrated Control Storage [*Data processing*] ... ICS
Integrated Control Unit (CAA) ... ICU
Integrated Corporate Database (IDA) ... ICDB
Integrated Data Acquisition System (MCD) ... IDAS
Integrated Data Base [*Data processing*] (TUT) ... IDB
Integrated Data Coding System (NG) ... IDCS
Integrated Data Communications Controller (CAA) ... IDCC
Integrated Data Dictionary (CAA) ... IDD
Integrated Data Display System ... IDDS
Integrated Data File ... IDF
Integrated Data Handling System (DDI) ... IDHS
Integrated Data Presentation ... IDP
Integrated Data Processing ... IDP
Integrated Data Processing Center ... IDPC
Integrated Data Processing System ... IDPS
Integrated Data Store [*or System*] [*Honeywell, Inc.*] [*Data processing*] ... IDS
Integrated Data Transmittal Package ... IDTP
Integrated Database Management System (CAA) ... IDBMS
Integrated Database Management System ... IDMS
Integrated Design and Engineering Automated System (IEEE) ... IDEAS
Integrated Digital Access [*Telecommunications*] ... IDA
Integrated Digital-Analog Converter (MCD) ... IDAC
Integrated Digital Logic Circuit ... IDLC
Integrated Digital Network [*Telecommunications*] ... IDN
Integrated Direct Numerical Control [*Burroughs Machines Ltd.*] [*Software package*] [*British*] (NCC) ... IDNC
Integrated Disk Adapter [*Sperry UNIVAC*] (CAA) ... IDA
Integrated Disk Control [*NCR Corp.*] (CAA) ... IDC
Integrated Display Situation ... IDS
Integrated Displays and Controls (MCD) ... IDC
Integrated Electronic Components (BUR) ... IEC
Integrated Electronic Signal Processor ... IESP
Integrated Feed Antenna ... IFA
Integrated File Adapter [*Data processing*] (BUR) ... IFA
Integrated File Processor (CAA) ... IFP
Integrated Financial Management System ... IFMS
Integrated Fluorescence Unit [*Image formation*] ... IFU
Integrated Force Administration System [*Bell System*] ... IFAMS
Integrated Graphics System [*Data processing*] (BUR) ... IGS
Integrated High-Frequency Antenna System ... IHFAS
Integrated Information Processing ... INTIP
Integrated Information Processing System [*Air Development Center, Rome, NY*] ... INTIPS
Integrated Information System (Operational) [*Marine Corps*] (DDI) ... I2S(OPS)
Integrated Injection Logic [*Microprocessing*] (BUR) ... IIL
Integrated Injection Logic [*Microprocessing*] ... I²L
Integrated Input/Output Processor (CAA) ... IIOP
Integrated Key Set [*Data processing*] ... IKS
Integrated Library System [*National Library of Medicine*] [*Information service*] (EISS) ... ILS
Integrated Library System Users Society (EANO) ... ILSUS
Integrated Logic Circuit ... ILC
Integrated Logistics Data System ... ILDS
Integrated Logistics Panel (NASA) ... ILP
Integrated Management Planning Information Systems [*Data processing*] ... IMPIS
Integrated Mass Storage Processor (CAA) ... IMSP
Integrated Memory Processor ... IMP
Integrated Microcomputer Systems, Inc. ... IMS
Integrated Microprocessor [*National Semiconductor*] (CAA) ... IMP
Integrated Mission Control Center (CDH) ... IMCC
Integrated MODEM (CAA) ... IM
Integrated Modular Panel System (CAA) ... IMPS
Integrated Motorists' Information System [*Computerized guidance system to speed traffic and avoid tie-ups*] ... IMIS
Integrated Multifunction Keyboard (MCD) ... IMFK
Integrated Multiplexer Channel (CAA) ... IMC
Integrated Network Architecture (CAA) ... INA
Integrated Network Fiber Optics (MCD) ... INFO
Integrated Network Processor (CAA) ... INP
Integrated Network Systems, Inc. ... INS
Integrated On-Line Non-Stop Manufacturing [*Safe Computing Ltd.*] [*Software package*] [*British*] (NCC) ... ION-M
Integrated On-Line Text Arrangement ... IOTA
Integrated Online Library Systems ... IOLS
Integrated Operator System [*Telecommunications*] ... IOS
Integrated Optical Circuit ... IOC
Integrated Optoelectronic Circuit ... IOC
Integrated Peripheral Adapter (CAA) ... IPA
Integrated Peripheral Channel (CAA) ... IPC
Integrated Plotting Package ... IPP
Integrated Printer Adapter (CAA) ... IPA
Integrated Processor Board (CAA) ... IPB
Integrated Radio Control (NVT) ... IRC
Integrated Radio Room (MCD) ... IRR
Integrated Random-Access Memory [*Data processing*] ... IRAM
Integrated Reliability Data System ... IRDS
Integrated Safeguard Information System ... ISIS
Integrated Schottky Logic (IEEE) ... ISL
Integrated Scientific Information System ... ISIS
Integrated Services Digital Network [*Telecommunications*] ... ISDN
Integrated Services Satellite Digital Network (MCD) ... ISSDN
Integrated Software Development System (CAA) ... ISDS
Integrated Software Functional Design (CAA) ... ISFD
Integrated Software Systems Corporation [*NASDAQ symbol*] (NQ) ... ISCX
Integrated Software Systems Corporation ... ISSCO
Integrated Storage Control ... ISC
Integrated Subrate Data Multiplexer (TEL) ... ISMX
Integrated Switched Data Service [*Telecommunications*] (TEL) ... ISDS
Integrated Switching and Multiplexing [*IBM Corp.*] ... ISAM
Integrated Switching and Transmission [*Telecommunications*] (TEL) ... IST
Integrated Switching and Transmission Network [*Telecommunications*] (TEL) ... ISTN
Integrated Symbolic Debugger [*Data processing*] (EISS) ... ISD
Integrated System for Automated Acquisition and Control ... ISAAC
Integrated System Definition Language [*Data processing*] (IEEE) ... IDEF
Integrated System Transformer (IEEE) ... IST
Integrated Systems Demonstrator (MCD) ... ISD
Integrated Telephone Recorder [*Telecommunications*] (TEL) ... ITR
Integrated Teleprocessing Network (CAA) ... ITN
Integrated Teleprocessing System (IEEE) ... ITPS
Integrated Test Block ... ITB
Integrated Test Facility [*Data processing*] ... ITF
Integrated Test Software (CAAL) ... ITS
Integrated Testing, Analysis, and Verification System (CAA) ... ITAVS
Integrated Trajectory Computations (SKY) ... ITC
Integrated Unit Record Processor (CAA) ... IURP
Integrated Vehicular Communication System (MCD) ... IVCS
Integrated Video Terminal (CAA) ... IVT
Integrated [*or Interior*] **Voice Communications System** (MCD) ... IVCS
Integrated Wideband Communications System/Southeast Asia (IEEE) ... IWCS/SEA
Integrating Digital Voltmeter ... IDVM
Integration Analog-to-Digital Converter (IEEE) ... IADIC
Integration Hardware and Software Review (MCD) ... IH/SR
Integriertes Statistisches Informationssystem [*Central Statistical Office*] [*Database*] [*Austrian*] (CUAD) ... ISIS
Intel Corporation [*NASDAQ symbol*] (NQ) ... INTC
Intelligence Automatic Data Processing Group ... IADPG
Intelligence Data Handling System (AFM) ... IDHS
Intelligence Data Input Packages (MCD) ... IDIPS
Intelligence Data System (DDI) ... IDS
Intelligence Finished Reports Information Subsystem [*Data processing*] ... IFRIS
Intelligence Industries Association [*Los Angeles, CA*] (EANO) ... IIA

Computer & Telecommunications Acronyms

Intelligence Reports Information Subsystem [Data processing]	IRIS
Intelligent Assistant [Data processing]	IA
Intelligent Communications Interface (IEEE)	ICI
Intelligent Computer-Assisted Instruction	ICAI
Intelligent Computer Systems Research Institute [University of Miami] [Research center] (RCD)	ICSRI
Intelligent Copier-Printer [Electrophotography]	IC-P
Intelligent Data Access (CAA)	IDA
Intelligent Data Network (CAA)	IDN
Intelligent Data Terminal (CAA)	IDT
Intelligent Digitizer (CAA)	ID
Intelligent Dual Interface (CAA)	IDI
Intelligent Gateway Processor [Data processing]	IGP
Intelligent Keyboard Device	IKBD
Intelligent Knowledge-Based System [Using artificial intelligence] [Data processing]	IKBS
Intelligent Line Adapter (CAA)	ILA
Intelligent Matrix Control [T-Bar, Inc.] (CAA)	IMC
Intelligent Memory Manager [Data processing]	IMM
Intelligent Microimage Terminal [Kodak]	IMT
Intelligent Network Processor (CAA)	INP
Intelligent Peripheral Controller [Data processing]	IPC
Intelligent Printer Interface (CAA)	IPI
Intelligent Printing System [Dataroyal, Inc.] (CAA)	IPS
Intelligent Remote Terminal Unit (CAA)	IRTU
Intelligent Support System (CAA)	ISS
Intelligent Systems Corporation (CAA)	ISC
Intelligent Television [Home video game] [Mattel, Inc.]	INTELLIVISION
Intelligent Terminal [Data processing]	IT
Intelligent Terminal System [IBM Corp.] (CAA)	ITS
Intelligent Time-Division Multiplexer	ITDM
INTELSAT [International Telecommunications Satellite] Operations Center (CBSS)	IOC
Intensity (MSA)	INTEN
Intensity Fluctuation Factor [Telecommunications] (TEL)	IFF
Inter-American Association of Broadcasters	IAAB
Inter-American Technical Council on Archives (DIT)	ITCA
Inter Block Gap	IBG
Inter-Institutional Integrated Services Information System (DEEC)	INSIS
Inter-Organization Board for Information Systems [United Nations] (EISS)	IOB
Inter-Record Gap [Data processing] [Telecommunications] (MCD)	IRG
Inter-Service Agency Automated Message Processing Exchange	IS/A AMPE
Inter-Tel, Inc. [NASDAQ symbol] (NQ)	INTL
Interaction Cross Talk [Telecommunications] (TEL)	IXT
Interaction Graphics Display	IGD
Interactive Algebraic Manipulation [Data processing]	IAM
Interactive Alphanumeric Television (CIT)	IATV
Interactive Applications Supervisor (CAH)	IAS
Interactive Array Computer (CAA)	IAC
Interactive Business Information Systems [Santa Ana, CA] [Software manufacturer] (DASOS)	IBIS
Interactive Business-Oriented Language (CAA)	IBOL
Interactive Cable Television	ICTV
Interactive COBOL Operating System (CAA)	ICOS
Interactive Communications Feature [IBM Corp.] (CAA)	ICF
Interactive Communications Software (CAA)	ICS
Interactive Computer-Aided Design Evaluation	ICADE
Interactive Computer Graphics	ICG
Interactive Computer System [Information science]	IACS
Interactive Computing [A publication]	Int Comp
Interactive Computing and Control Facility [IBM Corp. program product]	ICCF
Interactive Construction Industry System [NCR Ltd.] [Software package] [British] (NCC)	ICIS
Interactive Continuous Systems Modeling Program (OA)	ICSMP
Interactive Data Entry (CAA)	IDE
Interactive Data Entry Access [Data General Corp.] (CAA)	IDEA
Interactive Data Services, Incorporated [Database producer] [Information service] (EISS)	IDSI
Interactive Data System [Data processing]	IDS
Interactive Database Manipulator and Summarizer (CAA)	IDMAS
Interactive Debugging (IEEE)	ID
Interactive Debugging Aid	IDA
Interactive Dialogue Facility [Programing language] (CSR)	IDF
Interactive Digital Image Manipulation System [Minicomputer]	IDIMS
Interactive Direct Processing System [NCR Corp.] (CAA)	IDPS
Interactive Disk Operating System [Computer Associates, Inc.] (CAA)	IDOS
Interactive Display System (CAA)	IDS
Interactive Display Terminal (MCD)	IDT
Interactive Duct Sizing [Facet Ltd.] [Software package] [British] (NCC)	INDUS
Interactive Estimating [Camic Ltd.] [Software package] [British] (NCC)	INTEREST
Interactive Facility [Control Data Corp.] (CAA)	IAF
Interactive File Manager [Data processing] (CAA)	IFM
Interactive File Sharing	IFS
Interactive Financial Planning System [Harris Systems Ltd.] [Software package] [British] (NCC)	IFPS
Interactive Flow Simulator (TEL)	IFS
Interactive Grafics Digitizer [Data processing]	IGD
Interactive Graphic and Retrieval System (CAA)	INGRES
Interactive Graphics Analysis (CAA)	INGA
Interactive Graphics Language (CAA)	IGL
Interactive Graphics Packaging Program [Data processing]	IGPP
Interactive Graphics System [Data processing]	IGS
Interactive Graphics Terminal [Data processing]	IGT
Interactive Instructional System [IBM Corp.]	IIS
Interactive Job Submission [Data processing] (CAA)	IJS
Interactive Keyboard and Terminal [Data processing] (MCD)	IKAT
Interactive Man/Computer Augmentation System	IMCAS
Interactive Manufacturing Control System [NCR Ltd.] [Software package] [British] (NCC)	IMCS II
Interactive Market Systems, Inc. [Host] [Information service] (EISS)	IMS
Interactive Microprogramable Control (MCD)	IMP
Interactive Module Controller (CAA)	IMC
Interactive Multiprograming Operating System [NCR Corp.] (CAA)	IMOS
Interactive Operating System [Data processing] (CAA)	IOS
Interactive Operations Facility [Honeywell, Inc.] (CAA)	IOF
Interactive Problem-Control System [IBM Corp.]	IPCS
Interactive Programing [Data processing]	IAP
Interactive Query Facility [Data processing] (CAA)	IQF
Interactive Query Language [Digital Equipment Corp.] [Data processing] (CAA)	IQL
Interactive Query and Report Processor [IBM Corp.] [Data processing]	IQRP
Interactive Real-Time Information System	IRIS
Interactive Recorded Information Service [British] [Telecommunications] (TEL)	IRIS
Interactive Remote Job Entry (CAA)	IRJE
Interactive Resource Executive [NCR Corp.] (CAA)	IRX
Interactive Sciences Corporation [Information service] (EISS)	ISC
Interactive Search of Bibliographic Files (CAA)	ISBF
Interactive Simulation Language [Data processing] (IEEE)	ISL
Interactive Solids Modeling System [Gould Electronics Ltd. Computer Systems] [Software package] [British] (NCC)	ISMS
Interactive Structural Sizing and Analysis System [Data processing]	ISSAS
Interactive System Productivity Facility [Data processing]	ISPF
Interactive System Productivity Facility/Program Development Facility [Data processing]	ISPF/PDF
Interactive Systems Corporation [NASDAQ symbol] (NQ)	ISCO
Interactive Technology Laboratory [New York Institute of Technology] [Research center] (RCD)	ITL
Interactive Television Network [Dartmouth-Hitchcock Medical Center] [Hanover, NH] [Telecommunications] (TSSD)	INTERACT
Interactive Terminal Facility	ITF
Interactive Terminal Interface [Data processing] (IEEE)	ITI
Interactive Terminal Protocol (CAA)	ITP
Interactive Terminal Support (CAA)	ITS
Interactive Video Association [Evanston, IL] [Information service] (EISS)	IVA
Interactive Videodisc Consortium (EANO)	IVC
Interagency Committee on Automatic Data Processing [Office of Management and Budget]	IAC/ADP
Interagency Data Processing Committee	IADPC
Interagency Dialing System [Telephones]	IDS
Interarray Communications (NVT)	IAC
Interarray Processor (NVT)	IAP
Intercept [Telecommunications] (TEL)	ITC
Interceptor Distance Computer	IDC
Interchange File Separator [Data processing] (BUR)	IFS
Interchange Group Separator [Data processing] (BUR)	IGS
Interchange Record Separator [Data processing] (BUR)	IRS
Interchange of Scientific and Technical Information in Machine Language [Office of Science and Technology]	ISTIM
Interchange Unit Separator [Data processing] (BUR)	IUS
Interchannel Communicator (MCD)	ICC
Interchannel Time Displacement Error [Magnetic recording]	ITDE
Intercollegiate Broadcasting System	IBS
Intercom Information Resources, Inc. [Austin, TX] [Information service] (EISS)	IIR
Intercomm User Group [Later, SDAUG] (EANO)	IUG
Intercommunication (MSA)	ICM
Intercommunication Control Station (KSC)	ICS
Intercommunication Devices (MCD)	ID
Intercommunication Drum (MSA)	IC DRUM
Intercommunication Flip-Flop [Data processing]	ICF
Intercommunication Logic (CAA)	ICL
Intercommunication System	INTERCOM
Intercommunications	IC
Intercommunications System	ICS
Intercomp Design, Incorporated [Neshanic Station, NJ] [Telecommunications] (TSSD)	IDI
Intercompany Services Coordination [Telecommunications] (TEL)	ISC
Intercompany Services Coordination/Universal Service Order [Telecommunications] (TEL)	ISC/USO
Intercomputer (MCD)	IC
Intercomputer Adapter (CAA)	ICA
Intercomputer Channel (KSC)	IC
Intercomputer Channel (NASA)	ICC
Intercomputer Communication (MCD)	ICC
Intercomputer Communication System	ICCS
Intercomputer Compatibility Unit [Data processing]	ICCU

Computer & Telecommunications Acronyms

Interconnect Group (CAAL)	IG
Interconnecting Digital-Analog Converter (NG)	IDAC
Interconnection (KSC)	INTERCON
Interconnection Device (MCD)	ID
Intercontinental Data Control Corp. Ltd. [Ottawa, ON] [Telecommunications] (TSSD)	INTERDACO
Interdata Transaction Controller [Perkin-Elmer] (CAA)	ITC
Interdepartmental Dial System [Telephones]	IDS
Interdigit Pause [Telecommunications] (TEL)	IDP
Interdigital [Telecommunications] (IEEE)	ID
Interdigital Pause [Telecommunications] (TEL)	IP
Interdigital Transducer [Physics]	IDT
Interdisciplinary Machine Processing for Research and Education in Social Sciences [Dartmouth College, Hanover, NH] [Data processing system]	IMPRESS
Interdyne Co. [NASDAQ symbol] (NQ)	IDYN
Interexchange Carrier and Carrier Forum [Exchange Carriers Standards Association] [Telecommunications]	ICCF
Interface [Data processing] (KSC)	I/F
Interface Bus [Data processing]	IB
Interface Change Notice (MCD)	ICN
Interface Compatibility Record (NASA)	ICR
Interface Control Chart (NASA)	ICC
Interface Control Configuration List (DDI)	ICCL
Interface Control Documentation Log (KSC)	ICDL
Interface Control Panel (MCD)	ICP
Interface Control Word [Data processing] (CAA)	ICW
Interface Coordination and Control Procedure (NASA)	ICCP
Interface Coordination Memo (MCD)	ICM
Interface Data Sheet (NASA)	IDS
Interface Demonstration Unit (NASA)	IDU
Interface Design Specification (CAAL)	IDS
Interface Digital Processor (MCD)	IDPS
Interface and Display Electronics Assembly	IDEA
Interface Keying Unit [Data processing] (KSC)	IKU
Interface Latching Element (CAA)	ILE
Interface Message Processor [Data processing]	IMP
Interface Module (MCD)	IM
Interface Noise Inverter	INI
Interface and Priority Unit	IPU
Interface Problem Status Log (NASA)	IPSL
Interface Processor [Data processing] (CAA)	IP
Interface Program Plan (MCD)	IPP
Interface Register (CAA)	IFR
Interface Sharing Unit (CAA)	ISU
Interface Signal Chart	ISC
Interface Simulation System (CAAL)	ISS
Interface Specification Control Document (KSC)	ISCD
Interface Switching Unit (BUR)	ISU
Interface Systems [NASDAQ symbol] (NQ)	INTF
Interface Test Adapters (MCD)	ITA
Interface Unit [Data processing] (NASA)	I/FU
Interface Unit (CAA)	INTFU
Interface Unit [Data processing] (MCD)	IU
Interface Unit Adapter [Data processing] (MCD)	IUA
Interface Virtual Machine [Data processing] (CAA)	IVM
Interfaces in Computing [A publication]	IC
Interfaces in Computing [A publication]	Interfaces Comput
Interfacility Communication Network	IFCN
Interference [Broadcasting]	I
Interference [Telecommunications] (MDG)	INTEC
Interference [Telecommunications] (MSA)	INTRF
Interference Cancellation Equipment [Telecommunications]	ICE
Interference Control Monitor	ICM
Interference-to-Noise Ratio (IEEE)	IN
Interference-to-Noise Ratio	INR
Interference Suppressor (IEEE)	IS
Intergovernmental Bureau for Informatics [Rome, Italy] [Telecommunications] (EANO)	IBI
Intergovernmental Bureau for Informatics - International Computation Center	IBI-ICC
Intergovernmental Council for ADP [Automatic Data Processing]	ICA
Interim Circuit Order Control System [Bell System]	ICOCS
Interim Communications Satellite Committee	ICSC
Interim Data Communications Collection Center	IDCCC
Interim Digital-Analog Converter (VIT)	IDAC
Interim Equipment Order Control System [Bell System]	IEOCS
Interim High-Data Rate Terminal (CAAL)	IHDRT
Interim Operational Capability (CIT)	IOC
Interim Tactical ELINT [Electronic Intelligence] Processor	ITEP
Interim Tactical Information Processing and Interpretation	ITIPI
Interim Teleprinter System	ITS
Interior Communications Switchboard (VIT)	ICSWBD
Interlinked Computerized Storage and Processing System of Food and Agricultural Data [United Nations] [Databank] [Information service] (EISS)	ICS
Intermachine Trunk [Telecommunications] (TEL)	IMT
Intermec Corp. [NASDAQ symbol] (NQ)	INTR
Intermediate Amplifier	IA
Intermediate Cable Equalizers (IEEE)	ICE
Intermediate Configuration Control Board [Western Electric]	ICCB
Intermediate Dialing Center on a Toll Ticket [Telecommunications] (TEL)	D
Intermediate Digital Distribution Frame [Telecommunications] (TEL)	IDDF
Intermediate Distributing Frame [Telecommunications]	IDF
Intermediate Frame Memory [Data processing]	IFM
Intermediate Frequency [Electronics]	IF
Intermediate Frequency Transformer	IFT
Intermediate Language [Data processing] (BUR)	IL
Intermediate Language [Data processing] (TEL)	IML
Intermediate Language Machine (CAA)	ILM
Intermediate Language Processor [Data processing] (BUR)	ILP
Intermediate Language Program [Data processing] (CAA)	ILP
Intermediate Machine Instruction (CAA)	IMI
Intermediate Query Language [Data processing]	IQL
Intermediate Sideband (NATG)	ISB
Intermediate Storage Device (CAA)	ISD
Intermediate Tape [Telecommunications] (TEL)	IMT
Intermediate Text Block (CAA)	ITB
Intermediate Toll Center [Telecommunications] (TEL)	ITC
Intermediate Transfer Language (CAA)	ITL
Intermediate Transmission Block [Data processing] (BUR)	ITB
Intermetrics [NASDAQ symbol] (NQ)	IMET
Intermittent Drive Unit	IDU
Intermittent Operation during the Time Indicated [Broadcasting]	I
Intermittent Trouble Indication [Telecommunications] (TEL)	ITI
Internacia Postista kaj Telekomunikista Esperanto-Asocio [International Esperanto Association of Post and Telecommunication Workers] (EANO)	IPTEA
Internal Array Processor [Data General Corp.] (CAA)	IAP
Internal Bus [Data processing] (CAA)	IB
Internal Common Bus [Data processing] (CAA)	ICB
Internal Connection [Electronics]	IC
Internal Control Description Database (CAA)	ICDDB
Internal Control Description Language (CAA)	ICDL
Internal Data Channel (CAA)	IDC
Internal Delay Factor [Data processing]	IDF
Internal Distribution System [Television]	IDS
Internal Polarization Modulation (IEEE)	IPM
Internal Rate of Return [Telecommunications] (TEL)	IROR
Internal Revenue Service [Department of the Treasury] [Washington, DC]	IRS
Internal Routing Network (CAA)	IRN
Internal Standard Organization Code (CMD)	ISO
Internal Teleprocessing System (CMD)	ITPS
Internal Transfer Bus (CAA)	ITB
Internal Translation Information Subsystem [Data processing]	ITIS
Internal Translator [Carnegie Institute] [IBM Corp.]	IT
Internally Specified Index	ISI
Internally Stored Program	ISP
Internally Switched Interface System [Tymnet, Inc.] (CAA)	ISIS
International Accounting Center (TEL)	IAC
International Accounting and Traffic Analysis Equipment [Telecommunications] (TEL)	IATE
International Advanced Life Information System (BUR)	INTERALIS
International Advisory Committee [ANSI]	IAC
International Advisory Committee on Documentation, Libraries, and Archives [UNESCO] (DIT)	IACDLA
International Aeronautical Telecommunications Switching Center	IATSC
International Air Traffic Communications	IATC
International Air Traffic Communications Receiver Station	IATCR
International Air Traffic Communications Station	IATCS
International Air Traffic Communications System (MCD)	IATCS
International Air Traffic Communications Transmitter Station	IATCT
International Air Transport [formerly, Traffic] Association	IATA
International Airport Characteristics Data Bank [International Civil Aviation Organization] [Information service] (EISS)	ACDB
International Algebraic Language [Programing language] [Replaced by ALGOL]	IAL
International Algorithmic Language [Data processing] (BUR)	IAL
International Amateur Radio Union	IARU
International Apple Core	IAC
International Applications Group [IFIP]	IAG
International Association of Business Communicators	IABC
International Association of Computer Crime Investigators [Oakland, CA] (EANO)	IACCI
International Association of Computer Programmers (CAH)	IACP
International Association for Cybernetics [See also AIC] (EANO)	IAC
International Association for Mathematics and Computers in Simulation [Formerly, AICA] [Rutgers University] [New Brunswick, NJ] (CSR)	IMACS
International Association for Mathematics and Computers in Simulation (CAA)	IAMACS
International Association for Pattern Recognition (EANO)	IAPR
International Association of Satellite Users [Later, IASUS] (EANO)	IASU
International Association of Satellite Users and Suppliers [Mclean, VA] [Formerly, IASU] [Telecommunications] (EANO)	IASUS
International Association of Science and Technology for Development	IASTED
International Association for Social Science Information Service and Technology	IASSIST
International Association for Statistical Computing (EANO)	IASC
International Association of Telecomputer Networks [Winter Springs, FL] [Telecommunications] (EANO)	IATN

Computer & Telecommunications Acronyms

International Association of Word Processing Specialists [Formerly, NAWPS] (EANO) .... WPS
International Atomic Energy Agency [United Nations] [Vienna, Austria] [Database originator and operator] .... IAEA
International Atomic Time .... IAT
International Audio-Visual Technical Centre [Netherlands] (DIT) .... IAVTC
International Bank Information System (CAA) .... IBIS
International Bank for Reconstruction and Development [Also known as World Bank] .... IBRD
International Book Information Service (NITA) .... IBIS
International Broadcasting .... IB
International Brotherhood of Electrical Workers .... IBEW
International Bureau for Informatics .... IBI
International Bureau of Software Test .... IBST
International Business Earth Stations [Communications Satellite Corp.] .... IBES
International Business Forms Industries [Arlington, VA] .... IBFI
International Business Machines Corp. [White Plains, NY] [Computer manufacturer] [NYSE symbol] [Toronto Stock Exchange symbol] .... IBM
International Business Machine's Timesharing System (TEL) .... IBM TSS
International Business Unit [British] [Information service] (EISS) .... IBU
International Cancer Research Data Bank [National Cancer Institute] [Bethesda, MD] [Database producer] (EISS) .... ICRDB
International Chamber of Shipping .... ICS
International Civil Aviation Message Routing System .... ICAMRS
International Color Computer Club (EANO) ICCC
International Commission for Conformity of Certification of Electrical Equipment .... CEE
International Committee for Social Science Information and Documentation [France] [Information service] (EISS) .... ICSSID
International Communication Agency [Also, USICA] [Formerly called BECA and USIA, it later became known again as USIA] .... ICA
International Communication Association [Formerly, Industrial Communication Association] [Austin, TX] .... ICA
International [or Internal] Communication Unit [Telecommunications] (TEL) .... ICU
International Communications Association [Dallas, TX] [Telecommunications] (CSR) .... ICA
International Communications Corporation [Miami, FL] ICC
International Communications Satellite Consortium (MCD) .... ICSC
International Communications Sciences .... ICS
International Computaprint Corporation ICC
International Computation Center [Sponsored by UNESCO] [Rome, Italy] ICC
International Computer Bibliography [A publication of National Computing Center] .... ICB
International Computer Chess Association .... ICCA
International Computer Exhibition .... INCOMEX
International Computer Orphanage [Mississauga, ON] (EANO) .... ICO
International Computer Programs, Inc. [Information service] .... ICP
International Computer Symposium Proceedings [A publication] .... Intl Comp Symp
International Computer and Telecommunications Conference [International Conference Management, Inc.] [Dallas, TX] [Telecommunications] (TSSD) .... COMTEL
International Computers Limited [Great Britain] [Computer manufacturer] ICL
International Computers and Tabulators Ltd. [Later, ICL] .... ICT
International Computing Center's Preparatory Committee .... ICCPC
International Conference on Communications [IEEE] ICC
International Conference on Computer Applications [in developing countries] [1977] .... ICCA
International Conference on Computers and the Humanities .... ICCH
International Conference on Information Processing [Paris, 1959] .... ICIP
International Conference on Machine Searching and Translation .... ICMST
International Conference on Magnetics (MCD) .... INTERMAG
International Congress for Data Processing (CAA) .... ICD
International Congress of Electrical and Electronic Communications .... ICEEC
International Congress for Measurement and Automation (IEEE) .... INTERMAMA
International Congress of Publishers (DIT) .... ICP
International Construction Database [Information Centre for Regional Planning and Building Construction of the Fraunhofer-Society] [Database] (CUAD) .... ICONDA
International Consumer Reports [Consumers' Association] [London, England] [Information service] (EISS) .... ICR
International Council for Building Research, Studies, and Documentation (DIT) .... ICBRSD
International Council for Computer Communication [Washington, DC] (EANO) ICCC
International Council for Computers in Education [University of Oregon] [Eugene, OR] (EANO) .... ICCE
International Council of Scientific Unions [Paris, France] [Sponsors CODATA] .... ICSU
International Council for Technical Communication .... INTECOM
International Data Base [Bureau of Census] [Database] (FDB) .... IDB
International Data Collecting Platform (TEL) .... IDCP
International Data Corporation [Waltham, MA] [Information service] (EISS) .... IDC
International Data Group [Publisher of computer magazines] .... IDG
International Data Processing Institute (MCD) .... IDPI

International Data Sciences, Inc. [Lincoln, RI] [Hardware manufacturer] (DASO) .... IDS
International Data Technology, Inc. [Chicago, IL] [Software manufacturer] (DASOS) .... IDT
International Database Association [Defunct] (EANO) .... IDA
International Demographic Data Center [Bureau of the Census] [Washington, DC] [Database] [Information service] (EISS) .... IDDC
International Demographic Data Directory [Agency for International Development] (EISS) .... IDDD
International Development Education Documentation Service [University of Pittsburgh] (EISS) .... IDEDS
International Development Research Centre [Canada] [Information service] .... IDRC
International Digital Channel Service [Federal Trade Commission] (CAA) .... IDCS
International Digital Data Service [Western Union Corp.] [Data transmission service] .... IDDS
International Direct Dialing [Telecommunications] .... IDD
International Direct Distance Dialing [AT & T] .... IDDD
International Electronic Post [Postal service] .... INTELPOST
International Electronics Corporation (MUGU) .... IEC
International Electrotechnical Commission [Standards body] [Geneva, Switzerland] [See also CEI] .... IEC
International Facsimile Service [Telecommunications] (TEL) .... IFAX
International Federation of Associations of Computer Users in Engineering Architecture and Related Fields (EANO) .... FACE
International Federation on Automatic Control [Dusseldorf, WG] .... IFAC
International Federation of Computer Sciences .... IFCS
International Federation of Data Organizations for the Social Sciences [West Germany] [Information service] (EISS) .... IFDO
International Federation for Documentation [Also, FID] .... IFD
International Federation for Information Processing [Formerly, IFIPS] [London, England] .... IFIP
International Federation of Information Processing Societies [Later, IFIP] .... IFIPS
International Federation of Library Associations and Institutions [Tokyo, Japan] .... IFLA
International Federation of Operational Research Societies .... IFORS
International Federation of the Technical and Periodical Press (DIT) .... IFTPP
International Federation of Telephone Emergency Services (EANO) .... IFOTES
International Federation of Telephonic Emergency Services .... IFOTES
International Ferrocement Information Center (EISS) .... IFIC
International Fiber Optics and Communications [A publication] .... IFOC
International Film and Television Council [Rome, Italy] .... IFTC
International Frequency List (NATG) .... IFL
International Frequency Registration Board [ITU] .... IFRB
International Gravis Computer Technology, Inc. [Formerly, Gravis Computer Peripherals, Inc.] [Vancouver Stock Exchange symbol] .... IGV
International Group of Users of Information Systems (EISS) .... IGIS
International Information Centre for Terminology [Austria] [UNESCO] (EISS) .... INFOTERM
International Information Management Congress [Bethesda, MD] (EANO) .... IMC
International Information System on Research in Documentation [Paris, France] [UNESCO] (EISS) .... ISORID
International Information/Word Processing Association [Formerly, IWPA] [Later, IWP] (EANO) .... IIWPA
International Information/Word Processing Association [Formerly, IWPA] (EANO) .... IWP
International Irrigation Information Center (EISS) IIIC
International Joint Conference on Artificial Intelligence .... IJCAI
International Journal of Bio-Medical Computing [A publication] .... Internat J Bio-Med Comput
International Journal of Bio-Medical Computing [A publication] .... Int J Bio-M
International Journal of Bio-Medical Computing [A publication] .... Int J Bio-Med Comput
International Journal of Circuit Theory and Applications [A publication] .... Internat J Circuit Theory Appl
International Journal of Computer and Information Sciences [A publication] .... IJCIS
International Journal of Computer and Information Sciences [A publication] .... Internat J Comput Information Sci
International Journal of Computer and Information Sciences [A publication] .... Internat J Comput Inform Sci
International Journal of Computer and Information Sciences [A publication] .... Int J C Inf
International Journal of Computer and Information Sciences [A publication] .... Int J Comput & Inf Sci
International Journal of Computer Mathematics [A publication] .... Int J Com M
International Journal of Computer Mathematics [A publication] .... Int J Comput Math
International Journal of Computer Mathematics. Section A [A publication] .... Internat J Comput Math
International Journal of Computer Mathematics. Section A. Programming Languages. Theory and Methods [A publication] .... Int J Comput Math Sect A
International Journal of Computer Mathematics. Section B. Computational Methods [A publication] .... Int J Comput Math Sect B

Computer & Telecommunications Acronyms

International Journal. Computers and Fluids [A publication]................. Internat J Comput and Fluids
International Journal of Man-Machine Studies [A publication]................ Internat J Man-Machine Studies
International Journal of Man-Machine Studies [A publication]................ Internat J Man-Mach Stud
International Journal of Man-Machine Studies [A publication]...... Int J Man-M
International Journal of Man-Machine Studies [A publication]................ Int J Man-Mach Stud
International Journal of Micrographics and Video Technology [A publication]................ Int J Microgr and Video Technol
International Journal of Mini and Microcomputers [A publication]................ Int J Mini and Microcomput
International Labour Documentation [International Labour Office] [Geneva, Switzerland] [Bibliographic database] (OBD)........ LABORDOC
International Leased Telegraph Message Switching Service [British Telecom] [Telecommunications] (TEL)....... ILTMS
International Licensed Carrier [Telecommunications]................ ILC
International Line Selector (CAA)........ ILS
International Listening Association (EANO)........ ILA
International Luggage Registry [Computer system for recovery of airline luggage]................ ILR
International Machine Readable Catalogue (DEEC)....... INTERMARC
International Maintenance Control [Telecommunications]................ IMC
International Management Communications, Inc. [Database producer] (CUAD)........ IMC
International Management Services, Inc. [Information service] (EISS)...... IMS
International Maritime Satellite Organization [London, England] [Telecommunications] (TSSD)........ INMARSAT
International Maritime Satellite System [Department of Commerce]................ INMARISAT
International Maritime Satellite System [Department of Commerce]................ INMARSAT
International MarketNet [System of broker work stations created by IBM Corp. and Merrill Lynch & Co.]................ IMNET
International Mathematical and Statistical Libraries, Inc.................. IMSL
International Medical Informatics Association [IFIP special interest group] (EANO)........ IMIA
International Metered Communications................ IMCO
International Microcomputer Exposition (CAA)........ IME
International Micrographic Congress................ IMC
International Microprogramers' Society (CAA)........ IMPS
International MIDI [Musical Instrument Digital Interface] Association (EANO)........ IMA
International Minicomputer Accessories Corp. [Santa Clara, CA] [Hardware manufacturer] (DASO)........ INMAC
International Mobile Machines Corp.............. IMM
International Network Controlling Center [Telecommunications] (TEL)........ INCC
International Network Management Center [Telecommunications] (TEL)........ INMC
International Network Working Group [International Federation for Information Processing] (DEEC)........ INWG
International Nuclear Information System [International Atomic Energy Agency] [Vienna, Austria] [Bibliographic database] (OBD)........ INIS ATOMINDEX
International Number Dialing [Telecommunications] (TEL)........ IND
International Online Data Base [Chase Econometrics] [Database] (CUAD)........ INTLINE
International Online Information Meeting................ IOLIM
International Organization of Wo/Men in Telecommunications [Arlington, TX] (TSSD)........ IOWIT
International Organization for Standardization [Geneva, Switzerland] [United Nations]................ ISO
International Organization for Standardization Open Systems Interconnection Model................ IOS/OSI
International Organization of Wo/Men in Telecommunications [Arlington, TX] (EANO)........ IOWT
International Originating Toll Center [Bell System]................ IOTC
International Packaging Abstracts [Database] [Information retrieval] (ODIN)........ IPA
International Packet Switch Stream [Data processing]................ IPSS
International Packet-Switching Service [MCI International, Inc.] [Rye Brook, NY] [Telecommunications] (TSSD)........ IMPACS
International Packet Switching Service [British Post Office] (DEEC)........ IPSS
International Passenger Airline Reservations System................ IPARS
International Patent Agreement (IEEE)........ IPA
International Patent Documentation Center [Information service] [Austrian]................ INPADOC
International Patent Institute (DIT)........ IPI
International PBX [Private Branch Exchange] Telecommunicators [Richmond, VA] (EANO)........ IPC
International Petroleum Annual [Department of Energy] [Database] (FDB)........ IPA
International Pharmaceutical Abstracts [American Society of Hospital Pharmacists] [Bibliographic database] [A publication]........ IPA
International Phasor Telecom [NASDAQ symbol] (NQ)........ IPTLF
International Phototelegraph Position [Telecommunications] (TEL)........ IPP
International Polar Year................ IPY
International Press Telecommunications Council [See also CIPT] [London, England] [Telecommunications] [An association] (EANO)........ IPTC

International Program for the Development of Communications [UNESCO]................ IPDC
[The] International Project Management Group, Inc. [Glyndon, MD] [Telecommunications] (TSSD)........ TIPMG
International Radio Air Safety Association................ IRASA
International Radio Call Sign (DDI)........ IRCS
International Radio Frequency Board................ IRFB
International Record Carrier [Telecommunication companies providing international service] (TSSD)........ IRC
International Record Carrier, Inc. [New York, NY] [Telecommunications]................ IRC
International Reference Center for Abortion Research (EISS)........ IRCAR
International Referral Center for Information Handling Equipment [Yugoslavia] [UNESCO] (EISS)........ IRCIHE
International Rehabilitation Research Information System [National Institute of Handicapped Research] [Database] (CUAD)........ IRRIS
International Relations Information System [West Germany] (EISS)........ IRIS
International Relay, Incorporated [New York, NY] [Telecommunications] (TSSD)........ IRI
International Repeater Station [Telecommunications] (TEL)........ IRS
International Reporting and Information Services [International Private Intelligence Service] [Terminated, 1983]................ IRIS
International Reporting Information Systems................ IRIS
International Research Communications System [Electronic journal publisher] [British]................ IRCS
International Research & Evaluation [Information service] [Research center] (EISS)........ IRE
International Resource Development, Inc. [Norwalk, CT] [Telecommunications] [Information service] (EISS)........ IRD
International Road Research Documentation [OECD] [Bibliographic database] (OBD)........ IRRD
International Routing Plan [Telecommunications] (TEL)........ IRP
International Satellite for Ionospheric Studies [NASA-Canada]........ ISIS
International Science Information Services [Earth sciences data center] [Dallas, TX]................ ISIS
International Scientific Radio Union [Also, URSI]................ ISRU
International Secretariat of Arts, Communications Media, and Entertainment Trade Unions (EANO)........ ISACMETU
International Serials Data System [Paris, France] [Database] (EANO)........ ISDS
International Service Coordination Center [Communications] (CBSS)........ ISCC
International Simulation and Gaming Association (EANO)........ ISAGA
International Society for the Abolition of Data Processing Machines (EANO)........ ISADPM
International Society of Certified Electronics Technicians (EANO)........ ISCET
International Society of Mini- and Micro-Computers (EANO)........ ISMM
International Society of Wang Users [Lowell, MA] (EANO)........ ISWU
International Software AG Users Group [Reston, VA] (EANO)........ ISAGUG
International Software Network, Inc. [Milwaukee, WI] [Software manufacturer] (DASOS)........ ISN
International Solid State Circuits Conference................ ISSCC
International Sound Programing Center [Telecommunications] (CBSS)........ ISPC
International Special Commission on Radio Interference (MCD)........ ISPR
International Species Inventory System [Data processing for animal mating]................ ISIS
International Standard................ IS
International Standard Book Number [Library of Congress]........ ISBN
International Standard Book Number [Online database field identifier] (OBD)........ SB
International Standard Code for Information Interchange (NATG)........ ISCII
International Standard Program Number [Numbering system for software]................ ISPN
International Standard Serial Number [Library of Congress]........ ISSN
International Statistical Program Center [Agency for International Development] (EISS)........ ISPC
International Subscriber Dialing [Later, IDD] [Telecommunications]........ ISD
International Switching Center [Communications] (CBSS)........ ISC
International Switching Maintenance Center [Communications] (CBSS)........ ISMC
International Switching and Testing Center [Communications] (CBSS)........ ISTC
International Symposium on the Application of Computers and Operations Research in the Mineral Industries................ APCOM
International Symposium on Circuits and Systems [IEEE] (MCD)........ ISCAS
International Symposium on Subscribers' Loops and Services [Telecommunications] (TEL)........ ISSLS
International Systems Meeting [Data processing] (TUT)........ ISM
International Tandem Users' Group (EANO)........ ITUG
International Technical Communications Conference [Society for Technical Communication]................ ITCC
International Telecom Systems, Inc. [Madison, WI] [Telecommunications] (TSSD)........ ITS
International Telecommunications Satellite [Acronym is service mark and trade name of the International Telecommunications Satellite Organization and is used for communications services via satellite]................ INTELSAT
International Telecommunications Satellite Consortium [Superseded by International Telecommunications Satellite Organization]................ ITSC

Computer & Telecommunications Acronyms

International Telecommunications Union [*A specialized agency of the United Nations*] [*Geneva, Switzerland*] .... ITU
International Telecommunications Users Group [*Leatherhead, England*] [*Telecommunications*] [*Information service*] (EISS) .... INTUG
International Teleconferencing Association [*McLean, VA*] [*Telecommunications*] (EANO) .... IT/CA
International Telegraph Alphabet (NATG) .... ITA
International Telegraph and Telephonic Advisory Committee .... ITTAC
International Telegraphic Union [*United Nations*] .... ITU
International Telemetering Conference (CAA) .... ITC
International Telephone Exchange [*Telecommunications*] (TEL) .... ITE
International Telephone Services Center [*Telecommunications*] (TEL) .... ITSC
International Telephone and Telegraph Communication System .... ITTCS
International Telephone & Telegraph Corp. [*New York, NY*] .... IT and T
International Telephone & Telegraph Corp. [*NYSE symbol*] [*Wall Street slang name: "It Girl," the sobriquet for early movie star Clara Bow*] .... ITT
International Telephone and Telegraph Federal Laboratories .... ITTF
International Telephone and Telegraph Federal Laboratories .... ITTFL
International Telephone & Telegraph World Communications, Inc. .... ITTCOM
International Teletraffic Congress [*Telecommunications*] .... ITC
International Television Association [*Formerly, International Industrial Television Association*] [*Irving, TX*] [*Telecommunications*] [*Information service*] (EANO) .... ITVA
International Television Broadcasting .... ITVB
International Television Center [*Communications*] (CBSS) .... ITC
International Television Program Center [*Telecommunications*] (TEL) .... ITPC
International Thomson Library Services .... ITLS
International Tracts in Computer Science and Technology and Their Application [*A publication*] .... Int Tracts Comput Sci Technol Their Appl
International Trade Commission [*Databank originator*] .... ITC
International Transmission Maintenance Center [*Communications*] (CBSS) .... ITMC
International Tree-Ring Data Bank [*University of Arizona*] (EISS) .... ITRDB
International Union for Research of Communication (EANO) .... IURC
International Universal Time [*Telecommunications*] (TEL) .... UTI
International University of Communication [*Washington, DC*] ..... IUC
International University Consortium for Telecommunications in Learning [*Owings Mill, MD*] (EANO) .... IUC
International URSI [*Union Radio Scientifique Internationale*]-gram and World Day Service .... IUWDS
International Videotex Information Providers' Association [*British*] [*Information service*] (EISS) .... IVIPA
International Word Processing Association [*Later, IIWPA, IWP*] ...... IWPA
Internationale Messtechnische Konfoederation [*International Measurement Confederation*] [*Budapest, Hungary*] .... IMEKO
Internationale du Personnel des Postes, Telegraphes, et Telephones [*Postal, Telegraph, and Telephone International*] [*See also PTTI*] .... IPTT
Internet Protocol [*Facilitates data communications among networks*] (CCD) .... IP
Interphase Unit .... IPU
Interphone (FAAC) .... IFO
Interphone (VIT) .... INPH
Interphone (MDG) .... INT
Interphone (MCD) .... INTER
Interphone .... INTPH
Interphone Control Station .... ICS
Interphone Control System (DDI) .... ICS
Interplanetary Communications .... IPC
Interpolated Data and Speech Transmission [*Data processing*] ...... IDAST
Interpreter .... INTERP
Interpreter Generator (CAA) .... INTGEN
Interpretive Coding Language (CAA) ICL
Interpretive Computer Simulator .... ICS
Interpretive Programing System .... IPS
Interpretive Structural Modeling [*A computer-assisted learning process for structuring information*] .... ISM
Interprocess Communication Facility [*Digital Equipment Corp.*] (CAA) .... IPCF
Interprocess Controller (CAA) .... IPC
Interprocessor Buffer (CAA) .... IPB
Interprocessor Communication (BUR) .... IPC
Interprocessor Communication and Control Routine (MCD) ICC
Interprocessor Process [*Telecommunications*] (TEL) .... IPP
Interprocessor Signal Bus (CAA) .... IPSB
Interprocessor Signaling System [*Telecommunications*] (TEL) ...... IPSS
Interprocessor Unit (CAA) .... IPU
Interprogram Communication Facility [*Prime Computer, Inc.*] (CAA) ..... IPCF
Interrelated Logic Accumulating Scanner .... ILAS
Interrogate (MDG) .... INT
Interrogation, Recording, and Locating System [*Naval Oceanographic Office*] .... IRLS
Interrogation Sign [*Question mark*] [*Communications*] (FAAC) .... IMI
Interrupt (DEEC) .... INT
Interrupt [*Data processing*] [*Telecommunications*] .... INTR
Interrupt Acknowledge [*Data processing*] .... INTA
Interrupt Address to Bus [*Data processing*] (CAA) .... IAB
Interrupt Address Register (CAA) .... IAR
Interrupt Control Register [*Data processing*] .... ICR
Interrupt Control Register [*Data processing*] (MSA) .... INCR
Interrupt-Descriptor Table [*Data processing*] .... IDT
Interrupt Disk Operating System (CAA) .... IDOS
Interrupt Enable [*Data processing*] (CAA) .... IE
Interrupt Enable [*Data processing*] .... INTE
Interrupt Inhibit (CAA) II
Interrupt Level Subroutine (CMD) .... ILS
Interrupt Mask (CAA) .... IM
Interrupt-Mask Register [*Data processing*] .... IMR
Interrupt Priority Level (CAA) .... IPL
Interrupt Request [*Data processing*] .... IRQ
Interrupt Request Block (CMD) .... IRB
Interrupt Request Vector (CAA) .... IRV
Interrupt Return Register (CAA) .... IRR
Interrupt Service Routine (IEEE) .... ISR
Interrupt Service Subroutine (CMD) .... ISS
Interrupt Storage Area (OA) .... ISA
Interrupt System Enable (CAA) .... ISE
Interrupt and Timing [*Telecommunications*] (TEL) .... INTIM
Interrupt Vector Generator (CAA) .... IVG
Interrupted Continuous Waves [*Electronics*] .... ICW
Interrupted Ring Tone [*Telecommunications*] (TEL) .... IRT
Intersatellite Link (DEEC) .... ISL
Intersite Radio Communications System (MCD) .... IRCS
Interstate Airways Communications Station .... INSACS
Interstate Loan Library [*Council of State Governments*] (EISS) ILL
Interstate Organized Crime Index [*Computer databank*] .... IOCI
Interstate Settlement Information System [*AT & T*] .... ISIS
Interstation Noise Suppression .... INS
Interstation Transmission (KSC) .... IST
Interstellar Communications .... ISC
Interstellar Scattering [*of radio waves in the galaxy*] .... ISS
Intersubblock Gap (CAA) .... ISG
Intersymbol Interference .... ISI
Intersystem Link (CAA) .... ISL
Intertime Switch [*Connection or Call*] [*Telecommunications*] (TEL) .... ITS
Intertoll [*Trunk*] [*Telecommunications*] (TEL) .... IT
Intertype Fototronic Photographic System (DIT) .... IFPTS
Interunion Commission on Allocation of Frequencies [*Telecommunications*] .... IUCAF
Interuniversity Consortium for Political and Social Research [*University of Michigan*] [*Ann Arbor, MI*] .... ICPSR
Interval Pulse Time Modulation (OA) .... IPTM
Interval Selection Circuit .... ISC
Interval Service Value (BUR) .... ISV
Interval Timer [*Data processing*] (TUT) .... IT
Intervehicular Communication (KSC) IVC
Intervideo Network, Incorporated [*Los Angeles, CA*] [*Telecommunications*] (TSSD) .... INI
Intracommunication System (CIT) .... ICS
Intrasite Cabling (CET) .... ISC
Intrinsic Multiprocessing (IEEE) .... IMP
Introduction (MSA) .... INTRO
Intromogenous Computer Network .... ICN
Invalid Memory Address [*Data processing*] (CAA) .... IMA
Invention Marketing, Incorporated [*Information service*] (EISS) .... IMI
Inventory of Canadian Agri-Food Research [*Agriculture Canada*] [*Database*] (CUAD) .... ICAR
Inventory Control System [*Data processing*] (TUT) .... ICS
Inventory Forecasting and Replenishment Modules [*IBM Corp.*] .... INFOREM
Inventory Management & Production Control [*ISTEL*] [*Software package*] [*British*] (NCC) .... IMPCON
Inventory Management Program and Control Technique [*IBM Corp.*] [*Data processing*] .... IMPACT
Inventory Management and Simulator (CGC) .... IMS
Inventory Management System (NASA) .... IMS
Inventory of Sources for History of Twentieth Century Physics [*University of California, Berkeley*] [*Information service*] (EISS) .... ISHTCP
Inventory Validation Listing [*Data processing*] IVL
Inverse Discrete Fourier Transform [*Electronics*] (IEEE) .... IDFT
Inverted File Access Method (CAA) .... IFAM
Inverter (KSC) .... INV
Investigation on Teaching Using Microcomputers as an Aid .... ITMA
Investigative Support Information System [*Federal Bureau of Investigation*] .... ISIS
Investment Analysis Language [*Data processing*] (BUR) .... IAL
Investment Feasibility Studies (TEL) .... IFS
Invitation to Send [*Western Union*] [*Data communications*] .... ITS
Invitation to Transmit [*Communications*] (FAAC) .... K
Invitational Computer Conference (CAA) ICC
Inward Call Detail Recording [*Telecommunications*] (TEL) .... ICDR
Inward Wide Area Telephone Service [*Bell System*] .... INWATS
IOMEC Users Association [*Formerly, DUA*] [*Defunct*] .... IUA
Iomega Corp. [*NASDAQ symbol*] (NQ) .... IOMG
Ionospheric Forward Scatter (TEL) .... IFS
Ionospheric Prediction Service [*Telecommunications*] (TEL) .... IPS
Ionospheric Sounding Satellite [*Japan*] .... ISS
Iowa Library Information Teletype Exchange [*Des Moines, IA*] [*Telecommunications*] [*Library network*] .... I-LITE
IPL Systems, Inc. Cl A [*NASDAQ symbol*] (NQ) .... IPLSA

Iron Information Center [*Battelle Memorial Institute*] [*Information service*]   (EISS) IIC
Irregular Input Process [*Telecommunications*]   (TEL) .... I/P
ISI/Index to Scientific and Technical Proceedings and Books [*Institute for Scientific Information*] [*Philadelphia, PA*] [*Bibliographic database*]   (OBD) .... ISI/ISTP & B
Island Telephone Co. Ltd. [*Toronto Stock Exchange symbol*] .... IT
ISO [*International Organization for Standardization*] **Information Network** [*Information service*]   (EISS) .... ISONET
ISO [*International Organization for Standardization*] **Status Accumulating Binaries** [*Using*] **Extraordinary Logic** .... ISABEL
Isolated Fully Recessed Complementary Metal-Oxide Semiconductor   (TEL) .... ISO-CMOS
Isolated-Gate Field-Effect Transistor [*Electronics*] .... IGFET
Isolation Working Unit [*Telecommunications*]   (TEL) .... IWU
Isoplanar Integrated Injection Logic   (CAA) .... I³L
Israel Television .... ITV
ISSN [*International Standard Serial Number*] [*Online database field identifier*]   (OBD) .... IS
Issue Code [*Online database field identifier*]   (OBD) .... IS
Istituto Nazionale per lo Studio della Congiuntura [*Data Resources, Inc.*] [*Database*]   (CUAD) .... ISCO
Item Description .... ID
Item Logistics Data Transmittal .... ILDT
Item Logistics Data Transmittal Form   (NATG) .... ILDTF
Item Mark   (BUR) .... IM
Item Processing System   (BUR) .... IPS
Iterative Self-Organizing Data Analysis Technique A [*Data processing*] .... ISODATA
ITT [*International Telephone & Telegraph Corp.*] **Consumer Services Corp.** [*NYSE symbol*] [*Delisted*] .... ITS
ITT Corporate Communications Services, Inc.   (CAA) .... ITTCCS
ITT [*International Telephone & Telegraph Corp.*] **Secure Ranging and Communications System** .... ISRAC

J

J. H. Morgan Consultants [*Morristown, NJ*] [*Information service*]
  [*Telecommunications*]   (TSSD) .... JHMCO
Jack Morton Productions, Inc. [*New York, NY*]
  [*Telecommunications*]   (TSSD) .... JMP
Jail Accounting Microcomputer System .... JAM
Jam-Resistant Antenna .... JRA
Jam-Resistant Secure Communications .... JRSC
Jam-Resistant Secure Voice Communications   (MCD) .... JRSVC
Jam to Signal Ratio   (MCD) .... JSR
Jam Strobe   (IEEE) .... JS
Jamming Equipment .... JE
Janak-Botkin-Wallis [*Data processing program regarding forest growth; named for three men involved in program*] ..... JABOWA
Japan Annual Reviews in Electronics, Computers, and Telecommunications [*A publication*]
  .... Jpn Annu Rev Electron Comput Telecommun
Japan Electronics Buyers' Guide .... JEBG
Japan Information Center of Science and Technology [*Tokyo, Japan*] .... JICST
Japan Oceanographic Data Center [*Information service*]   (EISS) ..... JODC
Japan Online Information System [*Database*] .... JOIS
Japan Patent Information Organization [*Database producer*]
  (CUAD) .... JAPIO
Japan Patent Information Center [*Information service*]   (EISS) ..... JAPATIC
Japan Publications Guide Service [*Information service*]   (EISS) .... JPGS
Japan Telecommunications Engineering and Consultancy   (TEL) .... JTEC
Japan Telecommunications Review [*A publication*] .... JTR
Japanese Electronic Computer Company   (CAH) .... JECC
Japanese Electronic Industries Development Association .... JEIDA
Japanese Electronic Information Processing Automatic Computer .... JEIPAC
Japanese Industrial Standard .... JIS
Japanese Industrial Standards Committee [*Agency of Industrial Science and Technology, Ministry of International Trade and Industry*] [*Tokyo, Japan*] .... JISC
Japanese International Satellite Organization [*Cable-television system*] .... JISO
Japanese Keyword Indexing Simulator .... JAKIS
Jet Express Ticketing System   (TUT) .... JETS
Jet Propulsion Laboratory [*Renamed H. Allen Smith Jet Propulsion Laboratory, 1973, after a retiring congressman. However, name is not expected to be used officially*] [*California Institute of Technology*] [*NASA*] [*Research center*] .... JPL
Job   (IEEE) .... J
Job Accounting Facility   (CAA) .... JAF
Job Accounting Interface   (CAA) .... JAI
Job Accounting Table   (CAA) .... JAT
Job Analysis System [*Computer program*] .... JAS
Job Control Block [*Data processing*]   (BUR) .... JCB
Job Control Card   (MCD) .... JCC
Job Control Language [*High-level programing language*] [*1979*]
  [*Data processing*]   (CGC) .... JCL
Job Control Program   (CMD) .... JCP
Job Control Table   (CMD) .... JCT
Job Cylinder Map [*Data processing*]   (IBMDP) .... JCM
Job Data Sheet   (IEEE) .... JDS
Job Description Language [*Data processing*] .... JDL
Job Description Library   (CAA) .... JDL
Job Entry Central Services   (MCD) .... JECS
Job Entry Control Language   (CAA) .... JECL
Job Entry Peripheral Services [*IBM Corp.*]   (MCD) .... JEPS
Job Entry System [*or Subsystem*] [*IBM Corp.*] [*Data processing*] .. JES
Job Executive and Transport Satellite [*NCR Corp.*]   (CAA) .... JETS
Job File Control Block [*Data processing*]   (BUR) .... JFCB
Job File Number   (CAA) .... JFN
Job Information Block [*Data processing*]   (BUR) .... JIB
Job Information Service [*Department of Labor*] .... JIS
Job Memory Switch Matrix   (CAA) .... JMSX
Job Organization Language [*1979*] [*Data processing*]   (CSR) .... JOL
Job Pack Area [*Data processing*]   (IBMDP) .... JPA
Job Processing Unit   (CAA) .... JPU
Job Processing Word .... JPW
Job Processor   (CAA) .... JP

Job Services File   (CAA) .... JSF
Job Shop Simulation Program Generator   (KSC) .... JSSPG
Job Specification Language   (OA) .... JSL
Job Step Control Block [*Data processing*]   (BUR) .... JSCB
Job and Tape Planning System   (CAA) .... JTPS
John Crowe Productions, Inc. [*Houston, TX*] [*Telecommunications*]
  (TSSD) .... JCP
JOHNNIAC [*John's Integrator and Automatic Computer*] Open Shop System [*Time-sharing language*] [*Rand Corp.*] [*1962*]
  [*Data processing*] .... JOSS
John's [*Von Neumann*] Integrator and Automatic Computer [*An early computer*] .... JOHNNIAC
Joint Academic Network [*Proposed supercomputer network*] .... JANET
Joint Analog Numeric Understanding System .... JANUS
Joint Automatic Control Conference .... JACC
Joint Automatic Language Processing Group .... JALPG
Joint Center for Graduate Study [*Washington State University, University of Washington, and Oregon State University*]
  [*Research center*]   (RCD) .... JCGS
Joint Committee on Television Transmission .... CMTT
Joint Communications Center   (MCD) .... JCC
Joint Communications-Electronics Nomenclature System .... JCENS
Joint Communications and Electronics Working Group [*NATO*]
  (NATG) .... JCEWG
Joint Computer Conference .... JCC
Joint Coordination Center Communications Network .... JCCOMNET
Joint Council on Educational Telecommunications [*Corporation for Public Broadcasting*] [*Washington, DC*] .... JCET
Joint Council for Scientific and Technical Communication
  [*British*] .... JCSTC
Joint Electron Device Engineering Council [*Computer standards*] ..... JEDEC
Joint Electronics Information Agency .... JEIA
Joint Engineering Management Conference .... JEMC
Joint European Operations Communications Network .... JEOCN
Joint Industry Committee for Television Advertising Research
  [*Database producer*]   (CUAD) .... JICTAR
Joint Input Processing   (IEEE) .... JIP
Joint National Media Research [*Database producer*]   (CUAD) .... JNMR
Joint Telecommunications Standards Coordinating Committee
  [*American National Standards Institute*] [*Telecommunications*] ... JTSCC
Joint Track Data Storage .... JTDS
Joint User [*Telecommunications*]   (TEL) .... JU
Joint Users Group [*Data processing*] .... JUG
Joint Users Requirements Group   (NASA) .... JURG
Joint Utility Locating Information for Excavators
  [*Telecommunications*]   (TEL) .... JULIE
Joint WMO/IOC Group of Experts on Telecommunications .... ITEL
Joseph Guzman & Associates, Inc. [*Palatine, IL*]
  [*Telecommunications*]   (TSSD) .... JGA
Josephson AttoWeber Switch [*Data processor circuitry*] .... JAWS
Joule [*Symbol*] [*SI unit of energy*] .... J
Joule's Own Version of the International Algebraic [*or Algorithmic*] Language [*1958*] [*Data processing*] .... JOVIAL
Jour [*Day*] [*Telegram not to be delivered during the night time*] [*French*] .... J
Journal [*Online database field identifier*]   (OBD) .... JL
Journal. American Society for Information Science [*A publication*] .. JASIS
Journal. American Society for Information Science [*A publication*] .. JSI
Journal. Association for Computing Machinery [*A publication*] .... JACM
Journal. Association for Computing Machinery [*A publication*]
  .... J Ass Comput Mach
Journal. Association for Computing Machinery [*A publication*]
  .... J Assoc Comput Mach
Journal. Association of Personal Computers for Chemists [*A publication*] .... J Assoc Pers Comput Chem
Journal of Chemical Information and Computer Sciences [*A publication*] .... J Chem Inf Comp Sci
Journal of Chemical Information and Computer Sciences [*A publication*] .... JCICS
Journal Code [*Online database field identifier*]   (OBD) .... JC
Journal of Communication [*A publication*] .... JC
Journal of Communication [*A publication*] .... JCMNA
Journal of Communication [*A publication*] .... J Comm
Journal of Communication [*A publication*] .... J Communication

Journal of Computational and Applied Mathematics [A publication].. J Comput Appl Math
Journal of Computational Chemistry [A publication]................ J Comput Chem
Journal of Computational Physics [A publication].......... J Computational Phys
Journal of Computational Physics [A publication]..................... J Comput Ph
Journal of Computational Physics [A publication].................. J Comput Phys
Journal of Computer Assisted Tomography [A publication] .... J Comput Assisted Tomogr
Journal of Computer Assisted Tomography [A publication]... J Comput Assist Tomogr
Journal. Computer Society of India [A publication]............ J Comput Soc India
Journal of Computer and System Sciences [A publication].......... J Comput Sy
Journal of Computer and System Sciences [A publication].. J Comput Syst Sci
Journal of Computer and System Sciences [A publication].. J Comput and Syst Sci
Journal of Computer and System Sciences [A publication].................. JCSS
Journal of Current Laser Abstracts [A publication] .... J Curr Laser Abstr
Journal of Cybernetics and Information Science [A publication] .... J Cybern Inf Sci
Journal of Cybernetics and Information Science [A publication] .... J Cybern and Inf Sci
Journal of Data Education [A publication]............................. J Data Ed
Journal of Electronic Materials [A publication] .... J Elec Mat
Journal of Electronic Materials [A publication] .... J Electron Mater
Journal of Information Management [A publication]...................... J Info Mgmt
Journal of Information Processing [A publication]..... J Information Processing
Journal of Information Processing [A publication]................ J Inform Process
Journal. Institute of Electronics and Communication Engineers of Japan [A publication] .... J Inst Electron Commun Eng Jap
Journal. Institute of Electronics and Communication Engineers of Japan [A publication] .... J Inst Electron and Commun Eng Jpn
Journal. Institution of Electrical Engineers. Part 3. Radio and Communication Engineering [A publication].......... J Inst Electr Eng Part 3
Journal. Institution of Electronics and Telecommunication Engineers [A publication] .... J Inst Electron Telecommun Eng
Journal. Institution of Engineers (India). Electronics and Telecommunication Engineering Division [A publication] .... J Inst Eng (India) Electron Telecommun Eng Div
Journal. Institution of Engineers (India). Electronics and Telecommunication Engineering Division [A publication] .... J Inst (India) Electron Telecommun Eng Div
Journal. Institution of Telecommunication Engineers [A publication].. J Inst Telecommun Eng
Journal. Institution of Telecommunication Engineers (New Delhi) [A publication] .... J Inst Telecommun Eng (New Delhi)
Journal of Microcomputer Applications [A publication].. J Microcomput Appl
Journal of Micrographics [A publication]... J Microgr
Journal of Micrographics [A publication]................................... J Micrographics
Journal of Microwave Power [A publication]... JLMPA
Journal of Microwave Power [A publication] .... J Microwave Power
Journal of Microwave Power [A publication] .... J Microwave Pwr
Journal of Microwave Power [A publication].................................. JMPO
Journal Name [Online database field identifier] .... JN
Journal of Popular Film and Television [A publication] .... J Pop Film & TV
Journal of Popular Film and Television [A publication] .... J Pop Fi TV
Journal of Popular Film and Television [A publication] .... J Popular F
Journal of Systems Management [A publication].. JSM
Journal of Systems Management [A publication]............................ J Sys Mgmt
Journal of Systems Management [A publication]............................... J Sys Mgt
Journal of Systems Management [A publication]............................ J Systems Mgt
Journal of Systems Management [A publication]................................ J Syst Man
Journal of Systems Management [A publication]........................... J Syst Manage
Journal of Systems Management [A publication]............................... J Syst Mgt
Journal of Systems and Software [A publication] .... J Systems Software
Journal of Technical Writing and Communication [A publication] .... J Tech Writ Commun
Journal of Telecommunication Networks [A publication] .... J Telecommun Networks
JOVIAL [Joule's Own Version of the International Algorithmic Language] Compiler [Data processing] .... JC
JOVIAL [Joule's Own Version of the International Algorithmic Language] Compiler Implementation Tool [Data processing] (MCD)... JOCIT
JOVIAL [Joule's Own Version of the International Algorithmic Language] Compiler Validation System [Data processing]................ JCVS
JOVIAL [Joule's Own Version of the International Algorithmic Language] Control Program [Data processing].................................. JCP
Judiciously Efficient Fixed Frame [Data processing]   (MCD) .... JEFF
Jugoslovenska Radio-Televizija [Radio and television network] [Yugoslavia].. JRT
Jumbogroup Frequency Generator [Bell System].. JFG
Jumbogroup Frequency Supply [Bell System].. JFS
Jumbogroup Multiplex [Bell System].. JMX
Jump [Data processing]... JMP
Jump Address Register   (CAA) .... JAR
Jump on Condition [Data processing]   (BUR) .... JC
Jump on Condition [Data processing].. JCN
Jump Indirectly [Data processing].. JIN
Jump to Subroutine [Data processing]   (BUR) .... JSR
Jump to Subroutine Instruction [Data processing].................................. JMS
Jump Unconditionally [Data processing]... JUN

Junction   (AFM).. JCT
Junction Diode Circuit .... JDC
Junction Field-Effect Transistor .... JFET
Junction Frequency [Telecommunications]   (TEL) .... JF
Junction Gate Field-Effect Transistor   (TEL) .... JUGFET
Junction Grammar [Data processing]   (DEEC)... JG
Junction Panel [or Point] [Electronics]... JP
Junctor Frame [Telecommunications]   (TEL) .... JF
Junctor Grouping Frame [Telecommunications]   (TEL) .... JGF
Junctor Switch Frame [Telecommunications]   (TEL) .... JSF
Junior Participating Tactical Data System [Also known as "Jeep"]   (MCD).. JPTDS
Junk Acronyms When Speaking [Program] .... JAWS
Juristisches Informationssystem [Judicial Information System] [Federal Ministry of Justice] [Legal database] [West German]   (EISS).. JURIS
Just Perceptible Color Difference [Telecommunications]   (TEL)............ JPCD
Just Prior Condition [Data processing]... JPC
Justice Retrieval and Inquiry System [Department of Justice] [Legal databank] [Information service]   (EISS) .... JURIS
Justification Service Digit [Telecommunications]   (TEL) .... JSD
Justified   (CDH) .... J/S
Jute Protection [Telecommunications]   (TEL)... JP

K

K-Band Circulator	KBC
K-Band Feed	KBF
Karolinska Institutets Bibliotek och Informationscentral [*Karolinska Institute Library and Information Center*] [*Sweden*] [*Information service*] (EISS)	KIBIC
Kathode Pulse Modulation	KPM
Kaypro Corp. [*NASDAQ symbol*] (NQ)	KAYP
Keane, Inc. [*NASDAQ symbol*] (NQ)	KEAN
Keep-Alive Memory [*Data processing*]	KAM
Keep Cost Order [*Telecommunications*] (TEL)	KCO
Keep It Short and Sweet [*Radio messages*]	KISS
Keep It Simple, Sir [*Data processing*]	KISS
Keep It Simple Software Corp. [*Coral Gables, FL*] [*Software manufacturer*] (DASOS)	KISS
Keep It Straight and Simple [*Data processing*] (TUT)	KISS
Keller's Language [*1977*] [*Data processing*] (CSR)	KL
Kellogg Telecommunications Corporation [*Littleton, CO*] [*Telecommunications*] (TSSD)	KTC
Kentucky Economic Information System [*Database producer*] [*Information service*]	KEIS
Kernel Multiple Processing System [*Data processing*]	KMPS
Kerr Industrial Applications Center [*Southeastern Oklahoma State University, Durant, OK*] [*Information service*] (EISS)	KIAC
Key	K
Key-Auto-Key [*Data processing*]	KAK
Key Call Receiver [*Telecommunications*] (TEL)	KCR
Key Data Terminal (CAA)	KDT
Key Development Plan [*Telecommunications*] (TEL)	KDP
Key to Disc System (CAA)	KDS
Key to Disk Operating System (CAA)	KDOS
Key to Disk Software (CAA)	KTDS
Key Display Operating System (CAA)	KDOS
Key Display System [*Data processing*] (MDG)	KDS
Key Entry Processing (CAA)	KEP
Key Equipment [*Telecommunications*] (TEL)	KE
Key Field (CAA)	KF
Key Generator Module (CAA)	KGM
Key Issue Tracking [*Database*] (DEEC)	KIT
Key and Lamp Units [*Telecommunications*] (DEEC)	KLU
Key Length [*Data processing*] (BUR)	KL
Key Phrase in Context (DEEC)	KPIC
Key Pulse Adapter [*Telecommunications*] (TEL)	KPA
Key Pulse on Front Cord [*Telecommunications*] (TEL)	KPF
Key Pulsing	KP
Key Pulsing (MSA)	KPLS
Key Register (CAA)	KR
Key Sequenced Data Set (CMD)	KSDS
Key Station Terminal [*Data processing*]	KST
Key Strokes per Hour (CAA)	KSH
Key Symbol Out of Context [*Data processing*] (DIT)	KSOC
Key System Control Unit [*Telecommunications*]	KSU
Key Telephone Adapter [*Telecommunications*] (TEL)	KTA
Key Telephone System Modules	KTS
Key Telephone Unit	KTU
Key Transport Module (CAA)	KTM
Key Verifier [*Data processing*]	KV
Key Word [*Online database field identifier*] (OBD)	CLE
Key Word [*Online database field identifier*] (OBD)	KW
Key Word Adapted	KWA
Keyboard [*Data processing*]	KB
Keyboard (MSA)	KYBD
Keyboard Change Button [*Data processing*]	KCB
Keyboard Common Contact [*Data processing*]	KCC
Keyboard Control Unit (CAA)	KCU
Keyboard Data Entry	KDE
Keyboard Data Recorder [*Data processing*] (CGC)	KDR
Keyboard and Display [*Data processing*]	KAD
Keyboard, Display, and Printer (CAA)	KDP
Keyboard Encoder [*Data processing*]	KBE
Keyboard Entry [*Data processing*]	KBE
Keyboard Input Matrix [*Data processing*]	KIM
Keyboard Input Printout [*Data processing*] (IEEE)	KIPO
Keyboard Input Simulation [*Data processing*]	KIS
Keyboard Interface Control Unit (CAA)	KICU
Keyboard Interface Module (MCD)	KBIM
Keyboard Monitor [*Data processing*]	KBM
Keyboard Monitor [*Digital Equipment Corp.*] (CAA)	KMON
Keyboard Perforator	KP
Keyboard/Printer Control [*Data processing*]	KPC
Keyboard Process [*Data processing*]	KBP
Keyboard Send and Receive [*Data processing*]	KSR
Keyboard Simulated Lateral Telling [*Data processing*]	KSL
Keyboard Typing Reperforator [*Data processing*]	KTR
Keyboard Unit [*Data processing*] (NASA)	KBU
Keyed-Access, Erasable, Programable Read-Only Memory [*Data processing*]	KEPROM
Keyed Display Console	KDC
Keyed File Access System (CAA)	KFAS
Keyed Indexed Sequential Search (CAA)	KISS
Keyed Input Language (CAA)	KIL
Keyed Sequential Access Method [*Data processing*] (CMD)	KSAM
Keyed Sequential Access Mode [*Data processing*]	KSAM
Keying Material [*Data processing*] (NVT)	KEYMAT
Keying Relay	KR
Keying Switching Station	KSS
Keyletter-in-Context [*Data processing*]	KLIC
Keypunch [*Data processing*]	KP
Keypunch Cabinet [*Data processing*]	KPC
Keypunch Operator [*Data processing*]	KPO
Keyset Central Multiplexer (VIT)	KCMX
Keysort Multiple Selector	KMS
Keystation Adapter Unit [*Data processing*]	KAU
Keystation On-Line Business-Oriented Language [*Data processing*]	KOBOL
Keyword and Context [*Indexing*] (DIT)	KWAC
Keyword in Context [*Indexing*]	KWIC
Keyword out of Context [*Indexing*]	KWOC
Keyword in Title [*Indexing*]	KWIT
Keyword out of Title [*Indexing*]	KWOT
Keywords Permuted (DIT)	KEYPER
Kidsgrove ALGOL [*Algorithmic Language*] Digital Analogue Simulation [*Data processing*] [*British*]	KALDAS
Kienzle Input/Output Peripheral Interface (CAA)	KIOPI
Kilo [*A prefix meaning multiplied by 10^3*] [*SI symbol*]	k
Kilo-Instructions per Second	KIPS
Kiloampere	kA
KiloBIT [*Binary Digit*] [*Data processing*]	kb
KiloBITS [*Binary Digits*] per Second [*Transmission rate*] [*Data processing*] (TEL)	KBIT/S
KiloBITS [*Binary Digits*] per Second [*Transmission rate*] [*Data processing*]	kbps
KiloBITS [*Binary Digits*] per Second [*Transmission rate*] [*Data processing*]	kbs
Kilobyte [*Data processing*]	K
Kilobyte [*10^3 bytes*]	KB
Kilocharacter (BUR)	KC
Kilocycle [*Radio*]	kc
Kilocycles per Second	kcs
Kiloelectron Volt	keV
Kilogram [*Also, k*] [*Symbol*] [*SI unit for mass*]	kg
Kilohertz	Khz
Kilohm (MCD)	KOHM
Kilomegacycle	kMc
Kilometer	km
Kilometric Wavelength [*Radio astronomy*]	KOM
Kilovolt	kV
Kilovolt Ampere (CBSS)	kVA
Kilowatt	kW
Kilowatt-Hour	kWh
Kiloword (BUR)	KW
Kinetic Analysis Using Over-Relaxation [*FORTRAN computer program*] [*Physical chemistry*]	KORE
King Research, Incorporated [*Computer consultant*] [*Information service*] (EISS)	KRI
Kitchen Table International [*David D. Busch's vaporware software company*]	KTI

Kitchens Design Drawing and Costing [*Kitchens International DMS Electronics Ltd.*] [*Software package*] [*British*]   (NCC) .... KIDDCOS
Kite-Supported Antenna .... KSA
Klein Diversified Enterprises, Inc. [*Madison, WI*] [*Software manufacturer*]   (DASOS) .... KDE
KMW Systems Corp. [*NASDAQ symbol*]   (NQ) .... KMWS
Knotted List Structure   (BUR) .... KLS
Knowledge Engineer [*Data processing*] .... KE
Knowledge Engineering Environment [*An artificial intelligence system*] .... KEE
Knowledge Industry Publications, Incorporated [*White Plains, NY*] [*Telecommunications*] [*Information service*] .... KIPI
Knowledge Information Processing [*Data processing*] .... KIP
Knowledge Representation Language   (CAA) .... KRL
Kokusai Denshin Denwa Co. Ltd. [*Telegraph & Telephone Corp.*] [*Tokyo, Japan*] [*Telecommunications*] .... KDD
Konferenzberichte Kernforschung, Kerntechnik [*Information retrieval*]   (ODIN) .... KKK
Konyvtartudomanyi es Modszertani Kozpont [*Center for Library Science and Methodology*] [*Hungary*] [*Information service*]   (EISS) .... KMK
Koplar Communications Center [*St. Louis, MO*] [*Telecommunications*]   (TSSD) .... KCC
Korea Scientific and Technological Information Center [*INSPEC operator*] .... KORSTIC
Korean Institute for Science and Technology .... KIST
Kratos, Inc. [*NASDAQ symbol*]   (NQ) .... KTOS
Kurzberichte aus der Bauforschung [*Information retrieval*]   (ODIN) .... KBF
Kurzweil Data Entry Machine [*for optical character recognition*] .... KDEM
Kurzweil Reading Machine .... KRM

L

L-Band Transmitter	LBT
L. M. Ericsson [Swedish telecommunications company] (TEL)	LME
L-Type Multiplex [Telecommunications] (TEL)	LMX
Label (MDG)	L
Label Information Area (CMD)	LIA
Labor Information Database [International Labor Office] [Information service] (EISS)	LID
Labor Statistics [Database] [Department of Labor] (FDB)	LABSTAT
Laboratoire de Recherche en Sciences de l'Administration [Laval University] [Canada] [Research center] (RCD)	LRSA
Laboratories Low-Level Linked List Language [Bell Systems] (DIT)	L6
Laboratories Low-Level Linked List Language [Bell Systems] (MCD)	LLLLLL
Laboratory Animal Data Bank [Columbus Laboratories] [Columbus, OH] [Information service] (EISS)	LADB
Laboratory Automated Data Management	LADM
Laboratory for Computer and Communications Research [Simon Fraser University] [Canada] [Research center] (RCD)	LCCR
Laboratory Computer Online Inquiry	LACONIQ
Laboratory for Computer Science [Massachusetts Institute of Technology] [Research center] (RCD)	LCS
Laboratory for Computer Science Research [Rutgers University] [Research center] (RCD)	LCSR
Laboratory Data Management System [IBM Corp.]	LDMS
Laboratory of Electronics [Rockefeller University] [Research center] (RCD)	LE
Laboratory for Information and Decision Systems [Massachusetts Institute of Technology] [Research center] (RCD)	LIDS
Laboratory Instrument Computer [Medical analyzer]	LINC
Laboratory Module Computer Program	LMCP
Laboratory Peripheral System	LPS
Laboratory Vehicle Procedure Simulator	LVPS
L'Acquisition Numerique et Televisualisation d'Images Organisees en Pages d'Ecriture [French videotex system] (CAA)	ANTIOPE
Ladder Static Logic (OA)	LSL
Laminated Ferrite Memory System	LFMS
Lamp	L
Land-Based Test Site (VIT)	LBTS
Land-Line [Telecommunications] (TEL)	LL
Land Mobile Communications Council [Washington, DC] (EANO)	LMCC
Land Mobile Station [ITU designation] (NATG)	ML
Landesgewerbeamt [Nuremburg] [Information retrieval] (ODIN)	LGA
Landsat Earthnet Data Availability [ESA-Earthnet Programme Office] [Database] (CUAD)	LEDA
Langage de Programmation et de Gestion [French computer language] (IEEE)	LPG
Language [Online database field identifier] (CAA)	LA
Language [Online database field identifier] (OBD)	LG
Language Access to Distributed Data with Error Recovery (CAA)	LADDER
Language for ALGOL [Algorithmic Language] Compiler Extension [Data processing] (CSR)	LACE
Language for Automated Logic and System Design [Data processing] (CSR)	LALSD
Language Central Facility [Data processing] (IEEE)	LCF
Language Code [Online database field identifier] (OBD)	LC
Language for Computer Design (CSR)	LCD
Language for Conversational Computing (MDG)	LCC
Language Conversion Program [Data processing] (BUR)	LCP
Language Data Processing (MSA)	LDT
Language Dependent Translator (CAA)	LDL
Language Description Language [Data processing]	LDL
Language for Expressing Associative Procedures [Data processing]	LEAP
Language Information Network and Clearinghouse System [Center for Applied Linguistics] [Washington, DC]	LINCS
Language Interpretation Module (CAA)	LIM
Language Laboratory [University of California, Berkeley] [Research center] (RCD)	UCBLL
Language and Language Behavior Abstracts [Sociological Abstracts, Inc.] [Bibliographic database] [A publication]	LLBA
Language Media Format (CET)	LMF
Language and Mode Converter [Data processing] (TEL)	LAMC
Language for the On-Line Investigation and Transformation of Abstractions [Data processing] (TUT)	LOLITA
Language Processing and Debugging [Data processing] (BUR)	LPD
Language Processor Unit (CAA)	LPU
Language Research in Progress (DIT)	LRIP
Language for Simulation of Computer Architecture (CSR)	LASCAR
Language Specification (IEEE)	LS
Language Structure Group [CODASYL] (CAA)	LSG
Language for Symbolic Simulation (CAA)	LSS
Language for Systems Development (OA)	LSD
Language Translation [Data processing]	LT
Language Used to Communicate Information System Design	LUCID
Language for Utility Checkout and Instrumentation Development	LUCID
Language for Your Remote Instruction by Computer [Data processing] (MDG)	LYRIC
Langwelle [Long Wave] [German] (MCD)	LW
Lanier Business Products, Inc. [NYSE symbol] [Delisted]	LBP
Lanpar Technologies, Inc. [Toronto Stock Exchange symbol]	LPR
LARC Instruction Assembly	LISA
Large	LG
Large Aperture Scanning Telescope (TEL)	LAST
Large Automatic Research Computer	LARC
Large Base Unit [Telecommunications]	LBU
Large Capacity Core Storage [Data processing] (MDG)	LCCS
Large Capacity [or Core] Storage [Data processing] (CIT)	LCS
Large-Core Memory [Data processing]	LCM
Large Disk Storage [Data processing] (IEEE)	LDS
Large Integrated Monolithic Array Computer (MCD)	LIMAC
Large Interactive Surface [Automated drafting table that serves as a computer input and output device] (CCD)	LIS
Large Local Exchange [Telecommunications] (TEL)	LLE
Large Memory	LM
Large Off-Line Retrieval Text Base Access System	LORBAS
Large Print Video Terminal (CAA)	LPVT
Large-Scale Computer	LSC
Large-Scale Integrated Circuit [Electronics] (KSC)	LSIC
Large-Scale Integration [of circuits] [Electronics]	LSI
Large Table Electroplotter [Data processing]	LTE
Large Ultimate Size [Telecommunications] (TEL)	LUS
Larger Word [Data processing]	LWD
LASER Beam Recorder [or Recording]	LBR
LASER Communications (MCD)	LASERCOM
LASER Communications System	LCS
Laser Focus [A publication]	LAFOA
Laser Focus Buyers Guide [A publication]	Laser Foc
Laser Focus with Fiberoptic Communications [A publication]	Laser Focus Fiberoptic Commun
Laser Focus with Fiberoptic Technology [A publication]	Laser Focus Fiberoptic Technol
Laser Focus with Fiberoptic Technology [A publication]	LFFTD
LASER Relay Communication Equipment	LRCE
Laser Report [A publication]	Laser Rep
Lasers in Publishing Users Group (EANO)	LPUG
LaserVision	LV
Last (BUR)	LST
Last-Come, First-Served (CAA)	LCFS
Last Operation Completed [Data processing] (TUT)	LOP
Last Trunk Busy [Telecommunications] (TEL)	LTB
Last Word Address (NITA)	LWA
Latin American Data Bank [University of Florida] (EISS)	LADB
Lattice Screen Editor [Program editor]	LSE
Lauerer Markin Gibbs, Inc. [Toledo, OH] [Telecommunications] (TSSD)	LMG
Launch Data Bus [Data processing] (MCD)	LDB
Launch Guidance Computer (SKY)	LGC
Launch Numerical Aperture [Telecommunications] (TEL)	LNA
Law Enforcement Automated Data System (IEEE)	LEADS
Law Enforcement Computer Systems, Inc. [Sarasota, FL] [Software manufacturer] (DASOS)	LECS
Law Enforcement Information Network	LEIN
Law Enforcement Teletype [or Teletypewriter] Service [Phoenix, AZ]	LETS
Law School Computer Group [Southern Methodist University] [Dallas, TX] (EANO)	LSCG

Lawrence Berkeley Laboratory [Later, Lawrence Livermore Laboratory] [University of California] (EISS) ... LBL
Lawrence Livermore Laboratory [Also, LLNL] [University of California] ... LLL
Lawrence Livermore National Laboratory [Also, LLL] [University of California] ... LLNL
Lawrence Radiation Laboratory FORTRAN [Programing language] [1961] (CSR) ... LRLTRAN
Lawyers Co-Operative Publishing Co. [Rochester, NY] ... LCP
Lead Computing Gyro (MCD) ... LCG
Lead Computing Optical Sight ... LCOS
Lead Computing Optical Sighting System (MCD) ... LCOSS
Lead Covered Cable [Telecommunications] (TEL) ... LCC
Leading Ones Detector [Data processing] ... LOD
Leading Signal Unit [Telecommunications] (TEL) ... LSU
Leapfrog Configuration [Circuit theory] (IEEE) ... LF
Lear-Siegler, Incorporated [NYSE symbol] ... LSI
Learn, Execute, and Diagnose (CAA) ... LEAD
[The] Learning Channel [Cable-television system] ... TLC
Learning Research and Development Center [University of Pittsburgh] [Research center] ... LRDC
Learning Resources Network [Formerly, FUN] ... LERN
Learning Systems Institute [Florida State University] [Research center] (RCD) ... LSI
Lease Electronic Accounting System (IEEE) ... LEAS
Leased Line [Private telephone or Teletype line] [Telecommunications] ... LL
Leased Line Adapter [Telecommunications] (CAA) ... LLA
Leased Satellite Communications (NVT) ... LEASAT
Least Coincidence Voltage Detection (MDG) ... LCVD
Least Common BIT [Binary Digit] (MCD) ... LCB
Least Frequently Used [Data processing] (CAA) ... LFU
Least Recently Used [Replacement algorithm] [Data processing] ... LRU
Least Significant (IEEE) ... LS
Least Significant BIT [Binary Digit] [Data compaction] [Data processing] ... LSB
Least Significant Byte [Data processing] ... LSBY
Least Significant Character (IEEE) ... LSC
Least Significant Digit [Data compaction] (MUGU) ... LSD
Least Significant Position (CMD) ... LSP
Least Squares [Mathematical statistics] ... LS
Leave Message [Word processing] ... LM
Leave Word [Telecommunications] (TEL) ... LW
Lee Data Corp. [NASDAQ symbol] (NQ) ... LEDA
Left [Direction] ... L
Left-In Telephone [Telecommunications] (TEL) ... LEF
Left in Place [Telecommunications] (TEL) ... LI
Leg Multiple [Telegraph] [Telecommunications] (TEL) ... LM
Legal Information and Reference Services [General Accounting Office] (EISS) ... LIRS
Legal Research Service (EISS) ... LEXIS
Legal Resource Index [Information Access Corp.] [Bibliographic database] [Information service] (EISS) ... LRI
Legislative Authorization Program Information System [General Accounting Office] (EISS) ... LAPIS
Legislative Data Base [Department of Energy] [Information service] (EISS) ... LDB
Legislative Information and Status System [for House of Representatives] ... LEGIS
Legislative Information System [National Conference of State Legislatures] [Information service] (EISS) ... LIS
Lehigh Automatic Device for Efficient Retrieval [Center for Information Sciences, Lehigh University] [Bethlehem, PA] [Data processing] ... LEADER
Lehigh University Computing Center [Pennsylvania] [Research center] (RCD) ... LUCC
LeisureLine [Footscray, Vic.] [Database] [Information service] (EISS) ... LEIS
Length ... L
Length ... LEN
Less Than (IBMDP) ... LT
Lesson Assembly Program (IEEE) ... LAP
Letter ... LET
Letter [Online database field identifier] (OBD) ... LR
Letter (AFM) ... LTR
Letter Telegram ... LT
Letters Shift [Teleprinters] ... LTRS
Level (DDI) ... LEV
Level Control Function [Data processing] ... LCF
Level Measuring Set [for test signals] [Telecommunications] (TEL) ... LMS
Level of Study [Online database field identifier] (OBD) ... LV
Levin Computer Corp. [NASDAQ symbol] (NQ) ... LEVN
Lexical Functional Grammar [Artificial intelligence] ... LFG
Lexical-Graphical Composer Printer [Photocomposition] ... LGCP
Lexicography Information Service [West German] [Data processing] (DEEC) ... LEXIS
Lexicon Corp. [NASDAQ symbol] (NQ) ... LEXI
Lexidata Corp. [NASDAQ symbol] (NQ) ... LEXD
Liberty Bell Communications, Inc. [Detroit, MI] [Telecommunications] (TSSD) ... LBC
Librarian ... LIBR
Library (CDH) ... LIBR
Library Acquisition Program [Computer program] (CIT) ... LIBACC
Library Acquisition Services System Online [Suggested name for the Library of Cogress computer system] ... LASSO
Library Computer System ... LCS

Library of Congress [Online database field identifier] ... LC
Library of Congress Classification (CAH) ... LC
Library of Congress Information System [Information service] (EISS) ... LOCIS
Library of Congress Machine Readable Catalog [Library of Congress] [Washington, DC] [Bibliographic database] (OBD) ... LC MARC
Library Development Consultants, Inc. [Information service] (EISS) ... LDC
Library Experimental Automated Demonstration System [Data processing] ... LEADS
Library Hi Tech News [Published a bibliography using machine-readable datastrips] ... LHTN
Library Index Search and Transcribe (TUT) ... LIST
Library & Information Consultants Ltd. [Canada] [Information service] (EISS) ... LINC
Library Information Management System [Computerized library system] ... LIMS
Library Information and On-Line Network Service [New York Public Library] [Information service] (EISS) ... LIONS
Library and Information Research Group [Loughborough University] [British] [Information service] (EISS) ... LIRG
Library Information Retrieval System ... LIRS
Library and Information Science (IDA) ... LIS
Library and Information Science Abstracts [Library Association Publishing Ltd.] [Bibliographic database] [A publication] [British] ... LISA
Library Information Search and Retrieval Data System (IEEE) ... LIZARDS
Library Information Service [or System] [The Royal Library] [Sweden] [Database] [Information service] (EISS) ... LIBRIS
Library Information Services [Information service] (EISS) ... LIS
Library and Information Services Council [British] ... LISC
Library and Information Technology Association [Formerly, ISAD] [American Library Association] [Chicago, IL] ... LITA
Library Interface Systems, Incorporated [Information service] (EISS) ... LISI
Library Master File [FORTRAN program] ... LIBMAS
Library Merge Program [Computer program] (CIT) ... LIBMRG
Library On-Line Acquisitions [Washington State University] [Data processing system] ... LOLA
Library On-Line Information and Text Access [Oregon State University] [Corvallis, OR] [Data processing system] ... LOLITA
Library Order Information System [Computer system] [Library of Congress] [Obsolete] ... LOIS
Library Processes System [EDUCOMP] [Information service] (EISS) ... LPS
Library Reports & Research Service, Inc. [Denver, CO] [Information service] (EISS) ... LRRS
Library Research Center [University of Illinois] (EISS) ... LRC
Library Set [Computer program] (CIT) ... LIBSET
Library Software Package ... LSP
Library System [Computer program] (CIT) ... LIBSYS
Library Systems Analysis ... LISA
Licensing On-Line Retrieval Data System ... LORDS
Licensing Online Retrieval Data ... LORD
Licensure Information System [Public Health Service] (EISS) ... LIS
Liebert Corp. [NASDAQ symbol] (NQ) ... LIEB
Life Office Management Association [Atlanta, GA] ... LOMA
Life in One Position [Telecommunications] (TEL) ... LIOP
Light Amplification by Stimulated Emission of Radiation [Acronym was coined in 1957 by scientist Gordon Gould] ... LASER
Light Armor [Telecommunications] (TEL) ... LA
Light Detection and Ranging ... LIDAR
Light-Emitting Diode [Display component] ... LED
Light Energy Converter [Telecommunications] (TEL) ... LEC
Light Operated Typewriter (CAA) ... LOT
Light Pen (CAA) ... LP
Light Pulser Array ... LPA
Lighted Independent of Computer ... LIOC
Limb-Motion Sensor [System] ... LIMS
Limb Radiance Inversion Radiometer ... LRIR
Limit Address Register [Data processing] ... LAR
Limit Register (CAA) ... LR
Limit Signaling Comparator ... LSC
Limit of Stack Register (CAA) ... LOSR
Limited Amplifier Filter ... LAF
Limited Channel Logout (CAA) ... LCL
Limited Distance Line Adapter (CAA) ... LDLA
Limited-Distance MODEM [Data processing] ... LDM
Limited Frequency Band ... LFB
Limited Remote Communication Outlet ... LRCO
Limited Rights to Delivered Data ... LRDD
Lincoln Telecommunications [NASDAQ symbol] (NQ) ... LTEC
Line ... LN
Line Access Point [Telecommunications] (TEL) ... LAP
Line Adapter (CMD) ... LA
Line Addressable Random Access Memory [Data processing] (MDG) ... LARAM
Line Balancing Network [Telecommunications] (TEL) ... LBN
Line Buffer [Data processing] ... LB
Line Buffer System [Data processing] ... LBS
Line Building Out ... LBO
Line Circuit [Telecommunications] (DEEC) ... LC
Line Concentrator (CAA) ... LC
Line Concentrator Module (CAA) ... LCM
Line Control (CAA) ... LC
Line Control Adapter (CAA) ... LCA

Line Control Block [Data processing]	LCB
Line Control Module [Telecommunications] (TEL)	LCM
Line Control Unit [Data communications] (CAA)	LCU
Line Control Word (OA)	LCW
Line Driver-Receiver [Computer communication] (TEL)	LDR
Line Driver Unit [Computer communication] (MCD)	LDU
Line Embossing Device [Data processing]	LED
Line Equipment [Telecommunications] (TEL)	LE
Line of Equipment [Telecommunications] (TEL)	LEQ
Line Equipped [Telecommunications] (TEL)	LEQ
Line Exchange [Telecommunications] (CAA)	LEX
Line Expansion Function (CAA)	LEF
Line Fault Detector [Telecommunications] (TEL)	LFD
Line Feed [Control character] [Data processing]	LF
Line Finder [Teletype]	LF
Line Gate Number [Data processing]	LGN
Line Generator [Data processing] (CGC)	LG
Line Information Store [Telecommunications] (TEL)	LIS
Line Interface Handler (CAA)	LIH
Line Interface Module	LIM
Line Interface Unit [Data communications]	LIU
Line Intermediate Distributing Frame	LIDF
Line Leg [Telegraph] [Telecommunications] (TEL)	LL
Line Link Frame [Telecommunications] (TEL)	LLF
Line Link Network [Bell System]	LLN
Line Link Pulsing [Telecommunications]	LLP
Line Monitor Unit	LMU
Line Occupancy	LO
Line-Oriented Protocol (CAA)	LOP
Line Out of Service [Telecommunications] (TEL)	LOS
Line Printer [Data processing] (CGC)	LP
Line Printer [Data processing] (NASA)	LPR
Line Printer [Data processing] (MSA)	LPTR
Line Procedure Specifications (CMD)	LPS
Line Processing Unit (CAA)	LPU
Line Protection Switching System [Bell System]	LPSS
Line Removable Unit	LRU
Line Replaceable Unit (AFM)	LRU
Line Segment Block [Data processing]	LSB
Line Selection Module [Telecommunications] (TEL)	LSM
Line-Sharing Adapter (CAA)	LSA
Line-Sharing Device	LSD
Line-Sharing Unit (CAA)	LSU
Line of Sight	LOS
Line Signal Detector	LSD
Line Status Verifier [Telecommunications] (TEL)	LSV
Line Switch [Telecommunications] (TEL)	LS
Line Switch Frame [Telecommunications] (TEL)	LSF
Line Telecommunications	L/T
Line Telegraphy	LT
Line Term Buffer [Data processing]	LTB
Line and Terminal [Telecommunications] (TEL)	L & T
Line Terminating Unit (CET)	LTU
Line Termination Equipment [Telecommunications] (TEL)	LTE
Line Terminator (CAA)	LT
Line Time Clock (CAA)	LTC
Line Traffic Coordinator (CET)	LTD
Line Transfer Device (CAA)	LTD
Line Transient Suppression (CAA)	LTS
Line Type Modulation [Radio]	LTM
Line Unit [Data processing] (BUR)	LUT
Linear-Bounded Automaton	LBA
Linear Delta Modulation (CAA)	LDM
Linear Econometric Modeling System (BUR)	LEMS
Linear Elastic Analysis Program [SIA Computer Services] [Software package] [British] (NCC)	LEAP 5
Linear Feedback Shift Register (CAA)	LFSR
Linear Filter	LF
Linear Frequency Modulation on Pulse (MCD)	LFMOP
Linear Gate	LG
Linear Hybrid	LH
Linear Information Processing Language [High-order programing language] [Data processing] (IEEE)	LIPL
Linear Integrated Circuit	LIC
Linear Phase (CIT)	LP
Linear Phase Code Modulation (CAA)	LPCM
Linear Polarization	LP
Linear Power Amplifier	LPA
Linear Power Controller	LPC
Linear Predictive Coding [Digital coding technique] [Telecommunications]	LPC
Linear Programing [Data processing]	LP
Linear Programing Language [Intertechnique] [French] [Data processing] (BUR)	LPL
Linear Programing System [Data processing]	LPS
Linear Programing under Uncertainty [Data processing]	LPUU
Linear Stochastic Optimal Control and Estimation [Computer program]	LSOCE
Linear Threshold Element [Data processing]	LTE
Linear Transmission Channel	LTC
Linear Variable Differential Transformer	LVDT
Linearly Frequency-Modulated Pulse	LIFMOP
Linearly Organized Chemical Code for Use in Computer Systems (DIT)	LINCO
Linearly Polarized Mode [Telecommunications] (TEL)	LPM
Lines per Inch [Printing]	LPI
Lines per Minute [Data processing]	L/M
Lines per Minute [Data processing]	LPM
Lines per Second [Data processing]	LPS
Lingua Cosmica [Artificial language consisting of radio signals of varying lengths and frequencies]	LINCOS
Linguistics Research Center [University of Texas at Austin] [Research center] (RCD)	LRC
Link	L
Link Access Procedure [Telecommunications] (TEL)	LAP
Link Access Procedure Balanced [Data processing]	LAPB
Link Access Protocol (CCD)	LAP
Link Control Unit [Telecommunications] (TEL)	LCU
Link-Edit Language [Data processing]	LEL
Link Information Sciences (BUR)	LIS
Link Layer Service Access Point (CCD)	LSAP
Link Layer Service Data Unit (CCD)	LSDU
Link Level [Telecommunications] (CCD)	LL
Link Manager (CAA)	LM
Link Pack Area [Data processing] (MCD)	LPA
Link Retraction Unit (KSC)	LRU
Link and Selector Language (CAA)	LSL
Link Terminal [Telecommunications] (TEL)	LT
Link Utilization Efficiency (CAA)	LUE
Linkage Control Language [Data processing] (BUR)	LCL
Linked Compressor and Expander (NATG)	LINCOMPEX
Linked Indexed Sequential Access (CAA)	LISA
Linked Object Code	LOC
Linked Systems Project	LSP
Linked Term [Online database field identifier] (OBD)	LT
Linker Directive [Telecommunications] (TEL)	LD
Linking Relocating Loader (CAA)	LRL
Liquid Crystal Display	LCD
Liquid Crystal Shutter [Epson] [Printer technology]	LCS
Liquid Limit (IEEE)	LL
Liquid Phase Epitaxy [Magnetic film]	LPE
Liquified Petroleum Gas Report [American Petroleum Institute] [Database] (FDB)	LPGS
LISP Extended Algebraic Facility (CAH)	LEAF
List Assembly Programing [Data processing]	LAP
List Handling Facility (CAA)	LHF
List Management System (CAA)	LMS
List Processing [Programing language] [Data processing]	LISP
List Processing Language [Data processing] (IEEE)	LPL
List Processor [Standard programing language] [1958] [Data processing]	LISP
List Processor [Standard programing language] [Data processing] (BUR)	LP
Listed Address [Telecommunications] (TEL)	LA
Listed Directory Number [Bell System]	LDN
Lister Hill National Center for Biomedical Communications [National Library of Medicine] [Information service] (EISS)	LHNCBC
Listing of Oil and Gas Opportunities [Online Resource Exchange, Inc.] [Database] (CUAD)	PSI-LOGO
Literature Retrieval System [Data processing]	LIRES
Literature Retrieval System - Multiple Searching, Complete Text [Data processing]	LIRES-MC
Literaturnachweise [Literature References] [Informationszentrum Raum und Bau der Fraunhofer-Gesellschaft] [Database] (ODIN)	LINA
[The] Little Black Book [Cygnet Technologies, Inc.] [Database software]	LBB
Live Traffic Model [Telecommunications] (TEL)	LTM
Livermore Atomic Research Computer	LARC
Load (MDG)	L
Load Address Immediate (BUR)	LAI
Load Balance System [Telecommunications] (TEL)	LBS
Load Bank [Data processing] (KSC)	LB
Load Bank and Jump [Data processing]	LBJ
Load Buffer Memory [Data processing]	LBM
Load-Compensated Diode Transistor Logic [Data processing]	LCDTL
Load Computer [or Controller] (MCD)	LC
Load D-Bank and Jump [Data processing]	LDJ
Load Effective Address [Data processing]	LEA
Load External Memory Address Register (NITA)	LXMAR
Load and Go (BUR)	LAG
Load and Go FORTRAN [Data processing] (CDH)	GOTRAN
Load I-Bank and Jump [Data processing]	LIS
Load Interface Circuit (MCD)	LIC
Load Memory Lockout Register	LMLR
Load Module (MCD)	LM
Load On-Call [Data processing] (IDA)	LOCAL
Load Optimization and Passenger Acceptance Control [Airport computer]	LOPAC
Load Point (BUR)	LP
Load Storage Unit [Data processing] (CAA)	LSU
Loaded Program Request Block [Data processing] (BUR)	LPRB
Loader/Editor/Verifier [Telecommunications] (TEL)	LEV
Loading Coil [Telecommunications] (TEL)	LC
Loading Coil Case [Telecommunications] (TEL)	LCC
Loading Splice [Telecommunications] (TEL)	LS

Computer & Telecommunications Acronyms

Local	L
Local	LOC
Local Access Transport Area [Telecommunications]	LATA
Local Address (CAA)	LA
Local Address Space (CAA)	LAS
Local Area Broadcast	LAB
Local Area Data Set (CAA)	LADS
Local Area Data Transport [AT & T]	LADT
Local Area Network [Computer technology]	LAN
Local Area Network Reference Model (CCD)	LAN/RM
Local Area Telecommunications, Inc. [Digital microwave carrier] (TSSD)	LOCATE
Local Attached Support Processor (CAA)	LASP
Local Authorities Management Services and Computer Committee [British] (OA)	LAMSAC
Local Automatic Circuit Exchange [Telecommunications]	LACE
Local Automatic Message Accounting [Telecommunications] (TEL)	LAMA
Local-Battery Talking, Common-Battery Signaling [Telecommunications]	LBT CBS
Local Bus Adapter [Data processing] (CAA)	LBA
Local Bus Controller (CAA)	LBC
Local Call [Followed by telephone number]	LC
Local Circuit Switched Network (CCD)	LCSN
Local Communications Adapter [IBM Corp.] (CAA)	LCA
Local Communications Complex	LCC
Local Communications Console	LCC
Local Computer Network (CCD)	LCN
Local Concentrator Switching Unit [Telecommunications] (TEL)	LCSU
Local Control Point [Telecommunications] (TEL)	LCP
Local Data Administrator (CAA)	LDA
Local Data Distribution (CAA)	LDD
Local Data Manager (CAA)	LDM
Local Data Processor	LDP
Local Descriptor Table [Data processing]	LDT
Local Digital Message Exchange	LDMX
Local Digital Switch [Telecommunications] (TEL)	LDS
Local Display Controller (CAA)	LDC
Local Distribution System [Cable television] (MDG)	LDS
Local Engineering Control Office [Telecommunications] (TEL)	LECO
Local Exchange [Telecommunications] (TEL)	LE
Local Exchange Area Planning Simulation [Bell Laboratories]	LEAPS
Local Exchange Test Bed [Telecommunications] (TEL)	LETB
Local File Manager (CAA)	LFM
Local Format Storage (CAA)	LFS
Local Forms Control [Data processing] (CMD)	LFC
Local Frequency Distribution	LFD
Local Government Information Network [Commercial information service] [Control Data Corp.] [Database]	LOGIN
Local Graphics Library [Cambridge Computer Graphics Ltd.] [Software package] [British] (NCC)	LGL
Local Issue Data [Telecommunications] (TEL)	LID
Local Job Entry (CAA)	LJE
Local Junction Switching Unit [Telecommunications] (TEL)	LJSU
Local Line [Telecommunications] (CAA)	LL
Local Manual Attempt Recording (TEL)	LOMAR
Local Measured Service [Telecommunications] (TEL)	LMS
Local Memory (CAA)	LM
Local Memory Bus Interface [Data processing] (CAA)	LMBI
Local Memory Image (CAA)	LMI
Local Message Metering Service [Telecommunications] (TEL)	LMMS
Local Message Switched Network (CCD)	LMSN
Local Name Base [Data processing] (CAA)	LNB
Local Network Emulator (CAA)	LNE
Local Non-Switched Network (CCD)	LNSN
Local Number Dialed [Telecommunications] (TEL)	LND
Local Numbering Area [Telecommunications] (TEL)	LNA
Local Off-Net Access Line [Telecommunications] (TEL)	LONAL
Local Office Online Payment System [Unemployment insurance]	LOOPS
Local Origination [Television programing]	LO
Local Oscillator [Electronics]	LO
Local Oscillator Filter [Electronics]	LOF
Local Oscillator Frequency [Electronics]	LOF
Local Oxidation of Silicon [Transistor technology]	LOCOS
Local Packet Switched Network (CCD)	LPSN
Local Processor Link (CAA)	LPL
Local/Remote [Telecommunications] (TEL)	L/R
Local and Remote Printing [Data processing] (DEEC)	LARP
Local and Remote Printing Station [Data processing] (CAA)	LARPS
Local Service Planning System [Telecommunications] (TEL)	LSPS
Local Servicing Control Center [Telecommunications] (TEL)	LSCC
Local Servicing Control Unit [Telecommunications] (TEL)	LSCU
Local Session Identification [Data processing] (IBMDP)	LSID
Local Shared Resources [Data processing] (IBMDP)	LSR
Local Storage Function Register (CAA)	LSFR
Local Storage Unit [Data processing] (CAA)	LSU
Local Store (CAA)	LS
Local Store Data Register (CAA)	LSDR
Local Store Pointer (CAA)	LSP
Local Sunset	LS
Local Switching Replacement Planning [Telecommunications] (TEL)	LSRP
Local Switching Unit [Telecommunications] (TEL)	LSU
Local Synchronization Subsystem [Telecommunications] (TEL)	LSS
Local Synchronization Utility [Telecommunications] (TEL)	LSU
Local System Queue Area [Data processing] (BUR)	LSQA
Local Telephone Circuit [Telecommunications] (TEL)	LTC
Local Terminal Controller (CAA)	LTC
Local Test Desk (KSC)	LTD
Local User Terminal	LUT
Local Vertical/Relative Velocity Vector	LV/RVV
Local Virtual Address (CAA)	LVA
Locally Integrated Software Architecture [Apple microcomputer] [Data processing]	LISA
Location (AFM)	LOC
Location Counter [Data processing]	LC
Location Dependent (OA)	LOD
Lock-Out	LO
Locked Oscillator	LO
Locked Oscillator-Quadrature Grid [Data processing]	LO-QG
Lockheed Multiprocessor Simulation System (IEEE)	LOMUSS
Lodge-Pole Pine [Utility pole] [Telecommunications] (TEL)	LP
Log Analyzer Processor [Data processing]	LA
Log File Editor Processor [Data processing]	LOGFED
Log Periodic [Antenna] (NATG)	LP
Log Periodic Antenna	LPA
Log Periodic Array Antenna	LPAA
Log Periodic Broadband Antenna	LPBBA
Log Periodic V [Antenna]	LPV
Log Recording [Data processing]	LOGREC
Logarithm [Mathematics]	LOG
Logarithmic Amplifier	LA
Logarithmic Amplifier (IEEE)	LOAMP
Logarithmic Computing Instrument	LOCI
Logarithmic Feedback Element [Data processing]	LFE
Logarithmic Outline Processing System for Analog Data (IEEE)	LOPAD
Logic Bus Monitor [Data processing] (CET)	LBM
Logic Clock Pulse Generator [Data processing]	LCPG
Logic Control Block (CAA)	LCB
Logic and Control Simulator [Data processing] (BUR)	LOCS
Logic Design Data [Telecommunications] (TEL)	LDD
Logic Design Translator [Data processing] (TUT)	LDT
Logic Driver [Data processing]	LD
Logic Element (OA)	LE
Logic Enhanced Memory (CAA)	LEM
Logic Fault Simulator [Data processing]	LFS
Logic Flow Chart [Data processing]	LFC
Logic Function (OA)	LF
Logic Gate Expander [Data processing]	LGE
Logic Generating Language [Data processing]	LOGEL
Logic Level Driver [Data processing] (MCD)	LLD
Logic-in-Memory Array (CAA)	LIMA
Logic Module [Data processing] (MCD)	LM
Logic Probe (CAA)	LP
Logic Tables (IEEE)	LOGTAB
Logic and Test Function Drawer [Data processing] (MCD)	LTFD
Logic Theorist [or Theory] [Data processing]	LT
Logical Address (CAA)	LA
Logical Algorithmic Language [Data processing] (CSR)	LOGAL
Logical Algorithmic Language [Data processing]	LOGALGOL
Logical Analyzer of Hypothesis (IEEE)	LAH
Logical Aptitude Device (BUR)	LAD
Logical Block (CAA)	LB
Logical Channel [Data processing]	LCH
Logical Channel Fill (CAA)	LCF
Logical Channel Queue [Data processing] (BUR)	LCQ
Logical Channel Termination (CAA)	LCT
Logical Communications, Inc. [East Norwalk, CT] [Telecommunications] (TSSD)	LOGICOM
Logical Data Management, Inc. [Covina, CA] [Software manufacturer] (DASOS)	LDM
Logical Database (CAA)	LDB
Logical Design (CAA)	LD
Logical Device Address [Data processing] (IBMDP)	LDA
Logical Device Order [Data processing] (IBMDP)	LDO
Logical End of Media	LEM
Logical File [Data processing] (BUR)	LF
Logical File Name (CAA)	LFN
Logical Group Number [Data processing] (IBMDP)	LGN
Logical Inferences per Second [Data processing]	LIPS
Logical Input/Output Control System [Data processing]	LIOCS
Logical Inquiry and Update System (CAA)	LINUS
Logical Line Group [Data processing] (IBMDP)	LLG
Logical Link Control (CCD)	LLC
Logical Mapping Table (CAA)	LMT
Logical Memory Level (CAA)	LML
Logical Page Identifier (BUR)	LPID
Logical Page Number (BUR)	LPN
Logical Processor and Computer	LOGIPAC
Logical Record (CAA)	LR
Logical Record Length (CAA)	LRL
Logical Record Location	LRL
Logical Records of Fixed Length (MCD)	LRECL
Logical Shift Left [Data processing]	LSL
Logical Shift Right [Data processing]	LSR

Computer & Telecommunications Acronyms

Logical Structure: The Timing and the Sequencing of Synchronous/Asynchronous Machines [*Data processing*] (CSR) .... LOTIS
Logical Track Header (CAA) .... LTH
Logical Transient Area (CAA) .... LTA
Logical Unit [*Data processing*] .... LU
Logical Unit Block [*Data processing*] (TUT) .... LUB
Logical Unit to Logical Unit (CAA) .... LULU
Logical Unit Number (CAA) .... LUN
Logically Integrated FORTRAN Translator [*UNIVAC*] .... LIFT
Logically Organized Data Entry, Storage, and Recording .... LODESTAR
Logicheskii Yazyk dlia Predstavleniya Algoritmov Sinteza Releinykh Ustroistv [*A Programing Language for Logic and Coding Algorithm*] [*Book title*] .... LYpAS
Logicon, Inc. [*American Stock Exchange symbol*] .... LGN
Logistics Analysis Simulation System (CAA) .... LASS
Logistics Data Element Standardization and Management Process (IEEE) .... LODESMP
Logistics Intelligence Data Base .... LIDB
Logistics Management Engineering, Inc. [*Annapolis, MD*] [*Telecommunications*] (TSSD) .... LME
Lomas Data Products [*Marlboro, MA*] .... LDP
London Airport Cargo Electronic-Data-Processing Scheme .... LACES
Lone Signal Unit [*Telecommunications*] (TEL) .... LSU
Long Distance .... LD
Long-Distance Call (DDI) .... LDC
Long-Distance Communications .... LDC
Long-Distance Control System (IEEE) .... LDCS
Long Distance Transmission (BUR) .... LDT
Long Distance/USA, Inc. [*Honolulu, HI*] [*Telecommunications*] (TSSD) .... LD/USA
Long-Distance Xerography [*Xerox Corp.*] [*Communications facsimile system*] .... LDX
Long Feeder Route Analysis Program [*Bell System*] .... LFRAP
Long Island Sports Network [*Cable-television system*] .... LISN
Long Line [*Telecommunications*] (MCD) LL
Long Line Equipment [*Telecommunications*] (TEL) .... LLE
Long Pulse - Continuous Wave (NG) .... LP-CW
Long-Range Active Detection and Communications System .... LORADAC
Long-Range Earth Current Communications .... LOREC
Long-Range Facility [*Telecommunications*] (TEL) .... LRF
Long-Range Forecasting System (TEL) .... LRFS
Long-Range Planning Service [*Stanford Research Institute*] [*Assists businesses in investment activities*] (EISS) .... LRPS
Long-Range Proving Ground Automatic Computer (IEEE) .... LORPGAC
Long-Range Radiotelephone .... LRT
Long-Range Steerable Antenna (MCD) .... LORSA
Long-Range Very-High-Frequency/Ultrahigh-Frequency Communications (FAAC) .... LRCOM
Long-Route Engineering Study [*Bell System*] .... LORES
Long-Term Communications Improvement Plan (NATG) .... LOTCIP
Long-Term/Frequency Modulation .... LT/FM
Long-Term Memory .... LTM
Long-Term Procedural Language (CAH) .... LTPL
Long Term Projections [*Townsend-Greenspan & Co., Inc.*] [*Database*] (CUAD) .... LTP
Long-Term Storage [*Memory*] [*Data processing*] .... LTS
Long Wave [*Radio*] .... LW
Long Wire Antenna .... LWA
Longitudinal Parity [*Telecommunications*] (TEL) .... LP
Longitudinal Redundancy Check [*Data processing*] .... LRC
Longitudinal Redundancy Check Character [*Telecommunications*] (TEL) .... LRCC
Longitudinal Velocity Sorting Tube .... LVST
Longitudinal Video Recording .... LVR
Longitudinally Applied Paper Insulation [*Telecommunications*] (TEL) .... LPI
Lookahead Left to Right [*Data processing*] .... LALR
Looking for Party [*Telecommunications*] (TEL) .... LK
Lookup Dictionary Adaptor Program (IEEE) .... LADAPT
Lookup Dictionary Print Program (IEEE) .... LPRINT
Loop Activity Tracking Information System [*Telecommunications*] (TEL) .... LATIS
Loop Addition and Modification [*Data processing*] .... LAM
Loop Antenna (DEN) .... LA
Loop Carrier Analysis Program [*Bell System*] .... LCAP
Loop-Control [*Relay*] (IEEE) .... LPC
Loop Diagram (VIT) .... LD
Loop-Disconnect [*Telecommunications*] (TEL) .... LE
Loop Extender [*Telecommunications*] (TEL) .... LE
Loop Interface Address (CAA) .... LIA
Loop Maintenance Operations System [*Formerly, MLR*] [*Bell System*] .... LMOS
Loop Multiplexer (CAA) .... LM
Loop Regenerative Repeater (CAA) .... LRR
Loop Switching System [*Telecommunications*] (DEEC) .... LSS
Looper [*Data processing*] (MDG) L
Los Alamos Scientific Laboratory [*Also, LASL*] .... LA
Los Alamos Scientific Laboratory [*Also, LA*] .... LASL
Loss of Signal .... LOS
Lot-Size Inventory Management Interpolation Technique (BUR) .... LIMIT
Lotus Development Corp. [*NASDAQ symbol*] (NQ) .... LOTS
Loudspeaker (TEL) .... LSPK
Low L

Low (KSC) .... LO
Low-Altitude Satellite .... LAS
Low BIT [*Binary Digit*] Rate (MCD) .... LBR
Low BIT [*Binary Digit*] Test [*Data processing*] (IEEE) .... LBT
Low-Byte Enable (CAA) .... LBEN
Low Capacitance [*Cable*] [*Bell System*] .... LOCAP
Low-Cost Development System [*National Semiconductor Corp.*] (CAA) .... LCDS
Low Data Register [*Data processing*] .... LDR
Low Density (CIT) .... LD
Low Frequency .... LF
Low-Frequency Analysis and Recording .... LOFAR
Low-Frequency Beacon .... LFB
Low-Frequency Disturbance .... LFD
Low-Frequency Omnidirectional Radio Range .... LOR
Low-Frequency Phase Shifter [*Telecommunications*] (OA) .... LFPS
Low-Gain Antenna (CIT) .... LGA
Low-to-High (MDG) .... L/H
Low-Key Maintenance (CAA) .... LKM
Low-Level Interface (CAA) LLI
Low-Level Multiplexer (CAA) .... LLM
Low-Level Signaling Unit [*Telecommunications*] (TEL) .... LLSU
Low Noise .... LONO
Low-Noise Amplifier (CIT) .... LNA
Low-Noise Antenna .... LNA
Low-Noise Block [*Satellite communications*] .... LNB
Low-Noise Block Feed [*Satellite communications*] .... LNBF
Low-Noise Cable .... LNC
Low-Noise Converter [*Satellite communications*] .... LNC
Low-Noise Feed [*Satellite communications*] .... LNF
Low-Noise Level Margin .... LNLM
Low-Noise Receiver .... LNR
Low Pass [*Electronics*] .... LP
Low-Pass Filter [*Electronics*] .... LPF
Low-Pass Network [*Electronics*] .... LPN
Low-Power Amplifier (CET) .... LPA
Low-Power Schottky [*Electronics*] .... LPS
Low-Power Schottky [*Electronics*] .... LS
Low-Power Schottky Transistor-Transistor Logic [*Electronics*] .... LSTTL
Low-Power Television .... LPTV
Low-Power Transistor-Transistor Logic .... LPTTL
Low-Power Transistor-Transistor Logic (IEEE) .... LTTL
Low-Power Unit (CAAL) .... LPU
Low-Powered, Very-High-Frequency Omnirange .... LVOR
Low-Priority Key [*Data processing*] .... LK
Low Resolution [*Data processing*] .... LO-RES
Low-Resolution Facsimile [*Telecommunications*] (TEL) .... LRFAX
Low-Resolution Infrared Radiometer .... LRIR
Low-Resolution Infrared Radiometer (MSA) .... LRIRR
Low-Speed .... LS
Low-Speed Card Punch [*Data processing*] .... LSCP
Low-Speed Concentrator (CAA) .... LSC
Low-Speed Data Channel (CAA) .... LDC
Low-Speed Data Service [*RCA Global Communications, Inc.*] [*Telecommunications*] (TSSD) .... LSDS
Low-Speed Multiplexer Arrangement (CAA) .... LSMA
Low-Speed Paper Tape Punch [*Telecommunications*] .... LSPTP
Low-Speed Paper Tape Reader [*Telecommunications*] (TEL) .... LSPTR
Low-Speed Printer .... LSP
Low-Speed Reader (CAA) .... LSR
Low-Velocity Scanning .... LVS
Low-VHF [*Very-High-Frequency*] Transmitter-Receiver .... LVTR
Low-Voltage Drop (CET) .... LVD
Low-Voltage Plate .... LVP
Low-Voltage Power Supply .... LVPS
Low-Voltage Rack .... LVR
Low-Voltage Relay (DDI) .... LVR
Lower Echelon Automatic Switchboard .... LEAS
Lower Operator Rate [*Telecommunications*] [*British*] .... LOR
Lower Sideband [*Data transmission*] .... LSB
Lowercase [*i.e., small letters*] [*Typography*] LC
Lowest Usable [*or Useful*] Frequency [*Radio*] .... LUF
Lowest Usable [*or Useful*] High-Frequency [*Radio*] .... LUHF
Lubricate .... LUB
Lumen & Glare Calculations [*Facet Ltd.*] [*Software package*] [*British*] (NCC) .... LUGL
Lunar and Planetary Bibliography [*Lunar and Planetary Institute*] [*Information service*] (EISS) .... LPB
Lundy Electronics & Systems, Inc. [*American Stock Exchange symbol*] .... LDY
Lundy Electronics & Systems, Inc. Uts [*NASDAQ symbol*] (NQ) .... LNDEL
Luton Analogue Computing Engine [*British*] (DEN) .... LACE
Lynch, Young & Associates [*Newport Beach, CA*] [*Telecommunications*] (TSSD) .... LYA

M

Maastricht Automatic Data Processing and Display System [*Air traffic control*] .... MADAP
MAC [*Massive Algebraic Computation*] Symbolic Manipulator [*Programing language*] [*1969*] (CSR) .... MACSYMA
Mac [*Apple's Mackintosh computer*] Terminal Emulation Program .... MacTEP
Machinability Data Center [*Computerized search service*] [*DoD*] (EISS) .... MDC
Machine [*or Machinery*] .... MACH
Machine-Aided Cognition [*Computer project*] [*Massachusetts Institute of Technology*] .... MAC
Machine-Aided Composition and Editing .... MACE
Machine-Aided Drafting System (IEEE) .... MADS
Machine-Aided Graphics for Illustration and Composition [*Bell Telephone*] (NITA) .... MAGIC
Machine-Aided Information and Dissemination Systems .... MAIDS
Machine-Aided Manufacturing Information [*Data processing*] .... MAMI
Machine-Aided Program for Preparation of Instruction Data .... MAPID
Machine-Aided Technical Processing System [*Yale University Library*] [*New Haven, CT*] [*Data processing*] .... MATPS
Machine ANSI Data (OA) .... MAD
Machine-Assisted Educational System for Teaching by Remote Operation (IEEE) .... MAESTRO
Machine-Assisted Translation .... MAT
Machine-Assisted Vendor Information Network (CGC) .... MAVIN
Machine Automated Parts System (MCD) .... MAPS
Machine Automated Realty Service .... MARS
Machine for Automatic Graphics Interface to a Computer .... MAGIC
Machine Automatically Generating Production Inventory Evaluation [*Data processing*] (IEEE) .... MAGPIE
Machine Available Time [*Data processing*] .... MAT
Machine Check Analysis and Recording (BUR) .... MCAR
Machine Check Extended Logout (NITA) .... MCEL
Machine-Check Handler [*Data processing*] (MCD) .... MCH
Machine Check Interruption [*Data processing*] (BUR) .... MCI
Machine Check Interruption Code (NITA) .... MCIC
Machine Check Recording and Recovery [*Data processing*] (TUT) .... MCRR
Machine Communication with Digital Automatic Computer (OA) .... MACDAC
Machine Independent (NITA) .... MI
Machine Independent Microprograming Language (NITA) .... MIMOLA
Machine Independent Systems Effectiveness Data System (MCD) .... MISED
Machine-Independent Telemetry-Oriented Language [*Data processing*] (IEEE) .... MITOL
Machine Instruction Processor [*Data processing*] (BUR) .... MIP
Machine Interface Terminal D. N. C. [*Tangram Computer Aided Engineering*] [*Software package*] [*British*] (NCC) .... MIT
Machine Language [*Data processing*] .... ML
Machine Language Debugger [*National Computer Sharing Service*] (NITA) .... MLD
Machine Language Instruction (NITA) .... MLI
Machine Language Printed Circuit Boards [*Data processing*] (IEEE) .... MLPCB
Machine Language Program [*Data processing*] .... MLP
Machine Level Control [*Data processing*] (TUT) .... MLC
Machine Literature Searching [*Data processing*] (DIT) .... MLS
Machine-Oriented Language [*Programing language*] .... MOL
Machine-Prepared Wiring Data [*Telecommunications*] (TEL) .... MPWD
Machine Punch Card .... MPC
Machine-Readable Cards .... MARC
Machine-Readable Cataloging [*Library of Congress*] .... MARC
Machine Readable Cataloguing - Serials .... MARC-S
Machine-Readable Code .... MRC
Machine-Readable Data Files .... MRDF
Machine Readable Library Information [*British Library*] [*Information service*] (EISS) .... MERLIN
Machine-Readable Tapes [*Data processing*] (DDI) .... MRT
Machine Records Unit [*Data processing*] .... MRU
Machine Representation Language (NITA) .... MRL
Machine Specification Language (NITA) .... MSL
Machine Status Word [*Data processing*] .... MSW
Machine Survey and Installation Report (TUT) .... MSIR

Machine Translation [*Data processing*] .... MT
Machine Translation [*A publication*] .... MT
Machine Unit .... MU
Machine Utilization Index [*Data processing*] .... MUI
Machine Vision Association (EANO) .... MVA
Machinery .... MACHY
Machines for Coordinated Multiprocessing .... MCM
Machining Data Bank [*PERA*] [*Software package*] [*British*] (NCC) .... MACBANK
Machining Optimisation [*PERA*] [*Software package*] [*British*] (NCC) .... MACOPT
MacNeal-Schwendler Corp. [*American Stock Exchange symbol*] .... MNS
MacNeal-Schwendler Corporation [*NASDAQ symbol*] (NQ) .... MSCI
Macro Arithmetic Processors [*Data processing*] (MDG) .... MAP
Macro-Based Display Oriented Language [*Raytheon Co.*] (NITA) .... MACROL
Macro Description Language [*Data processing*] (BUR) .... MDL
Macro Operation Symbolic Assembler and Information Compiler [*Data processing*] (IEEE) .... MOSAIC
Macro-Oriented Business Language [*Data processing*] .... MOBL
[*A*] Macro Programing Language [*Data processing*] .... AMPL
Macro Read-Only Memory [*Data processing*] (NITA) .... MROM
Macro Selection Compiler [*Data processing*] (BUR) .... MSC
Macroaddress Bus (NITA) .... MAB
Macroaddress Register (NITA) .... MAR
Macroassembler (NITA) .... MAS
Macroassembly Language [*Data processing*] (BUR) .... MAL
Macroassembly Program [*Data processing*] .... MAP
Macrogenerator [*SEMIS*] (NITA) .... MAG
Macroinstruction Compiler Assembler [*Data processing*] .... MICA
Macromodular System [*Data processing*] (IEEE) .... MS
Macromodule and Digital Differential Analyzer Machine [*Data processing*] .... MADDAM
Macroprocessor (NITA) .... MP
MAD [*Magnetic Anomaly Detector*] Hunting Circle .... MHC
Madison Academic Computing Center [*University of Wisconsin - Madison*] [*Information service*] [*Research center*] .... MACC
Madison Square Garden Network [*Cable-television system*] .... MSG
Magazine Index [*Information Access Corp.*] [*Information service*] (EISS) .... MI
Magnetic (AFM) .... MAG
Magnetic Attitude Prediction .... MGAP
Magnetic Automatic Navigation [*System*] (RDA) .... MAN
Magnetic-Bubble Domain Device [*Data processing*] (IEEE) .... MBD
Magnetic Bubble Memory [*Data processing*] (IEEE) .... MBM
Magnetic Card [*Word processing*] .... MC
Magnetic Card Reader [*Data processing*] (NITA) .... MCR
Magnetic Card "Selectric" Typewriter [*IBM Corp.*] .... MCST
Magnetic Character Reader [*Data processing*] (IEEE) .... MCR
Magnetic Character Recognition [*Data processing*] (BUR) .... MCR
Magnetic Core Memory [*Data processing*] .... MCM
Magnetic Decision Element [*Data processing*] (BUR) .... MDE
Magnetic Device Evaluator [*Data processing*] .... MADE
Magnetic Disk [*Data processing*] (BUR) .... MD
Magnetic Disk Control Unit (NITA) .... MDCU
Magnetic Disk Drive (NITA) .... MDD
Magnetic Disk Storage Device [*Data processing*] .... MDSD
Magnetic Drum Module [*Data processing*] (CDH) .... DM
Magnetic Drum Receiving Equipment .... MADRE
Magnetic Drum Recorder .... MDR
Magnetic Drum Storage System .... MDSS
Magnetic Drum System .... MDS
Magnetic Energy Product .... MEP
Magnetic Field Calibration System .... MFCS
Magnetic Field Energy .... MFE
Magnetic Field Indicator .... MFI
Magnetic Field Intensity .... MFI
Magnetic Field Line .... MFL
Magnetic Field Perturbation .... MFP
Magnetic Field Strength .... MFS
Magnetic Film Counter .... MFC
Magnetic Film Handler (CMD) .... MFH
Magnetic Film Strip Recorder .... MFSR

Magnetic Flight Test Recording System ... MFTRS
Magnetic Flip-Flop [Data processing] ... MFF
Magnetic Flow Transmitter ... MFT
Magnetic Flux [Symbol] ... N
Magnetic Flux Density (CDH) ... b
Magnetic Forming Machine ... MFM
Magnetic Frequency Detector ... MFD
Magnetic Fusion Energy ... MFE
Magnetic Fusion Engineering Act ... MFEA
Magnetic Head [or Heading] ... MH
Magnetic Heading (FAAC) ... MHDG
Magnetic Heading System ... MHS
Magnetic Indicator Loop ... MIL
Magnetic Information Technology [NASDAQ symbol] (NQ) ... MITI
Magnetic Ink Character Recognition [Banking] [Data processing] ... MICR
Magnetic Ink Mark Recognition ... MIMR
Magnetic Ink Read ... MIR
Magnetic Insulation Test Experiment ... MITE
Magnetic Integrator Neuron Duplicator ... MIND
Magnetic Interaction Mechanism ... MIM
Magnetic Ledger Card (CMD) ... MLC
Magnetic Local Time ... MLT
Magnetic Logic Computer ... MAGLOC
Magnetic Phase Modulator ... MPM
Magnetic Recording Boresight [or Borescope] ... MRB
Magnetic Recording Head ... MRH
Magnetic Reed Rotary Switch ... MRRS
Magnetic Reed Switch ... MRS
Magnetic Storage [Data processing] ... MS
Magnetic Storage Drum [Data processing] ... MSD
Magnetic Storage Drum System [Data processing] ... MSDS
Magnetic Storage Ring [Data processing] ... MSR
Magnetic Tape ... MT
Magnetic Tape Accessory [General Electric Co.] (NITA) ... MTA
Magnetic Tape Cassette [Data processing] ... MTC
Magnetic Tape Channel [Data processing] (NITA) ... MTC
Magnetic Tape Control [Data processing] (TUT) ... MTC
Magnetic Tape Control Unit [Data processing] ... MTCU
Magnetic Tape Disk [Data processing] (NASA) ... MTDSK
Magnetic Tape Field Scan [Data processing] ... MFC
Magnetic Tape Field Search [Data processing] (CGC) ... MFS
Magnetic Tape Handler [Data processing] ... MTH
Magnetic Tape to Microfilm ... MT/MF
Magnetic Tape Operations System [Data processing] ... MTOS
Magnetic Tape Programing System [Data processing] (IEEE) ... MTPS
Magnetic Tape Recorder ... MTR
Magnetic Tape Recorder End ... MTRE
Magnetic Tape Recorder Start ... MTRS
Magnetic Tape Reformatting System [Hewlett-Packard Co.] ... MTRS
Magnetic Tape Search Unit [Data processing] ... MTSU
Magnetic Tape "Selectric" Composer [IBM Corp.] ... MTSC
Magnetic Tape "Selectric" Typewriter [IBM Corp.] ... MTST
Magnetic Tape Station [Data processing] (CET) ... MTS
Magnetic Tape Storage System ... MTSS
Magnetic Tape System [Data processing] ... MTS
Magnetic Tape and Telemetry (MCD) ... MTTM
Magnetic Tape Terminal [Data processing] ... MTT
Magnetic Tape Terminal Equipment [Data processing] (CET) ... MTTE
Magnetic Tape Transmissions (CET) ... MTM's
Magnetic Tape Transport [Data processing] (IEEE) ... MTT
Magnetic Tape Unit [Data processing] ... MTU
Magnetic Variation (MCD) ... M/V
Magnetic Video Camera [Sony Corp.] ... MAVICA
Magnetic Voltage Stabilizer ... MVS
Magnetic Wire Shift Register ... MWSR
Magnetically Insulated Diode [Physics] ... MID
Magnetizing Force [Symbol] (DEN) ... H
Magneto [Generator] ... MGN
Magnetohydrodynamics [Electric power] ... MHD
Magnetoionic Wave Component ... MWC
Magnetometer ... MGTMTR
Magnetomotive Force ... mmf
Magnetospheric Radio Burst ... MRB
Magnetostatic Backward Volume Wave [Telecommunications] (TEL) ... MSBVW
Magnetostatic Forward Volume Wave [Telecommunications] (TEL) ... MSFVW
Magnetostatic Surface Wave [Telecommunications] (TEL) ... MSSW
Magnetostatic Waves [Telecommunications] (TEL) ... MSW
Magnetron (MDG) ... M
Mail Boxes Etc. USA [Carlsbad, CA] [Telecommunications] (TSSD) ... MBE
Mail File Requirement [Code] [Data processing] ... MFR
Main Call Process [Telecommunications] (TEL) ... MCP
Main Channel (OA) ... MC
Main Communications Center ... MCC
Main Data Path (NITA) ... MDP
Main Display Console ... MDC
Main Distributing Frame [Bell System] ... MDF
Main Entry [Library Science] [Online database field identifier] (OBD) ... ME
Main Feed (MCD) ... MFD
Main Instrument Console and Readout Stations (NATG) ... MICRS
Main Lobe (IEEE) ... ML
Main Memory ... MM
Main Memory Address Register (NITA) ... MMAR
Main Memory Register (NITA) ... MMR
Main Memory Unit (NITA) ... MMU
Main Network [Telecommunications] (TEL) ... MN
Main Network Switching Center [Telecommunications] (TEL) ... MNSC
Main Storage (NITA) ... MS
Main Storage Control [Data processing] (BUR) ... MSC
Main Storage Control Element [Data processing] (IEEE) ... MSCE
Main Storage Database (NITA) ... MSDB
Main Storage Unit [Data processing] ... MSU
Main Traffic Group [Telecommunications] (TEL) ... MTG
Main Trunk Circuit [World Meteorological Organization] [Telecommunications] (TEL) ... MTC
Main Trunk System [Telecommunications] (TEL) ... MTS
Mainframe Termination [Telecommunications] (TEL) ... MFT
Maintain System History Program [IBM Corp.] ... MSHP
Maintenance (AFM) ... MAINT
Maintenance [Telecommunications] (TEL) ... MTCE
Maintenance Activities and Resources Simulation [Data processing] ... MARS
Maintenance and Administration Panel [Bell System] ... MAAP
Maintenance Analysis, Detection, and Reporting System [Data processing] (AFM) ... MADARS
Maintenance Analysis and Procedures System [Data processing] ... MAPS
Maintenance Automatic Integration Director [Data processing] ... MAID
Maintenance Busy [Telecommunications] (TEL) ... MB
Maintenance Computing and Recording System ... MCRS
Maintenance and Construction Management Information System [Data processing] ... MACMIS
Maintenance Control Center (AFM) ... MCC
Maintenance Control Module [Telecommunications] (TEL) ... MCM
Maintenance Control Section [DCE] ... MCS
Maintenance Control and Statistics Process [Telecommunications] (TEL) ... MCSP
Maintenance Control Unit [Data processing] (NITA) ... MCU
Maintenance Data System (MCD) ... MDS
Maintenance Demand Time (MCD) ... MDT
Maintenance Diagnostic Logic [Data processing] (BUR) ... MDL
Maintenance Diagnostic Unit (NITA) ... MDU
Maintenance Documentation System [Bell System] ... MDS
Maintenance Downtime (MCD) ... MDT
Maintenance Engineering Data Storage and Retrieval System (NG) ... MEDSARS
Maintenance Float Distribution Point [Data processing] (NATG) ... MFDP
Maintenance Information Retrieval Aid ... MIRAID
Maintenance Inventory Control System [Bell System] ... MICS
Maintenance Job Request ... MJR
Maintenance Management Software ... MMS
Maintenance Message Process [Telecommunications] (TEL) ... MMP
Maintenance and Operational Data Presentation Study ... MODAPS
Maintenance Panel ... MP
Maintenance Period ... MP
Maintenance Plan ... MP
Maintenance Point ... MP
Maintenance Prints ... MP
Maintenance Procedure (MCD) ... MP
Maintenance Program ... MP
Maintenance Signal Data Converter (MCD) ... MSDC
Maintenance Signal Data Recorder (MCD) ... MSDR
Maintenance Signal Data Recording Set [or System] (MCD) ... MSDRS
Maintenance Signal Unit [Telecommunications] (TEL) ... MSU
Maintenance and Status Unit [Telecommunications] (TEL) ... MSU
Maintenance Support Index ... MSI
Major Gain Control ... MGC
Major Incident Room Index and Action Management [Police computer] [British] ... MIRIAM
Major Item Data File ... MIDF
Major Subject Descriptor [Online database field identifier] (OBD) ... MJ
Major System Mode (CAAL) ... MSM
Malfunction Alert [Data processing] (BUR) ... MFA
Malfunction Analysis, Detection, and Recording [Data processing] ... MADAR
Malfunction Analysis, Detection, and Recording Subsystem [Data processing] (DDI) ... MADARS
Malfunction Investigation Laboratory ... MIL
Malfunction Rate ... MFR
Malicious Call Identification [Telecommunications] (TEL) ... MCI
Man and Computer (DIT) ... MAC
Man Computer Graphics [Data processing] ... MCG
Man-Hour Accounting Card (DDI) ... MHAC
Man In, Machine Out [Data processing] ... MIMO
Man-Machine Communication [Data processing] ... MMC
Man-Machine Interface ... MMI
Man-Machine Language [Data processing] (TEL) ... MML
Man-Machine Partnership Translation [Telecommunications] (IEEE) ... MMPT
Man-Machine System (MCD) ... MMS
Man-Vehicle Laboratory [Massachusetts Institute of Technology] [Research center] (RCD) ... MVL
Managed Data Network ... MDN
Management Access to Records (NITA) ... MATR
Management of Advanced Automation Technology Center [Worcester Polytechnic Institute] [Research center] (RCD) ... MAAT

Management Analysis Program (TUT) ... MAP
Management Analysis Reporting System [*Data processing*] ... MARS
Management Applications in a Computer Environment (IEEE) ... MACE
Management Assistance, Inc. [*NYSE symbol*] ... M
Management Assistance, Incorporated [*Tustin, CA*] [*Software manufacturer*] (DASOS) ... MAI
Management Automated Information Display System (KSC) ... MAIDS
Management & Computer Services, Inc. [*Information service*] (EISS) ... MACS
Management Consultants International, Inc. [*Canada*] [*Information service*] (EISS) ... MCI
Management Contents [*Information service*] (EISS) ... MC
Management Control Center [*Data processing*] (BUR) ... MCC
Management Control System (MCD) ... MCS
Management Data Online Status/Inquiry System (MCD) ... MDOSIS
Management Data Query System [*Data processing*] ... MDQS
Management Data Reporting System (MCD) ... MDRS
Management Data Service Center ... MDSC
Management Data System (NASA) ... MDS
Management Information Center ... MIC
Management Information Corporation [*Cherry Hill, NJ*] [*Information service*] (EISS) ... MIC
Management Information and Data Systems (NVT) ... MIDS
Management Information Report Access without Computer Languages [*Data processing*] (IEEE) ... MIRACL
Management Information Science (TUT) ... MIS
Management Information Service ... MIS
Management Information Specialist ... MIS
Management Information System Plan ... MISP
Management Information System Symbolic Interpretive Language [*Data processing*] ... MISSIL
Management Information Systems [*Corporation for Public Broadcasting*] [*Information service*] (EISS) ... MIS
Management Information and Text System (NITA) ... MITS
Management Integrated Control System (VIT) ... MICS
Management Integrated Data Accumulating System (VIT) ... MIDAS
Management Integrated System (TEL) ... MIS
Management Job Review [*LIMRA*] ... MJR
Management and Marketing Abstracts [*PIRA*] [*Bibliographic database*] [*British*] (OBD) ... MMA
Management On-Line Data System [*University of Syracuse*] ... MOLDS
Management Report Generator [*Randolph Data Services, Inc.*] [*Software package*] [*Data processing*] (IEEE) ... MARGEN
Management Scheduling and Control System [*Telecommunications*] (TEL) ... MSCS
Management Science [*Data processing*] (BUR) ... MS
Management Science of America [*NASDAQ symbol*] (NQ) ... MSAI
Management Science America, Inc. [*Atlanta, GA*] [*Software manufacturer*] (DASOS) ... MSA
Management Science Associates, Inc. [*Information service*] (EISS) ... MSA
Management Services Contractor [*INTELSAT*] (CBSS) ... MSC
Management Signal Unit [*Telecommunications*] (TEL) ... MSU
Management Statistics Subsystem (TEL) ... MSS
Management System Analysis ... MSA
Management Systems Laboratories [*Virginia Polytechnic Institute and State University*] [*Research center*] (RCD) ... MSL
Management Systems Unit (TUT) ... MSU
Management Update and Retrieval System ... MUR
Management Work Station [*Data processing*] (BUR) ... MWS
Manager Integrated Dictionary Week [*Manager Software Products*] [*Lexington, MA*] (EANO) ... MIDWEEK
Manchester Automatic Digital Machine [*Manchester University*] [*British*] (IEEE) ... MADM
Maneuver Control System [*Data processing*] ... MCS
Manhattan Cable TV, Inc. [*New York, NY*] [*Telecommunications*] (TSSD) ... MCTV
Manipulator Controller Interface Unit (NASA) ... MCIU
Manipulator Handset Controller (MCD) ... MHSC
Manitoba Research Council [*Winnipeg, MB*] [*Research center*] (RCD) ... MRC
Manned Interceptor Simulation Program ... MISP
Manned Satellite Inspection System ... MSIS
Manned Satellite Inspector ... MSI
Manpack Loop Antenna ... MLA
Manpower Information Retrieval System (IEEE) ... MIRS
Manpower Operations Data System [*Employment and Training Administration*] [*Department of Labor*] ... MODS
Manual (KSC) ... MAN
Manual (CDH) ... MN
Manual Clock [*Data processing*] (MDG) ... MK
Manual Communication Module [*Telecommunication device for the deaf*] ... MCM
Manual Data Input Function [*Data processing*] ... MDIF
Manual Data Input Section [*Data processing*] ... MDIS
Manual Data Input Unit [*Data processing*] ... MDIU
Manual Direction Finder [*Radio*] ... MDF
Manual Entry Subsystem (IEEE) ... MES
Manual Fault Isolation Test ... MFIT
Manual Frequency Control ... MFC
Manual Gain Control ... MGC
Manual High-Voltage Power Supply ... MHVPS
Manual Hold [*Telecommunications*] (DEEC) ... MH
Manual Input [*Data processing*] ... MANIP
Manual Input [*Data processing*] ... MI
Manual Input Buffer [*Data processing*] ... MIB
Manual Input Processing [*or Program*] [*Data processing*] ... MIP
Manual Intervention Facility ... MIF
Manual Pulser ... MP
Manual Ringdown [*Telecommunications*] (TEL) ... MRD
Manual Select Keyboard [*Data processing*] (KSC) ... MSK
Manual Wire Wrap ... MWW
Manual Wire Wrap Fixture ... MWWF
Manual Word ... MW
Manufacturers Data Services, Inc. [*Hendersonville, TN*] [*Software manufacturer*] (DASOS) ... MDS
Manufacturers' Radio Frequency Advisory Committee (EANO) ... MRFAC
Manufacturing, Accounting, and Production Information Control System [*IBM Corp.*] ... MAPICS
Manufacturing Activity Projection (TUT) ... MAP
Manufacturing Automation Protocol [*General Motors computer compatibility program*] ... MAP
Manufacturing Control System (TUT) ... MCS
Manufacturing Data Retrieval System (NASA) ... MDRS
Manufacturing Data Systems, Incorporated [*Ann Arbor, MI*] [*Software manufacturer*] (DASOS) ... MDSI
Manufacturing Information and Control System (OA) ... MIACS
Manufacturing Information System [*Data processing*] (BUR) ... MIS
[*A*] **Manufacturing Language** [*Data processing*] ... AML
Manufacturing Monitoring System [*Data processing*] (IBMDP) ... MMS
Manufacturing Operating System [*IBM Corp.*] ... MOS
Manufacturing Planning and Control [*Arthur Anderson & Co.*] [*Software package*] [*British*] (NCC) ... MAC-PAC
Manufacturing Process Control Document (KSC) ... MPCD
Manufacturing Research and Design Group [*McMaster University*] [*Canada*] [*Research center*] (RCD) ... MRDG
Manufacturing Resource Control [*Kongsberg UK*] [*Software package*] [*British*] (NCC) ... MRC
Manufacturing Resource Control System [*Deritend Computer Bureau Ltd.*] [*Software package*] [*British*] (NCC) ... MARC
Manufacturing Resource Planning [*Data processing*] ... MRP
Manufacturing & Resource Planning System [*Cincom Systems Ltd.*] [*Software package*] [*British*] (NCC) ... MRPS
[*The*] **Manufacturing System** [*Burroughs Machines Ltd.*] [*Software package*] [*British*] (NCC) ... TMS
Manufacturing Technology Centre of New Brunswick [*Fredericton, NB*] [*Research center*] (RCD) ... MTC
Manufacturing Test Data System (IEEE) ... MTDS
Map Analysis System [*Data processing*] ... MANS
Map Information Assembly and Display System ... MIADS
Mapped Real-Time Disk Operating System [*Data processing*] (MDG) ... MRDOS
Marconi Automatic Relay System (IEEE) ... MARS
Margaux Controls, Inc. [*NASDAQ symbol*] (NQ) ... MRGX
Marginal Check [*Computer*] ... MC
Marine Advisory Service [*National Oceanic and Atmospheric Administration*] [*Information service*] (EISS) ... MAS
Marine and Coastal Technology Information Service [*United Nations*] (EISS) ... MACTIS
Marine Information and Advisory Service [*Institute of Oceanographic Sciences*] [*Databank*] [*British*] (EISS) ... MIAS
Marine Pollution Information Centre [*Marine Biological Association of the United Kingdom*] (EISS) ... MARPIC
Marine Systems Operational Compiler ... MSOC
Marine Tactical Data System ... MTDS
Marine Toebreak Data System (NG) ... MTDS
Maritime Air Telecommunications Organization [*NATO*] (NATG) ... MATELO
Maritime Communications Satellite ... MARECS
Maritime Data Network [*Maritime Data Network Ltd.*] [*Database*] (CUAD) ... MARDATA
Maritime Mobile Telegraph Distress and Calling ... MMTDC
Maritime Mobile Telegraphy Calling ... MMTC
Maritime Satellite [*COMSAT*] ... MARSAT
Maritime Satellite System [*COMSAT*] ... MARISAT
Maritime Satellite System [*COMSAT*] ... MARSATS
Maritime Tactical Data Exchange (NATG) ... MTDE
Mark (KSC) ... MK
Mark Document Reader [*Trademark*] [*Bell & Howell*] ... MDR
Mark Sense Reading (NITA) ... MSR
Mark Sheet Reader [*Data processing*] (BUR) ... MSR
Marked [*Data processing*] (MDG) ... MRKD
Marked Stack Control Word (NITA) ... MSCW
Marker Pulse Conversion [*Telecommunications*] (TEL) ... MPC
Market Analysis Guide - Intercity Communications [*AT & T*] ... MAGIC
Market Analysis and Information Database [*Information service*] (EISS) ... MAID
Market Analysis and Reference System [*Vancouver stock exchange computer system*] [*Canada*] ... MARS
Market Analysis Report Generator [*Data processing*] ... MARG
Market Data Retrieval [*Westport, CT*] [*Originator, operator, and databank*] [*Information service*] (EISS) ... MDR
Market Identifiers [*Dun's Marketing Services*] ... MI
Market Research Information System [*Bell System*] ... MRIS
Marketing and Advertising General Information Centre [*Datasolve Ltd.*] [*Database*] (CUAD) ... MAGIC

Marketing and Advertising Reference Service [Predicats, Inc.] [Database] (CUAD)	MARS
Marketing Concepts, Incorporated [New York, NY] [Telecommunications] (TSSD)	MCI
Marketing, Engineering, and Business Services [Telecommunications] (TEL)	MEBS
Marketing Information Data Systems, Inc. [Information service] (EISS)	MIDS
Marketing Information System	MIS
Marketing Programs and Services Group, Inc. [Gaithersburg, MD] [Information service] [Telecommunications] (TSSD)	MPSG
Markov Game Planar Intercept-Evasion Package [Data processing]	MAGPIE
MARS [Military Affiliate Radio System] Technical Service (CET)	MTS
Marshall System for Aerospace Simulation [Programing language] [1966-68] (CSR)	MARSYAS
Martin Automatic Data-Reduction Equipment	MADRE
Martin Marietta Corporation (KSC)	MMC
Martin Marietta Data Systems (NITA)	MMDS
Maruzen Online Network [Maruzen Co. Ltd.] [Tokyo, Japan] [Telecommunications] (TSSD)	MARUNET
Maruzen Scientific Information Service Center [Maruzen Co. Ltd.] [Tokyo, Japan] [Telecommunications] (TSSD)	MASIS
Maryland Public Television [Owings Mills] [Information service] [Telecommunications] (TSSD)	MPT
Mask Programed Read-Only Memory (NITA)	MPROM
Mask Register (NITA)	MR
Mask Shop Information System [Bell Laboratories]	MSIS
Masked Read-Only Memory [Data processing]	MROM
Masking Parameter Printout [Data processing]	MAPP
Mass Data Storage Facility (SKY)	MDSF
Mass Digital Storage	MDS
Mass Digital Storage System	MDSS
Mass Memory (NASA)	MM
Mass Memory Control Subsystem (TEL)	MMCS
Mass Memory Store [Data processing] (IEEE)	MMS
Mass Model [Computer program]	MASMOD
Mass Random Access Data Storage [Data processing]	MRADS
Mass Random Access Disk [Data processing]	MRAD
Mass Service Mainline Cable Systems (OA)	MSMLCS
Mass Spectral Information System	MSIS
Mass Spectral Search System [National Bureau of Standards, Environmental Protection Agency, and National Institutes of Health] [Database]	MSSS
Mass Spectral Search System-Wiley [Cornell University] [Database] (CUAD)	MSSSW
Mass Spectrometry Bulletin [Mass Spectrometry Data Centre] [Bibliographic database] [British] (OBD)	MSB
Mass Spectrometry Data Centre [British] (EISS)	MSDC
Mass Storage [Data processing]	MS
Mass Storage Adapter (NITA)	MSA
Mass Storage Control [Data processing] (BUR)	MSC
Mass Storage Device [Data processing]	MSD
Mass Storage Editor [Data processing] (MCD)	MSE
Mass Storage Facility [Data processing] (IBMDP)	MSF
Mass Storage Input-Output [Data processing] (IEEE)	MSIO
Mass Storage Operating System [Control Data Corp.] [Data processing] (NVT)	MSOS
Mass Storage Processor [Honeywell, Inc.] (NITA)	MSP
Mass Storage Resident [Data processing] (IEEE)	MSR
Mass Storage System [Data processing]	MSS
Mass Storage System Communicator [Data processing] (IBMDP)	MSSC
Mass Storage System Control [Data processing] (BUR)	MSSC
Mass Storage Task Group [CODASYL] (NITA)	MSTG
Mass Storage Unit [Data processing] (NASA)	MSU
Mass Storage Volume (NITA)	MSV
Mass Storage Volume Control [Data processing] (BUR)	MSVC
Mass Tape Duplicator/Verifier [Data processing] (MCD)	MTD
Mass Termination System [Data processing] (IEEE)	MTS
Mass Unbalance Input [Data processing] (CIT)	MUI
Massachusetts General Hospital Utility Multiprograming System [Programing language]	MUMPS
Massachusetts Institute of Technology [Cambridge, MA]	MIT
Massachusetts Institute of Technology Information Laboratory Automatic Coding	MITILAC
Massive Algebraic Computation [Programing language] [1958] [Data processing] (CSR)	MAC
Massively Parallel Processor [Image processing]	MPP
Master	MSTR
Master Accession Document [Data processing] (BUR)	MAD
Master Acquisition Bus [Data processing] (MCD)	MAB
Master Air Data [Computer]	MAD
Master Antenna Television	MATV
Master Bus Controller [Data processing]	MBC
Master of Business Information Systems	MBIS
Master Clock	MCLK
Master Clock Unit (VIT)	MCU
Master Community Antenna	MCA
Master Control	MC
Master Control Center (NATG)	MCC
Master Control Console	MCC
Master Control and Data Buffer Storage Unit (NITA)	MCDBSU
Master Control Program [Burroughs Corp.]	MCP
Master Control Register (NITA)	MCR
Master Control Routine	MCR
Master Control System	MCS
Master Control Unit (NITA)	MCU
Master Data Center, Inc. [Southfield, MI] [Information service] (EISS)	MDC
Master Data File	MDF
Master Directory File [Data processing]	MDF
Master Document File [Data processing]	MDF
Master Driver Unit (VIT)	MDU
Master Drum Sender	MDS
Master Event Sequence Controller (KSC)	MESC
Master File	M/F
Master File Activities [Data processing]	MFA
Master File Change Activity [Data processing] (MCD)	MFCA
Master File Copy (KSC)	MFC
Master File Directory [Data processing]	MFD
Master File Maintenance	MFM
Master File Program [Data processing] (CIT)	MFP
Master File Replacement System [Data processing]	MFRS
Master Frequency Oscillator (NG)	MFO
Master Group Information System [AT & T]	MAGI
Master Group Multiplexer	MGM
Master-Group Translator [Telecommunications] (TEL)	MGT
Master History File	MHF
Master Index File	MIF
Master Instruction Tape [Data processing]	MIT
Master Instrumentation Timing Equipment (CET)	MITE
Master International Frequency List	MIFL
Master International Frequency Register	MIFR
Master Inventory File	MIF
Master Item File (MCD)	MIF
Master Item Identification Control System	MIICS
Master Library Tape [Data processing]	MLT
Master Measurement Database (NASA)	MMDB
Master Operating System [Sperry UNIVAC] (CAH)	MOS
Master Oscillator [Radio]	MO
Master Oscillator Power Amplifier [Radio]	MOPA
Master of Quantitative Systems	MQS
Master Radio Frequency List (NATG)	MRFL
Master of Radio and Television Engineering	MRTE
Master of Radio and Television Engineering	MRT Eng
Master Remote Query Interface System [Data processing]	MARQUIS
Master Reset (MCD)	MR
Master-Scale Television	MSTV
Master Scheduler (CMD)	MS
Master of Science in Computer-Based Information Systems	MSIS
Master of Science in Computer Information Systems	MSCIS
Master of Science in Computer Science	MSCS
Master of Science/Management Information Systems	MS/MIS
Master Sequence Controller (NASA)	MSC
Master Sequencer (DDI)	M/SEQ
Master Source File [Data processing] (BUR)	MSF
Master Source Program Library Tape [Data processing] (BUR)	MSPLT
Master Spares Positioning Resolver [Data processing]	MSPR
Master Standard Data	MSD
Master Switch	MSW
Master Switching Station (MCD)	MSS
Master Synchronization [Telecommunications] (TEL)	MSYNC
Master System Schedule (MCD)	MSS
Master Tape Control	MTC
Master Tape Data	MTD
Master Tape Loading	MTL
Master Tape Loading Program	MTLP
Master Tape Validation	MTVAL
Master Timer	MT
Master Timing and Control Circuit	MTCC
Master Training File [Data processing]	MTRF
Mastergroup Multiplex [AT & T]	MMX
Mastergroup Surveillance System [AT & T]	MSS
Masterspec 2 [Production Systems for Architects & Engineers, Inc.] [Information service] (EISS)	M2
Matching Available Student Time to Educational Resources [Data processing]	MASTER
Matching Logic and Adder (NITA)	MLA
Material Acquisition Management Application [Suggested name for the Library of Congress computer system]	MAMA
Material on Job Date [Telecommunications] (TEL)	MOJ
Material Properties Bibliographic Data System [Purdue University] [Database] (FDB)	MPBDS
Material Properties Numerical Data System [Purdue University] [Database] (FDB)	MPNDS
Material Requirements Planning [Tipdata Ltd.] [Software package] [British] (NCC)	MRP
Materials Acquisition Sub-System [Data processing]	MASS
Materials Business File [American Society for Metals, The Institute for Metals] [Information service] (EISS)	MBF
Mathematical Analysis without Programing [Data processing]	MAP
Mathematical Analyzer, Numerical Integrator and Computer	MANIAC
Mathematical Didactics [Fachinformationszentrum Energie, Physik, Mathematik GmbH] [Database] (CUAD)	MATHDI
Mathematical Laboratory [Programing language] (CSR)	MATHLAB
Mathematical Operations Computer	MOC

Mathematical Programing [*Data processing*] ... MP
Mathematical Programing System [*Data processing*] (CGC) ... MPS
Mathematical Programing System Control Language [*1974*] [*Data processing*] (CSR) ... MPSCL
Mathematical Programing System Extended [*IBM Corp.*] [*Data processing*] ... MPSX
Mathematical Programming Society ... MPS
Mathematical Tables and Other Aids to Computation ... MTAC
Mathematics ... MATH
Mathematics Abstracts [*Fachinformationszentrum Energie, Physik, Mathematik GmbH*] [*Database*] (CUAD) ... MATH
Mathematics of Computation (IEEE) ... MCOM
Mathematics and Computers in Simulation [*A publication*] ... Math Comput Simul
Mathematics and Computers in Simulation [*A publication*] ... Math Comput Simulation
Mathematics in Recognizable Form Automatically Compiled [*Data processing*] (TUT) ... MIRFAC
Matrix [*A publication*] ... Mat
Matrix (BUR) ... MX
Matrix Algebra General Interpretive Coding (IEEE) ... MAGIC
Matrix Algebra Interpretive Program (IEEE) ... MAIP
Matrix Connector Punched Card Programer [*Data processing*] (IEEE) ... MACON
Matrix Electrostatic Writing Technique (NITA) ... MEWT
Matrix of Environmental Residuals for Energy Systems [*Computerized information system*] ... MERES
Matrix Generator Language [*Data processing*] (BUR) ... MGL
Matrix Generator and Report Writer [*Data processing*] ... MGRW
Matrix Inversion Program [*Data processing*] (BUR) ... MIP
Matrix Iteration Method of Unfolding Spectra [*Data processing*] ... MIMUSA
Matrix Language [*Data processing*] (IEEE) ... MATLAN
Matrix Log-In Memory (NITA) ... MLIM
Maximum ... MAX
Maximum Available Power Gain (MSA) ... MAPG
Maximum Forward Voltage Drop ... MFVD
Maximum Interference Threshold [*Telecommunications*] (TEL) ... MAXIT
Maximum Likelihood [*Statistics*] ... ML
Maximum Likelihood Estimate [*or Estimator*] [*Statistics*] (CIT) ... MLE
Maximum Observed Frequency [*Radio*] ... MOF
Maximum Service Telecasters ... MST
Maximum Storage Bus Rate (NITA) ... MSBR
Maximum Time [*Telecommunications*] (TEL) ... TMAX
Maximum Undistorted Output ... MUO
Maximum Undistorted Power Output ... MUPO
Maximum Usable Frequency [*Signal transmission*] ... MUF
Maximum Usable Gain [*Bell System*] ... MUG
Maxwell [*Unit of magnetic flux*] [*Also, abWb*] ... Mx
Mayo Biotechnology Research Computer Facility [*Mayo Clinic*] [*Research center*] (RCD) ... MRCF
McCall Information Systems Company ... MISCO
McCarthy, Crisanti & Maffei, Inc. [*New York, NY*] [*Information service*] (EISS) ... MCM
McDonnell Automatic Checkout System [*McDonnell Douglas Corp.*] ... MACS
McDonnell Douglas Automated Voice Information System (MCD) ... MAVIS
McDonnell Douglas Automation Co. [*Robotics*] ... MCAUTO
McDonnell Douglas Corp. ... MCD
McDonnell Douglas Corporation ... MCDC
McDonnell Douglas Corporation ... MDC
McGill University System for Interactive Computing ... MUSIC
McGraw-Hill, Inc. [*NYSE symbol*] ... MHP
MCI Communications Corp. [*NASDAQ symbol*] (NQ) ... MCIC
MCS Telecommunications [*NASDAQ symbol*] (NQ) ... MTEL
MDS [*Multipoint Distribution System*] **Industry Association** [*Washington, DC*] [*Telecommunications*] (EANO) ... MDSIA
ME Compu Software, Inc. [*Vancouver Stock Exchange symbol*] ... CPU
Mead Data Central [*Dayton, OH*] ... MDC
Mean Active Maintenance Downtime [*Data processing*] ... M
Mean Corrective Downtime [*Data processing*] ... MCDT
Mean Cycles between Failures [*Quality control*] ... MCBF
Mean Delay Time (CAAL) ... MDT
Mean Detonating Time (NASA) ... MDT
Mean Downtime [*Data processing*] ... MDT
Mean Elapsed Downtime [*Data processing*] (MCD) ... MEDT
Mean Engine Operating Time between Failures [*Quality control*] ... MEOTBF
Mean One Way Propagation Time [*Telecommunications*] (TEL) ... MOPT
Mean Preventive Downtime [*Data processing*] ... MPDT
Mean Repair Time (DDI) ... MRT
Mean Square Error [*Statistics*] ... MSE
Mean Time between Degradations [*Quality control*] [*Telecommunications*] (TEL) ... MTBD
Mean Time to Diagnosis [*Quality control*] (BUR) ... MTTD
Mean Time between Errors [*Quality control*] (NITA) ... MTBE
Mean Time to Failure [*Quality control*] ... MTF
Mean Time to Failure [*Quality control*] ... MTTF
Mean Time between Failures [*Quality control*] ... MTBF
Mean Time between Interrupts [*Quality control*] (NITA) ... MTBI
Mean Time to Maintain [*Quality control*] (CMD) ... MTTM
Mean Time between Maintenance [*Quality control*] (AFM) ... MTBM
Mean Time between Outages [*Quality control*] [*Telecommunications*] (TEL) ... MTBO
Mean Time to Removal [*Quality control*] ... MTTR
Mean Time to Repair [*Quality control*] (CAAL) ... MTTR
Mean Time to Replacement [*Quality control*] ... MTTR
Mean Time to Restore [*Quality control*] (IEEE) ... MTTR
Mean Time to Restore Software [*Quality control*] (CAAL) ... MTTRS
Mean Time to Service Restoral [*Quality control*] [*Telecommunications*] (TEL) ... MTSR
Mean Time between Software Failures [*Quality control*] (CAAL) ... MTBSF
Mean Time between System Failures [*Quality control*] ... MTBSF
Meander Inverted Autocorrelated Function (OA) ... MIACF
Meaning Extraction [*Programing language*] [*1971*] (CSR) ... MEANINGEX
Measured Service Pricing [*Telecommunications*] (TEL) ... MS
Measured Time ... MT
Measurement of Air Pollution from Satellites ... MAPS
Measurement and Analysis Center [*Telecommunications*] (TEL) ... MAC
Measurement, Decision, and Actuation [*Data processing*] ... MDA
Measurement Facility [*Data processing*] (IBMDP) ... MF
Measurement Information Data Analytic System (IEEE) ... MIDAS
Measurement Requirements and Interface (MCD) ... MRI
Mechanical Aerospace Ground Equipment (TEL) ... MAGE
Mechanical Analog Computer (DEN) ... MAC
Mechanical Buffer Register [*Data processing*] ... MBR
Mechanical Engineering Data Services, Incorporated [*St. Louis, MO*] [*Software manufacturer*] (DASOS) ... MEDSI
Mechanical Failures Prevention Group ... MFPG
Mechanical Impulse (KSC) ... M/I
Mechanical and Numerical Integrator and Computer (IEEE) ... MANIAC
Mechanical Recording Head ... MRH
Mechanical Simulation [*of a computer-based directory assistance system*] ... MECHSIM
Mechanical Translation [*Data processing*] ... MT
Mechanical Translation [*A publication*] ... MT
Mechanically Despun Antenna (KSC) ... MDA
Mechanized Calling Card Service [*Formerly, ABC*] [*Telecommunications*] ... MCCS
Mechanized Customer Trouble Report Analysis Plan [*Telecommunications*] (TEL) ... MCTRAP
Mechanized Directory Assistance [*Telecommunications*] (TEL) ... MDA
Mechanized Equipment Assignment [*AT & T*] ... MEQA
Mechanized Line Records [*Later, LMOS*] [*Bell System*] ... MLR
Mechanized Line Testing [*Telecommunications*] (TEL) ... MLT
Mechanized Loop Testing (MCD) ... MLT
Mechanized Market Programing Procedures [*Data processing*] (TEL) ... MMPP
Mechanized Retrieval for Greater Efficiency [*Data processing*] ... MERGE
Mechanized Sales Office Record System [*Telecommunications*] (TEL) ... MSORS
Mechanized Scheduling [*Telecommunications*] (TEL) ... MS
Mechanized Storage and Retrieval [*Data processing*] ... MSR
Mechanized Teletypewriter Exchange (TEL) ... MTWX
Mechanized Unit Property System [*Telecommunications*] (TEL) ... MUPS
Mechanized Wire Centering/Cross Section [*AT & T*] [*Telecommunications*] (TEL) ... MWC/CS
Media ... MED
Media Access Unit (CCD) ... MAU
Media Conversion Program Generator (NITA) ... MCPG
Media Expenditure Analysis Ltd. [*Database producer*] (CUAD) ... MEAL
Media General Financial Services, Inc. [*Information service*] (EISS) ... MGFS
Media Processor [*Data processing*] (BUR) ... MP
Media Quality Unit [*Communications*] ... MQU
Media Report to Women [*A publication*] ... Media Rpt
Mediamark Research, Incorporated [*Database producer and database*] [*Information service*] (EISS) ... MRI
Median ... (M)
Medical Audit Program [*Computerized system of abstracted medical record information*] ... MAP
Medical Communications [*A publication*] ... MCOM
Medical Communications [*A publication*] ... Med Commun
Medical Computer Services (IEEE) ... MCS
Medical Display Analysis and Recording System ... MEDDARS
Medical Documentation Service [*College of Physicians*] [*Information service*] (EISS) ... MDS
Medical Documentation Systems [*Eli Lilly & Co.*] [*Information service*] (EISS) ... MEDDOC
Medical Documents [*Eccles Health Sciences Library - University of Utah*] [*Salt Lake City, UT*] [*Bibliographic database*] (OBD) ... MEDOC
Medical Electronic Data Aquisition and Control (OA) ... MEDAC
Medical Emergencies [*Computerized management course*] ... MEDEMG
Medical Evaluation Data System (IEEE) ... MEDS
Medical Information Bureau [*Databank*] ... MIB
Medical Information Network [*GTE Telenet Communications Corp.*] [*Reston, VA*] [*Telecommunications*] ... MINET
Medical Information Science Section [*National Institutes of Health*] [*Information service*] (EISS) ... MISS
Medical Information System via Telephone [*University of Alabama*] ... MIST
Medical Information Systems Program [*Data processing*] (BUR) ... MISP
Medical Information Technology, Inc. [*Westwood, MA*] [*Software manufacturer*] (DASOS) ... MEDITECH
Medical Literature Analysis and Retrieval System [*National Library of Medicine*] [*Bethesda, MD*] [*Database*] ... MEDLARS
Medical Subject Heading [*National Library of Medicine*] [*Thesaurus*] ... MeSH
Medically Oriented Data System (MCD) ... MODS
Medically Oriented Language ... MEDOL
Medium Access Control (CCD) ... MAC

Medium-Altitude Communications Satellite .... MACS
Medium-Altitude Communications Satellite System .... MACSS
Medium Data Utilization Station [*Australia*] [*Telecommunications*] (TEL) .... MDUS
Medium Frequency [*Radio electronics*] .... MF
Medium-Frequency Direction Finder [*or Finding*] .... MDF
Medium-Frequency Direction Finder [*or Finding*] .... MF/DF
Medium-Gain Antenna .... MGA
Medium-Gain Autotrack Antenna .... MGAA
Medium-High Frequency .... MHF
Medium- and High-Frequency Direction-Finding Station .... MHDF
Medium-, High-, and Very-High-Frequency Direction-Finding Station .... MHVDF
Medium Large Local Exchange [*Telecommunications*] (TEL) .... MLLE
Medium Local Exchange [*Telecommunications*] (TEL) .... MLE
Medium Low-BIT [*Binary Digit*] **Rate** [*Data processing*] (SKY) .... MLBR
Medium/Low Frequency (NATG) .... M/LF
Medium Power Traveling Wave Tube .... MPTWT
Medium-Powered Radio Range [*Loop radiators*] .... MRL
Medium-Powered Radio Range (Adcock) .... MRA
Medium-Scale Integration [*Circuit packaging*] .... MSI
Medium-Scale Integration Device [*Circuit packaging*] .... MSID
Medium-Sized Libraries/OCLC [*Online Computer Library Center*] **Users Group** .... MSLOUG
Medium-Speed DynaBIT [*Binary Digit*] **Memory** [*Data processing*] .... MSDM
Medium Standard Frequency (DEN) .... MSF
Medium- and Very-High-Frequency Direction-Finding Station .... MVDF
Medium-Voltage Mode .... MVM
Medium Wave Band .... MW
Medizinische Hochschule Hannover [*Information retrieval*] (ODIN) .... MHH
MEDLARS [*Medical Literature Analysis and Retrieval System*] **On-Line** [*National Library of Medicine*] [*Bibliographic database*] .... MEDLINE
Meeting Series [*Online database field identifier*] (OBD) .... MS
Meetings Industry Microcomputer Users Group [*Dallas, TX*] [*Information clearinghouse*] (EANO) .... MIMUG
Mega [*A prefix meaning multiplied by one million*] [*Symbol*] .... M
Mega [*A prefix meaning multiplied by one million*] .... MEG
MegaBIT [*Binary Digit*] [*Data processing*] .... MB
MegaBIT [*Binary Digit*] [*Data processing*] (MDG) .... MBIT
MegaBIT [*Binary Digit*] **Digital Troposcatter Subsystem** [*Communications*] (MCD) .... MDTS
MegaBITS [*Binary Digits*] **per Second** [*Transmission rate*] [*Data processing*] .... MBPS
MegaBITS [*Binary Digits*] **per Second** [*Transmission rate*] [*Data processing*] .... MB/S
MegaBITS [*Binary Digits*] **per Second** [*Transmission rate*] [*Data processing*] (MCD) .... MPS
Megabyte [*Data processing*] [*Data storage capacity*] .... M
Megabyte [*Data storage capacity*] [*Data processing*] .... Mb
Megacycle .... Mc
Megahertz [*Megacycles per Second*] [*See also MCPS, MCS, MC/S, MH*] .... MHz
Megaword (NITA) .... MWD
Megohm .... MEG
Melbourne University Dual-Package Analog Computer [*Australia*] .... MUDPAC
Melcom All Round Adaptive Consolidated Software [*Japanese*] (NITA) .... MARCS
Mellon Institute [*Carnegie-Mellon University*] [*Research center*] (RCD) .... MI
Mellonics Information Center [*Litton Systems, Inc.*] [*Information service*] (EISS) .... MIC
Memorex Corp. [*NYSE symbol*] [*Delisted*] .... MRX
Memorial Dose Distribution Computation Service [*Memorial Sloan-Kettering Cancer Center*] [*Information service*] (EISS) .... MDDCS
Memory .... M
Memory (MSA) .... MEM
Memory Access Controller (NITA) .... MAC
Memory Access Logic (NITA) .... MAL
Memory Access Unit (NITA) .... MAU
Memory Address [*Data processing*] .... MA
Memory-Address Register [*Data processing*] .... MAR
Memory-Address Register Storage [*Data processing*] .... MARS
Memory Address Test (NITA) .... MAT
Memory Allocation Manager (NITA) .... MAM
Memory Allocation and Protection (NITA) .... MAP
Memory Analysis, Response Generation, and Interference in English (NITA) .... MARGIE
Memory Bank Interface (NITA) .... MBI
Memory Base Register (NITA) .... MBR
Memory Buffer [*Data processing*] .... MB
Memory Buffer Register [*Data processing*] .... MBR
Memory Buffer Register, Even [*Data processing*] .... MBRE
Memory Buffer Register, Odd [*Data processing*] .... MBRO
Memory Buffer Unit [*Data processing*] (OA) .... MBU
Memory Bus [*Digital Equipment Corp.*] (NITA) .... MASSBUS
Memory Bus (NITA) .... MB
Memory Bus Controller (NITA) .... MBC
Memory Card Writer [*Telecommunications*] (TEL) .... MCW
Memory-Centered Processing [*or Processor*] [*System*] [*Data processing*] .... MCP
Memory Clock Pulse Amplifier .... MCPA
Memory Configuration [*Data processing*] (MCD) .... MC
Memory Control [*Unit*] [*Data processing*] .... MC
Memory Control and Logging [*Hewlett-Packard Co.*] (NITA) .... MCL
Memory Control Module (NITA) .... MCM
Memory Control Register (NITA) .... MCR
Memory Control Unit (OA) .... MCU
Memory Cycle Time [*Data processing*] (MCD) .... MCT
Memory-Data Bank .... MDB
Memory-Data Register .... MDR
Memory Disk Controller (NITA) .... MDC
Memory Disk System [*Data processing*] (IEEE) .... MDS
Memory Element [*Data processing*] (NITA) .... ME
Memory Excellence [*Brand name*] .... MEMOREX
Memory Expansion Unit (NITA) .... MEU
Memory Gate Generator [*Data processing*] .... MGG
Memory Implemented Data Acquisition Systems (NITA) .... MIDAS
Memory-Information Register [*Data processing*] .... MIR
Memory Input Register [*Data processing*] .... MIR
Memory Interface (NITA) .... MI
Memory Interface Connection [*Data processing*] .... MIC
Memory Lockout Register [*Data processing*] .... MLR
Memory Logic Unit [*Data processing*] .... MLU
Memory Management Controller (IEEE) .... MMC
Memory Management System (NITA) .... MMS
Memory Management Unit [*Data processing*] .... MMU
Memory Manager and Protect Unit (IEEE) .... MMPU
Memory-to-Memory Adapter [*Data processing*] .... MMA
Memory Module (MCD) .... MM
Memory Multiplexer [*Data processing*] (MDG) .... MM
Memory Multiplexer [*Data processing*] .... MMX
Memory Operating Characteristic [*Data processing*] (IEEE) .... MOC
Memory Operating Software [*Data processing*] .... MOS
Memory Organization Packet [*Artificial intelligence*] .... MOP
Memory-Oriented System (NITA) .... MOS
Memory Output [*Data processing*] (NITA) .... MO
Memory Output Register [*Data processing*] .... MOR
Memory Parity Error (NITA) .... MPE
Memory Printout [*Data processing*] .... MPO
Memory Processing Time (NITA) .... MPT
Memory Processor Switch .... MPS
Memory Protect Override (NITA) .... MPO
Memory Protection Unit (NITA) .... MPU
Memory Raster Display [*Data processing*] (TUT) .... MRD
Memory Read [*Data processing*] .... MR
Memory Reference Instruction (NITA) .... MRI
Memory Register [*Data processing*] .... MR
Memory Request Controller (NITA) .... MRC
Memory Service Unit [*Data processing*] .... MSU
Memory Storage Buffer [*Data processing*] (CAAL) .... MSB
Memory Storage Control [*Data processing*] .... MSC
Memory Storage Module (NITA) .... MSM
Memory System .... MS
Memory Test Computer [*SAGE*] .... MTC
Memory Unit [*Data processing*] (MCD) .... MU
Memory Unit Drum [*Data processing*] .... MUD
Memory Write [*Data processing*] .... MW
Menlo Park Applications Development [*IBM Corp.*] .... MPAD
Mental Measurements Yearbook Database [*University of Nebraska, Lincoln*] [*Database*] .... MMYD
Merge [*Data processing*] (IBMDP) .... M
Merge and Correlate Recorded Output [*Data processing*] (NASA) .... MACRO
Merged-Transistor Logic .... MTL
Merger Acquisition Improved Decision [*Data processing*] .... MAID
Merit of a Coil or Capacitor [*Electronics*] .... Q
Merritt and Miller's Own Block Structured Simulation Language, Unpronounceable Acronym For [*1969*] [*Data processing*] (CSR) .... MOBSSL-UAF
Mesa [*Type of transistor*] (MDG) .... MS
MeSH Heading [*Online database field identifier*] (OBD) .... MH
Meshless Storage Display Tube .... MSDT
Message (AFM) .... MSG
Message Access Method [*Honeywell, Inc.*] (NITA) .... MAM
Message Authentication Code (NITA) .... MAC
Message Center (DDI) .... MCTR
Message Composer [*Communications, data processing*] .... MC
Message Construction Unit .... MCU
Message Control Block (CET) .... MCB
Message Control Language [*Data processing*] .... MCL
Message Control Program [*Data processing*] .... MCP
Message Control System [*Burroughs Corp.*] [*Data processing*] (BUR) .... MCS
Message Control Task [*Data processing*] .... MCT
Message Data .... MD
Message Data Exchange Terminal (MCD) .... MEDAX
Message Decoder Unit .... MDU
Message Detail Recording [*Later, SMDR*] [*Telecommunications*] .... MDR
Message Discrimination Process [*Telecommunications*] (TEL) .... MDP
Message Element [*Telecommunications*] (TEL) .... ME
Message Encoder Unit .... MEU
Message Entry Device .... MED
Message Expediting Group (IEEE) .... MEG
Message Flow Graph (NITA) .... MFG
Message Format Service .... MFS
Message Generator .... MG

Message Generator (MSA) .... MSGG
Message Handler [*Data processing*] .... MH
Message Handling Processor (NITA) .... MHP
Message Has Been Misrouted [*Communications*] .... MSR
Message Identification Code [*Data processing*] (BUR) .... MIC
Message Input Description (NITA) .... MID
Message Input Device .... MID
Message Input Module [*Telecommunications*] (TEL) .... MIM
Message Input Processing (DDI) .... MIP
Message Interface Unit (CAAL) .... MIU
Message Multiplexer Operating System (NITA) .... MMOS
Message Output Description [*Data processing*] (NITA) .... MOD
Message Output Module [*Telecommunications*] (TEL) .... MOM
Message Output Processing (DDI) .... MOP
Message Processing Center .... MPC
Message Processing Interrupt Count .... MPIC
Message Processing Language [*Burroughs Corp.*] (NITA) .... MPL
Message Processing Modules (MCD) .... MPM
Message Processing Program [*Data processing*] (TUT) .... MPP
Message Processing Region [*IBM Corp.*] (NITA) .... MPR
Message Processing System (NVT) .... MPS
Message Queue Element [*Data processing*] (NITA) .... MQE
Message Refusal [*Telecommunications*] (TEL) .... MRF
Message Register .... MR
Message Repeat .... MR
Message Retransmission Unit .... MRU
Message Routing Process [*Telecommunications*] (TEL) .... MRP
Message Sequence Chart [*Telecommunications*] (TEL) .... MSC
Message Sequence Number (CAAL) .... MSN
Message Switching Center [*Telecommunications*] .... MSC
Message Switching Computer [*Telecommunications*] (TEL) .... MSC
Message Switching Concentration (NITA) .... MSC
Message Switching Data Service (NITA) .... MSDS
Message Switching Station [*Telecommunications*] (CET) .... MSS
Message Switching Unit .... MSU
Message Telecommunications Service .... MTS
Message Toll Service [*Communications*] .... MTS
Message Transmission Controller (NITA) .... MTC
Message Transmission Part [*Telecommunications*] (TEL) .... MTP
Message Transmission Subsystem [*Telecommunications*] (TEL) .... MTS
Message Waiting (MDG) .... MSG/WTG
Message-Waiting Indicator .... MWI
Messages per Day .... MD
Meta-Assembler Language [*Sperry UNIVAC computer language*] .... MASM
Meta Assembly Language (NITA) .... MAL
Meta LISP [*List Processor*] [*Programing language*] [*Data processing*] (CSR) .... MLISP
Metal Abstracts Index Data Base [*American Society for Metals*] [*Bibliographic database*] [*British*] (EISS) .... METADEX
Metal Data File [*National Research Council of Canada*] [*Database*] .... MDF
Metal-Insulator-Semiconductor .... MIS
Metal-Insulator-Semiconductor Field-Effect Transistor .... MISFET
Metal-Insulator-Semiconductor Inversion Layer [*Photovoltaic energy systems*] .... MIS/IL
Metal-Insulator-Semiconductor Metal (MCD) .... MISM
Metal Interface Amplifier .... MIA
Metal Matrix Composites Information Analysis Center [*DoD*] [*Information service*] (EISS) .... MMCIAC
Metal-Nitride-Oxide Silicon [*or Semiconductor*] .... MNOS
Metal-Oxide Semiconductor .... MOS
Metal-Oxide-Semiconductor Field-Effect Transistor .... MOSFET
Metal-Oxide-Semiconductor - Large-Scale Integration .... MOS-LSI
Metal-Oxide-Semiconductor Transistor .... MOST
Metal-Oxide-Semiconductor Transistor Logic (CET) .... MOSTL
Metal-Semiconductor Field-Effect Transistor .... MESFET
Metalanguage Symbol (CAH) .... METASYMBOL
Metallic Facility Terminal [*Telecommunications*] (TEL) .... MFT
Metallurgical and Thermochemical Data Service [*British*] [*Information service*] (EISS) .... MTDS
Metals and Ceramics Information Center [*Battelle Columbus Laboratories*] [*Columbus, OH*] [*Information service*] (EISS) .... MCIC
Metals Datafile/I [*American Society for Metals*] [*Database*] (CUAD) .... MDF/I
Meteorological Data Sounding System (IEEE) .... MDSS
Meteorological Data System .... MDS
Meteorological and Geoastrophysical Abstracts [*American Meteorological Society*] [*Bibliographic database*] [*A publication*] .... MGA
Meteorological and Geoastrophysical Abstracts [*American Meteorological Society*] [*Bibliographic database*] [*A publication*] .... M & GA
Meteorological Integrating Data Acquisition System .... MIDAS
Meteorological Office Computer [*British*] (DEN) .... COMET
Meteorological Operational Telecommunications Network Europe .... MOTNE
Meteorological Real-Time System [*Data processing*] (KSC) .... MRTS
Meteorological Satellite Section .... MSS
Meter [*SI unit of length*] .... m
Meter-Kilogram-Second [*System of units*] .... MKS
Meter-Reading Access Circuit [*Bell Laboratories*] .... MRAC
Metered Message Unit [*Telecommunications*] (TEL) .... MMU
Metering Head Differential (DDI) .... MHD
Metering over Junction [*Network administration*] [*Telecommunications*] (TEL) .... MOJ
Methodology for Unmanned Manufacture [*Robotics project*] [*Japanese*] .... MUM
Methods-of-Extracting-Text-Auto-Programing Language [*Data processing*] (IEEE) .... METAPLAN
Methods of Extracting Text Automatically [*General Electric Co.*] [*Text retrieval language*] (IEEE) .... META
Metrics Research Corporation [*Information service*] (EISS) .... MRC
Metrology Data Bank [*GIDEP*] .... MDB
Metropolitan Area Network (CCD) .... MAN
Metropolitan Area Transmission Facility Analysis Program [*AT & T*] [*Telecommunications*] (TEL) .... MATFAP
Metropolitan Area Trunk [*Telecommunications*] (TEL) .... MAT
Metropolitan Centrex [*Telephone network*] .... METREX
Metropolitan Interlibrary Cooperative System [*New York Public Library*] [*Information service*] .... MILCS
Metropolitan Statistical Area [*Census Bureau*] .... MSA
Mezhotraslevoi Naucho-Tekhni-Cheskii Kompleks [*Interdisciplinary Scientific-Technological Complex*] [*Russian*] .... MNTK
Michigan Algorithmic Decoder [*IBM Corp.*] [*University of Michigan*] [*Programing language*] [*1961*] .... MAD
Michigan Automatic General Integrated Computation (MCD) .... MAGIC
Michigan Automatic Scanning System (IEEE) .... MASS
Michigan [*University of*] **Digital Automatic Computer** .... MIDAC
Michigan Effectuation, Training, and Research Organization [*Computer-programed simulation game*] .... METRO
Michigan Information Transfer Source [*University of Michigan*] (EISS) .... MITS
Michigan Instructional Computer .... MIC
Michigan Natural Features Inventory [*Michigan State Department of Natural Resources*] [*Information service*] (EISS) .... MNFI
Michigan Products Information Exchange [*Menominee, MI*] [*Information service*] (EISS) .... MIPIE
Michigan Project for Computer-Assisted Biblical Studies [*University of Michigan*] [*Information service*] (EISS) .... MPCABS
Michigan State Integral Computer .... MISTIC
Michigan State University Discrete Computer .... MSUDC
Michigan Terminal System [*Data processing*] .... MTS
Micom Systems, Inc. [*NASDAQ symbol*] (NQ) .... MICS
Micro Aided Engineering 3D Visualisation [*Micro Aided Engineering Ltd. and Micro Aided Engineering Digital Microsystems Ltd.*] [*Software package*] [*British*] (NCC) .... MAEVIS
Micro Aided Engineering/Computer Aided Manufacturing [*Micro Aided Engineering Ltd. and Digital Microsystems Ltd.*] [*Software package*] [*British*] (NCC) .... MAECAM
Micro Aided Engineering/Drawing Office System [*Micro Aided Engineering Ltd.*] [*Software package*] [*British*] (NCC) .... MAEDOS
Micro Applications & Hardware [*Sausalito, CA*] [*Software manufacturer*] (DASOS) .... MICAH
Micro Computer Business Services .... MCBS
Micro Education Corporation of America .... MECA
Micro Measurement System [*3D Digital Design & Development Ltd.*] [*Software package*] [*British*] (NCC) .... MMS
Micro Online Library Information .... MOLLI
Micro Peripherals, Incorporated [*Salt Lake City, UT*] [*Hardware manufacturer*] (DASO) .... MPI
Micro Surface Mapping [*Software package*] [*British*] (NCC) .... MSM
Microalloy Transistor .... MAT
Microbalance Inverted Knudsen Effusion Recoil .... MIKER
Microband National System, Inc. [*New York, NY*] [*Telecommunications*] (TSSD) .... MNS
Microcircuit [*or Microwave*] **Device Reliability** (MCD) .... MDR
Microcoded Communications Line Adapter (NITA) .... MCLA
Microcomputer (MSA) .... MICMPTR
Microcomputer (DEEC) .... MICRO
Microcomputer Adaptation Procedures Corp. [*Indianapolis, IN*] [*Software manufacturer*] (DASOS) .... MAP
Microcomputer Board (NITA) .... MCB
Microcomputer Control Unit (NITA) .... MCU
Microcomputer Development Facilities (IEEE) .... MDF
Microcomputer Education Application Network [*Commercial firm*] [*Educational Turnkey Systems, Inc.*] [*Falls Church, VA*] (EANO) .... MEAN
Microcomputer Electronic Information Exchange [*Institute for Computer Science and Technology*] .... MEIE
Microcomputer Graphic System .... MGS
Microcomputer Industry Trade Association (NITA) .... MITA
Microcomputer-Interfaced Data Acquisition System [*Data processing*] .... MIDAS
Microcomputer Investors Association [*Fredericksburg, VA*] [*Database producer*] (EANO) .... MCIA
Microcomputer Numerical Control (MCD) .... MNC
Microcomputer Printout [*A publication*] .... Microcomput Printout
Microcomputer Software Association [*Arlington, VA*] (EANO) .... MCSA
Microcomputer Software Association [*Arlington, VA*] (EANO) .... MSA
Microcomputer System (NITA) .... MCS
Microcomputer Users in Education .... MUSE
Microcomputers and Primary Education .... MAPE
Microdynamic Angle and Rate Monitoring System .... MIDARM
Microelectric Logic Circuit .... MLC
Microelectronic and Computer Technology Research [*A research cooperative based in Austin, TX*] .... MCC
Microelectronic Integrated Test Equipment .... MITE
Microelectronic Radio Receiver .... MRR
Microelectronics (IEEE) .... MELEC

Microelectronics Center of North Carolina [Research Triangle Park, NC] [Research center] (RCD) ... MCNC
Microelectronics Innovation and Computer Science Research Program [University of California] [Research center] (RCD) ... MICRO
Microelectronics and Reliability [A publication] ... Microelectron Reliab
Microelectronics and Reliability [A publication] ... Microel Rel
Microelectronics Test and Evaluation [Raytheon Co.] ... MITE
Microelement (IEEE) ... MELEM
Microfarad ... MF
Microfarad ... MFD
Microfiche Image Transmission System (MCD) ... MITS
Microfiche Management System (DEEC) ... MMS
Microfilm Frame Card ... MFC
Microfilm Information Retrieval Access Code ... MIRACODE
Microfilm and Information Technology Center ... MITC
Microfilm Reader Recorder (TUT) ... MRR
Microfilm Recording Unit ... MRU
Microfilm Replacement System [Data processing] ... MRS
Microfilm Sequential Coding System [Bell System] ... MICROSECS
Microfilm Viewer ... MFV
Microfilmed Abstract System for Technical Information Retrieval [Illinois Institute of Technology] (EISS) ... MASTIR
Microfilming Corporation of America [Los Angeles, CA] [Information service] (EISS) ... MCA
Microforms International Marketing Corporation [Pergamon] ... MIMC
Microfunctional Circuit ... MFC
Microimaged Data Addition System [CAPS Equipment Ltd.] ... MIDAS
Microimplementation Language [Burroughs Corp.] (NITA) ... MIL
Microinstruction Bus [Data processing] (NITA) ... MIB
Microinstruction Read-Only Memory (NITA) ... MICROM
Microinstruction Register (NITA) ... MIR
Microinstruction Word (NITA) ... MIW
Microlayer Transistor ... MLT
Micromation Online Microfilmer ... MOM
Micrometer Frequency Meter ... MFM
Microminiature (IEEE) ... MICROMIN
Microminiature Relay ... MR
Micromodule (IEEE) ... MMOD
Micromodule Data Processor and Computer (IEEE) ... MICROPAC
Micron Corporation [NASDAQ symbol] (NQ) ... MICC
MicroNet Apple User's Group [CompuServe] [Database] ... MAUG
Microphone (MDG) ... MK
Micropolis Corp. [NASDAQ symbol] (NQ) ... MLIS
Microprint ... MP
Microprocedure Definition (NITA) ... MIDEF
Microprocessor (DEEC) ... MICRO
Microprocessor (MSA) ... MIPRCS
Microprocessor [Instrumentation] ... MP
Microprocessor Application Project [In manufacturing industry] [Department of the Interior] (DEEC) ... MAP
Microprocessor Automatic Testing [ASMAP Electronics Ltd.] [Software package] [British] (NCC) ... MATE
Microprocessor Control Unit ... MCU
Microprocessor Data Analyzer [Instrumentation] ... MIDAN
Microprocessor Development Aid ... MDA
Microprocessor Development Support System (NITA) ... MDSS
Microprocessor Development System [Motorola, Inc.] ... MDS
Microprocessor Host Loader [Electronics] ... MHL
Microprocessor Inertia and Communication System ... MICS
Microprocessor Interface (NITA) ... MPI
Microprocessor Language Assembler [Data processing] ... MLA
Microprocessor Language Editor [Data processing] ... MLE
Microprocessor [or Motorola's] Programing Language [1975] [Data processing] (CSR) ... MPL
Microprocessor Series [or System] (MDG) ... MPS
Microprocessor Unit [CPU of microcomputer] [Data processing] ... MPU
Microprogram (NITA) ... MP
Microprogram Address Register (NITA) ... MADR
Microprogram Address Register (NITA) ... MAR
Microprogram Address Register (NITA) ... MPAR
Microprogram Control (NITA) ... MPC
Microprogram Control Logic [Data processing] (MDG) ... MCL
Microprogram Control Memory (NITA) ... MPCM
Microprogram Design Description Language [1977] [Data processing] (CSR) ... MIDDLE
Microprogram Generating System (NITA) ... MPGS
Microprogram Location Counter (NITA) ... MLC
Microprogram Memory (NITA) ... MPM
Microprogram Operating System (NITA) ... MOS
Microprogram Storage [Data processing] (MDG) ... MS
Microprogramable Block Input/Output (NITA) ... MBIO
Microprogramable Computer Operating System (NITA) ... MCOS
Microprogramable Integrated Data Acquisition System (NITA) ... MIDAS
Microprogramed Array Processor (NITA) ... MAP
Microprogramed Communication Data Processor ... MCDP
Microprograming Design Aided System [RCA] (NITA) ... MIDAS
Microprograming Language (NITA) ... ML
Microprograming Technique ... MPT
Microprogrammed and Simulated Computer Organization ... MASCO
Microreciprocal Degrees ... MIRED
Microsecond Trip ... MST
Microsoft Disk Operating System [IBM Corp.] [Data processing] ... MS-DOS

Microstar Software Limited [Nepean, ON] [Telecommunications] (TSSD) ... MSL
Microswitch (KSC) ... MSW
Microunit ... mcU
Microwave ... MCRWV
Microwave ... MW
Microwave (DDI) ... MWAVE
Microwave Airborne Communications Relay (IEEE) ... MARCOM
Microwave Amplification by Stimulated Emission of Radiation ... MASER
Microwave Antenna Tower ... MAT
Microwave Attitude Control Sensor ... MACS
Microwave Automatic Vehicle Identification (MCD) ... MAVI
Microwave Carrier Supply ... MCS
Microwave Communication System ... MCS
Microwave Communications of America, Incorporated ... MCI
Microwave Communications Association [Washington, DC] [Telecommunications] (EANO) ... MCA
Microwave Delay Line ... MDL
Microwave Desorber [Instrumentation] ... MD
Microwave Detection and Ranging ... MIDAR
Microwave Dielectric Integrated Circuit (IEEE) ... MDIC
Microwave Emission Detector [Instrumentation] ... MED
Microwave Frequency Modulation Transmitter ... MFMT
Microwave Imager Sensor Study (MCD) ... MISS
Microwave Instantaneous Frequency Indication Receiver (MCD) ... MIFIR
Microwave Insular Line Integrated Circuit (IEEE) ... MILIC
Microwave Integrated Circuitry ... MIC
Microwave Interference Coordination ... MIC
Microwave Interference Protection ... MIP
Microwave Journal [A publication] ... Micro Jrl
Microwave Journal [A publication] ... Microwave J
Microwave Keying Switch ... MKS
Microwave Keying Switching Station ... MKSS
Microwave Line Stretcher ... MLS
Microwave Linear Accelerator ... MLA
Microwave Mixer Diode ... MMD
Microwave Phase Shifter ... MPS
Microwave Power Amplifier ... MPA
Microwave Power Meter ... MPM
Microwave Pressure Sounder (MCD) ... MPS
Microwave Pulse Shaping Network ... MPSN
Microwave Pulse Source ... MPS
Microwave Pulse Storage Subsystem (MCD) ... MIPS
Microwave Radiometer, Scatterometer, and Altimeter (MCD) ... MRSA
Microwave Relay Unit ... MRU
Microwave Rotary Joint ... MRJ
Microwave Scatterometer [Telecommunications] (TEL) ... MWS
Microwave Sensitivity Time Control [Circuit] ... MSTC
Microwave Services International, Inc. [Denville, NJ] [Telecommunications] (TSSD) ... MSI
Microwave Signal Generator ... MSG
Microwave Sounding Unit [Telecommunications] (TEL) ... MSU
Microwave Space Electronics Relay ... MISER
Microwave Space Relay [Electronics] ... MISRE
Microwave Space Research Facility ... MSRF
Microwave Spectra Data Center [National Bureau of Standards] ... MSDC
Microwave Spectrometer (TEL) ... MSW
Microwave Spectrum ... MS
Microwave Station ... MWS
Microwave Switch Control Assembly ... MSCA
Microwave Switching Station ... MSS
Microwave Systems News [A publication] ... Microwave Syst News
Microwave Systems News [A publication] ... Microw Syst News
Microwave Systems News [A publication] ... MSN
Microwave Target Designator ... MTD
Microwave Test Equipment ... MTE
Microwave Test Facility (CIT) ... MTF
Microwave Test Set (MCD) ... MTS
Microwave Theory and Technique (MCD) ... MTT
Microwave Ultrasonic Delay Line ... MUDL
Microwave Window Failure Mechanism ... MWFM
Mid-America Electronics Conference ... MAECON
Mid-Continent Telephone Corp. [NYSE symbol] [Delisted] ... MID
Midcontinental Regional Medical Library Program [University of Nebraska] [Library network] (EISS) ... MCRML
Midcourse Surveillance System (MCD) ... MSS
Middle East Database [New York Times Information Service, Inc.] (EISS) ... MEDAB
Middle East Electronic Communications Show and Conference [Arabian Exhibition Management WLL] [Manama, Bahrain] [Telecommunications] (TSSD) ... MECOM
Middle of the Road ... MOR
Mideast File [Tel-Aviv University] [Information service] (EISS) ... MEF
MIDI Processing Unit [Computer technology] ... MPU
Midwest Cable & Satellite, Inc. [Minneapolis, MN] [Telecommunications] (TSSD) ... MWCS
Midwestern Relay Company [Milwaukee, WI] [Telecommunications] (TSSD) ... MRC
Migent Software [Vancouver Stock Exchange symbol] ... MSC
Mile of Standard Cable ... MSC
Militarized Universal Digital Element Tester (MCD) ... MUDET
Miller Technology & Communications Corporation [NASDAQ symbol] (NQ) ... MECC

Computer & Telecommunications Acronyms

Milli- [*A prefix meaning divided by 1000*] [*SI symbol*] .... m
Milliampere .... mA
Millibyte [*Data processing*] .... mb
Millifarad (MCD) .... MFD
Milligram .... mg
Millihenry .... mH
Millimeter [*Metric*] .... mm
Millimeter Wave Communications Experiment .... MWCE
Millimeter Wave Contrast Seeker (MCD) .... MWCS
Millimeter Wave Device .... MWD
Millimeter Wave Experiment .... MWE
Millimeter Wave Mixer .... MWM
Millimeter Wave Propagation .... MWP
Millimeter Wave Tube .... MWT
Millimeter Wavelength Oscillator .... MWO
Million .... M
Million Bytes [*Data processing*] (BUR) .... MB
Million Dollar Directory [*Dun's Marketing Services*] [*Database*] .... MDD
Million Floating-Point Operations per Second [*Processing power units*] [*Data processing*] .... MFLOPS
Million Instructions per Second .... MIP
Million Operations per Second [*Processing power units*] [*Data processing*] .... MOPS
Million Pair Feet [*Telecommunications*] (TEL) .... MPF
Millions of Instructions per Second [*Facetiously translated as "Meaningless Indication of Performance"*] [*Processing power units*] [*Data processing*] .... MIPS
Millisecond [*Also, msec*] .... ms
Millisecond [*Also, ms*] .... msec
Millivolt .... mV
Millivolt Analog-Digital Instrumentation System .... MADIS
Milliwatt .... mW
Milliwatt Logic .... mWL
Mincomp Corp. [*NASDAQ symbol*] (NQ) .... MCOM
[*A*] Mind Forever Voyaging [*Infocom*] [*Computer gaming*] .... AMFV
Mind-Machine Interaction Research Center [*University of Florida*] [*Research center*] (RCD) .... MMIRC
Minerals Availability System/Minerals Industry Location Subsystem [*Bureau of Mines*] [*Database*] (FDB) .... MAS/MILS
Minerals Data System [*Database*] (FDB) .... MDS
Mini Core Processing Subsystem (TEL) .... MCPS
Miniature Data Acquisition System .... MIDAS
Miniature Electronic Auto-Collimator .... MINEAC
Miniature Fluxgate Magnetometer .... MFM
Miniature Gate Valve .... MGV
Miniature Individual Transmitter-Receiver Equipment (MCD) .... MITRE
Miniature Integrated Data System (MCD) .... MIDS
Miniature Protector Connector [*Telecommunications*] (TEL) .... MPC
Miniature Receiver Terminal .... MRT
Miniature Stepping Switch .... MSS
Miniaturized Instrumentation (MCD) .... MI
Miniaturized Integrated Telephone Equipment .... MITE
Miniaturized Integrated Telephone Equipment .... MINC
Minicomputer .... MNCMPTR
Minicomputer (MSA) .... MNCMPTR
Minicomputer Industry National Interchange [*An association*] (EANO) .... MINI
Minicomputer Interfacing Support System [*Data processing*] .... MISS
Minicomputer-Operated Retrieval (Partially Heuristic) System [*Data processing*] .... MORPHS
Minicomputer Review [*A publication*] .... Minicomput Rev
Minicomputer Users Interest Group [*Later, Mini/Micro Special Interest Group*] (EANO) .... MUIG
 .... MCL
Minimal Computer Load .... MCL
Minimal Terminal Communications System (NVT) .... MTCS
Minimal Total Processing Time (IEEE) .... MTPT
Minimum (AFM) .... MIN
Minimum Acceptable Performance [*Telecommunications*] (TEL) .... MAP
Minimum Automatic Computer (IEEE) .... MIAC
Minimum Call [*Television studio on standby*] .... MC
Minimum Discernible Signal [*Radio*] .... MDS
Minimum Discernible System (NASA) .... MDS
Minimum Hamming Distance [*Data processing*] ...... M/I
Minimum Impulse (KSC) ....
Minimum Impulse BIT [*Binary Digit*] [*Data processing*] (MCD) .... MIB
Minimum Independent Failure Element .... MIFE
Minimum Interference Threshold [*Telecommunications*] (TEL) .... MINIT
Minimum Material Condition [*Data processing*] (CDH) .... MIN MC
Minimum Mean Squared Error .... MMSE
Minimum Processing Time per Operation (DDI) .... MINPRT
Minimum Shift Keying .... MSK
Minimum Signal Element Duration [*Telecommunications*] (TEL) .... MSED
Minimum Size Executive Routines (NITA) .... MISER
Minimum Slack Time per Operation (DDI) .... MINSOP
Minimum Structure Module .... MIST
Minimum Teleprocessing Commmunications System (NITA) .... MTCS
Minimum Time [*Telecommunications*] (TEL) .... TMIN
Minimum Tracking Flux Density .... MTFD
Minimum Virtual Memory (OA) .... MVM
Mining Technology Clearing House [*British*] [*Information service*] (EISS) .... MTCH
Miniscribe Corp. [*NASDAQ symbol*] (NQ) .... MINY
Ministry of Communications .... MOC
Ministry of International Trade and Industry [*Japan*] .... MITI

Ministry of Posts and Telecommunications [*British*] .... MPT
Ministry of Supply Automatic Integrator and Computer [*British*] (DEN) .... MOSAIC
Minneapolis-Honeywell [*Minneapolis-Honeywell Regulator Co.*] [*Later, HON*] .... MH
Minneapolis-Honeywell Regulator Co. [*Later, HON*] .... M-H
Minnesota Computer-Aided Library System [*University of Minnesota*] .... MCALS
Minnesota Educational Computing Consortium .... MECC
Minnesota Instructional Language [*Data processing*] (CSR) .... MIL
Minnesota Interlibrary Telecommunications Exchange [*Library cooperative*] .... MINITEX
Minnesota Mining & Manufacturing Co. [*Also, MMM*] 3M
Minnesota Mining & Manufacturing Co. [*Also, 3M*] [*NYSE symbol*] .... MMM
Minnesota State Universities System Project for Automated Library Systems [*Information service*] .... MSUS/PALS
Minor Subject Descriptor [*Online database field identifier*] (OBD) .... MN
Minority Vendor Information Service [*National Minority Supplier Development Council, Inc.*] (EISS) .... VIS
Minute (AFM) .... MIN
Misalignment Estimation Software System (MCD) .... MESS
Miscellaneous Hardware .... MH
Miscellaneous Inputs Information Subsystem [*Data processing*] .... MIIS
Missed Message Rate (CAAL) .... MMR
Missing Interruption Checker (MCD) .... MIC
Missing Interruption Handler [*Data processing*] (IBMDP) .... MIH
Mission Analysis Computer Program .... MACP
Mission Interministerielle de l'Information Scientifique et Technique [*Interministerial Mission for Scientific and Technical Information*] [*France*] [*Information service*] (EISS) .... MIDIST
Missouri Institute of Psychiatry [*University of Missouri - Columbia*] [*Research center*] (RCD) .... MIP
Missouri Natural Heritage Inventory [*Missouri State Department of Conservation*] [*Information service*] (EISS) .... MoNHI
Mitel Corp. [*NYSE symbol*] [*Toronto Stock Exchange symbol*] .... MLT
Mitrol Industrial Management System [*Mitrol, Inc.*] [*Information service*] (EISS) .... MIMS
Mitsubishi Electric Corp. Literature and Information Search Service .... MELISS
Mixed Analog and Digital [*Telecommunications*] (TEL) .... MAD
Mixed Functional Block (IEEE) .... MFB
Mixed Integer Programing [*Data processing*] .... MIP
MLA [*Modern Language Association of America*] International Bibliography of Books and Articles on the Modern Languages and Literature [*Database*] [*A publication*] .... MLA
Mnemonic Assembly Language Translator [*Data processing*] (IEEE) .... MALT
Mobil Showcase Network [*Television*] .... MSN
Mobile Automatic Programed Checkout Equipment .... MAPCHE
Mobile Communication Terminal (OA) .... MCT
Mobile Communications Corp. of America Cl A [*NASDAQ symbol*] (NQ) .... MCCAA
Mobile Communications System (MCD) .... MCS
Mobile Data Terminal (MCD) .... MDT
Mobile Digital Computer [*Sylvania Electric Products Co.*] .... MOBIDIC
Mobile Doppler Tracking Station .... MDTS
Mobile Electronic Robot Manipulator and Underwater Television (IEEE) .... MERMUT
Mobile [*Truck-Mounted*] Ground Terminal .... MGT
Mobile Remote Handler .... MRH
Mobile Satellite Corp. [*King Of Prussia, PA*] [*Telecommunications*] (TSSD) .... MOBILESAT
Mobile Service [*Telecommunications*] (TEL) .... MS
Mobile Status Entry System .... MSES
Mobile Switching Office [*Bell System*] .... MSO
Mobile Telephone Exchange [*Nordic Mobile Telephone*] .... MTE
Mobile Telephone Service .... MTS
Mobile Telephone Switching Office [*Telecommunications*] .... MTSO
Mobile Terminal System [*IBM Corp.*] .... MTS
Mobile Utility Module System (IEEE) .... MUMS
Mobile Video Services Ltd. [*Washington, DC*] [*Telecommunications*] (TSSD) .... MVS
Modal Data Acquisition and Processing System ..... MODAPS
Mode .... M
Mode-Independent Unnumbered Information (CCD) .... MUI
Mode-Locked Surface-Acoustic Wave Oscillator [*Telecommunications*] (TEL) .... MLSO
Mode Selection Switch (KSC) .... MSS
Mode Selector Controller (MCD) .... MSC
Mode Suppressor (KSC) .... MDSPR
Mode Switch Chassis .... MSCH
Mode Transducer (MSA) .... MXDCR
Model (KSC) .... MOD
Model Building Language [*Programing language*] (IEEE) .... MOBULA
Model Experiment in Drug Indexing by Computer [*Rutgers University*] .... MEDICO
Model Incident Report [*Telecommunications*] (TEL) .... MIR
Model and Program [*Data processing*] (CGC) .... MAP
Model X-Y [*AEC computer code*] .... MOXY
Modeling Laboratory [*Programing language*] [*1970*] (CSR) .... MLAB
Modelling Systems [*Moss Systems Ltd.*] [*Software package*] [*British*] (NCC) .... MOSS
MODEM [*Modulator-Demodulator*] Executive [*Data processing*] .... MEX

MODEM Interface Modules [*Data processing*] (CGC) .... MIM
MODEM Sharing Device (NITA) .... MSD
Moderately Advanced Data Management [*Data processing*] .... MADAM
Modern Analytical Generator of Improved Circuits [*Data processing*] .... MAGIC
Modern Data Systems (IEEE) .... MDS
Modern Network Theory [*Electrical engineering computer*] .... MNT
Modern Satellite Network [*Cable-television system*] .... MSN
Modern Satellite Systems, Inc. [*Whitehouse Station, NJ*] [*Telecommunications*] (TSSD) .... MSS
Modern Telecommunications, Incorporated [*New York, NY*] (TSSD) .... MTI
Modernized Weather Teletypewriter Communication System (FAAC) .... MWTCS
Modification [*or Modify*] (AFM) .... MOD
Modification Review Board (AFM) .... MRB
Modified Alternate Mark Inversion [*Telecommunications*] (TEL) .... MAMI
Modified Binary-Coded Decimal (NITA) .... MBCD
Modified Biquinary Code [*Data processing*] .... MBQ
Modified Final Judgment [*Telecommunications*] .... MFJ
Modified Integration Digital Analog Simulator [*Data processing*] (MCD) .... MIDAS
Modified Intermediate Neglect of Differential Overlap [*Quantum mechanics*] .... MINDO
Modified Julian Date [*Telecommunications*] (TEL) .... MJD
Modified Link Pack Area (MCD) .... MLPA
Modified Modified Frequency Modulation (NITA) M2FM
Modified Random Phase Approximation .... MRPA
Modified Tape Armor [*Telecommunications*] (TEL) .... MT
Modify Address (IEEE) .... MA
Moding Sequencing and Control (MCD) .... MSC
Modular Advanced Graphics Generation System (IEEE) .... MAGGS
Modular Alphanumeric Graphics Generator (IEEE) .... MAGG
Modular Alter and Compose Console [*Data processing*] .... MACC
Modular Analysis Processor [*Applied Data Research, Inc.*] (NITA) .... MAP
Modular Application System [*Data processing*] .... MAP
Modular Application Systems [*Martin Marietta Data Systems*] (NITA) .... MAS
Modular Applications Executive [*Modular Computer Systems*] (NITA) .... MAX
Modular Applications Executive for Communications [*Modular Computer Systems*] (NITA) .... MAXCOM
Modular Approach to System Construction Operation and Test (MCD) .... MASCOT
Modular Arrangement of Predetermined Time Standards (TUT) .... MODAPTS
Modular Automatic Test Equipment .... MATE
Modular Building Distribution System [*Telecommunications*] (TEL) .... MBDS
Modular Computer .... MC
Modular Computer [*In company name, MODCOMP Systems, Inc.*] [*Fort Lauderdale, FL*] [*Software manufacturer*] (DASOS) .... MODCOMP
Modular Computer System (IEEE) .... MCS
Modular Computer System .... MODCOM
Modular Computer Systems, Inc. [*NYSE symbol*] .... MSY
Modular Data Acquisition and Control System [*or Subsystem*] [*Modular Computing Systems, Inc.*] (NITA) .... MODACS
Modular Data System (NITA) .... MDS
Modular Data Transaction System .... MDTS
Modular Design Language [*Data processing*] (CSR) .... MDL
Modular Digital Scan Converter (MCD) .... MDSC
Modular Display Tactical .... MDT
Modular Industrial Terminal (NITA) .... MIT
Modular Input/Output System (NITA) .... MINOS
Modular Input-Output System [*Telecommunications*] (TEL) .... MIOS
Modular Installation of Telecommunications Equipment Racks (TEL) .... MITER
Modular Integrated Circuit Package .... MICPAK
Modular Intelligent Terminal (NITA) .... MIT
Modular Interactive Network Designer (NITA) .... MIND
Modular Isodrive Memory Series .... MIMS
Modular Multiband Scanner (MCD) .... MMS
Modular Observation Device (RDA) .... MOD
Modular Operating System (BUR) .... MOS
Modular Opitical Digital Interface (NITA) .... MODI
Modular Output Unit for Talking to Humans (NITA) .... MOUTH
Modular Peripheral Interface Converter (NITA) .... MPC
Modular Power System (MCD) .... MPS
Modular Programing Language (CSR) .... MODULA
Modular Redundancy (NITA) .... MR
Modular Store Control Unit (NITA) .... MSCU
Modular System Programs [*IBM Corp.*] .... MSP
Modular Tactical Communications Center .... MTCC
Modular Thermal Analyzer Routine [*Data processing*] .... MOTAR
Modular Timing Terminal Unit .... MTTU
Modular Video Data System [*Sperry UNIVAC*] (NITA) .... MVDS
Modulate/Demodulate [*or Modulation/Demodulation or Modulator-Demodulator*] [*Data processing*] .... MODEM
Modulate-Demodulate Subsystem (CIT) .... MDS
Modulated Continuous Wave [*Radio signal transmission*] .... MCW
Modulated Noise Reference Unit [*Telecommunications*] (TEL) .... MNRU
Modulation [*Telecommunications*] (KSC) .... MOD
Modulation, Demodulation, Terminal, and Associated Equipment .... MDTA
Modulation Depth [*Broadcasting*] .... M
Modulation Response .... MR
Modulation Transfer Function [*Resolution measure*] .... MTF
Modulation Transfer Function Analyzer .... MTFA
Modulator (CET) .... MOD
Modulator-Demodulator [*Telecommunications*] (CET) .... M/D
Modulator-Demodulator [*Telecommunications*] (MCD) .... MOD
Modulator Isolation Diagnostic Analysis System (IEEE) .... MIDAS
Module Balance [*Data processing*] .... MB
Module Interconnection Language (NITA) .... MIL
Modus Operandi - Personal Appearance [*FBI computer procedure*] .... MOPA
Moessbauer Effect Data Center [*University of North Carolina*] [*Information service*] (EISS) .... MEDC
Mohawk Business-Oriented Language [*Mohawk Data Systems*] (NITA) .... MOBOL
Mohawk Data Sciences Corp. [*NYSE symbol*] .... MDS
Molecular Access System [*Computer program*] .... MACCS
Molecularized Digital Computer .... MOLECOM
Molten-Salt Reactor Information System .... MSRIS
Molten Salts Data Center [*National Bureau of Standards*] [*Rensselaer Polytechnic Institute*] [*Research center*] (EISS) .... MSDC
Moment Connections [*Computer Services Consultants Ltd.*] [*Software package*] [*British*] (NCC) .... MCON
Monchik-Weber Corporation [*NASDAQ symbol*] (NQ) .... MWCH
Money Market Services, Inc. [*Database producer*] (CUAD) .... MMS
Monitor (MDG) .... M
Monitor (MDG) .... MNTR
Monitor (DEN) .... MON
Monitor [*Data processing*] (BUR) .... MTR
Monitor and Alarm System (MCD) .... MAS
Monitor and Assembly System [*Data processing*] (BUR) .... MASS
Monitor Call [*Data processing*] (IBMDP) .... MC
Monitor and Control [*Data processing*] (BUR) .... MC
Monitor Displays [*Data processing*] (BUR) .... MD
Monitor Distribution System [*Television*] .... MDS
Monitor Event Simulation System (IEEE) .... MESS
Monitor Printing Unit [*Data processing*] (TUT) .... MPU
Monitor Unit [*Telecommunications*] (TEL) .... M/U
Monitoring and Control Station (NITA) .... MACS
Monocycle Position Modulation .... MPM
Monolithic Ferrite Memory Array .... MFMA
Monolithic Integrated Circuit .... MIC
Monolithic Quad Device .... MQD
Monolithic Systems Technology .... MST
Monopoly Information and Data Analysis System .... MIDAS
Monopulse Antenna Kit .... MAK
Monopulse Interference Filter .... MIF
Monopulse Resolution Improvement .... MRI
Monopulse Tracking Receiver .... MTR
Monroe Automatic Internal Diagnosis [*Data processing*] .... MAID
Monte-Carlo Inelastic Scattering [*Code*] [*Data processing*] .... MIS
Monte Carlo Method [*Data processing*] .... MCM
Month (AFM) .... MO
Monthly Availability Charge (BUR) .... MAC
Monthly Energy Review [*Department of Energy*] [*Database*] (FDB) .... MER
Moore School of Automatic Computers [*University of Pennsylvania*] .... MSAC
Morrison-Knudsen Technologies, Incorporated [*Boise, ID*] [*Telecommunications*] (TSSD) .... MKTI
Morse Telegraph Club .... MTC
[*The*] **Mortgage Index, Inc.** [*Remote Computing Corp.*] [*Information service*] (EISS) .... TMI
Moscow City Relay Network (OA) .... MCRN
Mosquito Data Bank of the University of Notre Dame .... MODABUND
Most Economical Route Selection [*Also, ARS*] [*Bell System*] [*Telecommunications*] .... MERS
Most Significant (CAH) .... MS
Most Significant BIT [*Binary Digit*] [*Data processing*] .... MSB
Most Significant Character [*Data processing*] (MDG) .... MSC
Most Significant Digit [*Data processing*] (CIT) .... MSD
Most Significant Position (CMD) .... MSP
Motional Feedback .... MFB
Motional Pickup Transducer (MCD) .... MPT
Motor Vehicle Information Management System [*Bell System*] .... MOVIMS
Motorized Antenna Switching Matrix .... MASM
Motorized Switching Matrix .... MSM
Motorola Automatic Sequential Computer Operated Tester .... MASCOT
Motorola Automatically Generated Integrated Circuits .... MAGIC
Motorola Disk Operating System (NITA) .... MDOS
Motorola Emitter-Coupled Logic (IEEE) .... MECL
Motorola Environmental Telemetry (DDI) .... MET
Motorola High-Threshold Logic .... MHTL
Motorola, Inc. [*NYSE symbol*] .... MOT
Motorola Processor Unit .... MPU
Mountain System Digital Automatic Computer .... MODAC
Move [*Telecommunications*] (TEL) .... MV
[*The*] **Movie Channel** [*Cable-television system*] .... TMC
Moving Domain Memories [*Data processing*] (MDG) .... MOD
Moving Head Disk [*Data processing*] (TEL) .... MHD
Moving Image [*A publication*] .... Mov Im
MSI Data Corp. [*American Stock Exchange symbol*] .... MSI
MTI Systems Corp. [*NASDAQ symbol*] (NQ) .... MTIS
MTS Systems Corporation [*NASDAQ symbol*] (NQ) .... MTSC
Muddle [*A computer language*] .... MDL
Muliple Instruction Streams Multiple Data Steams (NITA) .... MISMDS

Computer & Telecommunications Acronyms

Muller Data Corporation [Information service] (EISS)	MDC
Multi Address Asynchronous Communication System (OA)	MAACS
Multi-Indexed Sequential Access Method [Data processing]	MSAM
Multi-Input Standard Tape	MIST
Multi Solutions, Inc. [NASDAQ symbol] (NQ)	MULT
Multi-Tenant Telecommunications Association [Washington, DC] (EANO)	MTTA
Multi-User Dungeon [Computer game]	MUD
Multiaccess Real-Time Operating System [AEG Telefunken] [West German] (NITA)	MARTOS
Multiaction Computer	MAC
Multiaperture Reluctance Switch [Data storage unit]	MARS
Multiapplication Monitor (NITA)	MAM
Multiband (DEN)	MB
Multiband Direction Finder	MDF
Multiband Image Scanning System (SKY)	MISS
Multiband Infrared Filter Radiometer	MIFR
Multiband Infrared Radiometer	MIR
Multiband Spectral Observation Equipment	MSOE
Multibeam Antenna	MBA
Multibeam Radiometer Antenna	MBRA
Multiblock Synchronization Signal Unit [Telecommunications] (TEL)	MBS
Multiblock Synchronization Signal Unit [Telecommunications] (TEL)	MSU
Multibus Interface [Data processing] (MCD)	MBI
Multichannel	MCHAN
Multichannel Analog-to-Digital Data Encoder	MADE
Multichannel Analyzer	MCA
Multichannel Communications Controller	MCC
Multichannel Communications Program (IEEE)	MCP
Multichannel DIFAR [Directional Frequency Analysis and Recording System] Relay (NVT)	MCDR
Multichannel Fixed	MCF
Multichannel Memory System [Data processing]	MCMS
Multichannel Multipoint Distribution Service [Broadcasting term]	MMDS
Multichannel Receiver	MCR
Multichannel Signal Averager [Data processing]	MSA
Multichannel Voice Frequency [Telecommunications]	MCVF
Multichannel Voice Frequency Telegraphy [Telecommunications] (TEL)	MCVFT
Multichip [Circuit] [Electronics]	MC
Multicolor Automatic Projection System (IEEE)	MAPS
Multicommand Data System	MCDS
Multicomponent Circuits	MCC
Multicoupler (DDI)	MUC
Multicoupler Unit [Antenna] [Telecommunications] (TEL)	MCU
MULTICS Data Base Manager	MDBM
Multicultural Television	MTV
Multidimensional Access (OA)	MDA
Multidimensional Analysis (IEEE)	MDA
Multidimensional Array (OA)	MDA
Multidimensional Switching System [Instrumentation]	MDSS
Multidimensional Switching System - Packed Column Trap [Instrumentation]	MDSS-PCT
Multidimensional Tasking [Honeywell, Inc.] (NITA)	MDT
Multidisciplinary Integrated Research Activities in Complex Laboratory Environments [National Science Foundation]	MIRACLE
Multiemitter Transistor	MET
Multifile Linear Programing (NITA)	MFLP
Multiform Printer (NITA)	MFP
Multifrequency	MF
Multifrequency Key Pulsing	MFKP
Multifrequency Microwave Radiometer (MCD)	MFMR
Multifrequency Pulsing (MSA)	MFP
Multifrequency Receiver [Telecommunications]	MFR
Multifrequency Signal Detector [Telecommunications]	MSD
Multifrequency Signaling, Compelled [Telecommunications] (TEL)	MFC
Multifunction Antenna	MFA
Multifunction Card Machine (BUR)	MFCM
Multifunction Card Unit	MFCU
Multifunction CRT [Cathode-Ray Tube] Display System (NASA)	MCDS
Multifunction CRT [Cathode-Ray Tube] Display Unit (NASA)	MCDU
Multifunction Data Set Utility Language (NITA)	MFDSUL
Multifunction Display (MCD)	MFD
Multifunction Microwave Aperture	MMA
Multifunction Peripheral	MFP
Multifunction Protocol Converter (NITA)	MFPC
Multifunction Receiver System	MFRS
Multifunction Reference Unit (MCD)	MRU
Multifunction Sensor (MCD)	MFS
Multifunctional Information Distribution System [NATO] (MCD)	MIDS
Multifunctional Receiver (NASA)	MFR
Multigrounded Neutral [Telecommunications] (TEL)	MGN
Multihead Disk (NASA)	MHD
Multijunction Semiconductor Rectifier	MSR
Multijunction Unit [Data processing] (BUR)	MJU
Multilanguage System [Data processing] (IEEE)	MLS
Multilayer Ceramic Capacitor [Electronics]	MLCC
Multilayer Circuit	MLC
Multilayer Circuit Board	MLCB
Multilayer Printed Circuit	MLPC
Multilayer Printed Circuit Board	MPCB
Multilayer Printed-Wiring Board (IEEE)	MLPWB
Multilayer Printed Wiring Board	MPWB
Multilayer Wiring Board	MWB
Multileaving Remote Job Entry [IBM Corp.]	MRJE
Multilevel Amplitude Shift Keying	MASK
Multilevel Large-Scale Integration	MLSI
Multilevel Multiaccess (CCD)	MLMA
Multilevel Precedence and Preemption [Telecommunications] (TEL)	MLPP
Multiline Automatic Network Diagnostic and Transmission Equipment (NITA)	MANDATE
Multiline Communications Processor (NITA)	MLCP
Multiline Control (BUR)	MLC
Multilinear Array [In earth scanning]	MLA
Multimegabit Operation Multiplexer System	MOMS
Multimessage Unit [Telecommunications] (TEL)	MMU
Multimeter Wave Power Source	MWPS
Multimode Display	MMD
Multimode Information Distribution System (NITA)	MIDS
Multimode International Data Acquisition Service [Australia] [Information service] (EISS)	MIDAS
Multinational Communication-Electronics Working Group [Formerly, SGCEC] [NATO] (NATG)	MCEWG
Multiparameter Pulse Height Analyzer	MPPHA
Multiparty Connection Subsystem [Telecommunications] (TEL)	MPCS
Multiple	MULT
Multiple Access Computer	MAC
Multiple Access Control [Data processing] (DIT)	MAC
Multiple Access Facility [Data processing]	MAF
Multiple Access Interface (NITA)	MAI
Multiple Access to Memory [Data processing] (IEEE)	MAM
Multiple Access to Memory System [Data processing] (CIT)	MAMS
Multiple Access Retrieval System [Control Data Corp.] (NITA)	MARS
Multiple Access Sequential Selection [Data processing] (BUR)	MASS
Multiple Access Shared Time Executive Routine [Control Data Corp.] [Data processing]	MASTER
Multiple-Access Time-Division Experiment (IEEE)	MATE
Multiple Access Unit (NITA)	MAU
Multiple Address (DDI)	MX
Multiple Address Letter	MAL
Multiple Address Processing System	MAPS
Multiple Address Telegrams	MAT
Multiple Application Connector System	MACS
Multiple Array Processor	MAP
Multiple Audio Distribution [Communications]	MAD
Multiple Basic Channel (NITA)	MBC
Multiple Batch Station [Data processing] (OA)	MBS
Multiple Central Processing Unit (NITA)	MCPU
Multiple Channel Control Unit (NITA)	MCCU
Multiple Character Set (CMD)	MCS
Multiple-Chip Carrier [Computer technology]	MCC
Multiple Chip Package	MCP
Multiple Communications Control (BUR)	MCC
Multiple Communications Control Unit [Data processing]	MCCU
Multiple Computer Complex	MCC
Multiple Computer System	MCS
Multiple Concrete Duct [Telecommunications] (TEL)	MCD
Multiple Conductor, Heat and Flame Resistant, Armor [Cable]	MHFA
Multiple Console Support [Fujitsu Ltd.] [Data processing] (MCD)	MCS
Multiple Constraint Alternative Selector Program [Bell System]	MCASP
Multiple Control Program [Data processing]	MCP
Multiple Data Entry System (NITA)	MDES
Multiple Dataset System	MDS
Multiple Device Controller (NITA)	MDC
Multiple Digit Absorbing [Telecommunications] (TEL)	MDA
Multiple Dissemination	MD
Multiple Drop Wire [Telecommunications] (TEL)	MDW
Multiple-Electrode Flame Ionization Detector	MFID
Multiple Element Directional Universally Steerable Antenna	MEDUSA
Multiple Entry Multiple Exit (NITA)	MEME
Multiple External Line Control Unit (NITA)	MELCU
Multiple Filer Audit Program	MFA
Multiple-Frequency Shift Keying	MFSK
Multiple-Frequency Synthesizer	MFS
Multiple-Frequency X- and K-Band (CIT)	MXK
Multiple Goal Programing (NITA)	MGP
Multiple High-Speed Data Channel (NITA)	MHSDC
Multiple Host Support (NITA)	MHS
Multiple Index Data Access System [Prime Computer, Inc.] (NITA)	MIDAS
Multiple Index Sequential Access Method (NITA)	MISAM
Multiple Indexing and Console Retrieval Options [Information retrieval] [Data processing]	MICRO
Multiple Input/Output (NITA)	MIO
Multiple Input Terminal Equipment	MITE
Multiple Instantaneous Response File	MIRF
Multiple Instruction, Multiple Data (MCD)	MIMD
Multiple Instruction, Single Data [Processor configuration] (IEEE)	MISD
Multiple Key Hashing (NITA)	MKH
Multiple Level Indexing Scheme [Data processing] (TUT)	MLIS
Multiple-Line Encryption System	MLES
Multiple Line Printing (CMD)	MLP
Multiple Line Terminal Adapter [Data processing] (BUR)	MLTA
Multiple-Link Satellite Program (CIT)	MLSP

By Meaning

Computer & Telecommunications Acronyms

Multiple Logical Unit (NITA)	MLU
Multiple Match Resolver (OA)	MMR
Multiple Module Access	MMA
Multiple Negative [Circuit]	MUNE
Multiple Online Debugging System [Data processing] (IEEE)	MOLDS
Multiple Online Programing [Data processing] (DIT)	MOP
Multiple Operational Data Acquisition Program [Data processing]	MODAP
Multiple Peripheral Adapter (NITA)	MPA
Multiple Phase Shift Keying [Data processing] (TEL)	MPSK
Multiple Positive [Circuit]	MUPO
Multiple Processor [Data processing] (BUR)	MP
Multiple Projected Fibonacci [Microwave circuit]	MUPROF
Multiple-Purpose Communications (NG)	MPC
Multiple Quantum Well [Switch for an optical computer]	MQW
Multiple Read-Write Compute	MRWC
Multiple Report Creation System (NITA)	MRCS
Multiple Requesting [IBM Corp.] (NITA)	MR
Multiple-Response Enable (IEEE)	MRE
Multiple Response Resolver (NITA)	MRR
Multiple Scan Correlator	MSC
Multiple Sensor Display Group (MCD)	MSDG
Multiple Signal Unit [Telecommunications] (TEL)	MSU
Multiple Single Instruction, Multiple Data (MCD)	MSIMD
Multiple Sub-Nyquist Subsampling Encoding [Digital recording system introduced 1984]	MUSE
Multiple System Operator [Cable television]	MSO
Multiple Systems Coupling [Data processing]	MSC
Multiple-Technique Analytical Computer System	MACS
Multiple-Terminal Access [Data processing] (IBMDP)	MTA
Multiple-Terminal Communication Adapter [Data processing]	MTCA
Multiple Terminal Emulator (NITA)	MTE
Multiple Tile Duct [Telecommunications] (TEL)	MTD
Multiple Transmitter Duplicator	MXD
Multiple Unit Message [Telecommunications] (IEEE)	MUM
Multiple Unit Steerable Antenna [Electronics]	MUSA
Multiple Unit Terminal Test Set (MCD)	MUTTS
Multiple-Use MARC [Machine-Readable Cataloging] System [Library of Congress] [Online retrieval system] [Information service]	MUMS
Multiple Utility Peripheral System [Data processing]	MUPS
Multiple Virtual Storage [IBM Corp.] [Data processing]	MVS
Multiple Virtual Storage System Extension (NITA)	MVSSE
Multiple Virtual System [Data processing]	MVS
Multiple Wire Proportional Counter	MWPC
Multiplex [or Multiplexer] [Telecommunications]	MPX
Multiplex [or Multiplexer] [Telecommunications] (CIT)	MUX
Multiplex [or Multiplexer]	MX
Multiplex Data Bus [Data processing] (MCD)	MDB
Multiplex Interface Adapter (NASA)	MIA
Multiplex Interface Handler (NITA)	MIH
Multiplex Interferometric Fourier Spectroscopy	MIFS
Multiplex Interior Communications (NG)	MICS
Multiplex Line Adapter (SKY)	MLA
Multiplex Loop Interface Adapter (NITA)	MLIA
Multiplex Modulation (CIT)	MUXMOD
Multiplex Recording Photography	MRP
Multiplex Remote Terminal Unit (MCD)	MRTU
Multiplexed Analog Component [Satellite television] [British]	MAC
Multiplexed Information and Computing Service [Honeywell, Inc.]	MULTICS
Multiplexed Message Processor	MMP
Multiplexer	MPLX
Multiplexer	MPXR
Multiplexer (SKY)	MULTI
Multiplexer	MUXER
Multiplexer Analog-to-Digital Converter (MCD)	MADC
Multiplexer Control Unit (OA)	MCU
Multiplexer/Demultiplexer	MDM
Multiplexer/Demultiplexer [Bell Laboratories]	MULDEM
Multiplexer and Demultiplexer	MUX/DEMUX
Multiplexer Encoder Unit	MEU
Multiplexer and Terminal Unit	MTU
Multiplexer Unit [Telecommunications]	MXU
Multiplexes [or Multiplexers] [Telecommunications]	MUXES
Multiplexing Input-Output Processor [Data processing] (BUR)	MIOP
Multiplexing Unit (VIT)	MU
Multiplicative Noise Compensator [Telecommunications] (TEL)	MNC
Multiplier Decoder Gate [Data processing]	MDG
Multiplier Quotient [Data processing]	MQ
Multiplier Quotient Register [Data processing]	MQR
Multiplier Quotient Unit [Data processing]	MQU
Multiplier Register (NITA)	MR
Multiply (MDG)	MLY
Multiply (MDG)	MPY
Multiply (MDG)	MUL
Multiplying Digital-to-Analog Converter [Data processing] (IEEE)	MDAC
Multipoint Cross-Reference Index	MULDEX
Multipoint Distribution System [Line-of-sight relay system for electronic signals]	MDS
Multipoint Network Control System	MNCS
Multiport Memory Controller (NITA)	MMC
Multiport Memory Interface Unit (NITA)	MMIU
Multiport Programable Communications Interface (NITA)	MPCI
Multiprocessing [Data processing]	MP
Multiprocessing Control System [Data processing]	MPCS
Multiprocessing Monitor Control Program [Data processing]	MP/M
Multiprocessor Communications Adapter (NITA)	MCA
Multiprocessor Communications Unit (NITA)	MCU
Multiprocessor Computer	MPC
Multiprocessor Computer Complex	MPCC
Multiprocessor Experimental Computer Complex	MPECC
Multiprogram Control [Data processing]	MPC
Multiprogramed Computer System (IEEE)	MCS
Multiprograming Executive [Hewlett-Packard Co.] (NITA)	MPE
Multiprograming Executive [Data processing] (NITA)	MPX
Multiprograming with Fixed Number of Tasks [Data processing] (BUR)	MFT
Multiprograming Monitor (NITA)	MPM
Multiprograming Operating System (NITA)	MOS
Multiprograming System [Data processing] (CGC)	MPS
Multiprograming Utility System [Regnecentralen] [Denmark] (NITA)	MUS
Multiprograming Utility System Interpretive Language [Regnecentralen] [Denmark] (NITA)	MUSIL
Multiprograming with a Variable Number of Tasks [IBM Corp.] [Control program] [Data processing]	MVT
Multiprotocol Communications Controller	MPCC
Multipurpose	MP
Multipurpose Automatic Data Analysis Machine	MADAM
Multipurpose Communications and Signaling	MCS
Multipurpose Computer (CMD)	MPC
Multipurpose Display Repeater Indicator (MCD)	MDRI
Multipurpose and Generalized Interface to COBOL [Data processing] (TUT)	MAGIC
Multipurpose Optimization System [Data processing]	MPOS
Multipurpose Processing Language [Data processing] (IEEE)	MPPL
Multipurpose Programing Language	MPPL
Multipurpose Recorder (DDI)	MPR
Multiregional Input-Output	MRIO
Multischedule Private Line	MPL
Multisensor Display	MSD
Multisensor Processor (CAAL)	MSP
Multiservice Communications Systems (RDA)	MSCS
Multishare Network Architecture [Mitsubishi Corp.] (BUR)	MNA
Multispectral Scanner [or Sensor]	MSS
Multispectral Scanner and Data System	MSDS
Multistage Frequency Multiplexer (NITA)	MFM
Multistate Information System [Patient records]	MSIS
Multistation Interface Unit [Data processing]	MIU
Multistrip Coupler [Telecommunications] (TEL)	MSC
Multisubscriber Time-Sharing Systems [Computer system]	MSTS
Multisubsystem Adapter [Sperry UNIVAC] (NITA)	MSA
Multisystem Networking Facility (NITA)	MNF
Multisystem Networking Facility [Data processing]	MSNF
Multitarget Frequency	MTF
Multitask Terminal System (NITA)	MTTS
Multitasking (NITA)	MT
Multitasking BASIC [Data processing]	MTBASIC
Multiterminal Adapter (IEEE)	MTA
Multiterminal Unit (TEL)	MTU
Multitype Branching Process in a Random Environment [Data processing]	MBPRE
Multiuser Monitor (NITA)	MUM
Multiutility System (MCD)	MUS
Multivariable Control Unit [Data processing]	MVCU
Multiwork Station (NITA)	MWS
MUMPS [Massachusetts General Hospital Utility Multiprograming System] Users' Group [College Park, MD] (EANO)	MUG
Municipal Data Service [International City Management Association] [Information service] (EISS)	MDS
Museum Computer Network, Inc. [American Association of Museums] [Stony Brook, NY] [Research center] (RCD)	MCN
Museum Exchange for System's Help [National Museum of Natural History] (EISS)	MESH
Mush until No Good [Describes destruction of computer software]	MUNG
Music	MUS
Music Construction Set [Computer program designed by Will Harvey and published by Electronic Arts]	MCS
Music Information Retrieval	MIR
Music Television [Warner Amex Satellite Entertainment Co.] [Cable-television system]	MTV
Musical Instrument Digital Interface [Port] [Socket on an electronic synthesizer that permits a direct computer connection]	MIDI
Mutlifunction Communications Adapter (NITA)	MFCA
Mutliple Data Link Controller (NITA)	MDLC
Mutual Broadcasting System	MBS
Mutual Conductance (CDH)	Gm
Mutual Inductance [Symbol] [IUPAC]	M
Mutual Inductance Bridge	MIB
Mutual Institutions National Transfer System, Inc.	MINTS
Mutual Interference Chart (IEEE)	MIC
MUX [Multiplex] Terminal (MCD)	MT
My Compact Operating System [Toshiba] (NITA)	MYCOS
Mylar Insulation Material	MYIM

N

Nabu Network Corp. [Toronto Stock Exchange symbol] .... NBK
Name and Address .... N/A
Name and Address File [IRS] .... NAF
Nano [A prefix meaning divided by one billion] [SI symbol] .... n
Nanoampere .... nA
Nanosecond [100 billionth of a second] [Also, nsec] .... ns
Nanosecond [100 billionth of a second] [Also, ns] .... nsec
Narrow Beam   (NATG) .... NB
Narrowband .... NB
Narrowband Coherent Video   (IEEE) .... NBCV
Narrowband Conducted   (IEEE) .... NBC
Narrowband Detector .... NBD
Narrowband Dicke-Fix [Electronics]   (CET) .... NBDF
Narrowband Dicke-Fix [Electronics]   (MSA) .... NBDFX
Narrowband Filter .... NBF
Narrowband Frequency Modulation [Radio] .... NBFM
Narrowband Frequency Modulation [Radio] .... NFM
Narrowband Linear Detector   (MCD) .... NBLD
Narrowband Network .... NBN
Narrowband Noise .... NBN
Narrowband Phase Modulation   (MCD) .... NBPM
Narrowband Phase Modulation   (DEN) .... NPM
Narrowband Radiated   (IEEE) .... NBR
Narrowband Search   (MCD) .... NBS
Narrowband Subscriber Terminal   (CET) .... NBST
Narrowband Tape Recorder .... NBTR
Narrowband Voice Security .... NVS
Nashua Corp. [NYSE symbol] .... NSH
[The] Nashville Network [Cable-television system] .... TNN
Nassi-Schneiderman [Data processing] .... N-S
National Academy of Sciences [Washington, DC] .... NAS
National Account Management [Bell System] .... NAM
National Activity to Test Software .... NATS
National Aerometric Data Bank [Environmental Protection Agency] .... NADB
National Aerometric Data Information System [Environmental
  Protection Agency] .... NADIS
National Aeronautics and Space Administration [Washington, DC] .... NASA
National Aeronautics and Space Administration Remote Console ....
  .... NASA/RECON
National Aerospace Electronics Conference [IEEE] .... NAECON
National Air Communications [British] .... NAC
National Air Pollution Technical Information Center [of National
  Air Pollution Control Administration] [Also, APTIC]   (DIT) .... NAPTIC
National Airspace Data Interchange Network   (FAAC) .... NADIN
National Archives and Records Service [of GSA] [Washington, DC] ..... NARS
National Assessment of Educational Progress Information
  Retrieval System [National Institute of Education] [Database]
  (FDB) .... NAEPIRS
National Association of Aircraft and Communications Suppliers
  (EANO) .... NAACS
National Association for Better Broadcasting [Formerly, NAFBRAT] ...... NABB
National Association for Better Radio and Television [Later,
  NABB] .... NAFBRAT
National Association of Broadcast Unions and Guilds .... NABUG
National Association of Broadcasters [Telecommunications]   (TEL) .... NAB
National Association of Business and Educational Radio
  [Washington, DC] .... NABER
National Association of College and University Business Officers
  [Washington, DC] .... NACUBO
National Association of Computer Stores [Stamford, CT]   (EANO) .... NACS
National Association of Computerized Tax Processors [Annapolis,
  MD]   (EANO) .... NACTP
National Association of County Data Processing Administrators
  (EANO) .... NACDPA
National Association of Educational Broadcasters [Formerly,
  Association of College and University Broadcasting Stations
  (1934)] [Washington, DC] .... NAEB
National Association for Educational Computing   (EANO) .... NAEC
National Association of Electrical Distributors .... NAED
National Association of Electronic Keyboard Manufacturers
  (EANO) .... NAEKM
National Association of Farm Broadcasters .... NAFB

National Association of FM [Frequency Modulation] Broadcasters
  [Later, NRBA] .... NAFMB
National Association of Government Archives and Records
  Administrators   (EANO) .... NAGARA
National Association of Government Communicators   (EANO) .... NAGC
National Association of Independent Computer Companies
  (NITA) .... NAICC
National Association of Independent Television Producers and
  Distributors   (EANO) .... NAITPD
National Association of Industrial Technology   (EANO) .... NAIT
National Association of Instructional Leaders in Technical
  Education   (EANO) .... NAILTE
National Association of Professional Word Processing
  Technicians [Philadelphia, PA]   (EANO) .... NAPWPT
National Association of Radio and Telecommunications
  Engineers   (EANO) .... NARTE
National Association of Radiotelephone Systems [Later, Telocator
  Network of America]   (EANO) .... NARS
National Association of Regulatory Utility Commissioners
  [Telecommunications] [Information service] .... NARUC
National Association for Remotely Piloted Vehicles   (MCD) .... NARPV
National Association of Satellite Equipment Manufacturers [Tulsa,
  OK]   (EANO) .... NASEM
National Association of Securities Dealers .... NASD
National Association of Securities Dealers Automated Quotations
  [Over-the-counter stock quotations] [Bunker Ramo Corp.]
  [Trumbell, CT] .... NASDAQ
National Association for State Information Systems [Lexington,
  KY] .... NASIS
National Association of Telecommunications Officers and
  Advisors [National League of Cities] [Washington, DC]   (EANO) .... NATOA
National Association of Television Program Executives .... NATPE
National Association of Word Processing Specialists [Later, WPS]
  (EANO) .... NAWPS
National Automated Accounting Research System [American
  Institute of Certified Public Accountants] [Database]
  [Information service]   (EISS) .... NAARS
National Automated Clearing House Association   (EANO) .... NACHA
National Bibliographic Data Base [Deutsche Bibliothek] [Database]
  (ODIN) .... BIBLIO-DATA
National Biomedical Research Foundation [Georgetown
  University] [Research center] .... NBRF
National Black Network [A radio network] .... NBN
National Blood Data Center [American Blood Commission]
  [Information service]   (EISS) .... NBDC
National Broadcasting Company, Inc. [New York, NY] .... NBC
National Bureau of Economic Research [Cambridge, MA] .... NBER
National Bureau of Standards [Department of Commerce]
  [Washington, DC] .... NBS
National Bureau of Standards Center for Computer Sciences and
  Technology   (DIT) .... NBSCCST
National Bureau of Standards Frequency Standard   (IEEE) .... NBSFS
National Bureau of Standards Load Determination [Computer
  program] .... NBSLD
National Burn Information Exchange [Ann Arbor, MI] [Information
  service]   (EISS) .... NBIE
National Cable [formerly, Community] Television Association ...... NCTA
National Cable Television Institute   (EANO) .... NCTI
National Calling and Emergency Frequencies   (CET) .... NCEF
National Cancer Institute [of National Institutes of Health]
  [Database producer] .... NCI
National Captioning Institute [Falls Church, VA]
  [Telecommunications]   (EANO) .... NCI
National Cartographic and Geographic Information Center
  [Geological Survey] [Reston, VA] [Database]   (FDB) .... NCGIC
National Cash Register Co. [Later, NCR Corp.] [Computer
  manufacturer] .... NCR
National Cash Register Electronic Data Processing System
  (MCD) .... NATRON
National Center for Automated Information Retrieval   (EISS) ..... NCAIR
National Center for Business and Economic Communication
  [American University] [Research center]   (RCD) .... NCBEC

325

Computer & Telecommunications Acronyms

National Center for Computer Crime Data [Formerly, National Computer Crime Data Center (1979)] [Los Angeles, CA] [Database producer] (EANO)..... NCCCD
National Center for Health Statistics [Health Services and Mental Health Administration] [Rockville, MD] [Originator and database]..... NCHS
National Center of Scientific and Technological Information [National Council for Research and Development] [Tel Aviv, Israel] [Also, CSTI] (EISS)..... COSTI
National Center for Standards and Certification Information [National Bureau of Standards] [Database] (FDB)..... NCSCI
National Center for Supercomputing Applications [University of Illinois] [Research center] (RCD)..... NCSA
National Center for Telephone Research [Commercial firm] [Louis Harris and Associates] [New York, NY] (EANO)..... NCTR
National Centre for Information Media and Technology [British]..... CIMTECH
National Chemical Information System (DIT)..... NCIS
National Christian Network [Cable-television system]..... NCN
National Civil Defense Computer Facility..... NCDCF
National Clearing House of Rehabilitation Training Materials [Oklahoma State University] [Information service] (EISS)..... NCHRTM
National Clearinghouse for Alcohol Information [Rockville, MD] (EISS)..... NCALI
National Clearinghouse for Family Planning Information [Database] (FDB)..... NCFPI
National Clearinghouse for Human Genetic Diseases [Public Health Service] [Information service] (EISS)..... NCHGD
National Clearinghouse for Legal Services [Legal Services Corp.] [Information service] (EISS)..... NCLS
National Clearinghouse for Mental Health Information [Rockville, MD] [Database] [HEW]..... NCMHI
National Coal Resources Data System [Geological Survey] [Databank] [Information service] (EISS)..... NCRDS
National Commission on Electronic Fund Transfers..... NCEFT
National Commission on Libraries and Information Science..... NACLIS
National Commission on Libraries and Information Science [Washington, DC]..... NCLIS
National Commission on New Technological Uses of Copyrighted Works [Terminated, 1978] [Library of Congress]..... CONTU
National Communication System Instructions..... NCSI
National Communications [System]..... NACOM
National Communications Association [New York, NY] [Formerly, PCA] (EANO)..... NCA
National Communications Forum [National Engineering Consortium, Inc.] [Chicago, IL] [Telecommunications] (TSSD)..... NCF
National Communications Symposium [IEEE]..... NATCOM
National Communications System [GSA]..... NCS
National Computer Association [Littleton, CO] [Computer users group] (EANO)..... NCA
National Computer Center [IRS]..... NCC
National Computer Conference [United States] [A publication]..... Natl Comput Conf
National Computer Conference..... NCC
National Computer Graphics Association [Fairfax, VA] (EANO)..... NCGA
National Computer Institute (MCD)..... NCI
National Computer Network of Chicago, Inc. [Information service] (EISS)..... NCN
National Computer Program Abstract Service (EISS)..... NCPAS
National Computer Systems, Inc. (CAH)..... NCS
National Computer Systems, Inc. [NASDAQ symbol] (NQ)..... NLCS
National Computing Centre [Manchester, England]..... NCC
National Computing Industries, Inc. [Atlanta, GA] [Software manufacturer] (DASOS)..... NCI
National Conference on Communications (MCD)..... NATCOM
National Congressional Analysis Corp. (EISS)..... NCA
National Consortium for Computer Based Music Instruction [University of Delaware] [Newark, DE] [Research clearinghouse] (EANO)..... NCCBMI
National Conversational Software Systems, Inc. (NITA)..... NCSS
National Council for Families and Television (EANO)..... NCFT
National Credit Information Service [TRW, Inc.] [Long Beach, CA] [Credit-information databank] (EISS)..... NACIS
National Credit Information Service [TRW, Inc.] [Long Beach, CA] [Credit-information databank]..... NCIS
National Crime Information Center [FBI] [Washington, DC]..... NCIC
National Crime Survey [University of Michigan] [Database] (FDB)..... NCS
National Criminal Justice Reference Service [Later, ICJC] [Department of Justice] [Bibliographic database]..... NCJRS
National Data Communication (OA)..... NDC
National Data Corporation..... NDC
National Data Processing Service (NITA)..... NDPS
National Diabetes Information Clearinghouse [Public Health Service] (EISS)..... NDIC
National Diet Library [Tokyo, Japan] (DIT)..... NDL
National Diffusion Network [Department of Education] [Information service] (EISS)..... NDN
National Digestive Diseases Education and Information Clearinghouse [Public Health Service] (EISS)..... NDDEIC
National Driver Register..... NDR
National Earthquake Information Service [United States Geological Survey] (EISS)..... NEIS
National Education Computer Center..... NECC

National Educational Closed-Circuit Television Association [British]..... NECCTA
National Electrical Code..... NEC
National Electrical Manufacturers Association [Database producer and database]..... NEMA
National Electrical Safety Code..... NESC
National Electronic Information Corporation [Information service] (EISS)..... NEIC
National Electronic Injury Surveillance System [Consumer Product Safety Commission] [Washington, DC] [Databank]..... NEISS
National Electronic Packaging and Production Conference..... NEPCON
National Electronics Conference [Later, National Engineering Consortium]..... NEC
National Energy Information Center Affiliate [University of New Mexico] [Albuquerque, NM] (EISS)..... NEICA
National Energy Software Center [Department of Energy] [Information service] (EISS)..... NESC
National Engineering Information System (BUR)..... NEIS
National Engineering Laboratory [Superseded IAT] [National Bureau of Standards]..... NEL
National Engineering Laboratory's Thermophysical Properties Package [British] [Information service] (EISS)..... NELPAC
National Enterprise Board [Later, BTG] [British]..... NEB
National Environmental Data Referral Service [Online database]..... NEDRES
National Environmental Satellite, Data, and Information Service [National Oceanic and Atmospheric Administration]..... NESDIS
National Environmental Satellite Service [National Oceanic and Atmospheric Administration] [Telecommunications] (TEL)..... NESS
National Exchange Carriers Association..... NECA
National Exchange, Inc. [Los Angeles, CA] [Telecommunications] (TSSD)..... NEX
National Facsimile Network [National Weather Service]..... NAFAX
National Federation of Abstracting and Information [formerly, Indexing] Services [Pronounced "enface"] [Philadelphia, PA]..... NFAIS
National Federation of Citizen Band Radio Operators (EANO)..... NFCBRO
National Field Service Corp. [Suffern, NY] [Telecommunications] (TSSD)..... NFS
National Fire Prevention and Control Administration [Later, United States Fire Administration] [Department of Commerce]..... NFPCA
National Fire Protection Association [Boston, MA] [Databank originator]..... NFPA
National Geochemical Data Bank [Natural Environment Research Council] [British] [Information service] (EISS)..... NGDB
National Geodetic Information Center [National Oceanic and Atmospheric Administration] (EISS)..... NGIC
National Geodetic Survey Information Center [National Oceanic and Atmospheric Administration] (EISS)..... NGSIC
National Geographic Names Data Base [Geological Survey] [Database] (FDB)..... NGN
National Geophysical and Solar-Terrestrial Data Center [National Oceanic and Atmospheric Administration] [Boulder, CO] (EISS)..... NGSDC
National Graphical Association [British printers' union]..... NGA
National Health Information Clearinghouse [Public Health Service] (EISS)..... NHIC
National Health Planning Information Center [Hyattsville, MD] [HEW] [Database] (EISS)..... NHPIC
National Information Centre for Educational Media [Access Innovation database]..... NICEM
National Information Conference and Exposition [Associated Information Managers]..... NICE
National Information Retrieval Colloquium [Later, Benjamin Franklin Colloquium on Information Science]..... NIRC
National Information Sources on the Handicapped [Clearinghouse on the Handicapped] [Database] (FDB)..... NISH
National Information Storage and Retrieval Center..... NISARC
National Information System [Later, GIP] [UNESCO] (BUR)..... NIS
National Information Systems Task Force [Society of American Archivists] [Information service] (EISS)..... NISTF
National Institute for Computers in Engineering [Rockville, MD] (EANO)..... NICE
National Institute for Low Power Television (EANO)..... NILPT
National Institute for Telecommunications Research [South Africa] (CIT)..... NITR
National Institutes of Health [Public Health Service] [Bethesda, MD]..... NIH
National Instructional Television [Superseded by AIT] (EANO)..... NIT
National Jewish Television [Cable-television system]..... NJT
National Joint Computer Committee [of ACM, AIEE, IRE] [Superseded by AFIPS]..... NJCC
National Law Enforcement Telecommunications System..... NALECOM
National Law Enforcement Telecommunications System..... NLETS
National Lending Library for Science and Technology [Later, BLLD] [British Library]..... NLL
National Library of Medicine [Public Health Service] [Bethesda, MD] [Database producer]..... NLM
National Library of Science and Invention [British] (DIT)..... NLSI
National List of Scientific Plant Names [Department of Agriculture] (EISS)..... NLSPN
National Machine Accountants Association [Later, DPMA]..... NMAA
National Management Association [Dayton, OH]..... NMA
National Microfilm Association [Later, National Micrographics Association, now AIIM] [Trade association] (CAH)..... NMA

National Micrographics Association [*Later, AIIM*] [*Silver Spring, MD*] [*Trade association*] ... NMA
National Military Command System ... NMCS
National Mobile Radio Association (EANO) ... NMRA
National Mobile Radio System [*Later, Telocator Network of America*] ... NMRS
National Network Dialing [*Telecommunications*] (TEL) ... NND
National Newspaper Index [*Information Access Co.*] [*Bibliographic database*] [*Information service*] (EISS) ... NNI
National Nuclear Data Center [*Department of Energy*] (EISS) ... NNDC
National Number Routed [*Telecommunications*] (TEL) ... NNR
National Numerical Control Applications [*Buffalo, NY*] [*Software manufacturer*] (DASOS) ... NN/CA
National Nutrition Education Clearing House [*Society for Nutrition Education*] (EISS) ... NNECH
National Obscenity Law Center (EISS) ... NOLC
National Oceanic and Atmospheric Administration [*Pronounced "Noah"*] [*Rockville, MD*] [*Department of Commerce*] ... NOAA
National Oceanographic Data Center [*Washington, DC*] [*National Oceanic and Atmospheric Administration*] [*Databank originator*] ... NODC
National Office Computer Facility [*IRS*] ... NOCF
National Office Machine Dealers Association ... NOMDA
National Online Circuit [*Santa Barbara Public Library*] [*Santa Barbara, CA*] [*Online user group*] [*An association*] (EANO) ... NOC
National Organization of Telecommunications Engineers and Scientists [*Telecommunications*] (TSSD) ... NOTES
National Payphone Association (EANO) ... NPA
National Pesticide Information Retrieval System [*Database*] (FDB) ... NPIRS
National Pesticide Telecommunications Network (EANO) ... NPTN
National Physics Information System [*American Institute of Physics*] [*New York, NY*] (DIT) ... NPIS
National Planning Data Corporation [*Information service*] (EISS) ... NPDC
National Public Radio [*Washington, DC*] [*Telecommunications*] (TSSD) ... NPR
National Radio Broadcasters Association [*Formerly, FMDA, NAFMB*] ... NRBA
National Registry System for Chemical Compounds (DIT) ... NRSCC
National Regulatory Research Institute [*Ohio State University*] [*Research center*] (RCD) ... NRRI
National Rehabilitation Information Center [*Catholic University of America*] [*Bibliographic database*] (EANO) ... NARIC
National Rehabilitation Information Center [*Catholic University of America*] [*Database*] (FDB) ... NRIC
National Reprographic Centre for Documentation [*Hatfield Polytechnic Institute*] [*Hertfordshire, England*] [*Evaluation and information group*] [*Information service*] ... NRCd
National Research Council of Canada, Division of Mechanical Engineering [*Ottawa, ON*] [*Research center*] (RCD) ... NRC/DME
National Research Council Library (DIT) ... NRCL
National Research Library [*Canada*] (DIT) ... NRL
National Resource Inventory [*US database on erosion*] ... NRI
National Satellite Cable Association (EANO) ... NSCA
National Scholarship Research Service [*Information service*] (EISS) ... NSRS
National School Curriculum Center for Educational Computing (EANO) ... NSCEC
National Science Foundation [*Washington, DC*] [*Database originator*] ... NSF
National Science Library [*Later, Canada Institute for Scientific and Technical Information*] (DIT) ... NSL
National Semiconductor Corp. ... Nat Semi
National Semiconductor Corporation (NITA) ... NSC
National Semiconductor Corp. [*NYSE symbol*] ... NSM
National Society of Computer/Genealogists (EANO) ... NSC
National Society for Performance and Instruction [*Formerly, National Society for Programed Instruction*] [*Washington, DC*] ... NSPI
National Software Works (NITA) ... NSW
National Solar Technical Audience File [*Solar Energy Research Institute*] [*Database*] (FDB) ... NSTAF
National Sound and Communications Association (EANO) ... NSCA
National Sound-Program Center [*Telecommunications*] (TEL) ... NSPC
National Stock Number (MCD) ... NSN
National Strategic Target Data Base ... NSTDB
[*The*] **National Switchboard** [*Phoenix, AZ*] [*Telecommunications*] (TSSD) ... TNS
National Systems Corp. [*American Stock Exchange symbol*] [*Delisted*] ... NSY
National Technical Information Service [*Department of Commerce*] [*Springfield, VA*] [*Database producer and database*] ... NTIS
National Telecommunications Agency (NITA) ... NTA
National Telecommunications Conference [*IEEE*] ... NTC
National Telecommunications and Information Administration [*Department of Commerce*] ... NTIA
National Telecommunications Network [*Boca Raton, FL*] (TSSD) ... NTN
National Telecommunications & Technology Fund, Inc. [*New York, NY*] (TSSD) ... TELETECH
National Telephone Cooperative Association [*Washington, DC*] ... NTCA
National Television Center [*Telecommunications*] (TEL) ... NTC
National Television Standard Code [*Video equipment*] (RDA) ... NTSC
National Television Systems Committee ... NTSC
National Theater File [*Theater Sources, Inc.*] [*Information service*] (EISS) ... NTF
National Timesharing Council (EANO) ... NTC
National Traffic System [*Amateur radio*] ... NTS
National Training and Operational Technology Center [*Cincinnati, OH*] [*Environmental Protection Agency*] (EISS) ... NTOTC
National UHF [*Ultrahigh Frequency*] **Broadcasting Association** (EANO) ... NUBA
National University Consortium for Telecommunications in Teaching (EANO) ... NUC
National University Teleconference Network [*Stillwater, OK*] [*Telecommunications*] (TSSD) ... NUTN
National Video Clearinghouse, Inc. [*Information service*] (EISS) ... NVC
National Water Data Exchange [*United States Geological Survey*] [*Information service*] ... NAWDEX
National Water Quality Data Bank [*Canada*] [*Information service*] (EISS) ... NAQUADAT
National Yellow Pages Service ... NYPS
Nationality Broadcasting Network [*Cable-television system*] ... NBN
Nationwide Educational Computer Service (IEEE) ... NECS
Native American Public Broadcasting Consortium, Inc. [*Lincoln, NE*] [*Telecommunications*] [*An association*] (EANO) ... NAPBC
NATO Command, Control, and Information Systems and Automatic Data Processing Committee (NATG) ... NCCDPC
NATO Force Planning Data Base (NATG) ... NFPDB
NATO Integrated Communications System (NATG) ... NICS
NATO Integrated Communications System Organization (NATG) ... NICSO
NATO-Wide Communications System (NATG) ... NWCS
Natural Background Clutter ... NBC
Natural Binary-Coded Decimal (NITA) ... NBCD
Natural Convection in the Stationary Condition [*Computer program*] ... NAKOSTA
Natural Electronic Business User's Language [*International Computers Ltd.*] (CAH) ... NEBULA
Natural Language Data Base ... NLDB
Natural Language Operating System (NITA) ... NLOS
Natural Language Processing [*Data processing*] ... NLP
Natural Resource Management System [*Army Corps of Engineers*] [*Database*] (FDB) ... NRMS
Natural Wavelength ... NWL
Navy Numerical Weather Prediction [*Computer system*] [*Control Data Corp.*] (CAH) ... NANWEP
NBC Computer Service Corporation [*Lincoln, NE*] [*Software manufacturer*] (DASOS) ... NBC/CSC
NBI, Inc. [*NYSE symbol*] ... NBI
NCA Corporation [*NASDAQ symbol*] (NQ) ... NCAC
NCR [*NCR Corp.*] **Century Software** (NITA) ... NCS
NCR Corp. [*Formerly, National Cash Register Co.*] [*NYSE symbol*] ... NCR
NCR [*NCR Corp.*] **Electronic Autocoding Technique** [*Data processing*] (IDA) ... NEAT
NCR [*NCR Corp.*] **Optical Font** (MCD) ... NOF
NEA [*Nuclear Energy Agency*] **Data Bank** [*France*] [*Information service*] (EISS) ... NEA-DB
Near-End Crosstalk [*Bell System*] ... NEXT
Near Letter Quality [*Computer printer usage*] ... NLQ
Near Millimeter Wave System [*Telecommunications*] (TEL) ... NMMW
Nearest Neighbor [*Mathematics*] [*Computer search term*] ... NN
Nearly Instantaneous Compounding (MCD) ... NIC
Nebraska ETV [*Educational Television*] **Network** [*Lincoln, NE*] [*Telecommunications*] (TSSD) ... NETV
NEC Corp. ADR [*NASDAQ symbol*] (NQ) ... NIPNY
NEC [*Nippon Electric Company*]**-Toshiba Information Systems, Inc.** [*Japan*] (NITA) ... NTIS
Nederlands Genootschap voor Informatica [*Netherlands Society for Informatics*] [*Information service*] (EISS) ... NGI
Negate BCD [*Binary-Coded Decimal*] **Number** [*Data processing*] ... NBCD
Negate a Binary Number [*Data processing*] ... NEG
Negate a Binary Number with Extend [*Data processing*] ... NEGX
Negative [*Crystal*] ... n
Negative ... NEG
Negative Acknowledge [*or Acknowledgment*] [*Data communication*] ... NAK
Negative Channel Metal-Oxide Semiconductor ... NMOS
Negative Immittance Converter ... NIC
Negative Impedance Booster [*Electronics*] ... NIB
Negative Impedance Converter ... NIC
Negative-Positive-Negative [*Transistor*] (CET) ... N-P-N
Negative-Positive-Negative-Positive [*Transistor*] ... NPNP
Negotiated Critical Dates [*Telecommunications*] (TEL) ... NCD
Neiman-Marcus, Inc. ... NM
Nested Phrase Indexing System [*Automated indexing system*] (NITA) ... NEPHIS
Net Book Value [*Telecommunications*] (TEL) ... NBV
Net Control Station [*Communications*] [*Amateur radio*] ... NCS
Net Data Throughout ... NDT
Net Radio Interface [*Telecommunications*] (TEL) ... NRI
Net Switching Loss [*Telecommunications*] (TEL) ... NSL
Netherlands Information Combine [*Information service*] (EISS) ... NIC
Network [*Telecommunications*] ... NET
Network Access Controller (NITA) ... NAC
Network Access Device (CCD) ... NAD
Network Access Facility (NITA) ... NAF
Network Access Machine [*National Bureau of Standards*] [*Data processing*] ... NAM
Network Access Method [*Control Data Corp.*] [*Telecommunications*] (TEL) ... NAM
Network Access Pricing [*Telecommunications*] (TEL) ... NAP

Acronym Expansion	Acronym
Network Access Protocol (NITA)	NAP
Network Acknowledgment	NAK
Network Address Unit [Data processing] (BUR)	NAU
Network Application Node (NITA)	NAN
Network Building Out Capacitor [Telecommunications] (TEL)	NBOC
Network Building Out Resistor [Telecommunications] (TEL)	NBOR
Network Buildout (IEEE)	NBO
Network Busy Hour [Telecommunications] (TEL)	NBH
Network Communication Access Method (NITA)	NCAM
Network Communications Control Facility [IBM program product]	NCCF
Network Congestion [Telecommunications] (TEL)	NC
Network Connect	NC
Network Connection Element (NITA)	NCE
Network Connection Handler (NITA)	NCH
Network Control (CIT)	NETCON
Network Control Block (NITA)	NCB
Network Control Center (DEEC)	NCC
Network Control Language (NITA)	NCL
Network Control Module (NITA)	NCM
Network Control Node (NITA)	NCN
Network Control Office [Telecommunications] (TEL)	NCO
Network Control Program [IBM Corp.] [Telecommunications] (BUR)	NCP
Network Control Room [Television]	NCR
Network Control System (NITA)	NCS
Network Control Unit [Data processing]	NCU
Network Controller	NC
Network Countdown (SKY)	NC
Network Cryptographic Device (NITA)	NCD
Network Data Link Control (NITA)	NDLC
Network Database Management System (NITA)	NDBMS
Network Definition Language [Burroughs Corp.]	NDL
Network Design and Management System (NITA)	NDMS
Network Diagnostic Control (NITA)	NDC
Network Engineering Administrative Data System [AT & T]	NEADS
Network File Access Method (NITA)	NFAM
Network File Access Protocol (NITA)	NFAP
Network Front End (NITA)	NFE
Network Graphics Protocol (NITA)	NGP
Network Host Protocol (NITA)	NHP
Network In-Dial [Automatic Voice Network] (CET)	NID
Network In-Out Dial [Automatic Voice Network] (CET)	NIOD
Network Information Files [Burroughs Corp.] (NITA)	NIF
Network Information System [AT & T]	NIS
Network Input Processor [Data processing] (MCD)	NIP
Network Integrity Control System (NITA)	NICS
Network Interface Board (CCD)	NIB
Network Interface Card [Data processing]	NIC
Network Interface Control (NITA)	NIC
Network Interface Machine [Datapac] (NITA)	NIM
Network Interface Message Processing Host [NERComP]	NIMPH
Network Interface Monitor (NITA)	NIM
Network Interface Processor (MCD)	NIP
Network Interface System (NITA)	NIS
Network Interface Unit [Data processing] (CCD)	NIU
Network Job Control Language (NITA)	NJCL
Network Job Entry (NITA)	NJE
Network Job Interface (NITA)	NJI
Network Management Center [Data processing]	NMC
Network Management Services [Ohio Bell Communications, Inc.] [Cleveland, OH] [Telecommunications] (TSSD)	NMS
Network Management Signal [Telecommunications] (TEL)	NMS
Network Manager (MCD)	NM
Network Measurement Center (NITA)	NMC
Network Measurement System [Computer network]	NMS
Network Operating System (NITA)	NOS
Network Operating System/Batch Environment (NITA)	NOSBE
Network Operation Center [Bell System]	NOC
Network Operation Support Program [Data processing]	NOSP
Network Operations Forum [Exchange Carriers Standards Association] [Telecommunications]	NOF
Network Operations Trouble Information System [Telecommunications] (TEL)	NOTIS
Network Operator Control Program (NITA)	NOCP
Network-Oriented Data Acquisition Language (NITA)	NODAL
Network Out-Dial [Automatic Voice Network] (CET)	NOD
Network Planning [Data processing] (TUT)	NP
Network Planning Technique [Data processing] (IEEE)	NPT
Network Problem Determination Application [Data processing]	NPDA
Network Processing Supervisor [Honeywell, Inc.]	NPS
Network Processing Unit (NITA)	NPU
Network Protection Device [Telecommunications] (TEL)	NPD
Network Protocol Processor (NITA)	NPP
Network Pulse Forming	NPF
Network Restructuring Language (NITA)	NRL
Network Security Module (NITA)	NSM
Network Services Protocol [Digital Equipment Corp.] [Telecommunications] (TEL)	NSP
Network Signal Processor (NASA)	NSP
[A] Network of Social Security Information Resources [Canada] (EISS)	ANSSIR
Network Strategies, Incorporated [Burke, VA] [Telecommunications] (TSSD)	NSI
Network Supervisor System (NITA)	NSS
Network Support System [Data processing]	NSS
Network Switching Center [Telecommunications] (TEL)	NSC
Network Synchronization Subsystem [Telecommunications] (TEL)	NSS
Network Synthesis and Evaluation Technique [Data processing] (TUT)	NETSET
Network Systems Corporation [Brooklyn Park, MN] [Telecommunications] (TSSD)	NSC
Network Systems Corporation [NASDAQ symbol] (NQ)	NSCO
Network Technologies International, Inc. [Ann Arbor, MI] [Telecommunications] (TSSD)	NETI
Network Telecommunications [Denver, CO] [Telecommunications] (TSSD)	NETTEL
Network Terminal Option [Data processing]	NTO
Network Terminal Protocol (NITA)	NTP
Network Terminating Point [Telecommunications] (TEL)	NTP
Network Terminating Unit	NTU
Network Termination Processor (NITA)	NTP
Network User Address [Information retrieval] (ODIN)	NUA
Network User Identifier [Password] (DEEC)	NUI
Network Users Association (EANO)	NUA
Network Virtual Terminal (NITA)	NVT
Network Wide Directory (NITA)	NWD
Networking Advisory Group [Library of Congress]	NAG
[The] Networking Institute [Commercial firm] (EANO)	TNI
Networks File Transfer (NITA)	NFT
Neutron-Gamma Monte Carlo [Data processing]	NGM
Neutron Transmutation Doped [Silicon for semiconductor use]	NTD
Neutron Transport Computer Code	NTCC
Nevada Applied Ecology Information Center [Department of Energy] (EISS)	NAEIC
Nevada COBOL [Common Business-Oriented Language] Users Group [Norcross, GA] (EANO)	NCUG
Never Ever Mention Outside [Secret computer toy project of Axlon, Inc.]	NEMO
New Assembly Language (NITA)	NAL
New British Standard [Imperial wire gauge]	NBS
New Brunswick Telephone Co. Ltd. [Toronto Stock Exchange symbol]	NBT
New Computer Center [Social Security Administration]	NCC
New England Document Conservation Center [Andover, MA] [Information service] (EISS)	NEDCC
New England Energy Management Information System	NEEMIS
New England Regional Computing Program, Inc. [Boston, MA]	NERComP
New England Sports Network [Cable-television system]	NESN
New Era Technologies, Inc. [Washington, DC] [Telecommunications] (TSSD)	NET
New Information Systems and Services [United States] [A publication]	New Inf Syst Serv
New Integrated Computer Language (TUT)	NICOL
New Line [Data processing]	NL
New Line Character [Keyboard] [Data processing] (MDG)	NLC
New Master File (NITA)	NMF
New Mexico Institute of Mining and Technology Computer Center [Socorro, NM] [Research center] (RCD)	TCC
New Network Architecture (NITA)	NNA
New Product Announcements [Database]	NPA
New Product Line (CGC)	NPL
New Program Status Area (IEEE)	NPSA
New Program Status Word Location (NITA)	NPSWL
New Programing Language [1974] [Later, PL/1] [Data processing] (CGC)	NPL
New System [Data processing] (CGC)	NS
New World Computer [NASDAQ symbol] (NQ)	NEWW
New York Assembly Program [Data processing]	NYAP
New York New England Exchange [Telecommunications]	NYNEX
New York Racing Authority [Cable-television system]	NYRA
New York State Center for Advanced Technology in Computer Applications and Software Engineering [Syracuse University] [Research center] (RCD)	CASE
New York Stock Exchange	NYSE
New York Times Information Service, Inc. [Database originator and host] (EISS)	NYTIS
New Zealand Post Office [Telecommunications] (TEL)	NZPO
Newcorp, Inc. [American Stock Exchange symbol] [Delisted]	NWC
Newspaper Index [Bell & Howell Co.] [Database]	NDEX
Newspaper Systems Group [An association] (EANO)	NSG
Newton-Evans Research Company, Inc. [Ellicott City, MD] [Information service] (TSSD)	NERC
Next In, First Out (NITA)	NIFO
Next Most Significant Digit (OA)	NMSD
Next Most Significant Digit [Data processing]	NSD
Next Sequential Instruction (NITA)	NSI
Next System [Data processing] (CGC)	NS
Next Task Register (NITA)	NTR
Nicaraguan Telecommunication by Satellite [Commercial firm]	NICATELSAT
Night [Broadcasting term]	N
Night Alarm [Telecommunications] (TEL)	NA
Night Closing Trunks [Telecommunications] (TEL)	NCT
Night Letter [Telegraphic communications]	NLT
Night Message	NM
Night Message (MSA)	NTM
Night Telegraph Letter	NTL
Nihon Keizai Shimbun, Inc. (EISS)	NIKKEI

NIKKEI [*Nihon Keizai Shimbun, Inc.*] **Economic Electronic Databank Service - Information Retrieval** [*Japan*] [*Information service*] (EISS) ... NEEDS-IR
NIKKEI [*Nihon Keizai Shimbun, Inc.*] **Economic Electronic Databank Service - Time Sharing** [*Japan*] [*Information service*] (EISS) ... NEEDS-TS
Nimbus Automatic Programing System (IEEE) ... NAPS
Nims Associates, Incorporated [*Decatur, IL*] [*Software manufacturer*] (DASOS) ... NAI
Nineteen-Hundred Commercial Language (CAH) ... NICOL
Nineteen-Hundred Indexing and Cataloging (DIT) ... NIC
Nineteen-Hundred Integrated Modular Management System (NITA) ... NIMMS
Nippon Electric Automatic Computer (IEEE) ... NEAC
Nippon Electric Company [*Japan*] ... NEC
Nippon Gijutsu Boeki Co. Ltd. [*Japan*] [*Information service*] (EISS) ... NGB
Nippon Hoso Kyokai [*Japan National Broadcasting Corporation*] ... NHK
Nippon Information and Communication [*Joint venture of IBM Corp. Japan and Nippon Telegraph and Telephone*] ... NI & C
Nippon Information Processing System [*Nippon Shuppan Hanbai, Inc.*] [*Database*] (CUAD) ... NIPS
Nippon Telegraph and Telephone [*Telecommunications and videotex company*] [*Japan*] ... NTT
Nippon Television Network Corp. [*Japan*] ... NTV
Nixdorf Communications Network [*Nixdorf*] [*West German*] (NITA) ... NCN
No Access [*Telecommunications*] (TEL) ... NA
No-Address Instruction ... NAI
No Charge ... NC
No Checking Signal [*Telecommunications*] (TEL) ... NCS
No Connection [*Valve pins*] [*Technical drawings*] [*Radio*] ... NC
No Data Available [*Data processing*] ... NDA
No Input Acknowledge [*Data processing*] ... NIA
No Live Operator (NG) ... NOLO
No Operation (NITA) ... NOOP
No Operation [*Data processing*] ... NOP
No Parity (NITA) ... NP
No Print [*Telecommunications*] (TEL) ... NP
No Transmission [*Telecommunications*] (CDH) ... NT
No Transmitting Capability (FAAC) ... TMTNO
No Trouble Found (NITA) ... NTF
NOAA [*National Oceanic and Atmospheric Administration*] **Data Buoy Office** (EISS) ... NDBO
Nodal Switching Center (NITA) ... NSC
Node Compatibility List [*Telecommunications*] (TEL) ... NCL
Node Initialization Block [*Data processing*] (IBMDP) ... NIB
Noise [*Broadcasting*] ... N
Noise Analysis Program (NITA) ... NAP
Noise Balancing Circuit (DEN) ... NBC
Noise Bandwidth ... NBW
Noise Correlation (MSA) ... NC
Noise Criterion ... NC
Noise-Equivalent Bandwidth ... NEB
Noise-Equivalent Flux ... NEF
Noise-Equivalent Power ... NEP
Noise Factor ... NF
Noise Frequency (MSA) ... NF
Noise Improvement Factor (IEEE) ... NIF
Noise Index ... NI
Noise Information System [*Environmental Protection Agency*] (EISS) ... NIS
Noise to Interference Ratio [*Telecommunications*] (TEL) ... N/I
Noise Jammer Simulator [*Telecommunications*] (TEL) ... NJS
Noise Load Ratio ... NLR
Noise Measuring Set [*Telecommunications*] (TEL) ... NMS
Noise Meter (MSA) ... NM
Noise-Operated Automatic Level Adjustment ... NOALA
Noise-Operated Device for Antinoise [*Telecommunications*] (TEL) ... NODAN
Noise-Operated Gain-Adjusting Device ... NOGAD
Noise Output Device ... NOD
Noise Power/Bandwidth (CIT) ... N/B
Noise Power Ratio ... NPR
Noise Prediction and Reduction ... NPR
Noise Ratio ... NR
Noise Suppression Oscillator (MCD) ... NSO
Noise Suppressor System (MCD) ... NSS
Noise Temperature Ratio ... NTR
Noise Transmission Impairment [*Telecommunications*] ... NTI
Nomura Research Institute [*Database producer*] (CUAD) ... NRI
Non-Concurrent Operating System [*Sperry UNIVAC*] (CAH) ... NCOS
Non-Labeled [*Tape*] [*Data processing*] ... NL
Non-Traffic Sensitive [*Costs*] [*Telecommunications*] ... NTS
Nonacknowledgment Character [*Data processing*] ... NACK
Nonappropriated Funds Management Information System ... NAFMIS
Nonautomatic Relay Center ... NARC
Nonautomatic Self-Verification [*Data processing*] (MDG) ... NSV
Noncoded Information [*Data processing*] (IBMDP) ... NCI
Nondestructive Read [*Data processing*] ... NDR
Nondestructive Read/Write [*Data processing*] ... NDRW
Nondestructive Readout [*Data processing*] ... NDRO
Nondestructive Testing Information Center [*Battelle Memorial Institute*] [*Databank*] [*Information service*] (EISS) ... NTIC
Nondirectional Antenna ... ND
Nondirectional Beacon (Automatic Direction Finder) ... NDB(ADF)
Nondirectional Radio Beacon [*ITU designation*] (CET) ... RC
Nonerasable Storage [*Data processing*] ... NES
Nonimpact Off-Line Operating System [*Data processing*] ... NIPOLOS
Nonimpact Printer (NITA) ... NIP
Nonlinear Antenna System ... NAS
Nonlinear Circuit Analysis Program (MCD) ... NCAP
Nonlinear Distortion Analysis Program [*Bell System*] ... NODAP
Nonlinear Least Squares [*Computer program*] ... NLLSQ
Nonlinear Programing [*Algorithm*] ... NLP
Nonlinear Structural Analysis Program [*Data processing*] ... NONSAP
Nonlisted Name [*Telecommunications*] (TEL) ... NLST
Nonmasking Interrupt ... NMI
Nonmaster File [*Data processing*] ... NMF
Nonparametric Detection Scheme [*Communication signal*] ... NDS
Nonpolarized [*Data processing*] ... NP
Nonpolarized Return-to-Zero Recording [*Data processing*] (IBMDP) ... RZ(NP)
Nonprinting Character [*Data processing*] ... NPC
Nonprocedural Referencing Language (NITA) ... NPRL
Nonquaded [*Telecommunications*] (TEL) ... NQD
Nonrecurring Costs (KSC) ... NRC
Nonrecurring Installation Charge [*Telecommunications*] (TEL) ... NRI
Nonreturn to Zero [*Data transmission*] ... NRZ
Nonreturn to Zero Change ... NRZC
Nonreturn to Zero Change on One (BUR) ... NRZ1
Nonreturn to Zero Inverted [*Recording method*] ... NRZI
Nonreturn to Zero Level ... NRZL
Nonreturn to Zero Mark ... NRZM
Nonstandard Label [*Data processing*] ... NSL
Nonstandard Telephone Number [*Telecommunications*] (TEL) ... NSTN
Nonvolatile Metal-Oxide Semiconductor (MCD) ... NMOS
Nonvolatile Random-Access Memory [*Data processing*] ... NVRAM
Nonvolatile Semiconductor Memory (MCD) ... NVSM
Nonzero Transfer (NITA) ... NZT
Nora Eccles Harrison Cardiovascular Research and Training Center [*University of Utah*] [*Research center*] (RCD) ... CVRTC
Nordic Council for Scientific Information and Research Libraries [*Finland*] [*Information service*] (EISS) ... NORDINFO
Nordic Documentation Center for Mass Communication Research [*Finland*] [*Database originator*] [*Information service*] (EISS) ... NORDICOM
Nordic Energy Index [*Nordic Atomic Libraries Joint Secretariat*] [*Denmark*] [*Databank*] [*Information service*] (EISS) ... NEI
Nordic Mobile Telephone [*Radio-telephone system for car users*] [*Denmark, Finland, Norway, Sweden*] ... NMT
Nordiska Tele-Satelit Kommitton [*Norway*] (OA) ... NTSK
Norges Standardiseringsforbund [*Norwegian Standards Association*] [*Information service*] (EISS) ... NSF
Norges Teknisk-Naturvitenskapelige Forskningsraad [*Online database*] ... NTNF
Normal Digital Echo Suppressor [*Telecommunications*] (TEL) ... NDES
Normal Input-Output Control Executive [*Data processing*] ... NICE
Normal Response Mode (NITA) ... NRM
Normalisation, Automatisation de la Terminologie [*Standardization and Automation of Terminology*] [*Databank*] [*Information service*] [*France*] (EISS) ... NORMATERM
Normalized Alignment Score ... NAS
Normalized Device Coordinates [*Data processing*] ... NDC
Normally Closed [*Switch*] ... NC
Normally Open [*Switch*] ... NO
Normes et Reglements Informations Automatisees Accessibles en Ligne [*Automated Standards and Regulations Information Online*] [*Association Francaise de Normalisation*] [*Databank*] [*Information service*] [*France*] (EISS) ... NORIANE
Norsk Data [*Manufacturer and computer series*] [*Norway*] (NITA) ... NORD
Norsk Samfunnsvitenskapelig Datatjeneste [*Norwegian Social Science Data Services*] [*Information service*] (EISS) ... NSD
Norsk Selskap for Elektronisk Informasjonselskap [*Norwegian Computer Society*] [*Oslo, Norway*] ... NSEI
Norsk Senter for Informatikk [*Norwegian Center for Informatics*] [*Information broker, host, and database originator*] [*Information service*] (EISS) ... NSI
North [*or Northern*] ... N
North American Computer Service Association [*Casselberry, FL*] [*Absorbed International Association of Service Companies (1982)*] (EANO) ... NACSA
North American Data Airborne Recorder ... NADAR
North American Datamanager Users Group (EANO) ... NADUG
North American Honeywell Users Association [*Formerly, HUG-SMS*] (EANO) ... NAHU
North American Presentation Level Protocol Syntax [*Computer display system*] [*Pronounced "naplips"*] ... NAPLPS
North American Shortwave Association (EANO) ... NASWA
North American Simulation and Gaming Association (EANO) ... NASAGA
North American Stock Market [*I. P. Sharp*] [*Database*] ... NASTOCK
North American Telecommunications Association [*Washington, DC*] [*Information service*] (TSSD) ... NATA
North American Telephone Association [*Washington, DC*] (EANO) ... NATA
North American Vane Jump Angle Computer ... NAVJAC
North Atlantic Industries ... NA
North Atlantic Industries [*NASDAQ symbol*] (NQ) ... NATL
North Atlantic Radio System ... NARS
North Atlantic Radiotelephone ... NARTEL

North Atlantic Treaty Organization Satellite .... NATOSAT
North Central Computer Institute [*Madison, WI*] [*Research center*]
   (RCD) .... NCCI
North Central Regional Center for Rural Development [*Iowa State University*] [*Research center*]   (RCD) .... NCRCRD
North Star Computer Society [*Seattle, WA*]   (EANO) .... NSCS
Northeast .... NE
Northeast Regional Data Center [*University of Florida*] [*Research center*]   (RCD) .... NERDC
Northeast Satellite Systems [*Avoca, PA*] [*Telecommunications*]
   (TSSD) .... NESS
Northeast Water Resources Information Terminal   (EISS) .... NEWRIT
Northern Alberta Institute of Technology [*Edmonton, AB*] .... NAIT
Northern Area Communications System .... NACS
Northern Business Information, Inc. [*New York, NY*] [*Information service*]   (TSSD) .... NBI
Northern Pine [*Utility pole*] [*Telecommunications*]   (TEL) .... NP
Northern Telecom Ltd. [*NYSE symbol*] .... NT
Northern Telecom Limited [*Toronto Stock Exchange symbol*]
   [*Vancouver Stock Exchange symbol*] .... NTL
Northouse Industries, Incorporated [*Milwaukee, WI*] [*Software manufacturer*]   (DASOS) .... NII
Northwest .... NW
Northwest Computing Association .... NCA
Northwest Microfilm, Incorporated [*Information service*]   (EISS) .... NMI
Northwest Software Associates [*Spokane, WA*] [*Software manufacturer*]   (DASOS) .... NWSA
Northwest Telecommunications [*NASDAQ symbol*]   (NQ) .... NOWT
Northwestern On-Line Total Integrated System [*Northwestern University Library*] [*Evanston, IL*] [*Library automation project*]
   [*Information service*]   (EISS) .... NOTIS
Nortronics Automatic Test Equipment Language [*Data processing*] .... NATEL
Nortronics Corp.   (DDI) .... NORTR
Norwegian Telecommunications Administration [*Oslo*]   (TSSD) .... NTA
Norwegian Telecommunications Users Group [*Oslo*]   (TSSD) .... NORTEB
Norwesco, Inc. [*NASDAQ symbol*]   (NQ) .... NWES
Not at All .... NOTAL
Not And [*Logical operator*] [*Data processing*] .... NA
Not And [*Logical operator*] [*Data processing*] .... NAND
Not Assigned .... NA
Not Available .... NA
Not Equal [*Relational operator*] .... NE
Not Found [*Telephone listing*] [*Telecommunications*]   (TEL) .... NF
Not Heard [*Communications*] .... NHD
Not Invented Here [*Industrial term*] [*Data processing colloquialism*] .... NIH
Not Less Than .... NLT
Not to, nor Needed by, All .... NOTAL
Not Or [*Logical operator*] [*Data processing*] .... NO
Not Or [*Logical operator*] [*Data processing*] .... NOR
Not-Or-And [*Data processing*] .... N-O-A
Not Ready for Data   (NITA) .... NRFD
Not for Us [*Communications*] .... NFU
Not Yet in Library of Congress [*Suggested name for the Library of Congress computer system*] .... NYET LC
Note [*Online database field identifier*]   (OBD) .... NT
Notes [*Online database field identifier*]   (OBD) .... NO
Nothing Doing [*Amateur radio slang*] .... ND
Nothing but Initials [*Initialism is name of commercial word processor firm*] .... NBI
Notice of Information [*Data processing*] .... NI
Notified [*Telecommunications*]   (TEL) .... NFYD
Notify [*Telecommunications*]   (TEL) .... NFY
Notre Dame Translator [*Programing language*] [*1977*] [*Data processing*]   (CSR) .... NDTRAN
Nuclear Data, Incorporated [*American Stock Exchange symbol*] .... NDI
Nuclear Data Tape Program .... NDTP
Nuclear Data Unit [*International Atomic Energy Agency*]   (DIT) .... NDU
Nuclear Detonation Detection and Reporting System .... NUDETS
Nuclear Forces Communications Satellite .... NFCS
Nuclear Fuels Technology Information Center   (DIT) .... NUFTIC
Nuclear Magnetic Resonance Literature Search System [*National Institutes of Health*] [*Database*]   (FDB) .... NMRLIT
Nuclear Quadrupole Resonance [*Frequencies*] .... NQR
Nuclear Research Information Center [*American Nuclear Center*]
   [*Information service*]   (EISS) .... NRIC
Nuclear Structure References [*Database*]   (ODIN) .... NSR
Nucleotide Sequencing Search System .... NUCSEQ
Nucleus Initialization Program [*Data processing*] .... NIP
Null Character [*Keyboard*] [*Data processing*] .... NUL
Nullified Unpostable [*Data processing*] .... NU
Number .... N
Number   (KSC) .... NBR
Number .... NO
Number [*or Numerator, or Numeric*]   (CAH) .... NUM
Number-Controlled Oscillator   (CIT) .... NCO
Number of Document [*Online database field identifier*]   (OBD) .... ND
Number of Open Microphones .... NOM
Number of Terminals per Failure [*Data processing*] .... NTPF
Number Unobtainable [*Telecommunications*] .... NU
Number Unobtainable Tone [*Telecommunications*]   (TEL) .... NUT
Numbering Plan Area [*Bell System*] [*Telecommunications*] .... NPA
Numeral [*or Numerical*] .... NUM

Numeric .... N
Numeric Data Base [*INPADOC*] [*Data processing*] .... NDB
Numerical Aerodynamic Simulation Facility .... NASF
Numerical [*formerly, Nottingham*] Algorithms Group .... NAG
Numerical Analysis [*Data processing*]   (BUR) .... NA
Numerical Analysis Problem Solving System   (TUT) .... NAPSS
Numerical Analysis Research .... NAR
Numerical Analysis of Semiconductor Devices and Integrated Circuits [*Data processing*] .... NASECODE
Numerical Analysis Subroutines [*Data processing*]   (BUR) .... NAS
Numerical Analysis System   (BUR) .... NUMERALS
Numerical Aperture [*Microscopy*] .... NA
Numerical Control [*Data processing*] .... NC
Numerical Control Society [*Glenview, IL*] .... NCS
Numerical Data Advisory Board [*National Research Council*]
   [*Information service*]   (EISS) .... NDAB
Numerical Index   (BUR) .... NI
Numerical Plotting System .... NPS
Numerically Integrated Differential Analyzer [*Data processing*] .... NIDA
Numerically Integrated Elements System A [*Harris Systems Ltd.*]
   [*Software package*] [*British*]   (NCC) .... NISA
Nutrition Abstracts and Reviews [*Database*]   (ODIN) .... NAR
Nutritional Information and Analysis Center [*Illinois Institute of Technology and Institute of Food Technologists*]   (EISS) .... NIAC

O

Oak Ridge Automatic Computer and Logical Engine	ORACLE
Oak Ridge Binary Internal-Translator	ORBIT
Oak Ridge Computerized Hierarchical Information System [AEC] (EISS)	ORCHIS
Oak Ridge National Laboratory Library [AEC] (DIT)	ORNLL
Oak Ridge National Laboratory Nuclear Data Project [Database producer] (ODIN)	ORNLY-NDP
Object Module Assembly Program (NITA)	OMAP
Object-Oriented Design [Data processing]	OOD
Object Program Utility Routine (NITA)	OPUR
Objective Loudness Rating [of telephone connections] (IEEE)	OLR
Occupational Health Services, Inc. [Medical databank originator] [Information service]	OHS
Occupational Health Services Material Safety Data Sheets [Database] (CUAD)	OHS MSDS
Occurs (MDG)	OC
Ocean Data Systems, Incorporated [Rockville, MD] [Information service] (EISS)	ODSI
Oceanographic Datastation [Telecommunications] (TEL)	OD
Octal [Number system with a base of eight] [Data processing] (BUR)	O
Octal [Number system with a base of eight] [Data processing] (CET)	OCT
Octal [Data processing] (BUR)	OB
Octal-to-Binary [Data processing]	OCC
Octal Correction Cards [Data processing]	ODA
Octal Debugging Aid [Data processing]	ODT
Octal Debugging Technique (IEEE)	OD
Octal-to-Decimal [Data processing] (BUR)	O-H
Octal-to-Hexadecimal (IEEE)	OID
Octal Identifier [Data processing] (KSC)	OPP
Octal Print Punch [Data processing]	OTN
Octal Track Number [Data processing] (IBMDP)	ACK1
Odd Positive Acknowledgment [Data processing] (IBMDP)	ACK1
Oesterreichische Zeitschrift fuer Elektrizitaetswirtschaft [A publication]	Oesterr Z Elektrizitaetswirtsch
Off Frequency Rejection [Radio communications]	OFR
Off-Hook Service [Telecommunications] (TEL)	OHS
Off-Line Operating Simulator [Data processing]	OOPS
Off-Line Universal Command History [Data processing] (KSC)	OUCH
Off-Net Access Line [Telecommunications] (TEL)	ONAL
Off-Premise Extension	OPX
Off-Premise Station [Telecommunications] (TEL)	OPS
Off-the-Shelf System [Bell System]	OTSS
Offender Base Transaction Statistical System [Department of Justice] [Washington, DC] [Database] [Information service] (EISS)	OBTS
Office of Academic Computing [University of California, Los Angeles] [Research center] (RCD)	OAC
Office of Advanced Scientific Computing [National Science Foundation]	OASC
Office of Air Research Automatic Computer	OARAC
Office of the Assistant Secretary of Defense (Telecommunications)	OASD(T)
Office of Automated Data Management Services [General Services Administration]	OADMS
Office Automation Society International (EANO)	OASI
Office Automation System [Prime Computer Ltd.] [Software package] [British] (NCC)	OAS
Office Automation System (NITA)	OASYS
Office Balancing Network [Telecommunications] (TEL)	OBN
Office Busy Hour [Telecommunications] (TEL)	OBH
Office of Civil Defense	OCD
Office of Commercial Communications Management (AFM)	OCCM
Office of Computer Information [Department of Commerce] [Originator and database]	OCI
Office of Computer Processing Operations [Social Security Administration]	OCPO
Office of Computing Activities [Later, DCR] [National Science Foundation]	OCA
Office, Computing, and Accounting Machinery	OCAM
Office of Computing and Information Services [University of Georgia] [Research center] (RCD)	OCIS
Office of Computing Services [Georgia Institute of Technology] [Research center] (RCD)	OCS
Office of Cued Speech Programs [Gallaudet College] [Research center] (RCD)	OCSP
Office of Development Information and Utilization [Agency for International Development] [Information service] (EISS)	DIU
Office of Energy Information Services [Department of Energy] (EISS)	OEIS
Office Equipment Manufacturers Institute [Later, CBEMA]	OEMI
Office of Information Systems [Social and Rehabilitation Service, HEW]	OIS
Office Machines and Equipment Federation [British] (DIT)	OMEF
Office of Management and Budget [Washington, DC] [Formerly, Bureau of the Budget]	OMB
Office Master Frequency Supply [Telecommunications] (TEL)	OMFS
Office Network Exchange [Honeywell, Inc.]	ONE
Office of Public Trustee Information Management User System [Canada]	OPTIMUS
Office of Regulatory Information Systems [Energy Regulatory Commission] (EISS)	ORIS
Office for Remote Sensing of Earth Resources [Pennsylvania State University] [Research center]	ORSER
Office of Science Information Service [National Science Foundation]	OSIS
Office of Science and Technology Policy [Executive Office of the President]	OSTP
Office of Scientific and Technical Information [Later, BLR & DD] [British Library]	OSTI
Office of Software Improvement and Engineering [Social Security Administration]	OSIE
Office System (NITA)	OS
Office Technology Management Association [Milwaukee, WI] [Information service] (TSSD)	OTMA
Office of Telecommunications [Independent government agency] [British]	OFTEL
Office of Telecommunications [US government] (NITA)	OT
Office of Telecommunications Management [Later, OTP] [FCC]	OTM
Office of Telecommunications Policy [Terminated, 1978] [Executive Office of the President]	OTP
Office of Telecommunications Systems Operations [Social Security Administration]	OTSO
Official Airline Guide-Electronic Edition [Official Airline Guides, Inc.] [Database] (CUAD)	OAG-EE
Official Bulletin Station [Amateur radio]	OBS
Official Experimental Station [Amateur radio]	OES
Official Phone Station [Amateur radio]	OPS
Official Railway Equipment Register [National Railway Publication Company] [Information service] (EISS)	ORER
Official Relay Station [Amateur radio]	ORS
Offline Adaptive Computer [Data processing]	OLAC
Offline Data Generator (NITA)	ODG
Offline Recovery [Telecommunications] (TEL)	OLR
Offshore Lease Data System [Department of the Interior] [Information service] (EISS)	OLDS
Ohio Bell Communications, Inc. [Telecommunications] (TSSD)	OBC
Ohio University Cartographic Center [Research center] (RCD)	OUCC
Ohmmeter	OHM
Oil and Hazardous Materials Technical Assistance Data System [Environmental Protection Agency] [Databank] (EISS)	OHM-TADS
Old-Age-Pensioner CBer [Experienced citizens band radio operator]	OAPCB
Old Man [Communications operators' colloquialism]	OM
Old Master File (NITA)	OMF
Old Program Status Word Location (NITA)	OPSWL
Old Timer [Communications operators' colloquialism]	OT
Old Top [Communications operators' colloquialism]	OT
Omni Resources, Inc. [NASDAQ symbol] (NQ)	OMNRF
Omniantenna	OA
Omnibearing Indicator [Radio]	OBI
Omnibearing Selector [Radio]	OBS
Omnibus Computer Graphics, Inc. [Toronto Stock Exchange symbol]	OMI
Omnibus Program with Tabular Numerical Functions [Programing language] [1965] (CSR)	OMNITAB
Omnidirection Transmission	ODT
Omnidirectional (SKY)	OMNI
Omnidirectional Antenna	ODA

Computer & Telecommunications Acronyms

Omnidirectional Radio Range (MSA) ... OMNIRANGE
Omnidirectional Radio Range ... OR
Omnidirectional Range ... ODR
Omnidirectional Transmitter Antenna ... OTA
Omnirange Antenna ... OMNITENNA
Omnitronics Research Corporation [*NASDAQ symbol*] (NQ) ... ORCS
On-Board Computer (MCD) ... OBC
On-Board Digital Computer Control ... ODCC
On-Board Digital Data Handling ... ODDH
On-Board Experimental Data Support Facility ... OEDSF
On Call (BUR) ... OC
On Demand Analyzer Computer ... ODAC
On-the-Job Training ... OJT
On-Line Acquisitions Systems [*Brodart, Inc.*] [*Book acquisition system*] [*Information service*] (EISS) ... OLAS
On-Line Automated Reference Service [*Library science*] ... OARS
On-Line Business Systems, Inc. [*Information service*] (EISS) ... OBS
On-Line Encyclopedia [*Hypergraphics Corp.*] ... OLE
On-Line Hospital Management Information System [*Data processing*] ... OLHMIS
On-Line Process Synthesis [*Data processing*] ... OPS
On-Line Reactivity Computer [*Data processing*] ... ORC
On-Line, Real-Time, Branch Information Transmission [*IBM Corp.*] [*Data processing*] ... ORBIT
On-Line Reduced Bandwidth Information Transfer [*Data processing*] ... ORBIT
On-Line Remote Job Entry Terminal System [*Data processing*] ... ORJETS
On-Line Replacement Unit [*Data processing*] (MCD) ... ORU
On-Line Retrieval of Bibliographic Text [*Search system*] [*Data processing*] ... ORBIT
On-Line Retrieval and Computational Language for Economists [*Data processing*] ... ORACLE
On-Line Review [*A publication*] ... On-Line Rv
On-Line Software International [*NASDAQ symbol*] (NQ) ... OSII
On-Line Software International, Inc. [*Fort Lee, NJ*] [*Telecommunications*] (TSSD) ... OSI
On-Line System [*Stanford Research Institute*] [*Data processing*] ... NLS
On-Line Systems, Inc. [*American Stock Exchange symbol*] [*Delisted*] ... ONL
On-Line Test Executive Program [*IBM Corp.*] [*Data processing*] ... OLTEP
On-Line Training and Practice File [*Lockheed*] [*Data processing*] ... ONTAP
On-Line Wholesale Distribution System [*Data processing*] (BUR) ... OWD
On-Off Keying [*Data processing*] (IEEE) ... OOK
On-Shift Test (IEEE) ... OST
One Big Computer [*Proposed model for automation of the New York and American stock exchanges*] ... OBC
One-Digit Code Point [*Telecommunications*] (TEL) ... ODCP
One of the Firm [*Telecommunications*] (TEL) ... OF
One Hundred Call-Seconds [*Also, UC*] [*Bell System*] (TSSD) ... CCS
One-Sided Height Balanced [*Telecommunications*] (NITA) ... OSHB
One-Way Polar [*Telegraph*] ... OWP
Online (CAH) ... OL
Online-ADL-Nachrichten [*A publication*] ... OANAD
Online Circuit Analysis [*System*] [*Data processing*] ... OLCA
Online Computer [*System*] [*Data processing*] ... OLC
Online Computer Library Center [*Formerly, Ohio College Library Center. Initialism used in reference to cataloging system it developed*] [*Information service*] ... OCLC
Online Cryptanalytic Aid Language [*Data processing*] (TUT) ... OCAL
Online Cryptanalytic Aid System [*Data processing*] (IEEE) ... OCAS
Online Data Collection [*Data processing*] (MCD) ... OLDC
Online Data Entry System [*Burroughs Corp.*] (NITA) ... ODESY
Online Database (NITA) ... OLDB
Online Database Report [*A publication*] ... Online Database Rep
Online Database Search Assistance Machine [*Franklin Institute*] [*Information service*] (EISS) ... OL'SAM
Online Debugging Technique (NITA) ... ODT
Online Display System [*Data processing*] ... OLDS
Online Dokumentations- und Informationsverbund [*Online Documentation and Information Affiliation*] (ODIN) ... ODIN
Online Executive for Real Time [*Data processing*] (IEEE) ... OLERT
Online Image Forming Light Modulator (NITA) ... OLIFLM
Online Instrument and Control Program [*Data processing*] ... OIC
Online Instrument Package [*Data processing*] ... OLIP
Online without Limits (NITA) ... OWL
Online Logical Simulation System [*Data processing*] (KSC) ... OLLS
Online Manufacturing, Accounting, and Control System (NITA) ... OMAC
Online Monitor [*Data processing*] ... OLM
Online Operation [*Data processing*] ... OLO
Online Order Entry (NITA) ... OLOE
Online Pattern Analysis and Recognition System [*Data processing*] (MCD) ... OLPARS
Online Peripheral Test System (NITA) ... OPTS
Online Plotter Controller [*California Computer Products, Inc.*] (NITA) ... OPC
Online Processor (TEL) ... OLP
Online Programing (TEL) ... OLP
Online Programing System [*Data processing*] ... OLPS
Online Public Access Catalog ... OPAC
Online Query Language (NITA) ... OQL
Online Real Time [*Data processing*] ... OLRT
Online Retrieval of Information over a Network (IDA) ... ORION
Online Review [*A publication*] ... Online
Online Review [*A publication*] ... Online Rev
Online Scan [*Data processing*] (CAAL) ... OLS

Online Scientific Computer [*Data processing*] ... OLSC
Online Shared Cataloging System [*Data processing*] ... ONLICATS
Online Software System [*Data processing*] (IEEE) ... OLSS
Online Subsystem Facility [*Data processing*] (MCD) ... OLSF
Online System [*Data processing*] ... OLS
Online System Drivers [*NCR Corp.*] (NITA) ... OSD
Online Task Loader (NITA) ... OTL
Online Terminal Test [*Data processing*] (IBMDP) ... OLTT
Online Test [*Data processing*] ... OLT
Online Test System [*Data processing*] (BUR) ... OLTS
Online Time Share [*Data processing*] ... OLTS
Online Update (TEL) ... OLUD
Online Update Control Module (TEL) ... OLUM
Online Yield [*Data processing*] ... ONLY
Ontario Institute for Studies in Education [*University of Toronto*] [*Research center*] (RCD) ... OISE
Ontario Ministry of Transportation and Communications [*Downsview, ON*] [*Telecommunications*] (TSSD) ... OMTC
Onyx + IMI, Inc. [*NASDAQ symbol*] (NQ) ... ONIX
Open-Circuit Television ... OCTV
Open-Circuit Voltage (CIT) ... OCV
Open-Circuited Transmission Line ... OCTL
Open-Loop Bandwidth [*Also, OLBW*] ... OLB
Open-Loop Bandwidth [*Also, OLB*] ... OLBW
Open-Loop Receiver [*or Response*] (CIT) ... OLR
Open Macrodefinition (NITA) ... OMD
Open Protocol Enhanced Network [*Northern Telecom communications network*] [*Canada*] ... OPEN
Open Standards Interconnection [*International Standards Organisation*] ... OSI
Open System Interconnections [*Networking technique*] [*Data processing*] ... OSI
Open Systems Architecture [*Data processing*] ... OSA
Operand Address Register (NITA) ... OA
Operand Select Gate [*Data processing*] ... OSG
Operand Storage Register (NITA) ... OSR
Operating (MDG) ... OPERG
Operating Level (IEEE) ... OL
Operating Software (MCD) ... OS
Operating System (NITA) ... OPSYS
Operating System [*Data processing*] (BUR) ... OS
Operating System Command and Response Language (NITA) ... OSCRL
Operating System Communication Application Program [*Data processing*] (TUT) ... OSCAP
Operating System/Disk Operating System [*Software*] ... OS/DOS
Operating System Implementation Language (OA) ... OSIL
Operating System Interface (NITA) ... OSI
Operating System Language ... OSL
Operating System Monitor (NITA) ... OSM
Operating System/Multiprograming with a Fixed Number of Tasks [*IBM Corp.*] [*Data processing*] ... OS/MFT
Operating System/Multiprograming with a Variable Number of Tasks [*Data processing*] ... OS/MVT
Operating System/Multiprograming with Virtual Storage [*Data processing*] ... OS/MVS
Operating System Simulation Language [*1971*] [*Data processing*] (CSR) ... OSSL
Operating System Software [*Personal computers*] ... OSS
Operating System Supervisor (NITA) ... OSS
Operating System Table Loader [*Telecommunications*] (TEL) ... OSTL
Operating System Test [*Telecommunications*] (TEL) ... OSTEST
Operating System/Virtual Storage [*Data processing*] (MDG) ... OS/VS
Operating System Workstation [*Data processing*] ... OSWS
Operating Systems Review [*A publication*] ... Oper Syst Rev
Operating Telephone Company [*Bell System*] (TEL) ... OTC
Operation ... O
Operation Code (AFM) ... OP
Operation Code (NITA) ... OPC
Operation and Maintenance ... O & M
Operation Unit (NITA) ... OU
Operational Amplifier [*Telecommunications*] (TEL) ... OA
Operational Amplifier ... OP AMP
Operational Assistance and Instructive Data Equipment ... OAIDE
Operational Automatic Scheduling Information System (MUGU) ... OASIS
Operational Computer (IEEE) ... OC
Operational Computer Complex (KSC) ... OCC
Operational Control Unit ... OCU
Operational Cycle Time (OA) ... OCT
Operational Design and Analysis (IEEE) ... ODA
Operational Error Analysis Program (NITA) ... OEAP
Operational Management Information System [*Data processing*] ... OMIS
Operational Operating System [*Telecommunications*] (TEL) ... OOS
Operational Performance Analysis Language [*Data processing*] ... OPAL
Operational Programing Department [*Telecommunications*] (TEL) ... OPD
Operational Status BIT [*Binary Digit*] (NITA) ... OSB
Operational Synchronous Earth Observatory Satellite [*Telecommunications*] (TEL) ... OSEOS
Operational Taxonomic Unit [*Numerical taxonomy*] ... OTU
Operational Teletype Communications Subsystem (CIT) ... OTCS
Operational Teletype Message (CIT) ... OPS-X
Operational Teletype Network ... OTN
Operational Voice Communication Subsystem ... OVCS
Operations ... OPNS

332

Computer & Telecommunications Acronyms

Operations (MCD)	OPS
Operations-Communications	OP-COM
Operations Control Center [or Console] (AFM)	OCC
Operations Control System	OCS
Operations Manager (CIT)	OM
Operations per Minute [Performance measure]	OPM
Operations Monitor Alarm (NITA)	OMA
Operations Monitoring Computer	OMC
Operations Research [Data processing]	OR
Operations Research Center [Massachusetts Institute of Technology] [Research center] (KSC)	ORC
Operations Research or Management Science	OR/MS
Operations Research Society of America [Baltimore, MD]	ORSA
Operator	O
Operator Authorization Record [Data processing] (IBMDP)	OAR
Operator Call Handling Center [Telecommunications] (TEL)	OCHC
Operator Communication and Control Facility [IBM Corp.]	OCCF
Operator Console Facility [Data processing] (IBMDP)	OCF
Operator Control Command (BUR)	OCC
Operator Control Element [Data processing] (IBMDP)	OPCE
Operator Control Language [Data processing] (BUR)	OCL
Operator Data Register [Telecommunications] (TEL)	ODR
Operator Distance Dialing	ODD
Operator Interface Unit [Data processing]	OIU
Operator Number Identification [Bell System]	ONI
Operator-Oriented Language [Data processing]	OOL
Operator Override [Telecommunications] (TEL)	OOR
Operator Position Controller [Telecommunications]	OPC
Operator Programing Method [Data processing]	OPM
Operator Services Complex [Telecommunications] (TEL)	OSC
Operator Services Switching Unit [Telecommunications] (TEL)	OSSU
Operator's Subsystem [Telecommunications] (TEL)	OPS
Opisu Struktur Mikroprogramownych [Programing language] (CSR)	OSM
Optelecom, Inc. [NASDAQ symbol] (NQ)	OPTC
Optical Analog Matrix Processing	OAMP
Optical Bar Code	OBR
Optical Character Reader [Data processing]	OCR
Optical Character Recognition [Data processing]	OCR
Optical Character Recognition - ANSI Standard (Font A) (CAH)	OCRA
Optical Character Recognition - ANSI Standard (Font B) (CAH)	OCRB
Optical Character Recognition Equipment [Data processing]	OCRE
Optical Character Recognition Users Association [Later, RTUA] (EANO)	OCRUA
Optical Character Scanner [Data processing]	OCS
Optical Communicator System (MCD)	OCS
Optical Covert Communications Using LASER Transceivers (MCD)	OCCULT
Optical Data Digitizer [Data processing]	ODD
Optical Data Processing	ODP
Optical Data Transmission System	ODTS
Optical Digital Data Disc	ODD
Optical Disk Interface System [Data processing]	ODIS
Optical Display Memory [Data processing]	ODM
Optical Display Unit [Data processing] (MCD)	ODU
Optical Fiber Tube (NITA)	OFT
Optical Mark Page Reader [Data processing]	OMPR
Optical Mark Reader [Data processing]	OMAR
Optical Mark Reader [Data processing]	OMR
Optical Mark Recognition [Data processing] (MCD)	OMR
Optical Page Reader [Data processing] (CGC)	OPR
Optical Pattern Recognition (DEEC)	OPR
Optical Read-Only Storage [Data processing]	OROS
Optical Reader [Data processing] (BUR)	OR
Optical Reception of Announcements by Coded Line Electronics	ORACLE
Optical Scanning [Data processing]	OS
Optical Scanning Device [Data processing]	OSD
Optical Scanning Recognition [Data processing]	OSR
Optical Society of America [Washington, DC]	OSA
Optical Storage and Retrieval [Data processing]	OSAR
Optical Time-Domain Reflectometer [Data processing]	OTDR
Optical Transfer Function	OTF
Optical Video Disk (DEEC)	OVD
Optically Coupled Isolator (OA)	OCI
Optically Isolated Digital Input (NITA)	OIDI
Optically Scanned Character Automatic Reader [Data processing] (DIT)	OSCAR
Optimal Amplitude and Phase Modulation	OAPM
Optimal Code Generation	OCG
Optimal [or Orbital] Design Integration [Computer program]	ODIN
Optimal Real Storage (CMD)	ORS
Optimises Rectangles [AERE Harwell] [Software package] [British] (NCC)	OREC
Optimization-Oriented Language (NITA)	OPOL
Optimization of a Production Process by an Ordered Simulation and Iteration Technique (IEEE)	OPPOSIT
Optimization Program for Economical Remote Trunk Arrangement and TSPS [Traffic Service Positions System] Operator Arrangements [Telecommunications] (TEL)	OPERATORS
Optimized Processing Element (NITA)	OPE
Optimized Systems Software [San Jose, CA]	OSS
Optimum Phase Shift Keyed Signals [Telecommunications] (OA)	OPSKS
Optimum Systems Covariance Analysis Results (IEEE)	OSCAR
Optimum Traffic Frequency [Radio]	OTF
Optimum Working Frequency [Telecommunications]	OWF
Option Table Generator (NITA)	OTG
Optional	OPT
Optional Calling Measured Service [Telecommunications] (TEL)	OCMS
Optional Calling Plans [Telecommunications] (TEL)	OPC
Optional Residential Telephone Service [Telecommunications] (TEL)	ORTS
Optoelectronic Pulse Amplifier	OPA
Or Gate [Data processing]	OG
ORACLE Binary Internal Translator [Algebraic programing system]	ORBIT
Orbital Test Satellite [Communications satellite] [European Space Agency]	OTS
Orbital Very-Long Baseline Interferometer [Communications satellite] [Telecommunications] (IEEE)	OVLBI
Orbiting Radio Emission Observatory [Satellite]	OREO
Orbiting Satellite Carrying Amateur Radio [Telecommunications] (TEL)	OSCAR
Orbiting Solar Observatory [A satellite]	OSO
Order	ORD
Order Allocation System (CGC)	OASYS
Order Code Processor [International Computers Ltd.] (NITA)	OCP
Order Point Technique for Inventory Management (BUR)	OPTIM
Order Processing and Inventory Monitoring [Data processing]	OPIM
Order of Railroad Telegraphers [Later, Transportation-Communication Employees Union]	ORT
Order Status Control and Reporting [Telecommunications] (TEL)	OSCAR
Ordered Computer Collation of Unprepared Literary Texts	OCCULT
Ordered Random Access Talking Equipment	ORATE
Ordinal Memory Inspecting Binary Automatic Computer (IEEE)	OMIBAC
Ordinary National Certificate [British]	ONC
Ordnance Variable Automatic Computer	ORDVAC
Oregon Graduate Center for Study and Research [Beaverton, OR] [Research center] (RCD)	OGC
Oregon Legislative Information System [Information service]	OLIS
Oregon State Conversational Aid to Research [Data processing] (CSR)	OSCAR
Organisation Internationale de Radiodiffusion [International Radio Organization]	OIR
Organisation Internationale de Radiodiffusion et Television [International Radio and Television Organization]	OIRT
Organisation Meteorologique Mondiale [World Meteorological Organization - WMO]	OMM
Organizacion Meteorologica Mundial [World Meteorological Organization - WMO] [Spanish]	OMM
Organization	ORG
Organization of American States [Washington, DC]	OAS
Organization for Economic Cooperation and Development [Databank originator]	OECD
Organization for the Protection and Advancement of Small Telephone Companies [Washington, DC] [Telecommunications] (EANO)	OPASTCO
Organization for Use of the Telephone (EANO)	OUT
Organizational Source [Online database field identifier] [Data processing]	OS
Orientation and Access to Information and Documentation Sources in France [Commission de Coordination de la Documentation Administrative] [Database] (CUAD)	ORIADOC
Origin (MDG)	ORG
Origin Address Field [Data processing] (IBMDP)	OAF
Original Entry [Data processing]	OE
Original Equipment Manufacturer	OEM
Original Title [Online database field identifier] (OBD)	OTI
Originating Junctor [Telecommunications] (TEL)	OJ
Originating Station Treatment [Telecommunications] (TEL)	OST
Originating Toll Center [Telecommunications] (TEL)	OTC
Origination Screening Office [Telecommunications] (TEL)	OSO
Orthogonal Array Arithmetic Unit (NITA)	OAAU
Orthogonal Array Processor [Computer] (NITA)	OAP
Orthogonal Row Computer (NITA)	ORC
Orts-, Regional-, und Landesplanung Literaturinformationssystem [Literature Information System for Town and Regional Planning] [1974-1978] [Database] (ODIN)	ORLIS
Oscillate [or Oscillation, Oscillator, Oscillograph, Oscilloscope] (KSC)	OSC
Oscillating Doublet Antenna	ODA
Oscillator Activity Monitor [Telecommunications] (TEL)	OAM
Oscillator and Clock Module	OCM
Oscillator-Multiplier [Telecommunications] (TEL)	OSC-MULT
Oscillatory, Nonoscillatory Flip-Flop [Data processing]	ON-OFF
Oscillogram Trace Reader [Non-Linear Systems, Inc.] [Data processing]	OTRAC
Ostbayrisches Technologie-Transfer-Institut [Information retrieval] (ODIN)	OTTI
Other Common Carrier [Telecommunications]	OCC
Other Equipment Manufacturers (CMD)	OEM
Other Line [Telecommunications] (TEL)	OL
Other Military Teletypewriter Network (CET)	OMTN
Out of Band [Telecommunications] (TEL)	OOB
Out-of-Band Noise (CBSS)	OBN
Out of Order [Telecommunications] (TEL)	OOO
Out-of-Town [Word processing]	OOT
Outboard Data Manager (BUR)	ODM

By Meaning

Computer & Telecommunications Acronyms

Outboard Recorder (BUR)	OBR
Outer Lead Bond [Integrated circuit technology]	OLB
Outgoing [Data processing]	O/G
Outgoing Calls Barred [Telecommunications] (TEL)	OCB
Outgoing/Delay Dial [Telecommunications] (TEL)	OGDD
Outgoing Echo Suppressor [Telecommunications] (TEL)	OES
Outgoing/Immediate Dial [Telecommunications] (TEL)	OGID
Outgoing Junction [Telecommunications] (TEL)	OGJ
Outgoing Line	OGL
Outgoing Line Circuit	OLC
Outgoing Long-Wave Radiation [Satellite sensed]	OLR
Outgoing Matching Loss [Telecommunications] (TEL)	OML
Outgoing Message Process [Telecommunications] (TEL)	OGP
Outgoing Repeater	OGR
Outgoing Teletype	OTT
Outgoing Trunk	OGT
Outgoing Trunk Testing System [Telecommunications] (TEL)	OTTS
Outgoing Wide-Area Telephone Service [Telecommunications] (TEL)	OUTWATS
Outgoing/Wink Start [Telecommunications] (TEL)	OGWS
Outlook and Situation Information System [Department of Agriculture] (EISS)	OASIS
Outpulser, Identifier, Trunk Test	OITT
Output (BUR)	O
Output	OP
Output (NASA)	OUT
Output Amplitude	OA
Output Blocking Factor [Data processing] (IBMDP)	BO
Output Buffer [Data processing]	OB
Output Bus (NITA)	OB
Output Computer	OC
Output Control Program (NITA)	OCP
Output Control Register (NITA)	OCR
Output Control Subsystem (OA)	OCS
Output Data (IEEE)	OD
Output Data Buffer (NITA)	ODB
Output Data Control (NITA)	ODC
Output Data Strobe	ODS
Output Definition Register (NITA)	ODR
Output Disable (NITA)	OD
Output to Display Buffer [Data processing]	ODB
Output Display Unit [Data processing]	ODU
Output Enable [Semiconductor memory] (IEEE)	OE
Output Factor [Data processing] (IEEE)	OF
Output Latch (NITA)	OL
Output Limiting Facility [Data processing] (MDG)	OUTLIM
Output Logic Level	OLL
Output Measures for Public Libraries [Clarion University of Pennsylvania] [Information service] (EISS)	OUTPUTM
Output Module (NITA)	OM
Output Multiplex Synchronizer	OMS
Output Sequence Number (NITA)	OSN
Output Signal Distribution Unit (MCD)	OSDU
Output Terminal (NITA)	OT
Output Translator [IBM Corp.]	OUTRAN
Output Translator [IBM Corp.] (MSA)	OUTXLTR
Outside Broadcasts	OB
Outside Communications Cable Plant (CET)	OCCP
Outside Diameter	OD
Outside Plant [Telecommunications] (TEL)	OSP
Outstate Facility Network Planning System [Telecommunications] (TEL)	OFNPS
Over-Ocean Communications	OOC
Overall Connection Loss [Telecommunications] (TEL)	OCL
Overall Objective Loudness Rating [of telephone connections] (IEEE)	OOLR
Overall Rating [Broadcasting]	O
Overflow	OF
Overflow (DEEC)	OV
Overflow [Data processing]	OVF
Overflow Sequential Access Method [Data processing] (TUT)	OSAM
Overhead	OH
Overlapping Resolution Mapping [Data processing]	ORM
Overload Control Process [Telecommunications] (TEL)	OCP
Overload Control Subsystem [Telecommunications] (TEL)	OCS
Overload Detection [Telecommunications] (TEL)	OD
Overload Relay	OLR
Overnight Message Service [Diversified Data Processing and Consulting, Inc.] [Oak Park, MI] [Telecommunications] (TSSD)	OMS
Override Control BITS [Binary Digits] [Data processing]	OCB
Oversea Intelligence Data Processing System	OIDPS
Overseas Number Group Analysis [Telecommunications] (TEL)	ONGA
Overseas Telecommunications Commission [Australia] (TEL)	OTC
Own Exchange [Telecommunications] (TEL)	OE
Own Time Switch [Connection or call] [Telecommunications] (TEL)	OTS
Oxygen-Free, High-Conductivity [Copper]	OFHC

P

P-Register [*Data processing*] .... P
P-Type Intrinsic N-Type [*or Positive-Intrinsic-Negative*] .... PIN
Pacer Software, Incorporated [*La Jolla, CA*] [*Software manufacturer*] (DASOS) .... PSI
Pacific Aerospace Index (DIT) .... PAI
Pacific Coast Forest Research Information Network [*Later, WESTFORNET*] [*Forest Service*] (EISS) .... PACFORNET
Pacific Fleet Calls [*Radio call signs*] .... PACCALL
Pacific Islands Ecosystems [*Springfield, VA*] [*Department of the Interior*] [*Bibliographic database*] (OBD) .... PIE
Pacific Studies Center [*Mountain View, CA*] [*Research center*] (EANO) .... PSC
Pacific Telecommunications Council (EANO) .... PTC
Pacific Telephone & Telegraph Co. (FAAC) .... PTT
Pacing and Cardiac Electrophysiology Retrieval System [*Intermedics, Inc.*] [*Information service*] (EISS) .... PACERS
Package Transfer Unit (NITA) .... PTU
Packaged Assembly Circuit .... PAC
Packaged CRAM [*Card Random-Access Memory*] **Executive** [*NCR Corp.*] [*Data processing*] .... PACE
Packaging Science and Technology Abstracts [*International Food Information Service*] [*Database*] (CUAD) .... PSTA
Packed Switched Data (NITA) .... PSD
Packet Assembler/Disassembler [*Switching technique*] [*Data processing*] .... PAD
Packet Communications, Incorporated (NITA) .... PCI
Packet Multiplexer .... PMX
Packet Protocol Extension (NITA) .... PPX
Packet Radio Network (NITA) .... PRNET
Packet Radio Unit (NITA) .... PRU
Packet Switch Level Interface (NITA) .... PSLI
Packet Switched Data Service [*Telecommunications*] (TEL) .... PSDS
Packet-Switching Exchange .... PSE
Packet Switching Node (NITA) .... PSN
Packet Switching Processor (NITA) .... PSP
Packet Switching Service [*Telecommunications*] [*Information service*] [*British*] (EISS) .... PSS
Packet Switching Unit (NITA) .... PSU
PAFEC Interactive Graphics System [*PAFEC Ltd.*] [*Software package*] [*British*] (NCC) .... PIGS
Page [*or Pagination*] [*Online database field identifier*] .... PG
Page Address Field (NITA) .... PAF
Page Address Register (NITA) .... PAR
Page Control Block [*Data processing*] (IBMDP) .... PCB
Page Control Register (NITA) .... PCR
Page Data Register (NITA) .... PDR
Page Footing (BUR) .... PF
Page Formatter (MDG) .... PF
Page Frame Table (BUR) .... PFT
Page Heading (BUR) .... PH
Page Length Field (NITA) .... PLF
Page Map Address Register (NITA) .... PMAR
Page Printer (NVT) .... PP
Page Printer Control Block [*Data processing*] .... PPCB
Page Printer Spooling System [*Data processing*] .... PPSP
Page Printing System [*Honeywell, Inc.*] [*Data processing*] .... PPS
Page Reader Input System with Editing (NVT) .... PRISE
Page-Replacement Algorithm and Control Logic [*Data processing*] .... PRACL
Page Table [*Data processing*] (IBMDP) .... PGT
Page Table Entry (NITA) .... PTE
Page View Terminal [*Typography*] [*Videotex terminal*] .... PVT
Pageable Link-Pack Area (NITA) .... PLPA
Pageable Partition Queue Area [*Data processing*] (OA) .... PPQA
Pageable System Queue Area [*Data processing*] (MCD) .... PSQA
Paging Control Unit [*Telecommunications*] (TEL) .... PCU
Paid Service Indication [*Telecommunications*] (TEL) .... PSI
Pair Selected Ternary [*Data processing*] .... PST
Paired Wire [*Telecommunications*] (TEL) .... PRW
Pan-African Documentation and Information System [*United Nations*] (EISS) .... PADIS
Pan-African Telecommunications Network .... PANAFTEL
Pan American World Airways Communications System .... PANAMAC
Panel (KSC) .... PNL
Panel Call Indicator .... PCI
Pansophic Systems [*NASDAQ symbol*] (NQ) .... PANS
Paper Advance (BUR) .... PA
Paper Chemistry [*Institute of Paper Chemistry*] [*Appleton, WI*] [*Bibliographic database*] (OBD) .... PAPERCHEM
Paper-Insulated, Lead-Covered Cable [*Telecommunications*] .... PILC
Paper Tape .... PT
Paper Tape-to-Magnetic Tape Conversion System (DIT) .... PTS
Paper Tape Oriented Operating System (NITA) .... PTOS
Paper Tape Perforator .... PTP
Paper Tape Punch .... PTP
Paper Tape Reader .... PTR
Paper-Tape Sender .... PTS
Paper Tape and Transmission Code (NITA) .... PTTC
Paperless Entry Processing (CSR) .... PEP
Papiertechnische Stiftung [*Database producer*] (CUAD) .... PTS
Par Voie Telegraphique [*By Telegraph*] [*French*] .... PVT
Paradox Application Language [*ANSA*] [*Data processing*] .... PAL
Parallel .... P
Parallel Cascade Processor (IEEE) .... PCP
Parallel Communications Link (NITA) .... PCL
Parallel Data Controller .... PDC
Parallel Digital-to-Analog Converter (VIT) .... PARDAC
Parallel Digital Computing System .... PDCS
Parallel Digital Input/Output (NITA) .... PDIO
Parallel Element Processing Ensemble [*Burroughs Corp.*] (BUR) .... PEPE
Parallel Hardware Processing Language [*1977*] [*Data processing*] (CSR) .... PHPL
Parallel Head Disk (NITA) .... PHD
Parallel-In Parallel-Out [*Telecommunications*] (TEL) .... PIPO
Parallel-In Serial-Out [*Telecommunications*] (TEL) .... PISO
Parallel Input [*Data processing*] (BUR) .... PI
Parallel Input/Output (DEEC) .... PIO
Parallel Input-Output Unit [*Data processing*] (IEEE) .... PIOU
Parallel Instruction Control Unit (NITA) .... PICU
Parallel Instruction Execution [*Data processing*] (BUR) .... PIE
Parallel Instruction Queue (NITA) .... PIQ
Parallel Interface Element (NITA) .... PIE
Parallel Memory Address Counter [*Data processing*] .... PMAC
Parallel Memory-to-Memory Bus (NITA) .... PMMB
Parallel Microprogramed Processor [*Data processing*] .... PMP
Parallel Multiple Incremental Computer (NITA) .... PMIC
Parallel Multiplexer Interface Adapter (MCD) .... PMIA
Parallel Network Digital Computer (IEEE) .... PNDC
Parallel Optical Computer .... POC
Parallel Output [*Data processing*] (BUR) .... PO
Parallel Output (CIT) .... POT
Parallel Output Platform .... POP
Parallel Pattern Processor (NITA) .... PPP
Parallel Processing System [*Data processing*] (MDG) .... PPS
Parallel Processor (OA) .... PP
Parallel to Serial [*Converters*] (MCD) .... P/S
Parameter (VIT) .... PAR
Parameter (KSC) .... PARAM
Parameter .... PRMTR
Parameter Driven Software, Inc. [*Birmingham, MI*] [*Software manufacturer*] (DASOS) .... PDS
Parameter Entity Symbol Translator [*Elstree Computing Ltd.*] [*Software package*] [*British*] (NCC) .... PEST
Parameter Estimation by Sequential Testing [*Computer*] .... PEST
Parameter Processing System (CAAL) .... PPS
Parameter Sensitive Frequency Assignment Method (MCD) .... PSFAM
Parametric Amplifier (CIT) .... PARAMP
Parametric Integer Linear Program [*Data processing*] .... PILP
Parametric Semiconductor Amplifier (OA) .... PSA
Parametric Synthesis [*Data processing*] .... PARASYN
Parametric Synthesis [*Data processing*] .... PARSYN
Parametric Test Synthesis [*Data processing*] .... PATSY
Parity [*Atomic physics*] .... P
Parity BIT [*Binary Digit*] [*Data communications*] .... PBIT
Parity Check [*Data communications*] (TEL) .... PCHK
Parity Error (NITA) .... PE

Parity Odd (NITA) ... PO
Parkes Catalogue of Radio Sources [Australian National Radio Astronomy Observatory] [Information service] (EISS) ... PKSCAT
Parliamentary On-Line Information System [House of Commons Library] [Bibliographic database] [Information service] [British] (EISS) ... POLIS
Parliamentary On-Line Library Study [Atomic Energy Authority] [British] ... POLLS
Parsec Research Control Language [Pronounced "parkul"] [Robotics] ... PaRCL
Parser and Extensible Compiler [Programing language] (CSR) ... PARSEC
Part [Online database field identifier] (OBD) ... PT
Part and Assembly Description Language [Data processing] ... PADL
Partial Acceptance and Takeover Date [Telecommunications] (TEL) ... PATO
Partial Automatic Translation Technique ... PATT
Partial Differential Equation ... PDE
Partial Differential Equation Language [Data processing] ... PDEL
Partial Differential Equation Language [Data processing] (CSR) ... PDELAN
Partial Double Error Detection (NITA) ... PDED
Partial Network Control Center (NITA) ... PNCC
Partial Source Data Automation (NVT) ... PSDA
Participation Systems, Incorporated [Electronics Communications Co.] [Winchester, MA] [Telecommunications] (TSSD) ... PSI
Partitioned Access Method [Data processing] ... PAM
Partitioned Content Addressable Memory (NITA) ... PCAM
Partitioned Data Set [Data processing] (NASA) ... PDS
Partitioned Emulation Program [Data processing] (BUR) ... PEP
Partitioned Sequence Access Method (NITA) ... PSAM
Partnerships Data Net [Washington, DC] (EANO) ... PDN
Parts Control Automated Support System [Database] (FDB) ... PCASS
Parts Data Processing System [Bell Telephone] ... PDPS
Party Identity [Telecommunications] (TEL) ... PTI
Party Test [Telecommunications] (TEL) ... PTT
PASCAL/MT Users Group [Westmont, IL] (EANO) ... MTPUG
Pascal Software, Inc. [Moorhead, MN] [Hardware manufacturer] (DASO) ... PS
PASCAL Users' Group [Cleveland, OH] (EANO) ... PUG
Pass Card Reader [Telecommunications] (TEL) ... PCR
Passenger Airlines Reservation System (CGC) ... PARS
Passive Line Monitor [Datapoint] (NITA) ... PLM
Passive Optical Satellite Surveillance [System] (NATG) ... POSS
Passive Radio Frequency Acquisition System ... PARFAS
Password [Data processing] ... PASSWD
Patch Unit Radio [Bell System] ... PUR
Patchboard Programing System ... PPS
Patent Documentation Group (DIT) ... PDG
Patent Office [later, PTO] Data Retrieval System ... PODRS
Patent Office Techniques of Mechanized Access and Classification [Automation project, shut down in 1972] ... POTOMAC
Patent-Online-System [Bertelsmann Datenbankdienste GmbH] [Database] (CUAD) ... PATOS
Patent Search [Data processing] ... PATSEARCH
Patent Search System [Pergamon] [Database] [Data processing] [British] ... PSS
Patent, Trademark, and Copyright Institute [Franklin Pierce College] (EISS) ... PTC
Patentstelle fuer die Deutsche Forschung [Munich] [Information retrieval] (ODIN) ... PST
Path Control [Data processing] (IBMDP) ... PC
Path Independent Protocol (NITA) ... PIP
Path Information Unit [Data processing] ... PIU
Path Loss [Communications] (CBSS) ... PL
Path Loss, Downlink [Communications] (CBSS) ... PL)d
Path Loss, Uplink [Communications] (CBSS) ... PL)u
Path Selection Algorithm [Telecommunications] (TEL) ... PSA
Path Setup [Telecommunications] (TEL) ... PSU
Path Verification (NITA) ... PV
Patient Accounting, Census, and Statistics (TUT) ... PACS
Patient Automatic Data Recording Equipment (IEEE) ... PADRE
Patient Care Information System [Datacare, Inc.] (EISS) ... PCIS
Patient Computer Medical Record ... PCMR
Patient Data Automation ... PDA
Patient Data Management ... PDM
Patient Record Information for Education Requirements [Data processing] ... PRIMER
Pattern (MDG) ... PATN
Pattern Articulation Unit [Data processing] ... PAU
Pattern Correspondence Index ... PCI
Pattern Generation Language [Data processing] ... PAGAN
Pattern Information Processing System (NITA) ... PIPS
Pattern Recognition [A publication] ... Patt Recog
Pattern Recognition (BUR) ... PR
Pattern Recognition and Information Correlations [Police crime-detection computer] ... PATRIC
Pattern Recognition Interpretation and Correlation (CET) ... PATRIC
Pattern Recognition Society [Georgetown University Medical Center] [Washington, DC] ... PRS
Paul Kagan Associates, Inc. [Carmel, CA] [Information service] [Telecommunications] (EISS) ... PKA
Pay Actual Computer Time ... PACT
Pay-on-Answer [Telecommunications] [British] ... POA
Pay Television ... PTV

Pay Tone [Telecommunications] (TEL) ... PT
Pay-per-View [Pay-television service] ... PPV
Payment and Telecommunication Services Corp. [New York, NY] [Telecommunications] (TSSD) ... PATS
Peak-to-Average Ratio [Communications] ... PAR
Peak Envelope Power [Telecommunications] ... PEP
Peak Envelope Voltage [Telecommunications] (TEL) ... PEV
Peak Identification Computer ... PIC
Peak-to-Peak ... PP
Peak Power Control [Telecommunications] (TEL) ... PPC
Peak Selector Memory [Data processing] ... PSM
Peak Sideband Power (DEN) ... PSP
Pedagogic Algorithmic Language [Data processing] (TUT) ... PAL
Pedagogic Automatic Computer (IEEE) ... PAC
Peg Count [Telecommunications] (TEL) ... PC
Pencil Beam Antenna ... PBA
Pencil Tube (MDG) ... P
Penn State University Automatic Digital Computer ... PENNSTAC
Penril Corp. [American Stock Exchange symbol] ... PNL
Penta Systems International [NASDAQ symbol] (NQ) ... PSLI
Penta Users Group [Glen Burnie, MD] (EANO) ... PUG
Pentachlorophenol [Also, PCP] [Wood preservative] [Organic chemistry] (TEL) ... P
Penultimate Digit Storage [Telecommunications] (TEL) ... PDS
People's Message System [For Apple II computers] [Electronic bulletin boards] ... PMS
Perceived Noise ... PN
Perceived Noise Decibels ... PNdB
Perceived Noise Level ... PNL
Perceived Noise Level, Tone Corrected ... PNLT
PerfectData, Inc. [NASDAQ symbol] (NQ) ... PERF
Perforated Tape Reader ... PTR
Performance Analysis Routine [Data processing] ... PAR
Performance Data Computer ... PDC
Performance Data Computer System (MCD) ... PDCS
Performance Measurement System (MCD) ... PMS
Performance Monitor Unit [Communications] ... PMU
Performance Review for Operating Programs (BUR) ... PROP
Performing Artists Network [Electronic network] ... PAN
Performing Arts, Culture, and Entertainment [Proposed cable television system] ... PACE
Pergamon International Information Corporation [Information service] (EISS) ... PIIC
Periodic List of Data [Data processing] ... PLOD
Periodic Programs Termination [Data processing] ... PPT
Periodic Pulse Metering [Telecommunications] (TEL) ... PPM
Periodic Self-Test [Data processing] ... PST
Peripheral Adapter Module ... PAM
Peripheral Address Field (NITA) ... PAF
Peripheral Assignment Table (CMD) ... PAT
Peripheral Buffer ... PB
Peripheral Bus Computer [Bell System] ... PBC
Peripheral Communications (FAAC) ... PERCOM
Peripheral Control (BUR) ... PC
Peripheral Control Computer (OA) ... PCC
Peripheral Control Program ... PCP
Peripheral Control Pulse [Data processing] ... PCP
Peripheral Control Routine (CMD) ... PCR
Peripheral Control Terminal (NITA) ... PCT
Peripheral Control Unit (CMD) ... PCU
Peripheral Controller Interface (NITA) ... PCI
Peripheral Device (BUR) ... PD
Peripheral Equipment Tester [Data processing] (BUR) ... PET
Peripheral Event Processor [Data processing] ... PEP
Peripheral Input Tape [Data processing] ... PIT
Peripheral Interchange Program [Data processing] ... PIP
Peripheral Interface Adapter [Data processing] ... PIA
Peripheral Interface Module (CCD) ... PIM
Peripheral Interface Programer [Circuit] [Data processing] ... PIP
Peripheral Maintenance, Incorporated [Fairfield, NJ] [Hardware manufacturer] (DASO) ... PMI
Peripheral Processing Unit [Data processing] (CGC) ... PPU
Peripheral Processor [Data processing] (CGC) ... PP
Peripheral Unit [Computers] (MSA) ... PU
Peripheral Unit Processor [Data processing] ... PUP
Perkin-Elmer Corp. [NYSE symbol] ... PKN
Perkin-Elmer Processor [Computer] ... PEP
Permanent File Name (NITA) ... PFN
Permanent Glow [Telecommunications] (TEL) ... PG
Permanent Magnet [Loudspeaker] ... PM
Permanent Magnet Twistor [Memory] [Bell Laboratories] ... PMT
Permanent Scratch File [Data processing] ... PSCR
Permanent Signal [Telecommunications] (TEL) ... PS
Permanent Signal Detection [Telecommunications] (TEL) ... PSD
Permanent Signal Finder ... PSF
Permanent Sort Number [Data processing] ... PSN
Permanent Virtual Circuit (NITA) ... PVC
Permanently Associated [Telecommunications] (TEL) ... PA
Permanently Mounted User Set [Data processing] ... PMUS
Permutation Indexed Literature of Technology (IEEE) ... PILOT
Permuted on Subject Headings [Indexing technique] (DEEC) ... POSH
Permuterm Subject Index [Institute for Scientific Information] [A publication] (EISS) ... PSI

Pershing Instant Comment [*Donaldson, Lufkin & Jenrette*] [*Database*] (CUAD) ... PIC
Persistent Information Space Architecture [*Data processing*] ... PISA
Person to Person [*Telecommunications*] (TEL) ... P
Person to Person [*Word processing*] ... P-P
Person to Person: Collect and Special Instruction [*Telecommunications*] (TEL) ... PPCS
Personal Analog Computer ... PAC
Personal Applications Manager [*Hewlett-Packard Co.*] ... PAM
Personal Articulation Device [*Facetious term for pre-word-processing equipment*] ... PAD
Personal Computer ... PC
[*The*] **Personal Computer Book** ... TPCB
Personal Computer Management Association [*Commercial firm*] [*Orange, CA*] [*Information service*] (EANO) ... PCMA
Personal Computer Products [*San Diego, CA*] [*NASDAQ symbol*] (NQ) ... PCPI
Personal Computer World [*A publication*] ... Pers Comput World
Personal Computing System (DEEC) ... PCS
Personal Electronic Transactor [*Computer*] [*Commodore Business Machines*] ... PET
Personal Engineering Computer User's Society [*Boston, MA*] (EANO) ... PECUS
Personal Filing System [*Data-base program*] [*Software Publishing Corp.*] ... PFS
Personal Identification Number [*Banking*] ... PIN
Personal Identification Project [*Data processing*] ... PIP
Personal Information Retrieval System (DEEC) ... PIRS
Personal Portable Computer ... PPC
Personal Rapid Transit [*Computer-guided transit system*] ... PRT
Personal Rapid Transit System [*Computer-guided transit system*] ... PRTS
Personal Retrieval of Information by Microcomputer and Terminal Ensemble ... PRIMATE
Personal Systems Technology, Inc. [*Irvine, CA*] [*Hardware manufacturer*] (DASO) ... PERSYST
Personalcomputer Literaturnachweis [*Datendienst Weiss*] [*Database*] (CUAD) ... PCLN
Personalized Array Translator (IEEE) ... PAT
Personal'naia Elektronnaia Vychislitel'naia Mashina [*Personal Computer*] [*Russian*] ... PEVM
Personnel Information Communication [*or Control*] **System** [*Data processing*] ... PICS
Personnel Inventory Management System [*AT & T*] ... PIMS
Personnel/Payroll System (TUT) ... PPS
Personnel Simulation On-Line [*Department of State*] [*Computer program*] ... PERSON
PERT [*Program Evaluation and Review Technique*] **Automated Graphical Extension** (KSC) ... PAGE
Pertec Computer Corporation [*NYSE symbol*] [*Delisted*] ... PCC
Pest Control Literature Documentation [*Derwent Publications Ltd.*] [*Bibliographic database*] [*Information service*] (EISS) ... PESTDOC
Petroleum Data System [*University of Oklahoma*] [*Databank*] (EISS) ... PDS
Petroleum/Energy Business News Index [*American Petroleum Institute*] [*New York, NY*] [*Bibliographic database*] (OBD) ... P/E NEWS
Phantom Circuit [*Telecommunications*] (TEL) ... PH
Pharma-Dokumentations-Service [*Pharma Documentation Service*] [*West Germany*] [*Information service*] (EISS) ... PDS
Pharmaceutical Information Control System (DIT) ... PICS
Pharmaceutical News Index [*Data Courier, Inc.*] [*Louisville, KY*] [*Bibliographic database*] [*Information service*] ... PNI
Phase (KSC) ... PH
Phase Advance Pulse (NITA) ... PAP
Phase Alternation Line [*West German color television system*] ... PAL
Phase Alternation Line Delay (IEEE) ... PAL-D
Phase Alternation Line Simple [*TV decoding system*] (DEEC) ... PALS
Phase-Amplitude Modulation (CBSS) ... PAM
Phase Comparison Sinusoidal Frequency Shift Keying (NITA) ... PCSFSK
Phase Encoding [*Magnetic tape recording*] [*Data processing*] (MDG) ... PE
Phase-Exchange Keying [*Data processing*] (IEEE) ... PEK
Phase Lock Automatic Tuned Circuit Adjustment [*Telecommunications*] (OA) ... PATCA
Phase-Locked Automatic Frequency Control [*Telecommunications*] (OA) ... PAFC
Phase-Locked Oscillator ... PLO
Phase-Modulated Telemetry Transmission ... PMTT
Phase-Modulated Transmission ... PMT
Phase Modulation [*Radio data transmission*] (DEN) ... PHM
Phase Modulation [*Radio data transmission*] ... PM
Phase-Sensitive Converter (VIT) ... PSC
Phase-Sensitive Demodulator ... PSD
Phase-Sensitive Modulator (MCD) ... PSM
Phase-Sensitive Voltmeter ... PSVM
Phase Sequence Relay ... PSR
Phase-Shift ... PS
Phase-Shift Keying [*Data processing*] ... PSK
Phase-Shift Keying MODEM ... PSKM
Phase-Shift Keying - Pulse Code Modulation (DDI) ... PSK-PCM
Phase-Shift Modal Interference ... PSMI
Phase-Shifter, Electronic ... PSE
Phase-Shifter Module ... PSM
Phase Time Modulation ... PTM
Phased Array Antenna ... PAA
Phased Array Antenna System ... PAAS
Phased Array Antenna Technology Investigation ... PAATI
Phased Array Control Electronics ... PACE
Phased Array Module ... PAM
Phased Loading Entry [*Data processing*] ... PLE
Philco Automatic Circuit Tester ... PACT
Philippine Global Communications, Inc. [*Manila*] [*Telecommunications*] (TSSD) ... PHILCOM
Philippine Long Distance Telephone Co. [*American Stock Exchange symbol*] ... PHI
Philips Automatic Sequence Calculator ... PASCAL
Phone (MDG) ... PH
Phone Center Staffing and Sizing Program [*Telecommunications*] (TEL) ... PSSP
Photo-Data Card [*Trademark*] [*Data processing*] ... PDC
Photo-Digital Store (NITA) ... PDS
Photo Interpretive Program (BUR) ... PIP
Photo-Optical Terrain Simulator (MUGU) ... POTS
Photo-Selective Copper Reduction [*For circuit board manufacture*] ... PSCR
Photochromic Microimage [*Microfiche*] ... PCMI
Photochromic Microreproduction (DIT) ... PCMR
Photoconductive, Semiconductive Device ... PSD
Photoconductor ... PC
Photodiode Amplifier ... PA
Photoelectric Keyboard ... PKB
Photoelectric Tape Reader ... PTR
Photographic Reconnaissance System Analysis by Computer ... PRESAC
Photographically Stored Information Analog Comparator ... PHOSIAC
Photometric Determination of Equilibrium Constants [*Data processing*] ... PHODEC
Photomultiplier ... PM
Photomultiplier Tube ... PMT
Phototransistor Amplifier ... PTA
Phototypesetting and Composing [*AT & T*] ... PHOTAC
Photovoltaic Transient Analysis Computer Program ... PVTAP
Phrase Structure and Dependency Parser (DIT) ... PSDP
Phreakers, Hackers, and Laundry Service Employees [*East Coast group of computer trespassers raided by the FBI*] ... PHALSE
Physical Address Extension (NITA) ... PAX
Physical Block Number (NITA) ... PBN
Physical Device Address [*Data processing*] (IBMDP) ... PDA
Physical Input-Output Control System [*Data processing*] (BUR) ... PIOCS
Physical Memory Address (NITA) ... PMA
Physical Memory Level (NITA) ... PML
Physical Property Data Service [*Institution of Chemical Engineers*] [*Rugby, England*] [*Databank*] [*Information service*] (EISS) ... PPDS
Physical Sciences Laboratory [*University of Wisconsin - Madison, New Mexico State University*] [*Research center*] ... PSL
Physical Sciences Research Program [*North Carolina State University*] [*Research center*] (RCD) ... PSR
Physical Transaction Block (NITA) ... PTB
Physical Unit [*Data processing*] (IBMDP) ... PU
Physical Unit Block [*Data processing*] (TUT) ... PUB
Physicians Communication Service [*Database*] (CUAD) ... PHYCOM
Physics Briefs [*Database*] [*Information retrieval*] (ODIN) ... PB
Physikalische Berichte [*Physics Briefs*] [*Database*] [*Information retrieval*] (ODIN) ... PB
Pickup (FAAC) ... PUP
Pico [*A prefix meaning divided by one trillion*] [*SI symbol*] ... p
Picoampere ... pA
Picofarad (MDG) ... PUFF
Picojoule [*Logic gate efficiency measure*] (MDG) ... PJ
Picosecond ... ps
Pictorial and Artifact Retrieval and Information System [*Data processing*] ... PARIS
Pictorial Encoding Language [*Data processing*] (IEEE) ... PENCIL
Pictorial Information Digitizer [*Data processing*] (DIT) ... PID
Picture (MDG) ... PC
Picture Element [*Single element of resolution in image processing*] (IBMDP) ... PEL
Picture Element [*Single element of resolution in image processing*] (CIT) ... PIXEL
Picture-in-a-Picture [*Multi-Vision Products*] [*Video technology*] ... PIP
Picturephone Meeting Service [*AT & T*] ... PMS
Piece Identification Number (IDA) ... PIN
Piezoelectric Translator (DEEC) ... PZT
Piggyback Tape [*or Twistor*] [*Data processing*] ... PBT
Pill Box Antenna ... PBA
Pilot Direction Indicator [*Electronic communications*] ... PDI
Pilot [*or Public*] **Switched Digital Data Service** [*Telecommunications*] (TEL) ... PSDDS
Pinetree Computer Systems [*NASDAQ symbol*] (NQ) ... PNTR
Pioneer Television and Electronic Technicians Society [*Defunct*] ... PTETS
Piping & Instrumentation Diagrams [*Calcomp Ltd.*] [*Software package*] [*British*] (NCC) ... P & ID
Pitch Follow-Up Amplifier ... PFA
Pitch Ratio Adjust Device (MCD) ... PRAD
Pitney-Bowes, Inc. ... PB
Pitney-Bowes, Incorporated [*NYSE symbol*] ... PBI
Pitt Interpretive Language [*Data processing*] (DIT) ... PIL
PL/M Extended [*Programing language*] (CSR) ... PLMX
Plain Language Address [*Telecommunications*] (TEL) ... PLA
Plain Old Telephone [*Bell System's basic model*] ... POT

Computer & Telecommunications Acronyms

Plain Old Telephone Service [Humorous term for Long Lines Department of AT & T].................. POTS
Plan Position Indicator Mode [Data processing]........... PPI
Planar Array Antenna .... PAA
Planar Gas Discharge (MCD)................................ PGD
Plane Disagreement [Telecommunications] (TEL)....... PD
Plane Frame [Camutek] [Software package] [British] (NCC)........ PF
Plane Polarized [Telecommunications] (TEL)........... PP
Plane Stress Analysis and Plot [Data processing]...... PSAP
Planned Action with Constant Evaluation [Data processing]...... PACE
Planned Completion Date [Telecommunications] (TEL)........ PCD
Planned Maintenance [Contract Data Research] [Software package] [British] (NCC)...... PLANMAN
Planned Maintenance Systems [Falls Church, VA] [Software manufacturer] (DASOS)...... PMS
Planned Standard Programing [Data processing]........ PSP
Planned Start Installation [Telecommunications]...... PSI
Planning Aid for Retail Information System [IBM Corp.]...... PARIS
Planning, Control, and Decision Evaluation System [IBM Corp.]......... PLANCODE
[The] Planning Exchange Database [Pergamon InfoLine] [Glasgow, Scotland] [Database] [Information service] (EISS)........ PLANEX
Planning Research Corp. [In company name, PRC Realty Systems] [McLean, VA] [Software manufacturer] (DASOS)....... PRC
Planning through Retrieval of Information for Management Extrapolation........... PRIME
Planning Systems Generator .... PSG
Plant Computer .... PC
Plant Computer System .... PCS
Plant Design and Management System [Computer Aided Design Centre] [Software package] [British] (NCC)...... PDMS
Plant Information Network [Fish and Wildlife Service] (EISS)...... PIN
Plant Records Center [of the American Horticultural Society] (EISS)...... PRC
Plant Test Date [Telecommunications] (TEL)........... PTD
Plant Test Number [Telecommunications] (TEL)...... PTN
Plantronics, Inc. [NYSE symbol]............................ PLX
Plasma Display (NITA).. PD
Plasma Display Panel [Data processing].................. PDP
Plasma Display Terminal [Data processing].............. PDT
Plates on Elastic Foundations [Structures & Computers Ltd.] [Software package] [British] (NCC)............ PLONEF
Platinized Titanium Anode .... PTA
Playing to Win (EANO)...................................... PTW
Please (MDG)... PSE
Plesetsk [Satellite launch complex] [USSR] (CBSS)...... PLE
Plessey Co. Ltd. [NYSE symbol]............................ PLY
Plexus Corp. [NASDAQ symbol] (NQ)................... PLUSF
Plot Function [Data processing]............................. PF
Plot Points [Data processing]................................ PP
Plug Compatible [Data processing] (BUR)............... PC
Plug Compatible Ethernet (CCD).......................... PCE
Plug Compatible Mainframe [Data processing].......... PCM
Plug Compatible Manufacturer [Data processing]...... PCM
Plug Compatible Memory (NITA)......................... PCM
Plug-In Amplifier .... PIA
Plug-In Electronics .... PIE
Plug-In Inventory Control System [Bell System]........ PICS
Plug-In Inventory Control System/Detailed Continuing Property Record [Telecommunications] (TEL)...... PICS/DCPR
Plug-In Unit .... PIU
Plymouth Audioconferencing Network [Plymouth Polytechnic] [Plymouth, England] [Telecommunications] (TSSD)...... PACNET
Pneumatic Analog Computer .... PAC
PNP [Positive-Negative-Positive] Transistor Magnetic Logic (IEEE)...... PTML
Pockels Readout Optical Modulator........................ PROM
Pocket Computer .... PC
Pocket Select Language [Burroughs Corp.] (NITA)...... PSL
Point (CAH)... PT
Point-of-Failure [Data processing] (IBMDP)............. POF
Point-of-Last-Environment [Data processing] (IBMDP)...... POLE
Point-Positioning Data Base [Cartography] (RDA)...... PPDB
Point-of-Sale Terminal [Data transmission] (TSSD)...... POS
Point Spread Function .... PSF
Poison Control Data Base [Database] (FDB)............ PCDB
Polarization Angle [Telecommunications] (OA)......... POLANG
Polarization Modulation (MCD)............................ PM
Polarized Return-to-Zero Recording [Data processing] (IBMDP)...... RZ(P)
Polaroid Corp. [NYSE symbol]............................. PRD
Pole .... P
Pole Amplitude Modulation (IEEE)....................... PAM
Pole Broken [Telecommunications] (TEL)............... PBR
Police National Computer [British]........................ PNC
Political Information System [Databank of political strategist Richard Wirthlin]...... PINS
Politically Simulated World [Computer-assisted political science game]...... PSW
Pollable Data Terminal [Bell System]...................... PDT
Polled Access Circuit (NITA)............................... PAC
Polled Access Network (NITA)............................. PAN
PolyComputers, Inc. Uts [NASDAQ symbol] (NQ)...... POLYU
Polyethylene Insulated Conductor [Telecommunications]...... PIC
Polymorphic Programming Language [1971] [Data processing] (CSR)...... PPL
Polynomial Error Protection Code [Data processing]...... PEPC

Polyscope. Computer and Elektronik [A publication]............... Polyscope Comput and Elektron
Polytranslation Analysis and Programing (IEEE)...... POLYTRAN
Pool Maintenance Module [Telecommunications] (TEL)...... PMM
Pool Operational Module [Telecommunications] (TEL)...... POM
Poor Transmission [Telecommunications] (TEL)...... PTR
Popular Computing [A publication]....................... Pop Comput
Popular Electronics [A publication]....................... Pop Electr
Population Documentation Center [United Nations] [Information service] (EISS)...... PDC
Population Information On-Line [Population Information Program, Johns Hopkins University] [Bibliographic database] (EISS)...... POPLINE
Population Information Program [Johns Hopkins University] [Information service] (EISS)...... PIP
Population Research Service [Austin, TX] [Information service] (EISS)...... PRS
Port Check BIT [Binary Digit] [Telecommunications] (TEL)...... PCB
Port Command Area [Telecommunications] (TEL)...... PCM
Port Command Store [Telecommunications] (TEL)...... PCS
Port Communications Area [Telecommunications] (TEL)...... PCA
Port Control [Telecommunications] (TEL).............. PC
Port Control Diagnostic [Telecommunications] (TEL)...... PCD
Port Control Store [Telecommunications] (TEL)...... PCS
Port Control System [Telecommunications] (TEL)...... PCS
Port Expander Unit (NITA)................................. PEU
Port Group [Telecommunications] (TEL)................ PG
Port Group Control [Telecommunications] (TEL)...... PGC
Port Group Highway [Telecommunications] (TEL)...... PGH
Port Group Highway Timeslot [Telecommunications] (TEL)...... PGHTS
Port Group Interface [Telecommunications] (TEL)...... PGI
Port Identification [Telecommunications] (TEL)........ PID
Port Import Export Reporting Services [Journal of Commerce, Inc.] [Database] (CUAD)...... PIERS
Port Number [Telecommunications] (TEL)............. PT
Port Storage Area [Telecommunications] (TEL)....... PSA
Port Storage Utility [Telecommunications] (TEL)...... PSU
Port Store [Telecommunications] (TEL)................. PS
Port Strobe [Telecommunications] (TEL)............... PS
Portable (MDG).. P
Portable Code Processor .... PCP
Portable Computer .... PC
Portable Conference Telephone [Bell Laboratories]...... PCT
Portable Data Acquisition System.......................... PODAS
Portable Data Processing System (VIT).................. PODAPS
Portable Electronic Telephone .... PET
Portable Encoder/Illustrator [Facetious term for pre-word-processing equipment]...... PENCIL
Portable Keyboard .... PKB
Portable Magnetic Tape .... PMT
Portable Memory Unit [Data processing]............... PMU
Portable Propagation Recorder [Bell System]......... PPR
Portable Radio Telephone .... PRT
Portable Remote Terminal .... PRT
Portable Service Processor (IEEE)........................ PSP
Portable Traffic Monitor [Telecommunications] (TEL)...... PTM
Portable Voice Communications System .... PVCS
Position (KSC).. POS
Position Independent Code [Telecommunications] (TEL)...... PIC
Position Keeping Computer .... PKC
Position and Velocity Computer .... PVC
Positioning Arm Disk (NITA).............................. PAD
Positive [Crystal].. p
Positive (AFM)... POS
Positive-Channel Metal-Oxide Semiconductor [Telecommunications] (TEL)...... PMOS
Positive Feedback Circuit .... PFC
Positive Input - Negative Output [Data processing]...... PINO
Positive Interlace [Television]............................... PI
Positive/Negative... P/N
Positive-Negative-Positive [Transistor]................... PNP
Positive-Negative-Positive-Negative [Transistor] (MUGU)...... PNPN
Positron Computed Tomography .... PCT
Post-Deployment Software System (MCD)............ PDSS
Post Detection Filter [Telecommunications] (TEL)...... PDF
Post Dialing Delay [Telecommunications] (TEL)...... PDD
Post-Harvest Documentation Service [Kansas State University] (EISS)...... PHDS
Post Mortem Core Dump [Data processing]............ PMCD
Post Mortem Dump [Data processing]................... PMD
Post Mortem Tape Dump [Data processing]............ PMTD
Post Office Fast Facsimile [Transmission of documents] [British]...... POSTFAX
Post Office Processing Utility Subsystem [Telecommunications] (TEL)...... POPUS
Post Office Telecommunications [British]................ POT
Post Office Telecommunications Journal [A publication]...... P O Telecommun J
Post Office Work Unit [Computer performance measure] [British Telecom] (OA)...... POWU
Post Operation Data Analysis Facility .... PODAF
Post Sending Delay (DEEC).............................. PSD

Computer & Telecommunications Acronyms

Post und Telegraphenverwaltung [*Postal and Telegraph Administration*] [*Vienna, Austria*] [*Telecommunications*] (TSSD) .... PTT
Post, Telephon und Telegraphenbetriebe [*Berne, Switzerland*] [*Telecommunications*] (TSSD) .... PTT
Postal Telegraph Co. [*Terminated*] .... PT
Postal, Telegraph, and Telephone Administration (NATG) .... PTT
Postal, Telegraph, and Telephone International [*See also IPTT*] [*Brussels, Belgium*] .... PTTI
Posterior Probability [*Computations*] .... POSTP
Postes et Telecommunications .... P et T
Postes, Telegraphes, et Telediffusion [*Post, Telegraph, and Telephone*] [*General Post Office*] [*France*] .... PTT
Postpay Coin Telephone [*Telecommunications*] (TEL) .... PO
Posttuning Drift .... PTD
Potential (AFM) .... POT
Potential Difference [*Electricity*] .... PD
Potential Network Access Facility (NITA) .... PNAF
Potomac Pacific Engineering, Inc. .... PPE
Powder Diffraction Search-Match System [*International Data Center*] .... PDSM
Power [*Symbol*] [*IUPAC*] .... P
Power Amplifier .... PA
Power Amplifier Assembly .... PAA
Power Amplifier Klystron .... PAK
Power Amplifier Neutralizing Capacitor (DEN) .... PANC
Power Circuit Breaker (MSA) .... PCB
Power Conditioning System .... PCS
Power Control Unit .... PCU
Power Density Exceeding a Specified Level over an Area with an Assigned Frequency Band (IEEE) .... PODAF
Power Distribution System [*or Subsystem*] .... PDS
Power Distribution Unit .... PDU
Power Factor [*Radio*] .... PF
Power Fail Automatic Restart [*Data processing*] .... PFAR
Power Fail Recovery System [*Data processing*] (MDG) .... PFR
Power Fail/Restart (NITA) .... PFR
Power Flux Density [*Telecommunications*] (TEL) .... PFD
Power Frame [*Telecommunications*] (TEL) .... PF
Power Gain Antenna .... PGA
Power Industry Computer Applications .... PICA
Power Industry Computer Applications Conference (MCD) .... PICAC
Power Integrated Circuit [*Data processing*] .... PIC
Power Line Communications .... PLC
Power Line Transient (IEEE) .... PLT
Power On/Off Protection (CGC) .... POP
Power-On Self Test [*IBM-PC feature*] .... POST
Power-Plant and Process Design Management System [*Data processing*] .... PDMS
Power and Signal List [*Telecommunications*] (TEL) .... PSL
Power Signal-to-Noise Ratio (CIT) .... PSNR
Power Source Logic (CIT) .... PSL
Power Supply .... PS
Power Supply Unit (MSA) .... PSU
Power Switching and Logic (CIT) .... PS & L
Power System Optimization Program [*Data processing*] .... PSOP
Power Transformers (MCD) .... PTR
Powertec, Inc. [*NASDAQ symbol*] (NQ) .... PWTC
Practical Algorithm to Receive Information Coded in Alphanumeric [*Information retrieval*] (IDA) .... PATRICIA
Practical Computing [*A publication*] .... Pract Comput
Practical Data Manager [*Hitachi Ltd.*] [*Japan*] (NITA) .... PDM
Practical, Unpretentious, Nomographic Computer .... PUNC
Pre-Coordinate Indexing System (DEEC) .... PRECIS
Pre-Edited Interpretive System [*Data processing*] .... PRINT
Pre-Emption [*Telecommunications*] (TEL) .... PE
Preamplifier .... PA
Preamplifier Module Assembly .... PMA
Precedence Network In-Dialing [*Telecommunications*] (TEL) .... P-NID
Precise Tone Generator [*Telecommunications*] (TEL) .... PTG
Precision Analog Computing Equipment .... PACE
Precision Annotated Retrieval Display [*System*] [*Data processing*] .... PARD
Precision Artwork Language [*Data processing*] (TUT) .... PAL
Precision Encoding and Pattern Recognition Device [*Data processing*] .... PEPR
Precision Interactive Operation [*Data processing*] (CDH) .... PIO
Precision Methods, Incorporated [*Lorton, VA*] [*Hardware manufacturer*] (DASO) .... PMI
Precision Transmitter Receiver .... PTR
Precision Voltage Reference (MDG) .... PVR
Preclinical Literature Information System [*Data processing*] .... PLIS
Predefined Input Control Sequence (MCD) .... PICS
Predicasts Abstract Terminal System [*Data processing*] .... PATS
Predicasts Overview of Markets and Technology [*Predicasts, Inc.*] [*Cleveland, OH*] [*Bibliographic database*] (OBD) .... PTS PROMT
Predicasts Overviews of Marketing and Technology [*Business database*] .... PROMT
Predicasts Terminal Systems [*Predicasts, Inc.*] [*Cleveland, OH*] [*Database*] .... PTS
Prediction Error Filter [*Wave frequency and phase modifier*] .... PEF
Prediction, Simulation, Adaptation, Decision [*Data processing*] .... PSAD
Predictive Analyzer [*Data processing*] (DIT) .... PA
Prefix [*Indicating a private radiotelegram*] .... P
Prefix [*Indicating a private radiotelegram*] (BUR) .... PR

Prefix (NITA) .... PRE
Premature Release [*Telecommunications*] (TEL) .... PR
Premodulation Processor .... PMP
Premodulation Processor - Deep Space - Data .... PDD
Premodulation Processor - Near Earth Data (KSC) .... PND
Prenex Normal Form [*Logic*] .... PNF
Prentice-Hall Information Network [*New York, NY*] [*Information service*] (EISS) .... PHINet
Prepare Master Tape .... PMT
Prepare a New Perforated Tape for Message [*Communications*] (FAAC) .... PUN
Prepayment Coin Telephone [*Telecommunications*] (TEL) .... PRE
Preprocessor .... PP
Preprogramed Self-Instruction [*Data processing*] (IEEE) .... PSI
Preselected Alternate Master-Slave [*Telecommunications*] (TEL) .... PAMS
Present BIT [*Binary Digit*] [*Data processing*] .... P
Present Worth of Annual Charges [*Pronounced "p-wack"*] [*Bell System*] .... PWAC
Present Worth Expenditures [*Telecommunications*] (TEL) .... PWE
Presentation Graphic Feature [*Data processing*] .... PGF
Presentation Level Protocol [*AT & T Videotex System*] .... PLP
Presentation Services [*Data processing*] (IBMDP) .... PS
Pressure Modulation Radiometer .... PMR
Pressure Sensitive Identification (CAH) .... PSI
Prestel Advanced Network Design Architecture (DEEC) .... PANDA
Presunrise Authority .... PSA
Pretransmit Receiving .... PTR
Preventative Cyclic Retransmission [*Telecommunications*] (TEL) .... PCR
Previous to Appearance in MEDLINE [*Latham, NY*] [*Bibliographic database*] (OBD) .... PRE-MED
Previous Processor Mode (NITA) .... PPM
Priam Corp. [*NASDAQ symbol*] (NQ) .... PRIA
Price [*Online database field identifier*] (OBD) .... PR
Price Description Record (IBMDP) .... PDR
Price Index Numbers for Current Cost Accounting [*Service in Information and Analysis*] [*Databank*] [*British*] (EISS) .... PINCCA
Pricing Review to Intensify Competitive Environment [*Data processing*] .... PRICE
Primary Access Method [*Sperry UNIVAC*] (NITA) .... PAM
Primary Auxiliary Memory [*Unit*] [*Data processing*] (MCD) .... PAM
Primary Block Number [*Data processing*] .... PBN
Primary Bus [*Data processing*] (CAAL) .... PB
Primary Communications-Oriented System (IEEE) .... PCOS
Primary Control Program [*Data processing*] .... PCP
Primary Focus Feed [*Satellite communications*] .... PFF
Primary Frequency Supply [*Telecommunications*] (TEL) .... PFS
Primary Indicating Position Data Logger (IEEE) .... PIP
Primary Location Code [*Data processing*] .... PLC
Primary Long-Distance Carrier [*Telephone service*] .... PLDC
Primary Operating System (IEEE) .... POS
Primary Routing Center [*Telecommunications*] (TEL) .... PRC
Primary Waveform Generator [*Telecommunications*] (TEL) .... PWFG
Prime Computer, Inc. [*NYSE symbol*] .... PRM
Prime Network Software Package [*Prime Computer, Inc.*] (NITA) .... PRIMENET
Prime Operating System [*Prime Computer, Inc.*] (NITA) .... PRIMOS
Prime Users Group [*Natick, MA*] (EANO) .... PUG
Princeton Time Sharing Services, Inc. .... PTSS
Principal Register [*Data processing*] .... PR
Print .... P
Print Alphanumerically [*Data processing*] (MDG) .... PRA
Print Command Register (NITA) .... PCR
Print Contrast Scale (IEEE) .... PCS
Print Contrast Signal [*Data processing*] .... PCS
Print Contrast System (BUR) .... PCS
Print Control Language (NITA) .... PCL
Print Down Module .... PDM
Print Load Analyzer (NITA) .... PLA
Print Measurement Bureau [*Print Measurement Bureau*] [*Database*] (CUAD) .... PMB
Print Numerically (DEN) .... PRN
Print Out Effect .... POE
Print Position Counter (NITA) .... PPC
Print Positions (NITA) .... PP
Print-Punch [*Data processing*] (BUR) .... PP
Print Queue Processor [*Data processing*] .... PQUE
Print Screen [*Computer keyboard*] .... PrtSc
Print and Search Processor [*Data processing*] .... PANDS
Printed [*or Printer*] .... PR
Printed Circuit .... PC
Printed Circuit Assembly [*Telecommunications*] (TEL) .... PCA
Printed Circuit Board (MCD) .... PCB
Printed Circuit Board Socket .... PCBS
Printed Circuit Keyboard .... PCK
Printed Circuit Keyboard .... PCKB
Printed Circuit Patchboard .... PCP
Printed Wire Assembly [*Data processing*] .... PWA
Printed Wiring Board .... PWB
Printed Wiring Board Assembly (MCD) .... PWBA
Printed Wiring Cards [*Telecommunications*] .... PWC
Printed Wiring Master .... PWM
Printer .... PRNTR
Printer [*Data processing*] (MDG) .... PRT

By Meaning

Printer (DDI)	PRTR
Printer (MSA)	PTR
Printer Communications Adapter (NITA)	PCA
Printer Direction Optimizer (BUR)	PDO
Printer Driver	PRD
Printer Dump	PRD
Printer Interface Cartridge [Epson America, Inc.]	PIC
Printer Output Microfilm	POM
Printer Page [Data processing]	PP
Printer Systems Corporation [Gaithersburg, MD] [Hardware manufacturer] (DASO)	PSC
Printer Terminal (NITA)	PT
Printing Character [Data processing]	PCHAR
Printing Industry Computer Associates, Inc.	PICA
Printing Industry Language for Operations of Typesetting	PILOT
Printing-Out Paper	POP
Printing Request	PR
Printing Response-Time Monitor	PRTM
Printout (MSA)	PTOUT
Priority [Telecommunications] (TEL)	P
Priority (AFM)	PRI
Priority (CAH)	PRTY
Priority Interrupt (IEEE)	PI
Priority Interrupt Control Unit [Data processing] (MDG)	PICU
Priority Interrupt Controller (DEEC)	PIC
Priority Memory Access (NITA)	PMA
Priority Order Output System [Japan] (DIT)	POOS
Priority-Oriented Demand Assignment (NITA)	PODA
Priority Receiving with Inter-Departmental Efficiency [Data processing]	PRIDE
Priority Routine Organizer for Computer Transfers and Operations of Registers (CDH)	PROCTOR
Priority Selection Table [Data processing] (IBMDP)	PST
Priority Selection Table Extension [Data processing] (IBMDP)	PST-E
Priority Telegram	PT
Private (Automatic) Branch Exchange [Telecommunications] (DEN)	P(A)BX
Private Automatic Computer Exchange	PACX
Private Automatic Exchange [Telecommunications]	PAX
Private Branch Exchange [Telecommunications]	PBX
Private Circuit Control Module [Telecommunications] (TEL)	PCCM
Private Circuit Digital Data Service [Telecommunications] (TEL)	PCDDS
Private Communications Association [Later, NCA]	PCA
Private Exchange	PX
Private Input/Output [Telecommunications] (TEL)	PIO
Private Line	PL
Private Line Assured Service [Telecommunications] (TEL)	PLAS
Private Line Interface (NITA)	PLI
Private Line Service	PLS
Private Line Telephone	PLF
Private Line Telephone	PLT
Private Line Teletypewriter	PLT
Private Line Teletypewriter Service [Telecommunications] (TEL)	PLITTY
Private Manual Branch Exchange [Communications]	PMBX
Private Manual Exchange	PMX
Private Meter Check [Telecommunications] (TEL)	PMC
Private Microwave [System]	PMW
Private Packet Exchange (NITA)	PPX
Private Satellite Network, Inc. [New York, NY] [Telecommunications] (TSSD)	PSN
Private Switching Network [Telecoms]	PRISNET
Private Telecommunications Systems [Radio-Suisse Ltd.] [Berne, Switzerland] [Telecommunications] (TSSD)	PTS
Pro-Am Sports Systems [Cable-television network]	PASS
Probabilistic Automatic Pattern Analyzer [Data processing]	PAPA
Probabilistic Risk Assessment [Computer-based technique for accident prediction]	PRA
Probability Based-Matched [Database search techniques]	PBM
Probability Density Function [Statistics]	PDF
Probability Distribution Subprogram [Data processing] (BUR)	PDS
Probability Forecasting [Computer program] [Bell System]	PROBFOR
Problem Descriptor System	PDS
Problem Descriptor System/Matrix Generation [Programing language] [1965] (CSR)	PDS/MAGEN
Problem Determination Aid [Data processing] (MDG)	PDAID
Problem Identification Program (MCD)	PIP
Problem Input Preparation [Data processing] (BUR)	PIP
Problem Language Analyzer [Data processing] (CGC)	PLAN
Problem-Oriented Language [Data processing]	POL
Problem-Oriented Language Generator [Data processing] (BUR)	POLGEN
Problem-Oriented Medical Information System [Computerized patient-management system]	PROMIS
Problem-Oriented Routine (IEEE)	POR
Problem Program Efficiency (IEEE)	PPE
Problem Program Evaluator (NITA)	PPE
Problem Solution Engineering [Programing language] [Data processing] (CSR)	PROSE
Problem Specification (OA)	PS
Problem Specification Language (OA)	PSL
Problem Statement Language/Problem Specification Analyzer [Data processing]	PSL/PSA
Problem Tracking and Change Control [Data processing]	PT/CC
Problems of Control and Information Theory [A publication]	Probl Control Inf Theor
Problems of Control and Information Theory [A publication]	Probl Control and Inf Theory
Problems of Control and Information Theory (English Translation of the Papers in Russian) [A publication]	Probl Control and Inf Theory (Engl Transl Pap Rus)
Problems of Control and Information Theory. Problemy Upravlenija i Teorii Informacii [Budapest] [A publication]	Problems Control Inform Theory/Problemy Upravlen Teor Inform
Problems of Information Transmission [A publication]	Problems Inform Transmission
Problems of Information Transmission [A publication]	Probl Inf Transm
Problems of Information Transmission (USSR) [A publication]	Probl Inf Transm (USSR)
Procedural Control Language [1971] [Data processing] (CSR)	PCL
Procedural Language Implementing Analog Techniques [Data processing] (IEEE)	PLIANT
Procedural Language Processor (NITA)	PLP
Procedure	PROC
Procedure Definition Language [Data processing] (BUR)	PDL
Procedure Definition Processor [Data processing]	PDP
Procedure-Oriented Language [Data processing]	POL
Procedures Manual (IEEE)	PM
Proceed to Select [Telecommunications] (TEL)	PTS
Proceed to Send [Telecommunications] (TEL)	PTS
Proceedings	PROC
Proceedings. Computer Science and Statistics [A publication]	P Cmp Sc St
Proceedings. Institution of Electrical Engineers. Part E. Computers and Digital Techniques [A publication]	Proc Inst Elec Eng Pt E Computers Digital Tech
Proceedings. Institution of Electrical Engineers. Part F. Communications, Radar, and Signal Processing [A publication]	Proc Inst Elec Eng Pt F Commun Radar Signal Process
Process	PROC
Process Accessible Segment Table (NITA)	PAST
Process Allocator [Telecommunications] (TEL)	PA
Process Assembler Language	PAL
Process Assembly Case Evaluator Routine [Data processing] (TUT)	PACER
Process Automation (CMD)	PA
Process Automation & Computer Systems	PACS
Process Automation Monitor [Texas Instruments, Inc.] (OA)	PAM
Process Automation Monitor/Disk Version [Texas Instruments, Inc.] (NITA)	PAMD
Process Computer	PC
Process Computer [Data processing]	PROCOMP
Process Computer System	PCS
Process Control (DEN)	PC
Process Control Block	PCB
Process Control Computer	PCC
Process Control Interface (DEEC)	PCI
Process Control Language [Texas Instruments, Inc.] (NITA)	PCLA
Process Control Module [Telecommunications] (TEL)	PCM
Process Control Operating System (OA)	PCOS
Process Descriptor Base [Telecommunications] (TEL)	PDB
Process Evaluation Guide [Graphic Communications Association]	PEG
Process and Experiment Automation Real-Time Language [Data processing]	PEARL
Process Input Unit [Data processing] (BUR)	PIU
Process Instruments Digital Communication System [Beckman Industries] (NITA)	PIDCOM
Process Intelligent Control [A data processing system from LISP Machine, Inc.]	PICON
Process Interface Control (OA)	PIC
Process Interface Unit (NITA)	PIU
[A] Process Management and Information System [I. P. Sharp Associates Ltd.] [Software package] [British] (NCC)	PROMIS
Process Operating System [Toshiba Corp.] [Japan] (NITA)	POPS
Process Operator Console	POC
Process-Oriented Language [Data processing] (IEEE)	POL
Process-Oriented Real-Time Algorithmic Language [1978] [Data processing] (CSR)	PORTAL
Process Page Table [Telecommunications] (TEL)	PPT
Process Signal Interface Controller (NITA)	PSIC
Process Simulation Language [Data processing] (TEL)	PSL
Process Steering and Control Module [Telecommunications] (TEL)	PSCM
Process Subsystem [Telecommunications] (TEL)	PS
Process Systems Program (OA)	PROSPRO
Process and Test Control [Pendar Technical Association Ltd.] [Software package] [British] (NCC)	PROTECON
Process and Test Language (OA)	PTL
Process Variable Record (NITA)	PVR
Processed	PROCSD
Processed Language [Data processing]	PROLAN
Processing (MSA)	PRCSG
Processing Center [Telecommunications] (TEL)	PC
Processing Data Rate (IEEE)	PDR
Processing Element [of central processing unit]	PE
Processing Element Memory [Data processing]	PEM
Processing Information List [Data processing]	PIL

Processing Module [*Data processing*] .... PM
Processing Terminal Network Architecture [*Data processing*] (BUR) ..... PNA
Processing Time (NITA) .... PT
Processing Unit [*Data processing*] .... PU
Processing Unit Cabinet [*Data processing*] .... PUC
Procession Register Clock (NITA) .... PRC
Processor [*or Processing*] (NITA) .... PROC
Processor Common Communications System (NITA) .... PCCS
Processor Common Input/Output System [*Data processing*] .... PCIOS
Processor Control Console [*Telecommunications*] (TEL) .... PCC
Processor Control Unit (NITA) .... PCU
Processor Controller [*Data processing*] (MDG) .... PC
Processor Data Monitor (NASA) .... PDM
Processor Defined Function (NITA) .... PDF
Processor Emergency Recovery Circuit [*Bell System*] .... PERC
Processor Input-Output [*Data processing*] (MDG) .... PIO
Processor Interface (NITA) .... PI
Processor Interface Buffer [*Telecommunications*] (TEL) .... PIB
Processor Interface Module (NITA) .... PIM
Processor and Memory [*Data processing*] .... PAM
Processor Memory Enhancement (NITA) .... PME
Processor Memory Switch Matrix (NITA) .... PMSX
Processor Monitoring Instrument [*Data processing*] .... PMI
Processor Ready for Use [*Telecommunications*] (TEL) .... PRFU
Processor Request Flag [*Telecommunications*] (TEL) .... PRF
Processor Speed Up [*Computer memory core*] .... PSU
Processor State Register Main [*Data processing*] .... PSRM
Processor State Register Utility [*Data processing*] .... PSRU
Processor Status (OA) .... PS
Processor Status Word (DEEC) .... PSW
Processor Storage Control Function (NITA) .... PSCF
Processor System Modeling Language [*1976*] [*Data processing*] (CSR) .... PSML
Processor Tape Read .... PTR
Processor Technology Disk Operating System (NITA) .... PTDOS
Processor Utility [*Telecommunications*] (TEL) .... PU
Processor Utility Monitor [*Telecommunications*] (TEL) .... PUM
Processor Utility Subsystem [*Telecommunications*] (TEL) .... PUS
Processors, Memories, and Switches [*Programing language*] (CSR) .... PMS
Procurement Automated Source System [*Small Business Administration*] [*Information service*] (EISS) .... PASS
Procurement Operations Information System (MCD) .... POIS
Prodigy Systems, Inc. [*NASDAQ symbol*] (NQ) .... PDGY
Product [*or Production*] .... PROD
Product Definition Database (MCD) .... PDDB
Product Design Graphics System [*Prime Computer Ltd.*] [*Software package*] [*British*] (NCC) .... PDGS
Product Engineering Control Center [*Telecommunications*] (TEL) .... PECC
Product Information Network [*McGraw-Hill Information Systems Co.*] [*Information service*] (EISS) .... PIN
Product Output Reporting System .... PORS
Product and Support Requirements Request [*Data processing*] (IBMDP) .... PSRR
Production Acceptance Test (KSC) .... PAT
Production Adjustment Index [*Word processing*] .... PAI
Production Automated Riveting .... PAR
Production Control Information [*Sheffield, England*] [*Software supplier*] (NCC) .... PCI
Production Control System (BUR) .... PCS
Production Date [*Data processing*] .... PDATE
Production Engineering Productivity System [*Camtek Ltd.*] [*Software package*] [*British*] (NCC) .... PEPS
Production Information and Control System [*IBM Corp.*] [*Software package*] .... PICS
Production Inventory Control System (TUT) .... PICS
Production per Man-Hour .... PMH
Production Management System [*Safe Computing Ltd.*] [*Software package*] [*British*] (NCC) .... PMS
Production Planning System [*TDS Business Systems Ltd.*] [*Software package*] [*British*] (NCC) .... PPS
Production, Reviewing, Organizing, and Monitoring of Performance Techniques (BUR) .... PROMPT
Production Run Tape (IDA) .... PRT
Production System Simulator [*Data processing*] .... PROSIM
Production Training Indicator [*Data processing*] .... PTI
Productivity Improvement and Control System (BUR) .... PICS
Productivity Research and Extension Program [*North Carolina State University*] [*Research center*] (RCD) .... PREP
Produktivitaetszentrale Saar eV [*Saarbruecken*] [*Information retrieval*] (ODIN) .... PZ
Professional Abstracts Registries [*Database Innovations, Inc.*] .... PAR
Professional Group - Antennas and Propagation .... PGAP
Professional Group - Broadcast and Television Receivers .... PGBTR
Professional Group - Broadcast Transmission Systems .... PGBTS
Professional Group - Circuit Theory .... PGCT
Professional Group - Communications Systems .... PGCS
Professional Group - Electronic Devices .... PGED
Professional Group - Human Factors in Electronics .... PGHFE
Professional Group - Microwave Theory and Techniques .... PGMTT
Professional Group - Radio Frequency Interference .... PGRFI
Professional Group on Space Electronics and Telemetry .... PGSET
Professional Office System [*IBM Corp.*] .... PROFS
Professional Personal Computer .... PPC
Professional Resellers Organization (EANO) .... PRO
Professional Standards Review Organization [*Generic term for groups of physicians who may review the policies and decisions of their colleagues*] .... PSRO
Professional Technical Group on Antennas and Propagation [*of the IEEE*] .... PTGAP
Professional Technical Group on Electronic Computers [*Later, IEEE Computer Society*] .... PTGEC
Professional Video Services Corporation [*Washington, DC*] [*Telecommunications*] (TSSD) .... PVSC
Professional'naia Elektronnaia Vychislitel'naia Mashina [*Professional Computer*] [*Russian*] .... PEVM
Program (KSC) .... P
Program .... PGM
Program (AFM) .... PRGM
Program (KSC) .... PROG
Program Access (NITA) .... PA
Program Address .... PA
Program Address Register (NITA) .... PAR
Program Address Storage (IEEE) .... PAS
Program for Administrative Traffic Reports On-Line [*Computer program*] [*Bell System*] .... PATROL
Program Affinity Grouping and Evaluation System (NITA) .... PAGES
Program-Aid Routine [*Data processing*] .... PAR
Program Aid Software Systems [*Data processing*] (IEEE) .... PASS
Program for Algebraic Sequences Specifically of Input-Output Nature [*Data processing*] .... PASSION
Program Analysis [*Data processing*] (CGC) .... PA
Program Analysis Adaptable Control [*Data processing*] .... PAAC
Program Analysis for Documentation [*Data processing*] .... PAD
Program Analysis and Evaluation Model (IEEE) .... PAEM
Program for Analysis, Reporting, and Maintenance [*Data processing*] (TUT) .... PARMA
Program Application Instructions [*Telecommunications*] (TEL) .... PA
Program Applique a la Selection et a la Compilation Automatique de la Litterature [*Centre National de la Recherche Scientifique-Informascience*] [*Bibliographic database*] (OBD) .... PASCAL
Program Appraisal and Review (IEEE) .... PAR
Program Attention Key [*Data processing*] .... PA
Program Attention Key [*Data processing*] (BUR) .... PAK
Program. Automated Library and Information Systems [*England*] [*A publication*] .... Program Autom Libr Inf Syst
Program for Automatic Coding Techniques [*Data processing*] .... PACT
Program Booking Center [*Telecommunications*] (TEL) .... PBC
Program as Broadcast [*Radio*] (DEN) .... P-as-B
Program Check Interruption [*Data processing*] (MDG) .... PCI
Program Communication Block (NITA) .... PCB
Program Compiler [*Data processing*] (IEEE) .... PROCOMP
Program Control Block [*Data processing*] (BUR) .... PCB
Program Control Counter (NITA) .... PCC
Program Control Facility (NITA) .... PCF
Program Control Register .... PCR
Program Control Table [*Data processing*] .... PCT
Program Control Unit [*Data processing*] .... PCU
Program Control Word (NITA) .... PCW
Program Controlled Computer (DIT) .... PCC
Program-Controlled Interruption [*Data processing*] (IBMDP) .... PCI
Program Counter .... PC
Program Counter .... PCTR
Program Data Processing Section .... PDPS
Program Data Source (BUR) .... PDS
Program Design Data .... PDD
Program Design Language (NASA) .... PDL
Program Development System [*Data processing*] .... PDS
Program Development Tracking System [*Data processing*] .... PDTS
Program Document Requirement (BUR) .... PDR
Program Element (AFM) .... PE
Program Element Number [*Data processing*] (KSC) .... PEN
Program Error Note [*Data processing*] .... PEN
Program Evaluation for Repetitive Manufacture (IEEE) .... PERM
Program Evaluation Research Task (IEEE) .... PERT
Program Evaluation and Review Technique [*Data processing*] [*Computer performance management*] .... PERT
Program Evaluation and Review Technique Simulation [*Game*] .... PERTSIM
Program Evaluation and Review Technique/Time Analyzer [*Sperry UNIVAC*] (CDH) .... PERT/TIME
Program Evaluator and Tester [*Data processing*] .... PET
Program Event Recording [*Data processing*] (MDG) .... PER
Program Execution Request (NITA) .... PER
Program Execution System (NITA) .... PES
Program and File Analysis (NITA) .... PFA
Program File Processor (NITA) .... PFP
Program Function [*Data processing*] (IBMDP) .... PF
Program Generation System [*Data processing*] (MDG) .... PGS
Program Generic [*Data processing*] (TEL) .... PG
Program Identification Code (MUGU) .... PIC
Program Incident Report (NITA) .... PIR
Program Indicator Code (CMD) .... PI
Program Information Control and Retrieval System (NASA) .... PICRS
Program Information Coordination and Review Service (NASA) .... PICRS
Program Information File .... PIF
Program for Information Managers [*Later, AIM*] [*An association*] .... PRIM
Program Instruction [*Data processing*] (BUR) .... PI

Computer & Telecommunications Acronyms

Program Instruction, Calibration [*Marine Corps*] ... PIC
Program Instruction Tape [*Data processing*] (IEEE) ... PIT
Program Interface Control Plan (NASA) ... PICP
Program Interrupt ... PI
Program Interrupt Control [*Data processing*] ... PIC
Program Interrupt Entry [*Data processing*] ... PIE
Program Interrupt Word (NITA) ... PIW
Program Language Analyzer [*Data processing*] (IEEE) ... PLAN
Program for Learning in Accordance with Needs [*Westinghouse Learning Corp.*] ... PLAN
Program Level Change [*Data processing*] (IBMDP) ... PLC
Program Library Tape [*Data processing*] (IEEE) ... PLT
Program Library Update System (TUT) ... PLUS
Program for Linguistic Analysis of Natural Plants (IEEE) ... PLANT
Program Logic [*Data processing*] (TEL) ... PL
Program Logic Network (NASA) ... PLN
Program Logical Address Space (NITA) ... PLAS
Program Logistics and Network Scheduling System (IEEE) ... PLANS
Program Management Plan ... PMP
Program Management Responsibility Transfer (MCD) ... PMRT
Program Management System [*Data processing*] ... PMS
Program Master Tape ... PMT
Program Module Dictionary (OA) ... PMD
Program Monitoring (MUGU) ... PM
Program Monitoring and Diagnosis ... PMD
Program Monitoring and Planning Techniques (IEEE) ... PROMPT
Program Network Diagram [*Telecommunications*] (TEL) ... PND
Program. News of Computers in Libraries [*A publication*] ... Program News Comput Libr
Program for Numeric Tool Operation [*Data processing*] ... PRONTO
Program of Operation [*Data processing*] ... PROGOFOP
Program Operation Mode ... POM
Program for Operator Scheduling [*Bell System computer program*] ... POPS
Program for Optical System Design ... POSD
Program Performance Measurement Systems (IEEE) ... PPMS
Program Printout (MCD) ... PPO
Program in Process [*Data processing*] (BUR) ... PIP
Program Product [*Data processing*] ... PP
Program Production Library [*Data processing*] ... PPL
Program Reader Assembly [*Data processing*] ... PRA
Program Reference Table ... PRT
Program Register [*Data processing*] (BUR) ... PR
Program Requirements Package [*Data processing*] ... PRP
Program for Research in Information Systems Engineering [*University of Michigan*] [*Research center*] (RCD) ... PRIZE
Program Selection Key [*Data processing*] (BUR) ... PSK
Program-Sensitive Malfunction ... PSM
Program Specification Block [*IBM Corp.*] ... PSB
Program Standards Checker [*Data processing*] ... PSC
Program Start (KSC) ... PS
Program Status Chart [*Data processing*] ... PSC
Program Status Documents [*Data processing*] (TUT) ... PSD
Program Status Doubleword (NITA) ... PSD
Program Status Information [*Data processing*] (MCD) ... PSI
Program Status Register (NITA) ... PSR
Program Status Word [*Data processing*] ... PSW
Program Storage Unit [*Data processing*] (MDG) ... PSU
Program Store [*Data processing*] (IEEE) ... PS
Program Structure Code (AFM) ... PSC
Program Summary (NG) ... PS
Program Support Control System ... PSCS
Program Support Requirements (KSC) ... PSR
Program Synchronization Table (CMD) ... PST
Program Temporary Fix [*Data processing*] ... PTF
Program Test System [*Data processing*] (IEEE) ... PTS
Program Test Tape [*Data processing*] (IEEE) ... PTT
Program Transfer Interface (NITA) ... PTI
Program Unit Counter ... PUNC
Program Update Library (NITA) ... PUL
Program Update Tape (NITA) ... PUT
Program Utility Routines [*Data processing*] ... PUR
Program Validation Services [*Data processing*] ... PVS
Programable Algorithm Machine [*Data processing*] ... PAM
Programable Algorithm Machine Assembly Language [*Data processing*] ... PAL
Programable Algorithm Machine High-Level Language [*Data processing*] ... PHIL
Programable Array Logic [*Data processing*] (IEEE) ... PAL
Programable Array Logic Assembler [*Data processing*] (IEEE) ... PALASM
Programable Asynchronous Clustered Teleprocessing (NITA) ... PACT
Programable Asynchronous Dual Line Adapter (NITA) ... PADLA
Programable Asynchronous Line Adapter (NITA) ... PASLA
Programable Automatic Comparator ... PAC
Programable Automation ... PA
Programable Buffer Interface Card [*Data processing*] (NASA) ... PBIC
Programable Character Generator (NITA) ... PCG
Programable Communication Processor (OA) ... PCP
Programable Communications Interface (NITA) ... PCI
Programable Communications Subsystem (NITA) ... PCS
Programable Data Terminal [*Digital Equipment Corp.*] (IEEE) ... PDT
Programable Delay Unit (NITA) ... PDU
Programable Format [*Perforating keyboard*] ... PF
Programable Front-End Processor [*Data processing*] ... PFEP

Programable Gate Array (NITA) ... PGA
Programable Graphics Processor (NITA) ... PGP
Programable Hand-Held Calculator (RDA) ... PHHC
Programable Implantable Medication System ... PIMS
Programable Input Buffer ... PIB
Programable Integrated Control Equipment ... PICE
Programable Integrated Processor (IEEE) ... PIP
Programable Interval Clock (NASA) ... PIC
Programable Interval Timer (DEEC) ... PIT
Programable Keyboard and Display [*Data processing*] (NASA) ... PKD
Programable Line Adapter (NITA) ... PLA
Programable Logic Array [*Data processing*] ... PLA
Programable Logic Control [*Data processing*] ... PLC
Programable Machine Controller ... PMC
Programable Machine Interface (MCD) ... PMI
Programable Microcomputer Module (NITA) ... PMM
Programable Multiplex [*Data processing*] (TEL) ... PMUX
Programable Network (NITA) ... PN
Programable Network Telecommunications Operating System (NITA) ... PRONTO
Programable Peripheral Interface (MCD) ... PPI
Programable Peripheral Interface Unit (NITA) ... PPIU
Programable Power Supply ... PPS
Programable Protocol Interface Board (NITA) ... PPIB
Programable Read-Only Memory [*Data processing*] ... PROM
Programable Remote Operation [*Computer Devices, Inc.*] (NITA) ... PRO
Programable Sampling Network Switch (OA) ... PSNS
Programable Signal Processor (MCD) ... PSP
Programable Sound Generator [*Atari, Inc.*] ... PSG
Programable Synchronous/Asynchronous Receiver (IEEE) ... PSAR
Programable Synchronous/Asynchronous Transmitter (IEEE) ... PSAT
Programable Terminal Multiplexer [*Texas Instruments, Inc.*] (NITA) ... PTM
Programable Test Console ... PTC
Programable Text Processor [*Programing language*] (CSR) ... PTP
Programable Timer Module (NITA) ... PTM
Programable Transformer Converter (MCD) ... PRTRNS
Programable Translation Array (NITA) ... PTA
Programable Video Interface (NITA) ... PVI
Programed Access/Security System [*Card Key Systems*] (NITA) ... PASS
Programed Accounts Receivable Extra Service [*Data processing*] ... PAREX
Programed Analysis Computer Transfer (KSC) ... PACT
Programed Application Library [*IBM Corp.*] (CDH) ... PAL
Programed Automatic Circuit Evaluator and Recorder ... PACER
Programed Automatic Circuit Tester ... PACT
Programed Automatic Communications Equipment ... PACE
Programed Automatic Welding System ... PAWS
Programed Cryptographic Facility [*Data processing*] ... PCF
Programed Data Processor ... PDP
Programed Data Quantizer ... PDQ
Programed Digital Automatic Control [*Data processing*] ... PRODAC
Programed Digital Logic ... PDL
Programed Digital Processor (CIT) ... PDP
Programed Editor and Automated Resources for Learning (NITA) ... PEARL
Programed Extended Time Sharing [*Data processing*] ... PETS
Programed Film Reader [*System*] ... PFR
Programed Frequency Amplitude Modulation ... PFAM
Programed Function Keyboard [*Data processing*] ... PFK
Programed Information [*Data processing*] (CGC) ... PI
Programed Input/Output (NITA) ... PIO
Programed Instruction ... PI
Programed Instruction Language Learning [*Data processing*] ... PILL
Programed Instruction Text ... PIT
Programed International Computer Environment [*International relations simulation game*] ... PRINCE
Programed Introduction (MCD) ... PI
Programed Language-Based Enquiry System (NITA) ... PLANES
Programed Learning Aid ... PLAID
Programed Logic for Automatic Teaching [*or Training*] Operations [*University of Illinois*] [*Programing language*] ... PLATO
Programed Math Tutorial [*National Science Foundation*] ... PMT
Programed Multiline Controller (NITA) ... PMLC
Programed Operators and Primitives [*Data processing*] (CGC) ... POP
Programed Processor System ... PPS
Programed Reviewing, Ordering, and Forecasting Inventory Technique ... PROFIT
Programed Sequential Control Language (NITA) ... PSCL
Programed Temperature Gas Chromatography ... PTGC
Programed Test Input (MCD) ... PTI
Programed Test Input System (MCD) ... PTIS
Programed Transmission Control (BUR) ... PTC
Programed Turn Phase ... PTP
Programer ... PG
Programer (AFM) ... PRGMR
Programer [*or Programing*] (CAH) ... PROG
Programer Advanced Debugging System [*Data processing*] ... PADS
Programer Appraisal Instrument [*Data processing*] (IEEE) ... PAI
Programer Aptitude Test ... PAT
Programer Assistance and Liaison [*Data processing*] ... PAL
Programer Operating Standards Technique ... POST
Programer-Oriented Graphics Operation (IEEE) ... POGO
Programer and Probability Analyzer [*Data processing*] (IEEE) ... PAPA
Programer Reference Manual [*Data processing*] ... PRM
Programer Test Station ... PTS

Programer and Timer .... PT
Programer Training Center .... PTC
Programer Work Station (NITA) .... PWS
Programer's Automatic Testing System (DEEC) .... PATSY
Programer's Utility Filing System (DIT) .... PUFS
Programing (MSA) .... PRGMG
Programing .... PROGMG
Programing Analysis Consulting Education (IEEE) .... PACE
Programing Computer [*Data processing*] .... PROC
[*A*] **Programing Language** [*1960*] [*Data processing*] (CSR) .... APL
[*A*] **programing language** [*1963*] (CSR) .... MENTOR
Programing Language [*Data processing*] .... PL
Programing Language for Allocation and Network Scheduling [*1975*] [*Data processing*] (CSR) .... PLANS
Programing Language for Automatic Checkout Equipment .... PLACE
Programing Language Committee [*CODASYL*] (NITA) .... PLC
Programing Language for Interaction and Teaching [*1966*] [*Data processing*] .... PLANIT
Programing Language/Microcomputers [*Intel Corp.*] [*1973*] [*Data processing*] (CSR) .... PL/M
Programing Language Nineteen-Hundred [*Data processing*] .... PLAN
[*A*] **Programing Language Shared Variable** [*Data processing*] .... APLSV
[*A*] **Programing Language/Structured** [*Data processing*] (CSR) .... APL/S
Programing Language for UNIVAC [*Universal Automatic Computer*] **Systems** [*Data processing*] (CSR) .... PLUS
[*A*] **Programing Language/University of Massachusetts** [*Data processing*] (CSR) .... APLUM
Programing Language, Version One [*Data processing*] (MCD) PL/1
Programing Languages for Machine Tools [*Conference*] .... PROLAMAT
Programing Languages for the Zilog [*Data processing*] (CSR) .... PLZ
Programing in Logic [*Programing language*] [*1970*] .... PROLOG
Programing Logic Manual (TUT) .... PLM
Programing Panels and Decoding Circuits (OA) .... PPDC
Programing Program Strela [*Data processing*] (CDH) .... PPS
Programing Request for Price Quotation [*Data processing*] .... PRPQ
Programing Status Report [*Data processing*] (TUT) .... PSR
Programing Support Monitor [*Texas Instruments, Inc.*] (NITA) .... PSM
Programing Support Representative [*IBM Corp.*] .... PSR
Programing System (OA) .... PS
Programing System Activity Log [*Data processing*] (TUT) .... PSAL
Programme on Exchange and Transfer of Information on Community Water Supply and Sanitation [*World Health Organization*] [*Information service*] (EISS) .... POETRI
Programmed Learning and Educational Technology [*A publication*] .... Program Learn and Educ Technol
Programmed Learning and Educational Technology [*A publication*] .... Programmed Learning
Programming and Computer Software [*A publication*] .... Program and Comput Software
Programming and Computer Software [*A publication*] .... Programming and Comput Software
Progress in Quantum Electronics [*A publication*] .... Prog Quantum Electron
Project (AFM) .... PROJ
Project for the Advancement of Coding Techniques .... PACT
Project Control (NASA) .... PC
Project Control Sheet [*Data processing*] .... PCS
Project Control System [*Data processing*] .... PCS
Project Control Tool (BUR) .... PCT
Project Cost Model [*Project Software Ltd.*] [*Software package*] [*British*] (NCC) .... PCM
Project Data Control (MCD) .... PDC
Project Engineering Graphics System [*Computer Aided Design Centre*] [*Software package*] [*British*] (NCC) .... PEGS
Project Evaluation and Review with Graphic Output (IEEE) .... PERGO
Project Identification [*Data processing*] .... PROJID
Project on Information Processing (IEEE) .... PIP
Project on Information Technology and Education [*Carnegie Corp. of New York*] (EANO) .... PITE
Project for Integrated Catalogue Automation [*Royal Netherlands Library*] [*Cataloging cooperative*] (EISS) .... PICA
Project Literacy US [*Joint project of American Broadcasting Company and Public Broadcasting Service*] .... PLUS
Project Management and Production Team Technique [*Data processing*] .... PROMPT
Project Management System [*IBM Corp.*] [*Data processing*] .... PMS
Project Network Analysis (DEEC) .... PNA
Project Number [*Data processing*] [*Online database field identifier*] .... PN
Project, Programer Number .... PPN
Project Software & Development, Incorporated [*Cambridge, MA*] [*Software manufacturer*] (DASOS) .... PSDI
Project Systems Control (MCD) .... PSC
Project Work Schedule [*Data processing*] .... PWS
Projected Data Display .... PDD
Projected Inactive Time [*Data processing*] .... PIT
Projected Return on Open Office Facilities [*Computer program*] .... PROOF
PROM [*Programable Read-Only Memory*] **Memory Board** (NITA) .... PMB
PROM [*Programable Read-Only Memory*] **Programer Board** (NITA) .... PPB
Promisel & Korn, Inc. [*Bethesda, MD*] [*Information service*] (EISS) .... P & KI
Proof of Analog Results through a Numerical Equivalent Routine [*Data processing*] .... PARTNER
Propagation Distribution [*Broadcasting*] .... P
Propellant Utilization Data Translator .... PUDT
Property and Liability Information System (CGC) .... PALIS
Property Services Agency Information on Construction and Architecture [*Property Service Agency Library Service*] [*Database*] (CUAD) .... PICA
Proportional Band (NITA) .... PB
Proportional Bandwidth .... PBW
Proportional-Plus Integral [*Digital control*] .... PI
Proportional-Plus Integral-Plus Derivative [*Digital control algorithm*] .... PID
Proposed United States of America Standard (CGC) .... PUSAS
Proprietary Computer Systems, Inc. [*Information service*] (EISS) .... PCS
Proprietary Software Systems [*Data processing*] (IEEE) .... PSS
Protect [*or Protection*] (MSA) .... PROT
Protected Memory Address (NITA) .... PMA
Protected Message Exchange (NITA) .... PMX
Protected Queue Area [*Data processing*] (BUR) .... PQA
Protection Engineers Group [*United States Telephone Association*] [*Telecommunications*] .... PEG
Protective Clothing Arrangement [*Telecommunications*] (TEL) .... PCA
Protective Connecting Arrangement [*Telecommunications*] (TEL) .... PCA
Protective Device (BUR) .... PD
Protein Identification Resource [*National Biomedical Research Foundation*] [*Information service*] (EISS) .... PIR
Protocol Computers [*NASDAQ symbol*] (NQ) .... PCII
Protocol Data Query [*Database*] [*National Institutes of Health*] (FDB) .... PDQ
Protocol Data Unit (CCD) .... PDU
Prototype Communications Processor (CIT) .... PCP
Prototype Language for Economic Analysis [*Data processing*] (EISS) .... PLEA
Prototype On-Line Instrument Systems [*Data processing*] .... POIS
Prototype Real-Time Optical Tracker [*Data processing*] .... PRTOT
Provincial-Municipal Simulator [*Computer-based urban management system*] .... PROMUS
Provisional Frequency Board [*ITU*] .... PFB
Provisional System Feature [*Telecommunications*] (TEL) .... PSF
Pseudo Interrupt Device (OA) .... PID
Pseudo Machine Code [*Data processing*] (BUR) .... PMC
Pseudoadder Tree [*Data processing*] .... PAT
Pseudoline Control Block [*Data processing*] .... PLCB
Pseudonoise .... PN
Pseudorandom Binary Sequence [*Data processing*] .... PRBS
Pseudorandom Binary Sequence Generator [*Data processing*] .... PRBSG
Pseudorandom Frequency Modulated [*Data processing*] (DDI) .... PRFM
Pseudorandom Noise .... PRN
Pseudorandom Number .... PN
Pseudorandom Number .... PRN
Pseudorandom Pulse .... PRP
Pseudorandom Sequence .... PRS
Psychological Abstracts Information Services [*American Psychological Association*] (EISS) .... PsycINFO
PTS [*Predicasts*] **Marketing and Advertising Reference Service** [*Cleveland, OH*] [*Information service*] (EISS) .... MARS
PTS [*Predicasts*] **New Product Announcements** [*Cleveland, OH*] [*Information service*] (EISS) .... NPA
PTS [*Predicasts*] **Regional Business News** [*Cleveland, OH*] [*Database*] [*Information service*] (EISS) .... RBN
Public Access Message System .... PAMS
Public Address [*Amplification equipment*] [*Communications*] .... PA
Public Address Intercom System .... PAIC
Public Address System .... PAS
Public Affairs Information, Inc. [*Sacramento, CA*] [*Database producer*] [*Information service*] .... PAI
Public Affairs Information Service [*New York, NY*] [*Bibliographic database*] [*A publication*] .... PAIS
Public Broadcasting Service [*Sometimes facetiously translated "Petroleum Broadcasting Service," because of many grants from oil companies*] [*Washington, DC*] .... PBS
Public Coin Box [*Telecommunications*] (TEL) .... PCB
Public Data Network .... PDN
Public Demographics, Incorporated [*Information service*] (EISS) .... PDI
Public Interest Computer Association [*Washington, DC*] (EANO) .... PICA
Public Libraries Automation Network [*California State Library*] [*Sacramento, CA*] .... PLAN
Public Message Service [*Western Union Corp.*] .... PMS
Public Network [*Telecommunications*] .... PN
Public Opinion Laboratory [*Northern Illinois University*] [*Research center*] (RCD) .... POL
Public Relations Society of America Online Information Service (EISS) .... PRLINK
Public Safety Answering Point [*Telecommunications*] (TEL) .... PSAP
Public Service Announcement .... PSA
Public Service Commission [*Usually, of a specific state*] .... PSC
Public Service Satellite Consortium [*Washington, DC*] [*Telecommunications*] [*Information service*] (EANO) .... PSSC
Public Services Satellite .... PSS
Public Switched Network (BUR) .... PSN
Public Switched Telephone Circuits [*Telecommunications*] (TEL) .... PSTC
Public Switched Telephone Network .... PSTN
Public Technology, Inc. [*Washington, DC*] [*Research center*] (RCD) .... PTI
Public Telecommunications Facilities Program [*Department of Commerce*] .... PTFP
Public Telecommunications Review [*A publication*] .... Public TC Review
Public Telecommunications Trust [*Proposed replacement for Corporation for Public Broadcasting*] .... PTT
Public Telephone Service [*or System*] [*Telecommunications*] (TEL) .... PTS

By Meaning

Public Television .... PTV
Public Utilities Commission [*Data traffic regulator*] .... PUC
Public Utility Research Center [*University of Florida*] [*Research center*] (RCD) .... PURC
Publication Date [*Online database field identifier*] (OBD) .... PD
Publication Type [*Online database field identifier*] (OBD) .... PT
Publication Year [*Online database field identifier*] (OBD) .... PY
Publications. Modern Language Association of America [*Database*] [*A publication*] .... PMLA
Publications Reference File [*Government Printing Office*] [*Database*] (MCD) .... PRF
Publications and Technical Literature Research Section [*Environmental Protection Agency*] (EISS) .... PTLRS
Publisher [*Online database field identifier*] (OBD) .... PU
Publishers' Association [*London, England*] (DIT) .... PA
Publishers' Databases Limited [*Publishing consortium*] [*British*] ... PDL
Publishers' Information Card [*Later, IBIS*] [*British*] (DIT) .... PIC
Publisher's Name [*Online database field identifier*] (OBD) ..... PB
Publisher's Name [*Online database field identifier*] (OBD) ..... PN
Pulsating Current .... PC
Pulse-Address MODEM .... PAM
Pulse-Address Multiple Access [*Satellite communications*] ...... PAMA
Pulse Amplifier .... PA
Pulse Amplifier/Symbol Generator .... PASG
Pulse Amplitude Code Modulation [*Electronics*] .... PACM
Pulse Amplitude Modulation [*Electronics*] .... PAM
Pulse Amplitude Modulation - Frequency Modulation [*Electronics*] ... PAM-FM
Pulse Analysis-Recording Information System .... PARIS
Pulse Analyzer Signal Generator .... PASG
Pulse Averaging Discriminator .... PAD
Pulse Burst Waveform .... PBWF
Pulse Code Modulation [*Telecommunications*] .... PCM
Pulse Code Modulation Master Unit [*Electronics*] (NASA) ...... PCMMU
Pulse Code Modulation/Nonreturn to Zero (KSC) .... PCM/NRZ
Pulse Code Modulation - Phase-Shift .... PCM-PS
Pulse Code Modulation Shared (MCD) .... PCMS
Pulse-Coded Processing System .... PCPS
Pulse Comparator .... PC
Pulse Comparator .... PCP
Pulse Count [*Telecommunications*] (TEL) .... PCT
Pulse-Count Modulation .... PCM
Pulse-Count Modulation (MSA) .... PCTM
Pulse Counter [*Data processing*] (MDG) .... PC
Pulse Counter Adapter (NITA) .... PCA
Pulse Delay Binary Modulation (MCD) .... PDBM
Pulse Delay Device .... PDD
Pulse Delta Modulation (IEEE) .... PDM
Pulse-Duration Modulation [*Data transmission*] .... PDM
Pulse Encoding [*Data processing*] .... PE
Pulse-Forming Network .... PFN
Pulse Frequency (MDG) .... PFR
Pulse-Frequency Distortion Analyzer .... PFDA
Pulse-Frequency Diversity [*Electronics*] (NG) .... PFD
Pulse Generator .... PG
Pulse Height Analysis [*Spectroscopy*] .... PHA
Pulse Intensity Modulation .... PIM
Pulse Interference Emitting (MCD) .... PIE
Pulse Interval Modulation .... PIM
Pulse Length .... PL
Pulse-Length Discriminator (IEEE) .... PLD
Pulse-Length Modulation .... PLM
Pulse Link Relay [*Telecommunications*] (TEL) .... PLR
Pulse Link Repeater [*Telecommunications*] (TEL) .... PLR
Pulse Mode Multiplex .... PMM
Pulse-Modulated Communications System .... PMCS
Pulse Modulation .... PM
Pulse Number Modulation .... PNM
Pulse Output (NITA) .... PO
Pulse Pair Repetition Frequency (MCD) .... PPRF
Pulse Position Modulation [*Radio data transmission*] .... PPM
Pulse Rate Frequency (MUGU) .... PRF
Pulse Rate Modulation .... PRM
Pulse Ratio (IEEE) .... PR
Pulse Recurrence Frequency .... PRF
Pulse Recurrence Frequency Discrimination [*Telecommunications*] (TEL) .... PRFD
Pulse Recurrence [*or Repetition*] Period (CET) .... PRP
Pulse Recurrence [*or Repetition*] Rate (MUGU) .... PRR
Pulse Recurrence [*or Repetition*] Time (CET) .... PRT
Pulse Repetition Frequency [*Data processing*] (CDH) .... PRF
Pulse Repetition Rate Modulation [*Data transmission*] [*Data processing*] (TEL) .... PRRM
Pulse Sequence Generation [*Instrumentation*] .... PSG
Pulse Shape Discriminator .... PSD
Pulse Shift Keying (CAAL) .... PSK
Pulse Time Modulation [*Radio*] .... PTM
Pulse Time Multiplex .... PTM
Pulse Transmission Mode (MCD) .... PTM
Pulse-Type Phase Detector (OA) .... PPD
Pulse-Width Coded .... PWC
Pulse-Width Encoder .... PWE
Pulse-Width Modulation [*Electronic instrumentation*] .... PWM
Pulse-Width Multiplier (IEEE) .... PWM
Pulsed Avalanche Diode Oscillator [*Telecommunications*] (IEEE) ... PAO
Pulsed Carrier without Any Modulation Intended to Carry Information (IEEE) .... PO
Pulsed Continuous Wave (IEEE) .... PCW
Pulsed LASER Annealing [*Semiconductor technology*] .... PLA
Pulsed LASER System .... PLS
Pulsed Light Source .... PLS
Pulsed Microwave Power .... PMP
Pulsed Power Amplifier .... PPA
Pulsed Ultrasound Doppler Velocity Meter .... PUDVM
Pulses per Inch (CMD) .... PPI
Pulses per Second [*Data transmission*] .... PPS
Pulses per Second [*Data transmission*] (DEN) .... PS
Pumped Tunnel Diode Transistor Logic .... PTDTL
Punch .... P
Punch (KSC) .... PCH
Punch (CAH) .... PNCH
Punch Card Accounting System [*Data processing*] .... PCAS
Punch Card Equipment [*Data processing*] (AFM) .... PCE
Punch Card Machine [*Data processing*] .... PCM
Punch Feed Read (CMD) .... PFR
Punch Off [*Data processing*] (BUR) .... PF
Punch On (NITA) .... PN
Punched Card [*Data processing*] .... PC
Punched Card Accounting Machine [*Data processing*] .... PCAM
Punched Card Control Unit [*Data processing*] .... PCCU
Punched Card Data Processing .... PCDP
Punched Card Machine System [*Data processing*] .... PCMS
Punched Card Punch [*Data processing*] (IEEE) .... PCP
Punched Card Reader [*Data processing*] (BUR) .... PCR
Punched Card Requisition [*Data processing*] (MCD) .... PCR
Punched Card System [*Data processing*] .... PCS
Punched Card Utility [*Data processing*] (TUT) .... PCU
Punched Paper Tape [*Data processing*] .... PPT
Punched Paper Tape Reader [*Data processing*] .... PPTR
Punched Tape [*Data processing*] .... PT
Punched Tape Block Reader [*Data processing*] .... PTBR
Punched Tape Reader [*Data processing*] .... PTR
Punched Tape Verifier [*Data processing*] .... PTV
Pupil Registering and Operational Filing [*Data processing*] .... PROF
Purchase Information, Gifts, Loans, Exchanges Tracking [*Suggested name for the Library of Congress computer system*] .... PIGLET
Purdue University Fast FORTRAN [*Formula Translation*] Translator [*Data processing*] .... PUFFT
Pure Time Sharing [*Data processing*] (IEEE) .... PTS
Push Button .... PB
Push-Button Data Generator (IEEE) .... PBDG
Push-Button Telephone .... PBT
Push Down Memory [*Data processing*] .... PDM
Push Down Memory MODEM [*Data processing*] .... PDMM
Push Down Stack Automaton [*Data processing*] .... PSA
Push-Effective Address [*Data processing*] (IEEE) .... PEA
Push-On, Pull-Off [*Data processing*] .... POPO
Push-Pull .... P-P
Push-Pull Output (DEN) .... PPO
Push to Talk .... PTT

Q

Quad In-Line (DEEC) .... QIL
Quad In-Line Package (DEEC) .... QUIP
Quad in Line [*Electronics*] [*Telecommunications*] (TEL) .... QUIL
Quad-Phase Shift Key .... QPSK
Quad Synchronous Adapter [*Perkin-Elmer*] (NITA) .... QSA
Quadraphonic .... QUAD
Quadratic Programing [*Data processing*] (BUR) .... QP
Quadrature Amplitude Modulation .... QAM
Quadrature Amplitude Modulation (MCD) .... QTAM
Quadrature Amplitude Modulation (IEEE) .... QUAM
Quadrature Amplitude Shift Keying .... QASK
Quadrature Partial-Response System [*Telecommunications*] (TEL) ...... QPRS
Quadrature Sideband Amplitude Modulation .... QSAM
Quadrex Corp. [*NASDAQ symbol*] (NQ) .... QUAD
Quadriatic Arc Computer .... QUAC
Quadriplexer (SKY) .... QDXR
Quadrupole Flip-Flop [*Data processing*] .... QFF
Quadrupole Mass Spectrometer .... QMS
Quadrupole Resonance Response .... QRR
Quality (KSC) .... QUAL
Quality Assurance [*Data processing*] .... QA
Quality Assurance Data System .... QADS
Quality Assurance Systems Analysis Review (FAAC) .... QASAR
Quality Control [*or Controller*] .... QC
Quality Control Data .... QCD
Quality Data System (NASA) .... QDS
Quality Micro Systems [*Trademark*] .... QMS
Quality and Reliability Assurance .... Q & RA
Quality of Service [*Telecommunications*] (TEL) .... QOS
Quality Technology Information Service [*Atomic Energy Authority*]
    [*British*] (EISS) .... QUALTIS
Quantek Corporation [*Trademark*] .... QC
Quantile-Quantile [*Data processing*] .... Q-Q
Quantitative Computer Management (IEEE) .... QCM
Quantized Frequency Modulation .... QFM
Quantized Frequency Modulation Repeater .... QFMR
Quantized Pulse Modulation .... QPM
Quantizer (MDG) .... QNT
Quantizer, Analyzer, and Record Keeper [*Telecommunications*]
    (TEL) .... QUARK
Quantum Chemistry Program Exchange .... QCPE
Quantum Corp. [*NASDAQ symbol*] (NQ) .... QNTM
Quantum Counter .... QC
Quarter Word Designator [*Data processing*] .... Q
Quasi-Linear Sequential Machine .... QSM
Quasi-Stellar Source .... QSS
Quasi-Very-Long-Baseline Interferometry .... QVLBI
Quaternary Coherent Phase-Shift Keying .... QCPSK
Quaternary Differential Phase-Shift Keying (TEL) .... QDPSK
Quebec-Telephone [*Toronto Stock Exchange symbol*] .... QT
Query .... Q
Query .... QU
Query Analyzer (IEEE) .... QA
Query Evaluation and Search Technique (NITA) .... QUEST
Query by Example [*Data processing search method*] .... QBE
Query Formulation and Encoding .... QFE
Query Interactive Processor (IEEE) .... QUIP
Query Language [*1975*] (CSR) .... Q
Query Language [*Data processing*] (DIT) .... QL
Query Language Processor [*Data processing*] .... QLP
Query Normalization (NITA) .... QN
Query Online Terminal Assistance [*Data processing*] .... QUOTA
Query and Reporting Processor (NITA) .... QRP
[*A*] Query and Retrieval Interactive Utility System [*Data
    processing*] .... AQUARIUS
Query System [*Data processing*] (NITA) .... QS
Questar Corp. [*NYSE symbol*] .... STR
Question Analysis Transformation and Search [*Data processing*] ......
    .... QUANTRAS
Question-Answering System .... QAS
Questronics, Inc. [*NASDAQ symbol*] (NQ) .... QSTX
Queue (DEEC) .... Q
Queue Control Block [*Data processing*] .... QCB

Queue Entry (NITA) .... QE
Queue Full (NITA) .... QF
Queue Input/Output (NITA) .... QIO
Queue Length [*Telecommunications*] (TEL) .... QL
Queue Line Sharing Adapter [*Data processing*] (NITA) .... QLSA
Queue Manager [*Data processing*] (CMD) .... QM
Queue Run-Time [*Data processing*] (NITA) .... QRT
Queue Search Limit [*Data processing*] (NITA) .... QSL
Queue Select [*Data processing*] (NITA) .... QS
Queued Access Method [*Data processing*] .... QAM
Queued Indexed Sequential Access Method [*IBM Corp.*] [*Data
    processing*] (TUT) .... QISAM
Queued Sequential Access Method [*IBM Corp.*] [*Data processing*]
    (TUT) .... QSAM
Queued Telecommunications Access Method [*IBM Corp.*] [*Data
    processing*] (CGC) .... QTAM
Queued Terminal Access Method [*Data processing*] (NITA) .... QTAM
Queued Transaction Handling [*Data processing*] (NITA) .... QTH
Queuing Theory [*Telecommunications*] .... QT
Queuing Time [*Telecommunications*] (TEL) .... QT
Quick and Dirty [*Data processing*] (CGC) .... Q & D
Quick and Effective System to Enhance Retrieval [*Data
    processing*] .... QUESTER
Quick FORTRAN [*Programing language*] [*1979*] (DEEC) .... QUICKTRAN
Quick FORTRAN [*Programing language*] [*1979*] (CSR) .... QWIKTRAN
Quick Relocate and Link (NITA) .... QRL
Quick Text Editor .... QED
Quiesce-Completed [*Data processing*] (IBMDP) .... QC
Quiesce-at-End-of-Chain [*Data processing*] (IBMDP) .... QEC
Quiescent Aerial [*or Antenna*] .... QA
QUOTA [*Query Online Terminal Assistance*] Input Processor [*Data
    processing*] .... QUIP
Quotation Request .... QR

R

R-Register [Data processing]	R
RADAUS [Radio-Austria AG] Data-Service [Vienna] [Telecommunications] (TSSD)	RDS
Radiation Detection, Indication, and Computation [Radiological measuring instruments]	RADIAC
Radiation Experience Data [Food and Drug Administration] [Database] (FDB)	RED
Radiation Subprogramme Data Center	RSDC
Radically Tapered Antenna	RTA
Radio	RAD
Radio	RDO
Radio Acoustic Ranging	RAR
Radio Affiliate Replacement Plan [Canadian Broadcasting Corporation]	RARP
Radio Amateur Emergency Network (IEEE)	RAEN
Radio Amateur Satellite Corp. [An association] (EANO)	AMSAT
Radio Attenuation Measurement [Spacecraft for testing communications]	RAM
Radio Attenuation Measurement Project	RAMP
Radio Beacon	R/B
Radio Beam Communications	RBC
Radio Beam Communications Set	RBCS
Radio Bearing (DEN)	RB
Radio Berlin International	RBI
Radio Brenner [Radio network] [West Germany]	RB
Radio Canada International	RCI
Radio Club of America	RCA
Radio Club of America	RCOA
Radio Code Aptitude Area	RC
Radio Code Aptitude Test	RCAT
Radio Code Test, Speed of Response	RCTSR
Radio Collectors of America (EANO)	RCA
Radio Command [or Control] (KSC)	R/C
Radio Command Guidance	RCG
Radio Command Linkage	RCL
Radio Command System	RCS
Radio Common Carrier	RCC
Radio Common Channels	RCC
Radio Communications Center	RCC
Radio Communications and Electronic Engineers Association	RCEEA
Radio Communications Equipment	RCE
Radio Communications Instruction (MUGU)	RCI
Radio Communications Link Repeater (FAAC)	RCLR
Radio Communications Link Terminal (FAAC)	RCLT
Radio Communications Monitoring Association (EANO)	RCMA
Radio Communications Set	RCS
Radio Compass	RC
Radio Control Operator	RCO
Radio-Controlled Aerial Target	RCAT
Radio-Controlled Ultraviolet Measurement Program (MUGU)	RUMP
Radio Corporation of America Communications (MCD)	RCAC
Radio Digital Distance Magnetic Indicator (MCD)	RDDMI
Radio Digital System [Telecommunications] (TEL)	RDS
Radio Digital Terminal [Bell System]	RDT
Radio Direction Finder [or Finding]	RDF
Radio Direction Finder Station	RDFSTA
Radio Doppler Inertial	RDI
Radio Duties - Special	RS
Radio Electrician	RE
Radio Electrician	RELE
Radio and Electronic Component Manufacturers' Federation	RECMF
Radio Electronica [Netherlands] [A publication]	Radio Electron
Radio-Electronics [A publication]	Radio-Electr
Radio-Electronics [A publication]	Radio-Electron
Radio Electronics and Communications Systems [A publication]	Radio Electron Commun Syst
Radio and Electronics Measurements Committee [London, England] (DEN)	REMC
Radio-Electronics-Television Manufacturers Association [Later, Electronic Industries Association]	RETMA
Radio Emergency Associated Citizens Teams [Acronym alone is now used as official association name] (EANO)	REACT
Radio Emergency Search Communications Unit	RESCU
Radio Engineering and Electronic Physics [A publication]	Radio Eng Electron Phys
Radio Engineering and Electronic Physics [A publication]	Radio Engrg Electron Phys
Radio Engineering and Electronic Physics (USSR) [A publication]	Radio Eng Electron (USSR)
Radio Exposure	RE
Radio Facility Charts	RFC
Radio Free Europe	RFE
Radio Free Europe/Radio Liberty	RFE/RL
Radio Frequency [Transmission]	RF
Radio Frequency Amplifier	RFA
Radio Frequency Chart	RFC
Radio Frequency Choke	RFC
Radio Frequency Compatibility	RFC
Radio Frequency Crystal	RFC
Radio Frequency Horn Technique	RFHT
Radio Frequency Impedance Probe	RFIP
Radio Frequency Indicator	RFI
Radio Frequency Interchange (MDG)	RFI
Radio Frequency Interference	RFI
Radio Frequency Interference Meter	RFIM
Radio Frequency Interference Tests (KSC)	RFIT
Radio Frequency Joint	RFJ
Radio Frequency Noise	RFN
Radio Frequency Oscillator	RFO
Radio Frequency Seal	RFS
Radio-Frequency Shift (IEEE)	RFS
Radio Inertial (MCD)	RI
Radio Influence	RI
Radio-Influence Field (IEEE)	RIF
Radio Inspector	RI
Radio Interference (MCD)	RI
Radio Liberty	RL
Radio Maintenance Unit (DEN)	RMU
Radio Nacional de Espana [Radio network] [Spanish Sahara]	RNE
Radio Navigation	RN
Radio-Navigation Mobile	RNM
Radio Navigational Aids [NATO] (NATG)	RNA
Radio Network for Inter-American Telecommunications	RIT
Radio-Newsreel-Television Working Press Association	RNTWPA
Radio Noise Burst Monitor (MCD)	RNBM
Radio Noise Figure (CET)	RNF
Radio Noise Interference Test	RNIT
Radio Noise Voltage	RNV
Radio Noncontingent	RNC
Radio Operational Intercom System (KSC)	ROIS
Radio Operator	RO
Radio Operator/Maintenance Driver	ROMAD
Radio, Optical, Inertial	ROI
Radio Optical Observatory	ROO
Radio Positioning Mobile Station [ITU designation] [Telecommunications] (CET)	PO
Radio Projects Management Office	RPMO
Radio Proximity Fuze	RPF
Radio Range	RNG
Radio Range	RR
Radio Range Station Reported Unreliable [Message abbreviation]	RARU
Radio Readout	RDO
Radio Receiver Set	RRS
Radio Receptor Company	RRC
Radio Recognition	RR
Radio Recording Spectrophotometer	RRS
Radio Regulations	RR
Radio Relay	RR
Radio Relay Center (NATG)	RRC
Radio Relay Link (NATG)	RRL
Radio Relay Message Unit [Telecommunications] (TEL)	MUR
Radio Relay Pod	RRP
Radio Relay Station	RRS
Radio Relay System	RRS
Radio Remote Set (CAAL)	RRS
Radio Research	RR

Radio Research Board (DEN)	RRB
Radio Research Company	RRC
Radio Research and Development Establishment (MCD)	RRDE
Radio Research Laboratory	RRL
Radio Science [*A publication*]	Radio Sci
Radio Science [*A publication*]	RAS
Radio Science [*A publication*]	RASCA
Radio Set Control Group	RSCG
Radio Shack Computer Alumni Association (EANO)	RSCAA
Radio Simulation Patch Panel (CET)	RSPP
Radio Simulator	RS
Radio Solar Telescope Network (MCD)	RSTN
Radio Spectrum Measurement System [*National Telecommunications and Information Administration*]	RSMS
Radio Squadron Mobile (MUGU)	RSM
Radio Standards Laboratory [*National Bureau of Standards*]	RSL
Radio Subsystem (CIT)	RSS
Radio Switch Panel	RSP
Radio Switchboard (CAAL)	RS
Radio Technical Commission for Aeronautics [*Washington, DC*]	RTCA
Radio Technical Commission for Marine Services [*Later, RTCM*]	RTCMS
Radio Technical Commission for Maritime Services (EANO)	RTCM
Radio-Tele-Luxembourg	RTL
Radio Telefis Eireann [*Radio and television network*] [*Ireland*]	RTE
Radio Telegraph (MSA)	RTLG
Radio Telegraph Station	R Sta
Radio Telegraphy	RT
Radio Telemetry	RTel
Radio Telephone (MSA)	RT
Radio Telephony (MSA)	RTEL
Radio Telescope Network	RTN
Radio Telescope in Orbit (IEEE)	RATIO
Radio Teletype (IEEE)	RADIT
Radio and Teletype Control Center (DDI)	RATTC
Radio Teletypewriter (CET)	RADTT
Radio/Television Repair Program [*Association of Independent Colleges and Schools specialization code*]	RT
Radio and Television Research Council	RTRC
Radio Tower	R TR
Radio Tracking (KSC)	RT
Radio Tracking System Analyst (MUGU)	RTSA
Radio Trans-Europe	RTE
Radio Transmission Control (NATG)	RTC
Radio Transmission Control Panel (NATG)	RTCP
Radio Transmission Facility	RTF
Radio Transmission Frequency Measuring System (DDI)	RTFMS
Radio Transmitter	RT
Radio Trunk Extension (NATG)	RTE
Radio Tuned Circuit (DEN)	RTC
Radio Vehicle (DEN)	RV
Radio Wave Propagation	RWP
Radiobeacon Calibration Transmitter	RCT
Radiodiffusion Nationale Khmere [*Radio network*] [*Khmer Republic*]	RNK
Radiodiffusion-Television Belge [*Radio and television network*] [*Belgium*]	RTB
Radiodiffusion-Television Francaise [*Radio and television network*] [*France*]	RTF
Radiodiffusion Television Ivoirienne [*Radio and television network*] [*Ivory Coast*]	RTI
Radiodiffusion Television du Senegal [*Radio and television network*] [*Senegal*]	RTS
Radiodiffusion Television (Upper Volta) [*Radio and television network*]	RTV
Radiodifusion Argentina al Exterior [*Broadcasting organization*]	RAE
Radiolocation	RL
Radiolocation Mobile Station [*ITU designation*]	MR
Radiological Safety Analysis Computer (MCD)	RSAC
Radiometric Age Data Bank [*Geological Survey*] (EISS)	RADB
Radiotelegram	R
Radiotelegraph	RATG
Radiotelegraph	RTG
Radiotelegraphy	RT
Radiotelemetric Theodolite	RTT
Radiotelemetry and Remote Control (MCD)	RTRC
Radiotelemetry Subsystem (CIT)	RTS
Radiotelephone	RATEL
Radiotelephone	RT
Radiotelephone	RTF
Radiotelephone Operator	RATELO
Radiotelephone Operator	RTO
Radiotelephony	R/T
Radioteletype	RATT
Radioteletypewriter	RTT
Radioteletypewriter	RTTY
Radioteletypewriter Set	RTS
Radiotelevisao Portuguesa [*Radio and television network*] [*Portugal*]	RTP
Radiotelevisione Italiana [*Italian government-controlled radio and television company*]	RAI
Radiotelevisione Italiana [*Italian government-controlled radio and television company*]	RAITV
Rag Chewers' Club [*Amateur radio*]	RCC
Ragen Corp. [*NASDAQ symbol*] (NQ)	RAGN
Railroad Crossing [*Telecommunications*] (TEL)	RRX
Railroad Telegraphers Union	RTU
Railway Telegraph and Telephone Appliance Association	RTTAA
Rainbow Network Communications [*Floral Park, NY*] [*Telecommunications*] (TSSD)	RNC
RAM Address Register (OA)	RAAR
RAM Input/Output Timer (NITA)	RIOT
Rand Information Systems [*NASDAQ symbol*] (NQ)	RINS
Rand Intelligent Terminal Agent (DEEC)	RITA
Random Access [*Data processing*]	RA
Random Access Communications System	RACS
Random Access Computer Equipment	RACE
Random Access Control Equipment (IEEE)	RACE
Random Access and Correlation for Extended Performance	RACEP
Random Access Data (BUR)	RAD
Random Access Delta Modulation	RADEM
Random Access Device	RAD
Random Access Disc (MCD)	RAD
Random Access Discrete Address System	RADAS
Random Access Document Indexing and Retrieval	RADIR
Random Access Indestructive Advanced Memory [*Data processing*] (MSA)	RAIAM
Random Access Information Retrieval [*Data processing*] (IEEE)	RAIR
Random Access and Inquiry [*Data processing*]	RAI
Random Access Measurement [*System*] [*Data processing*]	RAM
Random Access Measurement System [*Data processing*]	RAMS
Random Access Memory [*Data processing*]	RAM
Random Access Memory Buffer [*Data processing*]	RAMB
Random Access Memory Device [*Data processing*]	RAMD
Random Access Memory Module [*Data processing*]	RAMM
Random Access Memory Store [*Data processing*] (TEL)	RAMS
Random Access Method of Accounting and Control [*Data processing*]	RAMAC
Random Access Nondestructive Advanced Memory [*Data processing*]	RANDAM
Random Access Parallel Tape	RAPTAP
Random Access Personnel Information Dissemination (IDA)	RAPID
Random Access Program [*Data processing*]	RAP
Random Access Programing and Checkout Equipment	RAPCOE
Random Access Projector	RAP
Random Access Secure Communications Antijam Link	RASCAL
Random Access Storage and Control [*Data processing*]	RASTAC
Random Access Storage and Display [*Data processing*]	RASTAD
Random Access Video Editing [*Computerized film editing*]	RAVE
Random Angle Modulation	RAM
Random Block Number [*Data processing*]	RBN
Random Communication Satellite	RANCOM
Random Communication Satellite System	RCSS
Random Digit Dialing [*Telecommunications*]	RDD
Random Evolutionary Operation	REVOP
Random Filing System (NITA)	RFS
Random House, Inc. [*NYSE symbol*] [*Delisted*]	RH
Random Input Describing Function [*Data processing*]	RIDF
Random Input Sampling [*Data processing*] (TUT)	RIP
Random Logic	RL
Random Mass Storage [*Data processing*] (TUT)	RMS
Random Multiple Access (NITA)	RMA
Random Splice [*Telecommunications*] (TEL)	RS
Range [*Maps and charts*] (MDG)	RGE
Range Automated Information System (KSC)	RAIS
Range Data Processor (MCD)	RDP
Range Endurance Speed and Time [*Computer*]	REST
Range Estimating and Evaluation Procedure [*Data processing*]	REEP
Range Extender with Gain [*Bell System*]	REG
Range Frequency Synthesizer	RFS
Range Information Display System (MCD)	RIDS
Range Instrumentation and Support Systems	RISS
Range of Jamming	ROJ
Range, Maximum	RMAX
Range and Range Rate	RRR
Range Rate Frequency Synthesizer	RRFS
Rank Annihilation Factor Analysis [*Data processing*]	RAFA
Rapid Access Data [*Xerox Corp.*] (NITA)	RAD
Rapid Access Device (NITA)	RAD
Rapid Access Disk	RAD
Rapid Access Drive (BUR)	RAD
Rapid Access Management Information System [*Data processing*] (CGC)	RAMIS
Rapid Access Recording (IEEE)	RAR
Rapid Access Tariff Expediting Service [*Journal of Commerce, Inc.*] [*Database*] (CUAD)	RATES
Rapid Alphanumeric Digital Indicating Device	RANDID
Rapid Automatic Checkout Equipment	RACE
Rapid Digital Automatic Computing	RADAC
Rapid Item Processor to Facilitate Complex Operations on Magnetic Tape Files [*Data processing*]	RIPFCOMTF
Rapid Serial Visual Presentation [*Data processing*]	RSVP
Rapid Transmission and Storage [*Goldmark Corp.*] [*TV system*]	RTS
Rapidata Interactive Text Editor (IEEE)	RITE
Rapidly Extensible Language System [*Data processing*] (CSR)	REL
Rapra Trade Names [*Rapra Technology Ltd.*] [*Information service*] (EISS)	RAPTN
Rare Disease Database [*National Organization for Rare Disorders*] [*Information service*] (EISS)	RDB

RASD [*Reference and Adult Services Division*] **Machine-Assisted Reference Section** ... RASD MARS
Raster Image Processor [*Printer technology*] ... RIP
Rate-Aided Tracking Computer ... RATC
Rate Center [*Telecommunications*] (TEL) ... RC
Rate of Information Throughput [*Data processing*] (BUR) ... RIT
Rate Input Form (NVT) ... RIF
Ratio Transformer [*Unit*] (CDH) ... RT
Rational FORTRAN [*Data processing*] ... RATFOR
Rational Number (MDG) ... R
Raumordnung, Stadtebau, Wohnungswesen, Bauwesen [*Regional Policy, Urban Development, Housing and Civil Engineering*] [*Database*] (ODIN) ... RSWB
Raw Data Recorder (NASA) ... RDR
Raw Data System (DDI) ... RADS
Raymond Engineering [*NASDAQ symbol*] (NQ) ... REIN
Raytheon Acoustic Telemetry and Control ... RATAC
Raytheon Airborne Microwave (MCD) ... RAM
Raytheon Airborne Microwave Platform [*Sky station*] ... RAMP
Raytheon Automatic Drafting Artwork Compiler ... RADAC
Raytheon Automatic Test Equipment Language [*Data processing*] (CSR) ... RATEL
Raytheon Communications Equipment [*Citizens band radio*] ... RAY-COM
Raytheon Controlled Inventory [*Data processing*] ... RAYCI
Raytheon Data Systems Co. ... RDS
Raytheon Digital Automatic Computer (MUGU) ... RAYDAC
Raytheon Resistor [*Electro-optical control device*] ... RAYSISTOR
Raytheon Spectrum Analyzer ... RAYSPAN
Raytheon Telephone [*Citizens band radio*] ... RAY-TEL
RCA Cable and Rockefeller Center Cable Pay-TV Program Service ... RCTV
RCA Corp. [*Formerly, Radio Corporation of America*] [*NYSE symbol*] ... RCA
RCA Corporation Communications ... RCC
Re-Entrant Process Allocator [*Telecommunications*] (TEL) ... RPA
Re-Entrant Processor (NITA) ... REP
Reaction Access System [*Computer program*] ... REACCS
Reactive Bias Circuit (MCD) ... RBC
Reactive Ion Etching [*Semiconductor technology*] ... RIE
Reactive Modulation Amplifier (OA) ... RMA
Reactive Terminal Service [*International Telephone & Telegraph computer*] ... RTS
Reactor and Plant Integrated Dynamics [*Data processing*] (KSC) ... RAPID
Read ... R
Read ... RD
Read Access Key (NITA) ... RAK
Read Address Counter ... RAC
Read Back [*Communications*] (FAAC) ... RB
Read Buffer ... RB
Read Channel Continue ... RCC
Read Channel Initialize ... RCI
Read and Compute ... RC
Read Data (NITA) ... RD
Read Data Check (CMD) ... RDC
Read Direct (OA) ... RD
Read Forward ... RF
Read-In (DEN) ... RI
Read-In Counter (NITA) ... RIC
Read Interrupt Mask [*Data processing*] ... RIM
Read/Modify/Write (OA) ... R/M/W
Read/Mostly [*Data processing*] (TEL) ... R/M
Read-Mostly Memory [*Data processing*] ... RMM
Read-Mostly Mode [*Data processing*] ... RMM
Read Only [*Data processing*] (IBMDP) ... RO
Read-Only Memory [*Computer memory*] [*Data processing*] ... ROM
Read-Only Memory Module [*Data processing*] ... ROMM
Read-Only Storage [*Data processing*] ... ROS
Read-Only Storage Address Register (NITA) ... ROSAR
Read-Only Storage Data Register (NITA) ... ROSDR
Read-Only Tape Handler (NITA) ... ROTH
Read Program Memory [*Data processing*] (MDG) ... RPM
Read, Punch, and Interpret (NITA) ... RPI
Read Tape Binary [*Data processing*] (IEEE) ... RTB
Read after Write (NITA) ... RAW
Read and Write [*Data processing*] ... RAW
Read-Write [*Data processing*] (MSA) ... R-W
Read, Write, and Compute ... RWC
Read-Write-Continue [*Data processing*] ... RWC
Read/Write Extend Delete (NITA) ... RWED
Read-Write-Initialize [*Data processing*] ... RWI
Read-Write Memory [*Data processing*] (MCD) ... RWM
Read/Write Register (NITA) ... RWR
Read-Write Tape [*Data processing*] ... RWT
Read-Write-Verify [*Data processing*] ... RWV
Readable (CDH) ... RDBL
Reader (MSA) ... RDR
Reader Action Service [*ZIP code computer*] ... REACTS
Reader Printer ... RP
Reader Punch (OA) ... RP
Reader/Sorter Processor (NITA) ... RSP
Reader Stop [*Data processing*] (BUR) ... RS
Reader Tape Contact ... RTC
Reader's Comment Form (IBMDP) ... RCF
Readiness Data ... RD
Readout ... RDOUT
Readout Matrix ... RM
Readout Memory (IEEE) ... ROM
Readout and Relay ... RR
Readout Technique ... RT
Ready ... RDY
Ready-Access [*Telecommunications*] (TEL) ... RA
Ready for Data (IEEE) ... RFD
Ready for Installation (MCD) ... RFI
Ready for Next Message (NITA) ... RFNM
Ready for Service (DDI) ... RFS
Real ... R
Real Circuit (NITA) ... RC
Real Estate Data, Incorporated [*Information service*] (EISS) ... REDI
Real Estate Information Network [*Electronic service*] ... REIN
Real Estate Management Information System (BUR) ... REMIS
Real and Not Corrected Input Data [*Data processing*] ... RANCID
Real Storage (NITA) ... RS
Real Storage Management [*Data processing*] (IBMDP) ... RSM
Real Storage Page Table [*Data processing*] (BUR) ... RSPT
Real Time [*Computer*] ... RT
Real-Time Acquisitions Management and Bibliographic Order System [*Suggested name for the Library of Congress computer system*] ... RAMBO
Real-Time Adaptive Control (NITA) ... RTAC
Real-Time Analyzer [*Electronics*] ... RTA
Real-Time Basic [*Data processing*] (MDG) ... RTE-B
Real-Time Batch Monitor [*Xerox Corp.*] (NITA) ... RBM
Real-Time BIT [*Binary Digit*] **Mapping** (DEEC) ... RTBM
Real-Time Cinetheodolite Data System ... RTCDS
Real-Time Clock [*Data processing*] (MCD) ... RTC
Real-Time Command [*Data processing*] ... RTC
Real-Time Communication System (NITA) ... RTCS
Real-Time Communications [*RCA*] ... REALCOM
Real-Time Communications Processor (NASA) ... RTCP
Real-Time Computer (CIT) ... RTC
Real-Time Computer Complex ... RCC
Real-Time Computer Complex ... RTCC
Real-Time Computer Facility (CIT) ... RTCF
Real-Time Computer Science Corp. [*Camarillo, CA*] [*Software manufacturer*] (DASOS) ... RTCS
Real-Time Computer System ... RTCS
Real-Time Control [*Data processing*] (MCD) ... RTC
Real-Time Counter [*Data processing*] (SKY) ... RTC
Real-Time Data Acquisition (NITA) ... REDAC
Real-Time Data Channel (IEEE) ... RTDC
Real-Time Data Distribution ... RTDD
Real-Time Data Handling System ... RTDHS
Real-Time Data Manager (MCD) ... RDM
Real-Time Data System ... RTDS
Real-Time Data Translator (CIT) ... RTDT
Real-Time Debugging Aid (NITA) ... RDA
Real-Time Digital Data Correction (MUGU) ... RTDDC
Real-Time Disk-Operating System [*Data processing*] ... RDOS
Real-Time Display ... RTD
Real-Time Electronic Access and Display [*System*] [*Data processing*] ... READ
Real-Time Event Monitor [*Data processing*] (IEEE) ... REMOS
Real-Time Executive [*Data processing*] (TUT) ... RTE
Real-Time Executive (OA) ... RTX
Real-Time Executive Routine [*Data processing*] ... REX
Real-Time Executive System [*SEMIS*] (NITA) ... RTES
Real-Time FORTRAN [*Data processing*] (CIT) ... RTF
Real-Time Graphic Display ... RTGD
Real-Time Information Retrieval System ... RTIRS
Real-Time Input/Output Controller [*Data processing*] (IEEE) ... RTI/OC
Real-Time Input-Output Transducer [*or Translator*] [*Data processing*] ... RIOT
Real-Time Language [*Data processing*] (IEEE) ... RTL
Real-Time Memory System (NITA) ... RTMS
Real-Time Monitor [*Systems Engineering Labs*] ... RTM
Real-Time Multiplexer Display ... RTMD
Real-Time Multiprograming Operating System [*Data processing*] (IEEE) ... RTMOS
Real-Time Multiprograming System (NITA) ... RTMS
Real-Time Operating System [*Control Data Corp.*] (CIT) ... RTOS
Real-Time Peripheral (IEEE) ... RTP
Real-Time Procedural Language [*Data processing*] (MDG) ... RTPL
Real-Time Profiler [*Instrumentation*] ... RTP
Real-Time Program Management (CIT) ... RTPM
Real-Time Programing System [*Data processing*] (IEEE) ... RPS
Real-Time Quality Control ... RTQC
Real-Time Readout ... RTR
Real-Time Readout ... RTRO
Real-Time Reconnaissance Cockpit Display System [*or Subsystem*] ... RTRCDS
Real-Time Rescheduling Subsystem ... RTRS
Real-Time Scheduling Display System (CIT) ... RTSDS
Real-Time Signal Processor (NVT) ... RTSP
Real-Time Simulation Facility (MCD) ... RTSF
Real-Time Subroutines (OA) ... RTS
Real-Time Switching System (SKY) ... RSS
Real-Time System ... RTS
Real-Time Telemetry Data ... RTTD

Computer & Telecommunications Acronyms

Real-Time Telemetry Data System	RTTDS
Real-Time Telemetry System (CIT)	RTTS
Real-Time Television	RTTV
Real-Time Terminal Application Program System [Data processing]	RTAPS
Real-Time Video	RTV
Real-Time Video Processing	RTVP
Realisations et Etudes Electronique [French computer manufacturer] (NITA)	R2E
Rearward Communications System (MDG)	RCS
Reason for Backlog [Telecommunications] (TEL)	RFB
Reason for Outage (FAAC)	RFO
Rebroadcast Link [Aerial]	RBL
Recall (MSA)	RCL
Receive (AFM)	RCV
Receive Clock Pulse (NITA)	RCP
Receive Data Register [Data processing] (MDG)	RDR
Receive Hub [Telegraph] [Telecommunications] (TEL)	RH
Receive Leg [Telecommunications] (TEL)	RL
Receive Not Ready [Data processing] (IEEE)	RNR
Receive Only	RO
Receive-Only Center (FAAC)	R/OC
Receive-Only Page Printer	ROPP
Receive-Only Printer [Data processing]	ROP
Receive-Only Typing Reperforator	ROTR
Receive-Only Typing Reperforator - Series to Parallel	ROTR-S/P
Receive Processor (NITA)	RP
Receive Ready [Data processing] (IEEE)	RR
Receive Reference Equivalent [Telecommunications] (TEL)	RRE
Receive-Transmit [Radio]	RT
Received Data (IEEE)	RD
Received Line Signal Detector	RLSD
Received Signal Level [Telecommunications] (TEL)	RSL
Received Text	RT
Receiver	R
Receiver	RCVR
Receiver	REC
Receiver	RECR
Receiver [or Reception] [Radio] (NATG)	RX
Receiver-Carrier Detector	RCD
Receiver Cuts Out [Telecommunications] (TEL)	RCO
Receiver and Data Processor (MCD)	RDP
Receiver Data from Unit Control (MCD)	RDUC
Receiver/Exciter (CIT)	RE
Receiver Holding Register (NITA)	RHR
Receiver Incremental Tuning	RIT
Receiver Intermodulation [Telecommunications] (TEL)	RIM
Receiver, Mobile	RM
Receiver Noise Figure	RNF
Receiver Off the Hook	R-O-H
Receiver-Off-Hook Tone Connecting Circuit	ROTCC
Receiver Only [Radio]	RONLY
Receiver Processor Unit [Electronics]	RPU
Receiver Station	RS
Receiver Threshold Test (CET)	RTT
Receiver/Transmitter [Radio] (KSC)	R/T
Receiver-Transmitter-Modulator	RTM
Receiver/Transmitter Unit	RTU
Receiving Inspection Data Status [Report]	RIDS
Receiving Memo	RM
Receiving Objective Loudness Rating [Telephones] (IEEE)	ROLR
Receiving-Only Monitor	ROMON
Receiving Ship [or Station]	RS
Receiving Station	RECSTA
Receiving Tube	RT
Reception Nil [Radio logs]	RN
Reception Node (NITA)	RN
Reception Poor [Radio logs]	RP
Reception Station	RS
Rechtswissenschaftliche Experten und Gutachter [NOMOS Datapool] [Database] (CUAD)	REX
Recognition and Control Processor [Data processing] (IBMDP)	RCP
Recognition Equipment, Inc. [NYSE symbol]	REC
Recognition Memory [Semionics Associates] [Data processing]	REM
Recognition Technologies Users Association (EANO)	RTUA
Recommended Standard [Telecommunications] (TEL)	RS
Recomp Algebraic Formula Translator [Data processing]	RAFT
Recomp Computer Interpretive Program Expediter [Data processing]	RECIPE
Recomp Users Group [Data processing]	RUG
Recomplement (CDH)	RECOMP
Reconfiguration and Fault Detection Unit (OA)	RFDU
Reconfiguration Maximum Theoretical Bandwidth (NITA)	RMTB
Reconnaissance Satellite	RS
Record	RCD
Record	REC
Record Carrier Competition Act [1981]	RCCA
Record Control Word [Data processing]	RCW
Record Count [Data processing]	RC
Record Definition Field [Data processing] (BUR)	RDF
Record Description [Data processing]	RD
Record Element Specification [Data processing]	RES
Record Extraction, Manipulation, and Print (DEEC)	REMAP
Record Length (NITA)	RL
Record Length Register (NITA)	RLR
Record Management System (NITA)	RMS
Record Mark (BUR)	RM
Record Number [Online database field identifier] (OBD)	RCN
Record Number [Online database field identifier] (OBD)	RN
Record/Retransmit (IEEE)	R/R
Record Select Program [Data processing] (TUT)	RSP
Record Separator [Control character] [Data processing]	RS
Recordak Automated Information Retrieval [System]	RAIR
Recorded Announcement [Telecommunications] (TEL)	R/A
Recorded Announcement [Telecommunications] (TEL)	RCAN
Recorded Information Service [Telecommunications] (TEL)	RIS
Recorded Voice Announcement [Telecommunications] (IBMDP)	RVA
Recorder and Communications Control (NASA)	R & CC
Recorder and Communications Control Panel (NASA)	RCCP
Recorder Switch Unit	RSU
Recording Completing [Trunk] [Telecommunications] (TEL)	RC
Recording Demand (DEN)	RD
Recording Industry Association of America [Formerly, Record Industry Association of America] [New York, NY]	RIAA
Records and Analysis Subsystem (TEL)	RAS
Records Arrival Date [Bell System] (TEL)	RAD
Records Issue Date [Bell System] (TEL)	RID
Records per Sector [Data processing] (NITA)	RPS
Recover [or Recovery]	REC
Recovery (KSC)	RECOV
Recovery Communications Network (SKY)	RCN
Recovery Management Support [Data processing]	RMS
Recovery Termination Management [Data processing]	RTM
Recreation Information Management [Department of Agriculture] [Database] (FDB)	RIM
Recreation Resources Center [University of Wisconsin] [Research center] (RCD)	RRC
Recreation Systems Analysis [Data processing]	RECSYS
Rectangular Concrete Columns [Jacys Computing Services] [Software package] [British] (NCC)	RCC
Rectangular Wave Modulation (IEEE)	RWM
Rectified Alternating Current [Radio]	RAC
Rectifier Enclosure Unit [Power supply] [Telecommunications] (TEL)	REU
Recurrent Fault Analysis [Telecommunications] (TEL)	RFA
Recursive Queue Analyzer (IEEE)	RQA
Red Especial de Transmision de Datos [Spanish telephone co.] (TEL)	RETD
Red Green Blue [Video monitor]	RGB
Red Green Blue Intensity [Video monitor]	RGBI
Redifon Analog-Digital Computer [British]	RADIC
Redstone Computer	RECOMP
Reduce [or Reduction]	RED
Reduced Delta Code Modulation [Digital memory]	RDCM
Reduced Instruction Set Computer	RISC
Reduced-Size Antenna Monopulse System	RAMS
Reduction of Electrical Demand Using Computer Equipment [Energy Management System]	REDUCE
Reed Switching Matrix	RSM
Reel	RL
Reel Sequence [Data processing]	RS
Reentrant Data Processing	REDAP
Reentry Antenna Test	RANT
Reeves Electronic Analog Computer	REAC
Reference [Online database field identifier] (OBD)	RE
Reference [Online database field identifier] (NATG)	REF
Reference [Online database field identifier] (OBD)	RF
Reference Clock [Telecommunications] (TEL)	RC
Reference Equivalent [Telecommunications] (TEL)	RE
Reference Indication Number	RIN
Reference Librarian Enhancement System [University of California] [Online microcomputer system]	REFLES
Reference Link Control Unit [Telecommunications] (TEL)	RLCU
Reference Our TWX [Teletypewriter communications] (FAAC)	ROTWX
Reference Radio	RERAD
Reference Register [Data processing]	RR
Reference Telegram	REFTEL
Reference Telephonic Power (DEN)	RTP
Reference Transmission Level Point [Telecommunications] (CBSS)	RTLP
Reference Your TWX [Teletypewriter Communications] (FAAC)	RUTWX
Referred-to-Input (CIT)	RTI
Referred-to-Output (CIT)	RTO
Reflect Array Pulse Compressor (RDA)	RAC
Reflecting Satellite Communication Antenna	RESCAN
Reflection Loss [Telecommunications] (TEL)	RL
Reflector Antenna System	RAS
Refractive Index Sounding System	RISS
Refractory Metal-Oxide Semiconductor (IEEE)	RMOS
Regeln fuer die Alphabetische Katalogisierung [Rules for Alphabetical Cataloging] [Information retrieval] (ODIN)	RAK
Region Control Block [Data processing] (BUR)	RCB
Region Control Task [Data processing] (BUR)	RCT
Region Internal Computer Code [Data processing]	RGICC
Regional Accounting Office [Telecommunications] (TEL)	RAO
Regional Data Associates [Information service] (EISS)	RDA
Regional Data Center	RDC
Regional Frequency Supplies [Telecommunications] (TEL)	RFS

Regional Highway Traffic Model [*Database*] [*No longer available online*] (CUAD) .... RHTM
Regional Operations Control Center [*AT & T*] .... ROCC
Regional Operations Control Centre Information Display System [*NORAD*] .... RIDS
Regional Processing Unit (NITA) .... RPU
Regional Telecommunications Hub [*Telecommunications*] (TEL) .... RTH
Regional User Group [*Data processing*] .... RUG
Register .... REG
Register .... REGIS
Register and Arithmetic/Logic Unit [*Data processing*] .... RALU
Register Enforced Automated Control Technique [*Cash register-computing system*] .... REACT
Register File (NITA) .... RF
Register and Indexed Storage (MCD) .... RX
Register for International Service in Education [*Information service*] (EISS) .... RISE
Register Memory (NITA) .... RM
Register Output (NITA) .... RO
Register to Register (MCD) .... RR
Register Select (NITA) .... RS
Register Sender Inward [*Telecommunications*] (TEL) .... RSI
Register Sender Outward [*Telecommunications*] (TEL) .... RSO
Register and Storage (MCD) .... RS
Register Storage Unit (NITA) .... RSU
Register Traffic [*Telecommunications*] (TEL) .... RT
Register Transfer [*Data processing*] .... RT
Register Transfer Language [*Data processing*] (CSR) .... RTL
Register Transfer Level (NITA) .... RTL
Register Transfer Module [*Data processing*] (MDG) .... RTM
Register-Transistor Logic [*Data processing*] .... RTL
Register Translator [*Telecommunications*] (TEL) .... R/T
Registered Business Programer [*Offered earlier by Data Processing Management Association, now discontinued*] (IEEE) .... RBP
Registered Organization Data Bank .... RODATA
Registered Protective Circuit .... RPC
Registry of Toxic Effects of Chemical Substances [*NIOSH*] [*Database*] .... RTECS
Reglement du Service International des Telecommunications de l'Aeronautique .... RSITA
Reglement Telegraphique [*Telegraph Regulations*] [*French*] .... RTG
Regression Testing [*Data processing*] (IEEE) .... RT
Regulatory Information Service [*Congressional Information Service, Inc.*] [*Bethesda, MD*] [*Telecommunications*] .... RIS
Rehabilitation Budgeting Program [*Telecommunications*] (TEL) .... REBUD
Rehabilitation Engineering Center for the Hearing Impaired [*Gallaudet College*] [*Research center*] (RCD) .... REC
Reinforced Concrete Column [*Camutek*] [*Software package*] [*British*] (NCC) .... RCCOL
Reinforced Concrete Design [*Camutek*] [*Software package*] [*British*] (NCC) .... RCB
Reject (MSA) .... REJ
Reject Sequence Number [*Data processing*] .... RSN
Rejection Message [*Communications*] (FAAC) .... RJT
Relational Algebraic Interpreter (NITA) .... RAIN
Relational Associative Processor (IEEE) .... RAP
Relational Database (NITA) .... RDB
Relational General Information System (NITA) .... REGIS
Relational Machine Language (NITA) .... RML
Relational Memory Systems [*San Jose, CA*] [*Hardware manufacturer*] (DASO) .... RELMS
Relative .... REL
Relative Address Programing Implementation Device [*Data processing*] .... RAPID
Relative Byte Address [*Data processing*] (MCD) .... RBA
Relative Performance Score [*Telecommunications*] (TEL) .... RPS
Relative Record Data Set (NITA) .... RRDS
Relative Record Number [*Data processing*] .... RRN
Relative Retention Time .... RRT
Relative Time Clock [*Data processing*] (MDG) .... RTC
Relative Velocity Computer .... RVC
Relative Virtual Address (NITA) .... RVA
Relativistic Electron Beam Accelerator .... REBA
Relay (FAAC) .... RLA
Relay .... RLY
Relay Block (MSA) .... RB
Relay Computer (BUR) .... RC
Relay Logic .... RL
Relay Rack [*Telecommunications*] (TEL) .... RR
Relay Set [*Telecommunications*] (TEL) .... R/S
Relay Storage Unit .... RSU
Relay Switch Group .... RSG
Relay Tester (VIT) .... RT
Relay Transmitter (DDI) .... RT
Release .... REL
Release Guard [*Telecommunications*] (TEL) .... RG
Release Guard [*Telecommunications*] (TEL) .... RLG
Release-Quiesce [*Data processing*] .... RELQ
Release Timer [*Telecommunications*] (TEL) .... RLST
Reliability, Availability, Maintainability, Safety, and Human Factors [*Telecommunications*] (TEL) .... RAMSH
Reliability, Availability, and Serviceability [*IBM Corp. slogan*] (MCD) .... RAS
Reliability and Configuration Accountability System .... RECON
Reliability Corporate Memory (IEEE) .... RCM
Reliability Data Center (KSC) .... RDC
Reliability Data Extractor (MCD) .... RDE
Reliability Improvement Factor .... RIF
Reliability Index .... RI
Reliability, Maintainability, and Availability [*Standards*] (DDI) .... RMA
Reliability and Maintainability Program (NITA) .... RAMP
Reliability Test Data Report .... RTDR
Reliability Verification Tests (NITA) .... RVT
Reliable Block Diagram (MCD) .... RBD
Reliable Test Analyzer [*Data processing*] .... RTA
Religion Index [*American Theological Library Association*] [*Chicago, IL*] [*Bibliographic database*] (OBD) .... RELI
Reloadable Control Storage [*Data processing*] .... RCS
Relocatable [*Data processing*] .... REL
Relocatable Assembly Language Floating Point (NITA) .... RALF
Relocatable Input/Output (NITA) .... RIO
Relocatable Library [*Data processing*] .... RLIB
Relocatable Output [*Data processing*] .... RO
Relocating Linking Loader (NITA) .... RLL
Relocation Address (NITA) .... RA
Relocation Dictionary (DEEC) .... RLD
Remedial Action Program Information Center [*Department of Energy*] [*Information service*] (EISS) .... RAPIC
Remington Rand Corp. [*NASDAQ symbol*] (NQ) .... REMR
Remington Rand Corp. [*Later, a division of Sperry-Rand*] .... REM-RAND
Remote [*Telecommunications*] (TEL) .... R
Remote [*Telecommunications*] (MSA) .... RMT
Remote Access [*Data processing*] [*Telecommunications*] .... RAX
Remote Access Computer Technique [*Data processing*] (IEEE) .... RACT
Remote Access Computing System [*Data processing*] .... RACS
Remote Access Editing System [*Data processing*] (IEEE) .... RAES
Remote Access Immediate Response [*Data processing*] (TUT) .... RAIR
Remote Access Interactive Debugger [*Data processing*] (IEEE) .... RAID
Remote Access Key (NITA) .... RAK
Remote Access Planning for Institutional Development [*Data processing*] .... RAPID
Remote Access Switching and Patching (NITA) .... RASP
Remote Analog Submultiplexer (MCD) .... RASM
Remote Automatic Control System (KSC) .... RACS
Remote Automatic Telemetry Equipment .... RATE
Remote Batch Entry (CMD) .... RBE
Remote Batch Facility (NITA) .... RBF
Remote Batch Module (NITA) .... RBM
Remote Batch System (NITA) .... RBS
Remote Batch Terminal .... RBT
Remote Bulletin Board System [*For IBM computers*] .... RBBS
Remote Call Forwarding [*Bell System*] .... RCF
Remote Circuit Breaker (MCD) .... RCB
Remote Communication Outlet [*ATCS*] .... RCO
Remote Communications Central .... RCC
Remote Communications Complex .... RCC
Remote Communications Concentrator (NITA) .... RCC
Remote Communications Console .... RCC
Remote Computer (NITA) .... RC
Remote Computer Access Communications Service .... RCAC
Remote Computer Interface Unit (NITA) .... RCIU
Remote Computing Service .... RCS
Remote Computing Supplies [*Downers Grove, IL*] [*Hardware manufacturer*] (DASO) .... RCS
Remote Concentrator (NITA) .... RC
Remote Continual Verification [*Telephonic monitoring system*] .... RECOVER
Remote Control .... RC
Remote Control Amplifier (MCD) .... RCA
Remote Control Bandwidth .... RCB
Remote Control Circuit Breaker (NASA) .... RCCB
Remote Control Equipment (DIT) .... RCE
Remote Control Indicator (CAAL) .... RCI
Remote Control Interface (NITA) .... RCI
Remote Control Location .... RCL
Remote Control Panel .... RCP
Remote Control (System) (DEN) .... RC(S)
Remote Control System .... RCS
Remote Control Unit .... RCU
Remote-Controlled Air-Ground Communication Site (MCD) .... RCAG
Remote-Controlled Vehicle (MCD) .... RCV
Remote Data Access (NASA) .... RDA
Remote Data Acquisition Unit .... RDAU
Remote Data Collection (MCD) .... RDC
Remote Data Concentrator .... RDC
Remote Data Processor .... RDP
Remote Data Transmitter .... RDT
Remote Device Interface Unit (NITA) .... RDIU
Remote Digital Multiplexer (MCD) .... RDM
Remote Digital Readout .... RDR
Remote Digital Readout .... RDRD
Remote Digital Submultiplexer (KSC) .... RDSM
Remote Display Control Panel (MCD) .... RDCP
Remote Display Link .... RDL
Remote Electronic Alphanumeric Display [*Data processing*] (IEEE) .... READ
Remote Electronic Microfilm Storage Transmission and Retrieval (NITA) .... REMSTA
Remote Enable (IEEE) .... REN

Computer & Telecommunications Acronyms

Remote Entry Acquisition Package (CGC) ... REAP
Remote Entry Services (MCD) ... RES
Remote Exchange [Telecommunications] (TEL) ... RX
Remote File Access (NITA) ... RFA
Remote File Management System ... RFMS
Remote Graphics Processor ... RGP
Remote Information Management System (NITA) ... RIMS
Remote Information Query System [Information retrieval service] [Data processing] ... RIQS
Remote Information Retrieval and Management System [Data processing] (BUR) ... RIRMS
Remote Information System (NITA) ... RIS
Remote Input/Output Terminal [Data processing] ... RIOT
Remote Intercomputer Communications Interface (MCD) ... RICC
Remote Job Entry [Data processing] ... RJE
Remote Job Entry Terminal System [Data processing] (MCD) ... RJETS
Remote Job Output [Data processing] (NITA) ... RJO
Remote Job Processing [Data processing] ... RJP
Remote Job System [Data processing] (MCD) ... RJS
Remote Line Adaptor (NITA) ... RLA
Remote Line Switch [Telecommunications] (TEL) ... RLS
Remote Line Unit [Telecommunications] ... RLU
Remote/Local (NASA) ... R/L
Remote Maintenance, Administration, and Traffic System-1 [Telecommunications] (TEL) ... RMATS-1
Remote Maintenance Line [Bell Laboratories] ... RML
Remote Maintenance Monitor [Data processing] (MCD) ... RMM
Remote Maintenance System ... RMS
Remote Memory Port Interface (NITA) ... RMPI
Remote Monitoring and Control System [Telecommunications] ... RMCS
Remote Multiplexer [Data processing] (CAAL) ... RM
Remote Multiplexer Unit [Data processing] (KSC) ... RMU
Remote Network Access Controller (NITA) ... RNAC
Remote Network Processor ... RNP
Remote Office Test Line [Bell Laboratories] ... ROTL
Remote On-Line Business Information Network [Data processing] (IEEE) ... ROBIN
Remote Online Print Executive System (NITA) ... ROPES
Remote Operated Radiographic Inspection System ... RORIS
Remote Operator Facility [Honeywell, Inc.] (NITA) ... ROF
Remote Operator's Console ... ROC
Remote Optical Character Recognition [Data processing] ... ROCR
Remote Peripheral Equipment (IEEE) ... RPE
Remote Pickup ... RP
Remote Position Control ... RPC
Remote Power Controller ... RPC
Remote Printer (BUR) ... RP
Remote Printing System (NITA) ... RPS
Remote Processing Service (BUR) ... RPS
Remote Program Load (NITA) ... RPL
Remote Query Update System [Data processing] (DDI) ... RQUS
Remote Receiver (FAAC) ... RRCVR
Remote Record Address (NITA) ... RRA
Remote Safing Switch (VIT) ... RSS
Remote Scanner-Encoder Unit [Bell Laboratories] ... RSEU
Remote Sensing Institute [South Dakota State University] [Research center] (RCD) ... RSI
Remote Sensing On-Line Retrieval System [Canada Centre for Remote Sensing] [Database] [Information service] (EISS) ... RESORS
Remote Sensing Society (EANO) ... RSS
Remote Service Unit (NASA) ... RSU
Remote Spooling Communications Subsystem [IBM Corp.] [Data processing] (IBMDP) ... RSCS
Remote Station Alarm ... RSA
Remote Storage Activities ... RSA
Remote Store Controller (NITA) ... RSC
Remote Support Facility (NITA) ... RSF
Remote Switching System [Telecommunications] ... RSS
Remote Switching Unit [Telecommunications] ... RSU
Remote System Verification Program (NITA) ... RSVP
Remote Technical Assistance and Information Network [Data processing] ... RETAIN
Remote Telecommunications Access Method [Data processing] ... RTAM
Remote Terminal [Data processing] ... RT
Remote Terminal Access Method [Data processing] (BUR) ... RTAM
Remote Terminal Controller (NITA) ... RTC
Remote Terminal Emulator [For teleprocessing validation] ... RTE
Remote Terminal Input/Output (NITA) ... RTIO
Remote Terminal Interactive Processor (MCD) ... RTIP
Remote Terminal Interface Package (NITA) ... RTIP
Remote Terminal Network ... RTN
Remote Terminal Supervisor (CMD) ... RTS
Remote Terminal Unit ... RTU
Remote Test Access [Telecommunications] (TEL) ... RTA
Remote Test System [Bell System] ... RTS
Remote Timing and Data Distribution ... RTDD
Remote Trunk Arrangement [Telecommunications] (TEL) ... RTA
Remote Tuning Technique ... RTT
Remote User Shared Hardware [Data processing] (DDI) ... RUSH
Remote User Terminal [Data processing] (CAAL) ... RUT
Remotely Accessible Management Systems [Data processing] ... RAMS
Removable Media Memory Units ... RMMU

Renton Electrical Analog for Solution of Thermal Analogous Networks ... REASTAN
Reorder Tone Trunks [Telecommunications] (TEL) ... ROTT
Repair of Repairables (MCD) ... ROFR
Repair Service Bureau [Telecommunications] (TEL) ... RSB
Repair Sevice Attendant [Telecommunications] (TEL) ... RSA
Repeat ... RPT
Repeat Attempt [Telecommunications] (TEL) ... R/A
Repeat Indication [Telecommunications] (TEL) ... RI
Repeated Back [Communications] (FAAC) ... RB
Repeater (CDH) ... RP
Reperforator [Telecommunications] (TEL) ... REPERF
Reperforator/Transmitter [Teletypewriter] [Data processing] ... R/T
Repertoire Analytique d'Articles de Revues de Quebec [Database] [A publication] ... RADAR
Repertoire des Banques de Donnees en Conversationnel [Database] (CUAD) ... REBK
Repetitive [Electronics] ... R
Repetitive Operation [Data processing] (MDG) ... REP-OP
Replacement Algorithm (OA) ... RA
Replication [Telecommunications] (TEL) ... REP
Replication Synchronization Process [Telecommunications] (TEL) ... RSP
Reply Paid ... RP
Reply Paid Telegram ... RPT
Reply by TWX [Teletypewriter communications] (FAAC) ... REPTWX
Report Collection Index [Studsvik Energiteknik AB] [Database] (CUAD) ... RECODEX
Report. Computer Centre. University of Tokyo [A publication] ... Rep Comput Centre Univ Tokyo
Report Format Generator (NITA) ... RFG
Report Generator (CMD) ... RG
Report Generator Language [Data processing] (IEEE) ... RGL
Report Heading (BUR) ... RH
Report of Observation/Samples Collected by Oceanographic Programs [Bureau National des Donnees Oceaniques] [Database] (CUAD) ... ROSCOPS
Report Program Generator [Programing language] [1962] ... RPG
Report Writer [Data processing] ... R/W
Reporting File (NITA) ... RF
Reporting Unit Code [Data processing] ... RUC
Reports Management System [Office of Management and Budget] [Database] (FDB) ... RMS
Representation Dependent Accessing Language (NITA) ... RDAL
Representation-Independent Programing Language (NITA) ... RIPL
Representation-Language Language [Data processing] ... RLL
Reproductive Toxicology [Database] ... REPROTOX
Reprogramable Programable Read-Only Memory [Data processing] (TEL) ... REPROM
Reprogramable Read-Only Memory [Data processing] (KSC) ... REPROM
Request ... REQ
Request Block (NITA) ... RB
Request for Data Services ... RDS
Request for Information ... RFI
Request Loading Entry [Data processing] ... RLE
Request Monitor Entry [Data processing] ... RME
Request Next Character (NITA) ... RNC
Request for Next Message (OA) ... RENM
Request Parameter List [Data processing] (BUR) ... RPL
Request for Price Quotation ... RPQ
Request for Programing [Data processing] (CIT) ... RFP
Request Programs Termination [Data processing] ... RPT
Request for Proposal ... RFP
Request for Quotation ... RFQ
Request-Response Header [Data processing] (BUR) ... RH
Request/Response Unit [Data processing] ... RU
Request, Retrieve, and Report [Data processing] (TUT) ... 3R
Request Select Entry [Data processing] ... RSE
Request to Send (NITA) ... RS
Request to Send ... RTS
Required ... REQD
Requirement ... REQT
Requirements Analysis Package [Data processing] ... RAP
Requirements Engineering and Validation System (NITA) ... REVS
Requirements Planning System [Data processing] (TUT) ... RPS
Requirements Statement Analyzer (NITA) ... RSA
Requirements Statement Language ... RSL
Requires ... REQS
Requisition Due Date (TEL) ... RDD
Requisition Received Date [Bell System] (TEL) ... RRD
Reroute [Telecommunications] (TEL) ... RR
Reroute Inhibit [Telecommunications] (TEL) ... RRI
Research in Advanced Communications in Europe [European Commission] ... RACE
Research and Advanced Development ... RAD
Research on Automatic Computation Electronics ... RACE
Research in Automatic Photocomposition and Information Dissemination ... RAPID
Research Computation Laboratory [University of Houston] [Research center] (RCD) ... RCL
Research Computing Center [University of New Hampshire] [Research center] (RCD) ... RCC
Research and Development ... R & D

Computer & Telecommunications Acronyms

Research and Development Information System [*Later, EPD/RDIS*] [*Electric Power Research Institute*] [*Information service*] (EISS) .... RDIS
Research and Engineering Information Services [*Exxon Research & Engineering Co.*] (EISS) .... REIS
Research and Evaluation Methods Program [*University of Massachusetts*] [*Research center*] (RCD) .... REMP
Research Highlights [*A publication*] (DIT) .... RH
Research Information Center and Library [*Foster Wheeler Corp.*] [*Information service*] (EISS) .... RICAL
Research Information Service [*John Crerar Library*] [*Information service*] (EISS) .... RIS
Research Information System [*Rehabilitation Services Administration*] (EISS) .... RIS
Research Institute for Advanced Computer Science [*University Space Research Association*] [*Research center*] (RCD) .... RIACS
Research Institute of America [*New York, NY*] [*Information service*] (EISS) .... RIA
Research Institute for Information Science and Engineering, Inc. [*Information service*] (EISS) .... RIISE
Research Laboratory of Electronics [*MIT*] [*Research center*] .... RLE
[*The*] Research Libraries Group, Inc. [*Database producer*] .... RLG
Research Libraries Information Network [*Pronounced "arlen"*] [*Formerly, BALLOTS*] [*Library network*] [*Information service*] .... RLIN
Research Referral Service [*International Federation for Documentation*] [*Information service*] (EISS) .... RRS
Research Services Ltd. [*Database producer*] (CUAD) .... RSL
Reset (MDG) .... R
Reset (MDG) .... RE
Reset [*Telecommunications*] (TEL) .... RST
Reset Control Circuit .... RCC
Reset-Set [*Data processing*] (CIT) .... RS
Reset-Set Trigger .... RST
Resident Access Methods (MCD) .... RAM
Resident Assembler Program (NITA) .... RAP
Resident Monitor (NITA) .... RMON
Resident Operating System (NITA) .... ROS
Resident Programer Analyst [*Data processing*] .... RPA
Resident Supervisor Call (BUR) .... RSVC
Resident Terminal Access Method [*Data processing*] .... RTAM
Residual Error Rate (DEEC) .... RER
Residual Master File [*Data processing*] .... RMF
Resistance [*Symbol*] [*IUPAC*] .... R
Resistance Capacitance .... RC
Resistance Coupled (CIT) .... RC
Resistance-Coupled Transistor Logic (DDI) .... RCTL
Resistance Temperature Detector .... RTD
Resistive Insulated-Gate Field Effect Transistor (NITA) .... RIGFET
Resistive Read-Only Storage (NITA) .... RROS
Resistor .... R
Resistor-Capacitor .... R-C
Resistor-Capacitor Transistor Logic .... RCTL
Resistor Color Code (DEN) .... RCC
Resistor Diode Logic (NITA) .... RDL
Resistor Diode Transistor Logic (IEEE) .... RDTL
Resistor Logic (IEEE) .... RL
Resistor Transistor .... RT
Resistor-Transistor Logic [*Data processing*] (BUR) .... RTL
Resolution of Initial Operational Techniques .... RIOT
Resolver/Quantizer (IEEE) .... R/Q
Resonant Frequency Tracking System .... REFTS
Resonant Gate Transistor .... RGT
Resource Access Control Facility [*IBM Corp.*] .... RACF
Resource Allocation Processor (CMD) .... RAP
Resource Control Block [*Data processing*] (IBMDP) .... RCB
Resource Definition Table [*Data processing*] (IBMDP) .... RDT
Resource Identification Table [*Data processing*] .... RSID
Resource Interface Module [*Datapoint*] (NITA) .... RIM
Resource Management Consultants [*Salem, NH*] [*Telecommunications*] (TSSD) .... RMC
Resource Manager (NITA) .... RM
Resource Measurement Facility [*Data processing*] .... RMF
Resource Request Generator (NITA) .... RRG
Resource-Sharing Time-Sharing System (NITA) .... RSTS
Resource Utilization Factor (NITA) .... RUF
Resource Utilization Monitor (NITA) .... RUM
Resource Vector Table [*Data processing*] (IBMDP) .... RVT
Resources in Computer Education [*Northwest Regional Educational Laboratory Microcomputer Software and Information for Teachers*] [*Database*] .... RICE
Resources in Education [*Formerly, Research in Education*] [*National Institute of Education*] [*Database*] .... RIE
Response Analysis Program [*Data processing*] (IBMDP) .... RAP
Response Data Word (MCD) .... RDW
Response Segmentation and Validation Program [*Donnelley Marketing Information Services*] [*Information service*] (EISS) .... RSVP
Response/Throughput Bias [*Data processing*] (BUR) .... RTB
Response Time [*Data processing*] .... RT
Response Time Module (OA) .... RTM
Response Time Reporting (NITA) .... RTR
Responsible Reporting Office [*Telecommunications*] (TEL) .... RRO
Responsive Environment Programed Laboratory (IEEE) .... REPLAB
Restoration Control Point [*Telecommunications*] (TEL) .... RCP

Restoration Priority (CET) .... RP
Restoration Priority [*Telecommunications*] (TEL) .... RSP
Restore (NITA) .... RES
Restricted Bandwidth Techniques (NG) .... REBAT
Retail Computer Facilities .... RCF
Retail Information System (BUR) .... RIS
Retape .... RETP
Retention Register [*Data processing*] .... RETR
Retention Time [*Data processing*] .... RT
Retired in Place [*Telecommunications*] (TEL) .... RIP
Retransmission Identity Signal [*Telecommunications*] (TEL) .... RIS
Retransmission Request Signal [*Telecommunications*] (TEL) .... RRS
Retrieval Analysis and Presentation System [*Data processing*] (TUT) .... RAPS
Retrieval through Automated Publication and Information Digest [*Data processing*] (DIT) .... RAPID
Retrieval Command Language [*Computer search language*] (DEEC) .... RECOL
Retrieval and Composition (DIT) .... RECOMP
Retrieval of Enriched Textual Abstracts [*Information retrieval program*] .... RETA
Retrieval of Information by On-Line Terminal [*Atomic Energy Authority*] [*Data processing*] [*British*] .... RIOT
Retrieval by Online Search [*Data processing*] .... ROSE
Retrieval and Processing Information for Display (DDI) .... RAPID
Retrieval and Sort Processor [*Data processing*] .... RASP
Retrieval by Title Words, Descriptors, and Classification (DIT) .... REWDAC
Retrieve (KSC) .... RETR
Retrieve (MCD) .... RETRV
Retrofit Installation Data (MCD) .... RID
Retrospective Bibliographies on Magnetic Tape (NASA) .... RBMT
Retrospective Machine Readable Catalog [*Carrollton Press, Inc.*] [*Arlington, VA*] [*Bibliographic database*] [*Online version of the US Library of Congress Shelflist*] (OBD) .... REMARC
Return Address (NITA) .... RA
Return Address Register (NITA) .... RAR
Return Beam Vidicon [*Satellite camera*] .... RBV
Return Beam Vidicon Camera .... RBVC
Return Control Word (NITA) .... RCW
Return Data Word (MCD) .... RDW
Return from Exception [*Data processing*] .... RTE
Return Loss .... RL
Return Rate (IEEE) .... RR
Return Register (NITA) .... RR
Return and Restore Status Register [*Data processing*] .... RTR
Return from Subroutine [*Data processing*] .... RTS
Return-to-Zero [*Recording scheme*] .... RTZ
Return-to-Zero Recording [*Data processing*] .... RZ
Revenue Analysis from Parametric Usage Descriptions [*Telecommunications*] (TEL) .... RAPUD
Reverse .... REV
Reverse Blocked .... RB
Reverse Current/Overcurrent (KSC) .... RC/OC
Reverse Half-Line [*Feed*] .... RHL
Reverse Interrupt Character [*Keyboard*] (NITA) .... RVI
Reverse Polish Notation [*Arithmetic evaluation*] [*Data processing*] (IEEE) .... RPN
Reversible Half-Wave .... RHW
Reversible Half-Wave Alternating Current .... RHWAC
Reversible Half-Wave Alternating Current - Direct Current .... RHWACDC
Reversible Half-Wave Direct Current .... RHWDC
Revised Unified New Compiler with Its Basic Language Extended [*Data processing*] .... RUNCIBLE
Revista de Telecomunicacion (Madrid) [*A publication*] .... Rev Telecomun (Madrid)
Revolution .... REV
Revolutions per Minute [*e.g., in reference to phonograph records*] .... RPM
Revolutions per Second (AFM) .... RPS
Revue des Telecommunications [*France*] [*A publication*] .... Rev Telecommun
Rewind (MDG) .... REW
Rewind (DEEC) .... RWD
Rewind (MSA) .... RWND
Rewind and Unload (OA) .... RUN
Reynolds & Reynolds [*NASDAQ symbol*] (NQ) .... REYNA
Right [*Direction*] .... R
Right Half Word .... RHW
Right-Hand Side .... RHS
Right to Left (CAH) .... RL
Right to Use [*Telecommunications*] (TEL) .... RTU
Rigid Waveguide .... RWG
RILM [*Repertoire International de la Litterature Musicale*] Abstracts of Music Literature [*City University of New York*] [*Database*] [*A publication*] .... RILM
Ring-Around Programing (CAAL) .... RAP
Ring Lead [*Telecommunications*] (TEL) .... RL
Ring Level (BUR) .... RL
Ring-Ring Trip [*Telecommunications*] (TEL) .... RRT
Ring Trip [*Telecommunications*] (TEL) .... RT
Ringback Tone [*Telecommunications*] (TEL) .... RBT
Ringdown [*Telecommunications*] (TEL) .... RD
Ringing Generator [*Telecommunications*] (TEL) .... RG
Ringing Tone [*Telecommunications*] (TEL) .... RT
Ringtone No Reply [*Telecommunications*] (TEL) .... RTNR

By Meaning

Ripple Adder (NITA) .... RA
Ripple-Blanking Input (IEEE) .... RBI
Ripple-Blanking Output (IEEE) .... RBO
RISC [Reduced-Instruction Set Computer] Technology [IBM Corp.] .... RT
Roadway Analysis and Design System [Data processing] .... ROADS
Roberts Information Services, Inc. [Fairfax, VA] [Information service] (EISS) .... ROBINS
Robotic Industries Association (EANO) .... RIA
Robotic Sample Processor [Automation] .... RSP
Robotics & Automation Research Laboratory [University of Toronto] [Research center] (RCD) .... RAL
Robotics Information [Cincinnati Milacron Industries, Inc.] [Database] .... RBOT
Robotics International (EANO) .... RI/SME
Robotics Today [A publication] .... Robotics T
Rochester Commercial and Industrial [Electronic service] .... RCI
Rock Analysis Storage System [United States Geological Survey] (EISS) .... RASS
Rock Information System [National Science Foundation] [Washington, DC] [Databank] (EISS) .... RKNFSYS
Rock-Oldies-News-Commercials Operation [Formula radio] .... RONCO
Rocketdyne Automatic Processing of Integrated Data [Data processing] .... RAPID
Rockwell International Corp. (MCD) .... RI
Rockwell International Corporation (NASA) .... RIC
Rockwell International Corp. [NYSE symbol] [Toronto Stock Exchange symbol] .... ROK
Rod Memory Computer [NCR Corp.] .... RMC
Roentgen Satellite [Space research] .... ROSAT
Roll-In/Roll-Out [Storage allocation] [Data processing] (NITA) .... RIRO
Rollback [Telecommunications] (TEL) .... RB
Rollback Module [Telecommunications] (TEL) .... RM
Rollback Process [Telecommunications] (TEL) .... RP
Rolm Corp. [NYSE symbol] [Delisted] .... RM
ROM [Read-Only Memory] Address Gate [Data processing] (NITA) .... RAG
ROM [Read-Only Memory] Address Register (NITA) .... RAR
ROM [Read-Only Memory] Instruction Register (NITA) .... RIR
ROM [Read-Only Memory] Location Counter (NITA) .... RLC
ROM Return Address Register (NITA) .... RRAR
Rome Air Development Center [ESD] .... RADC
Root Mean Square [of transmission waves] .... RMS
Root Mean Square Error .... RMSE
Roscoe User Group [Princeton, NJ] .... RUG
Rosner Television Systems, Inc. [New York, NY] [Telecommunications] (TSSD) .... RTS
Rotary Beam Antenna .... RBA
Rotary Digital Audio Tape .... RDAT
Rotary Dual Input for Analog Computation .... RODIAC
Rotary Out Trunk Switch [Telecommunications] (TEL) .... ROTS
Rotary Voice Coil [Computer technology] .... RVC
Rotate .... ROT
Rotate Left [Data processing] .... ROL
Rotate Right [Data processing] .... ROR
Rotate and Scale [Data processing] .... ROTSAL
Rotate through X Left [Data processing] .... ROXL
Rotate through X Right [Data processing] .... ROXR
Rotating Disc Electrode .... RDE
Rotating Phase Array Antenna .... RPAA
Rotational Position Sensing [Data processing] .... RPS
Rotor Blade Antenna .... RBA
Rotor Blade Homing Antenna .... RBHA
Route Accounting Subsystem [Telecommunications] (TEL) .... RAS
Route Control Digit [Telecommunications] (TEL) .... RCD
Route Digit Indicator [Telecommunications] (TEL) .... RDI
Route Monitoring Information [Telecommunications] (TEL) .... RMI
Route Relief Requirements System [Telecommunications] (TEL) .... RRRS
Route/Route Destination [Telecommunications] (TEL) .... RRD
Route Switching [Telecommunications] (TEL) .... RS
Route Treatment [Telecommunications] (TEL) .... RT
Routine for Executing Biological Unit Simulations [Computer program] .... REBUS
Routing Control Indicator [Telecommunications] (TEL) .... RCI
Routing Identifier [or Indicator] (AFM) .... RI
Routing Information Process [Telecommunications] (TEL) .... RIP
Row-Address Strobe (IEEE) .... RAS
Row Parity Check (IEEE) .... RPC
Royal Business Group [NASDAQ symbol] (NQ) .... RYBF
Royal Optimizing Assembly Routing [Royal McBee Corp.] [Data processing] .... ROAR
Royal Signals and Radar Establishment [Malvern, England] [Computer chip designer] .... RSRE
RSI [Resource Services, Inc.] Corporation [NASDAQ symbol] (NQ) .... RSIC
Rui Lopes Associates, Inc. [Sunnyvale, CA] [Telecommunications] (TSSD) .... RLA
Run Executive [Data processing] .... REX
Run Identification [Data processing] .... RUNID
Run Length Coding .... RLC
Run-Length-Limited [Data processing] .... RLL
Run-Time Library [Interdata] (NITA) .... RTL
Running Program Language [Data processing] .... RPL
Runstream [Data processing] .... RUN
Rural Automatic Exchange [Telecommunications] (TEL) .... RURAX
Rural Rehabilitation Technologies Database [University of North Dakota] [Information service] (EISS) .... RRTD
Rural Satellite Program [US Agency for International Development] [Washington, DC] [Telecommunications] (TSSD) .... RSP
Rush [on teletype messages] .... RX
Rutgers Computer and Technology Law Journal [A publication] .... Rutgers Comput and Technol Law J
Rutgers Journal of Computers and the Law [A publication] .... Rutgers J Computers & Law
Rutgers Journal of Computers and the Law [A publication] .... Rutgers J Comput & Law
Rutgers Journal of Computers, Technology, and the Law [A publication] .... Rutgers J Comput Technol and Law
Rutherford High Energy Laboratory (MCD) .... RHEL
Rutowski Optimization [Computer program] .... RUTOP
Ryerson International Development Centre [Ryerson Polytechnical Institute] [Canada] [Research center] (RCD) .... RIDC

S

S-Band (NASA)	S-BD
S-Band Antenna Switch (MCD)	SBAS
S-Band Exciter [System] [Also, SBES]	SBE
S-Band Exciter System [Also, SBE]	SBES
S-Band Feed System	SFS
S-Band Frequency Converter	SFC
S-Band Megawatt Transmit (CIT)	SMT
S-Band Multifrequency (CIT)	SMF
S-Band Polarization Diversity (CIT)	SPD
S-Band Power Amplifier (CIT)	SPA
S-Band Transponder	SBX
Safe Computing Chemical Factory System [Safe Computing Ltd.] [Software package] [British] (NCC)	CHEMSAFE
Safeguard Business Systems, Inc. [NYSE symbol]	SGB
Safety Data Sheet (KSC)	SDS
Safety Recommendation Information System [Database] (FDB)	SRIS
Safety-Related Display Instrumentation	SRDI
Safety Research Information Service [National Safety Council] [Chicago, IL] (EISS)	SRIS
SAL Cable Communications [NASDAQ symbol] (NQ)	SALC
Salary Information Retrieval System (IEEE)	SIRS
Sales and Business Reservations Done Electronically (CGC)	SABRE
Sales Catalog Index Project Input On-Line [Art Institute of Chicago, Cleveland Museum of Art, Metropolitan Museum of Art] [Information service] (EISS)	SCIPIO
Sales Environment Learning Laboratory [Computer-based marketing game]	SELL
Sales Processing Interactive Real-Time Inventory Technique [NCR Corp. trademark]	SPIRIT
Sales Profitability and Contribution Evaluator [Data processing]	SPACE
Salon International de l'Informatique, de la Communication, et de l'Organisation du Bureau [Business equipment exhibition] (NITA)	SICOB
Salton's Magical Automatic Retriever of Texts [Data processing]	SMART
Same Output Gate [Data processing]	SOG
Sample and Analysis Management System [Data processing]	SAM
Sample Control Tape [Data processing]	SCT
Sample Data (NG)	SD
Sample Data Control System (MCD)	SDCS
Sample and Hold (IEEE)	S/H
Sample Interval	SI
Sampled Data Simulator and Computer	SADSAC
Samples per Second	SPS
Sampling Analog Memory System	SAMS
Sanders Associates, Inc. [NYSE symbol]	SAA
Sanders Associates Video Input/Output Terminal Access Resource [Data processing] (IEEE)	SAVITAR
Santec Corp. [NASDAQ symbol] (NQ)	SNTE
Saperstein & Associates Limited [Vancouver, BC] [Telecommunications] (TSSD)	SAL
SAS [Statistical Analysis System] Users Group International (EANO)	SUGI
Satellite	SAT
Satellite	SATL
Satellite	STL
Satellite (CBSS)	STLT
Satellite (FAAC)	
Satellite-Aided Search and Rescue System [Telecommunications]	SASRS
Satellite Array for International and National Telecommunications (MCD)	SAINT
Satellite Attitude Acquisition	SAA
Satellite Automatic Monitoring System [Programing language]	SAMS
Satellite Automatic Tracking Antenna	SATAN
Satellite-Based Maritime Search and Rescue System [Telecommunications] (TEL)	SAMSARS
Satellite Broadcasters Association (EANO)	SBA
Satellite Business Systems [McLean, VA] [Telecommunications] (MCD)	SBS
Satellite Cable Audio Networks [Cable-television service]	SCAN
Satellite Communication Concentrator (NITA)	SCC
Satellite Communication Control Facility	SCCF
Satellite Communications [A publication]	Satell Commun
Satellite Communications [A publication]	Satellite
Satellite Communications Agency [AEC/DCA]	SATCOMA
Satellite Communications Contingency Planning Group (NATG)	SCCPG
Satellite Communications Control Centre [British]	SCCC
Satellite Communications Controller	SCC
Satellite Communications Network, Inc. [Edison, NJ] [Telecommunications] (TSSD)	SCN
Satellite Communications Overseas Transmission	SCOT
Satellite Computer (NITA)	SC
Satellite Configuration Control Element (MCD)	SCCE
Satellite Control Center	SCC
Satellite Control Satellite [Telecommunications] (TEL)	SCS
Satellite-Controlled Clock	SCC
Satellite Data (MCD)	SATDAT
Satellite Data Broadcast Networks, Inc. [New York, NY] [Telecommunications] (TSSD)	SATNET
Satellite Data Exchange (NITA)	SDX
Satellite Data Reduction [Processor system]	SADAR
Satellite Data Services Division [National Oceanic and Atmospheric Administration] [Information service] (EISS)	SDSD
Satellite Data Transmission System (DIT)	SDTS
Satellite Databank [European Space Agency] [Database] (CUAD)	SATELDATA
Satellite Digital and Display System	SDADS
Satellite Distribution Frame [Telecommunications] (TEL)	SDF
Satellite Grand Link System (NATG)	SGLS
Satellite Graphic Job Processor [Data processing]	SGJP
Satellite Ground Terminal	SGT
Satellite Ground Terminal System	SGTS
Satellite Inertial Navigation Determination (MCD)	SIND
Satellite Information Message Protocol	SIMP
Satellite Information Processor	SIP
Satellite Information Processor Operational Program (AFM)	SIPOP
Satellite Infrared Experiment (MCD)	SIRE
Satellite Input to Numerical Analysis and Prediction [National Weather Service]	SINAP
Satellite Inspector Program	SIP
Satellite Instructional Television Experiment [NASA/Indian Space Research Organization, 1974]	SITE
Satellite Interceptor System (AFM)	SIS
Satellite International Television Center [Telecommunications] (TEL)	SITC
Satellite Kill	SKILL
Satellite Master Antenna Television	SMATV
Satellite Networking Associates, Inc. [New York, NY] [Telecommunications] (TSSD)	SNA
Satellite News [A publication]	Satel News
Satellite News Channel [Cable-television system] [Went off the air October, 1983]	SNC
Satellite Observation System (DDI)	SOS
Satellite Operators and Users Technical Committee [McLean, VA] (EANO)	SOUTC
Satellite Paper Tape Transfer	SATPATT
Satellite Parametric Reduction	SPR
Satellite Photoelectric Analog Rectification System	SPEARS
Satellite Position Prediction and Display	SPAD
Satellite Positioning and Tracking	SPOT
Satellite Processor [Data transmission]	SP
Satellite Processor Access Method (OA)	SPAM
Satellite and Production Services [Tallahassee, FL] [Telecommunications] (TSSD)	SPS
Satellite Programming Network [Cable-television system]	SPN
Satellite Services, Incorporated [Houston, TX] [Telecommunications] (TSSD)	SSI
Satellite Situation Report	SSR
Satellite Surveillance Program [Canadian]	SURSAT
Satellite-Switched	SS
Satellite Switched Time Division Multiple Access (NITA)	SST-DMA
Satellite Syndicated Systems [Douglasville, GA] [Cable TV programing service] [Telecommunications]	SSS
Satellite System Monitoring Equipment	SSME
Satellite Systems Corporation [Virginia Beach, VA] [Telecommunications] (TSSD)	SSC
Satellite Systems Engineering, Inc. [Bethesda, MD] [Information service] (TSSD)	SSE
Satellite Systems Monitoring Group [INTELSAT] (CBSS)	SSMG

Satellite Systems Operations Guide [*INTELSAT*] (CBSS) ... SSOG
Satellite Technology Management, Inc. [*Torrance, CA*] [*Telecommunications*] (TSSD) ... STM
Satellite Telecommunications Analysis and Modeling Program ... STAMP
Satellite Telecommunications Company [*Japanese-American firm*] ... SATELCO
Satellite Television Corporation [*Washington, DC*] [*Telecommunications*] (TSSD) ... STC
Satellite Television Network [*Washington, DC*] [*Telecommunications*] (TSSD) ... STN
Satellite Transmission and Reception Specialists [*Houston, TX*] [*Telecommunications*] (TSSD) ... STARS
Satellite Transmissions Systems, Inc. [*Hauppauge, NY*] [*Telecommunications*] (TSSD) ... STS
Satellite Under Test ... SUT
Satellite Undetected Duds ... SUDS
Satellite Unfurlable Antenna ... SUA
Satellite Wildlife Research Project ... SWRP
Satisfactory Operation Factor [*Telecommunications*] (TEL) ... SOF
Saturn Kilometer-Wave Radiation [*Planetary science*] ... SKR
Satz Rechen Zentrum [*Computer Composition Center*] [*West German*] [*Information service*] (EISS) ... SRZ
Sausage Aerial [*Radio*] ... SA
Savage Information Services (EISS) ... SIS
Save Area Table [*Data processing*] (IBMDP) ... SAVT
Savings Comparative Analysis [*Federal Home Loan Bank Board*] [*Database*] (CUAD) ... SCAN
SBE, Incorporated [*NASDAQ symbol*] (NQ) ... SBEI
Scalar [*Mathematics*] ... S
Scale Factor ... SF
Scan Conversion Equipment [*Television*] ... SCE
Scan Converter and Display [*Systems*] ... SCAD
Scan Converter Display System (MCD) ... SCDS
Scan Converter [*or Counter*] **System** ... SCS
Scan Display Generator ... SDG
Scan-Optics, Inc. [*NASDAQ symbol*] (NQ) ... SOCR
Scan-Tron Corp. [*NASDAQ symbol*] (NQ) ... SCNN
Scandinavian Committee for Satellite Communications [*Telecommunications*] (TEL) ... STSK
Scandinavian Periodicals Index in Economics and Business [*Database*] [*Swedish*] (CUAD) ... SCANP
Scanner Association of North America (EANO) ... SCAN
Scanner Input Language (NITA) ... SIL
Scanner Keyed Input Language (NITA) ... SKIL
Scanning Analog-to-Digital Input Equipment [*National Bureau of Standards*] ... SADIE
Scanning Control Register ... SCR
Scanning Multichannel [*or Multifrequency or Multispectral*] **Microwave Radiometer** ... SMMR
Scanning Radiometer ... SR
Scatter Propagation Antenna ... SPA
Schedule ... SCH
Schedule Interface Log ... SIL
Scheduled Issue Date [*Telecommunications*] (TEL) ... SID
Scheduled Program Printout (NATG) ... SPPO
Scheduler Work Area [*Data processing*] (IBMDP) ... SWA
Scheduler Work Area Data Set [*IBM Corp.*] (MCD) ... SWADS
Scheduling Activity Control System [*PA Computers & Telecommunications Ltd.*] [*Software package*] [*British*] (NCC) ... SACS
Scheduling and Control by Automated Network System ... SCANS
Scheduling and Resource Management System [*Tymshare UK*] [*Software package*] [*British*] (NCC) ... SRMS
Schema Representation Language ... SRL
Schematic ... SCHM
Schematic Change Notice ... SCN
Schematic Diagram ... SD
Schering-Oriented Literature Analysis and Retrieval System [*Schering-Plough Corp.*] [*Information service*] (EISS) ... SCHOLAR
Schlumberger Ltd. [*NYSE symbol*] ... SLB
School Computer Use Plan (IEEE) ... SCUP
School Management Information Retrieval Service [*University of Oregon*] [*Eugene, OR*] ... SMIRS
School of Management and Strategic Studies [*Founded 1982 by Richard Farson, offers a two-year management program through GTE Telenet*] ... SMSS
School Practices Information File [*Educational testing service*] [*Database*] ... SPIF
School Practices Information Network [*Bibliographic Retrieval Services*] [*Information service*] (EISS) ... SPIN
Schottky Cell Array Technology (NITA) ... SCAT
Schottky Clamped Transistor ... SCT
Schottky Diode FET [*Field Effect Transistor*] **Logic** ... SDFL
Schottky Transistor Logic (IEEE) ... STL
Schottky Transistor-Transistor Logic (DEEC) ... S/TTL
Schwab Safe Co. [*American Stock Exchange symbol*] ... SS
Schweizerische Vereinigung fuer Operations Research [*Bern, Switzerland*] ... SVOR
Science Citation Index Search [*Institute for Scientific Information*] [*Philadelphia, PA*] [*Bibliographic database*] (OBD) ... SCISEARCH
Science Communication Division [*George Washington University Medical Center*] [*Information service*] (EISS) ... SCD
Science Dynamics Corp. [*NASDAQ symbol*] (NQ) ... SIDY
Science and Engineering Research Council Network [*Later, SERCNET*] (DEEC) ... SRCNET
Science Information Exchange [*Later, SSIE*] [*Smithsonian Institution*] ... SIE
Science Information Services Organization [*Franklin Institute*] (EISS) ... SISO
Science Management Corp. [*American Stock Exchange symbol*] ... SMG
Science and Mathematics Analysis Center [*ERIC*] ... SMAC
Science Research Associates, Inc. [*Chicago, IL*] [*Software manufacturer*] (DASOS) ... SRA
Science Research Council [*Later, SERC*] [*British*] ... SRC
Science and Technology Information Center [*China*] (EISS) ... STIC
Science and Technology Policies Information Exchange System [*UNESCO*] [*Paris, France*] [*Bibliographic database*] (EISS) ... SPINES
Sciences and Humanities Research Institute [*Iowa State University*] [*Research center*] (RCD) ... SHRI
Scientific Apparatus Makers Association ... SAMA
Scientific-Atlanta, Inc. [*NYSE symbol*] ... SFA
Scientific Communication and Technology Transfer [*System*] [*University of Pennsylvania*] ... SCATT
Scientific Computation of Optimal Programs (IEEE) ... SCOOP
Scientific Computers [*NASDAQ symbol*] (NQ) ... SCIE
Scientific Computers, Incorporated (MCD) ... SCI
Scientific Computing Facility (CIT) ... SCF
Scientific Computing Group [*University of Toronto*] [*Research center*] (RCD) ... SCG
Scientific Control Systems (DIT) ... SCS
Scientific Data Automation System (IEEE) ... SDAS
Scientific Data Center (MCD) ... SDC
Scientific Data System [*Later, XDS*] ... SDS
Scientific Elementary Basic Language [*1963*] [*Data processing*] (CSR) ... SCELBAL
Scientific and Engineering Computing Council (MCD) ... SECC
Scientific and Engineering Data Processing Center ... SEDPC
Scientific Information [*or Instruction*] **Processor** [*Honeywell, Inc.*] (NITA) ... SIP
Scientific Information Retrieval, Inc. [*Database management system*] [*Information service*] (EISS) ... SIR
Scientific Information Systems Department [*Merrell Dow Pharmaceuticals, Inc.*] [*Information service*] (EISS) ... SISD
Scientific Instruction Set (NITA) ... SIS
Scientific Library and Documentation Division [*National Science and Technology Authority*] [*Philippines*] [*Information service*] (EISS) ... SLDD
Scientific Machine Automation Corporation ... SMAC
Scientific Parameters for Health and the Environment, Retrieval and Estimation [*Environmental Protection Agency*] [*Database*] (CUAD) ... SPHERE
Scientific Processor (BUR) ... SP
Scientific Software [*NASDAQ symbol*] (NQ) ... SSFT
Scientific Software-Intercomp, Inc. [*Denver, CO*] [*Software manufacturer*] (DASOS) ... SSI
Scientific Subroutine Library (NITA) ... SSL
Scientific Subroutine Package [*Data processing*] ... SSP
Scientific Subroutine System [*Data processing*] (BUR) ... SSS
Scientific Systems Services, Inc. [*NASDAQ symbol*] (NQ) ... SSSV
Scientific and Technical Information Network ... STN
Scientific and Technical Information Processing [*A publication*] ... Sci Tech Inf Process
Scientific and Technical Information Processing (English Translation) [*A publication*] ... Sci Tech Inf Process (Engl Transl)
Scientific and Technical Information Processing (English Translation of Nauchno-Tekhnicheskaya Informatsiya Seriya I) [*A publication*] ... Sci Tech Inf Process (Eng Transl Nauchno-Tekh Inf Ser I)
Scientific & Technical Information Services, Inc. [*Information service*] (EISS) ... STIS
Scientific Time Sharing Corporation [*Host*] [*Information service*] (EISS) ... STSC
Scope, Inc. [*NASDAQ symbol*] (NQ) ... SCPE
Scorer and Analyzer [*Computerized educational testing*] ... SCORAN
Scotland to Iceland Submarine Cable System [*Telecommunications*] (TEL) ... SCOTICE
Scott Cable Communications [*NASDAQ symbol*] (NQ) ... JSCC
Scratch Pad Memory [*Data processing*] ... SPAD
Scratch Pad Memory [*Data processing*] (BUR) ... SPM
Screen Definition Facility [*Data processing*] ... SDF
Screen-Grid N-Channel Metal Oxide Semiconductor ... SGNMOS
Screen Management System [*Computer technology*] ... SMS
Screwed (MDG) ... SCD
Script Applier Mechanism [*Programing language*] [*1975*] (CSR) ... SAM
SDA [*Software Design Associates*] **Users' Group** ... SDAU
Sealed Cathode Ray Tube ... SCRT
Search Control (IEEE) ... SC
Search Decision Rule [*Data processing*] ... SDR
Search Jam System ... SJS
Search Mode Logic ... SML
Search Program for Infrared Spectra [*Canadian Scientific Numeric Database Service*] [*Database*] (CUAD) ... SPIR
Searchable Physics Information Notices [*American Institute of Physics*] [*New York, NY*] [*Bibliographic database*] ... SPIN
SEASAT Users Group of Europe ... SURGE
Seat of the Pants (CGC) ... SOP
Second [*or Secondary*] ... S

Computer & Telecommunications Acronyms

Second (AFM) .... SEC
Second Computer Inquiry (TSSD) CI2
Second Level Interrupt Handler (CMD) .... SLIH
Secondary Address Vector Table [Data processing] (IBMDP) .... SAVT
Secondary Data Display System (MCD) .... SDDS
Secondary Memory [Data processing] (BUR) .... SM
Secondary Multiplexing Unit (OA) .... SMU
Secondary Waveform Generator [Telecommunications] (TEL) .... SWFG
Section (MDG) .... SXN
Section Heading Code [Online database field identifier] (OBD) .... SH
Section Properties [Camutek] [Software package] [British] (NCC) .... SPROPS
Sectionalized Vertical Antenna .... SVA
Sector .... SEC
Sector Scan Indicator .... SSI
Sector/Subsector .... S/SS
Sector Switching Center [Telecommunications] (TEL) .... SSC
Sectored File Controller (NITA) .... SFC
Sectors per Track (NITA) .... SPT
Secure Automatic Communications Network .... SACNET
Secure Automatic Data Information Exchange [System] .... SADIE
Secure Systems Corporation [Manassas, VA] [Telecommunications] (TSSD) .... SSC
Secure Telephone Unit [Data processing] .... STU
Secure Transmission of Acoustic Data (NVT) .... SETAD
Secure Voice Cord Board [Telecommunications] (TEL) .... SECORD
Secure Voice Switch .... SVS
Secure Voice System [Telecommunications] .... SVS
Securities Data Base System [Capital Market Systems, Inc.] [Information service] (EISS) .... SDB
Securities Industry Automation Corporation [NYSE/ASE] .... SIAC
Securities Industry Communication [Western Union Corp.] [Information service] .... SICOM
Securities Order Matching [Data processing] .... SOM
Security Access Control [Data processing] .... SAC
Security Filter Processor (NITA) .... SFP
Security Log [Telecommunications] (TEL) .... SCLOG
Sedna Information Management System [Sedna Corp.] [Information service] (EISS) .... SIMS
See You Later [Telegrapher's slang] .... CUL
Seek Time per Track (NITA) .... STT
Segment .... SEG
Segment Address Field (NITA) .... SAF
Segment Address Register [Telecommunications] (NITA) .... SAR
Segment Base Register (BUR) .... SBR
Segment Control BIT [Binary Digit] (OA) .... SCB
Segment Descriptor Block (NITA) .... SDB
Segment Descriptor Word (NITA) .... SDW
Segment Frequency Algorithm (NITA) .... SFA
Segment Identification Register (NITA) .... SIR
Segment Limits Origin (NITA) .... SLO
Segment Search Argument [Data processing] (BUR) .... SSA
Segment Stack Number (NITA) .... SSN
Segment Table [Data processing] (IBMDP) .... SGT
Segment Table Entry [Data processing] (MDG) ..... STE
Segment Table Origin (NITA) .... STO
Segment Table Origin Register [Data processing] (BUR) .... STOR
Segment Table Register (NITA) .... STR
Segment Tag BITS [Binary Digits] (OA) .... STB
Segmented Level Programing [Data processing] (IEEE) .... SLP
Segmented Virtual Display File (NITA) .... SVDF
SEI Corporation [NASDAQ symbol] (NQ) .... SEIC
Seiler ALGOL Digitally Simulated Analog Computer .... SADSAC
Seiler Laboratory ALGOL Simulated Hybrid [Data processing] .... SLASH
Seismic Computerized Alert Network [For warning of an earthquake] .... SCAN
Seismological Data Center [Environmental Science Services Administration] .... SDC
Seizure [Telecommunications] (TEL) .... SZ
Seizures per Circuit per Hour [Telecommunications] (TEL) .... SCH
Sektion fuer Systementwicklung [GID] [Information retrieval] (ODIN) ..... SFS
Select ADC [Analog-to-Digital Converter] Register [Data processing] (MDG) .... SLAR
Select Frequency (NITA) .... SF
Select Information Exchange [Information service] (EISS) .... SIE
Select Standby (NITA) .... SS
Selectable Unit (BUR) .... SU
Selected Nodes List [Telecommunications] (TEL) .... SNL
Selected Water Resources Abstracts [Service of WRSIC] [Database] .... SWRA
Selective Automatic Computational Matching and Positioning (MCD) .... SACMAP
Selective Automatic Computational Matching and Positioning System ...... SACMAPS
Selective Calling [Radio] .... SELCAL
Selective Chopper Radiometer .... SCR
Selective Complement Accumulator .... SCM
Selective Dissemination of Information [System] [Data processing] .... SDI
Selective Dissemination of Information Online [National Library of Medicine] [Bethesda, MD] [Bibliographic database] (OBD) .... SDILINE
Selective Dissemination of Technical Information [Data processing] ...... SDTI
Selective Information Dissemination and Retrieval [Data processing] (DIT) .... SIDAR
Selective Information Retrieval [Data processing] .... SIR
Selective Letters [or Listing] in Combination .... SLIC
Selective Multiple Addresses Radio and Television Service [A program delivery service introduced by RCA] ..... SMARTS
Selective Notification of Information (NITA) .... SNI
Selective Paging Communications System .... SPCS
Selective Printing [Data processing] .... SPRINT
Selective Printing of Items from Tape [Data processing] .... SPIT
Selective Sequence Electronic Calculator [Data processing] .... SSEC
Selective Tape Print .... STP
Selective Top-to-Bottom Algorithm (DIT) .... STBA
Selector (DEN) .... SEL
Selector Channel (NITA) .... SLC
Selector Channel Emulation Unit (NITA) .... SCEU
Selector File Channel (NITA) .... SFC
Selector Group Matrix [Telecommunications] (TEL) .... SGX
Selector Input/Output Processor [Data processing] (IEEE) .... SIOP
Selenium Control Rectifier .... SCR
Self-Adaptive Flexible Format Retrieval and Storage System [Data processing] (EISS) .... SAFRAS
Self-Aligning Gate Metal Oxide Semiconductor (IEEE) .... SAGMOS
Self-Compensating Network [Telecommunications] (TEL) .... SCN
Self-Extending Translator (IEEE) .... SET
Self-Generating Dictionary (NITA) .... SGD
Self-Generating Master [Information management system] [Data processing] .... SELGEM
Self-Loading Tape (AFM) .... SLT
Self-Organizing Binary Logical Network [OTS] .... SOBLIN
Self-Organizing Large Information Dissemination System (IEEE) ...... SOLID
Self-Organizing Machine .... SOM
Self-Organizing Multiple-Access Discrete Address [Data processing] (IEEE) ..... SOMADA
Self-Phasing Array .... SPA
Self-Programed Electronic Equation Delineator ... SPEED
Self-Programed Individualized Education (IEEE) .... SPIE
Self-Programing Automatic Circuit Evaluator ...... SPACE
Self-Scaling Variable Metric [Algorithms] [Data processing] .... SSVM
Self-Test .... ST
Self-Test Automatic Readout .... STAR
Self-Test Program (MCD) .... STP
Self-Testing and Repairing [Computer self-repair] .... STAR
Self-Wiring Data [Telecommunications] (TEL) ..... SWD
Selling Areas-Marketing, Incorporated [Originator and database] [Information service] (EISS) ...... SAMI
Semantic Information Retrieval [Massachusetts Institute of Technology] [Data processing] (DIT) .... SIR
Semi-Micro Xerography (DEEC) .... SMX
Semiautomatic Analog Setting (IEEE) .... SATANAS
Semiautomatic Bibliographic Information Retrieval .... SABIR
Semiautomatic Bibliographic Information Retrieval System (DIT) ..... SABIRS
Semiautomatic Coding .... SAC
Semiautomatic Encoding of Chemistry for Information Retrieval (DIT) .... SECIR
Semiautomatic Mathematics (IEEE) .... SAM
Semiconductor .... SC
Semiconductor .... SCR
Semiconductor Bilateral Switch (MSA) .... SBS
Semiconductor-Controlled Rectifier .... SCT
Semiconductor Curve Tracer .... SDM
Semiconductor Disk Memory (NITA) .... SEMI
Semiconductor Equipment and Materials Institute .... SFB
Semiconductor Functional Block (IEEE) .... SIA
Semiconductor Industry Association (EANO) ..... SIS
Semiconductor-Insulator-Semiconductor .... SISS
Semiconductor-Insulator-Semiconductor System .... SCIC
Semiconductor Integrated Circuit .... SIC
Semiconductor Integrated Circuit .... SM
Semiconductor Memory (NITA) .... SMID
Semiconductor Memory Integrated Device (MCD) .... SMM
Semiconductor Memory Module (NITA) .... SMS
Semiconductor-Metal-Semiconductor .... SN
Semiconductor Network (IEEE) .... SCPR
Semiconductor Parameter Retrieval [Information Handling Services] [Database] (CUAD) ....
Semiconductor Storage Module (NITA) .... SSM
Semiconductor Storage Unit [Data processing] (TUT) .... SSU
Semiconductor Unilateral Switch (MSA) .... SUS
Semiconductors and Insulators [A publication] .. Semicond Insul
Semiconductors and Insulators [A publication] .. Semicond and Insul
Semiconductors and Semimetals [A publication] .. Semicond Semimet
Semiempirical Absorption Loss Formula [Radio] .... SEALF
Semifinal Splice [Telecommunications] (TEL) .... SS
Seminar Clearinghouse International, Inc. [Information service] (EISS) .... SCI
Semipermanently Associated [Telecommunications] (TEL) .... SPA
Semipost-Pay, Pay-Station [Telecommunications] (TEL) .... SPPAY
Semipost-Pay, Pay-Station [Telecommunications] (TEL) .... SPPS
Semipublic [Telecommunications] (TEL) .... SP
Semirandom Access Memory (NITA) .... SRAM
Send Digits [Telecommunications] (TEL) .... SD
Send Hub [Telegraphy] (TEL) .... SH
Send Leg [Telegraphy] (TEL) .... SL

357

By Meaning

Send Only ... SO
Send Priority and Route Digit [*Telecommunications*] (TEL) ... SPR
Send Processor (NITA) ... SP
Send and Receive ... SR
Send Register Control [*Data processing*] ... SRC
Send Test Message ... STM
Sending Complete [*Telecommunications*] (TEL) ... SC
Senior Management Forum [*Information Industry Association*] ... SMF
Senior Member of the Institution of Radio Engineers ... SMIRE
Sense Device Status Word (OA) ... SDSW
Sensible Policy in Information Resources and Information Technology (EANO) ... SPIRIT
Sensor Analog Relay System ... SARS
Sensor-Based Control Adapter (OA) ... SBCA
Sensor-Based Control Unit [*Data processing*] ... SBCU
Sensor Based System (BUR) ... SBS
Sensor Communication and Display System (MCD) ... SCDS
Sensor Data Record [*For spacecraft*] ... SDR
Sensor Interface Electronics Assembly (MCD) ... SIEA
Sensor Processor (BUR) ... SP
Sensor Referenced and Computer Controlled [*For remote manipulators*] ... SRCC
Sent [*Communications*] (FAAC) ... S
Sentence Appraiser and Diagrammer ... SAD
Sentinel Operating System (IEEE) ... SENTOS
Separate Absorption, Grading, and Multiplication Layers [*Semiconductor technology*] ... SAGM
Separate Index Access Method [*Data processing*] (BUR) ... SIAM
Separate Partition Option (NITA) ... SPO
Separate Telegram ... SEPTEL
Separation Designation Number ... SDN
Separation Parameter ... SEP
Sequence ... SEQ
Sequence Checking Tape ... SCT
Sequence Control Number Register [*Data processing*] ... SCNR
Sequence Control Unit (KSC) ... SCU
Sequence Controller (NITA) ... SC
Sequence Electronique Couleur avec Memoire [*Color Sequence with Memory*] [*French color television system*] ... SECAM
Sequence Information Data (DDI) ... SID
Sequence Initiate Update (SKY) ... SIU
Sequence Number (CIT) ... S/N
Sequence Programer [*Data processing*] ... SP
Sequency-Division Multiplexing (IEEE) ... SDM
Sequential Access Memory [*Data processing*] (IEEE) ... SAM
Sequential Access Method [*IBM Corp.*] [*Data processing*] (TUT) ... SAM
Sequential Analog-Digital Computer (DIT) ... SADC
Sequential Automatic Recorder and Annunciator ... SARA
Sequential Coding ... SECO
Sequential Control [*Teletype*] [*Data processing*] ... SECO
Sequential Control Counter [*Data processing*] (BUR) ... SCC
Sequential Control Logic (NITA) ... SCL
Sequential Events Recorder ... SER
Sequential Explicit Stochastic Linear Programing [*Data processing*] ... SESLP
Sequential and Iterative Operation Unit X (IEEE) ... SIOUX
Sequential Machine Controller [*Programing language*] [*1977-78*] (CSR) ... SMC
Sequential Position and Covariance Estimation (IEEE) ... SPACE
Sequential Processing Machine (DIT) ... SPM
Sequential Processor (NITA) ... SP
Sequential Programed Automatic Recording Transistor Analyzer ... SPARTA
Sequential Quadrature Inband [*Television system*] (DEN) ... SEQUIN
Sequential Single Frequency Code System [*Telecommunications*] (TEL) ... SSFC
Sequentially Controlled Automatic Transmitter Start ... SCATS
Sequentially Operated Teletypewriter Universal Selector ... SOTUS
Serial (AFM) ... SER
Serial Access Memory [*Data processing*] (DEEC) ... SAM
Serial BIT [*Binary Digit*] **Error Detector** ... SBED
Serial Communication Unit for Long Links (NITA) ... SCULL
Serial Data Transmission ... SDT
Serial Data Transmitter/Receiver [*Telecommunications*] (TEL) ... SDTR
Serial Digit Input/Output [*Data processing*] (NITA) ... SDIO
Serial Entry Printer ... SEP
Serial-In, Parallel-Out [*Telecommunications*] (TEL) ... SIPO
Serial Input (DEEC) ... SI
Serial Input Adapter (SKY) ... SIA
Serial Input Data [*Data processing*] ... SID
Serial Input/Output Channel (NITA) ... SIOC
Serial Interface Board (NITA) ... SIB
Serial Interface Chip ... SIC
Serial Line Unit (NITA) ... SLU
Serial Memory Address Counter [*Computer*] ... SMAC
Serial Number (MDG) ... SNO
Serial Output (NITA) ... SO
Serial Output Data [*Data processing*] ... SOD
Serial to Parallel (KSC) ... S/P
Serial Shift Counter [*Data processing*] ... SSC
Serialized Job Processor (NITA) ... SJP
Serialized On-Line Automatic Recording [*Data processing*] (IEEE) ... SOLAR
Serializer/Deserializer (NITA) ... SD
Serializer, Deserializer ... SERDES
Serials On-Line [*National Library of Medicine*] [*Bethesda, MD*] [*Database*] ... SERLINE
Series Computation of Reliability and Probability [*Data processing*] ... SCRAP
Series Mode Rejection (NITA) ... SMR
Series Number [*Online database field identifier*] (OBD) ... SR
Series Statement [*Online database field identifier*] (OBD) ... SE
Serveur Universitaire National de l'Information Scientifique et Technique [*Online service*] (CUAD) ... SUNIST
Service Access Point (CCD) ... SAP
Service Analysis Report [*Telecommunications*] (TEL) ... SAR
Service Analysis Request [*Telecommunications*] (TEL) ... SAR
Service Assistant [*Telecommunications*] (TEL) ... SA
Service Attitude Measurement [*Bell System*] ... SAM
Service Availability [*AT & T*] ... SAV
Service Bureau Corporation ... SBC
Service Center Internal Computer Code [*Data processing*] ... SCICC
Service Center Replacement System [*Data processing*] ... SCRS
Service Code [*Telecommunications*] (TEL) ... SC
Service Dealer's Newsletter [*Abington, PA*] [*A publication*] [*Information service*] (EISS) ... SDN
Service Evaluation System [*Telecommunications*] (TEL) ... SES
Service Indicator [*Telecommunications*] (TEL) ... SI
Service Indicator Associated Field [*Telecommunications*] (TEL) ... SIAF
Service in Information and Analysis [*Host*] [*British*] (BUR) ... SIA
Service Instructions Message [*Telecommunications*] (TEL) ... SIM
Service Interception [*Telecommunications*] (TEL) ... SVI
Service Level Reporter [*IBM Corp.*] ... SLR
Service Link Network [*Bell Laboratories*] ... SLN
Service Monitoring [*Telecommunications*] (TEL) ... SM
Service Observance Bureau [*A telephone-monitoring section of the Bell System*] ... SOB
Service Order Mechanization [*or Mechanized*] **System** [*AT & T*] ... SOMS
Service Order System [*Telecommunications*] (TEL) ... SOS
Service Priority List (BUR) ... SPL
Service Processor (BUR) ... SVP
Service Recording and Data Analysis System (IEEE) ... SRDAS
Service Request Block [*Data processing*] (BUR) ... SRB
Service by Satellite ... SATSERV
Service Software, Incorporated [*Cherry Hill, NJ*] [*Software manufacturer*] (DASOS) ... SSI
Service, Sort and Merge [*Data processing*] ... SESAME
Service, Sort, and Merge [*Data processing*] (IEEE) ... SESOME
Services Engineering Computer-Aided Design [*Pierce Management Services*] [*Software package*] [*British*] (NCC) ... SECAD
Servicing Control Unit [*Telecommunications*] (TEL) ... SCU
Servicing Log [*Telecommunications*] (TEL) ... SVLOG
Servicio de Consulta a Bancos de Informacion [*Data Base Consultation Service*] [*Mexico*] [*Information service*] (EISS) ... SECOBI
Serving Area Concept [*Bell System*] ... SAC
Serving Test Center [*Bell System*] ... STC
Servo Adapter Coupler ... SAC
Servomechanisms and Data Processing Laboratory [*Massachusetts Institute of Technology*] ... SDPL
Session Control [*Data processing*] (IBMDP) ... SC
Session Control Block [*Data processing*] (BUR) ... SCB
Session Handler (NITA) ... SH
Set ... S
Set (CDH) ... SE
Set Asynchronous Balanced Mode (CCD) ... SABM
Set Asynchronous Response Mode (NITA) ... SARM
Set/Clear [*Flip-flop*] [*Data processing*] ... SC
Set Clock ... SC
Set Conditionally [*Data processing*] ... SCC
Set Equation Transformation System [*1970*] [*Data processing*] (CSR) ... SETS
Set Interrupt Mask [*Data processing*] ... SIM
Set Location Counter (CMD) ... SLC
Set Mode (BUR) ... SM
Set-Oriented Retrieval Module (NITA) ... SORM
Set Overrides Clear (IEEE) ... SOC
Set-Reset [*Flip-Flop*] [*Data processing*] ... S-R
Set-Reset Clocked Data [*Data processing*] ... SRCD
Set-Reset Flip-Flop [*Data processing*] ... SRFF
Set-and-Test-Sequence-Number [*Data processing*] (IBMDP) ... STSN
Set Theoretic Language [*1971*] [*Data processing*] (CSR) ... SETL
Set Theoretic Language - BALM [*1973*] [*Data processing*] (CSR) ... SETB
Set-Up [*Control*] **Module** [*Telecommunications*] (TEL) ... SUM
Sets Tabular Material [*Phototypesetting computer*] ... SETAB
Settlement Problem-Oriented Language [*Data processing*] (IEEE) ... SEPOL
Settlement Register [*Data processing*] ... SR
Severe Environment Memory Series [*or System*] [*Data processing*] ... SEMS
Sewer Pipe [*Telecommunications*] (TEL) ... SP
Shakespeare Data Bank, Inc. [*Evanston, IL*] [*Information service*] (EISS) ... SDB
Share [*Business and trade*] ... SHR
Share Assembly Program [*Data processing*] ... SAP
Share Internal FORTRAN Translator [*Data processing*] (IEEE) ... SIFT
Share News on Automatic Coding Systems [*Data processing*] ... SNACS
Share Operating System [*Data processing*] ... SOS
Shared Batch Area [*Data processing*] (IBMDP) ... SBA

Computer & Telecommunications Acronyms

Shared Catalog Accessed Through Terminals [Data processing system] .... SCATT
Shared Data Set Integrity (NITA) .... SDSI
Shared Direct Memory Access [Sperry UNIVAC] (NITA) .... SDMA
Shared Hospital Accounting System [Data processing] .... SHAS
Shared Information Elicitation Facility [Data processing] .... SHIEF
Shared Information Service (CMD) .... SIS
Shared Laboratory Information System .... SLIS
Shared Line Adapter (NITA) .... SLA
Shared Mass Storage (NITA) .... SMS
Shared Medical Systems [NASDAQ symbol] (NQ) .... SMED
Shared Memory [Data processing] (BUR) .... SM
Shared Multiport Memory (NITA) .... SMM
Shared Peripheral Interface (NITA) .... SPI
Shared Tape Allocation Manager (NITA) .... STAM
Shared-Time Repair of Big Electronic Systems [Data processing] .... STROBES
Shared Virtual Area [Data processing] .... SVA
Shares Time with [Broadcasting term] .... ST
Sheffield Package Analysis and Identification of Data [Commercial & Industrial Development Bureau] [Software package] [British] (NCC) .... SPAID
Shelter Housed Automatic Digital Random Access [Data processing] .... SHADRAC
Shift (MSA) .... SHF
Shift Control Counter [Data processing] (MDG) .... SC
Shift-In Character [Keyboard] [Data processing] .... SI
Shift In, Shift Out (IEEE) .... SOSI
Shift Left and Count Instructions [Data processing] (MDG) .... SLC
Shift Left Out/Shift Right In (NITA) .... SLO/SRI
Shift-Out Character [Keyboard] [Data processing] .... SO
Shift Register .... SR
Shift Register Memory .... SRM
Shift Register Recognizer (IEEE) .... SRR
Shift and Select [Data processing] (MDG) .... SSL
Shift Word, Substituting .... SWS
Ship Abstracts [Helsinki University of Technology] [Bibliographic database] (OBD) .... SA
Ship Form Online Design System [British Ship Research Association] [Software package] [British] (NCC) .... SFOLDS
Ship Letter Telegram .... SLT
Ship Position Interpolation Computer (VIT) .... SPIC
Ship Station [ITU designation] (CET) .... MS
Shipboard Data Multiplex System (MCD) .... SDMS
Shipboard Impact Locator System .... SILS
Shipboard Satellite Communications System .... SSCS
Ships Integrated Communications System (MCD) .... SICS
Ship's Keyboard Display Unit .... SKDU
Shock Two-Dimensional Eulerian Elastic Plastic [Computer code] .... STEEP
Shock Wave Data Center [Lawrence Radiation Laboratory] .... SWDC
Shore Mode Data Transmitter (MCD) .... SMDT
Short Backfire [Antenna] .... SBF
Short Circuit .... S
Short Circuit .... SC
Short Circuit .... SCI
Short Circuit .... SHCRT
Short Circuit .... SCC
Short-Circuit Current .... SCAN
Short Current Abstracts and Notes (DIT) .... SF
Short Format (NITA) .... SIP
Short Irregular Pulses ....
Short LOFAR [Low-Frequency Acquisition and Ranging] Alerting Message (NVT) .... SLAM
Short Range MODEM (NITA) .... SRM
Short-Term Memory .... STM
Short Term Projections [Townsend-Greenspan & Co., Inc.] [Database] (CUAD) .... STP
Short Wave (FAAC) .... SHRTWV
Short Wavelength Limit .... SWL
Shortest Access Time First (NITA) .... SATF
Shortest Connected Network (OA) .... SCN
Shortest Job First [Data processing] .... SJF
Shortest Latency Time First .... SLTF
Shortest Remaining Time First [Data processing] .... SRTF
Shortest Seek Time First (NITA) .... SSTF
Shortwave [Electronics] .... SW
Shortwave Converter .... SWC
Shortwave Fadeouts .... SWF
Shortwave Infrared .... SWIR
Shortwave Listener [Radio] .... SWL
Shortwave Ratio (DEN) .... SWR
Shortwave Transmitter .... SWT
Shubert Entertainment and Arts Ticketing System [National computerized theatre-ticket selling system] .... SEATS
Shunt [Electricity] .... SH
SIAM [Society for Industrial and Applied Mathematics] Journal on Computing [A publication] .... SIAM J Comput
Side Frequency (DEN) .... SF
Sideband [Radio frequency] .... SB
Sideband Intermediate Frequency Communications System .... SIFCS
Sidetone [Telecommunications] (TEL) .... ST
Sidetone Objective Loudness Rating [of telephone connections] (IEEE) .... SOLR
Sidetone Path Loss [Telecommunications] (TEL) .... STPL
Sidetone Reduction [Telecommunications] (TEL) .... STR
Siebert Telecommunications Consulting, Incorporated [Cincinnati, OH] [Telecommunications] (TSSD) .... STCI
Sight and Sound [A publication] .... Sight & S
Sight and Sound [A publication] .... Si & So
Sight and Sound [A publication] .... SS
Sight and Sound [A publication] .... S & S
Sigma Center Information Storage and Retrieval System .... SCISRS
Sign-Filled Half-Word Designator [Data processing] .... XH
Sign Off [Data processing] (MDG) .... S/OFF
Sign On [Data processing] (MDG) .... S/ON
Signal [Telecommunications] (TEL) .... S
Signal .... SIG
Signal Amplitude Sampler and Totalizing Unit (IEEE) .... SASTU
Signal Comparator (VIT) .... SC
Signal Conditioning Amplifier .... SCAMP
Signal Conversion Electronics [Telecommunications] (TEL) .... SCE
Signal Conversion Relay [Telecommunications] (TEL) .... SCR
Signal Data Converter .... SDC
Signal Data Demodulator .... SDD
Signal Data Demodulator Set [or System] (CIT) .... SDDS
Signal Data Processing System .... SDPS
Signal Data Processor .... SDP
Signal Data Recording Set (MCD) .... SDRS
Signal Dispatch Point [Telecommunications] (TEL) .... SDP
Signal Distribution Unit .... SDU
Signal Frequency .... SF
Signal Generator .... SG
Signal Generator (IEEE) .... SIGGEN
Signal Ground (BUR) .... SG
Signal Information and Monitoring Service [American radio monitoring service] .... SIAM
Signal Intelligence [US surveillance satellite] .... SIGLINT
Signal Interface .... SI
Signal Interface Unit (MCD) .... SIU
Signal-to-Interference .... S/I
Signal-to-Interference Ratio .... SIR
Signal Messenger Service (NATG) .... SMS
Signal Node (NITA) .... SN
Signal-to-Noise Improvement [Data transmission] (IEEE) .... SNI
Signal-to-Noise Plus Interference Ratio .... SNIR
Signal to Noise Ratio [Unweighted] (CMD) .... S/N
Signal-to-Noise Ratio .... SNR
Signal-to-Noise Ratio Estimator (CIT) .... SNORE
Signal Plus Noise and Distortion .... SINAD
Signal Processing Language [Data processing] (CSR) .... SPL
Signal Processing Peripheral (NITA) .... SPP
Signal Processing System (KSC) .... SPS
Signal Processing Test Facility .... SPTF
Signal Processing Unit .... SPU
Signal Processor (NASA) .... S/P
Signal Processor Techniques Department .... SPTD
Signal Quality Detector .... SQD
Signal Routing and Interface (MCD) .... SRI
Signal Selection Switchboard (CAAL) S3
Signal Source Distribution Center .... SSDC
Signal Strength [Broadcasting] .... S
Signal Strength [Broadcasting] (KSC) .... SS
Signal Strength, Center Frequency [Broadcasting] .... SS/CF
Signal Strength Monitor [Broadcasting] .... SSM
Signal Transfer Point [Telecommunications] (TEL) .... STP
Signal Transfer Unit .... STU
Signal Transmission Reception and Distribution (IEEE) .... STRAD
Signal Word Index of Field and Title - Literature Abstract Specialized Search (DIT) .... SWIFT LASS
Signal Word Index of Field and Title - Scientific Information Retrieval (DIT) .... SWIFT SIR
Signaling Conversion Circuit [Telecommunications] (TEL) .... SCC
Signaling Ground [Telecommunications] (TEL) .... SGD
Signaling Information Field [Telecommunications] (TEL) .... SIF
Signaling Interworking Subsystem [Telecommunications] (TEL) .... SIS
Signaling Link Selection [Telecommunications] (TEL) .... SLS
Signaling Module [Telecommunications] (TEL) .... SM
Signaling Range Extender [Telecommunications] (TEL) .... SRE
Signaling and Supervisory Control (NITA) .... SSC
Signaling System [Telecommunications] (TEL) .... SS
Signaling Unit .... SU
Signals Operator .... SIGSOP
Signed Division [Data processing] .... DIVS
Signed Multiplication [Data processing] .... MULS
Significant Data Selection .... SIDASE
Significant Milestone Integration Lateral Evaluation [Data processing] .... SMILE
Significant Word in the Full Title [Data processing] (DIT) .... SWIFT
SIGPLAN Technical Committee on APL [A Programming Language] [Association for Computing Machinery] .... STAPL
SII [Systems Integrators, Incorporated] Eastern Regional Users Group [Scranton, PA] (EANO) .... SERUG
Silicon and Aluminum Metal-Oxide Semiconductor .... SAMOS
Silicon Bilateral Switch .... SBS
Silicon Diode Pellet .... SDP
Silicon Integrated Circuit .... SIC
Silicon Integrated Monolithic Circuit .... SIMC

Silicon Light Pulser Matrix ... SLPM
Silicon Multiplier Detector ... SMD
Silicon Pulser Array ... SPA
Silicon-on-Sapphire [*Integrated circuit*] ... SOS
Silicon-on-Something-Else [*Telecommunications*] (TEL) ... SOSE
Silicon Stud-Mounted Diode ... SSMD
Silicon Unilateral Switch ... SUS
Silicon Video Memory (OA) ... SVM
Silicon Voltage Reference Diode ... SVRD
Silver-Band Frequency Modulation (IEEE) ... SBFM
Simmons Market Research Bureau, Inc. [*Database producer*] (CUAD) ... SMRB
Simple Algebraic Language for Engineers [*Data processing*] ... SALE
Simple Analytical Interactive Language [*Data processing*] ... SAIL
Simple Electronic Computer [*Birkbeck College*] [*London, England*] (DEN) ... SEC
Simple Left to Right [*Data processing*] ... SLR
Simple-Minded Learning Machine (IEEE) ... SMLM
Simple Modeling and Planning [*SIMPLAN Users Group*] [*New York, NY*] ... SIMPLAN
Simple Output Format Translator (IEEE) ... SOFT
Simple Phrase Language [*Data processing*] ... SPL
Simple Programing Language [*Data processing*] ... SPL
[*A*] **Simple Systematic Integration of Statistical Techniques** (BUR) ... ASSIST
Simple Transition to Economical Processing (IEEE) ... STEP
Simple Transition to Electronic Processing ... STEP
Simplex [*Transmission direction*] (CET) ... SX
Simplex Circuit ... SPX
Simplex Remote Communications Central ... SRCC
Simplified Automatic Data Plotter ... SADAP
Simplified Computer Code ... SCC
Simplified Input for Toss [*Data processing*] ... SIFT
Simplified Language for Abstract Mathematical Structures [*Data processing*] (IEEE) ... SLAMS
Simplified Message Processing Simulation (IEEE) ... SMPS
Simplified Modeling and Planning [*Programing language*] [*1973*] (CSR) ... SIMPLAN
Simplified Modular Frame Assignment System [*Telecommunications*] (TEL) ... SMFA
Simplified Modular Frame Assignment System [*Bell System*] ... SMFAS
Simplified Needs Assessment Profile System [*Developed by Texas Instruments, Inc.*] ... SNAP
Simplified Neutron Transport Computer Code ... SNTCC
Simplified Numerical Automatic Programer [*Data processing*] ... SNAP
Simplified Programing for Acquisition and Control (IEEE) ... SIMPAC
Simplified Programing Language for Artists [*1978*] [*Data processing*] (CSR) ... SPLAT
Simplified User Logistics ... SUL
Simplify Obscure ALGOL [*Algorithmic Language*] **Programs** (MCD) ... SOAP
Simulated Data Generator ... SDG
Simulated Data Reduction Program ... SDRP
Simulated Data Tape ... SDT
Simulated Input Preparation System (IEEE) ... SIPS
Simulated Input Processor [*Data processing*] ... SIP
Simulated Linguistic Computer ... SLC
Simulated Message Analysis and Conversion Subsystem ... SMACS
Simulated Operational Computer (KSC) ... SOC
Simulated Output Program [*Data processing*] ... SOP
Simulated System (CAAL) ... SIMSYS
Simulated Tape Load ... STL
Simulated Video (MCD) ... SV
Simulating Digital Systems (CAH) ... SDS
Simulation of Analog and Hybrid Computers ... SAHYB
Simulation of Analog Methods [*Data processing*] ... SAM
Simulation and Assignment of Traffic to Urban Road Networks [*Kins Developments Ltd.*] [*Software package*] [*British*] (NCC) ... SATURN
Simulation as a Basis for Social Agents' Decisions [*Data processing*] ... SIMBAD
Simulation of the Columbia University Libraries [*Data processing research*] ... SCUL
Simulation of Combined Analog Digital Systems [*Data processing*] (IEEE) ... SCADS
Simulation and Computer [*Data processing*] ... SIMCOM
Simulation Councils, Incorporated ... SCI
Simulation Data Subsystem (KSC) ... SDS
Simulation and Evaluation of Chemical Synthesis [*Data processing*] ... SECS
Simulation Implementation Machine Programing Languages (KSC) ... SIMPL
Simulation of Industrial Management Problems [*Program*] [*1958*] [*Data processing*] (CSR) ... SIMPLE
Simulation Input Tape ... SIT
Simulation Interface Subsystem (KSC) ... SIS
Simulation Language [*1964*] [*Data processing*] (TUT) ... SIMULA
Simulation Language [*Data processing*] (BUR) ... SL
Simulation Language for Alternative Modeling [*Data processing*] (CSR) ... SLAM
Simulation Language Based on Programing Language, Version One ... SIMPL/1
Simulation of Logic Design ... SOLD
Simulation of Machine Indexing ... SMI
Simulation, Manual and Computerized ... SMAC
Simulation Mission Operation Computer (MCD) ... SMOC
Simulation Operation Computer (MCD) ... SOC
Simulation Oriented Language [*Data processing*] ... SOL
Simulation Package [*Data processing*] ... SIMPAC
[*A*] **Simulation Process Oriented Language** [*1972*] [*Data processing*] (CSR) ... ASPOL
Simulation Programing Language [*Data processing*] (NITA) ... SPL
Simulation Tape Conversion ... STC
Simulation Tape Print Program ... STAPP
Simulative Procedure Oriented Language (MCD) ... SIMUPOL
Simulator Compiler [*Computer*] ... SIMCOM
Simulator of Immediate Memory in Learning Experiments ... SIMILE
Simulator Test Set (CAAL) ... STS
Simultaneous ... SIMUL
Simultaneous Automatic Broadcast Homer (FAAC) ... SABH
Simultaneous Baseband Transmission [*of information*] ... SBT
Simultaneous Broadcast ... SB
Simultaneous Equation Solver [*Computer program*] ... SEQS
Simultaneous Operation Linked Ordinal Modular Network ... SOLOMON
Simultaneous Peripheral Operation Online [*Data processing*] (MCD) ... SPOOL
Simultaneous Processing Operation System [*Control Data Corp.*] [*Data processing*] ... SIPROS
Simultaneous Tape Read and Write ... STRAW
Simultaneous Transmission of Range Signals and Voice ... S
Simultaneous Voice/Data ... SVD
Sindacato Italiano Lavoratori Telecomunicazioni [*Italian Union of Telecommunications Workers*] ... SILTE
Sindacato Italiano Lavoratori Telefoni di Stato [*Italian Union of Government Telephone Workers*] ... SILTS
Sindacato Italiano Lavoratori Uffici Locali ed Agenzie Postelegrafonici [*Italian Union of Local Post and Telegraph Office Workers*] ... SILULAP
Sine-Kosine Multiplier ... SKM
Sine Wave Amplitude Modulation ... SWAM
Sine Wave Generator ... SWG
Sine Wave Inverter ... SWI
Singing Point [*Telecommunications*] (TEL) ... SP
Singing Return Loss [*Telecommunications*] (TEL) ... SRL
Single ... S
Single ... SNGL
Single-Actuated Voice Recorder ... SAVOR
Single Address Code ... SAC
Single Armor [*Telecommunications*] (TEL) ... SA
Single Assignment Mathematical Programing Language [*1971*] [*Data processing*] (CSR) ... SAMPLE
Single-BIT [*Binary Digit*] **Error Correction and Double-BIT** [*Binary Digit*] **Error Detection** (NITA) ... SECDED
Single Board Computer (DEEC) ... SBC
Single Byte Interleaved (NITA) ... SBI
Single Channel Amplitude Monopulse Processing ... SCAMP
Single Channel Analyzer ... SCA
Single-Channel-per-Carrier [*Telecommunications*] ... SCPC
Single-Channel-per-Carrier, Pulse-Code-Modulation, Multiple-Access, Demand-Assignment Equipment [*Telecommunications*] ... SPADE
Single Channel Control Unit (NITA) ... SCCU
Single Channel Ground and Airborne Radio System (MCD) ... SINCGARS
Single Channel Ground and Airborne Radio System, Very High Frequency ... SINCGARS-V
Single-Channel MODEM [*Telecommunications*] (TEL) ... SCM
Single Channel Simplex ... SCS
Single Character Recognition (NITA) ... SCR
Single Circuit [*Electricity*] ... SC
Single Conductor Cable (MSA) ... SCC
Single Contact [*Switch*] ... SC
Single Control Support (BUR) ... SCS
Single Copy Order Plan [*Later, STOP*] [*Bookselling*] ... SCOP
Single Cotton-Covered [*Wire insulation*] ... SCC
Single Degaussing Cable ... SDGA
Single Disk Storage Device [*Data processing*] (BUR) ... SDSD
Single Entry/Single Exit (NITA) ... SE/SE
Single Error Correcting (NITA) ... SEC
Single In-Line Memory Module [*Data processing*] ... SIMM
Single In-Line Package [*Data processing*] ... SIP
Single-Input, Single-Output [*Process engineering*] ... SISO
Single Instruction, Multiple Data (IEEE) ... SIMD
Single Instruction, Single Data (IEEE) ... SISD
Single Language Dedicated Time-Sharing System (NITA) ... SLDTSS
Single Line Control (BUR) ... SLC
Single Message Rate Timing ... SMRT
Single Mode Alignment (CAAL) ... SMAL
Single Number Access Plan [*Telecommunications*] (TEL) ... SNAP
Single Orbit Computation ... SOC
Single-Phase Full Wave ... SPFW
Single-Phase Half Wave ... SPHW
Single Photon Emission Computed Tomography ... SPECT
Single-Point Orbit Calculator ... SPOC
Single-Pole [*Switch*] ... SP
Single-Pole, Double-Throw [*Switch*] ... SPDT
Single-Pole, Double-Throw, Double-Break [*Switch*] (VIT) ... SPDTDB
Single-Pole, Double-Throw, Normally-Closed, Double-Break [*Switch*] (VIT) ... SPDTNCDB
Single-Pole, Double-Throw, Normally-Open [*Switch*] (VIT) ... SPDTNO

Computer & Telecommunications Acronyms

Single-Pole, Double-Throw, Normally-Open, Double-Break [Switch] (VIT) .... SPDTNODB
Single-Pole, Double-Throw Switch (VIT) .... SPDTSW
Single-Pole, Single-Throw [Switch] .... SPST
Single-Pole, Single-Throw, Normally-Closed [Switch] (VIT) .... SPSTNC
Single-Pole, Single-Throw, Normally-Open [Switch] (VIT) .... SPSTNO
Single-Pole, Single-Throw, Normally-Open, Double-Make [Switch] .... SPSTNODM
Single Precision Unpacked Rounded [floating-point package] [Computer program system] [Sperry Rand Corp.] .... SPUR
Single Processor Interface (NITA) .... SPI
Single Program Initiation [Data processing] (TUT) ..... SP
Single Programer .... SRE
Single Region Execution (NITA) .... SRE
Single Requesting Terminal [Data processing] (IBMDP) .... SRT
Single Sideband .... SSB
Single Sideband Amplitude Modulation (KSC) .... SSBAM
Single Sideband Filter .... SSF
Single Sideband Frequency Modulation (IEEE) .... SSBFM
Single Sideband Modulation .... SSM
Single Sideband Signal Multiplier [Telecommunications] (OA) .... SSM
Single Sideband Suppressed Carrier .... SSBSC
Single Sideband Suppressed Carrier Optical Modulator .... SSBSCOM
Single Sideband Transmission [Telecommunications] (TEL) .... SST
Single-Sideband Transmitted Carrier (IEEE) .... SSTC
Single-Sided, Double-Density Disk [Magnetic disk] [Data processing] .... SSDD
Single Sided Frame [Telecommunications] (TEL) ..... SSF
Single-Sided Pulse Width Modulation [Telecommunications] (OA) ..... SPWM
Single-Sided, Single-Density Disk [Magnetic disk] [Data processing] .... SSSD
Single Signal Superheterodyne [Radio] .... SSS
Single Signaling Unit [Telecommunications] (TEL) ... SSU
Single Silk-Covered [Wire insulation] .... SSC
Single Silk Covering over Enamel Insulation [Telecommunications] (TEL) .... SSE
Single Title Order Plan [Bookselling] .... STOP
Single Value (NITA) .... SV
Single Vibrations [Half cycles] .... SV
Single Vibrations [Half cycles] .... VS
Single Virtual Storage [IBM Corp.] [Data processing] .... SVS
Single Wire Armored [Cables] .... SWA
Single Word Dump (SKY) .... SWD
Singularity Analyzer [Data processing] .... SINGAN
Sinusoidal Input Describing Function [Data processing] .... SIDF
SIS Corp. [NASDAQ symbol] (NQ) .... SISB
Sistema Nacional de Informacion [National Information System] [Colombia] (EISS) .... SNI
Site Cutover Manager [Telecommunications] (TEL) .... SCOM
Site Data Processors .... SDP
Site Programer Course .... SPC
Site Resident Engineer [Telecommunications] (TEL) .... SRE
Situation Display Generator .... SDG
Six BIT [Binary Digit] Transcode (CMD) .... SBT
Six-BIT [Binary Digit] Universal Random Character Set [Data processing] .... SBURCS
Six Node Averaging Program [Data processing] ..... SNAP
Sixth Word Designator [Data processing] .... S
Size (MDG) .... SZ
Skaggs Telecommunications Service [Salt Lake City, UT] [Telecommunications] (TSSD) .... STS
Sketch-In-Depth [Parthorn] [Software package] [British] (NCC) ..... SID
Skew Buffer (NITA) .... SKB
Skip (BUR) .... SKP
Skip Flag [Data processing] (MDG) .... SF
Skyline Network Service [Satellite Business Systems] [McLean, VA] [Telecommunications] (TSSD) .... SNS
Slack Frame Program (OA) .... SFP
Slave Emulator Control Unit (NITA) .... SECU
Slave Processing Unit (NITA) .... SPU
Slave Programable Read-Only Memory (NITA) ...... S-P/ROM
Slave Register Set (NITA) .... SRS
Slewed [Antenna] .... S
Slide-In Unit [Telecommunications] (TEL) .... SIU
Slot Array Antenna .... SAA
Slotted Array X-Band Antenna .... SAXA
Slotted Waveguide .... SWG
Slow Operate [Relay] .... SO
Slow-Scan Television .... SSTV
Slow Write, Fast Read [Data processing] (IEEE) ..... SWFR
Small (FAAC) .... SML
Small Applications Satellite (KSC) .... SAS
Small Applications Technology Satellite (MCD) ...... SATS
Small Astronomy Satellite .... SAS
Small Automatic Exchange [Telecommunications] (TEL) ...... SAX
Small Base Unit [Telecommunications] .... SBU
Small Business Computer (BUR) .... SBC
Small Business Computer News [A publication] ...... Small Bus Comput News
Small Business Computers [A publication] .... Small Bus Comput
Small Business Systems Group [Westford, MA] [Telecommunications] (TSSD) .... SBSG
Small Computer Algorithmic Language .... SMALGOL
Small Computer Analytical and Mathematical Programing System (IEEE) .... SCAMPS
Small Computer Program Index [Allm Books] [Information service] [A publication] [British] (EISS) .... SCPI
Small Computer System (NITA) .... SCS
Small Computer System Interface .... SCSI
Small Computers in Libraries [A publication] .... SCIL
Small-Core Memory [Data processing] .... SCM
Small Library Computing, Inc. [Holbrook, NY] [Information service] (EISS) .... SLC
Small Local Exchange [Telecommunications] (TEL) .... SLE
Small-Medium Local Exchange [Telecommunications] (TEL) .... SMLE
Small Peripheral Controller (NITA) .... SPC
Small-Scale Integration .... SSI
Small Semiconductor Memory (NITA) .... SSM
Small Systems Software [A publication] .... Small Sys Soft
Small Systems Software [A publication] .... Small Syst Software
Small Systems World [A publication] .... Small Sys
Small Systems World [A publication] .... Small Syst World
Small Transportable Communications Stations ..... STRACS
Small Transportable Link Terminal .... STLT
Small Ultimate Size [Telecommunications] (TEL) ... SUS
Smallest Addressable Unit (NITA) .... SAU
Smart Front End (NITA) .... SFE
SMART's Own Concordance Constructor, Extremely Rapid [Cornell University] [Data processing] .... SOCCER
Smithsonian Institution Information Retrieval System (DIT) .... SIIRS
Smithsonian Science Information Exchange [Smithsonian Institution] [Washington, DC] [Database] .... SSIE
SNOBOL Implementation Language Reimplemented [1974] [Data processing] (CSR) .... SIL
Sociaal-Wetenschappelijk Informatie-en Documentatiecentrum [Social Science Information and Documentation Center] [Netherlands] [Information service] (EISS) .... SWIDOC
Social Data Exchange Association [Council for Community Services] [Information service] (EISS) .... SODEX
Social Planning, Policy & Development Abstracts [Sociological Abstracts, Inc.] [Database] (CUAD) .... SOPODA
Social Science Citation Index Search [Database] (ODIN) .... SOCIAL SCISEARCH
Social Science Data Archives [University of California, Los Angeles] [Information service] (EISS) .... SSDA
Social Science Data Center [University of Connecticut] [Research center] (EISS) .... SSDC
Social Science Data Center [Hunter College of City University of New York] [Research center] (RCD) .... SSDL
Social Science Documentation Centre [UNESCO] (EISS) ...... SSDC
Social Science Research Facilities Center [University of Minnesota] [Research center] (RCD) .... SSRFC
Social Science Research Institute [of CRESS] [University of Hawaii at Manoa] [Research center] (RDA) .... SSRI
Social Sciences Citation Index [Institute for Scientific Information] [Database] [A publication] .... SSCI
Social Sciences Literature Information System [Informationszentrum Sozialwissenschaften] [Database] (CUAD) .... SOLIS
Social Security Account Number .... SSAN
Social Security Administration [of HEW] .... SSA
Social Security Administration Data Acquisition and Response System .... SSADARS
Social Security Number .... SSN
Sociedad Espanola de Documentacion e Informacion Cientifica [Spanish Society for Documentation and Information Sciences] [Information service] (EISS) .... SEDIC
Societe Belge pour l'Application des Methodes Scientifiques de Gestion [Brussels, Belgium] .... SOGESCI
Societe d'Etudes et de Travaux Mecanographiques (OA) ...... SETM
Societe Europeenne pour le Traitement de l'Information [European Society for the Processing of Information] (CAH) .... SETI
Societe Francaise d'Etudes et de Realisations d'Equipements de Telecommunications [French communications engineering company] [Telecommunications] (TEL) .... SOFRECOM
Societe Internationale des Telecommunications Aeronautiques [International Society of Aeronautical Telecommunications] [London, England] .... SITA
Societe Mathematique de France (NITA) .... SMF
Societe de Microelectronique Industrielle de Sherbrooke, Inc. [University of Sherbrooke] [Canada] [Research center] (RCD) ... SMIS INC
Society for Applied Learning Technology [Warrenton, VA] (EANO) ..... SALT
Society of Broadcast Engineers (EANO) .... SBE
Society of Certified Data Processors (EANO) .... SCDP
Society of Communications Engineers and Analysts .... SCEA
Society for Computer Applications in Engineering, Planning, and Architecture [Rockville, MD] [Formerly, Civil Engineering Program Applications] [Later, SCAEPA] .... CEPA
Society for Computer Applications in Engineering, Planning, and Architecture [Formerly, CEPA] (EANO) .... SCAEPA
Society for Computer Medicine [Later, AAMSI] (EANO) .... SCM
Society for Computer Science in Biology and Medicine .... SCSBM
Society for Computer Simulation [La Jolla, CA] ...... SCS

By Meaning

361

Society for Conceptual and Content Analysis by Computer [*Bowling Green University*] [*Bowling Green, OH*] [*Association for Computers and the Humanities special interest group*] (EANO) ... SCCAC
Society of Data Educators [*Memphis, TN*] ... SDE
Society of Data Processing Machine Operators and Programmers ... DPMOAP
Society for Electro-Acoustic Music in the United States (EANO) ... SEAMUS
Society for General Systems Research [*Washington, DC*] ... SGSR
Society to Help Avoid Redundant Effort [*in data processing*] ... SHARE
Society of Indexers [*British*] (DIT) ... SI
Society for Industrial and Applied Mathematics [*Philadelphia, PA*] ... SIAM
Society for Information Display [*Playa Del Rey, CA*] ... SID
Society for Management Information Systems [*Chicago, IL*] (EANO) ... SMIS
Society of Manufacturing Engineers ... SME
Society of Motion Picture and Television Engineers [*Formerly, Society of Motion Picture Engineers*] [*Scarsdale, NY*] ... SMPTE
Society of Newspaper Design (EANO) ... SND
Society of Photo-Optical Instrumentation Engineers [*Bellingham, WA*] ... SPIE
Society for Private and Commercial Earth Stations [*Washington, DC*] [*Telecommunications*] [*Information service*] (EANO) ... SPACE
Society of Professional Management Consultants, Inc. [*New York, NY*] ... SPMC
Society of Reliability Engineers (EANO) ... SRE
Society of Satellite Professionals [*Washington, DC*] [*Telecommunications*] [*Information service*] [*An association*] (EANO) ... SSP
Society of Telecommunications Consultants [*New York, NY*] [*Telecommunications*] [*Information service*] [*An association*] (EANO) ... STC
Society for Wang Applications and Programs (CSR) ... SWAP
Society of Wireless Pioneers [*Santa Rosa, CA*] (EANO) ... SOWP
Society for Worldwide Interbank Financial Telecommunication [*La Hulpe, Belgium*] [*Banking network*] ... SWIFT
Socio-Economic Demographic Information System [*Lawrence Berkeley Laboratory*] [*Database*] (FDB) ... SEEDIS
Socony Mobil Automatic Real Time (DIT) ... SMART
SofTech, Inc. [*NASDAQ symbol*] (NQ) ... SOFT
Software [*Data processing*] (MCD) ... SFTWR
Software [*Data processing*] (CIT) ... SW
Software AG Systems Group [*NASDAQ symbol*] (NQ) ... SAGA
Software-Aided Multiform Input [*Software*] [*Data processing*] ... SWAMI
Software Career Link [*Database provider*] ... SCL
Software Conceptual Design [*Data processing*] ... SCD
Software Configuration Accounting and Reporting System (OA) ... SCARS
Software Configuration Control Board (KSC) ... SCCB
Software Configuration Management [*Data processing*] (IEEE) ... SCM
Software Correction Report (CAAL) ... SCR
Software Design Associates, Inc. [*New York, NY*] [*Software manufacturer*] (DASOS) ... SDA
Software Design Description [*Data processing*] (IEEE) ... SDD
Software Design Language (NITA) ... SDL
Software Design Review (MCD) ... SDR
Software Development Language [*Burroughs Corp.*] (NITA) ... SDL
Software Development System ... SDS
Software Development System (MCD) ... SWDS
Software Engineering (MCD) ... SE
Software Engineering Bibliographic Data Base [*Data and Analysis Center for Software*] [*Database*] (FDB) ... SEBD
Software Engineering Data [*Data Analysis Center for Software*] [*Database*] (FDB) ... SED
Software Engineering Facility (NITA) ... SEF
Software Engineering Institute [*DoD*] ... SEI
Software Engineering and Management (NITA) ... SEAM
Software Engineering Research Projects [*Data Analysis Center for Software*] [*Database*] (FDB) ... SERP
Software Engineering Technology ... SET
Software Engineering Terminology [*Data processing*] (IEEE) ... SET
Software Error Effects Analysis (NITA) ... SEEA
Software Error Notification [*Data processing*] ... SEN
Software Facilities and Standards [*Data processing*] (TEL) ... SFS
Software/Hardware Operational Control (NITA) ... SHOC
Software Implemented Friden Translator [*Data processing*] ... SWIFT
Software Institute of America [*Andover, MA*] [*Telecommunications*] (TSSD) ... SIA
Software Instrumentation Package [*Sperry UNIVAC*] [*Data processing*] ... SIP
Software Interrupt [*Data processing*] ... SWI
Software Life Cycle Management (NITA) ... SLCM
Software Maintenance Function [*Data processing*] (TEL) ... SMF
Software Management Plan (MCD) ... SMP
Software Master Library [*Data processing*] (TEL) ... SML
Software Message Generator [*Data processing*] (TEL) ... SMG
Software Newsletter [*A publication*] ... Softw Newsl
Software Parts List [*Data processing*] (TEL) ... SPL
Software: Practice and Experience [*A publication*] ... Software
Software: Practice and Experience [*A publication*] ... Software Pract Exper
Software: Practice and Experience [*A publication*] ... Software Pract and Exper
Software in Print [*Technique Learning*] [*Information service*] (EISS) ... SIP
Software Programing Language [*Data processing*] (IEEE) ... SPL
Software Publishers Association [*Washington, DC*] (EANO) ... SPA
Software Quality Assurance [*Data processing*] (IEEE) ... SQA
Software Recording Facility (NITA) ... SRF
Software Recovery Facility [*Data processing*] (IBMDP) ... SRF
Software Requirements Document [*Data processing*] (CIT) ... SRD
Software Requirements Engineering Methodology ... SREM
Software Research and Development Group [*University of Calgary*] [*Research center*] (RCD) ... SRDG
Software Review [*A publication*] ... Software Rev
Software Review [*A publication*] ... SSORD
Software Sciences Limited [*British*] (OA) ... SSL
Software Services of America [*NASDAQ symbol*] (NQ) ... SSOA
Software Slave Library [*Data processing*] (TEL) ... SSL
Software Specification Language (NITA) ... SSL
Software Staging Section [*Social Security Administration*] ... SSS
Software System Design [*Data processing*] (CIT) ... SSD
Software System Design Document (MCD) ... SSDD
Software Technology for Adaptable, Reliable Systems [*Data processing*] ... STARS
Software Timing and Control (NITA) ... STAC
Software Tools Communications [*A publication*] ... Software Tools Commun
Software World [*A publication*] ... Soft World
Soil Classification and Mapping Branch [*Department of Agriculture*] (EISS) ... SCAM
Soil Data Storage and Retrieval Unit [*Department of Agriculture*] (EISS) ... SDS & RU
Soil Engineering Problem-Oriented Language [*Data processing*] (TUT) ... SEPOL
Soil-Plant-Atmosphere [*Computer simulation model*] ... SPAM
Solar and Backscatter Ultraviolet Spectrometer (MCD) ... SBUV
Solar and Backscattered Ultraviolet and Total Ozone Mapping System ... SBUV/TOMS
Solar-Based Solar Power Satellite ... SSPS
Solar Communications ... SOCOM
Solar Energy Information Data Bank [*Department of Energy*] ... SEIDB
Solar Energy Information Services (EISS) ... SEIS
Solar Microwave Interferometer Imaging System ... SMIIS
Solar Proton Monitor ... SPM
Solar Radiation and Thermospheric Structure [*Japanese satellite*] ... SRATS
Solar System Data Processing System (CIT) ... SSDPS
Solar-Terrestrial Physics (EISS) ... STP
Solar Vacuum Telescope ... SVT
Solid Logic Dense (BUR) ... SLD
Solid Logic Technique [*Data processing*] (IEEE) ... SLT
Solid Logic Technology (DEEC) ... SLT
Solid State ... SS
Solid-State Analog-to-Digital Computer ... SADIC
Solid-State Circuit (MCD) ... SC
Solid State Communications [*A publication*] ... Solid State Commun
Solid State Communications [*A publication*] ... Solid St Commun
Solid State Communications [*A publication*] ... Sol St Comm
Solid-State Electric Logic (NG) ... SOSTEL
Solid-State Logic Timer ... SSLT
Solid-State Microwave Amplifier ... SSMA
Solid-State, Parallel, Expandable, Differential Analyzer Computer ... SPEDAC
Solid-State Storage Device [*Data processing*] ... SSD
Solid-State System ... SSS
Solid State Technology [*A publication*] ... Solid Stat
Solid State Technology [*A publication*] ... Solid State Technol
Solid State Technology [*A publication*] ... Sol St Tech
Some Remarks on Abstract Machines [*Data processing*] ... SRAM
SONAR Information Center (NVT) ... SIC
Sonic Telex System [*Sonicair*] [*Phoenix, AZ*] [*Telecommunications*] (TSSD) ... STS
Sony Corp. [*NYSE symbol*] [*Toronto Stock Exchange symbol*] [*Vancouver Stock Exchange symbol*] ... SNE
Sophisticated Operating System [*Apple III microcomputer*] [*Data processing*] ... SOS
Sophisticated String Editor (IEEE) ... SEDIT
Sort File Description [*Data processing*] (DDI) ... SD
Sort Generator (BUR) ... SG
Sort Key Edit [*Library of Congress*] ... SKED
Sort Merge and Reduction Tapes (CAAL) ... SMART
Sort Program Generator [*Data processing*] (BUR) ... SPG
Sorter Reader (OA) ... SR
Sorter Reader Buffer (OA) ... SRB
Sorter Reader Flow (OA) ... SRF
Sorting and Assembly of New Data ... SAND
Sorting, Updating, Report Generating, Etc. [*IBM Corp.*] [*Data processing*] ... SURGE
Sound Interface Device [*Computer chip*] ... SID
Source ... S
Source [*Online database field identifier*] (OBD) ... SO
Source Address (CCD) ... SA
Source Address Register [*Telecommunications*] (NITA) ... SAR
Source Code ... SC
Source Code Control System [*Data processing*] ... SCCS
Source Data Acquisition (BUR) ... SDA
Source Data Automation ... SDA
Source Data Automation Equipment ... SDAE
Source Data Automation System ... SDAS

Computer & Telecommunications Acronyms

Source Data Communication Retrieval (OA) .... SDCR
Source Data Entry (NITA) .... SDE
Source Data Information .... SDI
Source Data Operation (MDG) .... SDO
Source Data Processing (NITA) .... SDP
Source Data Utility (NITA) .... SDU
Source Document [*Data processing*] .... SD
Source Handshake (NITA) .... SH
Source Input Data Edit System (NITA) .... SIDES
Source Jamming (DDI) .... SJ
Source Language [*Data processing*] (BUR) .... SL
Source Language Debug [*Data processing*] (IEEE) .... SLD
Source Language Input Program (NITA) .... SLIPR
Source Language Processor [*Data processing*] (BUR) .... SLP
Source Library System (NITA) .... SLS
Source Library Update (NITA) .... SLU
Source Mail [*Electronic mail*] .... SMAIL
Source Program Library (NITA) .... SPL
Source Program Maintenance [*IBM Corp.*] .... SPM
Source Program Maintenance Online (NITA) .... SPMOL
Source Program Utility Routine (NITA) .... SPUR
Source Range Channel (IEEE) .... SRC
Source Range Neutron Flux Channel (IEEE) .... SRNFC
Source Record Punch .... SRP
Source Service Access Point (CCD) .... SSAP
Source/Sink [*Data processing*] (IBMDP) .... S/S
Source Statement Library [*Data processing*] .... SSL
Source Telecomputing Corporation [*McLean, VA*] [*Telecommunications*] (TSSD) .... STC
Sources de Financement des Entreprises [*CCMC Informatique de Gestion*] [*Database*] (CUAD) .... SOFIE
South Carolina Educational Television [*Columbia*] [*Telecommunications*] (TSSD) .... SCETV
South Central Research Library Council [*Ithaca, NY*] [*Library network*] (EISS) .... SCRLC
South Dakota Medical Information Exchange [*University of South Dakota*] [*Sioux Falls*] [*Telecommunications*] (TSSD) .... SDMIX
Southeast .... SE
Southeast Asia Telecommunications System .... SEATELCOM
Southeastern Regional Medical Library Program [*Emory University*] [*Atlanta, GA*] [*Library network*] (EISS) .... SERMLP
Southern Bell Telephone & Telegraph Co. (KSC) .... SBTT
Southern Center for Research and Innovation, Inc. [*University of Southern Mississippi*] [*Research center*] (RCD) .... SCRI
Southern Educational Communications Authority [*Television network*] .... SECA
Southern Forestry Information Network [*Forest Service*] (EISS) .... SOUTHFORNET
Southern New England Telephone Co. [*NYSE symbol*] .... SNG
Southern Pacific Communications Corp. (NITA) .... SPC
Southern Pacific Communications Corporation (CBSS) .... SPCC
Southern Pacific Communications' Switched Long Distance Service [*Telecommunications*] (TEL) .... SPRINT
Southern Pine [*Utility pole*] [*Telecommunications*] .... SP
Southern Satellite Systems, Inc. [*Tulsa, OK*] [*Telecommunications*] (TSSD) .... SSS
Southwest .... SW
Southwest Academic Library Consortium [*Library network*] (EISS) .... SWALC
Southwest Ohio Regional Data Center [*University of Cincinnati*] [*Research center*] (RCD) .... SORDC
Southwestern Order Retrieval and Distribution [*Southwest Bell Telephone Co.*] .... SORD
Soviet Automatic Control [*English Translation*] [*A publication*] .... SAUCB
Soviet Automatic Control [*A publication*] .... Sov Automat Contr
Soviet Automatic Control [*A publication*] .... Sov Autom Control
Soviet Automatic Control [*A publication*] .... Soviet Automat Control
Soviet Electrical Engineering [*English Translation*] [*A publication*] .... SOEEA
Soviet Electrical Engineering [*A publication*] .... Sov Elec Eng
Soviet Electrical Engineering [*English Translation of Elektrotekhnika*] [*A publication*] .... Sov Electr Eng
Soviet Power Engineering [*A publication*] .... Sov Power Eng
Soviet Power Engineering (English Translation of Elektricheskie Stantsii) [*A publication*] .... Sov Power Eng (Engl Transl)
Space Air Relay Communications (MCD) .... SPARC
Space Antennae Diversity [*Telecommunications*] (TEL) .... SAD
Space Character [*Keyboard*] .... SP
Space Communications .... SPACECOM
Space Communications Network .... SPAN
Space Communications Station Operation .... SCSO
Space Communications and Tracking .... SCAT
Space Division Multiple Access (CBSS) .... SDMA
Space Division Multiplexing [*Physics*] .... SDM
Space Division Switching [*Telecommunications*] .... SDS
Space Environment Laboratory [*National Oceanic and Atmospheric Administration*] .... SEL
Space Environment Laboratory Data Acquisition and Display System [*National Oceanic and Atmospheric Administration*] .... SELDADS
Space Management and Retail Tracking System [*Information Resources, Inc.*] .... SMART
Space Planning System [*Applied Research of Cambridge Ltd.*] [*Software package*] [*British*] (NCC) .... SPS
Space Program Language Implementation Tool (KSC) .... SPLIT
Space Programing Language [*Data processing*] .... SPL
Space Programing Language Machine .... SPLM
Space Switch [*Telecommunications*] (TEL) .... SS
Space Switch [*Telecommunications*] (TEL) .... SSW
Space-Time-Space [*Digital switching structure*] [*Telecommunications*] (TEL) .... STS
Space-Time Unit [*Computer*] .... STU
Space Ultrareliable Modular Computer .... SUMC
Spaceborne Computer .... SBC
Spaceborne Computer Engineering Conference (MCD) .... SCEC
Spaceborne Programer .... SBP
Spacecraft Antenna System .... SAS
Spacecraft Charging at High Altitudes [*Satellite*] .... SCATHA
Spacecraft Communicator (SKY) .... SCOM
Spacecraft Data Handling Equipment .... SDHE
Spacecraft Technical Control Center (MDG) .... STCC
Spacecraft Telecommunications System (CIT) .... STS
Spacecraft Telemetry Command Data Handling System (CIT) .... STCDHS
Spacecraft Television Video Data (CIT) .... STVD
Spacelab Support Module Simulator (MCD) .... SLSMS
Span Terminating Equipment [*Telecommunications*] (TEL) .... STE
Spanish International Network [*Cable-television system*] .... SIN
Spanish Universal Network [*Cable-television system*] .... SUN
Spare [*Telecommunications*] (TEL) .... SPR
Spare Band Surveillance System (MCD) .... SBSS
Spares Determination Method [*Bell System*] .... SDM
Spares Integrated Data System .... SIDS
Sparta Acquisition Digital Equipment .... SPADE
Spatial Computer .... SPAC
Special Advisory Committee on Telecommunications .... SCAT
Special Area Code [*Bell System*] .... SAC
Special Assembly for Fast Installations [*Telecommunications*] (TEL) .... SAFFI
Special Billing [*Telecommunications*] (TEL) .... SB
Special Characters Table [*Data processing*] (IBMDP) .... SCT
Special Circuit .... SC
Special Communications Alteration (DDI) .... SPECOMALT
Special Customer-Oriented Language (IDA) .... SPECOL
Special Education Instructional Materials Centers [*Office of Education*] [*Albany, NY*] [*Database producer*] (EISS) .... SEIMC
Special Exchange Service [*Telecommunications*] (TEL) .... SES
Special Function Key [*Calculators*] .... SFK
Special Function Unit (NITA) .... SFU
Special Industrial Radio Service Association [*Land Mobile Communications Council*] [*Rosslyn, VA*] .... SIRSA
Special Information Retrieval .... SIR
Special Instruction .... SI
Special Interest Committee (CGC) .... SIC
Special Interest Committee on Program Documentation [*Association for Computing Machinery*] .... SICDOC
Special Interest Group .... SIG
Special Interest Group on Academic and Associated Computing [*Formerly, SIGUCC*] [*Association for Computing Machinery*] .... SIGACC
Special Interest Group on Ada [*Association for Computing Machinery*] [*New York, NY*] (EANO) .... SIGADA
Special Interest Group on APL Programming Language [*Association for Computing Machinery*] [*New York, NY*] (EANO) .... SIGAPL
Special Interest Group for Architecture of Computer Systems [*Association for Computing Machinery*] [*New York, NY*] (CSR) .... SIGARCH
Special Interest Group on Artificial Intelligence [*Association for Computing Machinery*] [*New York, NY*] (EANO) .... SIGART
Special Interest Group on Automata and Computability Theory [*Association for Computing Machinery*] .... SIGACT
Special Interest Group/Automated Language Processing [*American Society for Information Science*] .... SIG/ALP
Special Interest Group on Biomedical Computing [*Association for Computing Machinery*] (EANO) .... SIGBIO
Special Interest Group on Business Data Processing and Management [*Association for Computing Machinery*] [*New York, NY*] (MCD) .... SIGBDP
Special Interest Group on Computer Graphics [*Association for Computing Machinery*] [*New York, NY*] .... SIGGRAPH
Special Interest Group on Computer and Human Interaction [*Association for Computing Machinery*] [*Northwestern University*] [*Evanston, IL*] (EANO) .... SIGCHI
Special Interest Group on Computer Personnel Research [*Association for Computing Machinery*] [*Indiana University*] [*Bloomington, IN*] .... SIGCPR
Special Interest Group for Computer Science Education [*Association for Computing Machinery*] [*New York, NY*] .... SIG/CSE
Special Interest Group on Computer Systems, Installation Management [*Association for Computing Machinery*] .... SIGCOSIM
Special Interest Group for Computer Uses in Education [*Association for Computing Machinery*] [*New York, NY*] .... SIGCUE
Special Interest Group for Computers and the Physically Handicapped [*Association for Computing Machinery*] [*New York, NY*] .... SIGCAPH
Special Interest Group on Computers and Society [*Association for Computing Machinery*] [*New York, NY*] .... SIGCAS
Special Interest Group for Computers and Society [*Association for Computing Machinery*] (EANO) .... SIGCS

Computer & Telecommunications Acronyms

Special Interest Group on Data Communication [*Association for Computing Machinery*] .... SIGCOMM
Special Interest Group for Design Automation [*Association for Computing Machinery*] [*New York, NY*] .... SIGDA
Special Interest Group on Documentation [*Association for Computing Machinery*] .... SIGDOC
Special Interest Group on File Description and Translation [*Association for Computing Machinery*] [*Later, Special Interest Group on the Management of Data*] .... SIGFIDET
Special Interest Group on Information Retrieval [*Association for Computing Machinery*] [*New York, NY*] .... SIGIR
Special Interest Group on Language Analysis and Studies in the Humanities [*Association for Computing Machinery*] .... SIGLASH
Special Interest Group on Management of Data [*Association for Computing Machinery*] .... SIGMOD
Special Interest Group for Mathematical Programing [*Association for Computing Machinery*] [*Washington, DC*] .... SIGMAP
Special Interest Group on Measurement and Evaluation [*Association for Computing Machinery*] (CSR) .... SIGMETRICS
Special Interest Group on Microprograming [*Association for Computing Machinery*] [*New York, NY*] .... SIGMICRO
Special Interest Group on Minicomputers [*Later, SIGSMALL*] [*Association for Computing Machinery*] .... SIGMINI
Special Interest Group for Numerical Mathematics [*Association for Computing Machinery*] (CSR) .... SIGNUM
Special Interest Group on Office Automation [*Association for Computing Machinery*] .... SIGOA
Special Interest Group on Operating Systems [*Association for Computing Machinery*] .... SIGOPS
Special Interest Group on Personal Computing [*Association for Computing Machinery*] .... SIGPC
Special Interest Group on Programing Languages [*Association for Computing Machinery*] [*New York, NY*] .... SIGPLAN
Special Interest Group on Real Time Processing [*Association for Computing Machinery*] .... SIGREAL
Special Interest Group on Security, Audit, and Control [*Association for Computing Machinery*] [*New York, NY*] .... SIGSAC
Special Interest Group/Selective Dissemination of Information [*American Society for Information Science*] .... SIG/SDI
Special Interest Group on Simulation [*Association for Computing Machinery*] [*New York, NY*] .... SIGSIM
Special Interest Group on Small Computing Systems and Applications [*Later, SIGSMALL*] [*Association for Computing Machinery*] [*New York, NY*] (EANO) .... SIGSCSA
Special Interest Group on Small Computing Systems and Applications [*Formerly, SIGSCSA*] [*Association for Computing Machinery*] (EANO) .... SIGSMALL
Special Interest Group on Social and Behavioral Science Computing [*Association for Computing Machinery*] .... SIGSOC
Special Interest Group on Software Engineering [*Association for Computing Machinery*] [*New York, NY*] .... SIGSOFT
Special Interest Group for Symbolic and Algebraic Manipulation [*Association for Computing Machinery*] .... SIGSAM
Special Interest Group for University and College Computing Services [*Association for Computing Machinery*] [*Later, Special Interest Group on Academic and Associated Computing*] [*Drake University*] [*Des Moines, IA*] .... SIGUCCS
Special Interest Group on Urban Data Systems, Planning, Architecture, and Civil Engineering [*Association for Computing Machinery*] .... SIGSPAC
Special Learning Education [*In company name, SLED Software*] [*Minneapolis, MN*] [*Software manufacturer*] (DASOS) .... SLED
Special Microwave Devices Operation [*Raytheon Co.*] .... SMDO
Special Monitor Output Generator (IEEE) .... SMOG
Special Operator Service Traffic [*Telecommunications*] (TEL) .... SOST
Special Police Radio Inquiry Network [*New York City*] .... SPRINT
Special-Purpose Cable Assembly .... SPCA
Special-Purpose Engineering Analysis Language (MCD) .... SPEAL
Special-Purpose Language [*Data processing*] .... SPL
Special-Purpose Multiprocessor [*Data processing*] .... SPMP
Special Purpose Processor (NITA) .... SPP
Special-Purpose Test Program (MCD) .... SPTP
Special Real-Time Command (KSC) .... SRTC
Special Register (NITA) .... SR
Special Safeguarding Measures [*Telecommunications*] (TEL) .... SSM
Special Service Center [*Bell System*] .... SSC
Special Service Work Order [*Telecommunications*] (TEL) .... SSWO
Special Services Forecasting System [*Telecommunications*] (TEL) .... SSFS
Special Services Management Bureau [*Telecommunications*] (TEL) .... SSMB
Special Services Protection [*Telecommunications*] (TEL) .... SSP
Special Warning Receiver (MCD) .... SWR
Special World Intervals .... SWI
Specialized Common Carrier [*Telecommunications*] .... SCC
Specialized Mobile Radio .... SMR
Specialized Technique for Efficient Typesetting .... STET
Specific Acoustic Capacitance .... SAC
Specific Inductive Capacity .... SIC
Specific Linear Optimal Control Program [*Hydrofoil*] [*Grumman Aerospace Corp.*] .... SLOCOP
Specification (AFM) .... SPEC
Specification Data Base .... SPECD
Specification and Description Language [*Telecommunications*] (TEL) .... SDL
Specification Information Retrieval System [*Data processing*] (MCD) .... SIR
Specification Verification [*Data processing*] (IEEE) .... SPECVER
Specifications for Web Offset Publications [*Printing technology*] .... SWOP
Specified Hours of Operation [*Broadcasting term*] .... SH
Specify Task Asynchronous Exit [*Data processing*] .... STAE
Specifying Queries as Relational Expressions [*Programing language*] [*1973*] [*Data processing*] (CSR) .... SQUARE
Specimen Input to Digital Automatic Computer (OA) .... SPIDAC
Spectral Bandwidth .... SBW
Spectral Matrix Method (KSC) .... SMM
Spectrometer Digital System .... SDS
Spectrum Clear Except Known Signals (MUGU) .... SCEKS
Spectrum Resources, Incorporated [*St. Charles, MO*] [*Telecommunications*] (TSSD) .... SRI
Specular Reflection Computer Program (MCD) .... SPREC
Speech Interference Level .... SIL
Speech Interpolation [*Telecommunications*] (TEL) .... SI
Speech/Noise [*Ratio*] [*Electronics*] .... S/N
Speech-Operated Noise Adjusting Device [*Telecommunications*] (TEL) .... SONAD
Speech Predictive Encoded Communications [*Telephone channels*] .... SPEC
Speech Processing Device .... SPD
Speech Recognition (NITA) .... SR
Speech Reinforcement System .... SRS
Speech Understanding System (NITA) .... SUS
Speed of Service [*Telecommunications*] (TEL) .... SOS
Speed Tolerant Recording [*Electronic Processors, Inc.*] (NITA) .... STR
Spencer Information Storage and Retrieval System (DIT) .... SPINSTRE
Sperry Air Data Equipment .... SPADE
Sperry Corp. [*NYSE symbol*] .... SY
Sperry Quick Updating of Internal Documentation (IEEE) .... SQUID
Sperry UNIVAC Material System .... SUMS
Sperry UNIVAC Minicomputer Management of Interactive Terminals (NITA) .... SUMMIT
Spherical Electrostatic Analyzer .... SEA
Spherical Wave Expansion [*Telecommunications*] (TEL) .... SWE
Spill Prevention Control and Countermeasure System [*Environmental Protection Agency*] [*Information service*] (EISS) .... SPCCS
Splice [*Telecommunications*] (TEL) .... SPL
Sponsoring Agency [*Online database field identifier*] (OBD) .... SN
Spool Multileaving [*Data processing*] (IBMDP) .... SML
Sport Information Resource Centre [*Coaching Association of Canada*] [*Database*] (EISS) .... SIRC
Sport und Sportwissenschaftliche Informationssystem [*Sport and Sports-Scientific Information System*] [*West Germany*] (EISS) .... SUSIS
[*The*] Sports Network [*Huntingdon Valley, PA*] [*Cable-television system*] [*Information service*] (EISS) .... TSN
Sprague Voltage-Sensitive Switch .... SVSS
Spread Spectrum (CET) .... SS
Spread Spectrum Modulation (NATG) .... SSM
Spread-Spectrum Multiple Access [*Satellite communications*] .... SSMA
Spread Spectrum Random Access System [*Telecommunications*] (TEL) .... SSRA
Spring Joint Computer Conference [*American Federation of Information Processing Societies*] .... SJCC
Square .... SQ
Square Loop Antenna .... SLA
Square Root [*Data processing*] .... SQR
Square Root Mode [*Data processing*] .... SRM
Squared Successive Differences [*Data processing*] .... SSD
Squarewave (MSA) .... SQW
Squarewave (DDI) .... SQWV
Squarewave Amplitude Modulation .... SAM
Squarewave Generator .... SWG
Staatsbibliothek Preussischer Kulturbesitz [*Berlin*] [*Information retrieval*] (ODIN) .... SBPK
Stability Return Loss [*Telecommunications*] (TEL) .... SRL
Stabilization Data Computer .... SDC
Stabilizer Gyro Circuit .... SGC
Stack (MSA) .... STK
Stack Access Block (NITA) .... SAB
[*A*] Stack Based Abstraction Language [*1978*] [*Data processing*] (CSR) .... ASBAL
Stack Control Block (NITA) .... SCB
Stack Pointer [*Data processing*] .... SP
Stack Segment [*Data processing*] .... SS
Stacked Dipole Aerial Array .... SDAA
Stadt- und Universitaetsbibliothek Frankfurt [*Database producer*] (ODIN) .... STUB
Stage Interface Substitute .... SIS
Standard (AFM) .... STD
Standard Address Generator (IEEE) .... SAG
Standard Buried Collector [*Circuit*] .... SBC
Standard Central Air Data Computer .... SCADC
Standard Computer Software Number .... SCSN
Standard COMSEC [*Communications Security*] Facility Equipment List .... SCFEL
Standard Cubic Feet per Day [*Of gasoline*] [*Telecommunications*] (TEL) .... SCFD
Standard Data Interface [*Data processing*] .... SDI

Standard Disk Filing System (NITA) ... SDFS
Standard Distribution Format [*Data processing*] ... SDF
Standard Drug File [*Derwent Publications Ltd.*] [*Database*] (CUAD) ... SDF
Standard Electronic Accounting Language [*Data processing*] (BUR) ... SEAL
Standard Electronic Module (CAAL) ... SEM
Standard Electronics Module Program (MCD) ... SEMP
Standard Estimating Module (IEEE) ... SEM
Standard External File (NITA) ... SEF
Standard Frequency and Time Signals (IEEE) ... SFTS
Standard Generalized Markup Language [*Electronic manuscript preparation and production*] ... SGML
Standard Hardware Interface Program ... SHIP
Standard Industrial Classification [*File indexing code*] ... SIC
Standard Industrial Trade Classification [*United Nations*] ... SITC
Standard Instruction Set (MSA) ... SIS
Standard Interface Adapter (NITA) ... SIA
Standard International Trade Classification ... SITC
Standard Label [*Data processing*] ... SL
Standard Level User Charges ... SLUC
Standard Markup Language [*Data processing*] ... SML
Standard Message Trunk Design System [*Telecommunications*] (TEL) ... SMETDS
Standard Metropolitan Statistical Area [*Later, MSA*] [*Census Bureau*] ... SMSA
Standard Modular System ... SMS
Standard Modular System Card [*Data processing*] (BUR) ... SMSC
Standard Navigation Computer ... SNC
Standard Network Access Protocol [*Data processing*] ... SNAP
Standard Network Interconnection [*Telecommunications*] ... SNI
Standard Notes and Parts Selection (TEL) ... SNAPS
Standard [*or Standing*] **Operating Procedure** ... SOP
Standard Pesticide File [*Derwent Publications Ltd.*] [*Database*] (CUAD) ... SPF
Standard Point Location Code [*American Trucking Association and Association of American Railroads*] ... SPLC
Standard Police Automated Resource Management Information System ... SPARMIS
Standard & Poor's Corp. ... S & P
Standard Program [*Data processing*] (BUR) ... SP
Standard Reference Data System (DIT) ... SRDS
Standard Reference Library (TUT) ... SRL
Standard Regional Route Transmitting Frequencies [*Communications*] (FAAC) ... RUT
Standard Serial Numbers (DIT) ... SSN
Standard Source Data Package ... SSDP
Standard Tape Executive Package [*or Program*] [*NCR Corp.*] (CGC) ... STEP
Standard Telecommunications Automatic Recognizer [*Data processing*] ... STAR
Standard Telegraph Level [*Telecommunications*] (TEL) ... STL
Standard Telephone and Cable [*IT & T affiliate*] [*British*] ... STC
Standard Terminal Program [*Data processing*] (IEEE) ... STEP
Standard Test Key [*Data processing*] ... STK
Standard Transmission Code [*Data processing*] ... STC
Standard Unit of Accounting [*Data processing*] ... SUA
Standard Unit of Processing [*Data processing*] ... SUP
Standard Universal Identifying Number (NITA) ... SUI
Standard User Labels [*Data processing*] ... SUL
Standard Utility Means for Information Transformation [*Data processing*] (TUT) ... SUMIT
Standard Wafer Array Programing (DEEC) ... SWAP
Standard Wire Gauge [*Telecommunications*] ... SWG
Standardization Data ... SD
Standardization Data Management Information System (DDI) ... SDMIS
Standardized Test Program (DDI) ... STP
Standards Eastern [*or Electronic*] **Automatic Computer** [*National Bureau of Standards*] ... SEAC
Standards Information Service [*National Bureau of Standards*] (EISS) ... SIS
Standards Planning and Requirements Committee [*ANSI*] ... SPARC
Standards Steering Committee [*ANSI*] ... SSC
Standards Western Automatic Computer [*National Bureau of Standards*] ... SWAC
Standing Wave Apparatus ... SWA
Standing Wave Area Monitor Indicator (MUGU) ... SWAMI
Standing Wave Detector ... SWD
Standing Wave Read-Only Memory [*Data processing*] ... SWROM
Stanford Artificial Intelligence Laboratory [*Stanford University*] ... SAIL
Stanford Center for Information Processing [*Stanford University*] [*Database*] ... SCIP
Stanford Electronics Laboratory [*Stanford University*] [*Research center*] ... SEL
Stanford Public Information Retrieval System [*Stanford University Libraries*] [*Stanford, CA*] [*Bibliographic database management system*] [*Information service*] ... SPIRES
Stanford Research Institute [*Later, SRI International*] [*Databank originator*] ... SRI
Stanford Telecommunications [*NASDAQ symbol*] (NQ) ... STII
Stanford University Medical Experimental Computer Project [*Stanford University*] [*Research center*] (RCD) ... SUMEX
STAR [*Self Testing and Reporting*] **Computer Assembly Language** (CIT) ... SCAL
STARAN Debug Module (OA) ... SDM
STARAN Evaluation and Training Facility (OA) ... SETF
Start of Address (NITA) ... SOA
Start Address [*Telecommunications*] (TEL) ... STAD
Start of Answer [*Telecommunications*] (TEL) ... AS
Start of Block (NITA) ... SOB
Start Computer (VIT) ... SC
Start Conversion [*Data processing*] ... SC
Start-Data-Traffic [*Data processing*] (IBMDP) ... SDT
Start of Entry [*Data processing*] ... SOE
Start of Frame (NITA) ... SOF
Start of Heading [*Transmission control character*] [*Data processing*] ... SOH
Start Input/Output (NITA) ... SIO
Start of Line Block (CET) ... SOLB
Start of Manual Message (BUR) ... SMM
Start-of-Message ... SOM
Start-of-Message - High Precedence (CET) ... SOM-H
Start-of-Message - Low Precedence (CET) ... SOM-L
Start-of-Message - Priority ... SOM-P
Start Sample Command Delayed ... SSCD
Start Signal Indicator [*Telecommunications*] (TEL) ... SSI
Start of Significance [*Data processing*] (BUR) ... SOS
Start/Stop (NITA) ... S/S
Start of Text (NITA) ... SOT
Start of Text Character [*Keyboard*] [*Data processing*] ... STX
Start Unload Address Register (SKY) ... SUAR
Start of Word ... SOW
Startover Data Transfer and Processing [*Program*] ... SDTP
State Alcoholism Profile Information System [*Public Health Service*] (EISS) ... SAPIS
State of the Art ... SOTA
State Change Algorithm Translator ... SCAT
State Energy Data System [*Department of Energy*] [*Database*] (FDB) ... SEDS
State Services Group [*Information service*] (EISS) ... SSG
State of Termination [*Telecommunications*] (TEL) ... SOT
State University Computation Center [*Iowa State University*] [*Research center*] (RCD) ... SUCC
State University of New York [*Computer retrieval and control projects*] [*Albany, NY*] ... SUNY
State University of New York Online Computer Library Center [*Library network*] ... SUNY/OCLC
Statement (AFM) ... STMT
Statement of Work (MCD) ... SOW
Statens Rad for Vetenskaplig Information och Dokumentation [*Swedish Council for Scientific Information and Documentation*] (EISS) ... SINFDOK
States Information Center [*Council of State Governments*] (EISS) ... SIC
Static ... S
Static Error Analysis (NITA) ... SEA
Static Induction Transistor [*Telecommunications*] (TEL) ... SIT
Static Memory Interface [*Data processing*] (MDG) ... SMI
Static Nonlinear Analysis of Shells of Revolution [*Computer program*] ... SNASOR
Static Pointer ... SP
Static Random Access Memory [*Data processing*] ... SRAM
Static Squelch Range ... SSR
Station [*Telecommunications*] ... STA
Station ... STN
Station Address [*Data processing*] (BUR) ... SA
Station Buffer Unit [*Data processing*] (OA) ... SBU
Station Communications Processor (CIT) ... SCP
Station Control Block [*Data processing*] (IBMDP) ... SCB
Station Control Unit (OA) ... SCU
Station Data Processing (CIT) ... SDP
Station Display Unit (NITA) ... SDU
Station Engineering Control Office [*Telecommunications*] (TEL) ... SECO
Station Engineering Manual [*Telecommunications*] (TEL) ... SEM
Station Identification Store [*Bell Laboratories*] ... SIS
Station Message Detail Recording [*Formerly, MDR*] [*Telecommunications*] ... SMDR
Station Open to Public Correspondence [*ITU designation*] ... CP
Station Program Identification [*Telecommunications*] (TEL) ... SPI
Station Selection Code (BUR) ... SSC
Station Signaling and Announcement Subsystem [*Telecommunications*] (TEL) ... SSAS
Station to Station ... S to S
Station to Station Send Paid [*Telecommunications*] (TEL) ... SSSP
Station Technical Control [*Telecommunications*] (TEL) ... STC
Stationery Digital Audio Tape ... SDAT
Statistical Analysis System [*Programing language*] [*1966*] ... SAS
Statistical Computing Library [*Bell System*] ... STATLIB
[*A*] **Statistical Computing Procedure** ... ASCOP
Statistical Context-Aided Testing [*North-Holland Publishing Co.*] [*Software package*] [*British*] (NCC) ... STATCAT
Statistical Data Recorder [*Data processing*] (MDG) ... SDR
Statistical Historical Input/Output Error Rate Utility [*Sperry UNIVAC*] (NITA) ... SHIOER
Statistical Interactive Programing System (NITA) ... SIPS
Statistical Interpretive Language [*Data processing*] (MDG) ... STIL
Statistical Multiplexing [*Telecommunications*] ... STM
Statistical Network Processor (NITA) ... SNP
Statistical Package for the Social Sciences [*Programing language*] [*1970*] ... SPSS

Statistical Processing and Analysis [Data processing]............... SPAN
Statistical Table Assembly and Retrieval System [Proposed for Social Security Administration] .... STAR
Statistical Time-Division Multiplexer [or Multiplexing] (NITA) ...... STDM
Statistical Utility Program .... SUP
Statistically Oriented Matrix Program (IEEE) .... STORM
Statistics Package [Computer program] (IEEE) .... STATPAC
Status .... ST
Status [Online database field identifier] .... STA
Status (MSA) .... STAT
Status Display Support (MCD) .... SDS
Status Entry Device [Telecommunications] (TEL) .... SED
Status Entry Device Multiplexer [Telecommunications] (TEL) .... SEDM
Status Fill-In Unit [Telecommunications] (TEL) .... SFU
Status Memory and Real Time System [AT & T] .... SMARTS
Status Register (NITA) .... SR
Status Statement [Online database field identifier] (OBD) .... SC
Status Valid (NITA) .... SV
Status Word Enable (NITA) .... SWE
Statutes and Cases Automated Legal Enquiry .... SCALE
Steady State Determining Routine (OA) .... SSDR
Steel, Aluminum, Polyethylene [Components of a type of telecommunications cable] .... STALPETH
Steel Beam Design [Modray Ltd.] [Software package] [British] (NCC) ..... SBD
Steel Column [Camutek] [Software package] [British] (NCC) .... STCOL
Steep-Spectrum Compact Sources [of galactic radio waves] .... SSCS
Steerable LASER Radiometer (MCD) .... SLAR
Steerable Null Antenna Processor (RDA) .... SNAP
Steering Damping System (MCD) .... SDS
Stellar Attitude Reference and Navigation .... STARAN
Step Adjustable Antenna .... SAA
Step Control Table (CMD) .... SCT
Step-Down and Step-Up (MSA) .... SDN & SU
Step-by-Step Monitor and Selector Hold [Telecommunications] (TEL) .... SMASH
Step-by-Step Switching System [Telecommunications] .... SxS
Stepped Electrode Transistor (NITA) .... SET
Stepped-Frequency Microwave Radiometer [For measuring rain rate and wind speed] .... SFMR
Sterba Curtain Antenna .... SCA
Stereo Broadcast [Radio] [British] .... S
Sterling and Decimal Invoicing Electronically (IEEE) .... SADIE
Stern Telecommunications Corporation [New York, NY] [Telecommunications] (TSSD) .... STC
Stiff Circuit Analysis Program [Data processing] .... STICAP
Still-Camera Video System [Canon, Inc.] .... SVS
Stimulated Learning by Automated Typewriter Environment .... SLATE
Sting Array [Computer system] (MCD) .... STAR
Stock Control and Analysis (BUR) .... SCAN
Stock Market Computer Answering Network [British] .... SCAN
Stock Technical Analysis Reports [Innovest Systems, Inc.] [Database] (CUAD) .... STAR
Stock Updating Sales Invoicing Electronically (IEEE) .... SUSIE
Stop Acknowledge (CMD) .... SAK
Stop-Start [Telecommunications] (TEL) .... STPST
Storage (NITA) .... S
Storage .... STGE
Storage (AFM) .... STOR
Storage Access Channel (CMD) .... SAC
Storage Access Control [Data processing] (NITA) .... SAC
Storage Address Register [Telecommunications] .... SAR
Storage Allocator [Telecommunications] (TEL) .... SA
Storage Buffer Register (NITA) .... SBR
Storage Bus in Register (NITA) .... SBIR
Storage Capacity .... SC
Storage Connecting Circuit [Teletype] .... SCC
Storage Control Unit .... SCU
Storage Data Bus (NITA) .... SDB
Storage Data Register (NITA) .... SDR
Storage, Handling, and Retrieval of Technical Data in Image Formation [Data processing] (IEEE) .... SHIRTDIF
Storage Immediate (CAH) .... SI
Storage and Information Retrieval System [IBM Corp.] .... STAIRS
Storage and Information Retrieval System/Virtual Storage [IBM Corp.] .... STAIRS/VS
Storage Instantaneous Audimeter [Measures television viewing] .... SIA
Storage Interface Facility (NITA) .... SIF
Storage Limits Register .... SLR
Storage Module Controller (NITA) .... SMC
Storage Module Drive (NITA) .... SMD
Storage Planning and Allocation [Data processing] .... SPAN
Storage and Processing Control System (NITA) .... SPCS
Storage Protect Violation (CMD) .... SPV
Storage Protection Register .... SPR
Storage Queue (NITA) .... STOQ
Storage Register (NITA) .... SR
Storage and Retrieval [Data processing] (DDI) .... S & R
Storage and Retrieval [Data processing] .... STORET
Storage and Retrieval for Water Quality Data [Environmental Protection Agency] [Databank] .... STORET
Storage to Storage (MCD) .... SS
Storage-to-Storage Instruction (IEEE) .... SSI
Storage Structure Language (NITA) .... SSL
Storage Technology Corporation [In company name, STC Systems, Inc.] [Waldwick, NJ] [Software manufacturer] (DASOS) .... STC
Storage Technology Corp. [NYSE symbol] .... STK
Storage Technology for Operational Readiness .... STORE
Storage Unit [Data processing] .... SU
Store (CDH) .... STR
Store Access Bus Recording Equipment [Telecommunications] (TEL) .... SABRE
Store Address Director (NITA) .... SAD
Store and Clear Accumulator [Data processing] (CDH) .... SAC
Store-and-Forward [Data communications] .... S/F
Store and Forward Element [Telecommunications] (TEL) .... SAFE
Store and Forward Facsimile (NITA) .... SAFF
Store Interface Link (NITA) .... SIL
Store Logical Word .... SLW
Store Monitor Unit (NITA) .... SMU
Stored .... STRD
Stored Address [Data processing] .... STORAD
Stored Data Definition Language .... SDDL
Stored Data Definition and Translation Task Group (OA) .... SDDTTG
Stored Data Description (NITA) .... SDD
Stored Index to Address .... SXA
Stored Information Loss Tree (NITA) .... SILT
Stored Logic Array (NITA) .... SLA
Stored Program Buffer (NITA) .... SPB
Stored Program CAMAC [Computer-Aided Measurement and Control] Channel [Data processing] .... SPCC
Stored Program Command [or Control] [Data processing] .... SPC
Stored Program Controlled Network [Telecommunications] .... SPCN
Stored Program Data Processor (KSC) .... SPDP
Stored Program Educational Computer .... SPEC
Stored Program Educational Transistorized Automatic Computer .... SPEDTAC
Stored Program Electronic Switching System [Telecommunications] (TEL) .... SPESS
Stored Program Element System [Data processing] (IEEE) .... SPES
Stored Program Real-Time Commands (MCD) .... SRTC
Storer Communications, Incorporated [NYSE symbol] .... SCI
Stores Keeping Unit .... SKU
Stores Management Multiplex Bus [Data processing] (MCD) .... SMMB
Stores Management System (MCD) .... SMS
Strachey and McIlroy [in SAM/76, a programing language named after its authors and developed in 1976] (CSR) .... SAM
Straight Binary Second .... SBS
Straight Channel Tape Print [Data processing] (KSC) .... SCTP
Straight Channel Tape Print Program [Data processing] (KSC) .... SCTPP
Straight Line Depreciation [Telecommunications] (TEL) .... SLD
Straight-Line Frequency .... SLF
Straight-Line Wavelength .... SLW
Straight-Line Wavelength (MSA) .... SLWL
Straight Wire Antenna .... SWA
Strategic Automatic Message-Switching Operational Network [Canada] (MCD) .... SAMSON
Stratified Indexing and Retrieval [Japan] [Data processing] (DIT) .... SIR
Stratospheric Sounding Unit [Telecommunications] (TEL) .... SSU
Stratus Computer, Inc. [NASDAQ symbol] (NQ) .... STRA
Stream Generation Statement [Data processing] .... SGS
Streamline Curvature Method [Computer program] .... SCM
Street Address Record [Telecommunications] (TEL) .... SAR
Strength Power and Communications Cable .... SPCC
Stress Wave Analysis Technique .... SWAT
Stress Wave Analyzing Program .... SWAP
Stress Wave Emission .... SWE
String Array Processor (NITA) .... STAR
String and Character Recording Oriented Logogrammatic Language [1970] [Data processing] (CSR) .... SCROLL
String Control Language [Data processing] .... SCL
String-Oriented Symbolic Language [1963] [Data processing] .... SNOBOL
String Processing Language [Data processing] (DIT) .... STRIP
String Processing System [Word processing software] (DEEC) .... SPS
Strip-Buried Heterostructure [Telecommunications] (TEL) .... SBH
Stromberg-Carlson Practices [Telecommunications] (TEL) .... SCP
Strowger Automatic Toll Ticketing [Telecommunications] .... SATT
Structural Analysis Program (MCD) .... SAP
Structural Analytical Interpreter (NITA) .... STRAIN
Structural Computer-Aided Logic Design (NITA) .... SCALD
Structural Design Language [Data processing] .... STRUDL
Structural Engineering Systems Solver [Programing language] [1962] .... STRESS
Structural Formula [Data processing] [Chemistry] .... STRUFO
Structural Macroassembly Language (NITA) .... SMAL
Structural Programing Technique (NITA) .... SPT
Structural Return Loss [Telecommunications] (TEL) .... SRL
Structure .... STRUC
Structure Memory (NITA) .... SM
Structure Memory Information Processor (NITA) .... SMIP
Structure-Oriented Description and Simulation (IEEE) .... SODAS
Structure and Parity Observing Output Function (NITA) .... SPOOF
Structured Analysis [Programing language] [1977] (CSR) .... SA
Structured Analysis, Design, and Programing [Data processing] .... SADP
Structured Analysis and Design Technique [Programing language] [1978] .... SADT
Structured Assembly Language (NITA) .... SAL

Computer & Telecommunications Acronyms

Structured Basic Language [*Data processing*] (CSR) ..... STRUBAL
Structured COBOL (NITA) ..... SCOBOL
Structured Document Handbook [*Data processing*] ..... SDH
Structured English Query Language [*1974*] [*Data processing*] (CSR) ..... SEQUEL
Structured Exploratory Data Analysis ..... SEDA
Structured Programing [*Data processing*] (BUR) ..... SP
Structured Programing Facility [*Data processing*] ..... SPF
Structured Query Language/Data System [*IBM Corp.*] ..... SQL/DS
Structures with Error Expurgation Program ..... SWEEP
Structures for Orbiting Radio Telescope ..... SORT
Student Career Automated Network (IEEE) ..... SCAN
Student Response System [*Automated group instruction*] (CGC) ..... SRS
Student Taskforce Against Telecommunication Information Concealment [*Student legal action organization*] ..... STATIC
Students for Data Education (IEEE) ..... SDE
Studio Location ..... SL
Study Organization Plan (BUR) ..... SOP
Sub BIT [*Binary Digit*] Encoder (MCD) ..... SBE
Subarchitectural Interface (NITA) ..... SAI
Subarray Electronics Module [*Data processing*] ..... SEM
Subcable (KSC) ..... S/C
Subcarrier Authorization (MSA) ..... SCA
Subcarrier Channel [*Telecommunications*] ..... SCA
Subcarrier Frequency Modulation [*Telecommunications*] (TEL) ..... SCFM
Subchannel Adapter ..... SCA
Subject [*Online database field identifier*] (OBD) ..... SU
Subject-Content-Oriented Retriever for Processing Information On-Line [*Congressional Research Service*] ..... SCORPIO
Subject Heading Authority List [*Data processing*] ..... SHAL
Subject Profile Index [*Computer-based*] ..... SPINDEX
Subject Word out of Context [*Data processing*] (DIT) ..... SWOC
Subminiature Integrated Antenna ..... SIA
Subminiature Microwave Delay Line ..... SMDL
Submodel ..... SBMDL
Submodule and Operator Controller [*For sequence of telephonic operations*] ..... SMOC
Submultiplexer Unit ..... SMX
Subprocessor with Dynamic Microprograming (NITA) ..... SPDM
Subrate Data Multiplexer [*Telecommunications*] (TEL) ..... SRDM
Subroutine [*Data processing*] ..... SR
Subroutine (NITA) ..... SUB
Subroutine Call Table [*Data processing*] (CDH) ..... SCT
Subsatellite Point [*Telecommunications*] (TEL) ..... SSP
Subscriber ..... Sub
Subscriber Busy [*Telecommunications*] (TEL) ..... SSB
Subscriber Carrier Terminal [*Telecommunications*] (TEL) ..... SCT
Subscriber Line Use [*Telecommunications*] ..... SLU
Subscriber Loop Analysis Program System [*Bell System*] ..... SLAPS
Subscriber Loop Carrier [*Telecommunications*] (TEL) ..... SLC
Subscriber Loop Multiplex [*Bell System*] ..... SLM
Subscriber Originating Trunk [*Telecommunications*] (TEL) ..... SOT
Subscriber Plant Factor [*Telecommunications*] ..... SPF
Subscriber-Response System [*Study of cable television*] [*Hughes Aircraft Co.*] ..... SRS
Subscriber Switching [*Telecommunications*] (TEL) ..... SSU
Subscriber Switching Unit [*Telecommunications*] (TEL) ..... SST
Subscriber Transferred [*Telecommunications*] (TEL) ..... STD
Subscriber Trunk Dialing [*Telephone communications*] ..... STD
Subscribers' Apparatus Line Tester [*Telecommunications*] (TEL) ..... SALT
Subscribers' Call Processing (Subsystem) [*Telecommunications*] (TEL) ..... SCP(S)
Subscribers' Circuit Routine Tester [*Telecommunications*] (TEL) ..... SCRT
Subscribers' Concentration Module [*Telecommunications*] (TEL) ..... SCM
Subscribers' Concentrator Unit [*Telecommunications*] (TEL) ..... SCU
Subscriber's Directory Number [*Telecommunications*] ..... SDN
Subscriber's Line Interface Circuit [*Telecommunications*] (TEL) ..... SLIC
Subscriber's Line Use System [*AT & T*] [*Telecommunications*] (TEL) ..... SLUS
Subscriber's Loop [*Telecommunications*] (TEL) ..... SL
Subscriber's Private Meter [*Telecommunications*] (TEL) ..... SPM
Subscribers' Switching Subsystem [*Telecommunications*] (TEL) ..... SSS
Subscribers' Trunk Unit [*Telecommunications*] (TEL) ..... STU
Subscription Television ..... STV
Subsequent Address Message [*Telecommunications*] (TEL) ..... SAM
Subsequent Signal Unit [*Group of BITS*] [*Telecommunications*] (TEL) ..... SSU
Subsidiary Communications Authorization [*Facilities used to transmit background music to subscribing customers*] ..... SCA
Subsidiary Communications Multiplex Operation [*FM radio frequency unused portion*] ..... SCMO
Substitute Character [*Keyboard*] (AFM) ..... SUB
Substrate Fed Logic (NITA) ..... SFL
Substructure [*Data processing*] ..... ss
Substructure and Nomenclature Searching System [*Chemical Information Systems, Inc.*] [*Database*] (CUAD) ..... SANSS
Subsystem Computer (MCD) ..... SSC
Subsystem Computer Application Software (MCD) ..... SCAS
Subsystem Controller Definition Record [*Data processing*] (IBMDP) ..... SCDR
Subsystem Design Manual (MCD) ..... SDM
Subsystem Library [*Data processing*] (IBMDP) ..... SLIB
Subsystem Program Preparation Support [*Programing language*] [*Data processing*] ..... SPPS
Subsystem Support Service (BUR) ..... SSS
Subtask ABEND [*Abnormal End*] Intercept [*Data processing*] (BUR) ..... STAI
Subtask Control Block [*Data processing*] (IBMDP) ..... STCB
Subtract BCD [*Binary Coded Decimal*] Number [*Data processing*] ..... SBCD
Subtract Binary Number [*Data processing*] ..... SUB
Successive Approximation Register [*Data processing*] ..... SAR
Sudanian Satellite (CBSS) ..... SUDOSAT
Sudden Cosmic-Noise Absorption ..... SCNA
Sudden Ionospheric Disturbance [*Telecommunications*] ..... SID
Suicide Information and Education Centre [*Canadian Mental Health Association*] [*Information service*] (EISS) ..... SIEC
Sumika Technical Information Service, Inc. [*Osaka, Japan*] [*Information service*] (EISS) ..... STIS
Summary of Component Control Status ..... SOCCS
Summary Message Enable Keyboard ..... SMEK
Summary of Proceedings and Debate [*of House of Representatives*] ..... SOPAD
Summary Punch IBM [*International Business Machines*] Collector (VIT) ..... SPIC
Summer Computer Simulation Conference ..... SCSC
Sun Co., Inc. [*NYSE symbol*] ..... SUN
Sun-Energy Collecting Satellite ..... SUNSAT
Sun-Improved Frequency Response ..... SIFR
Sunbeam Corp. [*NYSE symbol*] [*Delisted*] ..... SMB
Sundstrand Processing Language Internally Translated ..... SPLIT
Super Group (NATG) ..... SG
Super-Hard Extremely-Low Frequency (MCD) ..... SHELF
Super-High-Frequency [*Radio wave*] (NG) ..... SH
Super-High-Frequency [*Radio wave*] ..... SHF
Super Knowledge Information Processing Intelligence [*Data processing*] ..... SKIPI
Super Large-Scale Integration (DEEC) ..... SLSI
Super-Module Unit [*Telecommunications*] (TEL) ..... SMU
Super Video Recorder (DEEC) ..... SVR
Supercomputer Computations Research Institute [*Florida State University*] [*Research center*] (RCD) ..... SCRI
Supercomputer Project Research Experiment in Advanced Development [*Lawrence Livermore Laboratory, Los Alamos National Laboratory, and SRI*] ..... SPREAD
Superconducting Quantum Interference Detector [*or Device*] [*For studying changes in the Earth's magnetic field*] ..... SQUID
Superconductor-Insulator-Superconductor [*Transistor technology*] ..... SIS
Supergroup Connector [*Telecommunications*] (TEL) ..... SGC
Supergroup Distribution Frame [*Telecommunications*] (TEL) ..... SDF
Supergroup Distribution Frame [*Telecommunications*] (TEL) ..... SGDF
Superimpose (MDG) ..... SI
Superimposed Coding [*Data processing*] (DIT) ..... SC
Superimposed Current ..... SUPCUR
Superior Electric Co. [*NASDAQ symbol*] (NQ) ..... SUPE
Supermarket Subsystem Definition Record [*Data processing*] (IBMDP) ..... SSDR
Supervision Control Module [*Telecommunications*] (TEL) ..... SCM
Supervisor (TEL) ..... SR
Supervisor Call (NASA) ..... SVC
Supervisor of Multiprograming, Multiprocessing, Interactive Time Sharing [*Data processing*] (IEEE) ..... SUMMIT
Supervisor Program Over Other Kinds [*Data processing*] ..... SPOOK
Supervisor Request Block [*Data processing*] (BUR) ..... SVRB
Supervisory Control and Data Acquisition (IEEE) ..... SCADA
Supervisory Control Program [*Burroughs Corp.*] (NITA) ..... SCP
Supervisory Control of Program Execution (MCD) ..... SCOPE
Supervisory Process [*Telecommunications*] (TEL) ..... SP
Supervisory Tape Executive Program [*Data processing*] ..... STEP
Supervisory Time Frame (NITA) ..... STF
Supplementary Information [*Telecommunications*] (TEL) ..... SC
Supplementary Term [*Online database field identifier*] (OBD) ..... ST
Suppliers and Equipment Information Retrieval System [*International Civil Aviation Organization*] [*Databank*] [*Information service*] (EISS) ..... SEIRS
Supply Line Inventory Management System [*Bell System*] ..... SLIMS
Supply On-Line Option [*IMS America Ltd.*] [*Database*] (CUAD) ..... SOLO
Support Integrated Data System (MCD) ..... SIDS
Support Package for Aerospace Computer Emulation (MCD) ..... SPACE
Support of User Records and Files [*Data processing*] ..... SURF
Supporting Data Analysis ..... SDA
Suppress Leading Zero [*Data processing*] ..... SLZ
Suppress Length Indication (BUR) ..... SLI
Suppressed Carrier (IEEE) ..... SC
Suppressed-Carrier Double Sideband ..... SCDSB
Suppressing Line Operands and Translating to Hexadecimal [*Telecommunications*] (TEL) ..... SLOTH
Suppressor [*Electronics*] (MDG) ..... SU
Supreme Equipment & Systems [*NASDAQ symbol*] (NQ) ..... SEQP
Surface Acoustic Wave [*Microwave system*] ..... SAW
Surface Acoustic Wave Oscillator [*Telecommunications*] (TEL) ..... SAWO
Surface Barrier Transistor ..... SBT
Surface Coatings Abstracts [*Paint Research Association of Great Britain*] [*Bibliographic database*] (OBD) ..... SCA
Surface Electromagnetic Wave ..... SEW
Surface Mining and Environment Information System [*University of Arizona*] (EISS) ..... SEAMINFO

Computer & Telecommunications Acronyms

Surface Roughness Factor [*Telecommunications*] (TEL) .... SRF
Surface Ship Electromagnetic Jammer (DDI) .... SUREJ
Surface Water Automatic Computer .... SURWAC
Surface Wave Delay Line .... SWDL
Surface Wave Dielectrometer .... SWD
Surface Wave Mode .... SWM
Surface Wave Phenomena .... SWP
Surface Wave Transmission Line .... SWTL
Surge (MSA) .... SRG
Surveillance Calibration Satellite .... SURCAL
Surveillance and Control of Transmission Systems [*Bell Laboratories*] .... SCOTS
Surveillance Data Transmission .... SDT
Surveillance Television (AFM) .... STV
Survey Data Processing .... SDP
Survey of Doctorate Recipients [*National Research Council*] [*Database*] (FDB) .... SDR
Survey Methodology Information System [*Inter-University Consortium for Political & Social Research*] [*Database*] (FDB) .... SMIS
Survey Research Center [*University of Kentucky*] [*Research center*] (RCD) .... SRC
Survey Research Consultants International [*Information service*] (EISS) .... SRCI
Survey Sampling, Incorporated [*Information service*] (EISS) .... SSI
Survey Tabulation Services, Inc. [*Information service*] (EISS) .... STS
Survivable Satellite Communications System (MCD) .... SURVSA
Survivable Satellite Communications System (CBSS) .... SURVSATCOM
Swedish Drug Information System [*Swedish National Board of Health and Welfare*] [*Database*] [*Sweden*] (EISS) .... SWEDIS
Swedish Environmental Research Index [*Swedish National Environmental Protection Board*] [*Database*] (EISS) .... SERIX
Swedish Telecommunications Administration [*Farsta*] [*Telecommunications*] (TSSD) .... STA
Swedish Telecoms International AB [*Stockholm*] [*Telecommunications*] (TSSD) .... SWEDTEL
Sweep Frequency, Continuous Wave .... SFCW
Swept Frequency Jamming .... SFJ
Swept Frequency Radiometer System .... SFRS
SWIFT [*Society for Worldwide Interbank Financial Telecommunications*] Interface Device (NITA) .... SID
Swiss Broadcasting Corporation .... SBC
Swiss Institute for Technical Information [*Information service*] (EISS) .... SITI
Swiss Viewdata Information Providers Association [*Zurich*] [*Telecommunications*] (TSSD) .... SVIPA
Switch .... S
Switch .... SW
Switch (MCD) .... SWCH
Switch Busy Hour [*Telecommunications*] (IEEE) .... SBH
Switch Control Assembly .... SCA
Switch Handler [*Telecommunications*] (TEL) .... SH
Switch Maintenance Center [*Telecommunications*] (TEL) .... SMC
Switch Panel .... SP
Switch Register (NITA) .... SR
Switchband Wound [*Relay*] .... SW
Switchboard [*Telecommunications*] (TEL) .... S
Switchboard .... SWBD
Switchboard Panel [*Telecommunications*] (TEL) .... PAN
Switched Access Remote Test System [*Bell System*] .... SARTS
Switched Access System [*Telecommunications*] (TEL) .... SAS
Switched Data Access Line (NITA) .... SDAL
Switched Ground Discrete Input (MCD) .... SGDI
Switched Ground Discrete Output (MCD) .... SGDO
Switched Maintenance Access System [*Bell System*] .... SMAS
Switched Network Backup [*Data processing*] (IBMDP) .... SNBU
Switched Private Network Service [*ITT service mark*] .... SPNS
Switched Programable Read-Only Memory (NITA) .... SPROM
Switched Service Network [*Telecommunications*] .... SSN
Switched Telecommunications Network (NITA) .... STN
Switched Virtual Circuit .... SVC
Switching Central [*Telecommunications*] .... SWCENT
Switching Control Center [*Bell System*] .... SCC
Switching Control Center System [*Telecommunications*] (TEL) .... SCCS
Switching Equipment Congestion [*Telecommunications*] (TEL) .... SEC
Switching Logic Unit (CAAL) .... SLU
Switching and Maintenance Set .... SMS
Switching Mode Frequency Multipliers (OA) .... SFM
Switching Mode Regulator .... SMR
Switching Network Analysis Program [*Bell System*] .... SNAP
Switching Node and Processing Sites [*ITT*] (TEL) .... SNAPS
Switching Service Operations Center [*Telecommunications*] .... SSOC
Switching Unit (VIT) .... SU
Switching Unit .... SUN
Switchman's Local Test [*Telecommunications*] (TEL) .... SLT
Sydney Development Corp. [*Toronto Stock Exchange symbol*] .... SNY
SYFA Concurrent Logic Operating System (NITA) .... SYCLOPS
Sykes Datatronics [*NASDAQ symbol*] .... SYKE
Sylvania High-Intelligence Electronic Defense .... SHIELD
Sylvania Ultrahigh-Level Logic (IEEE) .... SUHL
Symbionics On-Line Information System [*Data processing*] (TUT) .... SOLIS
Symbol [*or Symbolic*] .... SYM
Symbol Generation and Storage [*Data processing*] .... SGS
Symbol Manipulation [*Data processing*] .... SYMAN

Symbol Processing Machine (IEEE) .... SPM
Symbol Programer (MUGU) .... SP
Symbol Sink - Matched Filter (CIT) .... SSMF
Symbol Technologies [*NASDAQ symbol*] (NQ) .... SMBL
Symbolic Algebraic Language [*Data processing*] (TUT) .... SYMBAL
Symbolic Algebraic Language Translator [*Data processing*] .... SALT
Symbolic and Algebraic Manipulation (IEEE) .... SAM
Symbolic Assembler (IEEE) .... SA
Symbolic Assembler for Binary Relocatable Programs (NITA) .... SABR
Symbolic Assembly Language [*Data processing*] (DIT) .... SAL
Symbolic Assembly Program [*Data processing*] .... SAP
Symbolic Automatic Integrator (CAH) .... SAINT
Symbolic Conversion Program (BUR) .... SCP
Symbolic Debugger [*Data processing*] .... SYMDEB
Symbolic Device Address (OA) .... SDA
Symbolic Disk Address (AFM) .... SDA
Symbolic File Support .... SFS
Symbolic Input [*Data processing*] .... SI
Symbolic Input Program [*Data processing*] (BUR) .... SIP
Symbolic Input Routine [*Data processing*] (DIT) .... SIR
Symbolic Integrator (NITA) .... SIN
Symbolic Language Adapted for Microcomputers (NITA) .... SLAM
Symbolic Language Assembly Program [*Data processing*] (KSC) .... SLAP
Symbolic List Processor (NITA) .... SLIP
Symbolic Machine Language [*Data processing*] .... SML
Symbolic Manipulation Language [*Data processing*] (CSR) .... SYMBOLANG
Symbolic Matrix Interpretation System (NITA) .... SMIS
Symbolic Operating System [*Data processing*] (CGC) .... SOS
Symbolic Optimum Assembly Programing [*IBM Corp.*] [*Data processing*] .... SOAP
Symbolic Output [*Data processing*] .... SO
Symbolic Program Assembly Routine [*Data processing*] .... SPAR
Symbolic Program for Automatic Control .... SYMPAC
Symbolic Program Tape [*Data processing*] (IEEE) .... SPT
Symbolic Program Translator [*Data processing*] (IEEE) .... SPT
Symbolic Programing Anyone Can Enjoy .... SPACE
Symbolic Programing System [*Data processing*] .... SPS
Symbolic Stream Generator [*Data processing*] .... SSG
Symbolic Utilities Revenue Environment [*IBM Corp.*] .... SURE
Symbols-Digits-Alphabetics .... SDA
Symbols per Second [*Data processing*] .... SPS
Symmetric List Interpretive Program [*Data processing*] (TUT) .... SLIP
Symmetric List Processor [*FORTRAN extension*] .... SLIP
Symmetric Multiprocessing (NITA) .... SMP
Symmetrical Switching Function (NITA) .... SSF
Symposium (MSA) .... SYMP
Symposium on Computer Applications in Medical Care [*Baltimore, MD*] .... SCAMC
Synagraphic Mapping System [*Computer-made maps*] .... SYMAP
Synchro-Digital/Digital-Synchro (CAAL) .... SD/DS
Synchro Loop Closure (VIT) .... SLC
Synchro Zeroing Procedure .... SZP
Synchromechanism (DDI) .... SYNC
Synchronization Separator and Digitizer .... SS & D
Synchronize .... SYNC
Synchronize (CBSS) .... SYNCH
Synchronized (MDG) .... SY
Synchronized .... SYNCD
Synchronized Digital Network [*Telecommunications*] (TEL) .... SDN
Synchronizer .... SYNCR
Synchronizing .... SYNCG
Synchronous .... SYN
Synchronous .... SYNCS
Synchronous Altitude Communications Satellite .... SACS
Synchronous Communications [*Satellite*] [*GSFC*] .... SYCOM
Synchronous Communications Access Method (NITA) .... SCAM
Synchronous Communications Adapter (NITA) .... SCA
Synchronous Communications Controller (NITA) .... SCC
Synchronous Continuous Orbital Three-Dimensional Tracking .... SCOTT
Synchronous Data-Link Control [*Data processing*] .... SDLC
Synchronous Data Modern Equipment .... SDME
Synchronous Digital Machine (NITA) .... SDM
Synchronous Identification System Study .... SISS
Synchronous Idle [*Transmission control character*] [*Data processing*] .... SYN
Synchronous Interface Module (NITA) .... SIM
Synchronous Line Adapter (NITA) .... SLA
Synchronous Line Control Unit (NITA) .... SLCU
Synchronous Line Driver (NITA) .... SLD
Synchronous Line Group (BUR) .... SLG
Synchronous Line Interface (NITA) .... SLI
Synchronous Line, Low, Load (BUR) .... SLLL
Synchronous Line Medium Speed (BUR) .... SL
Synchronous Line Medium Speed with Clock (BUR) .... SLC
Synchronous Line Module (NITA) .... SLM
Synchronous MODEM .... SM
Synchronous Modulator-Demodulator (MCD) .... SMD
Synchronous Network Processor (NITA) .... SNP
Synchronous, Operational Meteorological Satellite .... SOMS
Synchronous Orbit Communication Relay (MCD) .... SOCR
Synchronous Orbit Data Relay Satellite .... SODRS
Synchronous Phase Demodulator .... SPD
Synchronous Relay Satellite [*Telecommunications*] (TEL) .... SRS
Synchronous Remote Control (NITA) .... SRC

Computer & Telecommunications Acronyms

Synchronous Serial Data Adapter (NITA) ... SSDA
Synchronous Single-Line Controller (NITA) ... SSLC
Synchronous Stable Relaying (IEEE) ... SSR
Synchronous System Trap (NITA) ... SST
Synchronous Systems Interface (NITA) ... SSI
Synchronous Time-Division Multiplexing [Data processing] (MDG) ... STDM
Synchronous Transistor Logic (MDG) ... STL
Synchronous Transmission [Data processing] (TSSD) ... SYNCH
Synchronous Transmit Receive Access Method (CMD) ... STRAM
Synchronous Transmitter Receiver [Data processing] ... STR
Synchronous Wave Device ... SWD
Syncom Corporation [NASDAQ symbol] (NQ) ... SYCP
Syndicat Autonome des Agents de la Radiodiffusion du Togo
   [Autonomous Union of Radiobroadcasting Workers of Togo] ... SAARDT
Syndicat des Travailleurs en Telecommunications
   [Telecommunications Workers Union - TWU] [Canada] ... STT
Synergistic Communications [NASDAQ symbol] (NQ) ... SCGA
Syntactic Tracer Organized Retrospective Enquiry System
   [Instituut voor Wiskunde, Informatiewerk, en Statistiek] [Data processing] [Dutch] ... STORES
Syntagmatic Organization Language [Data processing] ... SYNTOL
Syntax Improving Device (IEEE) ... SID
Syntax-Oriented Translator (IEEE) ... SOT
Syntax and Semantics (IEEE) ... SYNSEM
Syntax Translation [Data processing] (DIT) ... SYNTRAN
Synthetic Array Data Processor ... SADP
Synthetic Phase Isolation [Telemetry] ... SPI
Syntrex, Inc. [NASDAQ symbol] (NQ) ... STRX
System (MDG) ... SYM
System (AFM) ... SYS
System ... SYST
System Access Technique [Sperry UNIVAC] (NITA) ... SAT
System to Accumulate and Retrieve Financial Information with Random Extraction [Data processing] ... STARFIRE
System Activity Monitor [Data processing] (CGC) ... SAM
System for Aiding Man-Machine Interaction [Prime Computer (UK) Ltd. and Prime Computers CAD/CAM Ltd.] [Software package] [British] (NCC) ... SAMMIE
System Analysis-Building Block Approach [Ge Cae International and Gen-Red Ltd.] [Software package] [British] (NCC) ... SABBA
System for Application [Data processing] ... SYFA
System Application Software [Data processing] (BUR) ... SAS
System Architecture Design Package (NITA) ... SADP
System for the Automated Management of Text from a Hierarchical Arrangement ... SAMANTHA
System for Automatic Value Exchange [Data processing] ... SAVE
System Automation Software, Incorporated ... SASI
System [or Subsystem] Availability Unit (NITA) ... SAU
System Balance Measure (BUR) ... SBM
System Change Request ... SCR
System Checkout Automatic Network Simulator ... SCANS
System Checkout Test Set (MCD) ... SCOTS
System of Circuit Analysis Program ... SYSCAP
System Circuit Test (VIT) ... SCT
System Command Language [Data processing] ... SCL
System Communication Pamphlet (IEEE) ... SCP
System Communications (CIT) ... SYSCOM
System Comparison Analysis [Bell System] ... SCA
System Compatibility Tests ... SCT
System Computerized for Economical Performance, Tracking, Recording and Evaluation [North Central Airlines] ... SCEPTRE
System for Computerized Olympic Results and Events [Texas Instruments, Inc.] (NITA) ... SCORE
System Consultants, Incorporated [Mason, MI] [Software manufacturer] (DASOS) ... SCI
System Control Area (NITA) ... SCA
System Control Audit Review File [Data processing] ... SCARF
System Control Interface (NITA) ... SCI
System Control Processor [Honeywell, Inc.] (NITA) ... SCP
System Control Programing [Data processing] ... SCP
System Control Unit ... SCU
System Controlling Research Image Processing Tasks (MCD) ... SCRIPT
System to Coordinate the Operation of Peripheral Equipment ... SCOPE
System for Data Calculation [Information retrieval] (ODIN) ... SDC
System Data Format [Data processing] ... SDF
System Data Link Control ... SDLC
System Data Record (CIT) ... SDR
System for Data Retrieval [Information retrieval] (ODIN) ... SDR
System Data Synthesizer (KSC) ... SDS
System Definition Record [Data processing] (IBMDP) ... SDR
System Definition Requirements ... SDR
System Descriptive Language [Data processing] (IEEE) ... SDL
System Design Kit (NITA) ... SDK
System Design Language (NITA) ... SDL
System Design Report [NATO] (NATG) ... SDR
System Design Specification ... SDS
System Developer Interface Activity [Data processing] ... SYDIA
System Development Corporation [Information service] ... SDC
System Development and Integration (MCD) ... SD & I
System Development Language [1971] [Data processing] (CSR) ... SDL
System Directory List [Data processing] (BUR) ... SDL
System Discrepancy Report ... SDR

System of Documentation and Information for Metallurgy [Commission of the European Communities] [Database] [Information service] (EISS) ... SDIM
System fuer Dokumentation und Information der Metallurgie [System for Documentation and Information in Metallurgy] [Fachinformationszentrum Werkstoffe] [Database] [German] (ODIN) ... SDIM1
System Effective Data Rate (BUR) ... SEDR
System for Electronic Analysis and Retrieval of Criminal Histories [Project succeeded by National Crime Information Center] [Department of Justice] ... SEARCH
System for Electronic Evaluation and Retrieval [Data processing] ... SEER
System Engineering Laboratories (MCD) ... SEL
System Environment Recording (BUR) ... SER
System Environment Recording, Editing, and Printing [Data processing] (TUT) ... SEREP
System Error Notification [Data processing] ... SEN
System Error Record Editing Program [Data processing] ... SEREP
System for Exploring Alternative Resource Commitments in Higher Education [Data processing] ... SEARCH
System External Storage (NITA) ... SES
System Failure Analysis Report (IEEE) ... SFAR
System Function Description (IEEE) ... SFD
System Gain (NITA) ... SG
System Industries [NASDAQ symbol] (NQ) ... SYSM
System for Information on Grey Literature in Europe [European Association for Grey Literature Exploitation] [Database] (EISS) ... SIGLE
System of Information Processing for Professional Societies ... SIPPS
System Information Processing Program (MCD) ... SIPP
System Information Reports Formatting (MCD) ... SIRF
System for Information Storage and Retrieval and Analysis ... SISTRAN
System Input [Data processing] (MDG) ... SYSIN
System Input/Output Adapter (CAAL) ... SIOA
System for Integrated Maintenance and Program Language Extension (NITA) ... SIMPLE
System Integration Receiver System (MCD) ... SIRS
System Integrators [NASDAQ symbol] (NQ) ... SINT
System for Interactive Guidance Information [Computerized career-counseling service offered by the Educational Testing Service] ... SIGI
System [or Subsystem] Interface Unit ... SIU
System for International Literature Information on Ceramics and Glass [Fachinformationszentrum Werkstoffe] [Database] (CUAD) ... SILICA
System Interrupt Supervisor (NITA) ... SIS
System Language (NITA) ... SL
System Library [Data processing] (MDG) ... SYSLIB
System Library File [Data processing] (BUR) ... SLF
System Life Cycle ... SLC
System Life Cycle Estimation (NITA) ... SLICE
System Log [Data processing] ... SYSLOG
System Logic and Algorithm Development ... SLAD
System and Logistics ... S & L
System Maintenance Unit [Data processing] ... SMU
System for Management and Allocation of Resources Technique [Data processing] ... SMART
System Management Facility [IBM Corp.] ... SMF
System Management Research Operation (DIT) ... SYMRO
System Measurement Facility [Data processing] (IEEE) ... SMF
System for the Mechanical Analysis and Retrieval of Text (DEEC) ... SMART
System Memory Interface [Data processing] (NITA) ... SMI
System Modification Program [Data processing] ... SMP
System Monitor Board (NITA) ... SMB
System Monitor Console (CAAL) ... SMC
System Monitoring Unit (NITA) ... SMU
System Network Activity Program [Sperry UNIVAC] (NITA) ... SNAP
System Network Computer Center [Louisiana State University] [Research center] (RCD) ... SNCC
System Network Online Operations Information [Suggested name for the Library of Congress computer system] ... SNOOPI
System Network Processor ... SNP
System Operator [Computer networking] ... SYSOP
System for Ordinary Life Operations [Insurance] ... SOLO
System Oriented Language ... SOL
System Output [Data processing] (IBMDP) ... SYSOUT
System Output Unit 1 [IBM Corp.] (MDG) ... SSOU1
System Override ... SO
System Package Plan [or Program] ... SPP
System Page Table [Telecommunications] (TEL) ... SPT
System Parameter Record [Data processing] (IBMDP) ... SPR
System Parameter Table [Data processing] (IBMDP) ... SPT
System Partitioning Unit [Data processing] ... SPU
System Performance and Activity Software Monitor [Data processing] (IEEE) ... SPASM
System Performance Factor [Telecommunications] (TEL) ... SPF
System Performance Rating ... SPR
System Performance Score [Telecommunications] (TEL) ... SPS
System for Processing Educational Data Electronically ... SPEDE
System Processor (IEEE) ... SP
System Productivity Facility [Data processing] ... SPF
System Program Loader (NITA) ... SPL
System Program Review ... SPR

Computer & Telecommunications Acronyms

System Programed Operators [Data processing] (MDG) .... SYSPOP
[A] System for Programers .... ASP
System Programing Language [Data processing] (NASA) .... SPL
System Queue Area [Data processing] (BUR) .... SQA
System Reaction Analysis [Bell System] .... SRA
System Residence [Data processing] (TUT) .... SYSRES
System Resource Manager [IBM Corp.] (BUR) .... SRM
System Run Control Record (NITA) .... SRCR
System Segment Table (NITA) .... SST
System Services Control Point [Data processing] .... SSCP
System Software (MCD) .... SS
System Specification Language (NITA) .... SSL
System Specification Verification (IEEE) .... SYSVER
System Status Display (SKY) .... SSD
System Status Indicator [Bell System] .... SSI
System Status Panel (NITA) .... SSP
System Status Report (NITA) .... SSR
System Summary Display (MCD) .... SSD
System Supervisor (NITA) .... SS
System Support Program (AFM) .... SSP
System Synthesizer and Evaluation Center .... SYSEC
System for Telephone Administrative Response [Data processing] .... STAR
System Test .... ST
System under Test .... SUT
System Test Complex Data System (CIT) .... STCDS
System Test Complex Equipment (CIT) .... STCE
System Test Loop (IEEE) .... STL
System Test Manufacturing Information System (IEEE) .... STMIS
System Test Objectives .... STO
System Test Software (CAAL) .... STS
System Transition Unit [Data processing] .... STU
System Utilization Monitor [Data processing] (TUT) .... SUM
System Validation Testing (NITA) .... SVT
System-Wide On-Line Network for Information Control [Data processing] .... SONIC
System Work Area (NITA) .... SWA
System Workshops in Forecasting Techniques [Bell System] .... SWIFT
Systematic Design Language [Data processing] .... SDL
Systematic Design Language [Data processing] (TUT) .... SDS
Systematic Plotting and Evaluation of Enumerated Data [National Bureau of Standards] [Data processing] .... SPEED
Systematics, Inc. [NASDAQ symbol] (NQ) .... SYST
Systeme de Documentation et d'Information en Metallurgie [System for Documentation and Information in Metallurgy] [Database] [French] (ODIN) SDIM1
Systeme Fundamental Europeen de Reference pour la Transmission Telephonique [European master telephone reference system] (DEN) .... SFERT
Systeme Informatique pour la Conjoncture [Information System for the Economy] [France] [Information service] [Databank] (EISS) .... SIC
Systeme Integre pour les Bibliotheques Universitaires de Lausanne [Integrated System for the University of Lausanne Libraries] [Switzerland] [Information service] (EISS) .... SIBIL
Systeme International d'Unites [International System of Units] [Also, SIU] .... SI
Systeme International d'Unites [International System of Units] [See also SI] .... SIU
Systeme de Reference pour la Determination de l'Affaiblissement Equivalent pour la Nettete [Master telephone transmission reference system] (DEN) .... SRAEN
Systems Adapter Module (NITA) .... SAM
Systems Adviser (CIT) .... SYSAD
Systems Analysis and Data Processing Office .... SADPO
Systems Analysis Module (IEEE) .... SAM
Systems Analysis and Resource Accounting [Data processing system] .... SARA
Systems Analysis Translator [Data processing] .... SYSTRAN
Systems Analyst (NITA) .... SA
Systems Assembly Language [Data processing] (IEEE) .... SAL
Systems Assurance Program [IBM Corp.] .... SAP
Systems Auditability and Control [Data processing] .... SAC
Systems Builders Association (EANO) .... SBA
Systems & Computer Technology Corporation [NASDAQ symbol] (NQ) .... SCTC
Systems-Computers-Controls [A publication] .... Syst-Comput-Controls
Systems and Computers Evaluation and Review Technique [Data processing] .... SCERT
Systems Control .... SYSCON
Systems Control Center .... SCC
Systems Control, Incorporated Computerized Library Operations [Information service] (EISS) .... SCICLOPS
Systems Control Language [Data processing] (NITA) .... SCL
Systems Data Analysis (CIT) .... SDA
Systems Data Analysis Section .... SDAS
Systems Development (MCD) .... SD
Systems Effectiveness Analyzer (IEEE) .... SEA
Systems Engineer [or Engineering] [Data processing] .... SE
Systems Equipment Engineer [Telecommunications] (TEL) ...... SEE
Systems Evaluation and Exchange of Knowledge [Data processing] (CGC) .... SEEK
Systems Generator [or Generation] [Data processing] (CGC) .... SYSGEN
Systems Information Bulletin [Data processing] .... SIB
Systems Integration and Deployment [Program] [Department of Transportation] .... SID
Systems Interface Test (NVT) .... SIT
Systems Language .... SLANG
Systems Library Subscription Service [Data processing] (IBMDP) .... SLSS
Systems Maintenance Management [Data processing] .... SMM
Systems Management Analysis Group (MCD) .... SMAG
Systems Management, Incorporated [Rosemont, IL] [Software manufacturer] (DASOS) .... SMI
Systems Manufacturing Division [IBM Corp.] .... SMD
Systems Measurement Instrument [Data processing] .... SMI
Systems Memory [Data processing] (BUR) .... SM
Systems Network Architecture [IBM Corp.] [Data processing] .... SNA
Systems Operational Description [or Design] .... SOD
Systems and Procedures Association [Later, ASM] .... SPA
Systems Requirement Review .... SRR
Systems Software Interface Processing (MCD) .... SSIP
Systems and Software Simulator S3
Systems Support Center (BUR) .... SSC
Systems Tape Addition and Maintenance Program [Data processing] (IEEE) .... STAMP
Systems Technology Forum [Burke, VA] [Telecommunications] (TSSD) .... STF
Systems Test and Operation Language (NITA) .... STOL
Systems for Test Output Consolidation [Data processing] .... STOC

T

T-Bar, Inc. [*American Stock Exchange symbol*]	TBR
T-Carrier [*Telecommunications*] (TEL)	TC
T-Carrier Administration System [*Minicomputer*] [*Bell System*]	TCAS
T-Carrier Restoration Control Center [*Bell System*]	TRCC
Tab Products Co. [*American Stock Exchange symbol*]	TBP
Tab-Tronic Recorder (DIT)	TTR
Table Base Register (NITA)	TBR
Table of Coincidences [*Telecommunications*] (TEL)	TOC
Table of Contents Editor Processor [*Data processing*]	TOCED
Table Editing Process	TEP
Table Input to Memory (NITA)	TIM
Table and Item Documentation System	TIDOS
Table Look Up [*Data processing*]	TLU
Table Mountain Radio Astronomy Observatory (CIT)	TMRAO
Table Producing Language [*1971*] [*Data processing*] (EISS)	TPL
Tabular Data (BUR)	TD
Tabular Language [*Data processing*] (IEEE)	TAB
Tabular Systems-Oriented Language [*General Electric Co.*] [*British*]	TABSOL
Tabulated Numerical Technical Data List	TNTDL
Tabulator Simulator	TABSIM
TACSATCOM [*Tactical Satellite Communications*] Management Office	TSMO
Tactical Automated Data Processing System	TACADS
Tactical Automatic Digital Switch	TADS
Tactical Automatic Digital Switching System	TADSS
Tactical Automatic Switch	TAS
Tactical Procedure Oriented Language [*Data processing*] (CSR)	TACPOL
Tactile Communicator [*Device which aids the deaf by translating certain sounds into coded vibrations*]	TC
Tactile Procedure-Oriented Language (CSR)	TACPOL
Taft Information System [*Provides information on private foundations*] (EISS)	TIS
Tag Vector Display Register (OA)	TVDR
Tailored Retrieval and Information Management (NITA)	TRIM
Taken Out of Service [*Telecommunications*] (TEL)	TOS
Talk/Listen (NASA)	T/L
Talk and Listen Beacon [*Radio*]	TALBE
Talk-between-Ships [*which are tactically maneuvering; also, the VHF radio equipment used for this purpose*]	TBS
Talking [*Telecommunications*] (TEL)	TLK
Tandem Computers [*NASDAQ symbol*] (NQ)	TNDM
Tandem Cross-Section Program [*Bell System*]	TCSP
Tandem Matching Loss [*Telecommunications*] (TEL)	TML
Tandem Signal Unit [*Telecommunications*] (TEL)	TSU
Tandon Corporation [*NASDAQ symbol*] (NQ)	TCOR
Tandy Corp. [*NYSE symbol*]	TAN
Tangent Latitude Computer	TLC
Tangent Latitude Computer Amplifier	TLCA
Tank Arrangement Thermal Efficiency [*Computer program*] (KSC)	TATE
Tank Fire Combat Computer	TFCC
Tano Corp. [*NASDAQ symbol*] (NQ)	TANO
Tape (BUR)	TP
Tape Armored [*Telecommunications*] (TEL)	TA
Tape Automated Bonding [*Integrated circuit technology*]	TAB
Tape Automatic Positioning and Control	TAPAC
Tape Block (CIT)	TPBK
Tape and Buffer System [*Data processing*]	TBS
Tape Cassette Recorder (NITA)	TCR
Tape Command (OA)	TC
Tape Compare Processor [*Data processing*]	TCOMP
Tape Control Unit	TCU
Tape-Controlled Automatic Testing	TCAT
Tape Conversion Program [*Data processing*] (MDG)	TCP
Tape Data Control Sheet [*Data processing*]	TDCS
Tape Data Handling System	TDHS
Tape Data Register (NITA)	TDR
Tape Data Selector	TDS
Tape Direct Memory Access (NITA)	TDMA
Tape Disk Operating System [*Data processing*] (TUT)	TDOS
Tape Dump and Utility Monitor [*Data processing*]	TDUM
Tape Edit Processor [*Data processing*]	TEP
Tape Editing Equipment	TEE
Tape Feed (NITA)	TF
Tape File Management (NITA)	TFM
Tape-to-File Recorder (DDI)	TFR
Tape File Supervisor (NITA)	TFS
Tape Handling Operational System [*Data processing*] (IEEE)	THOPS
Tape-Handling Optional Routines [*Honeywell, Inc.*]	THOR
Tape Identification Card	TIC
Tape Input - Tape Output [*Honeywell, Inc.*] [*Data processing*]	TIPTOP
Tape Interface Direct Memory Access (NITA)	TIDMA
Tape Intersystem Connection [*Data processing*]	TIC
Tape Inventory File (IEEE)	TIF
Tape Librarian System (NITA)	TLS
Tape Library (BUR)	TL
Tape Library Management System (NITA)	TLMS
Tape Management Catalog (NITA)	TMC
Tape Management System (MCD)	TMS
Tape Mark [*Data processing*] (BUR)	TM
Tape Operating System [*IBM Corp.*] [*Data processing*] (CGC)	TOS
Tape Output Test Rack Autonetics Diode	TOTRAD
Tape-Pack	TAPAK
Tape Playback BIT [*Binary Digit*] [*Data processing*]	TPB
Tape Post-Processing System (SKY)	TPPS
Tape-to-Print	TTP
Tape Processing Machine	TPM
Tape Processing System (CMD)	TPS
Tape Programed Automatic Tester	TAPAT
Tape Programed Row [*Data scanner*]	TPR
Tape Read Register	TRR
Tape Reader Emulator Module (NITA)	TREM
Tape-Reading Tripping Relay	TTR
Tape Record Coordinator [*Data processing*] (CGC)	TRC
Tape Register	TR
Tape Resident (NITA)	TR
Tape Resident Operating System [*Data processing*] (IEEE)	TROS
Tape Search Unit (CET)	TSU
Tape Serial Number [*Data processing*]	TSN
Tape Unit	TU
Tape Unit Group [*Telecommunications*] (TEL)	TUG
Tape Update of Formatted Files-Format Table Tape Updater and Generator [*Data processing*]	TUFF-TUG
Tape Velocity Fluctuation (OA)	TVF
Tape Write Register (NITA)	TWR
Tapeless Rotorless On-Line Cryptographic Equipment (NATG)	TROL
Tapered Aperture Horn Antenna	TAHA
Target Instruction Register (NITA)	TIR
Task Control Block [*Data processing*]	TCB
Task Control Character (CMD)	TCC
Task Control Program (NITA)	TCP
Task Execution Language (NITA)	TEL
Task Force for Community Broadcasting (EANO)	TCB
Task Group	TG
Task Input/Output Table [*Data processing*] (BUR)	TIOT
Task Input Queue [*Data processing*] (IBMDP)	TIQ
Task Level Controller (NITA)	TLC
Task-Oriented Costing [*Telecommunications*] (TEL)	TOC
Task Processing Unit (NITA)	TPU
Task Ready Queue (NITA)	TRQ
Taxicrinic Unit [*Data processing*]	TU
Taxonomic Information Retrieval [*Data processing*] (DIT)	TAXIR
TDK Corp. ADS [*NYSE symbol*]	TDK
TEAC Corporation of America [*Montebello, CA*] [*Hardware manufacturer*] (DASO)	TCA
Teach Cable Assembly [*Robot technology*]	TCA
Teach Information Processing Language	TIPL
Teach Yourself by Computer [*In company name, TYC Software*] [*Pittsford, NY*] [*Software manufacturer*] (DASOS)	TYC
Teacher Interactive Computer System (IEEE)	TICS
TEC, Inc. [*American Stock Exchange symbol*]	TCK
Technalysis Corp. [*NASDAQ symbol*] (NQ)	TECN
Technical [*or Technician*]	T
Technical	TECH
Technical Assistance Center [*Telecommunications*]	TAC
Technical Committee	TC

371

Technical Committee on Communications Satellites (DDI) .... TCCS
Technical Communication .... TC
Technical Communications [*NASDAQ symbol*] (NQ) .... TCCO
Technical Computing Center (IEEE) .... TCC
Technical Control Center .... TCC
Technical Control Facility [*or Function*] .... TCF
Technical Data Management Center [*Department of Energy*] [*Information service*] (EISS) .... TDMC
Technical Data Package .... TDP
Technical Data Package Automated System .... TEDPAS
Technical Data Relay (IEEE) .... TDR
Technical Database Services, Inc. [*New York, NY*] [*Information service*] (EISS) .... TDS
Technical Education Research Centers, Inc. [*Cambridge, MA*] [*Research center*] .... TERC
Technical Evaluation & Management Systems, Inc. [*Dallas, TX*] [*Software manufacturer*] (DASOS) .... TEAMS
Technical Information Division [*Romar Consultants, Inc.*] [*Information service*] (EISS) .... TID
Technical Information on Microfilm [*British*] (DIT) .... TIM
Technical Information Processing (IEEE) .... TIP
Technical Information Processing System [*Rockwell International Corp.*] (AFM) .... TIPS
Technical Information for Product Safety [*Consumer Product Safety Commission*] (EISS) .... TIPS
Technical Information Retrieval and Analysis System (CAAL) .... TIRAS
Technical Information Service (EISS) .... TIS
Technical Information Services [*Acurex Corp.*] (EISS) .... TIS
Technical Library Service (EISS) .... TLS
Technical Marketing Society of America (EANO) .... TMSA
Technical Newsletter (TUT) .... TNL
Technical and Office Protocol [*Boeing, MAP*] .... TOP
Technical and Operations Control Center [*INTELSAT*] (CBSS) .... TOCC
Technical Panel on the Earth Satellite Program .... TPESP
Technical Performance Measurement .... TPM
Technical Quality Control [*Telecommunications*] (TEL) .... TQC
Technical Reference Branch [*Department of Transportation*] (EISS) .... TRB
Technical Requirements Management System .... TRMS
Technical User Performance Specifications [*US Independent Telephone Association*] [*Telecommunications*] (TEL) .... TUPS
Technically Improved Interference Prediction System (IEEE) .... TIIPS
Technicolor (KSC) .... TC
Technicon Integrator/Calculator .... TIC
Technique for Econometric Modeling Program (BUR) .... TEMP
Technique for Extreme Point Optimization (BUR) .... TEMPO
Technique to Retrieve Information from Abstracts of Literature [*Data processing*] .... TRIAL
Technische Universitaet Muenchen [*Technical University of Munich*] [*Information retrieval*] (ODIN) .... TUM
Technological, Economic, Military, and Political Evaluation Routine [*Computer-based simulation model*] .... TEMPER
Technologically Advanced Family .... Taffie
Technology .... TECH
Technology-Assisted Learning Market Information Services [*Educational Programming Systems, Inc.*] .... TALMIS
Technology Communications, Incorporated .... TCI
Technology for Communications International [*NASDAQ symbol*] (NQ) .... TCII
Technology Concepts, Incorporated [*Sudbury, MA*] [*Telecommunications*] (TSSD) .... TCI
Technology Information Division [*Canada Centre for Mineral and Energy Technology*] [*Information service*] (EISS) .... TID
Technology Information Exchange [*of Public Technology, Inc.*] (EISS) .... TIE
Technology Information System [*Lawrence Livermore National Laboratory*] (EISS) .... TIS
Technology and Innovation Council [*Information Industry Association*] .... TIC
Technology Satellite .... TECHSAT
Technology Transfer Data Bank [*California State University*] [*Information service*] (EISS) .... TECTRA
Technology Transfer Institute [*Santa Monica, CA*] [*Telecommunications*] (TSSD) .... TTI
Techtran Industries, Inc. [*NASDAQ symbol*] (NQ) .... TECH
Tektronix, Inc. [*NYSE symbol*] .... TEK
Telamarketing Communications, Inc. [*Louisville, KY*] [*Telecommunications*] (TSSD) .... TMC
TelAutograph Corp. [*NYSE symbol*] [*Delisted*] .... TEL
Telcom Report [*A publication*] .... Telcom Rep
Tele-Communications Association [*Santa Ana, CA*] (EANO) .... TCA
Tele-Communications, Incorporated [*Brookpark, OH*] (TSSD) .... TCI
Tele-Communications, Inc. Cl A [*NASDAQ symbol*] (NQ) .... TCOMA
Tele-Communications, Inc. Cl B [*NASDAQ symbol*] (NQ) .... TCOMB
Tele-Communications, Inc. Wts [*NASDAQ symbol*] (NQ) .... TCOMW
Tele-Engineering Corporation [*Framingham, MA*] [*Telecommunications*] (TSSD) .... TEC
Tele-Tech Services [*Franklin, NJ*] [*Information service*] [*Telecommunications*] (TSSD) .... TTS
Tele-Typewriters for the Deaf [*An association*] .... TTYD
Tele-Universite (University of Quebec) [*Quebec, PQ*] [*Telecommunications*] (TSSD) .... TELUQ
Telebyte Technology [*NASDAQ symbol*] (NQ) .... TBTI
Telecom Australia Research Quarterly [*A publication*] .... Telecom Aust Res Q
Telecom Canada Remote Interface Monitoring and Management System .... TRIMMS
TeleCom Corp. [*NYSE symbol*] .... TEL
Telecommand (NASA) .... TLC
Telecommunication Alarm Surveillance and Control [*AT & T*] .... TASC
Telecommunication/Data Management System .... TCDMS
Telecommunication Engineering and Manufacturing Association [*British*] (NITA) .... TEMA
Telecommunication Information Control System (NITA) .... TICS
Telecommunication Journal [*A publication*] .... Telecomm J
Telecommunication Journal [*A publication*] .... Telecommun J
Telecommunication Journal of Australia [*A publication*] .... Telecom J
Telecommunication Journal of Australia [*A publication*] .... Telecom J Aust
Telecommunication Journal of Australia [*A publication*] .... Telecomm J Aust
Telecommunication Journal of Australia [*A publication*] .... Telecommun J Aust
Telecommunication Journal (English Edition) [*A publication*] .... Telecommun J (Engl Ed)
Telecommunication Laboratories [*Taiwan*] .... TCL
Telecommunication Management and Control [*AT & T*] .... TMAC
Telecommunication Program Generator (NITA) .... TPG
Telecommunication Switching System .... TSS
Telecommunication Training Centre [*Suva, Fiji*] [*Telecommunications*] (TSSD) .... TTC
Telecommunication Working Group .... TCWG
Telecommunications .... TC
Telecommunications (FAAC) .... TEL
Telecommunications (NASA) .... TELCOM
Telecommunications (AFM) .... TELECOM
Telecommunications [*A publication*] .... Telecom
Telecommunications [*A publication*] .... Telecomm
Telecommunications [*International Edition*] [*A publication*] .... Telecomms
Telecommunications Access Method (NITA) .... TAM
Telecommunications Access Method [*IBM Corp.*] [*Data processing*] .... TCAM
Telecommunications Advisory Board .... TAB
Telecommunications Authority Singapore (TEL) .... TAS
Telecommunications Center (CET) .... TCC
Telecommunications Consulting Group, Inc. [*Washington, DC*] (TSSD) .... TCG
Telecommunications Consumer Coalition (EANO) .... TCC
Telecommunications Control System [*Toshiba Corp.*] [*Data processing*] .... TCS
Telecommunications Cooperative Network (EANO) .... TCN
Telecommunications Coordinating Committee [*Department of State*] .... TCC
Telecommunications Data Interface .... TDI
Telecommunications Data-Link Monitor (CET) .... TDM
Telecommunications Dealers Association [*Formerly, Telephone Retailers Association*] [*Cincinnati, OH*] (EANO) .... TDA
Telecommunications Device for the Deaf .... TDD
Telecommunications Engineering Establishment [*British*] .... TEE
Telecommunications Engineering, Incorporated [*Dallas, TX*] (TSSD) .... TEI
Telecommunications Flying Unit [*British*] .... TFU
Telecommunications and Information Systems Laboratory [*University of Kansas*] [*Research center*] (RCD) .... TISL
Telecommunications International Union [*Hamden, CT*] [*Independent labor union*] (EANO) .... TIU
Telecommunications Management Corporation [*Dedham, MA*] (TSSD) .... TMC
Telecommunications Management, Incorporated [*Oakbrook, IL*] [*Telecommunications*] (TSSD) .... TMI
Telecommunications Managers Association [*Orpington, England*] (TSSD) .... TMA
Telecommunications Managers Association - Belgium [*Brussels*] (TSSD) .... TMAB
Telecommunications Marketing Corporation [*Bay Shore, NY*] (TSSD) .... TMC
Telecommunications Message Switcher .... TMS
Telecommunications Monitor (NITA) .... TCM
Telecommunications Planning Committee [*Civil Defense*] .... TPC
Telecommunications Processing Unit (NITA) .... TPU
Telecommunications Programing System (OA) .... TPS
Telecommunications and Radio Engineering [*A publication*] .... Telecommun Radio Eng
Telecommunications and Radio Engineering (USSR) [*A publication*] .... Tel Rad E R
Telecommunications and Radio Engineering (USSR). Part 2. Radio Engineering [*A publication*] .... Telecommun Radio Eng (USSR) Part 2
Telecommunications Research and Action Center [*Washington, DC*] [*Information service*] [*Telecommunications*] (TSSD) .... TRAC
Telecommunications Research Establishment [*British*] .... TRE
Telecommunications Research Group [*Culver City, CA*] [*Telecommunications*] (TSSD) .... TRG
Telecommunications Satellite .... TELESAT
Telecommunications Service Order [*Telecommunications*] (TEL) .... TSO
Telecommunications Service Request (CET) .... TSR
Telecommunications Software User's Network [*Telesun Corp.*] [*Salt Lake City, UT*] (TSSD) .... TELESUN
Telecommunications Study Unit [*American Topical Association*] [*Milwaukee, WI*] [*Telecommunications*] [*Information service*] [*An association*] (EANO) .... TSU
Telecommunications System (NITA) .... TCS
Telecommunications System (SKY) .... TS

Computer & Telecommunications Acronyms

Telecommunications Systems and Services Directory [*A publication*]	TSSD
Telecommunications Terminal Systems	TTS
Telecommunications Users Coalition (EANO)	TUC
Telecomputer Applications Group	TAG
Telecomputer Research, Incorporated [*Bala Cynwyd, PA*] [*Information service*] [*Telecommunications*] (TSSD)	TRI
Telecoms Authorities Cryptographic Algorithm [*Bell Telephone encryption chip*]	TACA
Telecoms On-Line Data System [*Telecommunications*] (TEL)	TOLD
Teleconcepts in Communications, Inc. [*New York, NY*] [*Telecommunications*] (TSSD)	TCC
Teleconference Association of Canada [*Toronto, ON*] [*Information service*] (TSSD)	TAC
Teleconference Network [*University of Nebraska Medical Center*] [*Omaha, NE*] [*Telecommunications*] (TSSD)	TCN
Teleconference Network of Texas [*University of Texas*] [*San Antonio*] [*Telecommunications*] (TSSD)	TNT
Teleconference System [*Memorial University of Newfoundland*] [*St. John's, NF*] [*Telecommunications*] (TSSD)	TCS
Teleconferencing Systems International, Inc. [*Elk Grove Village, IL*] [*Telecommunications*] (TSSD)	TCI
Teledata Processing	TDP
Teledata Processing	TeD
Telefunken-Decca [*Video disk system*]	T
Telegram	TE
Telegram	TEL
Telegram	TELE
Telegram	TELEG
Telegram	TELG
Telegram	TELM
Telegram	TG
Telegram	TGM
Telegram for Delivery by Telephone	TF
Telegram Identification Group [*Telecommunications*] (TEL)	TIG
Telegramme Multiple [*Telegram with Multiple Addresses*] [*French*]	TM
Telegraph	TEL
Telegraph	TELE
Telegraph	TELEG
Telegraph	TG
Telegraph	TLG
Telegraph	TB
Telegraph Bureau	
Telegraph and Data Message Generator (MCD)	TDMG
Telegraph and Data Signals Analyzer (MCD)	TDSA
Telegraph Delivery Order	TDO
Telegraph Department	TD
Telegraph Distortion Measuring System	TDMS
Telegraph Form	TF
Telegraph Line Pair (BUR)	TLP
Telegraph Money Order	TMO
Telegraph Office	Tel Off
Telegraph Office	TO
Telegraph Office	TOR
Telegraph on Radio [*Telecommunications*] (TEL)	TELRY
Telegraph Reply (FAAC)	TS
Telegraph System (MSA)	TSA
Telegraph System Analyzer	
Telegraphe Restant [*Telegram to Be Called for at a Telegraph Office*] [*French*]	TR
Telegraphic Address	TA
Telegraphic Approval Requested	TGARQ
Telegraphic Authority Requested	TGURQ
Telegraphic Automatic Relay [*or Routing*] Equipment (NG)	TARE
Telegraphic Automatic Routing in the Field (MCD)	TARIF
Telegraphic Message (MSA)	TWX
Telegraphic Transfer [*of funds*] [*Banking*]	TT
Telegraphic Transfers [*of funds*] [*Banking*]	TTS
Telegraphie sans Fil [*Wireless Telegraphy*] [*French*]	TSF
Telehop, Incorporated [*Fresno, CA*] [*Telecommunications*] (TSSD)	THI
Telemanagement Resources, Inc. [*Charlotte, NC*] [*Telecommunications*] (TSSD)	TMR
Telemation Program Services	TPS
Telemedia Communication Television [*Cable-television system*]	TCTV
Telemedicine for Ontario [*Toronto, ON*] [*Telecommunications*] (TSSD)	TFO
Telemeter [*or Telemetry*]	TLM
Telemeter Transmitter	TMX
Telemetered Data	TMD
Telemetered Data Reduction	TEDAR
Telemetering	TLMG
Telemetering Control Assembly	TCA
Telemetering Control Indicator (VIT)	TMCI
Telemetering Data Recording Set (CAAL)	TDRS
Telemetering Oscillator Voltage (VIT)	TOV
Telemetering Package	TELEPAK
Telemetric Automated Microbial Identification System	TAMIS
Telemetric Data Analyzer	TDA
Telemetric Data Converter	TELEDAC
Telemetric Data Monitor	TDM
Telemetric Universal Sensor	TELUS
Telemetry (KSC)	TEL
Telemetry (MSA)	TLMY
Telemetry	TM
Telemetry Acceptance Pattern (KSC)	TAP
Telemetry Analog to Digital [*Information converter*] (CDH)	TAD
Telemetry Analog-Digital Information Converter	TADIC
Telemetry Antenna	Telem Ant
Telemetry Antenna Pedestal	TAP
Telemetry Antenna Subsystem (NASA)	TAS
Telemetry Automatic Reduction Equipment	TARE
Telemetry Carrier Acquisition and Recovery (MCD)	TELECAR
Telemetry Checkout Equipment (KSC)	TCE
Telemetry Code Modulation	TCM
Telemetry and Command Data (KSC)	TCD
Telemetry Components Information (KSC)	TCI
Telemetry Compression Routine	TCR
Telemetry Computation	TMCOMP
Telemetry-Computer Translator [*Bell Laboratories*]	TCT
Telemetry Control and Monitoring (CIT)	TC & M
Telemetry Data Buffer (CIT)	TLMB
Telemetry Data Digitizer	TDD
Telemetry Data Evaluation System	TEDES
Telemetry Data Format Control Handbook (KSC)	TDFCHB
Telemetry Data Generation (SKY)	TDG
Telemetry Data Monitor Set	TDMS
Telemetry Data Processing Unit (CAAL)	TDPU
Telemetry Equipment Unit	TEU
Telemetry Evaluation Station	TES
Telemetry Format Load (MCD)	TFL
Telemetry Format Selection (NASA)	TFS
Telemetry Ground Station	TGS
Telemetry Ground System (NASA)	TGS
Telemetry Input System (CIT)	TIS
Telemetry Instruction Conference (KSC)	TIC
Telemetry Instrumentation Controller (SKY)	TIC
Telemetry Intelligence	TELINT
Telemetry Listing Submodule	TLS
Telemetry Modulation System	TMS
Telemetry Module Facility	TMF
Telemetry Multiplex System (SKY)	TMS
Telemetry On-Line Monitoring Compression and Transmission	TOMCAT
Telemetry On-Line Processing System [*Data processing*]	TOPS
Telemetry Online Processing System [*Data processing*]	TELOPS
Telemetry Output Buffer [*Data processing*]	TOB
Telemetry Processing	TMPROC
Telemetry Processor	TP
Telemetry Processor Module	TPM
Telemetry Range Instrumentation Aircraft	TRIA
Telemetry and Remote Control (IEEE)	TRC
Telemetry Simulation Program (CIT)	TSP
Telemetry Simulation Submodule	TSIMS
Telemetry Simulation Terminal (CIT)	TST
Telemetry Standards Coordination Committee	TSCC
Telemetry Subcarrier Spectrum Analyzer	TSSA
Telemetry-Surveillance-Communications	TELSCOM
Telemetry System Analysis Group (CIT)	TAG
Telemetry System Application Requirements (VIT)	TSAR
Telemetry, Tracking, Command, and Monitoring (CBSS)	TTC & M
Telemetry Transmission System	TTS
Telemetry Video Spectrum	TVS
Telemetry Working Group	TWG
TELENET Access Controller (NITA)	TAC
TELENET Communications Corp. [*GTE*] (TEL)	TELENET
TELENET Interface Processor (NITA)	TIP
Telephone (FAAC)	FONE
Telephone	T
Telephone	TEL
Telephone	TELE
Telephone	TELEPH
Telephone	TF
Telephone (NATG)	TN
Telephone (NATG)	TP
Telephone (CET)	TAD
Telephone Answering Device	
Telephone Answering Machine (IEEE)	TAM
Telephone Answering Service [*or System*]	TAS
Telephone Area Billing System	TABS
Telephone Artifacts Association (EANO)	TAA
Telephone Channel Monitor	TCM
Telephone Company Engineered [*Telecommunications*] (TEL)	TCE
Telephone Conference [*or Conversation*]	FONECON
Telephone Conference [*or Conversation*]	TELCON
Telephone [*or Teletype*] Conference [*or Conversation*] (AFM)	TELECON
Telephone Conference Summary	TCS
Telephone Consultants of America [*Bergenfield, NJ*] [*Telecommunications*] (TSSD)	TCA
Telephone Conversation (MCD)	FONCON
Telephone Conversation	TELECONV
Telephone, Data, and Special Audio (NASA)	TD & SA
Telephone Department	TD
Telephone Device for the Deaf	TDD
Telephone Directory	TD
Telephone Engineer and Management [*A publication*]	Teleph Eng & Manage
Telephone Engineer and Management [*A publication*]	Telephone

Computer & Telecommunications Acronyms

Telephone Engineer & Management [Harcourt Brace Jovanovich Publications, Inc.] [Geneva, IL] [Information service] [A publication]	TE & M
Telephone Engineering Center [Telecommunications] (TEL)	TEC
Telephone Equipment Order [Telecommunications] (TEL)	TEO
Telephone Exchange (Crossbar) [Telecommunications] (TEL)	TXK
Telephone Exchange (Digital) [Telecommunications] (TEL)	TXD
Telephone Exchange (Electronics) [Telecommunications] (IEEE)	TXE
Telephone Exchange (Strowger) [Telecommunications] (TEL)	TXS
Telephone Interference Factor (DEN)	TIF
Telephone Jack (DEN)	TJ
Telephone Line Interface (IEEE)	TLI
Telephone Line Patch (NITA)	TLP
Telephone Number	TN
Telephone Office	TO
Telephone Office Planning and Engineering System [Telecommunications] (TEL)	TOPES
Telephone Operating Company [Also, TELOP]	TELCO
Telephone Operating Co. [Also, TELCO]	TELOP
Telephone Operations and Standards Division [Rural Electrification Administration] [Telecommunications] (TEL)	TOSD
Telephone Order Processing System (OA)	TOPS
Telephone Package	TELPAK
Telephone Pickup Coil	TPC
Telephone Pickup Coil	TPUC
Telephone Pioneers of America [New York, NY]	TPA
Telephone Satellite, Experimental	TSX
Telephone Service Attitude Measurement [Telephone interviews] [AT & T]	TELSAM
Telephone Service Fitting	TSF
Telephone Service Observation [Telecommunications] (TEL)	TSO
Telephone Signal Unit [Telecommunications] (TEL)	TSU
Telephone Software Connection, Inc.	TSC
Telephone System	TEL-SYS
Telephone System Interface Unit (NITA)	TSIU
Telephone Terminal Cables (KSC)	TTC
Telephone Terminal Equipment	TTE
Telephone Trunk Call [British]	T
Telephone Video System [NEC America, Inc.] [Elk Grove Village, IL] [Telecommunications] (TSSD)	TVS
Telephonie sans Fil [Wireless telephony]	TPSF
Telephony Preprocessor [Telecommunications] (TEL)	TPP
Telephony User Part [Telecommunications] (TEL)	TUP
Telephotograph	TPHO
Teleprinter	TP
Teleprinter	TPR
Teleprinter Coordinator (SKY)	TPCO
Teleprinter Error Correction Equipment	TECE
Teleprinter Load Tables (KSC)	TLT
Teleprinter Message Pool (SKY)	TMP
Teleprinter Planning Table (SKY)	TPT
Teleprocessing [Data processing] (MCD)	TP
Teleprocessing Access Method (NITA)	TPAM
Teleprocessing Multiplexer Module (NITA)	TPMM
Teleprocessing Network Simulator	TPNS
Teleprocessing On-Line Test Executive [Data processing] (IBMDP)	TOTE
Teleprocessing On-Line Test Executive Program [IBM Corp.] (NITA)	TOLTEP
Teleprocessing Recording for Analysis by the Customer (IEEE)	TRACE
Teleram Communications [NASDAQ symbol] (NQ)	TELR
Teleram Users Group (EANO)	TUG
Teleregister Omni Processing and Switching [Data processing]	TOPS
TeleSciences, Inc. [American Stock Exchange symbol]	TSC
Teleteach Expanded Delivery System [US Air Force] [Wright-Patterson AFB, OH] [Telecommunications] (TSSD)	TEDS
Teletek, Inc. [NASDAQ symbol] (NQ)	TLTK
Teleterminals Expandable Added Memory (NITA)	TEAM
Teletype	T
Teletype	TT
Teletype (CAAL)	TTY
Teletype Alert Network (NVT)	TAN
Teletype Communications Unit (NVT)	TCU
Teletype Input Generator	TIG
Teletype Input Processing	TIP
Teletype Optical Projection System (IEEE)	TOPS
Teletype Page Printer	TPP
Teletype Preamble Generator (CIT)	TPG
Teletype Switching Facilities (FAAC)	TTS
Teletype Switching System [or Subsystem] (CIT)	TSS
Teletype Telling	TTL
Teletype Test Instruction (KSC)	TTI
Teletypesetter	TTS
Teletypewriter [Telecommunications]	TEL
Teletypewriter [Telecommunications]	TELETYPE
Teletypewriter [Telecommunications]	TT
Teletypewriter [Telecommunications]	TTY
Teletypewriter Assembly (CIT)	TTYA
Teletypewriter Automatic Dispatch System	TADS
Teletypewriter Buffer (CET)	TTB
Teletypewriter Communications Interrupted (FAAC)	TYPNO
Teletypewriter Communications Resumed (FAAC)	TYPOK
Teletypewriter Control Unit (CET)	TCU
Teletypewriter Control Unit	TTCU
Teletypewriter Distribution (NATG)	TELEDIS
Teletypewriter Exchange Service [Western Union] [Term also used generically for teletypewriter message]	TWX
Teletypewriter Integrated Display	TIDY
Teletypewriter Message (DDI)	TWIX
Teletypewriter, Private Line	TWPL
Teletypewriter Query-Reply Subsystem (CET)	TTYQ/RSS
Teletypewriter System (CIT)	TTS
Teletypewriter Technician	TTEC
Teletypewriter Terminal Assembly (CIT)	TTTA
Teletypewriter Translator (CET)	TTR
Televideo Consultants, Inc. [Evanston, IL] [Telecommunications] (TSSD)	TVC
TeleVideo Systems [NASDAQ symbol] (NQ)	TELV
Television	TV
Television Allocations Study Organization [Defunct]	TASO
Television Appliance Association	TAA
Television Automatic Sequence Control	TASCON
Television Briefing Console	TBC
Television Broadcasting (CET)	TELECAST
Television Broadcasting Station [ITU designation] (CET)	BCT
Television Camera (MDG)	TELECAMRA
Television Communications Subsystem (CIT)	TVCS
Television Confirming Sensor (MCD)	TECS
Television Control Center	TCC
Television Facility Test Position [Telecommunications] (TEL)	TFTP
Television Film Recorder	TFR
Television and Inertial Guidance	TVIG
Television Information Storage Tube	TVIST
Television Input Converter	TVIC
Television Interference [Communications]	TVI
Television LASER Link	TLL
Television Operating Center	TOC
Television Ordnance Scoring System (MCD)	TOSS
Television Picture Generator (MCD)	TEPIGEN
Television and Radio Political Action Committee [National Association of Broadcasters]	TARPAC
Television Receive Only [Telecommunications]	TVRO
Television Receiver/Monitor	TVRM
Television Remote Pickup	TRP
Television Scan Converter	TSC
Television Signal Generator	TVSG
Television Signal Tracer (DEN)	TST
Television, Sound Channel	TS
Television Space Observatory	TVSO
Television Subsystem [Spacecraft] (CIT)	TVS
Television System Monitor (SKY)	TVSM
Television Systems Section	TVSS
Television Terminal (CMD)	TVT
Television Typewriter (DEEC)	TVT
TELEX (CAH)	TEX
TELEX [Automated Teletypewriter Exchange Service] [Western Union Corp.]	TLX
TELEX (DEEC)	TX
TELEX Computer Inquiry Service (NITA)	TCIS
Telex Corporation [NYSE symbol]	TC
Tellabs [NASDAQ symbol] (NQ)	TLAB
Teller Register Unit Monitoring Program (IEEE)	TRUMP
Telocator Network of America [Formerly,, National Mobile Radio System (1977)] [Washington, DC] [Telecommunications] [An association] (TSSD)	TNA
Telxon Corp. [NASDAQ symbol] (NQ)	TLXN
Temperature	T
Temperature	TEMP
Temperature (BUR)	TMP
Temperature (MDG)	TMT
Temperature-Compensated Crystal Oscillator	TCXO
Temperature Control Circuit (CIT)	TCC
Temperature Density Computer	TDC
Temperature-Humidity Infrared Radiometer	THIR
Temperature Independent [Ferrite computer memory core]	TIN
Temperature Test Model (CIT)	TTM
Template Descriptor Memory (NITA)	TDM
Temporarily (MDG)	TMPRLY
Temporarily Disconnected at Subscriber's Request [Telecommunications] (TEL)	TDR
Temporarily Mounted User Set [Data processing]	TMUS
Temporarily Out of Service (DEN)	TOS
Temporarily Transferred [Telecommunications] (TEL)	TT
Temporary	TEMP
Temporary Assigned Skeleton [Data processing] (TUT)	TASK
Temporary Program File [Data processing]	TPF
Temporary Sort Number [Data processing]	TSN
Temporary Storage Register (NITA)	TSR
Temporary Text Delay (NITA)	TTD
Temps Atomique International [International Atomic Time] [Telecommunications] (TEL)	TAI
Ten Call Seconds [Telecommunications] (TEL)	XCS
Ten-Statement FORTRAN [Data processing] (IEEE)	TSF
Tenders Electronic Daily [Office for Official Publications of the European Communities] [Database] (CUAD)	TED
Tennessee Valley Authority [Knoxville, TN] [Databank originator]	TVA
Tension Truss Antenna Concept	TETRAC

Computer & Telecommunications Acronyms

Tera [*A prefix meaning multiplied by 10¹²*] [*SI symbol*]	T
TeraBIT [*Binary Digit*] [*10¹² BITs*]	Tb
TeraBIT [*Binary Digit*] **Memory** [*Data processing*]	TBM
Terabyte [*10¹² bytes*]	TB
Teracycle (BUR)	T
Terahertz	THz
Terak Corporation [*NASDAQ symbol*] (NQ)	TCGS
Termiflex Corp. [*NASDAQ symbol*] (NQ)	TFLX
Terminal	T
Terminal	TERM
Terminal	TML
Terminal	TRML
Terminal (AFM)	
Terminal Access to Batch Service [*Data processing*] (BUR)	TABS
Terminal Access Controller [*Advanced Research Projects Agency Network*] [*DoD*] (CCD)	TAC
Terminal Access Method (OA)	TAM
Terminal Access Processor (NITA)	TAP
Terminal Activated Channel Test (NITA)	TACT
Terminal Address Designator (NITA)	TAD
Terminal Address Register (NITA)	TAR
Terminal Address Selector	TAS
Terminal Application Language (NITA)	TAL
Terminal Application Program System [*Data processing*]	TAPS
Terminal Applications Package (IEEE)	TAP
Terminal Automatic Monitoring System (NITA)	TAMOS
Terminal-Based Electronic Mail (NITA)	TBEM
Terminal Buffer Unit [*Telecommunications*] (TEL)	TBU
Terminal Business-Oriented Language (NITA)	TEBOL
Terminal Command Language [*Applied Digital Data Systems*] (NITA)	TCL
Terminal Communication Adapter (NITA)	TCA
Terminal Communications (FAAC)	TCOM
Terminal Communications Subsystem (OA)	TCS
Terminal Computer (BUR)	TC
Terminal Computer Identification (KSC)	TCID
Terminal Computer Multiplexer	TCM
Terminal-to-Computer Multiplexer	TCS
Terminal Computer System (BUR)	TC
Terminal Concentrator (NITA)	TC
Terminal Congestion [*Telecommunications*] (TEL)	TCL
Terminal Control Language (NITA)	TCP
Terminal Control Program	TCS
Terminal Control System [*Hewlett-Packard Co.*] (SKY)	TCU
Terminal Control Unit (MCD)	TC
Terminal Controller	TERM
Terminal Data Corp. [*NASDAQ symbol*] (NQ)	TDIS
Terminal Data Input System (MCD)	TD
Terminal Digit [*Telecommunications*] (TEL)	TDFS
Terminal Digit Fitting System	TDR
Terminal Digit Requested [*Telecommunications*] (TEL)	TD
Terminal Display (BUR)	TED
Terminal Editor	TERPS
Terminal Enquiry/Response Programing System [*British*] (DIT)	TERP
Terminal Equipment Replacement Program [*Electronic communications system*] [*Department of State*]	TEP
Terminal Error Program (NITA)	TGEEP
Terminal Guidance Environmental Effects Program (MCD)	THP
Terminal Handling Processor (NITA)	TIC
Terminal Identification Code (NITA)	TIP
Terminal Impact Prediction (SKY)	TIF
Terminal Independent Format (NITA)	TIGS
Terminal Independent Graphics System (NITA)	TIOC
Terminal Input/Output Coordinator [*Data processing*] (IBMDP)	TIOM
Terminal Input/Output Module [*Data processing*] (TUT)	TIOWQ
Terminal Input/Output Wait Queue [*Data processing*] (NITA)	TERPS
Terminal Instrument Procedures	TI
Terminal Interface (NITA)	TIE
Terminal Interface Equipment (NITA)	TIP
Terminal Interface Package [*Data processing*]	TIS
Terminal Interface Subsystem [*Telecommunications*] (TEL)	TIU
Terminal Interface Unit [*Bell System*]	TJID
Terminal Job Identification (BUR)	TJS
Terminal Junction System (DDI)	TPL
Terminal per Line [*Telecommunications*]	TLU
Terminal Logic Unit [*Telecommunications*] (TEL)	TMP
Terminal Monitor Program [*Data processing*] (BUR)	TMT
Terminal Monitor Program [*Data processing*] (MDG)	TNL
Terminal Net Loss	TNC
Terminal Network Controller (NITA)	TN
Terminal Node (NITA)	TOLAR
Terminal On-Line Availability Reporting (NITA)	TOPP
Terminal-Operated Production Program (BUR)	TOADS
Terminal-Oriented Administrative Data System (NITA)	TOCS
Terminal-Oriented Computer System (NITA)	TOCAP
Terminal Oriented Control Applications Program	
Terminal Oriented Data Analysis and Retrieval System [*National Bureau of Standards*]	TODARS
Terminal-Oriented Service Language (NITA)	TOSL
Terminal-Oriented Software [*Data processing*] (IEEE)	TOS
Terminal-Oriented Support System (NITA)	TOSS
Terminal-Oriented System [*Data processing*] (IEEE)	TOS
Terminal Panel (NASA)	TMP
Terminal Pin Fault Insertion (NITA)	TPFI
Terminal Pole [*Telecommunications*] (TEL)	TP
Terminal Polling System (NITA)	TPS
Terminal Processing Language (NITA)	TPL
Terminal Processor (NITA)	TP
Terminal Protective Device (MSA)	TPD
Terminal Response Monitor (NITA)	TRM
Terminal Security System [*Data processing*]	TSS
Terminal Send Side (NITA)	TSS
Terminal Source Editor (NITA)	TSE
Terminal Status Block [*Data processing*] (IBMDP)	TSB
Terminal Support Module (NITA)	TSM
Terminal Tracking Telescope	TETRA
Terminal Unit	TU
Terminal Usage Reporting System [*Data processing*]	TURS
Terminal VHF [*Very-High Frequency*] **Omnirange** [*Radio*]	TVOR
Terminals per Station [*Telecommunications*]	TPS
Terminating Toll Center (DEN)	TTC
Terminating Toll Operator [*Telecommunications*] (TEL)	TX
Terminator Group (NITA)	TG
Terminology Evaluation and Acquisition Method (DEEC)	TEAM
Terrain	T
Terrestrial Microwave Link	TML
Terrestrial Radio System	TRS
Tesdata Systems Corporation [*NASDAQ symbol*] (NQ)	TDSC
Test (MSA)	T
Test	TST
Test Access [*Telecommunications*] (TEL)	TA
Test Access Control [*Telecommunications*] (TEL)	TAC
Test Access Control Interface [*Telecommunications*] (TEL)	TACI
Test Access Line Termination Circuit [*Telecommunications*] (TEL)	TALTC
Test Access Multiplexer [*Telecommunications*] (TEL)	TAM
Test Access Selector [*Telecommunications*] (TEL)	TAS
Test Access Signaling Conversion Circuit [*Telecommunications*] (TEL)	TASCC
Test Access Unit [*Telecommunications*] (TEL)	TAU
Test Assistance Program [*Sperry UNIVAC*] (NITA)	TAP
Test a BIT [*Binary Digit*] **and Change** [*Data processing*]	BCHG
Test a BIT [*Binary Digit*] **and Clear** [*Data processing*]	BCLR
Test a BIT [*Binary Digit*] **and Set**	BSET
Test Call Generator [*Telecommunications*] (TEL)	TCG
Test Call Module [*Telecommunications*] (TEL)	TCM
Test Collection [*Educational Testing Service*] [*Information service*] (EISS)	TC
Test Computer Unit (VIT)	TCU
Test Data Generator (BUR)	TDG
Test Distributor [*Telecommunications*] (TEL)	TD
Test Effectiveness Ratio [*Data processing*]	TER
Test Equipment	TE
Test File Generator [*Data processing*]	TFG
Test Frame [*Telecommunications*] (TEL)	TF
Test Generation and Simulation (NITA)	TEGAS
Test Input/Output [*Data processing*] (NITA)	TIO
Test Interface Summary (MCD)	TIS
Test Item Taker (NITA)	TIT
Test Maintenance Equipment [*Data processing*]	TME
Test Maintenance Panel [*Data processing*]	TMP
Test Maintenance Panel Subassembly [*Data processing*]	TMPS
Test Maintenance Unit [*Data processing*]	TMU
Test Message Monitor	TMM
Test Mode (NITA)	TM
Test-Oriented Disk System (IEEE)	TODS
Test-Oriented Language [*Data processing*]	TOL
Test-Oriented Operated Language [*Programing language*] [*Data processing*]	TOOL
Test-Oriented Paper-Tape System [*Data processing*] (IEEE)	TOPTS
Test Planning and Status Checker [*Data processing*]	TPSC
Test Point Algorithm Technique (MCD)	TPAT
Test Point Logic	TPL
Test Position	TP
Test Program Operating System (NITA)	TEPOS
Test and Repair Processor [*Data processing*]	TARP
Test Request Message [*Data processing*]	TRM
Test Retrieval and Memory Print [*Data processing*]	TRAMP
Test Run	TR
Test Scorer and Statistical Analyzer [*Data processing*]	TSSA
Test and Set [*Data processing*]	TAS
Test Set Computer	TSC
Test Set Logic	TSL
Test Signal Unit [*Telecommunications*] (TEL)	TSU
Test Software (MCD)	TSW
Test Source Library (NITA)	TSL
Test Switch	TSW
Test Tone to Noise Ratio [*Telecommunications*] (TEL)	TT/N
Test and Training Monitor	T/TM
Test Translator [*Data processing*]	TESTRAN
Test and Verify Programs [*Data processing*] (MDG)	T & V
Testing Methods and Techniques [*Telecommunications*] (TEL)	TMT
Testing and Operating System (CAH)	TOPS
Testing and Regulating Department [*Especially, in a wire communications maintenance division*]	T & R
Tethered Communications, Inc. [*Westinghouse subsidiary*]	TCOM
Tetrahedral Research Satellite	TRS
Tetrode [*Electronics*]	TET

Texas Christian University Computer Center [*Fort Worth, TX*] [*Research center*] (RCD) .... TCUCC
Texas Institute for Computational Mechanics [*University of Texas at Austin*] [*Research center*] (RCD) .... TICOM
Texas Instruments Automatic Computer .... TIAC
Texas Instruments Digital Analog Readout .... TIDAR
Texas Instruments, Inc. .... TI
Texas Instruments, Incorporated .... TII
Texas Instruments, Inc. [*NYSE symbol*] .... TXN
Texas Instruments, Inc. Index Access Method (NITA) .... TINDX
Texas Instruments Mini/Microcomputer Information Exchange [*Austin, TX*] (EANO) .... TI-MIX
Texas Instruments Planning and Control System .... TIPACS
Text .... TXT
Text Editing System (NITA) .... TES
Text Editor [*Data processing*] .... TE
Text and File Management System (NITA) .... TFMS
Text and Graphic System [*Savoy Software Science Ltd.*] [*Software package*] [*British*] (NCC) .... TAGS
Text Indexing and Retrieval [*Data processing*] .... TEXTIR
Text Information Processing System (NITA) .... TIPS
Text Processor (NITA) .... TP
Text Reckoning and Compiling [*Data processing*] .... TRAC
Textile Information Treatment Users' Service [*French Textile Institute*] [*Bibliographic database*] [*Information service*] (EISS) .... TITUS
Textile Operational Control System [*Data processing*] .... TOCS
Thai National Documentation Center (EISS) .... TNDC
Thank You [*Communications operator's procedural remark*] .... TU
Thanks [*Communications operator's procedural remark*] .... TNX
Theatre/Drama, and Speech Information Center (EISS) .... TDSIC
Thematic Mapper [*Satellite technology*] .... TM
Theoretical Computer Science [*A publication*] .... Theor Comput Sci
Theoretical Computer Science [*A publication*] .... Theoret Comput Sci
Theoretical Final Route [*Telecommunications*] (TEL) .... TFR
Thermal Analysis Data Station .... TADS
Thermal Analysis Software/Architects [*Amazon Energy Ltd.*] [*Software package*] [*British*] (NCC) .... ATAS
Thermal Analysis Software/Building Services [*Amazon Energy Ltd.*] [*Software package*] [*British*] (NCC) .... BTAS
Thermal Megawatt [*Also, TMW*] .... Mwt
Thermal Megawatt [*Also, Mwt*] .... TMW
Thermal Uplink Data Display [*Data processing*] .... THUDD
Thermionic Integrated Micromodule .... TIMM
Thermoplastic Photoconductor Device (NITA) .... TPD
Thin-Film Field-Effect Transistor .... TFT
Thin-Film Personal Communications and Telemetry System (MCD) .... TFPECTS
Thin-Film Transistor .... TFT
Thin-Line Communications Connectivity .... TLCC
Thin Solid Films (IEEE) .... TSF
Thinned Aperture Computed Lens (IEEE) .... TACOL
Third Normal Form [*Databases*] (NITA) .... TNF
Third Word Designator [*Data processing*] .... T
Thought Organizer [*Computer program produced by Fastware, Inc.*] .... THOR
Thousand .... K
Thousand Characters per Second .... KCS
Thousands of Operations per Second (NASA) .... KOPS
Threat Avoidance Receiver (MCD) .... TAR
Three-Axis Antenna Positioner .... TAAP
Three-Conductor, Heat and Flame Resistant, Radio Cable .... THFR
Three-Dimensional [*Pictures or films*] 3-D
Three-Dimensional Analog Computer [*British*] (MCD) .... TRIDAC
Three-Phase Full Wave .... TPFW
Three-Phase Half Wave .... TPHW
Three-State Control [*Data processing*] .... TSC
Threshold Logic Unit .... TLU
Threshold Signal-to-Interference Ratio (IEEE) .... TSI
Through-Connected Circuit [*Telecommunications*] (TEL) .... TCC
Through Group Filter [*Telecommunications*] (TEL) .... TGF
Thru-Mode [*or Tri-Mode*] **Tape Converter** .... TMTC
Ticker Tape Information Processing System [*Quote service*] .... TTIPS
Ticket Reservation Systems, Inc. .... TRS
Tidal Constants Data Base .... TC
Tidbinbilla Deep Space Communications Complex (CIT) .... TDSCC
Tie Communications [*American Stock Exchange symbol*] .... TIE
Tie Line [*Communication channel*] .... TL
Tieraerztliche Hochschule Hannover [*Information retrieval*] (ODIN) .... THH
Timber Information Keyword Retrieval [*Timber Research and Development Association*] [*Information service*] (EISS) .... TINKER
Time .... T
Time Analysis and Billing System (BUR) .... TABS
Time Analysis of Program Status (DDI) .... TAPS
Time Assignment Speech Interpolation [*Timesharing technique*] [*Telecommunications*] .... TASI
Time Automated Grid (NITA) .... TAG
Time-Bandwidth .... TB
Time Base Corrector [*Videotape recording element*] [*Early processing device*] .... TBC
Time and Charges [*Telecommunications*] (TEL) .... T & C
Time Clock (NITA) .... TC
Time Compression Tactical Communications .... TICTAC
Time to Computation .... TC
Time of Day .... TOD
Time in Deadband Digital Attitude Control .... TIDDAC
Time Delay Dropout [*Relay*] .... TDDO
Time Delay Relay .... TDR
Time Differential Phase-Shift Keying .... TDPSK
Time Display Unit (NASA) .... TDU
Time Division Circuit Switching [*Telecommunications*] (NITA) .... TDCS
Time-Division Data Link [*Radio*] .... TDDL
Time-Division Electronics Switching System (KSC) .... TIDES
Time Division Exchange (OA) .... TDX
Time-Division [*or Time-Domain*] **Multiple Access** [*Computer control system*] .... TDMA
Time-Division Multiplex Device [*Radio*] .... TDMD
Time-Division Multiplex - Variable Destination Multiple Access [*Telecommunications*] (TEL) .... TDM-VDMA
Time-Division Multiplexing [*Communications*] .... TDM
Time-Domain Reflectometry .... TDR
Time-Domain Reflectometry Microcomputer .... TDRM
Time Encoded Speech [*Telecommunications*] (TEL) .... TES
Time to Equipment Reset [*Data processing*] (MDG) .... TX
Time between Failures [*Quality control*] .... TBF
Time Generation and Simulation [*Telecommunications*] (TEL) .... TEGAS
Time Interval Error [*Telecommunications*] (TEL) .... TIE
Time and Materials .... T & M
Time-Modulated Antenna .... TMA
Time Modulation .... TM
Time Multiplexed Switching [*Telecommunications*] .... TMS
Time-Multiplexer Communications Channels .... TMCC
Time-Ordered System (MCD) .... TOS
Time of Origin [*Communications*] .... TOO
Time-Out .... TO
Time Prism Filter [*Telecommunications*] (TEL) .... TPF
Time Pulse .... TP
Time Series Analysis and Modeling [*Software*] (NITA) .... TSAM
Time Series Oriented Database (NITA) .... TSODB
Time Series Package [*Bell System*] .... TSPAK
Time-Shared Data Management [*System*] [*Data processing*] (IEEE) .... TSDM
Time-Shared Data Management System (TUT) .... TDMS
Time-Shared Disk Operating System [*Data processing*] (IEEE) .... TSDOS
Time-Shared Interactive Computer-Controlled Information Television [*System*] [*Mitre Corp.*] [*Brigham Young University*] [*1971*] .... TICCIT
Time-Shared Monitor System [*Data processing*] (IEEE) .... TMS
Time-Shared Monitor System [*Data processing*] (IEEE) .... TSM
Time-Shared Relational Associative Memory Program [*Data processing*] (IEEE) .... TRAMP
Time-Shared Routines for Analysis, Classification, and Evaluation (DIT) .... TRACE
Time Sharing [*Data processing*] (CGC) .... TS
Time-Sharing Assembly Program [*Data processing*] (DIT) .... TAP
Time Sharing Control Task [*Data processing*] (BUR) .... TSC
Time-Sharing Executive [*Modular Computer Systems*] [*Data processing*] .... TSX
Time-Sharing Job Control Block [*Data processing*] (IBMDP) .... TJB
Time-Sharing Operating System (NITA) .... TOPS
Time-Sharing Operating System [*Data processing*] (IEEE) .... TSOS
Time-Sharing Option [*Data processing*] .... TSO
Time-Sharing Programing System [*Data processing*] (IEEE) .... TSPS
Time Sharing Resources, Inc. [*Information service*] (EISS) .... TSR
Time-Sharing System [*Data processing*] .... TSS
Time-Sharing Terminals, Inc. .... TST
Time Sharing - Virtual System [*Data processing*] (MCD) .... TSVS
Time Shift Keying .... TSK
Time Slot [*Telecommunications*] (TEL) .... TS
Time Slot Access (NITA) .... TSA
Time Slot Access Unit [*Telecommunications*] (TEL) .... TSAU
Time Slot Assignment Circuit [*Telecommunications*] (TEL) .... TSAC
Time-Space-Space-Space-Time [*Telecommunications*] (TEL) .... TSSST
Time-Space-Time [*Digital switching*] [*Telecommunications*] (TEL) .... TST
Time Status Register .... TSR
Time Switch (MSA) .... TS
Time Switch [*Telecommunications*] (TEL) .... TSW
Time Variation of Gain .... TVG
Time Video Information Services, Inc. (EISS) .... TVIS
Time Wire Transmission .... TWX
Timed Environment Multipartitioned Operating System (NITA) .... TEMPOS
Timer Queue Element (NITA) .... TQE
Times Mirror Videotex Services, Inc. [*Information service*] (EISS) .... TMVS
Timeshare, Inc. Network [*Telecommunications*] (TEL) .... TYMNET
Timeslot Generator [*Telecommunications*] (TEL) .... TSG
Timeslot Interchange [*Telecommunications*] (TEL) .... TSI
Timing Control Unit (NITA) .... TCU
Timing Data Input-Output .... TDIO
Timing Selector .... TS
Timing System (MCD) .... TS
Timing and Telemetry .... T/T
Timing Unit .... TU
Tip [*Switchboard plug*] [*Telecommunications*] (TEL) .... T
Title [*Online database field identifier*] [*Data processing*] .... TI
Title [*Online database field identifier*] (OBD) .... TTL
TMA [*Tobacco Merchants Association*] **Bibliographic Index to the Tobacco Scene** [*Database*] (CUAD) .... TMA BITS
To Be Continued, Circuit Time Permitting (FAAC) .... TOC
Tocom, Inc. [*NASDAQ symbol*] (NQ) .... TOCM

Computer & Telecommunications Acronyms

Toggle ... TGL
Toggle ... TOG
Token Bus Controller [*Motorola, Inc.*] ... TBC
Tokyo Broadcasting System ... TBS
Tokyo Shibaura Electric Co. [*Computer manufacturer*] [*Japanese*] (CAH) ... TOSHIBA
Tokyo Shoko Research Ltd. [*Database producer*] (CUAD) ... TSR
Toll Alternatives Studies Program [*Telecommunications*] (TEL) ... TASP
Toll Center [*Telecommunications*] ... TC
Toll Centering and Metropolitan Sectoring [*AT & T*] [*Telecommunications*] (TEL) ... TCMS
Toll Circuit Layout [*Telecommunications*] (TEL) ... TCL
Toll Circuit Layout Record [*Telecommunications*] (TEL) ... TCLR
Toll Completing [*Telecommunications*] ... TC
Toll Connecting Trunk [*Telecommunications*] (TEL) ... TCT
Toll Dial Assistance [*Telecommunications*] (TEL) ... TDA
Toll Line Release ... TLR
Toll Point [*Telecommunications*] (TEL) ... TP
Toll Pole Line [*Telecommunications*] (TEL) ... TPL
Toll Prefix [*Telecommunications*] (TEL) ... TP
Toll Pulse Accepter [*Telecommunications*] (TEL) ... TPA
Toll Restricted [*Telecommunications*] (TEL) ... TOLR
Toll Room Switch [*Telecommunications*] (TEL) ... TRS
Toll Service Results Plan [*Bell System*] ... TSRP
Toll Switching [*Trunk*] [*Telecommunications*] (TEL) ... TS
Toll Switching System [*Telecommunications*] (TEL) ... TSS
Toll Testboard [*Telecommunications*] (TEL) ... TTB
Tolls Recording and Computing Equipment (IEEE) ... TRACE
Tone Burst (NITA) ... TB
Tone Burst Amplitude Modulation ... TBAM
Tone Burst Modulation (NITA) ... TBM
Tone Dial Receiver (NITA) ... TDR
Tone Off [*Telecommunications*] (TEL) ... TOF
Tone On [*Telecommunications*] (TEL) ... TON
Tone-Operated Net Loss Adjuster Receiving ... TONLAR
Tone Telegraph Filter ... TTF
Tool for Automatic Conversion of Operational Software (NITA) ... TACOS
Top Down (NITA) ... TD
Top-Down Parsing Language (NITA) ... TDPL
Top of Stack [*Data processing*] (NITA) ... TOS
Topic Indexing Matrix ... TIM
Toronto PET Users Group [*Canada*] ... TPUG
Toronto Region Aggregation of Computer Enthusiasts [*Canada*] ... TRACE
Torque-Differential Transmitter (MUGU) ... TDX
Torque Transmitter ... TX
Toshiba Minicomputer Complex System (NITA) ... TMCS
Toshiba Scientific and Business Automatic Computer [*Toshiba Corp.*] ... TOSBAC
Total ... TOT
Total Analysis System for Production, Accounting, and Control [*Data processing*] ... TAS-PAC
Total Automatic Banking System [*Trademark of Diebold, Inc.*] ... TABS
Total Bandwidth ... TBW
Total Data Entry (NITA) ... TDE
Total Data Network System (TEL) ... TDNS
Total Distributed Control [*Data processing*] ... TDC
Total Harmonic Distortion [*Electronics*] ... THD
Total Information for Educational Systems [*Saint Paul, MN*] (BUR) ... TIES
Total Information Gathering and Executive Reporting [*International Computers Ltd.*] (NITA) ... TIGER
Total Information Processing (BUR) ... TIP
Total Information System [*Data processing*] (CGC) ... TIS
Total Information System ... TIES
Total Integrated Engineering Systems ...
Total Language Processor [*Data processing*] (IEEE) ... TLP
Total Life Cycle Time (NITA) ... TLCT
Total Logic Solution ... TLS
Total Mean Downtime ... TMDT
Total Network Data System [*Bell System*] ... TNDS
Total Network Operations Plan [*Telecommunications*] (TEL) ... TNOP
Total On-Line Program and Information Control System [*Japan*] ... TOPICS
Total On-Line Searching and Cataloging Activities [*Information service*] ... TOSCA
Total On-Line Testing System [*Honeywell, Inc.*] (NITA) ... TOLTS
Total Operating Traffic System [*Bell System*] ... TOTS
Total Operations Processing System [*Data processing*] (CGC) ... TOPS
Total Service Life [*Telecommunications*] (TEL) ... TSL
Total Surface Tested (TUT) ... TST
Total Systems Performance [*MODCOMP*] (NITA) ... TSP
Total Time (MSA) ... TT
Totalized Interface Subroutine and Post Processor [*Data processing*] (BUR) ... TISAP
Totally Automated Programing Equipment (CIT) ... TAPE
Totally Self-Checking (NITA) ... TSC
Touch Calling Multifrequency (IEEE) ... TCMF
Touch and Learn Computer ... TLC
Touch-Tone Multifrequency (CET) ... TTMF
Tourism Reference and Data Centre [*Canada*] [*Information service*] (EISS) ... TRDC
Towed Buoy Antenna ... TBA
Toxic Materials Information Center [*Oak Ridge National Laboratory*] (EISS) ... TMIC
Toxic Substances Control Act Plant and Production Data ... TSCAPP
Toxic Substances Control Act Test Submissions [*Environmental Protection Agency*] [*Database*] (CUAD) ... TSCATS
Toxicology Data Bank [*Department of Energy*] [*Oak Ridge, TN*] [*Database*] (EISS) ... TDB
Toxicology Information Conversational On-Line Network [*National Library of Medicine*] [*Later, TOXLINE*] ... TOXICON
Toxicology On-Line [*National Library of Medicine*] [*Bethesda, MD*] [*Bibliographic database*] ... TOXLINE
TOXLINE Back-File [*Information retrieval*] (ODIN) ... TOXBACK
Track (DDI) ... TK
Track ... TR
Track ... TRK
Track Address Register ... TAR
Track Confirmation Word [*Data processing*] (TUT) ... TCW
Track Data Simulator ... TDS
Track Data Storage ... TDS
Track on Jamming ... TOJ
Track Navigation Computer ... TNC
Track-while-Scan [*Communications*] ... TWS
Track Sector Identification (NITA) ... TSID
Tracking Antenna System ... TAS
Tracking Computer Controls (MCD) ... TCC
Tracking and Data Acquisition (CET) ... T & DA
Tracking and Data Acquisition ... TDA
Tracking and Data Acquisition/Advanced Engineering (CIT) ... TDA/AE
Tracking and Data Acquisition System ... TDAS
Tracking Data Analysis (CIT) ... TDA
Tracking Data Processor ... TDP
Tracking and Data Relay Experiment [*Telecommunications*] (TEL) ... TDRE
Tracking and Display Processor (CAAL) ... TDP
Tracking and Guidance ... TG
Tracking Impact Prediction [*of satellites*] ... TIP
Tracking, Telemetry, and Command ... TT & C
Tracking, Telemetry, and Command ... TTC
Tracking, Telemetry, Command, and Voice ... TTCV
Tracking, Telemetry, and Control (MCD) ... TT & C
Tracking Telemetry Data Receiver ... TTDR
Tracks per Inch [*Magnetic storage devices*] [*Data processing*] (TUT) ... TPI
Trade and Industry Index [*Information Access Corp.*] [*Information service*] (EISS) ... TI
Trade Opportunity Referral Service [*Department of Agriculture*] [*Information service*] (EISS) ... TORS
Traditionally Administered Instruction (BUR) ... TAI
Traffic ... TRAF
Traffic Control Satellite ... TCS
Traffic Data Administration System [*Bell System*] ... TDAS
Traffic Data Processing ... TDP
Traffic Data Processing Program (MCD) ... TDPP
Traffic Data Recording System [*Bell System*] ... TDRS
Traffic Flow Security [*Telecommunications*] (TEL) ... TFS
Traffic Forecasting System [*Telecommunications*] (TEL) ... TFS
Traffic Measure and Path Search [*Telecommunications*] (TEL) ... TRAMPS
Traffic Measuring and Recording System [*Telecommunications*] (TEL) ... TMRS
Traffic Operator Position System [*Telecommunications*] (TEL) ... TOPS
Traffic Overload Reroute Control ... TORC
Traffic Retrieval Analysis Validation and Information System [*Telecommunications*] (TEL) ... TRAVIS
Traffic Route [*Telecommunications*] (TEL) ... TR
Traffic Route Testing [*Telecommunications*] (TEL) ... TRT
Traffic Service Position [*Telephone*] ... TSP
Traffic Service Position System [*Telecommunications*] ... TSPS
Traffic Service Position System Real-Time Capacity Program [*Telecommunications*] (TEL) ... TSPSCAP
Traffic Tester [*Telecommunications*] (TEL) ... TT
Traffic Trunk Administration [*Telecommunications*] (TEL) ... TTA
Traffic Trunk Order [*Telecommunications*] (TEL) ... TTO
Traffic Unit ... TU
Traffic Usage Recorder ... TUR
Trailing Edge ... TE
Trailing Wire Antenna [*on aircraft*] ... TWA
Trainer Control and Simulation Computer ... TCSC
Traitement Automatique des Donnees [*Automatic Data Processing*] [*French*] ... TAD
Trajectory Optimization and Linearized Pitch [*Computer program*] ... TOLIP
Tramiel Operating System ... TOS
Trans-Canada Telephone System (MCD) ... TCTS
Trans-Lux Corp. [*American Stock Exchange symbol*] ... TLX
Trans-World Radio ... TWR
TRANSAC [*Transistorized Automatic Computer*] Assembler Compiler ... TAC
TRANSAC [*Transistorized Automatic Computer*] Users Group ... TUG
Transaction Application Drive [*Computer Technology, Inc.*] (NITA) ... TAD
Transaction Application Program [*Data processing*] ... TAP
Transaction Control System [*Hitachi Ltd.*] (NITA) ... TCS
Transaction Definition Language (NITA) ... TDL
Transaction Distribution System (NITA) ... TDS
Transaction Driven System [*Honeywell, Inc.*] (NITA) ... TDS
Transaction Facility (NITA) ... TAF
Transaction Formatting Routines (NITA) ... TFR
Transaction Interface Package [*Sperry UNIVAC*] [*Data processing*] ... TIP
Transaction Interface Processor (NITA) ... TIP
Transaction Language (NITA) ... TL

Computer & Telecommunications Acronyms

Transaction Management, Incorporated [*Lexington, MA*] [*Hardware manufacturer*] (DASO) ..... TMI
Transaction Management System (BUR) ..... TMS
Transaction Network Service [*AT & T*] ..... TNS
Transaction Network Service Planning Model [*Telecommunications*] (TEL) ..... TRANSPLAN
Transaction Processing (NITA) ..... TP
Transaction Processing System (NITA) ..... TPS
Transaction Step Task (NITA) ..... TST
Transaction Terminal (BUR) ..... TT
Transaction Work Area (NITA) ..... TWA
Transactions. American Institute of Electrical Engineers. Part 1. Communication and Electronics [*A publication*] ..... Trans Am Inst Electr Eng Part 1
Transactions on Database Systems ..... TODS
Transactions. Institute of Electronics and Communication Engineers of Japan. Part A [*A publication*] ..... Trans Inst Electron & Commun Eng Jap A
Transactions. Institute of Electronics and Communication Engineers of Japan. Part B [*A publication*] ..... Trans Inst Electron Commun Eng Jpn Part B
Transactions. Institute of Electronics and Communication Engineers of Japan. Part B [*A publication*] ..... Trans Inst Electron and Commun Eng Jpn Part B
Transactions. Institute of Electronics and Communication Engineers of Japan. Part C [*A publication*] ..... Trans Inst Electron and Commun Eng Jpn Part C
Transactions. Institute of Electronics and Communication Engineers of Japan. Section J [*Japanese*] Part D [*A publication*] ..... Trans Inst Electron Commun Eng Jap Sect J Part D
Transactions on Mathematical Software ..... TOMS
Transactions on Programing Languages and Systems (MCD) ..... TOPLAS
Transamerica Electronic Scoring Technique [*Credit risk evaluation*] ..... TEST
Transatlantic Telephone [*Cable*] ..... TAT
Transatlantic Telephone Cable (IEEE) ..... TATC
Transborder Data Flows [*Also, TDF*] [*Telecommunications*] ..... TBDF
Transborder Data Flows [*Also, TBDF*] [*Telecommunications*] ..... TDF
Transceiver ..... TCR
Transceiver (CET) ..... TCVR
Transceiver ..... T/R
Transceiver (CET) ..... TRCVR
Transceiver ..... XCVR
Transcendental Network [*Centram Systems West, Inc.*] [*Berkeley, CA*] [*Telecommunications*] (TSSD) ..... TOPS
Transcontinental Corps [*Amateur radio*] ..... TCC
Transcribed Weather Broadcast ..... TWEB
Transfer ..... XFER
Transfer Channel Control (IEEE) ..... TCC
Transfer Charge [*Telecommunications*] (TEL) ..... XFC
Transfer Control Block (NITA) ..... TCB
Transfer Function Computer ..... TFC
Transfer-In Channel (CMD) ..... TIC
Transfer Rate of Information BITS [*Binary Digits*] [*Dial telephone network*] [*American National Standards Institute*] ..... TRIB
Transfer Switch ..... TSW
Transfer of Technology [*Telecommunications*] (TEL) ..... TOT
Transfer Unit ..... TU
Transfer Vector (NITA) ..... TV
Transferred-Electron-Device Logic (MSA) ..... TEDL
Transformation Definition Language [*Data processing*] (IBMDP) ..... TDL
Transformation and Identification Program [*Commercial & Industrial Development Bureau*] [*Software package*] [*British*] (NCC) ..... TRIP
Transformer ..... XFRMR
Transformer Analog Computer ..... TAC
Transformer Read Only Storage (NITA) ..... TROS
Transformer-Rectifier Unit (MCD) ..... TRU
Transhybrid Loss [*Telecommunications*] (TEL) ..... THL
Transient Circuit Analysis Program [*Data processing*] ..... TRACAP
Transient Intermodulation [*Distortion*] ..... TIM
Transient Program Area (DEEC) ..... TPA
Transient or Steady-State Analysis [*Data processing*] ..... TOSSA
Transient Voltage Suppressor ..... TVS
Transistor ..... TRANS
Transistor ..... TSTR
Transistor ..... XSTR
Transistor Analysis Recording Equipment ..... TARE
Transistor-Assisted Circuit ..... TAC
Transistor and Component Tester ..... TACT
Transistor Contact Land ..... TCL
Transistor Coupled Logic ..... TCL
Transistor Display and Data-Handling System [*Data processing*] (MDG) ..... TDS
Transistor Feedback Amplifier ..... TFA
Transistor Information Microfile ..... TIM
Transistor Photo Control ..... TPC
Transistor Qualification Program ..... TQP
Transistor Qualification Test ..... TQT
Transistor Qualification Test Program ..... TQTP
Transistor Resistor Logic ..... TRL
Transistor-Resistor-Transistor Logic (IEEE) ..... TRTL
Transistor under Test (IEEE) ..... TUT
Transistor-Transistor Logic [*Also, TTL*] ..... T²L
Transistor-Transistor Logic [*Also, T²L*] (VIT) ..... TTL
Transistor-Transistor Logic - Schottky (NITA) ..... TTL-S
Transistor-Transistor Logic Schottky Barrier (IEEE) ..... TTS
Transistorized (MSA) ..... TSTRZ
Transistorized Automatic Computer ..... TRANSAC
Transistorized Automatic Control ..... TAC
Transistorized Digital Readout ..... TDR
Transistorized High-Speed Operations Recorder ..... THOR
Transistorized Universal Logic Elements ..... TULE
Transistorized Voltmeter ..... TRVM
Transit Improvement Program [*Satellite*] (MCD) ..... TIP
Transit Simplified Receiver [*Satellite navigation system*] ..... TRANSIM
Transit Switching Center [*Telecommunications*] (TEL) ..... CT
Transit Switching Center [*Telecommunications*] (TEL) ..... TSC
Transit Time Modulation (DEN) ..... TTM
Transit Working [*Telecommunications*] (TEL) ..... TW
Transition State Analog ..... TSA
Translation Controller (SKY) ..... TC
Translation Definition Language ..... TDL
Translation Error Detector (DIT) ..... TED
Translation Lookaside Buffer [*Data processing*] (CMD) ..... TLAB
Translation Lookaside Buffer [*Data processing*] (BUR) ..... TLB
Translation Register (NITA) ..... TR
Translator, Assembler, Compiler ..... TAC
Translator Bail Switch ..... TBS
Translator and Code Treatment Frame (IEEE) ..... TCT
Translator Generator System (IEEE) ..... TGS
Translator Language [*Data processing*] ..... TRANSLANG
Transmission (FAAC) ..... TMTN
Transmission ..... TRANSMON
Transmission ..... XMSN
Transmission Adapter (MDG) ..... XA
Transmission Authenticator [*Telecommunications*] (TEL) ..... TA
Transmission Control Character [*Telecommunications*] (TEL) ..... TCC
Transmission Control Program (DEEC) ..... TCP
Transmission Control Protocol [*Advanced Research Projects Agency Network*] [*DoD*] (CCD) ..... TCP
Transmission Control Unit ..... TCU
Transmission Controlled Spark (MCD) ..... TCS
Transmission Controller ..... TC
Transmission Distortion Measuring Set ..... TDMS
Transmission and Distribution ..... T & D
Transmission Electron Microscope [*or Microscopy*] ..... TEM
Transmission Equivalent Resistance (IEEE) ..... TER
Transmission Fault Control [*Telecommunications*] (TEL) ..... TFC
Transmission Header [*Data processing*] (IBMDP) ..... TH
Transmission Impairment Measuring Set [*Telecommunications*] (TEL) ..... TIMS
Transmission Interface Converter XIC
Transmission Level [*or Line*] ..... TL
Transmission Level Point [*Telecommunications*] ..... TLP
Transmission Line Adapter [*or Assembly*] ..... TLA
Transmission Maintenance Center [*Telecommunications*] (TEL) ..... TMC
Transmission Matrix (IEEE) ..... TM
Transmission Measuring Set [*Bell Laboratories*] ..... TMS
Transmission Message Unit ..... TMU
Transmission Performance Index [*Telecommunications*] (TEL) ..... TPI
Transmission Report [*Telecommunications*] (TEL) ..... TR
Transmission Security [*Communications*] ..... TRANSEC
Transmission Set ..... TS
Transmission, Signaling, and Test Access ..... TSTA
Transmission and Signaling Test Plan and Analysis Concept [*Telecommunications*] ..... TSTPAC
Transmission Surveillance System [*Bell System*] ..... TSS
Transmission Surveillance System - Cable [*Telecommunications*] (TEL) ..... TSS-C
Transmission System Optimum Relief Tool [*Telecommunications*] (TEL) ..... TSORT
Transmission Test Set (IEEE) ..... TTS
Transmission Unit ..... TU
Transmit [*or Transmitting*] ..... T
Transmit ..... TRAN
Transmit (BUR) ..... TRN
Transmit (CDH) ..... TSMT
Transmit X
Transmit [*or Transmitter*] ..... XMIT
Transmit (MSA) ..... XMT
Transmit Carry and Clear ..... TCC
Transmit Data (IEEE) ..... TD
Transmit Data Register [*Data processing*] (MDG) ..... TDR
Transmit Frame Memory ..... TFM
Transmit Gain Control (MSA) ..... TGC
Transmit-Receive (CIT) ..... T-R
Transmit-Receive ..... XMT-REC
Transmit/Receive Control Unit (NITA) ..... TRC
Transmit/Receive Control Unit-Asynchronous Start/Stop (NITA) ..... TRC-AS
Transmit/Receive Control Unit-Synchronous Character (NITA) ..... TRC-SC
Transmit/Receive Control Unit-Synchronous Framing (NITA) ..... TRC-SF
Transmit, Receive, and Guard (MSA) ..... T/R & G
Transmit-Receive Unit ..... TRU
Transmits (FAAC) ..... TMTS
Transmittal (IEEE) ..... XMTL

Computer & Telecommunications Acronyms

Transmittal Control Record [Data processing]	TCR
Transmittal Header Record [Data processing]	THR
Transmittal Locator Number [Data processing]	TLN
Transmitted (FAAC)	TMTD
Transmitted (MCD)	XMTD
Transmitter	T
Transmitter	TMTR
Transmitter	TR
Transmitter (CDH)	TRNSMT
Transmitter	TX
Transmitter	XMTR
Transmitter Buffer Empty [Data processing]	TBE
Transmitter Buffer Empty [Data processing]	TBMT
Transmitter-Distributor (CIT)	T-D
Transmitter Experiment Package	TEP
Transmitter Frequency	TF
Transmitter Frequency Multiplier	TFM
Transmitter Holding Register (NITA)	THR
Transmitter Location	TL
Transmitter Off (BUR)	XOFF
Transmitter On (BUR)	XON
Transmitter Oscillator	TO
Transmitter Power Rating	TPR
Transmitter-Receiver	TXRX
Transmitter-Receiver	XMTR-REC
Transmitter Start Code [Bell System]	TSC
Transmitter Station	TS
Transmitter Turn-Off	TTO
Transmitter Underflow (NITA)	TUF
Transmitter Zone [Telecommunications] (TEL)	TZ
Transmitting (FAAC)	TMTG
Transmitting	TRANSMTG
Transmitting	XMTG
Transmitting Capability Returned to Service (FAAC)	TSMOK
Transmitting Objective Loudness Rating [of telephone connections] (IEEE)	TOLR
Transmitting Slide Wire	TSW
Transparent Intelligent Network (NITA)	TI-NET
Transparent Line Sharing Adapter (NITA)	TLSA
Transponder Access Program [Satellite Business Systems] [McLean, VA] [Telecommunications] (TSSD)	TAP
Transponder, Interrogator, Pinger, and Echo Sounder	TIPE
Transponder Interrogator Processor	TIP
Transponder On-Off	TROO
Transponder Receiver Isolation	TRI
Transponder Transmitter Detector	TTD
Transport Network Controller (NITA)	TNC
Transport Unit (MCD)	TU
Transportable Automated Intelligence Processing and Interpretation System (MCD)	TIPI
Transportable Communications	TRANSCOM
Transportable Communications System	TCS
Transportable Ground Communications Station	TGCS
Transportable Satellite Communications Link Terminal	TSCLT
Transportable Satellite Communications Terminal	TSCT
Transportable Satellite Earth Station	TSES
Transportable Telemetry Set	TTS
Transportable Very-Low-Frequency [Transmitter]	TVLF
Transportation and Communications Service [of GSA] [Abolished, 1972]	TCS
Transportation Concepts & Services [Metuchen, NJ] [Software manufacturer] (DASOS)	TCS
Transportation Data Coordinating Committee [Washington, DC]	TDCC
Transportation Management Services [Salt Lake City, UT] [Software manufacturer] (DASOS)	TMS
Transportation Planning Suite [MVA Systematica] [Software package] [British] (NCC)	TRIPS
Transportation Research Information Services [Transportation Research Board] [Bibliographic database]	TRIS
Transportation Safety Information System [Department of Transportation] (EISS)	TRANSIS
Transverse Electric [or Electrostatic] [Wave propagation mode]	TE
Transverse Electromagnetic [Wave] [Radio]	TEM
Transverse Magnetic	TM
Transverse Magnetic Wave [Radio]	TMW
Transverse Redundancy Check [Data processing] (IBMDP)	TRC
Trap on Overflow BIT [Binary Digit] Set [Data processing]	TRAPV
Trapped Plasma Avalanche Triggered Transit [Bell Laboratories]	TRAPATT
Travailleurs Unis du Telegraphe [United Telegraph Workers - UTW] [Canada]	TUT
Travel Agents Computer Society (EANO)	TACOS
Travel Industry Network, Inc. [Winter Springs, FL] [Telecommunications] (TSSD)	TINET
Traveling-Wave Amplifier	TWA
Traveling-Wave Amplifier Tube	TWAT
Traveling-Wave Cathode-Ray Tube (IEEE)	TWCRT
Traveling-Wave Phase Sifter	TWPS
Traveling-Wave Resonator	TWR
Traveling-Wave Tube [Radio]	TWT
Traveling-Wave Tube Amplifier [Radio]	TWTA
Travelwriter Marketletter [New York, NY] [Information service] (EISS)	TM
Treasury Computer Systems	TRECOMS
Treasury Enforcement Communications System [Customs Service]	TECS
Treasury Law Enforcement Information and Communications System	TLEICS
Tremendously High Frequency [Telecommunications] (TEL)	THF
Trend Analysis Program [American Council of Life Insurance] [Information service] (EISS)	TAP
Trent Resource Sharing Network [Ontario Library Service Trent] [Richmond Hill, ON] [Telecommunications] (TSSD)	TRESNET
Triad Systems Corporation [NASDAQ symbol] (NQ)	TRSC
Triangle Universities Computation Center [Durham, NC]	TUCC
Trigger Inverter Module (VIT)	TIM
Trigonometric Function Computer	TFC
Trinity Broadcasting Network [Cable-television system]	TBN
Triple Diffused Emitter-Follower Logic (MDG)	3DEFL
Triple-Diffusion Process (MDG)	3-D
Triple Erasure Correction (NITA)	TEC
Triple Frequency (DDI)	TF
Triple Modular Redundancy [Data processing]	TMR
Triple Pole [Switch]	TP
Triple-Pole, Double-Throw [Switch]	TPDT
Triple Pole and Neutral [Switch]	TP & N
Triple-Pole, Single-Throw [Switch]	TPST
Triple Throw [Switch]	3T
Triplex	TRX
Tristate Logic [Electronics]	TSL
Tropical [Broadcasting antenna]	TRO
Tropical Agriculture [Royal Tropical Institute] [Bibliographic database] [Dutch] (OBD)	TROPAG
Tropical Wind, Energy Conversion, and Reference Level [National Science Foundation]	TWERL
Tropical Wind, Energy Conversion, and Reference Level Experiment [National Science Foundation]	TWERLE
Troposcatter Communications Link	TCL
Troposcatter Communications System	TCS
Trouble [Telecommunications] (TEL)	TBL
Trouble Analysis System or Subsystem [Telecommunications] (TEL)	TASS
Trouble Report	TR
Troubleshooting Logic Diagram (NASA)	TSLD
True Airspeed Computer	TAC
True Airspeed Computer	TASC
True or Complement (OA)	T/C
Trunk Access Unit (NITA)	TAU
Trunk Block Connector	TBC
Trunk Class of Service [Telecommunications] (TEL)	TCOS
Trunk Control (NITA)	TC
Trunk Distribution Frame (DEN)	TDF
Trunk Encryption Device [Telecommunications] (TEL)	TED
Trunk Equipment [Telecommunications] (TEL)	TK
Trunk and Facilities Maintenance System [Telecommunications] (TEL)	TFMS
Trunk Forecasting System [Telecommunications] (TEL)	TFS
Trunk Frame [Telecommunications] (TEL)	TF
Trunk Group Identification [Telecommunications] (TEL)	TGID
Trunk Group Multiplexer [Telecommunications] (TEL)	TGM
Trunk Group Number [Telecommunications] (TEL)	TGN
Trunk Interface Handler (NITA)	TIH
Trunk Intermediate Distribution Frame [Telecommunications] (TEL)	TIDF
Trunk and Junction Routing [Telecommunications] (TEL)	TJR
Trunk Line Network (NITA)	TLN
Trunk Line Test Panel [Telecommunications] (TEL)	TLTP
Trunk Link Frame [Telecommunications] (TEL)	TLF
Trunk Maintenance Files [Telecommunications] (TEL)	TMF
Trunk Offer [Telecommunications] (TEL)	TKO
Trunk Processing Unit [Bell System]	TPU
Trunk Register Link [Telecommunications] (TEL)	TRL
Trunk Servicing Forecasting System [Telecommunications] (TEL)	TSFS
Trunk Servicing System [Bell System]	TSS
Trunks Integrated Record Keeping System [Bell System]	TIRKS
Trusco Data Systems [Atlanta, GA] [Software manufacturer] (DASOS)	TDS
TRW, Inc. [Formerly, Thompson Ramo Wooldridge, Inc.] [NYSE symbol]	TRW
Try Again [Telecommunications] (TEL)	AG
TS Communications [Springfield, IL] [Telecommunications] (TSSD)	TSCOM
TSCA Plant and Production [Environmental Protection Agency] [Database] (FDB)	TSCAPP
TSI, Incorporated [NASDAQ symbol] (NQ)	TSII
Tube Plate Drilling Program [Kongsberg UK] [Software package] [British] (NCC)	TUDRIP
Tulane Computer Laboratory [Tulane University] [Research center] (RCD)	TCL
Tunable Attribute Display Subsystem (CAAL)	TUNA
Tunable Control Frequency	TCF
Tunable Frequency Range (CIT)	TFR
Tunable Anode Tuned Grid (DEN)	TATG
Tuned Backward Wave Oscillator	TBWO
Tuned Integrated Circuit	TIC
Tuned Plate Tuned Grid [Electronic tube]	TPTG
Tuned Radio Frequency	TRF
Tuned Receiver Tuner	TRT
Tuning	TUN

By Meaning

Tuning Unit Member (IEEE)	TUM
Tunnel Diode	TD
Tunnel-Diode Amplifier	TDA
Tunnel-Diode Logic	TDL
Tunnel-Diode Mixer	TDM
Tunnel-Diode Transducer	TDT
Tunnel-Diode Transistor Logic	TDTL
Turbine Engine Monitoring and Control [*ASMAP Electronics Ltd.*] [*Software package*] [*British*] (NCC)	TEMAC
Turn-On Command (KSC)	TOC
Turnaround Index [*Data processing*]	TAI
Turnaround Ranging Station [*Telecommunications*] (TEL)	TARS
Turner Broadcasting System [*Cable-television system*]	TBS
Tutmonda Asocio pri Kibernetiko, Informatiko, kaj Sistemiko [*World Association of Cybernetics, Computer Science, and System Theory*] (EANO)	TAKIS
Tutorial Computer-Assisted Instruction (IEEE)	TCAI
[*A*] Tutorial System [*1971*] [*Data processing*] (CSR)	ATS
Twenty-Four-Hour Automatic Teller [*Trademark for self-service banking display panel*]	THAT
Twin Sideband	TSB
Twisted Nematic [*Telecommunications*] (TEL)	TN
Twisted Pair Cable	TPC
Twisted Telephone Radio, Shielded, Armored (VIT)	TTRSA
Twisted Wire Pair (NITA)	TWP
Two-Color Radiometer	TCR
Two-Dimensional	2-D
Two-Step Antenna	TSA
Two Terminal Series Parallel Networks (NITA)	TTSPN
Two-Tone Keying	TTK
Two-Tone Modulation	TTM
Two-Way/Delay Dial [*Telecommunications*] (TEL)	TWDD
Two-Way/Immediate Dial [*Telecommunications*] (TEL)	TWID
Two-Way/Wink Start [*Telecommunications*] (TEL)	TWWS
Tymnet DTS, Incorporated [*San Jose, CA*] [*Telecommunications*] (TSSD)	TDI
Tymshare, Inc. [*NYSE symbol*] [*Delisted*]	TYM
Typewriter	TW
Typewriter	TYPWRTR
Typewriter Buffer (OA)	TWB
Typewriter-Oriented Documentation-Aid System	TODAS
Typical	TYP
Typical Digital Automatic Computer	TYDAC
Typographic Communications Association [*Commercial firm*] (EANO)	TCA

U

UARCO, Inc. [*Formerly, United Autographic Register Company*] .... UARCO
UARCO, Inc. [*NYSE symbol*] [*Delisted*] .... URC
UDAM [*Universal Digital Avionics Module*] **Microprocessor Software Support System** (MCD) .... UMSSS
UHF [*Ultrahigh Frequency*] **Direction Finder** (FAAC) .... UDF
UHF [*Ultrahigh Frequency*] **Doppler System** .... UDOP
UK [*British Library*] **Machine Readable Catalogue** [*Bibliographic database*] (OBD) .... UK MARC
Ultimate Corp. [*American Stock Exchange symbol*] .... ULT
Ultimate Tensile Strength [*or Stress*] .... UTS
Ultimate User .... UU
Ultra-Intelligent Machine .... UIM
Ultra-Rapid Reader [*Data processing*] .... URR
Ultra-Violet Products, Inc. [*San Gabriel, CA*] [*Hardware manufacturer*] (DASO) .... UVP
Ultrahigh-Frequency [*Electricity of radio waves*] .... UHF
Ultrahigh-Frequency Direction Finder .... UHFDF
Ultrahigh-Frequency Filter .... UHFF
Ultrahigh-Frequency Generator .... UHFG
Ultrahigh-Frequency/High-Frequency (MCD) .... UHF/HF
Ultrahigh-Frequency Jammer .... UHFJ
Ultrahigh-Frequency Oscillator .... UHFO
Ultrahigh-Frequency Receiver .... UHFR
Ultrakurzwellenempfaenger [*Very-High-Frequency Receiver*] [*German*] .... UKWE
Ultralarge-Scale Integration [*of circuits*] [*Semiconductor technology*] .... ULSI
Ultralow Frequency .... ULF
Ultralow-Frequency Jammer .... ULFJ
Ultralow-Frequency Oscillator .... ULFO
Ultramicrowaves .... UMW
Ultrasmall Structures Research Office [*University of Michigan*] [*Research center*] (RCD) .... USRO
Ultrasonic Frequency (MSA) .... UF
Ultrasonic Frequency Transformer [*or Translator*] .... UFT
Ultrasonic Grating Constant .... UGC
Ultraviolet [*Electromagnetic spectrum range*] .... UV
Ultraviolet Communications .... ULTRACOM
Ultraviolet Communications System .... UVC
Ultraviolet-Erasable Programable Read-Only Memories [*Data processing*] .... UV-EPROMS
Ultraviolet Programable Read Only Memory (NITA) .... UVPROM
Umweltbundesamt [*Berlin*] [*Information retrieval*] (ODIN) .... UBA
Unassigned [*Telecommunications*] (TEL) .... UN
Unbalanced [*Telecommunications*] (TEL) .... UNBAL
Unbalanced Current Sensing (MCD) .... UCS
Unblocking [*Telecommunications*] (TEL) .... UBL
Unblocking Acknowledge [*Telecommunications*] (TEL) .... UBA
Uncertainty [*Standard deviation*] [*Data processing*] .... UNCERT
Uncommitted Logic Array [*Semiconductor technology*] .... ULA
Uncompensated Temperature Variation (TEL) .... UTV
Uncontrolled Term [*Online database field identifier*] (OBD) .... UT
Uncorrected Data Processor .... UCDP
Undefined .... UNDEF
Under Color Addition [*Printing technology*] .... UCA
Underfrequency .... UNDF
Undergraduate Computer Graphics Facility [*Stevens Institute of Technology*] [*Research center*] (RCD) .... UCGF
Underground [*Technical drawings*] .... UG
Underwater Cable System .... UCS
Underwater Communications System .... UCS
Underwater Integration Communication (VIT) .... UNICOM
Underwriters Laboratories, Inc. [*Also, ULI*] .... UL
Underwriters Laboratories, Incorporated [*Also, UL*] .... ULI
Ungermann-Bass, Inc. [*NASDAQ symbol*] (NQ) .... UNGR
Unibus Microchannel (NITA) .... UMC
Unichannel (NITA) .... UC
Unidad Informativa Computable [*Computerized Information Unit*] [*Mexico*] [*Information service*] (EISS) .... UNICOM
Unidata Systems, Inc. [*NASDAQ symbol*] (NQ) .... UDAT
Unified Automated Communication Network (NITA) .... UACN
Unified Communications [*Radio station*] .... UNICOM
Unified Data Base .... UDB
Unified Data System [*Data processing*] (TUT) .... UDS
Unified Direct Access System (BUR) .... UDAS
Unified S-Band System [*Radio*] .... USS
Unified Transfer System [*Computer to translate Russian to English*] .... UTS
Uniform Automated [*or Automatic*] **Data Processing** (VIT) .... UADP
Uniform Automated [*or Automatic*] **Data Processing System** .... UADPS
Uniform Automated [*or Automatic*] **Data Processing System/ Industrial Naval Air Station** .... UADPS/INAS
Uniform Call Distribution [*Telephone system*] .... UCD
Uniform Communications System .... UCS
Uniform Data Language (NITA) .... UDL
Uniform Fire Incident Reporting System [*National Fire Protection Association*] .... UFIRS
Uniform Inquiry Update Element (NITA) .... UNIQUE
Uniform Loop Clock (NITA) .... ULC
Uniform Random Numerator [*Data processing*] .... URN
Uniform Service Order Code [*Bell System*] (TEL) .... USOC
Uniform System of Accounts [*Telecommunications*] (TEL) .... USOA
Unijunction Transistor .... UJT
Uninet Japan Limited [*Telecommunications*] .... UJL
Uninterruptable Computer Power (NITA) .... UCP
Uninterrupted Automatic Control (NITA) .... UAC
Uninterruptible Power Supply [*or System*] .... UPS
Union Africaine et Malagache des Postes et Telecommunications .... UAMPT
Union Internationale des Organismes Touristiques et Culturels des Postes et des Telecommunications [*International Union of Tourist and Cultural Associations in the Postal and Telecommunications Services*] .... UTCPTT
Union Internationale de Producteurs et Distributeurs d'Energie Electrique [*International Union of Producers and Distributors of Electrical Energy*] .... UNIPEDE
Union Internationale des Telecommunications [*International Telecommunications Union*] .... UIT
Union Radio Scientifique Internationale [*International Union of Radio Science*] [*Also, ISRU*] [*Brussels, Belgium*] .... URSI
Union des Radio-Televisions Nationales Africaines [*Union of African National Radio and Television Stations*] .... URTNA
Union Telegraphique Internationale .... UTI
Uniprocessor (NITA) .... UP
Unique Data Item Description (MCD) .... UDID
Unique Record Number [*Data processing*] .... URN
Unique Sequential Access Method (NITA) .... USAM
UNISIST International Centre for Bibliographic Descriptions [*UNESCO*] [*Information service*] (EISS) .... UNIBID
Unit .... U
Unit Address Register (NITA) .... UAR
Unit Automatic Exchange .... UAX
Unit Control Block (MCD) .... UCB
Unit Control Word [*Data processing*] (BUR) .... UCW
Unit Exception (CMD) .... UE
Unit Ledger Card [*Data processing*] .... ULC
Unit Level Circuit Switch (CAAL) .... ULCS
Unit of Processing Capacity (NITA) .... UPC
Unit Record [*Data processing*] (CGC) .... UR
Unit Record Card .... URC
Unit Record Control (NITA) .... URC
Unit Record Processor (NITA) .... URP
Unit Register (NITA) .... UR
Unit Separator [*Control character*] [*Data processing*] .... US
Unit Time Coding .... UTC
Unit Transmission Loss .... UTL
United Aircraft Information Management System (DEEC) .... UAIMS
United Business Communications, Inc. [*Atlanta, GA*] [*Telecommunications*] (TSSD) .... UBC
United Business Network [*United Business Communications, Inc.*] [*Atlanta, GA*] [*Telecommunications*] (TSSD) .... UBN
United Computing Systems, Inc. .... UCS
United Data Processing (BUR) .... UDP
United Gas Laboratories Internally Programmed Automatic Computer .... UGLIAC
United Information Services, Inc. (EISS) .... UIS
United Kingdom Atomic Energy Authority [*London, England*] [*Databank originator and operator*] .... UKAEA
United Kingdom Automation Council [*London, England*] .... UKAC

United Kingdom Chemical Information Service [*University of Nottingham*] [*Nottingham, England*] [*Information broker, databank originator, and host*] ..... UKCIS
United Kingdom Information Technology Organization (DEEC) ..... UKITO
United Kingdom On-Line User Group [*Information service*] (EISS) ..... UKOLUG
United Kingdom Post Office [*Telecommunications*] (TEL) ..... UKPO
United Nations Bibliographic Information System [*New York, NY*] (EISS) ..... UNBIS
United Nations Center for Human Settlements [*Information broker*] [*Kenya*] ..... UNCHS
United Nations Educational, Scientific, and Cultural Organization [*Paris, France*] [*Database originator and operator*] ..... UNESCO
United Nations Environmental Program [*Nairobi, Kenya*] [*Database originator*] ..... UNEP
United Nations Standards Co-Ordinating Committee ..... UNSCC
United Press International ..... UPI
United Satellite Communications [*Cable TV programing service*] ..... USC
United Satellites Limited [*London, England*] [*Telecommunications*] (TSSD) ..... USL
United Software Systems & Services Corp. [*Los Angeles, CA*] [*Software manufacturer*] (DASOS) U3S
United States of America Standard (IEEE) ..... USAS
United States of America Standard Character Set for Optical Character Recognition [*Data processing*] ..... USASCOCR
United States of America Standard Character Set for Optical Character Recognition [*Data processing*] ..... USASCSOCR
United States of America Standard Code for Information Interchange ..... USASCII
United States of America Standards Institute [*Formerly, ASA*] [*Later, ANSI*] ..... USASI
United States Cellular Corporation [*Park Ridge, IL*] [*Telecommunications*] (TSSD) ..... USCC
United States Department of Agriculture [*Washington, DC*] [*Database originator*] ..... USDA
[*The*] **United States Electronic Mail Association** ..... USEMA
United States Establishment and Enterprise Microdata Base [*Brookings Institution*] ..... USEEM
United States Geological Survey [*Reston, VA*] [*Databank originator*] ..... USGS
United States Government Report Announcements (EISS) ..... USGRA
United States Independent Telephone Association [*Washington, DC*] ..... USITA
United States Information Agency ..... USIA
United States Information Service Library (DIT) ..... USISL
United States International Communication Agency [*Also, ICA*] [*Formerly called BECA and USIA, it later became known again as USIA*] ..... USICA
United States National Archives and Records Service (DIT) ..... USNARS
United States National Committee [*IEC*] ..... USNC
United States Political Science Documents [*University of Pittsburgh*] [*Bibliographic database*] [*Information service*] (EISS) ..... USPSD
United States Political Science Information Service [*University of Pittsburgh*] (EISS) ..... UPSIS
United States Postal Service ..... USPS
United States Robotics Society (CSR) ..... USRS
United States Satellite Broadcasting Co., Inc. [*Minneapolis, MN*] [*Telecommunications*] (TSSD) ..... USSB
United States Telephone Association [*Washington, DC*] (EANO) ..... USTA
United System of Electronic Computers (IEEE) ..... USEC
United System of Electronic Services (MCD) ..... USEC
United Technologies Corp. [*NYSE symbol*] ..... UTX
United Telecommunications, Inc. [*NYSE symbol*] ..... UT
United Telegraph Workers (EANO) ..... UTW
United Telephone Organizations ..... UTO
Unitized Digital Electronic Calculator (MCD) ..... UDEC
Unitized Microwave Devices ..... UMD
Units Consistency Analyzer [*Data processing*] ..... UCA
Unity Gain Bandwidth ..... UGB
Unity Gain Bandwidth ..... UGBW
UNIVAC Automated Documentation System [*Data processing*] ..... UNADS
UNIVAC Interactive Language [*Data processing*] (IEEE) ..... UIL
UNIVAC Scientific Exchange [*Later, UI, USE, Inc.*] ..... USE
UNIVAC Share Assembly Program [*Sperry UNIVAC*] [*Data processing*] (IEEE) ..... UNISAP
UNIVAC Storage and Retrieval System [*Sperry UNIVAC*] [*Data processing*] ..... UNISTAR
UNIVAC Users Association [*Later, AUUA*] ..... UUA
Universal Air Data Computer ..... UADC
Universal Asynchronous Receiver/Transmitter ..... UART
Universal Automatic Computer [*Remington Rand Corp.*] [*Early computer*] ..... UNIVAC
Universal Automatic Control and Test Equipment ..... UACTE
Universal Block Channel (DEEC) ..... UBC
Universal Bus [*Digital Equipment Corp.*] (NITA) ..... UNIBUS
Universal Cable Circuit Analysis Program [*Bell System*] ..... UNICCAP
Universal Call Sequence (NITA) ..... UCS
Universal Card Scanner [*Data processing*] (DIT) ..... UCS
Universal Character Buffer (NITA) ..... UCB
Universal Character Set [*Data processing*] (CGC) ..... UCS
Universal Circuit Board Tester ..... UCBT
Universal Classification System ..... UCS
Universal Clothing System [*Software package*] [*British*] (NCC) ..... UCS
Universal Code Synchronous Transmitter Receiver (NITA) ..... UCSTR
Universal Communications Monitor (NITA) ..... UCM
Universal Communications Switching Device ..... UCSD
Universal Compiler (IEEE) ..... UNICOMP
Universal Computer Oriented Language [*Programing language*] [*Data processing*] ..... UNCOL
Universal Copyright Convention ..... UCC
Universal Data Acquisition System ..... UDAS
Universal Data Entry (NITA) ..... UDE
Universal Data Set (CMD) ..... UDS
Universal Data Transfer Service [*ITT World Communications, Inc.*] [*Secaucus, NJ*] [*Telecommunications*] (TSSD) ..... UDTS
Universal Data Transmission System [*For international access*] ..... UDTS
Universal Decimal Classification [*Online database field identifier*] ..... UDC
Universal Development Laboratory [*Computer bug hunter*] [*Orion Instruments*] ..... UDL
Universal Digital Adaptive Recognizer (IEEE) ..... UDAR
Universal Digital Autopilot ..... UDAP
Universal Digital Avionics Module (MCD) ..... UDAM
Universal Digital Control (NITA) ..... UDC
Universal Digital Readout ..... UDR
Universal Digital Switch (MCD) ..... UDS
Universal Digital Transducer Indicator ..... UDTI
Universal Distributed System [*UNIVAC*] (NITA) ..... UDS
Universal Document Reader (BUR) ..... UDR
Universal Emulating Terminal (NITA) ..... UET
Universal File Access Method (NITA) ..... UFAM
Universal Flight Computer ..... UFC
Universal Flight Director Computer ..... UFDC
Universal Flip-Flop [*Data processing*] (CIT) ..... UF-F
Universal Frequency Counter (NITA) ..... UFC
Universal Gate for Logic Implementation [*Data processing*] (MCD) ..... UGLI
Universal Graphic Recorder [*Raytheon Co.*] ..... UGR
Universal Jamming System ..... UJS
Universal Job Control Language (NITA) ..... UJCL
Universal Keyboard [*Data processing*] ..... UKB
Universal Line Multiplexer (NITA) ..... ULM
Universal Locator Airborne Integrated Data System (MCD) ..... ULAIDS
Universal Logic Block (IEEE) ..... ULB
Universal Logic Circuit ..... ULC
Universal Logic Implementer ..... ULI
Universal Logic Module ..... ULM
Universal Memory System [*Intel Corp.*] (NITA) ..... UMS
Universal Micro Systems [*San Rafael, CA*] [*Software manufacturer*] (DASOS) ..... UMS
Universal Multiline Controller (NITA) ..... UMLC
Universal Navigation Computer ..... UNC
Universal Night Answering [*Telecommunications*] (TEL) ..... UNA
Universal Numerical Interchange Terminal ..... UNIT
Universal Output Computer ..... UOC
Universal Performance Assessment and Control System (NITA) ..... UPACS
Universal Peripheral Controller (NITA) ..... UPC
Universal Permissive Module (IEEE) ..... UPM
Universal Problem-Oriented Language [*Data processing*] (MCD) ..... UNIPOL
Universal Procedure-Oriented Language ..... UNIPOL
Universal Processing System (NITA) ..... UPS
Universal Processor [*Data processing*] ..... UNIPRO
Universal Product Code [*Grocery industry*] ..... UPC
Universal Programing Language [*Data processing*] (BUR) ..... UPL
Universal PROM Programer (NITA) ..... UPP
Universal Radio Group ..... URG
Universal Radio Relay ..... UNIRAR
Universal Satellite Corporation [*New York, NY*] [*Telecommunications*] (TSSD) ..... USATCO
Universal Service Order [*Bell System*] (TEL) ..... USO
Universal Signal Processor ..... USP
Universal Software Interface [*MRI Systems Corp.*] (NITA) ..... USI
Universal Software Market Identifier [*Technique Learning*] [*Information service*] (EISS) ..... USMI
Universal Synchronous/Asynchronous Receiver and Transmitter [*Data processing*] ..... USART
Universal Synchronous Receiver/Transmitter ..... USRT
Universal Tape Processor ..... UTP
Universal Tape-to-Tape Converter ..... UTTC
Universal Teleservice [*Satellite information service*] ..... UNITEL
Universal Terminal System [*Sperry UNIVAC*] [*Data processing*] ..... UTS
Universal Test Console (KSC) ..... UTC
Universal Test Equipment Compiler (KSC) ..... UTEC
Universal Time [*Astronomy*] ..... UT
Universal Time Code (CIT) ..... UTC
Universal Time Coordinated [*The Universal Time emitted by coordinated radio stations*] ..... UTC
Universal Time Sharing [*Data processing*] (IEEE) ..... UTS
Universal Trajector Compiler (IEEE) ..... UNITRAC
Universal Transfer Device (NITA) ..... UTD
Universal Translator Oriented Language (NITA) ..... UTOL
Universal Transmitter Clock ..... UTCLK
Universal Transversal Mercator Converter [*Computer program*] ..... MERCON
Universitaetsbibliothek [*University Library*] [*German*] [*Information retrieval*] (ODIN) ..... UB
Universitaetsbibliothek Karlsruhe [*Karlsruhe University Library*] [*Information retrieval*] (ODIN) ..... UBKA

Universitaetsbibliothek Muenchen [*Munich University Library*] [*Information retrieval*] (ODIN) .... UBM
University of Alaska Computer Network [*Fairbanks, AK*] [*Research center*] (RCD) .... UACN
University of California, Los Angeles [*Databank originator*] .... UCLA
University Center for Instructional Media and Technology [*University of Connecticut*] [*Research center*] (RCD) .... UCIMT
University Center for International Studies [*University of Pittsburgh*] [*Research center*] (EISS) .... UCIS
University College Computer [*London, England*] (DEN) .... UCC
University Computer Center [*North Dakota State University*] [*Research center*] (RCD) .... UCC
University Computer Center [*New Mexico State University*] [*Research center*] (RCD) .... UCC
University Computer Center [*Oklahoma State University*] [*Research center*] (RCD) .... UCC
University Computer Center [*San Diego State University*] [*Research center*] (RCD) .... UCC
University Computer Center [*University of Minnesota*] [*Research center*] (RCD) .... UCC
University Computer Services [*Ball State University*] [*Research center*] (RCD) .... UCS
University Computing Company [*International computer bureau*] (OA) .... UCC
University Computing and Information Services [*Villanova University*] [*Research center*] (RCD) .... UCIS
University Computing Services [*State University of New York at Buffalo*] [*Research center*] (RCD) .... UCS
University Computing Services [*University of Southern California*] [*Research center*] (RCD) .... UCS
University of Guelph Document Holdings [*Database*] [*No longer available online*] (CUAD) .... GDOC
University/Industry Cooperative Research Center for Communications and Signal Processing [*North Carolina State University*] [*Research center*] (RCD) .... CCSP
University of Kansas Center for Research, Incorporated [*Research center*] (RCD) .... CRINC
University of Manchester Institute of Science and Technology [*British*] [*Databank originator and research institute*] .... UMIST
University Microfilms International [*Commercial firm*] [*Ann Arbor, MI*] [*Microfilm and database producer*] .... UMI
University of Nevada System Computing Center [*Research center*] (RCD) .... UNSCC
University of New Haven Computer Center [*West Haven, CT*] [*Research center*] (RCD) .... UNHCC
University Science Statistics Project [*Moshman Associates, Inc.*] [*Information service*] (EISS) .... UNISTAT
University Statistics Center [*New Mexico State University*] [*Research center*] (RCD) .... USC
University of Tennessee at Knoxville Computer Center [*Research center*] (RCD) .... UTCC
Unix Systems Association (EANO) .... USA
Unknown [*Telecommunications*] (TEL) .... UN
Unlimited Machine Access from Scattered Sites [*Data processing*] .... UMASS
Unlimited Potential Data through Automation Technology in Education (IEEE) .... UPDATE
Unlimited Register Machine .... URM
Unlimited Sequential Input/Output (NITA) .... USIO
Unlimited Time [*Broadcasting term*] .... U
Unmanned Multifunction Satellite .... UMS
Unmanned Orbital Multifunction Satellite .... UOMS
Unmanned Orbital Satellite .... UOS
Unmanned Sensing Satellite System .... USSS
Unmanned Teleoperator Spacecraft (MCD) .... UTS
Unnumbered Acknowledge [*or Acknowledgment*] [*Telecommunications*] (IEEE) .... UA
Unpostable [*Data processing*] .... UNP
Unpostable [*Data processing*] .... UP
Unpostable Code [*Data processing*] .... UPC
Unprogramed Transfer Register .... UTR
Unsigned Division [*Data processing*] .... DIVU
Unsigned Multiplication [*Data processing*] .... MULU
Unusual End of Program [*Data processing*] .... UEP
Up Converter (NITA) .... UC
Up-Data Buffer [*Data processing*] .... UDB
Up-Data Link [*Data processing*] .... UDL
Up Link [*Data processing*] .... UL
Up Telecommunications Switch (SKY) .... UTL
Up Time (CAH) .... UT
Update [*Data processing*] (NASA) .... UD
Update [*Online database field identifier*] [*Data processing*] .... UP
Update Control Process [*Telecommunications*] (TEL) .... UCP
Update Report System (TEL) .... URS
Update State [*Online database field identifier*] (OBD) .... US
Update Transaction System (TEL) .... UTS
Upgraded Tactical Information Processing System [*Data processing*] .... UTIPS
Upgraded Third-Generation Enroute Software Program [*Data processing*] (MCD) .... UGT
Upper Limit .... UL
Upper Limiting Frequency .... ULF
Upper Sideband .... USB
Upper Terminal Area (NATG) .... UTA
Upper Turning Point .... UTP
Uppercase [*i.e., capital letters*] [*Typography*] .... UC
Uppercase and Lowercase [*i.e., capital and small letters*] [*Typography*] .... U & LC
Uprange Computer Input System .... UCIS
Uprange Computer Output System .... UCOS
Urban Data Service [*International City Management Association*] (EISS) .... UDS
Urban Information Interpreters, Incorporated (EISS) .... UIII
Urban Mass Transportation Research Information Service [*Department of Transportation*] [*Database*] .... UMTRIS
Urban and Regional Information Systems Association [*McLean, VA*] .... URISA
Urban Traffic Control System .... UTCS
Urgent Data Request [*GIDEP*] .... UDR
Urgent Postal Telegram .... UPT
US Design Corporation [*NASDAQ symbol*] (NQ) .... USDC
US Patent Data Base - Patent Technology Reports [*Patent and Trademark Office*] [*Database*] (FDB) .... PAT-PTR
US Patents Alert [*Derwent, Inc.*] [*Database*] .... USPA
US Telecommunications Suppliers Association [*Chicago, IL*] [*Telecommunications*] (EANO) .... USTSA
US Telecommunications Training Institute [*Washington, DC*] [*Telecommunications*] (TSSD) .... USTTI
US Telephone, Inc. [*Dallas, TX*] [*Telecommunications*] (TSSD) .... US TEL
Usage Data Report .... UDR
Usage Frequency Indicator (NITA) .... UFI
Usage Sensitive Pricing [*Telecommunications*] .... USP
Usage Sensitive Service [*Telecommunications*] .... USS
USE, Incorporated [*Acronym is now used as organization name*] .... UI
User Adaptive Language .... UAL
User Area [*Information storage*] (DEEC) .... UA
User Area Profile (NITA) .... UAP
User Attribute Data Set [*Data processing*] (MDG) .... UADS
User Block Handling Routine [*Data processing*] (IBMDP) .... UBHR
User Control Store (DEEC) .... UCS
User-Dependent-Type Code (CIT) .... UDTC
User Digital Analog Controller (NITA) .... UDAC
User Display Terminal (CIT) .... UDT
User Equipment (NITA) .... UE
User File Directory (NASA) .... UFD
User to File Manager (NITA) .... UFM
User Friendly Interface (NITA) .... UFI
User Header Label (CMD) .... UHL
User Identification [*Data processing*] .... USERID
User Identification Code (NITA) .... UIC
User Input/Output Devices [*Data processing*] (RDA) .... UIOD
User Instruction Group (NITA) .... UIG
User Instruction Register (NITA) .... UIR
User Interface (CIT) .... UI
User Language [*Data processing*] (DIT) .... UL
User Language [*Data processing*] .... ULANG
User Network Access Link Control (NITA) .... UNALC
User Network Control Machine (NITA) .... UNCM
User Network for Information Storage, Transfer Acquisition, and Retrieval (MCD) .... UNISTAR
User On-Line Interaction [*Data processing*] .... UOI
User-Oriented Data Display Language [*Data processing*] .... UODDL
User Process Table (NITA) .... UPT
User Program Sense Indicator (NITA) .... UPSI
User Program Switch Indicator [*Data processing*] (TUT) .... UPSI
User Programing Language [*Burroughs Corp.*] [*Data processing*] (IEEE) .... UPL
User Queue Table (NITA) .... UQT
User Requirements Analysis (NITA) .... URA
User Requirements Language [*Data processing*] .... URL
User Service Routine [*Digital Equipment Corp.*] (NITA) .... USR
User/System Interface (OA) .... USI
User Trailer Label (CMD) .... UTL
User Transfer Address (NITA) .... UTA
User Working Area (NITA) .... UWA
User Written Application Test [*Data processing*] .... UWAT
Users of Automatic Information Display Equipment .... UAIDE
User's Terminal (MCD) .... UT
USS Engineers & Consultants, Inc. [*Information service*] (EISS) .... UEC
Ustav Vedeckych Lekarskych Informaci [*Institute for Medical Information*] [*Czechoslovakia*] [*Database operator*] [*Information service*] (EISS) .... UVLI
Ustredi Vedeckych, Technickych, a Ekonomickych Informaci [*Central Office of Scientific, Technical, and Economic Information*] [*Prague, Czechoslovakia*] [*Information service*] (EISS) .... UVTEI
Utilitaire Logique Processor [*Programing language*] [*Data processing*] (CSR) .... ULP
Utilities Telecommunications Council (EANO) .... UTC
Utility (BUR) .... UT
Utility [*or Utilization*] (AFM) .... UTIL
Utility (BUR) .... UTLY
Utility Binary Dump [*Data processing*] .... UBD
Utility Compiler .... UCO
Utility Control Facility (NITA) .... UCF
Utility and Data Flow (NASA) .... UDF

Utility Data Institute [*Information service*] (EISS)	UDI
Utility Data Retrieval Control	UDRC
Utility Data Retrieval Output	UDRO
Utility Facilities Program [*Data processing*] (IBMDP)	UFP
Utility File (NITA)	UF
Utility Lead [*Telecommunications*] (TEL)	UL
Utility Octal Load	UOL
Utility-Oriented Language (MCD)	UOL
Utility Program Operating System (IEEE)	UPOS
Utility Radio Communication	URC
Utility Radio Transmitter	URT
Utility Tape Processor	UTP

V

V-Groove Metal-Oxide Semiconductor (MCD)	VMOS
Vacant National Number [*Telecommunications*] (TEL)	VNN
Vacuum-Tube (Voltmeter) (DEN)	VT(V)
Vacuum-Tube Voltmeter	VTVM
Valid Logic Systems [*NASDAQ symbol*] (NQ)	VLID
Valid Memory Address [*Data processing*]	VMA
Validation Control System (NITA)	VCS
Validation and Recovery (NITA)	VR
Validation Summary Report (NITA)	VSR
Validation/Verification (CAAL)	V/V
Valuable and Effective Network Utility Services (BUR)	VENUS
Value	VAL
Value-Added Carrier [*Telecommunications*]	VAC
Value-Added Common Carrier [*Telecommunications*]	VACC
Value Added and Data Services	VADS
Value-Added Network [*Data processing*] [*Telecommunications*]	VAN
Value Added Network Service [*Data processing*] [*Telecommunications*]	VANS
Value Added Service [*Telecommunications*] (TEL)	VAS
Value Engineering	VE
Valve Control Amplifier (MDG)	VCA
Van Houten Associates [*Information service*] (EISS)	VHA
Vapor Axial Deposition [*Optical fiber technology*]	VAD
Variable	V
Variable (AFM)	VAR
Variable, Attributes, Error Propagation (IEEE)	VAEP
Variable Axis Rotor Control System [*Telecommunications*] (TEL)	VARC
Variable Diode Circuit	VDC
Variable Diode Function Generator	VDFG
Variable Field Length (MCD)	VFL
Variable File Channel (NITA)	VFC
Variable Format Message Entry Device [*Data processing*] (MCD)	VFMED
Variable Frequency Oscillator	VFO
Variable Generator of Unfamiliar Stimuli [*Computer program*]	VARGUS
Variable Information Processing [*Naval Ordnance Laboratory*] [*Information retrieval*]	VIP
Variable Information Processing Package	VIPP
Variable Input-Output Code	VIOC
Variable Input Phototypesetter	VIP
Variable Instruction Computer	VIC
Variable Interlace System for Television Applications	VISTA
Variable Item Processing System (NITA)	VIPS
Variable Length Field (CAH)	VLF
Variable Length Word Symbolic Assembly System (IEEE)	VALSAS
Variable Level Access Method [*Data processing*] (TUT)	VLAM
Variable Message Cycle	VMC
Variable Mica Capacitor	VMC
Variable Microcycle Timing (NITA)	VMT
Variable Operating Frequency (NATG)	VOF
Variable Pulse Repetition Frequency (IEEE)	VPRF
Variable Random Access Memory [*Data processing*]	VRAM
Variable Rate Adaptive Multiplexing [*Telecommunications*] (TEL)	VRAM
Variable Slope Delta	VSD
Variable Slope Delta Modulation (NITA)	VSDM
Variable Specification List (NITA)	VSL
Variable Speech Control [*Device that permits distortion-free rapid playback of speech recorded on tape*]	VSC
Variable Speed Drive	VSD
Variable Threshold Digital Input (NITA)	VTDI
Variable Transmission	VT
Variable Word Size (NITA)	VWS
Variably Initialized Translator for Algorithmic Languages [*Data processing*]	VITAL
Varian Data Machines (NITA)	VDM
Variation	VAR
Varipolarization Beacon Antenna	VPBA
Varistor [*Telecommunications*] (TEL)	VRI
VAST [*Versatile Avionics Shop Test*] Interface Test Application Language (OA)	VITAL
VAST [*Versatile Avionics Shop Test*] Operating System Code (OA)	VOSC
VDI-Nachrichten [*VDI-Verlag GmbH*] [*Database*] (CUAD)	VDI-N
Vector [*Mathematics*]	V
Vector Addition System (NITA)	VAS
Vector Analog Computer	VAC
Vector Arithmetic Multiprocessor [*Data processing*] (IEEE)	VAMP
Vector Data Buffer (NITA)	VDB
Vector Graphic, Inc. [*NASDAQ symbol*] (NQ)	VCTR
Vector Graphics Access Method (NITA)	VGAM
Vector Instruction Processor (NITA)	VIP
Vector Instruction Set [*Data processing*]	VIS
Vector Processing Subsystem	VPSS
Vector Processor (NITA)	VP
Vehicle Inelastic Bending Response Analysis [*Computer program*]	VIBRA
Vehicle Origin Survey [*R. L. Polk & Co.*] [*Information service*] (EISS)	VOS
Vehicle Radio Remote Control	VRRC
Vehicle Scheduling Program [*Data processing*]	VSP
Vehicle Scheduling Program Extended [*Data processing*]	VSPX
Vehicular RADIAC [*Radioactivity Detection, Indication, and Computation*] System	VRS
Velocity Modulated Transistor [*Solid-state physics*]	VMT
Velocity Sensor Antenna (CIT)	VSA
Vendor Automated Data System (MCD)	VADS
Venture Development Corporation [*Natick, MA*] [*Telecommunications*] (TSSD)	VDC
Venture Evaluation and Review Technique	VERT
Verbal Information Storage and Text Analysis [*in FORTRAN computer language*]	VISTA
Verband Deutsche Elektrotechniker [*German*] [*Telecommunications*] (TEL)	VDE
Verbatim Corp. [*American Stock Exchange symbol*]	VRB
Verbit & Company, Consultants to Management [*Bala Cynwyd, PA*] [*Telecommunications*] (TSSD)	VCO
Verein Deutscher Giessereifachleute eV - Dokumentationsstelle und Bibliothek [*Dusseldorf*] [*Information retrieval*] (ODIN)	VDG-DOK
Vericom Test Application System [*Vericom Ltd.*] [*Software package*] [*British*] (NCC)	V-TAS
Verification Condition (NITA)	VC
Verification Condition Generator (NITA)	VCG
Verification and Validation [*Data processing*]	V & V
Verify (AFM)	VER
Verify Number If No Answer [*Telecommunications*] (TEL)	VN
Verifying Punch (CMD)	VP
Verkehrswasserbaubibliothek [*Bundesanstalt fuer Wasserbau*] [*Database*] (CUAD)	VtB
Vermont Information Processes, Inc. [*Middlebury, VT*] [*Information service*] (EISS)	VIP
Vermont Natural Heritage Program [*Montpelier, VT*] [*Information service*] (EISS)	VNHP
Vermont Research Corp. [*American Stock Exchange symbol*]	VRE
Vermont Telecommunications, Incorporated [*Burlington, VT*] [*Telecommunications*] (TSSD)	VTI
Versatile Automatic Data Exchange (MCD)	VADE
Versatile Automatic Test Equipment [*Computers*]	VATE
Versatile Information Processor [*Data processing*]	VIP
Version Description Document (KSC)	VDD
Vertical Anisotropic Etch [*Raytheon Co.*]	V-ATE
Vertical Arithmetic Unit (NITA)	VAU
Vertical Blanking Interval [*Telecommunications*]	VBI
Vertical Current Meter	VCM
Vertical Data Processing	VDP
Vertical Format Buffer (NITA)	VFB
Vertical Format Control (NITA)	VFC
Vertical Format Unit (BUR) [*Data processing*]	VFU
Vertical Injection Logic [*Data processing*]	VIL
Vertical Interval Reference [*Automatic color adjustment*] [*Television*]	VIR
Vertical Interval Test Signal (IEEE)	VITS
Vertical Polarization (AFM)	VERT
Vertical Receiving Hydrophone	VRH
Vertical Redundancy Check (BUR)	VRC
Vertical Side of Intermediate Distribution Frame [*Telecommunications*] (TEL)	VIDF
Vertical Side of Main Distribution Frame [*Telecommunications*] (TEL)	VMDF
Vertical Synchronous (DEEC)	VSYNC
Vertical Tabulation [*Data processing*]	VT
Vertical Tail	VT

Vertical Temperature Profile [*or Profiling*] **Radiometer** ... VTPR
Vertical Test Fixture ... VTF
Vertical Tracking Force [*of a phonograph cartridge*] ... VTF
Verwaltungslexikon [*NOMOS Datapool*] [*Database*] (CUAD) ... VLON
Very-High-Frequency [*Electronics*] ... VHF
Very-High-Frequency, Amplitude Modulated (NASA) ... VHF/AM
Very-High-Frequency Direction-Finding ... VDF
Very-High-Frequency Direction-Finding ... VHF/DF
Very-High-Frequency Filter ... VHFF
Very-High-Frequency, Frequency Modulated ... VHF-FM
Very-High-Frequency Generator ... VHFG
Very-High-Frequency Indeed [*Ultrahigh frequency*] [*British*] ... VHFI
Very-High-Frequency Jammer ... VHFJ
Very-High-Frequency Omnirange (AFM) ... VHFOR
Very-High-Frequency Oscillator ... VHFO
Very-High-Frequency Receiver ... VHFR
Very-High-Frequency Termination ... VHFT
Very-High-Order Language (NITA) ... VHOL
Very-High-Speed Integrated [*Electronics*] ... VHSI
Very-High-Speed Integrated Circuit [*Electronics*] ... VHSIC
Very-High-Speed Transit ... VHST
Very-High-Temperature Reactor ... VHTR
Very-Large-Scale Integrated Circuit [*Electronics*] ... VLSIC
Very Long Baseline Array ... VLBA
Very Long Baseline Interferometer [*or Interferometry*] ... VLBI
Very-Low-Frequency [*Electronics*] ... VLF
Very-Low-Frequency Jammer [*Electronics*] ... VLFJ
Very-Low-Frequency Receiver [*Electronics*] ... VLFR
Very Small Business System (NITA) ... VSBS
Very Small Local Exchange [*Telecommunications*] (TEL) ... VSLE
Vestigial Sideband [*Radio*] ... VSB
Vestigial Sideband Filter ... VSBF
Vestigial Sideband Filter ... VSF
Veteran Wireless Operators Association [*Clifton, NJ*] ... VWOA
Veterans Administration Libraries Online Resources ... VALOR
Veterinary Literature Documentation [*Derwent Publications Ltd.*] [*Bibliographic database*] (OBD) ... VETDOC
Veterinary Medical Data Program [*Association of Veterinary Medical Data Program Participants*] [*Information service*] (EISS) ... VMDP
VHF [*Very-High-Frequency*] **Aural Omnirange** ... VAOR
VHF [*Very-High-Frequency*] **Omnidirectional Range/Distance-Measuring for Air Coverage** ... VORDAC
VHF [*Very-High-Frequency*] **Omnirange - Distance-Measuring Equipment** (CET) ... VORDME
VHF [*Very-High-Frequency*] **Omnirange Localizer** (CET) ... VORLOC
Via Net Loss [*Telecommunications*] ... VNL
Via Net Loss Factor (TEL) ... VNLF
Vibration Data Accuracy Program ... VIDAP
Vibrational-Rotational [*Spectra*] [*Data processing*] ... VIBROT
Vicarm Arm Language ... VAL
Victor Analog Computer [*Data processing*] (CDH) ... VAC
Victor Technologies [*NASDAQ symbol*] (NQ) ... VICR
Video ... VID
Video Analog to Digital Converter (NITA) ... VADC
Video-Assisted Instruction (TUT) ... VAI
Video-Audio Range [*Radio*] ... VAR
Video Bandwidth ... VBW
Video Cassette Player ... VCP
Video Cassette Recorder ... VCR
Video Clutter Suppression (CAAL) ... VCS
Video Communications System ... VCS
Video Compact Cassette [*Video recorder*] [*Philips*] (DEEC) ... VCC
Video Computer System [*Atari, Inc.*] ... VCS
Video Concert Hall ... VCH
Video Contrast Seeker ... VCS
Video Data Collection Program ... VDCP
Video Data Link (NVT) ... VDL
Video Data Processor (NITA) ... VDP
Video Data Terminal [*Data processing*] ... VDT
Video Delta Modulation ... VDM
Video Detector Diode ... VDD
Video Digital Data Processing ... VDDP
Video Disc (DEEC) ... VISC
Video Disk (BUR) ... VD
Video Display Adapter with Digital Enhancement [*AT & T*] ... VDA/D
Video Display Board (NITA) ... VDB
Video Display Generator (NITA) ... VDG
Video Display Input (DEEC) ... VDI
Video Display Interface (NITA) ... VDI
Video Display System ... VDS
Video [*or Visual*] **Display Terminal** [*Data processing*] ... VDT
Video Display Unit [*Data processing*] ... VDU
Video Editing Terminal [*Data processing*] ... VET
Video Frequency ... VDF
Video Frequency (IEEE) ... VIDF
Video Frequency Carrier [*or Channel*] (CET) ... VFC
Video-to-Hardcopy Recorder ... VHR
Video Hits One [*Cable-television system*] ... VH-1
Video Home System ... VHS
Video Image Communication and Retrieval (NITA) ... VICAR
Video Image Processing System (SKY) ... VIPS
Video Input/Output (NITA) ... VIO
Video Integrator and Processor ... VIP
Video Interface Unit (MCD) ... VIU
Video Interface Unit Random Access Memory (NITA) ... VIURAM
Video Layout Terminal [*Data processing*] ... VLT
Video Logarithmic Amplifier ... VLA
Video Logic (IEEE) ... VL
Video Logic Unit (MCD) ... VLU
Video Long Player [*Video disk system*] [*Philips/MCA*] (DEEC) ... VLP
Video Mapping Group ... VMG
Video Matrix Terminal (OA) ... VMT
Video Mixer Group ... VMG
Video Output Impedance ... VOI
Video Output Voltage ... VOV
Video Processing and Electronic Reduction (IEEE) ... VIPER
Video Processor ... VP
Video Processor Control (MCD) ... VPC
Video Random Access Memory (DEEC) ... VRAM
Video Reception System ... VRS
Video Relay System ... VRS
Video Scroller Terminal [*Data processing*] ... VST
Video Select Switch (MCD) ... VSS
Video Signal Simulator (NATG) ... VSS
Video Simulation Interface (NASA) ... VSI
Video Software Dealers Association (EANO) ... VSDA
Video Storage System [*or Subsystem*] ... VSS
Video Sweep Integrator ... VSI
Video Switching Matrix (KSC) ... VSM
Video Switching Matrix System ... VSMS
Video Switching Network (MCD) ... VSN
Video Terminal Interface (NITA) ... VTI
Video Timing and Control (NITA) ... VTAC
Videocom Satellite Associates [*Dedham, MA*] [*Telecommunications*] (TSSD) ... VSA
Videofile Microwave System ... VMS
Videograph Display Control Unit ... VDCU
Videotape Recorder [*or Recording*] ... VTR
Videotex Industry Association [*Rosslyn, VA*] [*Telecommunications*] [*Information service*] (EANO) ... VIA
Videotex Information Service Providers Association of Canada (EISS) ... VISPAC
Vidion/International Association of Video (EANO) ... IAV
Vienna Definition Language [*1960*] [*Data processing*] (CSR) ... VDL
Viewdata Corporation of America, Inc. [*Miami Beach, FL*] [*Telecommunications*] (TSSD) ... VCA
VIEWDATA Terminal Program (NITA) ... VTP
Viewers for Quality Television (EANO) ... VQT
Viewing Instantly Security Transactions Automatically [*Wall Street*] ... VISTA
Viking Error Analysis Monte Carlo Program [*Data processing*] ... VEAMCOP
Violation Monitor and Remover [*Bell System*] ... VMR
Virco Manufacturing Corp. [*American Stock Exchange symbol*] ... VIR
Virginia Technical Library System [*Virginia Polytechnic Institute and State University Center for Library Automation*] [*Information service*] ... VTLS
Virtual Access Method (OA) ... VAM
Virtual Address (NITA) ... VA
Virtual Address Extension [*Data processing*] ... VAX
Virtual Address Translation ... VAT
Virtual Base Organization and Maintenance Processor (NITA) ... VBOMP
Virtual Block Processor (NITA) ... VBP
Virtual Channel to Channel Adapter (NITA) ... VCTCA
Virtual Circuit ... VC
Virtual City Associates Ltd. [*London, England*] [*Telecommunications*] (TSSD) ... VCA
Virtual Data (NITA) ... VD
Virtual Data Access Method (IEEE) ... VDAM
Virtual Device Interface [*Computer technology*] ... VDI
Virtual Hardware Monitor [*Data processing*] (IEEE) ... VHM
Virtual Information Storage (BUR) ... VIS
Virtual Input/Output [*Data processing*] (IBMDP) ... VIO
Virtual Integrated Communications Access Method [*Sperry UNIVAC*] (NITA) ... VICAM
Virtual Interaction Controller (NITA) ... VIC
Virtual Interactive Machine Test Program Generator (NITA) ... VIMTPG
Virtual Line Switch (NITA) ... VLSW
Virtual Linkage System [*or Subsystem*] (NITA) ... VLS
Virtual Machine [*Data processing*] ... VM
Virtual Machine Assist [*IBM Corp.*] (NITA) ... VMA
Virtual Machine Communication Facility (NITA) ... VMCF
Virtual Machine Control Block [*Data processing*] (IBMDP) ... VMBLOK
Virtual Machine Control Block (OA) ... VMCB
Virtual Machine/Conversational Monitor System [*Data processing*] ... VM/CMS
Virtual Machine Environment [*International Computers Ltd.*] (NITA) ... VME
Virtual Machine Identifier (OA) ... VMID
Virtual Machine Monitor [*Data processing*] (IEEE) ... VMM
Virtual Machine Time-Sharing System [*Data processing*] (IEEE) ... VMTSS
Virtual Memory [*Data processing*] (MCD) ... VM
Virtual Memory Allocation (OA) ... VMA
Virtual Memory Array Processing System (NITA) ... VMAPS
Virtual Memory Operating System [*Sperry UNIVAC*] [*Data processing*] (IEEE) ... VMOS
Virtual Memory Operating System [*Data processing*] ... VMS

Computer & Telecommunications Acronyms

Virtual Memory Technique [*Data processing*] (MDG)	VMT
Virtual Operating System (NITA)	VOS
Virtual Page Number (NITA)	VPN
Virtual Partitioned Access Method (OA)	VPAM
Virtual Processing Zero (NITA)	VPZ
Virtual Processor (OA)	VP
Virtual Program Status Word (OA)	VPSW
Virtual Redundancy Check [*Data processing*]	VRC
Virtual Resource Executive [*NCR Corp.*] (NITA)	VRX
Virtual Sequential Access Method (NITA)	VSAM
Virtual Storage [*Data processing*]	VS
Virtual Storage Access Method [*Data processing*]	VSAM
Virtual Storage Extension [*IBM Corp.*] [*Data processing*]	VSE
Virtual Storage Manager (BUR)	VSM
Virtual Storage Memory [*Data processing*] (MCD)	VSM
Virtual Storage Personal Computing [*IBM Corp.*] [*Data processing*]	VSPC
Virtual Storage System [*SEMIS*] (NITA)	VSS
Virtual Subscriber Computer (NITA)	VSC
Virtual Switching Point [*Telecommunications*] (TEL)	VSP
Virtual System (DEEC)	VS
Virtual System Access Method (NITA)	VSAM
Virtual Telecommunications [*or Teleprocessing*] Access Method [*IBM Corp.*] [*Data processing*]	VTAM
Virtual Telecommunications Access Method Entry	VTAME
Virtual Terminal Access Method (NITA)	VTAM
Virtual Terminal Protocol (NITA)	VTP
Virtual Unit Address (BUR)	VUA
Visible LASER Communication Experiment	VLCE
Vision Information Program (EISS)	VIP
Visual	VIS
Visual-Aural Digit Span Test	VADS
Visual-Aural Radio Range (MSA)	VARR
Visual-Aural Range [*Radio*]	VAR
Visual Average Speed Computer and Recorder [*Speed trap*]	VASCAR
Visual Call Sign [*Communications*]	VCS
Visual Communications Education	VICOED
Visual Data Entry On-Line [*Data processing*]	VIDEO
Visual Display Data	VDD
Visual Display Input (DEEC)	VDI
Visual Display Terminal (DEEC)	VDT
Visual Display Unit (IDA)	VDU
Visual Image Projection	VIP
Visual Information Display and Control	VIDAC
Visual Information Projection (CGC)	VIP
Visual Information for Satellite Telemetry Analysis	VISTA
Visual Input [*System*] [*AT & T*]	VIP
Visual Punch Card	VPC
Visual Radio Range	VRR
Visual Record Computer	VRC
Visual Record Printer (NITA)	VRP
Visual Search Microfilm File [*Trademark*] [*Data processing*]	VSMF
Visual Storage [*Data processing*]	VS
Visual Technology [*NASDAQ symbol*] (NQ)	VSAL
Visually Impaired Data Processors International [*Washington, DC*] (EANO)	VIDPI
Vital Bus Inverter [*Data processing*] (IEEE)	VBI
VLSI Technology, Inc. [*NASDAQ symbol*] (NQ)	VLSI
VMEbus International Trade Association (EANO)	VITA
VMI Research Laboratories [*Virginia Military Institute*] [*Research center*] (RCD)	VMIRL
VNR [*Van Nostrand Reinhold*] Information Services [*New York, NY*] (EISS)	VIS
Vocabulary	VOCAB
Vocabulary File Utility (NITA)	VFU
Vocabulary Read-Only Memory [*Data processing*]	VROM
Vocabulary Switching System [*Data processing*]	VSS
Vocal Synthesis (NITA)	VS
Vogelback Computing Center [*Northwestern University*] [*Research center*] (RCD)	VCC
Voice Access Arrangement (NITA)	VAA
Voice-Activated Typewriter	VAT
Voice of America	VOA
Voice Analyzer Data Converter (NITA)	VADAC
Voice Answer Back	VAB
Voice Band [*Telecommunications*] (NITA)	VB
Voice Band Compression (CET)	VOBANC
Voice Bank [*Telecommunications*] (TEL)	VB
Voice Code Translation (BUR)	VCT
Voice Coder	VOCODER
Voice Coder	VODER
Voice Communications	VOCOM
Voice Connecting Arrangement [*Telecommunications*] (TEL)	VCA
Voice Controlled Oscillator [*Telecommunications*] (TEL)	VCO
Voice/Data (BUR)	V/D
Voice Data Communications	VODACOM
Voice Data Entry Terminal System (NITA)	VDETS
Voice and Data Integrated System [*Telecommunications*] (TEL)	VADIS
Voice Data Processor System	VDPS
Voice & Data Resources, Inc. [*New York, NY*] [*Information service*] [*Telecommunications*] (TSSD)	VDR
Voice Data Switch (NITA)	VDS
Voice Digital Display	VDD
Voice Digitization Rate (NITA)	VDR
Voice Direct Line	VDL
Voice Frequency [*Communications*]	VF
Voice Frequency Carrier [*or Channel*]	VFC
Voice Frequency Carrier [*or Channel*] Telegraph [*or Teletype*]	VFCT
Voice Frequency Carrier Teletype (MSA)	VFCTT
Voice Frequency Facility Terminal [*Telecommunications*] (TEL)	VFFT
Voice Frequency Line [*Telecommunications*] (TEL)	VFL
Voice Frequency Signaling System	VFSS
Voice Frequency Telegraphy (NATG)	VFT
Voice Frequency Telegraphy	VFTG
Voice Frequency Terminal	VFT
Voice Gate Circuit Adaptors [*Data processing*] (MCD)	VGCA
Voice Grade [*Telecommunications*]	VG
Voice Input Module [*Cascade Graphics Development Ltd.*] [*Software package*] [*British*] (NCC)	VIM
Voice Integrated Presentations [*Telecommunications*] (RDA)	VIP
Voice Intercommunications Unit	VIU
Voice Interface Unit [*Telecommunications*] (TEL)	VIU
Voice Interruption Priority System	VIPS
Voice Messaging System [*Telecommunications*]	VMS
Voice Modulation	VM
Voice Numerical Control (NITA)	VNC
Voice Onset Time	VOT
Voice Operated Computer Systems [*St. Louis Park, MN*] [*Software manufacturer*] (DASOS)	VOCS
Voice-Operated Demonstrator	VODER
Voice-Operated Device Antising (CET)	VODAS
Voice-Operated Device for Automatic Transmission	VODAT
Voice-Operated Keying [*Data processing*]	VOX
Voice-Operated Loss Control and Suppressor	VOLCAS
Voice-Operated Relay	VOPR
Voice-Operated Relay	VOR
Voice-Operated Switch	VOS
Voice-Operated Switch	VOX
Voice-Operated Transmission	VOT
Voice Order Circuit (CET)	VOC
Voice Output Communications Aid	VOCA
Voice Response Unit	VRU
Voice plus Telegraph [*Telecommunications*] (TEL)	VPT
Voice plus Teleprinter Unit	V + TU
Voice Unit [*Signal amplitude measurement*]	VU
Voicemail International, Incorporated [*Santa Clara, CA*] [*Telecommunications*] (TSSD)	VMI
Volt [*Symbol*] [*SI unit of electric potential difference*]	V
Volt-Ampere	V-A
Volt-Ohm Meter (NITA)	VOM
Volt-Ohm-Milliammeter	VOM
Voltage (CET)	E
Voltage (CAH)	V
Voltage Control of Amplification	VCA
Voltage-Controlled Current Source [*Electronics*]	VCCS
Voltage Controlled Filter (NITA)	VCF
Voltage-Controlled Oscillator	VCO
Voltage-Controlled Voltage Source	VCVS
Voltage to Digital Converter	VDC
Voltage Doubler Circuit	VDC
Voltage to Frequency [*Converter*] [*Data processing*]	V/F
Voltage to Frequency Converter	VFC
Voltage Input (TEL)	VIN
Voltage-Logic-Current-Switching [*Electronics*]	VLCS
Voltage-Logic-Voltage-Switching [*Electronics*]	VLVS
Voltage Standing Wave	VSW
Voltage Standing-Wave Ratio	VSWR
Voltage to Substrate and Sources [*Microelectronics*] (DEEC)	VSS
Voltage Transformation Ratio [*Physics*]	VTR
Voltmeter	V
Voltmeter Analog-to-Digital Converter	VAD
Volts (SKY)	V
Volts Direct Current	VDC
Volume	VOL
Volume Indicator [*Radio equipment*]	VI
Volume Loadability Speed (IEEE)	VLS
Volume Sensitive Tariff [*Telecommunications*] (TEL)	VST
Volume Table of Contents [*Data processing*]	VOTC
Volume Table of Contents [*Data processing*]	VTOC
Volume Unit [*Signal amplitude measurement*]	VU
Voluntary Data Inquiry	VDI
Voluntary Hospitals of America [*Cable-television system*]	VHA
Volunteers in Technical Assistance [*Arlington, VA*] [*Telecommunications*]	VITA
VOR [*Very-High-Frequency Omnidirectional Range*] Test Signal (CET)	VOT
VORTEX [*Varian Omnitask Real-Time Executive*] Telecommunications Access Method (DEEC)	VTAM
Vsesoyuznyy Institut Nauchnoy i Tekhnicheskoy Informatsii [*All-Union Institute of Scientific and Technical Information*] [*USSR*]	VINITI

W

Wafer-Scale Integration [*Microelectronics*] ... WSI
Wait [*Morse telephony*] (FAAC) ... AS
Wait Acknowledge (NITA) ... WAK
Wait before Transmitting Positive Acknowledgment (DEEC) ... WACK
Walk-In Management Information System [*Data processing*] ... WIMIS
Walker Telecommunications Corp. [*NASDAQ symbol*] (NQ) ... WTEL
Wallace Communications Consultants [*Tampa, FL*] [*Telecommunications*] (TSSD) ... WCC
Wallace Computer Services [*NYSE symbol*] ... WCS
Wallingford Storm Sewer Package [*Hydraulics Research*] [*Software package*] [*British*] (NCC) ... WASSP
Walter Hinchman Associates, Incorporated [*Chevy Chase, MD*] [*Telecommunications*] (TSSD) ... WHAI
Wang Computer System (NITA) ... WCS
Wang Intersystem Exchange (NITA) ... WISE
Wang Laboratories, Inc. [*American Stock Exchange symbol*] ... WAN
Wang Office Systems User Society (CSR) ... WOSUS
Wang Software Vendors' Association [*Defunct*] (EANO) ... WSVA
War Operation Plan Response [*Pronounced "whopper"*] [*Name of NORAD computer in film "WarGames"*] ... WOPR
Warner Communications, Inc. [*NYSE symbol*] ... WCI
Warner-Eddison Associates, Inc. [*Information service*] (EISS) ... WEA
Warner-Lambert/Parke-Davis [*Computer files of chemical and biological data*] ... WL/PD
Washington Interagency Telecommunications System [*GSA*] ... WITS
Washington Library Network [*Washington State Library*] [*Olympia, WA*] [*Library network*] ... WLN
Washington Representative Services, Inc. [*Information service*] (EISS) ... WRS
Waste Management Information Bureau [*Atomic Energy Authority*] [*British*] [*Information service*] (EISS) ... WMIB
Watch Dog Timer (CIT) ... WDT
Water Resources Abstracts [*Database*] [*A publication*] ... WRA
Water Resources Document Reference Centre [*Canadian Department of Fisheries and the Environment*] [*Ottawa, ON*] [*Database*] (EISS) ... WATDOC
Water Resources Scientific Information Center [*Department of the Interior*] [*Washington, DC*] [*Database originator*] ... WRSIC
Water Use Information System [*Westinghouse Hanford Co.*] (EISS) ... WUIS
Waterloo FORTRAN [*University of Waterloo*] [*Canada*] ... WATFOR
Waterloo Interactive Direct Job Entry Terminal System [*IBM Corp.*] ... WIDJET
Waterloo Research Institute [*University of Waterloo*] [*Research center*] (RCD) ... WRI
Waters Computing Center [*Rose-Hulman Institute of Technology*] [*Research center*] (RCD) ... WCC
Watt [*Broadcasting term*] ... W
Watt-Hour ... WH
Watts per Candle [*Electricity*] ... WPC
Wave-Band ... WB
Wave Propagation Laboratory [*University of Houston*] [*National Oceanic and Atmospheric Administration*] [*Research center*] ... WPL
Waveform Distortion [*Telecommunications*] (TEL) ... WFD
Waveform Generator ... WFG
Waveguide below Cutoff (IEEE) ... WBCO
Waveguide Operating below Cutoff (IEEE) ... WGBC
Waveguide Slot Array Antenna ... WSAA
Wavelength [*Electronics*] ... WL
Wavelength Division Multiplex ... WDM
Way Control Block (NITA) ... WCB
We Have, Ready with Called Party [*Telecommunications*] (TEL) ... WH
Weak External Reference [*Data processing*] (BUR) ... WXTRN
Weak Signal Reception ... WSR
Weak Signals [*Radio*] ... WS
Weather Facsimile Experiment [*Environmental Science Services Administration*] ... WEFAX
Weather Services International Corp. [*Information service*] (EISS) ... WSI
Weekly Criminal Bulletin [*Canada Law Book*] [*Database*] ... WCB
Weight and Value Engineering System [*Data processing*] ... WAVES
Weldable Printed Circuit ... WPC
Welding Institute [*Cambridge, England*] [*Database originator and operator*] (EANO) ... WI
Well-Formed Formula [*Logic*] ... WFF
Well History Control System [*Petroleum Information Corp.*] [*Information service*] (EISS) ... WHCS
Well Information Network [*Database*] (CUAD) ... WIN
Wesley Bull & Associates, Incorporated [*Seattle, WA*] [*Telecommunications*] (TSSD) ... WBAI
Wespercorp [*American Stock Exchange symbol*] ... WP
West [*or Western*] ... W
West Virginia Network for Educational Telecomputing [*Morgantown, WV*] [*Research center*] (RCD) ... WVNET
Western Australia Institute of Technology [*Database originator and operator*] ... WAIT
Western Cedar [*Utility pole*] [*Telecommunications*] (TEL) ... WC
Western Data Processing Center [*University of California, Los Angeles*] ... WDPC
Western Digital Corporation [*American Stock Exchange symbol*] ... WDC
Western Digital Corporation [*NASDAQ symbol*] (NQ) ... WDCL
Western Educational Society for Telecommunications [*Arizona State University*] [*Tempe, AZ*] (EANO) ... WEST
Western Electric Co. ... WE
Western Electric Company ... WECO
Western Electronic Manufacturers Association [*Later, AEA*] ... WEMA
Western Electronics Show and Convention [*IEEE*] ... WESCON
Western Forest Research Information Network ... WESTFORNET
Western Hemlock [*Utility pole*] [*Telecommunications*] (TEL) ... WH
Western Information System for Energy Resources [*Dataline, Inc.*] [*Database*] (CUAD) ... WISER
Western Interstate Commission of Higher Education ... WICHE
Western Joint Computer Conference ... WJCC
Western Larch [*Utility pole*] [*Telecommunications*] (TEL) ... WL
Western Library Network [*Library of Congress*] [*Database*] (CUAD) ... WLN
Western Pennsylvania Advanced Technology Center [*University of Pittsburgh, Carnegie-Mellon University*] [*Research center*] (RCD) ... WPATC
Western Pine [*Utility pole*] [*Telecommunications*] (TEL) ... WP
Western Telecommunications Consulting Co. [*Los Angeles, CA*] [*Telecommunications*] (TSSD) ... WTC
Western Telecommunications, Incorporated [*Englewood, CO*] [*Telecommunications*] (CBSS) ... WTCI
Western Union Corp. [*Upper Saddle River, NJ*] [*NYSE symbol*] ... WU
Western Union Corporation (NITA) ... WUC
Western Union Electronic Mail, Incorporated [*McLean, VA*] [*Telecommunications*] (TSSD) ... WUEMI
Western Union Exchange [*Teleprinter*] ... WUX
Western Union International [*Division of WUI, Inc.*] ... WUI
Western Union Long Distance Service [*Western Union Telegraph Co.*] [*Upper Saddle River, NJ*] [*Telecommunications*] (TSSD) ... WULDS
Western Union Technical Review [*A publication*] ... West Union Tech Rev
Western Union Telegraph Co. [*Upper Saddle River, NJ*] [*NYSE symbol*] ... WUT
Western Union Telegraph Company [*Upper Saddle River, NJ*] (NITA) ... WUTC
Western Union Telegraph Company [*Upper Saddle River, NJ*] ... WUTELCO
Western Wisconsin Communications Cooperative [*Independence, WI*] [*Telecommunications*] (TSSD) ... WWCC
Westinghouse Broadcasting Company ... WBC
Westinghouse Digital Airborne Computer ... WEDAC
Westinghouse Electric Corporation ... WEC
Westinghouse Electric Corporation ... WECO
Westinghouse Electric Corp. [*NYSE symbol*] [*Wall Street slang name: "Wex"*] ... WX
Westinghouse Electronic Tubeless Analog Computer ... WETAC
Westinghouse Resolver/Quantizer (IEEE) ... WRQ
What You See Is What You Get [*Pronounced "whizziwig"*] [*Indicates that video display on word processor bears a high-quality resemblance to printed page that will result*] ... WYSIWYG
Whiskey-3 [*Shipboard radio*] ... AN-WSC-3
White House Conference on Library and Information Services [*Washington, DC, 1979*] ... WHCLIS
Who Are You? [*Communication*] ... WRU
Whole Word Designator [*Data processing*] ... W
Who's Who Resource File [*Minority Business Development Agency*] [*Database*] (FDB) ... WWRF
Wicat Systems, Inc. [*NASDAQ symbol*] (NQ) ... WCAT

Computer & Telecommunications Acronyms

Wide-Angle Display System ... WADS
Wide Application System Adapter (NITA) ... WASAR
Wide-Area Data Service [Data transmission service] ... WADS
Wide Area Network (CCD) ... WAN
Wide Range Analog Input Subsystem (NITA) ... WRAIS
Wideband [Radio transmission] ... WB
Wideband Antenna System ... WAS
Wideband Coherent Video (IEEE) ... WBCV
Wideband Communications Subsystem (CIT) ... WBCS
Wideband Frequency Modulation (CIT) ... WBFM
Wideband Limiting (IEEE) ... WBL
Wideband Multichannel Receiver ... WMR
Wideband Remote Switch (IEEE) ... WBRS
Wideband Signal Conditioner (MCD) ... WSC
Wideband Signal Processor ... WSP
Wideband Transformer [or Transmitter] ... WBT
Wideband Transmission Relay Acoustic Communications (MCD) ... WIDETRACK
Width ... W
Width ... WID
Width-to-Length [Ratio] (MDG) ... W/e
Will Talk [Telecommunications] (TEL) ... WT
Wind Electric System [Telecommunications] (TEL) ... WES
Wing Design Optimization with Aerolastic Constraints [Computer program] ... WIDOWAC
Winterhalter, Inc. [NASDAQ symbol] (NQ) ... WNTL
Wire Assembly (MSA) ... WA
Wire Chief [Test clerk] [Telecommunications] (TEL) ... WC
Wire Chief Test Panel [Telecommunications] (TEL) ... WCTP
Wire Relay Radio System ... WRRS
Wire Send [Telecommunications] (TEL) ... WS
Wire Way [Technical drawings] ... WW
Wire-Wound ... WW
Wired Program Computer ... WPC
Wired Shelf Group [Telecommunications] (TEL) ... WSG
Wireless Telegraphy [or Telephony] ... WT
Wisconsin Career Information System [Information service] ... WCIS
Wisconsin Center for Applied Microelectronics [University of Wisconsin - Madison] [Research center] (RCD) ... WCAM
Wisconsin Clinical Cancer Center [University of Wisconsin] [Research center] (RCD) ... WCCC
Wisconsin Information Science and Communications Consortium [University of Wisconsin - Madison] [Research center] (RCD) ... WISCOM
Wiswesser Line Notation [Information retrieval] (ODIN) ... WIN
With No Identification Columns [Intelligent assistant communication] ... WNIC
Without (AFM) ... WO
Wohl Associates [Bala Cynwyd, PA] [Telecommunications] (TSSD) ... WA
Women in Data Processing [San Diego, CA] (EANO) ... WDP
Women in Information Processing (EANO) ... WIP
Women in Telecommunications [San Francisco, CA] (EANO) ... WIT
Women's Computer Literacy Project [Commercial firm] [San Francisco, CA] (EANO) ... WCLP
Word ... W
Word ... WD
Word After [Message handling] ... WA
Word Control Logic (NITA) ... WCL
Word Count [Data processing] ... WC
Word Count Register (NITA) ... WCR
Word Image Processing System [Datacopy] ... WIPS
Word and Information Processing [A publication] ... Word and Inf Process
Word Line (NITA) ... WL
Word Mark (BUR) ... WM
Word-Oriented Random Access Memory [Data processing] (MCD) ... WORAM
Word Processing [Movement to improve secretarial/clerical function through a managed system of people, procedures, and modern office equipment] ... WP
Word Processing/Administrative Support [Extension of Word Processing] ... WP/AS
Word Processing Center ... WPC
Word Processing Now [A publication] ... Word Process Now
Word Processing Society, Incorporated (EANO) ... WPSI
Word Processing System (BUR) ... WPS
Word Processor ... WP
Word Terminal (NITA) ... WT
Word Terminal Synchronous ... WTS
Words and Authors Index [Computer-produced index] ... WADEX
Words a Minute ... WAM
Words per Minute ... WPM
Words per Second ... WPS
Work Analysis Program [Data processing] (BUR) ... WAP
Work Assignment Procedure ... WAP
Work Breakdown Structure [Data processing] ... WBS
Work Element Timer and Recorder for Automatic Computing ... WETARFAC
Work Flow Language [Data processing] (BUR) ... WFL
Work Planning and Control [Data processing] ... WP + C
Work in Progress (AFM) ... WIP
Work Queue Directory (OA) ... WKQDR
Work Station Facility (NITA) ... WSF
Working Group (FAAC) ... WG
Working Reference Telephone Circuit [Telecommunications] (TEL) ... WRTC
Working Register (NITA) ... WR
Working Space (NITA) ... WS
Working Storage [Data processing] (MDG) ... WS
Working Transmission Reference System [Telecommunications] (TEL) ... WRS
Working Voltage (MSA) ... WV
Working Voltage, Alternating Current (DEN) ... WVAC
Working Voltage, Direct Current ... WVDC
Workload Control File (NITA) ... WCF
Works Information and Management System [M & E White Consultants Ltd.] [Software package] [British] (NCC) ... WIMS
Workshop Computer Interface Unit (MCD) ... WCIU
World Administrative Radio Conference [Takes place every 20 years] [Held in 1979 in Geneva, Switzerland] [International Telecommunications Union] ... WARC
World Administrative Radio Conference for Maritime Mobile Telecommunications ... WARC-MAR
World Administrative Radio Conference for Space Telecommunications ... WARC-ST
World Aluminum Abstracts [American Society for Metals] [Metals Park, OH] [Database] [A publication] (EISS) ... WAA
World Computer Graphics Association [Washington, DC] (EANO) ... WCGA
World Coordinate (CCD) ... WC
World Data Center [National Academy of Sciences] [Data collection and exchange center] ... WDC
World Energy Data System [Department of Energy] [Information service] (EISS) ... WENDS
World Health Organization [The pronunciation "who" is not acceptable] [United Nations affiliate] [Geneva, Switzerland] [Databank originator] ... WHO
World Information Systems Exchange [Defunct] (EANO) ... WISE
World Intellectual Property Organization [Geneva, Switzerland] ... WIPO
World List of Scientific Periodicals [A publication] (DIT) ... WLSP
World Metal Index [Sheffield City Libraries] [British] [Information service] (EISS) ... WMI
World Meteorological Organization [See also OMM] [Geneva, Switzerland] (EANO) ... WMO
World Oceanographic Data Processing and Services Center ... WOPC
World Oil Project [National Science Foundation] (EISS) ... WOP
World Organization of General Systems and Cybernetics [Blackburn, England] ... WOGSC
World Patents Index [Derwent Publications Ltd.] [Database] ... WPI
World Studies Data Bank (EISS) ... WSDB
World Surface Coatings Abstracts [Paint Research Association] [Database] [A publication] ... WSCA
World Systems Division [of Communications Satellite Corp.] [Telecommunications] (TEL) ... WSD
World Teleport Association [New York, NY] [Telecommunications] (TSSD) ... WTA
World Textile Abstracts [Shirley Institute] [Database] [British] ... WTA
World Transindex [International Translations Centre] [Bibliographic database] [Dutch] (OBD) ... WTI
World Weather Watch [World Meteorological Office] [Databank] ... WWW
Worldwide Integrated Communications [Mohawk Data Sciences Corp.] [Parsippany, NJ] [Telecommunications] (TSSD) ... WINC
Writable Character Generation Module [Data processing] (BUR) ... WCGM
Writable Control Memory [Data processing] (BUR) ... WCM
Writable Control Storage [Data processing] ... WCS
Writable Diagnostic Control Store (NITA) ... WDCS
Write (NITA) ... W
Write (CAH) ... WR
Write Access Key (NITA) ... WAK
Write Data (NITA) ... WD
Write Data Check (CMD) ... WDC
Write Direct (OA) ... WD
Write Enable (IEEE) ... WE
Write Interface Unit (NITA) ... WRIU
Write Once, Read Mostly [Data processing] ... WORM
Write Only ... WO
Write-Only Memory [Data processing] (TUT) ... WOM
Write-Only Read-Only Memory [Data processing] (MDG) ... WOROM
Write-to-Operator [Data processing] (IBMDP) ... WTO
Write-to-Operator with Reply [Data processing] (IBMDP) ... WTOR
Write Optional Memory (IEEE) ... WOM
Write Program Memory [Data processing] ... WPM
Write Protect (NITA) ... WP
Write Protect Memory (NITA) ... WPM
Write Punch [Data processing] (MCD) ... WPN
Writing Pushdown Acceptor (NITA) ... WPDA
Wrong [Telecommunications] (TEL) ... WRG
Wrong Length Record [Data processing] (TUT) ... WLR
Wrong Number [Telecommunications] (TEL) ... WN
Wrong Number [Telecommunications] (TEL) ... WNO

X-Y-Z

X Automatic Code Translation   (IEEE) ... XACT
X-Band Antenna Feed Horn ... XAFH
X-Band Antenna System ... XAS
X-Band Communications Transponder ... XCT
X-Band Drive Amplifier ... XDA
X-Band Microwave Transmitter ... XMT
X-Band Parametric Amplifier ... XPA
X-Band Passive Array ... XPA
X-Band Phase Shifter ... XPS
X-Band Planar Array ... XPA
X-Band Planar Array Antenna ... XPAA
X-Band Power Amplifier ... XPA
X-Band Pseudopassive Array ... XPPA
X-Band Pulse Transmitter ... XPT
X-Band Pulsed Power Amplifier ... XPPA
X-Band Satellite Antenna ... XSA
X-Band Satellite Tracking Antenna ... XSTA
X-Band Stripline Tunnel Diode ... XSTD
X-Band Stripline Tunnel Diode Amplifier ... XSTDA
X-Band Tracking Antenna ... XTA
X-Band Transmitter   (CIT) ... XTX
X-Band Traveling Wave Amplifier ... XTWA
X-Band Traveling Wave MASER ... XTWM
X-Band Tunable Parametric Amplifier ... XTPA
XEBEC [NASDAQ symbol]   (NQ) ... XEBC
Xerox 9700 Users' Association   (EANO) ... XPLOR
Xerox Canada, Inc. [Toronto Stock Exchange symbol] ... XXC
Xerox Computer Services [Xerox Corp.]   (NITA) ... XCS
Xerox Corp. [NYSE symbol] ... XRX
Xerox Data Systems [Formerly, SDS] ... XDS
Xerox Graphic Printer [Xerox Corp.] ... XGP
Xerox Integrated Composition System [Xerox Corp.] [Computer typesetting system] ... XICS
Xerox Memory System   (NITA) ... XMS
Xerox Operating System   (CAH) ... XOS
Xerox Planning Model [A computerized representation of the Xerox Corp.'s operations] ... XPM
Xerox Telecommunications Network [Proposed]   (TSSD) ... XTEN
X*PRESS Information Services [Golden, CO]   (EISS) ... XIS
Xyvision Users Group [Richmond, VA]   (EANO) ... XUG
Yankee Group [Boston, MA] [Information service] [Telecommunications]   (TSSD) ... YG
Yaw Damper Computer   (TSSD) ... YDC
Year [Online database field identifier]   (TSSD) ... YR
Year to Date   (MCD) ... YTD
Yellow Page Rate Base Analysis Plan [Bell System]   (MCD) ... YRAP
Yellow Pages Datasystem [National Planning Data Corp.] [Database]   (CUAD) ... YPD
Yellow Pages Service [Telecommunications]   (TEL) ... YPS
Yes-No [Response prompt]   (TEL) ... YN
Yield Analysis Pattern [Data processing]   (TEL) ... YAP
You [Communications]   (FAAC) ... U
Youngest Empty Cell   (NITA) ... YEC
Yttrium Iron Garnet   (NITA) ... YIG
Yugoslav Committee for Electronics and Automation [Beograd, Yugoslavia]   (NITA) ... ETAN
Zeitschrift fuer Rundfunk und Fernsehen [NOMOS Datapool] [Database]   (CUAD) ... RUFE
Zeitschrift fuer Urheber und Medienrecht [NOMOS Datapool] [Database]   (CUAD) ... ZUM
Zenith Radio Corporation   (CUAD) ... ZRC
Zentec Corp. [NASDAQ symbol]   (NQ) ... ZENT
Zentralbibliothek der Medizin [Cologne] [Information retrieval] [West German]   (ODIN) ... ZBMED
Zentralblatt fuer Didaktik der Mathematik [Information retrieval]   (ODIN) ... ZDM
Zentralblatt fuer Mathematik und Ihre Grenzgebiete [Information retrieval]   (ODIN) ... ZFM
Zentralinstitut fuer Information und Dokumentation [Central Institute for Information and Documentation] [East Germany] [Information service]   (EISS) ... ZIID
Zentralstelle fuer Agrardokumentation und -Information [Center for Agricultural Documentation and Information] [Databank originator] [Information service] [West German]   (EISS) ... ZADI
Zentralstelle fuer Atomkernenergie-Dokumentation beim Gmelin-Institut [Central Agency for Atomic Energy Documentation of the Gmelin Institute] [Germany] [Database originator] [Also, AED]   (EISS) ... ZAED
Zentralstelle Dokumentation Elektrotechnik [Electrical Engineering Documentation Center] [Offenbach, WG] [Originator and database] [Information service]   (EISS) ... ZDE
Zentralstelle fuer Psychologische Information und Dokumentation [Center for Psychological Information and Documentation] [West Germany] [Database operator] [Information service]   (EISS) ... ZPID
Zero ... Z
Zero Access Storage ... ZAS
Zero-Base Budgeting ... ZBB
Zero Crossing Rate   (NITA) ... ZCR
Zero Express Dialing ... ZED
Zero Transmission Level Point   (IEEE) ... 0TLP
Ziegler Co., Inc. [NASDAQ symbol]   (NQ) ... ZEGL
Zilog List Processor [Programing language] [1979]   (CSR) ... ZLISP
Zone   (OA) ... ZN
Zone Wind Computer ... ZWC
Zoom In [Cinematography and Video] ... Z/I
Zork Interactive Language [Computer science] ... ZIL
Zurich, Mainz, Munich, Darmstadt [A joint European university effort on ALGOL processors] ... ZMMD
Zytec Computers [Vancouver Stock Exchange symbol] ... ZYT